Everyman, I will go with thee,
and be thy guide

THE EVERYMAN
LIBRARY

The Everyman Library was founded by J. M. Dent
in 1906. He chose the name Everyman because he wanted
to make available the best books ever written in every
field to the greatest number of people at the cheapest possible
price. He began with Boswell's 'Life of Johnson';
his one-thousandth title was Aristotle's 'Metaphysics',
by which time sales exceeded forty million.

Today Everyman paperbacks remain true to
J. M. Dent's aims and high standards, with a wide range
of titles at affordable prices in editions which address
the needs of today's readers. Each new text is reset to give
a clear, elegant page and to incorporate the latest thinking
and scholarship. Each book carries the pilgrim logo,
the character in 'Everyman', a medieval morality play,
a proud link between Everyman
past and present.

Charles Dickens

THE PICKWICK PAPERS

Edited by
MALCOLM ANDREWS
University of Kent

Series Editor
MICHAEL SLATER
University of London

with illustrations by
ROBERT SEYMOUR
R. W. BUSS
and
H. K. BROWNE ('PHIZ')

EVERYMAN
J. M. DENT · LONDON
CHARLES E. TUTTLE
VERMONT

Introduction and other critical apparatus
© J. M. Dent 1998

The Pickwick Papers first published
in Everyman in 1907
This text first published in Everyman in 1998

All rights reserved

J. M. Dent
Orion Publishing Group
Orion House,
5 Upper St Martin's Lane, London WC2H 9EA
and
Charles E. Tuttle Co. Inc.
28 South Main Street, Rutland,
Vermont 05701, USA

Typeset in Sabon by SetSystems Limited, Saffron Walden, Essex
Printed in Great Britain by
The Guernsey Press Co. Ltd, Guernsey, C.I.

This book if bound as a paperback is subject to
the condition that it may not be issued on loan or otherwise
except in its original binding.

British Library Cataloguing-in-Publication Data
is available upon request.

ISBN 0 460 87664 3

CONTENTS

ILLUSTRATIONS

(Except where otherwise indicated,
all illustrations are by H. K. Browne ['Phiz'])

NOTE ON THE AUTHOR, EDITOR
AND SERIES EDITOR

CHARLES DICKENS was born at Portsea, Portsmouth, on 7 February 1812. In 1817 the Dickens family settled in Chatham. These years, 1817-22, were the happiest of Dickens's early life. They came to an end when his father, John Dickens, was recalled to London and the family began its slow slide towards bankruptcy. In February 1824, John Dickens was imprisoned for debt in the Marshalsea and the twelve-year-old Charles was sent to work in a run-down warehouse off the Strand, labelling and packaging bottles of boot blacking. His sense of humiliation and thwarted ambition was acute, and the experience (which may have lasted a year) proved traumatic. His father was discharged from prison later in 1824, under the Insolvent Debtors' Act, and some months later Charles was removed from the warehouse and sent to school. In 1827 he was articled as a solicitor's clerk in Gray's Inn. He learned shorthand, became a reporter at Doctors' Commons and later a skilled reporter of Parliamentary debates. In the years from 1833 to 1836 he wrote a number of short stories and sketches which were published in various journals and collected in *Sketches by Boz* (1836), accompanied by illustrations by George Cruikshank. In April of the same year he married Catherine Hogarth, daughter of a newspaper editor. *Pickwick Papers*, begun in that year as a monthly instalment publication, soon became a great popular success. It was followed by *Oliver Twist* in 1837, *Nicholas Nickleby* in 1838-9 and (in his weekly periodical *Master Humphrey's Clock*) *The Old Curiosity Shop* and *Barnaby Rudge*, 1841. He made a triumphant tour of the United States in 1842 and in the same year published a critical account of his experience there in *American Notes*.

A Christmas Carol was published in 1843 and inaugurated the highly successful series of Christmas Books in the 1840s. *Martin Chuzzlewit* appeared in 1843-4 and *Dombey and Son* in 1846-8. *David Copperfield* was completed in 1850, the year in which he founded his own weekly magazine *Household Words*, a characteristically vivacious and imaginative family miscellany, which carried the serialised *Hard Times* in 1854. In that novel, as in its predecessor *Bleak House* (1852–3) and its successor *Little Dorrit* (1855–7), Dickens anatomised and satirised the social and political condition of England. In 1858 he and his wife formally separated and he moved to his new home at Gad's Hill in Kent. In the same year he began his career as a professional public reader of his work, a strenuous enterprise that proved highly lucrative as well as seriously harmful to his health. *A Tale of Two Cities* appeared in 1859 and *Great Expectations* in 1860–1, both serialised in Dickens's successor to *Household Words, All the Year Round*. His last novel to be completed in the old twenty-number monthly format was *Our Mutual Friend* (1864–5). In the winter of 1867–8 he toured the United States with his readings. In 1870 he began *The Mystery of Edwin Drood*, but had completed only half of it when he suffered a stroke at Gad's Hill and died on 9 June.

MALCOLM ANDREWS is Professor of Victorian and Visual Studies at the University of Kent at Canterbury. He is the author of *Dickens on England and the English, The Search for the Picturesque: Landscape Aesthetics and Tourism in Britain 1760–1800* and *Dickens and the Grown-up Child*, and is the Editor of *The Dickensian*.

MICHAEL SLATER is Professor of Victorian Literature at Birkbeck College, University of London, and a former Editor of *The Dickensian*. He is the author of *Dickens and Women* (1983) and has published a number of other books and articles relating to Dickens, as well as editions of *The Christmas Books* and *Nicholas Nickleby*. He is also Editor of the *Dent Uniform Edition of Dickens' Journalism*, of which two volumes have been published: *Sketches by Boz and Other Early Papers 1833–9* (1994) and *'The Amusements of the People' and Other Papers: Reports, Essays and Reviews 1834–51* (1996).

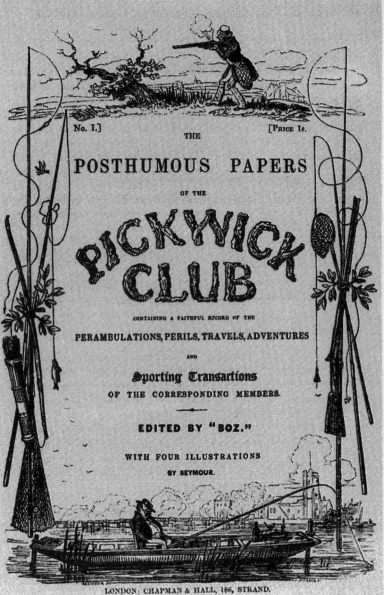

No. I.]   [Price 1s.

THE
POSTHUMOUS PAPERS
OF THE
PICKWICK CLUB

CONTAINING A FAITHFUL RECORD OF THE

PERAMBULATIONS, PERILS, TRAVELS, ADVENTURES

AND

Sporting Transactions

OF THE CORRESPONDING MEMBERS.

EDITED BY "BOZ."

WITH FOUR ILLUSTRATIONS
BY SEYMOUR.

LONDON: CHAPMAN & HALL, 186, STRAND.

MDCCCXXXVI.

Wrapper design for monthly parts

CHRONOLOGY OF DICKENS'S LIFE

Year	Age	Life
1812		Born in Portsea, Portsmouth, 7 February
1815	3	Dickens family moves to London
1817	5	Dickens family moves to Chatham
1822	10	Dickens family (now 6 children) moves to London
1824	12	Works at Warren's Blacking. John Dickens (father) in Marshalsea Debtors Prison for a few months
1825	13	Starts school at Wellington House Academy

CHRONOLOGY OF HIS TIMES

Year	Literary Context	Historical Events
1812	Byron, *Childe Harold* I & II	1811–20 Regency of George, Prince of Wales 1812–14 War with America
1813	Austen, *Pride and Prejudice* Southey becomes Poet Laureate	
1814	Austen, *Mansfield Park* Scott, *Waverley* Wordsworth, *The Excursion*	
1815		Battle of Waterloo
1816	Austen, *Emma*	Spa Fields Riots
1817	Keats, *Poems* Austen dies	
1818	Mary Shelley, *Frankenstein*	
1819	Byron, *Don Juan* I & II George Eliot born Whitman born	Peterloo Massacre The Six Acts
1820	Keats, *Lamia . . . and other Poems* Flaubert born	Accession of George IV Cato Street Conspiracy
1821	Keats dies De Quincey, *Confessions . . . Opium Eater*	Greek War of Liberation Napoleon dies
1822	Byron, *Vision of Judgement* Shelley dies	Suicide of Castlereagh
1823	Grimm Brothers, *German Popular Stories* (illus. G. Cruikshank)	Agricultural unrest
1824	Byron dies	
1825	Hazlitt, *Spirit of the Age*	Stockton–Darlington railway opens

Year	Age	Life
1827	15	Becomes junior clerk in solicitor's office
1829	17	Becomes a freelance reporter at Doctors' Commons
1830	18	Acquires British Museum Reader's Card
1831	19	Falls in love with Maria Beadnell. Appointed Parliamentary reporter
1833	21	First story written and published, 'A Dinner at Poplar Walk'
1834	22	Joins reporting staff of the *Morning Chronicle*
1835	23	Engaged to Catherine Hogarth
1836	24	*Sketches by Boz* published. Marries Catherine. *Pickwick Papers* begun. Resigns from the *Morning Chronicle*
1837	25	*Pickwick Papers* completed. Mary Hogarth (sister-in-law) dies. Becomes editor of *Bentley's Miscellany*
1838	26	*Oliver Twist* [dates given for publication of the novels refer to completion of their serialisation]
1839	27	*Nicholas Nickleby*
1840	28	Dickens begins *Master Humphrey's Clock*
1841	29	*The Old Curiosity Shop*; *Barnaby Rudge*
1842	30	Visits America (Jan.–June). *American Notes*
1843	31	*A Christmas Carol*
1844	32	Dickens and family stay in Genoa. *Martin Chuzzlewit*; *The Chimes*

Year	Literary Context	Historical Events
1826	Disraeli, *Vivian Gray*	
1827	Blake dies	University of London founded
1828	Meredith born D. G. Rossetti born	
1829	Jerrold, *Black-ey'd Susan*	Catholic Emancipation Act
1830	Tennyson, *Poems Chiefly Lyrical*	Accession of William IV July Revolution in France Wellington's ministry falls
1831		First cholera epidemic
1832	Lewis Carroll born Walter Scott dies	First Reform Bill
1833	Carlyle, *Sartor Resartus* Newman, *Tracts for the Times*	Abolition of slavery throughout British Empire State funding of schools begins
1834	Bulwer-Lytton, *Last Days of Pompeii* Coleridge and Lamb die	Tolpuddle Martyrs New Poor Law
1837	Carlyle, *The French Revolution* Lockhart, *Life of Scott*	Accession of Victoria
1838		Anti-Corn Law League Chartist petitions published London–Birmingham railway opens
1839	Carlyle, *Chartism*	First Factory Inspectors' Report
1840	Hardy born	Penny postage introduced
1841	Carlyle, *Heroes and Hero-Worship*	Peel becomes Prime Minister
1842	Tennyson, *Poems* Browning, *Dramatic Lyrics* Macaulay, *Lays of Ancient Rome*	Chartist riots Report on Sanitary Conditions of Labouring Population
1843	Carlyle, *Past and Present* Ruskin, *Modern Painters* I Wordsworth made Poet Laureate	
1844	Disraeli, *Coningsby* Elizabeth Barrett, *Poems*	Rochdale Pioneers found Co-operative Store

Year	Age	Life
1845	33	Dickens family returns from Italy. *The Cricket on the Hearth*
1846	34	Dickens family reside in Lausanne, Switzerland (June–Nov.). *Pictures from Italy.* Brief editorship of *Daily News. The Battle of Life*
1847	35	Dickens family, having moved to Paris in Nov. 1846, continue to reside there until March. Sets up Urania Cottage with Miss Burdett-Coutts.
1848	36	*Dombey and Son; The Haunted Man*
1850	38	Begins his weekly miscellany, *Household Words. David Copperfield*
1851	39	John Dickens dies
1853	41	*Bleak House.* Tours Italy and Switzerland with Wilkie Collins
1854	42	*Hard Times*
1855	43	Meets Maria Beadnell (now Mrs Winter) again. Spends several months in Paris
1856	44	Buys Gad's Hill Place

Year	Literary Context	Historical Events
1845	Disraeli, *Sybil*	Railway speculation Newman joins Catholic Church
1846		Repeal of Corn Laws
1847	Emily Brontë, *Wuthering Heights* Charlotte Brontë, *Jane Eyre* Tennyson, *The Princess*	
1848	Emily Brontë dies Thackeray, *Vanity Fair*	European Revolutions Chartist movement collapses after mass meeting in London Cholera epidemic Pre-Raphaelite Brotherhood founded
1849	Thackeray, *Pendennis* Ruskin, *Seven Lamps of Architecture*	
1850	Tennyson, *In Memoriam* Wordsworth dies Wordsworth, *The Prelude* Kingsley, *Alton Locke*	Pope appoints Catholic bishops to England
1851	Ruskin, *The Stones of Venice* Melville, *Moby-Dick*	Great Exhibition Gold discovered in New South Wales J. M. W. Turner dies
1852	Stowe, *Uncle Tom's Cabin* Thackeray, *Henry Esmond*	Napoleon III becomes Emperor of France Duke of Wellington dies
1853	Charlotte Brontë, *Villette*	Indian Civil Service open to competition
1854	Thoreau, *Walden*	Crimean War begins Newspaper Stamp Duty abolished Palmerston's premiership begins
1855	Browning, *Men and Women* Gaskell, *North and South* Kingsley, *Westward Ho!* Charlotte Brontë dies	
1856	Elizabeth Barrett Browning, *Aurora Leigh* Wilde and Shaw born	End of Crimean War

Year	Literary Context	Historical Events
1857	Trollope, *Barchester Towers* Flaubert, *Madame Bovary*	Indian Mutiny
1858	Eliot, *Scenes of Clerical Life*	Indian Viceroyalty established
1859	Tennyson, *Idylls of the King* Darwin, *Origin of Species* Mill, *On Liberty* Smiles, *Self-Help*	Rise of Fenianism in Ireland
1860	Collins, *The Woman in White* Eliot, *The Mill on the Floss*	
1861	Reade, *The Cloister and the Hearth*	Death of Prince Consort American Civil War begins
1862	Mill, *Utilitarianism*	
1863	Kingsley, *Water Babies* Eliot, *Romola* Thackeray dies	Gettysburg Address Slavery abolished in USA
1864	Newman, *Apologia Pro Vita Sua*	
1865	Carroll, *Alice's Adventures in Wonderland* Arnold, *Essays in Criticism*	President Lincoln assassinated Palmerston dies American Civil War ends
1866	Swinburne, *Poems and Ballads* Dostoyevsky, *Crime and Punishment*	First Barnardo Home Atlantic Cable laid
1867	Marx, *Das Kapital*	Disraeli's Reform Bill
1868	Browning, *The Ring and the Book* Collins, *The Moonstone*	Gladstone becomes Prime Minister
1869	Arnold, *Culture and Anarchy* Blackmore, *Lorna Doone*	Suez Canal opens Mill advocates emancipation of women
1870	D. G. Rossetti, *Poems*	Education Act: free public education in Board Schools Franco-Prussian War Fall of Napoleon III

SERIES EDITOR'S PREFACE

The Everyman Dickens is intended to be the most complete edition of Dickens's works so far published. It will be the first paperback edition to provide thorough and coherent coverage of all his shorter fiction as well as his extensive non-fictional writings. In addition to the fifteen novels and the five *Christmas Books*, the Everyman Dickens will include all the Christmas stories from *Household Words* and *All the Year Round*, all other short fiction, the two travel books and all Dickens's writings for children. Four volumes in the series will present the first-ever annotated edition of *Sketches by Boz, The Uncommercial Traveller* and other journalism, a substantial amount of which has been out of print for many years. Each volume will contain all the earliest illustrations to the work or works featured in it, kindly supplied by The Dickens House, and all Dickens's prefaces.

Every volume will be edited by a specialist in Victorian literature who has a particular interest in the work he or she is dealing with. Where appropriate, explanatory notes will be supplemented by a historical appendix giving more general background information on the text in question.

Throughout the series references to Dickens's published letters will be given as either 'Pilgrim' or 'Nonesuch'. 'Pilgrim' means *The Pilgrim Edition of the Letters of Charles Dickens*, eds M. House, G. Storey, K. Tillotson *et al.* (1965–in progress), and 'Nonesuch' means *The Letters of Charles Dickens*, ed. W. Dexter, 3 vols (1938), part of the Nonesuch Press Edition of Dickens's Works.

MICHAEL SLATER

INTRODUCTION

What kind of a book is *Pickwick Papers*, and where did it come from? The obvious answer – that it is a great comic novel written by the young Charles Dickens – can give a misleading impression both of the manner in which the book was originally constituted and of the impact it is likely to make on new readers.

Before considering these questions of genre and authorship, we might rehearse the famous historical account of the book's origins, which Dickens himself partly outlined in his Preface to the Cheap Edition, 1847, and repeated (with minor alterations) in the 1867 Preface. In 1836 Messrs Chapman and Hall, a recently established publishing partnership, and the artist Robert Seymour were developing a plan to publish a series of comic sporting prints, to be accompanied by some letterpress. The comedy was to turn on the ineptitude of a group of Londoners who fancy themselves as accomplished sportsmen and who, once in the country, prove abysmally incompetent in a variety of rural sports. The monthly wrapper design, with its border of fishing and shooting motifs, betrays these original intentions. The prints were to be issued as a popular monthly series. For the letterpress, the publishers approached the twenty-four-year-old Charles Dickens, who had made a name for himself (or for his pseudonymous self, 'Boz') as a sprightly writer of sketches of London life and scenery.

Dickens's agreement to the project was very much on his own terms: he would take the lead in deciding about the direction of the text and the artist would accommodate himself to the writer's requirements. 'I should like', he wrote in that later preface, 'to take my own way, with a freer range of English scenes and people . . . .' Dickens was to be paid 'nine guineas per sheet of 16 pages demy 8vo containing about 500 words in a page – of which we [the publishers] should require one sheet and a half every month', according to Chapman and Hall's letter of 12 February 1836. Dickens began to write Chapter 1 six days later. Near the end of March the first two monthly numbers were completed. Dickens was paid £29. Number 1 of *The Posthumous Papers of the Pickwick*

Club containing a Faithful Record of the Perambulations, Perils, Travels, Adventures and Sporting Transactions of the Corresponding Members was published on 31 March, price one shilling. On 2 April Dickens and Catherine Hogarth were married.

Seymour completed seven plates. On 20 April he took his own life. There the *Pickwick* project might have ended had not Dickens taken the initiative from near the start. As it was, a replacement for Seymour had to be found. R. W. Buss contributed two plates before the publishers settled on Hablot Knight Browne, whose pseudonym was 'Phiz'. Thus began the effervescent partnership of 'Boz' and 'Phiz'. *Pickwick* sold slowly to begin with, just a few hundred a month. By the summer of 1836 it had caught the public imagination, largely due to Dickens's decision (following encouragement by friends) to keep the character of Sam Weller firmly in the foreground as Mr Pickwick's manservant. The combination of Pickwick's genial and occasionally pompous innocence and Sam's boisterous, resourceful canniness struck many contemporaries as the repetition, in an English idiom, of the classic comic partnership of Don Quixote and Sancho Panza. As *The Metropolitan Magazine* commented in January 1837, 'The renowned Mr Pickwick is, himself, the legitimate successor to Don Quixote; indeed he is the Cockney Quixote of the nineteenth century.' A century later another classic master-servant relationship developed the same comic inversion whereby the naïve master is protected by the superior resourcefulness of his social subordinate: P. G. Wodehouse, who brought together Bertie Wooster and Jeeves, thought *Pickwick* the greatest humorous book in the language. Sam and the 'Cockney Quixote', together with Dickens's vivid sketches of London and country life through each episode, made *Pickwick* an extraordinary success. By the end of its run, in November 1837, its monthly circulation had reached 40,000. Dickens had catapulted himself into national, even international, celebrity.

These origins help in answering the questions about what kind of a book *Pickwick* is. In its earliest phases it was never designed as a novel. It was to be a monthly sequence of four comic prints with some accompanying narrative text. Then it became an illustrated episodic series of misadventures (the plates now reduced to two per number), involving three young members of a club presided over by a retired businessman. Later still, one particular comic episode, Mrs Bardell's mistaking Pickwick's talk of engaging Sam as a proposal of marriage to herself, generated two important changes of direction: Sam's retention as a major character, and Pickwick's entanglement with the law, leading to the trial and to his imprisonment. From that point on, more or less from Number 5 in August 1836, the centrifugal comic Adventures and Perambulations of the Pickwickians are counterpointed by the centripetal pull of London and the legal process. This development increasingly restricts that relatively aimless freedom of movement which had been the *raison d'être* of the original design, and it begins to turn an episodic literary ramble into a plotted novel. *Pickwick Papers* starts as a continuation of the *Sketches by Boz* and then turns into a comic novel. In February 1836, when Chapman and Hall and Dickens first agreed terms over *Pickwick*, neither party envisaged a novel. As Kathryn Chittick has persuasively shown (*Dickens and the 1830s* [1990], Chapter 4), Dickens was still planning to continue his series of sketches and tales for the *Morning Chronicle* and *Library of Fiction*. 'The Tuggs's at Ramsgate' was written in that February, and another tale was in planning stage. At the same time Dickens was writing the comic 'sketches' that constitute the opening few numbers of *Pickwick Papers*.

Pickwick as a literary genre belonged to 'periodical amusements' or 'magazines' as far as the contemporary reviews were concerned, not to 'Literature' or 'Novels'. It had no definite ending date: 'the series will be completed in about twenty numbers', announced an advertisement in *The Athenaeum* a few days before the first number was published. It was a free-wheeling, speculative literary enterprise, its ear close to the ground of public opinion and, through its serial format, quickly responsive to popular taste (hence the prominence of Sam Weller). Like a modern television soap opera, much of its direction and duration depended on the way it adjusted itself in mid-career to the public response.

From the start Dickens hedged his bets by offering his readers the sort of miscellany familiar in popular journalism as well as in the programmes of the popular theatre. Farce, satire and Grand Guignol followed each other erratically as the months went by. The staple comic misadventures were interrupted now and again by the recounting of gruesome tales of terminal alcoholism, murder and mania. Just as in plot terms Dickens developed the contrary pulls between the discursive rambling impulse of the Pickwickians and the legal snares laid for them in London, so he relied on tonal contrasts between his dark Gothic tales and his sunny farcical adventures. As the narrator observes at the end of the book: 'There are dark shadows on the earth, but its lights are stronger in contrast' (p. 775). All Dickens's early novels endorse this contrast as a principle of their design, the light and the dark, the benevolent and the wicked, countryside and metropolis, but none more so than *Pickwick Papers*. Most of the dark tales occur in the first half of the novel where the main narrative focuses on the high-spirited optimism of the club members. After the mid-point, the Dingley Dell Christmas, come the trial and imprisonment. The scenes in the Fleet introduce Pickwick and the reader to sombre and squalid experiences which render unnecessary any further interpolated tales of that kind. In fact, only two more tales appear in the second half, the legend of Prince Bladud and the Bagman's Uncle, neither of which dwells on the lurid sensational horrors of their predecessors.

At the end of its run, *Pickwick*'s twenty parts were bound into a single volume and sold for a guinea. As Kathryn Chittick has pointed out, Chapman and Hall had the option of issuing the finished book in a three-volume format, which would have made it eligible as a 'novel' for the lucrative circulating-library fiction market. But they didn't. 'Thus,' remarks Chittick, 'even in its binding, *Pickwick* belies its classification as a novel as the 1830s publishing world understood it' (*op. cit.*, pp. 69–70). Chittick also draws attention to a remark made some thirty-five years later by Edward Morgan, who was Richard Bentley's chief clerk at the time, in August 1836, when Dickens agreed a contract with Bentley for two three-volume novels. Morgan thought it rash of Bentley to commit himself to a writer 'then almost unknown, & who had certainly not yet written a novel – for the "Pickwick" papers, could not be then considered in that light' ('Brief Retrospect' [1873] in *Publisher's Archives: Richard Bentley & Son 1829–98* [Cambridge, 1976]). The 'then' refers to *Pickwick* after its first five monthly numbers had appeared, when it gave no indication of being planned as a novel.

So, to the question what kind of book is *Pickwick Papers*, the answer must be not only that it is in its finished form a hybrid – part magazine miscellany, part episodic adventure serial, part novel – but that it was always changing its generic identity as it evolved, just as its author was discovering his own literary métier as he improvised from month to month for over a year and a half.

This brings us to the second question posed at the beginning of this introduction: where did *Pickwick* come from? There are two aspects to this question, the nature of its authorship and the literary stock from which it grew.

At the end of the book Dickens writes: 'It is the fate of all authors or chroniclers to create imaginary friends, and lose them in the course of art' (pp. 775–6). 'Author', 'chronicler', 'art' – these terms have a cultural prestige which Dickens may well have felt he had earned by November 1837, when reviewers were seriously comparing him with Fielding and Smollett, and when he had signed up with Bentley as a professional novelist. But 'author' and 'art' seem somewhat remote from the way he styled himself and his literary function at the start of *Pickwick*. There, as in the wrapper title, he is the 'editor' of the papers recording the activities and reflections of the Pickwick Club. The merits he mock-grandiloquently claims for his role are 'the careful attention, indefatigable assiduity, and nice discrimination, with which his search among the multifarious documents confided to him has been conducted' (p. 3). These are specifically editorial merits which Boz is archly assuming as he introduces his project.

So Dickens starts as an 'editor' and ends as an 'author'. Both roles involve considerable stylistic posturing. Just as the substance of *Pickwick* is a medley of modes, so its creator tries out different voices. Most novice writers test out different voices, and experiment with a range of fictional modes, before establishing their own distinctive identity; but they do so in ways both more discrete and discreet. Their first few novels or short stories may differ stylistically from one another, but at least in each separate text the writer is likely to aim for a consistency of voice. They don't generally parade their changes of mind within a single work. But young Dickens does. Perhaps because he never initially thought of the project as a novel, his literary apprenticeship in *Pickwick Papers* is a multi-act spectacular on its own. He is a brilliantly versatile soloist, as his public readings twenty years later demonstrated in another kind of performance. As Paul Schlicke has shown (*Dickens and Popular Entertainment* [1985]), Dickens, in referring to himself as 'Mr Pickwick's Stage-Manager' ('Address' to Number 10, January 1837), saw his role as author as analogous to that of the great fairground manager, John Richardson. But Dickens is both manager and performer. He ranges from mock-portentous minuting of club proceedings to high-spirited satire of Parliamentary by-elections, from mannered melodramatic rhetoric in the tales to sententious reflections on human experience. The editorial detachment announced in the book's title and facetiously paraded in the opening chapters is not sustained for long. The indecision about the kind of narrator he is to be, about the relation of the narrator to his material and to his readership is both part of the problem with *Pickwick* and part of its fun. The narrator is as versatile an impersonator and improvisor as Alfred Jingle (he's also making his money by exploiting these talents). The fact that Dickens casts the vivacious and self-confidently improvising actor as his first villain is a delightful irony: Jingle, with much of his author's own extraordinary verbal energy, imagination and quick wit, steals both Rachael and the limelight in the early part of the book.

To see the author as a literary chameleon is one part of the response to the question where did *Pickwick* come from. The other part concerns its literary ancestry. Its original conception as a popular series of plates and accompanying letterpress about Cockney sportsmen meant that it was drawing on popular culture even before Dickens was approached as a writer. It was to exploit comically the divisions between city and country life, a stock resource in popular literature of the time. In chronicling the misadventures in the country of naïve Londoners, *Pickwick* was an interesting reversal of the more traditional comic confrontation between the gullible countryman and the astute city dweller. Once Dickens took on the idea, he developed the theme of 'innocents abroad', and the 'abroad' meant anywhere in England, town or country, that lay beyond the pale of the club's premises. He confronts the naïve Pickwick with not only wily London cabmen, lawyers and vagrant confidence tricksters, but also a range of experiences, directly or vicariously (through the dark tales told to Pickwick), of which he had very little idea, so sheltered evidently was his life as a businessman. As in the *Sketches by Boz*, part of Dickens's aim was to acquaint his middle-class readers with scenes and experiences increasingly unfamiliar to them. 'Newgate' and 'Gothic' fiction play their part in the resulting collage of *Pickwick*, side by side with efforts at documentary realism. As Terry Eagleton has remarked, each of Dickens's early novels 'is a veritable trafficjam of competing fictional modes – Gothic, Romance, moral fable, "social problem" novel, popular theatre, "short story", journalism, episodic "entertainment" – which permits "realism" no privileged status' (*Criticism and Ideology* [1976], p. 126). *Pickwick*'s literary ancestry is extraordinarily diverse. As already noted (and as the section on 'Dickens and his Critics' demonstrates), the early reviews recognised in *Pickwick* the reworking of several familiar veins of humour and picaresque adventure. Among Dickens's contemporaries they identified *Pickwick* prototypes in the work of Thomas Hood, John Poole's *Little Pedlington*, Pierce Egan, Theodore Hook, Washington Irving and others; and from the eighteenth century, Fielding, Smollett, Goldsmith and Sterne. Reviews sometimes made it sound as if *Pickwick* were little more than an expansive, vivacious mosaic, composed of dozens of bright pastiches. *The Athenaeum* gave what it thought to be the recipe: 'two pounds of Smollett, three ounces of Sterne, a handful of Hook, a dash of grammatical Pierce Egan' (3 December 1836, p. 841).

Dickens certainly was a brilliant pasticheur and ventriloquist. He came to *Pickwick* with his head full of the characters, settings, authorial self-assertions and stylistic cadences of his favourite childhood reading and theatre-going. It is not surprising that, given the generous publication space and relatively open brief of *Pickwick*, he should draw so much on all that stored miscellaneous material to produce something new, which was none the less rooted in traditional popular culture. Those roots are deep. Monthly publication makes Dickens into a professional story-teller of the old folk kind, gathering together his listeners at regular intervals to enjoy a potpourri of make-believe adventures. He repeats this pattern within the narrative itself when he gathers his fictional characters together to listen to stories told by other characters. This reflexivity is one of the delights of the book: an 'editor' self-consciously reports to his readers the experiences of characters who, as Members of a Corresponding Society, are supposedly *themselves* reporting on their experiences; and among those experiences are self-contained stories which give those Members almost identical status with the monthly readers of *Pickwick*. The whole enterprise is obsessed with the idea and practice of story-telling and reporting. Through such strategies, month by month, the book's events and characters threaded themselves into the real lives of the readers. The obituarist of the *Illustrated London News*, writing about 'The Late Charles Dickens' in June 1870, recalled the experience of reading serialised Dickens in the early days:

> It was just as if we received a letter or a visit, at regular intervals, from a kindly observant gossip, who was in the habit of watching the domestic life of the Nicklebys or the Chuzzlewits, and who would let us know from time to time how they were going on. There was no assumption in general, of having a complete and finished story to deliver . . . . The course of his narrative seemed to run on, somehow, almost simultaneously with the real progress of events . . . .

Pickwick Papers was the most popular comic novel of the most popular novelist of the Victorian age. It drew heavily on popular culture and ever since it has contributed generously to that culture. Over the last century and a half, it has gone in and out of critical fashion, as the later section on 'Dickens and his Critics' indicates; but that says more about critical fashion than about the novel. Perhaps, now at the end of Dickens's millennium, it is due for a critical come-back. *Pickwick*'s highly coloured, playful, pastiche-oriented, self-reflexive modes, *Pickwick* with all its jaunty *bricolage*, might seem particularly congenial to post-modern tastes. But oddly it has yet to attract much substantial critical attention of this kind.

It is one of those books whose colossal reputation nearly always precedes the reading. Long before I had known or cared much about Dickens I knew that my grandfather read it time and time again. I have the image of him, nestled into his armchair, pipe in mouth and sitting with legs crossed so that one slippered foot would wag vigorously in the air whenever a particular passage tickled him. It is hard to laugh with a lighted pipe in your mouth. When I inherited his copy of *Pickwick*, I discovered odd patches of powdery grey ash caught in the spine of certain pages, where a comic passage must have caused the pipe to erupt. I even thought it possible to gauge the comic power of *Pickwick* by comparing the size of the ash traces: the scale of spillage on some of the Weller pages was positively Vesuvian.

Dickens had a good idea of *Pickwick*'s immortality even before he had reached the halfway point in its composition. He wrote to his publishers on 1 November 1836:

> If I were to live a hundred years, and write three novels in each, I should never be so proud of any of them, as I am of Pickwick, feeling as I do, that it has made its own way, and hoping, as I must own I do hope, that long after my hand is withered as the pens it held, Pickwick will be found on many a dusty shelf with many a better work. [Pilgrim I, 189]

MALCOLM ANDREWS

NOTE ON THE TEXT AND ILLUSTRATIONS

The first edition of *Pickwick Papers* was in serial form. The full title was *The Posthumous Papers of the Pickwick Club containing a Faithful Record of the Perambulations, Perils, Travels, Adventures and Sporting Transactions of the Corresponding Members*: these *Papers* purported to be 'Edited by "Boz"'. It was published as twenty monthly instalments, selling for one shilling each, from April 1836 to November 1837. The last issue was a two-shilling double number. No issue appeared for June 1837, as a result of Dickens's grief over the sudden death of his sister-in-law, Mary Hogarth. Only about forty-five pages of the original manuscript survive, scattered in various libraries in Britain and America. The front-wrapper design for the monthly numbers was the work of Robert Seymour, who contributed the seven plates for the first two numbers before his suicide in April 1836. Seymour was replaced, briefly, by R. W. Buss, whose plates, 'The Cricket Match' (chosen to feature on the recent issue of the £10 note) and 'The Fat boy awake on this occasion only', appeared in Number 3. Both these plates are included in the present edition. Buss in turn was replaced by Hablot Knight Browne, who completed all the remaining ones and re-etched the second Buss plate. Browne redesigned and re-etched many of his earliest plates for the novels, and this edition includes, in Appendix C, four examples of 'second-state' plates which show substantial alterations. For detailed discussion of the original and subsequent illustrations, see Joseph Grego's *Pictorial Pickwickiana* (1899).

A cloth-bound single-volume edition was published in November 1837, priced at twenty-one shillings. Subsequent authoritative editions of this much pirated and parodied book appeared more or less every ten years: the Cheap Edition in 1847, was published both in serial and single-volume form and carried a substantial Preface; the Library Edition followed in 1858 and the Charles Dickens Edition of 1867 completed the main editions published during Dickens's lifetime.

The Charles Dickens Edition, which is the basis for this Everyman paperback edition of the text, reflects the changes which Dickens introduced to *Pickwick* over the thirty years following its original publication. These have been detailed in James Kinsley's Clarendon edition of the novel (1986). They included modifications in grammar and expression, the removal of profanities, colloquialisms and vulgarisms, and some reduction of the macabre.

In the present edition I have intervened very slightly, silently emending obvious misspellings and erroneous punctuation. In this work I am very grateful to my Research Assistant, Michael Flavin. The division of the monthly numbers is indicated in the table of contents.

TO

MR SERJEANT TALFOURD,[1] M.P.,

ETC., ETC

My Dear Sir,

If I had not enjoyed the happiness of your private friendship, I should still have dedicated this work to you, as a slight and most inadequate acknowledgment of the inestimable services you are rendering to the literature of your country, and of the lasting benefits you will confer upon the authors of this and succeeding generations, by securing to them and their descendants a permanent interest in the copyright[2] of their works.

Many a fevered head and palsied hand will gather new vigour in the hour of sickness and distress from your excellent exertions; many a widowed mother and orphan child, who would otherwise reap nothing from the fame of departed genius but its too frequent legacy of poverty and suffering, will bear, in their altered condition, higher testimony to the value of your labours than the most lavish encomiums from lip or pen could ever afford.

Beside such tributes, any avowal of feeling from me, on the question to which you have devoted the combined advantages of your eloquence, character, and genius, would be powerless indeed. Nevertheless, in thus publicly expressing my deep and grateful sense of your efforts in behalf of English literature, and of those who devote themselves to the most precarious of all pursuits, I do but imperfect justice to my own strong feelings on the subject, if I do no service to you.

These few sentences would have comprised all I should have had to say, if I had only known you in your public character. On the score of private feeling, let me add one word more.

Accept the dedication of this book, my dear Sir, as a mark of my warmest regard and esteem – as a memorial of the most gratifying friendship I have ever contracted, and of some of the pleasantest hours I have ever spent – as a token of my fervent admiration of every fine quality of your head and heart – as an assurance of the truth and sincerity with which I shall ever be,

My dear Sir,
Most faithfully and sincerely yours,
CHARLES DICKENS.

48, DOUGHTY STREET,
   SEPTEMBER 27, 1837.

Frontispiece to first volume edition

PREFACE TO THE FIRST EDITION (1837)

The author's object in this work, was to place before the reader a constant succession of characters and incidents; to paint them in as vivid colours as he could command; and to render them, at the same time, life-like and amusing.

Deferring to the judgment of others in the outset of the undertaking, he adopted the machinery of the club, which was suggested as that best adapted to his purpose; but, finding that it tended rather to his embarrassment than otherwise, he gradually abandoned it, considering it a matter of very little importance to the work whether strictly epic justice were awarded to the club, or not.

The publication of the book in monthly numbers, containing only thirty-two pages in each, rendered it an object of paramount importance that, while the different incidents were linked together by a chain of interest strong enough to prevent their appearing unconnected or impossible, the general design should be so simple as to sustain no injury from this detached and desultory form of publication, extending over no fewer than twenty months. In short, it was necessary – or it appeared so to the author – that every number should be, to a certain extent, complete in itself, and yet that the whole twenty numbers, when collected, should form one tolerably harmonious whole, each leading to the other by a gentle and not unnatural progress of adventure.

It is obvious that in a work published with a view to such considerations, no artfully interwoven or ingeniously complicated plot can with reason be expected. The author ventures to express a hope that he has successfully surmounted the difficulties of his undertaking. And if it be objected to the Pickwick Papers, that they are a mere series of adventures, in which the scenes are ever changing, and the characters come and go like the men and women we encounter in the real world, he can only content himself with the reflection, that they claim to be nothing else, and that the same objection has been made to the works of some of the greatest novelists in the English language.

The following pages have been written from time to time, almost as the periodical occasion arose. Having been written for the most part in the society of a very dear young friend,[1] who is now no more, they are connected in the author's mind at once with the happiest period of his life, and with its saddest and most severe affliction.

It is due to the gentleman,[2] whose designs accompany the letter-press, to state that the interval has been so short between the production of each number in manuscript and its appearance in print, that the greater portion of the Illustrations have been executed by the artist from the author's mere verbal description of what he intended to write.

The almost unexampled kindness and favour with which these papers have been received by the public will be a never-failing source of gratification and pleasant recollection while their author lives. He trusts that, throughout this book, no incident or expression occurs which could call a blush into the most delicate cheek, or wound the feelings of the most sensitive person. If any of his imperfect descriptions, while they afford amusement in the perusal, should induce only one reader to think better of his fellow men, and to look upon the brighter and more kindly side of human nature, he would indeed be proud and happy to have led to such a result.

PREFACE TO THE CHARLES DICKENS EDITION (1867)

It was observed, in the Preface to the original Edition of the 'Posthumous Papers of the Pickwick Club,' that they were designed for the introduction of diverting characters and incidents; that no ingenuity of plot was attempted, or even at that time considered very feasible by the author in connexion with the desultory mode of publication adopted; and that the machinery of the Club, proving cumbrous in the management, was gradually abandoned as the work progressed. Although, on one of these points, experience and study afterwards taught me something, and I could perhaps wish now that these chapters were strung together on a stronger thread of general interest, still, what they are they were designed to be.

I have seen various accounts of the origin of these Pickwick Papers, which have, at all events, possessed – for me – the charm of perfect novelty. As I may infer, from the occasional appearance of such histories, that my readers have an interest in the matter, I will relate how they came into existence.

I was a young man of two or three-and-twenty, when MESSRS.

CHAPMAN and HALL, attracted by some pieces I was at that time writing in the Morning Chronicle[1] newspaper, or had just written in the Old Monthly Magazine[2] (of which one series had lately been collected and published in two volumes,[3] illustrated by MR GEORGE CRUIKSHANK),[4] waited upon me to propose a something that should be published in shilling numbers – then only known to me, or, I believe, to anybody else, by a dim recollection of certain interminable novels in that form, which used to be carried about the country by pedlars, and over some of which I remember to have shed innumerable tears before I had served my apprenticeship to Life.

When I opened my door in Furnival's Inn[5] to the partner who represented the firm, I recognised in him the person from whose hands I had bought, two or three years previously, and whom I had never seen before or since, my first copy of the Magazine in which my first effusion – a paper in the 'Sketches,' called MR MINNS AND HIS COUSIN – dropped stealthily one evening at twilight, with fear and trembling, into a dark letter-box, in a dark office, up a dark court in Fleet Street – appeared in all the glory of print; on which occasion I walked down to Westminster Hall,[6] and turned into it for half-an-hour, because my eyes were so dimmed with joy and pride, that they could not bear the street, and were not fit to be seen there. I told my visitor of the coincidence, which we both hailed as a good omen; and so fell to business.

The idea propounded to me, was, that the monthly something should be a vehicle for certain plates to be executed by MR SEYMOUR;[7] and there was a notion, either on the part of that admirable humorous artist, or of my visitor, that a 'NIMROD CLUB,'[8] the members of which were to go out shooting, fishing, and so forth, and getting themselves into difficulties through their want of dexterity, would be the best means of introducing these. I objected, on consideration, that although born and partly bred in the country I was no great sportsman, except in regard to all kinds of locomotion; that the idea was not novel, and had been already much used; that it would be infinitely better for the plates to arise naturally out of the text; and that I would like to take my own way, with a freer range of English scenes and people, and was afraid I should ultimately do so in any case, whatever course I might prescribe to myself at starting. My views being deferred to, I thought of MR PICKWICK, and wrote the first number; from the proof sheets of which, MR SEYMOUR made his drawing of the Club, and his happy portrait of its founder: – the latter on MR

EDWARD CHAPMAN'S[9] description of the dress and bearing of a
real personage whom he had often seen. I connected MR PICKWICK
with a club, because of the original suggestion, and I put in Mr
Winkle expressly for the use of MR SEYMOUR. We started with a
number of twenty-four pages[10] instead of thirty-two, and four
illustrations in lieu of a couple. MR SEYMOUR's sudden and
lamented death before the second number was published, brought
about a quick decision upon a point already in agitation; the
number became one of thirty-two pages with only two illustrations,
and remained so to the end.

It is with great unwillingness that I notice some intangible and
incoherent assertions[11] which have been made, professedly on
behalf of MR SEYMOUR, to the effect that he had some share in the
invention of this book, or of anything in it, not faithfully described
in the foregoing paragraph. With the moderation that is due equally
to my respect for the memory of a brother-artist, and to my self-
respect, I confine myself to placing on record here the facts:

That, MR SEYMOUR never originated or suggested an incident, a
phrase, or a word, to be found in this book. That, MR SEYMOUR
died when only twenty-four pages[12] of this book were published,
and when assuredly not forty-eight were written. That, I believe I
never saw MR SEYMOUR's hand-writing in my life. That, I never saw
MR SEYMOUR but once in my life, and that was on the night but one
before his death, when he certainly offered no suggestion whatsoever. That I saw him then in presence of two persons, both living,
perfectly acquainted with all these facts, and whose written testimony to them I possess. Lastly, that MR EDWARD CHAPMAN (the
survivor of the original firm of CHAPMAN and HALL) has set down
in writing, for similar preservation, his personal knowledge of the
origin and progress of this book, of the monstrosity of the baseless
assertions in question, and (tested by details) even of the self-evident
impossibility of there being any truth in them. In the exercise of the
forbearance on which I have resolved, I do not quote MR EDWARD
CHAPMAN's account of his deceased partner's reception, on a certain
occasion, of the pretences in question.

'Boz,' my signature in the Morning Chronicle, and in the Old
Monthly Magazine, appended to the monthly cover of this book,
and retained long afterwards, was the nickname of a pet child, a
younger brother, whom I had dubbed Moses, in honour of the
Vicar of Wakefield; which being facetiously pronounced through
the nose, became Boses, and being shortened, became Boz. Boz was

a very familiar household word to me, long before I was an author, and so I came to adopt it.

It has been observed of Mr Pickwick, that there is a decided change in his character, as these pages proceed, and that he becomes more good and more sensible. I do not think this change will appear forced or unnatural to my readers, if they will reflect that in real life the peculiarities and oddities of a man who has anything whimsical about him, generally impress us first, and that it is not until we are better acquainted with him that we usually begin to look below these superficial traits, and to know the better part of him.

Lest there should be any well-intentioned persons who do not perceive the difference (as some such could not, when OLD MORTALITY[13] was newly published), between religion and the cant of religion, piety and the pretence of piety, a humble reverence for the great truths of Scripture and an audacious and offensive obtrusion of its letter and not its spirit in the commonest dissensions and meanest affairs of life, to the extraordinary confusion of ignorant minds, let them understand that it is always the latter, and never the former, which is satirized here. Further, that the latter is here satirized as being, according to all experience, inconsistent with the former, impossible of union with it, and one of the most evil and mischievous falsehoods existent in society – whether it establish its head-quarters, for the time being, in Exeter Hall, or Ebenezer Chapel,[14] or both. It may appear unnecessary to offer a word of observation on so plain a head. But it is never out of season to protest against that coarse familiarity with sacred things which is busy on the lip, and idle in the heart; or against the confounding of Christianity with any class of persons who, in the words of SWIFT,[15] have just enough religion to make them hate, and not enough to make them love, one another.

I have found it curious and interesting, looking over the sheets of this reprint, to mark what important social improvements have taken place about us, almost imperceptibly, since they were originally written. The licence of Counsel, and the degree to which Juries are ingeniously bewildered, are yet susceptible of moderation; while an improvement in the mode of conducting Parliamentary Elections (and even Parliaments too, perhaps) is still within the bounds of possibility. But legal reforms have pared the claws of Messrs. Dodson and Fogg; a spirit of self-respect, mutual forbearance, education, and co-operation for such good ends, has diffused itself among their clerks; places far apart are brought together, to the present convenience and advantage of the Public, and to the certain destruction, in time, of a host of petty jealousies, blindnesses, and prejudices, by which the Public alone have always been the sufferers; the laws relating to imprisonment for debt are altered; and the Fleet Prison[16] is pulled down!

Who knows, but by the time the series reaches its conclusion, it may be discovered that there are even magistrates in town and country, who should be taught to shake hands every day with Common-sense and Justice; that even Poor Laws[17] may have mercy on the weak, the aged, and unfortunate; that Schools, on the broad principles of Christianity,[18] are the best adornment for the length and breadth of this civilised land; that Prison-doors should be barred on the outside, no less heavily and carefully than they are barred within; that the universal diffusion of common means of decency and health is as much the right of the poorest of the poor, as it is indispensable to the safety of the rich, and of the State; that a few petty boards and bodies – less than drops in the great ocean of humanity, which roars around them – are not for ever to let loose Fever and Consumption on God's creatures at their will, or always to keep their jobbing little fiddles going, for a Dance of Death.*

* The Preface to the Charles Dickens Edition is substantially the same as the Preface to the Cheap Edition (1847) and the Library Edition (1858), with one major exception: in 1867 Dickens added the two paragraphs on the Seymour controversy, from 'It is with great unwillingness . . .' to '. . . of the pretences in question' (p. xl). See note 11 to this Preface. All the other changes to the Prefaces are recorded in James Kinsley's Clarendon edition of the novel, pp. 883–8.

THE

𝕻𝖔𝖘𝖙𝖍𝖚𝖒𝖔𝖚𝖘 𝕻𝖆𝖕𝖊𝖗𝖘

OF

THE PICKWICK CLUB.

BY CHARLES DICKENS.

WITH

FORTY-THREE ILLUSTRATIONS, BY R. SEYMOUR AND

PHIZ.

LONDON

CHAPMAN AND HALL, 186, STRAND

MDCCCXXXVII.

[The title page of the first edition, 1837]

THE PICKWICK PAPERS

THE

PICKWICK PAPERS

BY

CHARLES DICKENS.

PHIZ. fecit.

Title-page vignette

CHAPTER I

The Pickwickians

The first ray of light which illumines the gloom, and converts into a dazzling brilliancy that obscurity in which the earlier history of the public career of the immortal Pickwick would appear to be involved, is derived from the perusal of the following entry in the Transactions of the Pickwick Club, which the editor of these papers feels the highest pleasure in laying before his readers, as a proof of the careful attention, indefatigable assiduity, and nice discrimination, with which his search among the multifarious documents confided to him has been conducted.

'May 12, 1827.[1] Joseph Smiggers, Esq., PVPMPC,* presiding. The following resolutions unanimously agreed to: –

'That this Association has heard read, with feelings of unmingled satisfaction, and unqualified approval, the paper communicated by Samuel Pickwick, Esq., GCMPC,† entitled "Speculations on the Source of the Hampstead Ponds, with some Observations on the Theory of Tittlebats;"[2] and that this Association does hereby return its warmest thanks to the said Samuel Pickwick, Esq., GCMPC, for the same.

'That while this Association is deeply sensible of the advantages which must accrue to the cause of science from the production to which they have just adverted, – no less than from the unwearied researches of Samuel Pickwick, Esq., GCMPC, in Hornsey, Highgate, Brixton, and Camberwell,[3] – they cannot but entertain a lively sense of the inestimable benefits which must inevitably result from carrying the speculations of that learned man into a wider field, from extending his travels, and consequently enlarging his sphere of observation, to the advancement of knowledge,[4] and the diffusion of learning.

'That, with the view just mentioned, this Association has taken into its serious consideration a proposal, emanating from the aforesaid Samuel Pickwick, Esq., GCMPC, and three other Pickwickians hereinafter named, for forming a new branch of United

* Perpetual Vice-President – Member Pickwick-Club.
† General Chairman – Member Pickwick Club.

Pickwickians, under the title of The Corresponding Society of the Pickwick Club.

'That the said proposal has received the sanction and approval of this Association.

'That the Corresponding Society of the Pickwick Club is therefore hereby constituted; and that Samuel Pickwick, Esq., GCMPC, Tracy Tupman, Esq., MPC, Augustus Snodgrass, Esq., MPC, and Nathaniel Winkle, Esq., MPC, are hereby nominated and appointed members of the same; and that they be requested to forward, from time to time, authenticated accounts of their journeys and investigations, of their observations of character and manners, and of the whole of their adventures, together with all tales and papers to which local scenery or associations may give rise, to the Pickwick Club, stationed in London.

'That this Association cordially recognises the principle of every member of the Corresponding Society defraying his own travelling expenses; and that it sees no objection whatever to the members of the said society pursuing their inquiries for any length of time they please, upon the same terms.

'That the members of the aforesaid Corresponding Society be, and are, hereby informed, that their proposal to pay the postage of their letters, and the carriage of their parcels, has been deliberated upon by this Association: that this Association considers such proposal worthy of the great minds from which it emanated, and that it hereby signifies its perfect acquiescence therein.'

A casual observer, adds the secretary, to whose notes we are indebted for the following account – a casual observer might possibly have remarked nothing extraordinary in the bald head, and circular spectacles, which were intently turned towards his (the secretary's) face, during the reading of the above resolutions: to those who knew that the gigantic brain of Pickwick was working beneath that forehead, and that the beaming eyes of Pickwick were twinkling behind those glasses, the sight was indeed an interesting one. There sat the man who had traced to their source the mighty ponds of Hampstead, and agitated the scientific world with his Theory of Tittlebats, as calm and unmoved as the deep waters of the one on a frosty day, or as a solitary specimen of the other in the inmost recesses of an earthen jar. And how much more interesting did the spectacle become, when, starting into full life and animation, as a simultaneous call for 'Pickwick' burst from his followers, that illustrious man slowly mounted into the Windsor chair, on which he had been previously seated, and addressed the club himself had founded. What a study for an artist did that exciting scene present! The eloquent Pickwick, with one hand gracefully concealed behind his coat tails, and the other waving in air, to assist his glowing declamation; his elevated position revealing those tights and gaiters, which, had they clothed an ordinary man, might have passed without observation, but which, when Pickwick clothed them – if we may use the expression – inspired voluntary awe and respect; surrounded by the men who had volunteered to share the perils of his travels, and who were destined to participate in the glories of his discoveries. On his right hand sat Mr Tracy Tupman – the too susceptible Tupman, who to the wisdom and experience of maturer years superadded the enthusiasm and ardour of a boy, in the most interesting and pardonable of human weaknesses – love. Time and feeding had expanded that once romantic form; the black silk waistcoat had become more and more developed; inch by inch had the gold watch-chain beneath it disappeared from within the range of Tupman's vision; and gradually had the capacious chin encroached upon the borders of the white cravat: but the soul of Tupman had known no change – admiration of the fair sex was still its ruling passion. On the left of his great leader sat the poetic Snodgrass, and near him again the sporting Winkle, the former poetically enveloped in a mysterious blue cloak with a canine-skin collar, and the latter communicating additional lustre to a new green shooting coat, plaid neckerchief, and closely-fitted drabs.

Mr Pickwick's oration upon this occasion, together with the debate thereon, is entered on the Transactions of the Club. Both bear a strong affinity to the discussions of other celebrated bodies; and, as it is always interesting to trace a resemblance between the proceedings of great men, we transfer the entry to these pages.

'Mr Pickwick observed (says the Secretary) that fame was dear to the heart of every man. Poetic fame was dear to the heart of his friend Snodgrass; the fame of conquest was equally dear to his friend Tupman; and the desire of earning fame in the sports of the field, the air, and the water, was uppermost in the breast of his friend Winkle. He (Mr Pickwick) would not deny that he was influenced by human passions, and human feelings (cheers) – possibly by human weaknesses – (loud cries of 'No'); but this he would say, that if ever the fire of self-importance broke out in his bosom, the desire to benefit the human race in preference effectually quenched it. The praise of mankind was his Swing;[5] philanthropy was his insurance office. (Vehement cheering.) He had felt some pride – he acknowledged it freely, and let his enemies make the

Mr Pickwick addresses the Club

most of it – he had felt some pride when he presented his Tittlebatian Theory to the world; it might be celebrated or it might not. (A cry of 'It is,' and great cheering.) He would take the assertion of that honourable Pickwickian whose voice he had just heard – it was celebrated; but if the fame of that treatise were to extend to the furthest confines of the known world, the pride with which he should reflect on the authorship of that production would be as nothing compared with the pride with which he looked around him, on this, the proudest moment of his existence. (Cheers.) He was a humble individual. (No, no.) Still he could not but feel that they had selected him for a service of great honour, and of some danger. Travelling was in a troubled state, and the minds of coachmen were unsettled. Let them look abroad, and contemplate the scenes which were enacting around them. Stage coaches were upsetting in all directions, horses were bolting, boats were overturning, and boilers were bursting. (Cheers – a voice 'No.') No! (Cheers.) Let that honourable Pickwickian who cried 'No' so loudly come forward and deny it, if he could. (Cheers.) Who was it that cried 'No?' (Enthusiastic cheering.) Was it some vain and disappointed man – he would not say haberdasher – (loud cheers) – who, jealous of the praise which had been – perhaps undeservedly – bestowed on his (Mr Pickwick's) researches, and smarting under the censure which had been heaped upon his own feeble attempts at rivalry, now took this vile and calumnious mode of—

'Mr BLOTTON (of Aldgate) rose to order. Did the honourable Pickwickian allude to him? (Cries of 'Order,' 'Chair,' 'Yes,' 'No,' 'Go on,' 'Leave off,' &c.)

'Mr PICKWICK would not put up to be put down by clamour. He *had* alluded to the honourable gentleman. (Great excitement.)

'Mr BLOTTON would only say then, that he repelled the hon. gent.'s false and scurrilous accusation, with profound contempt. (Great cheering.) The hon. gent. was a humbug. (Immense confusion, and loud cries of 'Chair' and 'Order.')

'Mr A. SNODGRASS rose to order. He threw himself upon the chair. (Hear.) He wished to know whether this disgraceful contest between two members of that club should be allowed to continue. (Hear, hear.)

'The CHAIRMAN was quite sure the hon. Pickwickian would withdraw the expression he had just made use of.

'Mr BLOTTON, with all possible respect for the chair, was quite sure he would not.

'The CHAIRMAN felt it his imperative duty to demand of the

honourable gentleman, whether he had used the expression which had just escaped him in a common sense.

'Mr BLOTTON had no hesitation in saying that he had not – he had used the word in its Pickwickian sense.[6] (Hear, hear.) He was bound to acknowledge that, personally, he entertained the highest regard and esteem for the honourable gentleman; he had merely considered him a humbug in a Pickwickian point of view. (Hear, hear.)

'Mr PICKWICK felt much gratified by the fair, candid, and full explanation of his honourable friend. He begged it to be at once understood, that his own observations had been merely intended to bear a Pickwickian construction. (Cheers.)'

Here the entry terminates, as we have no doubt the debate did also, after arriving at such a highly satisfactory and intelligible point. We have no official statement of the facts which the reader will find recorded in the next chapter, but they have been carefully collated from letters and other MS. authorities[7] so unquestionably genuine as to justify their narration in a connected form.

CHAPTER 2

The first Day's Journey, and the first Evening's Adventures; with their Consequences

That punctual servant of all work, the sun, had just risen, and begun to strike a light on the morning of the thirteenth of May, one thousand eight hundred and twenty-seven, when Mr Samuel Pickwick burst like another sun from his slumbers, threw open his chamber window, and looked out upon the world beneath. Goswell Street was at his feet, Goswell Street was on his right hand – as far as the eye could reach, Goswell Street extended on his left; and the opposite side of Goswell Street was over the way. 'Such,' thought Mr Pickwick, 'are the narrow views of those philosophers who, content with examining the things that lie before them, look not to the truths which are hidden beyond. As well might I be content to gaze on Goswell Street for ever, without one effort to penetrate to the hidden countries which on every side surround it.' And having given vent to this beautiful reflection, Mr Pickwick proceeded to put himself into his clothes, and his clothes into his portmanteau. Great men are seldom over scrupulous in the arrangement of their attire; the operation of shaving, dressing, and coffee-imbibing was soon performed: and in another hour, Mr Pickwick, with his portmanteau in his hand, his telescope in his great-coat pocket, and his note-book in his waistcoat, ready for the reception of any discoveries worthy of being noted down, had arrived at the coach stand in St Martin's-le-Grand.[1]

'Cab!' said Mr Pickwick.

'Here you are sir,' shouted a strange specimen of the human race, in a sack-cloth coat, and apron of the same, who with a brass label and number round his neck, looked as if he were catalogued in some collection of rarities. This was the waterman. 'Here you are, sir. Now, then, fust cab!' And the first cab having been fetched from the public-house, where he had been smoking his first pipe, Mr Pickwick and his portmanteau were thrown into the vehicle.

'Golden Cross,'[2] said Mr Pickwick.

'Only a bob's vorth, Tommy,' cried the driver, sulkily, for the information of his friend the waterman, as the cab drove off.

'How old is that horse, my friend?' inquired Mr Pickwick, rubbing his nose with the shilling[3] he had reserved for the fare.

'Forty-two,' replied the driver, eyeing him askant.

'What!' ejaculated Mr Pickwick, laying his hand upon his note-book. The driver reiterated his former statement. Mr Pickwick looked very hard at the man's face, but his features were immovable, so he noted down the fact forthwith.

'And how long do you keep him out at a time?' inquired Mr Pickwick, searching for further information.

'Two or three veeks,' replied the man.

'Weeks!' said Mr Pickwick in astonishment – and out came the note-book again.

'He lives at Pentonwil[4] when he's at home,' observed the driver, coolly, 'but we seldom takes him home, on account of his veakness.'

'On account of his weakness!' reiterated the perplexed Mr Pickwick.

'He always falls down when he's took out o' the cab,' continued the driver, 'but when he's in it, we bears him up werry tight, and takes him in werry short, so as he can't werry well fall down; and we've got a pair o' precious large wheels on, so ven he *does* move, they run after him, and he must go on – he can't help it.'

Mr Pickwick entered every word of this statement in his note-book, with the view of communicating it to the club, as a singular instance of the tenacity of life in horses, under trying circumstances. The entry was scarcely completed when they reached the Golden

Cross. Down jumped the driver, and out got Mr Pickwick. Mr
Tupman, Mr Snodgrass, and Mr Winkle, who had been anxiously
waiting the arrival of their illustrious leader, crowded to welcome
him.

'Here's your fare,' said Mr Pickwick, holding out the shilling to
the driver.

What was the learned man's astonishment, when that unaccountable person flung the money on the pavement, and requested in
figurative terms to be allowed the pleasure of fighting him (Mr
Pickwick) for the amount!

'You are mad,' said Mr Snodgrass.

'Or drunk,' said Mr Winkle.

'Or both,' said Mr Tupman.

'Come on!' said the cab-driver, sparring away like clockwork.
'Come on – all four on you.'

'Here's a lark!' shouted half-a-dozen hackney coachmen. 'Go to
vork, Sam,' – and they crowded with great glee round the party.

'What's the row, Sam?' inquired one gentleman in black calico
sleeves.

'Row!' replied the cabman, 'what did he want my number for?'

'I didn't want your number,' said the astonished Mr Pickwick.

'What did you take it for, then?' inquired the cabman.

'I didn't take it,' said Mr Pickwick, indignantly.

'Would any body believe,' continued the cab-driver, appealing to
the crowd, 'would any body believe as an informer 'ud go about in
a man's cab, not only takin' down his number, but ev'ry word he
says into the bargain' (a light flashed upon Mr Pickwick – it was
the note-book).

'Did he though?' inquired another cabman.

'Yes, did he,' replied the first; 'and then arter aggerawatin' me to
assault him, gets three witnesses here to prove it. But I'll give it him,
if I've six months for it. Come on!' and the cabman dashed his hat
upon the ground, with a reckless disregard of his own private
property, and knocked Mr Pickwick's spectacles off, and followed
up the attack with a blow on Mr Pickwick's nose, and another on
Mr Pickwick's chest, and a third in Mr Snodgrass's eye, and a
fourth, by way of variety, in Mr Tupman's waistcoat, and then
danced into the road, and then back again to the pavement, and
finally dashed the whole temporary supply of breath out of Mr
Winkle's body; and all in half-a-dozen seconds.

'Where's an officer?' said Mr Snodgrass.

'Put'em under the pump,' suggested a hot-pieman.

The Pugnacious Cabman

'You shall smart for this,' gasped Mr Pickwick.

'Informers!' shouted the crowd.

'Come on,' cried the cabman, who had been sparring without cessation the whole time.

The mob had hitherto been passive spectators of the scene, but as the intelligence of the Pickwickians being informers was spread among them, they began to canvass with considerable vivacity the propriety of enforcing the heated pastry-vendor's proposition; and there is no saying what acts of personal aggression they might have committed had not the affray been unexpectedly terminated by the interposition of a new comer.

'What's the fun?' said a rather tall thin young man, in a green coat, emerging suddenly from the coach yard.

'Informers!' shouted the crowd again.

'We are not,' roared Mr Pickwick, in a tone which, to any dispassionate listener, carried conviction with it.

'Ain't you, though, – ain't you?' said the young man, appealing to Mr Pickwick, and making his way through the crowd by the infallible process of elbowing the countenances of its component members.

That learned man in a few hurried words explained the real state of the case.

'Come along, then' said he of the green coat, lugging Mr Pickwick after him by main force, and talking the whole way. 'Here, No. 924, take your fare, and take yourself off – respectable gentleman, – know him well – none of your nonsense – this way, sir, – where's your friends? – all a mistake, I see – never mind – accidents will happen – best regulated families – never say die – down upon your luck – pull him up – put that in his pipe – like the flavour – damned rascals.' And with a lengthened string of similar broken sentences, delivered with extraordinary volubility, the stranger led the way to the travellers' waiting-room, whither he was closely followed by Mr Pickwick and his disciples.

'Here, waiter!' shouted the stranger, ringing the bell with tremendous violence, 'glasses round, – brandy and water, hot and strong, and sweet, and plenty, – eye damaged, sir? Waiter! raw beef-steak for the gentleman's eye, – nothing like raw beef-steak for a bruise, sir; cold lamp-post very good, but lamp-post inconvenient – damned odd standing in the open street half-an-hour, with your eye against a lamp-post – eh, – very good – ha! ha!' And the stranger, without stopping to take breath, swallowed at a draught full half-a-pint of the reeking brandy and water, and flung himself into a chair with as much ease as if nothing uncommon had occurred.

While his three companions were busily engaged in proffering their thanks to their new acquaintance, Mr Pickwick had leisure to examine his costume and appearance.

He was about the middle height, but the thinness of his body, and the length of his legs, gave him the appearance of being much taller. The green coat had been a smart dress garment in the days of swallow-tails, but had evidently in those times adorned a much shorter man than the stranger, for the soiled and faded sleeves scarcely reached to his wrists. It was buttoned closely up to his chin, at the imminent hazard of splitting the back; and an old stock, without a vestige of shirt collar, ornamented his neck. His scanty black trousers displayed here and there those shiny patches which bespeak long service, and were strapped very tightly over a pair of patched and mended shoes, as if to conceal the dirty white stockings, which were nevertheless distinctly visible. His long black hair escaped in negligent waves from beneath each side of his old pinched up hat; and glimpses of his bare wrists might be observed between the tops of his gloves, and the cuffs of his coat sleeves. His face was thin and haggard; but an indescribable air of jaunty impudence and perfect self-possession pervaded the whole man.

Such was the individual on whom Mr Pickwick gazed through his spectacles (which he had fortunately recovered), and to whom he proceeded, when his friends had exhausted themselves, to return in chosen terms his warmest thanks for his recent assistance.

'Never mind,' said the stranger, cutting the address very short, 'said enough, – no more; smart chap that cabman – handled his fives⁵ well; but if I'd been your friend in the green jemmy – damn me – punch his head, – 'cod I would, – pig's whisper – pieman too, – no gammon.'⁶

This coherent speech was interrupted by the entrance of the Rochester coachman, to announce that 'The Commodore' was on the point of starting.

'Commodore!' said the stranger, starting up, 'my coach, – place booked, – one outside – leave you to pay for the brandy and water, – want change for a five, – bad silver – Brummagem buttons – won't do – no go – eh?' and he shook his head most knowingly.

Now it so happened that Mr Pickwick and his three companions had resolved to make Rochester their first halting place too; and having intimated to their new-found acquaintance that they were journeying to the same city, they agreed to occupy the seat at the back of the coach, where they could all sit together.

'Up with you,' said the stranger, assisting Mr Pickwick on to the roof with so much precipitation as to impair the gravity of that gentleman's deportment very materially.

'Any luggage, sir?' inquired the coachman.

'Who – I? Brown paper parcel here, that's all, – other luggage gone by water, – packing cases, nailed up – big as houses – heavy, heavy, damned heavy,' replied the stranger, as he forced into his pocket as much as he could of the brown paper parcel, which presented most suspicious indications of containing one shirt and a handkerchief.

'Heads, heads – take care of your heads!' cried the loquacious stranger, as they came out under the low archway, which in those days formed the entrance to the coach-yard. 'Terrible place – dangerous work – other day – five children – mother – tall lady, eating sandwiches – forgot the arch – crash – knock – children look round – mother's head off – sandwich in her hand – no mouth to put it in – head of a family off – shocking, shocking! Looking at Whitehall, sir? – fine place – little window – somebody else's head off there,[7] eh, sir? – he didn't keep a sharp look-out enough either – eh, sir, eh?'

'I am ruminating,' said Mr Pickwick; 'on the strange mutability of human affairs.'

'Ah! I see – in at the palace door one day, out at the window the next. Philosopher, sir?'

'An observer of human nature, sir,' said Mr Pickwick.

'Ah, so am I. Most people are when they've little to do and less to get. Poet, sir?'

'My friend Mr Snodgrass has a strong poetic turn,' said Mr Pickwick.

'So have I,' said the stranger. 'Epic poem, – ten thousand lines – revolution of July[8] – composed it on the spot – Mars by day, Apollo by night, – bang the field-piece, twang the lyre.'

'You were present at that glorious scene, sir?' said Mr Snodgrass.

'Present! think I was;* fired a musket, – fired with an idea, – rushed into wine shop – wrote it down – back again – whiz, bang – another idea – wine shop again – pen and ink – back again – cut

---

* A remarkable instance of the prophetic force of Mr Jingle's imagination; this dialogue occurring in the year 1827, and the Revolution in 1830.[9]

and slash – noble time, sir. Sportsman, sir?' abruptly turning to Mr Winkle.

'A little, sir,' replied that gentleman.

'Fine pursuit, sir, – fine pursuit. – Dogs, sir?'

'Not just now,' said Mr Winkle.

'Ah! you should keep dogs – fine animals – sagacious creatures – dog of my own once – Pointer – surprising instinct – out shooting one day – entering enclosure – whistled – dog stopped – whistled again – Ponto – no go; stock still – called him – Ponto, Ponto – wouldn't move – dog transfixed – staring at a board – looked up, saw an inscription – "Gamekeeper has orders to shoot all dogs found in this enclosure" – wouldn't pass it – wonderful dog – valuable dog that – very.'

'Singular circumstance that,' said Mr Pickwick. 'Will you allow me to make a note of it?'

'Certainly, sir, certainly – hundred more anecdotes of the same animal. – Fine girl, sir' (to Mr Tracy Tupman, who had been bestowing sundry anti-Pickwickian glances on a young lady by the roadside).

'Very!' said Mr Tupman.

'English girls not so fine as Spanish – noble creatures – jet hair – black eyes – lovely forms – sweet creatures – beautiful.'

'You have been in Spain, sir?' said Mr Tracy Tupman.

'Lived there – ages.'

'Many conquests, sir?' inquired Mr Tupman.

'Conquests! Thousands. Don Bolaro Fizzgig – Grandee – only daughter – Donna Christina – splendid creature – loved me to distraction – jealous father – high-souled daughter – handsome Englishman – Donna Christina in despair – prussic acid – stomach pump in my portmanteau – operation performed – old Bolaro in ecstasies – consent to our union – join hands and floods of tears – romantic story – very.'

'Is the lady in England now, sir?' inquired Mr Tupman, on whom the description of her charms had produced a powerful impression.

'Dead, sir – dead,' said the stranger, applying to his right eye the brief remnant of a very old cambric handkerchief. 'Never recovered the stomach pump – undermined constitution – fell a victim.'

'And her father?' inquired the poetic Snodgrass.

'Remorse and misery,' replied the stranger. 'Sudden disappearance – talk of the whole city – search made everywhere – without success – public fountain in the great square suddenly ceased playing – weeks elapsed – still a stoppage – workmen employed to clean it

NOTICE
THE
GAMEKEEPER
HAS ORDERS
TO SHOOT ALL
DOGS
FOUND IN
THIS
INCLOSURE

The Sagacious Dog

– water drawn off – father-in-law discovered sticking head first in the main pipe, with a full confession in his right boot – took him out, and the fountain played away again, as well as ever.'

'Will you allow me to note that little romance down, sir?' said Mr Snodgrass, deeply affected.

'Certainly, sir, certainly, – fifty more if you like to hear 'em – strange life mine – rather curious history – not extraordinary, but singular.'

In this strain, with an occasional glass of ale, by way of parenthesis, when the coach changed horses, did the stranger proceed, until they reached Rochester bridge, by which time the note-books, both of Mr Pickwick and Mr Snodgrass, were completely filled with selections from his adventures.

'Magnificent ruin!' said Mr Augustus Snodgrass, with all the poetic fervour that distinguished him, when they came in sight of the fine old castle.

'What a study for an antiquarian!' were the very words which fell from Mr Pickwick's mouth, as he applied his telescope to his eye.

'Ah! fine place,' said the stranger, 'glorious pile – frowning walls – tottering arches – dark nooks – crumbling staircases – Old cathedral too – earthy smell – pilgrims' feet worn away the old steps – little Saxon doors – confessionals like money-takers' boxes at theatres – queer customers those monks – Popes, and Lord Treasurers, and all sorts of old fellows, with great red faces, and broken noses, turning up every day – buff jerkins too – match-locks – Sarcophagus – fine place – old legends too – strange stories: capital;' and the stranger continued to soliloquise until they reached the Bull Inn, in the High Street, where the coach stopped.

'Do you remain here, sir?' inquired Mr Nathaniel Winkle.

'Here – not I – but you'd better – good house – nice beds – Wright's next house, dear – very dear – half-a-crown in the bill if you look at the waiter – charge you more if you dine at a friend's than they would if you dined in the coffee-room – rum fellows – very.'

Mr Winkle turned to Mr Pickwick, and murmured a few words; a whisper passed from Mr Pickwick to Mr Snodgrass, from Mr Snodgrass to Mr Tupman, and nods of assent were exchanged. Mr Pickwick addressed the stranger.

'You rendered us a very important service this morning, sir,' said he, 'will you allow us to offer a slight mark of our gratitude by begging the favour of your company at dinner?'

'Great pleasure – not presume to dictate, but broiled fowl and mushrooms – capital thing! what time?'

'Let me see,' replied Mr Pickwick, referring to his watch, 'it is now nearly three. Shall we say five?'

'Suit me excellently,' said the stranger, 'five precisely – till then – care of yourselves;' and lifting the pinched-up hat a few inches from his head, and carelessly replacing it very much on one side, the stranger, with half the brown paper parcel sticking out of his pocket, walked briskly up the yard, and turned into the High Street.

'Evidently a traveller in many countries, and a close observer of men and things,' said Mr Pickwick.

'I should like to see his poem,' said Mr Snodgrass.

'I should like to have seen that dog,' said Mr Winkle.

Mr Tupman said nothing; but he thought of Donna Christina, the stomach pump, and the fountain; and his eyes filled with tears.

A private sitting-room having been engaged, bed-rooms inspected, and dinner ordered, the party walked out to view the city and adjoining neighbourhood.

We do not find, from a careful perusal of Mr Pickwick's notes on the four towns, Stroud, Rochester, Chatham, and Brompton, that his impressions of their appearance differ in any material point from those of other travellers who have gone over the same ground. His general description is easily abridged.

'The principal productions of these towns,' says Mr Pickwick, 'appear to be soldiers, sailors, Jews, chalk, shrimps, officers, and dockyard men. The commodities chiefly exposed for sale in the public streets are marine stores, hard-bake, apples, flat-fish, and oysters. The streets present a lively and animated appearance, occasioned chiefly by the conviviality of the military. It is truly delightful to a philanthropic mind, to see these gallant men staggering along under the influence of an overflow, both of animal and ardent spirits; more especially when we remember that the following them about, and jesting with them, affords a cheap and innocent amusement for the boy population. Nothing (adds Mr Pickwick) can exceed their good humour. It was but the day before my arrival that one of them had been most grossly insulted in the house of a publican. The bar-maid had positively refused to draw him any more liquor; in return for which he had (merely in playfulness) drawn his bayonet, and wounded the girl in the shoulder. And yet this fine fellow was the very first to go down to the house next morning, and express his readiness to overlook the matter, and forget what had occurred.

'The consumption of tobacco in these towns (continues Mr Pickwick) must be very great: and the smell which pervades the streets must be exceedingly delicious to those who are extremely fond of smoking. A superficial traveller might object to the dirt which is their leading characteristic; but to those who view it as an indication of traffic and commercial prosperity, it is truly gratifying.'

Punctual to five o'clock came the stranger, and shortly afterwards the dinner. He had divested himself of his brown paper parcel, but had made no alteration in his attire; and was, if possible, more loquacious than ever.

'What's that?' he inquired, as the waiter removed one of the covers.

'Soles, sir.'

'Soles – ah! – capital fish – all come from London – stage-coach proprietors get up political dinners – carriage of soles – dozens of baskets – cunning fellows. Glass of wine, sir.'

'With pleasure,' said Mr Pickwick; and the stranger took wine, first with him, and then with Mr Snodgrass, and then with Mr Tupman, and then with Mr Winkle, and then with the whole party together, almost as rapidly as he talked.

'Devil of a mess on the staircase, waiter,' said the stranger. 'Forms going up – carpenters coming down – lamps, glasses, harps. What's going forward?'

'Ball, sir,' said the waiter.

'Assembly, eh?'

'No, sir, not Assembly, sir. Ball for the benefit of a charity, sir.'

'Many fine women in this town, do you know, sir?' inquired Mr Tupman, with great interest.

'Splendid – capital. Kent, sir – everybody knows Kent – apples, cherries, hops, and women. Glass of wine, sir?'

'With great pleasure,' replied Mr Tupman. The stranger filled, and emptied.

'I should very much like to go,' said Mr Tupman, resuming the subject of the ball, 'very much.'

'Tickets at the bar, sir,' interposed the waiter; 'half-a-guinea each, sir.'

Mr Tupman again expressed an earnest wish to be present at the festivity; but meeting with no response in the darkened eye of Mr Snodgrass, or the abstracted gaze of Mr Pickwick, he applied himself with great interest to the port wine and dessert, which had just been placed on the table. The waiter withdrew, and the party were left to enjoy the cosy couple of hours succeeding dinner.

'Beg your pardon, sir,' said the stranger, 'bottle stands – pass it round – way of the sun – through the button-hole – no heeltaps,'[10] and he emptied his glass, which he had filled about two minutes before, and poured out another, with the air of a man who was used to it.

The wine was passed, and a fresh supply ordered. The visitor talked, the Pickwickians listened. Mr Tupman felt every moment more disposed for the ball. Mr Pickwick's countenance glowed with an expression of universal philanthropy; and Mr Winkle and Mr Snodgrass fell fast asleep.

'They're beginning up-stairs,' said the stranger – 'hear the company – fiddles tuning – now the harp – there they go.' The various sounds which found their way down-stairs announced the commencement of the first quadrille.

'How I should like to go,' said Mr Tupman, again.

'So should I,' said the stranger, – 'confounded luggage – heavy smacks – nothing to go in – odd, an't it?'

Now general benevolence was one of the leading features of the Pickwickian theory, and no one was more remarkable for the zealous manner in which he observed so noble a principle than Mr Tracy Tupman. The number of instances, recorded on the Transactions of the Society, in which that excellent man referred objects of charity to the houses of other members for left-off garments or pecuniary relief is almost incredible.

'I should be very happy to lend you a change of apparel for the purpose,' said Mr Tracy Tupman, 'but you are rather slim, and I am – '

'Rather fat – grown up Bacchus[11] – cut the leaves – dismounted from the tub, and adopted kersey, eh? – not double distilled, but double milled – ha! ha! pass the wine.'

Whether Mr Tupman was somewhat indignant at the peremptory tone in which he was desired to pass the wine which the stranger passed so quickly away; or whether he felt very properly scandalised, at an influential member of the Pickwick club being ignominiously compared to a dismounted Bacchus, is a fact not yet completely ascertained. He passed the wine, coughed twice, and looked at the stranger for several seconds with a stern intensity; as that individual, however, appeared perfectly collected, and quite calm under his searching glance, he gradually relaxed, and reverted to the subject of the ball.

'I was about to observe, sir,' he said, 'that though my apparel would be too large, a suit of my friend Mr Winkle's would perhaps fit you better.'

The stranger took Mr Winkle's measure with his eye; and that feature glistened with satisfaction as he said – 'just the thing.'

Mr Tupman looked round him. The wine, which had exerted its somniferous influence over Mr Snodgrass and Mr Winkle, had stolen upon the senses of Mr Pickwick. That gentleman had gradually passed through the various stages which precede the lethargy produced by dinner, and its consequences. He had undergone the ordinary transitions from the height of conviviality to the depth of misery, and from the depth of misery to the height of conviviality. Like a gas lamp in the street, with the wind in the pipe, he had exhibited for a moment an unnatural brilliancy: then sunk so low as to be scarcely discernible: after a short interval he had burst out again, to enlighten for a moment, then flickered with an uncertain, staggering sort of light, and then gone out altogether. His head was sunk upon his bosom; and perpetual snoring, with a partial choke occasionally, were the only audible indications of the great man's presence.

The temptation to be present at the ball, and to form his first impressions of the beauty of the Kentish ladies, was strong upon Mr Tupman. The temptation to take the stranger with him was equally great. He was wholly unacquainted with the place, and its inhabitants; and the stranger seemed to possess as great a knowledge of both as if he had lived there from his infancy. Mr Winkle was asleep, and Mr Tupman had had sufficient experience in such matters to know, that the moment he awoke he would, in the ordinary course of nature, roll heavily to bed. He was undecided. 'Fill your glass, and pass the wine,' said the indefatigable visitor.

Mr Tupman did as he was requested; and the additional stimulus of the last glass settled his determination.

'Winkle's bed-room is inside mine,' said Mr Tupman; 'I couldn't make him understand what I wanted, if I woke him now, but I know he has a dress suit, in a carpet-bag, and supposing you wore it to the ball, and took it off when we returned, I could replace it without troubling him at all about the matter.'

'Capital,' said the stranger, 'famous plan – damned odd situation – fourteen coats in the packing cases, and obliged to wear another man's – very good notion, that – very.'

'We must purchase our tickets,' said Mr Tupman.

'Not worth while splitting a guinea,' said the stranger, 'toss who shall pay for both – I call; you spin – first time – woman – woman – bewitching woman,' and down came the sovereign, with the Dragon (called by courtesy a woman)[12] uppermost.

Mr Tupman rang the bell, purchased the tickets, and ordered chamber candle-sticks. In another quarter of an hour the stranger was completely arrayed in a full suit of Mr Nathaniel Winkle's.

'It's a new coat,' said Mr Tupman, as the stranger surveyed himself with great complacency in a cheval glass;[13] 'the first that's been made with our club button,' and he called his companion's attention to the large gilt button which displayed a bust of Mr Pickwick in the centre, and the letters 'P. C.' on either side.

'P. C.' said the stranger, – 'queer set out – old fellow's likeness, and "P. C." – What does "P. C." stand for – Peculiar Coat, eh?'

Mr Tupman, with rising indignation and great importance, explained the mystic device.

'Rather short in the waist, an't it?' said the stranger, screwing himself round to catch a glimpse in the glass of the waist buttons which were half way up his back. 'Like a general postman's coat – queer coats those – made by contract – no measuring – mysterious dispensations of Providence – all the short men get long coats – all the long men short ones.' Running on in this way, Mr Tupman's new companion adjusted his dress, or rather the dress of Mr Winkle; and, accompanied by Mr Tupman, ascended the staircase leading to the ball-room.

'What names, sir?' said the man at the door. Mr Tracy Tupman was stepping forward to announce his own titles, when the stranger prevented him.

'No names at all;' and then he whispered Mr Tupman, 'Names won't do – not known – very good names in their way, but not great ones – capital names for a small party, but won't make an impression in public assemblies – *incog.* the thing – Gentlemen from London – distinguished foreigners – anything.' The door was thrown open; and Mr Tracy Tupman, and the stranger, entered the ball-room.

It was a long room, with crimson-covered benches, and wax candles in glass chandeliers. The musicians were securely confined in an elevated den, and quadrilles[14] were being systematically got through by two or three sets of dancers. Two card-tables were made up in the adjoining card-room, and two pair of old ladies, and a corresponding number of stout gentlemen, were executing whist therein.

The finale concluded, the dancers promenaded the room, and Mr

Tupman and his companion stationed themselves in a corner, to observe the company.

'Charming women,' said Mr Tupman.

'Wait a minute,' said the stranger, 'fun presently – nobs[15] not come yet – queer place – Dock-yard people of upper rank don't know Dock-yard people of lower rank – Dock-yard people of lower rank don't know small gentry – small gentry don't know tradespeople – Commissioner don't know anybody.'

'Who's that little boy with the light hair and pink eyes, in a fancy dress?' inquired Mr Tupman.

'Hush, pray – pink eyes – fancy dress – little boy – nonsense – Ensign 97th – Honourable Wilmot Snipe – great family – Snipes – very.'

'Sir Thomas Clubber, Lady Clubber, and the Miss Clubbers!' shouted the man at the door in a stentorian voice. A great sensation was created throughout the room by the entrance of a tall gentleman in a blue coat and bright buttons, a large lady in blue satin, and two young ladies, on a similar scale, in fashionably-made dresses of the same hue.

'Commissioner – head of the yard[16] – great man – remarkably great man,' whispered the stranger in Mr Tupman's ear, as the charitable committee ushered Sir Thomas Clubber and family to the top of the room. The Honourable Wilmot Snipe, and other distinguished gentlemen crowded to render homage to the Miss Clubbers; and Sir Thomas Clubber stood bolt upright, and looked majestically over his black neckerchief at the assembled company.

'Mr Smithie, Mrs Smithie, and the Misses Smithie,' was the next announcement.

'What's Mr Smithie?' inquired Mr Tracy Tupman.

'Something in the yard,' replied the stranger. Mr Smithie bowed deferentially to Sir Thomas Clubber; and Sir Thomas Clubber acknowledged the salute with conscious condescension. Lady Clubber took a telescopic view of Mrs Smithie and family through her eye-glass, and Mrs Smithie stared in her turn at Mrs Somebody else, whose husband was not in the Dock-yard at all.

'Colonel Bulder, Mrs Colonel Bulder, and Miss Bulder,' were the next arrivals.

'Head of the Garrison,' said the stranger, in reply to Mr Tupman's inquiring look.

Miss Bulder was warmly welcomed by the Miss Clubbers; the greeting between Mrs Colonel Bulder and Lady Clubber was of the most affectionate description; Colonel Bulder and Sir Thomas

Clubber exchanged snuff-boxes, and looked very much like a pair of Alexander Selkirks[17] – 'Monarchs of all they surveyed.'

While the aristocracy of the place – the Bulders, and Clubbers, and Snipes – were thus preserving their dignity at the upper end of the room, the other classes of society were imitating their example in other parts of it. The less aristocratic officers of the 97th devoted themselves to the families of the less important functionaries from the Dock-yard. The solicitors' wives, and the wine-merchant's wife, headed another grade (the brewer's wife visited the Bulders); and Mrs Tomlinson, the post-office keeper, seemed by mutual consent to have been chosen the leader of the trade party.

One of the most popular personages, in his own circle, present was a little fat man, with a ring of upright black hair round his head, and an extensive bald plain on the top of it – Doctor Slammer, surgeon to the 97th. The Doctor took snuff with everybody, chatted with everybody, laughed, danced, made jokes, played whist, did everything, and was everywhere. To these pursuits, multifarious as they were, the little Doctor added a more important one than any – he was indefatigable in paying the most unremitting and devoted attention to a little old widow, whose rich dress and profusion of ornament bespoke her a most desirable addition to a limited income.

Upon the Doctor, and the widow, the eyes of both Mr Tupman and his companion had been fixed for some time, when the stranger broke silence.

'Lots of money – old girl – pompous Doctor – not a bad idea – good fun,' were the intelligible sentences which issued from his lips. Mr Tupman looked inquisitively in his face.

'I'll dance with the widow,' said the stranger.

'Who is she?' inquired Mr Tupman.

'Don't know – never saw her in all my life – cut out the Doctor – here goes.' And the stranger forthwith crossed the room; and, leaning against a mantel-piece, commenced gazing with an air of respectful and melancholy admiration on the fat countenance of the little old lady. Mr Tupman looked on, in mute astonishment. The stranger progressed rapidly; the little Doctor danced with another lady; the widow dropped her fan, the stranger picked it up, and presented it, – a smile – a bow – a curtsey – a few words of conversation. The stranger walked boldly up to, and returned with, the master of the ceremonies; a little introductory pantomime; and the stranger and Mrs Budger took their places in a quadrille.

The surprise of Mr Tupman at this summary proceeding, great as it was, was immeasurably exceeded by the astonishment of the Doctor. The stranger was young, and the widow was flattered. The Doctor's attentions were unheeded by the widow; and the Doctor's indignation was wholly lost on his imperturbable rival. Doctor Slammer was paralysed. He, Doctor Slammer, of the 97th, to be extinguished in a moment, by a man whom nobody had ever seen before, and whom nobody knew even now! Doctor Slammer – Doctor Slammer of the 97th rejected! Impossible! It could not be! Yes, it was; there they were. What! introducing his friend! Could he believe his eyes! He looked again, and was under the painful necessity of admitting the veracity of his optics; Mrs Budger was dancing with Mr Tracy Tupman, there was no mistaking the fact. There was the widow before him, bouncing bodily, here and there, with unwonted vigour; and Mr Tracy Tupman hopping about, with a face expressive of the most intense solemnity, dancing (as a good many people do) as if a quadrille were not a thing to be laughed at, but a severe trial to the feelings, which it requires inflexible resolution to encounter.

Silently and patiently did the Doctor bear all this, and all the handings of negus, and watching for glasses, and darting for biscuits, and coquetting, that ensued; but, a few seconds after the stranger had disappeared to lead Mrs Budger to her carriage, he darted swiftly from the room with every particle of his hitherto-bottled-up indignation effervescing, from all parts of his countenance, in a perspiration of passion.

The stranger was returning, and Mr Tupman was beside him. He spoke in a low tone, and laughed. The little Doctor thirsted for his life. He was exulting. He had triumphed.

'Sir!' said the Doctor, in an awful voice, producing a card, and retiring into an angle of the passage, 'my name is Slammer, Doctor Slammer, sir – 97th Regiment – Chatham Barracks – my card, sir, my card.' He would have added more, but his indignation choked him.

'Ah!' replied the stranger, coolly, 'Slammer – much obliged – polite attention – not ill now, Slammer – but when I am – knock you up.'[18]

'You – you're a shuffler! sir,' gasped the furious Doctor, 'a poltroon[19] – a coward – a liar – a – a – will nothing induce you to give me your card, sir!'

'Oh! I see,' said the stranger, half aside, 'negus too strong here – liberal landlord – very foolish – very – lemonade much better – hot rooms – elderly gentlemen – suffer for it in the morning – cruel – cruel;' and he moved on a step or two.

'You are stopping in this house, sir,' said the indignant little man; 'you are intoxicated now, sir; you shall hear from me in the morning, sir. I shall find you out, sir; I shall find you out.'

'Rather you found me out than found me at home,' replied the unmoved stranger.

Doctor Slammer looked unutterable ferocity, as he fixed his hat on his head with an indignant knock; and the stranger and Mr Tupman ascended to the bed-room of the latter to restore the borrowed plumage to the unconscious Winkle.

That gentleman was fast asleep; the restoration was soon made. The stranger was extremely jocose; and Mr Tracy Tupman, being quite bewildered with wine, negus, lights, and ladies, thought the whole affair an exquisite joke. His new friend departed; and, after experiencing some slight difficulty in finding the orifice in his night-cap, originally intended for the reception of his head, and finally overturning his candlestick in his struggles to put it on, Mr Tracy Tupman managed to get into bed by a series of complicated evolutions, and shortly afterwards sank into repose.

Seven o'clock had hardly ceased striking on the following morn-ing when Mr Pickwick's comprehensive mind was aroused from the state of unconsciousness, in which slumber had plunged it, by a loud knocking at his chamber door.

'Who's there?' said Mr Pickwick, starting up in bed.

'Boots,[20] sir.'

'What do you want?'

'Please, sir, can you tell me, which gentleman of your party wears a bright blue dress coat, with a gilt button with P. C. on it?'

'It's been given out to brush,' thought Mr Pickwick, and the man has forgotten whom it belongs to. 'Mr Winkle,' he called out, 'next room but two, on the right hand.'

'Thank'ee, sir,' said the Boots, and away he went.

'What's the matter?' cried Mr Tupman, as a loud knocking at *his* door roused *him* from his oblivious repose.

'Can I speak to Mr Winkle, sir?' replied the Boots from the outside.

'Winkle – Winkle!' shouted Mr Tupman, calling into the inner room.

'Hallo!' replied a faint voice from within the bed-clothes.

'You're wanted – some one at the door – ' and having exerted

Dr Slammer's defiance of Jingle

himself to articulate thus much, Mr Tracy Tupman turned round and fell fast asleep again.

'Wanted!' said Mr Winkle, hastily jumping out of bed, and putting on a few articles of clothing: 'wanted! at this distance from town – who on earth can want me?'

'Gentleman in the coffee-room, sir,' replied the Boots, as Mr Winkle opened the door, and confronted him; 'gentleman says he'll not detain you a moment, sir, but he can take no denial.'

'Very odd!' said Mr Winkle; 'I'll be down directly.'

He hurriedly wrapped himself in a travelling-shawl and dressing-gown, and proceeded down-stairs. An old woman and a couple of waiters were cleaning the coffee-room, and an officer in undress uniform was looking out of the window. He turned round as Mr Winkle entered, and made a stiff inclination of the head. Having ordered the attendants to retire, and closed the door very carefully, he said, 'Mr Winkle, I presume?'

'My name *is* Winkle, sir.'

'You will not be surprised, sir, when I inform you, that I have called here this morning on behalf of my friend, Dr Slammer, of the Ninety-seventh.'

'Doctor Slammer!' said Mr Winkle.

'Doctor Slammer. He begged me to express his opinion that your conduct of last evening was of a description which no gentleman could endure: and (he added) which no one gentleman would pursue towards another.'

Mr Winkle's astonishment was too real, and too evident, to escape the observation of Dr Slammer's friend; he therefore proceeded – 'My friend, Doctor Slammer, requested me to add, that he was firmly persuaded you were intoxicated during a portion of the evening, and possibly unconscious of the extent of the insult you were guilty of. He commissioned me to say, that should this be pleaded as an excuse for your behaviour, he will consent to accept a written apology, to be penned by you, from my dictation.'

'A written apology!' repeated Mr Winkle, in the most emphatic tone of amazement possible.

'Of course you know the alternative,' replied the visitor, coolly.

'Were you entrusted with this message to me, by name?' inquired Mr Winkle, whose intellects were hopelessly confused by this extraordinary conversation.

'I was not present myself,' replied the visitor, 'and in consequence of your firm refusal to give your card to Doctor Slammer, I was desired by that gentleman to identify the wearer of a very uncommon coat – a bright blue dress coat, with a gilt button displaying a bust, and the letter "P. C." '

Mr Winkle actually staggered with astonishment as he heard his own costume thus minutely described. Doctor Slammer's friend proceeded: – 'From the inquiries I made at the bar, just now, I was convinced that the owner of the coat in question arrived here, with three gentlemen, yesterday afternoon. I immediately sent up to the gentleman who was described as appearing the head of the party, and he at once referred me to you.'

If the principal tower of Rochester Castle had suddenly walked from its foundation, and stationed itself opposite the coffee-room window, Mr Winkle's surprise would have been as nothing compared with the profound astonishment with which he had heard this address. His first impression was, that his coat had been stolen. 'Will you allow me to detain you one moment?' said he.

'Certainly,' replied the unwelcome visitor.

Mr Winkle ran hastily up-stairs, and with a trembling hand opened the bag. There was the coat in its usual place, but exhibiting, on a close inspection, evident tokens of having been worn on the preceding night.

'It must be so,' said Mr Winkle, letting the coat fall from his hands. 'I took too much wine after dinner, and have a very vague recollection of walking about the streets and smoking a cigar afterwards. The fact is, I was very drunk; – I must have changed my coat – gone somewhere – and insulted somebody – I have no doubt of it; and this message is the terrible consequence.' Saying which, Mr Winkle retraced his steps in the direction of the coffee-room, with the gloomy and dreadful resolve of accepting the challenge of the warlike Doctor Slammer, and abiding by the worst consequences that might ensue.

To this determination Mr Winkle was urged by a variety of considerations; the first of which was, his reputation with the club. He had always been looked up to as a high authority on all matters of amusement and dexterity, whether offensive, defensive, or inoffensive; and if, on this very first occasion of being put to the test, he shrunk back from the trial, beneath his leader's eye, his name and standing were lost for ever. Besides, he remembered to have heard it frequently surmised by the uninitiated in such matters, that by an understood arrangement between the seconds, the pistols were seldom loaded with ball; and, furthermore, he reflected that if he applied to Mr Snodgrass to act as his second, and depicted the danger in glowing terms, that gentleman might possibly communicate the intelligence to Mr Pickwick, who would certainly lose no time in transmitting it to the local authorities, and thus prevent the killing or maiming of his follower.

Such were his thoughts when he returned to the coffee-room, and intimated his intention of accepting the Doctor's challenge.

'Will you refer me to a friend, to arrange the time and place of meeting?' said the officer.

'Quite unnecessary,' replied Mr Winkle; 'name them to me, and I can procure the attendance of a friend afterwards.'

'Shall we say – sunset this evening?' inquired the officer, in a careless tone.

'Very good,' replied Mr Winkle; thinking in his heart it was very bad.

'You know Fort Pitt?'

'Yes; I saw it yesterday.'

'If you will take the trouble to turn into the field which borders the trench, take the foot-path to the left when you arrive at an angle of the fortification, and keep straight on 'till you see me, I will precede you to a secluded place, where the affair can be conducted without fear of interruption.'

'*Fear* of interruption!' thought Mr Winkle.

'Nothing more to arrange, I think,' said the officer.

'I am not aware of anything more,' replied Mr Winkle.

'Good morning.'

'Good morning:' and the officer whistled a lively air as he strode away.

That morning's breakfast passed heavily off. Mr Tupman was not in a condition to rise, after the unwonted dissipation of the previous night; Mr Snodgrass appeared to labour under a poetical depression of spirits; and even Mr Pickwick evinced an unusual attachment to silence and soda-water. Mr Winkle eagerly watched his opportunity: it was not long wanting. Mr Snodgrass proposed a visit to the castle, and as Mr Winkle was the only other member of the party disposed to walk, they went out together.

'Snodgrass,' said Mr Winkle, when they had turned out of the public street, 'Snodgrass, my dear fellow, can I rely upon your secrecy?' As he said this, he most devoutly and earnestly hoped he could not.

'You can,' replied Mr Snodgrass. 'Hear me swear – '

'No, no,' interrupted Winkle, terrified at the idea of his companion's unconsciously pledging himself not to give information; 'don't swear, don't swear; it's quite unnecessary.'

Mr Snodgrass dropped the hand which he had, in the spirit of poesy, raised towards the clouds as he made the above appeal, and assumed an attitude of attention.

'I want your assistance, my dear fellow, in an affair of honour,' said Mr Winkle.

'You shall have it,' replied Mr Snodgrass, clasping his friend's hand.

'With a Doctor – Doctor Slammer, of the Ninety-seventh,' said Mr Winkle, wishing to make the matter appear as solemn as possible; 'an affair with an officer, seconded by another officer, at sunset this evening, in a lonely field beyond Fort Pitt.'

'I will attend you,' said Mr Snodgrass.

He was astonished, but by no means dismayed. It is extraordinary how cool any party but the principal can be in such cases. Mr Winkle had forgotten this. He had judged of his friend's feelings by his own.

'The consequences may be dreadful,' said Mr Winkle.

'I hope not,' said Mr Snodgrass.

'The Doctor, I believe, is a very good shot,' said Mr Winkle.

'Most of these military men are,' observed Mr Snodgrass, calmly; 'but so are you, an't you?'

Mr Winkle replied in the affirmative; and perceiving that he had not alarmed his companion sufficiently, changed his ground.

'Snodgrass,' he said, in a voice tremulous with emotion, 'if I fall, you will find in a packet which I shall place in your hands a note for my – for my father.'

This attack was a failure also. Mr Snodgrass was affected, but he undertook the delivery of the note as readily as if he had been a Twopenny Postman.[21]

'If I fall,' said Mr Winkle, 'or if the Doctor falls, you, my dear friend, will be tried as an accessory before the fact. Shall I involve my friend in transportation – possibly for life!'

Mr Snodgrass winced a little at this, but his heroism was invincible. 'In the cause of friendship,' he fervently exclaimed, 'I would brave all dangers.'

How Mr Winkle cursed his companion's devoted friendship internally, as they walked silently along, side by side, for some minutes, each immersed in his own meditations! The morning was wearing away; he grew desperate.

'Snodgrass,' he said, stopping suddenly, 'do *not* let me be baulked in this matter – do *not* give information to the local authorities – do *not* obtain the assistance of several peace officers, to take either me or Doctor Slammer, of the Ninety-seventh Regiment, at present quartered in Chatham Barracks, into custody, and thus prevent this duel; – I say, do *not*.'

Mr Snodgrass seized his friend's hand warmly, as he enthusiastically replied, 'Not for worlds!'

A thrill passed over Mr Winkle's frame as the conviction that he had nothing to hope from his friend's fears, and that he was destined to become an animated target, rushed forcibly upon him.

The state of the case having been formally explained to Mr Snodgrass, and a case of satisfaction pistols,[22] with the satisfactory accompaniments of powder, ball, and caps, having been hired from a manufacturer in Rochester, the two friends returned to their inn; Mr Winkle to ruminate on the approaching struggle, and Mr Snodgrass to arrange the weapons of war, and put them into proper order for immediate use.

It was a dull and heavy evening when they again sallied forth on their awkward errand. Mr Winkle was muffled up in a huge cloak to escape observation, and Mr Snodgrass bore under his the instruments of destruction.

'Have you got everything?' said Mr Winkle, in an agitated tone.

'Ev'rything,' replied Mr Snodgrass; 'plenty of ammunition, in case the shots don't take effect. There's a quarter of a pound of powder in the case, and I have got two newspapers in my pocket for the loadings.'[23]

These were instances of friendship for which any man might reasonably feel most grateful. The presumption is, that the gratitude of Mr Winkle was too powerful for utterance, as he said nothing, but continued to walk on – rather slowly.

'We are in excellent time,' said Mr Snodgrass, as they climbed the fence of the first field; 'the sun is just going down.' Mr Winkle looked up at the declining orb, and painfully thought of the probability of his 'going down' himself, before long.

'There's the officer,' exclaimed Mr Winkle, after a few minutes' walking.

'Where?' said Mr Snodgrass.

'There; – the gentleman in the blue cloak.' Mr Snodgrass looked in the direction indicated by the forefinger of his friend, and observed a figure, muffled up, as he had described. The officer evinced his consciousness of their presence by slightly beckoning with his hand; and the two friends followed him at a little distance, as he walked away.

The evening grew more dull every moment, and a melancholy

wind sounded through the deserted fields, like a distant giant whistling for his house-dog. The sadness of the scene imparted a sombre tinge to the feelings of Mr Winkle. He started as they passed the angle of the trench – it looked like a colossal grave.

The officer turned suddenly from the path, and after climbing a paling, and scaling a hedge, entered a secluded field. Two gentlemen were waiting in it; one was a little fat man, with black hair; and the other – a portly personage in a braided surtout – was sitting with perfect equanimity on a camp-stool.

'The other party, and a surgeon, I suppose,' said Mr Snodgrass; 'take a drop of brandy.' Mr Winkle seized the wicker bottle which his friend proffered, and took a lengthened pull at the exhilarating liquid.

'My friend, sir, Mr Snodgrass,' said Mr Winkle, as the officer approached. Doctor Slammer's friend bowed, and produced a case similar to that which Mr Snodgrass carried.

'We have nothing farther to say, sir, I think,' he coldly remarked, as he opened the case; 'an apology has been resolutely declined.'

'Nothing, sir,' said Mr Snodgrass, who began to feel rather uncomfortable himself.

'Will you step forward?' said the officer.

'Certainly,' replied Mr Snodgrass. The ground was measured, and preliminaries arranged.

'You will find these better than your own,' said the opposite second, producing his pistols. 'You saw me load them. Do you object to use them?'

'Certainly not,' replied Mr Snodgrass. The offer relieved him from considerable embarrassment, for his previous notions of loading a pistol were rather vague and undefined.

'We may place our men, then, I think,' observed the officer, with as much indifference as if the principals were chess-men, and the seconds players.

'I think we may,' replied Mr Snodgrass; who would have assented to any proposition, because he knew nothing about the matter. The officer crossed to Doctor Slammer, and Mr Snodgrass went up to Mr Winkle.

'It's all ready,' he said, offering the pistol. 'Give me your cloak.'

'You have got the packet, my dear fellow,' said poor Winkle.

'All right,' said Mr Snodgrass. 'Be steady, and wing him.'

It occurred to Mr Winkle that this advice was very like that which bystanders invariably give to the smallest boy in a street fight, namely, 'Go in, and win:' – an admirable thing to recommend, if you only know how to do it. He took off his cloak, however, in silence – it always took a long time to undo, that cloak – and accepted the pistol. The seconds retired, the gentleman on the camp-stool did the same, and the belligerents approached each other.

Mr Winkle was always remarkable for extreme humanity. It is conjectured that his unwillingness to hurt a fellow-creature intentionally was the cause of his shutting his eyes when he arrived at the fatal spot; and that the circumstance of his eyes being closed, prevented his observing the very extraordinary and unaccountable demeanour of Doctor Slammer. That gentleman started, stared, retreated, rubbed his eyes, stared again; and, finally, shouted 'Stop, stop!'

'What's all this?' said Doctor Slammer, as his friend and Mr Snodgrass came running up; 'That's not the man.'

'Not the man!' said Dr Slammer's second.

'Not the man!' said Mr Snodgrass.

'Not the man!' said the gentleman with the camp-stool in his hand.

'Certainly not,' replied the little Doctor. 'That's not the person who insulted me last night.'

'Very extraordinary!' exclaimed the officer.

'Very,' said the gentleman with the camp-stool. 'The only question is, whether the gentleman, being on the ground, must not be considered, as a matter of form, to be the individual who insulted our friend, Doctor Slammer, yesterday evening, whether he is really that individual or not:' and having delivered this suggestion, with a very sage and mysterious air, the man with the camp-stool took a large pinch of snuff, and looked profoundly round, with the air of an authority in such matters.

Now Mr Winkle had opened his eyes, and his ears too, when he heard his adversary call out for a cessation of hostilities; and perceiving by what he had afterwards said, that there was, beyond all question, some mistake in the matter, he at once foresaw the increase of reputation he should inevitably acquire by concealing the real motive of his coming out: he therefore stepped boldly forward, and said –

'I am not the person. I know it.'

'Then, that,' said the man with the camp-stool, 'is an affront to Dr Slammer, and a sufficient reason for proceeding immediately.'

'Pray be quiet, Payne,' said the Doctor's second. 'Why did you not communicate this fact to me this morning, sir?'

'To be sure – to be sure,' said the man with the camp-stool, indignantly.

'I entreat you to be quiet, Payne,' said the other. 'May I repeat my question, sir?'

'Because, sir,' replied Mr Winkle, who had had time to deliberate upon his answer, 'because, sir, you described an intoxicated and ungentlemanly person as wearing a coat which I have the honour, not only to wear, but to have invented – the proposed uniform, sir, of the Pickwick Club in London. The honour of that uniform I feel bound to maintain, and I therefore, without inquiry, accepted the challenge which you offered me.'

'My dear sir,' said the good-humoured little Doctor, advancing with extended hand, 'I honour your gallantry. Permit me to say, sir, that I highly admire your conduct, and extremely regret having caused you the inconvenience of this meeting, to no purpose.'

'I beg you won't mention it, sir,' said Mr Winkle.

'I shall feel proud of your acquaintance, sir,' said the little Doctor.

'It will afford me the greatest pleasure to know you, sir,' replied Mr Winkle. Thereupon the Doctor and Mr Winkle shook hands, and then Mr Winkle and Lieutenant Tappleton (the Doctor's second), and then Mr Winkle and the man with the camp-stool, and, finally, Mr Winkle and Mr Snodgrass – the last-named gentleman in an excess of admiration at the noble conduct of his heroic friend.

'I think we may adjourn,' said Lieutenant Tappleton.

'Certainly,' added the Doctor.

'Unless,' interposed the man with the camp-stool, 'unless Mr Winkle feels himself aggrieved by the challenge; in which case, I submit, he has a right to satisfaction.'

Mr Winkle, with great self-denial, expressed himself quite satisfied already.

'Or possibly,' said the man with the camp-stool, 'the gentleman's second may feel himself affronted with some observations which fell from me at an early period of this meeting: if so, I shall be happy to give *him* satisfaction immediately.'

Mr Snodgrass hastily professed himself very much obliged with the handsome offer of the gentleman who had spoken last, which he was only induced to decline by his entire contentment with the whole proceedings. The two seconds adjusted the cases, and the whole party left the ground in a much more lively manner than they had proceeded to it.

'Do you remain long here?' inquired Dr Slammer of Mr Winkle, as they walked on most amicably together.

'I think we shall leave here the day after to-morrow,' was the reply.

'I trust I shall have the pleasure of seeing you and your friend at my rooms, and of spending a pleasant evening with you, after this awkward mistake,' said the little Doctor; 'are you disengaged this evening?'

'We have some friends here,' replied Mr Winkle, 'and I should not like to leave them to-night. Perhaps you and your friend will join us at the Bull.'

'With great pleasure,' said the little Doctor; 'will ten o'clock be too late to look in for half an hour?'

'Oh dear, no,' said Mr Winkle. 'I shall be most happy to introduce you to my friends, Mr Pickwick and Mr Tupman.'

'It will give me great pleasure, I am sure,' replied Doctor Slammer, little suspecting who Mr Tupman was.

'You will be sure to come?' said Mr Snodgrass.

'Oh, certainly.'

By this time they had reached the road. Cordial farewells were exchanged, and the party separated. Doctor Slammer and his friends repaired to the barracks, and Mr Winkle, accompanied by his friend, Mr Snodgrass, returned to their inn.

CHAPTER 3

A new Acquaintance. The Stroller's Tale.
A Disagreeable Interruption, and an
unpleasant Encounter

Mr Pickwick had felt some apprehensions in consequence of the unusual absence of his two friends, which their mysterious behaviour during the whole morning had by no means tended to diminish. It was, therefore, with more than ordinary pleasure that he rose to greet them when they again entered; and with more than ordinary interest that he inquired what had occurred to detain them from his society. In reply to his questions on this point, Mr Snodgrass was about to offer an historical account of the circumstances just now detailed, when he was suddenly checked by observing that there were present, not only Mr Tupman and their stage-coach companion of the preceding day, but another stranger of equally singular appearance. It was a care-worn looking man, whose sallow face, and deeply sunken eyes, were rendered still more striking than nature had made them, by the straight black hair which hung in matted disorder half way down his face. His eyes were almost unnaturally bright and piercing; his cheek-bones were high and prominent; and his jaws were so long and lank, that an observer would have supposed that he was drawing the flesh of his face in, for a moment, by some contraction of the muscles, if his half-opened mouth and immovable expression had not announced that it was his ordinary appearance. Round his neck he wore a green shawl, with the large ends straggling over his chest, and making their appearance occasionally beneath the worn button-holes of his old waistcoat. His upper garment was a long black surtout; and below it he wore wide drab trousers, and large boots, running rapidly to seed.

It was on this uncouth-looking person that Mr Winkle's eye rested, and it was towards him that Mr Pickwick extended his hand, when he said 'A friend of our friend's here. We discovered this morning that our friend was connected with the theatre in this place, though he is not desirous to have it generally known, and this gentleman is a member of the same profession. He was about to favour us with a little anecdote connected with it, when you entered.'

'Lots of anecdote,' said the green-coated stranger of the day before, advancing to Mr Winkle and speaking in a low and confidential tone. 'Rum fellow – does the heavy business – no actor – strange man – all sorts of miseries – Dismal Jemmy, we call him on the circuit.' Mr Winkle and Mr Snodgrass politely welcomed the gentleman, elegantly designated as 'Dismal Jemmy;' and calling for brandy and water, in imitation of the remainder of the company, seated themselves at the table.

'Now, sir,' said Mr Pickwick, 'will you oblige us by proceeding with what you were going to relate?'

The dismal individual took a dirty roll of paper from his pocket, and turning to Mr Snodgrass, who had just taken out his note-book, said in a hollow voice perfectly in keeping with his outward man – 'Are you the poet?'

'I – I do a little in that way,' replied Mr Snodgrass, rather taken aback by the abruptness of the question.

'Ah! poetry makes life what lights and music do the stage – strip the one of its false embellishments, and the other of its illusions, and what is there real in either to live or care for?'

'Very true, sir,' replied Mr Snodgrass.

'To be before the footlights,' continued the dismal man, 'is like sitting at a grand, court show, and admiring the silken dresses of the gaudy throng – to be behind them is to be the people who make that finery, uncared for and unknown, and left to sink or swim, to starve or live, as fortune wills it.'

'Certainly,' said Mr Snodgrass: for the sunken eye of the dismal man rested on him, and he felt it necessary to say something.

'Go on, Jemmy,' said the Spanish traveller, 'like black-eyed Susan[1] – all in the Downs – no croaking – speak out – look lively.'

'Will you make another glass before you begin, sir?' said Mr Pickwick.

The dismal man took the hint, and having mixed a glass of brandy and water, and slowly swallowed half of it, opened the roll of paper and proceeded, partly to read, and partly to relate, the following incident, which we find recorded on the Transactions of the club as 'The Stroller's Tale.'

THE STROLLER'S TALE

'There is nothing of the marvellous in what I am going to relate,' said the dismal man; 'there is nothing even uncommon in it. Want and sickness are too common in many stations of life, to deserve more notice than is usually bestowed on the most ordinary vicissitudes of human nature. I have thrown these few notes together, because the subject of them was well known to me for many years. I traced his progress downwards, step by step, until at last he reached that excess of destitution from which he never rose again.

'The man of whom I speak was a low pantomime actor; and, like many people of his class, an habitual drunkard. In his better days, before he had become enfeebled by dissipation and emaciated by disease, he had been in the receipt of a good salary, which, if he had been careful and prudent, he might have continued to receive for some years – not many; because these men either die early, or, by unnaturally taxing their bodily energies, lose, prematurely, those physical powers on which alone they can depend for subsistence. His besetting sin gained so fast upon him, however, that it was found impossible to employ him in the situations in which he really was useful to the theatre. The public-house had a fascination for him which he could not resist. Neglected disease and hopeless poverty were as certain to be his portion as death itself, if he persevered in the same course; yet he *did* persevere, and the result may be guessed. He could obtain no engagement, and he wanted bread.

'Everybody who is at all acquainted with theatrical matters knows what a host of shabby, poverty-stricken men hang about the stage of a large establishment – not regularly engaged actors, but ballet people, procession men, tumblers, and so forth, who are taken on during the run of a pantomime, or an Easter piece, and are then discharged, until the production of some heavy spectacle occasions a new demand for their services. To this mode of life the man was compelled to resort; and taking the chair every night, at some low theatrical house, at once put him in possession of a few more shillings weekly, and enabled him to gratify his old propensity. Even this resource shortly failed him; his irregularities were too great to admit of his earning the wretched pittance he might thus have procured, and he was actually reduced to a state bordering on starvation, only procuring a trifle occasionally by borrowing it of some old companion, or by obtaining an appearance at one or other of the commonest of the minor theatres; and when he did earn anything, it was spent in the old way.

'About this time, and when he had been existing for upwards of a year no one knew how, I had a short engagement at one of the theatres on the Surrey side of the water, and here I saw this man whom I had lost sight of for some time; for I had been travelling in the provinces, and he had been skulking in the lanes and alleys of London. I was dressed to leave the house, and was crossing the stage on my way out, when he tapped me on the shoulder. Never shall I forget the repulsive sight that met my eye when I turned round. He was dressed for the pantomime, in all the absurdity of a clown's costume. The spectral figures in the Dance of Death,[2] the most frightful shapes that the ablest painter ever portrayed on canvas, never presented an appearance half so ghastly. His bloated body and shrunken legs – their deformity enhanced a hundred fold by the fantastic dress – the glassy eyes, contrasting fearfully with the thick white paint with which the face was besmeared; the grotesquely ornamented head, trembling with paralysis, and the long, skinny hands, rubbed with white chalk – all gave him a hideous and unnatural appearance, of which no description could convey an adequate idea, and which, to this day, I shudder to think of. His voice was hollow and tremulous, as he took me aside, and in broken words recounted a long catalogue of sickness and privations, terminating as usual with an urgent request for the loan of a trifling sum of money. I put a few shillings in his hand, and as I turned away I heard the roar of laughter which followed his first tumble on to the stage.

'A few nights afterwards, a boy put a dirty scrap of paper in my hand, on which were scrawled a few words in pencil, intimating that the man was dangerously ill, and begging me, after the performance, to see him at his lodging in some street – I forget the name of it now – at no great distance from the theatre. I promised to comply, as soon as I could get away; and, after the curtain fell, sallied forth on my melancholy errand.

'It was late, for I had been playing in the last piece; and as it was a benefit night,[3] the performances had been protracted to an unusual length. It was a dark cold night, with a chill damp wind, which blew the rain heavily against the windows and house fronts. Pools of water had collected in the narrow and little-frequented streets, and as many of the thinly-scattered oil-lamps had been blown out by the violence of the wind, the walk was not only a comfortless, but most uncertain one. I had fortunately taken the right course, however, and succeeded, after a little difficulty, in finding the house to which I had been directed – a coal-shed, with one story above it, in the back room of which lay the object of my search.

'A wretched-looking woman, the man's wife, met me on the stairs, and, telling me that he had just fallen into a kind of doze, led me softly in, and placed a chair for me at the bedside. The sick man was lying with his face turned towards the wall; and as he took no heed of my presence, I had leisure to observe the place in which I found myself.

'He was lying on an old bedstead, which turned up during the day. The tattered remains of a checked curtain were drawn round the bed's head, to exclude the wind, which however made its way into the comfortless room through the numerous chinks in the door, and blew it to and fro every instant. There was a low cinder fire in a rusty unfixed grate; and an old three-cornered stained table, with some medicine bottles, a broken glass, and a few other domestic articles, was drawn out before it. A little child was sleeping on a temporary bed which had been made for it on the floor, and the woman sat on a chair by its side. There were a couple of shelves, with a few plates and cups and saucers: and a pair of stage shoes and a couple of foils hung beneath them. With the exception of little heaps of rags and bundles which had been carelessly thrown into the corners of the room, these were the only things in the apartment.

'I had had time to note these little particulars, and to mark the heavy breathing and feverish startings of the sick man, before he was aware of my presence. In his restless attempts to procure some easy resting-place for his head, he tossed his hand out of the bed, and it fell on mine. He started up, and stared eagerly in my face.

'"Mr Hutley, John," said his wife; "Mr Hutley, that you sent for to-night, you know."

'"Ah!" said the invalid, passing his hand across his forehead; "Hutley – Hutley – let me see." He seemed endeavouring to collect his thoughts for a few seconds, and then grasping me tightly by the wrist said, 'Don't leave me – don't leave me, old fellow. She'll murder me; I know she will."

'"Has he been long so?" said I, addressing his weeping wife.

'"Since yesterday night," she replied. "John, John, don't you know me?"

'"Don't let her come near me," said the man, with a shudder, as she stooped over him. "Drive her away; I can't bear her near me." He stared wildly at her, with a look of deadly apprehension, and then whispered in my ear, "I beat her, Jem; I beat her yesterday, and many times before. I have starved her and the boy too; and now I am weak and helpless, Jem, she'll murder me for it; I know she will. If you'd seen her cry, as I have, you'd know it too. Keep her off." He relaxed his grasp, and sank back exhausted on the pillow.

'I knew but too well what all this meant. If I could have entertained any doubt of it, for an instant, one glance at the woman's pale face and wasted form would have sufficiently explained the real state of the case. "You had better stand aside," said I to the poor creature. "You can do him no good. Perhaps he will be calmer, if he does not see you." She retired out of the man's sight. He opened his eyes, after a few seconds, and looked anxiously round.

'"Is she gone?" he eagerly inquired.

'"Yes – yes," said I; "she shall not hurt you."

'"I'll tell you what, Jem," said the man, in a low voice, "she *does* hurt me. There's something in her eyes wakes such a dreadful fear in my heart, that it drives me mad. All last night, her large staring eyes and pale face were close to mine; wherever I turned, they turned; and whenever I started up from my sleep, she was at the bedside looking at me." He drew me closer to him, as he said in a deep, alarmed whisper – "Jem, she must be an evil spirit – a devil! Hush! I know she is. If she had been a woman she would have died long ago. No woman could have borne what she has."

'I sickened at the thought of the long course of cruelty and neglect which must have occurred to produce such an impression on such a man. I could say nothing in reply; for who could offer hope, or consolation, to the abject being before me?

'I sat there for upwards of two hours, during which time he tossed about, murmuring exclamations of pain or impatience, restlessly throwing his arms here and there, and turning constantly from side to side. At length he fell into that state of partial unconsciousness, in which the mind wanders uneasily from scene to scene, and from place to place, without the control of reason, but still without being able to divest itself of an indescribable sense of present suffering. Finding from his incoherent wanderings that this was the case, and knowing that in all probability the fever would not grow immediately worse, I left him, promising his miserable wife that I would repeat my visit next evening, and, if necessary, sit up with the patient during the night.

'I kept my promise. The last four-and-twenty hours had produced a frightful alteration. The eyes, though deeply sunk and heavy, shone with a lustre frightful to behold. The lips were parched, and cracked in many places: the dry hard skin glowed with a burning heat, and there was an almost unearthly air of wild anxiety in the man's face, indicating even more strongly the ravages of the disease. The fever was at its height.

'I took the seat I had occupied the night before, and there I sat for hours, listening to sounds which must strike deep to the heart of the most callous among human beings – the awful ravings of a dying man. From what I had heard of the medical attendant's opinion, I knew there was no hope for him: I was sitting by his death-bed. I saw the wasted limbs, which a few hours before had been distorted for the amusement of a boisterous gallery, writhing under the tortures of a burning fever – I heard the clown's shrill laugh, blending with the low murmurings of the dying man.

'It is a touching thing to hear the mind reverting to the ordinary occupations and pursuits of health, when the body lies before you weak and helpless; but when those occupations are of a character the most strongly opposed to anything we associate with grave or solemn ideas, the impression produced is infinitely more powerful. The theatre, and the public-house, were the chief themes of the wretched man's wanderings. It was evening, he fancied; he had a part to play that night; it was late, and he must leave home instantly. Why did they hold him, and prevent his going? – he should lose the money – he must go. No! they would not let him. He hid his face in his burning hands, and feebly bemoaned his own weakness, and the cruelty of his persecutors. A short pause, and he shouted out a few doggerel rhymes – the last he had ever learnt. He rose in bed, drew up his withered limbs, and rolled about in uncouth positions; he was acting – he was at the theatre. A minute's silence, and he murmured the burden of some roaring song. He had reached the old house at last: how hot the room was. He had been ill, very ill, but he was well now, and happy. Fill up his glass. Who was that, that dashed it from his lips? It was the same persecutor that had followed him before. He fell back upon his pillow and moaned aloud. A short period of oblivion, and he was wandering through a tedious maze of low arched-rooms – so low, sometimes, that he must creep upon his hands and knees to make his way along; it was close and dark, and every way he turned, some obstacle impeded his progress. There were insects too, hideous crawling things with eyes that stared upon him, and filled the very air around: glistening horribly amidst the thick darkness of the place. The walls and ceiling were alive with reptiles – the vault expanded to an enormous size – frightful figures flitted to and fro – and the faces of men he knew, rendered hideous by gibing[4] and mouthing, peered out from among them; they were searing him with heated irons, and binding his head with cords till the blood started; and he struggled madly for life.

'At the close of one of these paroxysms, when I had with great difficulty held him down in his bed, he sank into what appeared to be a slumber. Overpowered with watching and exertion, I had closed my eyes for a few minutes, when I felt a violent clutch on my shoulder. I awoke instantly. He had raised himself up, so as to seat himself in bed – a dreadful change had come over his face, but consciousness had returned, for he evidently knew me. The child who had been long since disturbed by his ravings, rose from its little bed, and ran towards its father, screaming with fright – the mother hastily caught it in her arms, lest he should injure it in the violence of his insanity; but, terrified by the alteration of his features, stood transfixed by the bed-side. He grasped my shoulder convulsively, and, striking his breast with the other hand, made a desperate attempt to articulate. It was unavailing – he extended his arm towards them, and made another violent effort. There was a rattling

The Dying Clown

noise in the throat – a glare of the eye – a short stifled groan – and he fell back – dead!'

———

It would afford us the highest gratification to be enabled to record Mr Pickwick's opinion of the foregoing anecdote. We have little doubt that we should have been enabled to present it to our readers, but for a most unfortunate occurrence.

Mr Pickwick had replaced on the table the glass which, during the last few sentences of the tale, he had retained in his hand; and had just made up his mind to speak – indeed, we have the authority of Mr Snodgrass's note-book for stating, that he had actually opened his mouth – when the waiter entered the room, and said –

'Some gentlemen, sir.'

It has been conjectured that Mr Pickwick was on the point of delivering some remarks which would have enlightened the world, if not the Thames, when he was thus interrupted: for he gazed sternly on the waiter's countenance, and then looked round on the company generally, as if seeking for information relative to the new comers.

'Oh!' said Mr Winkle, rising, 'some friends of mine – show them in. Very pleasant fellows,' added Mr Winkle, after the waiter had retired – 'Officers of the 97th, whose acquaintance I made rather oddly this morning. You will like them very much.'

Mr Pickwick's equanimity was at once restored. The waiter returned, and ushered three gentlemen into the room.

'Lieutenant Tappleton,' said Mr Winkle, 'Lieutenant Tappleton, Mr Pickwick – Doctor Payne, Mr Pickwick – Mr Snodgrass, you have seen before: my friend Mr Tupman, Doctor Payne – Dr Slammer, Mr Pickwick – Mr Tupman, Doctor Slam – .'

Here Mr Winkle suddenly paused; for strong emotion was visible on the countenance both of Mr Tupman and the Doctor.

'I have met *this* gentleman before,' said the Doctor, with marked emphasis.

'Indeed!' said Mr Winkle.

'And – and that person, too, if I am not mistaken,' said the Doctor, bestowing a scrutinising glance on the green-coated stranger. 'I think I gave that person a very pressing invitation last night, which he thought proper to decline.' Saying which the Doctor scowled magnanimously on the stranger, and whispered his friend Lieutenant Tappleton.

'You don't say so,' said that gentleman, at the conclusion of the whisper.

'I do, indeed,' replied Doctor Slammer.

'You are bound to kick him on the spot,' murmured the owner of the camp-stool with great importance.

'*Do* be quiet, Payne,' interposed the Lieutenant. 'Will you allow me to ask you, sir,' he said, addressing Mr Pickwick, who was considerably mystified by this very unpolite by-play, 'will you allow me to ask you, sir, whether that person belongs to your party?'

'No, sir,' replied Mr Pickwick, 'he is a guest of ours.'

'He is a member of your club, or I am mistaken?' said the Lieutenant, inquiringly.

'Certainly not,' responded Mr Pickwick.

'And never wears your club-button?' said the Lieutenant.

'No – never!' replied the astonished Mr Pickwick.

Lieutenant Tappleton turned round to his friend Doctor Slammer, with a scarcely perceptible shrug of the shoulder, as if implying some doubt of the accuracy of his recollection. The little Doctor looked wrathful, but confounded; and Mr Payne gazed with a ferocious aspect on the beaming countenance of the unconscious Pickwick.

'Sir,' said the Doctor, suddenly addressing Mr Tupman, in a tone which made that gentleman start as perceptibly as if a pin had been cunningly inserted in the calf of his leg, 'you were at the ball here last night!'

Mr Tupman gasped a faint affirmative, looking very hard at Mr Pickwick all the while.

'That person was your companion,' said the Doctor, pointing to the still unmoved stranger.

Mr Tupman admitted the fact.

'Now, sir,' said the Doctor to the stranger, 'I ask you once again, in the presence of these gentlemen, whether you choose to give me your card, and to receive the treatment of a gentleman; or whether you impose upon me the necessity of personally chastising you on the spot?'

'Stay, sir,' said Mr Pickwick, 'I really cannot allow this matter to go any further without some explanation. Tupman, recount the circumstances.'

Mr Tupman, thus solemnly abjured, stated the case in a few words; touched slightly on the borrowing of the coat; expatiated largely on its having been done 'after dinner;' wound up with a little penitence on his own account; and left the stranger to clear himself as he best could.

He was apparently about to proceed to do so, when Lieutenant

Tappleton, who had been eyeing him with great curiosity, said with considerable scorn – 'Haven't I seen you at the theatre, sir?'

'Certainly,' replied the unabashed stranger.

'He is a strolling actor,' said the Lieutenant, contemptuously; turning to Dr Slammer – 'He acts in the piece that the Officers of the 52nd get up at the Rochester Theatre to-morrow night. You cannot proceed in this affair, Slammer – impossible!'

'Quite!' said the dignified Payne.

'Sorry to have placed you in this disagreeable situation,' said Lieutenant Tappleton, addressing Mr Pickwick; 'allow me to suggest, that the best way of avoiding a recurrence of such scenes in future, will be to be more select in the choice of your companions. Good evening, sir!' and the Lieutenant bounced out of the room.

'And allow *me* to say, sir,' said the irascible Doctor Payne, 'that if I had been Tappleton, or if I had been Slammer, I would have pulled your nose, sir, and the nose of every man in this company. I would, sir, every man. Payne is my name, sir – Doctor Payne of the 43rd. Good evening, sir.' Having concluded this speech, and uttered the three last words in a loud key, he stalked majestically after his friend, closely followed by Doctor Slammer, who said nothing, but contented himself by withering the company with a look.

Rising rage and extreme bewilderment had swelled the noble breast of Mr Pickwick, almost to the bursting of his waistcoat, during the delivery of the above defiance. He stood transfixed to the spot, gazing on vacancy. The closing of the door recalled him to himself. He rushed forward with fury in his looks, and fire in his eye. His hand was upon the lock of the door; in another instant it would have been on the throat of Doctor Payne of the 43rd, had not Mr Snodgrass seized his revered leader by the coat tail, and dragged him back-wards.

'Restrain him,' cried Mr Snodgrass, 'Winkle, Tupman – he must not peril his distinguished life in such a cause as this.'

'Let me go,' said Mr Pickwick.

'Hold him tight,' shouted Mr Snodgrass; and by the united efforts of the whole company, Mr Pickwick was forced into an arm-chair.

'Leave him alone,' said the green-coated stranger – 'brandy and water – jolly old gentleman – lots of pluck – swallow this – ah! – capital stuff.' Having previously tested the virtues of a bumper, which had been mixed by the dismal man, the stranger applied the glass to Mr Pickwick's mouth; and the remainder of its contents rapidly disappeared.

There was a short pause; the brandy and water had done its

work; the amiable countenance of Mr Pickwick was fast recovering
its customary expression.

'They are not worth your notice,' said the dismal man.

'You are right, sir,' replied Mr Pickwick, 'they are not. I am
ashamed to have been betrayed into this warmth of feeling. Draw
your chair up to the table, sir.'

The dismal man readily complied: a circle was again formed
round the table, and harmony once more prevailed. Some lingering
irritability appeared to find a resting-place in Mr Winkle's bosom,
occasioned possibly by the temporary abstraction of his coat –
though it is scarcely reasonable to suppose that so slight a circumstance can have excited even a passing feeling of anger in a
Pickwickian breast. With this exception, their good humour was
completely restored; and the evening concluded with the conviviality with which it had begun.

CHAPTER 4

A Field-Day and Bivouac. More new Friends.
An Invitation to the Country

Many authors entertain, not only a foolish, but a really dishonest
objection to acknowledge the sources from whence they derive
much valuable information. We have no such feeling. We are merely
endeavouring to discharge, in an up-right manner, the responsible
duties of our editorial functions; and whatever ambition we might
have felt under other circumstances to lay claim to the authorship
of these adventures, a regard for truth forbids us to do more than
claim the merit of their judicious arrangement and impartial narration. The Pickwick papers are our New River Head;[1] and we may
be compared to the New River Company. The labours of others
have raised for us an immense reservoir of important facts. We
merely lay them on, and communicate them, in a clear and gentle
stream, through the medium of these numbers, to a world thirsting
for Pickwickian knowledge.

Acting in this spirit, and resolutely proceeding on our determination to avow our obligations to the authorities we have consulted,
we frankly say, that to the note-book of Mr Snodgrass are we
indebted for the particulars recorded in this, and the succeeding

chapter – particulars which, now that we have disburdened our conscience, we shall proceed to detail without further comment.

The whole population of Rochester and the adjoining towns rose from their beds at an early hour of the following morning, in a state of the utmost bustle and excitement. A grand review was to take place upon the Lines.[2] The manœuvres of half-a-dozen regiments were to be inspected by the eagle eye of the commander-in-chief; temporary fortifications had been erected, the citadel was to be attacked and taken, and a mine was to be sprung.[3]

Mr Pickwick was, as our readers may have gathered from the slight extract we gave from his description of Chatham, an enthusiastic admirer of the army. Nothing could have been more delightful to him – nothing could have harmonised so well with the peculiar feeling of each of his companions – as this sight. Accordingly they were soon a-foot, and walking in the direction of the scene of action, towards which crowds of people were already pouring from a variety of quarters.

The appearance of everything on the Lines denoted that the approaching ceremony was one of the utmost grandeur and importance. There were sentries posted to keep the ground for the troops, and servants on the batteries keeping places for the ladies, and sergeants running to and fro, with vellum-covered books under their arms, and Colonel Bulder, in full military uniform, on horseback, galloping first to one place and then to another, and backing his horse among the people, and prancing, and curvetting,[4] and shouting in a most alarming manner, and making himself very hoarse in the voice, and very red in the face, without any assignable cause or reason whatever. Officers were running backwards and forwards, first communicating with Colonel Bulder, and then ordering the sergeants, and then running away altogether; and even the very privates themselves looked from behind their glazed stocks with an air of mysterious solemnity, which sufficiently bespoke the special nature of the occasion.

Mr Pickwick and his three companions stationed themselves in the front rank of the crowd, and patiently awaited the commencement of the proceedings. The throng was increasing every moment; and the efforts they were compelled to make, to retain the position they had gained, sufficiently occupied their attention during the two hours that ensued. At one time there was a sudden pressure from behind; and then Mr Pickwick was jerked forward for several yards, with a degree of speed and elasticity highly inconsistent with the general gravity of his demeanour; at another moment there was a request to 'keep back' from the front, and then the butt end of a musket was either dropped upon Mr Pickwick's toe, to remind him of the demand, or thrust into his chest, to ensure its being complied with. Then some facetious gentlemen on the left, after pressing sideways in a body, and squeezing Mr Snodgrass into the very last extreme of human torture, would request to know 'vere he vos a shovin' to;' and when Mr Winkle had done expressing his excessive indignation at witnessing this unprovoked assault, some person behind would knock his hat over his eyes, and beg the favour of his putting his head in his pocket. These, and other practical witticisms, coupled with the unaccountable absence of Mr Tupman (who had suddenly disappeared, and was nowhere to be found), rendered their situation upon the whole rather more uncomfortable than pleasing or desirable.

At length that low roar of many voices ran through the crowd, which usually announces the arrival of whatever they have been waiting for. All eyes were turned in the direction of the sally-port.[5] A few moments of eager expectation, and colours were seen fluttering gaily in the air, arms glistened brightly in the sun, column after column poured on to the plain. The troops halted and formed; the word of command rung through the line, there was a general clash of muskets as arms were presented; and the commander-in-chief, attended by Colonel Bulder and numerous officers, cantered to the front. The military bands struck up altogether; the horses stood upon two legs each, cantered backwards, and whisked their tails about in all directions: the dogs barked, the mob screamed, the troops recovered, and nothing was to be seen on either side, as far as the eye could reach, but a long perspective of red coats and white trousers, fixed and motionless.

Mr Pickwick had been so fully occupied in falling about, and disentangling himself, miraculously, from between the legs of horses, that he had not enjoyed sufficient leisure to observe the scene before him, until it assumed the appearance we have just described. When he was at last enabled to stand firmly on his legs, his gratification and delight were unbounded.

'Can anything be finer or more delightful?' he inquired of Mr Winkle.

'Nothing,' replied that gentleman, who had had a short man standing on each of his feet for the quarter of an hour immediately preceding.

'It is indeed a noble and a brilliant sight,' said Mr Snodgrass, in whose bosom a blaze of poetry was rapidly bursting forth, 'to see the gallant defenders of their country drawn up in brilliant array before its peaceful citizens; their faces beaming – not with warlike ferocity, but with civilised gentleness; their eyes flashing – not with the rude fire of rapine or revenge, but with the soft light of humanity and intelligence.'

Mr Pickwick fully entered into the spirit of this eulogium, but he could not exactly re-echo its terms; for the soft light of intelligence burnt rather feebly in the eyes of the warriors, inasmuch as the command 'eyes front' had been given, and all the spectator saw before him was several thousand pair of optics, staring straight forward, wholly divested of any expression whatever.

'We are in a capital situation now,' said Mr Pickwick, looking round him. The crowd had gradually dispersed in their immediate vicinity, and they were nearly alone.

'Capital!' echoed both Mr Snodgrass and Mr Winkle.

'What are they doing now?' inquired Mr Pickwick, adjusting his spectacles.

'I – I – rather think,' said Mr Winkle, changing colour – 'I rather think they're going to fire.'

'Nonsense,' said Mr Pickwick, hastily.

'I – I – really think they are,' urged Mr Snodgrass, somewhat alarmed.

'Impossible,' replied Mr Pickwick. He had hardly uttered the word, when the whole half-dozen regiments levelled their muskets as if they had but one common object, and that object the Pickwickians, and burst forth with the most awful and tremendous discharge that ever shook the earth to its centre, or an elderly gentleman off his.

It was in this trying situation, exposed to a galling fire of blank cartridges, and harassed by the operations of the military, a fresh body of whom had begun to fall in on the opposite side, that Mr Pickwick displayed that perfect coolness and self-possession, which are the indispensable accompaniments of a great mind. He seized Mr Winkle by the arm, and placing himself between that gentleman and Mr Snodgrass, earnestly besought them to remember that beyond the possibility of being rendered deaf by the noise, there was no immediate danger to be apprehended from the firing.

'But – but – suppose some of the men should happen to have ball cartridges by mistake,' remonstrated Mr Winkle, pallid at the supposition he was himself conjuring up. 'I heard something whistle through the air just now – so sharp; close to my ear.'

'We had better throw ourselves on our faces, hadn't we?' said Mr Snodgrass.

'No, no – it's over now,' said Mr Pickwick. His lip might quiver, and his cheek might blanch, but no expression of fear or concern escaped the lips of that immortal man.

Mr Pickwick was right: the firing ceased; but he had scarcely time to congratulate himself on the accuracy of his opinion, when a quick movement was visible in the line: the hoarse shout of the word of command ran along it, and before either of the party could form a guess at the meaning of this new manœuvre, the whole of the half-dozen regiments, with fixed bayonets, charged at double quick time down upon the very spot on which Mr Pickwick and his friends were stationed.

Man is but mortal: and there is a point beyond which human courage cannot extend. Mr Pickwick gazed through his spectacles for an instant on the advancing mass, and then fairly turned his back and – we will not say fled; firstly, because it is an ignoble term, and, secondly, because Mr Pickwick's figure was by no means adapted for that mode of retreat – he trotted away, at as quick a rate as his legs would convey him; so quickly, indeed, that he did not perceive the awkwardness of his situation, to the full extent, until too late.

The opposite troops, whose falling-in had perplexed Mr Pickwick a few seconds before, were drawn up to repel the mimic attack of the sham besiegers of the citadel; and the consequence was that Mr Pickwick and his two companions found themselves suddenly inclosed between two lines of great length, the one advancing at a rapid pace, and the other firmly waiting the collision in hostile array.

'Hoi!' shouted the officers of the advancing line.

'Get out of the way,' cried the officers of the stationary one.

'Where are we to go to?' screamed the agitated Pickwickians.

'Hoi – hoi – hoi!' was the only reply. There was a moment of intense bewilderment, a heavy tramp of footsteps, a violent concussion, a smothered laugh; the half-dozen regiments were half a thousand yards off, and the soles of Mr Pickwick's boots were elevated in air.

Mr Snodgrass and Mr Winkle had each performed a compulsory somerset with remarkable agility, when the first object that met the eyes of the latter as he sat on the ground, staunching with a yellow silk handkerchief the stream of life which issued from his nose, was his venerated leader at some distance off, running after his own hat, which was gamboling playfully away in perspective.

There are very few moments in a man's existence when he experiences so much ludicrous distress, or meets with so little charitable commiseration, as when he is in pursuit of his own hat. A vast deal of coolness, and a peculiar degree of judgment, are requisite in catching a hat. A man must not be precipitate, or he runs over it; he must not rush into the opposite extreme, or he loses it altogether. The best way is, to keep gently up with the object of pursuit, to be wary and cautious, to watch your opportunity well, get gradually before it, then make a rapid dive, seize it by the crown, and stick it firmly on your head: smiling pleasantly all the time, as if you thought it as good a joke as anybody else.

There was a fine gentle wind, and Mr Pickwick's hat rolled sportively before it. The wind puffed, and Mr Pickwick puffed, and the hat rolled over and over as merrily as a lively porpoise in a strong tide; and on it might have rolled, far beyond Mr Pickwick's reach, had not its course been providentially stopped, just as that gentleman was on the point of resigning it to its fate.

Mr Pickwick, we say, was completely exhausted, and about to give up the chase, when the hat was blown with some violence against the wheel of a carriage, which was drawn up in a line with half-a-dozen other vehicles on the spot to which his steps had been directed. Mr Pickwick, perceiving his advantage, darted briskly forward, secured his property, planted it on his head, and paused to take breath. He had not been stationary half a minute, when he heard his own name eagerly pronounced by a voice, which he at once recognised as Mr Tupman's, and, looking upwards, he beheld a sight which filled him with surprise and pleasure.

In an open barouche, the horses of which had been taken out, the better to accommodate it to the crowded place, stood a stout old gentleman, in a blue coat and bright buttons, corduroy breeches and top boots, two young ladies in scarfs and feathers, a young gentleman apparently enamoured of one of the young ladies in scarfs and feathers, a lady of doubtful age, probably the aunt of the aforesaid, and Mr Tupman, as easy and unconcerned as if he had belonged to the family from the first moments of his infancy. Fastened up behind the barouche was a hamper of spacious dimensions – one of those hampers which always awakens in a contemplative mind associations connected with cold fowls, tongues, and bottles of wine – and on the box sat a fat and red-faced boy, in a state of somnolency, whom no speculative observer

Mr Pickwick in chase of his hat

could have regarded for an instant without setting down as the official dispenser of the contents of the before-mentioned hamper, when the proper time for their consumption should arrive.

Mr Pickwick had bestowed a hasty glance on these interesting objects, when he was again greeted by his faithful disciple.

'Pickwick – Pickwick,' said Mr Tupman: 'come up here. Make haste.'

'Come along, sir. Pray, come up,' said the stout gentleman. 'Joe! – damn that boy, he's gone to sleep again. – Joe, let down the steps.' The fat boy rolled slowly off the box, let down the steps, and held the carriage door invitingly open. Mr Snodgrass and Mr Winkle came up at the moment.

'Room for you all, gentlemen,' said the stout man. 'Two inside, and one out. Joe, make room for one of these gentlemen on the box. Now, sir, come along;' and the stout gentleman extended his arm, and pulled first Mr Pickwick, and then Mr Snodgrass, into the barouche by main force. Mr Winkle mounted to the box, the fat boy waddled to the same perch, and fell fast asleep instantly.

'Well, gentlemen,' said the stout man, 'very glad to see you. Know you very well, gentlemen, though you mayn't remember me. I spent some ev'nins at your club last winter – picked up my friend Mr Tupman here this morning, and very glad I was to see him. Well, sir, and how are you? You do look uncommon well, to be sure.'

Mr Pickwick acknowledged the compliment, and cordially shook hands with the stout gentleman in the top boots.

'Well, and how are you, sir?' said the stout gentleman, addressing Mr Snodgrass with paternal anxiety. 'Charming, eh? Well, that's right – that's right. And how are you, sir (to Mr Winkle)? Well, I am glad to hear you say you are well; very glad I am, to be sure. My daughters, gentlemen – my gals these are; and that's my sister, Miss Rachael Wardle. She's a Miss, she is; and yet she an't a Miss – eh, sir, eh?' And the stout gentleman playfully inserted his elbow between the ribs of Mr Pickwick, and laughed very heartily.

'Lor, brother?' said Miss Wardle, with a deprecating smile.

'True, true,' said the stout gentleman; 'no one can deny it. Gentlemen, I beg your pardon; this is my friend Mr Trundle. And now you all know each other, let's be comfortable and happy, and see what's going forward; that's what I say.' So the stout gentleman put on his spectacles, and Mr Pickwick pulled out his glass, and everybody stood up in the carriage, and looked over somebody else's shoulder at the evolutions of the military.

Astounding evolutions they were, one rank firing over the heads of another rank, and then running away; and then the other rank firing over the heads of another rank, and running away in their turn; and then forming squares, with officers in the centre; and then descending the trench on one side with scaling ladders, and ascending it on the other again by the same means; and knocking down barricades of baskets, and behaving in the most gallant manner possible. Then there was such a ramming down of the contents of enormous guns on the battery, with instruments like magnified mops; such a preparation before they were let off, and such an awful noise when they did go, that the air resounded with the screams of ladies. The young Miss Wardles were so frightened, that Mr Trundle was actually obliged to hold one of them up in the carriage, while Mr Snodgrass supported the other, and Mr Wardle's sister suffered under such a dreadful state of nervous alarm, that Mr Tupman found it indispensably necessary to put his arm round her waist, to keep her up at all. Everybody was excited, except the fat boy, and he slept as soundly as if the roaring of cannon were his ordinary lullaby.

'Joe, Joe!' said the stout gentleman, when the citadel was taken, and the besiegers and besieged sat down to dinner. 'Damn that boy, he's gone to sleep again. Be good enough to pinch him, sir – in the leg, if you please; nothing else wakes him – thank you. Undo the hamper, Joe.'

The fat boy, who had been effectually roused by the compression of a portion of his leg between the finger and thumb of Mr Winkle, rolled off the box once again, and proceeded to unpack the hamper, with more expedition than could have been expected from his previous inactivity.

'Now, we must sit close,' said the stout gentleman. After a great many jokes about squeezing the ladies' sleeves, and a vast quantity of blushing at sundry jocose proposals, that the ladies should sit in the gentlemen's laps, the whole party were stowed down in the barouche; and the stout gentleman proceeded to hand the things from the fat boy (who had mounted up behind for the purpose) into the carriage.

'Now, Joe, knives and forks.' The knives and forks were handed in, and the ladies and gentlemen inside, and Mr Winkle on the box, were each furnished with those useful instruments.

'Plates, Joe, plates.' A similar process employed in the distribution of the crockery.

'Now, Joe, the fowls. Damn that boy; he's gone to sleep again.

Joe! Joe!' (Sundry taps on the head with a stick, and the fat boy, with some difficulty, roused from his lethargy). 'Come, hand in the eatables.'

There was something in the sound of the last word which roused the unctuous boy. He jumped up: and the leaden eyes, which twinkled behind his mountainous cheeks, leered horribly upon the food as he unpacked it from the basket.

'Now make haste,' said Mr Wardle; for the fat boy was hanging fondly over a capon, which he seemed wholly unable to part with. The boy sighed deeply, and, bestowing an ardent gaze upon its plumpness, unwillingly consigned it to his master.

'That's right – look sharp. Now the tongue – now the pigeon-pie. Take care of that veal and ham – mind the lobsters – take the salad out of the cloth – give me the dressing.' Such were the hurried orders which issued from the lips of Mr Wardle, as he handed in the different articles described, and placed dishes in everybody's hands, and on everybody's knees, in endless number.

'Now, an't this capital?' inquired that jolly personage, when the work of destruction had commenced.

'Capital!' said Mr Winkle, who was carving a fowl on the box.

'Glass of wine?'

'With the greatest pleasure.'

'You'd better have a bottle to yourself, up there, hadn't you?'

'You're very good.'

'Joe!'

'Yes, sir.' (He wasn't asleep this time, having just succeeded in abstracting a veal patty.)

'Bottle of wine to the gentleman on the box. Glad to see you, sir.'

'Thankee.' Mr Winkle emptied his glass, and placed the bottle on the coach-box, by his side.

'Will you permit me to have the pleasure, sir?' said Mr Trundle to Mr Winkle.

'With great pleasure,' replied Mr Winkle to Mr Trundle: and then the two gentlemen took wine, after which they took a glass of wine round, ladies and all.

'How dear Emily is flirting with the strange gentleman,' whispered the spinster aunt, with true spinster-aunt-like envy, to her brother Mr Wardle.

'Oh! I don't know,' said the jolly old gentleman; 'all very natural, I dare say – nothing unusual. Mr Pickwick, some wine, sir?' Mr Pickwick, who had been deeply investigating the interior of the pigeon-pie, readily assented.

'Emily, my dear,' said the spinster aunt, with a patronising air, 'don't talk so loud, love.'

'Lor, aunt!'

'Aunt and the little old gentleman want to have it all to themselves, I think,' whispered Miss Isabella Wardle to her sister Emily. The young ladies laughed very heartily, and the old one tried to look amiable, but couldn't manage it.

'Young girls have *such* spirits,' said Miss Wardle to Mr Tupman, with an air of gentle commiseration, as if animal spirits were contraband, and their possession without a permit, a high crime and misdemeanour.

'Oh, they have,' replied Mr Tupman, not exactly making the sort of reply that was expected from him. 'It's quite delightful.'

'Hem!' said Miss Wardle, rather dubiously.

'Will you permit me,' said Mr Tupman, in his blandest manner, touching the enchanting Rachael's wrist with one hand, and gently elevating the bottle with the other. 'Will you permit me?'

'Oh, sir!' Mr Tupman looked most impressive; and Rachael expressed her fear that more guns were going off, in which case, of course, she would have required support again.

'Do you think my dear nieces pretty?' whispered their affectionate aunt to Mr Tupman.

'I should, if their aunt wasn't here,' replied the ready Pickwickian, with a passionate glance.

'Oh, you naughty man – but really, if their complexions were a *little* better, don't you think they would be nice-looking girls – by candle-light?'

'Yes; I think they would;' said Mr Tupman, with an air of indifference.

'Oh, you quiz[6] – I know what you were going to say.'

'What?' inquired Mr Tupman, who had not precisely made up his mind to say anything at all.

'You were going to say, that Isabella stoops – I know you were – you men are such observers. Well, so she does; it can't be denied; and, certainly, if there is one thing more than another that makes a girl look ugly, it is stooping. I often tell her, that when she gets a little older, she'll be quite frightful. Well, you *are* a quiz!'

Mr Tupman had no objection to earning the reputation at so cheap a rate: so he looked very knowing, and smiled mysteriously.

'What a sarcastic smile,' said the admiring Rachael; 'I declare I'm quite afraid of you.'

'Afraid of me!'

'Oh, you can't disguise anything from me – I know what that smile means, very well.'

'What?' said Mr Tupman, who had not the slightest notion himself.

'You mean,' said the amiable aunt, sinking her voice still lower – 'You mean, that you don't think Isabella's stooping is as bad as Emily's boldness. Well, she *is* bold! You cannot think how wretched it makes me sometimes – I'm sure I cry about it for hours together – my dear brother is *so* good and *so* unsuspicious, that he never sees it; if he did, I'm quite certain it would break his heart. I wish I could think it was only manner – I hope it may be – ' (here the affectionate relative heaved a deep sigh, and shook her head despondingly.)

'I'm sure aunt's talking about us,' whispered Miss Emily Wardle to her sister – 'I'm quite certain of it – she looks so malicious.'

'Is she?' replied Isabella – 'Hem! aunt, dear!'

'Yes, my dear love!'

'I'm *so* afraid you'll catch cold, aunt – have a silk handkerchief to tie round your dear old head – you really should take care of yourself – consider your age!'

However well deserved this piece of retaliation might have been, it was as vindictive a one as could well have been resorted to. There is no guessing in what form of reply the aunt's indignation would have vented itself, had not Mr Wardle unconsciously changed the subject, by calling emphatically for Joe.

'Damn that boy,' said the old gentleman, 'he's gone to sleep again.'

'Very extraordinary boy, that,' said Mr Pickwick, 'does he always sleep in this way?'

'Sleep!' said the old gentleman, 'he's always asleep. Goes on errands fast asleep, and snores as he waits at table.'

'How very odd!' said Mr Pickwick.

'Ah! odd indeed,' returned the old gentleman; 'I'm proud of that boy – wouldn't part with him on any account – he's a natural curiosity! Here, Joe – Joe – take these things away, and open another bottle – d'ye hear?'

The fat boy rose, opened his eyes, swallowed the huge piece of pie he had been in the act of masticating when he last fell asleep, and slowly obeyed his master's orders – gloating languidly over the remains of the feast, as he removed the plates, and deposited them in the hamper. The fresh bottle was produced, and speedily emptied: the hamper was made fast in its old place – the fat boy once more mounted the box – the spectacles and pocket-glass were again adjusted – and the evolutions of the military recommenced. There was a great fizzing and banging of guns, and starting of ladies – and then a mine was sprung, to the gratification of everybody – and when the mine had gone off, the military and the company followed its example, and went off too.

'Now, mind,' said the old gentleman, as he shook hands with Mr Pickwick at the conclusion of a conversation which had been carried on at intervals, during the conclusion of the proceedings – 'we shall see you all to-morrow.'

'Most certainly,' replied Mr Pickwick.

'You have got the address.'

'Manor Farm, Dingley Dell,' said Mr Pickwick, consulting his pocket-book.

'That's it,' said the old gentleman. 'I don't let you off, mind, under a week; and undertake that you shall see everything worth seeing. If you've come down for a country life, come to me, and I'll give you plenty of it. Joe – damn that boy, he's gone to sleep again – Joe, help Tom put in the horses.'

The horses were put in – the driver mounted – the fat boy clambered up by his side – farewells were exchanged – and the carriage rattled off. As the Pickwickians turned round to take a last glimpse of it, the setting sun cast a rich glow on the faces of their entertainers, and fell upon the form of the fat boy. His head was sunk upon his bosom; and he slumbered again.

CHAPTER 5

A short one. Showing, among other Matters, how
Mr Pickwick undertook to drive, and Mr Winkle to
ride; and how they both did it

Bright and pleasant was the sky, balmy the air, and beautiful the appearance of every object around, as Mr Pickwick leant over the balustrades of Rochester Bridge, contemplating nature, and waiting for breakfast. The scene was indeed one which might well have charmed a far less reflective mind, than that to which it was presented.

On the left of the spectator lay the ruined wall, broken in many places, and in some, overhanging the narrow beach below in rude and heavy masses. Huge knots of sea-weed hung upon the jagged and pointed stones, trembling in every breath of wind; and the green ivy clung mournfully round the dark and ruined battlements. Behind it rose the ancient castle, its towers roofless, and its massive walls crumbling away, but telling us proudly of its own might and strength, as when, seven hundred years ago, it rang with the clash of arms, or resounded with the noise of feasting and revelry. On either side, the banks of the Medway, covered with corn-fields and pastures, with here and there a windmill, or a distant church, stretched away as far as the eye could see, presenting a rich and varied landscape, rendered more beautiful by the changing shadows which passed swiftly across it, as the thin and half-formed clouds skimmed away in the light of the morning sun. The river, reflecting the clear blue of the sky, glistened and sparkled as it flowed noiselessly on; and the oars of the fishermen dipped into the water with a clear and liquid sound, as the heavy but picturesque boats glided slowly down the stream.

Mr Pickwick was roused from the agreeable reverie into which he had been led by the objects before him, by a deep sigh, and a touch on his shoulder. He turned round: and the dismal man was at his side.

'Contemplating the scene?' inquired the dismal man.

'I was,' said Mr Pickwick.

'And congratulating yourself on being up so soon?' Mr Pickwick nodded assent.

'Ah! people need to rise early, to see the sun in all his splendour, for his brightness seldom lasts the day through. The morning of day and the morning of life are but too much alike.'

'You speak truly, sir,' said Mr Pickwick.

'How common the saying,' continued the dismal man, '"The morning's too fine to last." How well might it be applied to our every-day existence. God! what would I forfeit to have the days of my childhood restored, or to be able to forget them for ever!'

'You have seen much trouble, sir,' said Mr Pickwick, compassionately.

'I have,' said the dismal man, hurriedly; 'I have. More than those who see me now would believe possible.' He paused for an instant, and then said, abruptly –

'Did it ever strike you, on such a morning as this, that drowning would be happiness and peace?'

'God bless me, no!' replied Mr Pickwick, edging a little from the balustrade, as the possibility of the dismal man's tipping him over, by way of experiment, occurred to him rather forcibly.

'*I* have thought so, often,' said the dismal man, without noticing the action. 'The calm, cool water seems to me to murmur an invitation to repose and rest. A bound, a splash, a brief struggle; there is an eddy for an instant, it gradually subsides into a gentle ripple; the waters have closed above your head, and the world has closed upon your miseries and misfortunes for ever.' The sunken eye of the dismal man flashed brightly as he spoke, but the momentary excitement quickly subsided; and he turned calmly away, as he said –

'There – enough of that. I wish to see you on another subject. You invited me to read that paper, the night before last, and listened attentively while I did so.'

'I did,' replied Mr Pickwick; 'and I certainly thought—'

'I asked for no opinion,' said the dismal man, interrupting him, 'and I want none. You are travelling for amusement and instruction. Suppose I forwarded you a curious manuscript – observe, not curious because wild or improbable, but curious as a leaf from the romance of real life. Would you communicate it to the club, of which you have spoken so frequently?'

'Certainly,' replied Mr Pickwick, 'if you wished it; and it would be entered on their transactions.'

'You shall have it,' replied the dismal man. 'Your address;' and, Mr Pickwick having communicated their probable route, the dismal man carefully noted it down in a greasy pocket-book, and, resisting Mr Pickwick's pressing invitation to breakfast, left that gentleman at his inn, and walked slowly away.

Mr Pickwick found that his three companions had risen, and were waiting his arrival to commence breakfast, which was ready laid in tempting display. They sat down to the meal; and broiled ham, eggs, tea, coffee, and sundries, began to disappear with a rapidity which at once bore testimony to the excellence of the fare, and the appetites of its consumers.

'Now, about Manor Farm,' said Mr Pickwick. 'How shall we go?'

'We had better consult the waiter, perhaps,' said Mr Tupman, and the waiter was summoned accordingly.

'Dingley Dell, gentlemen – fifteen miles, gentlemen – cross road – post-chaise, sir?'

'Post-chaise won't hold more than two,' said Mr Pickwick.

'True, sir – beg your pardon, sir. – Very nice four-wheeled chaise, sir – seat for two behind – one in front for the gentleman that drives – oh! beg your pardon, sir – that'll only hold three.'

'What's to be done?' said Mr Snodgrass.

'Perhaps one of the gentlemen would like to ride, sir?' suggested the waiter, looking towards Mr Winkle; 'very good saddle horses, sir – any of Mr Wardle's men coming to Rochester bring 'em back, sir.'

'The very thing,' said Mr Pickwick. 'Winkle, will you go on horseback?'

Mr Winkle did entertain considerable misgivings in the very lowest recesses of his own heart, relative to his equestrian skill; but, as he would not have them even suspected on any account, he at once replied with great hardihood, 'Certainly. I should enjoy it, of all things.'

Mr Winkle had rushed upon his fate; there was no resource. 'Let them be at the door by eleven,' said Mr Pickwick.

'Very well, sir,' replied the waiter.

The waiter retired; the breakfast concluded; and the travellers ascended to their respective bed-rooms, to prepare a change of clothing, to take with them on their approaching expedition.

Mr Pickwick had made his preliminary arrangements, and was looking over the coffee-room blinds at the passengers in the street, when the waiter entered, and announced that the chaise was ready – an announcement which the vehicle itself confirmed, by forthwith appearing before the coffee-room blinds aforesaid.

It was a curious little green box on four wheels, with a low place like a wine-bin for two behind, and an elevated perch for one in front, drawn by an immense brown horse, displaying great symmetry of bone. An hostler[1] stood near, holding by the bridle another immense horse – apparently a near relative of the animal in the chaise – ready saddled for Mr Winkle.

'Bless my soul!' said Mr Pickwick, as they stood upon the pavement while the coats were being put in. 'Bless my soul! who's to drive? I never thought of that.'

'Oh! you, of course,' said Mr Tupman.

'Of course,' said Mr Snodgrass.

'I!' exclaimed Mr Pickwick.

'Not the slightest fear, sir,' interposed the hostler. 'Warrant him quiet, sir; a hinfant in arms might drive him.'

'He don't shy, does he?' inquired Mr Pickwick.

'Shy, sir? – He wouldn't shy if he was to meet a vaggin-load of monkeys with their tails burnt off.'

The last recommendation was indisputable. Mr Tupman and Mr Snodgrass got into the bin; Mr Pickwick ascended to his perch, and deposited his feet on a floor-clothed shelf, erected beneath it for that purpose.

'Now, shiny Villiam,' said the hostler to the deputy hostler, 'give the gen'lm'n the ribbins.' 'Shiny Villiam' – so called, probably, from his sleek hair and oily countenance – placed the reins in Mr Pickwick's left hand; and the upper hostler thrust a whip into his right.

'Wo – o !' cried Mr Pickwick, as the tall quadruped evinced a decided inclination to back into the coffee-room window.

'Wo – o !' echoed Mr Tupman and Mr Snodgrass, from the bin.

'Only his playfulness, gen'lm'n,' said the head hostler encouragingly; 'jist kitch hold on him, Villiam.' The deputy restrained the animal's impetuosity, and the principal ran to assist Mr Winkle in mounting.

'T'other side, sir, if you please.'

'Blowed if the gen'lm'n worn't a gettin' up on the wrong side,' whispered a grinning post-boy to the inexpressibly gratified waiter.

Mr Winkle, thus instructed, climbed into his saddle, with about as much difficulty as he would have experienced in getting up the side of a first-rate man-of-war.

'All right?' inquired Mr Pickwick, with an inward presentiment that it was all wrong.

'All right,' replied Mr Winkle faintly.

'Let 'em go,' cried the hostler, – 'Hold him in, sir,' and away went the chaise, and the saddle-horse, with Mr Pickwick on the box of the one, and Mr Winkle on the back of the other, to the delight and gratification of the whole inn yard.

'What makes him go sideways?' said Mr Snodgrass in the bin, to Mr Winkle in the saddle.

'I can't imagine,' replied Mr Winkle. His horse was drifting up the street in the most mysterious manner – side first, with his head towards one side of the way, and his tail towards the other.

Mr Pickwick had no leisure to observe either this or any other particular, the whole of his faculties being concentrated in the management of the animal attached to the chaise, who displayed various peculiarities, highly interesting to a by-stander, but by no means equally amusing to any one seated behind him. Besides constantly jerking his head up, in a very unpleasant and uncomfortable manner, and tugging at the reins to an extent which rendered it a matter of great difficulty for Mr Pickwick to hold them, he had a singular propensity for darting suddenly every now and then to the side of the road, then stopping short, and then rushing forward for some minutes, at a speed which it was wholly impossible to control.

'What *can* he mean by this?' said Mr Snodgrass, when the horse had executed this manœuvre for the twentieth time.

'I don't know,' replied Mr Tupman; 'it *looks* very like shying, don't it?' Mr Snodgrass was about to reply, when he was interrupted by a shout from Mr Pickwick.

'Woo!' said that gentleman; 'I have dropped my whip.'

'Winkle,' said Mr Snodgrass, as the equestrian came trotting up on the tall horse, with his hat over his ears, and shaking all over, as if he would shake to pieces, with the violence of the exercise, 'pick up the whip, there's a good fellow.' Mr Winkle pulled at the bridle of the tall horse till he was black in the face; and having at length succeeded in stopping him, dismounted, handed the whip to Mr Pickwick, and grasping the reins, prepared to remount.

Now whether the tall horse, in the natural playfulness of his disposition, was desirous of having a little innocent recreation with Mr Winkle, or whether it occurred to him that he could perform the journey as much to his own satisfaction without a rider as with one, are points upon which, of course, we can arrive at no definite and distinct conclusion. By whatever motives the animal was actuated, certain it is that Mr Winkle had no sooner touched the reins, than he slipped them over his head, and darted backwards to their full length.

'Poor fellow,' said Mr Winkle, soothingly, – 'poor fellow – good old horse.' The 'poor fellow' was proof against flattery: the more Mr Winkle tried to get nearer him, the more he sidled away; and, notwithstanding all kinds of coaxing and wheedling, there were Mr Winkle and the horse going round and round each other for ten minutes, at the end of which time each was at precisely the same distance from the other as when they first commenced – an unsatisfactory sort of thing under any circumstances, but particularly so in a lonely road, where no assistance can be procured.

'What am I to do?' shouted Mr Winkle, after the dodging had been prolonged for a considerable time. 'What am I to do? I can't get on him.'

'You had better lead him till we come to a turnpike,' replied Mr Pickwick from the chaise.

'But he won't come!' roared Mr Winkle. 'Do come, and hold him.'

Mr Pickwick was the very personation of kindness and humanity: he threw the reins on the horse's back, and having descended from his seat, carefully drew the chaise into the hedge, lest anything should come along the road, and stepped back to the assistance of his distressed companion, leaving Mr Tupman and Mr Snodgrass in the vehicle.

The horse no sooner beheld Mr Pickwick advancing towards him with the chaise whip in his hand, than he exchanged the rotatory motion in which he had previously indulged, for a retrograde movement of so very determined a character, that it at once drew Mr Winkle, who was still at the end of the bridle, at a rather quicker rate than fast walking, in the direction from which they had just come. Mr Pickwick ran to his assistance, but the faster Mr Pickwick ran forward, the faster the horse ran backward. There was a great scraping of feet, and kicking up of the dust; and at last Mr Winkle, his arms being nearly pulled out of their sockets, fairly let go his hold. The horse paused, stared, shook his head, turned round, and quietly trotted home to Rochester, leaving Mr Winkle and Mr Pickwick gazing on each other with countenances of blank dismay. A rattling noise at a little distance attracted their attention. They looked up.

'Bless my soul!' exclaimed the agonized Mr Pickwick, 'there's the other horse running away!'

It was but too true. The animal was startled by the noise, and the reins were on his back. The result may be guessed. He tore off with the four-wheeled chaise behind him, and Mr Tupman and Mr Snodgrass in the four-wheeled chaise. The heat was a short one. Mr Tupman threw himself into the hedge, Mr Snodgrass followed his example, the horse dashed the four-wheeled chaise against a wooden bridge, separated the wheels from the body, and the bin from the perch; and finally stood stock still to gaze upon the ruin he had made.

The first care of the two unspilt friends was to extricate their unfortunate companions from their bed of quickset[2] – a process which gave them the unspeakable satisfaction of discovering that they had sustained no injury, beyond sundry rents in their garments, and various lacerations from the brambles. The next thing to be done was, to unharness the horse. This complicated process having been effected, the party walked slowly forward, leading the horse among them, and abandoning the chaise to its fate.

An hour's walking brought the travellers to a little road-side public-house, with two elm trees, a horse trough, and a sign-post,

Mr Winkle soothes the refractory Steed

in front; one or two deformed hay-ricks behind, a kitchen garden at the side, and rotten sheds and mouldering out-houses jumbled in strange confusion all about it. A red-headed man was working in the garden; and to him Mr Pickwick called lustily – 'Hallo there!'

The red-headed man raised his body, shaded his eyes with his hand, and stared, long and coolly, at Mr Pickwick and his companions.

'Hallo there!' repeated Mr Pickwick.

'Hallo!' was the red-headed man's reply.

'How far is it to Dingley Dell?'

'Better er seven mile.'

'Is it a good road?'

'No, t'ant.' Having uttered this brief reply, and apparently satisfied himself with another scrutiny, the red-headed man resumed his work.

'We want to put this horse up here,' said Mr Pickwick; 'I suppose we can, can't we?'

'Want to put that ere horse up, do ee?' repeated the red-headed man, leaning on his spade.

'Of course,' replied Mr Pickwick, who had by this time advanced, horse in hand, to the garden rails.

'Missus' – roared the man with the red head, emerging from the garden, and looking very hard at the horse – 'Missus!'

A tall bony woman – straight all the way down – in a coarse blue pelisse, with the waist an inch or two below her arm-pits, responded to the call.

'Can we put this horse up here, my good woman?' said Mr Tupman, advancing, and speaking in his most seductive tones. The woman looked very hard at the whole party; and the red-headed man whispered something in her ear.

'No,' replied the woman, after a little consideration, 'I'm afeerd on it.'

'Afraid!' exclaimed Mr Pickwick, 'what's the woman afraid of?'

'It got us in trouble last time,' said the woman, turning into the house; 'I woant have nothin' to say to 'un.'

'Most extraordinary thing I ever met with in my life,' said the astonished Mr Pickwick.

'I – I – really believe,' whispered Mr Winkle, as his friends gathered round him, 'that they think we have come by this horse in some dishonest manner.'

'What!' exclaimed Mr Pickwick, in a storm of indignation. Mr Winkle modestly repeated his suggestion.

'Hallo, you fellow!' said the angry Mr Pickwick, 'do you think we stole this horse?'

'I'm sure ye did,' replied the red-headed man, with a grin which agitated his countenance from one auricular organ to the other. Saying which, he turned into the house, and banged the door after him.

'It's like a dream,' ejaculated Mr Pickwick, 'a hideous dream. The idea of a man's walking about, all day, with a dreadful horse that he can't get rid of!' The depressed Pickwickians turned moodily away, with the tall quadruped, for which they all felt the most unmitigated disgust, following slowly at their heels.

It was late in the afternoon when the four friends and their four-footed companion turned into the lane leading to Manor Farm: and even when they were so near their place of destination, the pleasure they would otherwise have experienced was materially damped as they reflected on the singularity of their appearance, and the absurdity of their situation. Torn clothes, lacerated faces, dusty shoes, exhausted looks, and, above all, the horse. Oh, how Mr Pickwick cursed that horse: he had eyed the noble animal from time to time with looks expressive of hatred and revenge; more than once he had calculated the probable amount of the expense he would incur by cutting his throat; and now the temptation to destroy him, or to cast him loose upon the world, rushed upon his mind with tenfold force. He was roused from a meditation on these dire imaginings, by the sudden appearance of two figures at a turn of the lane. It was Mr Wardle, and his faithful attendant, the fat boy.

'Why, where *have* you been?' said the hospitable old gentleman; 'I've been waiting for you all day. Well, you *do* look tired. What! Scratches! Not hurt, I hope – eh? Well, I *am* glad to hear that – very. So you've been spilt, eh? Never mind. Common accident in these parts. Joe – he's asleep again! – Joe, take that horse from the gentleman, and lead it into the stable.'

The fat boy sauntered heavily behind them with the animal; and the old gentleman, condoling with his guests in homely phrase on so much of the day's adventures as they thought proper to communicate, led the way to the kitchen.

'We'll have you put to rights here,' said the old gentleman, 'and then I'll introduce you to the people in the parlour. Emma, bring out the cherry brandy; now, Jane, a needle and thread here; towels and water, Mary. Come, girls, bustle about.'

Three or four buxom girls speedily dispersed in search of the different articles in requisition, while a couple of large-headed, circular-visaged males rose from their seats in the chimney-corner (for although it was a May evening, their attachment to the wood fire appeared as cordial as if it were Christmas), and dived into some obscure recesses, from which they speedily produced a bottle of blacking, and some half-dozen brushes.

'Bustle!' said the old gentleman again, but the admonition was quite unnecessary, for one of the girls poured out the cherry brandy, and another brought in the towels, and one of the men suddenly seizing Mr Pickwick by the leg, at imminent hazard of throwing him off his balance, brushed away at his boot, till his corns were red-hot; while the other shampoo'd Mr Winkle with a heavy clothes-brush, indulging, during the operation, in that hissing sound which hostlers are wont to produce when engaged in rubbing down a horse.

Mr Snodgrass, having concluded his ablutions, took a survey of the room, while standing with his back to the fire, sipping his cherry brandy with heartfelt satisfaction. He describes it as a large apartment, with a red brick floor and a capacious chimney; the ceiling garnished with hams, sides of bacon, and ropes of onions. The walls were decorated with several hunting-whips, two or three bridles, a saddle and an old rusty blunderbuss, with an inscription below it, intimating that it was 'Loaded' – as it had been, on the same authority, for half a century at least. An old eight-day clock,[3] of solemn and sedate demeanour, ticked gravely in one corner; and a silver watch, of equal antiquity, dangled from one of the many hooks which ornamented the dresser.

'Ready?' said the old gentleman inquiringly, when his guests had been washed, mended, brushed, and brandied.

'Quite,' replied Mr Pickwick.

'Come along, then,' and the party having traversed several dark passages, and being joined by Mr Tupman, who had lingered behind to snatch a kiss from Emma, for which he had been duly rewarded with sundry pushings and scratchings, arrived at the parlour door.

'Welcome,' said their hospitable host, throwing it open and stepping forward to announce them, 'Welcome, gentlemen, to Manor Farm.'

An old-fashioned Card-party. The Clergyman's Verses. The Story of the Convict's Return

Several guests who were assembled in the old parlour rose to greet Mr Pickwick and his friends upon their entrance; and during the performance of the ceremony of introduction, with all due formalities, Mr Pickwick had leisure to observe the appearance, and speculate upon the characters and pursuits, of the persons by whom he was surrounded – a habit in which he in common with many other great men delighted to indulge.

A very old lady, in a lofty cap and faded silk gown – no less a personage than Mr Wardle's mother – occupied the post of honour on the right-hand corner of the chimney-piece; and various certificates of her having been brought up in the way she should go when young, and of her not having departed from it when old,[1] ornamented the walls, in the form of samplers of ancient date, worsted landscapes of equal antiquity, and crimson silk tea-kettle holders of a more modern period. The aunt, the two young ladies, and Mr Wardle, each vying with the other in paying zealous and unremitting attentions to the old lady, crowded round her easy-chair, one holding her ear-trumpet, another an orange, and a third a smelling-bottle, while a fourth was busily engaged in patting and punching the pillows which were arranged for her support. On the opposite side sat a bald-headed old gentleman, with a good-humoured benevolent face – the clergyman of Dingley Dell; and next him sat his wife, a stout blooming old lady, who looked as if she were well skilled, not only in the art and mystery of manufacturing home-made cordials greatly to other people's satisfaction, but of tasting them occasionally very much to her own. A little hard-headed, Ripstone-pippin-faced man, was conversing with a fat old gentleman in one corner; and two or three more old gentlemen, and two or three more old ladies, sat bolt upright and motionless on their chairs, staring very hard at Mr Pickwick and his fellow-voyagers.

'Mr Pickwick, mother,' said Mr Wardle, at the very top of his voice.

'Ah!' said the old lady, shaking her head; 'I can't hear you.'

'Mr Pickwick, grandma!' screamed both the young ladies together.

'Ah!' exclaimed the old lady. 'Well; it don't much matter. He don't care for an old'ooman like me, I dare say.'

'I assure you, ma'am,' said Mr Pickwick, grasping the old lady's hand, and speaking so loud that the exertion imparted a crimson hue to his benevolent countenance, 'I assure you, ma'am, that nothing delights me more than to see a lady of your time of life heading so fine a family, and looking so young and well.'

'Ah!' said the old lady, after a short pause; 'It's all very fine, I dare say; but I can't hear him.'

'Grandma's rather put out now,' said Miss Isabella Wardle, in a low tone; 'but she'll talk to you presently.'

Mr Pickwick nodded his readiness to humour the infirmities of age, and entered into a general conversation with the other members of the circle.

'Delightful situation this,' said Mr Pickwick.

'Delightful!' echoed Messrs. Snodgrass, Tupman, and Winkle.

'Well, I think it is,' said Mr Wardle.

'There an't a better spot o' ground in all Kent, sir,' said the hard-headed man with the pippin-face; 'there an't indeed, sir – I'm sure there an't, sir.' The hard-headed man looked triumphantly round, as if he had been very much contradicted by somebody, but had got the better of him at last.

'There an't a better spot o' ground in all Kent,' said the hard-headed man again, after a pause.

''Cept Mullins's Meadows,' observed the fat man solemnly.

'Mullins's Meadows!' ejaculated the other, with profound contempt.

'Ah, Mullins's Meadows,' repeated the fat man.

'Reg'lar good land that,' interposed another fat man.

'And so it is, sure-ly,' said a third fat man.

'Everybody knows that,' said the corpulent host.

The hard-headed man looked dubiously round, but finding himself in a minority, assumed a compassionate air, and said no more.

'What are they talking about?' inquired the old lady of one of her grand-daughters, in a very audible voice; for, like many deaf people, she never seemed to calculate on the possibility of other persons hearing what she said herself.

'About the land, grandma.'

'What about the land? – Nothing the matter, is there?'

'No, no. Mr Miller was saying our land was better than Mullins's Meadows.'

'How should he know anything about it?' inquired the old lady indignantly. 'Miller's a conceited coxcomb, and you may tell him I said so.' Saying which, the old lady, quite unconscious that she had spoken above a whisper, drew herself up, and looked carving-knives at the hard-headed delinquent.

'Come, come,' said the bustling host, with a natural anxiety to change the conversation, – 'What say you to a rubber,[2] Mr Pickwick?'

'I should like it of all things,' replied that gentleman; 'but pray don't make up one on my account.'

'Oh, I assure you, mother's very fond of a rubber,' said Mr Wardle; 'an't you, mother?'

The old lady, who was much less deaf on this subject than on any other, replied in the affirmative.

'Joe, Joe!' said the old gentleman; 'Joe – damn that – oh, here he is; put out the card-tables.'

The lethargic youth contrived without any additional rousing to set out two card-tables; the one for Pope Joan, and the other for whist.[3] The whist-players were Mr Pickwick and the old lady; Mr Miller and the fat gentleman. The round game comprised the rest of the company.

The rubber was conducted with all that gravity of deportment and sedateness of demeanour which befit the pursuit entitled 'whist' – a solemn observance, to which, as it appears to us, the title of 'game' has been very irreverently and ignominiously applied. The round-game table, on the other hand, was so boisterously merry as materially to interrupt the contemplations of Mr Miller, who, not being quite so much absorbed as he ought to have been, contrived to commit various high crimes and misdemeanours, which excited the wrath of the fat gentleman to a very great extent, and called forth the good-humour of the old lady in a proportionate degree.

'There!' said the criminal Miller triumphantly, as he took up the odd trick at the conclusion of a hand; 'that could not have been played better, I flatter myself; – impossible to have made another trick!'

'Miller ought to have trumped the diamond, oughtn't he, sir?' said the old lady.

Mr Pickwick nodded assent.

'Ought I, though?' said the unfortunate, with a doubtful appeal to his partner.

'You ought, sir,' said the fat gentleman, in an awful voice.

'Very sorry,' said the crest-fallen Miller.

'Much use that,' growled the fat gentleman.

'Two by honours makes us eight,' said Mr Pickwick.

Another hand. 'Can you one?' inquired the old lady.

'I can,' replied Mr Pickwick. 'Double, single, and the rub.'

'Never was such luck,' said Mr Miller.

'Never was such cards,' said the fat gentleman.

A solemn silence: Mr Pickwick humorous, the old lady serious, the fat gentleman captious, and Mr Miller timorous.

'Another double,' said the old lady: triumphantly making a memorandum of the circumstance, by placing one sixpence and a battered halfpenny under the candlestick.

'A double, sir,' said Mr Pickwick.

'Quite aware of the fact, sir,' replied the fat gentleman, sharply.

Another game, with a similar result, was followed by a revoke from the unlucky Miller; on which the fat gentleman burst into a state of high personal excitement which lasted until the conclusion of the game, when he retired into a corner, and remained perfectly mute for one hour and twenty-seven minutes; at the end of which time he emerged from his retirement, and offered Mr Pickwick a pinch of snuff with the air of a man who had made up his mind to a Christian forgiveness of injuries sustained. The old lady's hearing decidedly improved, and the unlucky Miller felt as much out of his element as a dolphin in a sentry-box.

Meanwhile the round game proceeded right merrily. Isabella Wardle and Mr Trundle 'went partners,' and Emily Wardle and Mr Snodgrass did the same; and even Mr Tupman and the spinster aunt established a joint-stock company of fish[4] and flattery. Old Mr Wardle was in the very height of his jollity; and he was *so* funny in his management of the board, and the old ladies were *so* sharp after their winnings, that the whole table was in a perpetual roar of merriment and laughter. There was one old lady who always had about half a dozen cards to pay for, at which everybody laughed, regularly every round; and when the old lady looked cross at having to pay, they laughed louder than ever; on which the old lady's face gradually brightened up, till at last she laughed louder than any of them. Then, when the spinster aunt got 'matrimony,' the young ladies laughed afresh, and the spinster aunt seemed disposed to be pettish; till, feeling Mr Tupman squeezing her hand under the table, *she* brightened up too, and looked rather knowing, as if matrimony in reality were not quite so far off as some people thought for; whereupon everybody laughed again, and especially old Mr Wardle, who enjoyed a joke as much as the youngest. As to Mr Snodgrass, he did nothing but whisper poetical sentiments into his partner's ear, which made one old gentleman facetiously sly, about partnerships at cards and partnerships for life, and caused the aforesaid old gentleman to make some remarks thereupon, accompanied with divers winks and chuckles, which made the company very merry and the old gentleman's wife especially so. And Mr Winkle came out with jokes which are very well known in town, but are not at all known in the country: and as everybody laughed at them very heartily, and said they were very capital, Mr Winkle was in a state of great honour and glory. And the benevolent clergyman looked pleasantly on; for the happy faces which surrounded the table made the good old man feel happy too; and though the merriment was rather boisterous, still it came from the heart and not from the lips: and this is the right sort of merriment, after all.

The evening glided swiftly away, in these cheerful recreations; and when the substantial though homely supper had been despatched, and the little party formed a social circle round the fire, Mr Pickwick thought he had never felt so happy in his life, and at no time so much disposed to enjoy, and make the most of, the passing moment.

'Now this,' said the hospitable host, who was sitting in great state next the old lady's arm-chair, with her hand fast clasped in his – 'This is just what I like – the happiest moments of my life have been passed at this old fire-side: and I am so attached to it, that I keep up a blazing fire here every evening, until it actually grows too hot to bear it. Why, my poor old mother, here, used to sit before this fire-place upon that little stool when she was a girl; didn't you, mother?'

The tear which starts unbidden to the eye when the recollection of old times and the happiness of many years ago is suddenly recalled, stole down the old lady's face as she shook her head with a melancholy smile.

'You must excuse my talking about this old place, Mr Pickwick,' resumed the host, after a short pause, 'for I love it dearly, and know no other – the old houses and fields seem like living friends to me: and so does our little church with the ivy, – about which, by-the-bye, our excellent friend there made a song when he first came amongst us. Mr Snodgrass, have you anything in your glass?'

'Plenty, thank you,' replied that gentleman, whose poetic curiosity had been greatly excited by the last observations of his entertainer. 'I beg your pardon, but you were talking about the song of the Ivy.'

'You must ask our friend opposite about that,' said the host knowingly: indicating the clergyman by a nod of his head.

'May I say that I should like to hear you repeat it, sir?' said Mr Snodgrass.

'Why really,' replied the clergyman, 'it's a very slight affair; and the only excuse I have for having ever perpetrated it is, that I was a young man at the time. Such as it is, however, you shall hear it if you wish.'

A murmur of curiosity was of course the reply; and the old gentleman proceeded to recite, with the aid of sundry promptings from his wife, the lines in question. 'I call them,' said he,

THE IVY GREEN

OH, a dainty plant is the Ivy green,
That creepeth o'er ruins old!
Of right choice food are his meals, I ween,
In his cell so lone and cold.
The wall must be crumbled, the stone decayed,
To pleasure his dainty whim:
And the mouldering dust that years have made,
Is a merry meal for him.
      Creeping where no life is seen,
      A rare old plant is the Ivy green.

Fast he stealeth on, though he wears no wings,
And a staunch old heart has he.
How closely he twineth, how tight he clings
To his friend the huge Oak Tree!
And slily he traileth along the ground,
And his leaves he gently waves,
As he joyously hugs and crawleth round
The rich mould of dead men's graves.
      Creeping where grim death has been,
      A rare old plant is the Ivy green.

Whole ages have fled and their works decayed,
And nations have scattered been;
But the stout old Ivy shall never fade,
From its hale and hearty green.
The brave old plant in its lonely days,
Shall fatten upon the past:
For the stateliest building man can raise,
Is the Ivy's food at last.
      Creeping on, where time has been,
      A rare old plant is the Ivy green.

While the old gentleman repeated these lines a second time, to enable Mr Snodgrass to note them down, Mr Pickwick perused the lineaments of his face with an expression of great interest. The old gentleman having concluded his dictation, and Mr Snodgrass having returned his note-book to his pocket, Mr Pickwick said:

'Excuse me, sir, for making the remark on so short an acquaintance; but a gentleman like yourself cannot fail, I should think, to have observed many scenes and incidents worth recording, in the course of your experience as a minister of the Gospel.'

'I have witnessed some certainly,' replied the old gentleman; 'but the incidents and characters have been of a homely and ordinary nature, my sphere of action being so very limited.'

'You *did* make some notes, I think, about John Edmunds, did you not?' inquired Mr Wardle, who appeared very desirous to draw his friend out, for the edification of his new visitors.

The old gentleman slightly nodded his head in token of assent, and was proceeding to change the subject, when Mr Pickwick said –

'I beg your pardon, sir; but pray, if I may venture to inquire, who was John Edmunds?'

'The very thing I was about to ask,' said Mr Snodgrass, eagerly.

'You are fairly in for it,' said the jolly host. 'You must satisfy the curiosity of these gentlemen, sooner or later; so you had better take advantage of this favourable opportunity, and do so at once.'

The old gentleman smiled good-humouredly as he drew his chair forward; – the remainder of the party drew their chairs closer together, especially Mr Tupman and the spinster aunt, who were possibly rather hard of hearing; and the old lady's ear-trumpet having been duly adjusted, and Mr Miller (who had fallen asleep during the recital of the verses) roused from his slumbers by an admonitory pinch, administered beneath the table by his ex-partner the solemn fat man, the old gentleman, without farther preface, commenced the following tale, to which we have taken the liberty of prefixing the title of

THE CONVICT'S RETURN

'WHEN I first settled in this village,' said the old gentleman, 'which is now just five-and-twenty years ago, the most notorious person among my parishioners was a man of the name of Edmunds, who leased a small farm near this spot. He was a morose, savage-hearted, bad man: idle and dissolute in his habits; cruel and ferocious in his disposition. Beyond the few lazy and reckless vagabonds with whom he sauntered away his time in the fields, or sotted in the ale-house, he had not a single friend or acquaintance; no one cared to speak to the man whom many feared, and every one detested – and Edmunds was shunned by all.

'This man had a wife and one son, who, when I first came here, was about twelve years old. Of the acuteness of that woman's sufferings, of the gentle and enduring manner in which she bore them, of the agony of solicitude with which she reared that boy, no one can form an adequate conception. Heaven forgive me the supposition, if it be an uncharitable one, but I do firmly and in my soul believe, that the man systematically tried for many years to break her heart; but she bore it all for her child's sake, and, however strange it may seem to many, for his father's too; for brute as he was and cruelly as he had treated her, she had loved him once; and the recollection of what he had been to her, awakened feelings of forbearance and meekness under suffering in her bosom, to which all God's creatures, but women, are strangers.

'They were poor – they could not be otherwise when the man pursued such courses; but the woman's unceasing and unwearied exertions, early and late, morning, noon, and night, kept them above actual want. Those exertions were but ill repaid. People who passed the spot in the evening – sometimes at a late hour of the night – reported that they had heard the moans and sobs of a woman in distress, and the sound of blows: and more than once, when it was past midnight, the boy knocked softly at the door of a neighbour's house, whither he had been sent, to escape the drunken fury of his unnatural father.

'During the whole of this time, and when the poor creature often bore about her marks of ill-usage and violence which she could not wholly conceal, she was a constant attendant at our little church. Regularly every Sunday, morning and afternoon, she occupied the same seat with the boy at her side; and though they were both poorly dressed – much more so than many of their neighbours who were in a lower station – they were always neat and clean. Every one had a friendly nod and a kind word for "poor Mrs Edmunds;" and sometimes, when she stopped to exchange a few words with a neighbour at the conclusion of the service in the little row of elm trees which leads to the church porch, or lingered behind to gaze with a mother's pride and fondness upon her healthy boy, as he sported before her with some little companions, her care-worn face would lighten up with an expression of heartfelt gratitude; and she would look, if not cheerful and happy, at least tranquil and contented.

'Five or six years passed away; the boy had become a robust and well-grown youth. The time that had strengthened the child's slight frame and knit his weak limbs into the strength of manhood had bowed his mother's form, and enfeebled her steps; but the arm that should have supported her was no longer locked in hers; the face that should have cheered her, no more looked upon her own. She occupied her old seat, but there was a vacant one beside her. The Bible was kept as carefully as ever, the places were found and folded down as they used to be: but there was no one to read it with her; and the tears fell thick and fast upon the book, and blotted the words from her eyes. Neighbours were as kind as they were wont to be of old, but she shunned their greetings with averted head. There was no lingering among the old elm trees now – no cheering anticipations of happiness yet in store. The desolate woman drew her bonnet closer over her face, and walked hurriedly away.

'Shall I tell you, that the young man, who, looking back to the earliest of his childhood's days to which memory and consciousness extended, and carrying his recollection down to that moment, could remember nothing which was not in some way connected with a long series of voluntary privations suffered by his mother for his sake, with ill-usage, and insult, and violence, and all endured for him; – shall I tell you, that he, with a reckless disregard of her breaking heart, and a sullen wilful forgetfulness of all she had done and borne for him, had linked himself with depraved and abandoned men, and was madly pursuing a headlong career, which must bring death to him, and shame to her? Alas for human nature! You have anticipated it long since.

'The measure of the unhappy woman's misery and misfortune was about to be completed. Numerous offences had been committed in the neighbourhood; the perpetrators remained undiscovered, and their boldness increased. A robbery of a daring and aggravated nature occasioned a vigilance of pursuit, and a strictness of search, they had not calculated on. Young Edmunds was suspected with three companions. He was apprehended – committed – tried – condemned – to die.

'The wild and piercing shriek from a woman's voice, which resounded through the court when the solemn sentence was pronounced, rings in my ears at this moment. That cry struck a terror to the culprit's heart, which trial, condemnation – the approach of death itself, had failed to awaken. The lips which had been compressed in dogged sullenness throughout, quivered and parted involuntarily; the face turned ashy pale as the cold perspiration broke forth from every pore; the sturdy limbs of the felon trembled, and he staggered in the dock.

'In the first transports of her mental anguish, the suffering mother threw herself upon her knees at my feet, and fervently besought the Almighty Being who had hitherto supported her in all her troubles, to release her from a world of woe and misery, and to spare the life of her only child. A burst of grief, and a violent struggle, such as I hope I may never have to witness again, succeeded. I knew that her heart was breaking from that hour; but I never once heard complaint or murmur escape her lips.

'It was a piteous spectacle to see that woman in the prison yard from day to day, eagerly and fervently attempting, by affection and entreaty, to soften the hard heart of her obdurate son. It was in vain. He remained moody, obstinate, and unmoved. Not even the unlooked-for commutation of his sentence to transportation for fourteen years, softened for an instant the sullen hardihood of his demeanour.

'But the spirit of resignation and endurance that had so long upheld her, was unable to contend against bodily weakness and infirmity. She fell sick. She dragged her tottering limbs from the bed to visit her son once more, but her strength failed her, and she sunk powerless on the ground.

'And now the boasted coldness and indifference of the young man were tested indeed; and the retribution that fell heavily upon him, nearly drove him mad. A day passed away and his mother was not there; another flew by, and she came not near him; a third evening arrived, and yet he had not seen her; and in four-and-twenty hours he was to be separated from her – perhaps for ever. Oh! how the long-forgotten thoughts of former days rushed upon his mind, as he almost ran up and down the narrow yard – as if intelligence would arrive the sooner for *his* hurrying – and how bitterly a sense of his helplessness and desolation rushed upon him, when he heard the truth! His mother, the only parent he had ever known, lay ill – it might be, dying – within one mile of the ground he stood on; were he free and unfettered, a few minutes would place him by her side. He rushed to the gate, and grasping the iron rails with the energy of desperation, shook it till it rang again, and threw himself against the thick wall as if to force a passage through the stone; but the strong building mocked his feeble efforts, and he beat his hands together and wept like a child.

'I bore the mother's forgiveness and blessing to her son in prison; and I carried his solemn assurance of repentance, and his fervent supplication for pardon, to her sick bed. I heard, with pity and compassion, the repentant man devise a thousand little plans for her comfort and support when he returned; but I knew that many months before he could reach his place of destination, his mother would be no longer of this world.

'He was removed by night. A few weeks afterwards the poor woman's soul took its flight, I confidently hope, and solemnly believe, to a place of eternal happiness and rest. I performed the burial service over her remains. She lies in our little churchyard. There is no stone at her grave's head. Her sorrows were known to man; her virtues to God.

'It had been arranged previously to the convict's departure, that he should write to his mother as soon as he could obtain permission, and that the letter should be addressed to me. The father had positively refused to see his son from the moment of his apprehension; and it was a matter of indifference to him whether he lived or died. Many years passed over without any intelligence of him; and when more than half his term of transportation had expired, and I had received no letter, I concluded him to be dead, as indeed, I almost hoped he might be.

'Edmunds, however, had been sent a considerable distance up the country on his arrival at the settlement; and to this circumstance, perhaps, may be attributed the fact, that though several letters were despatched, none of them ever reached my hands. He remained in the same place during the whole fourteen years. At the expiration of the term, steadily adhering to his old resolution and the pledge he gave his mother, he made his way back to England amidst innumerable difficulties, and returned, on foot, to his native place.

'On a fine Sunday evening, in the month of August, John Edmunds set foot in the village he had left with shame and disgrace seventeen years before. His nearest way lay through the churchyard. The man's heart swelled as he crossed the stile. The tall old elms, through whose branches the declining sun cast here and there a rich ray of light upon the shady path, awakened the associations of his earliest days. He pictured himself as he was then, clinging to his mother's hand, and walking peacefully to church. He remembered how he used to look up into her pale face; and how her eyes would sometimes fill with tears as she gazed upon his features – tears which fell hot upon his forehead as she stooped to kiss him, and made him weep too, although he little knew then what bitter tears hers were. He thought how often he had run merrily down that path with some childish playfellow, looking back, ever and again, to catch his mother's smile, or hear her gentle voice; and then a veil seemed lifted from his memory, and words of kindness unrequited, and warnings despised, and promises broken, thronged upon his recollection till his heart failed him, and he could bear it no longer.

'He entered the church. The evening service was concluded and the congregation had dispersed, but it was not yet closed. His steps echoed through the low building with a hollow sound, and he almost feared to be alone, it was so still and quiet. He looked round him. Nothing was changed. The place seemed smaller than it used to be, but there were the old monuments on which he had gazed with childish awe a thousand times; the little pulpit with its faded cushion; the Communion-table before which he had so often repeated the Commandments he had reverenced as a child, and forgotten as a man. He approached the old seat; it looked cold and desolate. The cushion had been removed, and the Bible was not there. Perhaps his mother now occupied a poorer seat, or possibly she had grown infirm and could not reach the church alone. He dared not think of what he feared. A cold feeling crept over him, and he trembled violently as he turned away.

'An old man entered the porch just as he reached it. Edmunds started back, for he knew him well; many a time he had watched him digging graves in the churchyard. What would *he* say to the returned convict?

'The old man raised his eyes to the stranger's face, bid him "good evening," and walked slowly on. He had forgotten him.

'He walked down the hill, and through the village. The weather was warm, and the people were sitting at their doors, or strolling in their little gardens as he passed, enjoying the serenity of the evening, and their rest from labour. Many a look was turned towards him, and many a doubtful glance he cast on either side to see whether any knew and shunned him. There were strange faces in almost every house; in some he recognised the burly form of some old schoolfellow – a boy when he last saw him – surrounded by a troop of merry children; in others he saw, seated in an easy-chair at a cottage door, a feeble and infirm old man, whom he only remembered as a hale and hearty labourer; but they had all forgotten him, and he passed on unknown.

'The last soft light of the setting sun had fallen on the earth, casting a rich glow on the yellow corn sheaves, and lengthening the shadows of the orchard trees, as he stood before the old house – the home of his infancy – to which his heart had yearned with an intensity of affection not to be described, through long and weary years of captivity and sorrow. The paling was low, though he well remembered the time when it had seemed a high wall to him: and he looked over into the old garden. There were more seeds and gayer flowers than there used to be, but there were the old trees still – the very tree, under which he had lain a thousand times when tired of playing in the sun, and felt the soft mild sleep of happy boyhood steal gently upon him. There were voices within the house. He listened, but they fell strangely upon his ear; he knew them not. They were merry too; and he well knew that his poor old mother could not be cheerful, and he away. The door opened, and a group of little children bounded out, shouting and romping. The father, with a little boy in his arms, appeared at the door, and they crowded round him, clapping their tiny hands, and dragging him out, to join their joyous sports. The convict thought on the many times he had shrunk from his father's sight in that very place. He remembered how often he had buried his trembling head beneath the bed-clothes, and heard the harsh word, and the hard stripe, and his mother's wailing; and though the man sobbed aloud with agony of mind as he left the spot, his fist was clenched, and his teeth were set, in fierce and deadly passion.

'And such was the return to which he had looked through the weary perspective of many years, and for which he had undergone so much suffering! No face of welcome, no look of forgiveness, no house to receive, no hand to help him – and this too in the old village. What was his loneliness in the wild thick woods, where man was never seen, to this!

'He felt that in the distant land of his bondage and infamy, he had thought of his native place as it was when he left it; not as it would be when he returned. The sad reality struck coldly at his heart, and his spirit sank within him. He had not courage to make inquiries, or to present himself to the only person who was likely to receive him with kindness and compassion. He walked slowly on; and shunning the road-side like a guilty man, turned into a meadow he well remembered; and covering his face with his hands, threw himself upon the grass.

'He had not observed that a man was lying on the bank beside him; his garments rustled as he turned round to steal a look at the new-comer; and Edmunds raised his head.

'The man had moved into a sitting posture. His body was much bent, and his face was wrinkled and yellow. His dress denoted him an inmate of the workhouse: he had the appearance of being very old, but it looked more the effect of dissipation or disease, than length of years. He was staring hard at the stranger, and though his eyes were lustreless and heavy at first, they appeared to glow with an unnatural and alarmed expression after they had been fixed upon him for a short time, until they seemed to be starting from their sockets. Edmunds gradually raised himself to his knees, and looked more and more earnestly upon the old man's face. They gazed upon each other in silence.

'The old man was ghastly pale. He shuddered and tottered to his feet. Edmunds sprang to his. He stepped back a pace or two. Edmunds advanced.

'"Let me hear you speak," said the convict, in a thick broken voice.

'"Stand off!" cried the old man, with a dreadful oath. The convict drew closer to him.

'"Stand off!" shrieked the old man. Furious with terror he raised his stick, and struck Edmunds a heavy blow across the face.

'"Father – devil!" murmured the convict, between his set teeth. He rushed wildly forward, and clenched the old man by the throat – but he was his father; and his arm fell powerless by his side.

'The old man uttered a loud yell which rang through the lonely fields like the howl of an evil spirit. His face turned black: the gore rushed from his mouth and nose, and dyed the grass a deep dark red, as he staggered and fell. He had ruptured a blood-vessel: and he was a dead man before his son could raise him.

*   *   *

'In that corner of the churchyard,' said the old gentleman, after a silence of a few moments, 'in that corner of the churchyard of which I have before spoken, there lies buried a man, who was in my employment for three years after this event: and who was truly contrite, penitent, and humbled, if ever man was. No one save myself knew in that man's lifetime who he was, or whence he came: – it was John Edmunds the returned convict.'

CHAPTER 7

How Mr Winkle, instead of shooting at the Pigeon
and killing the Crow, shot at the Crow and
wounded the Pigeon; how the Dingley Dell Cricket
Club played All-Muggleton, and how All-Muggleton
dined at the Dingley Dell expense: with other
interesting and instructive Matters

The fatiguing adventures of the day or the somniferous influence of
the clergyman's tale operated so strongly on the drowsy tendencies
of Mr Pickwick, that in less than five minutes after he had been
shown to his comfortable bed-room, he fell into a sound and
dreamless sleep, from which he was only awakened by the morning
sun darting his bright beams reproachfully into the apartment. Mr
Pickwick was no sluggard; and he sprang like an ardent warrior
from his tent – bedstead.

'Pleasant, pleasant country,' sighed the enthusiastic gentleman, as
he opened his lattice window. 'Who could live to gaze from day to
day on bricks and slates, who had once felt the influence of a scene
like this? Who could continue to exist, where there are no cows but
the cows on the chimney-pots; nothing redolent of Pan but pan-
tiles; no crop but stone crop?[1] Who could bear to drag out a life in
such a spot? Who I ask could endure it?' and, having cross-
examined solitude after the most approved precedents, at considerable length, Mr Pickwick thrust his head out of the lattice, and
looked around him.

The rich, sweet smell of the hayricks rose to his chamber window;
the hundred perfumes of the little flower-garden beneath scented
the air around; the deep-green meadows shone in the morning dew
that glistened on every leaf as it trembled in the gentle air; and the
birds sang as if every sparkling drop were a fountain of inspiration
to them. Mr Pickwick fell into an enchanting and delicious reverie.

'Hallo!' was the sound that roused him.

He looked to the right, but he saw nobody; his eyes wandered to
the left, and pierced the prospect; he stared into the sky, but he
wasn't wanted there; and then he did what a common mind would
have done at once – looked into the garden, and there saw Mr
Wardle.

'How are you?' said that good-humoured individual, out of
breath with his own anticipations of pleasure. 'Beautiful morning,

an't it? Glad to see you up so early. Make haste down, and come out. I'll wait for you here.'

Mr Pickwick needed no second invitation. Ten minutes sufficed for the completion of his toilet, and at the expiration of that time he was by the old gentleman's side.

'Hallo!' said Mr Pickwick in his turn: seeing that his companion was armed with a gun, and that another lay ready on the grass. 'What's going forward?'

'Why, your friend and I,' replied the host, 'are going out rook-shooting before breakfast. He's a very good shot, an't he?'

'I've heard him say he's a capital one,' replied Mr Pickwick; 'but I never saw him aim at anything.'

'Well,' said the host, 'I wish he'd come. Joe – Joe!'

The fat boy, who under the exciting influence of the morning did not appear to be more than three parts and a fraction asleep, emerged from the house.

'Go up, and call the gentleman, and tell him he'll find me and Mr Pickwick in the rookery. Show the gentleman the way there; d'ye hear?'

The boy departed to execute his commission; and the host, carrying both guns like a second Robinson Crusoe,[2] led the way from the garden.

'This is the place,' said the old gentleman, pausing after a few minutes walking, in an avenue of trees. The information was unnecessary; for the incessant cawing of the unconscious rooks sufficiently indicated their whereabout.

The old gentleman laid one gun on the ground, and loaded the other.

'Here they are,' said Mr Pickwick; and as he spoke, the forms of Mr Tupman, Mr Snodgrass, and Mr Winkle appeared in the distance. The fat boy, not being quite certain which gentleman he was directed to call, had with peculiar sagacity, and to prevent the possibility of any mistake, called them all.

'Come along,' shouted the old gentleman, addressing Mr Winkle; 'a keen hand like you ought to have been up long ago, even to such poor work as this.'

Mr Winkle responded with a forced smile, and took up the spare gun with an expression of countenance which a metaphysical rook, impressed with a foreboding of his approaching death by violence, may be supposed to assume. It might have been keenness, but it looked remarkably like misery.

The old gentleman nodded; and two ragged boys who had been

marshalled to the spot under the direction of the infant Lambert,[3] forthwith commenced climbing up two of the trees.

'What are those lads for?' inquired Mr Pickwick abruptly. He was rather alarmed; for he was not quite certain but that the distress of the agricultural interest, about which he had often heard a great deal, might have compelled the small boys attached to the soil to earn a precarious and hazardous subsistence by making marks of themselves for inexperienced sportsmen.

'Only to start the game,' replied Mr Wardle, laughing.

'To what?' inquired Mr Pickwick.

'Why, in plain English to frighten the rooks.'

'Oh! is that all?'

'You are satisfied?'

'Quite.'

'Very well. Shall I begin?'

'If you please,' said Mr Winkle, glad of any respite.

'Stand aside, then. Now for it.'

The boy shouted, and shook a branch with a nest on it. Half a dozen young rooks in violent conversation, flew out to ask what the matter was. The old gentleman fired by way of reply. Down fell one bird, and off flew the others.

'Take him up, Joe,' said the old gentleman.

There was a smile upon the youth's face as he advanced. Indistinct visions of rook-pie floated through his imagination. He laughed as he retired with the bird – it was a plump one.

'Now, Mr Winkle,' said the host, reloading his own gun. 'Fire away.'

Mr Winkle advanced, and levelled his gun. Mr Pickwick and his friends cowered involuntarily to escape damage from the heavy fall of rooks, which they felt quite certain would be occasioned by the devastating barrel of their friend. There was a solemn pause – a shout – a flapping of wings – a faint click.

'Hallo!' said the old gentleman.

'Won't it go?' inquired Mr Pickwick.

'Missed fire,' said Mr Winkle, who was very pale: probably from disappointment.

'Odd,' said the old gentleman, taking the gun. 'Never knew one of them miss fire before. Why, I don't see anything of the cap.'[4]

'Bless my soul,' said Mr Winkle. 'I declare I forgot the cap!'

The slight omission was rectified. Mr Pickwick crouched again. Mr Winkle stepped forward with an air of determination and resolution; and Mr Tupman looked out from behind a tree. The boy shouted; four birds flew out. Mr Winkle fired. There was a scream as of an individual – not a rook – in corporeal anguish. Mr Tupman had saved the lives of innumerable unoffending birds by receiving a portion of the charge in his left arm.

To describe the confusion that ensued would be impossible. To tell how Mr Pickwick in the first transports of his emotion called Mr Winkle 'Wretch!' how Mr Tupman lay prostrate on the ground; and how Mr Winkle knelt horror-stricken beside him; how Mr Tupman called distractedly upon some feminine Christian name, and then opened first one eye, and then the other, and then fell back and shut them both; – all this would be as difficult to describe in detail, as it would be to depict the gradual recovering of the unfortunate individual, the binding up of his arm with pocket-handkerchiefs, and the conveying him back by slow degrees supported by the arms of his anxious friends.

They drew near the house. The ladies were at the garden-gate, waiting for their arrival and their breakfast. The spinster aunt appeared; she smiled, and beckoned them to walk quicker. 'Twas evident she knew not of the disaster. Poor thing! there are times when ignorance is bliss indeed.

They approached nearer.

'Why, what *is* the matter with the little old gentleman?' said Isabella Wardle, The spinster aunt heeded not the remark; she thought it applied to Mr Pickwick. In her eyes Tracy Tupman was a youth; she viewed his years through a diminishing glass.

'Don't be frightened,' called out the old host, fearful of alarming his daughters. The little party had crowded so completely round Mr Tupman, that they could not yet clearly discern the nature of the accident.

'Don't be frightened,' said the host.

'What's the matter?' screamed the ladies.

'Mr Tupman has met with a little accident; that's all.'

The spinster aunt uttered a piercing scream, burst into an hysteric laugh, and fell backwards in the arms of her nieces.

'Throw some cold water over her,' said the old gentleman.

'No, no,' murmured the spinster aunt; 'I am better now. Bella, Emily – a surgeon! Is he wounded? – Is he dead? – Is he – ha, ha, ha!' Here the spinster aunt burst into fit number two, of hysteric laughter interspersed with screams.

'Calm yourself,' said Mr Tupman, affected almost to tears by this expression of sympathy with his sufferings. 'Dear, dear madam, calm yourself.'

'It is his voice!' exclaimed the spinster aunt; and strong symptoms of fit number three developed themselves forthwith.

'Do not agitate yourself, I entreat you, dearest madam,' said Mr Tupman soothingly. 'I am very little hurt, I assure you.'

'Then you are not dead!' ejaculated the hysterical lady. 'Oh, say you are not dead!'

'Don't be a fool, Rachael,' interposed Mr Wardle, rather more roughly than was quite consistent with the poetic nature of the scene. 'What the devil's the use of his *saying* he isn't dead?'

'No, no, I am not,' said Mr Tupman. 'I require no assistance but yours. Let me lean on your arm.' He added, in a whisper, 'Oh, Miss Rachael!' The agitated female advanced, and offered her arm. They turned into the breakfast parlour. Mr Tracy Tupman gently pressed her hand to his lips, and sank upon the sofa.

'Are you faint?' inquired the anxious Rachael.

'No,' said Mr Tupman. 'It is nothing. I shall be better presently.' He closed his eyes.

'He sleeps,' murmured the spinster aunt. (His organs of vision had been closed nearly twenty seconds). 'Dear – dear – Mr Tupman!'

Mr Tupman jumped up – 'Oh, say those words again!' he exclaimed.

The lady started. 'Surely you did not hear them!' she said, bashfully.

'Oh yes I did!' replied Mr Tupman; 'repeat them. If you would have me recover, repeat them.'

'Hush!' said the lady. 'My brother.'

Mr Tracy Tupman resumed his former position; and Mr Wardle, accompanied by a surgeon, entered the room.

The arm was examined, the wound dressed, and pronounced to be a very slight one; and the minds of the company having been thus satisfied, they proceeded to satisfy their appetites with countenances to which an expression of cheerfulness was again restored. Mr Pickwick alone was silent and reserved. Doubt and distrust were exhibited in his countenance. His confidence in Mr Winkle had been shaken – greatly shaken – by the proceedings of the morning.

'Are you a cricketer?' inquired Mr Wardle of the marksman.

At any other time, Mr Winkle would have replied in the affirmative. He felt the delicacy of his situation, and modestly replied, 'No.'

'Are you, sir?' inquired Mr Snodgrass.

'I was once upon a time,' replied the host; 'but I have given it up now. I subscribe to the club here, but I don't play.'

'The grand match is played to-day, I believe,' said Mr Pickwick.

'It is,' replied the host. 'Of course you would like to see it.'

'I, sir,' replied Mr Pickwick, 'am delighted to view any sports which may be safely indulged in, and in which the impotent effects of unskilful people do not endanger human life.' Mr Pickwick paused, and looked steadily on Mr Winkle, who quailed beneath his leader's searching glance. The great man withdrew his eyes after a few minutes, and added: 'Shall we be justified in leaving our wounded friend to the care of the ladies?'

'You cannot leave me in better hands,' said Mr Tupman.

'Quite impossible,' said Mr Snodgrass.

It was therefore settled that Mr Tupman should be left at home in charge of the females; and that the remainder of the guests, under the guidance of Mr Wardle, should proceed to the spot where was to be held that trial of skill, which had roused all Muggleton from its torpor, and inoculated Dingley Dell with a fever of excitement.

As their walk, which was not above two miles long, lay through shady lanes, and sequestered footpaths, and as their conversation turned upon the delightful scenery by which they were on every side surrounded, Mr Pickwick was almost inclined to regret the expedition they had used, when he found himself in the main street of the town of Muggleton.

Everybody whose genius has a topographical bent knows perfectly well that Muggleton is a corporate town, with a mayor, burgesses, and freemen; and anybody who has consulted the addresses of the mayor to the freemen, or the freemen to the mayor, or both to the corporation, or all three to Parliament, will learn from thence what they ought to have known before, that Muggleton is an ancient and loyal borough, mingling a zealous advocacy of Christian principles with a devoted attachment to commercial rights; in demonstration whereof, the mayor, corporation, and other inhabitants, have presented at divers times, no fewer than one thousand four hundred and twenty petitions against the continuance of negro slavery abroad, and an equal number against any interference with the factory system at home; sixty-eight in favour of the sale of livings in the Church, and eighty-six for abolishing Sunday trading[5] in the street.

Mr Pickwick stood in the principal street of this illustrious town, and gazed with an air of curiosity, not unmixed with interest, on the objects around him. There was an open square for the market-place; and in the centre of it, a large inn with a sign-post in front, displaying an object very common in art, but rarely met with in nature – to wit, a blue lion, with three bow legs in the air, balancing himself on the extreme point of the centre claw of his fourth foot. There were, within sight, an auctioneer's and fire-agency office, a corn-factor's,[6] a linen-draper's, a saddler's, a distiller's, a grocer's, and a shoe-shop – the last-mentioned warehouse being also appropriated to the diffusion of hats, bonnets, wearing apparel, cotton umbrellas, and useful knowledge.[7] There was a red brick house with a small paved court-yard in front, which anybody might have known belonged to the attorney; and there was, moreover, another red brick house with Venetian blinds, and a large brass door-plate, with a very legible announcement that it belonged to the surgeon. A few boys were making their way to the cricket-field; and two or three shop-keepers who were standing at their doors, looked as if they should like to be making their way to the same spot, as indeed to all appearance they might have done, without losing any great amount of custom thereby. Mr Pickwick having paused to make these observations, to be noted down at a more convenient period, hastened to rejoin his friends, who had turned out of the main street, and were already within sight of the field of battle.

The wickets were pitched, and so were a couple of marquees for the rest and refreshment of the contending parties. The game had not yet commenced. Two or three Dingley Dellers, and All-Muggletonians, were amusing themselves with a majestic air by throwing the ball carelessly from hand to hand; and several other gentlemen dressed like them, in straw hats, flannel jackets, and white trousers – a costume in which they looked very much like amateur stone-masons – were sprinkled about the tents, towards one of which Mr Wardle conducted the party.

Several dozen of 'How-are-you's?' hailed the old gentleman's arrival; and a general raising of the straw hats, and bending forward of the flannel jackets, followed his introduction of his guests as gentlemen from London, who were extremely anxious to witness the proceedings of the day, with which, he had no doubt, they would be greatly delighted.

'You had better step into the marquee, I think, sir,' said one very stout gentleman, whose body and legs looked like half a gigantic roll of flannel, elevated on a couple of inflated pillow-cases.

'You'll find it much pleasanter, sir,' urged another stout gentleman, who strongly resembled the other half of the roll of flannel aforesaid.

'You're very good,' said Mr Pickwick.

'This way,' said the first speaker; 'they notch[8] in here – it's the best place in the whole field;' and the cricketer, panting on before, preceded them to the tent.

'Capital game – smart sport – fine exercise – very,' were the words which fell upon Mr Pickwick's ear as he entered the tent; and the first object that met his eyes was his green-coated friend of the Rochester coach, holding forth, to the no small delight and edification of a select circle of the chosen of All-Muggleton. His dress was slightly improved, and he wore boots; but there was no mistaking him.

The stranger recognised his friends immediately: and, darting forward and seizing Mr Pickwick by the hand, dragged him to a seat with his usual impetuosity, talking all the while as if the whole of the arrangements were under his especial patronage and direction.

'This way – this way – capital fun – lots of beer – hogsheads; rounds of beef – bullocks; mustard – cart loads; glorious day – down with you – make yourself at home – glad to see you – very.'

Mr Pickwick sat down as he was bid, and Mr Winkle and Mr Snodgrass also complied with the directions of their mysterious friend. Mr Wardle looked on, in silent wonder.

'Mr Wardle – a friend of mine,' said Mr Pickwick.

'Friend of yours! – My dear sir, how are you? – Friend of *my* friend's – give me your hand, sir' – and the stranger grasped Mr Wardle's hand with all the fervour of a close intimacy of many years, and then stepped back a pace or two as if to take a full survey of his face and figure, and then shook hands with him again, if possible, more warmly than before.

'Well; and how came you here?' said Mr Pickwick, with a smile in which benevolence struggled with surprise.

'Come,' replied the stranger – 'stopping at Crown – Crown at Muggleton – met a party – flannel jackets – white trousers – anchovy sandwiches – devilled kidneys – splendid fellows – glorious.'

Mr Pickwick was sufficiently versed in the stranger's system of stenography to infer from this rapid and disjointed communication that he had, somehow or other, contracted an acquaintance with the All-Muggletons, which he had converted, by a process peculiar to himself, into that extent of good fellowship on which a general invitation may be easily founded. His curiosity was therefore satisfied, and putting on his spectacles he prepared himself to watch the play which was just commencing.

All-Muggleton had the first innings; and the interest became intense when Mr Dumkins and Mr Podder, two of the most renowned members of that most distinguished club, walked, bat in hand, to their respective wickets. Mr Luffey, the highest ornament of Dingley Dell, was pitched to bowl against the redoubtable Dumkins, and Mr Struggles was selected to do the same kind office for the hitherto unconquered Podder. Several players were stationed, to 'look out,' in different parts of the field, and each fixed himself into the proper attitude by placing one hand on each knee, and stooping very much as if he were 'making a back' for some beginner at leap-frog. All the regular players do this sort of thing; – indeed it's generally supposed that it is quite impossible to look out properly in any other position.

The umpires were stationed behind the wickets; the scorers were prepared to notch the runs; a breathless silence ensued. Mr Luffey retired a few paces behind the wicket of the passive Podder, and applied the ball to his right eye for several seconds. Dumkins confidently awaited its coming with his eyes fixed on the motions of Luffey.

'Play!' suddenly cried the bowler. The ball flew from his hand straight and swift towards the centre stump of the wicket. The wary Dumkins was on the alert; it fell upon the tip of the bat, and bounded far away over the heads of the scouts, who had just stooped low enough to let it fly over them.

'Run – run – another. – Now, then, throw her up – up with her – stop there – another – no – yes – no – throw her up, throw her up!' – Such were the shouts which followed the stroke; and, at the conclusion of which All-Muggleton had scored two. Nor was Podder behindhand in earning laurels wherewith to garnish himself and Muggleton. He blocked the doubtful balls, missed the bad ones, took the good ones, and sent them flying to all parts of the field. The scouts were hot and tired; the bowlers were changed and bowled till their arms ached; but Dumkins and Podder remained unconquered. Did an elderly gentleman essay to stop the progress of the ball, it rolled between his legs or slipped between his fingers. Did a slim gentleman try to catch it, it struck him on the nose, and bounded pleasantly off with redoubled violence, while the slim gentleman's eyes filled with water, and his form writhed with anguish. Was it thrown straight up to the wicket, Dumkins had reached it before the ball. In short, when Dumkins was caught out,

The Cricket Match

and Podder stumped out, All-Muggleton had notched some fifty-four, while the score of the Dingley Dellers was as blank as their faces. The advantage was too great to be recovered. In vain did the eager Luffey, and the enthusiastic Struggles, do all that skill and experience could suggest, to regain the ground Dingley Dell had lost in the contest; – it was of no avail; and in an early period of the winning game Dingley Dell gave in, and allowed the superior prowess of All-Muggleton.

The stranger, meanwhile, had been eating, drinking, and talking, without cessation. At every good stroke he expressed his satisfaction and approval of the player in a most condescending and patronising manner, which could not fail to have been highly gratifying to the party concerned; while at every bad attempt at a catch, and every failure to stop the ball, he launched his personal displeasure at the head of the devoted individual in such denunciations – as 'Ah, ah! – stupid' – 'Now, butter-fingers' – 'Muff' – 'Humbug' – and so forth – ejaculations which seemed to establish him in the opinion of all around, as a most excellent and undeniable judge of the whole art and mystery of the noble game of cricket.

'Capital game – well played – some strokes admirable,' said the stranger, as both sides crowded into the tent, at the conclusion of the game.

'You have played it, sir?' inquired Mr Wardle, who had been much amused by his loquacity.

'Played it! Think I have – thousands of times – not here – West Indies – exciting thing – hot work – very.'

'It must be rather a warm pursuit in such a climate,' observed Mr Pickwick.'

'Warm! – red hot – scorching – glowing. Played a match once – single wicket – friend the Colonel – Sir Thomas Blazo – who should get the greatest number of runs. – Won the toss – first innings – seven o'clock A.M. – six natives to look out – went in; kept in – heat intense – natives all fainted – taken away – fresh half-dozen ordered – fainted also – Blazo bowling – supported by two natives – couldn't bowl me out – fainted too – cleared away the Colonel – wouldn't give in – faithful attendant – Quanko Samba – last man left – sun so hot, bat in blisters, ball scorched brown – five hundred and seventy runs – rather exhausted – Quanko mustered up last remaining strength – bowled me out – had a bath, and went out to dinner.'

'And what became of what's-his-name, sir?' inquired an old gentleman.

'Blazo?'

'No – the other gentleman.'

'Quanko Samba?'

'Yes, sir.'

'Poor Quanko – never recovered it – bowled on, on my account – bowled off, on his own – died, sir.' Here the stranger buried his countenance in a brown jug, but whether to hide his emotion or imbibe its contents, we cannot distinctly affirm. We only know that he paused suddenly, drew a long and deep breath, and looked anxiously on, as two of the principal members of the Dingley Dell club approached Mr Pickwick, and said –

'We are about to partake of a plain dinner at the Blue Lion, sir; we hope you and your friends will join us.'

'Of course,' said Mr Wardle, 'among our friends we include Mr —;' and he looked towards the stranger.

'Jingle,' said that versatile gentleman, taking the hint at once. 'Jingle – Alfred Jingle, Esq., of No Hall, Nowhere.'

'I shall be very happy, I am sure,' said Mr Pickwick.

'So shall I,' said Mr Alfred Jingle, drawing one arm through Mr Pickwick's, and another through Mr Wardle's, as he whispered confidentially in the ear of the former gentleman: –

'Devilish good dinner – cold, but capital – peeped into the room this morning – fowls and pies, and all that sort of thing – pleasant fellows these – well behaved, too – very.'

There being no further preliminaries to arrange, the company straggled into the town in little knots of twos and threes; and within a quarter of an hour were all seated in the great room of the Blue Lion Inn, Muggleton – Mr Dumkins acting as chairman, and Mr Luffey officiating as vice.

There was a vast deal of talking and rattling of knives and forks, and plates: a great running about of three ponderous headed waiters, and a rapid disappearance of the substantial viands on the table; to each and every of which item of confusion, the facetious Mr Jingle lent the aid of half-a-dozen ordinary men at least. When everybody had eaten as much as possible, the cloth was removed, bottles, glasses, and dessert were placed on the table; and the waiters withdrew to 'clear away,' or in other words, to appropriate to their own private use and emolument whatever remnants of the eatables and drinkables they could contrive to lay their hands on.

Amidst the general hum of mirth and conversation that ensued, there was a little man with a puffy Say-nothing-to-me,-or-I'll-contradict-you sort of countenance, who remained very quiet;

occasionally looking round him when the conversation slackened, as if he contemplated putting in something very weighty; and now and then bursting into a short cough of inexpressible grandeur. At length, during a moment of comparative silence, the little man called out in a very loud, solemn voice –

'Mr Luffey!'

Everybody was hushed into a profound stillness as the individual addressed, replied –

'Sir!'

'I wish to address a few words to you, sir, if you will entreat the gentlemen to fill their glasses.'

Mr Jingle uttered a patronising 'hear, hear,' which was responded to by the remainder of the company: and the glasses having been filled the Vice-President assumed an air of wisdom in a state of profound attention; and said –

'Mr Staple.'

'Sir,' said the little man, rising, 'I wish to address what I have to say to *you* and not to our worthy chairman, because our worthy chairman is in some measure – I may say in a great degree – the subject of what I have to say, or I may say to – to – '

'State,' suggested Mr Jingle.

– 'Yes, to state,' said the little man, 'I thank my honourable friend, if he will allow me to call him so – (four hears, and one certainly from Mr Jingle) – for the suggestion. Sir, I am a Deller – a Dingley Deller (cheers.) I cannot lay claim to the honour of forming an item in the population of Muggleton; nor, sir, I will frankly admit, do I covet that honour: and I will tell you why, sir – (hear); to Muggleton I will readily concede all those honours and distinctions to which it can fairly lay claim – they are too numerous and too well known to require aid or recapitulation from me. But, sir, while we remember that Muggleton has given birth to a Dumkins and a Podder, let us never forget that Dingley Dell can boast a Luffey and a Struggles. (Vociferous cheering.) Let me not be considered as wishing to detract from the merits of the former gentlemen. Sir, I envy them the luxury of their own feelings on this occasion. (Cheers.) Every gentleman who hears me, is probably acquainted with the reply made by an individual, who – to use an ordinary figure of speech – "hung out" in a tub, to the emperor Alexander: – "If I were not Diogenes,"⁹ said he, "I would be Alexander." I can well imagine these gentlemen to say, "If I were not Dumkins I would be Luffey; if I were not Podder I would be Struggles." (Enthusiasm.) But, gentlemen of Muggleton, is it in cricket alone that your fellow-townsmen stand pre-eminent? Have you never heard of Dumkins and determination? Have you never been taught to associate Podder with property? (Great applause.) Have you never, when struggling for your rights, your liberties, and your privileges, been reduced, if only for an instant, to misgiving and despair? And when you have been thus depressed, has not the name of Dumkins laid afresh within your breast the fire which had just gone out; and has not a word from that man, lighted it again as brightly as if it had never expired? (Great cheering.) Gentlemen, I beg to surround with a rich halo of enthusiastic cheering the united names of "Dumkins and Podder."'

Here the little man ceased, and here the company commenced a raising of voices, and thumping of tables, which lasted with little intermission during the remainder of the evening. Other toasts were drunk. Mr Luffey and Mr Struggles, Mr Pickwick and Mr Jingle, were, each in his turn, the subject of unqualified eulogium; and each in due course returned thanks for the honour.

Enthusiastic as we are in the noble cause to which we have devoted ourselves, we should have felt a sensation of pride which we cannot express, and a consciousness of having done something to merit immortality of which we are now deprived, could we have laid the faintest outline of these addresses before our ardent readers. Mr Snodgrass, as usual, took a great mass of notes, which would no doubt have afforded most useful and valuable information, had not the burning eloquence of the words or the feverish influence of the wine made that gentleman's hand so extremely unsteady, as to render his writing nearly unintelligible, and his style wholly so. By dint of patient investigation, we have been enabled to trace some characters bearing a faint resemblance to the names of the speakers; and we can also discern an entry of a song[10] (supposed to have been sung by Mr Jingle), in which the words 'bowl' 'sparkling' 'ruby' 'bright,' and 'wine' are frequently repeated at short intervals. We fancy too, that we can discern at the very end of the notes, some indistinct reference to 'broiled bones;' and then the words 'cold' 'without' occur: but as any hypothesis we could found upon them must necessarily rest upon mere conjecture, we are not disposed to indulge in any of the speculations to which they may give rise.

We will therefore return to Mr Tupman; merely adding that within some few minutes before twelve o'clock that night, the convocation of worthies of Dingley Dell and Muggleton were heard to sing, with great feeling and emphasis, the beautiful and pathetic national air of

We won't go home 'till morning,
We won't go home 'till morning,
We won't go home 'till morning,
    'Till daylight doth appear.

CHAPTER 8

Strongly illustrative of the Position, that the Course of True Love is not a Railway

The quiet seclusion of Dingley Dell, the presence of so many of the gentler sex, and the solicitude and anxiety they evinced in his behalf, were all favourable to the growth and development of those softer feelings which nature had implanted deep in the bosom of Mr Tracy Tupman, and which now appeared destined to centre in one lovely object. The young ladies were pretty, their manners winning, their dispositions unexceptionable; but there was a dignity in the air, a touch-me-not-ishness in the walk, a majesty in the eye of the spinster aunt, to which, at their time of life, they could lay no claim, which distinguished her from any female on whom Mr Tupman had ever gazed. That there was something kindred in their nature, something congenial in their souls, something mysteriously sympathetic in their bosoms, was evident. Her name was the first that rose to Mr Tupman's lips as he lay wounded on the grass; and her hysteric laughter was the first sound that fell upon his ear when he was supported to the house. But had her agitation arisen from an amiable and feminine sensibility which would have been equally irrepressible in any case; or had it been called forth by a more ardent and passionate feeling, which he, of all men living, could alone awaken? These were the doubts which racked his brain as he lay extended on the sofa: these were the doubts which he determined should be at once and for ever resolved.

It was evening. Isabella and Emily had strolled out with Mr Trundle; the deaf old lady had fallen asleep in her chair; the snoring of the fat boy, penetrated in a low and monotonous sound from the distant kitchen; the buxom servants were lounging at the side-door, enjoying the pleasantness of the hour, and the delights of a flirtation, on first principles, with certain unwieldy animals attached to the farm; and there sat the interesting pair, uncared for by all, caring for none, and dreaming only of themselves; there they sat, in short, like a pair of carefully-folded kid-gloves – bound up in each other.

'I have forgotten my flowers,' said the spinster aunt.

'Water them now,' said Mr Tupman in accents of persuasion.

'You will take cold in the evening air,' urged the spinster aunt, affectionately.

'No, no,' said Mr Tupman rising; 'it will do me good. Let me accompany you.'

The lady paused to adjust the sling in which the left arm of the youth was placed, and taking his right arm led him to the garden.

There was a bower at the further end, with honeysuckle, jessamine,¹ and creeping plants – one of those sweet retreats which humane men erect for the accommodation of spiders.

The spinster aunt took up a large watering-pot which lay in one corner, and was about to leave the arbour. Mr Tupman detained her, and drew her to a seat beside him.

'Miss Wardle!' said he.

The spinster aunt trembled, till some pebbles which had accidentally found their way into the large watering-pot shook like an infant's rattle.

'Miss Wardle,' said Mr Tupman, 'you are an angel.'

'Mr Tupman!' exclaimed Rachael, blushing as red as the watering-pot itself.

'Nay,' said the eloquent Pickwickian – 'I know it but too well.'

'All women are angels, they say,' murmured the lady, playfully.

'Then what can *you* be; or to what, without presumption, can I compare you?' replied Mr Tupman. 'Where was the woman ever seen who resembled you? Where else could I hope to find so rare a combination of excellence and beauty? Where else could I seek to— Oh!' Here Mr Tupman paused, and pressed the hand which clasped the handle of the happy watering-pot.

The lady turned aside her head. 'Men are such deceivers,' she softly whispered.

'They are, they are,' ejaculated Mr Tupman; 'but not all men. There lives at least one being who can never change – one being who would be content to devote his whole existence to your happiness – who lives but in your eyes – who breathes but in your smiles – who bears the heavy burden of life itself only for you.'

'Could such an individual be found,' said the lady—

'But he *can* be found,' said the ardent Mr Tupman, interposing. 'He *is* found. He is here, Miss Wardle.' And ere the lady was aware of his intention, Mr Tupman had sunk upon his knees at her feet.

'Mr Tupman, rise,' said Rachael.

'Never!' was the valorous reply. 'Oh, Rachael!' – He seized her passive hand, and the watering-pot fell to the ground as he pressed it to his lips. – 'Oh, Rachael! say you love me.'

'Mr Tupman,' said the spinster aunt, with averted head – 'I can hardly speak the words; but – but – you are not wholly indifferent to me.'

Mr Tupman no sooner heard this avowal, than he proceeded to do what his enthusiastic emotions prompted, and what, for aught we know (for we are but little acquainted with such matters), people so circumstanced always do. He jumped up, and, throwing his arm round the neck of the spinster aunt, imprinted upon her lips numerous kisses, which after a due show of struggling and resistance, she received so passively, that there is no telling how many more Mr Tupman might have bestowed, if the lady had not given a very unaffected start and exclaimed in an affrighted tone –

'Mr Tupman, we are observed! – we are discovered!'

Mr Tupman looked round. There was the fat boy, perfectly motionless, with his large circular eyes staring into the arbour, but without the slightest expression on his face that the most expert physiognomist could have referred to astonishment, curiosity, or any other known passion that agitates the human breast. Mr Tupman gazed on the fat boy, and the fat boy stared at him; and the longer Mr Tupman observed the utter vacancy of the fat boy's countenance, the more convinced he became that he either did not know, or did not understand, anything that had been going forward. Under this impression, he said with great firmness –

'What do you want here, sir?'

'Supper's ready sir,' was the prompt reply.

'Have you just come here, sir?' inquired Mr Tupman, with a piercing look.

'Just,' replied the fat boy.

Mr Tupman looked at him very hard again; but there was not a wink in his eye, or a curve in his face.

Mr Tupman took the arm of the spinster aunt, and walked towards the house; the fat boy followed behind.

'He knows nothing of what has happened,' he whispered.

'Nothing,' said the spinster aunt.

There was a sound behind them, as of an imperfectly suppressed chuckle. Mr Tupman turned sharply round. No; it could not have been the fat boy; there was not a gleam of mirth, or anything but feeding in his whole visage.

The fat boy awake on this occasion only
Original illustration to the first issue of monthly part no. III by R. W. Buss

The fat boy awake on this occasion only
Replacement illustration by H. K. Browne ('Phiz') for later issues of part III

'He must have been fast asleep,' whispered Mr Tupman.

'I have not the least doubt of it,' replied the spinster aunt.

They both laughed heartily.

Mr Tupman was wrong. The fat boy, for once, had not been fast asleep. He was awake – wide awake – to what had been going forward.

The supper passed off without any attempt at a general conversation. The old lady had gone to bed; Isabella Wardle devoted herself exclusively to Mr Trundle; the spinster's attentions were reserved for Mr Tupman; and Emily's thoughts appeared to be engrossed by some distant object – possibly they were with the absent Snodgrass.

Eleven – twelve – one o'clock had struck, and the gentlemen had not arrived. Consternation sat on every face. Could they have been waylaid and robbed? Should they send men and lanterns in every direction by which they could be supposed likely to have travelled home? or should they—Hark! there they were. What could have made them so late? A strange voice, too! To whom could it belong? They rushed into the kitchen whither the truants had repaired, and at once obtained rather more than a glimmering of the real state of the case.

Mr Pickwick, with his hands in his pockets and his hat cocked completely over his left eye, was leaning against the dresser, shaking his head from side to side, and producing a constant succession of the blandest and most benevolent smiles without being moved thereunto by any discernible cause or pretence whatsoever; old Mr Wardle, with a highly-inflamed countenance, was grasping the hand of a strange gentleman muttering protestations of eternal friendship; Mr Winkle, supporting himself by the eight-day clock, was feebly invoking destruction upon the head of any member of the family who should suggest the propriety of his retiring for the night; and Mr Snodgrass had sunk into a chair, with an expression of the most abject and hopeless misery that the human mind can imagine, portrayed in every lineament of his expressive face.

'Is anything the matter?' inquired the three ladies.

'Nothing the matter,' replied Mr Pickwick. 'We – we're – all right. – I say, Wardle, we're all right, an't we?'

'I should think so,' replied the jolly host. – 'My dears, here's my friend, Mr Jingle – Mr Pickwick's friend, Mr Jingle, come 'pon – little visit.'

'Is anything the matter with Mr Snodgrass, sir?' inquired Emily, with great anxiety.

Mr Wardle & his friends under the influence of 'the salmon'

'Nothing the matter, ma'am,' replied the stranger. 'Cricket dinner – glorious party – capital songs – old port – claret – good – very good – wine, ma'am – wine.'

'It wasn't the wine,' murmured Mr Snodgrass, in a broken voice. 'It was the salmon.' (Somehow or other, it never *is* the wine, in these cases.)

'Hadn't they better go to bed, ma'am?' inquired Emma. 'Two of the boys will carry the gentlemen up stairs.'

'I won't go to bed,' said Mr Winkle, firmly.

'No living boy shall carry me,' said Mr Pickwick, stoutly; – and he went on smiling as before.

'Hurrah!' gasped Mr Winkle, faintly.

'Hurrah!' echoed Mr Pickwick, taking off his hat and dashing it on the floor, and insanely casting his spectacles into the middle of the kitchen. – At this humorous feat he laughed outright.

'Let's – have – 'nother – bottle,' cried Mr Winkle, commencing in a very loud key and ending in a very faint one. His head dropped upon his breast; and, muttering his invincible determination not to go to his bed, and a sanguinary regret that he had not 'done for old Tupman' in the morning, he fell fast asleep; in which condition he was borne to his apartment by two young giants under the personal superintendence of the fat boy, to whose protecting care Mr Snodgrass shortly afterwards confided his own person. Mr Pickwick accepted the proffered arm of Mr Tupman and quietly disappeared, smiling more than ever; and Mr Wardle, after taking as affectionate a leave of the whole family as if he were ordered for immediate execution, consigned to Mr Trundle the honour of conveying him up-stairs, and retired, with a very futile attempt to look impressively solemn and dignified.

'What a shocking scene!' said the spinster aunt.

'Dis – gusting!' ejaculated both the young ladies.

'Dreadful – dreadful!' said Jingle, looking very grave: he was about a bottle and a half ahead of any of his companions. 'Horrid spectacle – very!'

'What a nice man!' whispered the spinster aunt to Mr Tupman.

'Good-looking, too!' whispered Emily Wardle.

'Oh, decidedly,' observed the spinster aunt.

Mr Tupman thought of the widow at Rochester: and his mind was troubled. The succeeding half-hour's conversation was not of a nature to calm his perturbed spirit.[2] The new visitor was very talkative, and the number of his anecdotes was only to be exceeded by the extent of his politeness. Mr Tupman felt that as Jingle's popularity increased, he (Tupman) retired further into the shade. His laughter was forced – his merriment feigned; and when at last he laid his aching temples between the sheets, he thought, with horrid delight, on the satisfaction it would afford him to have Jingle's head at that moment between the feather bed and the mattress.

The indefatigable stranger rose betimes next morning, and, although his companions remained in bed overpowered with the dissipation of the previous night, exerted himself most successfully to promote the hilarity of the breakfast-table. So successful were his efforts, that even the deaf old lady insisted on having one or two of his best jokes retailed through the trumpet; and even she conde-scended to observe to the spinster aunt, that 'he' (meaning Jingle) 'was an impudent young fellow:' a sentiment in which all her relations then and there present thoroughly coincided.

It was the old lady's habit on the fine summer mornings to repair to the arbour in which Mr Tupman had already signalised himself, in form and manner following: first, the fat boy fetched from a peg behind the old lady's bed-room door, a close black satin bonnet, a warm cotton shawl, and a thick stick with a capacious handle; and the old lady having put on the bonnet and shawl at her leisure, would lean one hand on the stick and the other on the fat boy's shoulder, and walk leisurely to the arbour, where the fat boy would leave her to enjoy the fresh air for the space of half an hour; at the expiration of which time he would return and reconduct her to the house.

The old lady was very precise and very particular; and as this ceremony had been observed for three successive summers without the slightest deviation from the accustomed form, she was not a little surprised on this particular morning, to see the fat boy, instead of leaving the arbour, walk a few paces out of it, look carefully round him in every direction, and return towards her with great stealth and an air of the most profound mystery.

The old lady was timorous – most old ladies are – and her first impression was that the bloated lad was about to do her some grievous bodily harm with the view of possessing himself of her loose coin. She would have cried for assistance, but age and infirmity had long ago deprived her of the power of screaming; she, therefore, watched his motions with feelings of intense terror, which were in no degree diminished by his coming close up to her, and shouting in her ear in an agitated, and as it seemed to her, a threatening tone –

'Missus!'

Now it so happened that Mr Jingle was walking in the garden close to the arbour at this moment. He too heard the shout of 'Missus,' and stopped to hear more. There were three reasons for his doing so. In the first place, he was idle and curious; secondly, he was by no means scrupulous; thirdly, and lastly, he was concealed from view by some flowering shrubs. So there he stood, and there he listened.

'Missus!' shouted the fat boy.

'Well, Joe,' said the trembling old lady. 'I'm sure I have been a good mistress to you, Joe. You have invariably been treated very kindly. You have never had too much to do; and you have always had enough to eat.'

This last was an appeal to the fat boy's most sensitive feelings. He seemed touched, as he replied, emphatically –

'I knows I has.'

'Then what can you want to do now?' said the old lady, gaining courage.

'I wants to make your flesh creep,' replied the boy.

This sounded like a very bloodthirsty mode of showing one's gratitude; and as the old lady did not precisely understand the process by which such a result was to be attained, all her former horrors returned.

'What do you think I see in this very arbour last night?' inquired the boy.

'Bless us! What?' exclaimed the old lady, alarmed at the solemn manner of the corpulent youth.

'The strange gentleman – him as had his arm hurt – a kissin' and huggin'–'

'Who, Joe? None of the servants, I hope.'

'Worser than that,' roared the fat boy, in the old lady's ear.

'Not one of my grand-da'aters?'

'Worser than that.'

'Worse than *that*, Joe!' said the old lady, who had thought this the extreme limit of human atrocity. 'Who was it, Joe? I insist upon knowing.'

The fat boy looked cautiously round, and having concluded his survey, shouted in the old lady's ear:

'Miss Rachael.'

'What!' said the old lady, in a shrill tone. 'Speak louder.'

'Miss Rachael,' roared the fat boy.

'My da'ater!'

The train of nods which the fat boy gave by way of assent, communicated a *blanc-mange* like motion to his fat cheeks.

'And she suffered him!' exclaimed the old lady.

A grin stole over the fat boy's features as he said:

'I see her a kissin' of him agin.'

If Mr Jingle, from his place of concealment, could have beheld the expression which the old lady's face assumed at this communication, the probability is that a sudden burst of laughter would have betrayed his close vicinity to the summer-house. He listened attentively. Fragments of angry sentences such as, 'Without my permission!' – 'At her time of life' – 'Miserable old 'ooman like me' – 'Might have waited till I was dead,' and so forth, reached his ears; and then he heard the heels of the fat boy's boots crunching the gravel, as he retired and left the old lady alone.

It was a remarkable coincidence perhaps, but it was nevertheless a fact, that Mr Jingle within five minutes after his arrival at Manor Farm on the preceding night, had inwardly resolved to lay siege to the heart of the spinster aunt, without delay. He had observation enough to see, that his off-hand manner was by no means disagreeable to the fair object of his attack; and he had more than a strong suspicion that she possessed that most desirable of all requisites, a small independence. The imperative necessity of ousting his rival by some means or other, flashed quickly upon him, and he immediately resolved to adopt certain proceedings tending to that end and object, without a moment's delay. Fielding[3] tells us that man is fire, and woman tow, and the Prince of Darkness sets a light to 'em. Mr Jingle knew that young men, to spinster aunts, are as lighted gas to gunpowder, and he determined to essay the effect of an explosion without loss of time.

Full of reflections upon this important decision, he crept from his place of concealment, and, under cover of the shrubs before mentioned, approached the house. Fortune seemed determined to favour his design. Mr Tupman and the rest of the gentlemen left the garden by the side gate just as he obtained a view of it; and the young ladies, he knew, had walked out alone, soon after breakfast. The coast was clear.

The breakfast-parlour door was partially open. He peeped in. The spinster aunt was knitting. He coughed; she looked up and smiled. Hesitation formed no part of Mr Alfred Jingle's character. He laid his finger on his lips mysteriously, walked in, and closed the door.

'Miss Wardle,' said Mr Jingle, with affected earnestness, 'forgive intrusion – short acquaintance – no time for ceremony – all discovered.'

'Sir!' said the spinster aunt, rather astonished by the unexpected apparition and somewhat doubtful of Mr Jingle's sanity.

'Hush!' said Mr Jingle, in a stage whisper; – 'large boy – dumpling face – round eyes – rascal!' Here he shook his head expressively, and the spinster aunt trembled with agitation.

'I presume you allude to Joseph, sir?' said the lady, making an effort to appear composed.

'Yes, ma'am – damn that Joe! – treacherous dog, Joe – told the old lady – old lady furious – wild – raving – arbour – Tupman – kissing and hugging – all that sort of thing – eh, ma'am – eh?'

'Mr Jingle,' said the spinster aunt, 'if you come here, sir, to insult me –'

'Not at all – by no means,' replied the unabashed Mr Jingle; – 'overheard the tale – came to warn you of your danger – tender my services – prevent the hubbub. Never mind – think it an insult – leave the room' – and he turned, as if to carry the threat into execution.

'What *shall* I do!' said the poor spinster, bursting into tears. 'My brother will be furious.'

'Of course he will,' said Mr Jingle pausing – 'outrageous.'

'Oh, Mr Jingle, what *can* I say!' exclaimed the spinster aunt, in another flood of despair.

'Say he dreamt it,' replied Mr Jingle, coolly.

A ray of comfort darted across the mind of the spinster aunt at this suggestion. Mr Jingle perceived it, and followed up his advantage.

'Pooh, pooh! – nothing more easy – blackguard boy – lovely woman – fat boy horsewhipped – you believed – end of the matter – all comfortable.'

Whether the probability of escaping from the consequences of this ill-timed discovery was delightful to the spinster's feelings, or whether the hearing herself described as a 'lovely woman' softened the asperity of her grief, we know not. She blushed slightly, and cast a grateful look on Mr Jingle.

That insinuating gentleman sighed deeply, fixed his eyes on the spinster aunt's face for a couple of minutes, started melo-dramatically, and suddenly withdrew them.

'You seem unhappy, Mr Jingle,' said the lady, in a plaintive voice. 'May I show my gratitude for your kind interference, by inquiring into the cause, with a view, if possible, to its removal?'

'Ha!' exclaimed Mr Jingle, with another start – 'removal! remove *my* unhappiness, and your love bestowed upon a man who is insensible to the blessing – who even now contemplates a design upon the affections of the niece of the creature who – but no; he is my friend; I will not expose his vices. Miss Wardle – farewell!' At the conclusion of this address, the most consecutive he was ever known to utter, Mr Jingle applied to his eyes the remnant of a handkerchief before noticed, and turned towards the door.

'Stay, Mr Jingle!' said the spinster aunt emphatically. 'You have made an allusion to Mr Tupman – explain it.'

'Never!' exclaimed Jingle, with a professional (*i.e.* theatrical) air. 'Never!' and, by way of showing that he had no desire to be questioned further, he drew a chair close to that of the spinster aunt and sat down.

'Mr Jingle,' said the aunt, 'I entreat – I implore you, if there is any dreadful mystery connected with Mr Tupman, reveal it.'

'Can I,' said Mr Jingle, fixing his eyes on the aunt's face – 'Can I see – lovely creature – sacrificed at the shrine – heartless avarice!' He appeared to be struggling with various conflicting emotions for a few seconds, and then said in a low deep voice –

'Tupman only wants your money.'

'The wretch!' exclaimed the spinster, with energetic indignation. (Mr Jingle's doubts were resolved. She *had* money).

'More than that,' said Jingle – 'loves another.'

'Another!' ejaculated the spinster. 'Who?'

'Short girl – black eyes – niece Emily.'

There was a pause.

Now, if there were one individual in the whole world, of whom the spinster aunt entertained a mortal and deeply-rooted jealousy, it was this identical niece. The colour rushed over her face and neck, and she tossed her head in silence with an air of ineffable contempt. At last, biting her thin lips, and bridling up, she said –

'It can't be. I won't believe it.'

'Watch 'em,' said Jingle.

'I will,' said the aunt.

'Watch his looks.'

'I will.'

'His whispers.'

'I will.'

'He'll sit next her at table.'

'Let him.'

'He'll flatter her.'

'Let him.'

'He'll pay her every possible attention.'

'Let him.'

'And he'll cut[4] you.'

'Cut *me*!' screamed the spinster aunt. '*He* cut *me; – will* he!' and she trembled with rage and disappointment.

'You will convince yourself?' said Jingle.

'I will.'

'You'll show your spirit?'

'I will.'

'You'll not have him afterwards?'

'Never.'

'You'll take somebody else?'

'Yes.'

'You shall.'

Mr Jingle fell on his knees, remained thereupon for five minutes thereafter: and rose the accepted lover of the spinster aunt: conditionally upon Mr Tupman's perjury being made clear and manifest.

The burden of proof lay with Mr Alfred Jingle; and he produced his evidence that very day at dinner. The spinster aunt could hardly believe her eyes. Mr Tracy Tupman was established at Emily's side, ogling, whispering, and smiling, in opposition to Mr Snodgrass. Not a word, not a look, not a glance, did he bestow upon his heart's pride of the evening before.

'Damn that boy!' thought old Mr Wardle to himself. – He had heard the story from his mother. 'Damn that boy! He *must* have been asleep. It's all imagination.'

'Traitor!' thought the spinster aunt. 'Dear Mr Jingle was not deceiving me. Ugh! how I hate the wretch!'

The following conversation may serve to explain to our readers this apparently unaccountable alteration of deportment on the part of Mr Tracy Tupman.

The time was evening; the scene the garden. There were two figures walking in a side path; one was rather short and stout; the other rather tall and slim. They were Mr Tupman and Mr Jingle. The stout figure commenced the dialogue.

'How did I do it?' he inquired.

'Splendid – capital – couldn't act better myself – you must repeat the part tomorrow – every evening, till further notice.'

'Does Rachael still wish it?'

'Of course – she don't like it – but must be done – avert suspicion

– afraid of her brother – says there's no help for it – only a few days more – when old folks blinded – crown your happiness.'

'Any message?'

'Love – best love – kindest regards – unalterable affection. Can I say anything for you?'

'My dear fellow,' replied the unsuspicious Mr Tupman, fervently grasping his 'friend's' hand – 'carry my best love – say how hard I find it to dissemble – say anything that's kind: but add how sensible I am of the necessity of the suggestion she made to me, through you, this morning. Say I applaud her wisdom and admire her discretion.'

'I will. Anything more?'

'Nothing; only add how ardently I long for the time when I may call her mine, and all dissimulation may be unnecessary.'

'Certainly, certainly. Anything more?'

'Oh, my friend!' said poor Mr Tupman, again grasping the hand of his companion, 'receive my warmest thanks for your disinterested kindness; and forgive me if I have ever, even in thought, done you the injustice of supposing that you *could* stand in my way. My dear friend, can I ever repay you?'

'Don't talk of it,' replied Mr Jingle. He stopped short, as if suddenly recollecting something, and said – 'By-the-bye – can't spare ten pounds, can you? – very particular purpose – pay you in three days.'

'I dare say I can,' replied Mr Tupman, in the fulness of his heart. 'Three days, you say?'

'Only three days – all over then – no more difficulties.'

Mr Tupman counted the money into his companion's hand, and he dropped it piece by piece into his pocket, as they walked towards the house.

'Be careful,' said Mr Jingle – 'not a look.'

'Not a wink,' said Mr Tupman.

'Not a syllable.'

'Not a whisper.'

'All your attentions to the niece – rather rude, than otherwise, to the aunt – only way of deceiving the old ones.'

'I'll take care,' said Mr Tupman aloud.

'And *I'll* take care,' said Mr Jingle internally; and they entered the house.

The scene of that afternoon was repeated that evening, and on the three afternoons and evenings next ensuing. On the fourth, the host was in high spirits, for he had satisfied himself that there was no ground for the charge against Mr Tupman. So was Mr Tupman, for Mr Jingle had told him that his affair would soon be brought to a crisis. So was Mr Pickwick, for he was seldom otherwise. So was not Mr Snodgrass, for he had grown jealous of Mr Tupman. So was the old lady, for she had been winning at whist. So were Mr Jingle and Miss Wardle, for reasons of sufficient importance in this eventful history to be narrated in another chapter.

CHAPTER 9

A Discovery and a Chase

The supper was ready laid, the chairs were drawn round the table, bottles, jugs, and glasses were arranged upon the sideboard, and everything betokened the approach of the most convivial period in the whole four-and-twenty hours.

'Where's Rachael?' said Mr Wardle.

'Ay, and Jingle?' added Mr Pickwick.

'Dear me,' said the host, 'I wonder I haven't missed him before. Why, I don't think I've heard his voice for two hours at least. Emily, my dear, ring the bell.'

The bell was rung, and the fat boy appeared.

'Where's Miss Rachael?' He couldn't say.

'Where's Mr Jingle, then?' He didn't know.

Everybody looked surprised. It was late – past eleven o'clock. Mr Tupman laughed in his sleeve. They were loitering somewhere, talking about *him*. Ha, ha! capital notion that – funny.

'Never mind,' said Wardle, after a short pause, 'they'll turn up presently, I dare say. I never wait supper for anybody.'

'Excellent rule, that,' said Mr Pickwick, 'admirable.'

'Pray, sit down,' said the host.

'Certainly,' said Mr Pickwick: and down they sat.

There was a gigantic round of cold beef on the table, and Mr Pickwick was supplied with a plentiful portion of it. He had raised his fork to his lips, and was on the very point of opening his mouth for the reception of a piece of beef, when the hum of many voices suddenly arose in the kitchen. He paused, and laid down his fork. Mr Wardle paused too, and insensibly released his hold of the carving-knife, which remained inserted in the beef. He looked at Mr Pickwick. Mr Pickwick looked at him.

Heavy footsteps were heard in the passage; the parlour door was suddenly burst open; and the man who had cleaned Mr Pickwick's boots on his first arrival, rushed into the room, followed by the fat boy, and all the domestics.

'What the devil's the meaning of this?' exclaimed the host.

'The kitchen chimney ain't a-fire, is it, Emma?' inquired the old lady.

'Lor grandma! No,' screamed both the young ladies.

'What's the matter?' roared the master of the house.

The man gasped for breath, and faintly ejaculated –

'They ha' gone, Mas'r! – gone right clean off, sir!' (At this juncture Mr Tupman was observed to lay down his knife and fork, and to turn very pale.)

'Who's gone?' said Mr Wardle, fiercely.

'Mus'r Jingle and Miss Rachael, in a po'-chay, from Blue Lion, Muggleton. I was there; but I couldn't stop 'em; so I run off to tell'ee.'

'I paid his expenses!' said Mr Tupman, jumping up frantically. 'He's got ten pounds of mine! – stop him! – he's swindled me! – I won't bear it! – I'll have justice, Pickwick! – I won't stand it!' and with sundry incoherent exclamations of the like nature, the unhappy gentleman spun round and round the apartment, in a transport of frenzy.

'Lord preserve us!' ejaculated Mr Pickwick, eyeing the extraordinary gestures of his friend with terrified surprise. 'He's gone mad! What shall we do!'

'Do!' said the stout old host, who regarded only the last words of the sentence. 'Put the horse in the gig! I'll get a chaise at the Lion, and follow 'em instantly. Where' – he exclaimed, as the man ran out to execute the commission – 'Where's that villain, Joe?'

'Here I am; but I han't a willin,' replied a voice. It was the fat boy's.

'Let me get at him, Pickwick,' cried Wardle, as he rushed at the ill-starred youth. 'He was bribed by that scoundrel, Jingle, to put me on a wrong scent, by telling a cock-and-a-bull story of my sister and your friend Tupman!' (Here Mr Tupman sunk into a chair.) 'Let me get at him!'

'Don't let him!' screamed all the women, above whose exclamations the blubbering of the fat boy was distinctly audible.

'I won't be held!' cried the old man. 'Mr Winkle, take your hands off. Mr Pickwick, let me go, sir!'

It was a beautiful sight, in that moment of turmoil and confusion, to behold the placid and philosophical expression of Mr Pickwick's face, albeit somewhat flushed with exertion, as he stood with his arms firmly clasped round the extensive waist of their corpulent host, thus restraining the impetuosity of his passion, while the fat boy was scratched, and pulled, and pushed from the room by all the females congregated therein. He had no sooner released his hold, than the man entered to announce that the gig was ready.

'Don't let him go alone!' screamed the females. 'He'll kill somebody!'

'I'll go with him,' said Mr Pickwick.

'You're a good fellow, Pickwick,' said the host, grasping his hand. 'Emma, give Mr Pickwick a shawl to tie round his neck – make haste. Look after your grandmother, girls; she has fainted away. Now then, are you ready?'

Mr Pickwick's mouth and chin having been hastily enveloped in a large shawl: his hat having been put on his head, and his great coat thrown over his arm, he replied in the affirmative.

They jumped into the gig. 'Give her her head, Tom,' cried the host; and away they went, down the narrow lanes: jolting in and out of the cart-ruts, and bumping up against the hedges on either side, as if they would go to pieces every moment.

'How much are they a-head?' shouted Wardle, as they drove up to the door of the Blue Lion, round which a little crowd had collected, late as it was.

'Not above three-quarters of an hour,' was everybody's reply.

'Chaise and four directly! – out with 'em! Put up the gig afterwards.'

'Now, boys!' cried the landlord – 'chaise and four out – make haste – look alive there!'

Away ran the hostlers, and the boys. The lanterns glimmered, as the men ran to and fro; the horses' hoofs clattered on the uneven paving of the yard; the chaise rumbled as it was drawn out of the coach-house; and all was noise and bustle.

'Now then! – is that chaise coming out to-night?' cried Wardle.

'Coming down the yard now, sir,' replied the hostler.

Out came the chaise – in went the horses – on sprung the boys – in got the travellers.

'Mind – the seven-mile stage in less than half an hour!' shouted Wardle.

'Off with you!'

The boys applied whip and spur, the waiters shouted, the hostlers cheered, and away they went, fast and furiously.

'Pretty situation,' thought Mr Pickwick, when he had had a moment's time for reflection. 'Pretty situation for the General Chairman of the Pickwick Club. Damp chaise – strange horses – fifteen miles an hour – and twelve o'clock at night!'

For the first three or four miles, not a word was spoken by either of the gentlemen, each being too much immersed in his own reflections to address any observations to his companion. When they had gone over that much ground, however, and the horses getting thoroughly warmed began to do their work in really good style, Mr Pickwick became too much exhilarated with the rapidity of the motion, to remain any longer perfectly mute.

'We're sure to catch them, I think,' said he.

'Hope so,' replied his companion.

'Fine night,' said Mr Pickwick, looking up at the moon, which was shining brightly.

'So much the worse,' returned Wardle; 'for they'll have had all the advantage of the moonlight to get the start of us, and we shall lose it. It will have gone down in another hour.'

'It will be rather unpleasant going at this rate in the dark, won't it?' inquired Mr Pickwick.

'I dare say it will,' replied his friend drily.

Mr Pickwick's temporary excitement began to sober down a little, as he reflected upon the inconveniences and dangers of the expedition in which he had so thoughtlessly embarked. He was roused by a loud shouting of the post-boy on the leader.

'Yo—yo—yo—yo—yoe,' went the first boy.

'Yo—yo—yo—yoe!' went the second.

'Yo—yo—yo—yoe!' chimed in old Wardle himself, most lustily, with his head and half his body out of the coach window.

'Yo—yo—yo—yoe!' shouted Mr Pickwick, taking up the burden of the cry, though he had not the slightest notion of its meaning or object. And amidst the yo—yoing of the whole four, the chaise stopped.

'What's the matter?' inquired Mr Pickwick.

'There's a gate here,' replied old Wardle. 'We shall hear something of the fugitives.'

After a lapse of five minutes, consumed in incessant knocking and shouting, an old man in his shirt and trousers emerged from the turnpike-house, and opened the gate.

'How long is it since a post-chaise went through here?' inquired Mr Wardle.

'How long?'

'Ah!'

'Why, I don't rightly know. It worn't a long time ago, nor it worn't a short time ago – just between the two, perhaps.'

'Has any chaise been by at all?'

'Oh yes, there's been a shay by.'

'How long ago, my friend,' interposed Mr Pickwick, 'an hour?'

'Ah, I daresay it might be,' replied the man.

'Or two hours?' inquired the post-boy on the wheeler.

'Well, I shouldn't wonder if it was,' returned the old man doubtfully.

'Drive on, boys,' cried the testy old gentleman: 'don't waste any more time with that old idiot!'

'Idiot!' exclaimed the old man with a grin, as he stood in the middle of the road with the gate half-closed, watching the chaise which rapidly diminished in the increasing distance. 'No – not much o' that either; you've lost ten minutes here, and gone away as wise as you came, arter all. If every man on the line as has a guinea give him, earns it half as well, you won't catch t'other shay this side Mich'lmas,[1] old short-and-fat.' And with another prolonged grin, the old man closed the gate, re-entered his house, and bolted the door after him.

Meanwhile the chaise proceeded, without any slackening of pace, towards the conclusion of the stage. The moon, as Wardle had foretold, was rapidly on the wane; large tiers of dark heavy clouds, which had been gradually overspreading the sky for some time past, now formed one black mass over head; and large drops of rain which pattered every now and then against the windows of the chaise, seemed to warn the travellers of the rapid approach of a stormy night. The wind, too, which was directly against them, swept in furious gusts down the narrow road, and howled dismally through the trees which skirted the pathway. Mr Pickwick drew his coat closer about him, coiled himself more snugly up into the corner of the chaise, and fell into a sound sleep, from which he was only awakened by the stopping of the vehicle, the sound of the hostler's bell, and a loud cry of 'Horses on directly!'

But here another delay occurred. The boys were sleeping with such mysterious soundness, that it took five minutes a-piece to wake them. The hostler had somehow or other mislaid the key of the stable, and even when that was found, two sleepy helpers put the wrong harness on the wrong horses, and the whole process of harnessing had to be gone through afresh. Had Mr Pickwick been alone, these multiplied obstacles would have completely put an end to the pursuit at once, but old Wardle was not to be so easily daunted; and he laid about him with such hearty good-will, cuffing this man, and pushing that; strapping a buckle here, and taking in a link there, that the chaise was ready in a much shorter time than could reasonably have been expected, under so many difficulties.

They resumed their journey; and certainly the prospect before them was by no means encouraging. The stage was fifteen miles long, the night was dark, the wind high, and the rain pouring in torrents. It was impossible to make any great way against such obstacles united: it was hard upon one o'clock already; and nearly two hours were consumed in getting to the end of the stage. Here, however, an object presented itself, which rekindled their hopes, and re-animated their drooping spirits.

'When did this chaise come in?' cried old Wardle, leaping out of his own vehicle, and pointing to one covered with wet mud, which was standing in the yard.

'Not a quarter of an hour ago, sir;' replied the hostler, to whom the question was addressed.

'Lady and gentleman?' inquired Wardle, almost breathless with impatience.

'Yes, sir.'

'Tall gentleman – dress coat – long legs – thin body?'

'Yes, sir.'

'Elderly lady – thin face – rather skinny – eh?'

'Yes, sir.'

'By heavens, it's the couple, Pickwick,' exclaimed the old gentleman.

'Would have been here before,' said the hostler, 'but they broke a trace.'

'It is!' said Wardle, 'it is, by Jove! Chaise and four instantly! We shall catch them yet, before they reach the next stage. A guinea a-piece, boys – be alive there – bustle about – there's good fellows.'

And with such admonitions as these, the old gentleman ran up and down the yard, and bustled to and fro, in a state of excitement which communicated itself to Mr Pickwick also; and under the influence of which, that gentleman got himself into complicated entanglements with harness, and mixed up with horses and wheels of chaises, in the most surprising manner, firmly believing that by so doing he was materially forwarding the preparations for their resuming their journey.

'Jump in – jump in!' cried old Wardle, climbing into the chaise, pulling up the steps, and slamming the door after him. 'Come along! Make haste!' And before Mr Pickwick knew precisely what he was about, he felt himself forced in at the other door, by one pull from the old gentleman, and one push from the hostler; and off they were again.

'Ah! we *are* moving now,' said the old gentleman exultingly. They were indeed, as was sufficiently testified to Mr Pickwick, by his constant collisions either with the hard wood-work of the chaise, or the body of his companion.

'Hold up!' said the stout old Mr Wardle, as Mr Pickwick dived head foremost into his capacious waistcoat.

'I never did feel such a jolting in my life,' said Mr Pickwick.

'Never mind,' replied his companion, 'it will soon be over. Steady, steady.'

Mr Pickwick planted himself into his own corner, as firmly as he could; and on whirled the chaise faster than ever.

They had travelled in this way about three miles, when Mr Wardle, who had been looking out of the window for two or three minutes, suddenly drew in his face, covered with splashes, and exclaimed in breathless eagerness –

'Here they are!'

Mr Pickwick thrust his head out of his window. Yes: there was a chaise and four, a short distance before them, dashing along at full gallop.

'Go on, go on,' almost shrieked the old gentleman. 'Two guineas a-piece, boys – don't let 'em gain on us – keep it up – keep it up.'

The horses in the first chaise started on at their utmost speed; and those in Mr Wardle's galloped furiously behind them.

'I see his head,' exclaimed the choleric old man, 'Damme, I see his head.'

'So do I,' said Mr Pickwick, 'that's he.'

Mr Pickwick was not mistaken. The countenance of Mr Jingle, completely coated with the mud thrown up by the wheels, was plainly discernible at the window of his chaise; and the motion of his arm, which he was waving violently towards the postilions, denoted that he was encouraging them to increased exertion.

The interest was intense. Fields, trees, and hedges, seemed to rush past them with the velocity of a whirlwind, so rapid was the pace at which they tore along. They were close by the side of the first chaise. Jingle's voice could be plainly heard, even above the din of the wheels, urging on the boys. Old Mr Wardle foamed with rage and excitement. He roared out scoundrels and villains by the dozen, clenched his fist and shook it expressively at the object of his indignation; but Mr Jingle only answered with a contemptuous smile, and replied to his menaces by a shout of triumph, as his horses, answering the increased application of whip and spur, broke into a faster gallop, and left the pursuers behind.

Mr Pickwick had just drawn in his head, and Mr Wardle, exhausted with shouting, had done the same, when a tremendous jolt threw them forward against the front of the vehicle. There was a sudden bump – a loud crash – away rolled a wheel, and over went the chaise.

After a very few seconds of bewilderment and confusion, in which nothing but the plunging of horses, and breaking of glass, could be made out, Mr Pickwick felt himself violently pulled out from among the ruins of the chaise; and as soon as he had gained his feet, extricated his head from the skirts of his great coat, which materially impeded the usefulness of his spectacles, the full disaster of the case met his view.

Old Mr Wardle without a hat, and his clothes torn in several places, stood by his side, and the fragments of the chaise lay scattered at their feet. The post-boys, who had succeeded in cutting the traces, were standing, disfigured with mud and disordered by hard riding, by the horses' heads. About a hundred yards in advance was the other chaise, which had pulled up on hearing the crash. The postilions, each with a broad grin convulsing his countenance, were viewing the adverse party from their saddles, and Mr Jingle was contemplating the wreck from the coach-window, with evident satisfaction. The day was just breaking, and the whole scene was rendered perfectly visible by the grey light of the morning.

'Hallo!' shouted the shameless Jingle, 'anybody damaged? – elderly gentlemen – no light weights – dangerous work – very.'

'You're a rascal!' roared Wardle.

'Ha! ha!' replied Jingle; and then he added, with a knowing wink, and a jerk of the thumb towards the interior of the chaise – 'I say – she's very well – desires her compliments – begs you won't trouble yourself – love to *Tuppy* – won't you get up behind? – drive on, boys.'

The postilions resumed their proper attitudes, and away rattled the chaise, Mr Jingle fluttering in derision a white handkerchief from the coach-window.

Nothing in the whole adventure, not even the upset, had disturbed the calm and equable current of Mr Pickwick's temper. The villany, however, which could first borrow money of his faithful follower, and then abbreviate his name to 'Tuppy,' was more than

The Breakdown

he could patiently bear. He drew his breath hard, and coloured up to the very tips of his spectacles, as he said, slowly and emphatically –

'If ever I meet that man again, I'll—'

'Yes, yes,' interrupted Wardle, 'that's all very well: but while we stand talking here, they'll get their licence, and be married in London.'

Mr Pickwick paused, bottled up his vengeance, and corked it down.

'How far is it to the next stage?' inquired Mr Wardle, of one of the boys.

'Six mile, a'nt it, Tom?'

'Rayther better.'

'Rayther better nor six mile, sir.'

'Can't be helped,' said Wardle, 'we must walk it, Pickwick.'

'No help for it,' replied that truly great man.

So sending forward one of the boys on horseback, to procure a fresh chaise and horses, and leaving the other behind to take care of the broken one, Mr Pickwick and Mr Wardle set manfully forward on the walk, first tying their shawls round their necks, and slouching down their hats to escape as much as possible from the deluge of rain, which after a slight cessation had again begun to pour heavily down.

CHAPTER 10

Clearing up all Doubts (if any existed) of the Disinterestedness of Mr Jingle's Character

There are in London several old inns, once the head-quarters of celebrated coaches in the days when coaches performed their journeys in a graver and more solemn manner than they do in these times; but which have now degenerated into little more than the abiding and booking places of country waggons. The reader would look in vain for any of these ancient hostelries, among the Golden Crosses and Bull and Mouths, which rear their stately fronts in the improved streets of London. If he would light upon any of these old places, he must direct his steps to the obscurer quarters of the town; and there in some secluded nooks he will find several, still standing with a kind of gloomy sturdiness, amidst the modern innovations which surround them.

In the Borough[1] especially, there still remain some half dozen old inns, which have preserved their external features unchanged, and which have escaped alike the rage for public improvement, and the encroachments of private speculation. Great, rambling, queer, old places they are, with galleries, and passages, and staircases, wide enough and antiquated enough to furnish materials for a hundred ghost stories, supposing we should ever be reduced to the lamentable necessity of inventing any, and that the world should exist long enough to exhaust the innumerable veracious legends connected with old London Bridge, and its adjacent neighbourhood on the Surrey side.

It was in the yard of one of these inns – of no less celebrated a one than the White Hart – that a man was busily employed in brushing the dirt off a pair of boots, early on the morning succeeding the events narrated in the last chapter. He was habited in a coarse-striped waistcoat, with black calico sleeves, and blue glass buttons; drab breeches and leggings. A bright red handkerchief was wound in a very loose and unstudied style round his neck, and an old white hat was carelessly thrown on one side of his head. There were two rows of boots before him, one cleaned and the other dirty, and at every addition he made to the clean row, he paused from his work, and contemplated its results with evident satisfaction.

The yard presented none of that bustle and activity which are the usual characteristics of a large coach inn. Three or four lumbering waggons, each with a pile of goods beneath its ample canopy, about the height of the second-floor window of an ordinary house, were stowed away beneath a lofty roof which extended over one end of the yard; and another, which was probably to commence its journey that morning, was drawn out into the open space. A double tier of bed-room galleries, with old clumsy balustrades, ran round two sides of the straggling area, and a double row of bells to correspond, sheltered from the weather by a little sloping roof, hung over the door leading to the bar and coffee-room. Two or three gigs and chaise-carts were wheeled up under different little sheds and pent-houses; and the occasional heavy tread of a cart-horse, or rattling of a chain at the further end of the yard, announced to anybody who cared about the matter, that the stable lay in that direction. When we add that a few boys in smock frocks were lying asleep on heavy packages, woolpacks, and other articles that were scattered about on heaps of straw, we have described as fully as need be the general appearance of the yard of the White Hart Inn, High Street, Borough, on the particular morning in question.

A loud ringing of one of the bells, was followed by the appearance of a smart chambermaid in the upper sleeping gallery, who, after tapping at one of the doors, and receiving a request from within, called over the balustrades –

'Sam!'

'Hallo,' replied the man with the white hat.

'Number twenty-two wants his boots.'

'Ask number twenty-two, vether he'll have 'em now, or wait till he gets 'em,' was the reply.

'Come, don't be a fool, Sam,' said the girl, coaxingly, 'the gentleman wants his boots directly.'

'Well, you *are* a nice young 'ooman for a musical party, you are,' said the boot-cleaner. 'Look at these here boots – eleven pair o' boots; and one shoe as b'longs to number six, with the wooden leg. The eleven boots is to be called at half-past eight and the shoe at nine. Who's number twenty-two, that's to put all the others out? No, no; reg'lar rotation, as Jack Ketch² said, wen he tied the men up. Sorry to keep you a waitin', sir, but I'll attend to you directly.'

Saying which, the man in the white hat set to work upon a top-boot with increased assiduity.

There was another loud ring; and the bustling old landlady of the White Hart made her appearance in the opposite gallery.

'Sam,' cried the landlady, 'where's that lazy, idle – why, Sam – oh, there you are; why don't you answer?'

'Wouldn't be gen-teel to answer, till you'd done talking,' replied Sam, gruffly.

'Here, clean them shoes for number seventeen directly, and take 'em to private sitting-room, number five, first floor.'

The landlady flung a pair of lady's shoes into the yard, and bustled away.

'Number 5,' said Sam, as he picked up the shoes, and taking a piece of chalk from his pocket, made a memorandum of their destination on the soles – 'Lady's shoes and private sittin' room! I suppose *she* didn't come in the waggin.'

'She came in early this morning,' cried the girl, who was still leaning over the railing of the gallery, 'with a gentleman in a hackney-coach, and it's him as wants his boots, and you'd better do 'em, that's all about it.'

'Vy didn't you say so before,' said Sam, with great indignation, singling out the boots in question from the heap before him. 'For all I know'd he vas one o' the regular three-pennies. Private room! and a lady too! If he's anything of a gen'lm'n, he's vorth a shillin' a day, let alone the arrands.'

Stimulated by this inspiring reflection, Mr Samuel brushed away with such hearty good will, that in a few minutes the boots and shoes, with a polish which would have struck envy to the soul of the amiable Mr Warren (for they used Day and Martin[3] at the White Hart), had arrived at the door of number five.

'Come in,' said a man's voice, in reply to Sam's rap at the door.

Sam made his best bow, and stepped into the presence of a lady and gentleman seated at breakfast. Having officiously deposited the gentleman's boots right and left at his feet, and the lady's shoes right and left at hers, he backed towards the door.

'Boots,' said the gentleman.

'Sir,' said Sam, closing the door, and keeping his hand on the knob of the lock.

'Do you know – what's a-name – Doctors' Commons?'[4]

'Yes, sir.'

'Where is it?'

'Paul's Church-yard, sir; low archway on the carriage-side, bookseller's at one corner, hot-el on the other, and two porters in the middle as touts for licences.'

'Touts for licences!' said the gentleman.

'Touts for licences,' replied Sam. 'Two coves in vhite aprons – touches their hats wen you walk in – "Licence, sir, licence?" Queer sort, them, and their mas'rs too, sir – Old Bailey Proctors[5] – and no mistake.'

'What do they do?' inquired the gentleman.

'Do! *You*, sir! That a'nt the wost on it, neither. They puts things into old gen'lm'n's heads as they never dreamed of. My father, sir, wos a coachman. A widower he wos, and fat enough for anything – uncommon fat, to be sure. His missus dies, and leaves him four hundred pound. Down he goes to the Commons, to see the lawyer and draw the blunt[6] – wery smart – top boots on – nosegay in his button-hole – broad-brimmed tile – green shawl – quite the gen'lm'n. Goes through the archvay, thinking how he should invest the money – up comes the touter, touches his hat – "Licence, sir, licence?" – "What's that?" says my father. – "Licence, sir," says he. – "What licence?" says my father. – "Marriage licence," says the touter. – "Dash my veskit," says my father, "I never thought o' that." – "I think you wants one, sir," says the touter. My father pulls up, and thinks a bit – "No," says he, "damme, I'm too old, b'sides I'm a many sizes too large," says he. – "Not a bit on it, sir," says the touter. – "Think not?" says my father. – "I'm sure not," says he; "we married a gen'lm'n twice your size, last Monday." – "Did you, though," said my father. – "To be sure, we did," says the touter, "you're a babby to him – this way, sir – this way I!" – and sure enough my father walks arter him, like a tame monkey behind a horgan, into a little back office, vere a feller sat among dirty papers and tin boxes, making believe he was busy. "Pray take a seat, vile I makes out the affidavit, sir," says the lawyer. – "Thankee, sir," says my father, and down he sat, and stared with all his eyes, and his mouth vide open, at the names on the boxes. "What's your name, sir," says the lawyer. – "Tony Weller," says my father. – "Parish?" says the lawyer. – "Belle Savage," says my father; for he stopped there wen he drove up, and he know'd nothing about parishes, *he* didn't. – "And what's the lady's name?" says the lawyer. My father was struck all of a heap. "Blessed if I know," says he. – "Not know!" says the lawyer. – "No more nor you do," says my father, "can't I put that in arterwards?" – "Impossible!" says the lawyer. – "Wery well," says my father, after he'd thought a moment, "put down Mrs Clarke." – "What Clarke?" says the lawyer, dipping his pen in the ink. – "Susan Clarke, Markis o' Granby, Dorking," says my father; "she'll have me, if I ask, I des-say – I never said nothing to her, but she'll have me, I know." The licence was made out, and she *did* have him, and what's more she's got him now; and *I* never had any of the four hundred pound, worse luck. Beg your pardon, sir,' said Sam, when he had concluded, 'but wen I gets on this here grievance, I runs on like a new barrow vith the wheel greased.' Having said which, and having paused for an instant to see whether he was wanted for anything more, Sam left the room.

'Half-past nine – just the time – off at once;' said the gentleman, whom we need hardly introduce as Mr Jingle.

'Time – for what?' said the spinster aunt, coquettishly.

'Licence, dearest of angels – give notice at the church – call you mine, tomorrow' – said Mr Jingle, and he squeezed the spinster aunt's hand.

'The licence!' said Rachael, blushing.

'The licence,' repeated Mr Jingle –

> 'In hurry, post-haste for a licence,
> In hurry, ding dong I come back.'[7]

'How you run on,' said Rachael.

'Run on – nothing to the hours, days, weeks, months, years, when we're united – *run* on – they'll fly on – bolt – mizzle[8] – steam-engine – thousand-horse power – nothing to it.'

'Can't – can't we be married before to-morrow morning?' inquired Rachael.

'Impossible – can't be – notice at the church – leave the licence to-day – ceremony come off to-morrow.'

'I am so terrified, lest my brother should discover us!' said Rachael.

'Discover – nonsense – too much shaken by the break down – besides – extreme caution – gave up the post-chaise – walked on – took a hackney coach – came to the Borough – last place in the world that he'd look in – ha! ha! – capital notion that – very.'

'Don't be long,' said the spinster, affectionately, as Mr Jingle stuck the pinched-up hat on his head.

'Long away from *you*? – Cruel charmer,' and Mr Jingle skipped playfully up to the spinster aunt, imprinted a chaste kiss upon her lips, and danced out of the room.

'Dear man!' said the spinster as the door closed after him.

'Rum old girl,' said Mr Jingle, as he walked down the passage.

It is painful to reflect upon the perfidy of our species; and we will not, therefore, pursue the thread of Mr Jingle's meditations, as he wended his way to Doctors' Commons. It will be sufficient for our purpose to relate, that escaping the snares of the dragons in white aprons, who guard the entrance to that enchanted region, he reached the Vicar General's[9] office in safety, and having procured a highly flattering address on parchment, from the Archbishop of Canterbury, to his 'trusty and well-beloved Alfred Jingle and Rachael Wardle, greeting,' he carefully deposited the mystic document in his pocket, and retraced his steps in triumph to the Borough.

He was yet on his way to the White Hart, when two plump gentlemen and one thin one entered the yard, and looked round in search of some authorised person of whom they could make a few inquiries. Mr Samuel Weller happened to be at that moment engaged in burnishing a pair of painted tops, the personal property of a farmer who was refreshing himself with a slight lunch of two or three pounds of cold beef and a pot or two of porter, after the fatigues of the Borough market; and to him the thin gentleman straightway advanced.

'My friend,' said the thin gentleman.

'You're one o' the adwice gratis order,' thought Sam, 'or you wouldn't be so werry fond o' me all at once.' But he only said – 'Well, sir.'

'My friend,' said the thin gentleman, with a conciliatory hem – 'Have you got many people stopping here, now? Pretty busy. Eh?'

Sam stole a look at the inquirer. He was a little high-dried man, with a dark squeezed-up face, and small restless black eyes, that kept winking and twinkling on each side of his little inquisitive nose, as if they were playing a perpetual game of peep-bo with that feature. He was dressed all in black, with boots as shiny as his eyes, a low white neckcloth, and a clean shirt with a frill to it. A gold watch-chain, and seals, depended from his fob. He carried his black kid gloves *in* his hands, not *on* them; and as he spoke, thrust his wrists beneath his coat-tails, with the air of a man who was in the habit of propounding some regular posers.

'Pretty busy, eh?' said the little man.

'Oh, werry well, sir,' replied Sam, 'we shan't be bankrupts, and we shan't make our fort'ns. We eats our biled mutton without capers, and don't care for horse-radish wen ve can get beef.'

'Ah,' said the little man, 'you're a wag, a'nt you?'

'My eldest brother was troubled with that complaint,' said Sam; 'it may be catching – I used to sleep with him.'

'This is a curious old house of yours,' said the little man, looking round him.

'If you'd sent word you was a coming, we'd ha' had it repaired;' replied the imperturbable Sam.

The little man seemed rather baffled by these several repulses, and a short consultation took place between him and the two plump gentlemen. At its conclusion, the little man took a pinch of snuff from an oblong silver box, and was apparently on the point of renewing the conversation, when one of the plump gentlemen, who in addition to a benevolent countenance, possessed a pair of spectacles, and a pair of black gaiters, interfered –

'The fact of the matter is,' said the benevolent gentleman, 'that my friend here (pointing to the other plump gentleman) will give you half a guinea, if you'll answer one or two – '

'Now, my dear sir – my dear sir,' said the little man, 'pray, allow me – my dear sir, the very first principle to be observed in these cases, is this: if you place a matter in the hands of a professional man, you must in no way interfere in the progress of the business; you must repose implicit confidence in him. Really, Mr (he turned to the other plump gentleman, and said) – I forget your friend's name.'

First appearance of Mr Samuel Weller

'Pickwick,' said Mr Wardle, for it was no other than that jolly personage.

'Ah, Pickwick – really Mr Pickwick, my dear sir, excuse me – I shall be happy to receive any private suggestions of yours, as *amicus curiæ*,[10] but you must see the impropriety of your interfering with my conduct in this case, with such an *ad captandum*[11] argument as the offer of half a guinea. Really, my dear sir, really;' and the little man took an argumentative pinch of snuff, and looked very profound.

'My only wish, sir,' said Mr Pickwick, 'was to bring this very unpleasant matter to as speedy a close as possible.'

'Quite right – quite right,' said the little man.

'With which view,' continued Mr Pickwick, 'I made use of the argument which my experience of men has taught me is the most likely to succeed in any case.'

'Ay, ay,' said the little man, 'very good, very good, indeed; but you should have suggested it to *me*. My dear sir, I'm quite certain you cannot be ignorant of the extent of confidence which must be placed in professional men. If any authority can be necessary on such a point, my dear sir, let me refer you to the well-known case in Barnwell and – '

'Never mind George Barnwell,'[12] interrupted Sam, who had remained a wondering listener during this short colloquy; 'every body knows what sort of a case his was, tho' it's always been my opinion, mind you, that the young 'ooman deserved scragging[13] a precious sight more than he did. Hows'ever, that's neither here nor there. You want me to except of half a guinea. Werry well, I'm agreeable: I can't say no fairer than that, can I, sir? (Mr Pickwick smiled.) Then the next question is, what the devil do you want with me, as the man said wen he see the ghost?'

'We want to know – ' said Mr Wardle.

'Now my dear sir – my dear sir,' interposed the busy little man.

Mr Wardle shrugged his shoulders, and was silent.

'We want to know,' said the little man, solemnly; 'and we ask the question of you, in order that we may not awaken apprehensions inside – we want to know who you've got in this house, at present?'

'Who there is in the house!' said Sam, in whose mind the inmates were always represented by that particular article of their costume, which came under his immediate superintendence. 'There's a wooden leg in number six; there's a pair of Hessians in thirteen; there's two pair of halves in the commercial; there's these here painted tops in the snuggery inside the bar; and five more tops in the coffee-room.'

'Nothing more?' said the little man.

'Stop a bit,' replied Sam, suddenly recollecting himself. 'Yes; there's a pair of Wellingtons a good deal worn, and a pair o' lady's shoes, in number five.'

'What sort of shoes?' hastily inquired Wardle, who, together with Mr Pickwick, had been lost in bewilderment at the singular catalogue of visitors.

'Country make,' replied Sam.

'Any maker's name?'

'Brown.'

'Where of?'

'Muggleton.'

'It *is* them,' exclaimed Wardle. 'By Heavens, we've found them.'

'Hush!' said Sam. 'The Wellingtons has gone to Doctors' Commons.'

'No,' said the little man.

'Yes, for a licence.'

'We're in time,' exclaimed Wardle. 'Show us the room; not a moment is to be lost.'

'Pray, my dear sir – pray,' said the little man; 'caution, caution.' He drew from his pocket a red silk purse, and looked very hard at Sam as he drew out a sovereign.

Sam grinned expressively.

'Show us into the room at once, without announcing us,' said the little man, 'and it's yours.'

Sam threw the painted tops into a corner, and led the way through a dark passage, and up a wide staircase. He paused at the end of a second passage, and held out his hand.

'Here it is,' whispered the attorney, as he deposited the money in the hand of their guide.

The man stepped forward for a few paces, followed by the two friends and their legal adviser. He stopped at a door.

'Is this the room?' murmured the little gentleman.

Sam nodded assent.

Old Wardle opened the door; and the whole three walked into the room just as Mr Jingle, who had that moment returned, had produced the licence to the spinster aunt.

The spinster uttered a loud shriek, and, throwing herself in a chair, covered her face with her hands. Mr Jingle crumpled up the licence, and thrust it into his coat-pocket. The unwelcome visitors advanced into the middle of the room.

'You – you are a nice rascal, arn't you?' exclaimed Wardle, breathless with passion.

'My dear sir, my dear sir,' said the little man, laying his hat on the table. 'Pray, consider – pray. Defamation of character: action for damages. Calm yourself, my dear sir, pray – '

'How dare you drag my sister from my house?' said the old man.

'Ay – ay – very good,' said the little gentleman, 'you may ask that. How dare you, sir? – eh, sir?'

'Who the devil are you?' inquired Mr Jingle, in so fierce a tone, that the little gentleman involuntarily fell back a step or two.

'Who is he, you scoundrel,' interposed Wardle. 'He's my lawyer, Mr Perker, of Gray's Inn. Perker, I'll have this fellow prosecuted – indicted – I'll – I'll – I'll ruin him. And you,' continued Mr Wardle, turning abruptly round to his sister, 'you, Rachael, at a time of life when you ought to know better, what do *you* mean by running away with a vagabond, disgracing your family, and making yourself miserable. Get on your bonnet, and come back. Call a hackney-coach there, directly, and bring this lady's bill, d'ye hear – d'ye hear?'

'Cert'nly, sir,' replied Sam, who had answered Wardle's violent ringing of the bell with a degree of celerity which must have appeared marvellous to anybody who didn't know that his eye had been applied to the outside of the keyhole during the whole interview.

'Get on your bonnet,' repeated Wardle.

'Do nothing of the kind,' said Jingle. 'Leave the room, sir – no business here – lady's free to act as she pleases – more than one-and-twenty.'

'More than one-and-twenty!' ejaculated Wardle, contemptuously. 'More than one-and-forty!'

'I a'nt,' said the spinster aunt, her indignation getting the better of her determination to faint.

'You are,' replied Wardle, 'you're fifty if you're an hour.'

Here the spinster aunt uttered a loud shriek, and became senseless.

'A glass of water,' said the humane Mr Pickwick, summoning the landlady.

'A *glass* of water!' said the passionate Wardle. 'Bring a bucket, and throw it all over her; it'll do her good, and she richly deserves it.'

'Ugh, you brute!' ejaculated the kind-hearted landlady. 'Poor dear.' And with sundry ejaculations, of 'Come now, there's a dear – drink a little of this – it'll do you good – don't give way so – there's a love,' &c., &c., the landlady, assisted by a chamber-maid, proceeded to vinegar the forehead, beat the hands, titillate the nose, and unlace the stays of the spinster aunt, and to administer such other restoratives as are usually applied by compassionate females to ladies who are endeavouring to ferment themselves into hysterics.

'Coach is ready, sir,' said Sam, appearing at the door.

'Come along,' cried Wardle. 'I'll carry her down stairs.'

At this proposition, the hysterics came on with redoubled violence.

The landlady was about to enter a very violent protest against this proceeding, and had already given vent to an indignant inquiry whether Mr Wardle considered himself a lord of the creation, when Mr Jingle interposed –

'Boots,' said he, 'get me an officer.'

'Stay, stay,' said little Mr Perker. 'Consider, sir, consider.'

'I'll *not* consider,' replied Jingle. 'She's her own mistress – see who dares to take her away – unless she wishes it.'

'I *won't* be taken away,' murmured the spinster aunt. 'I *don't* wish it.' (Here there was a frightful relapse).

'My dear sir,' said the little man, in a low tone, taking Mr Wardle and Mr Pickwick apart: 'My dear sir, we're in a very awkward situation. It's a distressing case – very; I never knew one more so; but really, my dear sir, really we have no power to control this lady's action. I warned you before we came, my dear sir, that there was nothing to look to but a compromise.'

There was a short pause.

'What kind of compromise would you recommend?' inquired Mr Pickwick.

'Why, my dear sir, our friend's in an unpleasant position – very much so. We must be content to suffer some pecuniary loss.'

'I'll suffer any, rather than submit to this disgrace, and let her, fool as she is, be made miserable for life,' said Wardle.

'I rather think it can be done,' said the bustling little man. 'Mr Jingle, will you step with us into the next room for a moment?'

Mr Jingle assented, and the quartette walked into an empty apartment.

'Now, sir,' said the little man, as he carefully closed the door, 'is there no way of accommodating this matter – step this way, sir, for a moment – into this window, sir, where we can be alone – there, sir, there, pray sit down, sir. Now, my dear sir, between you and I, we know very well, my dear sir, that you have run off with this lady for the sake of her money. Don't frown, sir, don't frown; I say, between you and I, *we* know it. We are both men of the world, and *we* know very well that our friends here, are not – eh?'

Mr Jingle's face gradually relaxed; and something distantly resembling a wink quivered for an instant in his left eye.

'Very good, very good,' said the little man, observing the impression he had made. 'Now the fact is, that beyond a few hundreds, the lady has little or nothing till the death of her mother – fine old lady, my dear sir.'

'*Old*,' said Mr Jingle, briefly but emphatically.

'Why, yes,' said the attorney with a slight cough. 'You are right, my dear sir, she is *rather* old. She comes of an old family though, my dear sir; old in every sense of the word. The founder of that family came into Kent, when Julius Cæsar invaded Britain; – only one member of it, since, who hasn't lived to eighty-five, and *he* was beheaded by one of the Henrys. The old lady is not seventy-three now, my dear sir.' The little man paused, and took a pinch of snuff.

'Well,' cried Mr Jingle.

'Well, my dear sir – you don't take snuff! – ah! so much the better – expensive habit – well, my dear sir, you're a fine young man, man of the world – able to push your fortune, if you had capital, eh?'

'Well,' said Mr Jingle again.

'Do you comprehend me?'

'Not quite.'

'Don't you think – now, my dear sir, I put it to you, *don't* you think – that fifty pounds and liberty, would be better than Miss Wardle and expectation?'

'Won't do – not half enough!' said Mr Jingle rising.

'Nay, nay, my dear sir,' remonstrated the little attorney, seizing him by the button: 'Good round sum – a man like you could treble it in no time – great deal to be done with fifty pounds, my dear sir.'

'More to be done with a hundred and fifty,' replied Mr Jingle, coolly.

'Well, my dear sir, we won't waste time in splitting straws,' resumed the little man, 'say – say – seventy.'

'Won't do,' said Mr Jingle.

'Don't go away, my dear sir – pray don't hurry,' said the little man. 'Eighty; come: I'll write you a cheque at once.'

'Won't do,' said Mr Jingle.

'Well, my dear sir, well,' said the little man, still detaining him; 'just tell me what *will* do.'

'Expensive affair,' said Mr Jingle. 'Money out of pocket – posting, nine pounds; licence, three – that's twelve – compensation, a hundred – hundred and twelve – Breach of honour – and loss of the lady – '

'Yes, my dear sir, yes,' said the little man, with a knowing look, 'never mind the last two items. That's a hundred and twelve – say a hundred – come.'

'And twenty,' said Mr Jingle.

'Come, come, I'll write you a cheque,' said the little man; and down he sat at the table for that purpose.

'I'll make it payable the day after to-morrow,' said the little man, with a look towards Mr Wardle; 'and we can get the lady away, meanwhile.' Mr Wardle sullenly nodded assent.

'A hundred,' said the little man.

'And twenty,' said Mr Jingle.

'My dear sir,' remonstrated the little man.

'Give it him,' interposed Mr Wardle, 'and let him go.'

The cheque was written by the little gentleman, and pocketed by Mr Jingle.

'Now, leave this house instantly!' said Wardle, starting up.

'My dear sir,' urged the little man.

'And mind,' said Mr Wardle, 'that nothing should have induced me to make this compromise – not even a regard for my family – if I had not known that the moment you got any money in that pocket of yours, you'd go to the devil faster, if possible, than you would without it – '

'My dear sir,' urged the little man again.

'Be quiet, Perker,' resumed Wardle. 'Leave the room, sir.'

'Off directly,' said the unabashed Jingle. 'Bye bye, Pickwick.'

If any dispassionate spectator could have beheld the countenance of the illustrious man, whose name forms the leading feature of the title of this work, during the latter part of this conversation, he would have been almost induced to wonder that the indignant fire which flashed from his eyes, did not melt the glasses of his spectacles – so majestic was his wrath. His nostrils dilated, and his fists clenched involuntarily, as he heard himself addressed by the villain. But he restrained himself again – he did *not* pulverise him.

'Here,' continued the hardened traitor, tossing the licence at Mr Pickwick's feet; 'get the name altered – take home the lady – do for Tuppy.'

Mr Pickwick was a philosopher, but philosophers are only men in armour, after all. The shaft had reached him, penetrated through his philosophical harness, to his very heart. In the frenzy of his rage, he hurled the inkstand madly forward, and followed it up himself. But Mr Jingle had disappeared, and he found himself caught in the arms of Sam.

'Hallo,' said that eccentric functionary, 'furniter's cheap were you come from, sir. Self-acting ink, that 'ere; it's wrote your mark upon the wall, old gen'lm'n. Hold still, sir: wot's the use o' runnin' arter a man as has made his lucky, and got to t'other end of the Borough by this time.'

Mr Pickwick's mind, like those of all truly great men, was open to conviction. He was a quick, and powerful reasoner; and a moment's reflection sufficed to remind him of the impotency of his rage. It subsided as quickly as it had been roused. He panted for breath, and looked benignantly round upon his friends.

Shall we tell the lamentations that ensued, when Miss Wardle found herself deserted by the faithless Jingle? Shall we extract Mr Pickwick's masterly description of that heart-rending scene? His note-book, blotted with the tears of sympathising humanity, lies open before us; one word, and it is in the printer's hands. But, no! we will be resolute! We will not wring the public bosom, with the delineation of such suffering!

Slowly and sadly did the two friends and the deserted lady, return next day in the Muggleton heavy coach. Dimly and darkly had the sombre shadows of a summer's night fallen upon all around, when they again reached Dingley Dell, and stood within the entrance to Manor Farm.

CHAPTER II

Involving another Journey, and an Antiquarian
Discovery. Recording Mr Pickwick's Determination
to be present at an Election; and containing a
Manuscript of the old Clergyman's

A night of quiet and repose in the profound silence of Dingley Dell, and an hour's breathing of its fresh and fragrant air on the ensuing morning, completely recovered Mr Pickwick from the effects of his late fatigue of body and anxiety of mind. That illustrious man had been separated from his friends and followers, for two whole days; and it was with a degree of pleasure and delight, which no common imagination can adequately conceive, that he stepped forward to greet Mr Winkle and Mr Snodgrass, as he encountered those gentlemen on his return from his early walk. The pleasure was mutual; for who could ever gaze on Mr Pickwick's beaming face without experiencing the sensation? But still a cloud seemed to hang over his companions which that great man could not but be sensible of, and was wholly at a loss to account for. There was a mysterious air about them both, as unusual as it was alarming.

'And how,' said Mr Pickwick, when he had grasped his followers by the hand, and exchanged warm salutations of welcome; 'how is Tupman?'

Mr Winkle, to whom the question was more peculiarly addressed, made no reply. He turned away his head, and appeared absorbed in melancholy reflection.

'Snodgrass,' said Mr Pickwick, earnestly, 'How is our friend – he is not ill?'

'No,' replied Mr Snodgrass; and a tear trembled on his sentimental eye-lid, like a rain-drop on a window-frame. 'No; he is not ill.'

Mr Pickwick stopped, and gazed on each of his friends in turn.

'Winkle – Snodgrass,' said Mr Pickwick: 'what does this mean? Where is our friend? What has happened? Speak – I conjure, I entreat – nay, I command you, speak.'

There was a solemnity – a dignity – in Mr Pickwick's manner, not to be withstood.

'He is gone,' said Mr Snodgrass.

'Gone!' exclaimed Mr Pickwick. 'Gone!'

'Gone,' repeated Mr Snodgrass.

'Where!' ejaculated Mr Pickwick.

'We can only guess, from that communication,' replied Mr Snodgrass, taking a letter from his pocket, and placing it in his friend's hand. 'Yesterday morning, when a letter was received from Mr Wardle, stating that you would be home with his sister at night, the melancholy which had hung over our friend during the whole of the previous day, was observed to increase. He shortly afterwards disappeared: he was missing during the whole day, and in the evening this letter was brought by the hostler from the Crown, at Muggleton. It had been left in his charge in the morning, with a strict injunction that it should not be delivered until night.

Mr Pickwick opened the epistle. It was in his friend's hand-writing, and these were its contents: –

'My dear Pickwick,

'You, my dear friend, are placed far beyond the reach of many mortal frailties and weaknesses which ordinary people cannot overcome. You do not know what it is, at one blow, to be deserted by a lovely and fascinating creature, and to fall a victim to the artifices of a villain, who hid the grin of cunning, beneath the mask of friendship. I hope you never may.

'Any letter, addressed to me at the Leather Bottle, Cobham, Kent, will be forwarded – supposing I still exist. I hasten from the sight of that world, which has become odious to me. Should I hasten from it altogether, pity – forgive me. Life, my dear Pickwick, has become insupportable to me. The spirit which burns within us, is a porter's knot,[1] on which to rest the heavy load of worldly cares and troubles; and when that spirit fails us, the burden is too heavy to be borne. We sink beneath it. You may tell Rachael – Ah, that name! –

'TRACY TUPMAN.'

'We must leave this place, directly,' said Mr Pickwick, as he refolded the note. 'It would not have been decent for us to remain here, under any circumstances, after what has happened; and now we are bound to follow in search of our friend.' And so saying, he led the way to the house.

His intention was rapidly communicated. The entreaties to remain were pressing, but Mr Pickwick was inflexible. Business, he said, required his immediate attendance.

The old clergyman was present.

'You are not really going?' said he, taking Mr Pickwick aside.

Mr Pickwick reiterated his former determination.

'Then here,' said the old gentleman, 'is a little manuscript, which I had hoped to have the pleasure of reading to you myself. I found it on the death of a friend of mine – a medical man, engaged in our County Lunatic Asylum – among a variety of papers, which I had the option of destroying or preserving, as I thought proper. I can hardly believe that the manuscript is genuine, though it certainly is not in my friend's hand. However, whether it be the genuine production of a maniac, or founded upon the ravings of some unhappy being (which I think more probable), read it, and judge for yourself.'

Mr Pickwick received the manuscript, and parted from the

benevolent old gentleman with many expressions of good-will and esteem.

It was a more difficult task to take leave of the inmates of Manor Farm, from whom they had received so much hospitality and kindness. Mr Pickwick kissed the young ladies – we were going to say, as if they were his own daughters, only as he might possibly have infused a little more warmth into the salutation, the comparison would not be quite appropriate – hugged the old lady with filial cordiality: and patted the rosy cheeks of the female servants in a most patriarchal manner, as he slipped into the hands of each, some more substantial expression of his approval. The exchange of cordialities with their fine old host and Mr Trundle, were even more hearty and prolonged; and it was not until Mr Snodgrass had been several times called for, and at last emerged from a dark passage followed soon after by Emily (whose bright eyes looked unusually dim), that the three friends were enabled to tear themselves from their friendly entertainers. Many a backward look they gave at the Farm, as they walked slowly away: and many a kiss did Mr Snodgrass waft in the air, in acknowledgment of something very like a lady's handkerchief, which was waved from one of the upper windows, until a turn of the lane hid the old house from their sight.

At Muggleton they procured a conveyance to Rochester. By the time they reached the last-named place, the violence of their grief had sufficiently abated to admit of their making a very excellent early dinner; and having procured the necessary information relative to the road, the three friends set forward again in the afternoon to walk to Cobham.

A delightful walk it was: for it was a pleasant afternoon in June, and their way lay through a deep and shady wood, cooled by the light wind which gently rustled the thick foliage, and enlivened by the songs of the birds that perched upon the boughs. The ivy and the moss crept in thick clusters over the old trees, and the soft green turf overspread the ground like a silken mat. They emerged upon an open park, with an ancient hall, displaying the quaint and picturesque architecture of Elizabeth's time. Long vistas of stately oaks and elm trees appeared on every side: large herds of deer were cropping the fresh grass; and occasionally a startled hare scoured along the ground, with the speed of the shadows thrown by the light clouds which swept across a sunny landscape like a passing breath of summer.

'If this,' said Mr Pickwick, looking about him, 'if this were the place to which all who are troubled with our friend's complaint came, I fancy their old attachment to this world would very soon return.'

'I think so too,' said Mr Winkle.

'And really,' added Mr Pickwick, after half an hour's walking had brought them to the village, 'really, for a misanthrope's choice, this is one of the prettiest and most desirable places of residence I ever met with.'

In this opinion also, both Mr Winkle and Mr Snodgrass expressed their concurrence; and having been directed to the Leathern Bottle, a clean and commodious village ale-house, the three travellers entered, and at once inquired for a gentleman of the name of Tupman.

'Show the gentlemen into the parlour, Tom,' said the landlady.

A stout country lad opened a door at the end of the passage, and the three friends entered a long, low-roofed room, furnished with a large number of high-backed leather-cushioned chairs, of fantastic shapes, and embellished with a great variety of old portraits and roughly-coloured prints of some antiquity. At the upper end of the room was a table, with a white cloth upon it, well covered with a roast fowl, bacon, ale, and et ceteras; and at the table sat Mr Tupman, looking as unlike a man who had taken his leave of the world, as possible.

On the entrance of his friends, that gentleman laid down his knife and fork, and with a mournful air advanced to meet them.

'I did not expect to see you here,' he said, as he grasped Mr Pickwick's hand. 'It's very kind.'

'Ah!' said Mr Pickwick, sitting down, and wiping from his forehead the perspiration which the walk had engendered. 'Finish your dinner, and walk out with me. I wish to speak to you alone.'

Mr Tupman did as he was desired; and Mr Pickwick having refreshed himself with a copious draught of ale, waited his friend's leisure. The dinner was quickly despatched, and they walked out together.

For half an hour, their forms might have been seen pacing the churchyard to and fro, while Mr Pickwick was engaged in combatting his companion's resolution. Any repetition of his arguments would be useless; for what language could convey to them that energy and force which their great originator's manner communicated? Whether Mr Tupman was already tired of retirement, or whether he was wholly unable to resist the eloquent appeal which was made to him, matters not; he did *not* resist it at last.

'It mattered little to him,' he said, 'where he dragged out the miserable remainder of his days: and since his friend laid so much stress upon his humble companionship, he was willing to share his adventures.'

Mr Pickwick smiled; they shook hands; and walked back to rejoin their companions.

It was at this moment that Mr Pickwick made that immortal discovery, which has been the pride and boast of his friends, and the envy of every antiquarian in this or any other country. They had passed the door of their inn, and walked a little way down the village, before they recollected the precise spot in which it stood. As they turned back, Mr Pickwick's eye fell upon a small broken stone, partially buried in the ground, in front of a cottage door. He paused.

'This is very strange,' said Mr Pickwick.

'What is strange?' inquired Mr Tupman, staring eagerly at every object near him, but the right one. 'God bless me, what's the matter?'

This last was an ejaculation of irrepressible astonishment, occasioned by seeing Mr Pickwick, in his enthusiasm for discovery, fall on his knees before the little stone, and commence wiping the dust off it with his pocket-handkerchief.

'There is an inscription here,' said Mr Pickwick.

'Is it possible?' said Mr Tupman.

'I can discern,' continued Mr Pickwick, rubbing away with all his might, and gazing intently through his spectacles: 'I can discern a cross, and a B, and then a T. This is important,' continued Mr Pickwick, starting up. 'This is some very old inscription, existing perhaps long before the ancient alms-houses in this place. It must not be lost.'

He tapped at the cottage door. A labouring man opened it.

'Do you know how this stone came here, my friend?' inquired the benevolent Mr Pickwick.

'No, I doan't sir,' replied the man civilly. 'It was here long afore I war born, or any on us.'

Mr Pickwick glanced triumphantly at his companion.

'You – you – are not particularly attached to it, I dare say,' said Mr Pickwick, trembling with anxiety. 'You wouldn't mind selling it, now?'

'Ah! but who'd buy it?' inquired the man, with an expression of face which he probably meant to be very cunning.

'I'll give you ten shillings for it, at once,' said Mr Pickwick, 'if you would take it up for me.'

The astonishment of the village may be easily imagined, when (the little stone having been raised with one wrench of a spade), Mr Pickwick, by dint of great personal exertion, bore it with his own hands to the inn, and after having carefully washed it, deposited it on the table.

The exultation and joy of the Pickwickians knew no bounds, when their patience and assiduity, their washing and scraping, were crowned with success. The stone was uneven and broken, and the letters were straggling and irregular, but the following fragment of an inscription was clearly to be deciphered:

$$+$$
$$\text{BILST}$$
$$\text{UM}$$
$$\text{PSHI}$$
$$\text{S.M.}$$
$$\text{ARK}$$

Mr Pickwick's eyes sparkled with delight, as he sat and gloated over the treasure he had discovered. He had attained one of the greatest objects of his ambition. In a county known to abound in remains of the early ages; in a village in which there still existed some memorials of the olden time he – he, the Chairman of the Pickwick Club – had discovered a strange and curious inscription of unquestionable antiquity, which had wholly escaped the observation of the many learned men who had preceded him. He could hardly trust the evidence of his senses.

'This – this,' said he, 'determines me. We return to town, to-morrow.'

'To-morrow!' exclaimed his admiring followers.

'To-morrow,' said Mr Pickwick. 'This treasure must be at once deposited where it can be thoroughly investigated, and properly understood. I have another reason for this step. In a few days, an election is to take place for the borough of Eatanswill, at which Mr Perker, a gentleman whom I lately met, is the agent of one of the candidates. We will behold, and minutely examine, a scene so interesting to every Englishman.'

'We will,' was the animated cry of three voices.

Mr Pickwick looked round him. The attachment and fervour of his followers, lighted up a glow of enthusiasm within him. He was their leader, and he felt it.

'Let us celebrate this happy meeting with a convivial glass,' said he. This proposition, like the other, was received with unanimous applause. Having himself deposited the important stone in a small deal box, purchased from the landlady for the purpose, he placed himself in an arm-chair at the head of the table; and the evening was devoted to festivity and conversation.

It was past eleven o'clock – a late hour for the little village of Cobham – when Mr Pickwick retired to the bed-room which had been prepared for his reception. He threw open the lattice-window, and setting his light upon the table, fell into a train of meditation on the hurried events of the two preceding days.

The hour and the place were both favourable to contemplation; Mr Pickwick was roused by the church-clock striking twelve. The first stroke of the hour sounded solemnly in his ear, but when the bell ceased the stillness seemed insupportable; – he almost felt as if he had lost a companion. He was nervous and excited; and hastily undressing himself and placing his light in the chimney, got into bed.

Every one has experienced that disagreeable state of mind, in which a sensation of bodily weariness in vain contends against an inability to sleep. It was Mr Pickwick's condition at this moment: he tossed first on one side and then on the other; and perseveringly closed his eyes as if to coax himself to slumber. It was of no use. Whether it was the unwonted exertion he had undergone, or the heat, or the brandy and water, or the strange bed – whatever it was, his thoughts kept reverting very uncomfortably to the grim pictures down stairs, and the old stories to which they had given rise in the course of the evening. After half an hour's tumbling about, he came to the unsatisfactory conclusion, that it was of no use trying to sleep; so he got up and partially dressed himself. Anything, he thought, was better than lying there fancying all kinds of horrors. He looked out of the window – it was very dark. He walked about the room – it was very lonely.

He had taken a few turns from the door to the window, and from the window to the door, when the clergyman's manuscript for the first time entered his head. It was a good thought. If it failed to interest him, it might send him to sleep. He took it from his coat-pocket, and drawing a small table towards his bedside, trimmed the light, put on his spectacles, and composed himself to read. It was a strange hand-writing, and the paper was much soiled and blotted. The title gave him a sudden start, too; and he could not avoid casting a wistful glance round the room. Reflecting on the absurdity of giving way to such feelings, however, he trimmed the light again, and read as follows:

A MADMAN'S MANUSCRIPT

'Yes! – a madman's! How that word would have struck to my heart, many years ago! How it would have roused the terror that used to come upon me sometimes; sending the blood hissing and tingling through my veins, till the cold dew of fear stood in large drops upon my skin, and my knees knocked together with fright! I like it now though. It's a fine name. Shew me the monarch whose angry frown was ever feared like the glare of a madman's eye – whose cord and axe were ever half so sure as a madman's gripe. Ho! ho! It's a grand thing to be mad! to be peeped at like a wild lion through the iron bars – to gnash one's teeth and howl, through the long still night, to the merry ring of a heavy chain – and to roll and twine among the straw, transported with such brave music. Hurrah for the madhouse! Oh, it's a rare place!

'I remember days when I was *afraid* of being mad; when I used to start from my sleep, and fall upon my knees, and pray to be spared from the curse of my race; when I rushed from the sight of merriment or happiness, to hide myself in some lonely place, and spend the weary hours in watching the progress of the fever that was to consume my brain. I knew that madness was mixed up with my very blood, and the marrow of my bones; that one generation had passed away without the pestilence appearing among them, and that I was the first in whom it would revive. I knew it *must* be so: that so it always had been, and so it ever would be: and when I cowered in some obscure corner of a crowded room, and saw men whisper, and point, and turn their eyes towards me, I knew they were telling each other of the doomed madman; and I slunk away again to mope in solitude.

'I did this for years; long, long years they were. The nights here are long sometimes – very long; but they are nothing to the restless nights, and dreadful dreams I had at that time. It makes me cold to remember them. Large dusky forms with sly and jeering faces crouched in the corners of the room, and bent over my bed at night, tempting me to madness. They told me in low whispers, that the floor of the old house in which my father's father died, was stained with his own blood, shed by his own hand in raging madness. I drove my fingers into my ears, but they screamed into my head till the room rang with it, that in one generation before him the madness slumbered, but that his grandfather had lived for years with his hands fettered to the ground, to prevent his tearing himself to pieces. I knew they told the truth – I knew it well. I had found it out years before, though they had tried to keep it from me. Ha! ha! I was too cunning for them, madman as they thought me.

'At last it came upon me, and I wondered how I could ever have feared it. I could go into the world now, and laugh and shout with the best among them. I knew I was mad, but they did not even suspect it. How I used to hug myself with delight, when I thought of the fine trick I was playing them after their old pointing and leering, when I was not mad, but only dreading that I might one day become so! And how I used to laugh for joy, when I was alone, and thought how well I kept my secret, and how quickly my kind friends would have fallen from me, if they had known the truth. I could have screamed with ecstasy when I dined alone with some fine roaring fellow, to think how pale he would have turned, and how fast he would have run, if he had known that the dear friend who sat close to him, sharpening a bright glittering knife, was a madman with all the power, and half the will, to plunge it in his heart. Oh, it was a merry life!

'Riches became mine, wealth poured in upon me, and I rioted in pleasures enhanced a thousand fold to me by the consciousness of my well-kept secret. I inherited an estate. The law – the eagle-eyed law itself – had been deceived, and had handed over disputed thousands to a madman's hands. Where was the wit of the sharp-sighted men of sound mind? Where the dexterity of the lawyers, eager to discover a flaw? The madman's cunning had over-reached them all.

'I had money. How I was courted! I spent it profusely. How I was praised! How those three proud overbearing brothers humbled themselves before me! The old white-headed father, too – such deference – such respect – such devoted friendship – he worshipped me! The old man had a daughter, and the young men a sister; and all the five were poor. I was rich; and when I married the girl, I saw a smile of triumph play upon the faces of her needy relatives, as they thought of their well-planned scheme, and their fine prize. It was for me to smile. To smile! To laugh outright, and tear my hair, and roll upon the ground with shrieks of merriment. They little thought they had married her to a madman.

'Stay. If they had known it, would they have saved her? A sister's happiness against her husband's gold. The lightest feather I blow into the air, against the gay chain that ornaments my body!

'In one thing I was deceived with all my cunning. If I had not been mad – for though we madmen are sharp-witted enough, we get bewildered sometimes – I should have known that the girl would rather have been placed, stiff and cold in a dull leaden coffin, than borne an envied bride to my rich, glittering house. I should have known that her heart was with the dark-eyed boy whose name I once heard her breathe in her troubled sleep; and that she had been sacrificed to me, to relieve the poverty of the old white-headed man, and the haughty brothers.

'I don't remember forms or faces now, but I know the girl was beautiful. I *know* she was; for in the bright moonlight nights, when I start up from my sleep, and all is quiet about me, I see, standing still and motionless in one corner of this cell, a slight and wasted figure with long black hair, which streaming down her back, stirs with no earthly wind, and eyes that fix their gaze on me, and never wink or close. Hush! the blood chills at my heart as I write it down – that form is *her's*; the face is very pale, and the eyes are glassy bright; but I know them well. That figure never moves; it never frowns and mouths as others do, that fill this place sometimes; but it is much more dreadful to me, even than the spirits that tempted me many years ago – it comes fresh from the grave; and is so very death-like.

'For nearly a year I saw that face grow paler; for nearly a year I saw the tears steal down the mournful cheeks, and never knew the cause. I found it out at last though. They could not keep it from me long. She had never liked me; I had never thought she did: she despised my wealth, and hated the splendour in which she lived; – I had not expected that. She loved another. This I had never thought of. Strange feelings came over me, and thoughts, forced upon me by some secret power, whirled round and round my brain. I did not hate her, though I hated the boy she still wept for. I pitied – yes, I pitied – the wretched life to which her cold and selfish relations had doomed her. I knew that she could not live long, but the thought that before her death she might give birth to some ill-fated being, destined to hand down madness to its offspring, determined me. I resolved to kill her.

'For many weeks I thought of poison, and then of drowning, and then of fire. A fine sight the grand house in flames, and the madman's wife smouldering away to cinders. Think of the jest of a large reward, too, and of some sane man swinging in the wind for a deed he never did, and all through a madman's cunning! I thought often of this, but I gave it up at last. Oh! the pleasure of stropping the razor day after day, feeling the sharp edge, and thinking of the gash one stroke of its thin bright edge would make!

'At last the old spirits who had been with me so often before whispered in my ear that the time was come, and thrust the open razor into my hand. I grasped it firmly, rose softly from the bed, and leaned over my sleeping wife. Her face was buried in her hands. I withdrew them softly, and they fell listlessly on her bosom. She had been weeping; for the traces of the tears were still wet upon her cheek. Her face was calm and placid; and even as I looked upon it, a tranquil smile lighted up her pale features. I laid my hand softly on her shoulder. She started – it was only a passing dream. I leant forward again. She screamed, and woke.

'One motion of my hand, and she would never again have uttered cry or sound. But I was startled, and drew back. Her eyes were fixed on mine. I know not how it was, but they cowed and frightened me; and I quailed beneath them. She rose from the bed, still gazing fixedly and steadily on me. I trembled; the razor was in my hand, but I could not move. She made towards the door. As she neared it, she turned, and withdrew her eyes from my face. The spell was broken. I bounded forward, and clutched her by the arm. Uttering shriek upon shriek, she sunk upon the ground.

'Now I could have killed her without a struggle; but the house was alarmed. I heard the tread of footsteps on the stairs. I replaced the razor in its usual drawer, unfastened the door, and called loudly for assistance.

'They came, and raised her, and placed her on the bed. She lay bereft of animation for hours; and when life, look, and speech returned, her senses had deserted her, and she raved wildly and furiously.

'Doctors were called in – great men who rolled up to my door in easy carriages, with fine horses and gaudy servants. They were at her bedside for weeks. They had a great meeting, and consulted together in low and solemn voices in another room. One, the cleverest and most celebrated among them, took me aside, and bidding me prepare for the worst, told me – me, the madman! – that my wife was mad. He stood close beside me at an open window, his eyes looking in my face, and his hand laid upon my arm. With one effort, I could have hurled him into the street beneath. It would have been rare sport to have done it; but my secret was at stake, and I let him go. A few days after, they told me I must place her under some restraint: I must provide a keeper for her. I! I went into the open fields where none could hear me, and laughed till the air resounded with my shouts!

'She died next day. The white-headed old man followed her to the grave, and the proud brothers dropped a tear over the insensible corpse of her whose sufferings they had regarded in her lifetime with muscles of iron. All this was food for my secret mirth, and I laughed behind the white handkerchief which I held up to my face, as we rode home, till the tears came into my eyes.

'But though I had carried my object and killed her, I was restless and disturbed, and I felt that before long my secret must be known. I could not hide the wild mirth and joy which boiled within me, and made me when I was alone, at home, jump up and beat my hands together, and dance round and round, and roar aloud. When I went out, and saw the busy crowds hurrying about the streets; or to the theatre, and heard the sound of music, and beheld the people dancing, I felt such glee, that I could have rushed among them, and torn them to pieces limb from limb, and howled in transport. But I ground my teeth, and struck my feet upon the floor, and drove my sharp nails into my hands. I kept it down; and no one knew I was a madman yet.

'I remember – though it's one of the last things I *can* remember: for now I mix up realities with my dreams, and having so much to do, and being always hurried here, have no time to separate the two, from some strange confusion in which they get involved – I remember how I let it out at last. Ha! ha! I think I see their frightened looks now, and feel the ease with which I flung them from me, and dashed my clenched fist into their white faces, and then flew like the wind, and left them screaming and shouting far behind. The strength of a giant comes upon me when I think of it. There – see how this iron bar bends beneath my furious wrench. I could snap it like a twig, only there are long galleries here with many doors – I don't think I could find my way along them; and even if I could, I know there are iron gates below which they keep locked and barred. They know what a clever madman I have been, and they are proud to have me here, to show.

'Let me see; – yes, I had been out. It was late at night when I reached home, and found the proudest of the three proud brothers waiting to see me – urgent business he said: I recollect it well. I hated that man with all a madman's hate. Many and many a time had my fingers longed to tear him. They told me he was there. I ran swiftly up-stairs. He had a word to say to me. I dismissed the servants. It was late, and we were alone together – *for the first time*.

I kept my eyes carefully from him at first, for I knew what he little thought – and I gloried in the knowledge – that the light of madness gleamed from them like fire. We sat in silence for a few minutes. He spoke at last. My recent dissipation, and strange remarks, made so soon after his sister's death, were an insult to her memory. Coupling together many circumstances which had at first escaped his observation, he thought I had not treated her well. He wished to know whether he was right in inferring that I meant to cast a reproach upon her memory, and a disrespect upon her family. It was due to the uniform he wore, to demand this explanation.

'This man had a commission in the army – a commission, purchased with my money, and his sister's misery! This was the man who had been foremost in the plot to ensnare me, and grasp my wealth. This was the man who had been the main instrument in forcing his sister to wed me; well knowing that her heart was given to that puling boy. Due to *his* uniform! The livery of his degradation! I turned my eyes upon him – I could not help it – but I spoke not a word.

'I saw the sudden change that came upon him beneath my gaze. He was a bold man, but the colour faded from his face, and he drew back his chair. I dragged mine nearer to him; and as I laughed – I was very merry then – I saw him shudder. I felt the madness rising within me. He was afraid of me.

' "You were very fond of your sister when she was alive" – I said – "Very."

'He looked uneasily round him, and I saw his hand grasp the back of his chair: but he said nothing.

' "You villain," said I, "I found you out; I discovered your hellish plots against me; I know her heart was fixed on some one else before you compelled her to marry me. I know it – I know it."

'He jumped suddenly from his chair, brandished it aloft, and bid me stand back – for I took care to be getting closer to him all the time I spoke.

'I screamed rather than talked, for I felt tumultuous passions eddying through my veins, and the old spirits whispering and taunting me to tear his heart out.

' "Damn you," said I, starting up, and rushing upon him; "I killed her. I am a madman. Down with you. Blood, blood! I will have it!"

'I turned aside with one blow the chair he hurled at me in his terror, and closed with him; and with a heavy crash we rolled upon the floor together.

'It was a fine struggle that; for he was a tall strong man, fighting for his life; and I, a powerful madman, thirsting to destroy him. I knew no strength could equal mine, and I was right. Right again, though a madman! His struggles grew fainter. I knelt upon his chest, and clasped his brawny throat firmly with both hands. His face grew purple; his eyes were starting from his head, and with protruded tongue, he seemed to mock me. I squeezed the tighter.

'The door was suddenly burst open with a loud noise, and a crowd of people rushed forward, crying aloud to each other to secure the madman.

'My secret was out; and my only struggle now was for liberty and freedom. I gained my feet before a hand was on me, threw myself among my assailants, and cleared my way with my strong arm, as if I bore a hatchet in my hand, and hewed them down before me. I gained the door, dropped over the banisters, and in an instant was in the street.

'Straight and swift I ran, and no one dared to stop me. I heard the noise of feet behind, and redoubled my speed. It grew fainter and fainter in the distance, and at length died away altogether: but on I bounded, through marsh and rivulet, over fence and wall, with a wild shout which was taken up by the strange beings that flocked around me on every side, and swelled the sound, till it pierced the air. I was borne upon the arms of demons who swept along upon the wind, and bore down bank and hedge before them, and spun me round and round with a rustle and a speed that made my head swim, until at last they threw me from them with a violent shock, and I fell heavily upon the earth. When I woke I found myself here – here in this gay cell where the sun-light seldom comes, and the moon steals in, in rays which only serve to show the dark shadows about me, and that silent figure in its old corner. When I lie awake, I can sometimes hear strange shrieks and cries from distant parts of this large place. What they are, I know not; but they neither come from that pale form, nor does it regard them. For from the first shades of dusk till the earliest light of morning, it still stands motionless in the same place, listening to the music of my iron chain, and watching my gambols on my straw bed.'

At the end of the manuscript was written, in another hand, this note:

[The unhappy man whose ravings are recorded above, was a melancholy instance of the baneful results of energies misdirected in early life, and excesses prolonged until their consequences could never be repaired. The thoughtless riot, dissipation, and debauchery of his younger days, produced fever and delirium. The first effects of the latter was the strange delusion, founded upon a well-known medical theory, strongly contended for by some, and as strongly contested by others, that an hereditary madness existed in his family. This produced a settled gloom, which in time developed a morbid insanity, and finally terminated in raving madness. There is every reason to believe that the events he detailed, though distorted in the description by his diseased imagination, really happened. It is only matter of wonder to those who were acquainted with the vices of his early career, that his passions, when no longer controlled by reason, did not lead him to the commission of still more frightful deeds.]

Mr Pickwick's candle was just expiring in the socket, as he concluded the perusal of the old clergyman's manuscript; and when the light went suddenly out, without any previous flicker by way of warning, it communicated a very considerable start to his excited frame. Hastily throwing off such articles of clothing as he had put on when he rose from his uneasy bed, and casting a fearful glance around, he once more scrambled hastily between the sheets, and soon fell fast asleep.

The sun was shining brilliantly into his chamber when he awoke, and the morning was far advanced. The gloom which had oppressed him on the previous night, had disappeared with the dark shadows which shrouded the landscape, and his thoughts and feelings were as light and gay as the morning itself. After a hearty breakfast, the four gentlemen sallied forth to walk to Gravesend, followed by a man bearing the stone in its deal box. They reached that town about one o'clock (their luggage they had directed to be forwarded to the City, from Rochester), and being fortunate enough to secure places on the outside of a coach, arrived in London in sound health and spirits, on that same afternoon.

The next three or four days were occupied with the preparations which were necessary for their journey to the borough of Eatanswill. As any reference to that most important undertaking demands a separate chapter, we may devote the few lines which remain at the close of this, to narrate, with great brevity, the history of the antiquarian discovery.

It appears from the Transactions of the Club, then, that Mr Pickwick lectured upon the discovery at a General Club Meeting, convened on the night succeeding their return, and entered into a variety of ingenious and erudite speculations on the meaning of the inscription. It also appears that a skilful artist executed a faithful delineation of the curiosity, which was engraven on stone, and presented to the Royal Antiquarian Society, and other learned bodies – that heart-burnings and jealousies without number, were created by rival controversies which were penned upon the subject – and that Mr Pickwick himself wrote a Pamphlet, containing ninety-six pages of very small print, and twenty-seven different readings of the inscription. That three old gentlemen cut off their eldest sons with a shilling a-piece for presuming to doubt the antiquity of the fragment – and that one enthusiastic individual cut himself off prematurely, in despair at being unable to fathom its meaning. That Mr Pickwick was elected an honorary member of seventeen native and foreign societies, for making the discovery; that none of the seventeen could make anything of it; but that all the seventeen agreed it was very extraordinary.

Mr Blotton, indeed – and the name will be doomed to the undying contempt of those who cultivate the mysterious and the sublime – Mr Blotton, we say, with the doubt and cavilling peculiar to vulgar minds, presumed to state a view of the case, as degrading as ridiculous. Mr Blotton, with a mean desire to tarnish the lustre of the immortal name of Pickwick, actually undertook a journey to Cobham in person, and on his return, sarcastically observed in an oration at the club, that he had seen the man from whom the stone was purchased; that the man presumed the stone to be ancient, but solemnly denied the antiquity of the inscription – inasmuch as he represented it to have been rudely carved by himself in an idle mood, and to display letters intended to bear neither more nor less than the simple construction of – 'BILL STUMPS, HIS MARK;' and that Mr Stumps, being little in the habit of original composition, and more accustomed to be guided by the sound of words than by the strict rules of orthography, had omitted the concluding 'L' of his christian name.

The Pickwick Club (as might have been expected from so enlightened an Institution) received this statement with the contempt it deserved, expelled the presumptuous and ill-conditioned Blotton, and voted Mr Pickwick a pair of gold spectacles, in token of their confidence and approbation; in return for which, Mr Pickwick caused a portrait of himself to be painted, and hung up in the club room.

Mr Blotton though ejected was not conquered. He also wrote a pamphlet, addressed to the seventeen learned societies, native and foreign, containing a repetition of the statement he had already made, and rather more than half intimating his opinion that the seventeen learned societies were so many 'humbugs.' Hereupon the virtuous indignation of the seventeen learned societies, native and foreign, being roused, several fresh pamphlets appeared; the foreign learned societies corresponded with the native learned societies; the native learned societies translated the pamphlets of the foreign learned societies into English; the foreign learned societies translated the pamphlets of the native learned societies into all sorts of languages; and thus commenced that celebrated scientific discussion so well known to all men, as the Pickwick controversy.

But this base attempt to injure Mr Pickwick, recoiled upon the head of its calumnious author. The seventeen learned societies unanimously voted the presumptuous Blotton an ignorant meddler, and forthwith set to work upon more treatises than ever. And to this day the stone remains, an illegible monument of Mr Pickwick's greatness, and a lasting trophy to the littleness of his enemies.

CHAPTER 12

Descriptive of a very important Proceeding on the Part of Mr Pickwick; no less an Epoch in his Life, than in this History

Mr Pickwick's apartments in Goswell Street, although on a limited scale, were not only of a very neat and comfortable description, but peculiarly adapted for the residence of a man of his genius and observation. His sitting-room was the first floor front, his bed-room the second floor front; and thus, whether he were sitting at his desk in his parlour, or standing before the dressing-glass in his dormitory, he had an equal opportunity of contemplating human nature in all the numerous phases it exhibits, in that not more populous than popular thoroughfare. His landlady, Mrs Bardell – the relict and sole executrix of a deceased custom-house officer – was a comely woman of bustling manners and agreeable appearance, with a natural genius for cooking, improved by study and long practice, into an exquisite talent. There were no children, no servants, no fowls. The only other inmates of the house were a large man and a small boy; the first a lodger, the second a production of Mrs Bardell's. The large man was always home precisely at ten o'clock at night, at which hour he regularly condensed himself into the limits of a dwarfish French bedstead in the back parlour; and the infantine sports and gymnastic exercises of Master Bardell were exclusively confined to the neighbouring pavements and gutters. Cleanliness and quiet reigned throughout the house; and in it Mr Pickwick's will was law.

To any one acquainted with these points of the domestic economy of the establishment, and conversant with the admirable regulation of Mr Pickwick's mind, his appearance and behaviour on the morning previous to that which had been fixed upon for the journey to Eatanswill, would have been most mysterious and unaccountable. He paced the room to and fro with hurried steps, popped his head out of the window at intervals of about three minutes each, constantly referred to his watch, and exhibited many other manifestations of impatience very unusual with him. It was evident that something of great importance was in contemplation, but what that something was, not even Mrs Bardell herself had been enabled to discover.

'Mrs Bardell,' said Mr Pickwick, at last, as that amiable female approached the termination of a prolonged dusting of the apartment –

'Sir,' said Mrs Bardell.

'Your little boy is a very long time gone.'

'Why it's a good long way to the Borough, sir,' remonstrated Mrs Bardell.

'Ah,' said Mr Pickwick, 'very true; so it is.'

Mr Pickwick relapsed into silence, and Mrs Bardell resumed her dusting.

'Mrs Bardell,' said Mr Pickwick, at the expiration of a few minutes.

'Sir,' said Mrs Bardell again.

'Do you think it a much greater expense to keep two people, than to keep one?'

'La, Mr Pickwick,' said Mrs Bardell, colouring up to the very border of her cap, as she fancied she observed a species of matrimonial twinkle in the eyes of her lodger; 'La, Mr Pickwick, what a question!'

'Well, but *do* you?' inquired Mr Pickwick.

'That depends – ' said Mrs Bardell, approaching the duster very near to Mr Pickwick's elbow, which was planted on the table – 'that depends a good deal upon the person, you know, Mr Pickwick; and whether it's a saving and careful person, sir.'

'That's very true,' said Mr Pickwick, 'but the person I have in my eye (here he looked very hard at Mrs Bardell) I think possesses these qualities; and has, moreover, a considerable knowledge of the world, and a great deal of sharpness, Mrs Bardell; which may be of material use to me.'

'La, Mr Pickwick,' said Mrs Bardell; the crimson rising to her cap-border again.

'I do,' said Mr Pickwick, growing energetic, as was his wont in speaking of a subject which interested him, 'I do, indeed; and to tell you the truth, Mrs Bardell, I have made up my mind.'

'Dear me, sir,' exclaimed Mrs Bardell.

'You'll think it very strange now,' said the amiable Mr Pickwick, with a good-humoured glance at his companion, 'that I never consulted you about this matter, and never even mentioned it, till I sent your little boy out this morning – eh?'

Mrs Bardell could only reply by a look. She had long worshipped Mr Pickwick at a distance, but here she was, all at once, raised to a pinnacle to which her wildest and most extravagant hopes had never dared to aspire. Mr Pickwick was going to propose – a deliberate plan, too – sent her little boy to the Borough, to get him out of the way – how thoughtful – how considerate!

'Well,' said Mr Pickwick, 'what do you think?'

'Oh, Mr Pickwick,' said Mrs Bardell, trembling with agitation, 'you're very kind, sir.'

'It'll save you a good deal of trouble, won't it?' said Mr Pickwick.

'Oh, I never thought anything of the trouble, sir,' replied Mrs Bardell; 'and, of course, I should take more trouble to please you then, than ever; but it is so kind of you, Mr Pickwick, to have so much consideration for my loneliness.'

'Ah, to be sure,' said Mr Pickwick; 'I never thought of that. When I am in town, you'll always have somebody to sit with you. To be sure, so you will.'

'I'm sure I ought to be a very happy woman,' said Mrs Bardell.

'And your little boy – ' said Mr Pickwick.

'Bless his heart!' interposed Mrs Bardell, with a maternal sob.

'He, too, will have a companion,' resumed Mr Pickwick, 'a lively one, who'll teach him, I'll be bound, more tricks in a week than he would ever learn in a year.' And Mr Pickwick smiled placidly.

'Oh you dear – ' said Mrs Bardell.

Mr Pickwick started.

'Oh you kind, good, playful dear,' said Mrs Bardell; and without more ado, she rose from her chair, and flung her arms round Mr Pickwick's neck, with a cataract of tears and a chorus of sobs.

'Bless my soul,' cried the astonished Mr Pickwick; – 'Mrs Bardell my good woman – dear me, what a situation – pray consider. – Mrs Bardell, don't – if anybody should come – '

'Oh, let them come,' exclaimed Mrs Bardell, frantically; 'I'll never leave you – dear, kind, good, soul;' and, with these words, Mrs Bardell clung the tighter.

'Mercy upon me,' said Mr Pickwick, struggling violently, 'I hear somebody coming up the stairs. Don't, don't, there's a good creature, don't.' But entreaty and remonstrance were alike unavailing: for Mrs Bardell had fainted in Mr Pickwick's arms; and before he could gain time to deposit her on a chair, Master Bardell entered the room, ushering in Mr Tupman, Mr Winkle, and Mr Snodgrass.

Mr Pickwick was struck motionless and speechless. He stood with his lovely burden in his arms, gazing vacantly on the countenances of his friends, without the slightest attempt at recognition or explanation. They, in their turn, stared at him; and Master Bardell, in his turn, stared at everybody.

The astonishment of the Pickwickians was so absorbing, and the perplexity of Mr Pickwick was so extreme, that they might have remained in exactly the same relative situations until the suspended animation of the lady was restored, had it not been for a most beautiful and touching expression of filial affection on the part of her youthful son. Clad in a tight suit of corderoy, spangled with brass buttons of a very considerable size, he at first stood at the door astounded and uncertain; but by degrees, the impression that his mother must have suffered some personal damage, pervaded his partially developed mind, and considering Mr Pickwick as the aggressor, he set up an appalling and semi-earthly kind of howling, and butting forward with his head, commenced assailing that immortal gentleman about the back and legs, with such blows and pinches as the strength of his arm, and the violence of his excitement, allowed.

'Take this little villain away,' said the agonised Mr Pickwick, 'he's mad.'

'What *is* the matter?' said the three tongue-tied Pickwickians.

'I don't know,' replied Mr Pickwick, pettishly. 'Take away the boy' (here Mr Winkle carried the interesting boy, screaming and struggling, to the further end of the apartment). 'Now, help me, lead this woman down stairs.'

'Oh, I am better now,' said Mrs Bardell, faintly.

'Let me lead you down stairs,' said the ever gallant Mr Tupman.

'Thank you, sir – thank you;' exclaimed Mrs Bardell, hysterically. And down stairs she was led accordingly, accompanied by her affectionate son.

'I cannot conceive – ' said Mr Pickwick, when his friend returned – 'I cannot conceive what has been the matter with that woman. I

Mrs Bardell faints in Mr Pickwick's arms

had merely announced to her my intention of keeping a man servant, when she fell into the extraordinary paroxysm in which you found her. Very extraordinary thing.'

'Very,' said his three friends.

'Placed me in such an extremely awkward situation,' continued Mr Pickwick.

'Very,' was the reply of his followers, as they coughed slightly, and looked dubiously at each other.

This behaviour was not lost upon Mr Pickwick. He remarked their incredulity. They evidently suspected him.

'There is a man in the passage now,' said Mr Tupman.

'It's the man I spoke to you about,' said Mr Pickwick, 'I sent for him to the Borough this morning. Have the goodness to call him up, Snodgrass.'

Mr Snodgrass did as he was desired; and Mr Samuel Weller forthwith presented himself.

'Oh – you remember me, I suppose?' said Mr Pickwick.

'I should think so,' replied Sam, with a patronising wink. 'Queer start that 'ere, but he was one too many for you, warn't he? Up to snuff[1] and a pinch or two over – eh?'

'Never mind that matter now,' said Mr Pickwick hastily, 'I want to speak to you about something else. Sit down.'

'Thank 'ee, sir,' said Sam. And down he sat without farther bidding, having previously deposited his old white hat on the landing outside the door. 'Ta'nt a werry good 'un to look at,' said Sam, 'but it's an astonishin' 'un to wear; and afore the brim went, it was a werry handsome tile. Hows'ever it's lighter without it, that's one thing, and every hole lets in some air, that's another – wentilation gossamer I calls it.' On the delivery of this sentiment, Mr Weller smiled agreeably upon the assembled Pickwickians.

'Now with regard to the matter on which I, with the concurrence of these gentlemen, sent for you,' said Mr Pickwick.

'That's the pint, sir,' interposed Sam; 'out vith it, as the father said to the child, wen he swallowed a farden.'[2]

'We want to know, in the first place,' said Mr Pickwick, 'whether you have any reason to be discontented with your present situation.'

'Afore I answers that 'ere question, gen'lm'n,' replied Mr Weller, '*I* should like to know, in the first place, whether you're a goin' to purwide me with a better.'

A sunbeam of placid benevolence played on Mr Pickwick's features as he said, 'I have half made up my mind to engage you myself.'

'Have you, though?' said Sam.

Mr Pickwick nodded in the affirmative.

'Wages?' inquired Sam.

'Twelve pounds a year,' replied Mr Pickwick.

'Clothes?'

'Two suits.'

'Work?'

'To attend upon me; and travel about with me and these gentlemen here.'

'Take the bill down,' said Sam, emphatically. 'I'm let to a single gentleman, and the terms is agreed upon.'

'You accept the situation?' inquired Mr Pickwick.

'Cert'nly, replied Sam. 'If the clothes fits me half as well as the place, they'll do.'

'You can get a character of course?' said Mr Pickwick.

'Ask the landlady o' the White Hart about that, sir,' replied Sam.

'Can you come this evening?'

'I'll get into the clothes this minute, if they're here,' said Sam with great alacrity.

'Call at eight this evening,' said Mr Pickwick; 'and if the inquiries are satisfactory, they shall be provided.'

With the single exception of one amiable indiscretion, in which an assistant housemaid had equally participated, the history of Mr Weller's conduct was so very blameless, that Mr Pickwick felt fully justified in closing the engagement that very evening. With the promptness and energy which characterised not only the public proceedings, but all the private actions of this extraordinary man, he at once led his new attendant to one of those convenient emporiums where gentlemen's new and second-hand clothes are provided, and the troublesome and inconvenient formality of measurement dispensed with; and before night had closed in, Mr Weller was furnished with a grey coat with the P. C. button, a black hat with a cockade to it, a pink striped waistcoat, light breeches and gaiters, and a variety of other necessaries, too numerous to recapitulate.

'Well,' said that suddenly-transformed individual, as he took his seat on the outside of the Eatanswill coach next morning; 'I wonder whether I'm meant to be a footman, or a groom, or a gamekeeper, or a seedsman.[3] I looks like a sort of compo of every one on 'em. Never mind; there's change of air, plenty to see, and little to do; and all this suits my complaint uncommon; so long life to the Pickvicks, says I!'

Some Account of Eatanswill; of the State of Parties therein; and of the Election of a Member to serve in Parliament for that ancient, loyal, and patriotic Borough

We will frankly acknowledge, that up to the period of our being first immersed in the voluminous papers of the Pickwick Club, we had never heard of Eatanswill; we will with equal candour admit, that we have in vain searched for proof of the actual existence of such a place at the present day. Knowing the deep reliance to be placed on every note and statement of Mr Pickwick's, and not presuming to set up our recollection against the recorded declarations of that great man, we have consulted every authority, bearing upon the subject, to which we could possibly refer. We have traced every name in schedules A and B,[1] without meeting with that of Eatanswill;[2] we have minutely examined every corner of the Pocket County Maps issued for the benefit of society by our distinguished publishers,[3] and the same result has attended our investigation. We are therefore led to believe, that Mr Pickwick, with that anxious desire to abstain from giving offence to any, and with those delicate feelings for which all who knew him well know he was so eminently remarkable, purposely substituted a fictitious designation, for the real name of the place in which his observations were made. We are confirmed in this belief by a little circumstance, apparently slight and trivial in itself, but when considered in this point of view, not undeserving of notice. In Mr Pickwick's note-book, we can just trace an entry of the fact, that the places of himself and followers were booked by the Norwich coach; but this entry was afterwards lined through, as if for the purpose of concealing even the direction in which the borough is situated. We will not, therefore, hazard a guess upon the subject, but will at once proceed with this history; content with the materials which its characters have provided for us.

It appears, then, that the Eatanswill people, like the people of many other small towns, considered themselves of the utmost and most mighty importance, and that every man in Eatanswill, conscious of the weight that attached to his example, felt himself bound to unite, heart and soul, with one of the two great parties that divided the town – the Blues and the Buffs. Now the Blues lost no opportunity of opposing the Buffs, and the Buffs lost no opportunity of opposing the Blues; and the consequence was, that whenever the

Buffs and Blues met together at public meeting, Town-Hall, fair, or market, disputes and high words arose between them. With these dissensions it is almost superfluous to say that everything in Eatanswill was made a party question. If the Buffs proposed to new skylight the market-place,[4] the Blues got up public meetings, and denounced the proceeding; if the Blues proposed the erection of an additional pump in the High Street, the Buffs rose as one man and stood aghast at the enormity. There were Blue shops and Buff shops, Blue inns and Buff inns; – there was a Blue aisle and a Buff aisle, in the very church itself.

Of course it was essentially and indispensably necessary that each of these powerful parties should have its chosen organ and representative: and, accordingly, there were two newspapers in the town – the Eatanswill Gazette and the Eatanswill Independent; the former advocating Blue principles, and the latter conducted on grounds decidedly Buff. Fine newspapers they were. Such leading articles, and such spirited attacks! – 'Our worthless contemporary, the Gazette' – 'That disgraceful and dastardly journal, the Independent' – 'That false and scurrilous print, the Independent' – 'That vile and slanderous calumniator, the Gazette;' these, and other spirit-stirring denunciations were strewn plentifully over the columns of each, in every number, and excited feelings of the most intense delight and indignation in the bosoms of the townspeople.

Mr Pickwick, with his usual foresight and sagacity, had chosen a peculiarly desirable moment for his visit to the borough. Never was such a contest known. The Honourable Samuel Slumkey, of Slumkey Hall, was the Blue candidate; and Horatio Fizkin, Esq., of Fizkin Lodge, near Eatanswill, had been prevailed upon by his friends to stand forward on the Buff interest. The Gazette warned the electors of Eatanswill that the eyes not only of England, but of the whole civilised world, were upon them; and the Independent imperatively demanded to know, whether the constituency of Eatanswill were the grand fellows they had always taken them for, or base and servile tools, undeserving alike of the name of Englishmen and the blessings of freedom. Never had such a commotion agitated the town before.

It was late in the evening, when Mr Pickwick and his companions, assisted by Sam, dismounted from the roof of the Eatanswill coach. Large blue silk flags were flying from the windows of the Town Arms Inn, and bills were posted in every sash, intimating, in gigantic letters, that the honourable Samuel Slumkey's Committee sat there daily. A crowd of idlers were assembled in the road, looking at a hoarse man in the balcony, who was apparently talking himself very red in the face in Mr Slumkey's behalf; but the force and point of whose arguments were somewhat impaired by the perpetual beating of four large drums which Mr Fizkin's committee had stationed at the street corner. There was a busy little man beside him, though, who took off his hat at intervals and motioned to the people to cheer, which they regularly did, most enthusiastically; and as the red-faced gentleman went on talking till he was redder in the face than ever, it seemed to answer his purpose quite as well as if anybody had heard him.

The Pickwickians had no sooner dismounted, than they were surrounded by a branch mob of the honest and independent, who forthwith set up three deafening cheers, which being responded to by the main body (for it's not at all necessary for a crowd to know what they are cheering about) swelled into a tremendous roar of triumph, which stopped even the red-faced man in the balcony.

'Hurrah!' shouted the mob in conclusion.

'One cheer more,' screamed the little fugleman in the balcony, and out shouted the mob again, as if lungs were cast iron, with steel works.

'Slumkey for ever!' roared the honest and independent.

'Slumkey for ever!' echoed Mr Pickwick, taking off his hat.

'No Fizkin!' roared the crowd.

'Certainly not!' shouted Mr Pickwick.

'Hurrah!' And then there was another roaring, like that of a whole menagerie when the elephant has rung the bell for the cold meat.

'Who is Slumkey?' whispered Mr Tupman.

'I don't know,' replied Mr Pickwick in the same tone. 'Hush. Don't ask any questions. It's always best on these occasions to do what the mob do.'

'But suppose there are two mobs?' suggested Mr Snodgrass.

'Shout with the largest,' replied Mr Pickwick.

Volumes could not have said more.

They entered the house, the crowd opening right and left to let them pass, and cheering vociferously. The first object of consideration was to secure quarters for the night.

'Can we have beds here?' inquired Mr Pickwick, summoning the waiter.

'Don't know, sir,' replied the man; 'afraid we're full, sir – I'll inquire, sir.' Away he went for that purpose, and presently returned, to ask whether the gentlemen were 'Blue.'

As neither Mr Pickwick nor his companions took any vital interest in the cause of either candidate, the question was rather a difficult one to answer. In this dilemma Mr Pickwick bethought himself of his new friend, Mr Perker.

'Do you know a gentleman of the name of Perker?' inquired Mr Pickwick.

'Certainly, sir; honourable Mr Samuel Slumkey's agent.'

'He is Blue, I think?'

'Oh yes, sir.'

'Then *we* are Blue,' said Mr Pickwick; but observing that the man looked rather doubtful at this accommodating announcement, he gave him his card, and desired him to present it to Mr Perker forthwith, if he should happen to be in the house. The waiter retired; and re-appearing almost immediately with a request that Mr Pickwick would follow him, led the way to a large room on the first floor, where, seated at a long table covered with books and papers, was Mr Perker.

'Ah – ah, my dear sir,' said the little man, advancing to meet him; 'very happy to see you, my dear sir, very. Pray sit down. So you have carried your intention into effect. You have come down here to see an election – eh?'

Mr Pickwick replied in the affirmative.

'Spirited contest, my dear sir,' said the little man.

'I am delighted to hear it,' said Mr Pickwick, rubbing his hands. 'I like to see sturdy patriotism, on whatever side it is called forth; – and so it's a spirited contest?'

'Oh, yes,' said the little man, 'very much so indeed. We have opened all the public-houses in the place, and left our adversary nothing but the beer-shops – masterly stroke of policy that, my dear sir, eh?' – the little man smiled complacently, and took a large pinch of snuff.

'And what are the probabilities as to the result of the contest?' inquired Mr Pickwick.

'Why doubtful, my dear sir; rather doubtful as yet,' replied the little man. 'Fizkin's people have got three-and-thirty voters in the lock-up coach-house at the White Hart.'

'In the coach-house!' said Mr Pickwick, considerably astonished by this second stroke of policy.

'They keep 'em locked up there till they want 'em,' resumed the little man. 'The effect of that is, you see, to prevent our getting at them; and even if we could, it would be of no use, for they keep them very drunk on purpose. Smart fellow Fizkin's agent – very smart fellow indeed.'

Mr Pickwick stared, but said nothing.

'We are pretty confident, though,' said Mr Perker, sinking his voice almost to a whisper. 'We had a little tea-party here, last night – five-and-forty women, my dear sir – and gave every one of 'em a green parasol when she went away.'

'A parasol!' said Mr Pickwick.

'Fact, my dear sir, fact. Five-and-forty green parasols, at seven and sixpence a-piece. All women like finery, – extraordinary the effect of those parasols. Secured all their husbands, and half their brothers – beats stockings, and flannel, and all that sort of thing hollow. My idea, my dear sir, entirely. Hail, rain, or sunshine, you can't walk half a dozen yards up the street, without encountering half a dozen green parasols.'

Here the little man indulged in a convulsion of mirth, which was only checked by the entrance of a third party.

This was a tall, thin man, with a sandy-coloured head inclined to baldness, and a face in which solemn importance was blended with a look of unfathomable profundity. He was dressed in a long brown surtout, with a black cloth waistcoat, and drab trousers. A double eye-glass dangled at his waistcoat: and on his head he wore a very low-crowned hat with a broad brim. The new-comer was introduced to Mr Pickwick as Mr Pott, the editor of the Eatanswill Gazette. After a few preliminary remarks, Mr Pott turned round to Mr Pickwick, and said with solemnity –

'This contest excites great interest in the metropolis, sir?'

'I believe it does,' said Mr Pickwick.

'To which I have reason to know,' said Pott, looking towards Mr Perker for corroboration, – 'to which I have reason to know that my article of last Saturday in some degree contributed.'

'Not the least doubt of it,' said the little man.

'The press is a mighty engine, sir,' said Pott.

Mr Pickwick yielded his fullest assent to the proposition.

'But I trust, sir,' said Pott, 'that I have never abused the enormous power I wield. I trust, sir, that I have never pointed the noble instrument which is placed in my hands, against the sacred bosom of private life, or the tender breast of individual reputation; – I trust, sir, that I have devoted my energies to – to endeavours – humble they may be, humble I know they are – to instil those principles of – which – are –'

Here the editor of the Eatanswill Gazette, appearing to ramble, Mr Pickwick came to his relief, and said –

'Certainly.'

'And what, sir' – said Pott – 'what, sir, let me ask you as an impartial man, is the state of the public mind in London, with reference to my contest with the Independent?'

'Greatly excited, no doubt,' interposed Mr Perker, with a look of slyness which was very likely accidental.

'The contest,' said Pott, 'shall be prolonged so long as I have health and strength, and that portion of talent with which I am gifted. From that contest, sir, although it may unsettle men's minds and excite their feelings, and render them incapable for the discharge of the every-day duties of ordinary life; from that contest, sir, I will never shrink, till I have set my heel upon the Eatanswill Independent. I wish the people of London, and the people of this country to know, sir, that they may rely upon me; – that I will not desert them, that I am resolved to stand by them, sir, to the last.'

'Your conduct is most noble, sir,' said Mr Pickwick; and he grasped the hand of the magnanimous Pott.

'You are, sir, I perceive, a man of sense and talent,' said Mr Pott, almost breathless with the vehemence of his patriotic declaration. 'I am most happy, sir, to make the acquaintance of such a man.'

'And I,' said Mr Pickwick, 'feel deeply honoured by this expression of your opinion. Allow me, sir to introduce you to my fellow-travellers, the other corresponding members of the club I am proud to have founded.'

'I shall be delighted,' said Mr Pott.

Mr Pickwick withdrew, and returning with his friends, presented them in due form to the editor of the Eatanswill Gazette.

'Now my dear Pott,' said little Mr Perker, 'the question is, what are we to do with our friends here?'

'We can stop in this house, I suppose,' said Mr Pickwick.

'Not a spare bed in the house, my dear sir – not a single bed.'

'Extremely awkward,' said Mr Pickwick.

'Very;' said his fellow-voyagers.

'I have an idea upon this subject,' said Mr Pott, 'which I think may be very successfully adopted. They have two beds at the Peacock, and I can boldly say, on behalf of Mrs Pott, that she will be delighted to accommodate Mr Pickwick and any of his friends, if the other two gentlemen and their servant do not object to shifting, as they best can, at the Peacock.'

After repeated pressings on the part of Mr Pott, and repeated protestations on that of Mr Pickwick that he could not think of incommoding or troubling his amiable wife, it was decided that it was the only feasible arrangement that could be made. So it *was* made; and after dining together at the Town Arms, the friends separated, Mr Tupman and Mr Snodgrass repairing to the Peacock, and Mr Pickwick and Mr Winkle proceeding to the mansion of Mr Pott; it having been previously arranged that they should all re-assemble at the Town Arms in the morning, and accompany the honourable Samuel Slumkey's procession to the place of nomination.

Mr Pott's domestic circle was limited to himself and his wife. All men whom mighty genius has raised to a proud eminence in the world, have usually some little weakness which appears the more conspicuous from the contrast it presents to their general character. If Mr Pott had a weakness, it was, perhaps, that he was *rather* too submissive to the somewhat contemptuous control and sway of his wife. We do not feel justified in laying any particular stress upon the fact, because on the present occasion all Mrs Pott's most winning ways were brought into requisition to receive the two gentlemen.

'My dear,' said Mr Pott, 'Mr Pickwick – Mr Pickwick of London.'

Mrs Pott received Mr Pickwick's paternal grasp of the hand with enchanting sweetness: and Mr Winkle, who had not been announced at all, slided and bowed, unnoticed, in an obscure corner.

'P. my dear – ' said Mrs Pott.

'My life,' said Mr Pott.

'Pray introduce the other gentleman.'

'I beg a thousand pardons,' said Mr Pott. 'Permit me, Mrs Pott, Mr – '

'Winkle,' said Mr Pickwick.

'Winkle,' echoed Mr Pott; and the ceremony of introduction was complete.

'We owe you many apologies, ma'am,' said Mr Pickwick, 'for disturbing your domestic arrangements at so short a notice.'

'I beg you won't mention it, sir,' replied the feminine Pott, with vivacity. 'It is a high treat to me, I assure you, to see any new faces; living as I do, from day to day, and week to week, in this dull place, and seeing nobody.'

'Nobody, my dear!' exclaimed Mr Pott, archly.

'Nobody but *you*,' retorted Mrs Pott, with asperity.

'You see, Mr Pickwick,' said the host in explanation of his wife's lament, 'that we are in some measure cut off from many enjoyments and pleasures of which we might otherwise partake. My public station, as editor of the Eatanswill Gazette, the position which that paper holds in the country, my constant immersion in the vortex of politics – '

'P. my dear – ' interposed Mrs Pott.

'My life – ' said the editor.

'I wish, my dear, you would endeavour to find some topic of conversation in which these gentlemen might take some rational interest.'

'But my love,' said Mr Pott, with great humility, 'Mr Pickwick does take an interest in it.'

'It's well for him if he can,' said Mrs Pott, emphatically; 'I am wearied out of my life with your politics, and quarrels with the Independent, and nonsense. I am quite astonished P. at your making such an exhibition of your absurdity.'

'But my dear – ' said Mr Pott.

'Oh, nonsense, don't talk to me;' said Mrs Pott. 'Do you play écarté,⁵ sir?'

'I shall be very happy to learn under your tuition,' replied Mr Winkle.

'Well, then, draw that little table into this window, and let me get out of hearing of those prosy politics.'

'Jane,' said Mr Pott, to the servant who brought in candles, 'go down into the office, and bring me up the file of the Gazette for Eighteen Hundred and Twenty Eight.⁶ I'll read you – ' added the editor, turning to Mr Pickwick, 'I'll just read you a few of the leaders I wrote at that time upon the Buff job of appointing a new tollman to the turnpike here; I rather think they'll amuse you.'

'I should like to hear them very much, indeed,' said Mr Pickwick.

Up came the file, and down sat the editor, with Mr Pickwick at his side.

We have in vain pored over the leaves of Mr Pickwick's notebook, in the hope of meeting with a general summary of these beautiful compositions. We have every reason to believe that he was perfectly enraptured with the vigour and freshness of the style; indeed Mr Winkle has recorded the fact that his eyes were closed, as if with excess of pleasure, during the whole time of their perusal.

The announcement of supper put a stop both to the game at écarté, and the recapitulation of the beauties of the Eatanswill Gazette. Mrs Pott was in the highest spirits and the most agreeable humour. Mr Winkle had already made considerable progress in her good opinion, and she did not hesitate to inform him, confidentially, that Mr Pickwick was 'a delightful old dear.' These terms convey a familiarity of expression, in which few of those who were intimately acquainted with that colossal-minded man, would have presumed to indulge. We have preserved them, nevertheless, as affording at once a touching and a convincing proof of the estimation in which he was held by every class of society, and the ease with which he made his way to their hearts and feelings.

It was a late hour of the night – long after Mr Tupman and Mr Snodgrass had fallen asleep in the inmost recesses of the Peacock – when the two friends retired to rest. Slumber soon fell upon the senses of Mr Winkle, but his feelings had been excited, and his admiration roused; and for many hours after sleep had rendered him insensible to earthly objects, the face and figure of the agreeable Mrs Pott presented themselves again and again to his wandering imagination.

The noise and bustle which ushered in the morning, were sufficient to dispel from the mind of the most romantic visionary in existence, any associations but those which were immediately connected with the rapidly-approaching election. The beating of drums, the blowing of horns and trumpets, the shouting of men, and tramping of horses, echoed and re-echoed through the streets from the earliest dawn of day; and an occasional fight between the light skirmishers of either party at once enlivened the preparations and agreeably diversified their character.

'Well, Sam,' said Mr Pickwick, as his valet appeared at his bedroom door, just as he was concluding his toilet; 'all alive to-day, I suppose?'

'Reg'lar game, sir,' replied Mr Weller; 'our people's a col-lecting down at the Town Arms, and they're a hollering themselves hoarse already.'

'Ah,' said Mr Pickwick, 'do they seem devoted to their party, Sam?'

'Never see such dewotion in my life, sir.'

'Energetic, eh?' said Mr Pickwick.

'Uncommon,' replied Sam; 'I never see men eat and drink so much afore. I wonder they a'nt afeer'd o' bustin.'

'That's the mistaken kindness of the gentry here,' said Mr Pickwick.

'Wery likely,' replied Sam, briefly.

'Fine, fresh, hearty fellows they seem,' said Mr Pickwick, glancing from the window.

'Wery fresh,' replied Sam; 'me, and the two waiters at the Peacock, has been a pumpin' over the independent woters as supped there last night.'

'Pumping over independent voters!' exclaimed Mr Pickwick.

'Yes,' said his attendant, 'every man slept vere he fell down; we dragged 'em out, one by one, this mornin', and put 'em under the pump, and they're in reg'lar fine order, now. Shillin' a head the committee paid for that 'ere job.'

'Can such things be!' exclaimed the astonished Mr Pickwick.

'Lord bless your heart, sir,' said Sam, 'why where was you half baptized?[7] – that's nothin', that a'nt.'

'Nothing?' said Mr Pickwick.

'Nothin' at all, sir,' replied his attendant. 'The night afore the last day o' the last election here, the opposite party bribed the bar-maid at the Town Arms, to hocus the brandy and water of fourteen unpolled electors as was a stoppin' in the house.'

'What do you mean by "hocussing" brandy and water?' inquired Mr Pickwick.

'Puttin' laud'num in it,' replied Sam. 'Blessed if she didn't send 'em all to sleep till twelve hours arter the election was over. They took one man up to the booth, in a truck, fast asleep, by way of experiment, but it was no go – they wouldn't poll him; so they brought him back, and put him to bed again.'

'Strange practices, these,' said Mr Pickwick; half speaking to himself and half addressing Sam.

'Not half so strange as a miraculous circumstance as happened to my own father, at an election time, in this werry place, sir,' replied Sam.

'What was that?' inquired Mr Pickwick.

'Why he drove a coach down here once,' said Sam; ' 'lection time came on, and he was engaged by vun party to bring down woters from London. Night afore he was a going to drive up, committee on t'other side sends for him quietly, and away he goes vith the messenger, who shows him in; – large room – lots of gen'l'm'n – heaps of papers, pens and ink, and all that 'ere. "Ah, Mr Weller," says the gen'l'm'n in the chair, "glad to see you, sir; how are you?" – "Werry well, thank'ee, sir," says my father; "I hope *you're* pretty middlin," says he – "Pretty well, thank'ee, sir," says the gen'l'm'n; "sit down, Mr Weller – pray sit down, sir." So my father sits down, and he and the gen'l'm'n looks werry hard at each other. "You don't remember me?" says the gen'l'm'n. – "Can't say I do," says my father – "Oh, I know you," says the gen'l'm'n; "know'd you when you was a boy," says he. – "Well, I don't remember you,"

says my father – "That's very odd," says the gen'l'm'n – "Werry,"
says my father – "You must have a bad mem'ry, Mr Weller," says
the gen'l'm'n – "Well, it is a wery bad 'un," says my father – "I
thought so," says the gen'l'm'n. So then they pours him out a glass
of wine, and gammons him about his driving, and gets him into a
reg'lar good humour, and at last shoves a twenty pound note in his
hand. "It's a werry bad road between this and London," says the
gen'l'm'n – "Here and there it *is* a heavy road," says my father – .
'Specially near the canal, I think," says the gen'l'm'n – "Nasty bit
that 'ere," says my father – "Well, Mr Weller," says the gen'l'm'n,
"you're a wery good whip, and can do what you like with your
horses, we know. We're all wery fond o'you, Mr Weller, so in case
you *should* have an accident when you're a bringing these here
woters down, and *should* tip 'em over into the canal vithout hurtin'
of 'em, this is for yourself," says he – "Gen'l'm'n, you're wery
kind," says my father, "and I'll drink your health in another glass
of wine," says he; wich he did, and then buttons up the money, and
bows himself out. You wouldn't believe, sir,' continued Sam, with
a look of inexpressible impudence at his master, 'that on the wery
day as he came down with them woters, his coach *was* upset on that
'ere wery spot, and ev'ry man on 'em was turned into the canal.'

'And got out again?' inquired Mr Pickwick, hastily.

'Why,' replied Sam, very slowly, 'I rather think one old gen'l'm'n
was missin'; I know his hat was found, but I a'n't quite certain
whether his head was in it or not. But what I look at, is the hex-
traordinary, and wonderful coincidence, that arter what that
gen'l'm'n said, my father's coach should be upset in that wery place,
and on that wery day!'

'It is, no doubt, a very extraordinary circumstance indeed,' said
Mr Pickwick. 'But brush my hat, Sam, for I hear Mr Winkle calling
me to breakfast.'

With these words Mr Pickwick descended to the parlour, where
he found breakfast laid, and the family already assembled. The
meal was hastily despatched; each of the gentleman's hats was
decorated with an enormous blue favour, made up by the fair hands
of Mrs Pott herself; and as Mr Winkle had undertaken to escort
that lady to a house-top, in the immediate vicinity of the hustings,[8]
Mr Pickwick and Mr Pott repaired alone to the Town Arms, from
the back window of which, one of Mr Slumkey's committee was
addressing six small boys, and one girl, whom he dignified, at every
second sentence, with the imposing title of 'men of Eatanswill,'
whereat the six small boys aforesaid cheered prodigiously.

The stable-yard exhibited unequivocal symptoms of the glory and strength of the Eatanswill Blues. There was a regular army of blue flags, some with one handle, and some with two, exhibiting appropriate devices, in golden characters four feet high, and stout in proportion. There was a grand band of trumpets, bassoons and drums, marshalled four abreast, and earning their money, if ever men did, especially the drum beaters, who were very muscular. There were bodies of constables with blue staves, twenty committee-men with blue scarfs, and a mob of voters with blue cockades. There were electors on horseback, and electors a-foot. There was an open carriage and four, for the honourable Samuel Slumkey; and there were four carriages and pair, for his friends and supporters; and the flags were rustling, and the band was playing, and the constables were swearing, and the twenty committee-men were squabbling, and the mob were shouting, and the horses were backing, and the post-boys perspiring; and everybody, and everything, then and there assembled, was for the special use, behoof, honour, and renown, of the honourable Samuel Slumkey, of Slumkey Hall, one of the candidates for the representation of the Borough of Eatanswill, in the Commons House of Parliament of the United Kingdom.

Loud and long were the cheers, and mighty was the rustling of one of the blue flags, with 'Liberty of the Press' inscribed thereon, when the sandy head of Mr Pott was discerned in one of the windows, by the mob beneath; and tremendous was the enthusiasm when the honourable Samuel Slumkey himself, in top-boots, and a blue neckerchief, advanced and seized the hand of the said Pott, and melodramatically testified by gestures to the crowd, his ineffaceable obligations to the Eatanswill Gazette.

'Is everything ready?' said the honourable Samuel Slumkey to Mr Perker.

'Everything, my dear sir,' was the little man's reply.

'Nothing has been omitted, I hope?' said the honourable Samuel Slumkey.

'Nothing has been left undone, my dear sir – nothing whatever. There are twenty washed men at the street door for you to shake hands with; and six children in arms that you're to pat on the head, and inquire the age of; be particular about the children, my dear sir, – it has always a great effect, that sort of thing.'

'I'll take care,' said the honourable Samuel Slumkey.

'And, perhaps, my dear sir – ' said the cautious little man, 'perhaps if you *could* – I don't mean to say it's indispensable – but if you *could* manage to kiss one of 'em, it would produce a very great impression on the crowd.'

'Wouldn't it have as good an effect if the proposer or seconder did that?' said the honourable Samuel Slumkey.

'Why, I am afraid it wouldn't,' replied the agent; 'if it were done by yourself, my dear sir, I think it would make you very popular.'

'Very well,' said the honourable Samuel Slumkey, with a resigned air, 'then it must be done. That's all.'

'Arrange the procession,' cried the twenty committee-men.

Amidst the cheers of the assembled throng, the band, and the constables, and the committee-men, and the voters, and the horsemen, and the carriages, took their places – each of the two-horse vehicles being closely packed with as many gentlemen as could manage to stand upright in it; and that assigned to Mr Perker, containing Mr Pickwick, Mr Tupman, Mr Snodgrass, and about half a dozen of the committee beside.

There was a moment of awful suspense as the procession waited for the honourable Samuel Slumkey to step into his carriage. Suddenly the crowd set up a great cheering.

'He has come out,' said little Mr Perker, greatly excited; the more so as their position did not enable them to see what was going forward.

Another cheer, much louder.

'He has shaken hands with the men,' cried the little agent.

Another cheer, far more vehement.

'He has patted the babies on the head,' said Mr Perker, trembling with anxiety.

A roar of applause that rent the air.

'He has kissed one of 'em!' exclaimed the delighted little man.

A second roar.

'He has kissed another,' gasped the excited manager.

A third roar.

'He's kissing 'em all!' screamed the enthusiastic little gentleman. And hailed by the deafening shouts of the multitude, the procession moved on.

How or by what means it became mixed up with the other procession, and how it was ever extricated from the confusion consequent thereupon, is more than we can undertake to describe, inasmuch as Mr Pickwick's hat was knocked over his eyes, nose, and mouth, by one poke of a Buff flag-staff, very early in the proceedings. He describes himself as being surrounded on every side, when he could catch a glimpse of the scene, by angry and ferocious countenances, by a vast cloud of dust, and by a dense crowd of combatants. He represents himself as being forced from the carriage by some unseen power, and being personally engaged in a pugilistic encounter; but with whom, or how, or why, he is wholly unable to state. He then felt himself forced up some wooden steps by the persons from behind: and on removing his hat, found himself surrounded by his friends, in the very front of the left hand side of the hustings. The right was reserved for the Buff party, and the centre for the Mayor and his officers; one of whom – the fat crier[9] of Eatanswill – was ringing an enormous bell, by way of commanding silence, while Mr Horatio Fizkin, and the honourable Samuel Slumkey, with their hands upon their hearts, were bowing with the utmost affability to the troubled sea of heads that inundated the open space in front; and from whence arose a storm of groans, and shouts, and yells, and hootings, that would have done honour to an earthquake.

'There's Winkle,' said Mr Tupman, pulling his friend by the sleeve.

'Where?' said Mr Pickwick, putting on his spectacles, which he had fortunately kept in his pocket hitherto.

'There,' said Mr Tupman, 'on the top of that house.' And there, sure enough, in the leaden gutter of a tiled roof, were Mr Winkle and Mrs Pott, comfortably seated in a couple of chairs, waving their handkerchiefs in token of recognition – a compliment which Mr Pickwick returned by kissing his hand to the lady.

The proceedings had not yet commenced; and as an inactive crowd is generally disposed to be jocose, this very innocent action was sufficient to awaken their facetiousness.

'Oh you wicked old rascal,' cried one voice, 'looking arter the girls, are you?'

'Oh you wenerable sinner,' cried another.

'Putting on his spectacles to look at a married 'ooman!' said a third.

'I see him a winkin' at her, with his wicked old eye,' shouted a fourth.

'Look arter your wife, Pott,' bellowed a fifth; – and then there was a roar of laughter.

As these taunts were accompanied with invidious comparisons between Mr Pickwick and an aged ram, and several witticisms of the like nature; and as they moreover rather tended to convey reflections upon the honour of an innocent lady, Mr Pickwick's indignation was excessive; but as silence was proclaimed at the moment, he contented himself by scorching the mob with a look of pity for their misguided minds, at which they laughed more boisterously than ever.

'Silence!' roared the mayor's attendants.

'Whiffin, proclaim silence,' said the mayor, with an air of pomp befitting his lofty station. In obedience to this command the crier performed another concerto on the bell, whereupon a gentleman in the crowd called out 'muffins;' which occasioned another laugh.

'Gentlemen,' said the Mayor, at as loud a pitch as he could possibly force his voice to, 'Gentlemen. Brother electors of the Borough of Eatanswill. We are met here to-day for the purpose of choosing a representative in the room of our late – '

Here the Mayor was interrupted by a voice in the crowd.

'Suc-cess to the Mayor!' cried the voice, 'and may he never desert the nail and sarspan business, as he got his money by.'

This allusion to the professional pursuits of the orator was received with a storm of delight, which, with a bell-accompaniment, rendered the remainder of his speech inaudible, with the exception of the concluding sentence, in which he thanked the meeting for the patient attention with which they had heard him throughout, – an expression of gratitude which elicited another burst of mirth, of about a quarter of an hour's duration.

Next, a tall thin gentleman, in a very stiff white neckerchief, after being repeatedly desired by the crowd to 'send a boy home, to ask whether he hadn't left his woice under the pillow,' begged to nominate a fit and proper person to represent them in Parliament. And when he said it was Horatio Fizkin, Esquire, of Fizkin Lodge, near Eatanswill, the Fizkinites applauded, and the Slumkeyites groaned, so long, and so loudly, that both he and the seconder might have sung comic songs in lieu of speaking, without anybody's being a bit the wiser.

The friends of Horatio Fizkin, Esquire, having had their innings, a little choleric, pink-faced man stood forward to propose another fit and proper person to represent the electors of Eatanswill in Parliament; and very swimmingly the pink-faced gentleman would have got on, if he had not been rather too choleric to entertain a sufficient perception of the fun of the crowd. But after a very few sentences of figurative eloquence, the pink-faced gentleman got from denouncing those who interrupted him in the mob, to exchanging defiances with the gentlemen on the hustings; whereupon arose an uproar which reduced him to the necessity of expressing his feelings by serious pantomime, which he did, and then left the stage to his seconder, who delivered a written speech of half an hour's length, and wouldn't be stopped, because he had sent it all to the Eatanswill Gazette, and the Eatanswill Gazette had already printed it, every word.

Then Horatio Fizkin, Esquire, of Fizkin Lodge, near Eatanswill, presented himself for the purpose of addressing the electors; which he no sooner did, than the band employed by the honourable Samuel Slumkey, commenced performing with a power to which their strength in the morning was a trifle; in return for which, the Buff crowd belaboured the heads and shoulders of the Blue crowd; on which the Blue crowd endeavoured to dispossess themselves of their very unpleasant neighbours the Buff crowd; and a scene of struggling, and pushing, and fighting, succeeded, to which we can no more do justice than the Mayor could, although he issued imperative orders to twelve constables to seize the ring-leaders, who might amount in number to two hundred and fifty, or thereabouts. At all these encounters, Horatio Fizkin, Esquire, of Fizkin Lodge, and his friends, waxed fierce and furious; until at last Horatio Fizkin, Esquire, of Fizkin Lodge, begged to ask his opponent the honourable Samuel Slumkey, of Slumkey Hall, whether that band played by his consent; which question the honourable Samuel Slumkey declining to answer, Horatio Fizkin, Esquire, of Fizkin Lodge, shook his fist in the countenance of the honourable Samuel Slumkey, of Slumkey Hall; upon which the honourable Samuel Slumkey, his blood being up, defied Horatio Fizkin, Esquire, to mortal combat. At this violation of all known rules and precedents of order, the Mayor commanded another fantasia on the bell, and declared that he would bring before himself, both Horatio Fizkin, Esquire, of Fizkin Lodge, and the honourable Samuel Slumkey, of Slumkey Hall, and bind them over to keep the peace. Upon this terrific denunciation, the supporters of the two candidates interfered, and after the friends of each party had quarrelled in pairs, for three-quarters of an hour, Horatio Fizkin, Esquire, touched his hat to the honourable Samuel Slumkey: the honourable Samuel Slumkey touched his to Horatio Fizkin, Esquire: the band was stopped: the crowd were partially quieted: and Horatio Fizkin, Esquire, was permitted to proceed.

The speeches of the two candidates, though differing in every other respect, afforded a beautiful tribute to the merit and high worth of the electors of Eatanswill. Both expressed their opinion that a more independent, a more enlightened, a more public-spirited, a more noble-minded, a more disinterested set of men than

The Election at Eatanswill

those who had promised to vote for him, never existed on earth; each darkly hinted his suspicions that the electors in the opposite interest had certain swinish and besotted infirmities which rendered them unfit for the exercise of the important duties they were called upon to discharge. Fizkin expressed his readiness to do anything he was wanted; Slumkey, his determination to do nothing that was asked of him. Both said that the trade, the manufactures, the commerce, the prosperity of Eatanswill, would ever be dearer to their hearts than any earthly object; and each had it in his power to state, with the utmost confidence, that he was the man who would eventually be returned.

There was a show of hands; the Mayor decided in favour of the honourable Samuel Slumkey, of Slumkey Hall. Horatio Fizkin, Esquire, of Fizkin Lodge, demanded a poll, and a poll was fixed accordingly. Then a vote of thanks was moved to the Mayor for his able conduct in the chair; and the Mayor devoutly wishing that he had had a chair to display his able conduct in (for he had been standing during the whole proceedings), returned thanks. The processions reformed, the carriages rolled slowly through the crowd, and its members screeched and shouted after them as their feelings or caprice dictated.

During the whole time of the polling, the town was in a perpetual fever of excitement. Everything was conducted on the most liberal and delightful scale. Exciseable articles were remarkably cheap at all the public-houses; and spring vans paraded the streets for the accommodation of voters who were seized with any temporary dizziness in the head – an epidemic which prevailed among the electors, during the contest, to a most alarming extent, and under the influence of which they might frequently be seen lying on the pavements in a state of utter insensibility. A small body of electors remained unpolled on the very last day. They were calculating and reflecting persons, who had not yet been convinced by the arguments of either party, although they had had frequent conferences with each. One hour before the close of the poll, Mr Perker solicited the honour of a private interview with these intelligent, these noble, these patriotic men. It was granted. His arguments were brief, but satisfactory. They went in a body to the poll; and when they returned, the honourable Samuel Slumkey, of Slumkey Hall, was returned also.

Comprising a brief Description of the Company at the Peacock assembled; and a Tale told by a Bagman

It is pleasant to turn from contemplating the strife and turmoil of political existence, to the peaceful repose of private life. Although in reality no great partisan of either side, Mr Pickwick was sufficiently fired with Mr Pott's enthusiasm, to apply his whole time and attention to the proceedings, of which the last chapter affords a description compiled from his own memoranda. Nor while he was thus occupied was Mr Winkle idle, his whole time being devoted to pleasant walks and short country excursions with Mrs Pott, who never failed, when such an opportunity presented itself, to seek some relief from the tedious monotony she so constantly complained of. The two gentlemen being thus completely domesticated in the Editor's house, Mr Tupman and Mr Snodgrass were in a great measure cast upon their own resources. Taking but little interest in public affairs, they beguiled their time chiefly with such amusements as the Peacock afforded, which were limited to a bagatelle-board in the first floor, and a sequestered skittle-ground[1] in the back yard. In the science and nicety of both these recreations, which are far more abstruse than ordinary men suppose, they were gradually initiated by Mr Weller, who possessed a perfect knowledge of such pastimes. Thus, notwithstanding that they were in a great measure deprived of the comfort and advantage of Mr Pickwick's society, they were still enabled to beguile the time, and to prevent its hanging heavily on their hands.

It was in the evening, however, that the Peacock presented attractions which enabled the two friends to resist even the invitations of the gifted, though prosy, Pott. It was in the evening that the 'commercial room'[2] was filled with a social circle, whose characters and manners it was the delight of Mr Tupman to observe; whose sayings and doings it was the habit of Mr Snodgrass to note down.

Most people know what sort of places commercial rooms usually are. That of the Peacock differed in no material respect from the generality of such apartments; that is to say, it was a large bare-looking room, the furniture of which had no doubt been better when it was newer, with a spacious table in the centre, and a variety of smaller dittos in the corners: an extensive assortment of variously shaped chairs, and an old Turkey carpet, bearing about the same relative proportion to the size of the room, as a lady's pocket-handkerchief might to the floor of a watch-box.[3] The walls were garnished with one or two large maps; and several weather-beaten rough great coats, with complicated capes, dangled from a long row of pegs in one corner. The mantelshelf was ornamented with a wooden inkstand, containing one stump of a pen and half a wafer:[4] a road-book and directory: a county history minus the cover: and the mortal remains of a trout in a glass coffin. The atmosphere was redolent of tobacco-smoke, the fumes of which had communicated a rather dingy hue to the whole room, and more especially to the dusty red curtains which shaded the windows. On the sideboard a variety of miscellaneous articles were huddled together, the most conspicuous of which were some very cloudy fish-sauce cruets, a couple of driving-boxes, two or three whips, and as many travelling shawls, a tray of knives and forks, and the mustard.

Here it was that Mr Tupman and Mr Snodgrass were seated on the evening after the conclusion of the election, with several other temporary inmates of the house, smoking and drinking.

'Well, gents,' said a stout, hale personage of about forty, with only one eye – a very bright black eye, which twinkled with a roguish expression of fun and good humour, 'our noble selves, gents. I always propose that toast to the company, and drink Mary to myself. Eh, Mary!'

'Get along with you, you wretch,' said the hand-maiden, obviously not ill pleased with the compliment, however.

'Don't go away, Mary,' said the black-eyed man.

'Let me alone, imperence,'[5] said the young lady.

'Never mind,' said the one-eyed man, calling after the girl as she left the room. 'I'll step out by and by, Mary. Keep your spirits up, dear.' Here he went through the not very difficult process of winking upon the company with his solitary eye, to the enthusiastic delight of an elderly personage with a dirty face and a clay pipe.

'Rum creeters is women,' said the dirty-faced man, after a pause.

'Ah! no mistake about that,' said a very red-faced man, behind a cigar.

After this little bit of philosophy there was another pause.

'There's rummer things than women in this world though, mind you,' said the man with the black eye, slowly filling a large Dutch pipe,[6] with a most capacious bowl.

'Are you married?' inquired the dirty-faced man.

'Can't say I am.'

'I thought not.' Here the dirty-faced man fell into fits of mirth at his own retort, in which he was joined by a man of bland voice and placid countenance, who always made it a point to agree with everybody.

'Women, after all, gentlemen,' said the enthusiastic Mr Snodgrass, 'are the great props and comforts of our existence.'

'So they are,' said the placid gentleman.

'When they're in a good humour,' interposed the dirty-faced man.

'And that's very true,' said the placid one.

'I repudiate that qualification,' said Mr Snodgrass, whose thoughts were fast reverting to Emily Wardle, 'I repudiate it with disdain – with indignation. Show me the man who says anything against women, as women, and I boldly declare he is not a man.' And Mr Snodgrass took his cigar from his mouth, and struck the table violently with his clenched fist.

'That's good sound argument,' said the placid man.

'Containing a position which I deny,' interrupted he of the dirty countenance.

'And there's certainly a very great deal of truth in what you observe too, sir,' said the placid gentleman.

'Your health, sir,' said the bagman[7] with the lonely eye, bestowing an approving nod on Mr Snodgrass.

Mr Snodgrass acknowledged the compliment.

'I always like to hear a good argument,' continued the bagman, 'a sharp one, like this; it's very improving; but this little argument about women brought to my mind a story I have heard an old uncle of mine tell, the recollection of which, just now, made me say there were rummer things than women to be met with, sometimes.'

'I should like to hear that same story,' said the red-faced man with the cigar.

'Should you?' was the only reply of the bagman, who continued to smoke with great vehemence.

'So should I,' said Mr Tupman, speaking for the first time. He was always anxious to increase his stock of experience.

'Should *you*? Well then, I'll tell it. No I won't. I know you won't believe it,' said the man with the roguish eye, making that organ look more roguish than ever.

'If you say it's true, of course I shall,' said Mr Tupman.

'Well, upon that understanding I'll tell you,' replied the traveller. 'Did you ever hear of the great commercial house of Bilson and Slum? But it doesn't matter though, whether you did or not, because they retired from business long since. It's eighty years ago, since the circumstance happened to a traveller for that house, but he was a particular friend of my uncle's; and my uncle told the story to me. It's a queer name; but he used to call it

THE BAGMAN'S STORY,

and he used to tell it, something in this way.

'One winter's evening, about five o'clock, just as it began to grow dusk, a man in a gig might have been seen urging his tired horse along the road which leads across Marlborough Downs, in the direction of Bristol. I say he might have been seen, and I have no doubt he would have been, if any body but a blind man had happened to pass that way; but the weather was so bad and the night so cold and wet, that nothing was out but the water, and so the traveller jogged along in the middle of the road, lonesome and dreary enough. If any bagman of that day could have caught sight of the little neck-or-nothing sort of gig, with a clay-coloured body and red wheels, and the vixenish ill-tempered, fast-going bay mare, that looked like a cross between a butcher's horse and a two penny post-office pony,[8] he would have known at once, that this traveller could have been no other than Tom Smart, of the great house of Bilson and Slum, Cateaton Street, City. However, as there was no bagman to look on, nobody knew anything at all about the matter; and so Tom Smart and his clay-coloured gig with the red wheels, and the vixenish mare with the fast pace, went on together, keeping the secret among them: and nobody was a bit the wiser.

'There are many pleasanter places even in this dreary world, than Marlborough Downs when it blows hard; and if you throw in beside, a gloomy winter's evening, a miry and sloppy road, and a pelting fall of heavy rain, and try the effect, by way of experiment, in your own proper person, you will experience the full force of this observation.

'The wind blew – not up the road or down it, though that's bad enough, but sheer across it, sending the rain slanting down like the lines they used to rule in the copybooks at school, to make the boys slope well. For a moment it would die away, and the traveller would begin to delude himself into the belief that, exhausted with its previous fury, it had quietly lain itself down to rest, when, whoo! he would hear it growling and whistling in the distance, and on it would come rushing over the hill-tops, and sweeping along the plain, gathering sound and strength as it drew nearer, until it dashed with a heavy gust against horse and man, driving the sharp rain into their ears, and its cold damp breath into their very bones; and past them it would scour, far, far away, with a stunning roar, as if in ridicule of their weakness, and triumphant in the consciousness of its own strength and power.

'The bay mare splashed away, through the mud and water, with drooping ears; now and then tossing her head as if to express her disgust at this very ungentlemanly behaviour of the elements, but keeping a good pace notwithstanding, until a gust of wind, more furious than any that had yet assailed them, caused her to stop suddenly and plant her four feet firmly against the ground, to prevent her being blown over. It's a special mercy that she did this, for if she *had* been blown over, the vixenish mare was so light, and the gig was so light, and Tom Smart such a light weight into the bargain, that they must infallibly have all gone rolling over and over together, until they reached the confines of earth, or until the wind fell; and in either case the probability is, that neither the vixenish mare, nor the clay-coloured gig with the red wheels, nor Tom Smart, would ever have been fit for service again.

'"Well, damn my straps and whiskers," says Tom Smart, (Tom sometimes had an unpleasant knack of swearing), "Damn my straps and whiskers," says Tom, "if this ain't pleasant, blow me!"

'You'll very likely ask me why, as Tom Smart had been pretty well blown already, he expressed this wish to be submitted to the same process again. I can't say – all I know is, that Tom Smart said so – or at least he always told my uncle he said so, and it's just the same thing.

'"Blow me," says Tom Smart; and the mare neighed as if she were precisely of the same opinion.

'"Cheer up, old girl," said Tom, patting the bay mare on the neck with the end of his whip. "It won't do pushing on, such a night as this; the first house we come to we'll put up at, so the faster you go the sooner it's over. Soho, old girl – gently – gently."

'Whether the vixenish mare was sufficiently well acquainted with the tones of Tom's voice to comprehend his meaning, or whether she found it colder standing still than moving on, of course I can't say. But I can say that Tom had no sooner finished speaking, than she pricked up her ears, and started forward at a speed which made the clay-coloured gig rattle till you would have supposed every one of the red spokes were going to fly out on the turf of Marlborough Downs; and even Tom, whip as he was, couldn't stop or check her pace, until she drew up, of her own accord, before a road-side inn on the right-hand side of the way, about half a quarter of a mile from the end of the Downs.

'Tom cast a hasty glance at the upper part of the house as he threw the reins to the hostler, and stuck the whip in the box. It was a strange old place, built of a kind of shingle, inlaid, as it were, with cross-beams, with gabled-topped windows projecting completely over the pathway, and a low door with a dark porch, and a couple of steep steps leading down into the house, instead of the modern fashion of half a dozen shallow ones leading up to it. It was a comfortable-looking place though, for there was a strong cheerful light in the bar-window, which shed a bright ray across the road, and even lighted up the hedge on the other side; and there was a red flickering light in the opposite window, one moment but faintly discernible, and the next gleaming strongly through the drawn curtains, which intimated that a rousing fire was blazing within. Marking these little evidences with the eye of an experienced traveller, Tom dismounted with as much agility as his half-frozen limbs would permit, and entered the house.

'In less than five minutes' time, Tom was ensconced in the room opposite the bar – the very room where he had imagined the fire blazing – before a substantial matter-of-fact roaring fire, composed of something short of a bushel of coals, and wood enough to make half a dozen decent gooseberry bushes, piled half way up the chimney, and roaring and crackling with a sound that of itself would have warmed the heart of any reasonable man. This was comfortable, but this was not all, for a smartly dressed girl, with a bright eye and a neat ankle, was laying a very clean white cloth on the table; and as Tom sat with his slippered feet on the fender, and his back to the open door, he saw a charming prospect of the bar reflected in the glass over the chimney-piece, with delightful rows of green bottles and gold labels, together with jars of pickles and preserves, and cheeses and boiled hams, and rounds of beef, arranged on shelves in the most tempting and delicious array. Well, this was comfortable too; but even this was not all – for in the bar, seated at tea at the nicest possible little table, drawn close up before the brightest possible little fire, was a buxom widow of somewhere about eight and forty or thereabouts, with a face as comfortable as the bar, who was evidently the landlady of the house, and the supreme ruler over all these agreeable possessions. There was only one drawback to the beauty of the whole picture, and that was a tall man – a very tall man – in a brown coat and bright basket buttons, and black whiskers, and wavy black hair, who was seated at tea with the widow, and who it required no great penetration to discover was in a fair way of persuading her to be a widow no longer, but to confer upon him the privilege of sitting down in that bar, for and during the whole remainder of the term of his natural life.

'Tom Smart was by no means of an irritable or envious disposition, but somehow or other the tall man with the brown coat and the bright basket buttons did rouse what little gall he had in his composition, and did make him feel extremely indignant: the more especially as he could now and then observe, from his seat before the glass, certain little affectionate familiarities passing between the tall man and the widow, which sufficiently denoted that the tall man was as high in favour as he was in size. Tom was fond of hot punch – I may venture to say he was *very* fond of hot punch – and after he had seen the vixenish mare well fed and well littered down, and had eaten every bit of the nice little hot dinner which the widow tossed up for him with her own hands, he just ordered a tumbler of it, by way of experiment. Now, if there was one thing in the whole range of domestic art, which the widow could manufacture better than another, it was this identical article; and the first tumbler was adapted to Tom Smart's taste with such peculiar nicety, that he ordered a second with the least possible delay. Hot punch is a pleasant thing, gentlemen – an extremely pleasant thing under any circumstances – but in that snug old parlour, before the roaring fire, with the wind blowing outside till every timber in the old house creaked again, Tom Smart found it perfectly delightful. He ordered another tumbler, and then another – I am not quite certain whether he didn't order another after that – but the more he drank of the hot punch, the more he thought of the tall man.

'"Confound his impudence!" said Tom to himself, "what business has he in that snug bar? Such an ugly villain too!" said Tom. "If the widow had any taste, she might surely pick up some better fellow than that." Here Tom's eye wandered from the glass on the chimney-piece, to the glass on the table; and as he felt himself becoming gradually sentimental, he emptied the fourth tumbler of punch and ordered a fifth.

'Tom Smart, gentlemen, had always been very much attached to the public line. It had long been his ambition to stand in a bar of his own, in a green coat, knee-cords, and tops. He had a great notion of taking the chair at convivial dinners, and he had often thought how well he could preside in a room of his own in the talking way, and what a capital example he could set to his customers in the drinking department. All these things passed rapidly through Tom's mind as he sat drinking the hot punch by the roaring fire, and he felt very justly and properly indignant that the tall man should be in a fair way of keeping such an excellent house, while he, Tom Smart, was as far off from it as ever. So, after deliberating over the two last tumblers, whether he hadn't a perfect right to pick a quarrel with the tall man for having contrived to get into the good graces of the buxom widow, Tom Smart at last arrived at the satisfactory conclusion that he was a very ill-used and persecuted individual, and had better go to bed.

'Up a wide and ancient staircase the smart girl preceded Tom, shading the chamber candle with her hand, to protect it from the currents of air which in such a rambling old place might have found plenty of room to disport themselves in, without blowing the candle out, but which did blow it out nevertheless; thus affording Tom's enemies an opportunity of asserting that it was he, and not the wind, who extinguished the candle, and that while he pretended to be blowing it a-light again, he was in fact kissing the girl. Be this as it may, another light was obtained, and Tom was conducted through a maze of rooms, and a labyrinth of passages, to the apartment which had been prepared for his reception, where the girl bade him good night, and left him alone.

'It was a good large room with big closets, and a bed which might have served for a whole boarding-school, to say nothing of a couple of oaken presses that would have held the baggage of a small army; but what struck Tom's fancy most was a strange, grim-looking high-backed chair, carved in the most fantastic manner, with a flowered damask cushion, and the round knobs at the bottom of the legs carefully tied up in red cloth, as if it had got the gout in its toes. Of any other queer chair, Tom would only have thought it *was* a queer chair, and there would have been an end of the matter; but there was something about this particular chair, and yet he couldn't tell what it was, so odd and so unlike any other piece of furniture he had ever seen, that it seemed to fascinate him. He sat down before the fire, and stared at the old chair for half an hour; – Deuce take the chair, it was such a strange old thing, he couldn't take his eyes off it.

'"Well," said Tom, slowly undressing himself, and staring at the old chair all the while, which stood with a mysterious aspect by the bedside, "I never saw such a rum concern as that in my days. Very odd," said Tom, who had got rather sage with the hot punch, "Very odd." Tom shook his head with an air of profound wisdom, and looked at the chair again. He couldn't make anything of it though, so he got into bed, covered himself up warm, and fell asleep.

'In about half an hour, Tom woke up, with a start, from a

confused dream of tall men and tumblers of punch: and the first object that presented itself to his waking imagination was the queer chair.

'"I won't look at it any more," said Tom to himself, and he squeezed his eye-lids together, and tried to persuade himself he was going to sleep again. No use; nothing but queer chairs danced before his eyes, kicking up their legs, jumping over each other's backs, and playing all kinds of antics.

'"I may as well see one real chair, as two or three complete sets of false ones," said Tom, bringing out his head from under the bed-clothes. There it was, plainly discernible by the light of the fire, looking as provoking as ever.

'Tom gazed at the chair; and, suddenly as he looked at it, a most extraordinary change seemed to come over it. The carving of the back gradually assumed the lineaments and expression of an old shrivelled human face; the damask cushion became an antique, flapped waistcoat; the round knobs grew into a couple of feet, encased in red cloth slippers; and the old chair looked like a very ugly old man, of the previous century, with his arms a-kimbo. Tom sat up in bed, and rubbed his eyes to dispel the illusion. No. The chair was an ugly old gentleman; and what was more, he was winking at Tom Smart.

'Tom was naturally a headlong, careless sort of dog, and he had had five tumblers of hot punch into the bargain; so, although he was a little startled at first, he began to grow rather indignant when he saw the old gentleman winking and leering at him with such an impudent air. At length he resolved that he wouldn't stand it; and as the old face still kept winking away as fast as ever, Tom said, in a very angry tone:

'"What the devil are you winking at me for?"

'"Because I like it, Tom Smart," said the chair; or the old gentlemen, whichever you like to call him. He stopped winking though, when Tom spoke, and began grinning like a superannuated monkey.

'"How do you know my name, old nut-cracker face!" inquired Tom Smart, rather staggered; – though he pretended to carry it off so well.

'"Come, come Tom," said the old gentleman, "that's not the way to address solid Spanish Mahogany. Dam'me, you couldn't treat me with less respect if I was veneered." When the old gentleman said this, he looked so fierce that Tom began to grow frightened.

'"I didn't mean to treat you with any disrespect, sir," said Tom; in a much humbler tone than he had spoken in at first.

'"Well, well," said the old fellow, "perhaps not – perhaps not. Tom – ."

'"Sir – "

'"I know everything about you, Tom; everything. You're very poor, Tom."

'"I certainly am," said Tom Smart. "But how came you to know that?"

'"Never mind that," said the old gentleman; "you're much too fond of punch, Tom."

'Tom Smart was just on the point of protesting that he hadn't tasted a drop since his last birth-day, but when his eye encountered that of the old gentleman, he looked so knowing that Tom blushed, and was silent.

'"Tom," said the old gentleman, "the widow's a fine woman – remarkably fine woman – eh, Tom?" Here the old fellow screwed up his eyes, cocked up one of his wasted little legs, and looked altogether so unpleasantly amorous, that Tom was quite disgusted with the levity of his behaviour; – at his time of life, too!

'"I am her guardian, Tom," said the old gentleman.

'"Are you?" inquired Tom Smart.

'"I knew her mother, Tom," said the old fellow; "and her grandmother. She was very fond of me – made me this waistcoat, Tom."

'"Did she?" said Tom Smart.

'"And these shoes," said the old fellow, lifting up one of the red-cloth mufflers; "but don't mention it, Tom. I shouldn't like to have it known that she was so much attached to me. It might occasion some unpleasantness in the family." When the old rascal said this, he looked so extremely impertinent, that, as Tom Smart afterwards declared, he could have sat upon him without remorse.

'"I have been a great favourite among the women in my time, Tom," said the profligate old debauchee; "hundreds of fine women have sat in my lap for hours together. What do you think of that you dog, eh!" The old gentleman was proceeding to recount some other exploits of his youth, when he was seized with such a violent fit of creaking that he was unable to proceed.

'"Just serves you right, old boy," thought Tom Smart; but he didn't say anything.

'"Ah!" said the old fellow, "I am a good deal troubled with this now. I am getting old Tom, and have lost nearly all my rails. I have

had an operation performed, too – a small piece let into my back –
and I found it a severe trial, Tom."

'"I dare say you did, sir," said Tom Smart.

'"However," said the old gentleman, "that's not the point. Tom!
I want you to marry the widow."

'"Me, sir!" said Tom.

'"You;" said the old gentleman.

'"Bless your reverend locks," said Tom – (he had a few scattered
horse-hairs left) – "bless your reverend locks, she wouldn't have
me." And Tom sighed involuntarily, as he thought of the bar.

'"Wouldn't she?" said the old gentleman, firmly.

'"No, no," said Tom; "there's somebody else in the wind. A tall
man – a confoundedly tall man – with black whiskers."

'"Tom," said the old gentleman; "she will never have him."

'"Won't she?" said Tom. "If you stood in the bar, old gentleman,
you'd tell another story."

'"Pooh, pooh," said the old gentleman. "I know all about that."

'"About what?" said Tom.

'"The kissing behind the door, and all that sort of thing, Tom,"
said the old gentleman. And here he gave another impudent look,
which made Tom very wroth, because as you all know, gentlemen,
to hear an old fellow, who ought to know better, talking about
these things, is very unpleasant – nothing more so.

'"I know all about that, Tom," said the old gentleman. "I have
seen it done very often in my time, Tom, between more people than
I should like to mention to you; but it never came to anything after
all."

'"You must have seen some queer things," said Tom, with an
inquisitive look.

'"You may say that, Tom," replied the old fellow, with a very
complicated wink. "I am the last of my family, Tom," said the old
gentleman, with a melancholy sigh.

'"Was it a large one?" inquired Tom Smart.

'"There were twelve of us, Tom," said the old gentleman; "fine
straight-backed, handsome fellows as you'd wish to see. None of
your modern abortions – all with arms, and with a degree of polish,
though I say it that should not, which would have done your heart
good to behold."

'"And what's become of the others, sir?" asked Tom Smart.

'The old gentleman applied his elbow to his eye as he replied,
"Gone, Tom, gone. We had hard service, Tom, and they hadn't all
my constitution. They got rheumatic about the legs and arms, and

went into kitchens and other hospitals; and one of 'em, with long service and hard usage, positively lost his senses: – he got so crazy that he was obliged to be burnt. Shocking thing that, Tom."

'"Dreadful!" said Tom Smart.

'The old fellow paused for a few minutes, apparently struggling with his feelings of emotion, and then said:

'"However, Tom, I am wandering from the point. This tall man, Tom, is a rascally adventurer. The moment he married the widow, he would sell off all the furniture, and run away. What would be the consequence? She would be deserted and reduced to ruin, and I should catch my death of cold in some broker's shop."

'"Yes, but – "

'"Don't interrupt me," said the old gentleman. "Of you, Tom, I entertain a very different opinion; for I well know that if you once settled yourself in a public house, you would never leave it, as long as there was anything to drink within its walls."

'"I am very much obliged to you for your good opinion, sir," said Tom Smart.

'"Therefore," resumed the old gentleman, in a dictatorial tone; "you shall have her, and he shall not."

'"What is to prevent it?" said Tom Smart, eagerly.

'"This disclosure," replied the old gentleman; "he is already married."

'"How can I prove it?" said Tom, starting half out of bed.

'The old gentleman untucked his arm from his side, and having pointed to one of the oaken presses, immediately replaced it in its old position.

'"He little thinks," said the old gentleman, "that in the right hand pocket of a pair of trousers in that press, he has left a letter, entreating him to return to his disconsolate wife, with six – mark me, Tom – six babes, and all of them small ones."

'As the old gentleman solemnly uttered these words, his features grew less and less distinct, and his figure more shadowy. A film came over Tom Smart's eyes. The old man seemed gradually blending into the chair, the damask waist-coat to resolve into a cushion, the red slippers to shrink into little red cloth bags. The light faded gently away, and Tom Smart fell back on his pillow, and dropped asleep.

'Morning aroused Tom from the lethargic slumber, into which he had fallen on the disappearance of the old man. He sat up in bed, and for some minutes vainly endeavoured to recall the events of the preceding night. Suddenly they rushed upon him. He looked at the chair; it was a fantastic and grim-looking piece of furniture, certainly, but it must have been a remarkably ingenious and lively imagination, that could have discovered any resemblance between it and an old man.

'"How are you, old boy?" said Tom. He was bolder in the daylight – most men are.

'The chair remained motionless, and spoke not a word.

'"Miserable morning," said Tom. No. The chair would not be drawn into conversation.

'"Which press did you point to? – you can tell me that," said Tom. Devil a word, gentlemen, the chair would say.

'"It's not much trouble to open it, any how," said Tom, getting out of bed very deliberately. He walked up to one of the presses. The key was in the lock; he turned it, and opened the door. There *was* a pair of trousers there. He put his hand into the pocket, and drew forth the identical letter the old gentleman had described!

'"Queer sort of thing, this," said Tom Smart; looking first at the chair and then at the press, and then at the letter, and then at the chair again. "Very queer," said Tom. But, as there was nothing in either, to lessen the queerness, he thought he might as well dress himself, and settle the tall man's business at once – just to put him out of his misery.

'Tom surveyed the rooms he passed through, on his way down stairs, with the scrutinising eye of a landlord; thinking it not impossible, that before long, they and their contents would be his property. The tall man was standing in the snug little bar, with his hands behind him, quite at home. He grinned vacantly at Tom. A casual observer might have supposed he did it, only to show his white teeth; but Tom Smart thought that a consciousness of triumph was passing through the place where the tall man's mind would have been, if he had had any. Tom laughed in his face; and summoned the landlady.

'"Good morning, ma'am," said Tom Smart, closing the door of the little parlour as the widow entered.

'"Good morning, sir," said the widow. "What will you take for breakfast, sir?"

'Tom was thinking how he should open the case, so he made no answer.

'"There's a very nice ham," said the widow, "and a beautiful cold larded fowl.' Shall I send 'em in, sir?"

'These words roused Tom from his reflections. His admiration of the widow increased as she spoke. Thoughtful creature! Comfortable provider!

'"Who is that gentleman in the bar, ma'am?" inquired Tom.

'"His name is Jinkins, sir," said the widow, slightly blushing.

'"He's a tall man," said Tom.

'"He is a very fine man, sir," replied the widow, "and a very nice gentleman."

'"Ah!" said Tom.

'"Is there anything more you want, sir?" inquired the widow, rather puzzled by Tom's manner.

'"Why, yes," said Tom. "My dear ma'am, will you have the kindness to sit down for one moment?"

'The widow looked much amazed, but she sat down, and Tom sat down too, close beside her. I don't know how it happened, gentlemen – indeed my uncle used to tell me that Tom Smart said *he* didn't know how it happened either – but somehow or other the palm of Tom's hand fell upon the back of the widow's hand, and remained there while he spoke.

'"My dear ma'am," said Tom Smart – he had always a great notion of committing the amiable – "My dear ma'am, you deserve a very excellent husband; – you do indeed."

'"Lor, sir!" said the widow – as well she might: Tom's mode of commencing the conversation being rather unusual, not to say startling: the fact of his never having set eyes upon her before the previous night, being taken into consideration. "Lor, sir!"

'"I scorn to flatter, my dear ma'am," said Tom Smart. "You deserve a very admirable husband, and whoever he is, he'll be a very lucky man." As Tom said this his eye involuntarily wandered from the widow's face, to the comforts around him.

'The widow looked more puzzled than ever, and made an effort to rise. Tom gently pressed her hand, as if to detain her, and she kept her seat. Widows, gentlemen, are not usually timorous, as my uncle used to say.

'"I am sure I am very much obliged to you, sir, for your good opinion," said the buxom landlady, half laughing; "and if ever I marry again" –

'"*If*," said Tom Smart, looking very shrewdly out of the right-hand corner of his left eye. "*If*" –

'"Well," said the widow, laughing outright this time." "*When* I do, I hope I shall have as good a husband as you describe."

'"Jinkins to wit," said Tom.

'"Lor, sir!" exclaimed the widow.

'"Oh, don't tell me," said Tom, "I know him."

'"I am sure nobody who knows him, knows anything bad of him," said the widow, bridling up at the mysterious air with which Tom had spoken.

'"Hem!" said Tom Smart.

'The widow began to think it was high time to cry, so she took out her handkerchief, and inquired whether Tom wished to insult her: whether he thought it like a gentleman to take away the character of another gentleman behind his back: why, if he had got anything to say, he didn't say it to the man, like a man, instead of terrifying a poor weak woman in that way; and so forth.

'"I'll say it to him fast enough," said Tom, "only I want you to hear it first."

'"What is it?" inquired the widow, looking intently in Tom's countenance.

'"I'll astonish you," said Tom, putting his hand in his pocket.

'"If it is, that he wants money," said the widow, "I know that already, and you needn't trouble yourself."

'"Pooh, nonsense, that's nothing," said Tom Smart, "*I* want money. 'Tan't that."

'"Oh, dear, what can it be?" exclaimed the poor widow.

'"Don't be frightened," said Tom Smart. He slowly drew forth the letter, and unfolded it. "You won't scream?" said Tom, doubtfully.

'"No, no," replied the widow; "let me see it."

'"You won't go fainting away, or any of that nonsense?" said Tom.

'"No, no," returned the widow, hastily.

'"And don't run out, and blow him up," said Tom, "because I'll do all that for you; you had better not exert yourself."

'"Well, well," said the widow, "let me see it."

'"I will," replied Tom Smart; and, with these words, he placed the letter in the widow's hand.

'Gentlemen, I have heard my uncle say, that Tom Smart said, the widow's lamentations when she heard the disclosure would have pierced a heart of stone. Tom was certainly very tender-hearted, but they pierced his, to the very core. The widow rocked herself to and fro, and wrung her hands.

'"Oh, the deception and villainy of man!" said the widow.

'"Frightful, my dear ma'am; but compose yourself," said Tom Smart.

'"Oh, I can't compose myself," shrieked the widow. "I shall never find any one else I can love so much!"

'"Oh yes you will, my dear soul," said Tom Smart, letting fall a shower of the largest sized tears, in pity for the widow's misfortunes. Tom Smart, in the energy of his compassion, had put his arm round the widow's waist; and the widow, in a passion of grief, had clasped Tom's hand. She looked up in Tom's face, and smiled through her tears. Tom looked down in her's, and smiled through his.

'I never could find out, gentlemen, whether Tom did or did not kiss the widow at that particular moment. He used to tell my uncle he didn't, but I have my doubts about it. Between ourselves, gentlemen, I rather think he did.

'At all events, Tom kicked the very tall man out at the front door half an hour after, and married the widow a month after. And he used to drive about the country, with the clay-coloured gig with red wheels, and the vixenish mare with the fast pace, till he gave up business many years afterwards, and went to France with his wife; and then the old house was pulled down.'

————

'Will you allow me to ask you,' said the inquisitive old gentleman, 'what became of the chair?'

'Why,' replied the one-eyed bagman, 'it was observed to creak very much on the day of the wedding; but Tom Smart couldn't say for certain whether it was with pleasure or bodily infirmity. He rather thought it was the latter, though, for it never spoke afterwards.'

'Everybody believed the story, didn't they?' said the dirty-faced man, re-filling his pipe.

'Except Tom's enemies,' replied the bagman. 'Some of 'em said Tom invented it altogether; and others said he was drunk, and fancied it, and got hold of the wrong trousers by mistake before he went to bed. But nobody ever minded what *they* said.'

'Tom said it was all true?'

'Every word.'

'And your uncle?'

'Every letter.'

'They must have been very nice men, both of 'em;' said the dirty-faced man.

'Yes, they were,' replied the bagman; 'very nice men indeed!'

CHAPTER 15

In which is given a faithful Portraiture of two
distinguished Persons; and an accurate Description
of a Public Breakfast in their House and Grounds:
which Public Breakfast leads to the Recognition of
an old Acquaintance, and the commencement of
another Chapter

Mr Pickwick's conscience had been somewhat reproaching him for
his recent neglect of his friends at the Peacock; and he was just on
the point of walking forth in quest of them, on the third morning
after the election had terminated, when his faithful valet put into
his hand a card, on which was engraved the following inscription:

Mrs Leo Hunter
The Den. Eatanswill.

'Person's a waitin',' said Sam, epigrammatically.

'Does the person want me, Sam ?' inquired Mr Pickwick.

'He wants you particular ; and no one else'll do, as the Devil's
private secretary said ven he fetched avay Doctor Faustus,'[1] replied
Mr Weller.

'*He*. Is it a gentleman ?' said Mr Pickwick.

'A wery good imitation o' one, if it an't,' replied Mr Weller.

'But this is a lady's card,' said Mr Pickwick.

'Given me by a gen'lm'n, hows'ever,' replied Sam, 'and he's a
waitin' in the drawing-room – said he'd rather wait all day, than
not see you.'

Mr Pickwick, on hearing this determination, descended to the
drawing-room, where sat a grave man, who started up on his
entrance, and said, with an air of profound respect :

'Mr Pickwick, I presume ?'

'The same.'

'Allow me, sir, the honour of grasping your hand. Permit me, sir,
to shake it,' said the grave man.

'Certainly,' said Mr Pickwick.

The stranger shook the extended hand, and then continued.

'We have heard of your fame, sir. The noise of your antiquarian
discussion has reached the ears of Mrs Leo Hunter – my wife, sir; *I*
am *Mr* Leo Hunter' – the stranger paused, as if he expected that

Mr Pickwick would be overcome by the disclosure; but seeing that he remained perfectly calm, proceeded.

'My wife, sir – Mrs Leo Hunter – is proud to number among her acquaintance all those who have rendered themselves celebrated by their works and talents. Permit me, sir, to place in a conspicuous part of the list the name of Mr Pickwick, and his brother members of the club that derives its name from him.'

'I shall be extremely happy to make the acquaintance of such a lady, sir,' replied Mr Pickwick.

'You *shall* make it, sir,' said the grave man. 'To-morrow morning, sir, we give a public breakfast – a *fête champêtre*[2] – to a great number of those who have rendered themselves celebrated by their works and talents. Permit Mrs Leo Hunter, sir, to have the gratification of seeing you at the Den.'

'With great pleasure,' replied Mr Pickwick.

'Mrs Leo Hunter has many of these breakfasts, sir,' resumed the new acquaintance – ' "feasts of reason, sir, and flows of soul,"[3] as somebody who wrote a sonnet to Mrs Leo Hunter on her breakfasts, feelingly and originally observed.'

'Was *he* celebrated for his works and talents ?' inquired Mr Pickwick.

'He was, sir,' replied the grave man, 'all Mrs Leo Hunter's acquaintance are; it is her ambition, sir, to have no other acquaintance.'

'It is a very noble ambition,' said Mr Pickwick.

'When I inform Mrs Leo Hunter, that that remark fell from *your* lips, sir, she will indeed be proud,' said the grave man. 'You have a gentleman in your train, who has produced some beautiful little poems, I think, sir.'

'My friend Mr Snodgrass has a great taste for poetry,' replied Mr Pickwick.

'So has Mrs Leo Hunter, sir. She doats on poetry, sir. She adores it ; I may say that her whole soul and mind are wound up, and entwined with it. She has produced some delightful pieces, herself, sir. You may have met with her "Ode to an Expiring Frog," sir.'

'I don't think I have,' said Mr Pickwick.

'You astonish me, sir,' said Mr Leo Hunter. 'It created an immense sensation. It was signed with an "L" and eight stars, and appeared originally in a Lady's Magazine. It commenced

> "Can I view thee panting, lying
> On thy stomach, without sighing;

> Can I unmoved see thee dying
> > On a log,
> > Expiring frog !"'

'Beautiful !' said Mr Pickwick.

'Fine,' said Mr Leo Hunter, 'so simple.'

'Very,' said Mr Pickwick.

'The next verse is still more touching. Shall I repeat it ?'

'If you please,' said Mr Pickwick.

'It runs thus,' said the grave man, still more gravely.

> '"Say, have fiends in shape of boys,
> With wild halloo, and brutal noise,
> Hunted thee from marshy joys,
> > With a dog,
> > Expiring frog !"'

'Finely expressed,' said Mr Pickwick.

'All point, sir,' said Mr Leo Hunter, 'but you shall hear Mrs Leo Hunter repeat it. *She* can do justice to it, sir. She will repeat it, in character, sir, tomorrow morning.'

'In character !'

'As Minerva.[4] But I forgot – it's a fancy-dress breakfast.'

'Dear me,' said Mr Pickwick, glancing at his own figure – 'I can't possibly – '

'Can't, sir ; can't !' exclaimed Mr Leo Hunter. 'Solomon Lucas, the Jew in the High Street, has thousands of fancy dresses. Consider, sir, how many appropriate characters are open for your selection. Plato, Zeno, Epicurus, Pythagoras[5] – all founders of clubs.'

'I know that,' said Mr Pickwick, 'but as I cannot put myself in competition with those great men, I cannot presume to wear their dresses.'

The grave man considered deeply, for a few seconds, and then said,

'On reflection, sir, I don't know whether it would not afford Mrs Leo Hunter greater pleasure, if her guests saw a gentleman of your celebrity in his own costume, rather than in an assumed one. I may venture to promise an exception in your case, sir – yes, I am quite certain that on behalf of Mrs Leo Hunter, I may venture to do so.'

'In that case,' said Mr Pickwick, 'I shall have great pleasure in coming.'

'But I waste your time, sir,' said the grave man, as if suddenly recollecting himself. 'I know its value, sir. I will not detain you. I may tell Mrs Leo Hunter, then, that she may confidently expect you and your distinguished friends ? Good morning, sir, I am proud to have beheld so eminent a personage – not a step, sir ; not a word.' And without giving Mr Pickwick time to offer remonstrance or denial, Mr Leo Hunter stalked gravely away.

Mr Pickwick took up his hat, and repaired to the Peacock, but Mr Winkle had conveyed the intelligence of the fancy ball there, before him.

'Mrs Pott's going,' were the first words with which he saluted his leader.

'Is she ?' said Mr Pickwick.

'As Apollo,' replied Mr Winkle. 'Only Pott objects to the tunic.'

'He is right. He is quite right,' said Mr Pickwick emphatically.

'Yes; – so she's going to wear a white satin gown with gold spangles.'

'They'll hardly know what she's meant for; will they?' inquired Mr Snodgrass.

'Of course they will,' replied Mr Winkle indignantly. 'They'll see her lyre, won't they?'

'True; I forgot that,' said Mr Snodgrass.

'I shall go as a Bandit,' interposed Mr Tupman.

'What!' said Mr Pickwick, with a sudden start.

'As a bandit,' repeated Mr Tupman, mildly.

'You don't mean to say,' said Mr Pickwick, gazing with solemn sternness at his friend, 'You don't mean to say, Mr Tupman, that it is your intention to put yourself into a green velvet jacket, with a two-inch tail?'

'Such *is* my intention, sir,' replied Mr Tupman warmly. 'And why not, sir?'

'Because, sir,' said Mr Pickwick, considerably excited. 'Because you are too old, sir.'

'Too old!' exclaimed Mr Tupman.

'And if any further ground of objection be wanting,' continued Mr Pickwick, 'you are too fat, sir.'

'Sir,' said Mr Tupman, his face suffused with a crimson glow. 'This is an insult.'

'Sir,' replied Mr Pickwick in the same tone, 'It is not half the insult to you, that your appearance in my presence in a green velvet jacket, with a two-inch tail, would be to me.'

'Sir,' said Mr Tupman, 'you're a fellow.'

'Sir,' said Mr Pickwick, 'you're another!'

Mr Tupman advanced a step or two, and glared at Mr Pickwick.

Mr Pickwick returned the glare, concentrated into a focus by means of his spectacles, and breathed a bold defiance. Mr Snodgrass and Mr Winkle looked on, petrified at beholding such a scene between two such men.

'Sir,' said Mr Tupman, after a short pause, speaking in a low, deep voice, 'you have called me old.'

'I have,' said Mr Pickwick.

'And fat.'

'I reiterate the charge.'

'And a fellow.'

'So you are!'

There was a fearful pause.

'My attachment to your person, sir,' said Mr Tupman, speaking in a voice tremulous with emotion, and tucking up his wristbands meanwhile, 'is great – very great – but upon that person, I must take summary vengeance.'

'Come on, sir!' replied Mr Pickwick. Stimulated by the exciting nature of the dialogue, the heroic man actually threw himself into a paralytic attitude, confidently supposed by the two by-standers to have been intended as a posture of defence.

'What!' exclaimed Mr Snodgrass, suddenly recovering the power of speech, of which intense astonishment had previously bereft him, and rushing between the two, at the imminent hazard of receiving an application on the temple from each, 'What! Mr Pickwick, with the eyes of the world upon you! Mr Tupman! Who, in common with us all, derives a lustre from his undying name! For shame, gentlemen; for shame.'

The unwonted lines which momentary passion had ruled in Mr Pickwick's clear and open brow, gradually melted away, as his young friend spoke, like the marks of a black-lead pencil beneath the softening influence of India rubber. His countenance had resumed its usual benign expression, ere he concluded.

'I have been hasty,' said Mr Pickwick, 'very hasty. Tupman; your hand.'

The dark shadow passed from Mr Tupman's face, as he warmly grasped the hand of his friend.

'I have been hasty, too,' said he.

'No, no,' interrupted Mr Pickwick, 'the fault was mine. You will wear the green velvet jacket?'

'No, no,' replied Mr Tupman.

'To oblige me, you will,' resumed Mr Pickwick.

'Well, well, I will,' said Mr Tupman.

It was accordingly settled that Mr Tupman, Mr Winkle, and Mr Snodgrass, should all wear fancy dresses. Thus Mr Pickwick was led by the very warmth of his own good feelings to give his consent to a proceeding from which his better judgment would have recoiled – a more striking illustration of his amiable character could hardly have been conceived, even if the events recorded in these pages had been wholly imaginary.

Mr Leo Hunter had not exaggerated the resources of Mr Solomon Lucas. His wardrobe was extensive – very extensive – not strictly classical perhaps, nor quite new, nor did it contain any one garment made precisely after the fashion of any age or time, but everything was more or less spangled; and what *can* be prettier than spangles! It may be objected that they are not adapted to the daylight, but everybody knows that they would glitter if there were lamps; and nothing can be clearer than that if people give fancy balls in the day-time, and the dresses do not show quite as well as they would by night, the fault lies solely with the people who give the fancy balls, and is in no wise chargeable on the spangles. Such was the convincing reasoning of Mr Solomon Lucas; and influenced by such arguments did Mr Tupman, Mr Winkle, and Mr Snodgrass, engage to array themselves in costumes which his taste and experience induced him to recommend as admirably suited to the occasion.

A carriage was hired from the Town Arms, for the accommodation of the Pickwickians, and a chariot was ordered from the same repository, for the purpose of conveying Mr and Mrs Pott to Mrs Leo Hunter's grounds, which Mr Pott, as a delicate acknowledgment of having received an invitation, had already confidently predicted in the Eatanswill Gazette 'would present a scene of varied and delicious enchantment – a bewildering coruscation of beauty and talent – a lavish and prodigal display of hospitality – above all, a degree of splendour softened by the most exquisite taste; and adornment refined with perfect harmony and the chastest good keeping – compared with which, the fabled gorgeousness of Eastern Fairy-land itself, would appear to be clothed in as many dark and murky colours, as must be the mind of the splenetic and unmanly being who could presume to taint with the venom of his envy, the preparations making by the virtuous and highly distinguished lady, at whose shrine this humble tribute of admiration was offered.' This last was a piece of biting sarcasm against the Independent, who in consequence of not having been invited at all, had been through four numbers affecting to sneer at the whole affair, in his very largest type, with all the adjectives in capital letters.

The morning came: it was a pleasant sight to behold Mr Tupman in full Brigand's costume, with a very tight jacket, sitting like a pincushion over his back and shoulders: the upper portion of his legs encased in the velvet shorts, and the lower part thereof swathed in the complicated bandages to which all Brigands are peculiarly attached. It was pleasing to see his open and ingenuous countenance, well mustachioed and corked, looking out from an open shirt collar; and to contemplate the sugar-loaf hat, decorated with ribbons of all colours, which he was compelled to carry on his knee, inasmuch as no known conveyance with a top to it, would admit of any man's carrying it between his head and the roof. Equally humorous and agreeable was the appearance of Mr Snodgrass in blue satin trunks and cloak, white silk tights and shoes, and Grecian helmet: which everybody knows (and if they do not, Mr Solomon Lucas did) to have been the regular, authentic, every-day costume of a Troubadour, from the earliest ages down to the time of their final disappearance from the face of the earth. All this was pleasant, but this was as nothing compared with the shouting of the populace when the carriage drew up, behind Mr Pott's chariot, which chariot itself drew up at Mr Pott's door, which door itself opened, and displayed the great Pott accoutred as a Russian officer of justice, with a tremendous knout[6] in his hand – tastefully typical of the stern and mighty power of the Eatanswill Gazette, and the fearful lashings it bestowed on public offenders.

'Bravo!' shouted Mr Tupman and Mr Snodgrass from the passage, when they beheld the walking allegory.

'Bravo!' Mr Pickwick was heard to exclaim, from the passage.

'Hoo – roar Pott!' shouted the populace. Amid these salutations, Mr Pott, smiling with that kind of bland dignity which sufficiently testified that he felt his power, and knew how to exert it, got into the chariot.

Then there emerged from the house, Mrs Pott, who would have looked very like Apollo if she hadn't had a gown on: conducted by Mr Winkle, who in his light-red coat, could not possibly have been mistaken for anything but a sportsman, if he had not borne an equal resemblance to a general postman. Last of all came Mr Pickwick, whom the boys applauded as loud as anybody, probably under the impression that his tights and gaiters were some remnants of the dark ages; and then the two vehicles proceeded towards Mrs Leo Hunter's: Mr Weller (who was to assist in waiting) being stationed on the box of that in which his master was seated.

Every one of the men, women, boys, girls, and babies, who were assembled to see the visitors in their fancy dresses, screamed with delight and ecstasy, when Mr Pickwick, with the Brigand on one arm, and the Troubadour on the other, walked solemnly up the entrance. Never were such shouts heard, as those which greeted Mr Tupman's efforts to fix the sugar-loaf hat on his head, by way of entering the garden in style.

The preparations were on the most delightful scale; fully realising the prophetic Pott's anticipations about the gorgeousness of Eastern Fairy-land, and at once affording a sufficient contradiction to the malignant statements of the reptile Independent. The grounds were more than an acre and a quarter in extent, and they were filled with people! Never was such a blaze of beauty, and fashion, and literature. There was the young lady who 'did' the poetry in the Eatanswill Gazette, in the garb of a sultana, leaning upon the arm of the young gentleman who 'did' the review department, and who was appropriately habited in a field marshal's uniform – the boots excepted. There were hosts of these geniuses, and any reasonable person would have thought it honour enough to meet them. But more than these, there were half a dozen lions from London – authors, real authors, who had written whole books, and printed them afterwards – and here you might see 'em, walking about, like ordinary men, smiling, and talking – aye, and talking pretty considerable nonsense too, no doubt with the benign intention of rendering themselves intelligible to the common people about them. Moreover, there was a band of music in pasteboard caps; four something-ean singers in the costume of their country, and a dozen hired waiters in the costume of *their* country – and very dirty costume too. And above all, there was Mrs Leo Hunter in the character of Minerva, receiving the company, and overflowing with pride and gratification at the notion of having called such distinguished individuals together.

'Mr Pickwick, ma'am,' said a servant, as that gentleman approached the presiding goddess, with his hat in his hand, and the Brigand and Troubadour on either arm.

'What! Where!' exclaimed Mrs Leo Hunter, starting up, in an affected rapture of surprise.

'Here,' said Mr Pickwick.

'Is it possible that I have really the gratification of beholding Mr Pickwick himself!' ejaculated Mrs Leo Hunter.

'No other, ma'am,' replied Mr Pickwick, bowing very low. 'Permit me to introduce my friends – Mr Tupman – Mr Winkle – Mr Snodgrass – to the authoress of "The Expiring Frog."'

Very few people but those who have tried it, know what a difficult process it is, to bow in green velvet smalls, and a tight jacket, and high-crowned hat: or in blue satin trunks and white silks: or knee-cords and top-boots that were never made for the wearer, and have been fixed upon him without the remotest reference to the comparative dimensions of himself and the suit. Never were such distortions as Mr Tupman's frame underwent in his efforts to appear easy and graceful – never was such ingenious posturing, as his fancy-dressed friends exhibited.

'Mr Pickwick,' said Mrs Leo Hunter, 'I must make you promise not to stir from my side the whole day. There are hundreds of people here, that I must positively introduce you to.'

'You are very kind, ma'am,' said Mr Pickwick.

'In the first place, here are my little girls; I had almost forgotten them,' said Minerva, carelessly pointing towards a couple of full-grown young ladies, of whom one might be about twenty, and the other a year or two older, and who were dressed in very juvenile costumes – whether to make them look young, or their mamma younger, Mr Pickwick does not distinctly inform us.

'They are very beautiful,' said Mr Pickwick, as the juveniles turned away after being presented.

'They are very like their mamma, sir,' said Mr Pott, majestically.

'Oh you naughty man,' exclaimed Mrs Leo Hunter, playfully tapping the Editor's arm with her fan (Minerva with a fan!)

'Why now, my dear Mrs Hunter,' said Mr Pott, who was trumpeter in ordinary at the Den, 'you *know* that when your picture was in the Exhibition of the Royal Academy, last year, everybody inquired whether it was intended for you, or your youngest daughter; for you were so much alike that there was no telling the difference between you.'

'Well, and if they did, why need you repeat it, before strangers?' said Mrs Leo Hunter, bestowing another tap on the slumbering lion of the Eatanswill Gazette.

'Count, Count,' screamed Mrs Leo Hunter to a well-whiskered individual in a foreign uniform, who was passing by.

'Ah! you want me?' said the Count, turning back.

'I want to introduce two very clever people to each other,' said Mrs Leo Hunter. 'Mr Pickwick, I have great pleasure in introducing you to Count Smorltork.'[7] She added in a hurried whisper to Mr Pickwick – 'the famous foreigner – gathering materials for his great work on England – hem! – Count Smorltork, Mr Pickwick.'

Mrs Leo Hunter's Fancy-dress déjeuné

Mr Pickwick saluted the Count with all the reverence due to so great a man, and the Count drew forth a set of tablets.

'What you say, Mrs Hunt?' inquired the Count, smiling graciously on the gratified Mrs Leo Hunter, 'Pig Vig or Big Vig – what you call – Lawyer – eh? I see – that is it. Big Vig' – and the Count was proceeding to enter Mr Pickwick in his tablets, as a gentleman of the long robe, who derived his name from the profession to which he belonged, when Mrs Leo Hunter interposed.

'No, no, Count,' said the lady, 'Pick-wick.'

'Ah, ah, I see,' replied the Count. 'Peek – christian name; Weeks – surname; good, ver good. Peek Weeks. How you do Weeks?'

'Quite well, I thank you,' replied Mr Pickwick, with all his usual affability. 'Have you been long in England?'

'Long – ver long time – fortnight – more.'

'Do you stay here long?'

'One week.'

'You will have enough to do,' said Mr Pickwick, smiling, 'to gather all the materials you want, in that time.'

'Eh, they are gathered,' said the Count.

'Indeed!' said Mr Pickwick.

'They are here,' added the Count, tapping his forehead significantly. 'Large book at home – full of notes – music, picture, science, poetry, poltic; all tings.'

'The word politics, sir,' said Mr Pickwick, 'comprises, in itself, a difficult study of no inconsiderable magnitude.'

'Ah!' said the Count, drawing out the tablets again, 'ver good – fine words to begin a chapter. Chapter forty-seven. Poltics. The word poltic surprises by himself – ' And down went Mr Pickwick's remark, in Count Smorltork's tablets, with such variations and additions as the Count's exuberant fancy suggested, or his imperfect knowledge of the language, occasioned.

'Count,' said Mrs Leo Hunter.

'Mrs Hunt,' replied the Count.

'This is Mr Snodgrass, a friend of Mr Pickwick's and a poet.'

'Stop,' exclaimed the Count, bringing out the tablets once more. 'Head, potry – chapter, literary friends – name, Snowgrass; ver good. Introduced to Snowgrass – great poet, friend of Peek Weeks – by Mrs Hunt, which wrote other sweet poem – what is that name? – Fog – Perspiring Fog – ver good – ver good indeed.' And the Count put up his tablets, and with sundry bows and acknowledgments walked away, thoroughly satisfied that he had made the most important and valuable additions to his stock of information.

'Wonderful man, Count Smorltork,' said Mrs Leo Hunter.

'Sound philosopher,' said Mr Pott.

'Clear-headed, strong-minded person,' added Mr Snodgrass.

A chorus of by-standers took up the shout of Count Smorltork's praise, shook their heads sagely, and unanimously cried 'Very!'

As the enthusiasm in Count Smorltork's favour ran very high, his praises might have been sung until the end of the festivities, if the four something-ean singers had not ranged themselves in front of a small apple-tree, to look picturesque, and commenced singing their national songs, which appeared by no means difficult of execution, inasmuch as the grand secret seemed to be, that three of the something-ean singers should grunt, while the fourth howled. This interesting performance having concluded amidst the loud plaudits of the whole company, a boy forthwith proceeded to entangle himself with the rails of a chair, and to jump over it, and crawl under it, and fall down with it, and do everything but sit upon it, and then to make a cravat of his legs, and tie them round his neck, and then to illustrate the ease with which a human being can be made to look like a magnified toad – all which feats yielded high delight and satisfaction to the assembled spectators. After which, the voice of Mrs Pott was heard to chirp faintly forth, something which courtesy interpreted into a song, which was all very classical, and strictly in character, because Apollo was himself a composer, and composers can very seldom sing their own music or anybody else's, either. This was succeeded by Mrs Leo Hunter's recitation of her far-famed Ode to an Expiring Frog, which was encored once, and would have been encored twice, if the major part of the guests, who thought it was high time to get something to eat, had not said that it was perfectly shameful to take advantage of Mrs Hunter's good nature. So although Mrs Leo Hunter professed her perfect willingness to recite the ode again, her kind and considerate friends wouldn't hear of it on any account; and the refreshment room being thrown open, all the people who had ever been there before, scrambled in with all possible despatch: Mrs Leo Hunter's usual course of proceeding, being, to issue cards for a hundred, and breakfast for fifty, or in other words to feed only the very particular lions, and let the smaller animals take care of themselves.

'Where is Mr Pott?' said Mrs Leo Hunter, as she placed the aforesaid lions around her.

'Here I am,' said the editor, from the remotest end of the room; far beyond all hope of food, unless something was done for him by the hostess.

'Won't you come up here?'

'Oh pray don't mind him,' said Mrs Pott, in the most obliging voice – 'you give yourself a great deal of unnecessary trouble, Mrs Hunter. You'll do very well there, won't you – dear.'

'Certainly – love,' replied the unhappy Pott, with a grim smile. Alas for the knout! The nervous arm that wielded it, with such gigantic force, on public characters, was paralysed beneath the glance of the imperious Mrs Pott.

Mrs Leo Hunter looked round her in triumph. Count Smorltork was busily engaged in taking notes of the contents of the dishes; Mr Tupman was doing the honours of the lobster salad to several lionesses, with a degree of grace which no Brigand ever exhibited before; Mr Snodgrass having cut out the young gentleman who cut up the books for the Eatanswill Gazette, was engaged in an impassioned argument with the young lady who did the poetry: and Mr Pickwick was making himself universally agreeable. Nothing seemed wanting to render the select circle complete, when Mr Leo Hunter – whose department on these occasions, was to stand about in doorways, and talk to the less important people – suddenly called out –

'My dear; here's Mr Charles Fitz-Marshall.'

'Oh dear,' said Mrs Leo Hunter, 'how anxiously I have been expecting him. Pray make room, to let Mr Fitz-Marshall pass. Tell Mr Fitz-Marshall, my dear, to come up to me directly, to be scolded for coming so late.'

'Coming, my dear ma'am,' cried a voice, 'as quick as I can – crowds of people – full room – hard work – very.'

Mr Pickwick's knife and fork fell from his hand. He stared across the table at Mr Tupman, who had dropped *his* knife and fork, and was looking as if he were about to sink into the ground without further notice.

'Ah!' cried the voice, as its owner pushed his way among the last five and twenty Turks, officers, cavaliers, and Charles the Seconds, that remained between him and the table, 'regular mangle – Baker's patent[8] – not a crease in my coat, after all this squeezing – might have "got up my linen" as I came along – ha! ha! not a bad idea, that – queer thing to have it mangled when it's upon one, though – trying process – very.'

With these broken words, a young man dressed as a naval officer made his way up to the table, and presented to the astonished Pickwickians, the identical form and features of Mr Alfred Jingle.

The offender had barely time to take Mrs Leo Hunter's proffered hand, when his eyes encountered the indignant orbs of Mr Pickwick.

'Hallo!' said Jingle. 'Quite forgot – no directions to postilion – give 'em at once – back in a minute.'

'The servant, or Mr Hunter will do it in a moment, Mr Fitz-Marshall,' said Mrs Leo Hunter.

'No, no – I'll do it – shan't be long – back in no time,' replied Jingle. With these words he disappeared among the crowd.

'Will you allow me to ask you, ma'am,' said the excited Mr Pickwick, rising from his seat, 'who that young man is, and where he resides!'

'He is a gentleman of fortune, Mr Pickwick,' said Mrs Leo Hunter, 'to whom I very much want to introduce you. The Count will be delighted with him.'

'Yes, yes,' said Mr Pickwick, hastily. 'His residence – '

'Is at present at the Angel at Bury.'

'At Bury?'

'At Bury St Edmunds, not many miles from here. But dear me, Mr Pickwick, you are not going to leave us: surely Mr Pickwick you cannot think of going so soon.'

But long before Mrs Leo Hunter had finished speaking, Mr Pickwick had plunged through the throng, and reached the garden, whither he was shortly afterwards joined by Mr Tupman, who had followed his friend closely.

'It's of no use,' said Mr Tupman. 'He has gone.'

'I know it,' said Mr Pickwick, 'and I will follow him.'

'Follow him! Where?' inquired Mr Tupman.

'To the Angel at Bury,' replied Mr Pickwick, speaking very quickly. 'How do we know whom he is deceiving there? He deceived a worthy man once, and we were the innocent cause. He shall not do it again, if I can help it; I'll expose him! Where's my servant?'

'Here you are, sir,' said Mr Weller, emerging from a sequestered spot, where he had been engaged in discussing a bottle of Madeira, which he had abstracted from the breakfast-table, an hour or two before. 'Here's your servant, sir. Proud o' the title, as the Living Skellinton⁹ said, ven they show'd him.'

'Follow me instantly,' said Mr Pickwick. 'Tupman, if I stay at Bury, you can join me there, when I write. Till then, good-bye!'

Remonstrances were useless. Mr Pickwick was roused, and his mind was made up. Mr Tupman returned to his companions; and in another hour had drowned all present recollection of Mr Alfred Jingle, or Mr Charles Fitz-Marshall, in an exhilarating quadrille and a bottle of champagne. By that time, Mr Pickwick and Sam Weller, perched on the outside of a stage coach, were every succeeding minute placing a less and less distance between themselves and the good old town of Bury St Edmunds.

CHAPTER 16

Too full of Adventure to be briefly described

There is no month in the whole year, in which nature wears a more beautiful appearance than in the month of August. Spring has many beauties, and May is a fresh and blooming month, but the charms of this time of year, are enhanced by their contrast with the winter season. August has no such advantage. It comes when we remember nothing but clear skies, green fields, and sweet-smelling flowers – when the recollection of snow, and ice, and bleak winds, has faded from our minds as completely as they have disappeared from the earth, – and yet what a pleasant time it is! Orchards and corn-fields ring with the hum of labour; trees bend beneath the thick clusters of rich fruit which bow their branches to the ground; and the corn, piled in graceful sheaves, or waving in every light breath that sweeps above it, as if it wooed the sickle, tinges the landscape with a golden hue. A mellow softness appears to hang over the whole earth; the influence of the season seems to extend itself to the very waggon, whose slow motion across the well-reaped field, is perceptible only to the eye, but strikes with no harsh sound upon the ear.

As the coach rolls swiftly past the fields and orchards which skirt the road, groups of women and children, piling the fruit in sieves, or gathering the scattered ears of corn, pause for an instant from their labour, and shading the sun-burnt face with a still browner hand, gaze upon the passengers with curious eyes, while some stout urchin, too small to work, but too mischievous to be left at home, scrambles over the side of the basket in which he has been deposited for security, and kicks and screams with delight. The reaper stops in his work, and stands with folded arms, looking at the vehicle as it whirls past; and the rough cart horses bestow a sleepy glance upon the smart coach team, which says, as plainly as a horse's glance can, 'It's all very fine to look at, but slow going, over a heavy field, is better than warm work like that, upon a dusty road, after all.' You cast a look behind you, as you turn a corner of the road.

The women and children have resumed their labour: the reaper once more stoops to his work: the cart-horses have moved on: and all are again in motion.

The influence of a scene like this, was not lost upon the well-regulated mind of Mr Pickwick. Intent upon the resolution he had formed, of exposing the real character of the nefarious Jingle, in any quarter in which he might be pursuing his fraudulent designs, he sat at first taciturn and contemplative, brooding over the means by which his purpose could be best attained. By degrees his attention grew more and more attracted by the objects around him; and at last he derived as much enjoyment from the ride, as if it had been undertaken for the pleasantest reason in the world.

'Delightful prospect, Sam,' said Mr Pickwick.

'Beats the chimley pots, sir,' replied Mr Weller, touching his hat.

'I suppose you have hardly seen anything but chimney-pots and bricks and mortar all your life, Sam,' said Mr Pickwick, smiling.

'I worn't always a boots, sir,' said Mr Weller, with a shake of the head. 'I wos a wagginer's boy, once.'

'When was that?' inquired Mr Pickwick.

'When I wos first pitched neck and crop into the world, to play at leap-frog with its troubles,' replied Sam. 'I wos a carrier's boy at startin': then a vagginer's, then a helper, then a boots. Now I'm a gen'l'm'n's servant. I shall be a gen'l'm'n myself one of these days, perhaps, with a pipe in my mouth, and a summer-house in the back garden. Who knows? *I* shouldn't be surprised, for one.'

'You are quite a philosopher, Sam,' said Mr Pickwick.

'It runs in the family, I b'lieve, sir,' replied Mr Weller. 'My father's wery much in that line, now. If my mother-in-law[1] blows him up, he whistles. She flies in a passion, and breaks his pipe; he steps out, and gets another. Then she screams wery loud, and falls into 'sterics; and he smokes wery comfortably 'till she comes to agin. That's philosophy, sir, an't it?'

'A very good substitute for it, at all events,' replied Mr Pickwick, laughing. 'It must have been of great service to you, in the course of your rambling life, Sam.'

'Service, sir,' exclaimed Sam. 'You may say that. Arter I run away from the carrier, and afore I took up with the wagginer, I had unfurnished lodgin's for a fortnight.'

'Unfurnished lodgings?' said Mr Pickwick.

'Yes – the dry arches of Waterloo Bridge. Fine sleeping-place – within ten minutes' walk of all the public offices – only if there is any objection to it, it is that the sitivation's *rayther* too airy. I see some queer sights there.'

'Ah, I suppose you did,' said Mr Pickwick, with an air of considerable interest.

'Sights, sir,' resumed Mr Weller, 'as 'ud penetrate your benevolent heart, and come out on the other side. You don't see the reg'lar wagrants there; trust 'em, they knows better than that. Young beggars, male and female, as hasn't made a rise in their profession, takes up their quarters there sometimes; but it's generally the worn-out, starving, houseless creeturs as rolls themselves in the dark corners o' them lonesome places – poor creeturs as an't up to the twopenny rope.'

'And pray, Sam, what is the twopenny rope?' inquired Mr Pickwick.

'The twopenny rope, sir,' replied Mr Weller, 'is just a cheap lodgin' house, where the beds is twopence a night.'

'What do they call a bed a rope for?' said Mr Pickwick.

'Bless your innocence, sir, that a'nt it,' replied Sam. 'Wen the lady and gen'l'm'n as keeps the Hot-el first begun business they used to make the beds on the floor; but this wouldn't do at no price, 'cos instead o' taking a moderate two-penn'orth o' sleep, the lodgers used to lie there half the day. So now they has two ropes, 'bout six foot apart, and three from the floor, which goes right down the room; and the beds are made of slips of coarse sacking, stretched across 'em.'

'Well,' said Mr Pickwick.

'Well,' said Mr Weller, 'the adwantage o' the plan's hobvious. At six o'clock every mornin' they lets go the ropes at one end, and down falls all the lodgers. 'Consequence is, that being thoroughly waked, they get up wery quietly, and walk away! Beg your pardon, sir,' said Sam, suddenly breaking off in his loquacious discourse. 'Is this Bury St Edmunds?'

'It is,' replied Mr Pickwick.

The coach rattled through the well-paved streets of a handsome little town, of thriving and cleanly appearance, and stopped before a large inn situated in a wide open street, nearly facing the old abbey.

'And this,' said Mr Pickwick, looking up, 'is the Angel! We alight here, Sam. But some caution is necessary. Order a private room, and do not mention my name. You understand.'

'Right as a trivet,[2] sir,' replied Mr Weller, with a wink of intelligence; and having dragged Mr Pickwick's portmanteau from the hind boot, into which it had been hastily thrown when they joined the coach at Eatanswill, Mr Weller disappeared on his errand. A private room was speedily engaged; and into it Mr Pickwick was ushered without delay.

'Now Sam,' said Mr Pickwick, 'the first thing to be done is to – '

'Order dinner, sir,' interposed Mr Weller. 'It's wery late, sir.'

'Ah, so it is,' said Mr Pickwick, looking at his watch. 'You are right, Sam.'

'And if I might adwise, sir,' added Mr Weller, 'I'd just have a good night's rest arterwards, and not begin inquiring arter this here deep 'un 'till the mornin'. There's nothin' so refreshin' as sleep, sir, as the servant-girl said afore she drank the egg-cupful o' laudanum.'

'I think you are right, Sam,' said Mr Pickwick. 'But I must first ascertain that he is in the house, and not likely to go away.'

'Leave that to me, sir,' said Sam. 'Let me order you a snug little dinner, and make my inquiries below while it's a getting ready; I could worm ev'ry secret out o' the boots's heart, in five minutes, sir.'

'Do so,' said Mr Pickwick: and Mr Weller at once retired.

In half an hour, Mr Pickwick was seated at a very satisfactory dinner; and in three-quarters Mr Weller returned with the intelligence that Mr Charles Fitz-Marshall had ordered his private room to be retained for him, until further notice. He was going to spend the evening at some private house in the neighbourhood, had ordered the boots to sit up until his return, and had taken his servant with him.

'Now, sir,' argued Mr Weller, when he had concluded his report, 'if I can get a talk with this here servant in the mornin', he'll tell me all his master's concerns.'

'How do you know that?' interposed Mr Pickwick.

'Bless your heart, sir, servants always do,' replied Mr Weller.

'Oh, ah, I forgot that,' said Mr Pickwick. 'Well.'

'Then you can arrange what's best to be done, sir, and we can act according.'

As it appeared that this was the best arrangement that could be made, it was finally agreed upon. Mr Weller, by his master's permission, retired to spend the evening in his own way; and was shortly afterwards elected, by the unanimous voice of the assembled company, into the tap-room chair, in which honourable post he acquitted himself so much to the satisfaction of the gentlemen-frequenters, that their roars of laughter and approbation penetrated to Mr Pickwick's bedroom, and shortened the term of his natural rest by at least three hours.

Early on the ensuing morning, Mr Weller was dispelling all the feverish remains of the previous evening's conviviality, through the instrumentality of a halfpenny shower-bath (having induced a young gentleman attached to the stable-department, by the offer of that coin, to pump over his head and face, until he was perfectly restored), when he was attracted by the appearance of a young fellow in mulberry-coloured livery, who was sitting on a bench in the yard, reading what appeared to be a hymn-book, with an air of deep abstraction, but who occasionally stole a glance at the individual under the pump, as if he took some interest in his proceedings, nevertheless.

'You're a rum 'un to look at, you are!' thought Mr Weller, the first time his eyes encountered the glance of the stranger in the mulberry suit: who had a large, sallow, ugly face, very sunken eyes, and a gigantic head, from which depended a quantity of lank black hair. 'You're a rum 'un!' thought Mr Weller; and thinking this, he went on washing himself, and thought no more about him.

Still the man kept glancing from his hymn-book to Sam, and from Sam to his hymn-book, as if he wanted to open a conversation. So at last, Sam, by way of giving him an opportunity, said with a familiar nod –

'How are you, governor?'

'I am happy to say, I am pretty well, sir,' said the man, speaking with great deliberation, and closing the book. 'I hope you are the same, sir?'

'Why, if I felt less like a walking brandy-bottle, I shouldn't be quite so staggery this mornin',' replied Sam. 'Are you stoppin' in this house, old 'un?'

The mulberry man replied in the affirmative.

'How was it, you worn't one of us, last night?' inquired Sam, scrubbing his face with the towel. 'You seem one of the jolly sort – looks as conwivial as a live trout in a lime basket,' added Mr Weller, in an under tone.

'I was out last night, with my master,' replied the stranger.

'What's his name?' inquired Mr Weller, colouring up very red with sudden excitement, and the friction of the towel combined.

'Fitz-Marshall,' said the mulberry man.

'Give us your hand,' said Mr Weller, advancing; 'I should like to know you. I like your appearance, old fellow.'

'Well, that is very strange,' said the mulberry man, with great simplicity of manner. 'I like your's so much, that I wanted to speak to you, from the very first moment I saw you under the pump.'

'Did you though?'

'Upon my word. Now, isn't that curious.'

'Wery sing'ler,' said Sam, inwardly congratulating himself upon the softness of the stranger. 'What's your name, my patriarch?'

'Job.'

'And a wery good name it is – only one I know, that ain't got a nickname to it. What's the other name?'

'Trotter,' said the stranger. 'What is yours!'

Sam bore in mind his master's caution, and replied.

'My name's Walker; my master's name's Wilkins. Will you take a drop of somethin' this mornin', Mr Trotter?'

Mr Trotter acquiesced in this agreeable proposal: and having deposited his book in his coat-pocket, accompanied Mr Weller to the tap, where they were soon occupied in discussing an exhilarating compound, formed by mixing together, in a pewter vessel, certain quantities of British Hollands, and the fragrant essence of the clove.

'And what sort of a place have you got?' inquired Sam, as he filled his companion's glass, for the second time.

'Bad,' said Job, smacking his lips, 'very bad.'

'You don't mean that?' said Sam.

'I do, indeed. Worse than that, my master's going to be married.'

'No.'

'Yes; and worse than that, too, he's going to run away with an immense rich heiress, from boarding-school.'

'What a dragon!' said Sam, refilling his companion's glass. 'It's some boarding-school in this town, I suppose, a'nt it?'

Now, although this question was put in the most careless tone imaginable, Mr Job Trotter plainly showed by gestures, that he perceived his new friend's anxiety to draw forth an answer to it. He emptied his glass, looked mysteriously at his companion, winked both of his small eyes, one after the other, and finally made a motion with his arm, as if he were working an imaginary pump-handle: thereby intimating that he (Mr Trotter) considered himself as undergoing the process of being pumped, by Mr Samuel Weller.

'No, no,' said Mr Trotter, in conclusion, 'that's not to be told to everybody. That is a secret – a great secret, Mr Walker.'

As the mulberry man said this, he turned his glass upside down, as a means of reminding his companion that he had nothing left wherewith to slake his thirst. Sam observed the hint; and feeling the delicate manner in which it was conveyed, ordered the pewter vessel to be refilled, whereat the small eyes of the mulberry man glistened.

'And so it's a secret?' said Sam.

'I should rather suspect it was,' said the mulberry man, sipping his liquor, with a complacent face.

'I suppose your mas'r 's wery rich?' said Sam.

Mr Trotter smiled, and holding his glass in his left hand, gave four distinct slaps on the pocket of his mulberry indescribables with his right, as if to intimate that his master might have done the same without alarming anybody much, by the chinking of coin.

'Ah,' said Sam, 'that's the game, is it?'

The mulberry man nodded significantly.

'Well, and don't you think, old feller,' remonstrated Mr Weller, 'that if you let your master take in this here young lady, you're a precious rascal?'

'I know that,' said Job Trotter, turning upon his companion a countenance of deep contrition, and groaning slightly. 'I know that, and that's what it is that preys upon my mind. But what am I to do?'

'Do!' said Sam; 'di-wulge to the missis, and give up your master.'

'Who'd believe me?' replied Job Trotter. 'The young lady's considered the very picture of innocence and discretion. She'd deny it, and so would my master. Who'd believe me? I should lose my place, and get indicted for a conspiracy, or some such thing; that's all I should take by my motion.'

'There's somethin' in that,' said Sam, ruminating; 'there's somethin' in that.'

'If I knew any respectable gentleman who would take the matter up,' continued Mr Trotter, 'I might have some hope of preventing the elopement; but there's the same difficulty, Mr Walker, just the same. I know no gentleman in this strange place, and ten to one if I did, whether he would believe my story.'

'Come this way,' said Sam, suddenly jumping up, and grasping the mulberry man by the arm. 'My mas'r's the man you want, I see.' And after a slight resistance on the part of Job Trotter, Sam led his newly-found friend to the apartment of Mr Pickwick, to whom he presented him, together with a brief summary of the dialogue we have just repeated.

'I am very sorry to betray my master, sir,' said Job Trotter, applying to his eyes a pink checked pocket handkerchief about six inches square.

'The feeling does you a great deal of honour,' replied Mr Pickwick; 'but it is your duty, nevertheless.'

'I know it is my duty, sir,' replied Job, with great emotion. 'We should all try to discharge our duty, sir, and I humbly endeavour to discharge mine, sir; but it is a hard trial to betray a master, sir, whose clothes you wear, and whose bread you eat, even though he is a scoundrel, sir.'

'You are a very good fellow,' said Mr Pickwick, much affected, 'an honest fellow.'

'Come come,' interposed Sam, who had witnessed Mr Trotter's tears with considerable impatience, 'blow this here water-cart bis'ness. It won't do no good, this won't.'

'Sam,' said Mr Pickwick, reproachfully, 'I am sorry to find that you have so little respect for this young man's feelings.'

'His feelins is all wery well, sir,' replied Mr Weller; 'and as they're so wery fine, and it's a pity he should lose 'em, I think he'd better keep 'em in his own buzzum, than let 'em ewaporate in hot water, 'specially as they do no good. Tears never yet wound up a clock, or worked a steam ingen'. The next time you go out to a smoking party, young fellow, fill your pipe with that 'ere reflection; and for the present just put that bit of pink gingham into your pocket. 'T'an't so handsome that you need keep waving it about, as if you was a tight-rope dancer.'

'My man is in the right,' said Mr Pickwick, accosting Job, 'although his mode of expressing his opinion is somewhat homely, and occasionally incomprehensible.'

'He is, sir, very right,' said Mr Trotter, 'and I will give way no longer.'

'Very well,' said Mr Pickwick. 'Now, where is this boarding-school?'

'It is a large, old, red-brick house, just outside the town, sir,' replied Job Trotter.

'And when,' said Mr Pickwick, 'when is this villanous design to be carried into execution – when is this elopement to take place?'

'To-night, sir,' replied Job.

'To-night!' exclaimed Mr Pickwick.

'This very night, sir,' replied Job Trotter. 'That is what alarms me so much.'

'Instant measures must be taken,' said Mr Pickwick. 'I will see the lady who keeps the establishment immediately.'

'I beg your pardon, sir,' said Job, 'but that course of proceeding will never do.'

'Why not?' inquired Mr Pickwick.

'My master, sir, is a very artful man.'

'I know he is,' said Mr Pickwick.

'And he has so wound himself round the old lady's heart, sir,' resumed Job, 'that she would believe nothing to his prejudice, if you went down on your bare knees, and swore it; especially as you have no proof but the word of a servant, who, for anything she knows (and my master would be sure to say so), was discharged for some fault, and does this in revenge.'

'What had better be done, then?' said Mr Pickwick.

'Nothing but taking him in the very fact of eloping, will convince the old lady, sir,' replied Job.

'All them old cats *will* run their heads agin mile-stones,' observed Mr Weller in a parenthesis.

'But this taking him in the very act of elopement, would be a very difficult thing to accomplish, I fear,' said Mr Pickwick.

'I don't know, sir,' said Mr Trotter, after a few moments' reflection. 'I think it might be very easily done.'

'How?' was Mr Pickwick's inquiry.

'Why,' replied Mr Trotter, 'my master and I, being in the confidence of the two servants, will be secreted in the kitchen at ten o'clock. When the family have retired to rest, we shall come out of the kitchen, and the young lady out of her bed-room. A post-chaise will be waiting, and away we go.'

'Well?' said Mr Pickwick.

'Well, sir, I have been thinking that if you were in waiting in the garden behind, alone – '

'Alone,' said Mr Pickwick. 'Why alone?'

'I thought it very natural,' replied Job, 'that the old lady wouldn't like such an unpleasant discovery to be made before more persons than can possibly be helped. The young lady too, sir – consider her feelings.'

'You are very right,' said Mr Pickwick. 'The consideration evinces your delicacy of feeling. Go on; you are very right.'

'Well sir, I have been thinking that if you were waiting in the back garden alone, and I was to let you in, at the door which opens into it, from the end of the passage, at exactly half-past eleven o'clock, you would be just in the very moment of time to assist me in frustrating the designs of this bad man, by whom I have been unfortunately ensnared.' Here Mr Trotter sighed deeply.

'Don't distress yourself on that account,' said Mr Pickwick, 'if he had one grain of the delicacy of feeling which distinguishes you, humble as your station is, I should have some hopes of him.'

Job Trotter bowed low; and in spite of Mr Weller's previous remonstrance, the tears again rose to his eyes.

'I never see such a feller,' said Sam. 'Blessed if I don't think he's got a main in his head as is always turned on.'

'Sam,' said Mr Pickwick, with great severity. 'Hold your tongue.'

'Werry well, sir,' replied Mr Weller.

'I don't like this plan,' said Mr Pickwick, after deep meditation. 'Why cannot I communicate with the young lady's friends?'

'Because they live one hundred miles from here, sir,' responded Job Trotter.

'That's a clincher,' said Mr Weller, aside.

'Then this garden,' resumed Mr Pickwick. 'How am I to get into it?'

'The wall is very low, sir, and your servant will give you a leg up.'

'My servant will give me a leg up,' repeated Mr Pickwick, mechanically. 'You will be sure to be near this door that you speak of?'

'You cannot mistake it, sir; it's the only one that opens into the garden. Tap at it when you hear the clock strike, and I will open it instantly.'

'I don't like the plan,' said Mr Pickwick; 'but as I see no other, and as the happiness of this young lady's whole life is at stake, I adopt it. I shall be sure to be there.'

Thus, for the second time, did Mr Pickwick's innate good-feeling involve him in an enterprise from which he would most willingly have stood aloof.

'What is the name of the house?' inquired Mr Pickwick.

'Westgate House, sir. You turn a little to the right when you get to the end of the town; it stands by itself, some little distance off the high road, with the name on a brass plate on the gate.'

'I know it,' said Mr Pickwick. 'I observed it once before, when I was in this town. You may depend upon me.'

Mr Trotter made another bow, and turned to depart, when Mr Pickwick thrust a guinea into his hand.

'You're a fine fellow,' said Mr Pickwick, 'and I admire your goodness of heart. No thanks. Remember – eleven o'clock.'

'There is no fear of my forgetting it, sir,' replied Job Trotter. With these words he left the room, followed by Sam.

'I say,' said the latter, 'not a bad notion that 'ere crying. I'd cry like a rain-water spout in a shower on such good terms. How do you do it?'

'It comes from the heart, Mr Walker,' replied Job, solemnly. 'Good morning, sir.'

'You're a soft customer, you are; – we've got it all out o' you, any how,' thought Mr Weller, as Job walked away.

We cannot state the precise nature of the thoughts which passed through Mr Trotter's mind, because we don't know what they were.

The day wore on, evening came, and at a little before ten o'clock Sam Weller reported that Mr Jingle and Job had gone out together, that their luggage was packed up, and that they had ordered a chaise. The plot was evidently in execution, as Mr Trotter had foretold.

Half-past ten o'clock arrived, and it was time for Mr Pickwick to issue forth on his delicate errand. Resisting Sam's tender of his great-coat, in order that he might have no incumbrance in scaling the wall, he set forth, followed by his attendant.

There was a bright moon, but it was behind the clouds. It was a fine dry night, but it was most uncommonly dark. Paths, hedges, fields, houses, and trees, were enveloped in one deep shade. The atmosphere was hot and sultry, the summer lightning quivered faintly on the verge of the horizon, and was the only sight that varied the dull gloom in which everything was wrapped – sound there was none, except the distant barking of some restless house-dog.

They found the house; read the brass-plate, walked round the wall, and stopped at that portion of it which divided them from the bottom of the garden.

'You will return to the inn, Sam, when you have assisted me over,' said Mr Pickwick.

'Wery well, sir.'

'And you will sit up, till I return.'

'Cert'nly, sir.'

'Take hold of my leg; and, when I say "Over," raise me gently.'

'All right, sir.'

Having settled these preliminaries, Mr Pickwick grasped the top of the wall, and gave the word 'Over,' which was very literally obeyed. Whether his body partook in some degree of the elasticity of his mind, or whether Mr Weller's notions of a gentle push were of a somewhat rougher description than Mr Pickwick's, the immediate effect of his assistance was to jerk that immortal gentleman completely over the wall on to the bed beneath, where, after crushing three gooseberry-bushes and a rose-tree, he finally alighted at full length.

'You ha'n't hurt yourself, I hope, sir?' said Sam, in a loud whisper, as soon as he recovered from the surprise consequent upon the mysterious disappearance of his master.

'I have not hurt *myself*, Sam, certainly,' replied Mr Pickwick, from the other side of the wall, 'but I rather think that *you* have hurt me.'

'I hope not, sir,' said Sam.

'Never mind,' said Mr Pickwick, rising, 'it's nothing but a few scratches. Go away, or we shall be overheard.'

'Good-bye, sir.'

'Good-bye.'

With stealthy steps Sam Weller departed, leaving Mr Pickwick alone in the garden.

Lights occasionally appeared in the different windows of the house, or glanced from the staircases, as if the inmates were retiring to rest. Not caring to go too near the door, until the appointed time, Mr Pickwick crouched into an angle of the wall, and awaited its arrival.

It was a situation which might well have depressed the spirits of many a man. Mr Pickwick, however, felt neither depression nor misgiving. He knew that his purpose was in the main a good one, and he placed implicit reliance on the high-minded Job. It was dull, certainly; not to say, dreary; but a contemplative man can always employ himself in meditation. Mr Pickwick had meditated himself into a doze, when he was roused by the chimes of the neighbouring church ringing out the hour – half-past eleven.

'That is the time,' thought Mr Pickwick, getting cautiously on his feet. He looked up at the house. The lights had disappeared, and the shutters were closed – all in bed, no doubt. He walked on tip-toe to the door, and gave a gentle tap. Two or three minutes passing without any reply, he gave another tap rather louder, and then another rather louder than that.

At length the sound of feet was audible upon the stairs, and then the light of a candle shone through the key-hole of the door. There was a good deal of unchaining and unbolting, and the door was slowly opened.

Now the door opened outwards: and as the door opened wider and wider, Mr Pickwick receded behind it, more and more. What was his astonishment when he just peeped out, by way of caution, to see that the person who had opened it was – not Job Trotter, but a servant-girl with a candle in her hand! Mr Pickwick drew in his head again, with the swiftness displayed by that admirable melo-dramatic performer, Punch, when he lies in wait for the flat-headed comedian with the tin box of music.

'It must have been the cat, Sarah,' said the girl, addressing herself to some one in the house. 'Puss, puss, puss, – tit, tit, tit.'

But no animal being decoyed by these blandishments, the girl slowly closed the door, and re-fastened it; leaving Mr Pickwick drawn up straight against the wall.

'This is very curious,' thought Mr Pickwick. 'They are sitting up beyond their usual hour, I suppose. Extremely unfortunate, that they should have chosen this night, of all others, for such a purpose – exceedingly.' And with these thoughts, Mr Pickwick cautiously retired to the angle of the wall in which he had been before ensconced; waiting until such time as he might deem it safe to repeat the signal.

He had not been here five minutes, when a vivid flash of lightning was followed by a loud peal of thunder that crashed and rolled away in the distance with a terrific noise – then came another flash of lightning, brighter than the other, and a second peal of thunder louder than the first; and then down came the rain, with a force and fury that swept everything before it.

Mr Pickwick was perfectly aware that a tree is a very dangerous neighbour in a thunder-storm. He had a tree on his right, a tree on his left, a third before him, and a fourth behind. If he remained where he was, he might fall the victim of an accident; if he showed himself in the centre of the garden, he might be consigned to a constable; – once or twice he tried to scale the wall, but having no other legs this time, than those with which Nature had furnished him, the only effect of his struggles was to inflict a variety of very unpleasant gratings on his knees and shins, and to throw him into a state of the most profuse perspiration.

'What a dreadful situation,' said Mr Pickwick, pausing to wipe his brow after this exercise. He looked up at the house – all was dark. They must be gone to bed now. He would try the signal again.

He walked on tip-toe across the moist gravel, and tapped at the door. He held his breath, and listened at the key-hole. No reply: very odd. Another knock. He listened again. There was a low whispering inside, and then a voice cried –

'Who's there?'

'That's not Job,' thought Mr Pickwick, hastily drawing himself straight up against the wall again. 'It's a woman.'

He had scarcely had time to form this conclusion, when a window above stairs was thrown up, and three or four female voices repeated the query – 'Who's there?'

Mr Pickwick dared not move hand or foot. It was clear that the whole establishment was roused. He made up his mind to remain where he was, until the alarm had subsided: and then by a supernatural effort, to get over the wall, or perish in the attempt.

Like all Mr Pickwick's determinations, this was the best that could be made under the circumstances; but, unfortunately, it was founded upon the assumption that they would not venture to open the door again. What was his discomfiture, when he heard the chain and bolts withdrawn, and saw the door slowly opening, wider and wider! He retreated into the corner, step by step; but do what he would, the interposition of his own person, prevented its being opened to its utmost width.

'Who's there?' screamed a numerous chorus of treble voices from the staircase inside, consisting of the spinster lady of the establishment, three teachers, five female servants, and thirty boarders, all half-dressed, and in a forest of curlpapers.

Of course Mr Pickwick didn't say who *was* there: and then the burden of the chorus changed into – 'Lor'! I am so frightened.'

'Cook,' said the lady abbess, who took care to be on the top stair, the very last of the group – 'Cook, why don't you go a little way into the garden?'

'Please, ma'am, I don't like,' responded the cook.

'Lor', what a stupid thing that cook is!' said the thirty boarders.

'Cook,' said the lady abbess, with great dignity; 'don't answer me, if you please. I insist upon your looking into the garden immediately.'

Here the cook began to cry, and the house-maid said it was 'a shame!' for which partisanship she received a month's warning on the spot.

'Do you hear, cook?' said the lady abbess, stamping her foot impatiently.

'Don't you hear your missis, cook?' said the three teachers.

'What an impudent thing, that cook is!' said the thirty boarders.

The unfortunate cook, thus strongly urged, advanced a step or two, and holding her candle just where it prevented her from seeing anything at all, declared there was nothing there, and it must have been the wind. The door was just going to be closed in consequence,

The unexpected breaking up of the Seminary for young Ladies

when an inquisitive boarder, who had been peeping between the hinges, set up a fearful screaming, which called back the cook and the housemaid, and all the more adventurous, in no time.

'What is the matter with Miss Smithers?' said the lady abbess, as the aforesaid Miss Smithers proceeded to go into hysterics of four young lady power.

'Lor', Miss Smithers dear,' said the other nine-and-twenty boarders.

'Oh, the man – the man – behind the door!' screamed Miss Smithers.

The lady abbess no sooner heard this appalling cry, than she retreated to her own bed-room, double-locked the door, and fainted away comfortably. The boarders, and the teachers, and the servants, fell back upon the stairs, and upon each other; and never was such a screaming, and fainting, and struggling, beheld. In the midst of the tumult, Mr Pickwick emerged from his concealment, and presented himself amongst them.

'Ladies – dear ladies,' said Mr Pickwick.

'Oh, he says we're dear,' cried the oldest and ugliest teacher. 'Oh the wretch!'

'Ladies,' roared Mr Pickwick, rendered desperate by the danger of his situation. 'Hear me. I am no robber. I want the lady of the house.'

'Oh, what a ferocious monster!' screamed another teacher. 'He wants Miss Tomkins.'

Here there was a general scream.

'Ring the alarm bell, somebody!' cried a dozen voices.

'Don't – don't,' shouted Mr Pickwick. 'Look at me. Do I look like a robber! My dear ladies – you may bind me hand and leg, or lock me up in a closet, if you like. Only hear what I have got to say – only hear me.'

'How did you come in our garden?' faltered the housemaid.

'Call the lady of the house, and I'll tell her everything – everything:' said Mr Pickwick, exerting his lungs to the utmost pitch. 'Call her – only be quiet, and call her, and you shall hear everything.'

It might have been Mr Pickwick's appearance, or it might have been his manner, or it might have been the temptation – irresistible to a female mind – of hearing something at present enveloped in mystery, that reduced the more reasonable portion of the establishment (some four individuals) to a state of comparative quiet. By them it was proposed, as a test of Mr Pickwick's sincerity, that he should immediately submit to personal restraint; and that gentleman having consented to hold a conference with Miss Tomkins, from the interior of a closet in which the day boarders hung their bonnets and sandwich-bags, he at once stepped into it, of his own accord, and was securely locked in. This revived the others; and Miss Tomkins having been brought to, and brought down, the conference began.

'What did you do in my garden, Man?' said Miss Tomkins, in a faint voice.

'I came to warn you, that one of your young ladies was going to elope tonight,' replied Mr Pickwick, from the interior of the closet.

'Elope!' exclaimed Miss Tomkins, the three teachers, the thirty boarders, and the five servants. 'Who with?'

'Your friend, Mr Charles Fitz-Marshall.'

'*My* friend! I don't know any such person.'

'Well; Mr Jingle, then.'

'I never heard the name in my life.'

'Then, I have been deceived, and deluded,' said Mr Pickwick. 'I have been the victim of a conspiracy – a foul and base conspiracy. Send to the Angel, my dear ma'am, if you don't believe me. Send to the Angel for Mr Pickwick's man-servant, I implore you ma'am.'

'He must be respectable – he keeps a man-servant,' said Miss Tomkins to the writing and ciphering governess.

'It's my opinion, Miss Tomkins,' said the writing and ciphering governess, 'that his man-servant keeps him. *I* think he's a madman, Miss Tomkins, and the other's his keeper.'

'I think you are very right, Miss Gwynn,' responded Miss Tomkins. 'Let two of the servants repair to the Angel, and let the others remain here, to protect us.'

So two of the servants were despatched to the Angel in search of Mr Samuel Weller: and the remaining three stopped behind to protect Miss Tomkins, and the three teachers, and the thirty boarders. And Mr Pickwick sat down in the closet, beneath a grove of sandwich bags, and awaited the return of the messengers, with all the philosophy and fortitude he could summon to his aid.

An hour and a half elapsed before they came back, and when they did come, Mr Pickwick recognised, in addition to the voice of Mr Samuel Weller, two other voices, the tones of which struck familiarly on his ear; but whose they were, he could not for the life of him call to mind.

A very brief conversation ensued. The door was unlocked. Mr Pickwick stepped out of the closet, and found himself in the presence of the whole establishment of Westgate House, Mr Samuel Weller, and – old Wardle, and his destined son-in-law, Mr Trundle!

'My dear friend,' said Mr Pickwick, running forward and grasping Wardle's hand, 'my dear friend, pray, for Heaven's sake, explain to this lady the unfortunate and dreadful situation in which I am placed. You must have heard it from my servant; say, at all events, my dear fellow, that I am neither a robber nor a madman.'

'I have said so, my dear friend. I have said so already,' replied Mr Wardle, shaking the right hand of his friend, while Mr Trundle shook the left.

'And whoever says, or has said, he is,' interposed Mr Weller, stepping forward, 'says that which is not the truth, but so far from it, on the contrary, quite the rewerse. And if there's any number o' men on these here premises as has said so, I shall be wery happy to give 'em all a wery convincing proof o' their being mistaken, in this here wery room, if these wery respectable ladies'll have the goodness to retire, and order 'em up, one at a time.' Having delivered this defiance with great volubility, Mr Weller struck his open palm emphatically with his clenched fist, and winked pleasantly on Miss Tomkins: the intensity of whose horror at his supposing it within the bounds of possibility that there could be any men on the premises of Westgate House Establishment for Young Ladies, it is impossible to describe.

Mr Pickwick's explanation having already been partially made, was soon concluded. But neither in the course of his walk home with his friends, nor afterwards when seated before a blazing fire at the supper he so much needed, could a single observation be drawn from him. He seemed bewildered and amazed. Once, and only once, he turned round to Mr Wardle, and said

'How did you come here?'

'Trundle and I came down here, for some good shooting on the first,' replied Wardle. 'We arrived to-night, and were astonished to hear from your servant that you were here too. But I am glad you are,' said the old fellow, slapping him on the back. 'I am glad you are. We shall have a jovial party on the first, and we'll give Winkle another chance – eh, old boy?'

Mr Pickwick made no reply; he did not even ask after his friends at Dingley Dell, and shortly afterwards retired for the night, desiring Sam to fetch his candle when he rung.

The bell did ring in due course, and Mr Weller presented himself.

'Sam,' said Mr Pickwick, looking out from under the bed-clothes.

'Sir,' said Mr Weller.

Mr Pickwick paused, and Mr Weller snuffed the candle.

'Sam,' said Mr Pickwick again, as if with a desperate effort.

'Sir,' said Mr Weller, once more.

'Where is that Trotter?'

'Job, sir?'

'Yes.'

'Gone, sir.'

'With his master, I suppose?'

'Friend or master, or whatever he is, he's gone with him,' replied Mr Weller. 'There's a pair on 'em, sir.'

'Jingle suspected my design, and set that fellow on you, with this story, I suppose?' said Mr Pickwick, half choking.

'Just that, sir,' replied Mr Weller.

'It was all false, of course?'

'All, sir,' replied Mr Weller. 'Reg'lar do, sir; artful dodge.'

'I don't think he'll escape us quite so easily the next time, Sam?' said Mr Pickwick.

'I don't think he will, sir.'

'Whenever I meet that Jingle again, wherever it is,' said Mr Pickwick, raising himself in bed, and indenting his pillow with a tremendous blow, 'I'll inflict personal chastisement on him, in addition to the exposure he so richly merits. I will, or my name is not Pickwick.'

'And wenever I catches hold o' that there melan-cholly chap with the black hair,' said Sam, 'if I don't bring some real water into his eyes, for once in a way, my name a'nt Weller. Good night, sir!'

CHAPTER 17

Showing that an Attack of Rheumatism, in some cases, acts as a Quickener to Inventive Genius

The constitution of Mr Pickwick, though able to sustain a very considerable amount of exertion and fatigue, was not proof against such a combination of attacks as he had undergone on the memorable night, recorded in the last chapter. The process of being washed in the night air, and rough-dried in a closet, is as dangerous as it is peculiar. Mr Pickwick was laid up with an attack of rheumatism.

But although the bodily powers of the great man were thus impaired, his mental energies retained their pristine vigour. His spirits were elastic; his good humour was restored. Even the vexation consequent upon his recent adventure had vanished from his mind; and he could join in the hearty laughter which any allusion to it excited in Mr Wardle, without anger and without embarrassment. Nay, more. During the two days Mr Pickwick was confined to his bed, Sam was his constant attendant. On the first, he endeavoured to amuse his master by anecdote and conversation; on the second, Mr Pickwick demanded his writing-desk, and pen and ink, and was deeply engaged during the whole day. On the third, being able to sit up in his bed-chamber, he despatched his valet with a message to Mr Wardle and Mr Trundle, intimating that if they would take their wine there, that evening, they would greatly oblige him. The invitation was most willingly accepted; and when they were seated over their wine, Mr Pickwick with sundry blushes, produced the following little tale, as having been 'edited' by himself, during his recent indisposition, from his notes of Mr Weller's unsophisticated recital.

THE PARISH CLERK
A Tale of True Love

'Once upon a time in a very small country town, at a considerable distance from London, there lived a little man named Nathaniel Pipkin, who was the parish clerk of the little town, and lived in a little house in the little High Street, within ten minutes' walk of the little church; and who was to be found every day from nine till four, teaching a little learning to the little boys. Nathaniel Pipkin was a harmless, inoffensive, good-natured being, with a turned-up nose, and rather turned-in legs: a cast in his eye,[1] and a halt in his gait; and he divided his time between the church and his school, verily believing that there existed not, on the face of the earth, so clever a man as the curate, so imposing an apartment as the vestry-room, or so well-ordered a seminary as his own. Once, and only once, in his life, Nathaniel Pipkin had seen a bishop – a real bishop, with his arms in lawn sleeves, and his head in a wig. He had seen him walk, and heard him talk, at a confirmation, on which momentous occasion Nathaniel Pipkin was so overcome with reverence and awe, when the aforesaid bishop laid his hand on his head, that he fainted right clean away, and was borne out of church in the arms of the beadle.

'This was a great event, a tremendous era, in Nathaniel Pipkin's life, and it was the only one that had ever occurred to ruffle the smooth current of his quiet existence, when happening one fine afternoon, in a fit of mental abstraction, to raise his eyes from the slate on which he was devising some tremendous problem in compound addition for an offending urchin to solve, they suddenly rested on the blooming countenance of Maria Lobbs, the only daughter of old Lobbs, the great saddler over the way. Now, the eyes of Mr Pipkin had rested on the pretty face of Maria Lobbs many a time and oft before, at church and elsewhere; but the eyes of Maria Lobbs had never looked so bright, the cheeks of Maria Lobbs had never looked so ruddy, as upon this particular occasion. No wonder then, that Nathaniel Pipkin was unable to take his eyes from the countenance of Miss Lobbs; no wonder that Miss Lobbs, finding herself stared at by a young man, withdrew her head from the window out of which she had been peeping, and shut the casement and pulled down the blind; no wonder that Nathaniel Pipkin, immediately thereafter, fell upon the young urchin who had previously offended, and cuffed and knocked him about, to his heart's content. All this was very natural, and there's nothing at all to wonder at about it.

'It *is* matter of wonder, though, that any one of Mr Nathaniel Pipkin's retiring disposition, nervous temperament, and most particularly diminutive income, should from this day forth, have dared to aspire to the hand and heart of the only daughter of the fiery old Lobbs – of old Lobbs the great saddler, who could have bought up the whole village at one stroke of his pen, and never felt the outlay – old Lobbs, who was well known to have heaps of money, invested in the bank at the nearest market town – old Lobbs, who was reported to have countless and inexhaustible treasures, hoarded up in the little iron safe with the big key-hole, over the chimney-piece in the back parlour – old Lobbs, who it was well known, on festive occasions garnished his board with a real silver tea-pot, cream ewer,[2] and sugar-basin, which he was wont, in the pride of his heart, to boast should be his daughter's property when she found a man to her mind. I repeat it, to be matter of profound astonishment and intense wonder, that Nathaniel Pipkin should have had the temerity to cast his eyes in this direction. But love is blind: and Nathaniel had a cast in his eye: and perhaps these two circumstances, taken together, prevented his seeing the matter in its proper light.

'Now, if old Lobbs had entertained the most remote or distant idea of the state of the affections of Nathaniel Pipkin, he would just have razed the school-room to the ground, or exterminated its master from the surface of the earth, or committed some other outrage and atrocity of an equally ferocious and violent description; for he was a terrible old fellow, was Lobbs, when his pride was injured, or his blood was up. Swear! Such trains of oaths would come rolling and pealing over the way, sometimes, when he was denouncing the idleness of the bony apprentice with the thin legs, that Nathaniel Pipkin would shake in his shoes with horror, and the hair of the pupils' heads would stand on end with fright.

'Well! Day after day, when school was over, and the pupils gone, did Nathaniel Pipkin sit himself down at the front window, and while he feigned to be reading a book, throw sidelong glances over the way in search of the bright eyes of Maria Lobbs; and he hadn't sat there many days, before the bright eyes appeared at an upper window, apparently deeply engaged in reading too. This was delightful, and gladdening to the heart of Nathaniel Pipkin. It was something to sit there for hours together, and look upon that pretty face when the eyes were cast down; but when Maria Lobbs began to raise her eyes from her book, and dart their rays in the direction of Nathaniel Pipkin, his delight and admiration were perfectly boundless. At last, one day when he knew old Lobbs was out, Nathaniel Pipkin had the temerity to kiss his hand to Maria Lobbs; and Maria Lobbs, instead of shutting the window, and pulling down the blind, kissed *hers* to him, and smiled. Upon which, Nathaniel Pipkin determined, that, come what might, he would develop the state of his feelings, without further delay.

'A prettier foot, a gayer heart, a more dimpled face, or a smarter form, never bounded so lightly over the earth they graced, as did those of Maria Lobbs, the old saddler's daughter. There was a roguish twinkle in her sparkling eyes, that would have made its way to far less susceptible bosoms than that of Nathaniel Pipkin; and there was such a joyous sound in her merry laugh, that the sternest misanthrope must have smiled to hear it. Even old Lobbs himself, in the very height of his ferocity, couldn't resist the coaxing of his pretty daughter; and when she, and her cousin Kate – an arch, impudent-looking, bewitching little person – made a dead set upon the old man together, as, to say the truth, they very often did, he could have refused them nothing, even had they asked for a portion of the countless and inexhaustible treasures, which were hidden from the light, in the iron safe.

'Nathaniel Pipkin's heart beat high within him, when he saw this enticing little couple some hundred yards before him one summer's evening, in the very field in which he had many a time strolled about till night-time, and pondered on the beauty of Maria Lobbs.

But though he had often thought then, how briskly he would walk up to Maria Lobbs and tell her of his passion if he could only meet her, he felt now that she was unexpectedly before him, all the blood in his body mounting to his face, manifestly to the great detriment of his legs, which, deprived of their usual portion, trembled beneath him. When they stopped to gather a hedge-flower, or listen to a bird, Nathaniel Pipkin stopped too, and pretended to be absorbed in meditation, as indeed he really was; for he was thinking what on earth he should ever do, when they turned back, as they inevitably must in time, and meet him face to face. But though he was afraid to make up to them, he couldn't bear to lose sight of them; so when they walked faster, he walked faster, when they lingered he lingered, and when they stopped he stopped; and so they might have gone on, until the darkness prevented them, if Kate had not looked slyly back, and encouragingly beckoned Nathaniel to advance. There was something in Kate's manner that was not to be resisted, and so Nathaniel Pipkin complied with the invitation; and after a great deal of blushing on his part, and immoderate laughter on that of the wicked little cousin, Nathaniel Pipkin went down on his knees on the dewy grass, and declared his resolution to remain there for ever, unless he were permitted to rise the accepted lover of Maria Lobbs. Upon this, the merry laughter of Maria Lobbs rang through the calm evening air – without seeming to disturb it, though; it had such a pleasant sound – and the wicked little cousin laughed more immoderately than before, and Nathaniel Pipkin blushed deeper than ever. At length, Maria Lobbs being more strenuously urged by the love-worn little man, turned away her head, and whispered her cousin to say, or at all events Kate *did* say, that she felt much honoured by Mr Pipkin's addresses; that her hand and heart were at her father's disposal; but that nobody could be insensible to Mr Pipkin's merits. As all this was said with much gravity, and as Nathaniel Pipkin walked home with Maria Lobbs, and struggled for a kiss at parting, he went to bed a happy man, and dreamed all night long, of softening old Lobbs, opening the strong box, and marrying Maria.

'The next day, Nathaniel Pipkin saw old Lobbs go out upon his old grey poney, and after a great many signs at the window from the wicked little cousin, the object and meaning of which he could by no means understand, the bony apprentice with the thin legs came over to say that his master wasn't coming home all night, and that the ladies expected Mr Pipkin to tea, at six o'clock precisely. How the lessons were got through that day, neither Nathaniel

Pipkin nor his pupils knew any more than you do; but they were got through somehow, and, after the boys had gone, Nathaniel Pipkin took till full six o'clock to dress himself to his satisfaction. Not that it took long to select the garments he should wear, inasmuch as he had no choice about the matter; but the putting of them on to the best advantage, and the touching of them up previously, was a task of no inconsiderable difficulty or importance.

'There was a very snug little party, consisting of Maria Lobbs and her cousin Kate, and three or four romping, good-humoured, rosy-cheeked girls. Nathaniel Pipkin had ocular demonstration of the fact, that the rumours of old Lobbs's treasures were not exaggerated. There were the real solid silver tea-pot, cream-ewer, and sugar-basin, on the table, and real silver spoons to stir the tea with, and real china cups to drink it out of, and plates of the same, to hold the cakes and toast in. The only eye-sore in the whole place, was another cousin of Maria Lobbs's, and a brother of Kate, whom Maria Lobbs's called "Henry," and who seemed to keep Maria Lobbs all to himself, up in one corner of the table. It's a delightful thing to see affection in families, but it may be carried rather too far, and Nathaniel Pipkin could not help thinking that Maria Lobbs must be very particularly fond of her relations, if she paid as much attention to all of them as to this individual cousin. After tea, too, when the wicked little cousin proposed a game at blind man's buff, it somehow or other happened that Nathaniel Pipkin was nearly always blind, and whenever he laid his hand upon the male cousin, he was sure to find that Maria Lobbs was not far off. And though the wicked little cousin and the other girls pinched him, and pulled his hair, and pushed chairs in his way, and all sorts of things, Maria Lobbs never seemed to come near him at all; and once – once – Nathaniel Pipkin could have sworn he heard the sound of a kiss, followed by a faint remonstrance from Maria Lobbs, and a half-suppressed laugh from her female friends. All this was odd – very odd – and there is no saying what Nathaniel Pipkin might or might not have done, in consequence, if his thoughts had not been suddenly directed into a new channel.

'The circumstances which directed his thoughts into a new channel was a loud knocking at the street-door, and the person who made this loud knocking at the street-door, was no other than old Lobbs himself, who had unexpectedly returned, and was hammering away, like a coffin-maker: for he wanted his supper. The alarming intelligence was no sooner communicated by the bony apprentice with the thin legs, than the girls tripped up-stairs to

Maria Lobbs's bed-room, and the male cousin and Nathaniel Pipkin were thrust into a couple of closets in the sitting-room, for want of any better places of concealment; and when Maria Lobbs and the wicked little cousin had stowed them away, and put the room to rights, they opened the street door to old Lobbs, who had never left off knocking since he first began.

'Now it did unfortunately happen that old Lobbs being very hungry was monstrous cross. Nathaniel Pipkin could hear him growling away like an old mastiff with a sore throat; and whenever the unfortunate apprentice with the thin legs came into the room, so surely did old Lobbs commence swearing at him in a most Saracenic[3] and ferocious manner, though apparently with no other end or object than that of easing his bosom by the discharge of a few superfluous oaths. At length some supper, which had been warming up, was placed on the table, and then old Lobbs fell to, in regular style; and having made clear work of it in no time, kissed his daughter, and demanded his pipe.

'Nature had placed Nathaniel Pipkin's knees in very close juxta-position, but when he heard old Lobbs demand his pipe, they knocked together, as if they were going to reduce each other to powder; for, depending from a couple of hooks, in the very closet in which he stood, was a large brown-stemmed, silver-bowled pipe, which pipe he himself had seen in the mouth of old Lobbs, regularly every afternoon and evening, for the last five years. The two girls went down-stairs for the pipe, and up-stairs for the pipe, and everywhere but where they knew the pipe was, and old Lobbs stormed away meanwhile, in the most wonderful manner. At last he thought of the closet, and walked up to it. It was of no use a little man like Nathaniel Pipkin pulling the door inwards, when a great strong fellow like old Lobbs was pulling it outwards. Old Lobbs gave it one tug, and open it flew, disclosing Nathaniel Pipkin standing bolt upright inside, and shaking with apprehension from head to foot. Bless us! what an appalling look old Lobbs gave him, as he dragged him out by the collar, and held him at arm's length.

'"Why, what the devil do you want here?" said old Lobbs, in a fearful voice.

'Nathaniel Pipkin could make no reply, so old Lobbs shook him backwards and forwards, for two or three minutes, by way of arranging his ideas for him.

'"What do you want here?" roared Lobbs, "I suppose *you* have come after my daughter, now?"

'Old Lobbs merely said this as a sneer: for he did not believe that mortal presumption could have carried Nathaniel Pipkin so far. What was his indignation, when that poor man replied:

'"Yes, I did, Mr Lobbs. I did come after your daughter. I love her, Mr Lobbs."

'"Why, you snivelling, wry-faced, puny villain," gasped old Lobbs, paralysed by the atrocious confession; "what do you mean by that? Say this to my face! Damme, I'll throttle you!"

'It is by no means improbable that old Lobbs would have carried this threat into execution, in the excess of his rage, if his arm had not been stayed by a very unexpected apparition, to wit, the male cousin, who, stepping out of his closet, and walking up to old Lobbs, said:

'"I cannot allow this harmless person, sir, who has been asked here, in some girlish frolic, to take upon himself, in a very noble manner, the fault (if fault it is) which I am guilty of, and am ready to avow. *I* love your daughter, sir; and *I* am here for the purpose of meeting her."

'Old Lobbs opened his eyes very wide at this, but not wider than Nathaniel Pipkin.

'"You did?" said Lobbs, at last finding breath to speak.

'"I did."

'"And I forbade you this house, long ago."

'"You did, or I should not have been here, clandestinely, to-night."

'I am sorry to record it, of old Lobbs, but I think he would have struck the cousin, if his pretty daughter, with her bright eyes swimming in tears, had not clung to his arm.

'"Don't stop him, Maria," said the young man: "if he has the will to strike me, let him. I would not hurt a hair of his grey head, for the riches of the world."

'The old man cast down his eyes at this reproof, and they met those of his daughter. I have hinted once or twice before, that they were very bright eyes, and, though they were tearful now, their influence was by no means lessened. Old Lobbs turned his head away, as if to avoid being persuaded by them, when, as fortune would have it, he encountered the face of the wicked little cousin, who, half afraid for her brother, and half laughing at Nathaniel Pipkin, presented as bewitching an expression of countenance, with a touch of shyness in it too, as any man, old or young, need look upon. She drew her arm coaxingly through the old man's, and whispered something in his ear; and do what he would, old Lobbs couldn't help breaking out into a smile, while a tear stole down his cheek at the same time.

'Five minutes after this, the girls were brought down from the bed-room with a great deal of giggling and modesty; and while the young people were making themselves perfectly happy, old Lobbs got down the pipe, and smoked it: and it was a remarkable circumstance about that particular pipe of tobacco, that it was the most soothing and delightful one he ever smoked.

'Nathaniel Pipkin thought it best to keep his own counsel, and by so doing gradually rose into high favour with old Lobbs, who taught him to smoke in time; and they used to sit out in the garden on the fine evenings, for many years afterwards, smoking and drinking in great state. He soon recovered the effects of his attachment, for we find his name in the parish register, as a witness to the marriage of Maria Lobbs to her cousin; and it also appears, by reference to other documents, that on the night of the wedding he was incarcerated in the village cage, for having, in a state of extreme intoxication, committed sundry excesses in the streets, in all of which he was aided and abetted by the bony apprentice with the thin legs.'

CHAPTER 18

Briefly illustrative of two Points; – first, the Power of Hysterics, and, secondly, the Force of Circumstances

For two days after the breakfast at Mrs Hunter's the Pickwickians remained at Eatanswill, anxiously awaiting the arrival of some intelligence from their revered leader. Mr Tupman and Mr Snodgrass were once again left to their own means of amusement; for Mr Winkle, in compliance with a most pressing invitation, continued to reside at Mr Pott's house, and to devote his time to the companionship of his amiable lady. Nor was the occasional society of Mr Pott himself, wanting to complete their felicity. Deeply immersed in the intensity of his speculations for the public weal and the destruction of the Independent, it was not the habit of that great man to descend from his mental pinnacle to the humble level of ordinary minds. On this occasion, however, and as if expressly in compliment to any follower of Mr Pickwick's, he unbent, relaxed, stepped down from his pedestal, and walked upon the ground:

benignly adapting his remarks to the comprehension of the herd, and seeming in outward form, if not in spirit, to be one of them.

Such having been the demeanour of this celebrated public character towards Mr Winkle, it will be readily imagined that considerable surprise was depicted on the countenance of the latter gentleman, when, as he was sitting alone in the breakfast-room, the door was hastily thrown open, and as hastily closed, on the entrance of Mr Pott, who, stalking majestically towards him, and thrusting aside his proffered hand, ground his teeth, as if to put a sharper edge on what he was about to utter, and exclaimed, in a saw-like voice, –

'Serpent!'

'Sir!' exclaimed Mr Winkle, starting from his chair.

'Serpent, sir,' repeated Mr Pott, raising his voice, and then suddenly depressing it; 'I said, Serpent, sir – make the most of it.'

When you have parted with a man, at two o'clock in the morning, on terms of the utmost good fellowship, and he meets you again, at half-past nine, and greets you as a serpent, it is not unreasonable to conclude that something of an unpleasant nature has occurred meanwhile. So Mr Winkle thought. He returned Mr Pott's gaze of stone, and in compliance with that gentleman's request, proceeded to make the most he could of the 'serpent.' The most, however, was nothing at all; so, after a profound silence of some minutes' duration, he said, –

'Serpent, sir! Serpent, Mr Pott! What can you mean, sir? – this is pleasantry.'

'Pleasantry, sir!' exclaimed Pott, with a motion of the hand, indicative of a strong desire to hurl the Britannia metal[1] tea-pot at the head of his visitor. 'Pleasantry, sir! – but no, I will be calm; I will be calm, sir;' in proof of his calmness, Mr Pott flung himself into a chair, and foamed at the mouth.

'My dear sir,' interposed Mr Winkle.

'*Dear* sir!' replied Pott. 'How dare you address me, as dear sir, sir? How dare you look me in the face and do it, sir?'

'Well, sir, if you come to that,' responded Mr Winkle, 'how dare you look *me* in the face, and call me a serpent, sir?'

'Because you are one,' replied Mr Pott.

'Prove it, sir,' said Mr Winkle, warmly. 'Prove it.'

A malignant scowl passed over the profound face of the editor, as he drew from his pocket, the Independent of that morning; and laying his finger on a particular paragraph, threw the journal across the table to Mr Winkle.

That gentleman took it up, and read as follows: –

'Our obscure and filthy contemporary, in some disgusting observations on the recent election for this borough, has presumed to violate the hallowed sanctity of private life, and to refer, in a manner not to be misunderstood, to the personal affairs of our late candidate – aye, and notwithstanding his base defeat, we will add, our future member, Mr Fizkin. What does our dastardly contemporary mean? What would the ruffian say, if we, setting at naught, like him, the decencies of social intercourse, were to raise the curtain which happily conceals HIS private life from general ridicule, not to say from general execration? What, if we were even to point out, and comment on, facts and circumstances, which are publicly notorious, and beheld by every one, but our mole-eyed contemporary – what if we were to print the following effusion, which we received while we were writing the commencement of this article, from a talented fellow-townsman and correspondent!

'"LINES TO A BRASS POT.
'"Oh Pott! if you'd known
How false she'd have grown,
When you heard the marriage bells tinkle;
You'd have done then, I vow,
What you cannot help now,
And handed her over to W * * * * *"'

'What,' said Mr Pott, solemnly: 'what rhymes to "tinkle," villain?'

'What rhymes to tinkle?' said Mrs Pott, whose entrance at the moment forestalled the reply. 'What rhymes to tinkle? Why Winkle, I should conceive:' saying this, Mrs Pott smiled sweetly on the disturbed Pickwickian, and extended her hand towards him. The agitated young man would have accepted it, in his confusion, had not Pott indignantly interposed.

'Back, ma'am – back!' said the editor. 'Take his hand before my very face!'

'Mr P.!' said his astonished lady.

'Wretched woman, look here,' exclaimed the husband. 'Look here, ma'am – "Lines to a brass Pot." "Brass pot;" – that's me, ma'am. "False *she*'d have grown;" – that's you, ma'am – you.' With this ebullition of rage, which was not unaccompanied with something like a tremble, at the expression of his wife's face, Mr Pott dashed the current number of the Eatanswill Independent at her feet.

'Upon my word, sir,' said the astonished Mrs Pott, stooping to pick up the paper. 'Upon my word, sir!'

Mr Pott winced beneath the contemptuous gaze of his wife. He had made a desperate struggle to screw up his courage, but it was fast coming unscrewed again.

There appears nothing very tremendous in this little sentence, 'Upon my word, sir,' when it comes to be read; but the tone of voice in which it was delivered, and the look that accompanied it, both seeming to bear reference to some revenge to be thereafter visited upon the head of Pott, produced their full effect upon him. The most unskilful observer could have detected in his troubled countenance, a readiness to resign his Wellington boots to any efficient substitute who would have consented to stand in them at that moment.

Mrs Pott read the paragraph, uttered a loud shriek, and threw herself at full length on the hearth-rug, screaming, and tapping it with the heels of her shoes, in a manner which could leave no doubt of the propriety of her feelings on the occasion.

'My dear,' said the petrified Pott, – 'I didn't say I believed it; – I—' but the unfortunate man's voice was drowned in the screaming of his partner.

'Mrs Pott, let me entreat you, my dear ma'am, to compose yourself,' said Mr Winkle; but the shrieks and tappings were louder, and more frequent than ever.

'My dear,' said Mr Pott, 'I'm very sorry. If you won't consider your own health, consider me, my dear. We shall have a crowd round the house.' But the more strenuously Mr Pott entreated, the more vehemently the screams poured forth.

Very fortunately, however, attached to Mrs Pott's person was a body-guard of one, a young lady whose ostensible employment was to preside over her toilet, but who rendered herself useful in a variety of ways, and in none more so than in the particular department of constantly aiding and abetting her mistress in every wish and inclination opposed to the desires of the unhappy Pott. The screams reached this young lady's ears in due course, and brought her into the room with a speed which threatened to derange, materially, the very exquisite arrangement of her cap and ringlets.

'Oh, my dear, dear mistress!' exclaimed the body-guard, kneeling frantically by the side of the prostrate Mrs Pott. 'Oh, my dear mistress, what is the matter?'

'Your master – your brutal master,' murmured the patient.

Pott was evidently giving way.

'It's a shame,' said the body-guard, reproachfully. 'I know he'll be the death of you, ma'am. Poor dear thing!'

He gave way more. The opposite party followed up the attack.

'Oh don't leave me – don't leave me, Goodwin,' murmured Mrs Pott, clutching at the wrist of the said Goodwin with an hysteric jerk. 'You're the only person that's kind to me, Goodwin.'

At this affecting appeal, Goodwin got up a little domestic tragedy of her own, and shed tears copiously.

'Never, ma'am – never,' said Goodwin. 'Oh, sir, you should be careful – you should indeed; you don't know what harm you may do missis; you'll be sorry for it one day, I know – I've always said so.'

The unlucky Pott looked timidly on, but said nothing.

'Goodwin,' said Mrs Pott, in a soft voice.

'Ma'am,' said Goodwin.

'If you only knew how I have loved that man—'

'Don't distress yourself by recollecting it, ma'am,' said the body-guard.

Pott looked very frightened. It was time to finish him.

'And now,' sobbed Mrs Pott, 'now, after all, to be treated in this way; to be reproached and insulted in the presence of a third party, and that party almost a stranger. But I will not submit to it! Goodwin,' continued Mrs Pott, raising herself in the arms of her attendant, 'my brother, the Lieutenant, shall interfere. I'll be separated, Goodwin!'

'It would certainly serve him right, ma'am,' said Goodwin.

Whatever thoughts the threat of a separation might have awakened in Mr Pott's mind, he forebore to give utterance to them, and contented himself by saying, with great humility:

'My dear, will you hear me?'

A fresh train of sobs was the only reply, as Mrs Pott grew more hysterical, requested to be informed why she was ever born, and required sundry other pieces of information of a similar description.

'My dear,' remonstrated Mr Pott, 'do not give way to these sensitive feelings. I never believed that the paragraph had any foundation, my dear – impossible. I was only angry, my dear – I may say outrageous – with the Independent people for daring to insert it; that's all:' Mr Pott cast an imploring look at the innocent cause of the mischief, as if to entreat him to say nothing about the serpent.

'And what steps, sir, do you mean to take to obtain redress?' inquired Mr Winkle, gaining courage as he saw Pott losing it.

'Oh, Goodwin,' observed Mrs Pott, 'does he mean to horsewhip the editor of the Independent – does he, Goodwin?'

'Hush, hush, ma'am; pray keep yourself quiet,' replied the body-guard. 'I dare say he will, if you wish it, ma'am.'

'Certainly,' said Pott, as his wife evinced decided symptoms of going off again. 'Of course I shall.'

'When, Goodwin – when?' said Mrs Pott, still undecided about the going off.

'Immediately, of course,' said Mr Pott; 'before the day is out.'

'Oh, Goodwin,' resumed Mrs Pott, 'it's the only way of meeting the slander, and setting me right with the world.'

'Certainly, ma'am,' replied Goodwin. 'No man as is a man, ma'am, could refuse to do it.'

So, as the hysterics were still hovering about, Mr Pott said once more that he would do it; but Mrs Pott was so overcome at the bare idea of having ever been suspected, that she was half-a-dozen times on the very verge of a relapse, and most unquestionably would have gone off, had it not been for the indefatigable efforts of the assiduous Goodwin, and repeated entreaties for pardon from the conquered Pott; and finally, when that unhappy individual had been frightened and snubbed down to his proper level, Mrs Pott recovered, and they went to breakfast.

'You will not allow this base newspaper slander to shorten your stay here, Mr Winkle?' said Mrs Pott, smiling through the traces of her tears.

'I hope not,' said Mr Pott, actuated, as he spoke, by a wish that his visitor would choke himself with the morsel of dry toast which he was raising to his lips at the moment: and so terminate his stay effectually.

'I hope not.'

'You are very good,' said Mr Winkle; 'but a letter has been received from Mr Pickwick – so I learn by a note from Mr Tupman, which was brought up to my bed-room door, this morning – in which he requests us to join him at Bury today; and we are to leave by the coach at noon.'

'But you will come back?' said Mrs Pott.

'Oh, certainly,' replied Mr Winkle.

'You are quite sure?' said Mrs Pott, stealing a tender look at her visitor.

'Quite,' responded Mr Winkle.

The breakfast passed off in silence, for each member of the party was brooding over his, or her, own personal grievances. Mrs Pott was regretting the loss of a beau; Mr Pott his rash pledge to horsewhip the Independent; Mr Winkle his having innocently placed himself in so awkward a situation. Noon approached, and after many adieux and promises to return, he tore himself away.

'If he ever comes back, I'll poison him,' thought Mr Pott, as he turned into the little back office where he prepared his thunderbolts.

'If I ever do come back, and mix myself up with these people again,' thought Mr Winkle, as he wended his way to the Peacock, 'I shall deserve to be horse-whipped myself – that's all.'

His friends were ready, the coach was nearly so, and in half-an-hour they were proceeding on their journey, along the road over which Mr Pickwick and Sam had so recently travelled, and of which, as we have already said something, we do not feel called upon to extract Mr Snodgrass's poetical and beautiful description.

Mr Weller was standing at the door of the Angel, ready to receive them, and by that gentleman they were ushered to the apartment of Mr Pickwick, where, to the no small surprise of Mr Winkle and Mr Snodgrass, and the no small embarrassment of Mr Tupman, they found old Wardle and Trundle.

'How are you?' said the old man, grasping Mr Tupman's hand. 'Don't hang back, or look sentimental about it; it can't be helped, old fellow. For her sake, I wish you'd had her; for your own, I'm very glad you have not. A young fellow like you will do better one of these days – eh?' With this consolation, Wardle slapped Mr Tupman on the back, and laughed heartily.

'Well, and how are you, my fine fellows?' said the old gentleman, shaking hands with Mr Winkle and Mr Snodgrass at the same time. 'I have just been telling Pickwick that we must have you all down at Christmas. We're going to have a wedding – a real wedding this time.'

'A wedding!' exclaimed Mr Snodgrass, turning very pale.

'Yes, a wedding. But don't be frightened,' said the good-humoured old man; 'it's only Trundle there, and Bella.'

'Oh, is that all!' said Mr Snodgrass, relieved from a painful doubt which had fallen heavily on his breast. 'Give you joy, sir. How is Joe?'

'Very well,' replied the old gentleman. 'Sleepy as ever.'

'And your mother, and the clergyman, and all of 'em?'

'Quite well.'

'Where,' said Mr Tupman, with an effort – 'where is – *she*, sir?' and he turned away his head, and covered his eyes with his hand.

'*She*!' said the old gentleman, with a knowing shake of the head. 'Do you mean my single relative – eh?'

Mr Tupman, by a nod, intimated that his question applied to the disappointed Rachael.

'Oh, she's gone away,' said the old gentleman. 'She's living at a relation's, far enough off. She couldn't bear to see the girls, so I let her go. But come! Here's the dinner. You must be hungry after your ride. *I* am, without any ride at all; so let us fall to.'

Ample justice was done to the meal; and when they were seated round the table, after it had been disposed of, Mr Pickwick, to the intense horror and indignation of his followers, related the adventure he had undergone, and the success which had attended the base artifices of the diabolical Jingle.

'And the attack of rheumatism which I caught in that garden,' said Mr Pickwick, in conclusion, 'renders me lame at this moment.'

'I, too, have had something of an adventure,' said Mr Winkle, with a smile; and at the request of Mr Pickwick he detailed the malicious libel of the Eatanswill Independent, and the consequent excitement of their friend, the editor.

Mr Pickwick's brow darkened during the recital. His friends observed it, and, when Mr Winkle had concluded, maintained a profound silence. Mr Pickwick struck the table emphatically with his clenched fist, and spoke as follows:

'Is it not a wonderful circumstance,' said Mr Pickwick, 'that we seem destined to enter no man's house without involving him in some degree of trouble? Does it not, I ask, bespeak the indiscretion, or, worse than that, the blackness of heart – that I should say so! – of my followers, that, beneath whatever roof they locate, they disturb the peace of mind and happiness of some confiding female? Is it not, I say—'

Mr Pickwick would in all probability have gone on for some time, had not the entrance of Sam, with a letter, caused him to break off in his eloquent discourse. He passed his handkerchief across his forehead, took off his spectacles, wiped them, and put them on again; and his voice had recovered its wonted softness of tone when he said:

'What have you there, Sam?'

'Called at the Post-office just now, and found this here letter, as has laid there for two days,' replied Mr Weller. 'It's sealed with a vafer, and directed in round hand.'

'I don't know this hand,' said Mr Pickwick, opening the letter. 'Mercy on us! what's this? It must be a jest; it – it – can't be true.'

'What's the matter?' was the general inquiry.

'Nobody dead, is there?' said Wardle, alarmed at the horror in Mr Pickwick's countenance.

Mr Pickwick made no reply, but, pushing the letter across the table, and desiring Mr Tupman to read it aloud, fell back in his chair with a look of vacant astonishment quite alarming to behold.

Mr Tupman, with a trembling voice, read the letter, of which the following is a copy: –

Freeman's Court, Cornhill, August 28th, 1830.[2]
Bardell against Pickwick.

   Sir,
Having been instructed by Mrs Martha Bardell to commence
an action against you for a breach of promise of marriage, for
which the plaintiff lays her damages at fifteen hundred pounds,
we beg to inform you that a writ has been issued against you
in this suit in the Court of Common Pleas;[3] *and request to*
know, by return of post, the name of your attorney in London,
who will accept service thereof.
                        We are, Sir,
                            Your obedient servants,
                                Dodson and Fogg.
   Mr. Samuel Pickwick.

There was something so impressive in the mute astonishment with which each man regarded his neighbour, and every man regarded Mr Pickwick, that all seemed afraid to speak. The silence was at length broken by Mr Tupman.

'Dodson and Fogg,' he repeated mechanically.

'Bardell and Pickwick,' said Mr Snodgrass, musing.

'Peace of mind and happiness of confiding females,' murmured Mr Winkle, with an air of abstraction.

'It's a conspiracy,' said Mr Pickwick, at length recovering the power of speech; 'a base conspiracy between these two grasping attorneys, Dodson and Fogg. Mrs Bardell would never do it; – she hasn't the heart to do it; – she hasn't the case to do it. Ridiculous – ridiculous.'

'Of her heart,' said Wardle, with a smile, 'you should certainly be the best judge. I don't wish to discourage you, but I should certainly say that, of her case, Dodson and Fogg are far better judges than any of us can be.'

'It's a vile attempt to extort money,' said Mr Pickwick.

'I hope it is,' said Wardle, with a short, dry cough.

'Who ever heard me address her in any way but that in which a lodger would address his landlady?' continued Mr Pickwick, with great vehemence. 'Who ever saw me with her? Not even my friends here—'

'Except on one occasion,' said Mr Tupman.

Mr Pickwick changed colour.

'Ah,' said Mr Wardle. 'Well, that's important. There was nothing suspicious then, I suppose?'

Mr Tupman glanced timidly at his leader. 'Why,' said he, 'there was nothing suspicious; but – I don't know how it happened, mind – she certainly was reclining in his arms.'

'Gracious powers!' ejaculated Mr Pickwick, as the recollection of the scene in question struck forcibly upon him; 'what a dreadful instance of the force of circumstances! So she was – so she was.'

'And our friend was soothing her anguish,' said Mr Winkle, rather maliciously.

'So I was,' said Mr Pickwick. 'I won't deny it. So I was.'

'Hallo!' said Wardle; 'for a case in which there's nothing suspicious, this looks rather queer – eh, Pickwick? Ah, sly dog – sly dog!' and he laughed till the glasses on the side-board rang again.

'What a dreadful conjunction of appearances!' exclaimed Mr Pickwick, resting his chin upon his hands. 'Winkle – Tupman – I beg your pardon for the observations I made just now. We are all the victims of circumstances, and I the greatest.' With this apology Mr Pickwick buried his head in his hands, and ruminated; while Wardle measured out a regular circle of nods and winks, addressed to the other members of the company.

'I'll have it explained, though,' said Mr Pickwick, raising his head and hammering the table. 'I'll see this Dodson and Fogg! I'll go to London to-morrow.'

'Not to-morrow,' said Wardle; 'you're too lame.'

'Well, then, next day.'

'Next day is the first of September, and you're pledged to ride out with us, as far as Sir Geoffrey Manning's grounds, at all events, and to meet us at lunch, if you don't take the field.'

'Well, then, the day after,' said Mr Pickwick; 'Thursday. – Sam!'

'Sir,' replied Mr Weller.

'Take two places outside to London, on Thursday morning, for yourself and me.'

'Wery well, sir.'

Mr Weller left the room, and departed slowly on his errand, with his hands in his pocket, and his eyes fixed on the ground.

'Rum feller, the hemperor,' said Mr Weller, as he walked slowly up the street. 'Think o' his making up to that ere Mrs Bardell – vith a little boy, too! Always the vay vith these here old 'uns hows'ever, as is such steady goers to look at. I didn't think he'd ha' done it, though – I didn't think he'd ha' done it!' Moralising in this strain, Mr Samuel Weller bent his steps towards the booking-office.

CHAPTER 19

A pleasant Day, with an unpleasant Termination

The birds, who, happily for their own peace of mind and personal comfort, were in blissful ignorance of the preparations which had been making to astonish them, on the first of September, hailed it no doubt, as one of the pleasantest mornings they had seen that season. Many a young partridge who strutted complacently among the stubble, with all the finicking coxcombry of youth, and many an older one who watched his levity out of his little round eye, with the contemptuous air of a bird of wisdom and experience, alike unconscious of their approaching doom, basked in the fresh morning air with lively and blithesome feelings, and a few hours afterwards were laid low upon the earth. But we grow affecting: let us proceed.

In plain common-place matter-of-fact, then, it was a fine morning – so fine that you would scarcely have believed that the few months of an English summer had yet flown by. Hedges, fields, and trees, hill and moorland, presented to the eye their ever-varying shades of deep rich green; scarce a leaf had fallen, scarce a sprinkle of yellow mingled with the hues of summer, warned you that autumn had begun. The sky was cloudless; the sun shone out bright and warm; the songs of birds, and hum of myriads of summer insects, filled the air; and the cottage gardens, crowded with flowers of every rich and beautiful tint, sparkled, in the heavy dew, like beds of glittering jewels. Everything bore the stamp of summer, and none of its beautiful colours had yet faded from the die.

Such was the morning, when an open carriage, in which were three Pickwickians, (Mr Snodgrass having preferred to remain at home,) Mr Wardle, and Mr Trundle, with Sam Weller on the box beside the driver, pulled up by a gate at the road-side, before which stood a tall, raw-boned gamekeeper, and a half-booted, leather-legginned boy: each bearing a bag of capacious dimensions, and accompanied by a brace of pointers.

'I say,' whispered Mr Winkle to Wardle, as the man let down the steps, 'they don't suppose we're going to kill game enough to fill those bags, do they?'

'Fill them!' exclaimed old Wardle. 'Bless you, yes! You shall fill one, and I the other; and when we've done with them, the pockets of our shooting-jackets will hold as much more.'

Mr Winkle dismounted without saying anything in reply to this observation; but he thought within himself, that if the party remained in the open air, until he had filled one of the bags, they stood a considerable chance of catching colds in their heads.

'Hi, Juno, lass – hi, old girl; down, Daph, down,' said Wardle, caressing the dogs. 'Sir Geoffrey still in Scotland, of course, Martin?'

The tall gamekeeper replied in the affirmative, and looked with some surprise from Mr Winkle, who was holding his gun as if he wished his coat pocket to save him the trouble of pulling the trigger, to Mr Tupman, who was holding his as if he were afraid of it – as there is no earthly reason to doubt he really was.

'My friends are not much in the way of this sort of thing yet, Martin,' said Wardle, noticing the look. 'Live and learn, you know. They'll be good shots one of these days. I beg my friend Winkle's pardon, though; he has had some practice.'

Mr Winkle smiled feebly over his blue neckerchief in acknowledgment of the compliment, and got himself so mysteriously entangled with his gun, in his modest confusion, that if the piece had been loaded, he must inevitably have shot himself dead upon the spot.

'You mustn't handle your piece in that ere way, when you come to have the charge in it, sir,' said the tall gamekeeper, gruffly, 'or I'm damned if you won't make cold meat of some on us.'

Mr Winkle, thus admonished, abruptly altered its position, and in so doing, contrived to bring the barrel into pretty sharp contact with Mr Weller's head.

'Hallo!' said Sam, picking up his hat, which had been knocked off, and rubbing his temple. 'Hallo, sir! if you comes it this vay, you'll fill one o' them bags, and something to spare, at one fire.'

Here the leather-leggined boy laughed very heartily, and then tried to look as if it was somebody else, whereat Mr Winkle frowned majestically.

'Where did you tell the boy to meet us with the snack, Martin?' inquired Wardle.

'Side of One-tree Hill, at twelve o'clock, sir.'

'That's not Sir Geoffrey's land, is it?'

'No, sir; but it's close by it. It's Captain Boldwig's land; but there'll be nobody to interrupt us, and there's a fine bit of turf there.'

'Very well,' said old Wardle. 'Now the sooner we're off the better. Will you join us at twelve, then, Pickwick?'

Mr Pickwick was particularly desirous to view the sport, the more especially as he was rather anxious in respect of Mr Winkle's life and limbs. On so inviting a morning, too, it was very tantalising to turn back, and leave his friends to enjoy themselves. It was, therefore, with a very rueful air that he replied,

'Why, I suppose I must.'

'An't the gentleman a shot, sir?' inquired the long gamekeeper.

'No,' replied Wardle; 'and he's lame besides.'

'I should very much like to go,' said Mr Pickwick, 'very much.'

There was a short pause of commiseration.

'There's a barrow t'other side the hedge,' said the boy. 'If the gentleman's servant would wheel along the paths, he could keep nigh us, and we could lift it over the stiles, and that.'

'The wery thing,' said Mr Weller, who was a party interested, inasmuch as he ardently longed to see the sport. 'The wery thing. Well said, Smallcheck; I'll have it out in a minute.'

But here a difficulty arose. The long gamekeeper resolutely protested against the introduction into a shooting party, of a gentleman in a barrow, as a gross violation of all established rules and precedents.

It was a great objection, but not an insurmountable one. The gamekeeper having been coaxed and feed, and having, moreover, eased his mind by 'punching' the head of the inventive youth who had first suggested the use of the machine, Mr Pickwick was placed in it, and off the party set; Wardle and the long gamekeeper leading the way, and Mr Pickwick in the barrow, propelled by Sam, bringing up the rear.

'Stop, Sam,' said Mr Pickwick, when they had got half across the first field.

'What's the matter now?' said Wardle.

'I won't suffer this barrow to be moved another step,' said Mr

Pickwick, resolutely, 'unless Winkle carries that gun of his, in a different manner.'

'How *am* I to carry it?' said the wretched Winkle.

'Carry it with the muzzle to the ground,' replied Mr Pickwick.

'It's so unsportsman-like,' reasoned Winkle.

'I don't care whether it's unsportsman-like or not,' replied Mr Pickwick; 'I am not going to be shot in a wheelbarrow, for the sake of appearances, to please anybody.'

'I know the gentleman 'll put that ere charge into somebody afore he's done,' growled the long man.

'Well, well – I don't mind,' said poor Winkle, turning his gun-stock uppermost; – 'there.'

'Anythin' for a quiet life,' said Mr Weller; and on they went again.

'Stop!' said Mr Pickwick, after they had gone a few yards further.

'What now?' said Wardle.

'That gun of Tupman's is not safe: I know it isn't,' said Mr Pickwick.

'Eh? What! not safe?' said Mr Tupman, in a tone of great alarm.

'Not as you are carrying it,' said Mr Pickwick. 'I am very sorry to make any further objection, but I cannot consent to go on, unless you carry it as Winkle does his.'

'I think you had better, sir,' said the long gamekeeper, 'or you're quite as likely to lodge the charge in yourself as in anything else.'

Mr Tupman, with the most obliging haste, placed his piece in the position required, and the party moved on again; the two amateurs marching with reversed arms, like a couple of privates at a royal funeral.

The dogs suddenly came to a dead stop, and the party advancing stealthily a single pace, stopped too.

'What's the matter with the dogs' legs?' whispered Mr Winkle. 'How queer they're standing.'

'Hush, can't you?' replied Wardle, softly. 'Don't you see, they're making a point?'[1]

'Making a point!' said Mr Winkle, staring about him, as if he expected to discover some particular beauty in the landscape, which the sagacious animals were calling special attention to. 'Making a point! What are they pointing at?'

'Keep your eyes open,' said Wardle, not heeding the question in the excitement of the moment. 'Now then.'

There was a sharp whirring noise, that made Mr Winkle start back as if he had been shot himself. Bang, bang, went a couple of guns; – the smoke swept quickly away over the field, and curled into the air.

'Where are they?' said Mr Winkle, in a state of the highest excitement, turning round and round in all directions. 'Where are they? Tell me when to fire. Where are they – where are they?'

'Where are they?' said Wardle, taking up a brace of birds which the dogs had deposited at his feet. 'Why, here they are.'

'No, no; I mean the others,' said the bewildered Winkle.

'Far enough off, by this time,' replied Wardle, coolly reloading his gun.

'We shall very likely be up with another covey in five minutes,' said the long gamekeeper. 'If the gentleman begins to fire now, perhaps he'll just get the shot out of the barrel by the time they rise.'

'Ha! ha! ha!' roared Mr Weller.

'Sam,' said Mr Pickwick, compassionating his follower's confusion and embarrassment.

'Sir.'

'Don't laugh.'

'Certainly not, sir.' So, by way of indemnification, Mr Weller contorted his features from behind the wheelbarrow, for the exclusive amusement of the boy with the leggings, who thereupon burst into a boisterous laugh, and was summarily cuffed by the long gamekeeper, who wanted a pretext for turning round, to hide his own merriment.

'Bravo, old fellow!' said Wardle to Mr Tupman; 'you fired that time, at all events.'

'Oh yes,' replied Mr Tupman, with conscious pride. 'I let it off.'

'Well done. You'll hit something next time, if you look sharp. Very easy, ain't it?'

'Yes, it's very easy,' said Mr Tupman. 'How it hurts one's shoulder, though. It nearly knocked me backwards. I had no idea these small fire-arms kicked so.'

'Ah,' said the old gentleman, smiling; 'you'll get used to it in time. Now then – all ready – all right with the barrow there?'

'All right, sir,' replied Mr Weller.

'Come along then.'

'Hold hard, sir,' said Sam, raising the barrow.

'Aye, aye,' replied Mr Pickwick; and on they went, as briskly as need be.

'Keep that barrow back now,' cried Wardle when it had been

hoisted over a stile into another field, and Mr Pickwick had been deposited in it once more.

'All right, sir,' replied Mr Weller, pausing.

'Now, Winkle,' said the old gentleman, 'follow me softly, and don't be too late this time.'

'Never fear,' said Mr Winkle. 'Are they pointing?'

'No, no; not now. Quietly now, quietly.' On they crept, and very quietly they would have advanced, if Mr Winkle, in the performance of some very intricate evolutions with his gun, had not accidentally fired, at the most critical moment, over the boy's head, exactly in the very spot where the tall man's brain would have been, had he been there instead.

'Why, what on earth did you do that for?' said old Wardle, as the birds flew unharmed away.

'I never saw such a gun in my life,' replied poor Mr Winkle, looking at the lock, as if that would do any good. 'It goes off of its own accord. It *will* do it.'

'Will do it!' echoed Wardle, with something of irritation in his manner. 'I wish it would kill something of its own accord.'

'It'll do that afore long, sir,' observed the tall man, in a low, prophetic voice.

'What do you mean by that observation, sir?' inquired Mr Winkle, angrily.

'Never mind, sir, never mind,' replied the long gamekeeper; 'I've no family myself, sir; and this here boy's mother will get something handsome from Sir Geoffrey, if he's killed on his land. Load, again, sir, load again.'

'Take away his gun,' cried Mr Pickwick from the barrow, horror-stricken at the long man's dark insinuations. 'Take away his gun, do you hear, somebody?'

Nobody, however, volunteered to obey the command; and Mr Winkle, after darting a rebellious glance at Mr Pickwick, reloaded his gun, and proceeded onwards with the rest.

We are bound, on the authority of Mr Pickwick, to state, that Mr Tupman's mode of proceeding evinced far more of prudence and deliberation, than that adopted by Mr Winkle. Still, this by no means detracts from the great authority of the latter gentleman, on all matters connected with the field; because, as Mr Pickwick beautifully observes, it has somehow or other happened, from time immemorial, that many of the best and ablest philosophers, who have been perfect lights of science in matters of theory, have been wholly unable to reduce them to practice.

Mr Tupman's process, like many of our most sublime discoveries, was extremely simple. With the quickness and penetration of a man of genius, he had at once observed that the two great points to be attained were – first, to discharge his piece without injury to himself, and, secondly, to do so, without danger to the by-standers; – obviously, the best thing to do, after surmounting the difficulty of firing at all, was to shut his eyes firmly, and fire into the air.

On one occasion, after performing this feat, Mr Tupman, on opening his eyes, beheld a plump partridge in the act of falling wounded to the ground. He was on the point of congratulating Mr Wardle on his invariable success, when that gentleman advanced towards him, and grasped him warmly by the hand.

'Tupman,' said the old gentleman, 'you singled out that particular bird?'

'No,' said Mr Tupman – 'no.'

'You did,' said Wardle. 'I saw you do it – I observed you pick him out – I noticed you, as you raised your piece to take aim; and I will say this, that the best shot in existence could not have done it more beautifully. You are an older hand at this, than I thought you, Tupman; you have been out before.'

It was in vain for Mr Tupman to protest, with a smile of self-denial that he never had. The very smile was taken as evidence to the contrary; and from that time forth, his reputation was established. It is not the only reputation that has been acquired as easily, nor are such fortunate circumstances confined to partridge-shooting.

Meanwhile, Mr Winkle flashed, and blazed, and smoked away, without producing any material results worthy of being noted down; sometimes expending his charge in mid-air, and at others sending it skimming along so near the surface of the ground as to place the lives of the two dogs on a rather uncertain and precarious tenure. As a display of fancy shooting, it was extremely varied and curious; as an exhibition of firing with any precise object, it was, upon the whole, perhaps a failure. It is an established axiom, that 'every bullet has its billet.' If it apply in an equal degree to shot, those of Mr Winkle were unfortunate foundlings, deprived of their natural rights, cast loose upon the world, and billeted nowhere.

'Well,' said Wardle, walking up to the side of the barrow, and wiping the streams of perspiration from his jolly red face; 'smoking day, isn't it?'

'It is, indeed,' replied Mr Pickwick. 'The sun is tremendously hot, even to me. I don't know how you must feel it.'

'Why,' said the old gentleman, 'pretty hot. It's past twelve, though. You see that green hill there?'

'Certainly.'

'That's the place where we are to lunch; and, by Jove, there's the boy with the basket, punctual as clockwork!'

'So he is,' said Mr Pickwick, brightening up. 'Good boy, that. I'll give him a shilling, presently. Now, then, Sam, wheel away.'

'Hold on, sir,' said Mr Weller, invigorated with the prospect of refreshments. 'Out of the vay, young leathers. If you walley my precious life don't upset me, as the gen'l'm'n said to the driver when they was a carryin' him to Tyburn.'² And quickening his pace to a sharp run, Mr Weller wheeled his master nimbly to the green hill, shot him dexterously out by the very side of the basket, and proceeded to unpack it with the utmost dispatch.

'Weal pie,' said Mr Weller, soliloquising, as he arranged the eatables on the grass. 'Wery good thing is weal pie, when you know the lady as made it, and is quite sure it an't kittens; and arter all though, where's the odds, when they're so like weal that the wery piemen themselves don't know the difference?'

'Don't they, Sam?' said Mr Pickwick.

'Not they, sir,' replied Mr Weller, touching his hat. 'I lodged in the same house vith a pieman once, sir, and a wery nice man he was – reg'lar clever chap, too – make pies out o' anything, he could. "What a number o' cats you keep, Mr Brooks," says I, when I'd got intimate with him. "Ah," says he, "I do – a good many," says he. "You must be wery fond o' cats," says I. "Other people is," says he, a winkin' at me; "they an't in season till the winter though," says he. "Not in season!" says I. "No," says he, "fruits is in, cats is out." "Why, what do you mean?" says I. "Mean?" says he. "That I'll never be a party to the combination o' the butchers, to keep up the prices o' meat," says he. "Mr Weller," says he, a squeezing my hand wery hard, and vispering in my ear – "don't mention this here agin – but it's the seasonin' as does it. They're all made o' them noble animals," says he, a pointin' to a wery nice little tabby kitten, "and I seasons 'em for beefsteak, weal, or kidney, 'cordin to the demand. And more than that," says he, "I can make a weal a beef-steak, or a beef-steak a kidney, or any one on 'em a mutton, at a minute's notice, just as the market changes, and appetites wary!"'

'He must have been a very ingenious young man, that, Sam,' said Mr Pickwick, with a slight shudder.

'Just was, sir,' replied Mr Weller, continuing his occupation of emptying the basket, 'and the pies was beautiful. Tongue; well that's a wery good thing when it an't a woman's. Bread – knuckle o' ham, reg'lar picter – cold beef in slices, wery good. What's in them stone jars, young touch-and-go?'

'Beer in this one,' replied the boy, taking from his shoulder a couple of large stone bottles, fastened together by a leathern strap – 'cold punch in t'other.'

'And a wery good notion of a lunch it is, take it altogether,' said Mr Weller, surveying his arrangement of the repast with great satisfaction. 'Now, gen'l'm'n, "fall on," as the English said to the French when they fixed bagginets.'

It needed no second invitation to induce the party to yield full justice to the meal; and as little pressing did it require to induce Mr Weller, the long game-keeper, and the two boys, to station themselves on the grass, at a little distance, and do good execution upon a decent proportion of the viands. An old oak afforded a pleasant shelter to the group, and a rich prospect of arable and meadow land, intersected with luxuriant hedges, and richly ornamented with wood, lay spread out below them.

'This is delightful – thoroughly delightful!' said Mr Pickwick, the skin of whose expressive countenance was rapidly peeling off, with exposure to the sun.

'So it is: so it is, old fellow,' replied Wardle. 'Come; a glass of punch!'

'With great pleasure,' said Mr Pickwick; the satisfaction of whose countenance, after drinking it, bore testimony to the sincerity of the reply.

'Good,' said Mr Pickwick, smacking his lips. 'Very good. I'll take another. Cool; very cool. Come, gentlemen,' continued Mr Pickwick, still retaining his hold upon the jar, 'a toast. Our friends at Dingley Dell.'

The toast was drunk with loud acclamations.

'I'll tell you what I shall do, to get up my shooting again,' said Mr Winkle, who was eating bread and ham with a pocket-knife. 'I'll put a stuffed partridge on the top of a post, and practise at it, beginning at a short distance, and lengthening it by degrees. I understand it's capital practice.'

'I know a gen'l'man, sir,' said Mr Weller, 'as did that, and begun at two yards; but he never tried it on agin; for he blowed the bird right clean away at the first fire, and nobody ever seed a feather on him arterwards.'

'Sam,' said Mr Pickwick.

'Sir,' replied Mr Weller.

'Have the goodness to reserve your anecdotes till they are called for.'

'Cert'nly, sir.'

Here Mr Weller winked the eye which was not concealed by the beer-can he was raising to his lips with such exquisiteness, that the two boys went into spontaneous convulsions, and even the long man condescended to smile.

'Well, that certainly is most capital cold punch,' said Mr Pickwick, looking earnestly at the stone bottle; 'and the day is extremely warm, and – Tupman, my dear friend, a glass of punch?'

'With the greatest delight,' replied Mr Tupman; and having drank that glass, Mr Pickwick took another, just to see whether there was any orange peel in the punch, because orange peel always disagreed with him; and finding that there was not, Mr Pickwick took another glass to the health of their absent friend, and then felt himself imperatively called upon to propose another in honour of the punch-compounder, unknown.

This constant succession of glasses produced considerable effect upon Mr Pickwick; his countenance beamed with the most sunny smiles, laughter played around his lips, and good-humoured merriment twinkled in his eye. Yielding by degrees to the influence of the exciting liquid, rendered more so by the heat, Mr Pickwick expressed a strong desire to recollect a song which he had heard in his infancy, and the attempt proving abortive, sought to stimulate his memory with more glasses of punch, which appeared to have quite a contrary effect; for, from forgetting the words of the song, he began to forget how to articulate any words at all; and finally, after rising to his legs to address the company in an eloquent speech, he fell into the barrow, and fast asleep, simultaneously.

The basket having been repacked, and it being found perfectly impossible to awaken Mr Pickwick from his torpor, some discussion took place whether it would be better for Mr Weller to wheel his master back again, or to leave him where he was, until they should all be ready to return. The latter course was at length decided on; and as the further expedition was not to exceed an hour's duration, and as Mr Weller begged very hard to be one of the party, it was determined to leave Mr Pickwick asleep in the barrow, and to call for him on their return. So away they went, leaving Mr Pickwick snoring most comfortably in the shade.

That Mr Pickwick would have continued to snore in the shade until his friends came back, or, in default thereof, until the shades of evening had fallen on the landscape, there appears no reasonable cause to doubt; always supposing that he had been suffered to remain there in peace. But he was *not* suffered to remain there in peace. And this was what prevented him.

Captain Boldwig was a little fierce man in a stiff black neckerchief and blue surtout, who, when he did condescend to walk about his property, did it in company with a thick rattan[3] stick with a brass ferrule, and a gardener and sub-gardener with meek faces, to whom (the gardeners, not the stick) Captain Boldwig gave his orders with all due grandeur and ferocity: for Captain Boldwig's wife's sister had married a Marquis, and the Captain's house was a villa, and his land 'grounds,' and it was all very high, and mighty, and great.

Mr Pickwick had not been asleep half an hour when little Captain Boldwig, followed by the two gardeners, came striding along as fast as his size and importance would let him; and when he came near the oak tree, Captain Boldwig paused, and drew a long breath, and looked at the prospect as if he thought the prospect ought to be highly gratified at having him to take notice of it; and then he struck the ground emphatically with his stick, and summoned the head-gardener.

'Hunt,' said Captain Boldwig.

'Yes, sir,' said the gardener.

'Roll this place to-morrow morning – do you hear, Hunt?'

'Yes, sir.'

'And take care that you keep me this place in good order – do you hear, Hunt?'

'Yes, sir.'

And remind me to have a board done about trespassers, and spring guns,[4] and all that sort of thing, to keep the common people out. Do you hear, Hunt; do you hear?'

'I'll not forget it, sir.'

'I beg your pardon, sir,' said the other man, advancing, with his hand to his hat.

'Well, Wilkins, what's the matter with *you*?' said Captain Boldwig.

'I beg your pardon, sir – but I think there have been trespassers here to-day.'

'Ha!' said the Captain, scowling around him.

'Yes, sir – they have been dining here, I think, sir.'

'Why, confound their audacity, so they have,' said Captain Boldwig, as the crumbs and fragments that were strewn upon the grass met his eye. 'They have actually been devouring their food here. I wish I had the vagabonds here!' said the Captain, clenching the thick stick.

'I wish I had the vagabonds here,' said the Captain, wrathfully.

'Beg your pardon, sir,' said Wilkins, 'but – '

'But what? Eh?' roared the Captain; and following the timid glance of Wilkins, his eyes encountered the wheelbarrow and Mr Pickwick.

'Who are you, you rascal?' said the Captain, administering several pokes to Mr Pickwick's body with the thick stick. 'What's your name?'

'Cold punch,' murmured Mr Pickwick, as he sunk to sleep again.

'What?' demanded Captain Boldwig.

No reply.

'What did he say his name was?' asked the Captain.

'Punch, I think, sir,' replied Wilkins.

'That's his impudence, that's his confounded impudence,' said Captain Boldwig. 'He's only feigning to be asleep now,' said the Captain, in a high passion. 'He's drunk; he's a drunken plebeian.[5] Wheel him away, Wilkins, wheel him away directly.'

'Where shall I wheel him to, sir?' inquired Wilkins, with great timidity.

'Wheel him to the Devil,' replied Captain Boldwig.

'Very well, sir,' said Wilkins.

'Stay,' said the Captain.

Wilkins stopped accordingly.

'Wheel him,' said the Captain, 'wheel him to the pound;[6] and let us see whether he calls himself Punch when he comes to himself. He shall not bully me, he shall not bully me. Wheel him away.'

Away Mr Pickwick was wheeled in compliance with this imperious mandate; and the great Captain Boldwig, swelling with indignation, proceeded on his walk.

Inexpressible was the astonishment of the little party when they returned, to find that Mr Pickwick had disappeared, and taken the wheelbarrow with him. It was the most mysterious and unaccountable thing that was ever heard of. For a lame man to have got upon his legs without any previous notice, and walked off, would have been most extraordinary; but when it came to his wheeling a heavy barrow before him, by way of amusement, it grew positively miraculous. They searched every nook and corner round, together and separately; they shouted, whistled, laughed, called – and all with the same result. Mr Pickwick was not to be found. After some hours of fruitless search, they arrived at the unwelcome conclusion that they must go home without him.

Meanwhile Mr Pickwick had been wheeled to the Pound, and safely deposited therein, fast asleep in the wheelbarrow, to the immeasurable delight and satisfaction, not only of all the boys in the village, but three-fourths of the whole population, who had gathered round, in expectation of his waking. If their most intense gratification had been excited by seeing him wheeled in, how many hundredfold was their joy increased when, after a few indistinct cries of 'Sam!' he sat up in the barrow, and gazed with indescribable astonishment on the faces before him.

A general shout was of course the signal of his having woke up; and his involuntary inquiry of 'What's the matter?' occasioned another, louder than the first, if possible.

'Here's a game!' roared the populace.

'Where am I?' exclaimed Mr Pickwick.

'In the Pound,' replied the mob.

'How came I here? What was I doing? Where was I brought from?'

'Boldwig! Captain Boldwig!' was the only reply.

'Let me out,' cried Mr Pickwick. 'Where's my servant? Where are my friends?'

'You an't got no friends. Hurrah!' Then there came a turnip, then a potato, and then an egg: with a few other little tokens of the playful disposition of the many-headed.

How long this scene might have lasted, or how much Mr Pickwick might have suffered, no one can tell, had not a carriage, which was driving swiftly by, suddenly pulled up, from whence there descended old Wardle and Sam Weller, the former of whom, in far less time than it takes to write it, if not to read it, had made his way to Mr Pickwick's side, and placed him in the vehicle, just as the latter had concluded the third and last round of a single combat with the town-beadle.

'Run to the Justice's!' cried a dozen voices.

'Ah, run avay,' said Mr Weller, jumping up on the box. 'Give my compliments – Mr Veller's compliments – to the Justice, and tell him I've spiled his beadle, and that, if he'll svear in a new 'un, I'll come back agin to-morrow and spile him. Drive on, old feller.'

'I'll give directions for the commencement of an action for false imprisonment against this Captain Boldwig, directly I get to London,' said Mr Pickwick, as soon as the carriage turned out of the town.

Mr Pickwick in the Pound

'We were trespassing, it seems,' said Wardle.

'I don't care,' said Mr Pickwick, 'I'll bring the action.'

'No, you won't,' said Wardle.

'I will, by – ' but as there was a humorous expression in Wardle's face, Mr Pickwick checked himself, and said: 'Why not?'

'Because,' said old Wardle, half-bursting with laughter, 'because they might turn round on some of us, and say we had taken too much cold punch.'

Do what he would, a smile would come into Mr Pickwick's face; the smile extended into a laugh; the laugh into a roar; the roar became general. So, to keep up their good humour, they stopped at the first roadside tavern they came to, and ordered a glass of brandy and water all round, with a magnum of extra strength for Mr Samuel Weller.

CHAPTER 20

Showing how Dodson and Fogg were Men of
Business, and their Clerks Men of Pleasure; and how
an Affecting Interview took place between Mr
Weller and his long-lost Parent; showing also what
Choice Spirits assembled at the Magpie and Stump,
and what a capital Chapter the next one will be

In the ground-floor front of a dingy house, at the very furthest end of Freeman's Court, Cornhill, sat the four clerks of Messrs. Dodson and Fogg, two of his Majesty's Attorneys of the Courts of King's Bench and Common Pleas at Westminster, and solicitors of the High Court of Chancery:[1] the aforesaid clerks catching as favourable glimpses of Heaven's light and Heaven's sun, in the course of their daily labours, as a man might hope to do, were he placed at the bottom of a reasonably deep well; and without the opportunity of perceiving the stars in the day-time, which the latter secluded situation affords.

The clerks' office of Messrs. Dodson and Fogg was a dark, mouldy, earthy-smelling room, with a high wainscotted partition to screen the clerks from the vulgar gaze: a couple of old wooden chairs: a very loud-ticking clock: an almanack, an umbrella-stand, a row of hat-pegs, and a few shelves, on which were deposited several ticketed bundles of dirty papers, some old deal boxes[2] with paper labels, and sundry decayed stone ink bottles of various shapes and sizes. There was a glass door leading into the passage which formed the entrance to the court, and on the outer side of this glass door, Mr Pickwick, closely followed by Sam Weller, presented himself on the Friday morning succeeding the occurrence, of which a faithful narration is given in the last chapter.

'Come in, can't you!' cried a voice from behind the partition, in reply to Mr Pickwick's gentle tap at the door. And Mr Pickwick and Sam entered accordingly.

'Mr Dodson or Mr Fogg at home, sir?' inquired Mr Pickwick, gently, advancing, hat in hand, towards the partition.

'Mr Dodson ain't at home, and Mr Fogg's particularly engaged,' replied the voice; and at the same time the head to which the voice belonged, with a pen behind its ear, looked over the partition, and at Mr Pickwick.

It was a ragged head, the sandy hair of which, scrupulously parted on one side, and flattened down with pomatum,[3] was twisted into little semi-circular tails round a flat face ornamented with a pair of small eyes, and garnished with a very dirty shirt collar, and a rusty black stock.

'Mr Dodson ain't at home, and Mr Fogg's particularly engaged,' said the man to whom the head belonged.

'When will Mr Dodson be back, sir?' inquired Mr Pickwick.

'Can't say.'

'Will it be long before Mr Fogg is disengaged, sir?'

'Don't know.'

Here the man proceeded to mend his pen with great deliberation, while another clerk, who was mixing a Seidlitz powder, under cover of the lid of his desk, laughed approvingly.

'I think I'll wait,' said Mr Pickwick. There was no reply; so Mr Pickwick sat down unbidden, and listened to the loud ticking of the clock and the murmured conversation of the clerks.

'That was a game, wasn't it?' said one of the gentlemen, in a brown coat and brass buttons, inky drabs, and bluchers, at the conclusion of some inaudible relation of his previous evening's adventures.

'Devilish good – devilish good,' said the Seidlitz-powder man.

'Tom Cummins was in the chair,' said the man with the brown coat; 'It was half-past four when I got to Somers Town,[4] and then I was so uncommon lushey,[5] that I couldn't find the place where the latch-key went in, and was obliged to knock up[6] the old 'ooman. I say, I wonder what old Fogg 'ud say, if he knew it. I should get the sack, I s'pose – eh?'

At this humorous notion, all the clerks laughed in concert.

'There was such a game with Fogg here, this mornin',' said the man in the brown coat, 'while Jack was up stairs sorting the papers, and you two were gone to the stamp-office. Fogg was down here, opening the letters, when that chap as we issued the writ against at Camberwell, you know, came in – what's his name again?'

'Ramsey,' said the clerk who had spoken to Mr Pickwick.

'Ah, Ramsey – a precious seedy-looking customer. "Well, sir," says old Fogg, looking at him very fierce – you know his way – "well, sir, have you come to settle?" "Yes, I have, sir," said Ramsey, putting his hand in his pocket, and bringing out the money, "the debt's two pound ten, and the costs three pound five, and here it is, sir;" and he sighed like bricks, as he lugged out the money, done up in a bit of blotting-paper. Old Fogg looked first at the money, and then at him, and then he coughed in his rum way, so that I knew something was coming. "You don't know there's a declaration filed, which increases the costs materially, I suppose?" said Fogg. "You don't say that, sir," said Ramsey, starting back; "the time was only out last night, sir." "I do say it, though," said Fogg, "my clerk's just gone to file it. Hasn't Mr Jackson gone to file that declaration in Bullman and Ramsey, Mr Wicks?" Of course I said yes, and then Fogg coughed again, and looked at Ramsey. "My God!" said Ramsey; "and here have I nearly driven myself mad, scraping this money together, and all to no purpose." "None at all," said Fogg, coolly; "so you had better go back and scrape some more together, and bring it here in time." "I can't get it, by God!" said Ramsey, striking the desk with his fist. "Don't bully me, sir," said Fogg, getting into a passion on purpose. "I am not bullying you, sir," said Ramsey. "You are," said Fogg; "get out, sir; get out of this office, sir, and come back, sir, when you know how to behave yourself." Well, Ramsey tried to speak, but Fogg wouldn't let him, so he put the money in his pocket, and sneaked out. The door was scarcely shut, when old Fogg turned round to me, with a sweet smile on his face, and drew the declaration out of his coat pocket. "Here, Wicks," says Fogg, "take a cab, and go down to the Temple[7] as quick as you can, and file that. The costs are quite safe, for he's a steady man with a large family, at a salary of five-and-twenty shillings a week, and if he gives us a warrant of attorney,[8] as he must in the end, I know his employers will see it paid; so we may as well get all we can out of him, Mr Wicks; it's a Christian act to do it, Mr Wicks, for with his large family and small income, he'll be all the better for a good lesson against getting into debt, – won't he, Mr Wicks, won't he?" – and he smiled so good-naturedly as he went away, that it was delightful to see him. He is a capital man of business,' said Wicks, in a tone of the deepest admiration, 'capital, isn't he?'

The other three cordially subscribed to this opinion, and the anecdote afforded the most unlimited satisfaction.

'Nice men these here, sir,' whispered Mr Weller to his master; 'wery nice notion of fun they has, sir.'

Mr Pickwick nodded assent, and coughed to attract the attention of the young gentlemen behind the partition, who, having now relaxed their minds by a little conversation among themselves, condescended to take some notice of the stranger.

'I wonder whether Fogg's disengaged now?' said Jackson.

'I'll see,' said Wicks, dismounting leisurely from his stool. 'What name shall I tell Mr Fogg?'

'Pickwick,' replied the illustrious subject of these memoirs.

Mr Jackson departed up stairs on his errand, and immediately returned with a message that Mr Fogg would see Mr Pickwick in five minutes; and having delivered it, returned again to his desk.

'What did he say his name was?' whispered Wicks.

'Pickwick,' replied Jackson; 'it's the defendant in Bardell and Pickwick.'

A sudden scraping of feet, mingled with the sound of suppressed laughter, was heard from behind the partition.

'They're a twiggin' of you, sir,' whispered Mr Weller.

'Twigging of me, Sam!' replied Mr Pickwick; 'what do you mean by twigging me?'

Mr Weller replied by pointing with his thumb over his shoulder, and Mr Pickwick, on looking up, became sensible of the pleasing fact, that all the four clerks, with countenances expressive of the utmost amusement, and with their heads thrust over the wooden screen, were minutely inspecting the figure and general appearance of the supposed trifler with female hearts, and disturber of female happiness. On his looking up, the row of heads suddenly disappeared, and the sound of pens travelling at a furious rate over paper, immediately succeeded.

A sudden ring at the bell which hung in the office, summoned Mr Jackson to the apartment of Fogg, from whence he came back to say that he (Fogg) was ready to see Mr Pickwick if he would step up stairs.

Mr Pickwick & Sam in the attorney's office

Up stairs Mr Pickwick did step accordingly, leaving Sam Weller below. The room door of the one-pair back,[9] bore inscribed in legible characters the imposing words 'Mr Fogg;' and, having tapped thereat, and been desired to come in, Jackson ushered Mr Pickwick into the presence.

'Is Mr Dodson in?' inquired Mr Fogg.

'Just come in, sir,' replied Jackson.

'Ask him to step here.'

'Yes, sir.' Exit Jackson.

'Take a seat, sir,' said Fogg; 'there is the paper, sir; my partner will be here directly, and we can converse about this matter, sir.'

Mr Pickwick took a seat and the paper, but, instead of reading the latter, peeped over the top of it, and took a survey of the man of business, who was an elderly, pimply-faced, vegetable-diet sort of man, in a black coat, dark mixture trousers, and small black gaiters: a kind of being who seemed to be an essential part of the desk at which he was writing, and to have as much thought or sentiment.

After a few minutes' silence, Mr Dodson, a plump, portly, stern-looking man, with a loud voice, appeared; and the conversation commenced.

'This is Mr Pickwick,' said Fogg.

'Ah! You are the defendant, sir, in Bardell and Pickwick?' said Dodson.

'I am, sir,' replied Mr Pickwick.

'Well, sir,' said Dodson, 'and what do you propose?'

'Ah!' said Fogg, thrusting his hands into his trousers' pockets, and throwing himself back in his chair, 'what do you propose, Mr Pickwick?'

'Hush, Fogg,' said Dodson, 'let me hear what Mr Pickwick has to say.'

'I came, gentlemen,' said Mr Pickwick, gazing placidly on the two partners, 'I came here, gentlemen, to express the surprise with which I received your letter of the other day, and to inquire what grounds of action you can have against me.'

'Grounds of – ' Fogg had ejaculated thus much, when he was stopped by Dodson.

'Mr Fogg,' said Dodson, 'I am going to speak.'

'I beg your pardon, Mr Dodson,' said Fogg.

'For the grounds of action, sir,' continued Dodson, with moral elevation in his air, 'you will consult your own conscience and your own feelings. We, sir, we, are guided entirely by the statement of

our client. That statement, sir, may be true, or it may be false; it
may be credible, or it may be incredible; but, if it be true, and if it
be credible, I do not hesitate to say, sir, that our grounds of action,
sir, are strong, and not to be shaken. You may be an unfortunate
man, sir, or you may be a designing one; but if I were called upon,
as a juryman upon my oath, sir, to express an opinion of your
conduct, sir, I do not hesitate to assert that I should have but one
opinion about it.' Here Dodson drew himself up, with an air of
offended virtue, and looked at Fogg, who thrust his hands further
in his pockets, and, nodding his head sagely, said, in a tone of the
fullest concurrence, 'Most certainly.'

'Well, sir,' said Mr Pickwick, with considerable pain depicted in
his countenance, 'you will permit me to assure you, that I am a
most unfortunate man, so far as this case is concerned.'

'I hope you are, sir,' replied Dodson; 'I trust you may be, sir. If
you are really innocent of what is laid to your charge, you are more
unfortunate than I had believed any man could possibly be. What
do *you* say, Mr Fogg?'

'I say precisely what you say,' replied Fogg, with a smile of
incredulity.

'The writ, sir, which commences the action,' continued Dodson,
'was issued regularly. Mr Fogg, where is the *præcipe* book?'

'Here it is,' said Fogg, handing over a square book, with a
parchment cover.

'Here is the entry,' resumed Dodson. "'Middlesex, Capias[10]
Martha Bardell, widow, v. *Samuel Pickwick*. Damages, £1500.
Dodson and Fogg for the plaintiff, Aug. 28, 1830." All regular, sir;
perfectly.' Dodson coughed and looked at Fogg, who said 'Perfectly,' also. And then they both looked at Mr Pickwick.

'I am to understand, then,' said Mr Pickwick, 'that it really is
your intention to proceed with this action?'

'Understand, sir? That you certainly may,' replied Dodson, with
something as near a smile as his importance would allow.

'And that the damages are actually laid at fifteen hundred
pounds?' said Mr Pickwick.

'To which understanding you may add my assurance, that if we
could have prevailed upon our client, they would have been laid at
treble the amount, sir:' replied Dodson.

'I believe Mrs Bardell specially said, however,' observed Fogg,
glancing at Dodson, 'that she would not compromise for a farthing
less.'

'Unquestionably,' replied Dodson, sternly. For the action was only just begun; and it wouldn't have done to let Mr Pickwick compromise it then, even if he had been so disposed.

'As you offer no terms, sir,' said Dodson, displaying a slip of parchment in his right hand, and affectionately pressing a paper copy of it, on Mr Pickwick with his left, 'I had better serve you with a copy of this writ, sir. Here is the original, sir.'

'Very well, gentlemen, very well,' said Mr Pickwick, rising in person and wrath at the same time; 'you shall hear from my solicitor, gentlemen.'

'We shall be very happy to do so,' said Fogg, rubbing his hands.

'Very,' said Dodson, opening the door.

'And before I go, gentlemen,' said the excited Mr Pickwick, turning round on the landing, 'permit me to say, that of all the disgraceful and rascally proceedings – '

'Stay, sir, stay,' interposed Dodson, with great politeness. 'Mr Jackson! Mr Wicks!'

'Sir,' said the two clerks, appearing at the bottom of the stairs.

'I merely want you to hear what this gentleman says,' replied Dodson. 'Pray, go on, sir – disgraceful and rascally proceedings, I think you said?'

'I did,' said Mr Pickwick, thoroughly roused. 'I said, sir, that of all the disgraceful and rascally proceedings that ever were attempted, this is the most so. I repeat it, sir.'

'You hear that, Mr Wicks?' said Dodson.

'You won't forget these expressions, Mr Jackson?' said Fogg.

'Perhaps you would like to call us swindlers, sir,' said Dodson. 'Pray do, sir, if you feel disposed; now pray do, sir.'

'I do,' said Mr Pickwick. 'You *are* swindlers.'

'Very good,' said Dodson. 'You can hear down there, I hope, Mr Wicks?'

'Oh yes, sir,' said Wicks.

'You had better come up a step or two higher, if you can't,' added Mr Fogg. 'Go on, sir; do go on. You had better call us thieves, sir; or perhaps you would like to assault one of us. Pray do it, sir, if you would; we will not make the smallest resistance. Pray do it, sir.'

As Fogg put himself very temptingly within the reach of Mr Pickwick's clenched fist, there is little doubt that that gentleman would have complied with his earnest entreaty, but for the interposition of Sam, who, hearing the dispute, emerged from the office, mounted the stairs, and seized his master by the arm.

'You just come avay,' said Mr Weller. 'Battledore and

shuttlecock's[11] a wery good game, vhen you an't the shuttlecock and two lawyers the battledores, in which case it gets too excitin' to be pleasant. Come avay, sir. If you want to ease your mind by blowing up somebody, come out into the court and blow up me; but it's rayther too expensive work to be carried on here.'

And without the slightest ceremony, Mr Weller hauled his master down the stairs, and down the court, and having safely deposited him in Cornhill, fell behind, prepared to follow whithersoever he should lead.

Mr Pickwick walked on abstractedly, crossed opposite the Mansion House, and bent his steps up Cheapside. Sam began to wonder where they were going, when his master turned round, and said:

'Sam, I will go immediately to Mr Perker's.'

'That's just exactly the wery place vere you ought to have gone last night, sir,' replied Mr Weller.

'I think it is, Sam,' said Mr Pickwick.

'I *know* it is,' said Mr Weller.

'Well, well, Sam,' replied Mr Pickwick, 'we will go there at once, but first, as I have been rather ruffled, I should like a glass of brandy and water warm, Sam. Where can I have it, Sam?'

Mr Weller's knowledge of London was extensive and peculiar. He replied, without the slightest consideration:

'Second court on the right hand side – last house but vun on the same side the vay – take the box as stands in the first fire-place, 'cos there an't no leg in the middle o' the table, wich all the others has, and it's wery inconwenient.'

Mr Pickwick observed his valet's directions implicitly, and bidding Sam follow him, entered the tavern he had pointed out, where the hot brandy and water was speedily placed before him; while Mr Weller, seated at a respectful distance, though at the same table with his master, was accommodated with a pint of porter.

The room was one of a very homely description, and was apparently under the especial patronage of stage coachmen: for several gentlemen, who had all the appearance of belonging to that learned profession, were drinking and smoking in the different boxes. Among the number was one stout, red-faced, elderly man in particular, seated in an opposite box, who attracted Mr Pickwick's attention. The stout man was smoking with great vehemence, but between every half-dozen puffs, he took his pipe from his mouth, and looked first at Mr Weller and then at Mr Pickwick. Then, he would bury in a quart pot, as much of his countenance as the dimensions of the quart pot admitted of its receiving, and take another look at Sam and Mr Pickwick. Then he would take another half-dozen puffs with an air of profound meditation and look at them again. At last the stout man, putting up his legs on the seat, and leaning his back against the wall, began to puff at his pipe without leaving off at all, and to stare through the smoke at the new comers, as if he had made up his mind to see the most he could of them.

At first the evolutions of the stout man had escaped Mr Weller's observation, but by degrees, as he saw Mr Pickwick's eyes every now and then turning towards him, he began to gaze in the same direction, at the same time shading his eyes with his hand, as if he partially recognised the object before him, and wished to make quite sure of its identity. His doubts were speedily dispelled, however; for the stout man having blown a thick cloud from his pipe, a hoarse voice, like some strange effort of ventriloquism, emerged from beneath the capacious shawls which muffled his throat and chest, and slowly uttered these sounds – 'Wy, Sammy!'

'Who's that, Sam?' inquired Mr Pickwick.

'Why, I wouldn't ha' believed it, sir,' replied Mr Weller with astonished eyes. 'It's the old 'un.'

'Old one,' said Mr Pickwick. 'What old one?'

'My father, sir,' replied Mr Weller. 'How are you, my ancient?' With which beautiful ebullition of filial affection, Mr Weller made room on the seat beside him, for the stout man, who advanced pipe in mouth and pot in hand, to greet him.

'Wy, Sammy,' said the father, 'I han't seen you, for two year and better."

'Nor more you have, old codger,' replied the son. 'How's mother in law?'

'Wy, I'll tell you what, Sammy,' said Mr Weller, senior, with much solemnity in his manner; 'there never was a nicer woman as a widder, than that 'ere second wentur o'mine – a sweet creetur she was, Sammy; all I can say on her now, is, that as she was such an uncommon pleasant widder, it's a great pity she ever changed her con-dition. She don't act as a vife, Sammy.'

'Don't she, though?' inquired Mr Weller junior.

The elder Mr Weller shook his head, as he replied with a sigh, 'I've done it once too often, Sammy; I've done it once too often. Take example by your father, my boy, and be wery careful o' widders all your life, specially if they've kept a public-house, Sammy.' Having delivered this parental advice with great pathos, Mr Weller senior re-filled his pipe from a tin box he carried in his pocket, and, lighting his fresh pipe from the ashes of the old one, commenced smoking at a great rate.

'Beg your pardon, sir,' he said, renewing the subject, and addressing Mr Pickwick, after a considerable pause, 'nothin' personal, I hope, sir; I hope you han't got a widder, sir.'

'Not I,' replied Mr Pickwick, laughing; and while Mr Pickwick laughed, Sam Weller informed his parent in a whisper, of the relation in which he stood towards that gentleman.

'Beg your pardon, sir,' said Mr Weller, senior, taking off his hat, 'I hope you've no fault to find with Sammy, sir?'

'None whatever,' said Mr Pickwick.

'Wery glad to hear it, sir,' replied the old man; 'I took a good deal o' pains with his eddication, sir; let him run in the streets when he was wery young, and shift for his-self. It's the only way to make a boy sharp, sir.'

'Rather a dangerous process, I should imagine,' said Mr Pickwick, with a smile.

'And not a wery sure one, neither,' added Mr Weller; 'I got reg'larly done the other day.'

'No!' said his father.

'I did,' said the son; and he proceeded to relate, in as few words as possible how he had fallen a ready dupe to the stratagems of Job Trotter.

Mr Weller senior listened to the tale with the most profound attention, and, at its termination, said:

'Worn't one o' these chaps slim and tall, with long hair, and the gift o' the gab wery gallopin'?'

Mr Pickwick did not quite understand the last item of description, but, comprehending the first, said 'Yes,' at a venture.

'T'other's a black-haired chap in mulberry livery, with a wery large head?'

'Yes, yes, he is,' said Mr Pickwick and Sam, with great earnestness.

'Then I know where they are, and that's all about it,' said Mr Weller; 'they're at Ipswich, safe enough, them two.'

'No!' said Mr Pickwick.

'Fact,' said Mr Weller, 'and I'll tell you how I know it. I work an Ipswich coach now and then for a friend o' mine. I worked down the wery day arter the night as you caught the rheumatiz, and at the Black Boy at Chelmsford – the wery place they'd come to – I took 'em up, right through to Ipswich, where the man servant –

him in the mulberries – told me they was a goin' to put up for a long time.'

'I'll follow him,' said Mr Pickwick; 'we may as well see Ipswich as any other place. I'll follow him.'

'You're quite certain it was them, governor?' inquired Mr Weller, junior.

'Quite, Sammy, quite,' replied his father, 'for their appearance is wery sing'ler; besides that 'ere, I wondered to see the gen'lm'n so formiliar with his servant; and, more than that, as they sat in front, right behind the box, I heerd 'em laughing, and saying how they'd done old Fireworks.'

'Old who?' said Mr Pickwick.

'Old Fireworks, sir; by which, I've no doubt, they meant you, sir.'

There is nothing positively vile or atrocious in the appellation of 'old Fireworks,' but still it is by no means a respectful or flattering designation. The recollection of all the wrongs he had sustained at Jingle's hands had crowded on Mr Pickwick's mind, the moment Mr Weller began to speak: it wanted but a feather to turn the scale, and 'old Fireworks' did it.

'I'll follow him,' said Mr Pickwick, with an emphatic blow on the table.

'I shall work down to Ipswich the day arter to-morrow, sir,' said Mr Weller the elder, 'from the Bull in Whitechapel; and if you really mean go, you'd better go with me.'

'So we had,' said Mr Pickwick; 'very true; I can write to Bury, and tell them to meet me at Ipswich. We will go with you. But don't hurry away, Mr Weller; won't you take anything?'

'You're wery good, sir,' replied Mr W., stopping short; 'perhaps a small glass of brandy to drink your health, and success to Sammy, sir, wouldn't be amiss.'

'Certainly not,' replied Mr Pickwick. 'A glass of brandy here!' The brandy was brought: and Mr Weller, after pulling his hair to Mr Pickwick, and nodding to Sam, jerked it down his capacious throat as if it had been a small thimble-full.

'Well done, father,' said Sam, 'take care, old fellow, or you'll have a touch of your old complaint, the gout.'

'I've found a sov'rin' cure for that, Sammy,' said Mr Weller, setting down the glass.

'A sovereign cure for the gout,' said Mr Pickwick, hastily producing his notebook – 'what is it?'

'The gout, sir,' replied Mr Weller, 'the gout is a complaint as

arises from too much ease and comfort. If ever you're attacked with
the gout, sir, jist you marry a widder as has got a good loud woice,
with a decent notion of usin' it, and you'll never have the gout agin.
It's a capital prescription, sir. I takes it reg'lar, and I can warrant it
to drive away any illness as is caused by too much jollity.' Having
imparted this valuable secret, Mr Weller drained his glass once
more, produced a laboured wink, sighed deeply, and slowly retired.

'Well, what do you think of what your father says, Sam?' inquired
Mr Pickwick, with a smile.

'Think, sir!' replied Mr Weller; 'why, I think he's the wictim o'
connubiality, as Blue Beard's[12] domestic chaplain said, with a tear
of pity, ven he buried him.'

There was no replying to this very apposite conclusion, and,
therefore, Mr Pickwick, after settling the reckoning, resumed his
walk to Gray's Inn. By the time he reached its secluded groves,
however, eight o'clock had struck, and the unbroken stream of
gentlemen in muddy high-lows, soiled white hats, and rusty apparel,
who were pouring towards the different avenues of egress, warned
him that the majority of the offices had closed for that day.

After climbing two pairs of steep and dirty stairs, he found his
anticipations were realised. Mr Perker's 'outer door' was closed;
and the dead silence which followed Mr Weller's repeated kicks
thereat, announced that the officials had retired from business for
the night.

'This is pleasant, Sam,' said Mr Pickwick; 'I shouldn't lose an
hour in seeing him; I shall not be able to get one wink of sleep to-
night, I know, unless I have the satisfaction of reflecting that I have
confided this matter to a professional man.'

'Here's an old 'ooman comin' up-stairs, sir,' replied Mr Weller;
'p'raps she knows where we can find somebody. Hallo, old lady,
vere's Mr Perker's people?'

'Mr Perker's people,' said a thin, miserable-looking old woman,
stopping to recover breath after the ascent of the staircase, 'Mr
Perker's people's gone, and I'm a goin' to do the office out.'

'Are you Mr Perker's servant?' inquired Mr Pickwick.

'I am Mr Perker's laundress,' replied the old woman.

'Ah,' said Mr Pickwick, half aside to Sam, 'it's a curious
circumstance, Sam, that they call the old women in these inns,
laundresses. I wonder what's that for.'

''Cos they has a mortal awersion to washing anythin', I suppose,
sir,' replied Mr Weller.

'I shouldn't wonder,' said Mr Pickwick, looking at the old

woman, whose appearance, as well as the condition of the office, which she had by this time opened, indicated a rooted antipathy to the application of soap and water; 'do you know where I can find Mr Perker, my good woman?'

'No, I don't,' replied the old woman, gruffly; 'he's out o' town now.'

'That's unfortunate,' said Mr Pickwick; 'where's his clerk? Do you know?'

'Yes, I know where he is, but he won't thank me for telling you,' replied the laundress.

'I have very particular business with him,' said Mr Pickwick.

'Won't it do in the morning?' said the woman.

'Not so well,' replied Mr Pickwick.

'Well,' said the old woman, 'if it was anything very particular, I was to say where he was, so I suppose there's no harm in telling. If you just go to the Magpie and Stump, and ask at the bar for Mr Lowten, they'll show you in to him, and he's Mr Perker's clerk.'

With this direction, and having been furthermore informed that the hostelry in question was situated in a court, happy in the double advantage of being in the vicinity of Clare Market, and closely approximating to the back of New Inn, Mr Pickwick and Sam descended the ricketty staircase in safety, and issued forth in quest of the Magpie and Stump.

This favoured tavern, sacred to the evening orgies of Mr Lowten and his companions, was what ordinary people would designate a public-house. That the landlord was a man of a money-making turn, was sufficiently testified by the fact of a small bulk-head beneath the tap-room window, in size and shape not unlike a sedan-chair, being underlet to a mender of shoes: and that he was a being of a philanthropic mind, was evident from the protection he afforded to a pieman, who vended his delicacies without fear of interruption on the very door-step. In the lower windows, which were decorated with curtains of a saffron hue, dangled two or three printed cards, bearing reference to Devonshire cyder and Dantzic spruce, while a large black board, announcing in white letters to an enlightened public that there were 500,000 barrels of double stout in the cellars of the establishment, left the mind in a state of not unpleasing doubt and uncertainty as to the precise direction in the bowels of the earth, in which this mighty cavern might be supposed to extend. When we add, that the weather-beaten sign-board bore the half-obliterated semblance of a magpie intently eyeing a crooked streak of brown paint, which the neighbours had been taught from infancy to consider as the 'stump,' we have said all that need be said of the exterior of the edifice.

On Mr Pickwick's presenting himself at the bar, an elderly female emerged from behind a screen therein, and presented herself before him.

'Is Mr Lowten here, ma'am?' inquired Mr Pickwick.

'Yes he is, sir,' replied the landlady. 'Here, Charley, show the gentleman in, to Mr Lowten.'

'The gen'lm'n can't go in just now,' said a shambling pot-boy[13] with a red head, "cos Mr Lowten's a singin' a comic song, and he'll put him out. He'll be done d'rectly, sir.'

The red-headed pot-boy had scarcely finished speaking, when a most unanimous hammering of tables, and jingling of glasses, announced that the song had that instant terminated; and Mr Pickwick, after desiring Sam to solace himself in the tap,[14] suffered himself to be conducted into the presence of Mr Lowten.

At the announcement of 'gentleman to speak to you, sir,' a puffy-faced young man, who filled the chair at the head of the table, looked with some surprise in the direction from whence the voice proceeded: and the surprise seemed to be by no means diminished, when his eyes rested on an individual whom he had never seen before.

'I beg your pardon, sir,' said Mr Pickwick, 'and I am very sorry to disturb the other gentlemen, too, but I come on very particular business; and if you will suffer me to detain you at this end of the room for five minutes, I shall be very much obliged to you.'

The puffy-faced young man rose, and drawing a chair close to Mr Pickwick in an obscure corner of the room, listened attentively to his tale of woe.

'Ah,' he said, when Mr Pickwick had concluded, 'Dodson and Fogg – sharp practice their's – capital men of business, Dodson and Fogg, sir.'

Mr Pickwick admitted the sharp practice of Dodson and Fogg, and Lowten resumed.

'Perker ain't in town, and he won't be, neither, before the end of next week; but if you want the action defended, and will leave the copy with me, I can do all that's needful till he comes back.'

'That's exactly what I came here for,' said Mr Pickwick, handing over the document. 'If anything particular occurs, you can write to me at the post-office, Ipswich.'

'That's all right,' replied Mr Perker's clerk; and then seeing Mr Pickwick's eye wandering curiously towards the table, he added,

'Will you join us, for half-an-hour or so? We are capital company here to-night. There's Samkin and Green's managing-clerk, and Smithers and Price's chancery, and Pimkin and Thomas's out o' door[15] – sings a capital song, he does – and Jack Bamber, and ever so many more. You're come out of the country, I suppose. Would you like to join us?'

Mr Pickwick could not resist so tempting an opportunity of studying human nature. He suffered himself to be led to the table, where, after having been introduced to the company in due form, he was accommodated with a seat near the chairman, and called for a glass of his favourite beverage.

A profound silence, quite contrary to Mr Pickwick's expectation, succeeded.

'You don't find this sort of thing disagreeable, I hope, sir?' said his right hand neighbour, a gentleman in a checked shirt, and Mosaic[16] studs, with a cigar in his mouth.

'Not in the least,' replied Mr Pickwick, 'I like it very much, although I am no smoker myself.'

'I should be very sorry to say I wasn't,' interposed another gentleman on the opposite side of the table. 'It's board and lodging to me, is smoke.'

Mr Pickwick glanced at the speaker, and thought that if it were washing too, it would be all the better.

Here there was another pause. Mr Pickwick was a stranger, and his coming had evidently cast a damp upon the party.

'Mr Grundy's going to oblige the company with a song,' said the chairman.

'No he ain't,' said Mr Grundy.

'Why not?' said the chairman.

'Because he can't,' said Mr Grundy.

'You had better say he won't,' replied the chairman.

'Well, then, he won't,' retorted Mr Grundy. Mr Grundy's positive refusal to gratify the company, occasioned another silence.

'Won't anybody enliven us?' said the chairman, despondingly.

'Why don't you enliven us yourself, Mr Chairman?' said a young man with a whisker, a squint, and an open shirt collar (dirty), from the bottom of the table.

'Hear! hear!' said the smoking gentleman in the Mosaic jewellery.

'Because I only know one song, and I have sung it already, and it's a fine of "glasses round" to sing the same song twice in a night,' replied the chairman.

This was an unanswerable reply, and silence prevailed again.

'I have been to-night, gentlemen,' said Mr Pickwick, hoping to start a subject which all the company could take a part in discussing, 'I have been to-night in a place which you all know very well, doubtless, but which I have not been in before for some years, and know very little of; I mean Gray's Inn, gentlemen. Curious little nooks in a great place, like London, these old Inns are.'

'By Jove,' said the chairman, whispering across the table to Mr Pickwick, 'you have hit upon something that one of us, at least, would talk upon for ever. You'll draw old Jack Bamber out; he was never heard to talk about anything else but the Inns, and he has lived alone in them till he's half crazy.'

The individual to whom Lowten alluded, was a little yellow high-shouldered man, whose countenance, from his habit of stooping forward when silent, Mr Pickwick had not observed before. He wondered though, when the old man raised his shrivelled face, and bent his grey eye upon him, with a keen inquiring look, that such remarkable features could have escaped his attention for a moment. There was a fixed grim smile perpetually on his countenance; he leant his chin on a long skinny hand, with nails of extraordinary length; and as he inclined his head to one side, and looked keenly out from beneath his ragged grey eyebrows, there was a strange, wild slyness in his leer, quite repulsive to behold.

This was the figure that now started forward, and burst into an animated torrent of words. As this chapter has been a long one, however, and as the old man was a remarkable personage, it will be more respectful to him, and more convenient to us, to let him speak for himself in a fresh one.

CHAPTER 21

In which the Old Man launches forth into his favourite Theme, and relates a Story about a queer Client

'Aha!' said the old man, a brief description of whose manner and appearance concluded the last chapter, 'Aha! who was talking about the Inns?'

'I was, sir,' replied Mr Pickwick; 'I was observing what singular old places they are.'

'*You*!' said the old man, contemptuously, 'What do *you* know of the time when young men shut themselves up in those lonely rooms, and read and read, hour after hour, and night after night, till their reason wandered beneath their midnight studies; till their mental powers were exhausted; till morning's light brought no freshness or health to them; and they sank beneath the unnatural devotion of their youthful energies to their dry old books? Coming down to a later time, and a very different day, what do *you* know of the gradual sinking beneath consumption, or the quick wasting of fever – the grand results of "life" and dissipation – which men have undergone in these same rooms? How many vain pleaders for mercy, do you think have turned away heart-sick from the lawyer's office, to find a resting-place in the Thames, or a refuge in the gaol? They are no ordinary houses, those. There is not a pannel in the old wainscotting, but what, if it were endowed with the powers of speech and memory, could start from the wall, and tell its tale of horror – the romance of life, sir, the romance of life! Commonplace as they may seem now, I tell you they are strange old places, and I would rather hear many a legend with a terrific sounding name, than the true history of one old set of chambers.'

There was something so odd in the old man's sudden energy, and the subject which had called it forth, that Mr Pickwick was prepared with no observation in reply; and the old man checking his impetuosity, and resuming the leer, which had disappeared during his previous excitement, said:

'Look at them in another light: their most common-place and least romantic. What fine places of slow torture they are! Think of the needy man who has spent his all, beggared himself, and pinched his friends, to enter the profession, which will never yield him a morsel of bread. The waiting – the hope – the disappointment – the fear – the misery – the poverty – the blight on his hopes, and end to his career – the suicide perhaps, or the shabby, slipshod drunkard. Am I not right about them?' And the old man rubbed his hands, and leered as if in delight at having found another point of view in which to place his favourite subject.

Mr Pickwick eyed the old man with great curiosity, and the remainder of the company smiled, and looked on in silence.

'Talk of your German universities,'[1] said the little old man. 'Pooh, pooh! there's romance enough at home without going half a mile for it; only people never think of it.'

'I never thought of the romance of this particular subject before, certainly,' said Mr Pickwick, laughing.

'To be sure you didn't,' said the little old man, 'of course not. As a friend of mine used to say to me, "What is there in chambers, in particular?" "Queer old places," said I. "Not at all," said he. "Lonely," said I. "Not a bit of it," said he. He died one morning of apoplexy, as he was going to open his outer door. Fell with his head in his own letter-box, and there he lay for eighteen months. Every body thought he'd gone out of town.'

'And how was he found at last?' inquired Mr Pickwick.

'The benchers determined to have his door broken open, as he hadn't paid any rent for two years. So they did. Forced the lock; and a very dusty skeleton in a blue coat, black knee-shorts, and silks, fell forward in the arms of the porter who opened the door. Queer, that. Rather, perhaps?' The little old man put his head more on one side, and rubbed his hands with unspeakable glee.

'I know another case,' said the little old man, when his chuckles had in some degree subsided. 'It occurred in Clifford's Inn.[2] Tenant of a top set – bad character – shut himself up in his bed-room closet, and took a dose of arsenic. The steward thought he had run away; opened the door, and put a bill up. Another man came, took the chambers, furnished them, and went to live there. Somehow or other he couldn't sleep – always restless and uncomfortable. "Odd," says he. "I'll make the other room my bed-chamber, and this my sitting-room." He made the change, and slept very well at night, but suddenly found that, somehow, he couldn't read in the evening: he got nervous and uncomfortable, and used to be always snuffing his candles and staring about him. "I can't make this out," said he, when he came home from the play one night, and was drinking a glass of cold grog, with his back to the wall, in order that he mightn't be able to fancy there was any one behind him – "I can't make it out," said he; and just then his eyes rested on the little closet that had been always locked up, and a shudder ran through his whole frame from top to toe. "I have felt this strange feeling before," said he, "I cannot help thinking there's something wrong about that closet." He made a strong effort, plucked up his courage, shivered the lock with a blow or two of the poker, opened the door, and there, sure enough, standing bolt upright in the corner, was the last tenant, with a little bottle clasped firmly in his hand, and his face – well!' As the little old man concluded, he looked round on the attentive faces of his wondering auditory with a smile of grim delight.

'What strange things these are you tell us of, sir,' said Mr

Pickwick, minutely scanning the old man's countenance, by the aid of his glasses.

'Strange!' said the little old man. 'Nonsense; you think them strange, because you know nothing about it. They are funny, but not uncommon.'

'Funny!' exclaimed Mr Pickwick, involuntarily.

'Yes, funny, are they not?' replied the little old man, with a diabolical leer; and then, without pausing for an answer, he continued:

'I knew another man – let me see – forty years ago now – who took an old, damp, rotten set of chambers, in one of the most ancient Inns, that had been shut up and empty for years and years before. There were lots of old women's stories about the place, and it certainly was very far from being a cheerful one; but he was poor, and the rooms were cheap, and that would have been quite a sufficient reason for him, if they had been ten times worse than they really were. He was obliged to take some mouldering fixtures that were on the place, and, among the rest, was a great lumbering wooden press for papers, with large glass doors, and a green curtain inside; a pretty useless thing for him, for he had no papers to put in it; and as to his clothes, he carried them about with him, and that wasn't very hard work, either. Well, he had moved in all his furniture – it wasn't quite a truck-full – and had sprinkled it about the room, so as to make the four chairs look as much like a dozen as possible, and was sitting down before the fire at night, drinking the first glass of two gallons of whiskey he had ordered on credit, wondering whether it would ever be paid for, and if so, in how many years' time, when his eyes encountered the glass doors of the wooden press. "Ah" says he. "If I hadn't been obliged to take that ugly article at the old broker's valuation, I might have got something comfortable for the money. I'll tell you what it is, old fellow," he said, speaking aloud to the press, having nothing else to speak to: "if it wouldn't cost more to break up your old carcase, than it would ever be worth afterwards, I'd have a fire out of you in less than no time." He had hardly spoken the words, when a sound resembling a faint groan, appeared to issue from the interior of the case. It startled him at first, but thinking, on a moment's reflection, that it must be some young fellow in the next chamber, who had been dining out, he put his feet on the fender, and raised the poker to stir the fire. At that moment, the sound was repeated: and one of the glass doors slowly opening, disclosed a pale and emaciated figure in soiled and worn apparel, standing erect in the press. The figure was tall and thin, and the countenance expressive of care and anxiety; but there was something in the hue of the skin, and gaunt and unearthly appearance of the whole form, which no being of this world was ever seen to wear. "Who are you?" said the new tenant, turning very pale: poising the poker in his hand, however, and taking a very decent aim at the countenance of the figure. "Who are you?" "Don't throw that poker at me," replied the form; "If you hurled it with ever so sure an aim, it would pass through me, without resistance, and expend its force on the wood behind. I am a spirit." "And, pray, what do you want here?" faltered the tenant. "In this room," replied the apparition, "my wordly ruin was worked, and I and my children beggared. In this press, the papers in a long, long suit, which accumulated for years, were deposited. In this room, when I had died of grief, and long-deferred hope, two wily harpies divided the wealth for which I had contested during a wretched existence, and of which, at last, not one farthing was left for my unhappy descendants. I terrified them from the spot, and since that day have prowled by night – the only period at which I can re-visit the earth – about the scenes of my long-protracted misery. This apartment is mine: leave it to me." "If you insist upon making your appearance here," said the tenant, who had had time to collect his presence of mind during this prosy statement of the ghost's, "I shall give up possession with the greatest pleasure; but I should like to ask you one question, if you will allow me." "Say on," said the apparition, sternly. "Well," said the tenant, "I don't apply the observation personally to you, because it is equally applicable to most of the ghosts I ever heard of; but it does appear to me somewhat inconsistent, that when you have an opportunity of visiting the fairest spots of earth – for I suppose space is nothing to you – you should always return exactly to the very places where you have been most miserable." "Egad, that's very true; I never thought of that before," said the ghost. "You see, sir," pursued the tenant "this is a very uncomfortable room. From the appearance of that press, I should be disposed to say that it is not wholly free from bugs; and I really think you might find much more comfortable quarters: to say nothing of the climate of London, which is extremely disagreeable." "You are very right, sir," said the ghost, politely, "it never struck me till now; I'll try change of air directly." In fact, he began to vanish as he spoke: his legs, indeed, had quite disappeared. "And if, sir," said the tenant, calling after him, "if you *would* have the goodness to suggest to the other ladies and gentlemen who are now engaged in haunting old empty houses, that they might be much more comfortable elsewhere, you will confer a very great benefit on society." "I will," replied the ghost; "we must be dull fellows, very dull fellows, indeed; I can't imagine how we can have been so stupid." With these words, the spirit disappeared; and what is rather remarkable,' added the old man, with a shrewd look round the table, 'he never came back again.'

'That ain't bad, if it's true,' said the man in the Mosaic studs, lighting a fresh cigar.

'*If!*' exclaimed the old man, with a look of excessive contempt. 'I suppose,' he added, turning to Lowten, 'he'll say next, that my story about the queer client we had, when I was in an attorney's office, is not true, either – I shouldn't wonder.'

'I shan't venture to say anything at all about it, seeing that I never heard the story,' observed the owner of the Mosaic decorations.

'I wish you would repeat it, sir,' said Mr Pickwick.

'Ah, do,' said Lowten, 'nobody has heard it but me, and I have nearly forgotten it.'

The old man looked round the table, and leered more horribly than ever, as if in triumph, at the attention which was depicted in every face. Then rubbing his chin with his hand, and looking up to the ceiling as if to recal the circumstances to his memory, he began as follows:

THE OLD MAN'S TALE ABOUT THE QUEER CLIENT

'It matters little,' said the old man, 'where, or how, I picked up this brief history. If I were to relate it in the order in which it reached me, I should commence in the middle, and when I had arrived at the conclusion, go back for a beginning. It is enough for me to say that some of its circumstances passed before my own eyes. For the remainder I know them to have happened, and there are some persons yet living, who will remember them but too well.

'In the Borough High Street, near Saint George's Church, and on the same side of the way, stands, as most people know, the smallest of our debtors' prisons, the Marshalsea. Although in later times it has been a very different place from the sink of filth and dirt it once was, even its improved condition holds out but little temptation to the extravagant, or consolation to the improvident. The condemned felon has as good a yard for air and exercise in Newgate,[3] as the insolvent debtor in the Marshalsea Prison.*

'It may be my fancy, or it may be that I cannot separate the place

---

* Better. But this is past, in a better age, and the prison exists no longer.

from the old recollections associated with it, but this part of London I cannot bear. The street is broad, the shops are spacious, the noise of passing vehicles, the footsteps of a perpetual stream of people – all the busy sounds of traffic, resound in it from morn to midnight, but the streets around are mean and close; poverty and debauchery lie festering in the crowded alleys; want and misfortune are pent up in the narrow prison; an air of gloom and dreariness seems, in my eyes at least, to hang about the scene, and to impart to it a squalid and sickly hue.

'Many eyes, that have long since been closed in the grave, have looked round upon that scene lightly enough, when entering the gate of the old Marshalsea Prison for the first time: for despair seldom comes with the first severe shock of misfortune. A man has confidence in untried friends, he remembers the many offers of service so freely made by his boon companions when he wanted them not; he has hope – the hope of happy inexperience – and however he may bend beneath the first shock, it springs up in his bosom, and flourishes there for a brief space, until it droops beneath the blight of disappointment and neglect. How soon have those same eyes, deeply sunken in the head, glared from faces wasted with famine, and sallow from confinement, in days when it was no figure of speech to say that debtors rotted in prison, with no hope of release, and no prospect of liberty! The atrocity in its full extent no longer exists, but there is enough of it left to give rise to occurrences that make the heart bleed.

'Twenty years ago, that pavement was worn with the footsteps of a mother and child, who, day by day, so surely as the morning came, presented themselves at the prison gate; often after a night of restless misery and anxious thoughts, were they there, a full hour too soon, and then the young mother turning meekly away, would lead the child to the old bridge, and raising him in her arms to show him the glistening water, tinted with the light of the morning's sun, and stirring with all the bustling preparations for business and pleasure that the river presented at that early hour, endeavour to interest his thoughts in the objects before him. But she would quickly set him down, and hiding her face in her shawl, give vent to the tears that blinded her; for no expression of interest or amusement lighted up his thin and sickly face. His recollections were few enough, but they were all of one kind: all connected with the poverty and misery of his parents. Hour after hour had he sat on his mother's knee, and with childish sympathy watched the tears that stole down her face, and then crept quietly away into some dark corner, and sobbed himself to sleep. The hard realities of the world, with many of its worst privations – hunger and thirst, and cold and want – had all come home to him, from the first dawnings of reason; and though the form of childhood was there, its light heart, it merry laugh, and sparkling eyes, were wanting.

'The father and mother looked on upon this, and upon each other, with thoughts of agony they dared not breathe in words. The healthy, strong-made man, who could have borne almost any fatigue of active exertion, was wasting beneath the close confinement and unhealthy atmosphere of a crowded prison. The slight and delicate woman was sinking beneath the combined effects of bodily and mental illness. The child's young heart was breaking.

'Winter came, and with it weeks of cold and heavy rain. The poor girl had removed to a wretched apartment close to the spot of her husband's imprisonment; and though the change had been rendered necessary by their increasing poverty, she was happier now, for she was nearer him. For two months, she and her little companion watched the opening of the gate as usual. One day she failed to come, for the first time. Another morning arrived, and she came alone. The child was dead.

'They little know, who coldly talk of the poor man's bereavements, as a happy release from pain to the departed, and a merciful relief from expense to the survivor – they little know, I say, what the agony of those bereavements is. A silent look of affection and regard when all other eyes are turned coldly away – the consciousness that we possess the sympathy and affection of one being when all others have deserted us – is a hold, a stay, a comfort, in the deepest affliction, which no wealth could purchase, or power bestow. The child had sat at his parents' feet for hours together, with his little hands patiently folded in each other, and his thin wan face raised towards them. They had seen him pine away, from day to day; and though his brief existence had been a joyless one, and he was now removed to that peace and rest which, child as he was, he had never known in this world, they were his parents, and his loss sunk deep into their souls.

'It was plain to those who looked upon the mother's altered face, that death must soon close the scene of her adversity and trial. Her husband's fellow-prisoners shrunk from obtruding on his grief and misery, and left to himself alone, the small room he had previously occupied in common with two companions. She shared it with him: and lingering on without pain, but without hope, her life ebbed slowly away.

'She had fainted one evening in her husband's arms, and he had borne her to the open window, to revive her with the air, when the light of the moon falling full upon her face, shewed him a change upon her features, which made him stagger beneath her weight, like a helpless infant.

'"Set me down, George," she said faintly. He did so, and seating himself beside her, covered his face with his hands, and burst into tears.

'"It is very hard to leave you, George," she said, "but it is God's will, and you must bear it for my sake. Oh! how I thank Him for having taken our boy! He is happy, and in Heaven now. What would he have done here, without his mother!"

'"You shall not die, Mary, you shall not die;" said the husband, starting up. He paced hurriedly to and fro, striking his head with his clenched fists; then reseating himself beside her, and supporting her in his arms, added more calmly, "Rouse yourself, my dear girl. Pray, pray do. You will revive yet."

'"Never again, George; never again," said the dying woman. "Let them lay me by my poor boy now, but promise me, that if ever you leave this dreadful place, and should grow rich, you will have us removed to some quiet country churchyard, a long, long way off – very far from here – where we can rest in peace. Dear George, promise me you will."

'"I do, I do," said the man, throwing himself passionately on his knees before her. "Speak to me, Mary, another word; one look – but one!"

'He ceased to speak: for the arm that clasped his neck, grew stiff and heavy. A deep sigh escaped from the wasted form before him; the lips moved, and a smile played upon the face; but the lips were pallid, and the smile faded into a rigid and ghastly stare. He was alone in the world.

'That night, in the silence and desolation of his miserable room, the wretched man knelt down by the dead body of his wife, and called on God to witness a terrible oath, that from that hour, he devoted himself to revenge her death and that of his child; that thenceforth to the last moment of his life, his whole energies should be directed to this one object; that his revenge should be protracted and terrible; that his hatred should be undying and inextinguishable; and should hunt its object through the world.

'The deepest despair, and passion scarcely human, had made such fierce ravages on his face and form, in that one night, that his companions in misfortune shrunk affrighted from him as he passed by. His eyes were bloodshot and heavy, his face a deadly white, and his body bent as if with age. He had bitten his under lip nearly through in the violence of his mental suffering, and the blood which had flowed from the wound had trickled down his chin, and stained his shirt and neckerchief. No tear, or sound of complaint escaped him: but the unsettled look, and disordered haste with which he paced up and down the yard, denoted the fever which was burning within.

'It was necessary that his wife's body should be removed from the prison, without delay. He received the communication with perfect calmness, and acquiesced in its propriety. Nearly all the inmates of the prison had assembled to witness its removal; they fell back on either side when the widower appeared; he walked hurriedly forward, and stationed himself, alone, in a little railed area close to the lodge gate, from whence the crowd, with an instinctive feeling of delicacy, had retired. The rude coffin was borne slowly forward on men's shoulders. A dead silence pervaded the throng, broken only by the audible lamentations of the women, and the shuffling steps of the bearers on the stone pavement. They reached the spot where the bereaved husband stood: and stopped. He laid his hand upon the coffin, and mechanically adjusting the pall with which it was covered, motioned them onward. The turnkeys[4] in the prison lobby took off their hats as it passed through, and in another moment the heavy gate closed behind it. He looked vacantly upon the crowd, and fell heavily to the ground.

'Although for many weeks after this, he was watched, night and day, in the wildest ravings of fever, neither the consciousness of his loss, nor the recollection of the vow he had made, ever left him for a moment. Scenes changed before his eyes, place succeeded place, and event followed event, in all the hurry of delirium; but they were all connected in some way with the great object of his mind. He was sailing over a boundless expanse of sea, with a blood-red sky above, and the angry waters, lashed into fury beneath, boiling and eddying up, on every side. There was another vessel before them, toiling and labouring in the howling storm: her canvas fluttering in ribbons from the mast, and her deck thronged with figures who were lashed to the sides, over which huge waves every instant burst, sweeping away some devoted creatures into the foaming sea. Onward they bore, amidst the roaring mass of water, with a speed and force which nothing could resist; and striking the stern of the foremost vessel, crushed her, beneath their keel. From the huge whirlpool which the sinking wreck occasioned, arose a shriek so loud and shrill – the death-cry of a hundred drowning creatures, blended into one fierce yell – that it rung far above the war-cry of the elements, and echoed, and re-echoed till it seemed to pierce air, sky, and ocean. But what was that – that old grey-head that rose above the water's surface, and with looks of agony, and screams for aid, buffeted with the waves! One look, and he had sprung from the vessel's side, and with vigorous strokes was swimming towards it. He reached it; he was close upon it. They were *his* features. The old man saw him coming, and vainly strove to elude his grasp. But he clasped him tight, and dragged him beneath the water. Down, down with him, fifty fathoms down; his struggles grew fainter and fainter, until they wholly ceased. He was dead; he had killed him, and had kept his oath.

'He was traversing the scorching sands of a mighty desert, barefoot and alone. The sand choked and blinded him; its fine thin grains entered the very pores of his skin, and irritated him almost to madness. Gigantic masses of the same material, carried forward by the wind, and shone through, by the burning sun, stalked in the distance like pillars of living fire. The bones of men, who had perished in the dreary waste, lay scattered at his feet; a fearful light fell on everything around; so far as the eye could reach, nothing but objects of dread and horror presented themselves. Vainly striving to utter a cry of terror, with his tongue cleaving to his mouth, he rushed madly forward. Armed with supernatural strength, he waded through the sand, until exhausted with fatigue and thirst, he fell senseless on the earth. What fragrant coolness revived him; what gushing sound was that? Water! It was indeed a well; and the clear fresh stream was running at his feet. He drank deeply of it, and throwing his aching limbs upon the bank, sunk into a delicious trance. The sound of approaching footsteps roused him. An old grey-headed man tottered forward to slake his burning thirst. It was *he* again! He wound his arms round the old man's body, and held him back. He struggled, and shrieked for water, for but one drop of water to save his life! But he held the old man firmly, and watched his agonies with greedy eyes; and when his lifeless head fell forward on his bosom, he rolled the corpse from him with his feet.

'When the fever left him, and consciousness returned, he awoke to find himself rich and free: to hear that the parent who would have let him die in gaol – *would*! who *had* let those who were far dearer to him than his own existence, die of want and sickness of heart that medicine cannot cure – had been found dead on his bed of down. He had had all the heart to leave his son a beggar, but proud even of his health and strength, had put off the act till it was too late, and now might gnash his teeth in the other world, at the thought of the wealth his remissness had left him. He awoke to this, and he awoke to more. To recollect the purpose for which he lived, and to remember that his enemy was his wife's own father – the man who had cast him into prison, and who, when his daughter and her child sued at his feet for mercy, had spurned them from his door. Oh, how he cursed the weakness that prevented him from being up, and active, in his scheme of vengeance!

'He caused himself to be carried from the scene of his loss and misery, and conveyed to a quiet residence on the sea-coast; not in the hope of recovering his peace of mind or happiness, for both were fled for ever; but to restore his prostrate energies, and meditate on his darling object. And here, some evil spirit cast in his way the opportunity for his first, most horrible revenge.

'It was summer time; and wrapped in his gloomy thoughts, he would issue from his solitary lodgings early in the evening, and wandering along a narrow path beneath the cliffs, to a wild and lonely spot that had struck his fancy in his ramblings, seat himself on some fallen fragment of the rock, and burying his face in his hands, remain there for hours – sometimes until night had completely closed in, and the long shadows of the frowning cliffs above his head, cast a thick black darkness on every object near him.

'He was seated here, one calm evening in his old position, now and then raising his head to watch the flight of a sea-gull, or carry his eye along the glorious crimson path, which, commencing in the middle of the ocean, seemed to lead to its very verge where the sun was setting, when the profound stillness of the spot was broken by a loud cry for help; he listened, doubtful of his having heard aright, when the cry was repeated with even greater vehemence than before, and starting to his feet, he hastened in the direction whence it proceeded.

'The tale told itself at once: some scattered garments lay on the beach; a human head was just visible above the waves at a little distance from the shore; and an old man, wringing his hands in agony, was running to and fro, shrieking for assistance. The invalid, whose strength was now sufficiently restored, threw off his coat, and rushed towards the sea, with the intention of plunging in, and dragging the drowning man a-shore.

'"Hasten here, sir, in God's name; help, help, sir, for the love of Heaven. He is my son, sir, my only son!" said the old man, frantically, as he advanced to meet him. "My only son, sir, and he is dying before his father's eyes!"

'At the first word the old man uttered, the stranger checked himself in his career, and, folding his arms, stood perfectly motionless.

'"Great God!" exclaimed the old man, recoiling. "Heyling!"

'The stranger smiled, and was silent.

'"Heyling!" said the old man, wildly: "My boy, Heyling, my dear boy, look, look!" gasping for breath, the miserable father pointed to the spot where the young man was struggling for life.

'"Hark!" said the old man. "He cries once more. He is alive yet. Heyling, save him, save him!"

'The stranger smiled again, and remained immovable as a statue.

'"I have wronged you," shrieked the old man, falling on his knees, and clasping his hands together. "Be revenged; take my all, my life; cast me into the water at your feet, and, if human nature can repress a struggle, I will die, without stirring hand or foot. Do it, Heyling, do it, but save my boy, he is so young, Heyling, so young to die!"

'"Listen," said the stranger, grasping the old man fiercely by the wrist: "I will have life for life, and here is ONE. My child died, before his father's eyes, a far more agonising and painful death than that young slanderer of his sister's worth is meeting while I speak. You laughed – laughed in your daughter's face, where death had already set his hand – at our sufferings, then. What think you of them now? See there, see there!"

'As the stranger spoke, he pointed to the sea. A faint cry died away upon its surface: the last powerful struggle of the dying man agitated the rippling waves for a few seconds: and the spot where he had gone down into his early grave, was undistinguishable from the surrounding water.

*   *   *

'Three years had elapsed, when a gentleman alighted from a private carriage at the door of a London attorney, then well known as a man of no great nicety in his professional dealings: and requested a private interview on business of importance. Although evidently not past the prime of life, his face was pale, haggard, and dejected; and it did not require the acute perception of the man of business, to discern at a glance, that disease or suffering had done more to work a change in his appearance, than the mere hand of time could have accomplished in twice the period of his whole life.

'"I wish you to undertake some legal business for me," said the stranger.

'The attorney bowed obsequiously, and glanced at a large packet which the gentleman carried in his hand. His visitor observed the look, and proceeded.

'"It is no common business," said he; "nor have these papers reached my hands without long trouble and great expense."

'The attorney cast a still more anxious look at the packet: and his visitor, untying the string that bound it, disclosed a quantity of promissory notes, with copies of deeds, and other documents.

'"Upon these papers," said the client, "the man whose name they bear, has raised, as you will see, large sums of money, for some years past. There was a tacit understanding between him and the men into whose hands they originally went – and from whom I have by degrees purchased the whole, for treble and quadruple their nominal value – that these loans should be from time to time renewed, until a given period had elapsed. Such an understanding is nowhere expressed. He has sustained many losses of late; and these obligations accumulating upon him at once, would crush him to the earth."

'"The whole amount is many thousands of pounds," said the attorney, looking over the papers.

'"It is," said the client.

'"What are we to do?" inquired the man of business.

'"Do!" replied the client, with sudden vehemence. "Put every engine of the law in force, every trick that ingenuity can devise and rascality execute; fair means and foul; the open oppression of the law, aided by all the craft of its most ingenious practitioners. I would have him die a harassing and lingering death. Ruin him, seize and sell his lands and goods, drive him from house and home, and drag him forth a beggar in his old age, to die in a common gaol."

'"But the costs, my dear sir, the costs of all this," reasoned the attorney, when he had recovered from his momentary surprise. "If the defendant be a man of straw, who is to pay the costs, sir?"

'"Name any sum," said the stranger, his hand trembling so violently with excitement, that he could scarcely hold the pen he seized as he spoke; "Any sum, and it is yours. Don't be afraid to name it, man. I shall not think it dear, if you gain my object."

'The attorney named a large sum, at hazard, as the advance he should require to secure himself against the possibility of loss; but more with the view of ascertaining how far his client was really disposed to go, than with any idea that he would comply with the demand. The stranger wrote a cheque upon his banker, for the whole amount, and left him.

'The draft was duly honoured, and the attorney, finding that his strange client might be safely relied upon, commenced his work in earnest. For more than two years afterwards, Mr Heyling would sit whole days together, in the office, poring over the papers as they accumulated, and reading again and again, his eyes gleaming with joy, the letters of remonstrance, the prayers for a little delay, the representations of the certain ruin in which the opposite party must be involved, which poured in, as suit after suit, and process after process, was commenced. To all applications for a brief indulgence, there was but one reply – the money must be paid. Land, house, furniture, each in its turn, was taken under some one of the numerous executions which were issued; and the old man himself would have been immured in prison had he not escaped the vigilance of the officers, and fled.

'The implacable animosity of Heyling, so far from being satiated by the success of his persecution, increased a hundred-fold with the ruin he inflicted. On being informed of the old man's flight, his fury was unbounded. He gnashed his teeth with rage, tore the hair from his head, and assailed with horrid imprecations the men who had been entrusted with the writ. He was only restored to comparative calmness by repeated assurances of the certainty of discovering the fugitive. Agents were sent in quest of him, in all directions; every stratagem that could be invented was resorted to, for the purpose of discovering his place of retreat; but it was all in vain. Half a year had passed over, and he was still undiscovered.

'At length, late one night, Heyling, of whom nothing had been seen for many weeks before, appeared at his attorney's private residence, and sent up word that a gentleman wished to see him instantly. Before the attorney, who had recognised his voice from above stairs, could order the servant to admit him, he had rushed up the staircase, and entered the drawing-room pale and breathless. Having closed the door, to prevent being overheard, he sunk into a chair, and said, in a low voice:

'"Hush! I have found him at last."

'"No!" said the attorney. "Well done, my dear sir; well done."

'"He lies concealed in a wretched lodging in Camden Town," said Heyling. "Perhaps it is as well, we *did* lose sight of him, for he has been living alone there, in the most abject misery, all the time, and he is poor – very poor."

'"Very good," said the attorney. "You will have the caption
made to-morrow, of course?"

'"Yes," replied Heyling. "Stay! No! The next day. You are
surprised at my wishing to postpone it," he added, with a ghastly
smile; "but I had forgotten. The next day is an anniversary in his
life: let it be done then."

'"Very good," said the attorney. "Will you write down instructions for the officer?"

'"No; let him meet me here, at eight in the evening, and I will
accompany him, myself."

'They met on the appointed night, and, hiring a hackney coach,
directed the driver to stop at that corner of the old Pancras Road,
at which stands the parish workhouse. By the time they alighted
there, it was quite dark; and, proceeding by the dead wall in front
of the Veterinary Hospital, they entered a small by-street, which is,
or was at that time, called Little College Street, and which, whatever it may be now, was in those days a desolate place enough,
surrounded by little else than fields and ditches.

'Having drawn the travelling cap he had on half over his face,
and muffled himself in his cloak, Heyling stopped before the
meanest-looking house in the street, and knocked gently at the
door. It was at once opened by a woman, who dropped a curtesy of
recognition, and Heyling, whispering the officer to remain below,
crept gently up stairs, and, opening the door of the front room,
entered at once.

'The object of his search and his unrelenting animosity, now a
decrepid old man, was seated at a bare deal table, on which stood a
miserable candle. He started on the entrance of the stranger, and
rose feebly to his feet.

'"What now, what now?" said the old man. "What fresh misery
is this? What do you want here?"

'"A word with *you*," replied Heyling. As he spoke, he seated
himself at the other end of the table, and, throwing off his cloak
and cap, disclosed his features.

'The old man seemed instantly deprived of the power of speech.
He fell backward in his chair, and, clasping his hands together,
gazed on the apparition with a mingled look of abhorrence and
fear.

'"This day six years," said Heyling, "I claimed the life you owed
me for my child's. Beside the lifeless form of your daughter, old
man, I swore to live a life of revenge. I have never swerved from my
purpose for a moment's space; but if I had, one thought of her

The last visit of Heyling to the Old Man

uncomplaining, suffering look, as she drooped away, or of the starving face of our innocent child, would have nerved me to my task. My first act of requital you well remember: this is my last."

'The old man shivered, and his hands dropped powerless by his side.

'"I leave England to-morrow," said Heyling, after a moment's pause. "To-night I consign you to the living death to which you devoted her – a hopeless prison – "

'He raised his eyes to the old man's countenance, and paused. He lifted the light to his face, set it gently down, and left the apartment.

'"You had better see to the old man," he said to the woman, as he opened the door, and motioned the officer to follow him into the street. "I think he is ill." The woman closed the door, ran hastily up stairs, and found him lifeless.

*   *   *

'Beneath a plain grave-stone, in one of the most peaceful and secluded church yards in Kent, where wild flowers mingle with the grass, and the soft landscape around forms the fairest spot in the garden of England, lie the bones of the young mother and her gentle child. But the ashes of the father do not mingle with theirs; nor, from that night forward, did the attorney ever gain the remotest clue to the subsequent history of his queer client.'

————

As the old man concluded his tale, he advanced to a peg in one corner, and taking down his hat and coat, put them on with great deliberation; and, without saying another word, walked slowly away. As the gentleman with the Mosaic studs had fallen asleep, and the major part of the company were deeply occupied in the humorous process of dropping melted tallow-grease into his brandy and water, Mr Pickwick departed unnoticed, and having settled his own score, and that of Mr Weller, issued forth, in company with that gentleman, from beneath the portal of the Magpie and Stump.

Mr Pickwick journeys to Ipswich, and meets with a romantic Adventure with a middle-aged Lady in Yellow Curl Papers

'That 'ere your governor's luggage, Sammy?' inquired Mr Weller of his affectionate son, as he entered the yard of the Bull inn, Whitechapel, with a travelling bag and a small portmanteau.

'You might ha' made a worser guess than that, old feller,' replied Mr Weller the younger, setting down his burden in the yard, and sitting himself down upon it afterwards. 'The Governor hisself'll be down here presently.'

'He's a cabbin' it, I suppose?' said the father.

'Yes, he's a havin' two mile o' danger at eight-pence,' responded the son. 'How's mother-in-law this mornin'?'

'Queer, Sammy, queer,' replied the elder Mr Weller, with impressive gravity. 'She's been gettin' rayther in the Methodistical order lately, Sammy; and she is uncommon pious, to be sure. She's too good a creetur for me, Sammy. I feel I don't deserve her.'

'Ah,' said Mr Samuel, 'that's wery self-denyin' o' you.'

'Wery,' replied his parent, with a sigh. 'She's got hold o' some inwention for grown-up people being born again, Sammy; the new birth,[1] I thinks they calls it. I should wery much like to see that system in haction, Sammy. I should wery much like to see your mother-in-law born again. Wouldn't I put her out to nurse!'

'What do you think them women does t'other day,' continued Mr Weller, after a short pause, during which he had significantly struck the side of his nose with his fore-finger some half-dozen times. 'What do you think they does, t'other day, Sammy?'

'Don't know,' replied Sam, 'what?'

'Goes and gets up a grand tea drinkin' for a feller they calls their shepherd,' said Mr Weller. 'I was a standing starin' in at the pictur shop down at our place, when I sees a little bill about it; "tickets half-a-crown.[2] All applications to be made to the committee. Secretary, Mrs Weller;" and when I got home there was the committee a sittin' in our back parlour. Fourteen women; I wish you could ha' heard 'em, Sammy. There they was, a passin' resolutions, and wotin' supplies, and all sorts o' games. Well, what with your mother-in-law a worrying me to go, and what with my looking for'ard to seein' some queer starts if I did, I put my name down for a ticket; at six o'clock on the Friday evenin' I dresses my-

self out wery smart, and off I goes with the old 'ooman, and up we
walks into a fust floor where there was tea things for thirty, and a
whole lot o'women as begins whisperin' to one another, and lookin'
at me, as if they'd never seen a rayther stout gen'lm'n of eight-and-
fifty afore. By and bye, there comes a great bustle down stairs, and
a lanky chap with a red nose and a white neckcloth rushes up, and
sings out, "Here's the shepherd a coming to wisit his faithful flock;"
and in comes a fat chap in black, vith a great white face, a smilin'
avay like clockwork. Such goin's on, Sammy! "The kiss of peace,"
says the shepherd; and then he kissed the women all round, and ven
he'd done, the man vith the red nose began. I was just a thinkin'
whether I hadn't better begin too – 'specially as there was a wery
nice lady a sittin' next me – ven in comes the tea, and your mother-
in-law, as had been makin' the kettle bile down stairs. At it they
went, tooth and nail. Such a precious loud hymn, Sammy, while the
tea was a brewing; such a grace, such eatin' and drinkin'! I wish
you could ha' seen the shepherd walkin' into the ham and muffins.
I never see such a chap to eat and drink; never. The red-nosed man
warn't by no means the sort of person you'd like to grub[3] by
contract, but he was nothin' to the shepherd. Well; arter the tea
was over, they sang another hymn, and then the shepherd began to
preach: and wery well he did it, considerin' how heavy them muffins
must have lied on his chest. Presently he pulls up, all of a sudden,
and hollers out "Where is the sinner; where is the mis'rable sinner?"
Upon which, all the women looked at me, and began to groan as if
they was a dying. I thought it was rather sing'ler, but hows'ever, I
says nothing. Presently he pulls up again, and lookin' wery hard at
me, says, "Where is the sinner; where is the mis'rable sinner?" and
all the women groans again, ten times louder than afore. I got
rather wild at this, so I takes a step or two for'ard and says, "My
friend," says I, "did you apply that 'ere obserwation to me?" 'Stead
of begging my pardon as any gen'lm'n would ha' done, he got more
abusive than ever: called me a wessel, Sammy – a wessel of wrath[4]
– and all sorts o'names. So my blood being reg'larly up, I first give
him two or three for himself, and then two or three more to hand
over to the man with the red nose, and walked off. I wish you could
ha' heard how the women screamed, Sammy, ven they picked up
the shepherd from under the table—Hallo! here's the governor, the
size of life.'

As Mr Weller spoke, Mr Pickwick dismounted from a cab, and
entered the yard.

'Fine mornin' sir,' said Mr Weller senior.

'Beautiful indeed,' replied Mr Pickwick.

'Beautiful indeed,' echoed a red-haired man, with an inquisitive nose and blue spectacles, who had unpacked himself from a cab at the same moment as Mr Pickwick. 'Going to Ipswich, sir?'

'I am,' replied Mr Pickwick.

'Extraordinary coincidence. So am I.'

Mr Pickwick bowed.

'Going outside?' said the red-haired man.

Mr Pickwick bowed again.

'Bless my soul, how remarkable – I am going outside, too,' said the red-haired man: 'we are positively going together.' And the red-haired man, who was an important-looking, sharp-nosed, mysterious-spoken personage, with a bird-like habit of giving his head a jerk every time he said anything, smiled as if he had made one of the strangest discoveries that ever fell to the lot of human wisdom.

'I am happy in the prospect of your company, sir,' said Mr Pickwick.

'Ah,' said the new-comer, 'it's a good thing for both of us, isn't it? Company, you see – company is – is – it's a very different thing from solitude – ain't it?'

'There's no denying that 'ere,' said Mr Weller, joining in the conversation, with an affable smile. 'That's what I call a self-evident proposition, as the dog's-meat man⁵ said, when the house-maid told him he warn't a gentleman.'

'Ah,' said the red-haired man, surveying Mr Weller from head to foot with a supercilious look. 'Friend of yours, sir?'

'Not exactly a friend,' replied Mr Pickwick in a low tone. 'The fact is, he is my servant, but I allow him to take a good many liberties; for, between ourselves, I flatter myself he is an original, and I am rather proud of him.'

'Ah,' said the red-haired man, 'that, you see, is a matter of taste. I am not fond of anything original; I don't like it; don't see the necessity for it. What's your name, sir?'

'Here is my card, sir,' replied Mr Pickwick, much amused by the abruptness of the question, and the singular manner of the stranger.

'Ah,' said the red-haired man, placing the card in his pocket-book, 'Pickwick; very good. I like to know a man's name, it saves so much trouble. That's my card, sir. Magnus, you will perceive, sir – Magnus is my name. It's rather a good name, I think, sir?'

'A very good name, indeed,' said Mr Pickwick, wholly unable to repress a smile.

'Yes, I think it is,' resumed Mr Magnus. 'There's a good name before it, too, you will observe. Permit me, sir – if you hold the card a little slanting, this way, you catch the light upon the up-stroke. There – Peter Magnus – sounds well, I think, sir.'

'Very,' said Mr Pickwick.

'Curious circumstance about those initials, sir,' said Mr Magnus. 'You will observe – P.M. – post meridian. In hasty notes to intimate acquaintance, I sometimes sign myself "Afternoon." It amuses my friends very much, Mr Pickwick.'

'It is calculated to afford them the highest gratification, I should conceive,' said Mr Pickwick, rather envying the ease with which Mr Magnus's friends were entertained.

'Now, gen'lm'n,' said the hostler, 'coach is ready, if you please.'

'Is all my luggage in?' inquired Mr Magnus.

'All right, sir.'

'Is the red bag in?'

'All right, sir.'

'And the striped bag?'

'Fore boot, sir.'

'And the brown-paper parcel?'

'Under the seat, sir.'

'And the leather hat-box?'

'They're all in, sir.'

'Now, will you get up?' said Mr Pickwick.

'Excuse me,' replied Magnus, standing on the wheel. 'Excuse me, Mr Pickwick. I cannot consent to get up, in this state of uncertainty. I am quite satisfied from that man's manner, that that leather hat-box is *not* in.'

The solemn protestations of the hostler being wholly unavailing, the leather hat-box was obliged to be raked up from the lowest depth of the boot, to satisfy him that it had been safely packed; and after he had been assured on this head, he felt a solemn presentiment, first, that the red bag was mislaid, and next that the striped bag had been stolen, and then that the brown-paper parcel 'had come untied.' At length when he had received ocular demonstration of the groundless nature of each and every of these suspicions, he consented to climb up to the roof of the coach, observing that now he had taken every thing off his mind, he felt quite comfortable and happy.

'You're given to nervousness, an't you, sir?' inquired Mr Weller senior, eyeing the stranger askance, as he mounted to his place.

'Yes; I always am rather, about these little matters,' said the stranger, 'but I am all right now – quite right.'

'Well, that's a blessin',' said Mr Weller. 'Sammy, help your master up to the box: t'other leg, sir, that's it; give us your hand, sir. Up with you. You was a lighter weight when you was a boy, sir.'

'True enough, that, Mr Weller,' said the breathless Mr Pickwick, good humouredly, as he took his seat on the box beside him.

'Jump up in front, Sammy,' said Mr Weller. 'Now Villam, run 'em out. Take care o' the archvay, gen'lm'n. "Heads," as the pieman says.⁶ That'll do, Villam. Let 'em alone.' And away went the coach up Whitechapel, to the admiration of the whole population of that pretty-densely populated quarter.

'Not a wery nice neighbourhood this, sir,' said Sam, with a touch of the hat, which always preceded his entering into conversation with his master.

'It is not indeed, Sam,' replied Mr Pickwick, surveying the crowded and filthy street through which they were passing.

'It's a wery remarkable circumstance, sir,' said Sam, 'that poverty and oysters always seems to go together.'

'I don't understand you, Sam,' said Mr Pickwick.

'What I mean, sir,' said Sam, 'is, that the poorer a place is, the greater call there seems to be for oysters. Look here, sir; here's a oyster stall to every half-dozen houses. The street's lined vith 'em. Blessed if I don't think that ven a man's wery poor, he rushes out of his lodgings, and eats oysters in reg'lar desperation.'

'To be sure he does,' said Mr Weller senior; 'and it's just the same vith pickled salmon!'

'Those are two very remarkable facts, which never occurred to me before,' said Mr Pickwick. 'The very first place we stop at, I'll make a note of them.'

By this time they had reached the turnpike at Mile End; a profound silence prevailed until they had got two or three miles further on, when Mr Weller senior, turning suddenly to Mr Pickwick, said:

'Wery queer life is a pike-keeper's, sir.'

'A what?' said Mr Pickwick.

'A pike-keeper.'

'What do you mean by a pike-keeper?' inquired Mr Peter Magnus.

'The old 'un means a turnpike keeper, gen'lm'n,' observed Mr Samuel Weller, in explanation.

'Oh,' said Mr Pickwick, 'I see. Yes; very curious life. Very uncomfortable.'

'They're all on 'em men as has met vith some disappointment in life,' said Mr Weller senior.

'Ay, ay?' said Mr Pickwick.

'Yes. Consequence of vich, they retires from the world, and shuts themselves up in pikes; partly vith the view of being solitary, and partly to rewenge themselves on mankind, by takin' tolls.'

'Dear me,' said Mr Pickwick, 'I never knew that before.'

'Fact, sir,' said Mr Weller; 'if they was gen'lm'n you'd call 'em misanthropes, but as it is, they only takes to pike-keepin'.'

With such conversation, possessing the inestimable charm of blending amusement with instruction, did Mr Weller beguile the tediousness of the journey, during the greater part of the day. Topics of conversation were never wanting, for even when any pause occurred in Mr Weller's loquacity, it was abundantly supplied by the desire evinced by Mr Magnus to make himself acquainted with the whole of the personal history of his fellow-travellers, and his loudly-expressed anxiety at every stage, respecting the safety and well-being of the two bags, the leather hat-box, and the brown-paper parcel.

In the main street of Ipswich, on the left-hand side of the way, a short distance after you have passed through the open space fronting the Town Hall, stands an inn known far and wide by the appellation of The Great White Horse, rendered the more conspicuous by a stone statue of some rampacious animal with flowing mane and tail, distantly resembling an insane cart-horse, which is elevated above the principal door. The Great White Horse is famous in the neighbourhood, in the same degree as a prize ox, or county paper-chronicled turnip, or unwieldy pig – for its enormous size. Never were such labyrinths of uncarpeted passages, such clusters of mouldy, ill-lighted rooms, such huge numbers of small dens for eating or sleeping in, beneath any one roof, as are collected together between the four walls of the Great White Horse at Ipswich.

It was at the door of this overgrown tavern that the London coach stopped, at the same hour every evening; and it was from this same London coach, that Mr Pickwick, Sam Weller, and Mr Peter Magnus dismounted, on the particular evening to which this chapter of our history bears reference.

'Do you stop here, sir?' inquired Mr Peter Magnus, when the striped bag, and the red bag, and the brown-paper parcel, and the leather hat-box, had all been deposited in the passage. 'Do you stop here, sir?'

'I do,' said Mr Pickwick.

'Dear me,' said Mr Magnus, 'I never knew anything like these extraordinary coincidences. Why, I stop here too. I hope we dine together?'

'With pleasure,' replied Mr Pickwick. 'I am not quite certain whether I have any friends here or not, though. Is there any gentleman of the name of Tupman here, waiter?'

A corpulent man, with a fortnight's napkin under his arm, and coeval stockings[7] on his legs, slowly desisted from his occupation of staring down the street, on this question being put to him by Mr Pickwick; and, after minutely inspecting that gentleman's appearance, from the crown of his hat to the lowest button of his gaiters, replied emphatically:

'No.'

'Nor any gentleman of the name of Snodgrass?' inquired Mr Pickwick.

'No!'

'Nor Winkle?'

'No.'

'My friends have not arrived to-day, sir,' said Mr Pickwick. 'We will dine alone, then. Shew us a private room, waiter.'

On this request being preferred, the corpulent man condescended to order the boots to bring in the gentleman's luggage; and preceding them down a long dark passage, ushered them into a large badly-furnished apartment, with a dirty grate, in which a small fire was making a wretched attempt to be cheerful, but was fast sinking beneath the dispiriting influence of the place. After the lapse of an hour, a bit of fish and a steak were served up to the travellers, and when the dinner was cleared away, Mr Pickwick and Mr Peter Magnus drew their chairs up to the fire, and having ordered a bottle of the worst possible port wine, at the highest possible price, for the good of the house, drank brandy and water for their own.

Mr Peter Magnus was naturally of a very communicative disposition, and the brandy and water operated with wonderful effect in warming into life the deepest hidden secrets of his bosom. After sundry accounts of himself, his family, his connexions, his friends, his jokes, his business, and his brothers (most talkative men have a great deal to say about their brothers), Mr Peter Magnus took a blue view of Mr Pickwick through his coloured spectacles for several minutes, and then said, with an air of modesty:

'And what do you think – what *do* you think, Mr Pickwick – I have come down here for?'

'Upon my word,' said Mr Pickwick, 'it is wholly impossible for me to guess; on business, perhaps.'

'Partly right, sir,' replied Mr Peter Magnus, 'but partly wrong, at the same time: try again, Mr Pickwick.'

'Really,' said Mr Pickwick, 'I must throw myself on your mercy, to tell me or not, as you may think best; for I should never guess, if I were to try all night.'

'Why, then, he – he – he!' said Mr Peter Magnus, with a bashful titter, 'What should you think, Mr Pickwick, if I had come down here, to make a proposal, sir, eh? He – he – he!'

'Think! That you are very likely to succeed,' replied Mr Pickwick, with one of his beaming smiles.

'Ah!' said Mr Magnus. 'But do you really think so, Mr Pickwick? Do you, though?'

'Certainly,' said Mr Pickwick.

'No; but you're joking, though.'

'I am not, indeed.'

'Why, then,' said Mr Magnus, 'to let you into a little secret, *I* think so too. I don't mind telling you, Mr Pickwick, although I'm dreadful jealous by nature – horrid – that the lady is in this house.' Here Mr Magnus took off his spectacles, on purpose to wink, and then put them on again.

'That's what you were running out of the room for; before dinner, then, so often,' said Mr Pickwick, archly.

'Hush! Yes, you're right, that was it; not such a fool as to see her, though.'

'No!'

'No; wouldn't do, you know, after having just come off a journey. Wait till to-morrow, sir; double the chance then. Mr Pickwick, sir, there is a suit of clothes in that bag, and a hat in that box, which I expect, in the effect they will produce, will be invaluable to me, sir.'

'Indeed!' said Mr Pickwick.

'Yes; you must have observed my anxiety about them to-day. I do not believe that such another suit of clothes, and such a hat, could be bought for money, Mr Pickwick.'

Mr Pickwick congratulated the fortunate owner of the irresistible garments, on their acquisition; and Mr Peter Magnus remained for a few moments apparently absorbed in contemplation.

'She's a fine creature,' said Mr Magnus.

'Is she?' said Mr Pickwick.

'Very,' said Mr Magnus, 'very. She lives about twenty miles from here, Mr Pickwick. I heard she would be here to-night and all to-morrow forenoon, and came down to seize the opportunity. I think an inn is a good sort of a place to propose to a single woman in, Mr Pickwick. She is more likely to feel the loneliness of her situation in travelling, perhaps, than she would be at home. What do you think, Mr Pickwick?'

'I think it very probable,' replied that gentleman.

'I beg your pardon, Mr Pickwick,' said Mr Peter Magnus, 'but I am naturally rather curious; what may *you* have come down here for?'

'On a far less pleasant errand, sir,' replied Mr Pickwick, the colour mounting to his face at the recollection. 'I have come down here, sir, to expose the treachery and falsehood of an individual, upon whose truth and honour I placed implicit reliance.'

'Dear me,' said Mr Peter Magnus, 'that's very unpleasant. It is a lady, I presume? Eh? ah! Sly, Mr Pickwick, sly. Well, Mr Pickwick, sir, I wouldn't probe your feelings for the world. Painful subjects, these, sir, very painful. Don't mind me, Mr Pickwick, if you wish to give vent to your feelings. I know what it is to be jilted, sir; I have endured that sort of thing three or four times.'

'I am much obliged to you, for your condolence on what you presume to be my melancholy case,' said Mr Pickwick, winding up his watch, and laying it on the table, 'but – '

'No, no,' said Mr Peter Magnus, 'not a word more: it's a painful subject. I see, I see. What's the time Mr Pickwick?'

'Past twelve.'

'Dear me, it's time to go to bed. It will never do, sitting here. I shall be pale to-morrow, Mr Pickwick.'

At the bare notion of such a calamity, Mr Peter Magnus rang the bell for the chamber-maid; and the striped bag, the red bag, the leathern hat-box, and the brown-paper parcel, having been conveyed to his bed-room, he retired in company with a japanned[8] candlestick, to one side of the house, while Mr Pickwick, and another japanned candlestick, were conducted through a multitude of tortuous windings, to another.

'This is your room, sir,' said the chamber-maid.

'Very well,' replied Mr Pickwick, looking round him. It was a tolerably large double-bedded room, with a fire; upon the whole, a more comfortable-looking apartment than Mr Pickwick's short experience of the accommodations of the Great White Horse had led him to expect.

'Nobody sleeps in the other bed, of course,' said Mr Pickwick.

'Oh, no, sir.'

'Very good. Tell my servant to bring me up some hot water at half-past eight in the morning, and that I shall not want him any more to-night.'

'Yes, sir.' And bidding Mr Pickwick good night, the chamber-maid retired, and left him alone.

Mr Pickwick sat himself down in a chair before the fire, and fell into a train of rambling meditations. First he thought of his friends, and wondered when they would join him; then his mind reverted to Mrs Martha Bardell; and from that lady it wandered, by a natural process, to the dingy counting-house of Dodson and Fogg. From Dodson and Fogg's it flew off at a tangent, to the very centre of the history of the queer client; and then it came back to the Great White Horse at Ipswich, with sufficient clearness to convince Mr Pickwick that he was falling asleep. So he roused himself, and began to undress, when he recollected he had left his watch on the table down stairs.

Now, this watch was a special favourite with Mr Pickwick, having been carried about, beneath the shadow of his waistcoat, for a greater number of years than we feel called upon to state at present. The possibility of going to sleep, unless it were ticking gently beneath his pillow, or in the watch-pocket over his head, had never entered Mr Pickwick's brain. So as it was pretty late now, and he was unwilling to ring his bell at that hour of the night, he slipped on his coat, of which he had just divested himself, and taking the japanned candlestick in his hand, walked quietly down stairs.

The more stairs Mr Pickwick went down, the more stairs there seemed to be to descend, and again and again, when Mr Pickwick got into some narrow passage, and began to congratulate himself on having gained the ground-floor, did another flight of stairs appear before his astonished eyes. At last he reached a stone hall, which he remembered to have seen when he entered the house. Passage after passage did he explore; room after room did he peep into; at length, as he was on the point of giving up the search in despair, he opened the door of the identical room in which he had spent the evening, and beheld his missing property on the table.

Mr Pickwick seized the watch in triumph, and proceeded to re-trace his steps to his bed-chamber. If his progress downward had been attended with difficulties and uncertainty, his journey back was infinitely more perplexing. Rows of doors, garnished with boots of every shape, make, and size, branched off in every possible direction. A dozen times did he softly turn the handle of some bed-room door which resembled his own, when a gruff cry from within of 'Who the devil's that?' or 'What do you want here?' caused him to steal away, on tiptoe, with a perfectly marvellous celerity. He was reduced to the verge of despair, when an open door attracted his attention. He peeped in. Right at last! There were the two beds, whose situation he perfectly remembered, and the fire still burning. His candle, not a long one when he first received it, had flickered away in the drafts of air through which he had passed, and sank into the socket as he closed the door after him. 'No matter,' said Mr Pickwick, 'I can undress myself just as well by the light of the fire.'

The bedsteads stood one on each side of the door; and on the inner side of each was a little path, terminating in a rush-bottomed chair, just wide enough to admit of a person's getting into, or out of bed, on that side, if he or she thought proper. Having carefully drawn the curtains of his bed on the outside, Mr Pickwick sat down on the rush-bottomed chair, and leisurely divested himself of his shoes and gaiters. He then took off and folded up his coat, waistcoat, and neck-cloth, and slowly drawing on his tasseled night-cap, secured it firmly on his head, by tying beneath his chin the strings which he always had attached to that article of dress. It was at this moment that the absurdity of his recent bewilderment struck upon his mind. Throwing himself back in the rush-bottomed chair, Mr Pickwick laughed to himself so heartily, that it would have been quite delightful to any man of well-constituted mind to have watched the smiles that expanded his amiable features as they shone forth from beneath the night-cap.

'It is the best idea,' said Mr Pickwick to himself, smiling, till he almost cracked the night-cap strings: 'It is the best idea, my losing myself in this place, and wandering about those staircases, that I ever heard of. Droll, droll, very droll.' Here Mr Pickwick smiled again, a broader smile than before, and was about to continue the process of undressing, in the best possible humour, when he was suddenly stopped by a most unexpected interruption; to wit, the entrance into the room of some person with a candle, who, after locking the door, advanced to the dressing table, and set down the light upon it.

The smile that played on Mr Pickwick's features was instantaneously lost in a look of the most unbounded and wonder-stricken surprise. The person, whoever it was, had come in so suddenly and with so little noise, that Mr Pickwick had had no time to call out, or oppose their entrance. Who could it be? A robber? Some evil-minded person who had seen him come up stairs with a handsome watch in his hand, perhaps. What was he to do!

The only way in which Mr Pickwick could catch a glimpse of his mysterious visitor with the least danger of being seen himself, was by creeping on to the bed, and peeping out from between the curtains on the opposite side. To this manœuvre he accordingly resorted. Keeping the curtains carefully closed with his hand, so that nothing more of him could be seen than his face and night-cap, and putting on his spectacles, he mustered up courage, and looked out.

Mr Pickwick almost fainted with horror and dismay. Standing before the dressing-glass was a middle-aged lady, in yellow curl-papers, busily engaged in brushing what ladies call their 'back-hair.' However the unconscious middle-aged lady came into that room, it was quite clear that she contemplated remaining there for the night; for she had brought a rushlight[9] and shade with her, which, with praiseworthy precaution against fire, she had stationed in a basin on the floor, where it was glimmering away, like a gigantic light-house in a particularly small piece of water.

'Bless my soul,' thought Mr Pickwick, 'what a dreadful thing!'

'Hem!' said the lady; and in went Mr Pickwick's head with automaton-like rapidity.

'I never met with anything so awful as this,' thought poor Mr Pickwick, the cold perspiration starting in drops upon his night-cap. 'Never. This is fearful.'

It was quite impossible to resist the urgent desire to see what was going forward. So out went Mr Pickwick's head again. The prospect was worse than before. The middle-aged lady had finished arranging her hair; had carefully enveloped it in a muslin night-cap with a small plaited border; and was gazing pensively on the fire.

'This matter is growing alarming,' reasoned Mr Pickwick with himself. 'I can't allow things to go on in this way. By the self-possession of that lady it is clear to me that I must have come into the wrong room. If I call out she'll alarm the house; but if I remain here the consequences will be still more frightful.'

Mr Pickwick, it is quite unnecessary to say, was one of the most modest and delicate-minded of mortals. The very idea of exhibiting his night-cap to a lady overpowered him, but he had tied those confounded strings in a knot, and, do what he would, he couldn't get it off. The disclosure must be made. There was only one other way of doing it. He shrunk behind the curtains, and called out very loudly:

The middle-aged lady in the double-bedded Room

'Ha – hum!'

That the lady started at this unexpected sound was evident, by her falling up against the rushlight shade; that she persuaded herself it must have been the effect of imagination was equally clear, for when Mr Pickwick, under the impression that she had fainted away stone-dead from fright, ventured to peep out again, she was gazing pensively on the fire as before.

'Most extraordinary female this,' thought Mr Pickwick, popping in again. 'Ha – hum!'

These last sounds, so like those in which, as legends inform us, the ferocious giant Blunderbore[10] was in the habit of expressing his opinion that it was time to lay the cloth, were too distinctly audible to be again mistaken for the workings of fancy.

'Gracious Heaven!' said the middle-aged lady, 'what's that?'

'It's – it's – only a gentleman, Ma'am,' said Mr Pickwick from behind the curtains.

'A gentleman!' said the lady with a terrific scream.

'It's all over!' thought Mr Pickwick.

'A strange man!' shrieked the lady. Another instant and the house would be alarmed. Her garments rustled as she rushed towards the door.

'Ma'am,' said Mr Pickwick, thrusting out his head, in the extremity of his desperation, 'Ma'am!'

Now, although Mr Pickwick was not actuated by any definite object in putting out his head, it was instantaneously productive of a good effect. The lady, as we have already stated, was near the door. She must pass it, to reach the staircase and she would most undoubtedly have done so by this time, had not the sudden apparition of Mr Pickwick's night-cap driven her back into the remotest corner of the apartment, where she stood staring wildly at Mr Pickwick, while Mr Pickwick in his turn stared wildly at her.

'Wretch,' said the lady, covering her eyes with her hands, 'what do you want here?'

'Nothing, Ma'am; nothing, whatever, Ma'am;' said Mr Pickwick earnestly.

'Nothing!' said the lady, looking up.

'Nothing, Ma'am, upon my honour,' said Mr Pickwick, nodding his head so energetically that the tassel of his night-cap danced again. 'I am almost ready to sink, Ma'am, beneath the confusion of addressing a lady in my night-cap (here the lady hastily snatched off hers), but I can't get it off, Ma'am (here Mr Pickwick gave it a tremendous tug, in proof of the statement). It is evident to me,

Ma'am, now, that I have mistaken this bed-room for my own. I had not been here five minutes, Ma'am, when you suddenly entered it.'

'If this improbable story be really true, sir,' said the lady, sobbing violently, 'you will leave it instantly.'

'I will, Ma'am, with the greatest pleasure,' replied Mr Pickwick.

'Instantly, sir,' said the lady.

'Certainly, Ma'am,' interposed Mr Pickwick very quickly. 'Certainly, Ma'am. I – I – am very sorry, Ma'am,' said Mr Pickwick, making his appearance at the bottom of the bed, 'to have been the innocent occasion of this alarm and emotion; deeply sorry, Ma'am.'

The lady pointed to the door. One excellent quality of Mr Pickwick's character was beautifully displayed at this moment, under the most trying circumstances. Although he had hastily put on his hat over his night-cap, after the manner of the old patrol;[11] although he carried his shoes and gaiters in his hand, and his coat and waistcoat over his arm; nothing could subdue his native politeness.

'I am exceedingly sorry, Ma'am,' said Mr Pickwick, bowing very low.

'If you are, sir, you will at once leave the room,' said the lady.

'Immediately, Ma'am; this instant, Ma'am,' said Mr Pickwick, opening the door, and dropping both his shoes with a crash in so doing.

'I trust, Ma'am,' resumed Mr Pickwick, gathering up his shoes, and turning round to bow again: 'I trust, Ma'am, that my unblemished character, and the devoted respect I entertain for your sex, will plead as some slight excuse for this' – But before Mr Pickwick could conclude the sentence the lady had thrust him into the passage, and locked and bolted the door behind him.

Whatever grounds of self-congratulation Mr Pickwick might have for having escaped so quietly from his late awkward situation, his present position was by no means enviable. He was alone, in an open passage, in a strange house, in the middle of the night, half dressed; it was not to be supposed that he could find his way in perfect darkness to a room which he had been wholly unable to discover with a light, and if he made the slightest noise in his fruitless attempts to do so, he stood every chance of being shot at, and perhaps killed, by some wakeful traveller. He had no resource but to remain where he was until daylight appeared. So after groping his way a few paces down the passage, and, to his infinite alarm, stumbling over several pairs of boots in so doing, Mr

Pickwick crouched into a little recess in the wall, to wait for morning as philosophically as he might.

He was not destined, however, to undergo this additional trial of patience: for he had not been long ensconced in his present concealment when, to his unspeakable horror, a man, bearing a light, appeared at the end of the passage. His horror was suddenly converted into joy, however, when he recognised the form of his faithful attendant. It was indeed Mr Samuel Weller, who after sitting up thus late, in conversation with the Boots, who was sitting up for the mail, was now about to retire to rest.

'Sam,' said Mr Pickwick, suddenly appearing before him, 'Where's my bed-room?'

Mr Weller stared at his master with the most emphatic surprise; and it was not until the question had been repeated three several times, that he turned round, and led the way to the long-sought apartment.

'Sam,' said Mr Pickwick as he got into bed. 'I have made one of the most extraordinary mistakes to-night, that ever were heard of.'

'Wery likely, sir,' replied Mr Weller drily.

'But of this I am determined, Sam,' said Mr Pickwick; 'that if I were to stop in this house for six months, I would never trust myself about it, alone, again.'

'That's the wery prudentest resolution as you could come to, sir,' replied Mr Weller. 'You rayther want somebody to look arter you, sir, wen your judgment goes out a wisitin'.'

'What do you mean by that, Sam?' said Mr Pickwick. He raised himself in bed, and extended his hand, as if he were about to say something more; but suddenly checking himself, turned round, and bade his valet 'Good night.'

'Good night, sir,' replied Mr Weller. He paused when he got outside the door – shook his head – walked on – stopped – snuffed the candle – shook his head again – and finally proceeded slowly to his chamber, apparently buried in the profoundest meditation.

CHAPTER 23

In which Mr Samuel Weller begins to devote his
Energies to the Return Match between himself and
Mr Trotter

In a small room in the vicinity of the stable-yard, betimes in the morning, which was ushered in by Mr Pickwick's adventure with the middle-aged lady in the yellow curl-papers, sat Mr Weller senior, preparing himself for his journey to London. He was sitting in an excellent attitude for having his portrait taken.

It is very possible that at some earlier period of his career, Mr Weller's profile might have presented a bold and determined outline. His face, however, had expanded under the influence of good living, and a disposition remarkable for resignation; and its bold fleshy curves had so far extended beyond the limits originally assigned them, that unless you took a full view of his countenance in front, it was difficult to distinguish more than the extreme tip of a very rubicund nose. His chin, from the same cause, had acquired the grave and imposing form which is generally described by prefixing the word 'double' to that expressive feature; and his complexion exhibited that peculiarly mottled combination of colours which is only to be seen in gentlemen of his profession, and in underdone roast beef. Round his neck he wore a crimson travelling shawl, which merged into his chin by such imperceptible gradations, that it was difficult to distinguish the folds of the one, from the folds of the other. Over this, he mounted a long waistcoat of a broad pink-striped pattern, and over that again, a wide-skirted green coat, ornamented with large brass buttons, whereof the two which garnished the waist, were so far apart, that no man had ever beheld them both, at the same time. His hair, which was short, sleek, and black, was just visible beneath the capacious brim of a low-crowned brown hat. His legs were encased in knee-cord breeches, and painted top-boots: and a copper watch-chain, terminating in one seal, and a key of the same material, dangled loosely from his capacious waistband.

We have said that Mr Weller was engaged in preparing for his journey to London – he was taking sustenance, in fact. On the table before him, stood a pot of ale, a cold round of beef, and a very respectable-looking loaf, to each of which he distributed his favours in turn, with the most rigid impartiality. He had just cut a mighty slice from the latter, when the footsteps of somebody entering the room, caused him to raise his head; and he beheld his son.

'Mornin', Sammy!' said the father.

The son walked up to the pot of ale, and nodding significantly to his parent, took a long draught by way of reply.

'Werry good power o' suction, Sammy,' said Mr Weller the elder, looking into the pot, when his first-born had set it down half empty. 'You'd ha' made an uncommon fine oyster, Sammy, if you'd been born in that station o' life.'

'Yes, I des-say I should ha' managed to pick up a respectable livin',' replied Sam, applying himself to the cold beef, with considerable vigour.

'I'm werry sorry, Sammy,' said the elder Mr Weller, shaking up the ale, by describing small circles with the pot, preparatory to drinking. 'I'm werry sorry, Sammy, to hear from your lips, as you let yourself be gammoned by that 'ere mulberry man. I always thought, up to three days ago, that the names of Veller and gammon could never come into contract, Sammy, never.'

'Always exceptin' the case of a widder, of course,' said Sam.

'Widders, Sammy,' replied Mr Weller, slightly changing colour. 'Widders are 'ceptions to ev'ry rule. I *have* heerd how many ord'nary women, one widder's equal to, in pint o' comin' over you. I think it's five-and-twenty, but I don't rightly know vether it an't more.'

'Well; that's pretty well,' said Sam.

'Besides,' continued Mr Weller, not noticing the interruption, 'that's a wery different thing. You know what the counsel said, Sammy, as defended the gen'lem'n as beat his wife with the poker, venever he got jolly. "And arter all, my Lord," says he, "it's a amable weakness." So I says respectin' widders, Sammy, and so you'll say, ven you gets as old as me.'

'I ought to ha' know'd better, I know,' said Sam.

'Ought to ha' know'd better!' repeated Mr Weller, striking the table with his fist. 'Ought to ha' know'd better! why, I know a young 'un as hasn't had half nor quarter your eddication – as hasn't slept about the markets, no, not six months – who 'd ha' scorned to be let in, in such a vay; scorned it, Sammy.' In the excitement of feeling produced by this agonising reflection, Mr Weller rang the bell, and ordered an additional pint of ale.

'Well, it's no use talking about it now,' said Sam. 'It's over, and can't be helped, and that's one consolation, as they always says in Turkey, ven they cuts the wrong man's head off. It's my innings now, gov'rnor, and as soon as I catches hold o' this ere Trotter, I 'll have a good 'un.'

'I hope you will, Sammy. I hope you will,' returned Mr Weller. 'Here's your health, Sammy, and may you speedily vipe off the disgrace as you've inflicted on the family name.' In honour of this toast Mr Weller imbibed at a draught, at least two-thirds of the newly-arrived pint, and handed it over to his son, to dispose of the remainder, which he instantaneously did.

'And now, Sammy,' said Mr Weller, consulting the large double-faced silver watch that hung at the end of the copper chain. 'Now it's time I was up at the office to get my vay-bill, and see the coach loaded; for coaches, Sammy, is like guns – they requires to be loaded with wery great care, afore they go off.'

At this parental and professional joke, Mr Weller junior smiled a filial smile. His revered parent continued in a solemn tone:

'I'm a goin' to leave you, Samivel my boy, and there's no telling ven I shall see you again. Your mother-in-law may ha' been too much for me, or a thousand things may have happened by the time you next hears any news o' the celebrated Mr Veller o' the Bell Savage. The family name depends wery much upon you, Samivel, and I hope you'll do wot's right by it. Upon all little pints o' breedin', I know I may trust you as vell as if it was my own self. So I've only this here one little bit of adwice to give you. If ever you gets to up'ards o' fifty, and feels disposed to go a marryin' anybody – no matter who – jist you shut yourself up in your own room, if you've got one, and pison yourself off hand. Hangin's wulgar, so don't you have nothin' to say to that. Pison yourself, Samivel, my boy, pison yourself, and you'll be glad on it arterwards.' With these affecting words, Mr Weller looked stedfastly on his son, and turning slowly upon his heel, disappeared from his sight.

In the contemplative mood which these words had awakened, Mr Samuel Weller walked forth from the Great White Horse when his father had left him; and bending his steps towards St Clement's Church, endeavoured to dissipate his melancholy, by strolling among its ancient precincts. He had loitered about, for some time, when he found himself in a retired spot – a kind of court-yard of venerable appearance – which he discovered had no other outlet than the turning by which he had entered. He was about retracing his steps, when he was suddenly transfixed to the spot by a sudden appearance; and the mode and manner of this appearance, we now proceed to relate.

Mr Samuel Weller had been staring up, at the old brick houses now and then, in his deep abstraction, bestowing a wink upon some healthy-looking servant girl as she drew up a blind, or threw open a bed-room window, when the green gate of a garden at the bottom of the yard, opened, and a man having emerged therefrom, closed the green gate very carefully after him, and walked briskly towards the very spot where Mr Weller was standing.

Now, taking this, as an isolated fact, unaccompanied by any attendant circumstances, there was nothing very extraordinary in it; because in many parts of the world, men do come out of gardens, close green gates after them, and even walk briskly away, without attracting any particular share of public observation. It is clear, therefore, that there must have been something in the man, or in his manner, or both, to attract Mr Weller's particular notice. Whether there was, or not, we must leave the reader to determine, when we have faithfully recorded the behaviour of the individual in question.

When the man had shut the green gate after him, he walked, as we have said twice already, with a brisk pace up the court-yard; but he no sooner caught sight of Mr Weller, than he faltered, and stopped, as if uncertain, for the moment, what course to adopt. As the green gate was closed behind him, and there was no other outlet but the one in front, however, he was not long in perceiving that he must pass Mr Samuel Weller to get away. He therefore resumed his brisk pace, and advanced, staring straight before him. The most extraordinary thing about the man was, that he was contorting his face into the most fearful and astonishing grimaces that ever were beheld. Nature's handywork never was disguised with such extraordinary artificial carving, as the man had overlaid his countenance with, in one moment.

'Well!' said Mr Weller to himself, as the man approached. 'This is wery odd. I could ha' swore it was him.'

Up came the man, and his face became more frightfully distorted than ever, as he drew nearer.

'I could take my oath to that 'ere black hair, and mulberry suit,' said Mr Weller; 'only I never see such a face as that, afore.'

As Mr Weller said this, the man's features assumed an unearthly twinge, perfectly hideous. He was obliged to pass very near Sam, however, and the scrutinising glance of that gentleman enabled him to detect, under all these appalling twists of feature, something too like the small eyes of Mr Job Trotter, to be easily mistaken.

'Hallo, you sir!' shouted Sam, fiercely.

The stranger stopped.

'Hallo!' repeated Sam, still more gruffly.

The man with the horrible face, looked, with the greatest surprise, up the court, and down the court, and in at the windows of the houses – everywhere but at Sam Weller – and took another step forward, when he was brought to again, by another shout.

'Hallo, you sir!' said Sam, for the third time.

There was no pretending to mistake where the voice came from now, so the stranger, having no other resource, at last looked Sam Weller full in the face.

'It won't do, Job Trotter,' said Sam. 'Come! None o' that 'ere nonsense. You ain't so wery 'andsome that you can afford to throw avay many o' your good looks. Bring them 'ere eyes o' your'n back into their proper places, or I'll knock 'em out of your head. Dy'e hear?'

As Mr Weller appeared fully disposed to act up to the spirit of this address, Mr Trotter gradually allowed his face to resume its natural expression; and then giving a start of joy, exclaimed, 'What do I see? Mr Walker!'

'Ah,' replied Sam. 'You're wery glad to see me, ain't you?'

'Glad!' exclaimed Job Trotter; 'oh, Mr Walker, if you had but known how I have looked forward to this meeting! It is too much, Mr Walker; I cannot bear it, indeed I cannot.' And with these words, Mr Trotter burst into a regular inundation of tears, and, flinging his arms around those of Mr Weller, embraced him closely, in an ecstasy of joy.

'Get off!' cried Sam, indignant at this process, and vainly endeavouring to extricate himself from the grasp of his enthusiastic acquaintance. 'Get off, I tell you. What are you crying over me for, you portable ingine?'

'Because I am so glad to see you,' replied Job Trotter, gradually releasing Mr Weller, as the first symptoms of his pugnacity disappeared. 'Oh, Mr Walker, this is too much.'

'Too much!' echoed Sam, 'I think it is too much – rayther! Now what have you got to say to me, eh?'

Mr Trotter made no reply; for the little pink pocket handkerchief was in full force.

'What have you got to say to me, afore I knock your head off?' repeated Mr Weller, in a threatening manner.

'Eh!' said Mr Trotter, with a look of virtuous surprise.

'What have you got to say to me?'

'I, Mr Walker!'

'Don't call me Valker; my name's Veller; you know that vell enough. What have you got to say to me?'

'Bless you, Mr Walker – Weller I mean – a great many things, if you will come away somewhere, where we can talk comfortably. If you knew how I have looked for you, Mr Weller – '

'Wery hard, indeed, I s'pose?' said Sam, drily.

'Very, very sir,' replied Mr Trotter, without moving a muscle of his face. 'But shake hands, Mr Weller.'

Sam eyed his companion for a few seconds, and then, as if actuated by a sudden impulse, complied with his request.

'How,' said Job Trotter, as they walked away, 'How is your dear, good master? Oh, he is a worthy gentleman, Mr Weller! I hope he didn't catch cold, that dreadful night, sir.'

There was a momentary look of deep slyness in Job Trotter's eye, as he said this, which ran a thrill through Mr Weller's clenched fist as he burnt with a desire to make a demonstration on his ribs. Sam constrained himself, however, and replied that his master was extremely well.

'Oh, I am so glad,' replied Mr Trotter, 'is he here?'

'Is your'n?' asked Sam, by way of reply.

'Oh, yes, he is here, and I grieve to say, Mr Weller, he is going on, worse than ever.'

'Ah, ah?' said Sam.

'Oh, shocking – terrible!'

'At a boarding-school?' said Sam.

'No, not at a boarding-school,' replied Job Trotter, with the same sly look which Sam had noticed before; 'Not at a boarding-school.'

'At the house with the green gate?' said Sam, eyeing his companion closely.

'No, no – oh, not there,' replied Job, with a quickness very unusual to him, 'not there.'

'What was *you* a doin' there?' asked Sam, with a sharp glance. 'Got inside the gate by accident, perhaps?'

'Why, Mr Weller,' replied Job, 'I don't mind telling you my little secrets, because, you know, we took such a fancy for each other when we first met. You recollect how pleasant we were that morning?'

'Oh yes,' said Sam, impatiently. 'I remember. Well.'

'Well,' replied Job, speaking with great precision, and in the low tone of a man who communicates an important secret; 'In that house with the green gate, Mr Weller, they keep a good many servants.'

'So I should think, from the look on it,' interposed Sam.

'Yes,' continued Mr Trotter, 'and one of them is a cook, who has saved up a little money, Mr Weller, and is desirous, if she can establish herself in life, to open a little shop in the chandlery way, you see.'

'Yes.'

'Yes, Mr Weller. Well, sir, I met her at a chapel that I go to: a very neat little chapel in this town, Mr Weller, where they sing the number four collection of hymns,[1] which I generally carry about with me, in a little book, which you may perhaps have seen in my hand – and I got a little intimate with her, Mr Weller, and from that, an acquaintance sprung up between us, and I may venture to say, Mr Weller, that I am to be the chandler.'

'Ah, and a wery amiable chandler you'll make,' replied Sam, eyeing Job with a side look of intense dislike.

'The great advantage of this, Mr Weller,' continued Job, his eyes filling with tears as he spoke, 'will be, that I shall be able to leave my present disgraceful service with that bad man, and to devote myself to a better and more virtuous life; more like the way in which I was brought up, Mr Weller.'

'You must ha' been wery nicely brought up,' said Sam.

'Oh, very, Mr Weller, very,' replied Job. At the recollection of the purity of his youthful days, Mr Trotter pulled forth the pink handkerchief, and wept copiously.

'You must ha' been an uncommon nice boy, to go to school vith,' said Sam.

'I was, sir,' replied Job, heaving a deep sigh. 'I was the idol of the place.'

'Ah,' said Sam, 'I don't wonder at it. What a comfort you must ha' been to your blessed mother.'

At these words, Mr Job Trotter inserted an end of the pink handkerchief into the corner of each eye, one after the other, and began to weep copiously.

'Wot's the matter vith the man,' said Sam, indignantly. 'Chelsea water-works[2] is nothin' to you. What are you melting vith now? The consciousness o' willainy?'

'I cannot keep my feelings down, Mr Weller,' said Job, after a short pause. 'To think that my master should have suspected the conversation I had with yours, and so dragged me away in a post-chaise, and after persuading the sweet young lady to say she knew nothing of him, and bribing the school-mistress to do the same, deserted her for a better speculation! Oh! Mr Weller, it makes me shudder.'

'Oh, that was the vay, was it?' said Mr Weller.

'To be sure it was,' replied Job.

'Vell,' said Sam, as they had now arrived near the Hotel, 'I vant to have a little bit o'talk with you, Job; so if you're not partickler engaged, I should like to see you at the Great White Horse to-night, somewheres about eight o'clock.'

'I shall be sure to come,' said Job.

'Yes, you'd better,' replied Sam, with a very meaning look, 'or else I shall perhaps be asking arter you, at the other side of the green gate, and then I might cut you out, you know.'

'I shall be sure to be with you, sir,' said Mr Trotter; and wringing Sam's hand with the utmost fervour, he walked away.

'Take care, Job Trotter, take care,' said Sam, looking after him, 'or I shall be one too many for you this time. I shall, indeed.' Having uttered this soliloquy, and looked after Job till he was to be seen no more, Mr Weller made the best of his way to his master's bed-room.

'It's all in training, sir,' said Sam.

'What's in training, Sam?' inquired Mr Pickwick.

'I have found 'em out, sir,' said Sam.

'Found out who?'

'That 'ere queer customer, and the melan-cholly chap with the black hair.'

'Impossible, Sam!' said Mr Pickwick, with the greatest energy. 'Where are they, Sam; where are they?'

'Hush, hush!' replied Mr Weller; and as he assisted Mr Pickwick to dress, he detailed the plan of action on which he proposed to enter.

'But when is this to be done, Sam?' inquired Mr Pickwick.

'All in good time, sir,' replied Sam.

Whether it was done in good time, or not, will be seen hereafter.

CHAPTER 24

Wherein Mr Peter Magnus grows jealous, and the
middle-aged Lady apprehensive, which brings the
Pickwickians within the grasp of the Law

When Mr Pickwick descended to the room in which he and Mr Peter Magnus had spent the preceding evening, he found that gentleman with the major part of the contents of the two bags, the leathern hat-box, and the brown-paper parcel, displayed to all possible advantage on his person, while he himself was pacing up and down the room in a state of the utmost excitement and agitation.

'Good morning, sir,' said Mr Peter Magnus. 'What do you think of this, sir?'

'Very effective indeed,' replied Mr Pickwick, surveying the garments of Mr Peter Magnus with a good-natured smile.

'Yes, I think it'll do,' said Mr Magnus. 'Mr Pickwick, sir, I have sent up my card.'

'Have you?' said Mr Pickwick.

'And the waiter brought back word, that she would see me at eleven – at eleven, sir; it only wants a quarter now.'

'Very near the time,' said Mr Pickwick.

'Yes, it is rather near,' replied Mr Magnus, 'rather too near to be pleasant – eh! Mr Pickwick, sir?'

'Confidence is a great thing in these cases,' observed Mr Pickwick.

'I believe it is, sir,' said Mr Peter Magnus. 'I am very confident, sir. Really, Mr Pickwick, I do not see why a man should feel any fear in such a case as this, sir. What is it, sir? There's nothing to be ashamed of; it's a matter of mutual accommodation, nothing more. Husband on one side, wife on the other. That's my view of the matter, Mr Pickwick.'

'It is a very philosophical one,' replied Mr Pickwick. 'But breakfast is waiting, Mr Magnus. Come.'

Down they sat to breakfast, but it was evident, notwithstanding the boasting of Mr Peter Magnus, that he laboured under a very considerable degree of nervousness, of which loss of appetite, a propensity to upset the tea-things, a spectral attempt at drollery, and an irresistible inclination to look at the clock, every other second, were among the principal symptoms.

'He – he – he,' tittered Mr Magnus, affecting cheerfulness, and gasping with agitation. 'It only wants two minutes, Mr Pickwick. Am I pale, sir?'

'Not very,' replied Mr Pickwick.

There was a brief pause.

'I beg your pardon, Mr Pickwick; but have you ever done this sort of thing in your time?' said Mr Magnus.

'You mean proposing?' said Mr Pickwick.

'Yes.'

'Never,' said Mr Pickwick, with great energy, 'never.'

'You have no idea, then, how it's best to begin?' said Mr Magnus.

'Why,' said Mr Pickwick, 'I may have formed some ideas upon the subject, but, as I have never submitted them to the test of experience, I should be sorry if you were induced to regulate your proceedings by them.'

'I should feel very much obliged to you, for any advice, sir,' said Mr Magnus, taking another look at the clock: the hand of which was verging on the five minutes past.

'Well, sir,' said Mr Pickwick, with the profound solemnity with which that great man could, when he pleased, render his remarks so deeply impressive: 'I should commence, sir, with a tribute to the lady's beauty and excellent qualities; from them, sir, I should diverge to my own unworthiness.'

'Very good,' said Mr Magnus.

'Unworthiness for *her* only, mind, sir,' resumed Mr Pickwick; 'for to shew that I was not wholly unworthy, sir, I should take a brief review of my past life, and present condition. I should argue, by analogy, that to anybody else, I must be a very desirable object. I should then expatiate on the warmth of my love, and the depth of my devotion. Perhaps I might then be tempted to seize her hand.'

'Yes, I see,' said Mr Magnus; 'that would be a very great point.'

'I should then, sir,' continued Mr Pickwick, growing warmer as the subject presented itself in more glowing colours before him: 'I should then, sir, come to the plain and simple question, "Will you have me?" I think I am justified in assuming that upon this, she would turn away her head.'

'You think that may be taken for granted?' said Mr Magnus; 'because if she did not do that at the right place, it would be embarrassing.'

'I think she would,' said Mr Pickwick. 'Upon this, sir, I should squeeze her hand, and I think – I *think*, Mr Magnus – that after I had done that, supposing there was no refusal, I should gently draw away the handkerchief, which my slight knowledge of human nature leads me to suppose the lady would be applying to her eyes at the moment, and steal a respectful kiss. I think I should kiss her, Mr Magnus; and at this particular point, I am decidedly of opinion that if the lady were going to take me at all, she would murmur into my ears a bashful acceptance.'

Mr Magnus started; gazed on Mr Pickwick's intelligent face, for a short time in silence; and then (the dial pointing to the ten minutes past) shook him warmly by the hand, and rushed desperately from the room.

Mr Pickwick had taken a few strides to and fro ; and the small hand of the clock following the latter part of his example, had arrived at the figure which indicates the half hour, when the door suddenly opened. He turned round to meet Mr Peter Magnus, and encountered, in his stead, the joyous face of Mr Tupman, the serene countenance of Mr Winkle, and the intellectual lineaments of Mr Snodgrass. As Mr Pickwick greeted them, Mr Peter Magnus tripped into the room.

'My friends, the gentleman I was speaking of – Mr Magnus,' said Mr Pickwick.

'Your servant, gentlemen,' said Mr Magnus, evidently in a high state of excitement; 'Mr Pickwick, allow me to speak to you, one moment, sir.'

As he said this, Mr Magnus harnessed his forefinger to Mr Pickwick's button-hole, and, drawing him to a window recess, said:

'Congratulate me, Mr Pickwick ; I followed your advice to the very letter.'

'And it was all correct, was it?' inquired Mr Pickwick.

'It was, sir. Could not possibly have been better,' replied Mr Magnus. 'Mr Pickwick, she is mine.'

'I congratulate you with all my heart,' replied Mr Pickwick, warmly shaking his new friend by the hand.

'You must see her, sir,' said Mr Magnus; 'this way, if you please. Excuse us for one instant, gentlemen.' Hurrying on in this way, Mr Peter Magnus drew Mr Pickwick from the room. He paused at the next door in the passage, and tapped gently thereat.

'Come in,' said a female voice. And in they went.

'Miss Witherfield,' said Mr Magnus, 'Allow me to introduce my very particular friend, Mr Pickwick. Mr Pickwick, I beg to make you known to Miss Witherfield.'

The lady was at the upper end of the room. As Mr Pickwick bowed, he took his spectacles from his waistcoat pocket, and put them on ; a process which he had no sooner gone through, than, uttering an exclamation of surprise, Mr Pickwick retreated several paces, and the lady, with a half-suppressed scream, hid her face in her hands, and dropped into a chair; whereupon Mr Peter Magnus was stricken motionless on the spot, and gazed from one to the other, with a countenance expressive of the extremities of horror and surprise.

This certainly was, to all appearance, very unaccountable behaviour, but the fact is, that Mr Pickwick no sooner put on his spectacles, than he at once recognised in the future Mrs Magnus the lady into whose room he had so unwarrantably intruded on the previous night; and the spectacles had no sooner crossed Mr Pickwick's nose, than the lady at once identified the countenance which she had seen surrounded by all the horrors of a night-cap. So the lady screamed, and Mr Pickwick started.

'Mr Pickwick!' exclaimed Mr Magnus, lost in astonishment, 'What is the meaning of this, sir? What is the meaning of it, sir?' added Mr Magnus, in a threatening, and a louder tone.

'Sir,' said Mr Pickwick, somewhat indignant at the very sudden manner in which Mr Peter Magnus had conjugated himself into the imperative mood, 'I decline answering that question.'

'You decline it, sir?' said Mr Magnus.

'I do, sir,' replied Mr Pickwick: 'I object to saying anything which may compromise that lady, or awaken unpleasant recollections in her breast, without her consent and permission.'

'Miss Witherfield,' said Mr Peter Magnus, 'do you know this person?'

'Know him!' repeated the middle-aged lady, hesitating.

'Yes, know him, ma'am. I said know him,' replied Mr Magnus, with ferocity.

'I have seen him,' replied the middle-aged lady.

'Where?' inquired Mr Magnus, 'where?'

'That,' said the middle-aged lady, rising from her seat, and averting her head, 'that I would not reveal for worlds.'

'I understand you, ma'am,' said Mr Pickwick, 'and respect your delicacy; it shall never be revealed by *me*, depend upon it.'

'Upon my word, ma'am,' said Mr Magnus, 'considering the situation in which I am placed with regard to yourself, you carry this matter off with tolerable coolness – tolerable coolness, ma'am.'

'Cruel Mr Magnus!' said the middle-aged lady; here she wept very copiously indeed.

'Address your observations to me, sir,' interposed Mr Pickwick; 'I alone am to blame, if anybody be.'

'Oh! you alone are to blame, are you, sir?' said Mr Magnus, 'I – I – see through this, sir. You repent of your determination now, do you?'

'My determination!' said Mr Pickwick.

'Your determination, sir. Oh! don't stare at me, sir,' said Mr Magnus; 'I recollect your words last night, sir. You came down here, sir, to expose the treachery and falsehood of an individual on whose truth and honour you had placed implicit reliance – eh?' Here Mr Peter Magnus indulged in a prolonged sneer; and taking off his green spectacles – which he probably found superfluous in his fit of jealousy – rolled his little eyes about, in a manner frightful to behold.

'Eh?' said Mr Magnus; and then he repeated the sneer with increased effect. 'But you shall answer it, sir.'

'Answer what?' said Mr Pickwick.

'Never mind, sir,' replied Mr Magnus, striding up and down the room. 'Never mind.'

There must be something very comprehensive in this phrase of 'Never mind,' for we do not recollect to have ever witnessed a quarrel in the street, at a theatre, public room, or elsewhere, in which it has not been the standard reply to all belligerent inquiries. 'Do you call yourself a gentleman, sir?' – 'Never mind, sir.' 'Did I offer to say anything to the young woman, sir?' – 'Never mind, sir?' 'Do you want your head knocked up against that wall, sir?' – 'Never mind, sir.' It is observable, too, that there would appear to be some hidden taunt in this universal 'Never mind,' which rouses more indignation in the bosom of the individual addressed, than the most lavish abuse could possibly awaken.

We do not mean to assert that the application of this brevity to himself, struck exactly that indignation to Mr Pickwick's soul, which it would infallibly have roused in a vulgar breast. We merely record the fact that Mr Pickwick opened the room door, and abruptly called out, 'Tupman, come here!'

Mr Tupman immediately presented himself, with a look of very considerable surprise.

'Tupman,' said Mr Pickwick, 'a secret of some delicacy, in which that lady is concerned, is the cause of a difference which has just arisen between this gentleman and myself. When I assure him, in your presence, that it has no relation to himself, and is not in any way connected with his affairs, I need hardly beg you to take notice that if he continue to dispute it, he expresses a doubt of my veracity, which I shall consider extremely insulting.' As Mr Pickwick said this, he looked encyclopædias at Mr Peter Magnus.

Mr Pickwick's upright and honourable bearing, coupled with that force and energy of speech which so eminently distinguished him, would have carried conviction to any reasonable mind; but unfortunately at that particular moment, the mind of Mr Peter Magnus was in anything but reasonable order. Consequently, instead of receiving Mr Pickwick's explanation as he ought to have done, he forthwith proceeded to work himself into a red-hot, scorching, consuming, passion, and to talk about what was due to his own feelings, and all that sort of thing: adding force to his declamation by striding to and fro, and pulling his hair – amusements which he would vary occasionally, by shaking his fist in Mr Pickwick's philanthropic countenance.

Mr Pickwick, in his turn, conscious of his own innocence and rectitude, and irritated by having unfortunately involved the middle-aged lady in such an unpleasant affair, was not so quietly disposed as was his wont. The consequence was, that words ran high, and voices higher; and at length Mr Magnus told Mr Pickwick he should hear from him; to which Mr Pickwick replied, with laudable politeness, that the sooner he heard from him the better; whereupon the middle-aged lady rushed in terror from the room, out of which Mr Tupman dragged Mr Pickwick, leaving Mr Peter Magnus to himself and meditation.

If the middle-aged lady had mingled much with the busy world, or had profited at all, by the manners and customs of those who make the laws and set the fashions, she would have known that this sort of ferocity is the most harmless thing in nature ; but as she had lived for the most part in the country, and never read the parliamentary debates, she was little versed in these particular refinements of civilised life. Accordingly, when she had gained her bed-chamber, bolted herself in, and begun to meditate on the scene she had just witnessed, the most terrific pictures of slaughter and destruction presented themselves to her imagination; among which, a full-length portrait of Mr Peter Magnus borne home by four men, with the embellishment of a whole barrel-full of bullets in his left side, was among the very least. The more the middle-aged lady meditated, the more terrified she became; and at length she determined to repair to the house of the principal magistrate of the town, and request him to secure the persons of Mr Pickwick and Mr Tupman without delay.

To this decision the middle-aged lady was impelled by a variety of considerations, the chief of which, was the incontestable proof it would afford of her devotion to Mr Peter Magnus, and her anxiety for his safety. She was too well acquainted with his jealous temperament to venture the slightest allusion to the real cause of her agitation on beholding Mr Pickwick; and she trusted to her own influence and power of persuasion with the little man, to quell his boisterous jealousy, supposing that Mr Pickwick were removed, and no fresh quarrel could arise. Filled with these reflections, the middle-aged lady arrayed herself in her bonnet and shawl, and repaired to the Mayor's dwelling straightway.

Now George Nupkins, Esquire, the principal magistrate aforesaid, was as grand a personage as the fastest walker would find out, between sunrise and sunset, on the twenty-first of June, which being, according to the almanacs, the longest day in the whole year, would naturally afford him the longest period for his search. On this particular morning, Mr Nupkins was in a state of the utmost excitement and irritation, for there had been a rebellion in the town; all the day scholars at the largest day-school had conspired to break the windows of an obnoxious apple-seller, and had hooted the beadle, and pelted the constabulary – an elderly gentleman in top-boots, who had been called out to repress the tumult, and who had been a peace-officer, man and boy, for half a century at least. And Mr Nupkins was sitting in his easy chair, frowning with majesty, and boiling with rage, when a lady was announced on pressing, private, and particular business. Mr Nupkins looked calmly terrible, and commanded that the lady should be shown in: which command, like all the mandates of emperors, and magistrates, and other great potentates of the earth, was forthwith obeyed; and Miss Witherfield, interestingly agitated, was ushered in accordingly.

'Muzzle!' said the magistrate.

Muzzle was an undersized footman, with a long body and short legs.

'Muzzle!'

'Yes, your worship.'

'Place a chair, and leave the room.'

'Yes, your worship.'

'Now, ma'am, will you state your business?' said the magistrate.

'It is of a very painful kind, sir,' said Miss Witherfield.

'Very likely, ma'am,' said the magistrate. 'Compose your feelings, ma'am.' Here Mr Nupkins looked benignant. 'And then tell me what legal business brings you here, ma'am.' Here the magistrate triumphed over the man; and he looked stern again.

'It is very distressing to me, sir, to give this information,' said Miss Witherfield, 'but I fear a duel is going to be fought here.'

'Here, ma'am?' said the magistrate. 'Where, ma'am?'

'In Ipswich.'

'In Ipswich, ma'am! A duel in Ipswich!' said the magistrate, perfectly aghast at the notion. 'Impossible, ma'am; nothing of the kind can be contemplated in this town, I am persuaded. Bless my soul, ma'am, are you aware of the activity of our local magistracy? Do you happen to have heard, ma'am, that I rushed into a prizering on the fourth of May last, attended by only sixty special constables; and, at the hazard of falling a sacrifice to the angry passions of an infuriated multitude, prohibited a pugilistic contest between the Middlesex Dumpling and the Suffolk Bantam? A duel in Ipswich, ma'am! I don't think – I do *not* think,' said the magistrate, reasoning with himself, 'that any two men can have had the hardihood to plan such a breach of the peace in this town.'

'My information is unfortunately but too correct,' said the middle-aged lady, 'I was present at the quarrel.'

'It's a most extraordinary thing,' said the astounded magistrate. 'Muzzle!'

'Yes, your worship.'

'Send Mr Jinks here, directly! Instantly.'

'Yes, your worship.'

Muzzle retired; and a pale, sharp-nosed, half-fed, shabbily-clad clerk, of middle age, entered the room.

'Mr Jinks,' said the magistrate. 'Mr Jinks.'

'Sir,' said Mr Jinks.

'This lady, Mr Jinks, has come here, to give information of an intended duel in this town.'

Mr Jinks not knowing exactly what to do, smiled a dependent's smile.

'What are you laughing at, Mr Jinks?' said the magistrate.

Mr Jinks looked serious, instantly.

'Mr Jinks,' said the magistrate, 'you're a fool.'

Mr Jinks looked humbly at the great man, and bit the top of his pen.

'You may see something very comical in this information, sir; but I can tell you this, Mr Jinks; that you have very little to laugh at,' said the magistrate.

The hungry-looking Jinks sighed, as if he were quite aware of the fact of his having very little indeed, to be merry about; and, being ordered to take the lady's information, shambled to a seat, and proceeded to write it down.

'This man, Pickwick, is the principal, I understand,' said the magistrate, when the statement was finished.

'He is,' said the middle-aged lady.

'And the other rioter – what's his name, Mr Jinks?'

'Tupman, sir.'

'Tupman is the second?'

'Yes.'

'The other principal you say, has absconded, ma'am?'

'Yes,' replied Miss Witherfield, with a short cough.

'Very well,' said the magistrate. 'These are two cut-throats from London, who have come down here to destroy his Majesty's population: thinking that at this distance from the capital, the arm of the law is weak and paralysed. They shall be made an example of. Draw up the warrants, Mr Jinks. Muzzle!'

'Yes, your worship.'

'Is Grummer down stairs?'

'Yes, your worship.'

'Send him up.'

The obsequious Muzzle retired, and presently returned, introducing the elderly gentleman in the top-boots, who was chiefly remarkable for a bottle-nose, a hoarse voice, a snuff-coloured surtout, and a wandering eye.

'Grummer,' said the magistrate.

'Your wash-up.'

'Is the town quiet now?'

'Pretty well, your wash-up,' replied Grummer. 'Pop'lar feeling has in a measure subsided, consekens o' the boys having dispersed to cricket.'

'Nothing but vigorous measures will do in these times, Grummer,' said the magistrate, in a determined manner. 'If the authority of the king's officers is set at nought, we must have the riot act read. If the civil power cannot protect these windows, Grummer, the military must protect the civil power, and the windows too. I believe that is a maxim of the constitution, Mr Jinks?'

'Certainly, sir,' said Jinks.

'Very good,' said the magistrate, signing the warrants. 'Grummer, you will bring these persons before me, this afternoon. You will find them at the Great White Horse. You recollect the case of the Middlesex Dumpling and the Suffolk Bantam, Grummer?'

Mr Grummer intimated, by a retrospective shake of the head, that he should never forget it – as indeed it was not likely he would, so long as it continued to be cited daily.

'This is even more unconstitutional,' said the magistrate; 'this is even a greater breach of the peace, and a grosser infringement of his Majesty's prerogative. I believe duelling is one of his Majesty's most undoubted prerogatives, Mr Jinks?'

'Expressly stipulated in Magna Charta, sir,' said Mr Jinks.

'One of the brightest jewels in the British crown, wrung from his Majesty by the Barons, I believe, Mr Jinks?' said the magistrate.

'Just so, sir,' replied Mr Jinks.

'Very well,' said the magistrate, drawing himself up proudly, 'it shall not be violated in this portion of his dominions. Grummer, procure assistance, and execute these warrants with as little delay as possible. Muzzle!'

'Yes, your worship.'

'Show the lady out.'

Miss Witherfield retired, deeply impressed with the magistrate's learning and research; Mr Nupkins retired to lunch; Mr Jinks retired within himself – that being the only retirement he had, except the sofa-bedstead in the small parlour which was occupied by his landlady's family in the daytime – and Mr Grummer retired, to wipe out, by his mode of discharging his present commission, the insult which had been fastened upon himself, and the other representative of his Majesty – the beadle – in the course of the morning.

While these resolute and determined preparations for the conservation of the King's peace, were pending, Mr Pickwick and his friends, wholly unconscious of the mighty events in progress, had sat quietly down to dinner; and very talkative and companionable they all were. Mr Pickwick was in the very act of relating his adventure of the preceding night, to the great amusement of his followers, Mr Tupman especially, when the door opened, and a somewhat forbidding countenance peeped into the room. The eyes in the forbidding countenance looked very earnestly at Mr Pickwick, for several seconds, and were to all appearance satisfied with their investigation; for the body to which the forbidding countenance belonged, slowly brought itself into the apartment, and presented the form of an elderly individual in top-boots – not to keep the reader any longer in suspense, in short, the eyes were the wandering eyes of Mr Grummer, and the body was the body of the same gentleman.

Mr Grummer's mode of proceeding was professional, but peculiar. His first act was to bolt the door on the inside; his second, to polish his head and countenance very carefully with a cotton handkerchief; his third, to place his hat, with the cotton handkerchief in it, on the nearest chair; and his fourth, to produce from the breast-pocket of his coat a short truncheon, surmounted by a brazen crown,[1] with which he beckoned to Mr Pickwick with a grave and ghost-like air.

Mr Snodgrass was the first to break the astonished silence. He looked steadily at Mr Grummer for a brief space, and then said emphatically: 'This is a private room, sir. A private room.'

Mr Grummer shook his head, and replied, 'No room's private to his Majesty when the street door's once passed. That's law. Some people maintains that an Englishman's house is his castle. That's gammon.'[2]

The Pickwickians gazed on each other with wondering eyes.

'Which is Mr Tupman?' inquired Mr Grummer. He had an intuitive perception of Mr Pickwick; he knew *him* at once.

'My name's Tupman,' said that gentleman.

'My name's Law,' said Mr Grummer.

'What?' said Mr Tupman.

'Law,' replied Mr Grummer, 'law, civil power, and exekative; them's my titles; here's my authority. Blank Tupman, blank Pickvick – against the peace of our sufferin Lord the King – stattit in that case made and purwided – and all regular. I apprehend you Pickvick! Tupman – the aforesaid.'

'What do you mean by this insolence?' said Mr Tupman, starting up: 'Leave the room!'

'Halloo,' said Mr Grummer, retreating very expeditiously to the door, and opening it an inch or two, 'Dubbley.'

'Well,' said a deep voice from the passage.

'Come for'ard, Dubbley.'

At the word of command, a dirty-faced man, something over six feet high, and stout in proportion, squeezed himself through the half-open door (making his face very red in the process), and entered the room.

'Is the other specials outside, Dubbley?' inquired Mr Grummer.

Mr Dubbley, who was a man of few words, nodded assent.

'Order in the diwision under your charge, Dubbley,' said Mr Grummer.

Mr Dubbley did as he was desired; and half a dozen men, each with a short truncheon and a brass crown, flocked into the room. Mr Grummer pocketed his staff, and looked at Mr Dubbley; Mr Dubbley pocketed *his* staff and looked at the division; the division pocketed *their* staves and looked at Messrs. Tupman and Pickwick.

Mr Pickwick and his followers rose as one man.

'What is the meaning of this atrocious intrusion upon my privacy?' said Mr Pickwick.

'Who dares apprehend me?' said Mr Tupman.

'What do you want here, scoundrels?' said Mr Snodgrass.

Mr Winkle said nothing, but he fixed his eyes on Grummer, and bestowed a look upon him, which, if he had had any feeling, must have pierced his brain. As it was, however, it had no visible effect upon him whatever.

When the executive perceived that Mr Pickwick and his friends were disposed to resist the authority of the law, they very significantly turned up their coat sleeves, as if knocking them down in the first instance, and taking them up afterwards, were a mere professional act which had only to be thought of, to be done, as a matter of course. This demonstration was not lost upon Mr Pickwick. He conferred a few moments with Mr Tupman apart, and then signified his readiness to proceed to the Mayor's residence, merely begging the parties then and there assembled, to take notice, that it was his firm intention to resent this monstrous invasion of his privileges as an Englishman, the instant he was at liberty; whereat the parties then and there assembled laughed very heartily, with the single exception of Mr Grummer, who seemed to consider that any slight cast upon the divine right of magistrates, was a species of blasphemy, not to be tolerated.

But when Mr Pickwick had signified his readiness to bow to the laws of his country; and just when the waiters, and hostlers, and chamber-maids, and post-boys, who had anticipated a delightful commotion from his threatened obstinacy, began to turn away, disappointed and disgusted, a difficulty arose which had not been foreseen. With every sentiment of veneration for the constituted authorities, Mr Pickwick resolutely protested against making his appearance in the public streets, surrounded and guarded by the officers of justice, like a common criminal. Mr Grummer, in the then disturbed state of public feeling (for it was half-holiday, and the boys had not yet gone home), as resolutely protested against walking on the opposite side of the way, and taking Mr Pickwick's parole that he would go straight to the magistrate's; and both Mr Pickwick and Mr Tupman as strenuously objected to the expense of a post-coach, which was the only respectable conveyance that could be obtained. The dispute ran high, and the dilemma lasted long; and just as the executive were on the point of overcoming Mr Pickwick's objection to walking to the magistrate's, by the trite expedient of carrying him thither, it was recollected that there stood in the inn yard, an old sedan-chair, which having been originally built for a gouty gentleman with funded property, would hold Mr Pickwick and Mr Tupman, at least as conveniently as a modern post-chaise. The chair was hired, and brought into the hall; Mr Pickwick and Mr Tupman squeezed themselves inside, and pulled down the blinds; a couple of chairmen were speedily found; and the procession started in grand order. The specials surrounded the body of the vehicle; Mr Grummer and Mr Dubbley marched triumphantly in front; Mr Snodgrass and Mr Winkle walked arm-in-arm behind; and the unsoaped of Ipswich brought up the rear.

The shopkeepers of the town, although they had a very indistinct notion of the nature of the offence, could not but be much edified and gratified by this spectacle. Here was the strong arm of the law, coming down with twenty gold-beater force, upon two offenders from the metropolis itself; the mighty engine was directed by their own magistrate, and worked by their own officers; and both the criminals by their united efforts, were securely shut up, in the narrow compass of one sedan-chair. Many were the expressions of approval and admiration which greeted Mr Grummer, as he headed the cavalcade, staff in hand; loud and long were the shouts raised by the unsoaped; and amidst these united testimonials of public approbation, the procession moved slowly and majestically along.

Mr Weller, habited in his morning jacket with the black calico sleeves, was returning in a rather desponding state from an unsuccessful survey of the mysterious house with the green gate, when, raising his eyes, he beheld a crowd pouring down the street, surrounding an object which had very much the appearance of a sedan-chair. Willing to divert his thoughts from the failure of his enterprise, he stepped aside to see the crowd pass; and finding that they were cheering away, very much to their own satisfaction, forthwith began (by way of raising his spirits) to cheer too, with all his might and main.

Mr Grummer passed, and Mr Dubbley passed, and the sedan passed, and the body-guard of specials passed, and Sam was still responding to the enthusiastic cheers of the mob, and waving his hat about as if he were in the very last extreme of the wildest joy (though, of course, he had not the faintest idea of the matter in hand), when he was suddenly stopped by the unexpected appearance of Mr Winkle and Mr Snodgrass.

'What's the row, gen'l'm'n?' cried Sam. 'Who have they got in this here watch-box in mournin'?'

Both gentlemen replied together, but their words were lost in the tumult.

'Who?' cried Sam again.

Once more was a joint reply returned; and, though the words were inaudible, Sam saw by the motion of the two pairs of lips that they had uttered the magic word 'Pickwick.'

This was enough. In another minute Mr Weller had made his way through the crowd, stopped the chairmen, and confronted the portly Grummer.

'Hallo, old gen'l'm'n!' said Sam. 'Who have you got in this here conwayance?'

'Stand back,' said Mr Grummer, whose dignity, like the dignity of a great many other men, had been wondrously augmented by a little popularity.

'Knock him down, if he don't,' said Mr Dubbley.

'I'm wery much obliged to you, old gen'l'm'n,' replied Sam, 'for consulting my conwenience, and I'm still more obliged to the other gen'l'm'n, who looks as if he'd just escaped from a giant's carrywan, for his wery 'ansome suggestion; but I should perfer your givin' me a answer to my question, if it's all the same to you. – How are you, sir?' This last observation was addressed with a patronising air to Mr Pickwick, who was peeping through the front window.

Mr Grummer, perfectly speechless with indignation, dragged the truncheon with the brass crown from its particular pocket, and flourished it before Sam's eyes.

'Ah,' said Sam, 'it's wery pretty, 'specially the crown, which is uncommon like the real one.'

'Stand back!' said the outraged Mr Grummer. By way of adding force to the command, he thrust the brass emblem of royalty into Sam's neckcloth with one hand, and seized Sam's collar with the other: a compliment which Mr Weller returned by knocking him down out of hand: having previously, with the utmost consideration, knocked down a chairman for him to lie upon.

Whether Mr Winkle was seized with a temporary attack of that species of insanity which originates in a sense of injury, or animated by this display of Mr Weller's valour, is uncertain; but certain it is, that he no sooner saw Mr Grummer fall than he made a terrific onslaught on a small boy who stood next him; whereupon Mr Snodgrass, in a truly christian spirit, and in order that he might take no one unawares, announced in a very loud tone that he was going to begin, and proceeded to take off his coat with the utmost deliberation. He was immediately surrounded and secured; and it is but common justice both to him and Mr Winkle to say, that they did not make the slightest attempt to rescue either themselves or Mr Weller: who, after a most vigorous resistance, was overpowered by numbers and taken prisoner. The procession then re-formed; the chairmen resumed their stations; and the march was re-commenced.

Mr Pickwick's indignation during the whole of this proceeding was beyond all bounds. He could just see Sam upsetting the specials, and flying about in every direction; and that was all he could see, for the sedan doors wouldn't open, and the blinds wouldn't pull

Mr Weller attacks the Executive of Ipswich

up. At length, with the assistance of Mr Tupman, he managed to push open the roof; and mounting on the seat, and steadying himself as well as he could, by placing his hand on that gentleman's shoulder, Mr Pickwick proceeded to address the multitude; to dwell upon the unjustifiable manner in which he had been treated; and to call upon them to take notice that his servant had been first assaulted. In this order they reached the magistrate's house; the chairmen trotting, the prisoners following, Mr Pickwick oratorising, and the crowd shouting.

CHAPTER 25

Showing, among a variety of pleasant Matters, how majestic and impartial Mr Nupkins was; and how Mr Weller returned Mr Job Trotter's Shuttlecock as heavily as it came. With another Matter, which will be found in its Place

Violent was Mr Weller's indignation as he was borne along; numerous were the allusions to the personal appearance and demeanour of Mr Grummer and his companion: and valorous were the defiances to any six of the gentlemen present: in which he vented his dissatisfaction. Mr Snodgrass and Mr Winkle listened with gloomy respect to the torrent of eloquence which their leader poured forth from the sedan-chair, and the rapid course of which not all Mr Tupman's earnest entreaties to have the lid of the vehicle closed, were able to check for an instant. But Mr Weller's anger quickly gave way to curiosity when the procession turned down the identical court-yard in which he had met with the runaway Job Trotter: and curiosity was exchanged for a feeling of the most gleeful astonishment, when the all-important Mr Grummer, commanding the sedan-bearers to halt, advanced with dignified and portentous steps to the very green gate from which Job Trotter had emerged, and gave a mighty pull at the bell-handle which hung at the side thereof. The ring was answered by a very smart and pretty-faced servant-girl, who, after holding up her hands in astonishment at the rebellious appearance of the prisoners, and the impassioned language of Mr Pickwick, summoned Mr Muzzle. Mr Muzzle opened one half of the carriage gate, to admit the sedan, the captured ones, and the specials; and immediately slammed it in the faces of the mob, who, indignant at being excluded, and anxious to see what followed, relieved their feelings by kicking at the gate and ringing the bell, for an hour or two afterwards. In this amusement they all took part by turns, except three or four fortunate individuals, who, having discovered a grating in the gate which commanded a view of nothing, stared through it with the indefatigable perseverance with which people will flatten their noses against the front windows of a chemist's shop, when a drunken man, who has been run over by a dog-cart in the street, is undergoing a surgical inspection in the back-parlour.

At the foot of a flight of steps, leading to the house door, which was guarded on either side by an American aloe[1] in a green tub, the sedan-chair stopped. Mr Pickwick and his friends were conducted into the hall, whence, having been previously announced by Muzzle, and ordered in by Mr Nupkins, they were ushered into the worshipful presence of that public-spirited officer.

The scene was an impressive one, well calculated to strike terror to the hearts of culprits, and to impress them with an adequate idea of the stern majesty of the law. In front of a big book-case, in a big chair, behind a big table, and before a big volume, sat Mr Nupkins, looking a full size larger than any one of them, big as they were. The table was adorned with piles of papers: and above the further end of it, appeared the head and shoulders of Mr Jinks, who was busily engaged in looking as busy as possible. The party having all entered, Muzzle carefully closed the door, and placed himself behind his master's chair to await his orders. Mr Nupkins threw himself back, with thrilling solemnity, and scrutinised the faces of his unwilling visitors.

'Now, Grummer, who is that person?' said Mr Nupkins, pointing to Mr Pickwick, who, as the spokesman of his friends, stood hat in hand, bowing with the utmost politeness and respect.

'This here's Pickvick, your wash-up,' said Grummer.

'Come, none o'that 'ere, old Strike-a-light,' interposed Mr Weller, elbowing himself into the front rank. 'Beg your pardon, sir, but this here officer o' yourn in the gambooge tops, 'ull never earn a decent livin' as a master o' the ceremonies any vere. This here, sir,' continued Mr Weller, thrusting Grummer aside, and addressing the magistrate with pleasant familiarity, 'This here is S. Pickvick, Esquire; this here's Mr Tupman; that 'ere's Mr Snodgrass; and furder on, next him on the t'other side, Mr Winkle – all wery nice genl'm'n, sir, as you'll be wery happy to have the acquaintance on;

so the sooner you commits these here officers o' yourn to the tread-mill for a month or two, the sooner we shall begin to be on a pleasant understanding. Business first, pleasure arterwards, as King Richard the Third said wen he stabbed the t'other king in the Tower, afore he smothered the babbies.'

At the conclusion of this address, Mr Weller brushed his hat with his right elbow, and nodded benignly to Jinks, who had heard him throughout, with unspeakable awe.

'Who is this man, Grummer?' said the magistrate.

'Wery desp'rate ch'racter, your wash-up,' replied Grummer. 'He attempted to rescue the prisoners, and assaulted the officers; so we took him into custody, and brought him here.'

'You did quite right,' replied the magistrate. 'He is evidently a desperate ruffian.'

'He is my servant, sir,' said Mr Pickwick, angrily.

'Oh! he is your servant, is he?' said Mr Nupkins. 'A conspiracy to defeat the ends of justice, and murder its officers. Pickwick's servant. Put that down, Mr Jinks.'

Mr Jinks did so.

'What's your name, fellow?' thundered Mr Nupkins.

'Veller,' replied Sam.

'A very good name for the Newgate Calendar,'[2] said Mr Nupkins.

This was a joke; so Jinks, Grummer, Dubbley, all the specials, and Muzzle, went into fits of laughter of five minutes' duration.

'Put down his name, Mr Jinks,' said the magistrate.

'Two L's, old feller,' said Sam.

Here an unfortunate special laughed again, whereupon the magistrate threatened to commit him, instantly. It is a dangerous thing to laugh at the wrong man, in these cases.

'Where do you live?' said the magistrate.

'Vare-ever I can,' replied Sam.

'Put down that, Mr Jinks,' said the magistrate, who was fast rising into a rage.

'Score it under,' said Sam.

'He is a vagabond, Mr Jinks,' said the magistrate. 'He is a vagabond on his own statement; is he not, Mr Jinks?'

'Certainly, sir.'

'Then I'll commit him. I'll commit him as such,' said Mr Nupkins.

'This is a wery impartial country for justice,' said Sam. 'There ain't a magistrate goin' as don't commit himself, twice as often as he commits other people.'

At this sally another special laughed, and then tried to look so

supernaturally solemn, that the magistrate detected him immediately.

'Grummer,' said Mr Nupkins, reddening with passion, 'how dare
you select such an inefficient and disreputable person for a special
constable, as that man? How dare you do it, sir?'

'I am very sorry, your wash-up,' stammered Grummer.

'Very sorry!' said the furious magistrate. 'You shall repent of this
neglect of duty, Mr Grummer; you shall be made an example of.
Take that fellow's staff away. He's drunk. You're drunk, fellow.'

'I am not drunk, your worship,' said the man.

'You *are* drunk,' returned the magistrate. 'How dare you say you
are not drunk, sir, when I say you are? Doesn't he smell of spirits,
Grummer?'

'Horrid, your wash-up,' replied Grummer, who had a vague
impression that there was a smell of rum somewhere.

'I knew he did,' said Mr Nupkins. 'I saw he was drunk when he
first came into the room, by his excited eye. Did you observe his
excited eye, Mr Jinks?'

'Certainly, sir.'

'I haven't touched a drop of spirits this morning,' said the man,
who was as sober a fellow as need be.

'How dare you tell me a falsehood?' said Mr Nupkins. 'Isn't he
drunk at this moment, Mr Jinks?'

'Certainly, sir,' replied Jinks.

'Mr Jinks,' said the magistrate, 'I shall commit that man, for
contempt. Make out his committal, Mr Jinks.'

And committed the special would have been, only Jinks, who was
the magistrate's adviser (having had a legal education of three years
in a country attorney's office) whispered the magistrate that he
thought it wouldn't do; so the magistrate made a speech, and said,
that in consideration of the special's family, he would merely
reprimand and discharge him. Accordingly, the special was abused,
vehemently, for a quarter of an hour, and sent about his business:
and Grummer, Dubbley, Muzzle, and all the other specials murmured their admiration of the magnanimity of Mr Nupkins.

'Now, Mr Jinks,' said the magistrate, 'swear Grummer.'

Grummer was sworn directly; but as Grummer wandered, and
Mr Nupkins' dinner was nearly ready, Mr Nupkins cut the matter
short, by putting leading questions to Grummer, which Grummer
answered as nearly in the affirmative as he could. So the examination went off, all very smooth and comfortable, and two assaults
were proved against Mr Weller, and a threat against Mr Winkle,

and a push against Mr Snodgrass. When all this was done to the magistrate's satisfaction, the magistrate and Mr Jinks consulted in whispers.

The consultation having lasted about ten minutes, Mr Jinks retired to his end of the table; and the magistrate, with a preparatory cough, drew himself up in his chair, and was proceeding to commence his address, when Mr Pickwick interposed.

'I beg your pardon, sir, for interrupting you,' said Mr Pickwick; 'but before you proceed to express, and act upon, any opinion you may have formed on the statements which have been made here, I must claim my right to be heard, so far as I am personally concerned.'

'Hold your tongue, sir,' said the magistrate, peremptorily.

'I must submit to you, sir,' said Mr Pickwick.

'Hold your tongue, sir,' interposed the magistrate, 'or I shall order an officer to remove you.'

'You may order your officers to do whatever you please, sir,' said Mr Pickwick; 'and I have no doubt, from the specimen I have had of the subordination preserved amongst them, that whatever you order, they will execute, sir; but I shall take the liberty, sir, of claiming my right to be heard, until I am removed by force.'

'Pickwick and principle!' exclaimed Mr Weller, in a very audible voice.

'Sam, be quiet,' said Mr Pickwick.

'Dumb as a drum vith a hole in it, sir,' replied Sam.

Mr Nupkins looked at Mr Pickwick with a gaze of intense astonishment, at his displaying such unwonted temerity; and was apparently about to return a very angry reply, when Mr Jinks pulled him by the sleeve, and whispered something in his ear. To this, the magistrate returned a half-audible answer, and then the whispering was renewed. Jinks was evidently remonstrating.

At length the magistrate, gulping down, with a very bad grace, his disinclination to hear anything more, turned to Mr Pickwick, and said sharply: 'What do you want to say?'

'First,' said Mr Pickwick, sending a look through his spectacles, under which even Nupkins quailed. 'First, I wish to know what I and my friend have been brought here for?'

'Must I tell him?' whispered the magistrate to Jinks.

'I think you had better, sir,' whispered Jinks to the magistrate.

'An information has been sworn before me,' said the magistrate, 'that it is apprehended you are going to fight a duel, and that the other man, Tupman, is your aider and abettor in it. Therefore – eh, Mr Jinks?'

'Certainly, sir.'

'Therefore, I call upon you both, to – I think that's the course, Mr Jinks?'

'Certainly, sir."

'To – to – what Mr Jinks?' said the magistrate, pettishly.

'To find bail, sir.'

'Yes. Therefore, I call upon you both – as I was about to say, when I was interrupted by my clerk – to find bail.'

'Good bail,' whispered Mr Jinks,

'I shall require good bail,' said the magistrate.

'Town's-people,' whispered Jinks.

'They must be town's-people,' said the magistrate.

'Fifty pounds each,' whispered Jinks, 'and householders, of course.'

'I shall require two sureties of fifty pounds each,' said the magistrate aloud, with great dignity, 'and they must be house-holders, of course.'

'But, bless my heart, sir,' said Mr Pickwick, who, together with Mr Tupman, was all amazement and indignation; 'we are perfect strangers in this town. I have as little knowledge of any house-holders here, as I have intention of fighting a duel with anybody.'

'I dare say,' replied the magistrate, 'I dare say – don't you, Mr Jinks?'

'Certainly, sir.'

'Have you anything more to say?' inquired the magistrate.

Mr Pickwick *had* a great deal more to say, which he would no doubt have said, very little to his own advantage, or the magistrate's satisfaction, if he had not, the moment he ceased speaking, been pulled by the sleeve by Mr Weller, with whom he was immediately engaged in so earnest a conversation, that he suffered the magis-trate's inquiry to pass wholly unnoticed. Mr Nupkins was not the man to ask a question of the kind twice over; and so, with another preparatory cough, he proceeded, amidst the reverential and admir-ing silence of the constables, to pronounce his decision.

He should fine Weller two pounds for the first assault, and three pounds for the second. He should fine Winkle two pounds, and Snodgrass one pound, besides requiring them to enter into their own recognizances to keep the peace towards all his Majesty's subjects, and especially towards his liege servant, Daniel Grummer. Pickwick and Tupman he had already held to bail.

Immediately on the magistrate ceasing to speak, Mr Pickwick, with a smile mantling on his again good-humoured countenance, stepped forward, and said:

'I beg the magistrate's pardon, but may I request a few minutes' private conversation with him, on a matter of deep importance to himself?'

'What?' said the magistrate.

Mr Pickwick repeated his request.

'This is a most extraordinary request,' said the magistrate. 'A private interview?'

'A private interview,' replied Mr Pickwick, firmly; 'only, as a part of the information which I wish to communicate is derived from my servant, I should wish him to be present.'

The magistrate looked at Mr Jinks; Mr Jinks looked at the magistrate; the officers looked at each other in amazement. Mr Nupkins turned suddenly pale. Could the man Weller, in a moment of remorse, have divulged some secret conspiracy for his assassination? It was a dreadful thought. He was a public man: and he turned paler, as he thought of Julius Cæsar and Mr Perceval.[3]

The magistrate looked at Mr Pickwick again, and beckoned Mr Jinks.

'What do you think of this request, Mr Jinks?' murmured Mr Nupkins.

Mr Jinks, who didn't exactly know what to think of it, and was afraid he might offend, smiled feebly, after a dubious fashion, and, screwing up the corners of his mouth, shook his head slowly from side to side.

'Mr Jinks,' said the magistrate, gravely, 'you are an ass.'

At this little expression of opinion, Mr Jinks smiled again – rather more feebly than before – and edged himself by degrees, back into his own corner.

Mr Nupkins debated the matter within himself for a few seconds, and then, rising from his chair, and requesting Mr Pickwick and Sam to follow him, led the way into a small room which opened into the justice parlour. Desiring Mr Pickwick to walk to the upper end of the little apartment, and holding his hand upon the half-closed door, that he might be able to effect an immediate escape, in case there was the least tendency to a display of hostilities, Mr Nupkins expressed his readiness to hear the communication, whatever it might be.

'I will come to the point at once, sir,' said Mr Pickwick; 'it affects yourself, and your credit, materially. I have every reason to believe, sir, that you are harbouring in your house, a gross impostor!'

'Two,' interrupted Sam. 'Mulberry agin all natur, for tears and willainny!'

'Sam,' said Mr Pickwick, 'if I am to render myself intelligible to this gentleman, I must beg you to control your feelings.'

'Wery sorry, sir,' replied Mr Weller; 'but when I think o' that ere Job, I can't help opening the walve a inch or two.'

'In one word, sir,' said Mr Pickwick, 'is my servant right in suspecting that a certain Captain Fitz-Marshall is in the habit of visiting here? Because,' added Mr Pickwick, as he saw that Mr Nupkins was about to offer a very indignant interruption, 'because, if he be, I know that person to be a – '

'Hush, hush,' said Mr Nupkins, closing the door. 'Know him to be what, sir?'

'An unprincipled adventurer – a dishonourable character – a man who preys upon society, and makes easily-deceived people his dupes, sir; his absurd, his foolish, his wretched dupes, sir,' said the excited Mr Pickwick.

'Dear me,' said Mr Nupkins, turning very red, and altering his whole manner directly, 'Dear me, Mr – '

'Pickwick,' said Sam.

'Pickwick,' said the magistrate, 'dear me, Mr Pickwick – pray take a seat – you cannot mean this? Captain Fitz-Marshall?'

'Don't call him a cap'en,' said Sam, 'nor Fitz-Marshall neither; he ain't neither one nor t'other. He's a strolling actor, he is, and his name's Jingle; and if ever there was a wolf in a mulberry suit, that ere Job Trotter's him.'

'It is very true, sir,' said Mr Pickwick, replying to the magistrate's look of amazement; 'my only business in this town, is to expose the person of whom we now speak.'

Mr Pickwick proceeded to pour into the horror-stricken ear of Mr Nupkins, an abridged account of Mr Jingle's atrocities. He related how he had first met him; how he had eloped with Miss Wardle; how he had cheerfully resigned the lady for a pecuniary consideration; how he had entrapped himself into a lady's boarding-school at midnight; and how he (Mr Pickwick) now felt it his duty to expose his assumption of his present name and rank.

As the narrative proceeded, all the warm blood in the body of Mr Nupkins tingled up into the very tips of his ears. He had picked up the captain at a neighbouring race-course. Charmed with his long list of aristocratic acquaintance, his extensive travel, and his fashionable demeanour, Mrs Nupkins and Miss Nupkins had exhibited Captain Fitz-Marshall, and quoted Captain Fitz-Marshall, and hurled Captain Fitz-Marshall at the devoted heads of their select circle of acquaintance, until their bosom friends, Mrs Porkenham and the Miss Porkenhams, and Mr Sidney Porkenham, were ready to burst with jealousy and despair. And now, to hear, after all, that he was a needy adventurer, a strolling player, and if not a swindler, something so very like it, that it was hard to tell the difference! Heavens! What would the Porkenhams say! What would be the triumph of Mr Sidney Porkenham when he found that his addresses had been slighted for such a rival! How should he, Nupkins, meet the eye of old Porkenham at the next Quarter Sessions! And what a handle would it be for the opposition magisterial party, if the story got abroad!

'But after all,' said Mr Nupkins, brightening for a moment, after a long pause; 'after all, this is a mere statement. Captain Fitz-Marshall is a man of very engaging manners, and, I dare say, has many enemies. What proof have you of the truth of these representations?'

'Confront me with him,' said Mr Pickwick, 'that is all I ask, and all I require. Confront him with me and my friends here; you will want no further proof.'

'Why,' said Mr Nupkins, 'that might be very easily done, for he will be here to-night, and then there would be no occasion to make the matter public, just – just – for the young man's own sake, you know. I – I – should like to consult Mrs Nupkins on the propriety of the step, in the first instance, though. At all events, Mr Pickwick, we must despatch this legal business before we can do anything else. Pray step back into the next room.'

Into the next room they went.

'Grummer,' said the magistrate, in an awful voice.

'Your wash-up,' replied Grummer, with the smile of a favourite.

'Come, come, sir,' said the magistrate, sternly, 'don't let me see any of this levity here. It is very unbecoming, and I can assure you that you have very little to smile at. Was the account you gave me just now strictly true? Now be careful, sir?'

'Your wash-up,' stammered Grummer, 'I – '

'Oh, you are confused, are you?' said the magistrate. 'Mr Jinks, you observe this confusion?'

'Certainly, sir,' replied Jinks.

'Now,' said the magistrate, 'repeat your statement, Grummer, and again I warn you to be careful. Mr Jinks, take his words down.'

The unfortunate Grummer proceeded to re-state his complaint, but, what between Mr Jinks's taking down his words, and the magistrate's taking them up; his natural tendency to rambling, and his extreme confusion; he managed to get involved, in something under three minutes, in such a mass of entanglement and contradiction, that Mr Nupkins at once declared he didn't believe him. So the fines were remitted, and Mr Jinks found a couple of bail in no time. And all these solemn proceedings having been satisfactorily concluded, Mr Grummer was ignominiously ordered out – an awful instance of the instability of human greatness, and the uncertain tenure of great men's favour.

Mrs Nupkins was a majestic female in a pink gauze turban and a light brown wig. Miss Nupkins possessed all her mamma's haughtiness without the turban, and all her ill-nature without the wig; and whenever the exercise of these two amiable qualities involved mother and daughter in some unpleasant dilemma, as they not unfrequently did, they both concurred in laying the blame on the shoulders of Mr Nupkins. Accordingly, when Mr Nupkins sought Mrs Nupkins, and detailed the communication which had been made by Mr Pickwick, Mrs Nupkins suddenly recollected that she had always expected something of the kind; that she had always said it would be so; that her advice was never taken; that she really did not know what Mr Nupkins supposed she was; and so forth.

'The idea!' said Miss Nupkins, forcing a tear of very scanty proportions into the corner of each eye; 'the idea of my being made such a fool of!'

'Ah! you may thank your papa, my dear,' said Mrs Nupkins; 'how have I implored and begged that man to inquire into the Captain's family connections; how have I urged and entreated him to take some decisive step! I am quite certain nobody would believe it – quite.'

'But, my dear,' said Mr Nupkins.

'Don't talk to me, you aggravating thing, don't!' said Mrs Nupkins.

'My love,' said Mr Nupkins, 'you professed yourself very fond of Captain Fitz-Marshall. You have constantly asked him here, my dear, and you have lost no opportunity of introducing him elsewhere.'

'Didn't I say so, Henrietta?' cried Mrs Nupkins, appealing to her daughter, with the air of a much-injured female. 'Didn't I say that your papa would turn round and lay all this at my door? Didn't I say so?' Here Mrs Nupkins sobbed.

'Oh pa!' remonstrated Miss Nupkins. And here she sobbed too.

'Isn't it too much, when he has brought all this disgrace and ridicule upon us, to taunt *me* with being the cause of it?' exclaimed Mrs Nupkins.

'How can we ever show ourselves in society!' said Miss Nupkins.

'How can we face the Porkenhams!' cried Mrs Nupkins.

'Or the Griggs's!' cried Miss Nupkins.

'Or the Slummintowkens!' cried Mrs Nupkins. 'But what does your papa care! What is it to *him*!' At this dreadful reflection, Mrs Nupkins wept with mental anguish, and Miss Nupkins followed on the same side.

Mrs Nupkins's tears continued to gush forth, with great velocity, until she had gained a little time to think the matter over: when she decided, in her own mind, that the best thing to do would be to ask Mr Pickwick and his friends to remain until the Captain's arrival, and then to give Mr Pickwick the opportunity he sought. If it appeared that he had spoken truly, the Captain could be turned out of the house without noising the matter abroad, and they could easily account to the Porkenhams for his disappearance, by saying that he had been appointed, through the Court influence of his family, to the Governor-Generalship of Sierra Leone, or Saugur Point,[4] or any other of those salubrious climates which enchant Europeans so much that, when they once get there, they can hardly ever prevail upon themselves to come back again.

When Mrs Nupkins dried up her tears, Miss Nupkins dried up *hers*, and Mr Nupkins was very glad to settle the matter as Mrs Nupkins had proposed. So Mr Pickwick and his friends, having washed off all marks of their late encounter, were introduced to the ladies, and soon afterwards to their dinner; and Mr Weller, whom the magistrate with his peculiar sagacity had discovered in half an hour to be one of the finest fellows alive, was consigned to the care and guardianship of Mr Muzzle, who was specially enjoined to take him below, and make much of him.

'How de do, sir?' said Mr Muzzle, as he conducted Mr Weller down the kitchen stairs.

'Why, no con-siderable change has taken place in the state of my system, since I see you cocked up behind your governor's chair in the parlour, a little vile ago,' replied Sam.

'You will excuse my not taking more notice of you then,' said Mr Muzzle. 'You see, master hadn't introduced us, then. Lord, how fond he is of you, Mr Weller, to be sure!'

'Ah,' said Sam, 'what a pleasant chap he is!'

'Ain't he?' replied Mr Muzzle.

'So much humour,' said Sam.

'And such a man to speak,' said Mr Muzzle. 'How his ideas flow, don't they?'

'Wonderful,' replied Sam; 'they come's a pouring out, knocking each other's heads so fast, that they seems to stun one another; you hardly know what he's arter, do you?'

'That's the great merit of his style of speaking,' rejoined Mr Muzzle. 'Take care of the last step, Mr Weller. Would you like to wash your hands, sir, before we join the ladies? Here's a sink, with the water laid on, sir, and a clean jack towel behind the door.'

'Ah! perhaps I may as wel have a rinse,' replied Mr Weller, applying plenty of yellow soap to the towel, and rubbing away, till his face shone again. 'How many ladies are there?'

'Only two in our kitchen,' said Mr Muzzle, 'cook and 'ousemaid. We keep a boy to do the dirty work, and a gal besides, but they dine in the washus.'

'Oh, they dines in the washus, do they?' said Mr Weller.

'Yes,' replied Mr Muzzle, 'we tried 'em at our table when they first come, but we couldn't keep 'em. The gal's manners is dreadful vulgar; and the boy breathes so very hard while he's eating, that we found it impossible to sit at table with him.'

'Young grampus!'⁵ said Mr Weller.

'Oh, dreadful,' rejoined Mr Muzzle; 'but that is the worst of country service, Mr Weller; the juniors is always so very savage. This way, sir, if you please; this way.'

Preceding Mr Weller, with the utmost politeness, Mr Muzzle conducted him into the kitchen.

'Mary,' said Mr Muzzle to the pretty servant-girl, 'this is Mr Weller: a gentleman as master has sent down, to be made as comfortable as possible.'

'And your master's a knowin' hand, and has just sent me to the right place,' said Mr Weller, with a glance of admiration at Mary. 'If I wos master o' this here house, I should alvays find the materials for comfort vere Mary wos.'

'Lor, Mr Weller!' said Mary, blushing.

'Well, I never!' ejaculated the cook.

'Bless me, cook, I forgot you,' said Mr Muzzle. 'Mr Weller, let me introduce you.'

'How are you, ma'am,' said Mr Weller. 'Werry glad to see you, indeed, and hope our acquaintance may be a long 'un, as the gen'lm'n said to the fi' pun' note.'

When this ceremony of introduction had been gone through, the cook and Mary retired into the back kitchen to titter, for ten minutes; then returning, all giggles and blushes, they sat down to dinner.

Mr Weller's easy manners and conversational powers had such irresistible influence with his new friends, that before the dinner was half over, they were on a footing of perfect intimacy, and in possession of a full account of the delinquency of Job Trotter.

'I never could a-bear that Job,' said Mary.

'No more you never ought to, my dear,' replied Mr Weller.

'Why not?' inquired Mary.

'Cos ugliness and svindlin' never ought to be formiliar vith elegance and wirtew,' replied Mr Weller. 'Ought they, Mr Muzzle?'

'Not by no means,' replied that gentleman.

Here Mary laughed, and said the cook had made her; and the cook laughed, and said she hadn't.

'I han't got a glass,' said Mary.

'Drink with me, my dear,' said Mr Weller. 'Put your lips to this here tumbler, and then I can kiss you by deputy.'

'For shame, Mr Weller!' said Mary.

'What's a shame, my dear?'

'Talkin' in that way.'

'Nonsense; it ain't no harm. It's natur; ain't it, cook?'

'Don't ask me imperence,' replied the cook in a high state of delight: and hereupon the cook and Mary laughed again, till what between the beer, and the cold meat, and the laughter combined, the latter young lady was brought to the verge of choking – an alarming crisis from which she was only recovered by sundry pats on the back, and other necessary attentions, most delicately administered by Mr Samuel Weller.

In the midst of all this jolity and conviviality, a loud ring was heard at the garden-gate: to which the young gentleman who took his meals in the wash-house, immediately responded. Mr Weller was in the height of his attentions to the pretty house-maid; Mr Muzzle was busy doing the honours of the table; and the cook had just paused to laugh, in the very act of raising a huge morsel to her lips; when the kitchen-door opened, and in walked Mr Job Trotter.

We have said in walked Mr Job Trotter, but the statement is not distinguished by our usual scrupulous adherence to fact. The door opened and Mr Trotter appeared. He *would* have walked in, and was in the very act of doing so, indeed, when catching sight of Mr Weller, he involuntarily shrank back a pace or two, and stood

Job Trotter encounters Sam in Mr Muzzle's Kitchen

gazing on the unexpected scene before him, perfectly motionless with amazement and terror.

'Here he is!' said Sam, rising with great glee. 'Why we were that wery moment a speaking o' you. How are you? Where *have* you been? Come in.'

Laying his hand on the mulberry collar of the unresisting Job, Mr Weller dragged him into the kitchen; and, locking the door, handed the key to Mr Muzzle, who very coolly buttoned it up in a side-pocket.

'Well, here's a game!' cried Sam. 'Only think o' my master havin' the pleasure o' meeting your'n, up stairs, and me havin' the joy o' meetin' you down here. How *are* you gettin' on, and how *is* the chandlery bis'ness likely to do? Wel, I am so glad to see you. How happy you look. It's quite a treat to see you; ain't it, Mr Muzzle?'

'Quite,' said Mr Muzzle.

'So cheerful he is!' said Sam.

'In such good spirits!' said Muzzle.

'And so glad to see *us* – that makes it so much more comfortable,' said Sam. 'Sit down; sit down.'

Mr Trotter suffered himself to be forced into a chair by the fireside. He cast his small eyes, first on Mr Weller, and then on Mr Muzzle, but said nothing.

'Well, now,' said Sam, 'afore these here ladies, I should jest like to ask you, as a sort of curiosity, wether you don't con-sider yourself as nice and well-behaved a young gen'lm'n, as ever used a pink check pocket-handkerchief, and the number four collection?'

'And as was ever a-going to be married to a cook,' said that lady, indignantly, 'The willin!'

'And leave off his evil ways, and set up in the chandlery line, arterwards,' said the house-maid.

'Now, I'll tell you what it is, young man,' said Mr Muzzle, solemnly, enraged at the last two allusions, 'this here lady (pointing to the cook) keeps company with me; and when you presume, sir, to talk of keeping chandlers' shops with her, you injure me in one of the most delicatest points in which one man can injure another. Do you understand me, sir?'

Here Mr Muzzle, who had a great notion of his eloquence, in which he imitated his master, paused for a reply.

But Mr Trotter made no reply. So Mr Muzzle proceeded in a solemn manner:

'It's very probable, sir, that you won't be wanted up stairs for several minutes, sir, because *my* master is at this moment particularly engaged in settling the hash of *your* master, sir; and therefore you'll have leisure, sir, for a little private talk with me, sir. Do you understand me, sir?'

Mr Muzzle again paused for a reply; and again Mr Trotter disappointed him.

'Well, then,' said Mr Muzzle, 'I'm very sorry to have to explain myself before ladies, but the urgency of the case will be my excuse. The back kitchen's empty, sir. If you will step in there, sir, Mr Weller will see fair, and we can have mutual satisfaction till the bell rings. Follow me, sir!'

As Mr Muzzle uttered these words, he took a step or two towards the door; and by way of saving time, began to pull off his coat as he walked along.

Now, the cook no sooner heard the concluding words of this desperate challenge, and saw Mr Muzzle about to put it into execution, than she uttered a loud and piercing shriek, and rushing on Mr Job Trotter, who rose from his chair on the instant, tore and buffeted his large flat face, with an energy peculiar to excited females, and twining her hands in his long black hair, tore therefrom about enough to make five or six dozen of the very largest-sized mourning-rings. Having accomplished this feat with all the ardour which her devoted love for Mr Muzzle inspired, she staggered back; and being a lady of very excitable and delicate feelings, she instantly fell under the dresser, and fainted away.

At this moment, the bell rang.

'That's for you, Job Trotter,' said Sam; and before Mr Trotter could offer remonstrance or reply – even before he had time to stanch the wounds inflicted by the insensible lady – Sam seized one arm and Mr Muzzle the other; and one pulling before, and the other pushing behind, they conveyed him up stairs, and into the parlour.

It was an impressive tableau. Alfred Jingle, Esquire, alias Captain Fitz-Marshall, was standing near the door with his hat in his hand, and a smile on his face, wholly unmoved by his very unpleasant situation. Confronting him, stood Mr Pickwick, who had evidently been inculcating some high moral lesson; for his left hand was beneath his coat tail, and his right extended in air, as was his wont when delivering himself of an impressive address. At a little distance, stood Mr Tupman with indignant countenance, carefully held back by his two younger friends; at the further end of the room were Mr Nupkins, Mrs Nupkins, and Miss Nupkins, gloomily grand, and savagely vexed.

'What prevents me,' said Mr Nupkins, with magisterial dignity, as Job was brought in: 'What prevents me from detaining these men as rogues and impostors? It is a foolish mercy. What prevents me?'

'Pride, old fellow, pride,' replied Jingle, quite at his ease. 'Wouldn't do – no go – caught a captain, eh? – ha! ha! very good – husband for daughter – biter bit – make it public – not for worlds – look stupid – very!'

'Wretch,' said Mrs Nupkins, 'we scorn your base insinuations.'

'I always hated him,' added Henrietta.

'Oh, of course,' said Jingle. 'Tall young man – old lover – Sidney Porkenham – rich – fine fellow – not so rich as captain, though? – turn him away – off with him – anything for captain – nothing like captain anywhere – all the girls – raving mad – eh, Job?'

Here Mr Jingle laughed very heartily; and Job, rubbing his hands with delight, uttered the first sound he had given vent to, since he entered the house – a low noiseless chuckle, which seemed to intimate that he enjoyed his laugh too much, to let any of it escape in sound.

'Mr Nupkins,' said the elder lady, 'this is not a fit conversation for the servants to overhear. Let these wretches be removed.'

'Certainly, my dear,' said Mr Nupkins. 'Muzzle!'

'Your worship.'

'Open the front door.'

'Yes, your worship.'

'Leave the house!' said Mr Nupkins, waving his hand emphatically.

Jingle smiled, and moved towards the door.

'Stay!' said Mr Pickwick.

Jingle stopped.

'I might,' said Mr Pickwick, 'have taken a much greater revenge for the treatment I have experienced at your hands, and that of your hypocritical friend there.'

Job Trotter bowed with great politeness, and laid his hand upon his heart.

'I say,' said Mr Pickwick, growing gradually angry, 'that I might have taken a greater revenge, but I content myself with exposing you, which I consider a duty I owe to society. This is a leniency, sir, which I hope you will remember.'

When Mr Pickwick arrived at this point, Job Trotter, with facetious gravity, applied his hand to his ear, as if desirous not to lose a syllable he uttered.

'And I have only to add, sir,' said Mr Pickwick, now thoroughly

angry, 'that I consider you a rascal, and a – a ruffian – and – and
worse than any man I ever saw, or heard of, except that pious and
sanctified vagabond in the mulberry livery.'

'Ha! ha!' said Jingle, 'good fellow, Pickwick – fine heart – stout
old boy – but must *not* be passionate – bad thing, very – bye, bye –
see you again some day – keep up your spirits – now, Job – trot!'

With these words, Mr Jingle stuck on his hat in the old fashion,
and strode out of the room. Job Trotter paused, looked round,
smiled, and then with a bow of mock solemnity to Mr Pickwick,
and a wink to Mr Weller, the audacious slyness of which baffles all
description, followed the footsteps of his hopeful master.

'Sam,' said Mr Pickwick, as Mr Weller was following.

'Sir.'

'Stay here.'

Mr Weller seemed uncertain.

'Stay here,' repeated Mr Pickwick.

'Mayn't I polish that ere Job off, in the front garden?' said Mr
Weller.

'Certainly not,' replied Mr Pickwick.

'Mayn't I kick him out o' the gate, sir?' said Mr Weller.

'Not on any account,' replied his master.

For the first time since his engagement, Mr Weller looked, for a
moment, discontented and unhappy. But his countenance immediately cleared up; for the wily Mr Muzzle, by concealing himself
behind the street door, and rushing violently out, at the right
instant, contrived with great dexterity to overturn both Mr Jingle
and his attendant, down the flight of steps, into the American aloe
tubs that stood beneath.

'Having discharged my duty, sir,' said Mr Pickwick to Mr
Nupkins, 'I will, with my friends, bid you farewell. While we thank
you for such hospitality as we have received, permit me to assure
you, in our joint names, that we should not have accepted it, or
have consented to extricate ourselves in this way, from our previous
dilemma, had we not been impelled by a strong sense of duty. We
return to London to-morrow. Your secret is safe with us.'

Having thus entered his protest against their treatment of the
morning, Mr Pickwick bowed low to the ladies, and notwithstanding the solicitations of the family, left the room with his friends.

'Get your hat, Sam,' said Mr Pickwick.

'It's below stairs, sir,' said Sam, and he ran down after it.

Now, there was nobody in the kitchen, but the pretty house-
maid; and as Sam's hat was mislaid, he had to look for it; and the

pretty house-maid lighted him. They had to look all over the place for the hat. The pretty house-maid, in her anxiety to find it, went down on her knees, and turned over all the things that were heaped together in a little corner by the door. It was an awkward corner. You couldn't get at it without shutting the door first.

'Here it is,' said the pretty house-maid. 'This is it, ain't it?'

'Let me look,' said Sam.

The pretty house-maid had stood the candle on the floor; as it gave a very dim light, Sam was obliged to go down on *his* knees before he could see whether it really was his own hat or not. It was a remarkably small corner, and so – it was nobody's fault but the man's who built the house – Sam and the pretty house-maid were necessarily very close together.

'Yes, this is it,' said Sam. 'Good bye!'

'Good bye!' said the pretty house-maid.

'Good bye!' said Sam; and as he said it, he dropped the hat that had cost so much trouble in looking for.

'How awkward you are,' said the pretty house-maid. 'You'll lose it again, if you don't take care.'

So, just to prevent his losing it again, she put it on for him.

Whether it was that the pretty house-maid's face looked prettier still, when it was raised towards Sam's, or whether it was the accidental consequence of their being so near to each other, is matter of uncertainty to this day; but Sam kissed her.

'You don't mean to say you did that on purpose,' said the pretty house-maid, blushing.

'No, I didn't then,' said Sam; 'but I will now.'

So he kissed her again.

'Sam!' said Mr Pickwick, calling over the banisters.

'Coming, sir,' replied Sam, running up stairs.

'How long you have been!' said Mr Pickwick.

'There was something behind the door, sir, which perwented our getting it open, for ever so long, sir,' replied Sam.

And this was the first passage of Mr Weller's first love.

Which contains a brief Account of the Progress of the Action of Bardell against Pickwick

Having accomplished the main end and object of his journey, by the exposure of Jingle, Mr Pickwick resolved on immediately returning to London, with the view of becoming acquainted with the proceedings which had been taken against him, in the mean time, by Messrs. Dodson and Fogg. Acting upon this resolution with all the energy and decision of his character, he mounted to the back seat of the first coach which left Ipswich on the morning after the memorable occurrences detailed at length in the two preceding chapters; and accompanied by his three friends, and Mr Samuel Weller, arrived in the metropolis, in perfect health and safety, the same evening.

Here, the friends, for a short time, separated. Messrs. Tupman, Winkle, and Snodgrass repaired to their several homes to make such preparations as might be requisite for their forthcoming visit to Dingley Dell; and Mr Pickwick and Sam took up their present abode in very good, old-fashioned, and comfortable quarters: to wit, the George and Vulture Tavern and Hotel, George Yard, Lombard Street.

Mr Pickwick had dined, finished his second pint of particular port, pulled his silk handkerchief over his head, put his feet on the fender, and thrown himself back in an easy chair, when the entrance of Mr Weller with his carpet bag, aroused him from his tranquil meditations.

'Sam,' said Mr Pickwick.

'Sir,' said Mr Weller.

'I have just been thinking, Sam,' said Mr Pickwick, 'that having left a good many things at Mrs Bardell's, in Goswell Street, I ought to arrange for taking them away, before I leave town again.'

'Wery good, sir,' replied Mr Weller.

'I could send them to Mr Tupman's, for the present, Sam,' continued Mr Pickwick, 'but before we take them away, it is necessary that they should be looked up, and put together. I wish you would step up to Goswell Street, Sam, and arrange about it.'

'At once, sir?' inquired Mr Weller.

'At once,' replied Mr Pickwick. 'And stay, Sam,' added Mr Pickwick, pulling out his purse, 'There is some rent to pay. The quarter is not due till Christmas, but you may pay it, and have done with it. A month's notice terminates my tenancy. Here it is, written out. Give it, and tell Mrs Bardell she may put a bill up, as soon as she likes.'

'Wery good, sir,' replied Mr Weller; 'anythin' more, sir?'

'Nothing more, Sam.'

Mr Weller stepped slowly to the door, as if he expected something more; slowly opened it, slowly stepped out, and had slowly closed it within a couple of inches, when Mr Pickwick called out,

'Sam.'

'Sir,' said Mr Weller, stepping quickly back, and closing the door behind him.

'I have no objection, Sam, to your endeavouring to ascertain how Mrs Bardell herself seems disposed towards me, and whether it is really probable that this vile and groundless action is to be carried to extremity. I say I do not object to your doing this, if you wish it, Sam,' said Mr Pickwick.

Sam gave a short nod of intelligence, and left the room. Mr Pickwick drew the silk handkerchief once more over his head, and composed himself for a nap. Mr Weller promptly walked forth, to execute his commission.

It was nearly nine o'clock when he reached Goswell Street. A couple of candles were burning in the little front parlour, and a couple of caps were reflected on the window-blind. Mrs Bardell had got company.

Mr Weller knocked at the door, and after a pretty long interval – occupied by the party without, in whistling a tune, and by the party within, in persuading a refractory flat candle[2] to allow itself to be lighted – a pair of small boots pattered over the floor-cloth, and Master Bardell presented himself.

'Well, young townskip,' said Sam, 'how's mother?'

'She's pretty well,' replied Master Bardell, 'so am I.'

'Well, that's a mercy,' said Sam; 'tell her I want to speak to her, will you my hinfant fernomenon?'[1]

Master Bardell, thus adjured, placed the refractory flat candle on the bottom stair, and vanished into the front parlour with his message.

The two caps, reflected on the window-blind, were the respective head-dresses of a couple of Mrs Bardell's most particular acquaintance, who had just stepped in, to have a quiet cup of tea, and a little warm supper of a couple of sets of pettitoes and some toasted cheese. The cheese was simmering and browning away, most delightfully, in a little Dutch oven[3] before the fire; the pettitoes were getting on deliciously in a little tin saucepan on the hob; and Mrs Bardell and her two friends were getting on very well, also, in a little quiet conversation about and concerning all their particular friends and acquaintance; when Master Bardell came back from answering the door, and delivered the message intrusted to him by Mr Samuel Weller.

'Mr Pickwick's servant!' said Mrs Bardell, turning pale.

'Bless my soul!' said Mrs Cluppins.

'Well, I raly would *not* ha' believed it, unless I had ha' happened to ha' been here!' said Mrs Sanders.

Mrs Cluppins was a little brisk, busy-looking woman; Mrs Sanders was a big, fat, heavy-faced personage; and the two were the company.

Mrs Bardell felt it proper to be agitated; and as none of the three exactly knew whether, under existing circumstances, any communication, otherwise than through Dodson and Fogg, ought to be held with Mr Pickwick's servant, they were all rather taken by surprise. In this state of indecision, obviously the first thing to be done, was to thump the boy for finding Mr Weller at the door. So his mother thumped him, and he cried melodiously.

'Hold your noise – do – you naughty creetur!' said Mrs Bardell.

'Yes; don't worrit your poor mother,' said Mrs Sanders.

'She's quite enough to worrit her, as it is, without you, Tommy,' said Mrs Cluppins, with sympathising resignation.

'Ah! worse luck, poor lamb!' said Mrs Sanders.

At all which moral reflections, Master Bardell howled the louder.

'Now, what *shall* I do?' said Mrs Bardell to Mrs Cluppins.

'*I* think you ought to see him,' replied Mrs Cluppins. 'But on no account without a witness.'

'*I* think two witnesses would be more lawful,' said Mrs Sanders, who, like the other friend, was bursting with curiosity.

'Perhaps he'd better come in here,' said Mrs Bardell.

'To be sure,' replied Mrs Cluppins, eagerly catching at the idea; 'Walk in, young man; and shut the street door first, please.'

Mr Weller immediately took the hint; and presenting himself in the parlour, explained his business to Mrs Bardell thus:

'Werry sorry to 'casion any personal inconwenience, ma'am, as the housebreaker said to the old lady when he put her on the fire; but as me and my governor's only jest come to town, and is jest going away agin, it can't be helped you see.'

'Of course, the young man can't help the faults of his master,' said Mrs Cluppins, much struck by Mr Weller's appearance and conversation.

'Certainly not,' chimed in Mrs Sanders, who, from certain wistful glances at the little tin saucepan, seemed to be engaged in a mental calculation of the probable extent of the pettitoes, in the event of Sam's being asked to stop supper.

'So all I've come about, is jest this here,' said Sam, disregarding the interruption; 'First, to give my governor's notice – there it is. Secondly, to pay the rent – here it is. Thirdly, to say as all his things is to be put together, and give to anybody as we sends for 'em. Fourthly, that you may let the place as soon as you like – and that's all.'

'Whatever has happened,' said Mrs Bardell, 'I always have said, and always will say, that in every respect but one, Mr Pickwick has always behaved himself like a perfect gentleman. His money always was as good as the bank: always.'

As Mrs Bardell said this, she applied her handkerchief to her eyes, and went out of the room to get the receipt.

Sam well knew that he had only to remain quiet, and the women were sure to talk; so he looked alternately at the tin saucepan, the toasted cheese, the wall, and the ceiling, in profound silence.

'Poor dear!' said Mrs Cluppins.

'Ah, poor thing!' replied Mrs Sanders.

Sam said nothing. He saw they were coming to the subject.

'I raly cannot contain myself,' said Mrs Cluppins, 'when I think of such perjury. I don't wish to say anything to make you uncomfortable, young man, but your master's an old brute, and I wish I had him here to tell him so.'

'I wish you had,' said Sam.

'To see how dreadful she takes on, going moping about, and taking no pleasure in nothing, except when her friends comes in, out of charity, to sit with her, and make her comfortable,' resumed Mrs Cluppins, glancing at the tin saucepan and the Dutch oven, 'it's shocking!'

'Barbareous,' said Mrs Sanders.

'And your master, young man! A gentleman with money, as could never feel the expense of a wife, no more than nothing,' continued Mrs Cluppins, with great volubility; 'why there ain't the faintest shade of an excuse for his behaviour! Why don't he marry her?'

'Ah,' said Sam, 'to be sure; that's the question.'

'Question, indeed,' retorted Mrs Cluppins; 'she'd question him, if she'd my spirit. Hows'ever, there *is* law for us women, mis'rable creeturs as they'd make us, if they could; and that your master will find out, young man, to his cost, afore he's six months older.'

At this consolatory reflection, Mrs Cluppins bridled up, and smiled at Mrs Sanders, who smiled back again.

'The action's going on, and no mistake,' thought Sam, as Mrs Bardell re-entered with the receipt.

'Here's the receipt, Mr Weller,' said Mrs Bardell, 'and here's the change, and I hope you'll take a little drop of something to keep the cold out, if it's only for old acquaintance' sake, Mr Weller.'

Sam saw the advantage he should gain, and at once acquiesced; whereupon Mrs Bardell produced, from a small closet, a black bottle and a wine glass; and so great was her abstraction, in her deep mental affliction, that, after filling Mr Weller's glass, she brought out three more wine glasses, and filled them too.

'Lauk, Mrs Bardell,' said Mrs Cluppins, 'see what you've been and done!'

'Well, that is a good one!' ejaculated Mrs Sanders.

'Ah, my poor head!' said Mrs Bardell, with a faint smile.

Sam understood all this, of course, so he said at once, that he never could drink before supper, unless a lady drank with him. A great deal of laughing ensued, and Mrs Sanders volunteered to humour him, so she took a slight sip out of her glass. Then, Sam said it must go all round, so they all took a slight sip. Then, little Mrs Cluppins proposed as a toast, 'Success to Bardell agin Pick-wick;' and then the ladies emptied their glasses in honour of the sentiment, and got very talkative directly.

'I suppose you've heard what's going forward, Mr Weller?' said Mrs Bardell.

'I've heerd somethin' on it,' replied Sam.

'It's a terrible thing to be dragged before the public, in that way, Mr Weller,' said Mrs Bardell; 'but I see now, that it's the only thing I ought to do, and my lawyers, Mr Dodson and Fogg, tell me, that with the evidence as we shall call, we must succeed. I don't know what I should do, Mr Weller, if I didn't.'

The mere idea of Mrs Bardell's failing in her action, affected Mrs Sanders so deeply, that she was under the necessity of re-filling and re-emptying her glass immediately; feeling, as she said afterwards, that if she hadn't had the presence of mind to do so, she must have dropped.

'Ven is it expected to come on?' inquired Sam.

'Either in February or March,' replied Mrs Bardell.

'What a number of witnesses there'll be, won't there?' said Mrs Cluppins.

'Ah, won't there!' replied Mrs Sanders.

'And won't Mr Dodson and Fogg be wild if the plaintiff shouldn't get it?' added Mrs Cluppins, 'when they do it all on speculation!'

'Ah! won't they!' said Mrs Sanders.

'But the plaintiff must get it,' resumed Mrs Cluppins.

'I hope so,' said Mrs Bardell.

'Oh, there can't be any doubt about it,' rejoined Mrs Sanders.

'Vell,' said Sam, rising and setting down his glass, 'All I can say is, that I wish you *may* get it.'

'Thank'ee, Mr Weller,' said Mrs Bardell fervently.

'And of them Dodson and Foggs, as does these sort o'things on spec,' continued Mr Weller, 'as well as for the other kind and gen'rous people o' the same purfession, as sets people by the ears, free gratis for nothin', and sets their clerks to work to find out little disputes among their neighbours and acquaintances as vants settlin' by means o' law-suits – all I can say o' them is, that I vish they had the revard I'd give 'em.'

'Ah, I wish they had the reward that every kind and generous heart would be inclined to bestow upon them!' said the gratified Mrs Bardell.

'Amen to that,' replied Sam, 'and a fat and happy livin' they'd get out of it! Wish you good night, ladies.'

To the great relief of Mrs Sanders, Sam was allowed to depart without any reference, on the part of the hostess, to the pettitoes and toasted cheese: to which the ladies, with such juvenile assistance as Master Bardell could afford, soon afterwards rendered the amplest justice – indeed they wholly vanished before their strenuous exertions.

Mr Weller went his way back to the George and Vulture, and faithfully recounted to his master, such indications of the sharp practice of Dodson and Fogg, as he had contrived to pick up in his visit to Mrs Bardell's. An interview with Mr Perker, next day, more than confirmed Mr Weller's statement; and Mr Pickwick was fain to prepare for his Christmas visit to Dingley Dell, with the pleasant anticipation that some two or three months afterwards, an action brought against him for damages sustained by reason of a breach of promise of marriage, would be publicly tried in the Court of Common Pleas: the plaintiff having all the advantages derivable, not only from the force of circumstances, but from the sharp practice of Dodson and Fogg to boot.

CHAPTER 27

Samuel Weller makes a Pilgrimage to Dorking, and beholds his Mother-in-Law

There still remaining an interval of two days before the time agreed upon for the departure of the Pickwickians to Dingley Dell, Mr Weller sat himself down in a back room at the George and Vulture, after eating an early dinner, to muse on the best way of disposing of his time. It was a remarkably fine day; and he had not turned the matter over in his mind ten minutes, when he was suddenly stricken filial and affectionate; and it occurred to him so strongly that he ought to go down and see his father, and pay his duty to his mother-in-law, that he was lost in astonishment at his own remissness in never thinking of this moral obligation before. Anxious to atone for his past neglect without another hour's delay, he straightway walked up stairs to Mr Pickwick, and requested leave of absence for this laudable purpose.

'Certainly, Sam, certainly,' said Mr Pickwick, his eyes glistening with delight at this manifestation of filial feeling on the part of his attendant; 'certainly, Sam.'

Mr Weller made a grateful bow.

'I am very glad to see that you have so high a sense of your duties as a son, Sam,' said Mr Pickwick.

'I always had, sir,' replied Mr Weller.

'That's a very gratifying reflection, Sam,' said Mr Pickwick, approvingly.

'Wery, sir,' replied Mr Weller; 'if ever I wanted anythin' o' my father, I always asked for it in a wery 'spectful and obligin' manner. If he didn't give it me, I took it, for fear I should be led to do anythin' wrong, through not havin' it. I saved him a world o' trouble in this vay, sir.'

'That's not precisely what I meant, Sam,' said Mr Pickwick, shaking his head, with a slight smile.

'All good feelin', sir – the wery best intentions, as the gen'lm'n said ven he run away from his wife 'cos she seemed unhappy with him,' replied Mr Weller.

'You may go, Sam,' said Mr Pickwick.

'Thank'ee, sir,' replied Mr Weller; and having made his best bow, and put on his best clothes, Sam planted himself on the top of the Arundel coach, and journeyed on to Dorking.

The Marquis of Granby[1] in Mrs Weller's time was quite a model of a road-side public-house of the better class – just large enough to be convenient, and small enough to be snug. On the opposite side of the road was a large sign-board on a high post, representing the head and shoulders of a gentleman with an apoplectic countenance, in a red coat with deep blue facings, and a touch of the same blue over his three-cornered hat, for a sky. Over that again were a pair of flags; beneath the last button of his coat were a couple of cannon; and the whole formed an expressive and undoubted likeness of the Marquis of Granby of glorious memory.

The bar window displayed a choice collection of geranium plants, and a well-dusted row of spirit phials. The open shutters bore a variety of golden inscriptions, eulogistic of good beds and neat wines; and the choice group of countrymen and hostlers lounging about the stable-door and horse-trough, afforded presumptive proof of the excellent quality of the ale and spirits which were sold within. Sam Weller paused, when he dismounted from the coach, to note all these little indications of a thriving business, with the eye of an experienced traveller; and having done so, stepped in at once, highly satisfied with everything he had observed.

'Now, then!' said a shrill female voice the instant Sam thrust his head in at the door, 'what do you want, young man?'

Sam looked round in the direction whence the voice proceeded. It came from a rather stout lady of comfortable appearance, who was seated beside the fire-place in the bar, blowing the fire to make the kettle boil for tea. She was not alone; for on the other side of the fire-place, sitting bolt upright in a high-backed chair, was a man in thread-bare black clothes, with a back almost as long and stiff as that of the chair itself, who caught Sam's most particular and especial attention at once.

He was a prim-faced, red-nosed man, with a long, thin countenance, and a semi-rattlesnake sort of eye – rather sharp, but decidedly bad. He wore very short trousers, and black-cotton stockings, which, like the rest of his apparel, were particularly rusty. His looks were starched, but his white neckerchief was not, and its long limp ends straggled over his closely-buttoned waistcoat in a very uncouth and unpicturesque fashion. A pair of old, worn beaver gloves, a broad-brimmed hat, and a faded green umbrella, with plenty of whalebone sticking through the bottom, as if to counterbalance the want of a handle at the top, lay on a chair beside him, and, being disposed in a very tidy and careful manner, seemed to imply that the red-nosed man, whoever he was, had no intention of going away in a hurry.

To do the red-nosed man justice, he would have been very far from wise if he had entertained any such intention; for, to judge from all appearances, he must have been possessed of a most desirable circle of acquaintance, if he could have reasonably expected to be more comfortable anywhere else. The fire was blazing brightly under the influence of the bellows, and the kettle was singing gaily under the influence of both. A small tray of tea things was arranged on the table, a plate of hot buttered toast was gently simmering before the fire, and the red-nosed man himself was busily engaged in converting a large slice of bread into the same agreeable edible, through the instrumentality of a long brass toasting-fork. Beside him stood a glass of reeking hot pine-apple rum and water, with a slice of lemon in it; and every time the red-nosed man stopped to bring the round of toast to his eye, with the view of ascertaining how it got on, he imbibed a drop or two of the hot pine-apple rum and water, and smiled upon the rather stout lady, as she blew the fire.

Sam was so lost in the contemplation of this comfortable scene, that he suffered the first inquiry of the rather stout lady to pass unheeded. It was not until it had been twice repeated, each time in a shriller tone, that he became conscious of the impropriety of his behaviour.

'Governor in?' inquired Sam, in reply to the question.

'No, he isn't,' replied Mrs Weller; for the rather stout lady was no other than the quondam relict and sole executrix of the dead-and-gone Mr Clarke; 'No, he isn't, and I don't expect him, either.'

'I suppose he's a drivin' up to-day?' said Sam.

'He may be, or he may not,' replied Mrs Weller, buttering the round of toast which the red-nosed man had just finished. 'I don't know, and, what's more, I don't care. Ask a blessin', Mr Stiggins.'

The red-nosed man did as he was desired, and instantly commenced on the toast with fierce voracity.

The appearance of the red-nosed man had induced Sam, at first sight, to more than half suspect that he was the deputy shepherd of whom his estimable parent had spoken. The moment he saw him eat, all doubt on the subject was removed, and he perceived at once that if he purposed to take up his temporary quarters where he was, he must make his footing good without delay. He therefore commenced proceedings by putting his arm over the half-door of the bar, coolly unbolting it, and leisurely walking in.

'Mother-in-law,' said Sam, 'how are you?'

'Why, I do believe he is a Weller!' said Mrs W., raising her eyes to Sam's face, with no very gratified expression of countenance.

'I rayther think he is,' said the imperturbable Sam; 'and I hope this here reverend gen'lm'n 'll excuse me saying that I wish I was *the* Weller as owns you, mother-in-law.'

This was a double-barrelled compliment. It implied that Mrs Weller was a most agreeable female, and also that Mr Stiggins had a clerical appearance. It made a visible impression at once; and Sam followed up his advantage by kissing his mother-in-law.

'Get along with you!' said Mrs Weller, pushing him away.

'For shame, young man!' said the gentleman with the red nose.

'No offence, sir, no offence,' replied Sam; 'you're wery right, though; it ain't the right sort o'thing, wen mothers-in-law is young and good looking, is it, sir?'

'It's all vanity,'[2] said Mr Stiggins.

'Ah, so it is,' said Mrs Weller, setting her cap to rights.

Sam thought it was, too, but he held his peace.

The deputy shepherd seemed by no means best pleased with Sam's arrival; and when the first effervescence of the compliment had subsided, even Mrs Weller looked as if she could have spared him without the smallest inconvenience. However, there he was; and as he couldn't be decently turned out, they all three sat down to tea.

'And how's father?' said Sam.

At this inquiry, Mrs Weller raised her hands, and turned up her eyes, as if the subject were too painful to be alluded to.

Mr Stiggins groaned.

'What's the matter with that 'ere gen'lm'n?' inquired Sam.

'He's shocked at the way your father goes on in,' replied Mrs Weller.

'Oh, he is, is he?' said Sam.

'And with too good reason,' added Mrs Weller, gravely.

Mr Stiggins took up a fresh piece of toast, and groaned heavily.

'He is a dreadful reprobate,' said Mrs Weller.

'A man of wrath!'[3] exclaimed Mr Stiggins. He took a large semi-circular bite out of the toast, and groaned again.

Sam felt very strongly disposed to give the reverend Mr Stiggins something to groan for, but he repressed his inclination, and merely asked, 'What's the old 'un up to, now?'

'Up to, indeed!' said Mrs Weller. 'Oh, he has a hard heart. Night after night does this excellent man – don't frown, Mr Stiggins: I *will* say you *are* an excellent man – come and sit here, for hours together, and it has not the least effect upon him.'

'Well, that is odd,' said Sam; 'it 'ud have a wery considerable effect upon me, if I wos in his place; I know that.'

'The fact is, my young friend,' said Mr Stiggins, solemnly, 'he has an obderrate bosom. Oh, my young friend, who else could have resisted the pleading of sixteen of our fairest sisters, and withstood their exhortations to subscribe to our noble society for providing the infant negroes in the West Indies with flannel waistcoats and moral pocket handkerchiefs?'[4]

'What's a moral pocket ankercher?' said Sam; 'I never see one o' them articles o' furniter.'

'Those which combine amusement with instruction, my young friend,' replied Mr Stiggins: 'blending select tales with wood-cuts.'

'Oh, I know,' said Sam; 'them as hangs up in the linen-drapers' shops, with beggars' petitions and all that 'ere upon 'em?'

Mr Stiggins began a third round of toast, and nodded assent.

'And he wouldn't be persuaded by the ladies, wouldn't he?' said Sam.

'Sat and smoked his pipe, and said the infant negroes were – what did he say the infant negroes were?' said Mrs Weller.

'Little humbugs,' replied Mr Stiggins, deeply affected.

'Said the infant negroes were little humbugs,' repeated Mrs Weller. And they both groaned at the atrocious conduct of the old gentleman.

A great many more iniquities of a similar nature might have been disclosed, only the toast being all eaten, the tea having got very weak, and Sam holding out no indications of meaning to go, Mr Stiggins suddenly recollected that he had a most pressing appointment with the shepherd, and took himself off accordingly.

The tea-things had been scarcely put away, and the hearth swept up, when the London coach deposited Mr Weller senior at the door; his legs deposited him in the bar; and his eyes showed him his son.

'What, Sammy!' exclaimed the father.

'What, old Nobs!' ejaculated the son. And they shook hands heartily.

'Werry glad to see you, Sammy,' said the elder Mr Weller, 'though how you've managed to get over your mother-in-law, is a mystery to me. I only vish you'd write me out the receipt, that's all.'

'Hush!' said Sam, 'she's at home, old feller.'

'She ain't vithin hearin',' replied Mr Weller; 'she always goes and blows up, down stairs, for a couple of hours arter tea; so we'll just give ourselves a damp, Sammy.'

Saying this, Mr Weller mixed two glasses of spirits and water, and produced a couple of pipes. The father and son sitting down opposite each other: Sam on one side of the fire, in the high-backed chair, and Mr Weller senior on the other, in an easy ditto: they proceeded to enjoy themselves with all due gravity.

'Anybody been here, Sammy?' asked Mr Weller senior, drily, after a long silence.

Sam nodded an expressive assent.

'Red-nosed chap?' inquired Mr Weller.

Sam nodded again.

'Amiable man that 'ere, Sammy,' said Mr Weller, smoking violently.

'Seems so,' observed Sam.

'Good hand at accounts,' said Mr Weller.

'Is he?' said Sam.

'Borrows eighteenpence on Monday, and comes on Tuesday for a shillin' to make it up half a crown; calls again on Vensday for another half crown to make it five shillin's; and goes on, doubling, till he gets it up to a five pund note in no time, like them sums in the 'rithmetic book 'bout the nails in the horse's shoes,⁵ Sammy.'

Sam intimated by a nod that he recollected the problem alluded to by his parent.

'So you vouldn't subscribe to the flannel veskits?' said Sam, after another interval of smoking.

'Cert'nly not,' replied Mr Weller; 'what's the good o' flannel veskits to the young niggers abroad? But I'll tell you what it is, Sammy,' said Mr Weller, lowering his voice, and bending across the fire-place; 'I'd come down wery handsome towards strait veskits for some people at home.'

As Mr Weller said this, he slowly recovered his former position, and winked at his first-born, in a profound manner.

'It cert'nly seems a queer start to send out pocket ankerchers to people as don't know the use on 'em,' observed Sam.

'They're alvays a doin' some gammon of that sort, Sammy,' replied his father. 'T'other Sunday I wos walkin' up the road, wen who should I see, a standin' at a chapel-door, with a blue soup-plate in her hand, but your mother-in-law! I werily believe there was change for a couple o' suv'rins in it, then, Sammy, all in ha'pence; and as the people come out, they rattled the pennies in it, till you'd ha' thought that no mortal plate as ever was baked, could ha' stood the wear and tear. What d'ye think it was all for?'

'For another tea-drinkin', perhaps,' said Sam.

'Not a bit on it,' replied the father; 'for the shepherd's water-rate, Sammy.'

'The shepherd's water-rate!' said Sam.

'Ay,' replied Mr Weller, 'there was three quarters owin', and the shepherd hadn't paid a farden, not he – perhaps it might be on account that the water warn't o' much use to him, for it's wery little o' that tap he drinks, Sammy, wery; he knows a trick worth a good half dozen of that, he does. Hows'ever, it warn't paid, and so they cuts the water off. Down goes the shepherd to chapel, gives out as he's a persecuted saint, and says he hopes the heart of the turncock[6] as cut the water off, 'll be softened, and turned in the right vay: but he rayther thinks he's booked for somethin' uncomfortable. Upon this, the women calls a meetin', sings a hymn, wotes your mother-in-law into the chair, wolunteers a col-lection next Sunday, and hands it all over to the shepherd. And if he ain't got enough out on 'em, Sammy, to make him free of the water company for life,' said Mr Weller, in conclusion, 'I'm one Dutchman, and you're another, and that's all about it.'

Mr Weller smoked for some minutes in silence, and then resumed:

'The worst o' these here shepherds is, my boy, that they reg'larly turns the heads of all the young ladies, about here. Lord bless their little hearts, they thinks it's all right, and don't know no better; but they're the wictims o' gammon, Samivel, they're the wictims o' gammon.'

'I s'pose they are,' said Sam.

'Nothin' else,' said Mr Weller, shaking his head gravely; 'and wot aggrawates me, Samivel, is to see 'em a wastin' all their time and labour in making clothes for copper-coloured people as don't want 'em, and taking no notice of flesh-coloured Christians as do. If I'd my vay, Samivel, I'd just stick some o' these here lazy shepherds behind a heavy wheelbarrow, and run 'em up and down a fourteen-inch-wide plank all day. That 'ud shake the nonsense out of 'em, if anythin' vould.'

Mr Weller having delivered this gentle recipe with strong emphasis, eked out by a variety of nods and contortions of the eye, emptied his glass at a draught, and knocked the ashes out of his pipe, with native dignity.

He was engaged in this operation, when a shrill voice was heard in the passage.

'Here's your dear relation, Sammy,' said Mr Weller; and Mrs W. hurried into the room.

'Oh, you've come back, have you!' said Mrs Weller.

'Yes, my dear,' replied Mr Weller, filling a fresh pipe.

'Has Mr Stiggins been back?' said Mrs Weller.

'No, my dear, he hasn't,' replied Mr Weller, lighting the pipe by the ingenious process of holding to the bowl thereof, between the tongs, a red-hot coal from the adjacent fire; 'and what's more, my dear, I shall manage to surwive it, if he don't come back at all.'

'Ugh, you wretch!' said Mrs Weller.

'Thank'ee, my love,' said Mr Weller.

'Come, come, father,' said Sam, 'none o' these little lovins afore strangers. Here's the reverend gen'lm'n a comin' in now.'

At this announcement, Mrs Weller hastily wiped off the tears which she had just begun to force on; and Mr W. drew his chair sullenly into the chimney corner.

Mr Stiggins was easily prevailed on, to take another glass of the hot pine-apple rum and water, and a second, and a third, and then to refresh himself with a slight supper, previous to beginning again. He sat on the same side as Mr Weller senior; and every time he could contrive to do so, unseen by his wife, that gentleman indicated to his son the hidden emotions of his bosom, by shaking his fist over the deputy shepherd's head: a process which afforded his son the most unmingled delight and satisfaction, the more especially as Mr Stiggins went on, quietly drinking the hot pine-apple rum and water, wholly unconscious of what was going on.

The major part of the conversation was confined to Mrs Weller and the reverend Mr Stiggins; and the topics principally descanted on, were the virtues of the shepherd, the worthiness of his flock, and the high crimes and misdemeanors of everybody beside; dissertations which the elder Mr Weller occasionally interrupted by half-suppressed references to a gentleman of the name of Walker,[7] and other running commentaries of the same kind.

At length Mr Stiggins, with several most indubitable symptoms of having quite as much pine-apple rum and water about him, as he could comfortably accommodate, took his hat, and his leave: and Sam was, immediately afterwards, shown to bed by his father. The respectable old gentleman wrung his hand fervently, and seemed disposed to address some observation to his son; but on Mrs Weller advancing towards him, he appeared to relinquish that intention, and abruptly bade him good night.

Sam was up betimes next day, and having partaken of a hasty

breakfast, prepared to return to London. He had scarcely set foot without the house, when his father stood before him.

'Goin', Sammy?' inquired Mr Weller.

'Off at once,' replied Sam.

'I vish you could muffle that 'ere Stiggins, and take him with you,' said Mr Weller.

'I am ashamed on you!' said Sam, reproachfully; 'what do you let him show his red nose in the Markis o' Granby at all, for?'

Mr Weller the elder fixed on his son an earnest look, and replied, ' 'Cause I'm a married man, Samivel, 'cause I'm a married man. Wen you're a married man, Samivel, you'll understand a good many things as you don't understand now; but vether it's worth while goin' through so much, to learn so little, as the charity-boy said ven he got to the end of the alphabet, is a matter o' taste. *I* rayther think it isn't.'

'Well,' said Sam, 'good bye.'

'Tar, tar, Sammy,' replied his father.

'I've only got to say this here,' said Sam, stopping short, 'that if *I* was the properiator o' the Markis o' Granby, and that 'ere Stiggins came and made toast in *my* bar, I'd – '

'What?' interposed Mr Weller, with great anxiety. 'What?'

' – Pison his rum and water,' said Sam.

'No!' said Mr Weller, shaking his son eagerly by the hand, 'would you raly, Sammy; would you, though?'

'I would,' said Sam. 'I wouldn't be too hard upon him at first. I'd drop him in the water-butt, and put the lid on; and if I found he was insensible to kindness, I'd try the other persvasion.'

The elder Mr Weller bestowed a look of deep, unspeakable admiration on his son: and, having once more grasped his hand, walked slowly away, revolving in his mind the numerous reflections to which his advice had given rise.

Sam looked after him, until he turned a corner of the road: and then set forward on his walk to London. He meditated, at first, on the probable consequences of his own advice, and the likelihood and unlikelihood of his father's adopting it. He dismissed the subject from his mind, however, with the consolatory reflection that time alone would show; and this is the reflection we would impress upon the reader.

CHAPTER 28

A good-humoured Christmas Chapter, containing an
Account of a Wedding, and some other Sports
beside: which although in their way, even as good
Customs as Marriage itself, are not quite so
religiously kept up, in these degenerate Times

As brisk as bees, if not altogether as light as fairies, did the four
Pickwickians assemble on the morning of the twenty-second day of
December, in the year of grace in which these, their faithfully-
recorded adventures, were undertaken and accomplished.
Christmas was close at hand, in all his bluff and hearty honesty; it
was the season of hospitality, merriment, and open-heartedness; the
old year was preparing, like an ancient philosopher, to call his
friends around him, and amidst the sound of feasting and revelry to
pass gently and calmly away. Gay and merry was the time, and gay
and merry were at least four of the numerous hearts that were
gladdened by its coming.

And numerous indeed are the hearts to which Christmas brings a
brief season of happiness and enjoyment. How many families,
whose members have been dispersed and scattered far and wide, in
the restless struggles of life, are then reunited, and meet once again
in that happy state of companionship and mutual good-will, which
is a source of such pure and unalloyed delight, and one so
incompatible with the cares and sorrows of the world, that the
religious belief of the most civilised nations, and the rude traditions
of the roughest savages, alike number it among the first joys of a
future condition of existence, provided for the blest and happy!
How many old recollections, and how many dormant sympathies,
does Christmas time awaken!

We write these words now, many miles distant from the spot at
which, year after year, we met on that day, a merry and joyous
circle. Many of the hearts that throbbed so gaily then, have ceased
to beat; many of the looks that shone so brightly then, have ceased
to glow; the hands we grasped, have grown cold; the eyes we
sought, have hid their lustre in the grave; and yet the old house, the
room, the merry voices and smiling faces, the jest, the laugh, the
most minute and trivial circumstances connected with those happy
meetings, crowd upon our mind at each recurrence of the season,
as if the last assemblage had been but yesterday! Happy, happy

Christmas, that can win us back to the delusions of our childish
days; that can recal to the old man the pleasures of his youth; that
can transport the sailor and the traveller, thousands of miles away,
back to his own fire-side and his quiet home!

But we are so taken up and occupied with the good qualities of
this saint Christmas, that we are keeping Mr Pickwick and his
friends waiting in the cold on the outside of the Muggleton coach,
which they have just attained, well wrapped up in great-coats,
shawls, and comforters. The portmanteaus and carpet-bags have
been stowed away, and Mr Weller and the guard are endeavouring
to insinuate into the fore-boot a huge cod-fish several sizes too large
for it – which is snugly packed up, in a long brown basket, with a
layer of straw over the top, and which has been left to the last, in
order that he may repose in safety on the half-dozen barrels of real
native oysters, all the property of Mr Pickwick, which have been
arranged in regular order at the bottom of the receptacle. The
interest displayed in Mr Pickwick's countenance is most intense, as
Mr Weller and the guard try to squeeze the cod-fish into the boot,
first head first, and then tail first, and then top upward, and then
bottom upward, and then side-ways, and then long-ways, all of
which artifices the implacable cod-fish sturdily resists, until the
guard accidentally hits him in the very middle of the basket,
whereupon he suddenly disappears into the boot, and with him, the
head and shoulders of the guard himself, who, not calculating upon
so sudden a cessation of the passive resistance of the cod-fish,
experiences a very unexpected shock, to the unsmotherable delight
of all the porters and bystanders. Upon this, Mr Pickwick smiles
with great good-humour, and drawing a shilling from his waistcoat
pocket, begs the guard, as he picks himself out of the boot, to drink
his health in a glass of hot brandy and water; at which the guard
smiles too, and Messrs. Snodgrass, Winkle, and Tupman, all smile
in company. The guard and Mr Weller disappear for five minutes:
most probably to get the hot brandy and water, for they smell very
strongly of it, when they return, the coachman mounts to the box,
Mr Weller jumps up behind, the Pickwickians pull their coats round
their legs and their shawls over their noses, the helpers pull the
horse-cloths off, the coachman shouts out a cheery 'All right,' and
away they go.

They have rumbled through the streets, and jolted over the
stones, and at length reach the wide and open country. The wheels
skim over the hard and frosty ground: and the horses, bursting into
a canter at a smart crack of the whip, step along the road as if the

load behind them: coach, passengers, cod-fish, oyster barrels, and all: were but a feather at their heels. They have descended a gentle slope, and enter upon a level, as compact and dry as a solid block of marble, two miles long. Another crack of the whip, and on they speed, at a smart gallop: the horses tossing their heads and rattling the harness, as if in exhilaration at the rapidity of the motion: while the coachman, holding whip and reins in one hand, takes off his hat with the other, and resting it on his knees, pulls out his handkerchief, and wipes his forehead: partly because he has a habit of doing it, and partly because it's as well to show the passengers how cool he is, and what an easy thing it is to drive four-in-hand, when you have had as much practice as he has. Having done this very leisurely (otherwise the effect would be materially impaired), he replaces his handkerchief, pulls on his hat, adjusts his gloves, squares his elbows, cracks the whip again, and on they speed, more merrily than before.

A few small houses, scattered on either side of the road, betoken the entrance to some town or village. The lively notes of the guard's key-bugle[1] vibrate in the clear cold air, and wake up the old gentleman inside, who, carefully letting down the window-sash half-way, and standing sentry over the air, takes a short peep out, and then carefully pulling it up again, informs the other inside that they're going to change directly; on which the other inside wakes himself up, and determines to postpone his next nap until after the stoppage. Again the bugle sounds lustily forth, and rouses the cottager's wife and children, who peep out at the house-door, and watch the coach till it turns the corner, when they once more crouch round the blazing fire, and throw on another log of wood against father comes home; while father himself, a full mile off, has just exchanged a friendly nod with the coachman, and turned round to take a good long stare at the vehicle as it whirls away.

And now the bugle plays a lively air as the coach rattles through the ill-paved streets of a country-town; and the coachman, undoing the buckle which keeps his ribands together, prepares to throw them off the moment he stops. Mr Pickwick emerges from his coat collar, and looks about him with great curiosity; perceiving which, the coachman informs Mr Pickwick of the name of the town, and tells him it was market-day yesterday, both of which pieces of information Mr Pickwick retails to his fellow-passengers; whereupon they emerge from their coat collars too, and look about them also. Mr Winkle, who sits at the extreme edge, with one leg dangling in the air, is nearly precipitated into the street, as the coach twists round the sharp corner by the cheesemonger's shop, and turns into the market-place; and before Mr Snodgrass, who sits next to him, has recovered from his alarm, they pull up at the inn yard, where the fresh horses, with cloths on, are already waiting. The coachman throws down the reins and gets down himself, and the other outside passengers drop down also: except those who have no great confidence in their ability to get up again: and they remain where they are, and stamp their feet against the coach to warm them – looking, with longing eyes and red noses, at the bright fire in the inn bar, and the sprigs of holly with red berries which ornament the window.

But the guard has delivered at the corn-dealer's shop the brown paper packet he took out of the little pouch which hangs over his shoulder by a leathern strap; and has seen the horses carefully put to; and has thrown on the pavement the saddle which was brought from London on the coach-roof; and has assisted in the conference between the coachman and the hostler about the grey mare that hurt her off-fore-leg last Tuesday; and he and Mr Weller are all right behind, and the coachman is all right in front, and the old gentleman inside, who has kept the window down full two inches all this time, has pulled it up again, and the cloths are off, and they are all ready for starting, except the 'two stout gentlemen,' whom the coachman inquires after with some impatience. Hereupon the coachman, and the guard, and Sam Weller, and Mr Winkle, and Mr Snodgrass, and all the hostlers, and every one of the idlers, who are more in number than all the others put together, shout for the missing gentlemen as loud as they can bawl. A distant response is heard from the yard, and Mr Pickwick and Mr Tupman come running down it, quite out of breath, for they have been having a glass of ale a-piece, and Mr Pickwick's fingers are so cold that he has been full five minutes before he could find the sixpence to pay for it. The coachman shouts an admonitory 'Now then, gen'lm'n!' the guard re-echoes it; the old gentleman inside thinks it a very extraordinary thing that people *will* get down when they know there isn't time for it; Mr Pickwick struggles up on one side, Mr Tupman on the other; Mr Winkle cries 'All right;' and off they start. Shawls are pulled up, coat collars are re-adjusted, the pavement ceases, the houses disappear, and they are once again dashing along the open road, with the fresh clear air blowing in their faces, and gladdening their very hearts within them.

Such was the progress of Mr Pickwick and his friends by the Muggleton Telegraph, on their way to Dingley Dell; and at three o'clock that afternoon they all stood, high and dry, safe and sound, hale and hearty, upon the steps of the Blue Lion, having taken on the road quite enough of ale and brandy to enable them to bid defiance to the frost that was binding up the earth in its iron fetters, and weaving its beautiful net-work upon the trees and hedges. Mr Pickwick was busily engaged in counting the barrels of oysters and superintending the disinterment of the cod-fish, when he felt himself gently pulled by the skirts of the coat. Looking round, he discovered that the individual who resorted to this mode of catching his attention was no other than Mr Wardle's favourite page, better known to the readers of this unvarnished history, by the distinguishing appellation of the fat boy.

'Aha!' said Mr Pickwick.

'Aha!' said the fat boy.

As he said it, he glanced from the cod-fish to the oyster-barrels, and chuckled joyously. He was fatter than ever.

'Well, you look rosy enough, my young friend,' said Mr Pickwick.

'I've been asleep, right in front of the tap-room fire,' replied the fat boy, who had heated himself to the colour of a new chimney-pot, in the course of an hour's nap. 'Master sent me over with the shay-cart, to carry your luggage up to the house. He'd ha' sent some saddle-horses, but he thought you'd rather walk, being a cold day.'

'Yes, yes,' said Mr Pickwick, hastily, for he remembered how they had travelled over nearly the same ground on a previous occasion. 'Yes, we would rather walk. Here, Sam!'

'Sir,' said Mr Weller.

'Help Mr Wardle's servant to put the packages into the cart, and then ride on with him. We will walk forward at once.'

Having given this direction, and settled with the coachman, Mr Pickwick and his three friends struck into the footpath across the fields, and walked briskly away, leaving Mr Weller and the fat boy confronted together for the first time. Sam looked at the fat boy with great astonishment, but without saying a word; and began to stow the luggage rapidly away in the cart, while the fat boy stood quietly by, and seemed to think it a very interesting sort of thing to see Mr Weller working by himself.

'There,' said Sam, throwing in the last carpet-bag. 'There they are!'

'Yes,' said the fat boy, in a very satisfied tone, 'there they are.'

'Vell, young twenty stun,' said Sam, 'you're a nice specimen of a prize boy, you are!'

'Thank'ee,' said the fat boy.

'You ain't got nothin' on your mind as makes you fret yourself, have you?' inquired Sam.

'Not as I knows on,' replied the fat boy.

'I should rayther ha' thought, to look at you, that you was a labourin' under an unrequited attachment to some young 'ooman,' said Sam.

The fat boy shook his head.

'Vell,' said Sam, 'I'm glad to hear it. Do you ever drink anythin'?'

'I likes eating, better,' replied the boy.

'Ah,' said Sam, 'I should ha' s'posed that; but what I mean is, should you like a drop of anythin' as 'd warm you? but I s'pose you never was cold, with all them elastic fixtures, was you?'

'Sometimes,' replied the boy; 'and I likes a drop of something, when it's good.'

'Oh, you do, do you?' said Sam, 'come this way, then!'

The Blue Lion tap was soon gained, and the fat boy swallowed a glass of liquor without so much as winking; a feat which considerably advanced him in Mr Weller's good opinion. Mr Weller having transacted a similar piece of business on his own account, they got into the cart.

'Can you drive?' said the fat boy.

'I should rayther think so,' replied Sam.

'There, then,' said the fat boy, putting the reins in his hand, and pointing up a lane, 'it's as straight as you can go; you can't miss it.'

With these words, the fat boy laid himself affectionately down by the side of the cod-fish: and placing an oyster-barrel under his head for a pillow, fell asleep instantaneously.

'Well,' said Sam, 'of all the cool boys ever I set my eyes on, this here young gen'l'm'n is the coolest. Come, wake up young dropsy!'²

But as young dropsy evinced no symptoms of returning animation, Sam Weller sat himself down in front of the cart, and starting the old horse with a jerk of the rein, jogged steadily on, towards Manor Farm.

Meanwhile, Mr Pickwick and his friends having walked their blood into active circulation, proceeded cheerfully on. The paths were hard; the grass was crisp and frosty; the air had a fine, dry, bracing coldness; and the rapid approach of the grey twilight (slate-coloured is a better term in frosty weather) made them look forward with pleasant anticipation to the comforts which awaited them at their hospitable entertainer's. It was the sort of afternoon that might induce a couple of elderly gentlemen, in a lonely field, to take off

their great-coats and play at leap-frog in pure lightness of heart and
gaiety; and we firmly believe that had Mr Tupman at that moment
proffered 'a back,' Mr Pickwick would have accepted his offer with
the utmost avidity.

However, Mr Tupman did not volunteer any such accommodation, and the friends walked on, conversing merrily. As they
turned into a lane they had to cross, the sound of many voices burst
upon their ears; and before they had even had time to form a guess
to whom they belonged, they walked into the very centre of the
party who were expecting their arrival – a fact which was first
notified to the Pickwickians, by the loud 'Hurrah,' which burst
from old Wardle's lips, when they appeared in sight.

First, there was Wardle himself, looking, if possible, more jolly
than ever; then there were Bella and her faithful Trundle; and,
lastly, there were Emily and some eight or ten young ladies, who
had all come down to the wedding, which was to take place next
day, and who were in as happy and important a state as young
ladies usually are, on such momentous occasions; and they were,
one and all, startling the fields and lanes, far and wide, with their
frolic and laughter.

The ceremony of introduction, under such circumstances, was
very soon performed, or we should rather say that the introduction
was soon over, without any ceremony at all. In two minutes
thereafter, Mr Pickwick was joking with the young ladies who
wouldn't come over the stile while he looked – or who, having
pretty feet and unexceptionable ankles, preferred standing on the
top-rail for five minutes or so, declaring that they were too
frightened to move – with as much ease and absence of reserve or
constraint, as if he had known them for life. It is worthy of remark,
too, that Mr Snodgrass offered Emily far more assistance than the
absolute terrors of the stile (although it was full three feet high, and
had only a couple of stepping-stones) would seem to require; while
one black-eyed young lady in a very nice little pair of boots with
fur round the top, was observed to scream very loudly, when Mr
Winkle offered to help her over.

All this was very snug and pleasant. And when the difficulties of
the stile were at last surmounted, and they once more entered on
the open field, old Wardle informed Mr Pickwick how they had all
been down in a body to inspect the furniture and fittings-up of the
house, which the young couple were to tenant, after the Christmas
holidays; at which communication Bella and Trundle both coloured
up, as red as the fat boy after the tap-room fire; and the young lady

with the black eyes and the fur round the boots, whispered something in Emily's ear, and then glanced archly at Mr Snodgrass: to which Emily responded that she was a foolish girl, but turned very red, notwithstanding; and Mr Snodgrass, who was as modest as all great geniuses usually are, felt the crimson rising to the crown of his head, and devoutly wished in the inmost recesses of his own heart that the young lady aforesaid, with her black eyes, and her archness, and her boots with the fur round the top, were all comfortably deposited in the adjacent county.

But if they were social and happy outside the house, what was the warmth and cordiality of their reception when they reached the farm! The very servants grinned with pleasure at sight of Mr Pickwick; and Emma bestowed a half-demure, half-impudent, and all pretty, look of recognition, on Mr Tupman, which was enough to make the statue of Bonaparte in the passage, unfold his arms, and clasp her within them.

The old lady was seated in customary state in the front parlour, but she was rather cross, and, by consequence, most particularly deaf. She never went out herself, and like a great many other old ladies of the same stamp, she was apt to consider it an act of domestic treason, if anybody else took the liberty of doing what she couldn't. So, bless her old soul, she sat as upright as she could, in her great chair, and looked as fierce as might be – and that was benevolent after all.

'Mother,' said Wardle, 'Mr Pickwick. You recollect him?'

'Never mind,' replied the old lady with great dignity. 'Don't trouble Mr Pickwick about an old creetur like me. Nobody cares about me now, and it's very nat'ral they shouldn't.' Here the old lady tossed her head, and smoothed down her lavender-coloured silk dress, with trembling hands.

'Come, come, ma'am,' said Mr Pickwick, 'I can't let you cut an old friend in this way. I have come down expressly to have a long talk, and another rubber with you; and we'll show these boys and girls how to dance a minuet, before they're eight-and-forty hours older.'

The old lady was rapidly giving way, but she did not like to do it all at once; so she only said, 'Ah! I can't hear him!'

'Nonsense, mother,' said Wardle. 'Come, come, don't be cross, there's a good soul. Recollect Bella; come, you must keep her spirits up, poor girl.'

The good old lady heard this, for her lip quivered as her son said it. But age has its little infirmities of temper, and she was not quite brought round yet. So, she smoothed down the lavender-coloured dress again, and turning to Mr Pickwick said, 'Ah, Mr Pickwick, young people was very different, when I was a girl.'

'No doubt of that, ma'am,' said Mr Pickwick, 'and that's the reason why I would make much of the few that have any traces of the old stock,' – and saying this, Mr Pickwick gently pulled Bella towards him, and bestowing a kiss upon her forehead, bade her sit down on the little stool at her grandmother's feet. Whether the expression of her countenance, as it was raised towards the old lady's face, called up a thought of old times, or whether the old lady was touched by Mr Pickwick's affectionate good nature, or whatever was the cause, she was fairly melted; so she threw herself on her grand-daughter's neck, and all the little ill-humour evaporated in a gush of silent tears.

A happy party they were, that night. Sedate and solemn were the score of rubbers in which Mr Pickwick and the old lady played together; uproarious was the mirth of the round table. Long after the ladies had retired, did the hot elder wine, well qualified with brandy and spice, go round, and round, and round again; and sound was the sleep and pleasant were the dreams that followed. It is a remarkable fact that those of Mr Snodgrass bore constant reference to Emily Wardle; and that the principal figure in Mr Winkle's visions was a young lady with black eyes, an arch smile, and a pair of remarkably nice boots with fur round the tops.

Mr Pickwick was awakened, early in the morning, by a hum of voices and a pattering of feet, sufficient to rouse even the fat boy from his heavy slumbers. He sat up in bed and listened. The female servants and female visitors were running constantly to and fro; and there were such multitudinous demands for hot water, such repeated outcries for needles and thread, and so many half-suppressed entreaties of 'Oh, do come and tie me, there's a dear!' that Mr Pickwick in his innocence began to imagine that something dreadful must have occurred: when he grew more awake, and remembered the wedding. The occasion being an important one he dressed himself with peculiar care, and descended to the breakfast room.

There were all the female servants in a bran new uniform of pink muslin gowns with white bows in their caps, running about the house in a state of excitement and agitation which it would be impossible to describe. The old lady was dressed out in a brocaded gown which had not seen the light for twenty years, saving and excepting such truant rays as had stolen through the chinks in the box in which it had been lain by, during the whole time. Mr Trundle was in high feather and spirits, but a little nervous withal. The hearty old landlord was trying to look very cheerful and unconcerned, but failing signally in the attempt. All the girls were in tears and white muslin, except a select two or three who were being honoured with a private view of the bride and bridesmaids, up stairs. All the Pickwickians were in most blooming array; and there was a terrific roaring on the grass in front of the house, occasioned by all the men, boys, and hobbledehoys[3] attached to the farm, each of whom had got a white bow in his button-hole, and all of whom were cheering with might and main: being incited thereunto, and stimulated therein, by the precept and example of Mr Samuel Weller, who had managed to become mighty popular already, and was as much at home as if he had been born on the land.

A wedding is a licensed subject to joke upon, but there really is no great joke in the matter after all; – we speak merely of the ceremony, and beg it to be distinctly understood that we indulge in no hidden sarcasm upon a married life. Mixed up with the pleasure and joy of the occasion, are the many regrets at quitting home, the tears of parting between parent and child, the consciousness of leaving the dearest and kindest friends of the happiest portion of human life, to encounter its cares and troubles with others still untried and little known: natural feelings which we would not render this chapter mournful by describing, and which we should be still more unwilling to be supposed to ridicule.

Let us briefly say, then, that the ceremony was performed by the old clergyman, in the parish church of Dingley Dell, and that Mr Pickwick's name is attached to the register, still preserved in the vestry thereof; that the young lady with the black eyes signed her name in a very unsteady and tremulous manner; that Emily's signature, as the other bridesmaid, is nearly illegible; that it all went off in very admirable style; that the young ladies generally thought it far less shocking than they had expected; and that although the owner of the black eyes and the arch smile informed Mr Winkle that she was sure she could never submit to anything so dreadful, we have the very best reasons for thinking she was mistaken. To all this, we may add, that Mr Pickwick was the first who saluted the bride, and that in so doing, he threw over her neck a rich gold watch and chain, which no mortal eyes but the jeweller's had ever beheld before. Then, the old church bell rang as gaily as it could, and they all returned to breakfast.

'Vere does the mince pies go, young opium eater?' said Mr Weller to the fat boy, as he assisted in laying out such articles of consumption as had not been duly arranged on the previous night.

The fat boy pointed to the destination of the pies.

'Wery good,' said Sam, 'stick a bit o' Christmas in 'em. T'other dish opposite. There; now we look compact and comfortable, as the father said ven he cut his little boy's head off, to cure him o' squintin'.'

As Mr Weller made the comparison, he fell back a step or two, to give full effect to it, and surveyed the preparation with the utmost satisfaction.

'Wardle,' said Mr Pickwick, almost as soon as they were all seated, 'a glass of wine, in honour of this happy occasion!'

'I shall be delighted, my boy,' said Wardle. 'Joe – damn that boy, he's gone to sleep.'

'No, I ain't, sir,' replied the fat boy, starting up from a remote corner, where, like the patron saint of fat boys – the immortal Horner[4] – he had been devouring a Christmas pie: though not with the coolness and deliberation which characterised that young gentleman's proceedings.

'Fill Mr Pickwick's glass.'

'Yes, sir.'

The fat boy filled Mr Pickwick's glass, and then retired behind his master's chair, from whence he watched the play of the knives and forks, and the progress of the choice morsels from the dishes to the mouths of the company, with a kind of dark and gloomy joy that was most impressive.

'God bless you, old fellow!' said Mr Pickwick.

'Same to you, my boy,' replied Wardle; and they pledged each other, heartily.

'Mrs Wardle,' said Mr Pickwick, 'we old folks must have a glass of wine together, in honour of this joyful event.'

The old lady was in a state of great grandeur just then, for she was sitting at the top of the table in the brocaded gown, with her newly-married granddaughter on one side and Mr Pickwick on the other, to do the carving. Mr Pickwick had not spoken in a very loud tone, but she understood him at once, and drank off a full glass of wine to his long life and happiness; after which the worthy old soul launched forth into a minute and particular account of her own wedding, with a dissertation on the fashion of wearing high-heeled shoes, and some particulars concerning the life and adventures of the beautiful Lady Tollimglower, deceased: at all of which the old lady herself laughed very heartily indeed, and so did the young ladies too, for they were wondering among themselves what on earth grandma was talking about. When they laughed, the old lady laughed ten times more heartily, and said that these always had been considered capital stories: which caused them all to laugh again, and put the old lady into the very best of humours. Then, the cake was cut, and passed through the ring;⁵ the young ladies saved pieces to put under their pillows to dream of their future husbands on; and a great deal of blushing and merriment was thereby occasioned.

'Mr Miller,' said Mr Pickwick to his old acquaintance the hard-headed gentleman, 'a glass of wine?'

'With great satisfaction, Mr Pickwick,' replied the hard-headed gentleman, solemnly.

'You'll take me in?' said the benevolent old clergyman.

'And me,' interposed his wife.

'And me, and me,' said a couple of poor relations at the bottom of the table, who had eaten and drank very heartily, and laughed at everything.

Mr Pickwick expressed his heartfelt delight at every additional suggestion; and his eyes beamed with hilarity and cheerfulness.

'Ladies and gentlemen,' said Mr Pickwick, suddenly rising.

'Hear, hear! Hear, hear! Hear, hear!' cried Mr Weller, in the excitement of his feelings.

'Call in all the servants,' cried old Wardle, interposing to prevent the public rebuke which Mr Weller would otherwise most indubitably have received from his master. 'Give them a glass of wine each, to drink the toast in. Now, Pickwick.'

Amidst the silence of the company, the whispering of the women servants, and the awkward embarrassment of the men, Mr Pickwick proceeded.

'Ladies and gentlemen – no, I won't say ladies and gentlemen, I'll call you my friends, my dear friends, if the ladies will allow me to take so great a liberty' —

Here Mr Pickwick was interrupted by immense applause from the ladies, echoed by the gentlemen, during which the owner of the eyes was distinctly heard to state that she could kiss that dear Mr Pickwick. Whereupon Mr Winkle gallantly inquired if it couldn't be done by deputy: to which the young lady with the black eyes replied, 'Go away' – and accompanied the request with a look which said as plainly as a look could do—'if you can.'

'My dear friends,' resumed Mr Pickwick, 'I am going to propose the health of the bride and bridegroom – God bless 'em (cheers and tears). My young friend, Trundle, I believe to be a very excellent and manly fellow; and his wife I know to be a very amiable and lovely girl, well qualified to transfer to another sphere of action the happiness which for twenty years she has diffused around her, in her father's house. (Here, the fat boy burst forth into stentorian blubberings, and was led forth by the coat collar, by Mr Weller). I wish,' added Mr Pickwick, 'I wish I was young enough to be her sister's husband (cheers), but, failing that, I am happy to be old enough to be her father; for, being so, I shall not be suspected of any latent designs when I say, that I admire, esteem, and love them both (cheers and sobs). The bride's father, our good friend there, is a noble person, and I am proud to know him (great uproar). He is a kind, excellent, independent-spirited, fine-hearted, hospitable, liberal man (enthusiastic shouts from the poor relations, at all the adjectives; and especially at the two last). That his daughter may enjoy all the happiness, even he can desire; and that he may derive from the contemplation of her felicity all the gratification of heart and peace of mind which he so well deserves, is, I am persuaded, our united wish. So, let us drink their healths, and wish them prolonged life, and every blessing!'

Mr Pickwick concluded amidst a whirlwind of applause; and once more were the lungs of the supernumeraries, under Mr Weller's command, brought into active and efficient operation. Mr Wardle proposed Mr Pickwick; Mr Pickwick proposed the old lady. Mr Snodgrass proposed Mr Wardle; Mr Wardle proposed Mr Snodgrass. One of the poor relations proposed Mr Tupman, and the other poor relation proposed Mr Winkle; all was happiness and festivity, until the mysterious disappearance of both the poor relations beneath the table, warned the party that it was time to adjourn.

At dinner they met again, after a five-and-twenty mile walk, undertaken by the males at Wardle's recommendation, to get rid of the effects of the wine at breakfast. The poor relations had kept in bed all day, with the view of attaining the same happy consummation, but, as they had been unsuccessful, they stopped there. Mr Weller kept the domestics in a state of perpetual hilarity; and the fat boy divided his time into small alternate allotments of eating and sleeping.

The dinner was as hearty an affair as the breakfast, and was quite as noisy, without the tears. Then came the dessert and some more toasts. Then came the tea and coffee; and then, the ball.

The best sitting room at Manor Farm was a good, long, dark-panelled room with a high chimney-piece, and a capacious chimney, up which you could have driven one of the new patent cabs, wheels and all. At the upper end of the room, seated in a shady bower of holly and evergreens, were the two best fiddlers, and the only harp, in all Muggleton. In all sorts of recesses, and on all kinds of brackets, stood massive old silver candlesticks with four branches each. The carpet was up, the candles burnt bright, the fire blazed and crackled on the hearth, and merry voices and light-hearted laughter rang through the room. If any of the old English yeomen had turned into fairies when they died, it was just the place in which they would have held their revels.

If anything could have added to the interest of this agreeable scene, it would have been the remarkable fact of Mr Pickwick's appearing without his gaiters, for the first time within the memory of his oldest friends.

'You mean to dance?' said Wardle.

'Of course I do,' replied Mr Pickwick. 'Don't you see I am dressed for the purpose?' Mr Pickwick called attention to his speckled silk stockings, and smartly tied pumps.

'*You* in silk stockings!' exclaimed Mr Tupman jocosely.

'And why not, sir – why not?' said Mr Pickwick, turning warmly upon him.

'Oh, of course there is no reason why you shouldn't wear them,' responded Mr Tupman.

'I imagine not sir, I imagine not,' said Mr Pickwick in a very peremptory tone.

Mr Tupman had contemplated a laugh, but he found it was a serious matter; so he looked grave, and said they were a pretty pattern.

'I hope they are,' said Mr Pickwick fixing his eyes upon his friend. 'You see nothing extraordinary in the stockings, *as* stockings, I trust sir?'

'Certainly not. Oh certainly not,' replied Mr Tupman. He walked away; and Mr Pickwick's countenance resumed its customary benign expression.

'We are all ready, I believe,' said Mr Pickwick, who was stationed with the old lady at the top of the dance, and had already made four false starts, in his excessive anxiety to commence.

'Then begin at once,' said Wardle. 'Now!'

Up struck the two fiddles and the one harp, and off went Mr

Pickwick into hands across, when there was a general clapping of hands, and a cry of 'Stop, stop!'

'What's the matter!' said Mr Pickwick, who was only brought to, by the fiddles and harp desisting, and could have been stopped by no other earthly power, if the house had been on fire.

'Where's Arabella Allen?' cried a dozen voices.

'And Winkle?' added Mr Tupman.

'Here we are!' exclaimed that gentleman, emerging with his pretty companion from the corner; as he did so, it would have been hard to tell which was the redder in the face, he or the young lady with the black eyes.

'What an extraordinary thing it is, Winkle,' said Mr Pickwick, rather pettishly, 'that you couldn't have taken your place before.'

'Not at all extraordinary,' said Mr Winkle.

'Well,' said Mr Pickwick, with a very expressive smile, as his eyes rested on Arabella, 'well, I don't know that it *was* extraordinary, either, after all.'

However, there was no time to think more about the matter, for the fiddles and harp began in real earnest. Away went Mr Pickwick – hands across – down the middle to the very end of the room, and half-way up the chimney, back again to the door – poussette[6] everywhere – loud stamp on the ground – ready for the next couple – off again – all the figure over once more – another stamp to beat out the time – next couple, and the next, and the next again – never was such going! At last, after they had reached the bottom of the dance, and full fourteen couple after the old lady had retired in an exhausted state, and the clergyman's wife had been substituted in her stead, did that gentleman, when there was no demand whatever on his exertions, keep perpetually dancing in his place, to keep time to the music: smiling on his partner all the while with a blandness of demeanour which baffles all description.

Long before Mr Pickwick was weary of dancing, the newly-married couple had retired from the scene. There was a glorious supper down-stairs, notwithstanding, and a good long sitting after it; and when Mr Pickwick awoke, late the next morning, he had a confused recollection of having, severally and confidentially, invited somewhere about five-and-forty people to dine with him at the George and Vulture, the very first time they came to London; which Mr Pickwick rightly considered a pretty certain indication of his having taken something besides exercise, on the previous night.

'And so your family has games in the kitchen to-night, my dear, has they?' inquired Sam of Emma.

'Yes, Mr Weller,' replied Emma; 'we always have on Christmas eve. Master wouldn't neglect to keep it up on any account.'

'Your master's a wery pretty notion of keepin' anythin' up, my dear,' said Mr Weller; 'I never see such a sensible sort of man as he is, or such a reg'lar gen'l'm'n.'

'Oh, that he is!' said the fat boy, joining in the conversation; 'don't he breed nice pork!' The fat youth gave a semi-cannibalic leer at Mr Weller, as he thought of the roast legs and gravy.

'Oh, you've woke up, at last, have you?' said Sam.

The fat boy nodded.

'I'll tell you what it is, young boa constructer,' said Mr Weller, impressively; 'if you don't sleep a little less, and exercise a little more, wen you comes to be a man you'll lay yourself open to the same sort of personal inconwenience as was inflicted on the old gen'l'm'n as wore the pigtail.'

'What did they do to him?' inquired the fat boy, in a faltering voice.

'I'm a-goin' to tell you,' replied Mr Weller; 'he was one o' the largest patterns as was ever turned out – reg'lar fat man, as hadn't caught a glimpse of his own shoes for five-and-forty-year.'

'Lor!' exclaimed Emma.

'No, that he hadn't, my dear,' said Mr Weller; 'and if you'd put an exact model of his own legs on the dinin' table afore him, he wouldn't ha' known 'em. Well, he always walks to his office with a wery handsome gold watch-chain hanging out, about a foot and a quarter; and a gold watch in his fob pocket as was worth – I'm afraid to say how much, but as much as a watch can be – a large, heavy, round manafacter, as stout for a watch, as he was for a man, and with a big face in proportion. "You'd better not carry that 'ere watch," says the old gen'l'm'n's friends, "you'll be robbed on it," says they. "Shall I?" says he. "Yes, you will," says they. "Vell," says he, "I should like to see the thief as could get this here watch out, for I'm blest if *I* ever can, it's such a tight fit," says he; "and venever I wants to know what's o'clock, I'm obliged to stare into the bakers' shops," he says. Well, then he laughs as hearty as if he was a goin' to pieces, and out he walks agin with his powdered head and pigtail, and rolls down the Strand vith the chain hangin' out furder than ever, and the great round watch almost bustin' through his grey kersey smalls. There warn't a pickpocket in all London as didn't take a pull at that chain, but the chain 'ud never break, and the watch 'ud never come out, so they soon got tired o' dragging such a heavy old gen'l'm'n along the pavement, and he'd go home and laugh till the pigtail wibrated like the penderlum of a Dutch clock.[7] At last, one day the old gen'l'm'n was a rollin' along, and he sees a pickpocket as he know'd by sight, a-comin' up, arm in arm vith a little boy vith a wery large head. "Here's a game," says the old gen'l'm'n to himself, "they're a-goin' to have another try, but it won't do!" So he begins a-chucklin' wery hearty, wen, all of a sudden, the little boy leaves hold of the pickpocket's arm, and rushes headforemost straight into the old gen'l'm'n's stomach, and for a moment doubles him right up vith the pain. "Murder!" says the old gen'l'm'n. "All right, sir," says the pickpocket, a wisperin' in his ear. And wen he come straight agin, the watch and chain was gone, and what's worse than that, the old gen'l'm'n's digestion was all wrong ever artervards, to the wery last day of his life; so just you look about you, young feller, and take care you don't get too fat.'

As Mr Weller concluded this moral tale, with which the fat boy appeared much affected, they all three repaired to the large kitchen, in which the family were by this time assembled, according to annual custom on Christmas eve, observed by old Wardle's forefathers from time immemorial.

From the centre of the ceiling of this kitchen, old Wardle had just suspended, with his own hands, a huge branch of mistletoe, and this same branch of mistletoe instantaneously gave rise to a scene of general and most delightful struggling and confusion; in the midst of which, Mr Pickwick, with a gallantry that would have done honour to a descendant of Lady Tollimglower herself, took the old lady by the hand, led her beneath the mystic branch; and saluted her in all courtesy and decorum. The old lady submitted to this piece of practical politeness with all the dignity which befitted so important and serious a solemnity, but the younger ladies, not being so thoroughly imbued with a superstitious veneration for the custom: or imagining that the value of a salute is very much enhanced if it cost a little trouble to obtain it: screamed and struggled, and ran into corners, and threatened and remonstrated, and did everything but leave the room, until some of the less adventurous gentlemen were on the point of desisting, when they all at once found it useless to resist any longer, and submitted to be kissed with a good grace. Mr Winkle kissed the young lady with the black eyes, and Mr Snodgrass kissed Emily, and Mr Weller, not being particular about the form of being under the mistletoe, kissed Emma and the other female servants, just as he caught them. As to the poor relations, they kissed everybody, not even excepting the

Christmas Eve at Mr Wardle's

plainer portions of the young-lady visitors, who, in their excessive confusion, ran right under the mistletoe, as soon as it was hung up, without knowing it! Wardle stood with his back to the fire, surveying the whole scene, with the utmost satisfaction; and the fat boy took the opportunity of appropriating to his own use, and summarily devouring, a particularly fine mince-pie, that had been carefully put by, for somebody else.

Now, the screaming had subsided, and faces were in a glow, and curls in a tangle, and Mr Pickwick, after kissing the old lady as before mentioned, was standing under the mistletoe, looking with a very pleased countenance on all that was passing around him, when the young lady with the black eyes, after a little whispering with the other young ladies, made a sudden dart forward, and, putting her arm round Mr Pickwick's neck, saluted him affectionately on the left cheek; and before Mr Pickwick distinctly knew what was the matter, he was surrounded by the whole body, and kissed by every one of them.

It was a pleasant thing to see Mr Pickwick in the centre of the group, now pulled this way, and then that, and first kissed on the chin, and then on the nose, and then on the spectacles: and to hear the peals of laughter which were raised on every side; but it was a still more pleasant thing to see Mr Pickwick, blinded shortly afterwards with a silk handkerchief, falling up against the wall, and scrambling into corners, and going through all the mysteries of blind-man's buff, with the utmost relish for the game, until at last he caught one of the poor relations, and then had to evade the blind-man himself, which he did with a nimbleness and agility that elicited the admiration and applause of all beholders. The poor relations caught the people who they thought would like it, and, when the game flagged, got caught themselves. When they were all tired of blind-man's buff, there was a great game at snap-dragon,[8] and when fingers enough were burned with that, and all the raisins were gone, they sat down by the huge fire of blazing logs to a substantial supper, and a mighty bowl of wassail,[9] something smaller than an ordinary wash-house copper, in which the hot apples were hissing and bubbling with a rich look, and a jolly sound, that were perfectly irresistible.

'This,' said Mr Pickwick, looking round him, 'this is, indeed, comfort.'

'Our invariable custom,' replied Mr Wardle. 'Everybody sits down with us on Christmas eve, as you see them now – servants and all; and here we wait, until the clock strikes twelve, to usher

Christmas in, and beguile the time with forfeits and old stories. Trundle, my boy, rake up the fire.'

Up flew the bright sparks in myriads as the logs were stirred. The deep red blaze sent forth a rich glow, that penetrated into the furthest corner of the room, and cast its cheerful tint on every face.

'Come,' said Wardle, 'a song – a Christmas song! I'll give you one, in default of a better.'

'Bravo!' said Mr Pickwick.

'Fill up,' cried Wardle. 'It will be two hours, good, before you see the bottom of the bowl through the deep rich colour of the wassail; fill up all round, and now for the song.'

Thus saying, the merry old gentleman, in a good, round, sturdy voice, commenced without more ado:

A CHRISTMAS CAROL

I care not for Spring; on his fickle wing
Let the blossoms and buds be borne:
He woos them amain with his treacherous rain,
And he scatters them ere the morn.
An inconstant elf, he knows not himself,
Nor his own changing mind an hour,
He'll smile in your face, and, with wry grimace,
He'll wither your youngest flower.

Let the Summer sun to his bright home run,
He shall never be sought by me;
When he's dimmed by a cloud I can laugh aloud,
And care not how sulky he be!
For his darling child is the madness wild
That sports in fierce fever's train;
And when love is too strong, it don't last long,
As many have found to their pain.

A mild harvest night, by the tranquil light
Of the modest and gentle moon,
Has a far sweeter sheen, for me, I ween,
Than the broad and unblushing noon.
But every leaf awakens my grief,
As it lieth beneath the tree;
So let Autumn air be never so fair,
It by no means agrees with me.

But my song I troll out, for CHRISTMAS stout,
The hearty, the true, and the bold;

A bumper I drain, and with might and main
Give three cheers for this Christmas old!
We'll usher him in with a merry din
That shall gladden his joyous heart,
And we'll keep him up, while there's bite or sup,
And in fellowship good, we'll part.

In his fine honest pride, he scorns to hide,
One jot of his hard-weather scars;
They're no disgrace, for there's much the same trace
On the cheeks of our bravest tars.
Then again I sing 'till the roof doth ring,
And it echoes from wall to wall –
To the stout old wight, fair welcome to-night,
As the King of the Seasons all!

This song was tumultuously applauded – for friends and dependents make a capital audience – and the poor relations, especially, were in perfect ecstasies of rapture. Again was the fire replenished, and again went the wassail round.

'How it snows!' said one of the men, in a low tone.

'Snows, does it?' said Wardle.

'Rough, cold night, sir,' replied the man; 'and there's a wind got up, that drifts it across the fields, in a thick white cloud.'

'What does Jem say?' inquired the old lady. 'There ain't anything the matter, is there?'

'No, no, mother,' replied Wardle; 'he says there's a snow-drift, and a wind that's piercing cold. I should know that, by the way it rumbles in the chimney.'

'Ah!' said the old lady, 'there was just such a wind, and just such a fall of snow, a good many years back, I recollect – just five years before your poor father died. It was a Christmas eve, too; and I remember that on that very night he told us the story about the goblins that carried away old Gabriel Grub.'

'The story about what?' said Mr Pickwick.

'Oh, nothing, nothing,' replied Wardle. 'About an old sexton, that the good people down here suppose to have been carried away by goblins.'

'Suppose!' ejaculated the old lady. 'Is there any body hardy enough to disbelieve it? Suppose! Haven't you heard ever since you were a child, that he *was* carried away by the goblins, and don't you know he was?'

'Very well, mother, he was, if you like,' said Wardle, laughing.

'He *was* carried away by goblins, Pickwick; and there's an end of the matter.'

'No, no,' said Mr Pickwick, 'not an end of it, I assure you; for I must hear how, and why, and all about it.'

Wardle smiled, as every head was bent forward to hear; and filling out the wassail with no stinted hand, nodded a health to Mr Pickwick, and began as follows:

But bless our editorial heart, what a long chapter we have been betrayed into! We had quite forgotten all such petty restrictions as chapters, we solemnly declare. So here goes, to give the goblin a fair start in a new one! A clear stage and no favour for the goblins, ladies and gentlemen, if you please.

CHAPTER 29

The Story of the Goblins who stole a Sexton

'In an old abbey town, down in this part of the country, a long, long while ago – so long, that the story must be a true one, because our great grandfathers implicitly believed it – there officiated as sexton and grave-digger in the churchyard, one Gabriel Grub. It by no means follows that because a man is a sexton, and constantly surrounded by the emblems of mortality, therefore he should be a morose and melancholy man; your undertakers are the merriest fellows in the world; and I once had the honour of being on intimate terms with a mute, who in private life, and off duty, was as comical and jocose a little fellow as ever chirped out a devil-may-care song, without a hitch in his memory, or drained off the contents of a good stiff glass without stopping for breath. But, notwithstanding these precedents to the contrary, Gabriel Grub was an ill-conditioned, cross-grained, surly fellow – a morose and lonely man, who consorted with nobody but himself, and an old wicker bottle which fitted into his large deep waistcoat pocket – and who eyed each merry face, as it passed him by, with such a deep scowl of malice and ill-humour, as it was difficult to meet, without feeling something the worse for.

'A little before twilight, one Christmas Eve, Gabriel shouldered his spade, lighted his lantern, and betook himself towards the old churchyard; for he had got a grave to finish by next morning, and, feeling very low, he thought it might raise his spirits, perhaps, if he went on with his work at once. As he went his way, up the ancient street, he saw the cheerful light of the blazing fires gleam through the old casements, and heard the loud laugh and the cheerful shouts of those who were assembled around them; he marked the bustling preparations for next day's cheer, and smelt the numerous savoury odours consequent thereupon, as they steamed up from the kitchen windows in clouds. All this was gall and wormwood[1] to the heart of Gabriel Grub; and when groups of children, bounded out of the houses, tripped across the road, and were met, before they could knock at the opposite door, by half a dozen curly-headed little rascals who crowded round them as they flocked up-stairs to spend the evening in their Christmas games, Gabriel smiled grimly, and clutched the handle of his spade with a firmer grasp, as he thought of measles, scarlet-fever, thrush, hooping-cough, and a good many other sources of consolation besides.

'In this happy frame of mind, Gabriel strode along: returning a short, sullen growl to the good-humoured greetings of such of his neighbours as now and then passed him: until he turned into the dark lane which led to the churchyard. Now, Gabriel had been looking forward to reaching the dark lane, because it was, generally speaking, a nice, gloomy, mournful place, into which the towns-people did not much care to go, except in broad day-light, and when the sun was shining; consequently, he was not a little indignant to hear a young urchin roaring out some jolly song about a merry Christmas, in this very sanctuary, which had been called Coffin Lane ever since the days of the old abbey, and the time of the shaven-headed monks. As Gabriel walked on, and the voice drew nearer, he found it proceeded from a small boy, who was hurrying along, to join one of the little parties in the old street, and who, partly to keep himself company, and partly to prepare himself for the occasion, was shouting out the song at the highest pitch of his lungs. So Gabriel waited until the boy came up, and then dodged him into a corner, and rapped him over the head with his lantern five or six times, to teach him to modulate his voice. And as the boy hurried away with his hand to his head, singing quite a different sort of tune, Gabriel Grub chuckled very heartily to himself, and entered the churchyard: locking the gate behind him.

'He took off his coat, put down his lantern, and getting into the unfinished grave, worked at it for an hour or so, with right good will. But the earth was hardened with the frost, and it was no very easy matter to break it up, and shovel it out; and although there was a moon, it was a very young one, and shed little light upon the grave, which was in the shadow of the church. At any other time, these obstacles would have made Gabriel Grub very moody and miserable, but he was so well pleased with having stopped the small boy's singing, that he took little heed of the scanty progress he had made, and looked down into the grave, when he had finished work for the night, with grim satisfaction: murmuring as he gathered up his things:

> Brave lodgings for one, brave lodgings for one,
> A few feet of cold earth, when life is done;
> A stone at the head, a stone at the feet,
> A rich, juicy meal for the worms to eat;
> Rank grass over head, and damp clay around,
> Brave lodgings for one, these, in holy ground!

'"Ho! ho!" laughed Gabriel Grub, as he sat himself down on a flat tombstone which was a favourite resting-place of his; and drew forth his wicker bottle. "A coffin at Christmas! A Christmas Box. Ho! ho! ho!"

'"Ho! ho! ho!" repeated a voice which sounded close behind him.

'Gabriel paused, in some alarm, in the act of raising the wicker bottle to his lips: and looked round. The bottom of the oldest grave about him, was not more still and quiet, than the churchyard in the pale moonlight. The cold hoar-frost glistened on the tombstones, and sparkled like rows of gems, among the stone carvings of the old church. The snow lay hard and crisp upon the ground; and spread over the thickly-strewn mounds of earth, so white and smooth a cover, that it seemed as if corpses lay there, hidden only by their winding sheets. Not the faintest rustle broke the profound tranquillity of the solemn scene. Sound itself appeared to be frozen up, all was so cold and still.

'"It was the echoes," said Gabriel Grub, raising the bottle to his lips again.

'"It was *not*," said a deep voice.

'Gabriel started up, and stood rooted to the spot with astonishment and terror; for his eyes rested on a form that made his blood run cold.

'Seated on an upright tombstone, close to him, was a strange unearthly figure, whom Gabriel felt at once, was no being of this world. His long fantastic legs which might have reached the ground, were cocked up, and crossed after a quaint, fantastic fashion; his sinewy arms were bare; and his hands rested on his knees. On his

The Goblin and the Sexton

short round body, he wore a close covering, ornamented with small slashes; a short cloak dangled at his back; the collar was cut into curious peaks, which served the goblin in lieu of ruff or neckerchief; and his shoes curled up at his toes into long points. On his head, he wore a broad-brimmed sugar-loaf hat, garnished with a single feather. The hat was covered with the white frost; and the goblin looked as if he had sat on the same tombstone very comfortably, for two or three hundred years. He was sitting perfectly still; his tongue was put out, as if in derision; and he was grinning at Gabriel Grub with such a grin as only a goblin could call up.

'"It was *not* the echoes," said the goblin.

'Gabriel Grub was paralysed, and could make no reply.

'"What do you do here on Christmas Eve?" said the goblin sternly.

'"I came to dig a grave, sir," stammered Gabriel Grub.

'"What man wanders among graves and churchyards on such a night as this?" cried the goblin.

'"Gabriel Grub! Gabriel Grub!" screamed a wild chorus of voices that seemed to fill the churchyard. Gabriel looked fearfully round – nothing was to be seen.

'"What have you got in that bottle?" said the goblin.

'"Hollands, sir," replied the sexton, trembling more than ever; for he had bought it of the smugglers, and he thought that perhaps his questioner might be in the excise department of the goblins.

'"Who drinks Hollands alone, and in a churchyard, on such a night as this?" said the goblin.

'"Gabriel Grub! Gabriel Grub!" exclaimed the wild voices again.

'The goblin leered maliciously at the terrified sexton, and then raising his voice, exclaimed:

'"And who, then, is our fair and lawful prize?"

'To this inquiry the invisible chorus replied, in a strain that sounded like the voices of many choristers singing to the mighty swell of the old church organ – a strain that seemed borne to the sexton's ears upon a wild wind, and to die away as it passed onward; but the burden of the reply was still the same, "Gabriel Grub! Gabriel Grub!"

'The goblin grinned a broader grin than before, as he said, "Well, Gabriel, what do you say to this?"

'The sexton gasped for breath.

'"What do you think of this, Gabriel?" said the goblin, kicking up his feet in the air on either side of the tombstone, and looking at the turned-up points with as much complacency as if he had been contemplating the most fashionable pair of Wellingtons in all Bond Street.

'"It's – it's – very curious, sir," replied the sexton, half dead with fright; "very curious, and very pretty, but I think I'll go back and finish my work, sir, if you please."

'"Work!" said the goblin, "what work?"

'"The grave, sir; making the grave," stammered the sexton.

'"Oh, the grave, eh?" said the goblin; "who makes graves at a time when all other men are merry, and takes a pleasure in it?"

'Again the mysterious voices replied, "Gabriel Grub! Gabriel Grub!"

'"I'm afraid my friends want you, Gabriel," said the goblin, thrusting his tongue further into his cheek than ever – and a most astonishing tongue it was – "I'm afraid my friends want you, Gabriel," said the goblin.

'"Under favour, sir," replied the horror-stricken sexton, "I don't think they can, sir; they don't know me, sir; I don't think the gentlemen have ever seen me, sir."

'"Oh yes they have," replied the goblin; "we know the man with the sulky face and grim scowl, that came down the street to-night, throwing his evil looks at the children, and grasping his burying spade the tighter. We know the man who struck the boy in the envious malice of his heart, because the boy could be merry, and he could not. We know him, we know him."

'Here, the goblin gave a loud shrill laugh, which the echoes returned twenty-fold: and throwing his legs up in the air, stood upon his head, or rather upon the very point of his sugar-loaf hat, on the narrow edge of the tomb-stone: whence he threw a somerset[2] with extraordinary agility, right to the sexton's feet, at which he planted himself in the attitude in which tailors generally sit upon the shopboard.

'"I – I – am afraid I must leave you, sir," said the sexton, making an effort to move.

'"Leave us!" said the goblin, "Gabriel Grub going to leave us. Ho! ho! ho!"

'As the goblin laughed, the sexton observed, for one instant, a brilliant illumination within the windows of the church, as if the whole building were lighted up; it disappeared, the organ pealed forth a lively air, and whole troops of goblins, the very counterpart of the first one, poured into the church-yard, and began playing at leap-frog with the tomb-stones: never stopping for an instant to take breath, but "overing" the highest among them, one after the other, with the utmost marvellous dexterity. The first goblin was a most astonishing leaper, and none of the others could come near him; even in the extremity of his terror the sexton could not help observing, that while his friends were content to leap over the common-sized gravestones, the first one took the family vaults, iron railings and all, with as much ease as if they had been so many street posts.

'At last the game reached to a most exciting pitch; the organ played quicker and quicker; and the goblins leaped faster and faster: coiling themselves up, rolling head over heels upon the ground, and bounding over the tombstones like foot-balls. The sexton's brain whirled round with the rapidity of the motion he beheld, and his legs reeled beneath him, as the spirits flew before his eyes: when the goblin king, suddenly darting towards him, laid his hand upon his collar, and sank with him through the earth.

'When Gabriel Grub had had time to fetch his breath, which the rapidity of his descent had for the moment taken away, he found himself in what appeared to be a large cavern, surrounded on all sides by crowds of goblins, ugly and grim; in the centre of the room, on an elevated seat, was stationed his friend of the churchyard; and close beside him stood Gabriel Grub himself, without power of motion.

'"Cold to-night," said the king of the goblins, "very cold. A glass of something warm, here!"

'At this command, half a dozen officious goblins, with a perpetual smile upon their faces, whom Gabriel Grub imagined to be courtiers, on that account, hastily disappeared, and presently returned with a goblet of liquid fire, which they presented to the king.

'"Ah!" cried the goblin, whose cheeks and throat were transparent, as he tossed down the flame, "This warms one, indeed! Bring a bumper of the same, for Mr Grub."

'It was in vain for the unfortunate sexton to protest that he was not in the habit of taking anything warm at night; one of the goblins held him while another poured the blazing liquid down his throat; the whole assembly screeched with laughter as he coughed and choked, and wiped away the tears which gushed plentifully from his eyes, after swallowing the burning draught.

'"And now," said the king, fantastically poking the taper corner of his sugar-loaf hat into the sexton's eye, and thereby occasioning him the most exquisite pain: "And now, show the man of misery and gloom, a few of the pictures from our own great storehouse!"

'As the goblin said this, a thick cloud which obscured the remoter end of the cavern, rolled gradually away, and disclosed, apparently at a great distance, a small and scantily furnished, but neat and clean apartment. A crowd of little children were gathered round a bright fire, clinging to their mother's gown, and gambolling around her chair. The mother occasionally rose, and drew aside the window-curtain, as if to look for some expected object; a frugal meal was ready spread upon the table; and an elbow chair was placed near the fire. A knock was heard at the door: the mother opened it, and the children crowded round her, and clapped their hands for joy, as their father entered. He was wet and weary, and shook the snow from his garments, as the children crowded round him, and seizing his cloak, hat, stick, and gloves, with busy zeal, ran with them from the room. Then, as he sat down to his meal before the fire, the children climbed about his knee, and the mother sat by his side, and all seemed happiness and comfort.

'But a change came upon the view, almost imperceptibly. The scene was altered to a small bed-room, where the fairest and youngest child lay dying; the roses had fled from his cheek, and the light from his eye; and even as the sexton looked upon him with an interest he had never felt or known before, he died. His young brothers and sisters crowded round his little bed, and seized his tiny hand, so cold and heavy; but they shrunk back from its touch, and looked with awe on his infant face; for calm and tranquil as it was, and sleeping in rest and peace as the beautiful child seemed to be, they saw that he was dead, and they knew that he was an Angel looking down upon, and blessing them, from a bright and happy Heaven.

'Again the light cloud passed across the picture, and again the subject changed. The father and mother were old and helpless now, and the number of those about them was diminished more than half; but content and cheerfulness sat on every face, and beamed in every eye, as they crowded round the fireside, and told and listened to old stories of earlier and bygone days. Slowly and peacefully, the father sank into the grave, and, soon after, the sharer of all his cares and troubles followed him to a place of rest. The few, who yet survived them, knelt by their tomb, and watered the green turf which covered it, with their tears; then rose, and turned away: sadly and mournfully, but not with bitter cries, or despairing lamentations, for they knew that they should one day meet again; and once more they mixed with the busy world, and their content and cheerfulness were restored. The cloud settled upon the picture, and concealed it from the sexton's view.

"'What do you think of *that*?" said the goblin, turning his large face towards Gabriel Grub.

'Gabriel murmured out something about its being very pretty, and looked somewhat ashamed, as the goblin bent his fiery eyes upon him.

"'*You* a miserable man!" said the goblin, in a tone of excessive contempt. "You!" He appeared disposed to add more, but indignation choked his utterance, so he lifted up one of his very pliable legs, and flourishing it above his head a little, to insure his aim, administered a good sound kick to Gabriel Grub; immediately after which, all the goblins in waiting, crowded round the wretched sexton, and kicked him without mercy: according to the established and invariable custom of courtiers upon earth, who kick whom royalty kicks, and hug whom royalty hugs.

'"Show him some more!" said the king of the goblins.

'At these words, the cloud was dispelled, and a rich and beautiful landscape was disclosed to view – there is just such another, to this day, within half a mile of the old abbey town. The sun shone from out the clear blue sky, the water sparkled beneath his rays, and the trees looked greener, and the flowers more gay, beneath his cheering influence. The water rippled on, with a pleasant sound; the trees rustled in the light wind that murmured among their leaves; the birds sang upon the boughs; and the lark carolled on high, her welcome to the morning. Yes, it was morning: the bright, balmy morning of summer; the minutest leaf, the smallest blade of grass, was instinct with life. The ant crept forth to her daily toil, the butterfly fluttered and basked in the warm rays of the sun; myriads of insects spread their transparent wings, and revelled in their brief but happy existence. Man walked forth, elated with the scene; and all was brightness and splendour.

'"*You* a miserable man!" said the king of the goblins, in a more contemptuous tone than before. And again the king of the goblins gave his leg a flourish; again it descended on the shoulders of the sexton; and again the attendant goblins imitated the example of their chief.

'Many a time the cloud went and came, and many a lesson it taught to Gabriel Grub, who, although his shoulders smarted with pain from the frequent applications of the goblin's feet, looked on with an interest that nothing could diminish. He saw that men who worked hard, and earned their scanty bread with lives of labour, were cheerful and happy; and that to the most ignorant, the sweet face of nature was a never-failing source of cheerfulness and joy.

He saw those who had been delicately nurtured, and tenderly brought up, cheerful under privations, and superior to suffering, that would have crushed many of a rougher grain, because they bore within their own bosoms the materials of happiness, content-ment, and peace. He saw that women, the tenderest and most fragile of all God's creatures, were the oftenest superior to sorrow, adversity, and distress; and he saw that it was because they bore, in their own hearts, an inexhaustible well-spring of affection and devotion. Above all, he saw that men like himself, who snarled at the mirth and cheerfulness of others, were the foulest weeds on the fair surface of the earth; and setting all the good of the world against the evil, he came to the conclusion that it was a very decent and respectable sort of world after all. No sooner had he formed it, than the cloud which closed over the last picture, seemed to settle on his senses, and lull him to repose. One by one, the goblins faded from his sight; and as the last one disappeared, he sunk to sleep.

'The day had broken when Gabriel Grub awoke, and found himself lying, at full length on the flat grave-stone in the churchyard, with the wicker bottle lying empty by his side, and his coat, spade, and lantern, all well whitened by the last night's frost, scattered on the ground. The stone on which he had first seen the goblin seated, stood bolt upright before him, and the grave at which he had worked, the night before, was not far off. At first, he began to doubt the reality of his adventures, but the acute pain in his shoulders when he attempted to rise, assured him that the kicking of the goblins was certainly not ideal. He was staggered again, by observing no traces of footsteps in the snow on which the goblins had played at leap-frog with the grave-stones, but he speedily accounted for this circumstance when he remembered that, being spirits, they would leave no visible impression behind them. So, Gabriel Grub got on his feet as well as he could, for the pain in his back; and brushing the frost off his coat, put it on, and turned his face towards the town.

'But he was an altered man, and he could not bear the thought of returning to a place where his repentance would be scoffed at, and his reformation disbelieved. He hesitated for a few moments; and then turned away to wander where he might, and seek his bread elsewhere.

'The lantern, the spade, and the wicker bottle, were found, that day, in the churchyard. There were a great many speculations about the sexton's fate, at first, but it was speedily determined that he had been carried away by the goblins; and there were not wanting some very credible witnesses who had distinctly seen him whisked through the air on the back of a chestnut horse blind of one eye, with the hind-quarters of a lion, and the tail of a bear. At length all this was devoutly believed; and the new sexton used to exhibit to the curious, for a trifling emolument, a good-sized piece of the church weathercock which had been accidentally kicked off by the aforesaid horse in his aërial flight, and picked up by himself in the churchyard, a year or two afterwards.

'Unfortunately, these stories were somewhat disturbed by the unlooked-for reappearance of Gabriel Grub himself, some ten years afterwards, a ragged, contented, rheumatic old man. He told his story to the clergyman, and also to the mayor; and in course of time it began to be received, as a matter of history, in which form it has continued down to this very day. The believers in the weathercock tale, having misplaced their confidence once, were not easily prevailed upon to part with it again, so they looked as wise as they could, shrugged their shoulders, touched their foreheads, and murmured something about Gabriel Grub having drunk all the Hollands, and then fallen asleep on the flat tombstone; and they affected to explain what he supposed he had witnessed in the goblin's cavern, by saying that he had seen the world, and grown wiser. But this opinion, which was by no means a popular one at any time, gradually died off; and be the matter how it may, as Gabriel Grub was afflicted with rheumatism to the end of his days, this story has at least one moral, if it teach no better one – and that is, that if a man turn sulky and drink by himself at Christmas time, he may make up his mind to be not a bit the better for it: let the spirits be never so good, or let them be even as many degrees beyond proof, as those which Gabriel Grub saw in the goblin's cavern.'

CHAPTER 30

How the Pickwickians made and cultivated the
Acquaintance of a couple of nice Young Men
belonging to one of the Liberal Professions; how
they disported themselves on the Ice; and how their
first Visit came to a conclusion

'Well, Sam,' said Mr Pickwick as that favoured servitor entered his
bed-chamber with his warm water, on the morning of Christmas
Day, 'Still frosty?'

'Water in the wash-hand basin's a mask o' ice, sir,' responded
Sam.

'Severe weather, Sam,' observed Mr Pickwick.

'Fine time for them as is well wropped up, as the Polar Bear said
to himself, ven he was practising his skating,' replied Mr Weller.

'I shall be down in a quarter of an hour, Sam,' said Mr Pickwick,
untying his nightcap.

'Wery good, sir,' replied Sam. 'There's a couple o' Sawbones
down stairs.'

'A couple of what!' exclaimed Mr Pickwick, sitting up in bed.

'A couple o' Sawbones,' said Sam.

'What's a Sawbones?' inquired Mr Pickwick, not quite certain
whether it was a live animal, or something to eat.

'What! Don't you know what a Sawbones is, sir?' inquired Mr
Weller. 'I thought everybody know'd as a Sawbones was a Surgeon.'

'Oh, a Surgeon, eh?' said Mr Pickwick, with a smile.

'Just that, sir,' replied Sam. 'These here ones as is below, though,
aint reg'lar thorough-bred Sawbones; they're only in trainin'.'

'In other words they're Medical Students, I suppose?' said Mr
Pickwick.

Sam Weller nodded assent.

'I am glad of it,' said Mr Pickwick, casting his nightcap energetically on the counterpane. 'They are fine fellows; very fine fellows;
with judgments matured by observation and reflection; tastes
refined by reading and study. I am very glad of it.'

'They're a smokin' cigars by the kitchen fire,' said Sam.

'Ah!' observed Mr Pickwick, rubbing his hands, 'overflowing
with kindly feelings and animal spirits. Just what I like to see.'

'And one on 'em,' said Sam, not noticing his master's interruption, 'one on 'em's got his legs on the table, and is a drinkin' brandy

neat, vile the tother one – him in the barnacles[1] – has got a barrel o' oysters atween his knees, wich he's a openin' like steam, and as fast as he eats 'em, he takes a aim vith the shells at young dropsy, who's a sittin' down fast asleep, in the chimbley corner.'

'Eccentricities of genius, Sam,' said Mr Pickwick. 'You may retire.'

Sam did retire accordingly; Mr Pickwick, at the expiration of the quarter of an hour, went down to breakfast.

'Here he is at last!' said old Mr Wardle. 'Pickwick, this is Miss Allen's brother, Mr Benjamin Allen. Ben we call him, and so may you if you like. This gentleman is his very particular friend, Mr —'

'Mr Bob Sawyer,' interposed Mr Benjamin Allen; whereupon Mr Bob Sawyer and Mr Benjamin Allen laughed in concert.

Mr Pickwick bowed to Bob Sawyer, and Bob Sawyer bowed to Mr Pickwick; Bob and his very particular friend then applied themselves most assiduously to the eatables before them; and Mr Pickwick had an opportunity of glancing at them both.

Mr Benjamin Allen was a coarse, stout, thick-set young man, with black hair cut rather short, and a white face cut rather long. He was embellished with spectacles, and wore a white neckerchief. Below his single-breasted black surtout, which was buttoned up to his chin, appeared the usual number of pepper-and-salt coloured legs, terminating in a pair of imperfectly polished boots. Although his coat was short in the sleeves, it disclosed no vestige of a linen wristband; and although there was quite enough of his face to admit of the encroachment of a shirt collar, it was not graced by the smallest approach to that appendage. He presented, altogether, rather a mildewy appearance, and emitted a fragrant odour of full-flavoured Cubas.[2]

Mr Bob Sawyer, who was habited in a coarse blue coat, which, without being either a great-coat or a surtout, partook of the nature and qualities of both, had about him that sort of slovenly smartness, and swaggering gait, which is peculiar to young gentlemen who smoke in the streets by day, shout and scream in the same by night, call waiters by their Christian names, and do various other acts and deeds of an equally facetious description. He wore a pair of plaid trousers, and a large rough double-breasted waistcoat; out of doors, he carried a thick stick with a big top. He eschewed gloves, and looked, upon the whole, something like a dissipated Robinson Crusoe.

Such were the two worthies to whom Mr Pickwick was introduced, as he took his seat at the breakfast table on Christmas morning.

'Splendid morning, gentlemen,' said Mr Pickwick.

Mr Bob Sawyer slightly nodded his assent to the proposition, and asked Mr Benjamin Allen for the mustard.

'Have you come far this morning, gentlemen?' inquired Mr Pickwick.

'Blue Lion at Muggleton,' briefly responded Mr Allen.

'You should have joined us last night,' said Mr Pickwick.

'So we should,' replied Bob Sawyer, 'but the brandy was too good to leave in a hurry: wasn't it, Ben?'

'Certainly,' said Mr Benjamin Allen; 'and the cigars were not bad, or the pork chops either: were they, Bob?'

'Decidedly not,' said Bob. The particular friends resumed their attack upon the breakfast, more freely than before, as if the recollection of last night's supper had imparted a new relish to the meal.

'Peg away, Bob,' said Mr Allen to his companion, encouragingly.

'So I do,' replied Bob Sawyer. And so, to do him justice, he did.

'Nothing like dissecting, to give one an appetite,' said Mr Bob Sawyer, looking round the table.

Mr Pickwick slightly shuddered.

'By the bye, Bob,' said Mr Allen, 'have you finished that leg yet?'

'Nearly,' replied Sawyer, helping himself to half a fowl as he spoke. 'It's a very muscular one for a child's.'

'Is it?' inquired Mr Allen, carelessly.

'Very,' said Bob Sawyer, with his mouth full.

'I've put my name down for an arm, at our place,' said Mr Allen. 'We're clubbing for a subject, and the list is nearly full, only we can't get hold of any fellow that wants a head. I wish you'd take it.'

'No,' replied Bob Sawyer; 'can't afford expensive luxuries.'

'Nonsense!' said Allen.

'Can't indeed,' rejoined Bob Sawyer. 'I wouldn't mind a brain, but I couldn't stand a whole head.'

'Hush, hush, gentlemen, pray,' said Mr Pickwick, 'I hear the ladies.'

As Mr Pickwick spoke, the ladies, gallantly escorted by Messrs. Snodgrass, Winkle, and Tupman, returned from an early walk.

'Why, Ben!' said Arabella, in a tone which expressed more surprise than pleasure at the sight of her brother.

'Come to take you home to-morrow,' replied Benjamin.

Mr Winkle turned pale.

'Don't you see Bob Sawyer, Arabella?' inquired Mr Benjamin Allen, somewhat reproachfully. Arabella gracefully held out her hand, in acknowledgment of Bob Sawyer's presence. A thrill of hatred struck to Mr Winkle's heart, as Bob Sawyer inflicted on the proffered hand a perceptible squeeze.

'Ben, dear!' said Arabella, blushing; 'have – have – you been introduced to Mr Winkle?'

'I have not been, but I shall be very happy to be, Arabella,' replied her brother gravely. Here Mr Allen bowed grimly to Mr Winkle, while Mr Winkle and Mr Bob Sawyer glanced mutual distrust out of the corners of their eyes.

The arrival of the two new visitors, and the consequent check upon Mr Winkle and the young lady with the fur round her boots, would in all probability have proved a very unpleasant interruption to the hilarity of the party, had not the cheerfulness of Mr Pickwick, and the good humour of the host, been exerted to the very utmost for the common weal. Mr Winkle gradually insinuated himself into the good graces of Mr Benjamin Allen, and even joined in a friendly conversation with Mr Bob Sawyer; who, enlivened with the brandy, and the breakfast, and the talking, gradually ripened into a state of extreme facetiousness, and related with much glee an agreeable anecdote, about the removal of a tumour on some gentleman's head: which he illustrated by means of an oyster-knife and a half-quartern loaf, to the great edification of the assembled company. Then, the whole train went to church, where Mr Benjamin Allen fell fast asleep: while Mr Bob Sawyer abstracted his thoughts from worldly matters, by the ingenious process of carving his name on the seat of the pew, in corpulent letters of four inches long.

'Now,' said Wardle, after a substantial lunch, with the agreeable items of strong-beer and cherry-brandy, had been done ample justice to; 'what say you to an hour on the ice? We shall have plenty of time.'

'Capital!' said Mr Benjamin Allen.

'Prime!' ejaculated Mr Bob Sawyer.

'You skate, of course, Winkle?' said Wardle.

'Ye-yes; oh, yes,' replied Mr Winkle. 'I – I – am *rather* out of practice.'

'Oh, *do* skate, Mr Winkle,' said Arabella. 'I like to see it so much.'

'Oh, it is *so* graceful,' said another young lady.

A third young lady said it was elegant, and a fourth expressed her opinion that it was 'swan-like.'

'I should be very happy, I'm sure,' said Mr Winkle, reddening; 'but I have no skates.'

This objection was at once overruled. Trundle had a couple of pair, and the fat boy announced that there were half-a-dozen more down stairs: whereat Mr Winkle expressed exquisite delight, and looked exquisitely uncomfortable.

Old Wardle led the way to a pretty large sheet of ice; and the fat boy and Mr Weller, having shovelled and swept away the snow which had fallen on it during the night, Mr Bob Sawyer adjusted his skates with a dexterity which to Mr Winkle was perfectly marvellous, and described circles with his left leg, and cut figures of eight, and inscribed upon the ice, without once stopping for breath, a great many other pleasant and astonishing devices, to the excessive satisfaction of Mr Pickwick, Mr Tupman, and the ladies: which reached a pitch of positive enthusiasm, when old Wardle and Benjamin Allen, assisted by the aforesaid Bob Sawyer, performed some mystic evolutions, which they called a reel.

All this time, Mr Winkle, with his face and hands blue with the cold, had been forcing a gimlet into the soles of his feet, and putting his skates on, with the points behind, and getting the straps into a very complicated and entangled state, with the assistance of Mr Snodgrass, who knew rather less about skates than a Hindoo. At length, however, with the assistance of Mr Weller, the unfortunate skates were firmly screwed and buckled on, and Mr Winkle was raised to his feet.

'Now, then, sir,' said Sam, in an encouraging tone; 'off vith you, and show 'em how to do it.'

'Stop, Sam, stop!' said Mr Winkle, trembling violently, and clutching hold of Sam's arms with the grasp of a drowning man. 'How slippery it is, Sam!'

'Not an uncommon thing upon ice, sir,' replied Mr Weller. 'Hold up, sir!'

This last observation of Mr Weller's bore reference to a demonstration Mr Winkle made at the instant, of a frantic desire to throw his feet in the air, and dash the back of his head on the ice.

'These – these – are very awkward skates; ain't they, Sam?' inquired Mr Winkle, staggering.

'I'm afeerd there's a orkard gen'l'm'n in 'em, sir,' replied Sam.

'Now, Winkle,' cried Mr Pickwick, quite unconscious that there was anything the matter. 'Come; the ladies are all anxiety.'

'Yes, yes,' replied Mr Winkle, with a ghastly smile. 'I'm coming.'

'Just a goin' to begin,' said Sam, endeavouring to disengage himself. 'Now, sir, start off!'

'Stop an instant, Sam,' gasped Mr Winkle, clinging most affectionately to Mr Weller. 'I find I've got a couple of coats at home that I don't want, Sam. You may have them, Sam.'

'Thank'ee, sir,' replied Mr Weller.

'Never mind touching your hat, Sam,' said Mr Winkle, hastily. 'You needn't take your hand away to do that. I meant to have given you five shillings this morning for a Christmas-box, Sam. I'll give it you this afternoon, Sam.'

'You're wery good, sir,' replied Mr Weller.

'Just hold me at first, Sam; will you?' said Mr Winkle. 'There – that's right. I shall soon get in the way of it, Sam. Not too fast, Sam; not too fast.'

Mr Winkle stooping forward, with his body half doubled up, was being assisted over the ice by Mr Weller, in a very singular and unswan-like manner, when Mr Pickwick most innocently shouted from the opposite bank:

'Sam!'

'Sir?'

'Here. I want you.'

'Let go, sir,' said Sam. 'Don't you hear the governor a callin'? Let go, sir.'

With a violent effort, Mr Weller disengaged himself from the grasp of the agonised Pickwickian, and, in so doing, administered a considerable impetus to the unhappy Mr Winkle. With an accuracy which no degree of dexterity or practice could have insured, that unfortunate gentleman bore swiftly down into the centre of the reel, at the very moment when Mr Bob Sawyer was performing a flourish of unparalleled beauty. Mr Winkle struck wildly against him, and with a loud crash they both fell heavily down. Mr Pickwick ran to the spot. Bob Sawyer had risen to his feet, but Mr Winkle was far too wise to do anything of the kind, in skates. He was seated on the ice, making spasmodic efforts to smile; but anguish was depicted on every lineament of his countenance.

'Are you hurt?' inquired Mr Benjamin Allen, with great anxiety.

'Not much,' said Mr Winkle, rubbing his back very hard.

'I wish you'd let me bleed you,' said Mr Benjamin, with great eagerness.

'No, thank you,' replied Mr Winkle hurriedly.

'I really think you had better,' said Allen.

'Thank you,' replied Mr Winkle; 'I'd rather not.'

'What do *you* think, Mr Pickwick?' inquired Bob Sawyer.

Mr Pickwick was excited and indignant. He beckoned to Mr Weller, and said in a stern voice, 'Take his skates off.'

'No; but really I had scarcely begun,' remonstrated Mr Winkle.

'Take his skates off,' repeated Mr Pickwick firmly.

The command was not to be resisted. Mr Winkle allowed Sam to obey it in silence.

'Lift him up,' said Mr Pickwick. Sam assisted him to rise.

Mr Pickwick retired a few paces apart from the by-standers; and, beckoning his friend to approach, fixed a searching look upon him, and uttered in a low, but distinct and emphatic tone, these remarkable words:

'You're a humbug, sir.'

'A what?' said Mr Winkle, starting.

'A humbug, sir. I will speak plainer, if you wish it. An impostor, sir.'

With those words, Mr Pickwick turned slowly on his heel, and rejoined his friends.

While Mr Pickwick was delivering himself of the sentiment just recorded, Mr Weller and the fat boy, having by their joint endeavours cut out a slide, were exercising themselves thereupon, in a very masterly and brilliant manner. Sam Weller, in particular, was displaying that beautiful feat of fancy-sliding which is currently denominated 'knocking at the cobbler's door,' and which is achieved by skimming over the ice on one foot, and occasionally giving a postman's knock upon it with the other. It was a good long slide, and there was something in the motion which Mr Pickwick, who was very cold with standing still, could not help envying.

'It looks a nice warm exercise that, doesn't it?' he inquired of Wardle, when that gentleman was thoroughly out of breath, by reason of the indefatigable manner in which he had converted his legs into a pair of compasses, and drawn complicated problems on the ice.

'Ah, it does indeed,' replied Wardle. 'Do you slide?'

'I used to do so, on the gutters, when I was a boy,' replied Mr Pickwick.

'Try it now,' said Wardle.

'Oh do please, Mr Pickwick!' cried all the ladies.

'I should be very happy to afford you any amusement,' replied Mr Pickwick, 'but I haven't done such a thing these thirty years.'

'Pooh! pooh! Nonsense!' said Wardle, dragging off his skates with the impetuosity which characterised all his proceedings. 'Here;

I'll keep you company; come along!' And away went the good tempered old fellow down the slide, with a rapidity which came very close upon Mr Weller, and beat the fat boy all to nothing.

Mr Pickwick paused, considered, pulled off his gloves and put them in his hat: took two or three short runs, baulked himself as often, and at last took another run, and went slowly and gravely down the slide, with his feet about a yard and a quarter apart, amidst the gratified shouts of all the spectators.

'Keep the pot a bilin', sir!' said Sam; and down went Wardle again, and then Mr Pickwick, and then Sam, and then Mr Winkle, and then Mr Bob Sawyer, and then the fat boy, and then Mr Snodgrass, following closely upon each other's heels, and running after each other with as much eagerness as if all their future prospects in life depended on their expedition.

It was the most intensely interesting thing, to observe the manner in which Mr Pickwick performed his share in the ceremony; to watch the torture of anxiety with which he viewed the person behind, gaining upon him at the imminent hazard of tripping him up; to see him gradually expend the painful force he had put on at first, and turn slowly round on the slide, with his face towards the point from which he had started; to contemplate the playful smile which mantled on his face when he had accomplished the distance, and the eagerness with which he turned round when he had done so, and ran after his predecessor: his black gaiters tripping pleas-antly through the snow, and his eyes beaming cheerfulness and gladness through his spectacles. And when he was knocked down (which happened upon the average every third round), it was the most invigorating sight that can possibly be imagined, to behold him gather up his hat, gloves, and handkerchief, with a glowing countenance, and resume his station in the rank, with an ardour and enthusiasm that nothing could abate.

The sport was at its height, the sliding was at the quickest, the laughter was at the loudest, when a sharp smart crack was heard. There was a quick rush towards the bank, a wild scream from the ladies, and a shout from Mr Tupman. A large mass of ice disap-peared; the water bubbled up over it; Mr Pickwick's hat, gloves, and handkerchief were floating on the surface; and this was all of Mr Pickwick that anybody could see.

Dismay and anguish were depicted on every countenance, the males turned pale, and the females fainted, Mr Snodgrass and Mr Winkle grasped each other by the hand, and gazed at the spot where their leader had gone down, with frenzied eagerness: while Mr

Mr Pickwick slides

Tupman, by way of rendering the promptest assistance, and at the same time conveying to any persons who might be within hearing, the clearest possible notion of the catastrophe, ran off across the country at his utmost speed, screaming 'Fire!' with all his might.

It was at this moment, when old Wardle and Sam Weller were approaching the hole with cautious steps, and Mr Benjamin Allen was holding a hurried consultation with Mr Bob Sawyer, on the advisability of bleeding the company generally, as an improving little bit of professional practice – it was at this very moment, that a face, head, and shoulders, emerged from beneath the water, and disclosed the features and spectacles of Mr Pickwick.

'Keep yourself up for an instant – for only one instant!' bawled Mr Snodgrass.

'Yes, do; let me implore you – for my sake!' roared Mr Winkle, deeply affected. The adjuration was rather unnecessary; the probability being, that if Mr Pickwick had declined to keep himself up for anybody else's sake, it would have occurred to him that he might as well do so, for his own.

'Do you feel the bottom there, old fellow?' said Wardle.

'Yes, certainly,' replied Mr Pickwick, wringing the water from his head and face, and gasping for breath. 'I fell upon my back. I couldn't get on my feet at first.'

The clay upon so much of Mr Pickwick's coat as was yet visible, bore testimony to the accuracy of this statement; and as the fears of the spectators were still further relieved by the fat boy's suddenly recollecting that the water was nowhere more than five feet deep, prodigies of valour were performed to get him out. After a vast quantity of splashing, and cracking, and struggling, Mr Pickwick was at length fairly extricated from his unpleasant position, and once more stood on dry land.

'Oh, he'll catch his death of cold,' said Emily.

'Dear old thing!' said Arabella. 'Let me wrap this shawl round you, Mr Pickwick.'

'Ah, that's the best thing you can do,' said Wardle; 'and when you've got it on, run home as fast as your legs can carry you, and jump into bed directly.'

A dozen shawls were offered on the instant. Three or four of the thickest having been selected, Mr Pickwick was wrapped up, and started off, under the guidance of Mr Weller: presenting the singular phenomenon of an elderly gentleman, dripping wet, and without a hat, with his arms bound down to his sides, skimming over the ground, without any clearly defined purpose, at the rate of six good English miles an hour.

But Mr Pickwick cared not for appearances in such an extreme case, and urged on by Sam Weller, he kept at the very top of his speed until he reached the door of Manor Farm, where Mr Tupman had arrived some five minutes before, and had frightened the old lady into palpitations of the heart by impressing her with the unalterable conviction that the kitchen chimney was on fire – a calamity which always presented itself in glowing colours to the old lady's mind, when anybody about her evinced the smallest agitation.

Mr Pickwick paused not an instant until he was snug in bed. Sam Weller lighted a blazing fire in the room, and took up his dinner; a bowl of punch was carried up afterwards, and a grand carouse held in honour of his safety. Old Wardle would not hear of his rising, so they made the bed the chair, and Mr Pickwick presided. A second and a third bowl were ordered in; and when Mr Pickwick awoke next morning, there was not a symptom of rheumatism about him : which proves, as Mr Bob Sawyer very justly observed, that there is nothing like hot punch in such cases: and that if ever hot punch did fail to act as a preventive, it was merely because the patient fell into the vulgar error of not taking enough of it.

The jovial party broke up next morning. Breakings up are capital things in our school days, but in after life they are painful enough. Death, self-interest, and fortune's changes, are every day breaking up many a happy group, and scattering them far and wide; and the boys and girls never come back again. We do not mean to say that it was exactly the case in this particular instance; all we wish to inform the reader is, that the different members of the party dispersed to their several homes; that Mr Pickwick and his friends once more took their seats on the top of the Muggleton coach; and that Arabella Allen repaired to her place of destination, wherever it might have been – we dare say Mr Winkle knew, but we confess we don't – under the care and guardianship of her brother Benjamin, and his most intimate and particular friend, Mr Bob Sawyer.

Before they separated, however, that gentleman and Mr Benjamin Allen drew Mr Pickwick aside with an air of some mystery: and Mr Bob Sawyer thrusting his forefinger between two of Mr Pickwick's ribs, and thereby displaying his native drollery, and his knowledge of the anatomy of the human frame, at one and the same time, inquired:

'I say, old boy, where do you hang out?'

Mr Pickwick replied that he was at present suspended at the George and Vulture.

'I wish you'd come and see me,' said Bob Sawyer.

'Nothing would give me greater pleasure,' replied Mr Pickwick.

'There's my lodgings,' said Mr Bob Sawyer, producing a card. 'Lant Street, Borough; it's near Guy's,[3] and handy for me, you know. Little distance after you've passed Saint George's Church – turns out of the High Street on the right hand side the way.'

'I shall find it,' said Mr Pickwick.

'Come on Thursday fortnight, and bring the other chaps with you,' said Mr Bob Sawyer, 'I'm going to have a few medical fellows that night.'

Mr Pickwick expressed the pleasure it would afford him to meet the medical fellows; and after Mr Bob Sawyer had informed him that he meant to be very cosey, and that his friend Ben was to be one of the party, they shook hands and separated.

We feel that in this place we lay ourself open to the inquiry whether Mr Winkle was whispering, during this brief conversation, to Arabella Allen; and if so, what he said; and furthermore, whether Mr Snodgrass was conversing apart with Emily Wardle; and if so, what *he* said. To this, we reply, that whatever they might have said to the ladies, they said nothing at all to Mr Pickwick or Mr Tupman for eight-and-twenty miles, and that they sighed very often, refused ale and brandy, and looked gloomy. If our observant lady readers can deduce any satisfactory inferences from these facts, we beg them by all means to do so.

CHAPTER 31

Which is all about the Law, and sundry Great
Authorities learned therein

Scattered about, in various holes and corners of the Temple, are certain dark and dirty chambers, in and out of which, all the morning in Vacation, and half the evening too in Term time, there may be seen constantly hurrying with bundles of papers under their arms, and protruding from their pockets, an almost uninterrupted succession of Lawyers' Clerks. There are several grades of Lawyers' Clerks. There is the Articled Clerk, who has paid a premium, and is an attorney in perspective, who runs a tailor's bill, receives invitations to parties, knows a family in Gower Street, and another in Tavistock Square:[1] who goes out of town every Long Vacation to see his father, who keeps live horses innumerable; and who is, in short, the very aristocrat of clerks. There is the salaried clerk – out of door, or in door, as the case may be – who devotes the major part of his thirty shillings a week to his personal pleasure and adornment, repairs half-price to the Adelphi Theatre[2] at least three times a week, dissipates majestically at the cider cellars afterwards, and is a dirty caricature of the fashion which expired six months ago. There is the middle-aged copying clerk, with a large family, who is always shabby, and often drunk. And there are the office lads in their first surtouts, who feel a befitting contempt for boys at day-schools: club as they go home at night, for saveloys and porter: and think there's nothing like 'life.' There are varieties of the genus, too numerous to recapitulate, but however numerous they may be, they are all to be seen, at certain regulated business hours, hurrying to and from the places we have just mentioned.

These sequestered nooks are the public offices of the legal profession, where writs are issued, judgments signed, declarations filed, and numerous other ingenious machines put in motion for the torture and torment of His Majesty's liege subjects, and the comfort and emolument of the practitioners of the law. They are, for the most part, low-roofed, mouldy rooms, where innumerable rolls of parchment, which have been perspiring in secret for the last century, send forth an agreeable odour, which is mingled by day with the scent of the dry rot, and by night with the various exhalations which arise from damp cloaks, festering umbrellas, and the coarsest tallow candles.

About half-past seven o'clock in the evening, some ten days or a fortnight after Mr Pickwick and his friends returned to London, there hurried into one of these offices, an individual in a brown coat and brass buttons, whose long hair was scrupulously twisted round the rim of his napless hat, and whose soiled drab trousers were so tightly strapped over his Blucher boots, that his knees threatened every moment to start from their concealment. He produced from his coat pockets a long and narrow strip of parchment, on which the presiding functionary impressed an illegible black stamp. He then drew forth four scraps of paper, of similar dimensions, each containing a printed copy of the strip of parchment with blanks for a name; and having filled up the blanks, put all the five documents in his pocket, and hurried away.

The man in the brown coat, with the cabalistic documents in his pocket, was no other than our old acquaintance Mr Jackson, of the house of Dodson and Fogg, Freeman's Court, Cornhill. Instead of returning to the office from whence he came, however, he bent his steps direct to Sun Court, and walking straight into the George and Vulture, demanded to know whether one Mr Pickwick was within.

'Call Mr Pickwick's servant, Tom,' said the barmaid of the George and Vulture.

'Don't trouble yourself,' said Mr Jackson, 'I've come on business. If you'll show me Mr Pickwick's room I'll step up myself.'

'What name, sir?' said the waiter.

'Jackson,' replied the clerk.

The waiter stepped up stairs to announce Mr Jackson; but Mr Jackson saved him the trouble by following close at his heels, and walking into the apartment before he could articulate a syllable.

Mr Pickwick had, that day, invited his three friends to dinner; they were all seated round the fire, drinking their wine, when Mr Jackson presented himself, as above described.

'How de do, sir?' said Mr Jackson, nodding to Mr Pickwick.

That gentleman bowed, and looked somewhat surprised, for the physiognomy of Mr Jackson dwelt not in his recollection.

'I have called from Dodson and Fogg's,' said Mr Jackson, in an explanatory tone.

Mr Pickwick roused at the name. 'I refer you to my attorney, sir: Mr Perker, of Gray's Inn,' said he. 'Waiter, show this gentleman out.'

'Beg your pardon, Mr Pickwick,' said Jackson, deliberately depositing his hat on the floor, and drawing from his pocket the strip of parchment. 'But personal service, by clerk or agent, in these cases, you know, Mr Pickwick – nothing like caution, sir, in all legal forms?'

Here Mr Jackson cast his eye on the parchment; and, resting his hands on the table, and looking round with a winning and persuasive smile, said: 'Now, come; don't let's have no words about such a little matter as this. Which of you gentlemen's name's Snodgrass?'

At this inquiry Mr Snodgrass gave such a very undisguised and palpable start, that no further reply was needed.

'Ah! I thought so,' said Mr Jackson, more affably than before. 'I've got a little something to trouble you with, sir.'

'Me!' exclaimed Mr Snodgrass.

'It's only a *subpœna* in Bardell and Pickwick on behalf of the plaintiff,' replied Jackson, singling out one of the slips of paper, and producing a shilling from his waistcoat pocket.³ 'It'll come on, in the settens⁴ after Term; fourteenth of Febooary, we expect; we've marked it a special jury cause, and it's only ten down the paper. That's your's, Mr Snodgrass.' As Jackson said this he presented the parchment before the eyes of Mr Snodgrass, and slipped the paper and the shilling into his hand.

Mr Tupman had witnessed this process in silent astonishment, when Jackson, turning sharply upon him, said:

'I think I ain't mistaken when I say your name's Tupman, am I?'

Mr Tupman looked at Mr Pickwick; but, perceiving no encouragement in that gentleman's widely-opened eyes to deny his name, said:

'Yes, my name *is* Tupman, sir.'

'And that other gentleman's Mr Winkle, I think?' said Jackson.

Mr Winkle faltered out a reply in the affirmative; and both gentlemen were forthwith invested with a slip of paper, and a shilling each, by the dexterous Mr Jackson.

'Now,' said Jackson, 'I'm afraid you'll think me rather troublesome, but I want somebody else, if it ain't inconvenient. I *have* Samuel Weller's name here, Mr Pickwick.'

'Send my servant here, waiter,' said Mr Pickwick. The waiter retired, considerably astonished, and Mr Pickwick motioned Jackson to a seat.

There was a painful pause, which was at length broken by the innocent defendant.

'I suppose, sir,' said Mr Pickwick, his indignation rising while he spoke; 'I suppose, sir, that it is the intention of your employers to seek to criminate me upon the testimony of my own friends?'

Mr Jackson struck his forefinger several times against the left side of his nose, to intimate that he was not there to disclose the secrets of the prison-house,⁵ and playfully rejoined:

'Not knowin', can't say.'

'For what other reason, sir,' pursued Mr Pickwick, 'are these subpoenas served upon them, if not for this?'

'Very good plant, Mr Pickwick,' replied Jackson, slowly shaking his head. 'But it won't do. No harm in trying, but there's little to be got out of me.'

Here Mr Jackson smiled once more upon the company, and, applying his left thumb to the tip of his nose, worked a visionary coffee-mill with his right hand: thereby performing a very graceful piece of pantomime (then much in vogue, but now, unhappily, almost obsolete) which was familiarly denominated 'taking a grinder.'

'No, no, Mr Pickwick,' said Jackson, in conclusion; 'Perker's people must guess what we've served these subpoenas for. If they can't, they must wait till the action comes on, and then they'll find out.'

Mr Pickwick bestowed a look of excessive disgust on his unwelcome visitor, and would probably have hurled some tremendous anathema at the heads of Messrs. Dodson and Fogg, had not Sam's entrance at the instant interrupted him.

'Samuel Weller?' said Mr Jackson, inquiringly.

'Vun o' the truest things as you've said for many a long year,' replied Sam, in a most composed manner.

'Here's a subpoena for you, Mr Weller,' said Jackson.

'What's that in English?' inquired Sam.

'Here's the original,' said Jackson, declining the required explanation.

'Which?' said Sam.

'This,' replied Jackson, shaking the parchment.

'Oh, that's the 'rig'nal, is it?' said Sam. 'Well, I'm wery glad I've seen the 'rig'nal, 'cos it's a gratifyin' sort o' thing, and eases vun's mind so much.'

'And here's the shilling,' said Jackson. 'It's from Dodson and Fogg's.'

'And it's uncommon handsome o' Dodson and Fogg, as knows so little of me, to come down vith a present,' said Sam. 'I feel it as a wery high compliment, sir; it's a wery hon'rable thing to them, as they knows how to reward merit werever they meets it. Besides wich, it's affectin' to one's feelin's.'

As Mr Weller said this, he inflicted a little friction on his right eye-lid, with the sleeve of his coat, after the most approved manner of actors when they are in domestic pathetics.

Mr Jackson seemed rather puzzled by Sam's proceedings; but, as he had served the subpoenas, and had nothing more to say, he made a feint of putting on the one glove which he usually carried in his hand, for the sake of appearances; and returned to the office to report progress.

Mr Pickwick slept little that night; his memory had received a very disagreeable refresher on the subject of Mrs Bardell's action. He breakfasted betimes next morning, and, desiring Sam to accompany him, set forth towards Gray's Inn Square.

'Sam!' said Mr Pickwick, looking round, when they got to the end of Cheapside.

'Sir?' said Sam, stepping up to his master.

'Which way?'

'Up Newgate Street.'

Mr Pickwick did not turn round immediately, but looked vacantly in Sam's face for a few seconds, and heaved a deep sigh.

'What's the matter, sir?' inquired Sam.

'This action, Sam,' said Mr Pickwick, 'is expected to come on, on the fourteenth of next month.'

'Remarkable coincidence that 'ere, sir,' replied Sam.

'Why, remarkable, Sam?' inquired Mr Pickwick.

'Walentine's day, sir,' responded Sam; 'reg'lar good day for a breach o' promise trial.'

Mr Weller's smile awakened no gleam of mirth in his master's countenance. Mr Pickwick turned abruptly round, and led the way in silence.

They had walked some distance: Mr Pickwick trotting on before, plunged in profound meditation, and Sam following behind, with a countenance expressive of the most enviable and easy defiance of everything and everybody: when the latter, who was always especially anxious to impart to his master any exclusive information he possessed, quickened his pace until he was close at Mr Pickwick's heels; and, pointing up at a house they were passing, said:

'Wery nice pork-shop that 'ere, sir.'

'Yes, it seems so,' said Mr Pickwick.

'Celebrated Sassage factory,' said Sam.

'Is it?' said Mr Pickwick.

'Is it!' reiterated Sam, with some indignation; 'I should rayther think it was. Why, sir, bless your innocent eyebrows, that's were the mysterious disappearance of a 'spectable tradesman took place four year ago.'

'You don't mean to say he was burked,⁶ Sam?' said Mr Pickwick, looking hastily round.

'No, I don't indeed, sir,' replied Mr Weller, 'I wish I did; far worse than that. He was the master o' that 'ere shop, sir, and the inwenter o' the patent-never-leavin'-off sassage steam ingine, as ud swaller up a pavin' stone if you put it too near, and grind it into sassages as easy as if it was a tender young babby. Wery proud o' that machine he was, as it was nat'ral he should be, and he'd stand down in the celler a lookin' at it wen it was in full play, till he got quite melancholy with joy. A wery happy man he'd ha' been, sir, in the procession o' that 'ere ingine and two more lovely hinfants besides, if it hadn't been for his wife, who was a most ow-dacious wixin. She was always a follerin' him about, and dinnin' in his ears, till at last he couldn't stand it no longer. "I'll tell you what it is, my dear," he says one day; "if you persewere in this here sort of amusement," he says, "I'm blessed if I don't go away to 'Merriker; and that's all about it." "You're a idle willin," says she, "and I wish the 'Merrikins joy of their bargain." Arter wich she keeps on abusin' of him for half an hour, and then runs into the little parlour behind the shop, sets to a screamin'', says he'll be the death on her, and falls in a fit, which lasts for three good hours – one o' them fits wich is all screamin' and kickin'. Well, next mornin', the husband was missin'. He hadn't taken nothin' from the till, – hadn't even put on his great-coat – so it was quite clear he warn't gone to 'Merriker. Didn't come back next day; didn't come back next week; Missis had bills printed, sayin' that, if he'd come back, he should be forgiven everythin' (which was very liberal, seein' that he hadn't done nothin' at all); the canals was dragged, and for two months artervards, wenever a body turned up, it was carried, as a reg'lar thing, straight off to the sassage shop. Hows'ever, none on'em answered; so they gave out that he'd run avay, and she kep on the bis'ness. One Saturday night, a little thin old gen'l'm'n comes into the shop in a great passion and says, "Are you the missis o' this here shop?" "Yes, I am," says she. "Well, ma'am," says he, "then I've just looked in to say that me and my family ain't a goin' to be choked for nothin'; and more than that, ma'am," he says, "you'll allow me to observe, that as you don't use the primest parts of the meat in the manafacter o' sassages, I think you'd find beef come nearly as cheap as buttons." "As buttons, sir!" says she. "Buttons, ma'am," says the little old gentleman, unfolding a bit of paper, and shewin' twenty or thirty halves o' buttons. "Nice seasonin' for sassages, is trousers' buttons, ma'am." "They're my husband's buttons!" says the widder, beginnin' to faint. "What!" screams the little old gen'l'm'n, turnin' wery pale. "I see it all," says the widder; "in a fit of temporary insanity he rashly converted his-self into sassages!" And so he had, sir,' said Mr Weller, looking steadily into Mr Pickwick's horror-stricken countenance, 'or else he'd been draw'd into the ingine; but however that might ha' been, the little old gen'l'm'n, who had been remarkably partial to sassages all his life, rushed out o' the shop in a wild state, and was never heerd on artervards!'

The relation of this affecting incident of private life brought master and man to Mr Perker's chambers. Lowten, holding the door half open, was in conversation with a rustily-clad, miserable-looking man, in boots without toes and gloves without fingers. There were traces of privation and suffering – almost of despair – in his lank and care-worn countenance; he felt his poverty, for he shrunk to the dark side of the staircase as Mr Pickwick approached.

'It's very unfortunate,' said the stranger, with a sigh.

'Very,' said Lowten, scribbling his name on the door-post with his pen, and rubbing it out again with the feather. 'Will you leave a message for him?'

'When do you think he'll be back?' inquired the stranger.

'Quite uncertain,' replied Lowten, winking at Mr Pickwick, as the stranger cast his eyes towards the ground.

'You don't think it would be of any use my waiting for him?' said the stranger, looking wistfully into the office.

'Oh no, I'm sure it wouldn't,' replied the clerk, moving a little more into the centre of the door-way. 'He's certain not to be back this week, and it's a chance whether he will be next; for when Perker once gets out of town, he's never in a hurry to come back again.'

'Out of town!' said Mr Pickwick; 'dear me, how unfortunate!'

'Don't go away, Mr Pickwick,' said Lowten, 'I've got a letter for you.' The stranger seeming to hesitate, once more looked towards the ground, and the clerk winked slily at Mr Pickwick, as if to intimate that some exquisite piece of humour was going forward, though what it was Mr Pickwick could not for the life of him divine.

'Step in, Mr Pickwick,' said Lowten. 'Well, will you leave a message, Mr Watty, or will you call again?'

'Ask him to be so kind as to leave out word what has been done in my business,' said the man; 'for God's sake don't neglect it, Mr Lowten.'

'No, no; I won't forget it,' replied the clerk. 'Walk in, Mr Pickwick. Good morning, Mr Watty; it's a fine day for walking, isn't it?' Seeing that the stranger still lingered, he beckoned Sam Weller to follow his master in, and shut the door in his face.

'There never was such a pestering bankrupt as that since the world began, I do believe!' said Lowten, throwing down his pen with the air of an injured man. 'His affairs haven't been in Chancery quite four years yet, and I'm d – d if he don't come worrying here twice a week. Step this way, Mr Pickwick. Perker *is* in, and he'll see you, I know. Devilish cold,' he added, pettishly, 'standing at that

door, wasting one's time with such seedy vagabonds!' Having very
vehemently stirred a particularly large fire with a particularly small
poker, the clerk led the way to his principal's private room, and
announced Mr Pickwick.

'Ah, my dear sir,' said little Mr Perker, bustling up from his chair.
'Well, my dear sir, and what's the news about your matter, eh?
Anything more about our friends in Freeman's Court? They've not
been sleeping, *I* know that. Ah, they're very smart fellows; very
smart, indeed.'

As the little man concluded, he took an emphatic pinch of snuff,
as a tribute to the smartness of Messrs. Dodson and Fogg.

'They are great scoundrels,' said Mr Pickwick.

'Aye, aye,' said the little man; 'that's a matter of opinion, you
know, and we won't dispute about terms; because of course you
can't be expected to view these subjects with a professional eye.
Well, we've done everything that's necessary. I have retained
Serjeant Snubbin.'[7]

'Is he a good man?' inquired Mr Pickwick.

'Good man!' replied Perker; 'bless your heart and soul, my dear
sir, Serjeant Snubbin is at the very top of his profession. Gets treble
the business of any man in court – engaged in every case. You
needn't mention it abroad; but we say – we of the profession – that
Serjeant Snubbin leads the court by the nose.'

The little man took another pinch of snuff as he made this
communication, and nodded mysteriously to Mr Pickwick.

'They have subpœna'd my three friends,' said Mr Pickwick.

'Ah! of course they would,' replied Perker. 'Important witnesses;
saw you in a delicate situation.'

'But she fainted of her own accord,' said Mr Pickwick. 'She threw
herself into my arms.'

'Very likely, my dear sir,' replied Perker; 'very likely and very
natural. Nothing more so, my dear sir, nothing. But who's to prove
it?'

'They have subpœna'd my servant too,' said Mr Pickwick,
quitting the other point; for there Mr Perker's question had
somewhat staggered him.

'Sam?' said Perker.

Mr Pickwick replied in the affirmative.

'Of course, my dear sir; of course. I knew they would. I could
have told *you* that, a month ago. You know, my dear sir, if you
will take the management of your affairs into your own hands
after intrusting them to your solicitor, you must also take the

consequences.' Here Mr Perker drew himself up with conscious dignity, and brushed some stray grains of snuff from his shirt frill.

'And what do they want him to prove?' asked Mr Pickwick, after two or three minutes' silence.

'That you sent him up to the plaintiff's to make some offer of a compromise, I suppose,' replied Perker. 'It don't matter much, though; I don't think many counsel could get a great deal out of *him*.'

'I don't think they could,' said Mr Pickwick; smiling, despite his vexation, at the idea of Sam's appearance as a witness. 'What course do we pursue?'

'We have only one to adopt, my dear sir,' replied Perker; 'cross-examine the witnesses; trust to Snubbin's eloquence; throw dust in the eyes of the judge; throw ourselves on the jury.'

'And suppose the verdict is against me?' said Mr Pickwick.

Mr Perker smiled, took a very long pinch of snuff, stirred the fire, shrugged his shoulders, and remained expressively silent.

'You mean that in that case I must pay the damages?' said Mr Pickwick, who had watched this telegraphic answer with considerable sternness.

Perker gave the fire another very unnecessary poke, and said 'I am afraid so.'

'Then I beg to announce to you, my unalterable determination to pay no damages whatever,' said Mr Pickwick, most emphatically. 'None, Perker. Not a pound, not a penny, of my money, shall find its way into the pockets of Dodson and Fogg. That is my deliberate and irrevocable determination.' Mr Pickwick gave a heavy blow on the table before him, in confirmation of the irrevocability of his intention.

'Very well, my dear sir, very well,' said Perker. 'You know best, of course.'

'Of course,' replied Mr Pickwick hastily. 'Where does Serjeant Snubbin live?'

'In Lincoln's Inn Old Square,'[8] replied Perker.

'I should like to see him,' said Mr Pickwick.

'See Serjeant Snubbin, my dear sir!' rejoined Perker, in utter amazement. 'Pooh, pooh, my dear sir, impossible. See Serjeant Snubbin! Bless you, my dear sir, such a thing was never heard of, without a consultation fee being previously paid, and a consultation fixed. It couldn't be done, my dear sir; it couldn't be done.'

Mr Pickwick, however, had made up his mind not only that it could be done, but that it should be done; and the consequence was, that within ten minutes after he had received the assurance that the thing was impossible, he was conducted by his solicitor into the outer office of the great Serjeant Snubbin himself.

It was an uncarpeted room of tolerable dimensions, with a large writing-table drawn up near the fire: the baize top of which had long since lost all claim to its original hue of green, and had gradually grown grey with dust and age, except where all traces of its natural colour were obliterated by ink-stains. Upon the table were numerous little bundles of papers tied with red tape; and behind it, sat an elderly clerk, whose sleek appearance, and heavy gold watch-chain, presented imposing indications of the extensive and lucrative practice of Mr Serjeant Snubbin.

'Is the Serjeant in his room, Mr Mallard?' inquired Perker, offering his box with all imaginable courtesy.

'Yes he is,' was the reply, 'but he's very busy. Look here; not an opinion given yet, on any one of these cases; and an expedition fee paid with all of 'em.' The clerk smiled as he said this, and inhaled the pinch of snuff with a zest which seemed to be compounded of a fondness for snuff and a relish for fees.

'Something like practice that,' said Perker.

'Yes,' said the barrister's clerk, producing his own box, and offering it with the greatest cordiality; 'and the best of it is, that as nobody alive except myself can read the Serjeant's writing, they are obliged to wait for the opinions, when he has given them, till I have copied 'em, ha – ha – ha!'

'Which makes good for we know who, besides the Serjeant, and draws a little more out of the clients, eh?' said Perker; 'Ha, ha, ha!' At this the Serjeant's clerk laughed again; not a noisy boisterous laugh, but a silent, internal chuckle, which Mr Pickwick disliked to hear. When a man bleeds inwardly, it is a dangerous thing for himself; but when he laughs inwardly, it bodes no good to other people.

'You haven't made me out that little list of the fees that I'm in your debt, have you?' said Perker.

'No, I have not,' replied the clerk.

'I wish you would,' said Perker. 'Let me have them, and I'll send you a cheque. But I suppose you're too busy pocketing the ready money, to think of the debtors, eh? ha, ha, ha!' This sally seemed to tickle the clerk amazingly, and he once more enjoyed a little quiet laugh to himself.

'But, Mr Mallard, my dear friend,' said Perker, suddenly recovering his gravity, and drawing the great man's great man into a corner, by the lappel of his coat; 'you must persuade the Serjeant to see me, and my client here.'

'Come, come,' said the clerk, 'that's not bad either. See the Serjeant! come, that's too absurd.' Notwithstanding the absurdity of the proposal, however, the clerk allowed himself to be gently drawn beyond the hearing of Mr Pickwick; and after a short conversation conducted in whispers, walked softly down a little dark passage, and disappeared into the legal luminary's sanctum: whence he shortly returned on tiptoe, and informed Mr Perker and Mr Pickwick that the Serjeant had been prevailed upon, in violation of all established rules and customs, to admit them at once.

Mr Serjeant Snubbin was a lantern-faced, sallow-complexioned man, of about five-and-forty, or – as the novels say – he might be fifty. He had that dull-looking boiled eye which is often to be seen in the heads of people who have applied themselves during many years to a weary and laborious course of study; and which would have been sufficient, without the additional eye-glass which dangled from a broad black riband round his neck, to warn a stranger that he was very near-sighted. His hair was thin and weak, which was partly attributable to his having never devoted much time to its arrangement, and partly to his having worn for five-and-twenty years the forensic⁹ wig which hung on a block beside him. The marks of hair-powder on his coat-collar, and the ill-washed and worse tied white neckerchief round his throat, showed that he had not found leisure since he left the court to make any alteration in his dress: while the slovenly style of the remainder of his costume warranted the inference that his personal appearance would not have been very much improved if he had. Books of practice, heaps of papers, and opened letters, were scattered over the table, without any attempt at order or arrangement; the furniture of the room was old and ricketty; the doors of the book-case were rotting in their hinges; the dust flew out from the carpet in little clouds at every step; the blinds were yellow with age and dirt; the state of everything in the room showed, with a clearness not to be mistaken, that Mr Serjeant Snubbin was far too much occupied with his professional pursuits to take any great heed or regard of his personal comforts.

The Serjeant was writing when his clients entered; he bowed abstractedly when Mr Pickwick was introduced by his solicitor; and then, motioning them to a seat, put his pen carefully in the inkstand, nursed his left leg, and waited to be spoken to.

'Mr Pickwick is the defendant in Bardell and Pickwick, Serjeant Snubbin,' said Perker.

'I am retained in that, am I?' said the Serjeant.

'You are, sir,' replied Perker.

The Serjeant nodded his head, and waited for something else.

'Mr Pickwick was anxious to call upon you, Serjeant Snubbin,' said Perker, 'to state to you, before you entered upon the case, that he denies there being any ground or pretence whatever for the action against him; and that unless he came into court with clean hands, and without the most conscientious conviction that he was right in resisting the plaintiff's demand, he would not be there at all. I believe I state your views correctly; do I not, my dear sir?' said the little man, turning to Mr Pickwick.

'Quite so,' replied that gentleman.

Mr Serjeant Snubbin unfolded his glasses, raised them to his eyes; and, after looking at Mr Pickwick for a few seconds with great curiosity, turned to Mr Perker, and said, smiling slightly as he spoke:

'Has Mr Pickwick a strong case?'

The attorney shrugged his shoulders.

'Do you purpose calling witnesses?'

'No.'

The smile on the Serjeant's countenance became more defined; he rocked his leg with increased violence; and, throwing himself back in his easy-chair, coughed dubiously.

These tokens of the Serjeant's presentiments on the subject, slight as they were, were not lost on Mr Pickwick. He settled the spectacles, through which he had attentively regarded such demonstrations of the barrister's feelings as he had permitted himself to exhibit, more firmly on his nose; and said with great energy, and in utter disregard of all Mr Perker's admonitory winkings and frownings:

'My wishing to wait upon you, for such a purpose as this, sir, appears, I have no doubt, to a gentleman who sees so much of these matters as you must necessarily do, a very extraordinary circumstance.'

The Serjeant tried to look gravely at the fire, but the smile came back again.

'Gentlemen of your profession, sir,' continued Mr Pickwick, 'see the worst side of human nature. All its disputes, all its ill-will and bad blood, rise up before you. You know from your experience of juries (I mean no disparagement to you, or them) how much depends upon *effect* : and you are apt to attribute to others, a desire to use, for purposes of deception and self-interest, the very instruments which you, in pure honesty and honour of purpose, and with a laudable desire to do your utmost for your client, know the temper and worth of so well, from constantly employing them yourselves. I really believe that to this circumstance may be attributed the vulgar but very general notion of your being, as a body, suspicious, distrustful, and over-cautious. Conscious as I am, sir, of the disadvantage of making such a declaration to you, under such circumstances, I have come here, because I wish you distinctly to understand, as my friend Mr Perker has said, that I am innocent of the falsehood laid to my charge; and although I am very well aware of the inestimable value of your assistance, sir, I must beg to add, that unless you sincerely believe this, I would rather be deprived of the aid of your talents than have the advantage of them.'

Long before the close of this address, which we are bound to say was of a very prosy character for Mr Pickwick, the Serjeant had relapsed into a state of abstraction. After some minutes, however, during which he had reassumed his pen, he appeared to be again aware of the presence of his clients; raising his head from the paper, he said, rather snappishly,

'Who is with me in this case?'

'Mr Phunky, Serjeant Snubbin,' replied the attorney.

'Phunky, Phunky,' said the Serjeant, 'I never heard the name before. He must be a very young man.'

'Yes, he is a very young man,' replied the attorney. 'He was only called the other day. Let me see – he has not been at the Bar eight years yet.'

'Ah, I thought not,' said the Serjeant, in that sort of pitying tone in which ordinary folks would speak of a very helpless little child. 'Mr Mallard, send round to Mr – Mr – .'

'Phunky's – Holborn Court, Gray's Inn,' interposed Perker. (Holborn Court, by the bye, is South Square now). 'Mr Phunky, and say I should be glad if he'd step here, a moment.'

Mr Mallard departed to execute his commission; and Serjeant Snubbin relapsed into abstraction until Mr Phunky himself was introduced.

Although an infant barrister, he was a full-grown man. He had a very nervous manner, and a painful hesitation in his speech; it did not appear to be a natural defect, but seemed rather the result of timidity, arising from the consciousness of being 'kept down' by want of means, or interest, or connexion, or impudence, as the case might be. He was overawed by the Serjeant, and profoundly courteous to the attorney.

The first interview with Mr Serjeant Snubbin

'I have not had the pleasure of seeing you before, Mr Phunky,' said Serjeant Snubbin, with haughty condescension.

Mr Phunky bowed. He *had* had the pleasure of seeing the Serjeant, and of envying him too, with all a poor man's envy, for eight years and a quarter.

'You are with me in this case, I understand?' said the Serjeant.

If Mr Phunky had been a rich man, he would have instantly sent for his clerk to remind him; if he had been a wise one, he would have applied his fore-finger to his forehead, and endeavoured to recollect, whether, in the multiplicity of his engagements he had undertaken this one, or not; but as he was neither rich nor wise (in this sense at all events) he turned red, and bowed.

'Have you read the papers, Mr Phunky?' inquired the Serjeant.

Here again, Mr Phunky should have professed to have forgotten all about the merits of the case; but as he had read such papers as had been laid before him in the course of the action, and had thought of nothing else, waking or sleeping, throughout the two months during which he had been retained as Mr Serjeant Snubbin's junior, he turned a deeper red, and bowed again.

'This is Mr Pickwick,' said the Serjeant, waving his pen in the direction in which that gentleman was standing.

Mr Phunky bowed to Mr Pickwick with a reverence which a first client must ever awaken; and again inclined his head towards his leader.

'Perhaps you will take Mr Pickwick away,' said the Serjeant, 'and – and – and – hear anything Mr Pickwick may wish to communicate. We shall have a consultation, of course.' With this hint that he had been interrupted quite long enough, Mr Serjeant Snubbin, who had been gradually growing more and more abstracted, applied his glass to his eyes for an instant, bowed slightly round, and was once more deeply immersed in the case before him: which arose out of an interminable lawsuit, originating in the act of an individual, deceased a century or so ago, who had stopped up a pathway leading from some place which nobody ever came from, to some other place which nobody ever went to.

Mr Phunky would not hear of passing through any door until Mr Pickwick and his solicitor had passed through before him, so it was some time before they got into the Square; and when they did reach it, they walked up and down, and held a long conference, the result of which was, that it was a very difficult matter to say how the verdict would go; that nobody could presume to calculate on the issue of an action; that it was very lucky they had prevented the other party from getting Serjeant Snubbin; and other topics of doubt and consolation, common in such a position of affairs.

Mr Weller was then roused by his master from a sweet sleep of an hour's duration; and, bidding adieu to Lowten, they returned to the City.

CHAPTER 32

Describes, far more fully than the Court Newsman ever did, a Bachelor's Party, given by Mr Bob Sawyer at his Lodgings in the Borough

There is a repose about Lant Street, in the borough, which sheds a gentle melancholy upon the soul. There are always a good many houses to let in the street: it is a bye-street too, and its dulness is soothing. A house in Lant Street would not come within the denomination of a first-rate residence, in the strict acceptation of the term; but it is a most desirable spot nevertheless. If a man wished to abstract himself from the world – to remove himself from within the reach of temptation – to place himself beyond the possibility of any inducement to look out of the window – he should by all means go to Lant Street.

In this happy retreat are colonised a few clear-starchers,[1] a sprinkling of journeymen bookbinders, one or two prison agents for the Insolvent Court, several small housekeepers who are employed in the Docks, a handful of mantua-makers,[2] and a seasoning of jobbing tailors. The majority of the inhabitants either direct their energies to the letting of furnished apartments, or devote themselves to the healthful and invigorating pursuit of mangling.[3] The chief features in the still life of the street are green shutters, lodging-bills, brass door-plates, and bell-handles; the principal specimens of animated nature, the pot-boy, the muffin youth, and the baked-potato man. The population is migratory, usually disappearing on the verge of quarter-day,[4] and generally by night. His majesty's revenues are seldom collected in this happy valley; the rents are dubious; and the water communication is very frequently cut off.

Mr Bob Sawyer embellished one side of the fire, in his first-floor front, early on the evening for which he had invited Mr Pickwick; and Mr Ben Allen the other. The preparations for the reception of visitors appeared to be completed. The umbrellas in the passage had been heaped into the little corner outside the backparlour door; the bonnet and shawl of the landlady's servant had been removed from the banisters; there were not more than two pairs of pattens on the street-door mat, and a kitchen candle, with a very long snuff, burnt cheerfully on the ledge of the staircase window. Mr Bob Sawyer had himself purchased the spirits at a wine vaults in High Street, and had returned home preceding the bearer thereof, to preclude the possibility of their delivery at the wrong house. The punch was ready-made in a red pan in the bed-room; a little table, covered with a green baize cloth, had been borrowed from the parlour, to play at cards on; and the glasses of the establishment, together with those which had been borrowed for the occasion from the public-house, were all drawn up in a tray, which was deposited on the landing outside the door.

Notwithstanding the highly satisfactory nature of all these arrangements, there was a cloud on the countenance of Mr Bob Sawyer, as he sat by the fire-side. There was a sympathising expression, too, in the features of Mr Ben Allen, as he gazed intently on the coals; and a tone of melancholy in his voice, as he said, after a long silence:

'Well, it *is* unlucky she should have taken it in her head to turn sour, just on this occasion. She might at least have waited till to-morrow.'

'That's her malevolence, that's her malevolence,' returned Mr Bob Sawyer, vehemently. 'She says that if I can afford to give a party I ought to be able to pay her confounded "little bill."'

'How long has it been running?' inquired Mr Ben Allen. A bill, by the bye, is the most extraordinary locomotive engine that the genius of man ever produced. It would keep on running during the longest lifetime, without ever once stopping of its own accord.

'Only a quarter, and a month or so,' replied Mr Bob Sawyer.

Ben Allen coughed hopelessly, and directed a searching look between the two top bars of the stove.

'It'll be a deuced unpleasant thing if she takes it into her head to let out, when those fellows are here, won't it?' said Mr Ben Allen at length.

'Horrible,' replied Bob Sawyer, 'horrible.'

A low tap was heard at the room door. Mr Bob Sawyer looked expressively at his friend, and bade the tapper come in; whereupon a dirty slipshod girl in black cotton stockings, who might have passed for the neglected daughter of a superannuated dustman in very reduced circumstances, thrust in her head, and said,

'Please, Mister Sawyer, Missis Raddle wants to speak to *you*.'

Before Mr Bob Sawyer could return any answer, the girl suddenly disappeared with a jerk, as if somebody had given her a violent pull behind; this mysterious exit was no sooner accomplished, than there was another tap at the door – a smart pointed tap, which seemed to say, 'Here I am, and in I'm coming.'

Mr Bob Sawyer glanced at his friend with a look of abject apprehension, and once more cried 'Come in.'

The permission was not at all necessary, for, before Mr Bob Sawyer had uttered the words, a little fierce woman bounced into the room, all in a tremble with passion, and pale with rage.

'Now Mr Sawyer,' said the little fierce woman, trying to appear very calm, 'if you'll have the kindness to settle that little bill of mine I'll thank you, because I've got my rent to pay this afternoon, and my landlord's a waiting below now.' Here the little woman rubbed her hands, and looked steadily over Mr Bob Sawyer's head, at the wall behind him.

'I am very sorry to put you to any inconvenience, Mrs Raddle,' said Bob Sawyer, deferentially, 'but—'

'Oh, it isn't any inconvenience,' replied the little woman, with a shrill titter. 'I didn't want it particular before to-day; leastways, as it has to go to my landlord directly, it was as well for you to keep it as me. You promised me this afternoon, Mr Sawyer, and every gentleman as has ever lived here, has kept his word, sir, as of course anybody as calls himself a gentleman, does.' Mrs Raddle tossed her head, bit her lips, rubbed her hands harder, and looked at the wall more steadily than ever. It was plain to see, as Mr Bob Sawyer remarked in a style of eastern allegory on a subsequent occasion, that she was 'getting the steam up.'

'I am very sorry, Mrs Raddle,' said Bob Sawyer with all imaginable humility, 'but the fact is, that I have been disappointed in the City to-day.' – Extraordinary place that City. An astonishing number of men always *are* getting disappointed there.

'Well, Mr Sawyer,' said Mrs Raddle, planting herself firmly on a purple cauliflower in the Kidderminster carpet, 'and what's that to me, sir?'

'I – I – have no doubt, Mrs Raddle,' said Bob Sawyer, blinking this last question, 'that before the middle of next week we shall be able to set ourselves quite square, and go on, on a better system, afterwards.'

This was all Mrs Raddle wanted. She had bustled up to the apartment of the unlucky Bob Sawyer, so bent upon going into a passion, that, in all probability, payment would have rather disappointed her than otherwise. She was in excellent order for a little relaxation of the kind: having just exchanged a few introductory compliments with Mr R. in the front kitchen.

'Do you suppose, Mr Sawyer,' said Mrs Raddle, elevating her voice for the information of the neighbours, 'do you suppose that I'm a-going day after day to let a fellar occupy my lodgings as never thinks of paying his rent, nor even the very money laid out for the fresh butter and lump sugar that's bought for his breakfast, and the very milk that's took in, at the street door? Do you suppose a hardworking and industrious woman as has lived in this street for twenty year (ten year over the way, and nine year and three quarter in this very house) has nothing else to do but to work herself to death after a parcel of lazy idle fellars, that are always smoking and drinking, and lounging, when they ought to be glad to turn their hands to anything that would help 'em to pay their bills? Do you—'

'My good soul,' interposed Mr Benjamin Allen, soothingly.

'Have the goodness to keep your observashuns to yourself, sir, I beg,' said Mrs Raddle, suddenly arresting the rapid torrent of her speech, and addressing the third party with impressive slowness and solemnity. 'I am not aweer, sir, that you have any right to address your conversation to me. I don't think I let these apartments to you, sir.'

'No, you certainly did not,' said Mr Benjamin Allen.

'Very good, sir,' responded Mrs Raddle, with lofty politeness. 'Then p'raps, sir, you'll confine yourself to breaking the arms and legs of the poor people in the hospitals, and keep yourself *to* yourself, sir, or there may be some persons here as will make you, sir.'

'But you are such an unreasonable woman,' remonstrated Mr Benjamin Allen.

'I beg your parding, young man,' said Mrs Raddle, in a cold perspiration of anger. 'But will you have the goodness just to call me that again, sir?'

'I didn't make use of the word in any invidious sense, ma'am,' replied Mr Benjamin Allen, growing somewhat uneasy on his own account.

'I beg your parding, young man,' demanded Mrs Raddle in a

louder and more imperative tone. 'But who do you call a woman? Did you make that remark to me, sir?'

'Why, bless my heart!' said Mr Benjamin Allen.

'Did you apply that name to me, I ask of you, sir?' interrupted Mrs Raddle, with intense fierceness, throwing the door wide open.

'Why, of course I did,' replied Mr Benjamin Allen.

'Yes, of course you did,' said Mrs Raddle, backing gradually to the door, and raising her voice to its loudest pitch, for the special behoof of Mr Raddle in the kitchen. 'Yes, of course you did! And everybody knows that they may safely insult me in my own 'ouse while my husband sits sleeping down stairs, and taking no more notice than if I was a dog in the streets. He ought to be ashamed of himself (here Mrs Raddle sobbed) to allow his wife to be treated in this way by a parcel of young cutters and carvers of live people's bodies, that disgraces the lodgings (another sob), and leaving her exposed to all manner of abuse; a base, faint-hearted, timorous wretch, that's afraid to come up stairs, and face the ruffinly creatures – that's afraid – that's afraid to come!' Mrs Raddle paused to listen whether the repetition of the taunt had roused her better half; and, finding that it had not been successful, proceeded to descend the stairs with sobs innumerable: when there came a loud double knock at the street door: whereupon she burst into an hysterical fit of weeping, accompanied with dismal moans, which was prolonged until the knock had been repeated six times, when, in an uncontrollable burst of mental agony, she threw down all the umbrellas, and disappeared into the back parlour, closing the door after her with an awful crash.

'Does Mr Sawyer live here?' said Mr Pickwick, when the door was opened.

'Yes,' said the girl, 'first floor. It's the door straight afore you, when you gets to the top of the stairs.' Having given this instruction, the handmaid, who had been brought up among the aboriginal inhabitants of Southwark, disappeared, with the candle in her hand, down the kitchen stairs: perfectly satisfied that she had done everything that could possibly be required of her under the circumstances.

Mr Snodgrass, who entered last, secured the street door, after several ineffectual efforts, by putting up the chain; and the friends stumbled up stairs, where they were received by Mr Bob Sawyer, who had been afraid to go down, lest he should be waylaid by Mrs Raddle.

'How are you?' said the discomfited student. 'Glad to see you, –

take care of the glasses.' This caution was addressed to Mr
Pickwick, who had put his hat in the tray.

'Dear me,' said Mr Pickwick, 'I beg your pardon.'

'Don't mention it, don't mention it,' said Bob Sawyer. 'I'm rather
confined for room here, but you must put up with all that, when
you come to see a young bachelor. Walk in. You've seen this
gentleman before, I think?' Mr Pickwick shook hands with Mr
Benjamin Allen, and his friends followed his example. They had
scarcely taken their seats when there was another double knock.

'I hope that's Jack Hopkins!' said Mr Bob Sawyer. 'Hush. Yes, it
is. Come up, Jack; come up.'

A heavy footstep was heard upon the stairs, and Jack Hopkins
presented himself. He wore a black velvet waistcoat, with thunder-
and-lightning buttons; and a blue striped shirt, with a white false
collar.

'You're late, Jack?' said Mr Benjamin Allen.

'Been detained at Bartholomew's,'[5] replied Hopkins.

'Anything new?'

'No, nothing particular. Rather a good accident brought into the
casualty ward.'

'What was that, sir?' inquired Mr Pickwick.

'Only a man fallen out of a four pair of stairs' window;[6] – but it's
a very fair case – very fair case indeed.'

'Do you mean that the patient is in a fair way to recover?'
inquired Mr Pickwick.

'No,' replied Hopkins, carelessly. 'No, I should rather say he
wouldn't. There must be a splendid operation though, to-morrow –
magnificent sight if Slasher does it.'

'You consider Mr Slasher a good operator?' said Mr Pickwick.

'Best alive,' replied Hopkins. 'Took a boy's leg out of the socket
last week – boy ate five apples and a gingerbread cake – exactly two
minutes after it was all over, boy said he wouldn't lie there to be
made game of, and he'd tell his mother if they didn't begin.'

'Dear me!' said Mr Pickwick, astonished.

'Pooh! That's nothing, that ain't,' said Jack Hopkins. 'Is it, Bob?'

'Nothing at all,' replied Mr Bob Sawyer.

'By the bye, Bob,' said Hopkins, with a scarcely perceptible
glance at Mr Pickwick's attentive face, 'we had a curious accident
last night. A child was brought in, who had swallowed a necklace.'

'Swallowed what, sir?' interrupted Mr Pickwick.

'A necklace,' replied Jack Hopkins. 'Not all at once, you know,
that would be too much – *you* couldn't swallow that, if the child

did – eh, Mr Pickwick, ha! ha!' Mr Hopkins appeared highly gratified with his own pleasantry; and continued. 'No, the way was this. Child's parents were poor people who lived in a court. Child's eldest sister bought a necklace; common necklace, made of large black wooden beads. Child, being fond of toys, cribbed[7] the necklace, hid it, played with it, cut the string, and swallowed a bead. Child thought it capital fun, went back next day, and swallowed another bead.'

'Bless my heart,' said Mr Pickwick, 'what a dreadful thing! I beg your pardon, sir. Go on.'

'Next day, child swallowed two beads; the day after that, he treated himself to three, and so on, till in a week's time he had got through the necklace – five-and-twenty beads in all. The sister, who was an industrious girl, and seldom treated herself to a bit of finery, cried her eyes out, at the loss of the necklace; looked high and low for it; but, I needn't say, didn't find it. A few days afterwards, the family were at dinner – baked shoulder of mutton, and potatoes under it – the child, who wasn't hungry, was playing about the room, when suddenly there was heard a devil of a noise, like a small hail storm. "Don't do that, my boy," said the father. "I ain't a doin' nothing," said the child. "Well, don't do it again," said the father. There was a short silence, and then the noise began again, worse than ever. "If you don't mind what I say, my boy," said the father, "you'll find yourself in bed, in something less than a pig's whisper." He gave the child a shake to make him obedient, and such a rattling ensued as nobody ever heard before. "Why, damme, it's *in* the child!" said the father, "he's got the croup[8] in the wrong place!" "No I haven't, father," said the child, beginning to cry, "it's the necklace; I swallowed it, father." – The father caught the child up, and ran with him to the hospital: the beads in the boy's stomach rattling all the way with the jolting; and the people looking up in the air, and down in the cellars, to see where the unusual sound came from. He's in the hospital now,' said Jack Hopkins, 'and he makes such a devil of a noise when he walks about, that they're obliged to muffle him in a watchman's coat, for fear he should wake the patients!'

'That's the most extraordinary case I ever heard of,' said Mr Pickwick, with an emphatic blow on the table.

'Oh, that's nothing,' said Jack Hopkins; 'is it, Bob?'

'Certainly not,' replied Mr Bob Sawyer.

'Very singular things occur in our profession, I can assure you, sir,' said Hopkins.

'So I should be disposed to imagine,' replied Mr Pickwick.

Another knock at the door, announced a large-headed young man in a black wig, who brought with him a scorbutic[9] youth in a long stock. The next comer was a gentleman in a shirt emblazoned with pink anchors, who was closely followed by a pale youth with a plated watchguard. The arrival of a prim personage in clean linen and cloth boots rendered the party complete. The little table with the green baize cover was wheeled out; the first instalment of punch was brought in, in a white jug; and the succeeding three hours were devoted to *vingt-et-un* at sixpence a dozen, which was only once interrupted by a slight dispute between the scorbutic youth and the gentleman with the pink anchors; in the course of which, the scorbutic youth intimated a burning desire to pull the nose of the gentleman with the emblems of hope: in reply to which, that individual expressed his decided unwillingness to accept of any 'sauce' on gratuitous terms, either from the irascible young gentleman with the scorbutic countenance, or any other person who was ornamented with a head.

When the last 'natural'[10] had been declared, and the profit and loss account of fish and sixpences adjusted, to the satisfaction of all parties, Mr Bob Sawyer rang for supper, and the visitors squeezed themselves into corners while it was getting ready.

It was not so easily got ready as some people may imagine. First of all, it was necessary to awaken the girl, who had fallen asleep with her face on the kitchen table; this took a little time, and, even when she did answer the bell, another quarter of an hour was consumed in fruitless endeavours to impart to her a faint and distant glimmering of reason. The man to whom the order for the oysters had been sent, had not been told to open them; it is a very difficult thing to open an oyster with a limp knife or a two-pronged fork; and very little was done in this way. Very little of the beef was done either; and the ham (which was also from the German-sausage shop round the corner) was in a similar predicament. However, there was plenty of porter in a tin can; and the cheese went a great way, for it was very strong. So upon the whole, perhaps, the supper was quite as good as such matters usually are.

After supper, another jug of punch was put upon the table, together with a paper of cigars, and a couple of bottles of spirits. Then, there was an awful pause; and this awful pause was occasioned by a very common occurrence in this sort of places, but a very embarrassing one notwithstanding.

The fact is, the girl was washing the glasses. The establishment boasted four; we do not record the circumstance as at all derogatory to Mrs Raddle, for there never was a lodging-house yet, that was not short of glasses. The landlady's glasses were little thin blown glass tumblers, and those which had been borrowed from the public-house were great, dropsical, bloated articles, each supported on a huge gouty leg.[11] This would have been in itself sufficient to have possessed the company with the real state of affairs; but the young woman of all work had prevented the possibility of any misconception arising in the mind of any gentleman upon the subject, by forcibly dragging every man's glass away, long before he had finished his beer, and audibly stating, despite the winks and interruptions of Mr Bob Sawyer, that it was to be conveyed down stairs, and washed forthwith.

It is a very ill wind that blows nobody any good. The prim man in the cloth boots, who had been unsuccessfully attempting to make a joke during the whole time the round game lasted, saw his opportunity, and availed himself of it. The instant the glasses disappeared, he commenced a long story about a great public character, whose name he had forgotten, making a particularly happy reply to another eminent and illustrious individual whom he had never been able to identify. He enlarged at some length and with great minuteness upon divers collateral circumstances, distantly connected with the anecdote in hand, but for the life of him he couldn't recollect at that precise moment what the anecdote was, although he had been in the habit of telling the story with great applause for the last ten years.

'Dear me,' said the prim man in the cloth boots, 'it is a very extraordinary circumstance.'

'I am sorry you have forgotten it,' said Mr Bob Sawyer, glancing eagerly at the door, as he thought he heard the noise of glasses jingling; 'very sorry.'

'So am I,' responded the prim man, 'because I know it would have afforded so much amusement. Never mind; I dare say I shall manage to recollect it, in the course of half-an-hour or so.'

The prim man arrived at this point, just as the glasses came back, when Mr Bob Sawyer, who had been absorbed in attention during the whole time, said he should very much like to hear the end of it, for, so far as it went, it was, without exception, the very best story he had ever heard.

The sight of the tumblers restored Bob Sawyer to a degree of equanimity which he had not possessed since his interview with his landlady. His face brightened up, and he began to feel quite convivial.

'Now, Betsy,' said Mr Bob Sawyer, with great suavity, and dispersing, at the same time, the tumultuous little mob of glasses the girl had collected in the centre of the table: 'now, Betsy, the warm water: be brisk, there's a good girl.'

'You can't have no warm water,' replied Betsy.

'No warm water!' exclaimed Mr Bob Sawyer.

'No,' said the girl, with a shake of the head which expressed a more decided negative than the most copious language could have conveyed. 'Missis Raddle said you warn't to have none.'

The surprise depicted on the countenances of his guests imparted new courage to the host.

'Bring up the warm water instantly – instantly!' said Mr Bob Sawyer, with desperate sternness.

'No. I can't,' replied the girl; 'Missis Raddle raked out the kitchen fire afore she went to bed, and locked up the kittle.'

'Oh, never mind; never mind. Pray don't disturb yourself about such a trifle,' said Mr Pickwick, observing the conflict of Bob Sawyer's passions, as depicted in his countenance, 'cold water will do very well.'

'Oh, admirably,' said Mr Benjamin Allen.

'My landlady is subject to some slight attacks of mental derangement,' remarked Bob Sawyer with a ghastly smile; 'and I fear I must give her warning.'

'No, don't,' said Ben Allen.

'I fear I must,' said Bob with heroic firmness. 'I'll pay her what I owe her, and give her warning to-morrow morning.' Poor fellow! how devoutly he wished he could!

Mr Bob Sawyer's heart-sickening attempts to rally under this last blow, communicated a dispiriting influence to the company, the greater part of whom, with the view of raising their spirits, attached themselves with extra cordiality to the cold brandy and water, the first perceptible effects of which were displayed in a renewal of hostilities between the scorbutic youth and the gentleman in the shirt. The belligerents vented their feelings of mutual contempt, for some time, in a variety of frownings and snortings, until at last the scorbutic youth felt it necessary to come to a more explicit understanding on the matter; when the following clear understanding took place.

'Sawyer,' said the scorbutic youth, in a loud voice.

'Well, Noddy,' replied Mr Bob Sawyer.

'I should be very sorry, Sawyer,' said Mr Noddy, 'to create any unpleasantness at any friend's table, and much less at yours, Sawyer – very; but I must take this opportunity of informing Mr Gunter that he is no gentleman.'

'And *I* should be very sorry, Sawyer, to create any disturbance in the street in which you reside,' said Mr Gunter, 'but I'm afraid I shall be under the necessity of alarming the neighbours by throwing the person who has just spoken, out o' window.'

'What do you mean by that, sir?' inquired Mr Noddy.

'What I say, sir,' replied Mr Gunter.

'I should like to see you do it, sir,' said Mr Noddy.

'You shall *feel* me do it in half a minute, sir,' replied Mr Gunter.

'I request that you'll favour me with your card, sir,' said Mr Noddy.

'I'll do nothing of the kind, sir,' replied Mr Gunter.

'Why not, sir?' inquired Mr Gunter.

'Because you'll stick it up over your chimney-piece, and delude your visitors into the false belief that a gentleman has been to see you, sir,' replied Mr Gunter.

'Sir, a friend of mine shall wait on you in the morning,' said Mr Noddy.

'Sir, I'm very much obliged to you for the caution, and I'll leave particular directions with the servant to lock up the spoons,' replied Mr Gunter.

At this point the remainder of the guests interposed, and remonstrated with both parties on the impropriety of their conduct; on which Mr Noddy begged to state that his father was quite as respectable as Mr Gunter's father; to which Mr Gunter replied that his father was to the full as respectable as Mr Noddy's father, and that his father's son was as good a man as Mr Noddy, any day in the week. As this announcement seemed the prelude to a recommencement of the dispute, there was another interference on the part of the company; and a vast quantity of talking and clamouring ensued, in the course of which Mr Noddy gradually allowed his feelings to overpower him, and professed that he had ever entertained a devoted personal attachment towards Mr Gunter. To this Mr Gunter replied that, upon the whole, he rather preferred Mr Noddy to his own brother; on hearing which admission, Mr Noddy magnanimously rose from his seat, and proffered his hand to Mr Gunter. Mr Gunter grasped it with affecting fervour; and everybody said that the whole dispute had been conducted in a manner which was highly honourable to both parties concerned.

'Now,' said Jack Hopkins, 'just to set us going again, Bob, I don't mind singing a song.' And Hopkins, incited thereto, by tumultuous applause, plunged himself at once into "The King, God bless him," which he sang as loud as he could, to a novel air, compounded of the "Bay of Biscay," and "A Frog he would." The chorus was the essence of the song; and, as each gentleman sang it to the tune he knew best, the effect was very striking indeed.

It was at the end of the chorus to the first verse, that Mr Pickwick held up his hand in a listening attitude, and said, as soon as silence was restored:

'Hush! I beg your pardon. I thought I heard somebody calling from up stairs.'

A profound silence immediately ensued; and Mr Bob Sawyer was observed to turn pale.

'I think I hear it now,' said Mr Pickwick. 'Have the goodness to open the door.'

The door was no sooner opened than all doubt on the subject was removed.

'Mr Sawyer! Mr Sawyer!' screamed a voice from the two-pair landing.

'It's my landlady,' said Bob Sawyer, looking round him with great dismay. 'Yes, Mrs Raddle.'

'What do you mean by this, Mr Sawyer?' replied the voice, with great shrillness and rapidity of utterance. 'Ain't it enough to be swindled out of one's rent, and money lent out of pocket besides, and abused and insulted by your friends that dares to call themselves men: without having the house turned out of window, and noise enough made to bring the fire-engines here, at two o'clock in the morning? – Turn them wretches away.'

'You ought to be ashamed of yourselves,' said the voice of Mr Raddle, which appeared to proceed from beneath some distant bed-clothes.

'Ashamed of themselves!' said Mrs Raddle. 'Why don't you go down and knock 'em every one down stairs? You would if you was a man.'

'I should if I was a dozen men, my dear,' replied Mr Raddle, pacifically, 'but they've the advantage of me in numbers, my dear.'

'Ugh, you coward!' replied Mrs Raddle, with supreme contempt. 'Do you mean to turn them wretches out, or not, Mr Sawyer?'

'They're going, Mrs Raddle, they're going,' said the miserable Bob. 'I am afraid you'd better go,' said Mr Bob Sawyer to his friends. 'I *thought* you were making too much noise.'

'It's a very unfortunate thing,' said the prim man. 'Just as we were getting so comfortable too!' The prim man was just beginning to have a dawning recollection of the story he had forgotten.

'It's hardly to be borne,' said the prim man, looking round. 'Hardly to be borne, is it?'

'Not to be endured,' replied Jack Hopkins; 'let's have the other verse, Bob. Come, here goes!'

'No, no, Jack, don't,' interposed Bob Sawyer; 'it's a capital song, but I am afraid we had better not have the other verse. They are very violent people, the people of the house.'

'Shall I step up stairs, and pitch into the landlord?' inquired Hopkins, 'or keep on ringing the bell, or go and groan on the staircase? You may command me, Bob.'

'I am very much indebted to you for your friendship and good nature, Hopkins,' said the wretched Mr Bob Sawyer, 'but I think the best plan to avoid any further dispute is for us to break up at once.'

'Now, Mr Sawyer!' screamed the shrill voice of Mrs Raddle, 'are them brutes going?'

'They're only looking for their hats, Mrs Raddle,' said Bob; 'they are going directly.'

'Going!' said Mrs Raddle, thrusting her night-cap over the banisters just as Mr Pickwick, followed by Mr Tupman, emerged from the sitting-room. 'Going! what did they ever come for?'

'My dear ma'am,' remonstrated Mr Pickwick, looking up.

'Get along with you, you old wretch!' replied Mrs Raddle, hastily withdrawing the night-cap. 'Old enough to be his grandfather, you willin! You're worse than any of 'em.'

Mr Pickwick found it in vain to protest his innocence, so hurried down stairs into the street, whither he was closely followed by Mr Tupman, Mr Winkle, and Mr Snodgrass. Mr Ben Allen, who was dismally depressed with spirits and agitation, accompanied them as far as London Bridge, and in the course of the walk confided to Mr Winkle, as an especially eligible person to intrust the secret to, that he was resolved to cut the throat of any gentleman except Mr Bob Sawyer who should aspire to the affections of his sister Arabella. Having expressed his determination to perform this painful duty of a brother with proper firmness, he burst into tears, knocked his hat over his eyes, and, making the best of his way back, knocked double knocks at the door of the Borough Market office, and took short naps on the steps alternately, until daybreak, under the firm impression that he lived there, and had forgotten the key.

The visitors having all departed, in compliance with the rather pressing request of Mrs Raddle, the luckless Mr Bob Sawyer was left alone, to meditate on the probable events of to-morrow, and the pleasures of the evening.

CHAPTER 33

Mr Weller the elder delivers some Critical Sentiments respecting Literary Composition; and, assisted by his son Samuel, pays a small Instalment of Retaliation to the Account of the Reverend Gentleman with the Red Nose

The morning of the thirteenth of February, which the readers of this authentic narrative know, as well as we do, to have been the day immediately preceding that which was appointed for the trial of Mrs Bardell's action, was a busy time for Mr Samuel Weller, who was perpetually engaged in travelling from the George and Vulture to Mr Perker's chambers and back again, from and between the hours of nine o'clock in the morning and two in the afternoon, both inclusive. Not that there was anything whatever to be done, for the consultation had taken place, and the course of proceeding to be adopted, had been finally determined on; but Mr Pickwick being in a most extreme state of excitement, persevered in constantly sending small notes to his attorney, merely containing the inquiry, 'Dear Perker. Is all going on well?' to which Mr Perker invariably forwarded the reply, 'Dear Pickwick. As well as possible;' the fact being, as we have already hinted, that there was nothing whatever to go on, either well or ill, until the sitting of the court on the following morning.

But people who go voluntarily to law, or are taken forcibly there, for the first time, may be allowed to labour under some temporary irritation and anxiety: and Sam, with a due allowance for the frailties of human nature, obeyed all his master's behests with that imperturbable good humour and unruffable composure which formed one of his most striking and amiable characteristics.

Sam had solaced himself with a most agreeable little dinner, and was waiting at the bar for the glass of warm mixture in which Mr Pickwick had requested him to drown the fatigues of his morning's walks, when a young boy of about three feet high, or thereabouts, in a hairy cap and fustian over-alls, whose garb bespoke a laudable ambition to attain in time the elevation of an hostler, entered the passage of the George and Vulture, and looked first up the stairs, and then along the passage, and then into the bar, as if in search of somebody to whom he bore a commission; whereupon the barmaid, conceiving it not improbable that the said commission might be directed to the tea or table spoons of the establishment, accosted the boy with

'Now, young man, what do *you* want?'

'Is there anybody here, named Sam?' inquired the youth, in a loud voice of treble quality.

'What's the t'other name?' said Sam Weller, looking round.

'How should I know?' briskly replied the young gentleman below the hairy cap.

'You're a sharp boy, you are,' said Mr Weller; 'only I wouldn't show that wery fine edge too much, if I was you, in case anybody took it off. What do you mean by comin' to a hot-el, and asking arter Sam, vith as much politeness as a vild Indian?'

' 'Cos an old gen'l'm'n told me to,' replied the boy.

'What old gen'l'm'n?' inquired Sam, with deep disdain.

'Him as drives a Ipswich coach, and uses our parlour,' rejoined the boy. 'He told me yesterday mornin' to come to the George and Wultur this arternoon, and ask for Sam.'

'It's my father, my dear,' said Mr Weller, turning with an explanatory air to the young lady in the bar; 'blessed if I think he hardly knows wot my other name is. Vell, young brockiley sprout, wot then?'[1]

'Why, then,' said the boy, 'you was to come to him at six o'clock to our ouse, 'cos he wants to see you – Blue Boar, Leaden'all Markit. Shall I say you're comin'?'

'You *may* wenture on that 'ere statement, sir,' replied Sam. And thus empowered, the young gentleman walked away, awakening all the echoes in George Yard as he did so, with several chaste and extremely correct imitations of a drover's whistle, delivered in a tone of peculiar richness and volume.

Mr Weller having obtained leave of absence from Mr Pickwick, who, in his then state of excitement and worry was by no means displeased at being left alone, set forth, long before the appointed hour, and having plenty of time at his disposal, sauntered down as far as the Mansion House,[2] where he paused and contemplated, with a face of great calmness and philosophy, the numerous cads and drivers of short stages[3] who assemble near that famous place of resort, to the great terror and confusion of the old-lady population of these realms. Having loitered here, for half an hour or so, Mr Weller turned, and began wending his way towards Leadenhall Market, through a variety of bye-streets and courts. As he was sauntering away his spare time, and stopped to look at almost every object that met his gaze, it is by no means surprising that Mr Weller should have paused before a small stationer's and print-seller's window; but without further explanation it does appear surprising that his eyes should have no sooner rested on certain pictures which were exposed for sale therein, than he gave a sudden start, smote his right leg with great vehemence, and exclaimed with energy, 'If it hadn't been for this, I should ha' forgot all about it, till it was too late!'

The particular picture on which Sam Weller's eyes were fixed, as he said this, was a highly coloured representation of a couple of human hearts skewered together with an arrow, cooking before a cheerful fire, while a male and female cannibal in modern attire: the gentleman being clad in a blue coat and white trousers, and the lady in a deep red pelisse with a parasol of the same: were approaching the meal with hungry eyes, up a serpentine gravel path leading there-unto. A decidedly indelicate young gentleman, in a pair of wings and nothing else, was depicted as superintending the cooking; a representation of the spire of the church in Langham Place,[4] London, appeared in the distance; and the whole formed a 'valentine,' of which, as a written inscription in the window testified, there was a large assortment within, which the shopkeeper pledged himself to dispose of, to his countrymen generally, at the reduced rate of one and sixpence each.

'I should ha' forgot it; I should certainly ha' forgot it!' said Sam; so saying, he at once stepped into the stationer's shop, and requested to be served with a sheet of the best gilt-edged letter-paper, and a hard-nibbed pen which could be warranted not to splutter. These articles having been promptly supplied, he walked on direct towards Leadenhall Market at a good round pace, very different from his recent lingering one. Looking round him, he there beheld a sign-board on which the painter's art had delineated something remotely resembling a cerulean elephant[5] with an aquiline nose in lieu of trunk. Rightly conjecturing that this was the Blue Boar himself, he stepped into the house, and inquired concerning his parent.

'He won't be here this three quarters of an hour or more,' said the young lady who superintended the domestic arrangements of the Blue Boar.

'Wery good, my dear,' replied Sam. 'Let me have nine penn'orth o' brandy and water luke, and the inkstand, will you miss?'

The brandy and water luke, and the inkstand, having been carried into the little parlour, and the young lady having carefully flattened down the coals to prevent their blazing, and carried away the poker to preclude the possibility of the fire being stirred, without the full privity and concurrence of the Blue Boar being first had and obtained, Sam Weller sat himself down in a box near the stove, and pulled out the sheet of gilt-edged letter-paper, and the hard-nibbed pen. Then looking carefully at the pen to see that there were no hairs in it, and dusting down the table, so that there might be no crumbs of bread under the paper, Sam tucked up the cuffs of his coat, squared his elbows, and composed himself to write.

To ladies and gentlemen who are not in the habit of devoting themselves practically to the science of penmanship, writing a letter is no very easy task; it being always considered necessary in such cases for the writer to recline his head on his left arm, so as to place his eyes as nearly as possible on a level with the paper, while glancing sideways at the letters he is constructing, to form with his tongue imaginary characters to correspond. These motions, although unquestionably of the greatest assistance to original composition, retard in some degree the progress of the writer; and Sam had unconsciously been a full hour and a half writing words in small text, smearing out wrong letters with his little finger, and putting in new ones which required going over very often to render them visible through the old blots, when he was roused by the opening of the door and the entrance of his parent.

'Vell, Sammy,' said the father.

'Vell, my Prooshan Blue,'[6] responded the son, laying down his pen. 'What's the last bulletin about mother-in-law?'

'Mrs Veller passed a very good night, but is uncommon perwerse, and unpleasant this mornin'. Signed upon oath, S. Veller, Esquire, Senior. That's the last vun as was issued, Sammy,' replied Mr Weller, untying his shawl.

'No better yet?' inquired Sam.

'All the symptoms aggerawated,' replied Mr Weller, shaking his head. 'But wot's that, you're a doin' of? Pursuit of knowledge under difficulties, Sammy?'

'I've done now,' said Sam with slight embarrassment; 'I've been a writin'.'

'So I see,' replied Mr Weller. 'Not to any young 'ooman, I hope, Sammy?'

'Why it's no use a sayin' it ain't,' replied Sam, 'It's a walentine.'

'A what!' exclaimed Mr Weller, apparently horror-stricken by the word.

'A walentine,' replied Sam.

'Samivel, Samivel,' said Mr Weller, in reproachful accents, 'I didn't think you'd ha' done it. Arter the warnin' you've had o' your father's wicious propensities; arter all I've said to you upon this here wery subject; arter actiwally seein' and bein' in the company o' your own mother-in-law, vich I should ha' thought wos a moral lesson as no man could never ha' forgotten to his dyin' day! I didn't think you'd ha' done it, Sammy, I didn't think you'd ha' done it!' These reflections were too much for the good old man. He raised Sam's tumbler to his lips and drank off its contents.

'Wot's the matter now?' said Sam.

'Nev'r mind, Sammy,' replied Mr Weller, 'it'll be a wery agonizin' trial to me at my time of life, but I'm pretty tough, that's vun consolation, as the wery old turkey remarked wen the farmer said he wos afeerd he should be obliged to kill him for the London market.'

'Wot'll be a trial?' inquired Sam.

'To see you married, Sammy – to see you a dilluded wictim, and thinkin' in your innocence that it's all wery capital,' replied Mr Weller, 'It's a dreadful trial to a father's feelin's, that 'ere, Sammy.'

'Nonsense,' said Sam. 'I ain't a goin' to get married, don't you fret yourself about that; I know you're a judge of these things. Order in your pipe, and I'll read you the letter. There!'

We cannot distinctly say whether it was the prospect of the pipe, or the consolatory reflection that a fatal disposition to get married ran in the family and couldn't be helped, which calmed Mr Weller's feelings, and caused his grief to subside. We should be rather disposed to say that the result was attained by combining the two sources of consolation, for he repeated the second in a low tone, very frequently; ringing the bell meanwhile, to order in the first. He then divested himself of his upper coat; and lighting the pipe and placing himself in front of the fire with his back towards it, so that he could feel its full heat, and recline against the mantelpiece at the same time, turned towards Sam, and, with a countenance greatly mollified by the softening influence of tobacco, requested him to 'fire away.'

Sam dipped his pen into the ink to be ready for any corrections, and began with a very theatrical air:

'"Lovely—."'

'Stop,' said Mr Weller, ringing the bell. 'A double glass o' the inwariable, my dear.'

'Very well, sir,' replied the girl; who with great quickness appeared, vanished, returned, and disappeared.

'They seem to know your ways here,' observed Sam.

'Yes,' replied his father, 'I've been here before, in my time. Go on, Sammy.'

'"Lovely creetur,"' repeated Sam.

' 'Tain't in poetry, is it?' interposed his father.

'No, no,' replied Sam.

'Werry glad to hear it,' said Mr Weller. 'Poetry's unnat'ral; no man ever talked poetry 'cept a beadle on boxin' day, or Warren's blackin', or Rowland's oil,[7] or some o' them low fellows; never you let yourself down to talk poetry, my boy. Begin agin, Sammy.'

Mr Weller resumed his pipe with critical solemnity, and Sam once more commenced, and read as follows.

'"Lovely creetur i feel myself a dammed" – .'

'That ain't proper,' said Mr Weller, taking his pipe from his mouth.

'No; it ain't "dammed",' observed Sam, holding the letter up to the light, 'it's "shamed," there's a blot there – "I feel myself ashamed."'

'Werry good,' said Mr Weller. 'Go on.'

'"Feel myself ashamed, and completely cir – " I forget what this here word is,' said Sam, scratching his head with the pen, in vain attempts to remember.

'Why don't you look at it, then?' inquired Mr Weller.

'So I *am* a lookin' at it,' replied Sam, 'but there's another blot. Here's a "c," and a "i," and a "d."'

'Circumwented, p'haps,' suggested Mr Weller.

'No, it ain't that,' said Sam, 'circumscribed; that's it.'

'That ain't as good a word as circumwented, Sammy,' said Mr Weller, gravely.

'Think not?' said Sam.

'Nothin' like it,' replied his father.

'But don't you think it means more?' inquired Sam.

'Vell p'raps it is a more tenderer word,' said Mr Weller, after a few moments' reflection. 'Go on, Sammy.'

The Valentine

'"Feel myself ashamed and completely circumscribed in a dressin'
of you, for you *are* a nice gal and nothin' but it."'

'That's a werry pretty sentiment,' said the elder Mr Weller,
removing his pipe to make way for the remark.

'Yes, I think it is rayther good,' observed Sam, highly flattered.

'Wot I like in that 'ere style of writin',' said the elder Mr Weller,
'is, that there ain't no callin' names in it, – no Wenuses, nor nothin'
o' that kind. Wot's the good o' callin' a young 'ooman a Wenus or
a angel, Sammy?'

'Ah! what, indeed?' replied Sam.

'You might jist as well call her a griffin, or a unicorn, or a king's
arms at once, which is werry well known to be a col-lection o'
fabulous animals,' added Mr Weller.

'Just as well,' replied Sam.

'Drive on, Sammy,' said Mr Weller.

Sam complied with the request, and proceeded as follows; his
father continuing to smoke, with a mixed expression of wisdom
and complacency, which was particularly edifying.

'"Afore I see you, I thought all women was alike."'

'So they are,' observed the elder Mr Weller, parenthetically.

'"But now," continued Sam, "now I find what a reg'lar soft-
headed, ink-red'lous turnip I must ha' been; for there ain't nobody
like you, though *I* like you better than nothin' at all." I thought it
best to make that rayther strong,' said Sam, looking up.

Mr Weller nodded approvingly, and Sam resumed.

'"So I take the privilidge of the day, Mary, my dear – as the
gen'l'm'n in difficulties did, ven he valked out of a Sunday, – to tell
you that the first and only time I see you, your likeness was took on
my hart in much quicker time and brighter colours than ever a
likeness was took by the profeel macheen[8] (wich p'raps you may
have heerd on Mary my dear) altho it *does* finish a portrait and put
the frame and glass on complete, with a hook at the end to hang it
up by, and all in two minutes and a quarter."'

'I am afeerd that werges on the poetical, Sammy,' said Mr Weller,
dubiously.

'No it don't,' replied Sam, reading on very quickly, to avoid
contesting the point:

'"Except of me Mary my dear as your walentine and think over
what I've said. – My dear Mary I will now conclude." That's all,'
said Sam.

'That's rather a sudden pull up, ain't it, Sammy?' inquired Mr
Weller.

'Not a bit on it,' said Sam; 'she'll vish there wos more, and that's the great art o'letter writin'.'

'Well,' said Mr Weller, 'there's somethin' in that; and I wish your mother-in-law'ud only conduct her conwersation on the same genteel principle. Ain't you a goin' to sign it?'

'That's the difficulty,' said Sam; 'I don't know what *to* sign it.'

'Sign it, Veller,' said the oldest surviving proprietor of that name.

'Won't do,' said Sam. 'Never sign a walentine with your own name.'

'Sign it "Pickvick," then,' said Mr Weller; 'it's a werry good name, and a easy one to spell.'

'The wery thing,' said Sam. 'I *could* end with a werse; what do you think?'

'I don't like it, Sam,' rejoined Mr Weller. 'I never know'd a respectable coachman as wrote poetry, 'cept one, as made an affectin' copy o' werses the night afore he wos hung for a highway robbery; and *he* wos only a Cambervell man, so even that's no rule.'

But Sam was not to be dissuaded from the poetical idea that had occurred to him, so he signed the letter,

> Your love-sick
> Pickwick.'

And having folded it, in a very intricate manner, squeezed a down-hill direction in one corner: 'To Mary, Housemaid, at Mr Nupkins's Mayor's, Ipswich, Suffolk;' and put it into his pocket, wafered, and ready for the General Post. This important business having been transacted, Mr Weller the elder proceeded to open that, on which he had summoned his son.

'The first matter relates to your governor, Sammy,' said Mr Weller. 'He's a goin' to be tried to-morrow, ain't he?'

'The trial's a comin' on,' replied Sam.

'Vell,' said Mr Weller, 'Now I s'pose he'll want to call some witnesses to speak to his character, or p'haps to prove a alleybi. I've been a turnin' the bis'ness over in my mind, and he may make hisself easy, Sammy. I've got some friends as'll do either for him, but my adwice 'ud be this here – never mind the character, and stick to the alleybi. Nothing like a alleybi, Sammy, nothing.' Mr Weller looked very profound as he delivered this legal opinion; and burying his nose in his tumbler, winked over the top thereof, at his astonished son.

'Why, what do you mean?' said Sam; 'you don't think he's a goin' to be tried at the Old Bailey, do you?'

'That ain't no part of the present con-sideration, Sammy,' replied Mr Weller. 'Verever he's a goin' to be tried, my boy, a alleybi's the thing to get him off. Ve got Tom Vildspark off that 'ere manslaughter, with a alleybi, ven all the big vigs to a man said as nothing couldn't save him. And my 'pinion is, Sammy, that if your governor don't prove a alleybi, he'll be what the Italians call reg'larly flummoxed, and that's all about it.'

As the elder Mr Weller entertained a firm and unalterable conviction that the Old Bailey was the supreme court of judicature in this country, and that its rules and forms of proceeding regulated and controlled the practice of all other courts of justice whatsoever, he totally disregarded the assurances and arguments of his son, tending to show that the alibi was inadmissible; and vehemently protested that Mr Pickwick was being 'wictimised.' Finding that it was of no use to discuss the matter further, Sam changed the subject, and inquired what the second topic was, on which his revered parent wished to consult him.

'That's a pint o' domestic policy, Sammy,' said Mr Weller. 'This here Stiggins – '

'Red-nosed man?' inquired Sam.

'The wery same,' replied Mr Weller. 'This here red-nosed man, Sammy, wisits your mother-in-law vith a kindness and constancy as I never see equalled. He's sitch a friend o' the family, Sammy, that wen he's away from us, he can't be comfortable unless he has somethin' to remember us by.'

'And I'd give him somethin' as 'ud turpentine and bees'-vax[9] his memory for the next ten years or so, if I wos you,' interposed Sam.

'Stop a minute,' said Mr Weller; 'I wos a going to say, he always brings now, a flat bottle as holds about a pint and a-half, and fills it vith the pine-apple rum afore he goes avay.'

'And empties it afore he comes back, I s'pose?' said Sam.

'Clean!' replied Mr Weller; 'never leaves nothin' in it but the cork and the smell; trust him for that, Sammy. Now, these here fellows, my boy, are a goin' to-night to get up the monthly meetin' o' the Brick Lane Branch o' the United Grand Junction Ebenezer Temperance Association. Your mother-in-law *wos* a goin', Sammy, but she's got the rheumatics, and can't; and I, Sammy – I've got the two tickets as wos sent her.' Mr Weller communicated this secret with great glee, and winked so indefatigably after doing so, that Sam began to think he must have got the *tic douloureux*[10] in his right eye-lid.

'Well?' said that young gentleman.

'Well,' continued his progenitor, looking round him very cautiously, 'you and I'll go, punctiwal to the time. The deputy shepherd won't, Sammy; the deputy shepherd won't.' Here Mr Weller was seized with a paroxysm of chuckles, which gradually terminated in as near an approach to a choke as an elderly gentleman can, with safety, sustain.

'Well, I never see sitch an old ghost in all my born days,' exclaimed Sam, rubbing the old gentleman's back, hard enough to set him on fire with the friction. 'What are you a laughin' at, corpilence?'[11]

'Hush! Sammy,' said Mr Weller, looking round him with increased caution, and speaking in a whisper: 'Two friends o' mine, as works the Oxford Road, and is up to all kinds o' games, has got the deputy shepherd safe in tow, Sammy; and ven he does come to the Ebenezer Junction, (vich he's sure to do: for they'll see him to the door, and shove him in if necessary) he'll be as far gone in rum and water, as ever he wos at the Markis o' Granby, Dorkin', and that's not sayin' a little neither.' And with this, Mr Weller once more laughed immoderately, and once more relapsed into a state of partial suffocation, in consequence.

Nothing could have been more in accordance with Sam Weller's feelings, than the projected exposure of the real propensities and qualities of the red-nosed man; and it being very near the appointed hour of meeting, the father and son took their way at once to Brick Lane: Sam not forgetting to drop his letter into a general post-office as they walked along.

The monthly meetings of the Brick Lane Branch of the United Grand Junction Ebenezer Temperance Association, were held in a large room, pleasantly and airily situated at the top of a safe and commodious ladder. The president was the straight-walking Mr Anthony Humm, a converted fireman, now a schoolmaster, and occasionally an itinerant preacher; and the secretary was Mr Jonas Mudge, chandler's shop-keeper, an enthusiastic and disinterested vessel, who sold tea to the members. Previous to the commencement of business, the ladies sat upon forms, and drank tea, till such time as they considered it expedient to leave off; and a large wooden money-box was conspicuously placed upon the green baize cloth of the business table, behind which the secretary stood, and acknowledged, with a gracious smile, every addition to the rich vein of copper which lay concealed within.

On this particular occasion the women drank tea to a most alarming extent; greatly to the horror of Mr Weller senior, who, utterly regardless of all Sam's admonitory nudgings, stared about him in every direction with the most undisguised astonishment.

'Sammy,' whispered Mr Weller, 'if some o' these here people don't want tappin' to-morrow mornin', I ain't your father, and that's wot it is. Why, this here old lady next me is a drowndin' herself in tea.'

'Be quiet, can't you?' murmured Sam.

'Sam,' whispered Mr Weller, a moment afterwards, in a tone of deep agitation, 'mark my vords, my boy. If that 'ere secretary fellow keeps on for only five minutes more, he'll blow hisself up with toast and water.'

'Well, let him, if he likes,' replied Sam; 'it ain't no bis'ness o' yourn.'

'If this here lasts much longer, Sammy,' said Mr Weller, in the same low voice, 'I shall feel it my duty, as a human bein', to rise and address the cheer. There's a young 'ooman on the next form but two, as has drunk nine breakfast cups and a half; and she's a swellin' wisibly before my wery eyes.'

There is little doubt that Mr Weller would have carried his benevolent intention into immediate execution, if a great noise, occasioned by putting up the cups and saucers, had not very fortunately announced that the tea-drinking was over. The crockery having been removed, the table with the green baize cover was carried out into the centre of the room, and the business of the evening was commenced by a little emphatic man, with a bald head, and drab shorts, who suddenly rushed up the ladder, at the imminent peril of snapping the two little legs encased in the drab shorts, and said:

'Ladies and gentlemen, I move our excellent brother, Mr Anthony Humm, into the chair.'

The ladies waved a choice collection of pocket handkerchiefs at this proposition; and the impetuous little man literally moved Mr Humm into the chair, by taking him by the shoulders and thrusting him into a mahogany-frame which had once represented that article of furniture. The waving of handkerchiefs was renewed; and Mr Humm, who was a sleek, white-faced man, in a perpetual perspiration, bowed meekly, to the great admiration of the females, and formally took his seat. Silence was then proclaimed by the little man in the drab shorts, and Mr Humm rose and said – That, with the permission of his Brick Lane Branch brothers and sisters, then and there present, the secretary would read the report of the Brick Lane Branch committee; a proposition which was again received with a demonstration of pocket-handkerchiefs.

The secretary having sneezed in a very impressive manner, and the cough which always seizes an assembly, when anything particular is going to be done, having been duly performed, the following document was read:

'REPORT OF THE COMMITTEE OF THE BRICK LANE
BRANCH OF THE UNITED GRAND JUNCTION EBENEZER
TEMPERANCE ASSOCIATION

'Your committee have pursued their grateful labours during the past month, and have the unspeakable pleasure of reporting the following additional cases of converts to Temperance.

'H. Walker, tailor, wife, and two children. When in better circumstances, owns to having been in the constant habit of drinking ale and beer; says he is not certain whether he did not twice a week, for twenty years, taste "dog's nose," which your committee find upon inquiry, to be compounded of warm porter, moist sugar, gin, and nutmeg (a groan, and "So it is!" from an elderly female.) Is now out of work and pennyless; thinks it must be the porter (cheers) or the loss of the use of his right hand; is not certain which, but thinks it very likely that, if he had drank nothing but water all his life, his fellow work-man would never have stuck a rusty needle in him, and thereby occasioned his accident (tremendous cheering). Has nothing but cold water to drink, and never feels thirsty (great applause).

'Betsy Martin, widow, one child, and one eye. Goes out charing and washing, by the day; never had more than one eye, but knows her mother drank bottled stout, and shouldn't wonder if that caused it (immense cheering). Thinks it not impossible that if she had always abstained from spirits, she might have had two eyes by this time (tremendous applause). Used, at every place she went to, to have eighteen pence a day, a pint of porter, and a glass of spirits; but since she became a member of the Brick Lane Branch, has always demanded three and sixpence instead (the announcement of this most interesting fact was received with deafening enthusiasm).

'Henry Beller was for many years toast-master at various corporation dinners, during which time he drank a great deal of foreign wine; may sometimes have carried a bottle or two home with him;

is not quite certain of that, but is sure if he did, that he drank the contents. Feels very low and melancholy, is very feverish, and has a constant thirst upon him; thinks it must be the wine he used to drink (cheers). Is out of employ now: and never touches a drop of foreign wine by any chance (tremendous plaudits).

'Thomas Burton[12] is purveyor of cat's meat to the Lord Mayor and Sheriffs, and several members of the Common Council (the announcement of this gentleman's name was received with breathless interest). Has a wooden leg; finds a wooden leg expensive, going over the stones; used to wear second-hand wooden legs, and drink a glass of hot gin and water regularly every night – sometimes two (deep sighs). Found the second-hand wooden legs split and rot very quickly; is firmly persuaded that their constitution was undermined by the gin and water (prolonged cheering). Buys new wooden legs now, and drinks nothing but water and weak tea. The new legs last twice as long as the others used to do, and he attributes this solely to his temperate habits (triumphant cheers).'

Anthony Humm now moved that the assembly do regale itself with a song. With a view to their rational and moral enjoyment, brother Mordlin had adapted the beautiful words of 'Who hasn't heard of a Jolly Young Waterman?' to the tune of the Old Hundredth, which he would request them to join him in singing (great applause). He might take that opportunity of expressing his firm persuasion that the late Mr Dibdin,[13] seeing the errors of his former life, had written that song to show the advantages of abstinence. It was a temperance song (whirlwinds of cheers). The neatness of the young man's attire, the dexterity of his feathering, the enviable state of mind which enabled him in the beautiful words of the poet, to

'Row along, thinking of nothing at all,'

all combined to prove that he must have been a water-drinker (cheers). Oh, what a state of virtuous jollity! (rapturous cheering.) And what was the young man's reward? Let all young men present mark this:

'The maidens all flock'd to his boat so readily.'

(Loud cheers, in which the ladies joined.) What a bright example! The sisterhood, the maidens, flocking round the young waterman, and urging him along the stream of duty and of temperance. But, was it the maidens of humble life only, who soothed, consoled, and supported him? No!

'He was always first oars with the fine city ladies.'

(immense cheering.) The soft sex to a man – he begged pardon, to a female – rallied round the young waterman, and turned with disgust from the drinker of spirits (cheers). The Brick Lane Branch brothers were watermen (cheers and laughter). That room was their boat; that audience were the maidens; and he (Mr Anthony Humm), however unworthily, was 'first oars' (unbounded applause).

'Wot does he mean by the soft sex, Sammy?' inquired Mr Weller, in a whisper.

'The womin,' said Sam, in the same tone.

'He ain't far out there, Sammy,' replied Mr Weller; 'they *must* be a soft sex, – a wery soft sex, indeed – if they let themselves be gammoned by such fellers as him.'

Any further observations from the indignant old gentleman were cut short by the announcement of the song, which Mr Anthony Humm gave out, two lines at a time, for the information of such of his hearers as were unacquainted with the legend. While it was being sung, the little man with the drab shorts disappeared; he returned immediately on its conclusion, and whispered Mr Anthony Humm, with a face of the deepest importance.

'My friends,' said Mr Humm, holding up his hand in a deprecatory manner, to bespeak the silence of such of the stout old ladies as were yet a line or two behind; 'my friends, a delegate from the Dorking branch of our society, Brother Stiggins, attends below.'

Out came the pocket-handkerchiefs again, in greater force than ever; for Mr Stiggins was excessively popular among the female constituency of Brick Lane.

'He may approach, I think,' said Mr Humm, looking round him, with a fat smile. 'Brother Tadger, let him come forth and greet us.'

The little man in the drab shorts who answered to the name of Brother Tadger, bustled down the ladder with great speed, and was immediately afterwards heard tumbling up with the reverend Mr Stiggins.

'He's a comin', Sammy,' whispered Mr Weller, purple in the countenance with suppressed laughter.

'Don't say nothin' to me,' replied Sam, 'for I can't bear it. He's close to the door. I heard him a-knockin' his head again the lath and plaster[14] now.'

As Sam Weller spoke, the little door flew open, and brother Tadger appeared, closely followed by the reverend Mr Stiggins, who no sooner entered, than there was a great clapping of hands, and stamping of feet, and flourishing of handkerchiefs; to all of which manifestations of delight, Brother Stiggins returned no other acknowledgment than staring with a wild eye, and a fixed smile, at the extreme top of the wick of the candle on the table: swaying his body to and fro, meanwhile, in a very unsteady and uncertain manner.

'Are you unwell, brother Stiggins?' whispered Mr Anthony Humm.

'I am all right, sir,' replied Mr Stiggins, in a tone in which ferocity was blended with an extreme thickness of utterance; 'I am all right, sir.'

'Oh, very well,' rejoined Mr Anthony Humm, retreating a few paces.

'I believe no man here, has ventured to say that I am *not* all right, sir?' said Mr Stiggins.

'Oh, certainly not,' said Mr Humm.

'I should advise him not to, sir; I should advise him not,' said Mr Stiggins.

By this time the audience were perfectly silent, and waited with some anxiety for the resumption of business.

'Will you address the meeting brother?' said Mr Humm, with a smile of invitation.

'No, sir,' rejoined Mr Stiggins; 'No, sir. I will not, sir.'

The meeting looked at each other with raised eye-lids; and a murmur of astonishment ran through the room.

'It's my opinion, sir,' said Mr Stiggins, unbuttoning his coat, and speaking very loudly; 'it's my opinion, sir, that this meeting is drunk, sir. Brother Tadger, sir!' said Mr Stiggins, suddenly increasing in ferocity, and turning sharp round on the little man in the drab shorts, '*you* are drunk, sir!' With this, Mr Stiggins, entertaining a praiseworthy desire to promote the sobriety of the meeting, and to exclude therefrom all improper characters, hit brother Tadger on the summit of the nose with such unerring aim, that the drab shorts disappeared like a flash of lightning. Brother Tadger had been knocked, head first, down the ladder.

Upon this, the women set up a loud and dismal screaming; and rushing in small parties before their favourite brothers, flung their arms around them to preserve them from danger. An instance of affection, which had nearly proved fatal to Humm, who, being extremely popular, was all but suffocated, by the crowd of female devotees that hung about his neck, and heaped caresses upon him.

The greater part of the lights were quickly put out, and nothing but noise and confusion resounded on all sides.

'Now Sammy,' said Mr Weller, taking off his great coat with much deliberation, 'just you step out, and fetch in a watchman.'

'And wot are you a goin' to do, the while?' inquired Sam.

'Never you mind me, Sammy,' replied the old gentleman; 'I shall ockipy myself in havin' a small settlement with that 'ere Stiggins.' Before Sam could interfere to prevent it, his heroic parent had penetrated into a remote corner of the room, and attacked the reverend Mr Stiggins with manual dexterity.

'Come off!' said Sam.

'Come on!' cried Mr Weller; and without further invitation he gave the reverend Mr Stiggins a preliminary tap on the head, and began dancing round him in a buoyant and cork-like manner, which in a gentleman at his time of life was a perfect marvel to behold.

Finding all remonstrance unavailing, Sam pulled his hat firmly on, threw his father's coat over his arm, and taking the old man round the waist, forcibly dragged him down the ladder, and into the street; never releasing his hold, or permitting him to stop, until they reached the corner. As they gained it, they could hear the shouts of the populace, who were witnessing the removal of the reverend Mr Stiggins to strong lodgings for the night: and could hear the noise occasioned by the dispersion in various directions of the members of the Brick Lane Branch of the United Grand Junction Ebenezer Temperance Association.

CHAPTER 34

Is wholly devoted to a full and faithful Report of the memorable Trial[1] of Bardell against Pickwick

'I wonder what the foreman of the jury, whoever he'll be, has got for breakfast' said Mr Snodgrass, by way of keeping up a conversation on the eventful morning of the fourteenth of February.

'Ah!' said Perker, 'I hope he's got a good one.'

'Why so?' inquired Mr Pickwick.

'Highly important; very important, my dear sir,' replied Perker. 'A good, contented, well-breakfasted juryman, is a capital thing to get hold of. Discontented or hungry jurymen, my dear sir, always find for the plaintiff.'

'Bless my heart,' said Mr Pickwick, looking very blank; 'what do they do that for?'

'Why, I don't know,' replied the little man, coolly; 'saves time, I suppose. If it's near dinner-time, the foreman takes out his watch when the jury has retired, and says, "Dear me, gentlemen, ten minutes to five, I declare! I dine at five, gentlemen." "So do I," says every body else, except two men who ought to have dined at three, and seem more than half disposed to stand out in consequence. The foreman smiles, and puts up his watch: – "Well, gentlemen, what do we say, plaintiff or defendant, gentlemen? I rather think, so far as I am concerned, gentlemen, – I say, I rather think, – but don't let that influence you – I *rather* think the plaintiff's the man." Upon this, two or three other men are sure to say that they think so too – as of course they do; and then they get on very unanimously and comfortably. Ten minutes past nine!' said the little man, looking at his watch. 'Time we were off, my dear sir; breach of promise trial – court is generally full in such cases. You had better ring for a coach, my dear sir, or we shall be rather late.'

Mr Pickwick immediately rang the bell; and a coach having been procured, the four Pickwickians and Mr Perker ensconced themselves therein, and drove to Guildhall;[2] Sam Weller, Mr Lowten, and the blue bag,[3] following in a cab.

'Lowten,' said Perker, when they reached the outer hall of the court, 'put Mr Pickwick's friends in the students' box;[4] Mr Pickwick himself had better sit by me. This way, my dear sir, this way.' Taking Mr Pickwick by the coat-sleeve, the little man led him to the low seat just beneath the desks of the King's Counsel, which is constructed for the convenience of attorneys, who from that spot can whisper into the ear of the leading counsel in the case, any instructions that may be necessary during the progress of the trial. The occupants of this seat are invisible to the great body of spectators, inasmuch as they sit on a much lower level than either the barristers or the audience, whose seats are raised above the floor. Of course they have their backs to both, and their faces towards the judge.

'That's the witness-box, I suppose?' said Mr Pickwick, pointing to a kind of pulpit, with a brass rail, on his left hand.

'That's the witness-box, my dear sir,' replied Perker, disinterring a quantity of papers from the blue bag, which Lowten had just deposited at his feet.

'And that,' said Mr Pickwick, pointing to a couple of enclosed seats on his right, 'that's where the jurymen sit, is it not?'

'The identical place, my dear sir,' replied Perker, tapping the lid of his snuff-box.

Mr Pickwick stood up in a state of great agitation, and took a glance at the court. There were already a pretty large sprinkling of spectators in the gallery, and a numerous muster of gentlemen in wigs, in the barristers' seats: who presented, as a body, all that pleasing and extensive variety of nose and whisker for which the bar of England is so justly celebrated. Such of the gentlemen as had a brief to carry, carried it in as conspicuous a manner as possible, and occasionally scratched their noses therewith, to impress the fact more strongly on the observation of the spectators. Other gentlemen, who had no briefs to show, carried under their arms goodly octavos, with a red label behind, and that underdone-pie-crust-coloured cover, which is technically known as 'law calf.' Others, who had neither briefs nor books, thrust their hands into their pockets, and looked as wise as they conveniently could; others, again, moved here and there with great restlessness and earnestness of manner, content to awaken thereby the admiration and astonishment of the uninitiated strangers. The whole, to the great wonderment of Mr Pickwick, were divided into little groups, who were chatting and discussing the news of the day in the most unfeeling manner possible, – just as if no trial at all were coming on.

A bow from Mr Phunky, as he entered, and took his seat behind the row appropriated to the King's Counsel, attracted Mr Pickwick's attention; and he had scarcely returned it, when Mr Serjeant Snubbin appeared, followed by Mr Mallard, who half hid the Serjeant behind a large crimson bag which he placed on his table, and, after shaking hands with Perker, withdrew. Then there entered two or three more Serjeants; and among them, one with a fat body and a red face, who nodded in a friendly manner to Mr Serjeant Snubbin, and said it was a fine morning.

'Who's that red-faced man, who said it was a fine morning, and nodded to our counsel?' whispered Mr Pickwick.

'Mr Serjeant Buzfuz,' replied Perker. 'He's opposed to us; he leads on the other side. That gentleman behind him is Mr Skimpin, his junior.'

Mr Pickwick was on the point of inquiring, with great abhorrence of the man's cold-blooded villany, how Mr Serjeant Buzfuz, who was counsel for the opposite party, dared to presume to tell Mr Serjeant Snubbin, who was counsel for him, that it was a fine morning, when he was interrupted by a general rising of the barristers, and a loud cry of 'Silence!' from the officers of the court.

Looking round, he found that this was caused by the entrance of
the judge.

Mr Justice Stareleigh (who sat in the absence of the Chief Justice,
occasioned by indisposition,) was a most particularly short man,
and so fat, that he seemed all face and waistcoat. He rolled in, upon
two little turned legs, and having bobbed gravely to the bar, who
bobbed gravely to him, put his little legs underneath his table and
his little three-cornered hat upon it; and when Mr Justice Stareleigh
had done this, all you could see of him was two queer little eyes,
one broad pink face and somewhere about half of a big and very
comical-looking wig.

The judge had no sooner taken his seat, than the officer on the
floor of the court called out 'Silence!' in a commanding tone, upon
which another officer in the gallery cried 'Silence!' in an angry
manner, whereupon three or four more ushers shouted 'Silence!' in
a voice of indignant remonstrance. This being done, a gentleman in
black, who sat below the judge, proceeded to call over the names of
the jury; and after a great deal of bawling, it was discovered that
only ten special jurymen were present. Upon this, Mr Sergeant
Buzfuz prayed a *tales*;[5] the gentleman in black then proceeded to
press into the special jury, two of the common jurymen; and a
green-grocer and a chemist were caught directly.

'Answer to your names, gentlemen, that you may be sworn,' said
the gentleman in black. 'Richard Upwitch.'

'Here,' said the green-grocer.

'Thomas Groffin.'

'Here,' said the chemist.

'Take the book, gentlemen. You shall well and truly try – '

'I beg this court's pardon,' said the chemist, who was a tall, thin,
yellow-visaged man, 'but I hope this court will excuse my
attendance.'

'On what grounds, sir?' said Mr Justice Stareleigh.

'I have no assistant, my Lord,' said the chemist.

'I can't help that, sir,' replied Mr Justice Stareleigh. 'You should
hire one.'

'I can't afford it, my Lord,' rejoined the chemist.

'Then you ought to be able to afford it, sir,' said the judge,
reddening; for Mr Justice Stareleigh's temper bordered on the
irritable, and brooked not contradiction.

'I know I *ought* to do, if I got on as well as I deserved, but I
don't, my Lord,' answered the chemist.

'Swear the gentleman,' said the judge, peremptorily.

The officer had got no further than the 'You shall well and truly try,' when he was again interrupted by the chemist.

'I am to be sworn, my Lord, am I?' said the chemist.

'Certainly, sir,' replied the testy little judge.

'Very well, my Lord,' replied the chemist, in a resigned manner. 'Then there'll be murder before this trial's over; that's all. Swear me, if you please, sir;' and sworn the chemist was, before the judge could find words to utter.

'I merely wanted to observe, my Lord,' said the chemist, taking his seat with great deliberation, 'that I've left nobody but an errand-boy in my shop. He is a very nice boy, my Lord, but he is not acquainted with drugs; and I know that the prevailing impression on his mind is, that Epsom salts means oxalic acid; and syrup of senna, laudanum.[6] That's all, my Lord.' With this, the tall chemist composed himself into a comfortable attitude, and, assuming a pleasant expression of countenance, appeared to have prepared himself for the worst.

Mr Pickwick was regarding the chemist with feelings of the deepest horror, when a slight sensation was perceptible in the body of the court; and immediately afterwards Mrs Bardell, supported by Mrs Cluppins, was led in, and placed, in a drooping state, at the other end of the seat on which Mr Pickwick sat. An extra sized umbrella was then handed in by Mr Dodson, and a pair of pattens by Mr Fogg, each of whom had prepared a most sympathising and melancholy face for the occasion. Mrs Sanders then appeared, leading in Master Bardell. At sight of her child, Mrs Bardell started; suddenly recollecting herself, she kissed him in a frantic manner; then relapsing into a state of hysterical imbecility, the good lady requested to be informed where she was. In reply to this, Mrs Cluppins and Mrs Sanders turned their heads away and wept, while Messrs. Dodson and Fogg intreated the plaintiff to compose herself. Serjeant Buzfuz rubbed his eyes very hard with a large white handkerchief, and gave an appealing look towards the jury, while the judge was visibly affected, and several of the beholders tried to cough down their emotions.

'Very good notion that, indeed,' whispered Perker to Mr Pickwick. 'Capital fellows those Dodson and Fogg; excellent ideas of effect, my dear sir, excellent.'

As Perker spoke, Mrs Bardell began to recover by slow degrees, while Mrs Cluppins, after a careful survey of Master Bardell's buttons and the button-holes to which they severally belonged, placed him on the floor of the court in front of his mother, – a

The Trial

commanding position in which he could not fail to awaken the full commiseration and sympathy of both judge and jury. This was not done without considerable opposition, and many tears, on the part of the young gentleman himself, who had certain inward misgivings that the placing him within the full glare of the judge's eye was only a formal prelude to his being immediately ordered away for instant execution, or for transportation beyond the seas, during the whole term of his natural life, at the very least.

'Bardell and Pickwick,' cried the gentleman in black, calling on the case, which stood first on the list.

'I am for the plaintiff, my Lord,' said Mr Serjeant Buzfuz.

'Who is with you, brother Buzfuz?' said the judge. Mr Skimpin bowed, to intimate that he was.

'I appear for the defendant, my Lord,' said Mr Serjeant Snubbin.

'Anybody with you, brother Snubbin?' inquired the court.

'Mr Phunky, my Lord,' replied Serjeant Snubbin.

'Serjeant Buzfuz and Mr Skimpin for the plaintiff,' said the judge, writing down the names in his note-book, and reading as he wrote; 'for the defendant, Serjeant Snubbin and Mr Monkey.'

'Beg your Lordship's pardon, Phunky.'

'Oh, very good,' said the judge; 'I never had the pleasure of hearing the gentleman's name before.' Here Mr Phunky bowed and smiled, and the judge bowed and smiled too, and then Mr Phunky, blushing into the very whites of his eyes, tried to look as if he didn't know that everybody was gazing at him: a thing which no man ever succeeded in doing yet, or in all reasonable probability, ever will.

'Go on,' said the judge.

The ushers again called silence, and Mr Skimpin proceeded to 'open the case;' and the case appeared to have very little inside it when he had opened it, for he kept such particulars as he knew, completely to himself, and sat down, after a lapse of three minutes, leaving the jury in precisely the same advanced stage of wisdom as they were in before.

Serjeant Buzfuz then rose with all the majesty and dignity which the grave nature of the proceedings demanded, and having whispered to Dodson, and conferred briefly with Fogg, pulled his gown over his shoulders, settled his wig, and addressed the jury.

Serjeant Buzfuz began by saying, that never, in the whole course of his professional experience – never, from the very first moment of his applying himself to the study and practice of the law – had he approached a case with feelings of such deep emotion, or with such a heavy sense of the responsibility imposed upon him – a responsibility, he would say, which he could never have supported, were he not buoyed up and sustained by a conviction so strong, that it amounted to positive certainty that the cause of truth and justice, or, in other words, the cause of his much-injured and most oppressed client, must prevail with the high-minded and intelligent dozen of men whom he now saw in that box before him.

Counsel usually begin in this way, because it puts the jury on the very best terms with themselves, and makes them think what sharp fellows they must be. A visible effect was produced immediately; several jurymen beginning to take voluminous notes with the utmost eagerness.

'You have heard from my learned friend, gentlemen,' continued Serjeant Buzfuz, well knowing that, from the learned friend alluded to, the gentlemen of the jury had heard just nothing at all – 'you have heard from my learned friend, gentlemen, that this is an action for a breach of promise of marriage, in which the damages are laid at £1,500. But you have not heard from my learned friend, inasmuch as it did not come within my learned friend's province to tell you, what are the facts and circumstances of the case. Those facts and circumstances, gentlemen, you shall hear detailed by me, and proved by the unimpeachable female whom I will place in that box before you.'

Here Mr Serjeant Buzfuz, with a tremendous emphasis on the word 'box,' smote his table with a mighty sound, and glanced at Dodson and Fogg, who nodded admiration of the serjeant, and indignant defiance of the defendant.

'The plaintiff, gentlemen,' continued Serjeant Buzfuz, in a soft and melancholy voice, 'the plaintiff is a widow; yes, gentlemen, a widow. The late Mr Bardell, after enjoying, for many years, the esteem and confidence of his sovereign, as one of the guardians of his royal revenues, glided almost imperceptibly from the world, to seek elsewhere for that repose and peace which a custom-house can never afford.'

At this pathetic description of the decease of Mr Bardell, who had been knocked on the head with a quart-pot in a public-house cellar, the learned serjeant's voice faltered, and he proceeded with emotion:

'Some time before his death, he had stamped his likeness upon a little boy. With this little boy, the only pledge of her departed exciseman, Mrs Bardell shrunk from the world, and courted the retirement and tranquillity of Goswell Street; and here she placed in her front parlour-window a written placard, bearing this inscription

– "Apartments furnished for a single gentleman. Inquire within."'
Here Serjeant Buzfuz paused, while several gentlemen of the jury
took a note of the document.

'There is no date to that, is there, sir?' inquired a juror.

'There is no date, gentlemen,' replied Serjeant Buzfuz; 'but I am
instructed to say that it was put in the plaintiff's parlour-window
just this time three years. I intreat the attention of the jury to the
wording of this document. "Apartments furnished for a single
gentleman"! Mrs Bardell's opinions of the opposite sex, gentlemen,
were derived from a long contemplation of the inestimable qualities
of her lost husband. She had no fear, she had no distrust, she had
no suspicion, all was confidence and reliance. "Mr Bardell," said
the widow; "Mr Bardell was a man of honour, Mr Bardell was a
man of his word, Mr Bardell was no deceiver, Mr Bardell was once
a single gentleman himself; to single gentlemen I look for protection,
for assistance, for comfort, and for consolation; in single gentlemen
I shall perpetually see something to remind me of what Mr Bardell
was, when he first won my young and untried affections; to a single
gentleman, then, shall my lodgings be let." Actuated by this
beautiful and touching impulse (among the best impulses of our
imperfect nature, gentlemen,) the lonely and desolate widow dried
her tears, furnished her first floor, caught the innocent boy to her
maternal bosom, and put the bill up in her parlour-window. Did it
remain there long? No. The serpent was on the watch, the train was
laid, the mine was preparing, the sapper and miner was at work.
Before the bill had been in the parlour-window three days – three
days – gentlemen – a Being, erect upon two legs, and bearing all the
outward semblance of a man, and not of a monster, knocked at the
door of Mrs Bardell's house. He inquired within; he took the
lodgings; and on the very next day he entered into possession of
them. This man was Pickwick – Pickwick, the defendant.'

Serjeant Buzfuz, who had proceeded with such volubility that his
face was perfectly crimson, here paused for breath. The silence
awoke Mr Justice Stareleigh, who immediately wrote down something with a pen without any ink in it, and looked unusually
profound, to impress the jury with the belief that he always thought
most deeply with his eyes shut. Serjeant Buzfuz proceeded.

'Of this man Pickwick I will say little; the subject presents but
few attractions; and I, gentlemen, am not the man, nor are you,
gentlemen, the men, to delight in the contemplation of revolting
heartlessness, and of systematic villany.'

Here Mr Pickwick, who had been writhing in silence for some

time, gave a violent start, as if some vague idea of assaulting Serjeant Buzfuz, in the august presence of justice and law, suggested itself to his mind. An admonitory gesture from Perker restrained him, and he listened to the learned gentleman's continuation with a look of indignation, which contrasted forcibly with the admiring faces of Mrs Cluppins and Mrs Sanders.

'I say systematic villany, gentlemen,' said Serjeant Buzfuz, looking through Mr Pickwick, and talking *at* him; 'and when I say systematic villany, let me tell the defendant Pickwick, if he be in court, as I am informed he is, that it would have been more decent in him, more becoming, in better judgment, and in better taste, if he had stopped away. Let me tell him, gentlemen, that any gestures of dissent or disapprobation in which he may indulge in this court will not go down with you; that you will know how to value and how to appreciate them; and let me tell him further, as my lord will tell you, gentlemen, that a counsel, in the discharge of his duty to his client, is neither to be intimidated nor bullied, nor put down; and that any attempt to do either the one or the other, or the first, or the last, will recoil on the head of the attempter, be he plaintiff or be he defendant, be his name Pickwick, or Noakes, or Stoakes, or Stiles, or Brown, or Thompson.'

This little divergence from the subject in hand, had of course, the intended effect of turning all eyes to Mr Pickwick. Sergeant Buzfuz, having partially recovered from the state of moral elevation into which he had lashed himself, resumed:

'I shall show you, gentlemen, that for two years Pickwick continued to reside constantly, and without interruption or intermission, at Mrs Bardell's house. I shall show you that Mrs Bardell, during the whole of that time, waited on him, attended to his comforts, cooked his meals, looked out his linen for the washerwoman when it went abroad, darned, aired, and prepared it for wear, when it came home, and, in short, enjoyed his fullest trust and confidence. I shall show you that, on many occasions, he gave halfpence, and on some occasions even sixpences, to her little boy; and I shall prove to you, by a witness whose testimony it will be impossible for my learned friend to weaken or controvert, that on one occasion he patted the boy on the head, and, after inquiring whether he had won any *alley tors* or *commoneys*[7] lately (both of which I understand to be a particular species of marbles much prized by the youth of this town), made use of this remarkable expression: "How should you like to have another father?" I shall prove to you, gentlemen, that about a year ago, Pickwick suddenly began to absent himself from home, during long intervals, as if with the intention of gradually breaking off from my client; but I shall show you also, that his resolution was not at that time sufficiently strong, or that his better feelings conquered, if better feelings he has, or that the charms and accomplishments of my client prevailed against his unmanly intentions; by proving to you, that on one occasion, when he returned from the country, he distinctly and in terms, offered her marriage: previously however, taking special care that there should be no witness to their solemn contract; and I am in a situation to prove to you, on the testimony of three of his own friends, – most unwilling witnesses, gentlemen – most unwilling witnesses – that on that morning he was discovered by them holding the plaintiff in his arms, and soothing her agitation by his caresses and endearments.'

A visible impression was produced upon the auditors by this part of the learned serjeant's address. Drawing forth two very small scraps of paper, he proceeded:

'And now, gentlemen, but one word more. Two letters have passed between these parties, letters which are admitted to be in the hand-writing of the defendant, and which speak volumes indeed. These letters, too, bespeak the character of the man. They are not open, fervent, eloquent epistles, breathing nothing but the language of affectionate attachment. They are covert, sly, underhanded communications, but, fortunately, far more conclusive than if couched in the most glowing language and the most poetic imagery – letters that must be viewed with a cautious and suspicious eye – letters that were evidently intended at the time, by Pickwick, to mislead and delude any third parties into whose hands they might fall. Let me read the first: – "Garraway's,[8] twelve o'clock. Dear Mrs B. – Chops and Tomata sauce. Yours, PICKWICK. Gentlemen, what does this mean? Chops and Tomata sauce. Yours, Pickwick! Chops! Gracious heavens! and Tomata sauce! Gentlemen, is the happiness of a sensitive and confiding female to be trifled away, by such shallow artifices as these? The next has no date whatever, which is in itself suspicious. "Dear Mrs B., I shall not be at home till to-morrow. Slow coach." And then follows this very remarkable expression. "Don't trouble yourself about the warming-pan."[9] The warming pan! Why, gentlemen, who *does* trouble himself about a warming-pan? When was the peace of mind of man or woman broken or disturbed by a warming-pan, which is in itself a harmless, a useful, and I will add, gentlemen, a comforting article of domestic furniture? Why is Mrs Bardell so earnestly entreated not to agitate

herself about this warming-pan, unless (as is no doubt the case) it is
a mere cover for hidden fire – a mere substitute for some endearing
word or promise, agreeably to a preconcerted system of correspondence, artfully contrived by Pickwick with a view to his contemplated desertion, and which I am not in a condition to explain? And
what does this allusion to the slow coach mean? For aught I know,
it may be a reference to Pickwick himself, who has most unquestionably been a criminally slow coach during the whole of this transaction, but whose speed will now be very unexpectedly accelerated,
and whose wheels, gentlemen, as he will find to his cost, will very
soon be greased by you!'

Mr Serjeant Buzfuz paused in this place, to see whether the jury
smiled at his joke; but as nobody took it but the green-grocer,
whose sensitiveness on the subject was very probably occasioned by
his having subjected a chaise-cart to the process in question on that
identical morning, the learned serjeant considered it advisable to
undergo a slight relapse into the dismals before he concluded.

'But enough of this, gentlemen,' said Mr Serjeant Buzfuz, 'it is
difficult to smile with an aching heart; it is ill jesting when our
deepest sympathies are awakened. My client's hopes and prospects
are ruined, and it is no figure of speech to say that her occupation
is gone indeed. The bill is down – but there is no tenant. Eligible
single gentlemen pass and repass – but there is no invitation for
them to inquire within or without. All is gloom and silence in the
house; even the voice of the child is hushed; his infant sports are
disregarded when his mother weeps; his "alley tors' and his
"commoneys" are alike neglected; he forgets the long familiar cry
of "knuckle down,"[10] and at tip-cheese,[11] or odd and even, his hand
is out. But Pickwick, gentlemen, Pickwick, the ruthless destroyer of
this domestic oasis in the desert of Goswell Street – Pickwick, who
has choked up the well, and thrown ashes on the sward – Pickwick,
who comes before you to-day with his heartless Tomata sauce and
warming-pans – Pickwick still rears his head with unblushing
effrontery, and gazes without a sigh on the ruin he has made.
Damages, gentlemen – heavy damages – is the only punishment
with which you can visit him; the only recompence you can award
to my client. And for those damages she now appeals to an
enlightened, a high-minded, a right-feeling, a conscientious, a
dispassionate, a sympathising, a contemplative jury of her civilised
countrymen.' With this beautiful peroration, Mr Serjeant Buzfuz
sat down, and Mr Justice Stareleigh woke up.

'Call Elizabeth Cluppins,' said Serjeant Buzfuz, rising a minute afterwards, with renewed vigour.

The nearest usher called for Elizabeth Tuppins; another one, at a little distance off, demanded Elizabeth Jupkins; and a third rushed in a breathless state into King Street, and screamed for Elizabeth Muffins till he was hoarse.

Meanwhile Mrs Cluppins, with the combined assistance of Mrs Bardell, Mrs Sanders, Mr Dodson, and Mr Fogg, was hoisted into the witness-box; and when she was safely perched on the top step, Mrs Bardell stood on the bottom one, with the pocket-handkerchief and pattens in one hand, and a glass bottle that might hold about a quarter of a pint of smelling salts in the other, ready for any emergency. Mrs Sanders, whose eyes were intently fixed on the judge's face, planted herself close by, with the large umbrella: keeping her right thumb pressed on the spring with an earnest countenance, as if she were fully prepared to put it up at a moment's notice.

'Mrs Cluppins,' said Serjeant Buzfuz, 'pray compose yourself, ma'am.' Of course, directly Mrs Cluppins was desired to compose herself she sobbed with increased vehemence, and gave divers alarming manifestations of an approaching fainting fit, or, as she afterwards said, of her feelings being too many for her.

'Do you recollect, Mrs Cluppins?' said Serjeant Buzfuz, after a few unimportant questions, 'do you recollect being in Mrs Bardell's back one pair of stairs,[12] on one particular morning in July last, when she was dusting Pickwick's apartment?'

'Yes, my Lord and Jury, I do,' replied Mrs Cluppins.

'Mr Pickwick's sitting-room was the first-floor front, I believe?'

'Yes, it were, sir,' replied Mrs Cluppins.

'What were you doing in the back room, ma'am?' inquired the little judge.

'My Lord and Jury,' said Mrs Cluppins, with interesting agitation, 'I will not deceive you.'

'You had better not, ma'am,' said the little judge.

'I was there,' resumed Mrs Cluppins, 'unbeknown to Mrs Bardell; I had been out with a little basket, gentlemen, to buy three pound of red kidney purtaties, which was three pound tuppense ha'penny, when I see Mrs Bardell's street door on the jar.'

'On the what?' exclaimed the little judge.

'Partly open, my Lord.' said Serjeant Snubbin.

'She *said* on the jar,' said the little judge, with a cunning look.

'It's all the same, my Lord,' said Serjeant Snubbin. The little judge looked doubtful, and said he'd make a note of it. Mrs Cluppins then resumed:

'I walked in, gentlemen, just to say good mornin', and went, in a permiscuous manner, up stairs, and into the back room. Gentlemen, there was the sound of voices in the front room, and—'

'And you listened, I believe, Mrs Cluppins?' said Serjeant Buzfuz.

'Beggin' your pardon, sir,' replied Mrs Cluppins, in a majestic manner, 'I would scorn the haction. The voices was very loud sir, and forced themselves upon my ear.'

'Well, Mrs Cluppins, you were not listening, but you heard the voices. Was one of those voices, Pickwick's?'

'Yes, it were, sir.'

And Mrs Cluppins, after distinctly stating that Mr Pickwick addressed himself to Mrs Bardell, repeated, by slow degrees, and by dint of many questions, the conversation with which our readers are already acquainted.

The jury looked suspicious, and Mr Serjeant Buzfuz smiled and sat down. They looked positively awful when Serjeant Snubbin intimated that he should not cross-examine the witness, for Mr Pickwick wished it to be distinctly stated that it was due to her to say, that her account was in substance correct.

Mrs Cluppins having once broken the ice, thought it a favourable opportunity for entering into a short dissertation on her own domestic affairs; so, she straight-way proceeded to inform the court that she was the mother of eight children at that present speaking, and that she entertained confident expectations of presenting Mr Cluppins with a ninth, somewhere about that day six months. At this interesting point, the little judge interposed most irascibly; and the effect of the interposition was, that both the worthy lady and Mrs Sanders were politely taken out of court, under the escort of Mr Jackson, without further parley.

'Nathaniel Winkle!' said Mr Skimpin.

'Here!' replied a feeble voice. Mr Winkle entered the witness-box, and having been duly sworn, bowed to the judge with considerable deference.

'Don't look at me, sir,' said the judge, sharply, in acknowledgment of the salute; 'look at the jury.'

Mr Winkle obeyed the mandate, and looked at the place where he thought it most probable the jury might be; for seeing anything in his then state of intellectual complication was wholly out of the question.

Mr Winkle was then examined by Mr Skimpin, who, being a

promising young man of two or three and forty, was of course anxious to confuse a witness who was notoriously predisposed in favour of the other side, as much as he could.

'Now, sir,' said Mr Skimpin, 'have the goodness to let his Lordship and the jury know what your name is, will you?' and Mr Skimpin inclined his head on one side to listen with great sharpness to the answer, and glanced at the jury meanwhile, as if to imply that he rather expected Mr Winkle's natural taste for perjury would induce him to give some name which did not belong to him.

'Winkle,' replied the witness.

'What's your Christian name, sir?' angrily inquired the little judge.

'Nathaniel, sir.'

'Daniel, – any other name?'

'Nathaniel, sir – my Lord, I mean.'

'Nathaniel Daniel, or Daniel Nathaniel?'

'No, my Lord, only Nathaniel; not Daniel at all.'

'What did you tell me it was Daniel for, then, sir?' inquired the judge.

'I didn't, my Lord,' replied Mr Winkle.

'You did, sir,' replied the judge, with a severe frown. 'How could I have got Daniel on my notes, unless you told me so, sir?'

This argument, was, of course, unanswerable.

'Mr Winkle has rather a short memory, my Lord,' interposed Mr Skimpin, with another glance at the jury. 'We shall find means to refresh it before we have quite done with him, I dare say.'

'You had better be careful, sir,' said the little judge, with a sinister look at the witness.

Poor Mr Winkle bowed, and endeavoured to feign an easiness of manner, which, in his then state of confusion, gave him rather the air of a disconcerted pickpocket.

'Now, Mr Winkle,' said Mr Skimpin, 'attend to me, if you please, sir; and let me recommend you, for your own sake, to bear in mind his Lordship's injunction to be careful. I believe you are a particular friend of Pickwick, the defendant, are you not?'

'I have known Mr Pickwick now, as well as I recollect at this moment, nearly—'

'Pray, Mr Winkle, do not evade the question. Are you, or are you not, a particular friend of the defendant's?'

'I was just about to say, that—'

'Will you, or will you not, answer my question, sir?'

'If you don't answer the question you'll be committed, sir,' interposed the little judge, looking over his note-book.

'Come, sir,' said Mr Skimpin, 'yes or no, if you please.'

'Yes, I am,' replied Mr Winkle.

'Yes, you are. And why couldn't you say that at once, sir? Perhaps you know the plaintiff, too? Eh, Mr Winkle?'

'I don't know her; I've seen her.'

'Oh, you don't know her, but you've seen her? Now, have the goodness to tell the gentlemen of the jury what you mean by *that*, Mr Winkle.'

'I mean that I am not intimate with her, but I have seen her when I went to call on Mr Pickwick in Goswell Street.'

'How often have you seen her, sir?'

'How often?'

'Yes, Mr Winkle, how often? I'll repeat the question for you a dozen times, if you require it, sir.' And the learned gentleman, with a firm and steady frown, placed his hands on his hips, and smiled suspiciously at the jury.

On this question there arose the edifying brow-beating, customary on such points. First of all, Mr Winkle said it was quite impossible for him to say how many times he had seen Mrs Bardell. Then he was asked if he had seen her twenty times, to which he replied, 'Certainly, – more than that.' Then he was asked whether he hadn't seen her a hundred times – whether he couldn't swear that he had seen her more than fifty times – whether he didn't know that he had seen her at least seventy-five times – and so forth; the satisfactory conclusion which was arrived at, at last, being, that he had better take care of himself, and mind what he was about. The witness having been by these means reduced to the requisite ebb of nervous perplexity, the examination was continued as follows:

'Pray, Mr Winkle, do you remember calling on the defendant Pickwick at these apartments in the plaintiff's house in Goswell Street, on one particular morning, in the month of July last?'

'Yes, I do.'

'Were you accompanied on that occasion by a friend of the name of Tupman, and another of the name of Snodgrass?'

'Yes, I was.'

'Are they here?'

'Yes, they are,' replied Mr Winkle, looking very earnestly towards the spot where his friends were stationed.

'Pray attend to me, Mr Winkle, and never mind your friends,' said Mr Skimpin, with another expressive look at the jury. 'They must tell their stories without any previous consultation with you, if none has yet taken place (another look at the jury). Now, sir, tell the gentlemen of the jury what you saw on entering the defendant's room, on this particular morning. Come; out with it, sir; we must have it, sooner or later.'

'The defendant, Mr Pickwick, was holding the plaintiff in his arms, with his hands clasping her waist,' replied Mr Winkle with natural hesitation, 'and the plaintiff appeared to have fainted away.'

'Did you hear the defendant say anything?'

'I heard him call Mrs Bardell a good creature, and I heard him ask her to compose herself, for what a situation it was, if any body should come, or words to that effect.'

'Now, Mr Winkle, I have only one more question to ask you, and I beg you to bear in mind his lordship's caution. Will you undertake to swear that Pickwick, the defendant, did not say on the occasion in question, "My dear Mrs Bardell, you're a good creature; compose yourself to this situation, for to this situation you must come, or words to *that* effect?'

'I – I didn't understand him so, certainly,' said Mr Winkle, astounded at this ingenious dove-tailing of the few words he had heard. 'I was on the staircase, and couldn't hear distinctly; the impression on my mind is – '

'The gentlemen of the jury want none of the impressions on your mind, Mr Winkle, which I fear would be of little service to honest, straightforward men,' interposed Mr Skimpin. 'You were on the staircase, and didn't distinctly hear; but you will not swear that Pickwick did not make use of the expressions I have quoted? Do I understand that?'

'No, I will not,' replied Mr Winkle; and down sat Mr Skimpin with a triumphant countenance.

Mr Pickwick's case had not gone off in so particularly happy a manner, up to this point, that it could very well afford to have any additional suspicion cast upon it. But as it could afford to be placed in a rather better light, if possible, Mr Phunky rose for the purpose of getting something important out of Mr Winkle in cross-examination. Whether he did get anything important out of him, will immediately appear.

'I believe, Mr Winkle,' said Mr Phunky, 'that Mr Pickwick is not a young man?'

'Oh no,' replied Mr Winkle; 'old enough to be my father.'

'You have told my learned friend that you have known Mr

Pickwick a long time. Had you ever any reason to suppose or believe that he was about to be married?'

'Oh no; certainly not;' replied Mr Winkle with so much eagerness, that Mr Phunky ought to have got him out of the box with all possible dispatch. Lawyers hold that there are two kinds of particularly bad witnesses: a reluctant witness, and a too-willing witness; it was Mr Winkle's fate to figure in both characters.

'I will even go further than this, Mr Winkle,' continued Mr Phunky in a most smooth and complacent manner. 'Did you ever see anything in Mr Pickwick's manner and conduct towards the opposite sex, to induce you to believe that he ever contemplated matrimony of late years, in any case?'

'Oh no; certainly not,' replied Mr Winkle.

'Has his behaviour, when females have been in the case, always been that of a man, who, having attained a pretty advanced period of life, content with his own occupations and amusements, treats them only as a father might his daughters?'

'Not the least doubt of it,' replied Mr Winkle, in the fulness of his heart. 'That is – yes – oh yes – certainly.'

'You have never known anything in his behaviour towards Mrs Bardell, or any other female, in the least degree suspicious?' said Mr Phunky, preparing to sit down; for Serjeant Snubbin was winking at him.

'N – n – no,' replied Mr Winkle, 'except on one trifling occasion, which, I have no doubt, might be easily explained.'

Now, if the unfortunate Mr Phunky had sat down when Serjeant Snubbin winked at him, or if Serjeant Buzfuz had stopped this irregular cross-examination at the outset (which he knew better than to do; observing Mr Winkle's anxiety, and well knowing it would, in all probability, lead to something serviceable to him), this unfortunate admission would not have been elicited. The moment the words fell from Mr Winkle's lips, Mr Phunky sat down, and Serjeant Snubbin rather hastily told him he might leave the box, which Mr Winkle prepared to do with great readiness, when Serjeant Buzfuz stopped him.

'Stay, Mr Winkle, stay!' said Serjeant Buzfuz, 'will your lordship have the goodness to ask him, what this one instance of suspicious behaviour towards females on the part of this gentleman, who is old enough to be his father, was?'

'You hear what the learned counsel says, sir,' observed the judge, turning to the miserable and agonized Mr Winkle. 'Describe the occasion to which you refer.'

'My lord,' said Mr Winkle, trembling with anxiety, 'I – I'd rather not.'

'Perhaps so,' said the little judge; 'but you must.'

Amid the profound silence of the whole court, Mr Winkle faltered out, that the trifling circumstance of suspicion was Mr Pickwick's being found in a lady's sleeping apartment at midnight; which had terminated, he believed, in the breaking off of the projected marriage of the lady in question, and had led, he knew, to the whole party being forcibly carried before George Nupkins, Esq., magistrate and justice of the peace, for the borough of Ipswich!

'You may leave the box, sir,' said Serjeant Snubbin. Mr Winkle *did* leave the box, and rushed with delirious haste to the George and Vulture, where he was discovered some hours after, by the waiter, groaning in a hollow and dismal manner, with his head buried beneath the sofa cushions.

Tracy Tupman, and Augustus Snodgrass, were severally called into the box; both corroborated the testimony of their unhappy friend; and each was driven to the verge of desperation by excessive badgering.

Susannah Sanders was then called, and examined by Serjeant Buzfuz, and cross-examined by Serjeant Snubbin. Had always said and believed that Pickwick would marry Mrs Bardell; knew that Mrs Bardell's being engaged to Pickwick was the current topic of conversation in the neighbourhood, after the fainting in July; had been told it herself by Mrs Mudberry which kept a mangle, and Mrs Bunkin which clear-starched, but did not see either Mrs Mudberry or Mrs Bunkin in court. Had heard Pickwick ask the little boy how he should like to have another father. Did not know that Mrs Bardell was at that time keeping company with the baker, but did know that the baker was then a single man and is now married. Couldn't swear that Mrs Bardell was not very fond of the baker, but should think that the baker was not very fond of Mrs Bardell, or he wouldn't have married somebody else. Thought Mrs Bardell fainted away on the morning in July, because Pickwick asked her to name the day; knew that she (witness) fainted away stone dead when Mr Sanders asked *her* to name the day, and believed that everybody as called herself a lady would do the same, under similar circumstances. Heard Pickwick ask the boy the question about the marbles, but upon her oath did not know the difference between an alley tor and a commoney.

By the COURT. – During the period of her keeping company with Mr Sanders, had received love letters, like other ladies. In the course of their correspondence Mr Sanders had often called her a 'duck,' but never 'chops,' nor yet 'tomata sauce.' He was particularly fond of ducks. Perhaps if he had been as fond of chops and tomata sauce, he might have called her that, as a term of affection.

Serjeant Buzfuz now rose with more importance than he had yet exhibited, if that were possible, and vociferated: 'Call Samuel Weller.'

It was quite unnecessary to call Samuel Weller; for Samuel Weller stepped briskly into the box the instant his name was pronounced; and placing his hat on the floor, and his arms on the rail, took a bird's-eye view of the bar, and a comprehensive survey of the bench, with a remarkably cheerful and lively aspect.

'What's your name, sir?' inquired the judge.

'Sam Weller, my lord,' replied that gentleman.

'Do you spell it with a "V" or a "W?"' inquired the judge.

'That depends upon the taste and fancy of the speller, my lord,' replied Sam, 'I never had occasion to spell it more than once or twice in my life, but I spells it with a "V."'

Here a voice in the gallery exclaimed aloud, 'Quite right too, Samivel, quite right. Put it down a we, my lord, put it down a we.'

'Who is that, who dares to address the court?' said the little judge, looking up. 'Usher.'

'Yes, my lord.'

'Bring that person here instantly.'

'Yes, my lord.'

But as the usher didn't find the person, he didn't bring him; and, after a great commotion, all the people who had got up to look for the culprit, sat down again. The little judge turned to the witness as soon as his indignation would allow him to speak, and said,

'Do you know who that was, sir?'

'I rayther suspect it was my father, my lord,' replied Sam.

'Do you see him here now?' said the judge.

'No, I don't, my lord,' replied Sam, staring right up into the lantern in the roof of the court.

'If you could have pointed him out, I would have committed him instantly,' said the judge.

Sam bowed his acknowledgments and turned, with unimpaired cheerfulness of countenance, towards Serjeant Buzfuz.

'Now, Mr Weller,' said Serjeant Buzfuz.

'Now, sir,' replied Sam.

'I believe you are in the service of Mr Pickwick, the defendant in this case. Speak up, if you please, Mr Weller.'

'I mean to speak up, sir,' replied Sam; 'I am in the service o' that 'ere gen'l'man, and a wery good service it is.'

'Little to do, and plenty to get, I suppose?' said Serjeant Buzfuz, with jocularity.

'Oh, quite enough to get, sir, as the soldier said ven they ordered him three hundred and fifty lashes,' replied Sam.

'You must not tell us what the soldier, or any other man, said, sir,' interposed the judge; 'it's not evidence.'

'Wery good, my lord,' replied Sam.

'Do you recollect anything particular happening on the morning when you were first engaged by the defendant; eh, Mr Weller?' said Serjeant Buzfuz.

'Yes I do sir,' replied Sam.

'Have the goodness to tell the jury what it was.'

'I had a reg'lar new fit out o' clothes that mornin', gen'l'men of the jury,' said Sam, 'and that was a wery partickler and uncommon circumstance vith me in those days.'

Hereupon there was a general laugh; and the little judge, looking with an angry countenance over his desk, said, 'You had better be careful, sir.'

'So Mr Pickwick said at the time, my lord,' replied Sam; 'and I was wery careful o' that 'ere suit o' clothes; wery careful indeed, my lord.'

The judge looked sternly at Sam for full two minutes, but Sam's features were so perfectly calm and serene that the judge said nothing, and motioned Serjeant Buzfuz to proceed.

'Do you mean to tell me, Mr Weller,' said Serjeant Buzfuz, folding his arms emphatically, and turning half-round to the jury, as if in mute assurance that he would bother the witness yet: 'Do you mean to tell me, Mr Weller, that you saw nothing of this fainting on the part of the plaintiff in the arms of the defendant, which you have heard described by the witnesses?'

'Certainly not,' replied Sam, 'I was in the passage till they called me up, and then the old lady was not there.'

'Now, attend, Mr Weller,' said Serjeant Buzfuz, dipping a large pen into the inkstand before him, for the purpose of frightening Sam with a show of taking down his answer. 'You were in the passage, and yet saw nothing of what was going forward. Have you a pair of eyes, Mr Weller?'

'Yes, I have a pair of eyes,' replied Sam, 'and that's just it. If they wos a pair o' patent double million magnifyin' gas microscopes[13] of hextra power, p'raps I might be able to see through a flight o' stairs and a deal door; but bein' only eyes, you see, my wision's limited.'

At this answer, which was delivered without the slightest appearance of irritation, and with the most complete simplicity and equanimity of manner, the spectators tittered, the little judge smiled, and Serjeant Buzfuz looked particularly foolish. After a short consultation with Dodson and Fogg, the learned Serjeant again turned towards Sam, and said, with a painful effort to conceal his vexation, 'Now, Mr Weller, I'll ask you a question on another point, if you please.'

'If you please, sir,' rejoined Sam, with the utmost good-humour.

'Do you remember going up to Mrs Bardell's house, one night in November last?'

'Oh yes, wery well.'

'Oh, you *do* remember that, Mr Weller,' said Serjeant Buzfuz, recovering his spirits; 'I thought we should get at something at last.'

'I rayther thought that, too, sir,' replied Sam; and at this the spectators tittered again.

'Well; I suppose you went up to have a little talk about this trial – eh, Mr Weller?' said Serjeant Buzfuz, looking knowingly at the jury.

'I went up to pay the rent; but we *did* get a talkin' about the trial,' replied Sam.

'Oh, you did get a talking about the trial,' said Serjeant Buzfuz, brightening up with the anticipation of some important discovery. 'Now what passed about the trial; will you have the goodness to tell us, Mr Weller?'

'Vith all the pleasure in life, sir,' replied Sam. 'Arter a few unimportant obserwations from the two wirtuous females as has been examined here to-day, the ladies gets into a very great state o' admiration at the honourable conduct of Mr Dodson and Fogg – them two gen'l'men as is settin' near you now.' This, of course, drew general attention to Dodson and Fogg, who looked as virtuous as possible.

'The attorneys for the plaintiff,' said Mr Serjeant Buzfuz. 'Well! They spoke in high praise of the honourable conduct of Messrs. Dodson and Fogg, the attorneys for the plaintiff, did they?'

'Yes,' said Sam, 'they said what a wery gen'rous thing it was o' them to have taken up the case on spec, and to charge nothing at all for costs, unless they got 'em out of Mr Pickwick.'

At this very unexpected reply, the spectators tittered again, and

Dodson and Fogg, turning very red, leant over to Serjeant Buzfuz, and in a hurried manner whispered something in his ear.

'You are quite right,' said Serjeant Buzfuz aloud, with affected composure. 'It's perfectly useless, my lord, attempting to get at any evidence through the impenetrable stupidity of this witness. I will not trouble the court by asking him any more questions. Stand down, sir.'

'Would any other gen'l'man like to ask me anythin'?' inquired Sam, taking up his hat, and looking round most deliberately.

'Not I, Mr Weller, thank you,' said Serjeant Snubbin, laughing.

'You may go down, sir,' said Serjeant Buzfuz, waving his hand impatiently. Sam went down accordingly, after doing Messrs. Dodson and Fogg's case as much harm as he conveniently could, and saying just as little respecting Mr Pickwick as might be, which was precisely the object he had had in view all along.

'I have no objection to admit, my lord,' said Serjeant Snubbin, 'if it will save the examination of another witness, that Mr Pickwick has retired from business, and is a gentleman of considerable independent property.'

'Very well,' said Serjeant Buzfuz, putting in the two letters to be read, 'Then that's my case, my lord.'

Serjeant Snubbin then addressed the jury on behalf of the defendant; and a very long and a very emphatic address he delivered, in which he bestowed the highest possible eulogiums on the conduct and character of Mr Pickwick; but inasmuch as our readers are far better able to form a correct estimate of that gentleman's merits and deserts, than Serjeant Snubbin could possibly be, we do not feel called upon to enter at any length into the learned gentleman's observations. He attempted to show that the letters which had been exhibited, merely related to Mr Pickwick's dinner, or to the preparations for receiving him in his apartments on his return from some country excursion. It is sufficient to add in general terms, that he did the best he could for Mr Pickwick; and the best, as every body knows, on the infallible authority of the old adage, could do no more.

Mr Justice Stareleigh summed up, in the old-established and most approved form. He read as much of his notes to the jury as he could decipher on so short a notice, and made running comments on the evidence as he went along. If Mrs Bardell were right, it was perfectly clear that Mr Pickwick was wrong, and if they thought the evidence of Mrs Cluppins worthy of credence they would believe it, and, if they didn't, why they wouldn't. If they were satisfied that a breach of promise of marriage had been committed, they would find for the plaintiff with such damages as they thought proper; and if, on the other hand, it appeared to them that no promise of marriage had ever been given, they would find for the defendant with no damages at all. The jury then retired to their private room to talk the matter over, and the judge retired to *his* private room, to refresh himself with a mutton chop and a glass of sherry.

An anxious quarter of an hour elapsed; the jury came back; the judge was fetched in. Mr Pickwick put on his spectacles, and gazed at the foreman with an agitated countenance and a quickly beating heart.

'Gentlemen,' said the individual in black, 'are you all agreed upon your verdict?'

'We are,' replied the foreman.

'Do you find for the plaintiff, gentlemen, or for the defendant?'

'For the plaintiff.'

'With what damages, gentlemen?'

'Seven hundred and fifty pounds.'

Mr Pickwick took off his spectacles, carefully wiped the glasses, folded them into their case, and put them in his pocket; then having drawn on his gloves with great nicety, and stared at the foreman all the while, he mechanically followed Mr Perker and the blue bag out of court.

They stopped in a side room while Perker paid the court fees; and here, Mr Pickwick was joined by his friends. Here, too, he encountered Messrs. Dodson and Fogg, rubbing their hands with every token of outward satisfaction.

'Well, gentlemen,' said Mr Pickwick.

'Well, sir,' said Dodson: for self and partner.

'You imagine you'll get your costs, don't you, gentlemen?' said Mr Pickwick.

Fogg said they thought it rather probable. Dodson smiled, and said they'd try.

'You may try, and try, and try again, Messrs. Dodson and Fogg,' said Mr Pickwick vehemently, 'but not one farthing of costs or damages do you ever get from me, if I spend the rest of my existence in a debtor's prison.'

'Ha, ha!' laughed Dodson. 'You'll think better of that, before next term, Mr Pickwick.'

'He, he, he! We'll soon see about that Mr Pickwick,' grinned Fogg.

Speechless with indignation, Mr Pickwick allowed himself to be led by his solicitor and friends to the door, and there assisted into a hackney-coach, which had been fetched for the purpose, by the ever watchful Sam Weller.

Sam had put up the steps, and was preparing to jump upon the box, when he felt himself gently touched on the shoulder; and looking round, his father stood before him. The old gentleman's countenance wore a mournful expression, as he shook his head gravely, and said, in warning accents:

'I know'd what 'ud come 'o this here mode 'o doin' bisness. Oh Sammy, Sammy, vy worn't there a alleybi!'

CHAPTER 35

In which Mr Pickwick thinks he had better go to Bath; and goes accordingly

'But surely, my dear sir,' said little Perker, as he stood in Mr Pickwick's apartment on the morning after the trial: 'Surely you don't really mean – really and seriously now, and irritation apart – that you won't pay these costs and damages?'

'Not one halfpenny,' said Mr Pickwick, firmly; 'not one halfpenny.'

'Hooroar for the principle, as the money-lender said ven he vouldn't renew the bill,' observed Mr Weller, who was clearing away the breakfast things.

'Sam,' said Mr Pickwick, 'have the goodness to step down stairs.'

'Cert'nly, sir,' replied Mr Weller; and acting on Mr Pickwick's gentle hint, Sam retired.

'No, Perker,' said Mr Pickwick, with great seriousness of manner, 'my friends here, have endeavoured to dissuade me from this determination, but without avail. I shall employ myself as usual, until the opposite party have the power of issuing a legal process of execution against me; and if they are vile enough to avail themselves of it, and to arrest my person, I shall yield myself up with perfect cheerfulness and content of heart. When can they do this?'

'They can issue execution, my dear sir, for the amount of the damages and taxed costs, next term,' replied Perker, 'just two months hence, my dear sir.'

'Very good,' said Mr Pickwick. 'Until that time, my dear fellow, let me hear no more of the matter. And now,' continued Mr

Pickwick, looking round on his friends with a good-humoured smile, and a sparkle in the eye which no spectacles could dim or conceal, 'the only question is, Where shall we go next?'

Mr Tupman and Mr Snodgrass were too much affected by their friend's heroism to offer any reply. Mr Winkle had not yet sufficiently recovered the recollection of his evidence at the trial, to make any observation on any subject, so Mr Pickwick paused in vain.

'Well,' said that gentleman, 'if you leave me to suggest our destination, I say Bath. I think none of us have ever been there.'

Nobody had; and as the proposition was warmly seconded by Perker, who considered it extremely probable that if Mr Pickwick saw a little change and gaiety he would be inclined to think better of his determination, and worse of a debtor's prison, it was carried unanimously: and Sam was at once dispatched to the White Horse Cellar,[1] to take five places by the half-past seven o'clock coach, next morning.

There were just two places to be had inside, and just three to be had out; so Sam Weller booked for them all, and having exchanged a few compliments with the booking-office clerk on the subject of a pewter half-crown[2] which was tendered him as a portion of his 'change,' walked back to the George and Vulture, where he was pretty busily employed until bed-time in reducing clothes and linen into the smallest possible compass, and exerting his mechanical genius in constructing a variety of ingenious devices for keeping the lids on boxes which had neither locks nor hinges.

The next was a very unpropitious morning for a journey – muggy, damp, and drizzly. The horses in the stages that were going out, and had come through the city, were smoking so, that the outside passengers were invisible. The newspaper-sellers looked moist, and smelt mouldy; the wet ran off the hats of the orange-venders as they thrust their heads into the coach windows, and diluted the insides in a refreshing manner. The Jews with the fifty-bladed penknives shut them up in despair; the men with the pocket-books made pocket-books of them. Watch-guards and toasting-forks were alike at a discount, and pencil-cases and sponge were a drug in the market.

Leaving Sam Weller to rescue the luggage from the seven or eight porters who flung themselves savagely upon it, the moment the coach stopped: and finding that they were about twenty minutes too early: Mr Pickwick and his friends went for shelter into the travellers' room – the last resource of human dejection.

The travellers' room at the White Horse Cellar is of course uncomfortable; it would be no travellers' room if it were not. It is the right-hand parlour, into which an aspiring kitchen fire-place appears to have walked, accompanied by a rebellious poker, tongs, and shovel. It is divided into boxes, for the solitary confinement of travellers, and is furnished with a clock, a looking-glass, and a live waiter: which latter article is kept in a small kennel for washing glasses, in a corner of the apartment.

One of these boxes was occupied, on this particular occasion, by a stern-eyed man of about five-and-forty, who had a bald and glossy forehead, with a good deal of black hair at the sides and back of his head, and large black whiskers. He was buttoned up to the chin in a brown coat; and had a large seal-skin travelling cap, and a great-coat and cloak, lying on the seat beside him. He looked up from his breakfast as Mr Pickwick entered, with a fierce and peremptory air, which was very dignified; and having scrutinised that gentleman and his companions to his entire satisfaction, hummed a tune, in a manner which seemed to say that he rather suspected somebody wanted to take advantage of him, but it wouldn't do.

'Waiter,' said the gentleman with the whiskers.

'Sir?' replied a man with a dirty complexion, and a towel of the same, emerging from the kennel before mentioned.

'Some more toast.'

'Yes, sir.'

'Buttered toast, mind,' said the gentleman, fiercely.

'D'rectly, sir,' replied the waiter.

The gentleman with the whiskers hummed a tune in the same manner as before, and pending the arrival of the toast, advanced to the front of the fire, and, taking his coat tails under his arms, looked at his boots, and ruminated.

'I wonder whereabouts in Bath this coach puts up,' said Mr Pickwick, mildly addressing Mr Winkle.

'Hum – eh – what's that?' said the strange man.

'I made an observation to my friend, sir,' replied Mr Pickwick, always ready to enter into conversation. 'I wondered at what house the Bath coach put up. Perhaps you can inform me.'

'Are you going to Bath?' said the strange man.

'I am, sir,' replied Mr Pickwick.

'And those other gentlemen?'

'They are going also,' said Mr Pickwick.

'Not inside – I'll be damned if you're going inside,' said the strange man.

'Not all of us,' said Mr Pickwick.

'No, not all of you,' said the strange man emphatically. 'I've taken two places. If they try to squeeze six people into an infernal box that only holds four, I'll take a post-chaise and bring an action. I've paid my fare. It won't do; I told the clerk when I took my places that it wouldn't do. I know these things have been done. I know they are done every day; but *I* never was done, and I never will be. Those who know me best, best know it; crush me!' Here the fierce gentleman rang the bell with great violence, and told the waiter he'd better bring the toast in five seconds, or he'd know the reason why.

'My good sir,' said Mr Pickwick, 'you will allow me to observe that this is a very unnecessary display of excitement. I have only taken places inside for two.'

'I am glad to hear it,' said the fierce man. 'I withdraw my expressions. I tender an apology. There's my card. Give me your acquaintance.'

'With great pleasure, sir,' replied Mr Pickwick. 'We are to be fellow travellers, and I hope we shall find each other's society mutually agreeable.'

'I hope we shall,' said the fierce gentleman. 'I know we shall. I like your looks; they please me. Gentlemen, your hands and names. Know me.'

Of course, an interchange of friendly salutations followed this gracious speech; and the fierce gentleman immediately proceeded to inform the friends, in the same short, abrupt, jerking sentences, that his name was Dowler; that he was going to Bath on pleasure; that he was formerly in the army; that he had now set up in business as a gentleman; that he lived upon the profits; and that the individual for whom the second place was taken, was a personage no less illustrious than Mrs Dowler his lady wife.

'She's a fine woman,' said Mr Dowler. 'I am proud of her. I have reason.'

'I hope I shall have the pleasure of judging,' said Mr Pickwick, with a smile.

'You shall,' replied Dowler. 'She shall know you. She shall esteem you. I courted her under singular circumstances. I won her through a rash vow. Thus. I saw her; I loved her; I proposed; she refused me. – "You love another?" – "Spare my blushes." – "I know him." – "You do." – "Very good; if he remains here, I'll skin him."'

'Lord bless me!' exclaimed Mr Pickwick, involuntarily.

'Did you skin the gentleman, sir?' inquired Mr Winkle, with a very pale face.

'I wrote him a note. I said it was a painful thing. And so it was.'

'Certainly,' interposed Mr Winkle.

'I said I had pledged my word as a gentleman to skin him. My character was at stake. I had no alternative. As an officer in His Majesty's service, I was bound to skin him. I regretted the necessity, but it must be done. He was open to conviction. He saw that the rules of the service were imperative. He fled. I married her. Here's the coach. That's her head.'

As Mr Dowler concluded, he pointed to a stage which had just driven up, from the open window of which a rather pretty face in a bright blue bonnet was looking among the crowd on the pavement: most probably for the rash man himself. Mr Dowler paid his bill and hurried out with his travelling-cap, coat, and cloak; and Mr Pickwick and his friends followed to secure their places.

Mr Tupman and Mr Snodgrass had seated themselves at the back part of the coach; Mr Winkle had got inside; and Mr Pickwick was preparing to follow him, when Sam Weller came up to his master, and whispering in his ear, begged to speak to him, with an air of the deepest mystery.

'Well, Sam,' said Mr Pickwick, 'what's the matter now?'

'Here's rayther a rum go, sir,' replied Sam.

'What?' inquired Mr Pickwick.

'This here, sir,' rejoined Sam. 'I'm wery much afeerd, sir, that the properiator o' this here coach is a playin' some imperence vith us.'

'How is that, Sam?' said Mr Pickwick; 'aren't the names down on the way-bill?'[3]

'The names is not only down on the vay-bill, sir,' replied Sam, 'but they've painted vun on 'em up, on the door o' the coach.' As Sam spoke, he pointed to that part of the coach door on which the proprietor's name usually appears; and there, sure enough, in gilt letters of a goodly size, was the magic name of PICKWICK![4]

'Dear me,' exclaimed Mr Pickwick, quite staggered by the coincidence; 'what a very extraordinary thing!'

'Yes, but that ain't all,' said Sam, again directing his master's attention to the coach door; 'not content vith writin' up Pickwick, they puts "Moses" afore it, vich I call addin' insult to injury, as the parrot said ven they not only took him from his native land, but made him talk the English langwidge arterwards.'

'It's odd enough certainly, Sam,' said Mr Pickwick; 'but if we stand talking here, we shall lose our places.'

'Wot, ain't nothin' to be done in consequence, sir?' exclaimed Sam, perfectly aghast at the coolness with which Mr Pickwick prepared to ensconce himself inside.

'Done!' said Mr Pickwick. 'What should be done?'

'Ain't nobody to be whopped for takin' this here liberty, sir?' said Mr Weller, who had expected that at least he would have been commissioned to challenge the guard and coachman to a pugilistic encounter on the spot.

'Certainly not,' replied Mr Pickwick eagerly; 'not on any account. Jump up to your seat directly.'

'I'm wery much afeerd,' muttered Sam to himself, as he turned away, 'that somethin' queer's come over the governor, or he'd never ha' stood this so quiet. I hope that 'ere trial hasn't broke his spirit, but it looks bad, wery bad.' Mr Weller shook his head gravely; and it is worthy of remark, as an illustration of the manner in which he took this circumstance to heart, that he did not speak another word until the coach reached the Kensington turnpike.[5] Which was so long a time for him to remain taciturn, that the fact may be considered wholly unprecedented.

Nothing worthy of special mention occurred during the journey. Mr Dowler related a variety of anecdotes, all illustrative of his own personal prowess and desperation, and appealed to Mrs Dowler in corroboration thereof: when Mrs Dowler invariably brought in, in the form of an appendix, some remarkable fact or circumstance which Mr Dowler had forgotten, or had perhaps through modesty omitted: for the addenda in every instance went to show that Mr Dowler was even a more wonderful fellow than he made himself out to be. Mr Pickwick and Mr Winkle listened with great admiration, and at intervals conversed with Mrs Dowler, who was a very agreeable and fascinating person. So, what between Mr Dowler's stories, and Mrs Dowler's charms, and Mr Pickwick's good humour, and Mr Winkle's good listening, the insides contrived to be very companionable all the way.

The outsides did as outsides always do. They were very cheerful and talkative at the beginning of every stage, and very dismal and sleepy in the middle, and very bright and wakeful again towards the end. There was one young gentleman in an India-rubber cloak, who smoked cigars all day; and there was another young gentleman in a parody upon a great coat, who lighted a good many, and feeling obviously unsettled after the second whiff, threw them away when he thought nobody was looking at him. There was a third young man on the box who wished to be learned in cattle; and an old one behind, who was familiar with farming. There was a constant succession of Christian names in smock frocks and white coats, who were invited to have a 'lift' by the guard, and who knew every horse and hostler on the road and off it; and there was a dinner which would have been cheap at half-a-crown a mouth, if any moderate number of mouths could have eaten it in the time. And at seven o'clock P.M., Mr Pickwick and his friends, and Mr Dowler and his wife, respectively retired to their private sitting-rooms at the White Hart hotel, opposite the Great Pump Room, Bath, where the waiters, from their costume, might be mistaken for Westminster boys,⁶ only they destroy the illusion by behaving themselves much better.

Breakfast had scarcely been cleared away on the succeeding morning, when a waiter brought in Mr Dowler's card, with a request to be allowed permission to introduce a friend. Mr Dowler at once followed up the delivery of the card, by bringing himself and the friend also.

The friend was a charming young man of not much more than fifty, dressed in a very bright blue coat with resplendent buttons, black trousers, and the thinnest possible pair of highly-polished boots. A gold eye-glass was suspended from his neck by a short broad black ribbon; a gold snuff-box was lightly clasped in his left hand; gold rings innumerable, glittered on his fingers; and a large diamond pin set in gold glistened in his shirt frill. He had a gold watch, and a gold curb chain⁷ with large gold seals; and he carried a pliant ebony cane with a heavy gold top. His linen was of the very whitest, finest, and stiffest; his wig of the glossiest, blackest, and curliest. His snuff was princes' mixture; his scent *bouquet du roi*. His features were contracted into a perpetual smile; and his teeth were in such perfect order that it was difficult at a small distance to tell the real from the false.

'Mr Pickwick,' said Mr Dowler; 'my friend, Angelo Cyrus Bantam, Esquire, M.C. Bantam; Mr Pickwick. Know each other.'

'Welcome to Ba – ath, sir. This is indeed an acquisition. Most welcome to Ba – ath, sir. It is long – very long, Mr Pickwick, since you drank the waters. It appears an age, Mr Pickwick. Re – markable!'

Such were the expressions with which Angelo Cyrus Bantam, Esquire, M.C., took Mr Pickwick's hand; retaining it in his, meantime, and shrugging up his shoulders with a constant succession of bows, as if he really could not make up his mind to the trial of letting it go again.

'It is a very long time since I drank the waters, certainly,' replied Mr Pickwick; 'for to the best of my knowledge, I was never here before.'

'Never in Ba – ath, Mr Pickwick!' exclaimed the Grand Master, letting the hand fall in astonishment. 'Never in Ba – ath! He! he! Mr Pickwick, you are a wag. Not bad, not bad. Good, good. He! he! he! Re – markable!'

'To my shame, I must say that I am perfectly serious,' rejoined Mr Pickwick. 'I really never was here before.'

'Oh, I see,' exclaimed the Grand Master, looking extremely pleased; 'Yes, yes – good, good – better and better. You are the gentleman of whom we have heard. Yes; we know you, Mr Pickwick; we know you.'

'The reports of the trial in those confounded papers,' thought Mr Pickwick. 'They have heard all about me.'

'You are the gentleman residing on Clapham Green,' resumed Bantam, 'who lost the use of his limbs from imprudently taking cold after port wine; who could not be moved in consequence of acute suffering, and who had the water from the King's Bath bottled at one hundred and three degrees, and sent by waggon to his bed-room in town, where he bathed, sneezed, and same day recovered. Very re-markable!'

Mr Pickwick acknowledged the compliment which the supposition implied, but had the self-denial to repudiate it, notwithstanding; and taking advantage of a moment's silence on the part of the M. C., begged to introduce his friends, Mr Tupman, Mr Winkle, and Mr Snodgrass. An introduction which overwhelmed the M. C. with delight and honour.

'Bantam,' said Mr Dowler, 'Mr Pickwick and his friends are strangers. They must put their names down. Where's the book?'

'The register of the distinguished visitors in Ba – ath will be at the Pump Room this morning at two o'clock,'* replied the M. C. 'Will you guide our friends to that splendid building, and enable me to procure their autographs?'

'I will,' rejoined Dowler. 'This is a long call. It's time to go. I shall be here again in an hour. Come.'

'This is a ball night,' said the M. C., again taking Mr Pickwick's hand, as he rose to go. 'The ball-nights in Ba – ath are moments snatched from Paradise; rendered bewitching by music, beauty, elegance, fashion, etiquette, and – and – above all, by the absence of tradespeople, who are quite inconsistent with Paradise; and who have an amalgamation of themselves at the Guildhall every fortnight, which is, to say the least, remarkable. Good bye, good bye!' and protesting all the way down stairs that he was most satisfied, and most delighted, and most overpowered, and most flattered, Angelo Cyrus Bantam, Esquire, M. C., stepped into a very elegant chariot that waited at the door, and rattled off.

At the appointed hour, Mr Pickwick and his friends, escorted by Dowler, repaired to the Assembly Rooms, and wrote their names down in a book. An instance of condescension at which Angelo Bantam was even more overpowered than before. Tickets of admission to that evening's assembly were to have been prepared for the whole party, but as they were not ready, Mr Pickwick undertook, despite all the protestations to the contrary of Angelo Bantam, to send Sam for them at four o'clock in the afternoon, to the M. C.'s house in Queen Square. Having taken a short walk through the city, and arrived at the unanimous conclusion that Park Street was very much like the perpendicular streets a man sees in a dream, which he cannot get up for the life of him, they returned to the White Hart, and dispatched Sam on the errand to which his master had pledged him.

Sam Weller put on his hat in a very easy and graceful manner, and thrusting his hands in his waistcoat pockets, walked with great deliberation to Queen Square, whistling as he went along, several of the most popular airs of the day, as arranged with entirely new movements for that noble instrument the organ, either mouth or barrel. Arriving at the number in Queen Square to which he had been directed, he left off whistling, and gave a cheerful knock, which was instantaneously answered by a powdered-headed footman in gorgeous livery, and of symmetrical stature.

'Is this here Mr Bantam's, old feller?' inquired Sam Weller, nothing abashed by the blaze of splendour which burst upon his sight, in the person of the powdered-headed footman with the gorgeous livery.

'Why, young man?' was the haughty inquiry of the powdered-headed footman.

' 'Cos if it is, jist you step into him with that 'ere card, and say Mr Veller's a waitin', will you?' said Sam. And saying it, he very coolly walked into the hall, and sat down.

The powdered-headed footman slammed the door very hard, and scowled very grandly; but both the slam and the scowl were lost upon Sam, who was regarding a mahogany umbrella stand with every outward token of critical approval.

Apparently, his master's reception of the card had impressed the powdered-headed footman in Sam's favour, for when he came back from delivering it, he smiled in a friendly manner, and said that the answer would be ready directly.

'Werry good,' said Sam. 'Tell the old gen'l'm'n not to put himself in a perspiration. No hurry, six-foot. I've had my dinner.'

'You dine early, sir,' said the powdered-headed footman.

'I find I gets on better at supper when I does,' replied Sam.

'Have you been long in Bath, sir?' inquired the powdered-headed footman. 'I have not had the pleasure of hearing of you before.'

'I haven't created any wery surprisin' sensation here, as yet,' rejoined Sam, 'for me and the other fash'nables only come last night.'

'Nice place, sir,' said the powdered-headed footman.

'Seems so,' observed Sam.

'Pleasant society, sir,' remarked the powdered-headed footman. 'Very agreeable servants, sir.'

'I should think they wos,' replied Sam. 'Affable, unaffected, say-nothin'-to-nobody sort o' fellers.'

'Oh, very much so, indeed, sir,' said the powdered-headed footman, taking Sam's remark as a high compliment. 'Very much so indeed. Do you do anything in this way, sir?' inquired the tall footman, producing a small snuff-box with a fox's head on the top of it.

'Not without sneezing,' replied Sam.

'Why, it *is* difficult, sir, I confess,' said the tall footman. 'It may be done by degrees, sir. Coffee is the best practice. I carried coffee, sir, for a long time. It looks very like rappee,[9] sir.'

Here, a sharp peal at the bell, reduced the powdered-headed footman to the ignominious necessity of putting the fox's head in his pocket, and hastening with a humble countenance to Mr Bantam's 'study.' By the by, who ever knew a man who never read or wrote either, who hadn't got some small back parlour which he *would* call a study!

'There is the answer sir,' said the powdered-headed footman. 'I am afraid you'll find it inconveniently large.'

'Don't mention it,' said Sam, taking a letter with a small enclosure. 'It's just possible as exhausted nature may manage to surwive it.'

'I hope we shall meet again, sir,' said the powdered-headed

footman, rubbing his hands, and following Sam out to the door-step.

'You are wery obligin', sir,' replied Sam. 'Now, don't allow yourself to be fatigued beyond your powers; there's a amiable bein'. Consider what you owe to society, and don't let yourself be injured by too much work. For the sake o' your feller creeturs, keep your self as quiet as you can; only think what a loss you would be!' With these pathetic words, Sam Weller departed.

'A very singular young man that,' said the powdered-headed footman, looking after Mr Weller, with a countenance which clearly showed he could make nothing of him.

Sam said nothing at all. He winked, shook his head, smiled, winked again; and with an expression of countenance which seemed to denote that he was greatly amused with something or other, walked merrily away.

At precisely twenty minutes before eight o'clock that night, Angelo Cyrus Bantam, Esq., the Master of the Ceremonies, emerged from his chariot at the door of the Assembly Rooms in the same wig, the same teeth, the same eye-glass, the same watch and seals, the same rings, the same shirt-pin, and the same cane. The only observable alterations in his appearance were, that he wore a brighter blue coat, with a white silk lining: black tights, black silk stockings, and pumps, and a white waistcoat, and was, if possible, just a thought more scented.

Thus attired, the Master of the Ceremonies, in strict discharge of the important duties of his all-important office, planted himself in the rooms to receive the company.

Bath being full, the company and the sixpences for tea, poured in, in shoals. In the ball-room, the long card-room, the octagonal card-room, the staircases, and the passages, the hum of many voices, and the sound of many feet, were perfectly bewildering. Dresses rustled, feathers waved, lights shone, and jewels sparkled. There was the music – not of the quadrille band, for it had not yet commenced; but the music of soft tiny footsteps, with now and then a clear merry laugh – low and gentle, but very pleasant to hear in a female voice, whether in Bath or elsewhere. Brilliant eyes, lighted up with pleasurable expectation, gleamed from every side; and look where you would, some exquisite form glided gracefully through the throng, and was no sooner lost, than it was replaced by another as dainty and bewitching.

In the tea-room, and hovering round the card-tables, were a vast number of queer old ladies and decrepid old gentlemen, discussing all the small talk and scandal of the day, with a relish and gusto which sufficiently bespoke the intensity of the pleasure they derived from the occupation. Mingled with these groups, were three or four matchmaking mammas, appearing to be wholly absorbed by the conversation in which they were taking part, but failing not from time to time to cast an anxious sidelong glance upon their daughters, who, remembering the maternal injunction to make the best use of their youth, had already commenced incipient flirtations in the mislaying of scarves, putting on gloves, setting down cups, and so forth; slight matters apparently, but which may be turned to surprisingly good account by expert practitioners.

Lounging near the doors, and in remote corners, were various knots of silly young men, displaying various varieties of puppyism and stupidity; amusing all sensible people near them with their folly and conceit; and happily thinking themselves the objects of general admiration. A wise and merciful dispensation which no good man will quarrel with.

And lastly, seated on some of the back benches, where they had already taken up their positions for the evening, were divers unmarried ladies past their grand climacteric,[10] who, not dancing because there were no partners for them, and not playing cards lest they should be set down as irretrievably single, were in the favourable situation of being able to abuse everybody without reflecting on themselves. In short, they could abuse everybody, because everybody was there. It was a scene of gaiety, glitter, and show; of richly-dressed people, handsome mirrors, chalked floors, girandoles,[11] and in all parts of the scene, gliding from spot to spot in silent softness, bowing obsequiously to this party, nodding familiarly to that, and smiling complacently on all, was the sprucely attired person of Angelo Cyrus Bantam, Esquire, Master of the Ceremonies.

'Stop in the tea-room. Take your sixpenn'orth. They lay on hot water, and call it tea. Drink it,' said Mr Dowler, in a loud voice, directing Mr Pickwick, who advanced at the head of the little party, with Mrs Dowler on his arm. Into the tea-room Mr Pickwick turned; and catching sight of him, Mr Bantam corkscrewed his way through the crowd, and welcomed him with ecstasy.

'My dear sir, I am highly honoured. Ba – ath is favoured. Mrs Dowler, you embellish the rooms. I congratulate you on your feathers. Re – markable!'

'Any body here?' inquired Dowler, suspiciously.

'Any body! The *élite* of Ba – ath. Mr Pickwick, do you see the lady in the gauze turban?'

'The fat old lady?' inquired Mr Pickwick, innocently.

'Hush, my dear sir – nobody's fat or old in Ba – ath. That's the Dowager Lady Snuphanuph.'

'Is it indeed?' said Mr Pickwick.

'No less a person, I assure you,' said the Master of the Ceremonies. 'Hush. Draw a little nearer, Mr Pickwick. You see the splendidly dressed young man coming this way?'

'The one with the long hair, and the particularly small forehead?' inquired Mr Pickwick.

'The same. The richest young man in Ba – ath at this moment. Young Lord Mutanhed.'

'You don't say so?' said Mr Pickwick.

'Yes. You'll hear his voice in a moment, Mr Pickwick. He'll speak to me. The other gentleman with him, in the red under waistcoat and dark moustache, is the Honourable Mr Crushton, his bosom friend. How do you do, my lord?'

'Veway hot, Bantam,' said his lordship.

'It *is* very warm, my lord,' replied the M. C.

'Confounded,' assented the Honourable Mr Crushton.

'Have you seen his lordship's mail cart, Bantam?' inquired the Honourable Mr Crushton, after a short pause, during which young Lord Mutanhed had been endeavouring to stare Mr Pickwick out of countenance, and Mr Crushton had been reflecting what subject his lordship could talk about best.

'Dear me, no,' replied the M. C. 'A mail cart! What an excellent idea. Re – markable!'

'Gwacious heavens!' said his lordship, 'I thought evewebody had seen the new mail cart; it's the neatest, pwettiest, gwacefullest thing that ever wan upon wheels. Painted wed, with a cweam piebald.'

'With a real box for the letters, and all complete,' said the Honourable Mr Crushton.

'And a little seat in fwont, with an iwon wail, for the dwiver,' added his lordship. 'I dwove it over to Bwistol the other morning, in a cwimson coat, with two servants widing a quarter of a mile behind; and confound me if the people didn't wush out of their cottages, and awest my pwogwess, to know if I wasn't the post. Glowious, glowious!'

At this anecdote his lordship laughed very heartily, as did the listeners, of course. Then, drawing his arm through that of the obsequious Mr Crushton, Lord Mutanhed walked away.

'Delightful young man, his lordship,' said the Master of the Ceremonies.

'So I should think,' rejoined Mr Pickwick, drily.

The dancing having commenced, the necessary introductions having been made, and all preliminaries arranged, Angelo Bantam rejoined Mr Pickwick, and led him into the card-room.

Just at the very moment of their entrance, the Dowager Lady Snuphanuph and two other ladies of an ancient and whist-like appearance, were hovering over an unoccupied card-table; and they no sooner set eyes upon Mr Pickwick under the convoy of Angelo Bantam, than they exchanged glances with each other, seeing that he was precisely the very person they wanted, to make up the rubber.

'My dear Bantam,' said the Dowager Lady Snuphanuph, coaxingly, 'find us some nice creature to make up this table; there's a good soul.' Mr Pickwick happened to be looking another way at the moment, so her ladyship nodded her head towards him, and frowned expressively.

'My friend Mr Pickwick, my lady, will be most happy, I am sure, re – markably so,' said the M. C., taking the hint. 'Mr Pickwick, Lady Snuphanuph – Mrs Colonel Wugsby – Miss Bolo.'

Mr Pickwick bowed to each of the ladies, and, finding escape impossible, cut. Mr Pickwick and Miss Bolo against Lady Snuphanuph and Mrs Colonel Wugsby.

As the trump card was turned up, at the commencement of the second deal, two young ladies hurried into the room, and took their stations on either side of Mrs Colonel Wugsby's chair, where they waited patiently until the hand was over.

'Now, Jane,' said Mrs Colonel Wugsby, turning to one of the girls, 'what is it?'

'I came to ask, ma, whether I might dance with the youngest Mr Crawley,' whispered the prettier and younger of the two.

'Good God, Jane, how can you think of such things?' replied the mamma, indignantly. 'Haven't you repeatedly heard that his father has eight hundred a-year, which dies with him? I am ashamed of you. Not on any account.'

'Ma,' whispered the other, who was much older than her sister, and very insipid and artificial, 'Lord Mutanhed has been introduced to me. I said I *thought* I wasn't engaged, ma.'

'You're a sweet pet, my love,' replied Mrs Colonel Wugsby, tapping her daughter's cheek with her fan, 'and are always to be trusted. He's immensely rich, my dear. Bless you!' With these words

The Card Room at Bath

Mrs Colonel Wugsby kissed her eldest daughter most affectionately, and, frowning in a warning manner upon the other, sorted her cards.

Poor Mr Pickwick! he had never played with three thorough-paced female card-players before. They were so desperately sharp, that they quite frightened him. If he played a wrong card, Miss Bolo looked a small armoury of daggers; if he stopped to consider which was the right one, Lady Snuphanuph would throw herself back in her chair, and smile with a mingled glance of impatience and pity to Mrs Colonel Wugsby: at which Mrs Colonel Wugsby would shrug up her shoulders, and cough, as much as to say she wondered whether he ever would begin. Then, at the end of every hand, Miss Bolo would inquire with a dismal countenance and reproachful sigh, why Mr Pickwick had not returned that diamond, or led the club, or roughed the spade, or finessed the heart, or led through the honour, or brought out the ace, or played up to the king, or some such thing; and in reply to all these grave charges, Mr Pickwick would be wholly unable to plead any justification whatever, having by this time forgotten all about the game. People came and looked on, too, which made Mr Pickwick nervous. Besides all this, there was a great deal of distracting conversation near the table, between Angelo Bantam and the two Miss Matinters, who, being single and singular, paid great court to the Master of the Ceremonies, in the hope of getting a stray partner now and then. All these things, combined with the noises and interruptions of constant comings in and goings out, made Mr Pickwick play rather badly; the cards were against him, also; and when they left off at ten minutes past eleven, Miss Bolo rose from the table considerably agitated, and went straight home, in a flood of tears, and a sedan-chair.

Being joined by his friends, who one and all protested that they had scarcely ever spent a more pleasant evening, Mr Pickwick accompanied them to the White Hart, and having soothed his feelings with something hot, went to bed, and to sleep, almost simultaneously.

The chief features of which, will be found to be an authentic Version of the Legend of Prince Bladud, and a most extraordinary Calamity that befel Mr Winkle

As Mr Pickwick contemplated a stay of at least two months in Bath, he deemed it advisable to take private lodgings for himself and friends for that period; and as a favourable opportunity offered for their securing, on moderate terms, the upper portion of a house in the Royal Crescent, which was larger than they required, Mr and Mrs Dowler offered to relieve them of a bed-room and sitting-room. This proposition was at once accepted, and in three days' time they were all located in their new abode, when Mr Pickwick began to drink the waters with the utmost assiduity. Mr Pickwick took them systematically. He drank a quarter of a pint before breakfast, and then walked up a hill; and another quarter of a pint after breakfast, and then walked down a hill; and after every fresh quarter of a pint, Mr Pickwick declared, in the most solemn and emphatic terms, that he felt a great deal better: whereat his friends were very much delighted, though they had not been previously aware that there was anything the matter with him.

The great pump-room[1] is a spacious saloon, ornamented with Corinthian pillars, and a music gallery, and a Tompion clock,[2] and a statue of Nash,[3] and a golden inscription, to which all the water-drinkers should attend, for it appeals to them in the cause of a deserving charity.[4] There is a large bar with a marble vase, out of which the pumper gets the water; and there are a number of yellow-looking tumblers, out of which the company get it; and it is a most edifying and satisfactory sight to behold the perseverance and gravity with which they swallow it. There are baths near at hand, in which a part of the company wash themselves; and a band plays afterwards, to congratulate the remainder on their having done so. There is another pump-room, into which infirm ladies and gentle-men are wheeled, in such an astonishing variety of chairs and chaises, that any adventurous individual who goes in with the regular number of toes, is in imminent danger of coming out without them; and there is a third, into which the quiet people go, for it is less noisy than either. There is an immensity of promenad-ing, on crutches and off, with sticks and without, and a great deal of conversation, and liveliness, and pleasantry.

Every morning, the regular water-drinkers, Mr Pickwick among the number, met each other in the pump-room, took their quarter of a pint, and walked constitutionally. At the afternoon's promenade, Lord Mutanhed, and the Honourable Mr Crushton, the Dowager Lady Snuphanuph, Mrs Colonel Wugsby, and all the great people, and all the morning water-drinkers, met in grand assemblage. After this, they walked out, or drove out, or were pushed out in bath chairs, and met one another again. After this, the gentlemen went to the reading-rooms and met divisions of the mass. After this, they went home. If it were theatre night, perhaps they met at the theatre; if it were assembly night, they met at the rooms; and if it were neither, they met the next day. A very pleasant routine, with perhaps a slight tinge of sameness.

Mr Pickwick was sitting up by himself, after a day spent in this manner, making entries in his journal: his friends having retired to bed: when he was roused by a gentle tap at the room door.

'Beg your pardon, sir,' said Mrs Craddock, the landlady, peeping in; 'but *did* you want anything more, sir?'

'Nothing more, ma'am,' replied Mr Pickwick.

'My young girl is gone to bed, sir,' said Mrs Craddock; 'and Mr Dowler is good enough to say that he'll sit up for Mrs Dowler, as the party isn't expected to be over till late; so I was thinking if you wanted nothing more, Mr Pickwick, I would go to bed.'

'By all means, ma'am,' replied Mr Pickwick.

'Wish you good night, sir,' said Mrs Craddock.

'Good night, ma'am,' rejoined Mr Pickwick.

Mrs Craddock closed the door, and Mr Pickwick resumed his writing.

In half an hour's time the entries were concluded. Mr Pickwick carefully rubbed the last page on the blotting-paper, shut up the book, wiped his pen on the bottom of the inside of his coat-tail, and opened the drawer of the inkstand to put it carefully away. There were a couple of sheets of writing-paper, pretty closely written over, in the inkstand drawer, and they were folded so that the title, which was in a good round hand, was fully disclosed to him. Seeing from this, that it was no private document: and as it seemed to relate to Bath, and was very short: Mr Pickwick unfolded it, lighted his bed-room candle that it might burn up well by the time he finished; and drawing his chair nearer the fire, read as follows:

THE TRUE LEGEND OF PRINCE BLADUD

'Less than two hundred years agone, on one of the public baths in this city, there appeared an inscription in honour of its mighty founder, the renowned Prince Bladud. That inscription is now erased.

'For many hundred years before that time, there had been handed down, from age to age, an old legend, that the illustrious Prince being afflicted with leprosy, on his return from reaping a rich harvest of knowledge in Athens, shunned the court of his royal father, and consorted moodily with husbandmen and pigs. Among the herd (so said the legend) was a pig of grave and solemn countenance, with whom the Prince had a fellow feeling – for he too was wise – a pig of thoughtful and reserved demeanour; an animal superior to his fellows, whose grunt was terrible, and whose bite was sharp. The young Prince sighed deeply as he looked upon the countenance of the majestic swine; he thought of his royal father, and his eyes were bedewed with tears.

'This sagacious pig was fond of bathing in rich, moist mud. Not in summer, as common pigs do, now, to cool themselves, and did even in those distant ages (which is a proof that the light of civilisation had already begun to dawn, though feebly), but in the cold sharp days of winter. His coat was ever so sleek, and his complexion so clear, that the Prince resolved to essay the purifying qualities of the same water that his friend resorted to. He made the trial. Beneath that black mud, bubbled the hot springs of Bath. He washed, and was cured. Hastening to his father's court, he paid his best respects, and returning quickly hither, founded this city, and its famous baths.

'He sought the pig with all the ardour of their early friendship – but, alas! the waters had been his death. He had imprudently taken a bath at too high a temperature, and the natural philosopher was no more! He was succeeded by Pliny,[5] who also fell a victim to his thirst for knowledge.

'This *was* the legend. Listen to the true one.

'A great many centuries since, there flourished, in great state, the famous and renowned Lud Hudibras, king of Britain. He was a mighty monarch. The earth shook when he walked: he was so very stout. His people basked in the light of his countenance: it was so red and glowing. He was, indeed, every inch a king. And there were a good many inches of him too, for although he was not very tall, he was a remarkable size round, and the inches that he wanted in height, he made up in circumference. If any degenerate monarch of modern times could be in any way compared with him, I should say the venerable King Cole would be that illustrious potentate.

'This good king had a queen, who eighteen years before, had had a son, who was called Bladud. He was sent to a preparatory seminary in his father's dominions until he was ten years old, and was then dispatched, in charge of a trusty messenger, to a finishing school at Athens; and as there was no extra charge for remaining during the holidays, and no notice required previous to the removal of a pupil, there he remained for eight long years, at the expiration of which time, the king his father sent the lord chamberlain over, to settle the bill, and to bring him home: which, the lord chamberlain doing, was received with shouts, and pensioned immediately.

'When King Lud saw the Prince his son, and found he had grown up such a fine young man, he perceived at once what a grand thing it would be to have him married without delay, so that his children might be the means of perpetuating the glorious race of Lud, down to the very latest ages of the world. With this view, he sent a special embassy, composed of great noblemen who had nothing particular to do, and wanted lucrative employment, to a neighbouring king, and demanded his fair daughter in marriage for his son: stating at the same time that he was anxious to be on the most affectionate terms with his brother and friend, but that if they couldn't agree in arranging this marriage, he should be under the unpleasant necessity of invading his kingdom, and putting his eyes out. To this, the other king (who was the weaker of the two) replied, that he was very much obliged to his friend and brother for all his goodness and magnanimity, and that his daughter was quite ready to be married, whenever Prince Bladud liked to come and fetch her.

'This answer no sooner reached Britain, than the whole nation were transported with joy. Nothing was heard, on all sides, but the sounds of feasting and revelry, – except the chinking of money as it was paid in by the people to the collector of the Royal Treasures, to defray the expenses of the happy ceremony. It was upon this occasion that King Lud, seated on the top of his throne in full council, rose, in the exuberance of his feelings, and commanded the lord chief justice to order in the richest wines and the court minstrels: an act of graciousness which has been, through the ignorance of traditionary historians, attributed to King Cole, in those celebrated lines in which his majesty is represented as

> Calling for his pipe, and calling for his pot,
> And calling for his fiddlers three.

Which is an obvious injustice to the memory of King Lud, and a dishonest exaltation of the virtues of King Cole.

'But, in the midst of all this festivity and rejoicing, there was one individual present, who tasted not when the sparkling wines were poured forth, and who danced not, when the minstrels played. This was no other than Prince Bladud himself, in honour of whose happiness a whole people were at that very moment, straining alike their throats and purse-strings. The truth was, that the Prince, forgetting the undoubted right of the minister for foreign affairs to fall in love on his behalf, had, contrary to every precedent of policy and diplomacy, already fallen in love on his own account, and privately contracted himself unto the fair daughter of a noble Athenian.

'Here we have a striking example of one of the manifold advantages of civilisation and refinement. If the Prince had lived in later days, he might at once have married the object of his father's choice, and then set himself seriously to work, to relieve himself of the burden which rested heavily upon him. He might have endeavoured to break her heart by a systematic course of insult and neglect; or, if the spirit of her sex, and a proud consciousness of her many wrongs had upheld her under this ill treatment, he might have sought to take her life, and so get rid of her effectually. But neither mode of relief suggested itself to Prince Bladud; so he solicited a private audience, and told his father.

'It is an old prerogative of kings to govern everything but their passions. King Lud flew into a frightful rage, tossed his crown up to the ceiling, and caught it again – for in those days kings kept their crowns on their heads, and not in the Tower – stamped the ground, rapped his forehead, wondered why his own flesh and blood rebelled against him, and, finally, calling in his guards, ordered the Prince away to instant confinement in a lofty turret; a course of treatment which the kings of old very generally pursued towards their sons, when their matrimonial inclinations did not happen to point to the same quarter as their own.

'When Prince Bladud had been shut up in the lofty turret for the greater part of a year, with no better prospect before his bodily eyes than a stone wall, or before his mental vision than prolonged imprisonment, he naturally began to ruminate on a plan of escape, which, after months of preparation, he managed to accomplish; considerately leaving his dinner knife in the heart of his gaoler, lest the poor fellow (who had a family) should be considered privy to his flight, and punished accordingly by the infuriated king.

'The monarch was frantic at the loss of his son. He knew not on whom to vent his grief and wrath, until fortunately bethinking himself of the Lord Chamberlain who had brought him home, he struck off his pension and his head together.

'Meanwhile, the young Prince, effectually disguised, wandered on foot through his father's dominions, cheered and supported in all his hardships by sweet thoughts of the Athenian maid, who was the innocent cause of his weary trials. One day he stopped to rest in a country village; and seeing that there were gay dances going forward on the green, and gay faces passing to and fro, ventured to inquire of a reveller who stood near him; the reason for this rejoicing.

'"Know you not, O stranger," was the reply, "of the recent proclamation of our gracious king?"

'"Proclamation! No. What proclamation?" rejoined the Prince – for he had travelled along the bye and little-frequented ways, and knew nothing of what had passed upon the public roads, such as they were.

'"Why," replied the peasant, "the foreign lady that our Prince wished to wed, is married to a foreign noble of her own country; and the king proclaims the fact, and a great public festival besides; for now, of course, Prince Bladud will come back and marry the lady his father chose, who they say is as beautiful as the noon-day sun. Your health, sir. God save the King!"

'The Prince remained to hear no more. He fled from the spot, and plunged into the thickest recesses of a neighbouring wood. On, on, he wandered, night and day: beneath the blazing sun, and the cold pale moon: through the dry heat of noon, and the damp cold of night: in the grey light of morn, and the red glare of eve. So heedless was he of time or object, that being bound for Athens, he wandered as far out of his way as Bath.

'There was no city where Bath stands, then. There was no vestige of human habitation, or sign of man's resort, to bear the name; but there was the same noble country, the same broad expanse of hill and dale, the same beautiful channel stealing on, far away: the same lofty mountains which, like the troubles of life, viewed at a distance, and partially obscured by the bright mist of its morning, lose their ruggedness and asperity, and seem all ease and softness. Moved by the gentle beauty of the scene, the Prince sank upon the green turf, and bathed his swollen feet in his tears.

'"Oh!" said the unhappy Bladud, clasping his hands, and mournfully raising his eyes towards the sky, "would that my wanderings might end here! Would that these grateful tears with which I now mourn hope misplaced, and love despised, might flow in peace for ever!"

'The wish was heard. It was in the time of the heathen deities, who used occasionally to take people at their words, with a promptness, in some cases extremely awkward. The ground opened beneath the Prince's feet; he sunk into the chasm; and instantaneously it closed upon his head for ever, save where his hot tears welled up through the earth, and where they have continued to gush forth ever since.

'It is observable that, to this day, large numbers of elderly ladies and gentlemen who have been disappointed in procuring partners, and almost as many young ones who are anxious to obtain them repair, annually, to Bath to drink the waters, from which they derive much strength and comfort. This is most complimentary to the virtue of Prince Bladud's tears, and strongly corroborative of the veracity of this legend.'

———

Mr Pickwick yawned, several times, when he had arrived at the end of this little manuscript: carefully refolded, and replaced it in the inkstand drawer: and then, with a countenance expressive of the utmost weariness, lighted his chamber candle, and went up stairs to bed.

He stopped at Mr Dowler's door, according to custom, and knocked to say good night.

'Ah!' said Dowler, 'going to bed? I wish I was. Dismal night. Windy; isn't it?'

'Very,' said Mr Pickwick. 'Good night.'

'Good night.'

Mr Pickwick went to his bed-chamber, and Mr Dowler resumed his seat before the fire, in fulfilment of his rash promise to sit up till his wife came home.

There are few things more worrying than sitting up for somebody, especially if that somebody be at a party. You cannot help thinking how quickly the time passes with them, which drags so heavily with you; and the more you think of this, the more your hopes of their speedy arrival decline. Clocks tick so loud, too, when you are sitting up alone, and you seem as if you had an under garment of cobwebs on. First, something tickles your right knee, and then the same sensation irritates your left. You have no sooner changed your position, than it comes again in the arms; when you have fidgeted your limbs into all sorts of odd shapes, you have a sudden relapse in the nose, which you rub as if to rub it off – as there is no doubt you would, if you could. Eyes, too, are mere personal inconveniences; and the wick of one candle gets an inch and a half long, while you are snuffing the other. These, and various other little nervous annoyances, render sitting up for a length of time after everybody else has gone to bed, anything but a cheerful amusement.

This was just Mr Dowler's opinion, as he sat before the fire, and felt honestly indignant with all the inhuman people at the party who were keeping him up. He was not put into better humour either, by the reflection that he had taken it into his head, early in the evening, to think he had got an ache there, and so stopped at home. At length, after several droppings asleep, and fallings forward towards the bars, and catchings backward soon enough to prevent being branded in the face, Mr Dowler made up his mind that he would throw himself on the bed in the back-room and *think* – not sleep, of course.

'I'm a heavy sleeper,' said Mr Dowler, as he flung himself on the bed. 'I must keep awake. I suppose I shall hear a knock here. Yes. I thought so. I can hear the watchman. There he goes. Fainter now though. A little fainter. He's turning the corner. Ah!' When Mr Dowler arrived at this point, *he* turned the corner at which he had been long hesitating, and fell fast asleep.

Just as the clock struck three, there was blown into the crescent a sedan-chair with Mrs Dowler inside, borne by one short fat chairman, and one long thin one, who had had much ado to keep their bodies perpendicular: to say nothing of the chair. But on that high ground, and in the crescent, which the wind swept round and round as if it were going to tear the paving stones up, its fury was tremendous. They were very glad to set the chair down, and give a good round loud double-knock at the street door.

They waited some time, but nobody came.

'Servants is in the arms o' Porpus,[6] I think,' said the short chairman, warming his hands at the attendant link-boy's[7] torch.

'I wish he'd give 'em a squeeze and wake 'em,' observed the long one.

'Knock again, will you, if you please,' cried Mrs Dowler from the chair. 'Knock two or three times, if you please.'

The short man was quite willing to get the job over, as soon as possible; so he stood on the step, and gave four or five most startling double-knocks, of eight or ten knocks a piece: while the long man went into the road, and looked up at the windows for a light.

Nobody came. It was all as silent and dark as ever.

'Dear me!' said Mrs Dowler. 'You must knock again, if you please.'

'Their ain't a bell, is there, ma'am?' said the short chairman.

'Yes, there is,' interposed the link-boy, 'I've been a ringing at it ever so long.'

'It's only a handle,' said Mrs Dowler, 'the wire's broken.'

'I wish the servants' heads wos,' growled the long man.

'I must trouble you to knock again, if you please,' said Mrs Dowler with the utmost politeness.

The short man did knock again several times, without producing the smallest effect. The tall man, growing very impatient, then relieved him, and kept on perpetually knocking double-knocks of two loud knocks each, like an insane postman.

At length Mr Winkle began to dream that he was at a club, and that the members being very refractory, the chairman was obliged to hammer the table a good deal to preserve order; then, he had a confused notion of an auction room where there were no bidders, and the auctioneer was buying everything in; and ultimately he began to think it just within the bounds of possibility that somebody might be knocking at the street door. To make quite certain, however, he remained quiet in bed for ten minutes or so, and listened; and when he had counted two or three and thirty knocks, he felt quite satisfied, and gave himself a great deal of credit for being so wakeful.

'Rap rap – rap rap – rap rap – ra, ra, ra, ra, ra, rap!' went the knocker.

Mr Winkle jumped out of bed, wondering very much what could possibly be the matter, and hastily putting on his stockings and slippers, folded his dressing gown round him, lighted a flat candle from the rush-light that was burning in the fire-place, and hurried down stairs.

'Here's somebody comin' at last, ma'am,' said the short chairman.

'I wish I wos behind him vith a bradawl,'[8] muttered the long one.

'Who's there?' cried Mr Winkle, undoing the chain.

'Don't stop to ask questions, cast-iron head,' replied the long man, with great disgust, taking it for granted that the inquirer was a footman; 'but open the door.'

'Come, look sharp, timber eye-lids,' added the other encouragingly.

Mr Winkle, being half asleep, obeyed the command mechanically, opened the door a little, and peeped out. The first thing he saw, was the red glare of the link-boy's torch. Startled by the sudden fear that the house might be on fire, he hastily threw the door wide open, and holding the candle above his head, stared eagerly before him, not quite certain whether what he saw was a sedan-chair or a fire engine. At this instant there came a violent gust of wind; the light was blown out; Mr Winkle felt himself irresistibly impelled on to the steps; and the door blew to, with a loud crash.

'Well, young man, now you *have* done it!' said the short chairman.

Mr Winkle, catching sight of a lady's face at the window of the sedan, turned hastily round, plied the knocker with all his might and main, and called frantically upon the chairman to take the chair away again.

'Take it away, take it away,' cried Mr Winkle. 'Here's somebody coming out of another house; put me into the chair. Hide me! Do something with me!'

All this time he was shivering with cold; and every time he raised his hand to the knocker, the wind took the dressing gown in a most unpleasant manner.

'The people are coming down the Crescent now. There are ladies with 'em; cover me up with something. Stand before me!' roared Mr Winkle. But the chairmen were too much exhausted with laughing to afford him the slightest assistance, and the ladies were every moment approaching nearer and nearer.

Mr Winkle gave a last hopeless knock; the ladies were only a few doors off. He threw away the extinguished candle, which, all this time, he had held above his head, and fairly bolted into the sedan-chair where Mrs Dowler was.

Now, Mrs Craddock had heard the knocking and the voices at last; and, only waiting to put something smarter on her head than her night-cap, ran down into the front drawing-room to make sure that it was the right party. Throwing up the window-sash as Mr Winkle was rushing into the chair, she no sooner caught sight of what was going forward below, than she raised a vehement and dismal shriek, and implored Mr Dowler to get up directly, for his wife was running away with another gentleman.

Upon this, Mr Dowler bounced off the bed as abruptly as an India-rubber ball,[9] and rushing into the front room, arrived at one window just as Mr Pickwick threw up the other: when the first object that met the gaze of both, was Mr Winkle bolting into the sedan-chair.

'Watchman,' shouted Dowler furiously; 'stop him – hold him – keep him tight – shut him in, till I come down. I'll cut his throat – give me a knife – from ear to ear, Mrs Craddock – I will!' And

Mr Winkle's situation when the door blew to

breaking from the shrieking landlady, and from Mr Pickwick, the indignant husband seized a small supper-knife, and tore into the street.

But Mr Winkle didn't wait for him. He no sooner heard the horrible threat of the valorous Dowler, than he bounced out of the sedan, quite as quickly as he had bounced in, and throwing off his slippers into the road, took to his heels and tore round the Crescent, hotly pursued by Dowler and the watchman. He kept ahead; the door was open as he came round the second time; he rushed in, slammed it in Dowler's face, mounted to his bed-room, locked the door, piled a washhand-stand,[10] chest of drawers, and table against it, and packed up a few necessaries ready for flight with the first ray of morning.

Dowler came up to the outside of the door; avowed, through the key-hole, his stedfast determination of cutting Mr Winkle's throat next day; and, after a great confusion of voices in the drawing-room, amidst which that of Mr Pickwick was distinctly heard endeavouring to make peace, the inmates dispersed to their several bed-chambers, and all was quiet once more.

It is not unlikely that the inquiry may be made, where Mr Weller was, all this time? We will state where he was, in the next chapter.

CHAPTER 37

Honourably accounts for Mr Weller's Absence, by
describing a Soirée to which he was invited and
went; also relates how he was entrusted by
Mr Pickwick with a Private Mission of Delicacy
and Importance

'Mr Weller,' said Mrs Craddock, upon the morning of this very eventful day, 'here's a letter for you.'

'Wery odd that,' said Sam, 'I'm afeerd there must be somethin' the matter, for I don't recollect any gen'lm'n in my circle of acquaintance as is capable o'writin' one.'

'Perhaps something uncommon has taken place,' observed Mrs Craddock.

'It must be somethin' wery uncommon indeed, as could produce a letter out o' any friend o' mine,' replied Sam, shaking his head dubiously; 'nothin' less than a nat'ral conwulsion, as the young gen'lm'n observed ven he wos took with fits. It can't be from the gov'ner,' said Sam, looking at the direction. 'He always prints, I know, 'cos he learnt writin' from the large bills[1] in the bookin' offices. It's a wery strange thing now, where this here letter can ha' come from.'

As Sam said this, he did what a great many people do when they are uncertain about the writer of a note, – looked at the seal, and then at the front, and then at the back, and then at the sides, and then at the superscription;[2] and, as a last resource, thought perhaps he might as well look at the inside, and try to find out from that.

'It's wrote on gilt-edged paper,' said Sam, as he unfolded it, 'and sealed in bronze vax vith the top of a door-key. Now for it.' And, with a very grave face, Mr Weller slowly read as follows:

'A select company of the Bath footmen presents their compliments to Mr Weller, and requests the pleasure of his company this evening, to a friendly swarry,[3] consisting of a boiled leg of mutton with the usual trimmings. The swarry to be on table at half-past nine o'clock punctually.'

This was inclosed in another note, which ran thus –

'Mr John Smauker, the gentleman who had the pleasure of meeting Mr Weller at the house of their mutual acquaintance, Mr Bantam, a few days since, begs to enclose Mr Weller the herewith invitation. If Mr Weller will call on Mr John Smauker at nine o'clock, Mr John Smauker will have the pleasure of introducing Mr Weller.

(Signed) 'JOHN SMAUKER.'

The envelope was directed to blank Weller, Esq., at Mr Pickwick's; and in a parenthesis, in the left hand corner, were the words 'airy bell,'[4] as an instruction to the bearer.

'Vell,' said Sam, 'this is comin' it rayther powerful, this is. I never heerd a biled leg o' mutton called a swarry afore. I wonder wot they'd call a roast one.'

However, without waiting to debate the point, Sam at once betook himself into the presence of Mr Pickwick, and requested leave of absence for that evening, which was readily granted. With this permission, and the street-door key, Sam Weller issued forth a little before the appointed time, and strolled leisurely towards Queen Square, which he no sooner gained than he had the satisfaction of beholding Mr John Smauker leaning his powdered head against a lamp post at a short distance off, smoking a cigar through an amber tube.

'How do you do, Mr Weller?' said Mr John Smauker, raising his hat gracefully with one hand, while he gently waved the other in a condescending manner. 'How do you do, sir?'

'Why, reasonably conwalessent,' replied Sam. 'How do *you* find yourself, my dear feller?'

'Only so so,' said Mr John Smauker.

'Ah, you've been a workin' too hard,' observed Sam. 'I was fearful you would; it won't do, you know; you must not give way to that 'ere uncompromisin' spirit o' your'n.'

'It's not so much that, Mr Weller,' replied Mr John Smauker, 'as bad wine; I'm afraid I've been dissipating.'

'Oh! that's it, is it?' said Sam; 'that's a wery bad complaint, that.'

'And yet the temptation, you see, Mr Weller,' observed Mr John Smauker.

'Ah, to be sure,' said Sam.

'Plunged into the very vortex of society, you know, Mr Weller,' said Mr John Smauker with a sigh.

'Dreadful indeed!' rejoined Sam.

'But it's always the way,' said Mr John Smauker; 'if your destiny leads you into public life, and public station, you must expect to be subjected to temptations which other people is free from, Mr Weller.'

'Precisely what my uncle said, ven *he* vent into the public line,' remarked Sam, 'and wery right the old gen'lm'n wos, for he drank hisself to death in somethin' less than a quarter.'

Mr John Smauker looked deeply indignant at any parallel being drawn between himself and the deceased gentleman in question; but as Sam's face was in the most immoveable state of calmness, he thought better of it, and looked affable again.

'Perhaps we had better be walking,' said Mr Smauker, consulting a copper time-piece[5] which dwelt at the bottom of a deep watch-pocket, and was raised to the surface by means of a black string, with a copper key at the other end.

'P'raps we had,' replied Sam, 'or they'll overdo the swarry, and that'll spile it.'

'Have you drank the waters, Mr Weller?' inquired his companion, as they walked towards High Street.

'Once,' replied Sam.

'What did you think of 'em, sir?'

'I thought they wos particklery unpleasant,' replied Sam.

'Ah,' said Mr John Smauker, 'you disliked the killibeate taste,[6] perhaps?'

'I don't know much about that 'ere,' said Sam. 'I thought they'd a wery strong flavour o' warm flat irons.'

'That *is* the killibeate, Mr Weller,' observed Mr John Smauker, contemptuously.

'Well, if it is, it's a wery inexpressive word, that's all,' said Sam. 'It may be, but I ain't much in the chimical line myself, so I can't say.' And here, to the great horror of Mr John Smauker, Sam Weller began to whistle.

'I beg your pardon, Mr Weller,' said Mr John Smauker, agonized at the exceedingly ungenteel sound, 'Will you take my arm?'

'Thankee, you're wery good, but I won't deprive you of it,' replied Sam. 'I've rayther a way o' puttin' my hands in my pockets, if it's all the same to you.' As Sam said this, he suited the action to the word, and whistled far louder than before.

'This way,' said his new friend, apparently much relieved as they turned down a bye street; 'we shall soon be there.'

'Shall we?' said Sam, quite unmoved by the announcement of his close vicinity to the select footmen of Bath.

'Yes,' said Mr John Smauker. 'Don't be alarmed, Mr Weller.'

'Oh no,' said Sam.

'You'll see some very handsome uniforms, Mr Weller,' continued Mr John Smauker; 'and perhaps you'll find some of the gentlemen rather high at first, you know, but they'll soon come round.'

'That's wery kind on 'em,' replied Sam.

'And you know,' resumed Mr John Smauker, with an air of sublime protection; 'you know, as you're a stranger, perhaps they'll be rather hard upon you at first.'

'They won't be wery cruel, though, will they?' inquired Sam.

'No, no,' replied Mr John Smauker, pulling forth the fox's head, and taking a gentlemanly pinch. 'There are some funny dogs among us, and they will have their joke, you know; but you mustn't mind 'em, you mustn't mind 'em.'

'I'll try and bear up agin such a reg'lar knock down o' talent,' replied Sam.

'That's right,' said Mr John Smauker, putting up the fox's head, and elevating his own; 'I'll stand by you.'

By this time they had reached a small greengrocer's shop, which Mr John Smauker entered, followed by Sam: who, the moment he got behind him, relapsed into a series of the very broadest and most unmitigated grins, and manifested other demonstrations of being in a highly enviable state of inward merriment.

Crossing the greengrocer's shop, and putting their hats on the stairs in the little passage behind it, they walked into a small parlour; and here the full splendour of the scene burst upon Mr Weller's view.

A couple of tables were put together in the middle of the parlour, covered with three or four cloths of different ages and dates of washing, arranged to look as much like one as the circumstances of the case would allow. Upon these were laid knives and forks for six or eight people. Some of the knife handles were green, others red, and a few yellow; and as all the forks were black, the combination of colours was exceedingly striking. Plates for a corresponding number of guests were warming behind the fender; and the guests themselves were warming before it: the chief and most important of whom appeared to be a stoutish gentleman in a bright crimson coat with long tails, vividly red breeches, and a cocked hat, who was standing with his back to the fire, and had apparently just entered, for besides retaining his cocked hat on his head, he carried in his hand a high stick, such as gentlemen of his profession usually elevate in a sloping position over the roofs of carriages.

'Smauker, my lad, your fin,' said the gentleman with the cocked hat.

Mr Smauker dovetailed the top joint of his right hand little finger into that of the gentleman with the cocked hat, and said he was charmed to see him looking so well.

'Well, they tell me I am looking pretty blooming,' said the man with the cocked hat, 'and it's a wonder, too. I've been following our old woman about, two hours a-day, for the last fortnight; and if a constant contemplation of the manner in which she hooks-and-eyes that infernal lavender coloured old gown of her's behind, isn't enough to throw any body into a low state of despondency for life, stop my quarter's salary.'

At this, the assembled selections laughed very heartily; and one gentleman in a yellow waistcoat, with a coach trimming border, whispered a neighbour in green foil smalls, that Tuckle was in spirits to-night.

'By the bye,' said Mr Tuckle, 'Smauker, my boy, you —' The remainder of the sentence was forwarded into Mr John Smauker's ear, by whisper.

'Oh, dear me, I quite forgot,' said Mr John Smauker. 'Gentlemen, my friend Mr Weller.'

'Sorry to keep the fire off you, Weller,' said Mr Tuckle, with a familiar nod. 'Hope you're not cold, Weller.'

'Not by no means, Blazes,' replied Sam. 'It 'ud be a wery chilly subject as felt cold wen you stood opposit. You'd save coals if they put you behind the fender in the waitin' room at a public office, you would.'

As this retort appeared to convey rather a personal allusion to Mr Tuckle's crimson livery, that gentleman looked majestic for a few seconds, but gradually edging away from the fire, broke into a forced smile, and said it wasn't bad.

'Wery much obliged for your good opinion, sir,' replied Sam. 'We shall get on by degrees, I des-say. We'll try a better one, bye-and-bye.'

At this point the conversation was interrupted by the arrival of a gentleman in orange-coloured plush, accompanied by another selection in purple cloth, with a great extent of stocking. The new comers having been welcomed by the old ones, Mr Tuckle put the question that supper be ordered in, which was carried unanimously.

The greengrocer and his wife then arranged upon the table a boiled leg of mutton, hot, with caper sauce, turnips, and potatoes. Mr Tuckle took the chair, and was supported at the other end of the board by the gentleman in orange plush. The greengrocer put on a pair of wash-leather gloves to hand the plates with, and stationed himself behind Mr Tuckle's chair.

'Harris,' said Mr Tuckle, in a commanding tone.

'Sir,' said the greengrocer.

'Have you got your gloves on?'

'Yes, sir.'

'Then take the kiver,[7] off.'

'Yes, sir.'

The greengrocer did as he was told, with a show of great humility, and obsequiously handed Mr Tuckle the carving knife; in doing which, he accidentally gaped.[8]

'What do you mean by that, sir?' said Mr Tuckle, with great asperity.

'I beg your pardon, sir,' replied the crest-fallen greengrocer, 'I didn't mean to do it, sir; I was up very late last night, sir.'

'I tell you what my opinion of you is, Harris,' said Mr Tuckle with a most impressive air, 'you're a wulgar beast.'

'I hope, gentlemen,' said Harris, 'that you won't be severe with me, gentlemen. I'm very much obliged to you indeed, gentlemen, for your patronage, and also for your recommendations, gentlemen, whenever additional assistance in waiting is required. I hope, gentlemen, I give satisfaction.'

'No, you don't sir,' said Mr Tuckle. 'Very far from it, sir.'

'We consider you an inattentive reskel,' said the gentleman in the orange plush.

'And a low thief,' added the gentleman in the green-foil smalls.

'And an unreclaimable blaygaird,' added the gentleman in purple.

The poor greengrocer bowed very humbly while these little epithets were bestowed upon him, in the true spirit of the very smallest tyranny; and when every body had said something to show his superiority, Mr Tuckle proceeded to carve the leg of mutton, and to help the company.

This important business of the evening had hardly commenced, when the door was thrown briskly open, and another gentleman in a light-blue suit, and leaden buttons, made his appearance.

'Against the rules,' said Mr Tuckle. 'Too late, too late.'

'No, no; positively I couldn't help it,' said the gentleman in blue. 'I appeal to the company. An affair of gallantry now, an appointment at the theayter.'

'Oh, that indeed,' said the gentleman in the orange plush.

'Yes; raly now, honour bright,' said the man in blue. 'I made a promese to fetch our youngest daughter at half-past ten, and she is such an uncauminly fine gal, that I raly hadn't the art to disappint her. No offence to the present company, sir, but a petticut, sir, a petticut, sir, is irrevokeable.'

'I begin to suspect there's something in that quarter,' said Tuckle, as the new comer took his seat next Sam. 'I've remarked, once or twice, that she leans very heavy on your shoulder when she gets in and out of the carriage.'

'Oh raly, raly, Tuckle, you shouldn't,' said the man in blue. 'It's not fair. I may have said to one or two friends that she was a very divine creechure, and had refused one or two offers without any hobvus cause, but – no, no, no, indeed, Tuckle – before strangers, too – it's not right – you shouldn't. Delicacy, my dear friend, delicacy!' And the man in blue, pulling up his neckerchief, and adjusting his coat cuffs, nodded and frowned as if there were more behind, which he could say if he liked, but was bound in honour to suppress.

The man in blue being a light-haired, stiff-necked, free and easy sort of footman, with a swaggering air and pert face, had attracted Mr Weller's especial attention at first, but when he began to come out in this way, Sam felt more than ever disposed to cultivate his acquaintance; so he launched himself into the conversation at once, with characteristic independence.

'Your health, sir,' said Sam. 'I like your conwersation much. I think it's wery pretty.'

At this the man in blue smiled, as if it were a compliment he was well used to; but looked approvingly on Sam at the same time, and said he hoped he should be better acquainted with him, for without any flattery at all he seemed to have the makings of a very nice fellow about him, and to be just the man after his own heart.

'You're wery good, sir,' said Sam. 'What a lucky feller you are!'

'How do you mean?' inquired the gentleman in blue.

'That 'ere young lady,' replied Sam. 'She knows wot's wot, she does. Ah! I see.' Mr Weller closed one eye, and shook his head from side to side, in a manner which was highly gratifying to the personal vanity of the gentleman in blue.

'I'm afraid you're a cunning fellow, Mr Weller,' said that individual.

'No, no,' said Sam. 'I leave all that 'ere to you. It's a great deal more in your way than mine, as the gen'l'm'n on the right side o' the garden vall said to the man on the wrong 'un, ven the mad bull wos a comin' up the lane.'

'Well, well, Mr Weller,' said the gentleman in blue, 'I think she has remarked my air and manner, Mr Weller.'

'I should think she couldn't wery well be off o' that,' said Sam.

'Have you any little thing of that kind in hand, sir?' inquired the favoured gentleman in blue, drawing a toothpick from his waistcoat pocket.

'Not exactly,' said Sam. 'There's no daughters at my place, else o' course I should ha' made up to vun on 'em. As it is, I don't think I can do with any thin' under a female markis. I might take up with a young ooman o' large property as hadn't a title, if she made wery fierce love to me. Not else.'

'Of course not, Mr Weller,' said the gentleman in blue, 'one can't be troubled, you know; and *we* know, Mr Weller – we, who are men of the world – that a good uniform must work its way with the women, sooner or later. In fact, that's the only thing, between you and me, that makes the service worth entering into.'

'Just so,' said Sam. 'That's it, o' course.'

When this confidential dialogue had gone thus far, glasses were placed round, and every gentleman ordered what he liked best, before the public-house shut up. The gentleman in blue, and the man in orange, who were the chief exquisites of the party, ordered 'cold srub and water,' but with the others, gin and water, sweet, appeared to be the favourite beverage. Sam called the greengrocer a 'desp'rate willin,' and ordered a large bowl of punch: two circumstances which seemed to raise him very much in the opinion of the selections.

'Gentlemen,' said the man in blue, with an air of the most consummate dandyism, 'I'll give you the ladies; come.'

'Hear, hear!' said Sam, 'The young mississes.'

Here there was a loud cry of 'Order,' and Mr John Smauker, as the gentleman who had introduced Mr Weller into that company, begged to inform him that the word he had just made use of, was unparliamentary.

'Which word was that 'ere, sir?' inquired Sam.

'Mississes, sir,' replied Mr John Smauker, with an alarming frown. 'We don't recognise such distinctions here.'

'Oh, wery good,' said Sam; 'then I'll amend the obserwation, and call 'em the dear creeturs, if Blazes vill allow me.'

Some doubt appeared to exist in the mind of the gentleman in the green-foil smalls, whether the chairman could be legally appealed to, as 'Blazes,' but as the company seemed more disposed to stand upon their own rights than his, the question was not raised. The man with the cocked hat, breathed short, and looked long at Sam, but apparently thought it as well to say nothing, in case he should get the worst of it.

After a short silence, a gentleman in an embroidered coat reaching down to his heels, and a waistcoat of the same which kept one half of his legs warm, stirred his gin and water with great energy, and putting himself upon his feet, all at once, by a violent effort, said he was desirous of offering a few remarks to the company: whereupon the person in the cocked hat, had no doubt that the company would be very happy to hear any remarks that the man in the long coat might wish to offer.

'I feel a great delicacy, gentlemen, in coming for'ard,' said the man in the long coat, 'having the misforchune to be a coachman, and being only admitted as a honorary member of these agreeable swarrys, but I do feel myself bound, gentlemen – drove into a corner, if I may use the expression – to make known an afflicting circumstance which has come to my knowledge; which has happened I may say within the soap of my every day contemplation. Gentlemen, our friend Mr Whiffers (everybody looked at the individual in orange), our friend Mr Whiffers has resigned.'

Universal astonishment fell upon the hearers. Each gentleman looked in his neighbour's face, and then transferred his glance to the upstanding coachman.

'You may well be sapparised, gentlemen,' said the coachman. 'I will not wenchure to state the reasons of this irrepairabel loss to the service, but I will beg Mr Whiffers to state them himself, for the improvement and imitation of his admiring friends.'

The suggestion being loudly approved of, Mr Whiffers explained. He said he certainly could have wished to have continued to hold the appointment he had just resigned. The uniform was extremely rich and expensive, the females of the family was most agreeable, and the duties of the situation was not, he was bound to say, too heavy: the principal service that was required of him, being, that he should look out of the hall window as much as possible, in company with another gentleman, who had also resigned. He could have wished to have spared that company the painful and disgusting detail on which he was about to enter, but as the explanation had been demanded of him, he had no alternative but to state, boldly and distinctly, that he had been required to eat cold meat.

It is impossible to conceive the disgust which this avowal awakened in the bosoms of the hearers. Loud cries of 'Shame!' mingled with groans and hisses, prevailed for a quarter of an hour.

Mr Whiffers then added that he feared a portion of this outrage might be traced to his own forbearing and accommodating disposition. He had a distinct recollection of having once consented to eat salt butter, and he had, moreover, on an occasion of sudden sickness in the house, so far forgotten himself as to carry a coal scuttle up to the second floor. He trusted he had not lowered himself in the good opinion of his friends by this frank confession of his faults; and he hoped the promptness with which he had resented the last unmanly outrage on his feelings, to which he had referred, would reinstate him in their good opinion, if he had.

Mr Whiffers' address was responded to, with a shout of admiration, and the health of the interesting martyr was drunk in a most enthusiastic manner; for this, the martyr returned thanks, and proposed their visitor, Mr Weller; a gentleman whom he had not the pleasure of an intimate acquaintance with, but who was the friend of Mr John Smauker, which was a sufficient letter of recommendation to any society of gentlemen whatever, or wherever. On this account, he should have been disposed to have given Mr Weller's health with all the honours, if his friends had been drinking wine; but as they were taking spirits by way of a change, and as it might be inconvenient to empty a tumbler at every toast, he should propose that the honours be understood.

At the conclusion of this speech, everybody took a sip in honour of Sam; and Sam having ladled out, and drunk, two full glasses of punch in honour of himself, returned thanks in a neat speech.

'Wery much obliged to you, old fellers,' said Sam, ladling away at the punch in the most unembarrassed manner possible, 'for this here compliment; wich comin' from sich a quarter, is wery overvelmin'. I've heerd a good deal on you as a body, but I will say, that I never thought you was sich uncommon nice men as I find you air. I only hope you'll take care o' yourselves, and not compromise nothin' o' your dignity, which is a wery charmin' thing to see, when one's out a walkin', and has always made me wery happy to look at, ever since I was a boy about half as high as the brass-headed stick o' my wery respectable friend, Blazes, there. As to the wictim of oppression in the suit o' brimstone, all I can say of him, is, that I hope he'll get jist as good a berth as he deserves: in vich case it's wery little cold swarry as ever he'll be troubled with agin.'

Here Sam sat down with a pleasant smile, and his speech having been vociferously applauded, the company broke up.

'Wy, you don't mean to say you're a goin', old feller?' said Sam Weller to his friend Mr John Smauker.

'I must indeed,' said Mr Smauker; 'I promised Bantam.'

'Oh, wery well,' said Sam; 'that's another thing. P'raps *he'd* resign if you disappinted him. You ain't a goin', Blazes?'

'Yes, I am,' said the man with the cocked hat.

'Wot, and leave three quarters of a bowl of punch behind you!' said Sam; 'nonsense, set down agin.'

Mr Tuckle was not proof against this invitation. He laid aside the cocked hat and stick which he had just taken up, and said he would have one glass, for good fellowship's sake.

As the gentleman in blue went home the same way as Mr Tuckle, he was prevailed upon to stop too. When the punch was about half gone, Sam ordered in some oysters from the greengrocer's shop; and the effect of both was so extremely exhilarating, that Mr Tuckle, dressed out with the cocked hat and stick, danced the frog hornpipe[9] among the shells on the table: while the gentleman in blue played an accompaniment upon an ingenious musical instrument formed of a hair comb and a curl-paper. At last, when the punch was all gone, and the night nearly so, they sallied forth to see each other home. Mr Tuckle no sooner got into the open air, than he was seized with a sudden desire to lie on the curb-stone; Sam thought it would be a pity to contradict him, and so let him have his own way. As the cocked hat would have been spoilt if left there, Sam very considerately flattened it down on the head of the gentleman in blue, and putting the big stick in his hand, propped him up against his own street-door, rang the bell, and walked quietly home.

At a much earlier hour next morning than his usual time of rising, Mr Pickwick walked down stairs completely dressed, and rang the bell.

'Sam,' said Mr Pickwick, when Mr Weller appeared in reply to the summons, 'shut the door.'

Mr Weller did so.

'There was an unfortunate occurrence here, last night, Sam,' said Mr Pickwick, 'which gave Mr Winkle some cause to apprehend violence from Mr Dowler.'

'So I've heerd from the old lady down stairs, sir,' replied Sam.

'And I'm sorry to say, Sam,' continued Mr Pickwick, with a most perplexed countenance, 'that in dread of this violence, Mr Winkle has gone away.'

'Gone avay!' said Sam.

'Left the house early this morning, without the slightest previous communication with me,' replied Mr Pickwick. 'And is gone, I know not where.'

'He should ha' stopped and fought it out, sir,' replied Sam, contemptuously. 'It wouldn't take much to settle that 'ere Dowler, sir.'

'Well, Sam,' said Mr Pickwick, 'I may have my doubts of his great bravery and determination, also. But however that may be, Mr Winkle is gone. He must be found, Sam. Found and brought back to me.'

'And s'pose he won't come back, sir?' said Sam.

'He must be made, Sam,' said Mr Pickwick.

'Who's to do it, sir?' inquired Sam with a smile.

'You,' replied Mr Pickwick.

'Wery good, sir.'

With these words Mr Weller left the room, and immediately afterwards was heard to shut the street door. In two hours' time he returned with as much coolness as if he had been despatched on the most ordinary message possible, and brought the information that an individual, in every respect answering Mr Winkle's description, had gone over to Bristol that morning, by the branch coach from the Royal Hotel.

'Sam,' said Mr Pickwick, grasping his hand, 'you're a capital fellow; an invaluable fellow. You must follow him, Sam.'

'Cert'nly, sir,' replied Mr Weller.

'The instant you discover him, write to me immediately, Sam,' said Mr Pickwick. 'If he attempts to run away from you, knock him down, or lock him up. You have my full authority, Sam.'

'I'll be wery careful, sir,' rejoined Sam.

'You'll tell him,' said Mr Pickwick, 'that I am highly excited, highly displeased, and naturally indignant, at the very extraordinary course he has thought proper to pursue.'

'I will, sir,' replied Sam.

'You'll tell him,' said Mr Pickwick, 'that if he does not come back to this very house, with you, he will come back with me, for I will come and fetch him.'

'I'll mention that 'ere, sir,' rejoined Sam.

'You think you can find him, Sam?' said Mr Pickwick, looking earnestly in his face.

'Oh, I'll find him if he's any vere,' rejoined Sam, with great confidence.

'Very well,' said Mr Pickwick. 'Then the sooner you go the better.'

With these instructions, Mr Pickwick placed a sum of money in the hands of his faithful servitor, and ordered him to start for Bristol immediately, in pursuit of the fugitive.

Sam put a few necessaries in a carpet bag, and was ready for starting. He stopped when he had got to the end of the passage, and walking quietly back, thrust his head in at the parlour door.

'Sir,' whispered Sam.

'Well, Sam,' said Mr Pickwick.

'I fully understands my instructions, do I, sir?' inquired Sam.

'I hope so,' said Mr Pickwick.

'It's reg'larly understood about the knockin' down, is it sir?' inquired Sam.

'Perfectly,' replied Mr Pickwick. 'Thoroughly. Do what you think necessary. You have my orders.'

Sam gave a nod of intelligence, and withdrawing his head from the door, set forth on his pilgrimage with a light heart.

How Mr Winkle, when he stepped out of the Frying-Pan, walked gently and comfortably into the Fire

The ill-starred gentleman who had been the unfortunate cause of the unusual noise and disturbance which alarmed the inhabitants of the Royal Crescent in manner and form already described, after passing a night of great confusion and anxiety, left the roof beneath which his friends still slumbered, bound he knew not whither. The excellent and considerate feelings which prompted Mr Winkle to take this step can never be too highly appreciated or too warmly extolled. 'If,' reasoned Mr Winkle with himself, 'if this Dowler attempts (as I have no doubt he will) to carry into execution his threat of personal violence against myself, it will be incumbent on me to call him out. He has a wife; that wife is attached to, and dependent on him. Heavens! If I should kill him in the blindness of my wrath, what would be my feelings ever afterwards!' This painful consideration operated so powerfully on the feelings of the humane young man, as to cause his knees to knock together, and his countenance to exhibit alarming manifestations of inward emotion. Impelled by such reflections, he grasped his carpet-bag, and creeping stealthily down stairs, shut the detestable street-door with as little noise as possible, and walked off. Bending his steps towards the Royal Hotel, he found a coach on the point of starting for Bristol, and, thinking Bristol as good a place for his purpose as any other he could go to, he mounted the box, and reached his place of destination in such time as the pair of horses, who went the whole stage and back again twice a day or more, could be reasonably supposed to arrive there.

He took up his quarters at The Bush,[1] and, designing to postpone any communication by letter with Mr Pickwick until it was probable that Mr Dowler's wrath might have in some degree evaporated, walked forth to view the city, which struck him as being a shade more dirty than any place he had ever seen. Having inspected the docks and shipping, and viewed the cathedral, he inquired his way to Clifton, and being directed thither, took the route which was pointed out to him. But, as the pavements of Bristol are not the widest or cleanest upon earth, so its streets are not altogether the straightest or least intricate; Mr Winkle being greatly puzzled by their manifold windings and twistings, looked about him for a decent shop in which he could apply afresh, for counsel and instruction.

His eye fell upon a newly-painted tenement which had been recently converted into something between a shop and a private-house, and which a red lamp, projecting over the fan-light of the street-door, would have sufficiently announced as the residence of a medical practitioner, even if the word 'Surgery' had not been inscribed in golden characters on a wainscot ground, above the window of what, in times bygone, had been the front parlour. Thinking this an eligible place wherein to make his inquiries, Mr Winkle stepped into the little shop where the gilt-labelled drawers and bottles were; and finding nobody there, knocked with a half-crown on the counter, to attract the attention of anybody who might happen to be in the back parlour, which he judged to be the innermost and peculiar sanctum of the establishment, from the repetition of the word surgery on the door – painted in white letters this time, by way of taking off the monotony.

At the first knock, a sound, as of persons fencing with fire-irons,[2] which had until now been very audible, suddenly ceased; at the second, a studious-looking young gentleman in green spectacles, with a very large book in his hand, glided quietly into the shop, and stepping behind the counter, requested to know the visitor's pleasure.

'I am sorry to trouble you, sir,' said Mr Winkle, 'but will you have the goodness to direct me to—'

'Ha! ha! ha!' roared the studious young gentleman, throwing the large book up into the air, and catching it with great dexterity at the very moment when it threatened to smash to atoms all the bottles on the counter. 'Here's a start!'

There was, without doubt; for Mr Winkle was so very much astonished at the extraordinary behaviour of the medical gentleman, that he involuntarily retreated towards the door, and looked very much disturbed at his strange reception.

'What, don't you know me?' said the medical gentleman.

Mr Winkle murmured, in reply, that he had not that pleasure.

'Why, then,' said the medical gentleman, 'there are hopes for me yet; I may attend half the old women in Bristol if I've decent luck. Get out, you mouldy old villain, get out!' With this adjuration, which was addressed to the large book, the medical gentleman kicked the volume with remarkable agility to the further end of the shop, and, pulling off his green spectacles, grinned the identical grin of Robert Sawyer, Esquire, formerly of Guy's Hospital in the Borough, with a private residence in Lant Street.

'You don't mean to say you weren't down upon me!' said Mr Bob Sawyer, shaking Mr Winkle's hand with friendly warmth.

'Upon my word I was not,' replied Mr Winkle, returning the pressure.

'I wonder you didn't see the name,' said Bob Sawyer, calling his friend's attention to the outer door, on which, in the same white paint, were traced the words 'Sawyer, late Nockemorf.'

'It never caught my eye,' returned Mr Winkle.

'Lord, if I had known who you were, I should have rushed out, and caught you in my arms,' said Bob Sawyer; 'but upon my life, I thought you were the King's-taxes.'[3]

'No!' said Mr Winkle.

'I did, indeed,' responded Bob Sawyer, 'and I was just going to say that I wasn't at home, but if you'd leave a message I'd be sure to give it to myself; for he don't know me; no more does the Lighting and Paving. I think the Church-rates[4] guesses who I am, and I know the Water-works does, because I drew a tooth of his when I first came down here. But come in, come in!' Chattering in this way, Mr Bob Sawyer pushed Mr Winkle into the back room, where, amusing himself by boring little circular caverns in the chimney-piece with a red-hot poker, sat no less a person than Mr Benjamin Allen.

'Well!' said Mr Winkle. 'This is indeed a pleasure I did not expect. What a very nice place you have here!'

'Pretty well, pretty well,' replied Bob Sawyer. 'I *passed*, soon after that precious party, and my friends came down with the needful for this business; so I put on a black suit of clothes, and a pair of spectacles, and came here to look as solemn as I could.'

'And a very snug little business you have, no doubt?' said Mr Winkle, knowingly.

'Very,' replied Bob Sawyer. 'So snug, that at the end of a few years you might put all the profits in a wine glass, and cover 'em over with a gooseberry leaf.'

'You cannot surely mean that?' said Mr Winkle. 'The stock it-self – '

'Dummies, my dear boy,' said Bob Sawyer; 'half the drawers have nothing in 'em, and the other half don't open.'

'Nonsense!' said Mr Winkle.

'Fact – honor!' returned Bob Sawyer, stepping out into the shop, and demonstrating the veracity of the assertion by divers hard pulls at the little gilt knobs on the counterfeit drawers. 'Hardly anything real in the shop but the leeches, and *they* are second-hand.'

'I shouldn't have thought it!' exclaimed Mr Winkle, much surprised.

'I hope not,' replied Bob Sawyer, 'else where's the use of appearances, eh? But what will you take? Do as we do? That's right. Ben, my fine fellow, put your hand into the cupboard, and bring out the patent digester.'

Mr Benjamin Allen smiled his readiness, and produced from the closet at his elbow a black bottle half full of brandy.

'You don't take water, of course?' said Bob Sawyer.

'Thank you,' replied Mr Winkle. 'It's *rather* early. I should like to qualify it,[5] if you have no objection.'

'None in the least, if you can reconcile it to your conscience,' replied Bob Sawyer; tossing off, as he spoke, a glass of the liquor with great relish. 'Ben, the pipkin!'

Mr Benjamin Allen drew forth, from the same hiding-place, a small brass pipkin, which Bob Sawyer observed he prided himself upon, particularly because it looked so business-like. The water in the professional pipkin[6] having been made to boil, in course of time, by various little shovelsfull of coal, which Mr Bob Sawyer took out of a practicable window-seat, labelled 'Soda Water,' Mr Winkle adulterated his brandy; and the conversation was becoming general, when it was interrupted by the entrance into the shop of a boy, in a sober grey livery and a gold-laced hat, with a small covered basket under his arm: whom Mr Bob Sawyer immediately hailed with, 'Tom, you vagabond, come here.'

The boy presented himself accordingly.

'You've been stopping to over all the posts in Bristol, you idle young scamp!'said Mr Bob Sawyer.

'No, sir, I haven't,' replied the boy.

'You had better not!' said Mr Bob Sawyer, with a threatening aspect. 'Who do you suppose will ever employ a professional man, when they see his boy playing at marbles in the gutter, or flying the garter[7] in the horse-road? Have you no feeling for your profession, you groveller? Did you leave all the medicine?'

'Yes, sir.'

'The powders for the child, at the large house with the new family, and the pills to be taken four times a day at the ill-tempered old gentleman's with the gouty leg?'

'Yes, sir.'

'Then shut the door, and mind the shop.'

'Come,' said Mr Winkle, as the boy retired, 'things are not quite so bad as you would have me believe, either. There is *some* medicine to be sent out.'

Mr Bob Sawyer peeped into the shop to see that no stranger was within hearing, and leaning forward to Mr Winkle, said, in a low tone:

'He leaves it all, at the wrong houses.'

Mr Winkle looked perplexed, and Bob Sawyer and his friend laughed.

'Don't you see?' said Bob. 'He goes up to a house, rings the area bell, pokes a packet of medicine without a direction into the servant's hand, and walks off. Servant takes it into the dining-parlour; master opens it, and reads the label: "Draught to be taken at bed-time – pills as before – lotion as usual – *the* powder. From Sawyer's, late Nockemorf's. Physicians' prescriptions carefully pre-pared, and all the rest of it. Shows it to his wife – *she* reads the label; it goes down to the servants – *they* read the label. Next day, boy calls: "Very sorry – his mistake – immense business – great many parcels to deliver – Mr Sawyer's compliments – late Nocke-morf." The name gets known, and that's the thing, my boy, in the medical way. Bless your heart, old fellow, it's better than all the advertising in the world. We have got one four-ounce bottle that's been to half the houses in Bristol, and hasn't done yet.'

'Dear me, I see,' observed Mr Winkle; 'what an excellent plan!'

'Oh, Ben and I have hit upon a dozen such,' replied Bob Sawyer, with great glee. 'The lamplighter has eighteenpence a week to pull the night-bell for ten minutes every time he comes round; and my boy always rushes into church, just before the psalms, when the people have got nothing to do but look about 'em, and calls me out, with horror and dismay depicted on his countenance. "Bless my soul," everybody says, "somebody taken suddenly ill! Sawyer, late Nockemorf, sent for. What a business that young man has!"'

At the termination of this disclosure of some of the mysteries of medicine, Mr Bob Sawyer and his friend, Ben Allen, threw them-selves back in their respective chairs, and laughed boisterously. When they had enjoyed the joke to their hearts' content, the discourse changed to topics in which Mr Winkle was more immedi-ately interested.

We think we have hinted elsewhere, that Mr Benjamin Allen had a way of becoming sentimental after brandy. The case is not a peculiar one, as we ourself can testify: having, on a few occasions, had to deal with patients who have been afflicted in a similar manner. At this precise period of his existence, Mr Benjamin Allen had perhaps a greater predisposition to maudlinism than he had ever known before; the cause of which malady was briefly this. He had been staying nearly three weeks with Mr Bob Sawyer; Mr Bob Sawyer was not remarkable for temperance, nor was Mr Benjamin Allen for the ownership of a very strong head; the consequence was, that, during the whole space of time just mentioned, Mr Benjamin Allen had been wavering between intoxication partial, and intoxication complete.

'My dear friend,' said Mr Ben Allen, taking advantage of Mr Bob Sawyer's temporary absence behind the counter, whither he had retired to dispense some of the second-hand leeches, previously referred to: 'my dear friend, I am very miserable.'

Mr Winkle professed his heartfelt regret to hear it, and begged to know whether he could do anything to alleviate the sorrows of the suffering student.

'Nothing, my dear boy, nothing,' said Ben. 'You recollect Arabella, Winkle? My sister Arabella – a little girl, Winkle, with black eyes – when we were down at Wardle's? I don't know whether you happened to notice her, a nice little girl, Winkle. Perhaps my features may recal her countenance to your recollection?'

Mr Winkle required nothing to recal the charming Arabella to his mind; and it was rather fortunate he did not, for the features of her brother Benjamin would unquestionably have proved but an indifferent refresher to his memory. He answered, with as much calmness as he could assume, that he perfectly remembered the young lady referred to, and sincerely trusted she was in good health.

'Our friend Bob is a delightful fellow, Winkle,' was the only reply of Mr Ben Allen.

'Very,' said Mr Winkle; not much relishing this close connexion of the two names.

'I designed 'em for each other; they were made for each other, sent into the world for each other, born for each other, Winkle,' said Mr Ben Allen, setting down his glass with emphasis. 'There's a special destiny in the matter, my dear sir; there's only five years' difference between 'em, and both their birthdays are in August.'

Mr Winkle was too anxious to hear what was to follow, to express much wonderment at this extraordinary coincidence, marvellous as it was; so Mr Ben Allen, after a tear or two, went on to say, that, notwithstanding all his esteem and respect and veneration for his friend, Arabella had unaccountably and undutifully evinced the most determined antipathy to his person.

'And I think,' said Mr Ben Allen, in conclusion,'I think there's a prior attachment.'

'Have you any idea who the object of it might be?' asked Mr Winkle, with great trepidation.

Mr Ben Allen seized the poker, flourished it in a warlike manner above his head, inflicted a savage blow on an imaginary skull, and wound up by saying, in a very expressive manner, that he only wished he could guess; that was all.

'I'd show him what I thought of him,' said Mr Ben Allen. And round went the poker again, more fiercely than before.

All this was, of course, very soothing to the feelings of Mr Winkle, who remained silent for a few minutes; but at length mustered up resolution to inquire whether Miss Allen was in Kent.

'No, no,' said Mr Ben Allen, laying aside the poker, and looking very cunning; 'I didn't think Wardle's exactly the place for a headstrong girl; so, as I am her natural protector and guardian, our parents being dead, I have brought her down into this part of the country to spend a few months at an old aunt's, in a nice dull close place. I think that will cure her, my boy. If it doesn't, I'll take her abroad for a little while, and see what that'll do.'

'Oh, the aunt's is in Bristol, is it?' faltered Mr Winkle.

'No, no, not in Bristol,' replied Mr Ben Allen, jerking his thumb over his right shoulder: 'over that way; down there. But, hush, here's Bob. Not a word, my dear friend, not a word.'

Short as this conversation was, it roused in Mr Winkle the highest degree of excitement and anxiety. The suspected prior attachment rankled in his heart. Could he be the object of it? Could it be for him that the fair Arabella had looked scornfully on the sprightly Bob Sawyer, or had he a successful rival? He determined to see her, cost what it might; but here an insurmountable objection presented itself, for whether the explanatory 'over that way,' and 'down there,' of Mr Ben Allen, meant three miles off, or thirty, or three hundred, he could in no wise guess.

But he had no opportunity of pondering over his love just then, for Bob Sawyer's return was the immediate precursor of the arrival of a meat pie from the baker's, of which that gentleman insisted on his staying to partake. The cloth was laid by an occasional charwoman, who officiated in the capacity of Mr Bob Sawyer's house-keeper; and a third knife and fork having been borrowed from the mother of the boy in the grey livery (for Mr Sawyer's domestic arrangements were as yet conducted on a limited scale), they sat down to dinner; the beer being served up, as Mr Sawyer remarked, 'in its native pewter.'

After dinner, Mr Bob Sawyer ordered in the largest mortar in the shop, and proceeded to brew a reeking jorum[8] of rum-punch therein: stirring up and amalgamating the materials with a pestle in a very creditable and apothecary-like manner. Mr Sawyer, being a bachelor, had only one tumbler in the house, which was assigned to Mr Winkle as a compliment to the visitor: Mr Ben Allen being accommodated with a funnel with a cork in the narrow end: and Bob Sawyer contented himself with one of those wide-lipped crystal vessels inscribed with a variety of cabalistic characters, in which chemists are wont to measure out their liquid drugs in compounding prescriptions. These preliminaries adjusted, the punch was tasted, and pronounced excellent; and it having been arranged that Bob Sawyer and Ben Allen should be considered at liberty to fill twice to Mr Winkle's once, they started fair, with great satisfaction and good-fellowship.

There was no singing, because Mr Bob Sawyer said it wouldn't look professional; but to make amends for this deprivation there was so much talking and laughing that it might have been heard, and very likely was, at the end of the street. Which conversation materially lightened the hours and improved the mind of Mr Bob Sawyer's boy, who, instead of devoting the evening to his ordinary occupation of writing his name on the counter, and rubbing it out again, peeped through the glass door, and thus listened and looked on at the same time.

The mirth of Mr Bob Sawyer was rapidly ripening into the furious; Mr Ben Allen was fast relapsing into the sentimental, and the punch had well-nigh disappeared altogether, when the boy hastily running in, announced that a young woman had just come over, to say that Sawyer late Nockemorf was wanted directly, a couple of streets off. This broke up the party. Mr Bob Sawyer, understanding the message, after some twenty repetitions, tied a wet cloth round his head to sober himself, and, having partially succeeded, put on his green spectacles and issued forth. Resisting all entreaties to stay till he came back, and finding it quite impossible to engage Mr Ben Allen in any intelligible conversation on the subject nearest his heart, or indeed on any other, Mr Winkle took his departure, and returned to the Bush.

The anxiety of his mind, and the numerous meditations which Arabella had awakened, prevented his share of the mortar of punch

Conviviality at Bob Sawyer's

producing that effect upon him which it would have had, under other circumstances. So, after taking a glass of soda-water and brandy at the bar, he turned into the coffee-room, dispirited rather than elevated by the occurrences of the evening.

Sitting in the front of the fire, with his back towards him, was a tallish gentleman in a great-coat: the only other occupant of the room. It was rather a cool evening for the season of the year, and the gentleman drew his chair aside to afford the new comer a sight of the fire. What were Mr Winkle's feelings when, in doing so, he disclosed to view the face and figure of the vindictive and sanguinary Dowler!

Mr Winkle's first impulse was to give a violent pull at the nearest bell-handle, but that unfortunately happened to be immediately behind Mr Dowler's head. He had made one step towards it, before he checked himself. As he did so, Mr Dowler very hastily drew back.

'Mr Winkle, sir. Be calm. Don't strike me. I won't bear it. A blow! Never!' said Mr Dowler, looking meeker than Mr Winkle had expected in a gentleman of his ferocity.

'A blow, sir?' stammered Mr Winkle.

'A blow, sir,' replied Dowler. 'Compose your feelings. Sit down. Hear me.'

'Sir,' said Mr Winkle, trembling from head to foot, 'before I consent to sit down beside, or opposite you, without the presence of a waiter, I must be secured by some further understanding. You used a threat against me last night, sir, a dreadful threat, sir.' Here Mr Winkle turned very pale indeed, and stopped short.

'I did,' said Dowler, with a countenance almost as white as Mr Winkle's. 'Circumstances were suspicious. They have been explained. I respect your bravery. Your feeling is upright. Conscious innocence. There's my hand. Grasp it.'

'Really sir,' said Mr Winkle, hesitating whether to give his hand or not, and almost fearing that it was demanded in order that he might be taken at an advantage, 'really sir, I—'

'I know what you mean,' interposed Dowler. 'You feel aggrieved. Very natural. So should I. I was wrong. I beg your pardon. Be friendly. Forgive me.' With this, Dowler fairly forced his hand upon Mr Winkle, and shaking it with the utmost vehemence, declared he was a fellow of extreme spirit, and he had a higher opinion of him than ever.

'Now,' said Dowler, 'sit down. Relate it all. How did you find me? When did you follow? Be frank. Tell me.'

'It's quite accidental,' replied Mr Winkle, greatly perplexed by the curious and unexpected nature of the interview, 'Quite.'

'Glad of it,' said Dowler. 'I woke this morning. I had forgotten my threat. I laughed at the accident. I felt friendly. I said so.'

'To whom?' inquired Mr Winkle.

'To Mrs Dowler. "You made a vow," said she. "I did," said I. "It was a rash one," said she. "It was," said I. "I'll apologise. Where is he?"'

'Who?' inquired Mr Winkle.

'You,' replied Dowler. 'I went down stairs. You were not to be found. Pickwick looked gloomy. Shook his head. Hoped no violence would be committed. I saw it all. You felt yourself insulted. You had gone, for a friend perhaps. Possibly for pistols. "High spirit," said I. "I admire him."'

Mr Winkle coughed, and beginning to see how the land lay, assumed a look of importance.

'I left a note for you,' resumed Dowler. 'I said I was sorry. So I was. Pressing business called me here. You were not satisfied. You followed. You required a verbal explanation. You were right. It's all over now. My business is finished. I go back to-morrow. Join me.'

As Dowler progressed in his explanation, Mr Winkle's countenance grew more and more dignified. The mysterious nature of the commencement of their conversation was explained; Mr Dowler had as great an objection to duelling as himself; in short, this blustering and awful personage was one of the most egregious cowards in existence, and interpreting Mr Winkle's absence through the medium of his own fears, had taken the same step as himself, and prudently retired until all excitement of feeling should have subsided.

As the real state of the case dawned upon Mr Winkle's mind, he looked very terrible, and said he was perfectly satisfied; but at the same time, said so, with an air that left Mr Dowler no alternative but to infer that if he had not been, something most horrible and destructive must inevitably have occurred. Mr Dowler appeared to be impressed with a becoming sense of Mr Winkle's magnanimity and condescension; and the two belligerents parted for the night, with many protestations of eternal friendship.

About half-past twelve o'clock, when Mr Winkle had been revelling some twenty minutes in the full luxury of his first sleep, he was suddenly awakened by a loud knocking at his chamber-door, which, being repeated with increased vehemence, caused him to start up in bed, and inquire who was there, and what the matter was.

'Please, sir, here's a young man which says he must see you directly,' responded the voice of the chambermaid.

'A young man!' exclaimed Mr Winkle.

'No mistake about that 'ere, sir,' replied another voice through the keyhole; 'and if that wery same interestin' young creetur ain't let in vithout delay, it's wery possible as his legs vill enter afore his countenance.' The young man gave a gentle kick at one of the lower panels of the door, after he had given utterance to this hint, as if to add force and point to the remark.

'Is that you, Sam?' inquired Mr Winkle, springing out of bed.

'Quite unpossible to identify any gen'l'm'n with any degree o' mental satisfaction, vithout lookin' at him, sir,' replied the voice, dogmatically.

Mr Winkle, not much doubting who the young man was, unlocked the door; which he had no sooner done, than Mr Samuel Weller entered with great precipitation, and carefully re-locking it on the inside, deliberately put the key in his waistcoat pocket: and, after surveying Mr Winkle from head to foot, said:

'You're a wery humorous young gen'l'm'n, you air, sir!'

'What do you mean by this conduct, Sam?' inquired Mr Winkle, indignantly. 'Get out, sir, this instant. What do you mean, sir?'

'What do I mean,' retorted Sam; 'come, sir, this is rayther too rich, as the young lady said, wen she remonstrated with the pastry-cook, arter he'd sold her a pork-pie as had got nothin' but fat inside. What do I mean! Well, that ain't a bad 'un, that ain't.'

'Unlock that door, and leave this room immediately, sir,' said Mr Winkle.

'I shall leave this here room, sir, just precisely at the wery same moment as you leaves it,' responded Sam, speaking in a forcible manner, and seating himself with perfect gravity. 'If I find it necessary to carry you away, pick-a-back,[9] o' course I shall leave it the least bit o' time possible afore you; but allow me to express a hope as you won't reduce me to ex-tremities; in saying wich, I merely quote wot the nobleman said to the fractious pennywinkle,[10] ven he vouldn't come out of his shell by means of a pin, and he consequently began to be afeered that he should be obliged to crack him in the parlour-door.' At the end of this address, which was unusually lengthy for him, Mr Weller planted his hands on his knees, and looked full in Mr Winkle's face, with an expression of countenance which showed that he had not the remotest intention of being trifled with.

'You're a amiably-disposed young man, sir, I don't think,' resumed Mr Weller, in a tone of moral reproof, 'to go inwolving our precious governor in all sorts o' fanteegs,[11] wen he's made up his mind to go through every think for principle. You're far worse nor Dodson, sir; and as for Fogg, I consider him a born angel to you!' Mr Weller having accompanied this last sentiment with an emphatic slap on each knee, folded his arms with a look of great disgust, and threw himself back in his chair, as if awaiting the criminal's defence.

'My good fellow,' said Mr Winkle, extending his hand; his teeth chattering all the time he spoke, for he had been standing, during the whole of Mr Weller's lecture, in his night-gear; 'My good fellow, I respect your attachment to my excellent friend, and I am very sorry indeed, to have added to his causes for disquiet. There, Sam, there!'

'Well,' said Sam, rather sulkily, but giving the proffered hand a respectful shake at the same time: 'Well, so you ought to be, and I am very glad to find you air; for, if I can help it, I won't have him put upon by nobody, and that's all about it.'

'Certainly not, Sam,' said Mr Winkle. 'There! Now go to bed, Sam, and we'll talk further about this, in the morning.'

'I'm wery sorry,' said Sam, 'but I can't go to bed.'

'Not go to bed!' repeated Mr Winkle.

'No,' said Sam, shaking his head. 'Can't be done.'

'You don't mean to say you're going back to-night, Sam?' urged Mr Winkle, greatly surprised.

'Not unless you particklerly wish it,' replied Sam; 'but I musn't leave this here room. The governor's orders wos peremptory.'

'Nonsense, Sam,' said Mr Winkle, 'I must stop here two or three days; and more than that, Sam, you must stop here too, to assist me in gaining an interview with a young lady – Miss Allen, Sam; you remember her – whom I must and will see before I leave Bristol.'

But in reply to each of these positions, Sam shook his head with great firmness, and energetically replied, 'It can't be done.'

After a great deal of argument and representation on the part of Mr Winkle, however, and a full disclosure of what had passed in the interview with Dowler, Sam began to waver; and at length a compromise was effected, of which the following were the main and principal conditions:

That Sam should retire, and leave Mr Winkle in the undisturbed possession of his apartment, on the condition that he had permission to lock the door on the outside, and carry off the key; provided always, that in the event of an alarm of fire, or other dangerous contingency, the door should be instantly unlocked. That a letter should be written to Mr Pickwick early next morning, and forwarded per Dowler, requesting his consent to Sam and Mr Winkle's remaining at Bristol, for the purpose, and with the object, already assigned, and begging an answer by the next coach; if favourable, the aforesaid parties to remain accordingly, and if not, to return to Bath immediately on the receipt thereof. And, lastly, that Mr Winkle should be understood as distinctly pledging himself not to resort to the window, fire-place, or other surreptitious mode of escape, in the meanwhile. These stipulations having been concluded, Sam locked the door and departed.

He had nearly got down stairs, when he stopped, and drew the key from his pocket.

'I quite forgot about the knockin' down,' said Sam, half turning back. 'The governor distinctly said it was to be done. Amazin' stupid o' me, that 'ere! Never mind,' said Sam, brightening up, 'it's easily done to-morrow, anyways.'

Apparently much consoled by this reflection, Mr Weller once more deposited the key in his pocket, and descending the remainder of the stairs without any fresh visitations of conscience, was soon, in common with the other inmates of the house, buried in profound repose.

CHAPTER 39

Mr Samuel Weller, being entrusted with a Mission of Love, proceeds to execute it; with what success will hereinafter appear

During the whole of next day, Sam kept Mr Winkle steadily in sight, fully determined not to take his eyes off him for one instant, until he should receive express instructions from the fountain-head. However disagreeable Sam's very close watch and great vigilance were to Mr Winkle, he thought it better to bear with them, than, by any act of violent opposition, to hazard being carried away by force, which Mr Weller more than once strongly hinted was the line of conduct that a strict sense of duty prompted him to pursue.

There is little reason to doubt that Sam would very speedily have quieted his scruples, by bearing Mr Winkle back to Bath, bound hand and foot, had not Mr Pickwick's prompt attention to the note, which Dowler had undertaken to deliver, forestalled any such proceeding. In short, at eight o'clock in the evening, Mr Pickwick himself walked into the coffee-room of the Bush tavern, and told Sam with a smile, to his very great relief, that he had done quite right, and it was unnecessary for him to mount guard any longer.

'I thought it better to come myself,' said Mr Pickwick, addressing Mr Winkle, as Sam disencumbered him of his great-coat and travelling shawl, 'to ascertain, before I gave my consent to Sam's employment in this matter, that you are quite in earnest and serious, with respect to this young lady.'

'Serious, from my heart – from my soul!' returned Mr Winkle, with great energy.

'Remember,' said Mr Pickwick, with beaming eyes, 'we met her at our excellent and hospitable friend's, Winkle. It would be an ill return to tamper, lightly, and without due consideration, with this young lady's affections. I'll not allow that, sir. I'll not allow it.'

'I have no such intention, indeed,' exclaimed Mr Winkle, warmly. 'I have considered the matter well, for a long time, and I feel that my happiness is bound up in her.'

'That's wot we call tying it up in a small parcel, sir,' interposed Mr Weller, with an agreeable smile.

Mr Winkle looked somewhat stern at this interruption, and Mr Pickwick angrily requested his attendant not to jest with one of the best feelings of our nature; to which Sam replied, 'That he wouldn't, if he was aware on it; but there were so many on 'em, that he hardly know'd which was the best ones wen he heerd 'em mentioned.'

Mr Winkle then recounted what had passed between himself and Mr Ben Allen, relative to Arabella; stated that his object was to gain an interview with the young lady, and make a formal disclosure of his passion; and declared his conviction, founded on certain dark hints and mutterings of the aforesaid Ben, that, wherever she was at present immured, it was somewhere near the Downs. And this was his whole stock of knowledge or suspicion on the subject.

With this very slight clue to guide him, it was determined that Mr Weller should start next morning on an expedition of discovery; it was also arranged that Mr Pickwick and Mr Winkle, who were less confident of their powers, should parade the town meanwhile, and accidentally drop in upon Mr Bob Sawyer in the course of the day, in the hope of seeing or hearing something of the young lady's whereabout.

Accordingly, next morning, Sam Weller issued forth upon his quest, in no way daunted by the very discouraging prospect before him; and away he walked, up one street and down another – we were going to say, up one hill and down another, only it's all uphill at Clifton – without meeting with anything or anybody that tended to throw the faintest light on the matter in hand. Many were the colloquies into which Sam entered with grooms who were airing horses on roads, and nursemaids who were airing children in lanes; but nothing could Sam elicit from either the first-mentioned or the last, which bore the slightest reference to the object of his artfully-prosecuted inquiries. There were a great many young ladies in a great many houses, the greater part whereof were shrewdly suspected by the male and female domestics to be deeply attached to somebody, or perfectly ready to become so, if opportunity offered. But as none among these young ladies was Miss Arabella Allen, the information left Sam at exactly the old point of wisdom at which he had stood before.

Sam struggled across the Downs against a good high wind, wondering whether it was always necessary to hold your hat on with both hands in that part of the country, and came to a shady by-place about which were sprinkled several little villas of quiet and secluded appearance. Outside a stable-door at the bottom of a long back lane without a thoroughfare, a groom in undress was idling about, apparently persuading himself that he was doing something with a spade and a wheelbarrow. We may remark, in this place, that we have scarcely ever seen a groom near a stable, in his lazy moments, who has not been, to a greater or less extent, the victim of this singular delusion.

Sam thought he might as well talk to this groom as to any one else, especially as he was very tired with walking, and there was a good large stone just opposite the wheelbarrow; so he strolled down the lane, and, seating himself on the stone, opened a conversation with the ease and freedom for which he was remarkable.

'Mornin', old friend,' said Sam.

'Arternoon, you mean,' replied the groom, casting a surly look at Sam.

'You're wery right, old friend,' said Sam; 'I *do* mean arternoon. How are you?'

'Why, I don't find myself much the better for seeing of you,' replied the ill-tempered groom.

'That's wery odd – that is,' said Sam, 'for you look so uncommon cheerful, and seem altogether so lively, that it does vun's heart good to see you.'

The surly groom looked surlier still at this, but not sufficiently so to produce any effect upon Sam, who immediately inquired, with a countenance of great anxiety, whether his master's name was not Walker.

'No, it ain't,' said the groom.

'Nor Brown, I s'pose?' said Sam.

'No, it ain't.'

'Nor Vilson?'

'No; nor that neither,' said the groom.

'Vell,' replied Sam, 'then I'm mistaken, and he hasn't got the honor o' my acquaintance, which I thought he had. Don't wait here out o' compliment to me,' said Sam, as the groom wheeled in the barrow, and prepared to shut the gate. 'Ease afore ceremony, old boy; I'll excuse you.'

'I'd knock your head off for half-a-crown,' said the surly groom, bolting one half of the gate.

'Couldn't afford to have it done on those terms,' rejoined Sam. 'It 'ud be worth a life's board vages at least, to you, and 'ud be cheap at that. Make my compliments in doors. Tell 'em not to vait dinner for me, and say they needn't mind puttin' any by, for it'll be cold afore I come in.'

In reply to this, the groom waxing very wrath, muttered a desire to damage somebody's person; but disappeared without carrying it into execution, slamming the door angrily after him, and wholly unheeding Sam's affectionate request, that he would leave him a lock of his hair before he went.

Sam continued to sit on the large stone, meditating upon what was best to be done, and revolving in his mind a plan for knocking at all the doors within five miles of Bristol, taking them at a hundred and fifty or two hundred a day, and endeavouring to find Miss Arabella by that expedient, when accident all of a sudden threw in his way what he might have sat there for a twelvemonth and yet not found without it.

Into the lane where he sat, there opened three or four garden-gates, belonging to as many houses, which though detached from each other, were only separated by their gardens. As these were large and long, and well planted with trees, the houses were not only at some distance off, but the greater part of them were nearly concealed from view. Sam was sitting with his eyes fixed upon the dust-heap outside the next gate to that by which the groom had disappeared, profoundly turning over in his mind the difficulties of his present undertaking, when the gate opened, and a female servant came out into the lane to shake some bed-side carpets.

Sam was so very busy with his own thoughts, that it is probable he would have taken no more notice of the young woman than just raising his head and remarking that she had a very neat and pretty figure, if his feelings of gallantry had not been most strongly roused by observing that she had no one to help her, and that the carpets seemed too heavy for her single strength. Mr Weller was a gentleman of great gallantry in his own way, and he no sooner remarked this circumstance than he hastily rose from the large stone, and advanced towards her.

'My dear,' said Sam, sliding up with an air of great respect, 'You'll spile that wery pretty figure out o' all perportion if you shake them carpets by yourself. Let me help you.'

The young lady, who had been coyly affecting not to know that a gentleman was so near, turned round as Sam spoke – no doubt (indeed she said so, afterwards) to decline this offer from a perfect stranger – when instead of speaking, she started back, and uttered a half-suppressed scream. Sam was scarcely less staggered, for in the countenance of the well-shaped female servant, he beheld the very features of his Valentine, the pretty housemaid from Mr Nupkins's.

'Wy, Mary my dear!' said Sam.

'Lauk, Mr Weller,' said Mary, 'how you do frighten one!'

Sam made no verbal answer to this complaint, nor can we precisely say what reply he *did* make. We merely know that after a short pause Mary said, 'Lor do adun,¹ Mr Weller!' and that his hat had fallen off a few moments before – from both of which tokens we should be disposed to infer that one kiss or more, had passed between the parties.

'Why, how did you come here?' said Mary, when the conversation to which this interruption had been offered, was resumed.

'O' course I came to look arter you, my darlin,' replied Mr Weller; for once permitting his passion to get the better of his veracity.

'And how did you know I was here?' inquired Mary. 'Who could have told you that I took another service at Ipswich, and that they afterwards moved all the way here? Who *could* have told you that, Mr Weller?'

'Ah to be sure,' said Sam with a cunning look, 'that's the pint. Who could ha' told me?'

'It wasn't Mr Muzzle, was it?' inquired Mary.

'Oh, no,' replied Sam, with a solemn shake of the head, 'it warn't him.'

'It must have been the cook,' said Mary.

'O' course it must,' said Sam.

'Well, I never heard the like of that!' exclaimed Mary.

'No more did I,' said Sam. 'But Mary, my dear:' here Sam's manner grew extremely affectionate: 'Mary, my dear, I've got another affair in hand as is wery pressin'. There's one o' my governor's friends – Mr Winkle, you remember him.'

'Him in the green coat?' said Mary. 'Oh, yes, I remember him.'

'Well,' said Sam, 'he's in a horrid state o' love; reg'larly comfoozled, and done over with it.'

'Lor!' interposed Mary.

'Yes,' said Sam: 'but that's nothin' if we could find out the young 'ooman;' and here Sam, with many digressions upon the personal beauty of Mary, and the unspeakable tortures he had experienced since he last saw her, gave a faithful account of Mr Winkle's present predicament.

'Well,' said Mary, 'I never did!'

'O' course not,' said Sam, 'and nobody never did, nor never vill neither; and here am I a walkin' about like the wandering Jew[2] – a sportin' character you have perhaps heerd on Mary, my dear, as wos alvays doin' a match agin' time, and never vent to sleep – looking arter this here Miss Arabella Allen.'

'Miss who?' said Mary, in great astonishment.

'Miss Arabella Allen,' said Sam.

'Goodness gracious!' said Mary, pointing to the garden door which the sulky groom had locked after him. 'Why, it's that very house; she's been living there these six weeks. Their upper housemaid, which is lady's maid too, told me all about it over the wash-house palin's before the family was out of bed, one mornin'.'

'Wot, the wery next door to you?' said Sam.

'The very next,' replied Mary.

Mr Weller was so deeply overcome on receiving this intelligence that he found it absolutely necessary to cling to his fair informant for support; and divers little love passages had passed between them, before he was sufficiently collected to return to the subject.

'Vell,' said Sam at length, 'if this don't beat cock-fightin', nothin' never vill, as the Lord Mayor said, ven the chief secretary o' state proposed his missis's health arter dinner. That wery next house! Wy, I've got a message to her as I've been a tryin' all day to deliver.'

'Ah,' said Mary, 'but you can't deliver it now, because she only walks in the garden in the evening, and then only for a very little time; she never goes out, without the old lady.'

Sam ruminated for a few moments, and finally hit upon the following plan of operations; that he should return just at dusk – the time at which Arabella invariably took her walk – and, being admitted by Mary into the garden of the house to which she belonged, would contrive to scramble up the wall, beneath the over-hanging boughs of a large pear-tree, which would effectually screen him from observation; would there deliver his message, and arrange, if possible, an interview on behalf of Mr Winkle for the ensuing evening at the same hour. Having made this arrangement with great dispatch, he assisted Mary in the long-deferred occupation of shaking the carpets.

It is not half as innocent a thing as it looks, that shaking little pieces of carpet – at least, there may be no great harm in the shaking, but the folding is a very insidious process. So long as the shaking lasts, and the two parties are kept the carpet's length apart, it is as innocent an amusement as can well be devised; but when the folding begins, and the distance between them gets gradually lessened from one half its former length to a quarter, and then to an eighth, and then to a sixteenth, and then to a thirty-second, if the carpet be long enough: it becomes dangerous. We do not know, to a nicety, how many pieces of carpet were folded in this instance, but we can venture to state that as many pieces as there were, so many times did Sam kiss the pretty housemaid.

Mr Weller regaled himself with moderation at the nearest tavern until it was nearly dusk, and then returned to the lane without the thoroughfare. Having been admitted into the garden by Mary, and having received from that lady sundry admonitions concerning the safety of his limbs and neck, Sam mounted into the pear-tree, to wait until Arabella should come in sight.

He waited so long without this anxiously expected event occur-ring that he began to think it was not going to take place at all, when he heard light footsteps upon the gravel, and immediately afterwards beheld Arabella walking pensively down the garden. As soon as she came nearly below the tree, Sam began, by way of gently indicating his presence, to make sundry diabolical noises similar to those which would probably be natural to a person of middle age who had been afflicted with a combination of inflammatory sore throat, croup, and hooping-cough, from his earliest infancy.

Upon this, the young lady cast a hurried glance towards the spot from whence the dreadful sounds proceeded; and her previous alarm being not at all diminished when she saw a man among the branches, she would most certainly have decamped, and alarmed the house, had not fear fortunately deprived her of the power of moving, and caused her to sink down on a garden seat; which happened by good luck to be near at hand.

'She's a goin' off,' soliloquised Sam in great perplexity. 'Wot a thing it is, as these here young creeturs *will* go a faintin' avay just wen they oughtn't to. Here, young 'ooman, Miss Sawbones,³ Mrs Vinkle, don't!'

Whether it was the magic of Mr Winkle's name, or the coolness of the open air, or some recollection of Mr Weller's voice, that revived Arabella, matters not. She raised her head and languidly inquired 'Who's that, and what do you want?'

'Hush,' said Sam, swinging himself on to the wall, and crouching there in as small a compass as he could reduce himself to, 'only me, miss, only me.'

'Mr Pickwick's servant;' said Arabella, earnestly.

'The wery same, miss,' replied Sam. 'Here's Mr Vinkle reg'larly sewed up vith desperation, miss.'

'Ah!' said Arabella, drawing nearer the wall.

'Ah indeed,' said Sam. 'Ve thought ve should ha' been obliged to straight-veskit him last night; he's been a ravin' all day; and he says if he can't see you afore to-morrow night's over, he vishes he may be somethin'-unpleasanted if he don't drownd hisself.'

'Oh no, no, Mr Weller!' said Arabella, clasping her hands.

'That's wot he says, miss,' replied Sam. 'He's a man of his word, and it's my opinion he'll do it, miss. He's heerd all about you from the Sawbones in barnacles.'

'From my brother!' said Arabella, having some faint recognition of Sam's description.

'I don't rightly know which is your brother miss,' replied Sam. 'Is it the dirtiest vun o' the two?'

'Yes, yes, Mr Weller,' returned Arabella, 'go on. Make haste, pray.'

'Well miss,' said Sam, 'he's heerd all about it from him; and it's the gov'nor's opinion that if you don't see him wery quick, the Sawbones as we've been a speaking on, 'ull get as much extra lead in his head[4] as'll damage the dewelopment o' the orgins if they ever put it in spirits artervards.'

'Oh, what can I do to prevent these dreadful quarrels!' exclaimed Arabella.

'It's the suspicion of a priory 'tachment as is the cause of it all,' replied Sam. 'You'd better see him, miss.'

'But how? – where?' cried Arabella. 'I dare not leave the house alone. My brother is so unkind, so unreasonable! I know how strange my talking thus to you must appear, Mr Weller, but I am very, very unhappy – ' and here poor Arabella wept so bitterly, that Sam grew chivalrous.

'It may seem very strange talkin' to me about these here affairs, miss,' said Sam with great vehemence: 'but all I can say is, that I'm not only ready but villin' to do anythin' as'll make matters agreeable; and if chuckin' either o' them Sawboneses out o' winder 'ull do it, I'm the man.' As Sam Weller said this, he tucked up his wristbands, at the imminent hazard of falling off the wall in so doing, to intimate his readiness to set to work immediately.

Flattering as these professions of good feeling were, Arabella resolutely declined (most unaccountably as Sam thought,) to avail herself of them. For some time she strenuously refused to grant Mr Winkle the interview Sam had so pathetically requested; but at length, when the conversation threatened to be interrupted by the unwelcome arrival of a third party, she hurriedly gave him to understand, with many professions of gratitude, that it was barely possible she might be in the garden an hour later, next evening. Sam understood this perfectly well; and Arabella bestowing upon him one of her sweetest smiles, tripped gracefully away, leaving Mr Weller in a state of very great admiration of her charms, both personal and mental.

Having descended in safety from the wall, and not forgotten to devote a few moments to his own particular business in the same department, Mr Weller then made the best of his way back to the Bush, where his prolonged absence had occasioned much speculation and some alarm.

'We must be careful,' said Mr Pickwick, after listening attentively to Sam's tale, 'not for our own sakes, but for that of the young lady. We must be very cautious.'

'*We!*' said Mr Winkle, with marked emphasis.

Mr Pickwick's momentary look of indignation at the tone of this remark, subsided into his characteristic expression of benevolence, as he replied:

'*We*, sir! I shall accompany you.'

'You!' said Mr Winkle.

'I,' replied Mr Pickwick, mildly. 'In affording you this interview, the young lady has taken a natural, perhaps, but still a very imprudent step. If I am present at the meeting, a mutual friend, who is old enough to be the father of both parties, the voice of calumny can never be raised against her hereafter.'

Mr Pickwick's eyes lightened with honest exultation at his own foresight, as he spoke thus. Mr Winkle was touched by this little trait of his delicate respect for the young *protégée* of his friend, and took his hand with a feeling of regard, akin to veneration.

'You *shall* go,' said Mr Winkle.

'I will,' said Mr Pickwick. 'Sam, have my great-coat and shawl ready, and order a conveyance to be at the door to-morrow evening, rather earlier than is absolutely necessary, in order that we may be in good time.'

Mr Weller touched his hat, as an earnest of his obedience, and withdrew to make all needful preparations for the expedition.

The coach was punctual to the time appointed; and Mr Weller, after duly installing Mr Pickwick and Mr Winkle inside, took his seat on the box by the driver. They alighted, as had been agreed on, about a quarter of a mile from the place of rendezvous, and desiring the coachman to await their return, proceeded the remaining distance on foot.

It was at this stage of the undertaking that Mr Pickwick, with many smiles and various other indications of great self satisfaction, produced from one of his coat pockets a dark lantern,[5] with which he had specially provided himself for the occasion, and the great mechanical beauty of which, he proceeded to explain to Mr Winkle as they walked along, to the no small surprise of the few stragglers they met.

'I should have been the better for something of this kind, in my last garden expedition, at night; eh, Sam?' said Mr Pickwick, looking good-humouredly round at his follower, who was trudging behind.

'Wery nice things, if they're managed properly, sir,' replied Mr Weller; 'but when you don't want to be seen, I think they're more useful arter the candle's gone out, than wen it's alight.'

Mr Pickwick appeared struck by Sam's remarks, for he put the lantern into his pocket again, and they walked on in silence.

'Down here, sir,' said Sam. 'Let me lead the way. This is the lane, sir.'

Down the lane they went, and dark enough it was. Mr Pickwick brought out the lantern, once or twice, as they groped their way along, and threw a very brilliant little tunnel of light before them, about a foot in diameter. It was very pretty to look at, but seemed to have the effect of rendering surrounding objects rather darker than before.

At length they arrived at the large stone. Here Sam recommended his master and Mr Winkle to seat themselves, while he reconnoitred, and ascertained whether Mary was yet in waiting.

After an absence of five or ten minutes, Sam returned, to say that the gate was opened, and all quiet. Following him with stealthy tread, Mr Pickwick and Mr Winkle soon found themselves in the garden. Here everybody said 'Hush!' a good many times; and that being done, no one seemed to have any very distinct apprehension of what was to be done next.

'Is Miss Allen in the garden yet, Mary?' inquired Mr Winkle, much agitated.

'I don't know, sir,' replied the pretty housemaid. 'The best thing to be done, sir, will be for Mr Weller to give you a hoist up into the tree, and perhaps Mr Pickwick will have the goodness to see that nobody comes up the lane, while I watch at the other end of the garden. Goodness gracious, what's that!'

'That 'ere blessed lantern' ull be the death on us all,' exclaimed Sam, peevishly. 'Take care wot you're a doin' on, sir; you're sendin' a blaze o'light, right into the back parlor winder.'

'Dear me!' said Mr Pickwick, turning hastily aside, 'I didn't mean to do that.'

'Now, it's in the next house, sir,' remonstrated Sam.

'Bless my heart!' exclaimed Mr Pickwick, turning round again.

'Now, it's in the stable, and they'll think the place is a' fire,' said Sam. 'Shut it up, sir, can't you?'

'It's the most extraordinary lantern I ever met with, in all my life!' exclaimed Mr Pickwick, greatly bewildered by the effects he had so unintentionally produced. 'I never saw such a powerful reflector.'

'It'll be vun too powerful for us, if you keep blazin' away in that manner, sir,' replied Sam, as Mr Pickwick, after various unsuccessful efforts, managed to close the slide. 'There's the young lady's footsteps. Now, Mr Vinkle, sir, up vith you.'

'Stop, stop!' said Mr Pickwick, 'I must speak to her first. Help me up, Sam.'

'Gently, sir,' said Sam, planting his head against the wall, and making a platform of his back. 'Step a top o' that' ere flower-pot, sir. Now then, up vith you.'

'I'm afraid I shall hurt you, Sam,' said Mr Pickwick.

'Never mind me, sir,' replied Sam. 'Lend him a hand, Mr Vinkle, sir. Steady, sir, steady! That's the time o' day!'

As Sam spoke, Mr Pickwick, by exertions almost supernatural in a gentleman of his years and weight, contrived to get upon Sam's back; and Sam gently raising himself up, and Mr Pickwick holding on fast by the top of the wall, while Mr Winkle clasped him tight by the legs, they contrived by these means to bring his spectacles just above the level of the coping.[6]

'My dear,' said Mr Pickwick, looking over the wall, and catching sight of Arabella, on the other side, 'Don't be frightened, my dear, it's only me.'

'Oh pray go away, Mr Pickwick,' said Arabella. 'Tell them all to go away. I am so dreadfully frightened. Dear, dear Mr Pickwick, don't stop there. You'll fall down and kill yourself, I know you will.'

'Now, pray don't alarm yourself, my dear,' said Mr Pickwick, soothingly. 'There is not the least cause for fear, I assure you. Stand firm Sam,' said Mr Pickwick, looking down.

'All right, sir,' replied Mr Weller. 'Don't be longer than you can conweniently help, sir. You're rayther heavy.'

'Only another moment, Sam,' replied Mr Pickwick. 'I merely wished you to know, my dear, that I should not have allowed my young friend to see you in this clandestine way, if the situation in which you are placed, had left him any alternative; and lest the impropriety of this step should cause you any uneasiness, my love, it may be a satisfaction to you, to know that I am present. That's all, my dear.'

'Indeed, Mr Pickwick, I am very much obliged to you for your kindness and consideration,' replied Arabella, drying her tears with her handkerchief. She would probably have said much more, had not Mr Pickwick's head disappeared with great swiftness, in consequence of a false step on Sam's shoulder, which brought him suddenly to the ground. He was up again in an instant, however, and bidding Mr Winkle make haste and get the interview over, ran out into the lane to keep watch, with all the courage and ardour of youth. Mr Winkle himself, inspired by the occasion, was on the wall in a moment, merely pausing to request Sam to be careful of his master.

'I'll take care on him, sir,' replied Sam. 'Leave him to me.'

'Where is he? What's he doing, Sam?' inquired Mr Winkle.

'Bless his old gaiters,' rejoined Sam, looking out at the garden-door. 'He's a keepin' guard in the lane vith that 'ere dark lantern, like a amiable Guy Fawkes![7] I never see such a fine creetur in my days. Blessed if I don't think his heart must ha' been born five-and twenty year arter his body, at least!'

Mr Winkle stayed not to hear the encomium upon his friend. He had dropped from the wall; thrown himself at Arabella's feet; and by this time was pleading the sincerity of his passion with an eloquence worthy even of Mr Pickwick himself.

While these things were going on in the open air, an elderly gentleman of scientific attainments was seated in his library, two or three houses off, writing a philosophical treatise, and ever and anon moistening his clay[8] and his labours with a glass of claret from a venerable-looking bottle which stood by his side. In the agonies of composition, the elderly gentleman looked sometimes at the carpet, sometimes at the ceiling, and sometimes at the wall; and when neither carpet, ceiling, nor wall, afforded the requisite degree of inspiration, he looked out of the window.

In one of these pauses of invention, the scientific gentleman was gazing abstractedly on the thick darkness outside, when he was very much surprised by observing a most brilliant light glide through the air, at a short distance above the ground, and almost instantaneously vanish. After a short time the phenomenon was repeated, not once or twice, but several times: at last the scientific gentleman, laying down his pen, began to consider to what natural causes these appearances were to be assigned.

They were not meteors; they were too low. They were not glow-worms; they were too high. They were not will-o'-the-wisps; they were not fire-flies; they were not fire-works. What could they be? Some extraordinary and wonderful phenomenon of nature, which no philosopher had ever seen before; something which it had been reserved for him alone to discover, and which he should immortalise his name by chronicling for the benefit of posterity. Full of this idea, the scientific gentleman seized his pen again, and committed to paper sundry notes of these unparalleled appearances, with the date, day, hour, minute, and precise second at which they were visible: all of which were to form the data of a voluminous treatise of great research and deep learning, which should astonish all the atmospherical sages that ever drew breath in any part of the civilised globe.

He threw himself back in his easy chair, wrapped in contemplations of his future greatness. The mysterious light appeared more brilliantly than before: dancing, to all appearance, up and down the lane, crossing from side to side, and moving in an orbit as eccentric as comets themselves.

The scientific gentleman was a bachelor. He had no wife to call in and astonish, so he rang the bell for his servant.

'Pruffle,' said the scientific gentleman, 'there is something very extraordinary in the air to-night. Did you see that?' said the scientific gentleman, pointing out of the window, as the light again became visible.

'Yes, I did, sir.'

'What do you think of it, Pruffle?'

'Think of it, sir?'

'Yes. You have been bred up in this country. What should you say was the cause of those lights, now?'

The scientific gentleman smilingly anticipated Pruffle's reply that he could assign no cause for them at all. Pruffle meditated.

'I should say it was thieves, sir,' said Pruffle at length.

'You're a fool, and may go down stairs,' said the scientific gentleman.

'Thank you, sir,' said Pruffle. And down he went.

But the scientific gentleman could not rest under the idea of the ingenious treatise he had projected being lost to the world, which must inevitably be the case if the speculation of the ingenious Mr Pruffle were not stifled in its birth. He put on his hat and walked quickly down the garden, determined to investigate the matter to the very bottom.

Now, shortly before the scientific gentleman walked out into the garden, Mr Pickwick had run down the lane as fast as he could, to convey a false alarm that somebody was coming that way; occasionally drawing back the slide of the dark lantern to keep himself from the ditch. The alarm was no sooner given, than Mr Winkle scrambled back over the wall, and Arabella ran into the house; the garden-gate was shut, and the three adventurers were making the best of their way down the lane, when they were startled by the scientific gentleman unlocking his garden-gate.

'Hold hard,' whispered Sam, who was, of course, the first of the party. 'Show a light for just vun second, sir.'

Mr Pickwick did as he was desired, and Sam, seeing a man's head peeping out very cautiously within half-a-yard of his own, gave it a gentle tap with his clenched fist, which knocked it, with a hollow sound, against the gate. Having performed this feat with great suddenness and dexterity, Mr Weller caught Mr Pickwick up on his back, and followed Mr Winkle down the lane at a pace which, considering the burden he carried, was perfectly astonishing.

'Have you got your vind back agin, sir,' inquired Sam, when they had reached the end.

'Quite. Quite, now,' replied Mr Pickwick.

'Then come along, sir,' said Sam, setting his master on his feet again. 'Come between us, sir. Not half a mile to run. Think you 're vinnin a cup, sir. Now for it.'

Thus encouraged, Mr Pickwick made the very best use of his legs. It may be confidently stated that a pair of black gaiters never got over the ground in better style than did those of Mr Pickwick on this memorable occasion.

The coach was waiting, the horses were fresh, the roads were good, and the driver was willing. The whole party arrived in safety at the Bush before Mr Pickwick had recovered his breath.

'In with you at once, sir,' said Sam, as he helped his master out. 'Don't stop a second in the street, arter that 'ere exercise. Beg your pardon, sir,' continued Sam, touching his hat as Mr Winkle descended. 'Hope there warn't a priory 'tachment, sir?'

Mr Winkle grasped his humble friend by the hand, and whispered in his ear, 'It's all right, Sam; quite right.' Upon which Mr Weller struck three distinct blows upon his nose in token of intelligence, smiled, winked, and proceeded to put the steps up, with a countenance expressive of lively satisfaction.

As to the scientific gentleman, he demonstrated, in a masterly treatise, that these wonderful lights were the effect of electricity; and clearly proved the same by detailing how a flash of fire danced before his eyes when he put his head out of the gate, and how he received a shock which stunned him for a quarter of an hour afterwards; which demonstration delighted all the Scientific Associations[9] beyond measure, and caused him to be considered a light of science ever afterwards.

CHAPTER 40

Introduces Mr Pickwick to a new and not
uninteresting Scene in the great Drama of Life

The remainder of the period which Mr Pickwick had assigned as the duration of the stay at Bath, passed over without the occurrence of anything material. Trinity Term commenced. On the expiration of its first week, Mr Pickwick and his friends returned to London; and the former gentleman, attended of course by Sam, straightway repaired to his old quarters at the George and Vulture.

On the third morning after their arrival, just as all the clocks in the city were striking nine individually, and somewhere about nine hundred and ninety-nine collectively, Sam was taking the air in George Yard, when a queer sort of fresh painted vehicle drove up, out of which there jumped with great agility, throwing the reins to a stout man who sat beside him, a queer sort of gentleman, who seemed made for the vehicle, and the vehicle for him.

The vehicle was not exactly a gig, neither was it a stanhope. It was not what is currently denominated a dog-cart, neither was a taxed-cart, nor a chaise-cart, nor a guillotined cabriolet; and yet it had something of the character of each and every of these machines. It was painted a bright yellow, with the shafts and wheels picked out in black; and the driver sat, in the orthodox sporting style, on cushions piled about two feet above the rail. The horse was a bay, a well-looking animal enough; but with something of a flash and dog-fighting air about him, nevertheless, which accorded both with the vehicle and his master.

The master himself was a man of about forty, with black hair, and carefully combed whiskers. He was dressed in a particularly gorgeous manner, with plenty of articles of jewellery about him – all about three sizes larger than those which are usually worn by gentlemen – and a rough great-coat to crown the whole. Into one pocket of this great-coat, he thrust his left hand the moment he dismounted, while from the other he drew forth, with his right, a very bright and glaring silk handkerchief, with which he whisked a speck or two of dust from his boots, and then, crumpling it in his hand, swaggered up the court.

It had not escaped Sam's attention that, when this person dismounted, a shabby-looking man in a brown great-coat shorn of divers buttons, who had been previously slinking about, on the opposite side of the way, crossed over, and remained stationary close by. Having something more than a suspicion of the object of the gentleman's visit, Sam preceded him to the George and Vulture, and, turning sharp round, planted himself in the centre of the doorway.

'Now, my fine fellow!' said the man in the rough coat, in an imperious tone, attempting at the same time to push his way past.

'Now, sir, wot's the matter!' replied Sam, returning the push with compound interest.

'Come, none of this, my man; this won't do with me,' said the owner of the rough coat, raising his voice, and turning white. 'Here, Smouch!'

'Well, wot's amiss here?' growled the man in the brown coat, who had been gradually sneaking up the court during this short dialogue.

'Only some insolence of this young man's,' said the principal, giving Sam another push.

'Come, none o' this gammon,' growled Smouch, giving him another, and a harder one.

This last push had the effect which it was intended by the experienced Mr Smouch to produce; for while Sam, anxious to return the compliment, was grinding that gentleman's body against the doorpost, the principal crept past, and made his way to the bar: whither Sam, after bandying a few epithetical remarks with Mr Smouch, followed at once.

'Good morning, my dear,' said the principal, addressing the young lady at the bar, with Botany Bay[1] ease, and New South Wales gentility; 'which is Mr Pickwick's room, my dear?'

'Show him up,' said the bar-maid to a waiter, without deigning another look at the exquisite, in reply to his inquiry.

The waiter led the way up stairs as he was desired, and the man in the rough coat followed, with Sam behind him: who, in his progress up the staircase, indulged in sundry gestures indicative of supreme contempt and defiance: to the unspeakable gratification of the servants and other lookers-on. Mr Smouch, who was troubled with a hoarse cough, remained below, and expectorated in the passage.

Mr Pickwick was fast asleep in bed, when his early visitor, followed by Sam, entered the room. The noise they made, in so doing, awoke him.

'Shaving water, Sam,' said Mr Pickwick, from within the curtains.

'Shave you directly, Mr Pickwick,' said the visitor, drawing one of them back from the bed's head. 'I've got an execution against you, at the suit of Bardell. – Here's the warrant. – Common Pleas. – Here's my card. I suppose you'll come over to my house.' Giving Mr Pickwick a friendly tap on the shoulder, the sheriff's officer (for such he was) threw his card on the counterpane, and pulled a gold toothpick from his waistcoat pocket.

'Namby's the name,' said the sheriff's deputy, as Mr Pickwick took his spectacles from under the pillow, and put them on, to read the card. 'Namby, Bell Alley, Coleman Street.'

At this point, Sam Weller, who had had his eyes fixed hitherto on Mr Namby's shining beaver, interfered:

'Are you a Quaker?' said Sam.

'I'll let you know who I am, before I've done with you,' replied the indignant officer. 'I'll teach you manners, my fine fellow, one of these fine mornings.'

'Thankee,' said Sam. 'I'll do the same to you. Take your hat off.' With this, Mr Weller, in the most dexterous manner, knocked Mr Namby's hat to the other side of the room: with such violence, that he had very nearly caused him to swallow the gold tooth-pick into the bargain.

'Observe this, Mr Pickwick,' said the disconcerted officer, gasping for breath. 'I've been assaulted in the execution of my dooty by your servant in your chamber. I'm in bodily fear. I call you to witness this.'

'Don't witness nothin', sir,' interposed Sam. 'Shut your eyes up tight, sir. I'd pitch him out o' winder, only he couldn't fall far enough, 'cause o' the leads outside.'

'Sam,' said Mr Pickwick in an angry voice, as his attendant made various demonstrations of hostilities, 'if you say another word, or offer the slightest interference with this person, I discharge you that instant.'

'But, sir!' said Sam.

'Hold your tongue,' interposed Mr Pickwick. 'Take that hat up again.'

But this Sam flatly and positively refused to do; and, after he had been severely reprimanded by his master, the officer, being in a hurry, condescended to pick it up himself: venting a great variety of threats against Sam meanwhile, which that gentleman received with perfect composure: merely observing that if Mr Namby would have the goodness to put his hat on again, he would knock it into the latter end of next week. Mr Namby, perhaps thinking that such a process might be productive of inconvenience to himself, declined to offer the temptation, and, soon after, called up Smouch. Having informed him that the capture was made, and that he was to wait for the prisoner until he should have finished dressing, Namby then swaggered out, and drove away. Smouch, requesting Mr Pickwick in a surly manner 'to be as alive as he could, for it was a busy time,' drew up a chair by the door, and sat there, until he had finished dressing. Sam was then dispatched for a hackney coach, and in it the triumvirate proceeded to Coleman Street. It was fortunate the distance was short; for Mr Smouch, besides possessing no very enchanting conversational powers, was rendered a decidedly unpleasant companion in a limited space, by the physical weakness to which we have elsewhere adverted.

The coach having turned into a very narrow and dark street, stopped before a house with iron bars to all the windows; the door-posts of which were graced by the name and title of 'Namby, Officer to the Sheriffs of London:' the inner gate having been opened by a gentleman who might have passed for a neglected twin brother of Mr Smouch, and who was endowed with a large key for the purpose, Mr Pickwick was shown into the 'coffee-room.'

This coffee-room was a front parlour: the principal features of which were fresh sand and stale tobacco smoke. Mr Pickwick bowed to the three persons who were seated in it when he entered; and having dispatched Sam for Perker, withdrew into an obscure corner, and from thence looked with some curiosity upon his new companions.

One of these was a mere boy of nineteen or twenty, who, though it was yet barely ten o'clock, was drinking gin and water, and smoking a cigar: amusements to which, judging from his inflamed countenance, he had devoted himself pretty constantly for the last year or two of his life. Opposite him, engaged in stirring the fire with the toe of his right boot, was a coarse vulgar young man of about thirty, with a sallow face and harsh voice: evidently possessed of that knowledge of the world, and captivating freedom of manner, which is to be acquired in public-house parlours, and at low billiard-tables. The third tenant of the apartment was a middle-aged man in a very old suit of black, who looked pale and haggard, and paced up and down the room incessantly: stopping, now and then, to look with great anxiety out of the window as if he expected somebody, and then resuming his walk.

'You'd better have the loan of my razor this morning, Mr Ayresleigh,' said the man who was stirring the fire, tipping the wink to his friend the boy.

'Thank you, no, I shan't want it; I expect I shall be out, in the course of an hour or so,' replied the other in a hurried manner. Then, walking again up to the window, and once more returning disappointed, he sighed deeply, and left the room; upon which the other two burst into a loud laugh.

'Well, I never saw such a game as that,' said the gentleman who had offered the razor, whose name appeared to be Price. 'Never!' Mr Price confirmed the assertion with an oath, and then laughed again, when of course the boy (who thought his companion one of the most dashing fellows alive) laughed also.

'You'd hardly think, would you now,' said Price, turning towards Mr Pickwick, 'that that chap's been here a week yesterday, and never once shaved himself yet, because he feels so certain he's going out in half an hour's time, that he thinks he may as well put it off till he gets home?'

'Poor man!' said Mr Pickwick. 'Are his chances of getting out of his difficulties really so great?'

'Chances be d – d,' replied Price; 'he hasn't half the ghost of one. I wouldn't give *that* for his chance of walking about the streets this time ten years.' With this Mr Price snapped his fingers contemptuously, and rang the bell.

'Give me a sheet of paper, Crookey,' said Mr Price to the attendant, who in dress and general appearance looked something between a bankrupt grazier,[2] and a drover[3] in a state of insolvency; 'and a glass of brandy and water, Crookey, d'ye hear? I'm going to write to my father, and I must have a stimulant, or I shan't be able to pitch it strong enough into the old boy.' At this facetious speech, the young boy, it is almost needless to say, was fairly convulsed.

'That's right,' said Mr Price. 'Never say die. All fun, ain't it?'

'Prime!' said the young gentleman.

'You've some spirit about you, you have,' said Price. 'You've seen something of life.'

'I rather think I have!' replied the boy. He had looked at it through the dirty panes of glass in a bar door.

Mr Pickwick feeling not a little disgusted with this dialogue, as well as with the air and manner of the two beings by whom it had been carried on, was about to inquire whether he could not be accommodated with a private sitting-room, when two or three strangers of genteel appearance entered, at sight of whom the boy threw his cigar into the fire, and whispering to Mr Price that they had come to 'make it all right' for him, joined them at a table in the further end of the room.

It would appear, however, that matters were not going to be

made all right quite so speedily as the young gentleman anticipated; for a very long conversation ensued, of which Mr Pickwick could not avoid hearing certain angry fragments regarding dissolute conduct, and repeated forgiveness. At last, there were very distinct allusions made by the oldest gentleman of the party to one Whitecross Street,[4] at which the young gentleman, notwithstanding his primeness and his spirit and his knowledge of life into the bargain, reclined his head upon the table, and howled dismally.

Very much satisfied with this sudden bringing down of the youth's valour, and this effectual lowering of his tone, Mr Pickwick rang the bell, and was shown, at his own request, into a private room furnished with a carpet, table, chairs, sideboard and sofa, and ornamented with a looking-glass, and various old prints. Here, he had the advantage of hearing Mrs Namby's performance on a square piano over head, while the breakfast was getting ready; when it came, Mr Perker came too.

'Aha, my dear sir,' said the little man, 'nailed at last, eh? Come, come, I'm not sorry for it either, because now you'll see the absurdity of this conduct. I've noted down the amount of the taxed costs and damages for which the ca-sa[5] was issued, and we had better settle at once and lose no time. Namby is come home by this time, I dare say. What say you, my dear sir? Shall I draw a cheque, or will you?' The little man rubbed his hands with affected cheerfulness as he said this, but glancing at Mr Pickwick's countenance, could not forbear at the same time casting a desponding look towards Sam Weller.

'Perker,' said Mr Pickwick, 'let me hear no more of this, I beg. I see no advantage in staying here, so I shall go to prison to-night.'

'You can't go to Whitecross Street, my dear sir,' said Perker. 'Impossible! There are sixty beds in a ward; and the bolt's on, sixteen hours out of the four-and-twenty.'

'I would rather go to some other place of confinement if I can,' said Mr Pickwick. 'If not, I must make the best I can of that.'

'You can go to the Fleet,[6] my dear sir, if you're determined to go somewhere,' said Perker.

'That'll do,' said Mr Pickwick. 'I'll go there directly I have finished my breakfast.'

'Stop, stop, my dear sir; not the least occasion for being in such a violent hurry to get into a place that most other men are as eager to get out of,' said the good-natured little attorney. 'We must have a habeas corpus.[7] There'll be no judge at chambers till four o'clock this afternoon. You must wait till then.'

'Very good,' said Mr Pickwick, with unmoved patience. 'Then we will have a chop, here, at two. See about it, Sam, and tell them to be punctual.'

Mr Pickwick remaining firm, despite all the remonstrances and arguments of Perker, the chops appeared and disappeared in due course; he was then put into another hackney-coach, and carried off to Chancery Lane, after waiting half an hour or so for Mr Namby, who had a select dinner party and could on no account be disturbed before.

There were two judges in attendance at Sergeant's Inn – one King's Bench, and one Common Pleas – and a great deal of business appeared to be transacting before them, if the number of lawyers' clerks who were hurrying in and out with bundles of papers, afforded any test. When they reached the low archway which forms the entrance to the Inn, Perker was detained a few moments parleying with the coachman about the fare and the change; and Mr Pickwick, stepping to one side to be out of the way of the stream of people that were pouring in and out, looked about him with some curiosity.

The people that attracted his attention most, were three or four men of shabby-genteel appearance, who touched their hats to many of the attorneys who passed, and seemed to have some business there, the nature of which Mr Pickwick could not divine. They were curious-looking fellows. One, was a slim and rather lame man in rusty black, and a white neckerchief; another, was a stout burly person, dressed in the same apparel, with a great reddish-black cloth round his neck; a third, was a little weazen drunken-looking body with a pimply face. They were loitering about, with their hands behind them, and now and then with an anxious countenance whispered something in the ear of some of the gentlemen with papers, as they hurried by. Mr Pickwick remembered to have very often observed them lounging under the archway when he had been walking past; and his curiosity was quite excited to know to what branch of the profession these dingy-looking loungers could possibly belong.

He was about to propound the question to Namby, who kept close beside him, sucking a large gold ring on his little finger, when Perker bustled up, and observing that there was no time to lose, led the way into the Inn. As Mr Pickwick followed, the lame man stepped up to him, and civilly touching his hat, held out a written card, which Mr Pickwick, not wishing to hurt the man's feelings by refusing, courteously accepted and deposited in his waistcoat-pocket.

'Now,' said Perker, turning round before he entered one of the offices, to see that his companions were close behind him. 'In here, my dear sir. Hallo, what do *you* want?'

This last question was addressed to the lame man, who, unobserved by Mr Pickwick, made one of the party. In reply to it, the lame man touched his hat again, with all imaginable politeness, and motioned towards Mr Pickwick.

'No, no,' said Perker with a smile. 'We don't want you, my dear friend, we don't want you.'

'I beg your pardon, sir,' said the lame man. 'The gentleman took my card. I hope you will employ me, sir. The gentleman nodded to me. I'll be judged by the gentleman himself. You nodded to me, sir?'

'Pooh, pooh, nonsense. You didn't nod to any body, Pickwick? A mistake, a mistake,' said Perker.

'The gentleman handed me his card,' replied Mr Pickwick, producing it from his waistcoat-pocket. 'I accepted it, as the gentleman seemed to wish it – in fact I had some curiosity to look at it when I should be at leisure. I—'

The little attorney burst into a loud laugh, and returning the card to the lame man, informing him it was all a mistake, whispered to Mr Pickwick as the man turned away in dudgeon, that he was only a bail.

'A what!' exclaimed Mr Pickwick.

'A bail,' replied Perker.

'A bail!'

'Yes, my dear sir – half a dozen of 'em here. Bail you to any amount, and only charge half-a-crown. Curious trade isn't it?' said Perker, regaling himself with a pinch of snuff.

'What! Am I to understand that these men earn a livelihood by waiting about here, to perjure themselves before the judges of the land, at the rate of half-a-crown a crime!' exclaimed Mr Pickwick, quite aghast at the disclosure.

'Why, I don't exactly know about perjury, my dear sir,' replied the little gentleman. 'Harsh word, my dear sir, very harsh word indeed. It's a legal fiction, my dear sir, nothing more.' Saying which, the attorney shrugged his shoulders, smiled, took a second pinch of snuff, and led the way into the office of the judge's clerk.

This was a room of a specially dirty appearance, with a very low ceiling and old panneled walls; and so badly lighted, that although it was broad day outside, great tallow candles were burning on the desks. At one end, was a door leading to the judge's private apartment, round which were congregated a crowd of attorneys and managing clerks, who were called in, in the order in which their respective appointments stood upon the file. Every time this door was opened to let a party out, the next party made a violent rush to get in; and, as in addition to the numerous dialogues which passed between the gentlemen who were waiting to see the judge, a variety of personal squabbles ensued between the greater part of those who had seen him, there was as much noise as could well be raised in an apartment of such confined dimensions.

Nor were the conversations of these gentlemen the only sounds that broke upon the ear. Standing on a box behind a wooden bar at another end of the room, was a clerk in spectacles, who was 'taking the affidavits:' large batches of which were, from time to time, carried into the private room by another clerk for the judge's signature. There were a large number of attorneys' clerks to be sworn, and it being a moral impossibility to swear them all at once, the struggles of these gentlemen to reach the clerk in spectacles, were like those of a crowd to get in at the pit door of a theatre when Gracious Majesty honours it with its presence. Another functionary, from time to time, exercised his lungs in calling over the names of those who had been sworn, for the purpose of restoring to them their affidavits after they had been signed by the judge: which gave rise to a few more scuffles; and all these things going on at the same time, occasioned as much bustle as the most active and excitable person could desire to behold. There were yet another class of persons – those who were waiting to attend summonses their employers had taken out, which it was optional to the attorney on the opposite side to attend or not – and whose business it was, from time to time, to cry out the opposite attorney's name; to make certain that he was not in attendance without their knowledge.

For example. Leaning against the wall, close beside the seat Mr Pickwick had taken, was an office-lad of fourteen, with a tenor voice; near him, a common-law clerk with a bass one.

A clerk hurried in with a bundle of papers, and stared about him.

'Sniggle and Blink,' cried the tenor.

'Porkin and Snob,' growled the bass.

'Stumpy and Deacon,' said the new comer.

Nobody answered; the next man who came in, was hailed by the whole three; and he in his turn shouted for another firm; and then somebody else roared in a loud voice for another; and so forth.

All this time, the man in the spectacles was hard at work, swearing the clerks: the oath being invariably administered, without any effort at punctuation, and usually in the following terms:

'Take the book in your right hand this is your name and hand-writing you swear that the contents of this your affidavit are true so help you God a shilling you must get change I haven't got it.'

'Well, Sam,' said Mr Pickwick, 'I suppose they are getting the *habeas corpus* ready.'

'Yes,' said Sam, 'and I wish they'd bring out the have-his-carcase. It's wery unpleasant keepin' us vaitin' here. I'd ha' got half a dozen have-his-carcases ready, pack'd up and all, by this time.'

What sort of cumbrous and unmanageable machine, Sam Weller imagined a habeas corpus to be, does not appear; for Perker, at that moment, walked up, and took Mr Pickwick away.

The usual forms having been gone through, the body of Samuel Pickwick was soon afterwards confided to the custody of the tipstaff,[8] to be by him taken to the Warden of the Fleet Prison, and there detained until the amount of the damages and costs in the action of Bardell against Pickwick was fully paid and satisfied.

'And that,' said Mr Pickwick, laughing, 'will be a very long time. Sam, call another hackney-coach. Perker, my dear friend, good bye.'

'I shall go with you, and see you safe there,' said Perker.

'Indeed,' replied Mr Pickwick, 'I would rather go without any other attendant than Sam. As soon as I get settled, I will write and let you know, and I shall expect you immediately. Until then, good bye.'

As Mr Pickwick said this, he got into the coach which had by this time arrived: followed by the tipstaff. Sam having stationed himself on the box, it rolled away.

'A most extraordinary man that!' said Perker, as he stopped to pull on his gloves.

'What a bankrupt he'd make, sir,' observed Mr Lowten, who was standing near. 'How he would bother the commissioners! He'd set 'em at defiance if they talked of committing him, sir.'

The attorney did not appear very much delighted with his clerk's professional estimate of Mr Pickwick's character, for he walked away without deigning any reply.

The hackney-coach jolted along Fleet Street, as hackney-coaches usually do. The horses 'went better,' the driver said, when they had anything before them, (they must have gone at a most extraordinary pace when there was nothing,) and so the vehicle kept behind a cart; when the cart stopped, it stopped; and when the cart went on again, it did the same. Mr Pickwick sat opposite the tipstaff; and the tipstaff sat with his hat between his knees, whistling a tune, and looking out of the coach window.

Time performs wonders. By the powerful old gentleman's aid, even a hackney-coach gets over half a mile of ground. They stopped at length, and Mr Pickwick alighted at the gate of the Fleet.

The tipstaff, looking over his shoulder to see that his charge was following close at his heels, preceded Mr Pickwick into the prison; turning to the left, after they had entered, they passed through an open door into a lobby, from which a heavy gate: opposite to that by which they had entered, and which was guarded by a stout turnkey with the key in his hand: led at once into the interior of the prison.

Here they stopped, while the tipstaff delivered his papers; and here Mr Pickwick was apprised that he would remain, until he had undergone the ceremony, known to the initiated as 'sitting for your portrait.'

'Sitting for my portrait!' said Mr Pickwick.

'Having your likeness taken, sir,' replied the stout turnkey. 'We're capital hands at likenesses here. Take 'em in no time, and always exact. Walk in, sir, and make yourself at home.'

Mr Pickwick complied with the invitation, and sat himself down: when Mr Weller, who stationed himself at the back of the chair, whispered that the sitting was merely another term for undergoing an inspection by the different turnkeys, in order that they might know prisoners from visitors.

'Well, Sam,' said Mr Pickwick, 'then I wish the artists would come. This is rather a public place.'

'They vont be long, sir, I des-say,' replied Sam. 'There's a Dutch clock,' sir.'

'So I see,' observed Mr Pickwick.

'And a bird-cage, sir,' says Sam. 'Veels vithin veels, a prison in a prison. Ain't it, sir?'

As Mr Weller made this philosophical remark, Mr Pickwick was aware that his sitting had commenced. The stout turnkey having been relieved from the lock, sat down, and looked at him carelessly, from time to time, while a long thin man who had relieved him, thrust his hands beneath his coat-tails, and planting himself opposite, took a good long view of him. A third rather surly-

Mr Pickwick sits for his Portrait

looking gentleman: who had apparently been disturbed at his tea, for he was disposing of the last remnant of a crust and butter when he came in: stationed himself close to Mr Pickwick; and, resting his hands on his hips, inspected him narrowly; while two others mixed with the group, and studied his features with most intent and thoughtful faces. Mr Pickwick winced a good deal under the operation, and appeared to sit very uneasily in his chair; but he made no remark to anybody while it was being performed, not even to Sam, who reclined upon the back of the chair, reflecting, partly on the situation of his master, and partly on the great satisfaction it would have afforded him to make a fierce assault upon all the turnkeys there assembled, one after the other, if it were lawful and peaceable so to do.

At length the likeness was completed, and Mr Pickwick was informed, that he might now proceed into the prison.

'Where am I to sleep to-night?' inquired Mr Pickwick.

'Why I don't rightly know about to-night,' replied the stout turnkey. 'You'll be chummed[10] on somebody to-morrow, and then you'll be all snug and comfortable. The first night's generally rather unsettled, but you'll be set all squares to-morrow.'

After some discussion, it was discovered that one of the turnkeys had a bed to let, which Mr Pickwick could have for that night. He gladly agreed to hire it.

'If you'll come with me, I'll show it you at once,' said the man. 'It ain't a large 'un; but it's an out-and-outer[11] to sleep in. This way, sir.'

They passed through the inner gate, and descended a short flight of steps. The key was turned after them; and Mr Pickwick found himself, for the first time in his life, within the walls of a debtor's prison.

CHAPTER 41

What befel Mr Pickwick when he got into the Fleet; what Prisoners he saw there; and how he passed the Night

Mr Tom Roker, the gentleman who had accompanied Mr Pickwick into the prison, turned sharp round to the right when he got to the bottom of the little flight of steps, and led the way, through an iron gate which stood open, and up another short flight of steps, into a long narrow gallery, dirty and low, paved with stone, and very dimly lighted by a window at each remote end.

'This,' said the gentleman, thrusting his hands into his pockets, and looking carelessly over his shoulder to Mr Pickwick, 'This here is the hall flight.'

'Oh,' replied Mr Pickwick, looking down a dark and filthy staircase, which appeared to lead to a range of damp and gloomy stone vaults, beneath the ground, 'and those, I suppose, are the little cellars where the prisoners keep their small quantities of coals. Unpleasant places to have to go down to; but very convenient, I dare say.'

'Yes, I shouldn't wonder if they was convenient,' replied the gentleman, 'seeing that a few people live there, pretty snug. That's the Fair, that is.'

'My friend,' said Mr Pickwick, 'you don't really mean to say that human beings live down in those wretched dungeons?'

'Don't I?' replied Mr Roker, with indignant astonishment; 'why shouldn't I?'

'Live! Live down there!' exclaimed Mr Pickwick.

'Live down there! Yes, and die down there, too, wery often!' replied Mr Roker; 'and what of that? Who's got to say anything agin it? Live down there! Yes, and a wery good place it is to live in, ain't it?'

As Roker turned somewhat fiercely upon Mr Pickwick in saying this, and, moreover muttered in an excited fashion certain unpleasant invocations concerning his own eyes, limbs, and circulating fluids, the latter gentleman deemed it advisable to pursue the discourse no further. Mr Roker then proceeded to mount another staircase, as dirty as that which led to the place which had just been the subject of discussion, in which ascent he was closely followed by Mr Pickwick and Sam.

'There,' said Mr Roker, pausing for breath when they reached another gallery of the same dimensions as the one below, 'this is the coffee-room flight; the one above's the third, and the one above that's the top; and the room where you're a-going to sleep to-night is the warden's room, and it's this way – come on.' Having said all this in a breath, Mr Roker mounted another flight of stairs, with Mr Pickwick and Sam Weller following at his heels.

These staircases received light from sundry windows placed at some little distance above the floor, and looking into a gravelled area bounded by a high brick wall, with iron *chevaux-de-frise* at the top. This area, it appeared from Mr Roker's statement, was the racket-ground; and it further appeared, on the testimony of the same gentleman, that there was a smaller area in that portion of the prison which was nearest Farringdon Street, denominated and called 'the Painted Ground,' from the fact of its walls having once displayed the semblances of various men-of-war in full sail, and other artistical effects achieved in bygone times by some imprisoned draughtsman in his leisure hours.

Having communicated this piece of information, apparently more for the purpose of discharging his bosom of an important fact, than with any specific view of enlightening Mr Pickwick, the guide, having at length reached another gallery, led the way into a small passage at the extreme end: opened a door: and disclosed an apartment of an appearance by no means inviting, containing eight or nine iron bedsteads.

'There,' said Mr Roker, holding the door open, and looking triumphantly round at Mr Pickwick, 'there's a room!'

Mr Pickwick's face, however, betokened such a very trifling portion of satisfaction at the appearance of his lodging, that Mr Roker looked for a reciprocity of feeling into the countenance of Samuel Weller, who, until now, had observed a dignified silence.

'There's a room, young man,' observed Mr Roker.

'I see it,' replied Sam, with a placid nod of the head.

'You wouldn't think to find such a room as this in the Farringdon Hotel, would you?' said Mr Roker, with a complacent smile.

To this Mr Weller replied with an easy and unstudied closing of one eye; which might be considered to mean, either that he would have thought it, or that he would not have thought it, or that he had never thought anything at all about it: as the observer's imagination suggested. Having executed this feat, and re-opened his eye, Mr Weller proceeded to inquire which was the individual bedstead that Mr Roker had so flatteringly described as an out-an-outer to sleep in.

'That's it,' replied Mr Roker, pointing to a very rusty one in a corner. 'It would make any one go to sleep, that bedstead would, whether they wanted to or not.'

'I should think,' said Sam, eyeing the piece of furniture in question with a look of excessive disgust, 'I should think poppies was nothing to it.'

'Nothing at all,' said Mr Roker.

'And I s'pose,' said Sam, with a sidelong glance at his master, as if to see whether there were any symptoms of his determination being shaken by what passed, 'I s'pose the other gen'l'men as sleeps here, *are* gen'l'men.'

'Nothing but it,' said Mr Roker. 'One of 'em takes his twelve pints of ale a-day, and never leaves off smoking even at his meals.'

'He must be a first-rater,' said Sam.

'A, 1,' replied Mr Roker.

Nothing daunted, even by this intelligence, Mr Pickwick smilingly announced his determination to test the powers of the narcotic bedstead for that night; and Mr Roker, after informing him that he could retire to rest at whatever hour he thought proper, without any further notice or formality, walked off, leaving him standing with Sam in the gallery.

It was getting dark; that is to say, a few gas jets were kindled in this place which was never light, by way of compliment to the evening, which had set in outside. As it was rather warm, some of the tenants of the numerous little rooms which opened into the gallery on either hand, had set their doors ajar. Mr Pickwick peeped into them as he passed along, with great curiosity and interest. Here four or five great hulking fellows, just visible through a cloud of tobacco-smoke, were engaged in noisy and riotous conversation over half-emptied pots of beer, or playing at all-fours¹ with a very greasy pack of cards. In the adjoining room, some solitary tenant might be seen, poring, by the light of a feeble tallow candle, over a bundle of soiled and tattered papers, yellow with dust and dropping to pieces from age: writing, for the hundredth time, some lengthened statement of his grievances, for the perusal of some great man whose eyes it would never reach, or whose heart it would never touch. In a third, a man, with his wife and a whole crowd of children, might be seen making up a scanty bed on the ground, or upon a few chairs, for the younger ones to pass the night in. And in a fourth, and a fifth, and a sixth, and a seventh, the noise, and the beer, and the tobacco-smoke, and the cards, all came over again in greater force than before.

In the galleries themselves, and more especially on the staircases, there lingered a great number of people, who came there, some because their rooms were empty and lonesome, others because their rooms were full and hot: the greater part because they were restless and uncomfortable, and not possessed of the secret of exactly knowing what to do with themselves. There were many classes of people here, from the labouring man in his fustian jacket, to the broken-down spendthrift in his shawl dressing-gown, most appropriately out at elbows, but there was the same air about them all –

a listless jail-bird careless swagger, a vagabondish who's-afraid sort of bearing, which is wholly indescribable in words, but which any man can understand in one moment if he wish, by setting foot in the nearest debtor's prison, and looking at the very first group of people he sees there, with the same interest as Mr Pickwick did.

'It strikes me, Sam,' said Mr Pickwick, leaning over the iron-rail at the stair-head, 'It strikes me, Sam, that imprisonment for debt is scarcely any punishment at all.'

'Think not, sir?' inquired Mr Weller.

'You see how these fellows drink, and smoke, and roar,' replied Mr Pickwick. 'It's quite impossible that they can mind it much.'

'Ah, that's just the wery thing, sir,' rejoined Sam, '*they* don't mind it; it's a regular holiday to them – all porter and skittles. It's the t'other vuns as gets done over, vith this sort o' thing: them down-hearted fellers as can't svig away at the beer, nor play at skittles neither; them as vould pay if they could, and gets low by being boxed up. I'll tell you wot it is, sir; them as is always a idlin' in public houses it don't damage at all, and them as is alvays a workin' wen they can, it damages too much. "It's unekal," as my father used to say wen his grog worn't made half-and-half: "It's unekal, and that's the fault on it."'

'I think you're right, Sam,' said Mr Pickwick, after a few moments' reflection, 'quite right.'

'P'raps, now and then, there's some honest people as likes it,' observed Mr Weller, in a ruminative tone, 'but I never heerd o' one as I can call to mind, 'cept the little dirty-faced man in the brown coat; and that was force of habit.'

'And who was he?' inquired Mr Pickwick.

'Wy, that's just the wery point as nobody never know'd,' replied Sam.

'But what did he do?'

'Wy he did wot many men as has been much better know'd has done in their time, sir,' replied Sam, 'he run a match agin the constable, and vun it.'

'In other words, I suppose,' said Mr Pickwick, 'he got into debt.'

'Just that, sir,' replied Sam, 'and in course o' time he come here in consekens. It warn't much – execution for nine pound nothin', multiplied by five for costs; but hows'ever here he stopped for seventeen year. If he got any wrinkles in his face, they was stopped up vith the dirt, for both the dirty face and the brown coat wos just the same at the end o' that time as they wos at the beginnin'. He wos a wery peaceful inoffendin' little creetur, and wos alvays a bustlin' about for somebody, or playin' rackets² and never vinnin'; till at last the turnkeys they got quite fond on him, and he wos in the lodge ev'ry night, a chattering vith 'em, and tellin' stories, and all that 'ere. Vun night he wos in there as usual, along vith a wery old friend of his, as wos on the lock, ven he says all of a sudden, "I ain't seen the market outside, Bill," he says (Fleet Market wos there at that time) – "I ain't seen the market outside, Bill," he says, "for seventeen year." "I know you ain't," says the turnkey, smoking his pipe. "I should like to see it for a minit, Bill," he says. "Wery probable," says the turnkey, smoking his pipe wery fierce, and making believe he warn't up to wot the little man wanted. "Bill," says the little man, more abrupt than afore, "I've got the fancy in my head. Let me see the public streets once more afore I die; and if I ain't struck with apoplexy, I'll be back in five minits by the clock." "And wot 'ud become o' me if you *wos* struck with apoplexy?" said the turnkey. "Wy," says the little creetur, "whoever found me, 'ud bring me home, for I've got my card in my pocket, Bill," he says, "No. 20, Coffee-room Flight:" and that wos true, sure enough, for wen he wanted to make the acquaintance of any new comer, he used to pull out a little limp card vith them words on it and nothin' else; in consideration of vich, he wos alvays called Number Tventy. The turnkey takes a fixed look at him, and at last he says in a solemn manner, "Tventy," he says, "I'll trust you; you won't get your old friend into trouble." "No, my boy; I hope I've somethin' better behind here," says the little man; and as he said it he hit his little veskit wery hard, and then a tear started out o' each eye, which wos wery extraordinary, for it wos supposed as water never touched his face. He shook the turnkey by the hand; out he vent—'

'And never came back again,' said Mr Pickwick.

'Wrong for vunce, sir,' replied Mr Weller, 'for back he come, two minits afore the time, a bilin' with rage: sayin' how he'd been nearly run over by a hackney-coach: that he warn't used to it: and he was blowed if he wouldn't write to the Lord Mayor. They got him pacified at last; and for five years arter that, he never even so much as peeped out o' the lodge-gate.'

'At the expiration of that time he died, I suppose,' said Mr Pickwick.

'No he didn't, sir,' replied Sam. 'He got a curiosity to go and taste the beer at a new public-house over the way, and it wos such a wery nice parlour, that he took it into his head to go there every night, wich he did for a long time, always comin' back reg'lar about a quarter of an hour afore the gate shut, wich wos all wery snug and comfortable. At last he began to get so precious jolly, that he used to forget how the time vent, or care nothin' at all about it, and he vent on gettin' later and later, till vun night his old friend wos just a shuttin' the gate – had turned the key in fact – wen he come up. "Hold hard, Bill," he says. "Wot, ain't you come home yet, Tventy?" says the turnkey, "I thought you wos in, long ago." "No I wasn't," says the little man, vith a smile. "Well then, I'll tell you wot it is, my friend," says the turnkey, openin' the gate wery slow and sulky, "it's my 'pinion as you've got into bad company o' late, which I'm wery sorry to see. Now, I don't wish to do nothing harsh," he says, "but if you can't confine yourself to steady circles, and find your vay back at reglar hours, as sure as you're a standin' there, I'll shut you out altogether!" The little man was seized vith a wiolent fit o' tremblin', and never vent outside the prison walls artervards!'

As Sam concluded, Mr Pickwick slowly retraced his steps down stairs. After a few thoughtful turns in the Painted Ground, which, as it was now dark, was nearly deserted, he intimated to Mr Weller that he thought it high time for him to withdraw for the night; requesting him to seek a bed in some adjacent public-house, and return early in the morning, to make arrangements for the removal of his master's wardrobe from the George and Vulture. This request Mr Samuel Weller prepared to obey, with as good a grace as he could assume, but with a very considerable show of reluctance nevertheless. He even went so far as to essay sundry ineffectual hints regarding the expediency of stretching himself on the gravel for that night; but finding Mr Pickwick obstinately deaf to any such suggestions, finally withdrew.

There is no disguising the fact that Mr Pickwick felt very low-spirited and uncomfortable; not for lack of society, for the prison was very full, and a bottle of wine would at once have purchased the utmost good-fellowship of a few choice spirits, without any more formal ceremony of introduction; but he was alone in the coarse vulgar crowd, and felt the depression of spirit and sinking of heart, naturally consequent on the reflection that he was cooped and caged up, without a prospect of liberation. As to the idea of releasing himself by ministering to the sharpness of Dodson and Fogg, it never for an instant entered his thoughts.

In this frame of mind he turned again into the coffee-room gallery, and walked slowly to and fro. The place was intolerably dirty, and the smell of tobacco-smoke perfectly suffocating. There was a perpetual slamming and banging of doors as the people went in and out; and the noise of their voices and footsteps echoed and re-echoed through the passages constantly. A young woman, with a child in her arms, who seemed scarcely able to crawl, from emaciation and misery, was walking up and down the passage in conversation with her husband, who had no other place to see her in. As they passed Mr Pickwick, he could hear the female sob; and once she burst into such a passion of grief, that she was compelled to lean against the wall for support, while the man took the child in his arms, and tried to soothe her.

Mr Pickwick's heart was really too full to bear it, and he went up stairs to bed.

Now, although the warden's room was a very uncomfortable one (being, in every point of decoration and convenience, several hundred degrees inferior to the common infirmary of a county gaol), it had at present the merit of being wholly deserted save by Mr Pickwick himself. So, he sat down at the foot of his little iron bedstead, and began to wonder how much a year the warden made out of the dirty room. Having satisfied himself, by mathematical calculation, that the apartment was about equal in annual value to the freehold of a small street in the suburbs of London, he took to wondering what possible temptation could have induced a dingy-looking fly that was crawling over his pantaloons, to come into a close prison, when he had the choice of so many airy situations – a course of meditation which led him to the irresistible conclusion that the insect was mad. After settling this point, he began to be conscious that he was getting sleepy; whereupon he took his nightcap out of the pocket in which he had had the precaution to stow it in the morning, and, leisurely undressing himself, got into bed, and fell asleep.

'Bravo! Heel over toe – cut³ and shuffle – pay away at it, Zephyr! I'm smothered if the Opera House isn't your proper hemisphere. Keep it up! Hooray!' These expressions, delivered in a most boisterous tone, and accompanied with loud peals of laughter, roused Mr Pickwick from one of those sound slumbers which, lasting in reality some half hour, seem to the sleeper to have been protracted for three weeks or a month.

The voice had no sooner ceased than the room was shaken with such violence that the windows rattled in their frames, and the bed-steads trembled again. Mr Pickwick started up, and remained for some minutes fixed in mute astonishment at the scene before him.

On the floor of the room, a man in a broad-skirted green coat, with corderoy knee smalls and grey cotton stockings, was perform-ing the most popular steps of a hornpipe, with a slang and burlesque

The Warden's Room

caricature of grace and lightness, which, combined with the very appropriate character of his costume, was inexpressibly absurd. Another man, evidently very drunk, who had probably been tumbled into bed by his companions, was sitting up between the sheets, warbling as much as he could recollect of a comic song, with the most intensely sentimental feeling and expression; while a third, seated on one of the bedsteads, was applauding both performers with the air of a profound connoisseur, and encouraging them by such ebullitions of feeling as had already roused Mr Pickwick from his sleep.

This last man was an admirable specimen of a class of gentry which never can be seen in full perfection but in such places; – they may be met with, in an imperfect state, occasionally about stable-yards and public-houses; but they never attain their full bloom except in these hot-beds, which would almost seem to be considerately provided by the Legislature for the sole purpose of rearing them.

He was a tall fellow, with an olive complexion, long dark hair, and very thick bushy whiskers meeting under his chin. He wore no neckerchief, as he had been playing rackets all day, and his open shirt collar displayed their full luxuriance. On his head he wore one of the common eighteenpenny French skull-caps, with a gawdy tassel dangling therefrom, very happily in keeping with a common fustian coat. His legs: which, being long, were afflicted with weakness: graced a pair of Oxford-mixture trousers, made to show the full symmetry of those limbs. Being somewhat negligently braced, however, and, moreover, but imperfectly buttoned, they fell in a series of not the most graceful folds over a pair of shoes sufficiently down at heel to display a pair of very soiled white stockings. There was a rakish, vagabond smartness, and a kind of boastful rascality, about the whole man, that was worth a mine of gold.

This figure was the first to perceive that Mr Pickwick was looking on; upon which he winked to the Zephyr, and entreated him, with mock gravity, not to wake the gentleman.

'Why, bless the gentleman's honest heart and soul!' said the Zephyr, turning round and affecting the extremity of surprise; 'the gentleman *is* awake. Hem, Shakespeare! How do you do, sir? How is Mary and Sarah, sir? and the dear old lady at home, sir? Will you have the kindness to put my compliments into the first little parcel you're sending that way, sir, and say that I would have sent 'em before, only I was afraid they might be broken in the waggon, sir?'

'Don't overwhelm the gentleman with ordinary civilities when you see he's anxious to have something to drink,' said the gentleman with the whiskers, with a jocose air. 'Why don't you ask the gentleman what he'll take?'

'Dear me, I quite forgot,' replied the other. 'What *will* you take, sir? Will you take port wine, sir, or sherry wine, sir? I can recommend the ale, sir; or perhaps you'd like to taste the porter, sir? Allow me to have the felicity of hanging up your nightcap, sir.'

With this, the speaker snatched that article of dress from Mr Pickwick's head, and fixed it in a twinkling on that of the drunken man, who, firmly impressed with the belief that he was delighting a numerous assembly, continued to hammer away at the comic song in the most melancholy strains imaginable.

Taking a man's nightcap from his brow by violent means, and adjusting it on the head of an unknown gentleman of dirty exterior, however ingenious a witticism in itself, is unquestionably one of those which come under the denomination of practical jokes. Viewing the matter precisely in this light, Mr Pickwick, without the slightest intimation of his purpose, sprang vigorously out of bed, struck the Zephyr so smart a blow in the chest as to deprive him of a considerable portion of the commodity which sometimes bears his name, and then, recapturing his nightcap, boldly placed himself in an attitude of defence.

'Now,' said Mr Pickwick, gasping no less from excitement than from the expenditure of so much energy, 'come on – both of you – both of you!' With this liberal invitation the worthy gentleman communicated a revolving motion to his clenched fists, by way of appalling his antagonists with a display of science.

It might have been Mr Pickwick's very unexpected gallantry, or it might have been the complicated manner in which he had got himself out of bed, and fallen all in a mass upon the hornpipe man, that touched his adversaries. Touched they were; for, instead of then and there making an attempt to commit manslaughter, as Mr Pickwick implicitly believed they would have done, they paused, stared at each other a short time, and finally laughed outright.

'Well; you're a trump, and I like you all the better for it,' said the Zephyr. 'Now jump into bed again, or you'll catch the rheumatics. No malice, I hope?' said the man, extending a hand the size of the yellow clump of fingers which sometimes swings over a glover's door.

'Certainly not,' said Mr Pickwick with great alacrity; for, now that the excitement was over, he began to feel rather cool about the legs.

'Allow me the *h*onour,' said the gentleman with the whiskers, presenting his dexter hand, and aspirating the h.

'With much pleasure, sir,' said Mr Pickwick; and having executed a very long and solemn shake, he got into bed again.

'My name is Smangle, sir,' said the man with the whiskers.

'Oh,' said Mr Pickwick.

'Mine is Mivins,' said the man in the stockings.

'I am delighted to hear it, sir,' said Mr Pickwick.

'Hem,' coughed Mr Smangle.

'Did you speak, sir?' said Mr Pickwick.

'No, I did not, sir?' said Mr Smangle.

'I thought you did, sir,' said Mr Pickwick.

All this was very genteel and pleasant; and, to make matters still more comfortable, Mr Smangle assured Mr Pickwick a great many times that he entertained a very high respect for the feelings of a gentleman; which sentiment, indeed, did him infinite credit, as he could be in no wise supposed to understand them.

'Are you going through the Court, sir?' inquired Mr Smangle.

'Through the what?' said Mr Pickwick.

'Through the Court – Portugal Street[4] – the Court for the Relief of—you know.'

'Oh, no,' replied Mr Pickwick. 'No, I am not.'

'Going out, perhaps?' suggested Mivins.

'I fear not,' replied Mr Pickwick. 'I refuse to pay some damages, and am here in consequence.'

'Ah,' said Mr Smangle, 'paper has been my ruin.'

'A stationer, I presume, sir?' said Mr Pickwick, innocently.

'Stationer! No, no; confound and curse me! Not so low as that. No trade. When I say paper, I mean bills.'

'Oh, you use the word in that sense. I see,' said Mr Pickwick.

'Damme! A gentleman must expect reverses,' said Smangle. 'What of that? Here am I in the Fleet Prison. Well; good. What then? I'm none the worse for that, am I?'

'Not a bit,' replied Mr Mivins. And he was quite right; for, so far from Mr Smangle being any the worse for it, he was something the better, inasmuch as to qualify himself for the place, he had attained gratuitous possession of certain articles of jewellery, which, long before that, had found their way to the pawnbroker's.

'Well; but come,' said Mr Smangle; 'this is dry work. Let's rinse our mouths with a drop of burnt sherry; the last comer shall stand it, Mivins shall fetch it, and I'll help to drink it. That's a fair and gentlemanlike division of labour, any how. Curse me!'

Unwilling to hazard another quarrel, Mr Pickwick gladly assented to the proposition, and consigned the money to Mr Mivins, who, as it was nearly eleven o'clock, lost no time in repairing to the coffee-room on his errand.

'I say,' whispered Smangle, the moment his friend had left the room; 'what did you give him?'

'Half a sovereign,' said Mr Pickwick.

'He's a devilish pleasant gentlemanly dog,' said Mr Smangle; – 'infernal pleasant. I don't know anybody more so, but—' Here Mr Smangle stopped short, and shook his head dubiously.

'You don't think there is any probability of his appropriating the money to his own use?' said Mr Pickwick.

'Oh, no! Mind, I don't say that; I expressly say that he's a devilish gentlemanly fellow,' said Mr Smangle. 'But I think, perhaps, if somebody went down, just to see that he didn't dip his beak into the jug by accident, or make some confounded mistake in losing the money as he came up stairs, it would be as well. Here, you sir, just run down stairs, and look after that gentleman, will you?'

This request was addressed to a little timid-looking nervous man, whose appearance bespoke great poverty, and who had been crouching on his bedstead all this while, apparently stupified by the novelty of his situation.

'You know where the coffee-room is,' said Smangle; 'just run down, and tell that gentleman you've come to help him up with the jug. Or – stop – I'll tell you what – I'll tell you how we'll do him,' said Smangle, with a cunning look.

'How?' said Mr Pickwick.

'Send down word that he's to spend the change in cigars. Capital thought. Run and tell him that; d'ye hear? They shan't be wasted,' continued Smangle, turning to Mr Pickwick. '*I'll* smoke em.'

This manœuvering was so exceedingly ingenious, and, withal, performed with such immovable composure and coolness, that Mr Pickwick would have had no wish to disturb it, even if he had had the power. In a short time Mr Mivins returned, bearing the sherry, which Mr Smangle dispensed in two little cracked mugs: considerately remarking, with reference to himself, that a gentleman must not be particular under such circumstances, and that, for his part, he was not too proud to drink out of the jug. In which, to show his sincerity, he forthwith pledged the company in a draught which half emptied it.

An excellent understanding having been by these means promoted, Mr Smangle proceeded to entertain his hearers with a
relation of divers romantic adventures in which he had been from
time to time engaged, involving various interesting anecdotes of a
thorough-bred horse, and a magnificent Jewess, both of surpassing
beauty, and much coveted by the nobility and gentry of these
kingdoms.

Long before these elegant extracts from the biography of a
gentleman, were concluded, Mr Mivins had betaken himself to bed,
and had set in snoring for the night: leaving the timid stranger and
Mr Pickwick to the full benefit of Mr Smangle's experiences.

Nor were the two last-named gentlemen as much edified as they
might have been, by the moving passages narrated. Mr Pickwick
had been in a state of slumber for some time, when he had a faint
perception of the drunken man bursting out afresh with the comic
song, and receiving from Mr Smangle a gentle intimation, through
the medium of the water jug, that his audience were not musically
disposed. Mr Pickwick then once again dropped off to sleep, with a
confused consciousness that Mr Smangle was still engaged in
relating a long story, the chief point of which appeared to be, that,
on some occasion particularly stated and set forth, he had 'done' a
bill and a gentleman at the same time.

CHAPTER 42

Illustrative, like the preceding one, of the old
Proverb, that Adversity brings a Man acquainted
with strange Bed-fellows. Likewise containing Mr
Pickwick's extraordinary and startling
announcement to Mr Samuel Weller

When Mr Pickwick opened his eyes next morning, the first object
upon which they rested, was Samuel Weller, seated upon a small
black portmanteau, intently regarding, apparently in a condition of
profound abstraction, the stately figure of the dashing Mr Smangle:
while Mr Smangle himself, who was already partially dressed, was
seated on his bedstead, occupied in the desperately hopeless attempt
of staring Mr Weller out of countenance. We say desperately
hopeless, because Sam, with a comprehensive gaze which took in

Mr Smangle's cap, feet, head, face, legs, and whiskers, all at the same time, continued to look steadily on, with every demonstration of lively satisfaction, but with no more regard to Mr Smangle's personal sentiments on the subject than he would have displayed had he been inspecting a wooden statue, or a straw-embowelled Guy Faux.

'Well; will you know me again?' said Mr Smangle, with a frown.

'I'd svear to you anyveres, sir,' replied Sam, cheerfully.

'Don't be impertinent to a gentleman, sir,' said Mr Smangle.

'Not on no account,' replied Sam. 'If you'll tell me wen he wakes, I'll be upon the wery best extra-super behaviour!' This observation, having a remote tendency to imply that Mr Smangle was no gentleman, kindled his ire.

'Mivins!' said Mr Smangle, with a passionate air.

'What's the office?' replied that gentleman from his couch.

'Who the devil is this fellow?'

''Gad,' said Mr Mivins, looking lazily out from under the bed-clothes, 'I ought to ask *you* that. Hasn't he any business here?'

'No,' replied Mr Smangle.

'Then knock him down stairs, and tell him not to presume to get up till I come and kick him,' rejoined Mr Mivins; with this prompt advice that excellent gentleman again betook himself to slumber.

The conversation exhibiting these unequivocal symptoms of verging on the personal, Mr Pickwick deemed it a fit point at which to interpose.

'Sam,' said Mr Pickwick.

'Sir,' rejoined that gentleman.

'Has anything new occurred since last night?'

'Nothin' partickler, sir,' replied Sam, glancing at Mr Smangle's whiskers; 'the late prewailance of a close and confined atmosphere has been rayther favorable to the growth of veeds, of an alarmin' and sangvinary natur; but vith that 'ere exception things is quiet enough.'

'I shall get up,' said Mr Pickwick; 'give me some clean things.'

Whatever hostile intentions Mr Smangle might have entertained, his thoughts were speedily diverted by the unpacking of the portmanteau; the contents of which, appeared to impress him at once with a most favourable opinion, not only of Mr Pickwick, but of Sam also, who, he took an early opportunity of declaring in a tone of voice loud enough for that eccentric personage to overhear, was a regular thorough-bred original, and consequently the very man after his own heart. As to Mr Pickwick, the affection he conceived for him knew no limits.

'Now is there anything I can do for you, my dear sir?' said Smangle.

'Nothing that I am aware of, I am obliged to you,' replied Mr Pickwick.

'No linen that you want sent to the washerwoman's? I know a delightful washerwoman outside, that comes for my things twice a week; and, by Jove! – how devilish lucky! – this is the day she calls. Shall I put any of those little things up with mine? Don't say anything about the trouble. Confound and curse it! if one gentleman under a cloud, is not to put himself a little out of the way to assist another gentleman in the same condition, what's human nature?'

Thus spake Mr Smangle, edging himself meanwhile as near as possible to the portmanteau, and beaming forth looks of the most fervent and disinterested friendship.

'There's nothing you want to give out for the man to brush, my dear creature, is there?' resumed Smangle.

'Nothin' whatever, my fine feller,' rejoined Sam, taking the reply into his own mouth. 'P'raps if vun of us wos to brush, without troubling the man, it 'ud be more agreeable for all parties, as the schoolmaster said wen the young gentleman objected to being flogged by the butler.'

'And there's nothing that I can send in my little box to the washerwoman's, is there?' said Smangle, turning from Sam to Mr Pickwick, with an air of some discomfiture.

'Nothin' whatever, sir,' retorted Sam; 'I'm afeerd the little box must be chock full o' your own as it is.'

This speech was accompanied with such a very expressive look at that particular portion of Mr Smangle's attire, by the appearance of which the skill of laundresses in getting up gentlemen's linen is generally tested, that he was fain to turn upon his heel, and, for the present at any rate, to give up all design on Mr Pickwick's purse and wardrobe. He accordingly retired in dudgeon to the racket-ground, where he made a light and wholesome breakfast on a couple of the cigars which had been purchased on the previous night.

Mr Mivins, who was no smoker, and whose account for small articles of chandlery had also reached down to the bottom of the slate, and been 'carried over' to the other side, remained in bed, and, in his own words, 'took it out in sleep.'

After breakfasting in a small closet attached to the coffee-room, which bore the imposing title of the Snuggery; the temporary inmate of which, in consideration of a small additional charge, had the unspeakable advantage of overhearing all the conversation in the coffee-room aforesaid; and after dispatching Mr Weller on some necessary errands, Mr Pickwick repaired to the Lodge, to consult Mr Roker concerning his future accommodation.

'Accommodation, eh?' said that gentleman, consulting a large book. 'Plenty of that, Mr Pickvick. Your chummage ticket will be on twenty-seven, in the third.'

'Oh,' said Mr Pickwick. 'My what, did you say?'

'Your chummage ticket,' replied Mr Roker; 'you're up to that?'

'Not quite,' replied Mr Pickwick, with a smile.

'Why,' said Mr Roker, 'it's as plain as Salisbury. You'll have a chummage ticket upon twenty-seven in the third, and them as is in the room will be your chums.'

'Are there many of them?' inquired Mr Pickwick, dubiously.

'Three,' replied Mr Roker.

Mr Pickwick coughed.

'One of'em's a parson,' said Mr Roker, filling up a little piece of paper as he spoke; 'another's a butcher.'

'Eh?' exclaimed Mr Pickwick.

'A butcher,' repeated Mr Roker, giving the nib of his pen a tap on the desk to cure it of a disinclination to mark. 'What a thorough-paced goer he used to be sure-ly! You remember Tom Martin, Neddy?' said Roker, appealing to another man in the lodge, who was paring the mud off his shoes with a five-and-twenty bladed pocket knife.

'*I* should think so,' replied the party addressed, with a strong emphasis on the personal pronoun.

'Bless my dear eyes!' said Mr Roker, shaking his head slowly from side to side, and gazing abstractedly out of the grated windows before him, as if he were fondly recalling some peaceful scene of his early youth; 'it seems but yesterday that he whopped the coal-heaver down Fox-under-the-Hill[1] by the wharf there. I think I can see him now, a coming up the Strand between the two street-keepers,[2] a little sobered by the bruising, with a patch o' winegar and brown paper over his right eyelid, and that 'ere lovely bulldog, as pinned the little boy arterwards, a following at his heels. What a rum thing Time is, ain't it, Neddy?'

The gentleman to whom these observations were addressed, who appeared of a taciturn and thoughtful cast, merely echoed the inquiry; Mr Roker, shaking off the poetical and gloomy train of thought into which he had been betrayed, descended to the common business of life, and resumed his pen.

'Do you know what the third gentleman is?' inquired Mr Pickwick, not very much gratified by this description of his future associates.

'What is that Simpson, Neddy?' said Mr Roker, turning to his companion.

'What Simpson?' said Neddy.

'Why him in twenty-seven in the third, that this gentleman's going to be chummed on.'

'Oh, him!' replied Neddy: 'he's nothing exactly. He *was* a horse chaunter: he's a leg now.'[3]

'Ah, so I thought,' rejoined Mr Roker, closing the book, and placing the small piece of paper in Mr Pickwick's hands. 'That's the ticket, sir.'

Very much perplexed by this summary disposition of his person, Mr Pickwick walked back into the prison, revolving in his mind what he had better do. Convinced, however, that before he took any other steps it would be advisable to see, and hold personal converse with, the three gentlemen with whom it was proposed to quarter him, he made the best of his way to the third flight.

After groping about in the gallery for some time, attempting in the dim light to decipher the numbers on the different doors, he at length appealed to a potboy, who happened to be pursuing his morning occupation of gleaning for pewter.[4]

'Which is twenty-seven, my good fellow?' said Mr Pickwick.

'Five doors further on,' replied the potboy. 'There's the likeness of a man being hung, and smoking a pipe the while, chalked outside the door.'

Guided by this direction, Mr Pickwick proceeded slowly along the gallery until he encountered the 'portrait of a gentleman,' above described, upon whose countenance he tapped, with the knuckle of his fore-finger – gently at first, and then audibly. After repeating this process several times without effect, he ventured to open the door and peep in.

There was only one man in the room, and he was leaning out of window as far as he could without overbalancing himself, endeavouring, with great perseverance, to spit upon the crown of the hat of a personal friend on the parade below. As neither speaking, coughing, sneezing, knocking, nor any other ordinary mode of attracting attention, made this person aware of the presence of a visitor, Mr Pickwick, after some delay, stepped up to the window, and pulled him gently by the coat-tail. The individual brought in his head and shoulders with great swiftness, and surveying Mr Pickwick from head to foot, demanded in a surly tone what the – something beginning with a capital H – he wanted.

'I believe,' said Mr Pickwick, consulting his ticket, 'I believe this is twenty-seven in the third?'

'Well?' replied the gentleman.

'I have come here in consequence of receiving this bit of paper,' rejoined Mr Pickwick.

'Hand it over,' said the gentleman.

Mr Pickwick complied.

'I think Roker might have chummed you somewhere else,' said Mr Simpson (for it was the leg), after a very discontented sort of a pause.

Mr Pickwick thought so also; but, under all the circumstances, he considered it a matter of sound policy to be silent.

Mr Simpson mused for a few moments after this, and then, thrusting his head out of the window, gave a shrill whistle, and pronounced some word aloud, several times. What the word was, Mr Pickwick could not distinguish; but he rather inferred that it must be some nickname which distinguished Mr Martin: from the fact of a great number of gentlemen on the ground below, immediately proceeding to cry 'Butcher!' in imitation of the tone in which that useful class of society are wont, diurnally, to make their presence known at area railings.

Subsequent occurrences confirmed the accuracy of Mr Pickwick's impression; for, in a few seconds, a gentleman, prematurely broad for his years: clothed in a professional blue jean frock, and top-boots with circular toes: entered the room nearly out of breath, closely followed by another gentleman in very shabby black, and a seal-skin cap. The latter gentleman, who fastened his coat all the way up to his chin by means of a pin and a button alternately, had a very coarse red face, and looked like a drunken chaplain; which, indeed, he was.

These two gentlemen having by turns perused Mr Pickwick's billet, the one expressed his opinion that it was 'a rig,'[5] and the other his conviction that it was 'a go.' Having recorded their feelings in these very intelligible terms, they looked at Mr Pickwick and each other in awkward silence.

'It's an aggravating thing, just as we got the beds so snug,' said the chaplain, looking at three dirty mattresses, each rolled up in a blanket: which occupied one corner of the room during the day, and formed a kind of slab, on which were placed an old cracked basin, ewer, and soap-dish, of common yellow earthenware, with a blue flower: 'Very aggravating.'

Mr Martin expressed the same opinion in rather stronger terms; Mr Simpson, after having let a variety of expletive adjectives loose upon society without any substantive to accompany them, tucked up his sleeves, and began to wash the greens for dinner.

While this was going on, Mr Pickwick had been eyeing the room, which was filthily dirty, and smelt intolerably close. There was no vestige of either carpet, curtain, or blind. There was not even a closet in it. Unquestionably there were but few things to put away, if there had been one; but, however few in number, or small in individual amount, still, remnants of loaves and pieces of cheese, and damp towels, and scrags of meat, and articles of wearing apparel, and mutilated crockery, and bellows without nozzles, and toasting-forks without prongs, *do* present somewhat of an uncomfortable appearance when they are scattered about the floor of a small apartment, which is the common sitting and sleeping room of three idle men.

'I suppose this can be managed somehow,' said the butcher, after a pretty long silence. 'What will you take to go out?'

'I beg your pardon,' replied Mr Pickwick. 'What did you say? I hardly understand you.'

'What will you take to be paid out?' said the butcher. 'The regular chummage is two-and-six. Will you take three bob?'

' – And a bender,'⁶ suggested the clerical gentleman.

'Well, I don't mind that; it's only twopence a-piece more,' said Mr Martin.

'What do you say, now? We'll pay you out for three-and-sixpence a week. Come!'

'And stand a gallon of beer down,' chimed in Mr Simpson. 'There!'

'And drink it on the spot,' said the chaplain. 'Now!'

'I really am so wholly ignorant of the rules of this place,' returned Mr Pickwick, 'that I do not yet comprehend you. *Can* I live anywhere else? I thought I could not.'

At this inquiry Mr Martin looked, with a countenance of excessive surprise, at his two friends, and then each gentleman pointed with his right thumb over his left shoulder. This action, imperfectly described in words by the very feeble term of 'over the left,' when performed by any number of ladies or gentlemen who are accustomed to act in unison, has a very graceful and airy effect; its expression is one of light and playful sarcasm.

'*Can* you!' repeated Mr Martin, with a smile of pity.

'Well, if I knew as little of life as that, I'd eat my hat and swallow the buckle whole,' said the clerical gentleman.

'So would I,' added the sporting one, solemnly.

After this introductory preface, the three chums informed Mr Pickwick, in a breath, that money was, in the Fleet, just what money was out of it; that it would instantly procure him almost anything he desired; and that, supposing he had it, and had no objection to spend it, if he only signified his wish to have a room to himself, he might take possession of one, furnished and fitted to boot, in half an hour's time.

With this, the parties separated, very much to their common satisfaction: Mr Pickwick once more retracing his steps to the lodge: and the three companions adjourning to the coffee-room, there to spend the five shillings which the clerical gentleman had, with admirable prudence and foresight, borrowed of him for the purpose.

'I knowed it!' said Mr Roker, with a chuckle, when Mr Pickwick stated the object with which he had returned. 'Didn't I say so, Neddy?'

The philosophical owner of the universal penknife, growled an affirmative.

'I knowed you'd want a room for yourself, bless you!' said Mr Roker. 'Let me see. You'll want some furnitur. You'll hire that of me, I suppose? That's the reg'lar thing.'

'With great pleasure,' replied Mr Pickwick.

'There's a capital room up in the coffee-room flight, that belongs to a Chancery prisoner,' said Mr Roker. 'It'll stand you in a pound a-week. I suppose you don't mind that?'

'Not at all,' said Mr Pickwick.

'Just step there with me,' said Roker, taking up his hat with great alacrity; 'the matters's settled in five minutes. Lord! why didn't you say at first that you was willing to come down handsome?'

The matter was soon arranged, as the turnkey had foretold. The Chancery prisoner had been there long enough to have lost friends, fortune, home, and happiness, and to have acquired the right of having a room to himself. As he laboured, however, under the inconvenience of often wanting a morsel of bread, he eagerly listened to Mr Pickwick's proposal to rent the apartment, and readily covenanted and agreed to yield him up the sole and undisturbed possession thereof, in consideration of the weekly payment of twenty shillings; from which fund he furthermore contracted to pay out any person or persons that might be chummed upon it.

As they struck the bargain, Mr Pickwick surveyed him with a painful interest. He was a tall, gaunt, cadaverous man, in an old great-coat and slippers: with sunken cheeks, and a restless, eager eye. His lips were bloodless, and his bones sharp and thin. God help him! the iron teeth of confinement and privation had been slowly filing him down for twenty years.

'And where will you live meanwhile, sir?' said Mr Pickwick, as he laid the amount of the first week's rent, in advance, on the tottering table.

The man gathered up the money with a trembling hand, and replied that he didn't know yet; he must go and see where he could move his bed to.

'I am afraid sir,' said Mr Pickwick, laying his hand gently and compassionately on his arm; 'I am afraid you will have to live in some noisy crowded place. Now, pray, consider this room your own when you want quiet, or when any of your friends come to see you.'

'Friends!' interposed the man, in a voice which rattled in his throat. 'If I lay dead at the bottom of the deepest mine in the world; tight screwed down and soldered in my coffin; rotting in the dark and filthy ditch that drags its slime along, beneath the foundations of this prison; I could not be more forgotten or unheeded than I am here. I am a dead man; dead to society, without the pity they bestow on those whose souls have passed to judgment. Friends to see *me*! My God! I have sunk, from the prime of life into old age, in this place, and there is not one to raise his hand above my bed when I lie dead upon it, and say, "It is a blessing he is gone!"'

The excitement, which had cast an unwonted light over the man's face, while he spoke, subsided as he concluded; and, pressing his withered hands together in a hasty and disordered manner, he shuffled from the room.

'Rides rather rusty,' said Mr Roker, with a smile. 'Ah! they're like the elephants. They feel it now and then, and it makes 'em wild!'

Having made this deeply-sympathising remark, Mr Roker entered upon his arrangements with such expedition, that in a short time the room was furnished with a carpet, six chairs, a table, a sofa bedstead, a tea-kettle, and various small articles, on hire, at the very reasonable rate of seven-and-twenty shillings and sixpence per week.

'Now, is there anything more we can do for you?' inquired Mr Roker, looking round with great satisfaction, and gaily chinking the first week's hire in his closed fist.

'Why, yes,' said Mr Pickwick, who had been musing deeply for some time. 'Are there any people here, who run on errands, and so forth?'

'Outside, do you mean?' inquired Mr Roker.

'Yes. I mean who are able to go outside. Not prisoners.'

'Yes, there is,' said Roker. 'There's an unfortunate devil, who has got a friend on the poor side, that's glad to do anything of that sort. He's been running odd jobs, and that, for the last two months. Shall I send him?'

'If you please,' rejoined Mr Pickwick. 'Stay; no. The poor side, you say? I should like to see it. I'll go to him myself.'

The poor side of a debtor's prison, is, as its name imports, that in which the most miserable and abject class of debtors are confined. A prisoner having declared upon the poor side, pays neither rent nor chummage. His fees, upon entering and leaving the gaol, are reduced in amount, and he becomes entitled to a share of some small quantities of food: to provide which, a few charitable persons have, from time to time, left trifling legacies in their wills. Most of our readers will remember, that, until within a very few years past, there was a kind of iron cage in the wall of the Fleet Prison, within which was posted some man of hungry looks, who, from time to time, rattled a money-box, and exclaimed in a mournful voice, 'Pray, remember the poor debtors; pray, remember the poor debtors.' The receipts of this box, when there were any, were divided among poor prisoners; and the men on the poor side relieved each other in this degrading office.

Although this custom has been abolished, and the cage is now boarded up, the miserable and destitute condition of these unhappy persons remains the same. We no longer suffer them to appeal at the prison gates to the charity and compassion of the passers by; but we still leave unblotted in the leaves of our statute book, for the reverence and admiration of succeeding ages, the just and wholesome law which declares that the sturdy felon shall be fed and clothed, and that the penniless debtor shall be left to die of starvation and nakedness. This is no fiction. Not a week passes over our heads, but, in every one of our prisons for debt, some of these men must inevitably expire in the slow agonies of want, if they were not relieved by their fellow-prisoners.

Turning these things in his mind, as he mounted the narrow staircase at the foot of which Roker had left him, Mr Pickwick gradually worked himself to the boiling-over point; and so excited was he with his reflections on this subject, that he had burst into the room to which he had been directed, before he had any distinct recollection, either of the place in which he was, or of the object of his visit.

The general aspect of the room recalled him to himself at once; but he had no sooner cast his eyes on the figure of a man who was brooding over the dusty fire than, letting his hat fall on the floor, he stood perfectly fixed, and immoveable with astonishment.

Yes; in tattered garments, and without a coat; his common calico shirt, yellow and in rags; his hair hanging over his face; his features changed with suffering, and pinched with famine; there sat Mr Alfred Jingle: his head resting on his hand, his eyes fixed upon the fire, and his whole appearance denoting misery and dejection!

Near him, leaning listlessly against the wall, stood a strong-built countryman flicking with a worn-out hunting-whip the top-boot that adorned his right foot – his left being (for he dressed by easy stages) thrust into an old slipper. Horses, dogs, and drink, had brought him there, pell-mell. There was a rusty spur on the solitary boot, which he occasionally jerked into the empty air, at the same time giving the boot a smart blow, and muttering some of the sounds by which a sportsman encourages his horse. He was riding, in imagination, some desperate steeple-chase at that moment. Poor wretch! He never rode a match on the swiftest animal in his costly stud, with half the speed at which he had torn along the course that ended in the Fleet.

On the opposite side of the room an old man was seated on a small wooden box, with his eyes rivetted on the floor, and his face settled into an expression of the deepest and most hopeless despair. A young girl – his little grand-daughter – was hanging about him: endeavouring, with a thousand childish devices, to engage his attention; but the old man neither saw nor heard her. The voice that had been music to him, and the eyes that had been light, fell coldly on his senses. His limbs were shaking with disease, and the palsy had fastened on his mind.

There were two or three other men in the room, congregated in a little knot, and noisily talking among themselves. There was a lean and haggard woman, too – a prisoner's wife – who was watering,

Discovery of Jingle in the Fleet

with great solicitude, the wretched stump of a dried-up, withered plant, which, it was plain to see, could never send forth a green leaf again; – too true an emblem, perhaps, of the office she had come there to discharge.

Such were the objects which presented themselves to Mr Pickwick's view, as he looked round him in amazement. The noise of some one stumbling hastily into the room, roused him. Turning his eyes towards the door, they encountered the new comer; and in him, through his rags and dirt, he recognised the familiar features of Mr Job Trotter.

'Mr Pickwick!' exclaimed Job aloud.

'Eh?' said Jingle, starting from his seat. 'Mr —! So it is – queer place – strange thing – serves me right – very.' Mr Jingle thrust his hands into the place where his trousers pockets used to be, and, dropping his chin upon his breast, sank back into his chair.

Mr Pickwick was affected; the two men looked so very miserable. The sharp involuntary glance Jingle had cast at a small piece of raw loin of mutton, which Job had brought in with him, said more of their reduced state than two hours' explanation could have done. Mr Pickwick looked mildly at Jingle, and said:

'I should like to speak to you in private. Will you step out for an instant?'

'Certainly,' said Jingle, rising hastily. 'Can't step far – no danger of over-walking yourself here – Spike park – grounds pretty – romantic, but not extensive – open for public inspection – family always in town – housekeeper desperately careful – very.'

'You have forgotten your coat,' said Mr Pickwick, as they walked out to the staircase, and closed the door after them.

'Eh?' said Jingle. 'Spout[7] – dear relation – uncle Tom – couldn't help it – must eat, you know. Wants of nature – and all that.'

'What do you mean?'

'Gone, my dear sir – last coat – can't help it. Lived on a pair of boots – whole fortnight. Silk umbrella – ivory handle – week – fact – honour – ask Job – knows it.'

'Lived for three weeks upon a pair of boots, and a silk umbrella with an ivory handle!' exclaimed Mr Pickwick, who had only heard of such things in shipwrecks, or read of them in Constable's Miscellany.[8]

'True,' said Jingle, nodding his head. 'Pawnbroker's shop – duplicates here – small sums – mere nothing – all rascals.'

'Oh,' said Mr Pickwick, much relieved by this explanation; 'I understand you. You have pawned your wardrobe.'

'Everything – Job's too – all shirts gone – never mind – saves washing. Nothing soon – lie in bed – starve – die – Inquest – little bone-house – poor prisoner – common necessaries – hush it up – gentlemen of the jury – warden's tradesmen – keep it snug – natural death – coroner's order – workhouse funeral – serve him right – all over – drop the curtain.'

Jingle delivered this singular summary of his prospects in life, with his accustomed volubility, and with various twitches of the countenance to counterfeit smiles. Mr Pickwick easily perceived that his recklessness was assumed, and looking him full, but not unkindly, in the face, saw that his eyes were moist with tears.

'Good fellow,' said Jingle, pressing his hand, and turning his head away. 'Ungrateful dog – boyish to cry – can't help it – bad fever – weak – ill – hungry. Deserved it all – but suffered much – very.' Wholly unable to keep up appearances any longer, and perhaps rendered worse by the effort he had made, the dejected stroller sat down on the stairs, and, covering his face with his hands, sobbed like a child.

'Come, come,' said Mr Pickwick, with considerable emotion, 'we 'll see what can be done, when I know all about the matter. Here, Job; where is that fellow?'

'Here, sir,' replied Job, presenting himself on the staircase. We have described him, by-the-bye, as having deeply-sunken eyes, in the best of times. In his present state of want and distress, he looked as if those features had gone out of town altogether.

'Here, sir,' cried Job.

'Come here, sir,' said Mr Pickwick, trying to look stern, with four large tears running down his waistcoat. 'Take that, sir.'

Take what? In the ordinary acceptation of such language, it should have been a blow. As the world runs, it ought to have been a sound, hearty cuff; for Mr Pickwick had been duped, deceived, and wronged by the destitute outcast who was now wholly in his power. Must we tell the truth? It was something from Mr Pickwick's waistcoat-pocket, which chinked as it was given into Job's hand, and the giving of which, somehow or other imparted a sparkle to the eye, and a swelling to the heart, of our excellent old friend, as he hurried away.

Sam had returned when Mr Pickwick reached his own room, and was inspecting the arrangements that had been made for his comfort, with a kind of grim satisfaction which was very pleasant to look upon. Having a decided objection to his master's being there at all, Mr Weller appeared to consider it a high moral duty not to appear too much pleased with anything that was done, said, suggested, or proposed.

'Well, Sam,' said Mr Pickwick.

'Well, sir,' replied Mr Weller.

'Pretty comfortable now, eh, Sam?'

'Pretty vell, sir,' responded Sam, looking round him in a disparaging manner.

'Have you seen Mr Tupman and our other friends?'

'Yes, I *have* seen 'em, sir, and they're a comin' to-morrow, and wos wery much surprised to hear they warn't to come to-day,' replied Sam.

'You have brought the things I wanted?'

Mr Weller in reply pointed to various packages which he had arranged, as neatly as he could, in a corner of the room.

'Very well, Sam,' said Mr Pickwick, after a little hesitation; 'listen to what I am going to say, Sam.'

'Cert'nly, sir,' rejoined Mr Weller, 'fire away, sir.'

'I have felt from the first, Sam,' said Mr Pickwick, with much solemnity, 'that this is not the place to bring a young man to.'

'Nor an old 'un neither, sir,' observed Mr Weller.

'You're quite right, Sam,' said Mr Pickwick; 'but old men may come here, through their own heedlessness and unsuspicion: and young men may be brought here by the selfishness of those they serve. It is better for those young men, in every point of view, that they should not remain here. Do you understand me, Sam?'

'Vy no, sir, I do NOT,' replied Mr Weller, doggedly.

'Try, Sam,' said Mr Pickwick.

'Vell, sir,' rejoined Sam, after a short pause, 'I think I see your drift; and if I do see your drift, it's my 'pinion that you're a comin' it a great deal too strong, as the mail-coachman said to the snowstorm, ven it overtook him.'

'I see you comprehend me, Sam,' said Mr Pickwick. 'Independently of my wish that you should not be idling about a place like this, for years to come, I feel that for a debtor in the Fleet to be attended by his man-servant is a monstrous absurdity. Sam,' said Mr Pickwick, 'for a time, you must leave me.'

'Oh, for a time, eh, sir?' rejoined Mr Weller, rather sarcastically.

'Yes, for the time that I remain here,' said Mr Pickwick. 'Your wages I shall continue to pay. Any one of my three friends will be happy to take you, were it only out of respect to me. And if I ever do leave this place, Sam,' added Mr Pickwick, with assumed cheerfulness: 'if I do, I pledge you my word that you shall return to me instantly.'

'Now I'll tell you wot it is, sir,' said Mr Weller, in a grave and solemn voice, 'This here sort o' thing won't do at all, so don't let's hear no more about it.'

'I am serious, and resolved, Sam,' said Mr Pickwick.

'You air, air you, sir?' inquired Mr Weller, firmly. 'Wery good, sir. Then so am I.'

Thus speaking, Mr Weller fixed his hat on his head with great precision, and abruptly left the room.

'Sam!' cried Mr Pickwick, calling after him, 'Sam! Here!'

But the long gallery ceased to re-echo the sound of footsteps. Sam Weller was gone.

CHAPTER 43

Showing how Mr Samuel Weller got into Difficulties

In a lofty room, ill-lighted and worse ventilated, situate in Portugal Street, Lincoln's Inn Fields, there sit nearly the whole year round, one, two, three, or four gentlemen in wigs, as the case may be, with little writing desks before them, constructed after the fashion of those used by the judges of the land, barring the French polish. There is a box of barristers on their right hand; there is an inclosure of insolvent debtors on their left; and there is an inclined plane of most especially dirty faces in their front. These gentlemen are the Commissioners of the Insolvent Court,[1] and the place in which they sit, is the Insolvent Court itself.

It is, and has been, time out of mind, the remarkable fate of this Court to be, somehow or other, held and understood, by the general consent of all the destitute shabby-genteel people in London, as their common resort, and place of daily refuge. It is always full. The steams of beer and spirits perpetually ascend to the ceiling, and, being condensed by the heat, roll down the walls like rain; there are more old suits of clothes in it at one time, than will be offered for sale in all Houndsditch[2] in a twelvemonth; more unwashed skins and grizzly beards than all the pumps and shaving-shops between Tyburn and Whitechapel could render decent, between sunrise and sunset.

It must not be supposed that any of these people have the least shadow of business in, or the remotest connection with, the place they so indefatigably attend. If they had, it would be no matter of surprise, and the singularity of the thing would cease. Some of them sleep during the greater part of the sitting; others carry small portable dinners wrapped in pocket-handkerchiefs or sticking out of their worn-out pockets, and munch and listen with equal relish; but no one among them was ever known to have the slightest personal interest in any case that was ever brought forward. Whatever they do, there they sit from the first moment to the last. When it is heavy rainy weather, they all come in, wet through; and at such times the vapours of the Court are like those of a fungus-pit.

A casual visitor might suppose this place to be a Temple dedicated to the Genius of Seediness. There is not a messenger or process-server attached to it, who wears a coat that was made for him; not a tolerably fresh, or wholesome-looking man in the whole establishment, except a little white-headed apple-faced tipstaff, and even he, like an ill-conditioned cherry preserved in brandy, seems to have artificially dried and withered up into a state of preservation to which he can lay no natural claim. The very barristers' wigs are ill-powdered, and their curls lack crispness.

But the attorneys, who sit at a large bare table below the Commissioners, are, after all, the greatest curiosities. The professional establishment of the more opulent of these gentlemen, consists of a blue bag and a boy: generally a youth of the Jewish persuasion. They have no fixed offices, their legal business being transacted in the parlours of public-houses, or the yards of prisons: whither they repair in crowds, and canvass for customers after the manner of omnibus cads. They are of a greasy and mildewed appearance; and if they can be said to have any vices at all, perhaps drinking and cheating are the most conspicuous among them. Their residences are usually on the outskirts of 'the Rules,'[3] chiefly lying within a circle of one mile from the obelisk in St George's Fields.[4] Their looks are not prepossessing, and their manners are peculiar.

Mr Solomon Pell, one of this learned body, was a fat flabby pale man, in a surtout which looked green one minute and brown the next: with a velvet collar of the same cameleon tints. His forehead was narrow, his face wide, his head large, and his nose all on one side, as if Nature, indignant with the propensities she observed in him in his birth, had given it an angry tweak which it had never recovered. Being short-necked and asthmatic, however, he respired principally through this feature; so, perhaps, what it wanted in ornament, it made up in usefulness.

'I'm sure to bring him through it,' said Mr Pell.

'Are you though?' replied the person to whom the assurance was pledged.

'Certain sure,' replied Pell; 'but if he'd gone to any irregular practitioner, mind you, I wouldn't have answered for the consequences.'

'Ah!' said the other, with open mouth.

'No, that I wouldn't,' said Mr Pell; and he pursed up his lips, frowned, and shook his head mysteriously.

Now, the place where this discourse occurred, was the public-house just opposite to the Insolvent Court; and the person with whom it was held, was no other than the elder Mr Weller, who had come there, to comfort and console a friend, whose petition to be discharged under the act, was to be that day heard, and whose attorney he was at that moment consulting.

'And vere is George?' inquired the old gentleman.

Mr Pell jerked his head in the direction of a back parlour: whither Mr Weller at once repairing, was immediately greeted in the warmest and most flattering manner by some half-dozen of his professional brethren, in token of their gratification at his arrival. The insolvent gentleman, who had contracted a speculative but imprudent passion for horsing long stages, which had led to his present embarrassments, looked extremely well, and was soothing the excitement of his feelings with shrimps and porter.

The salutation between Mr Weller and his friends was strictly confined to the freemasonry of the craft; consisting of a jerking round of the right wrist, and a tossing of the little finger into the air at the same time. We once knew two famous coachmen (they are dead now, poor fellows) who were twins, and between whom an unaffected and devoted attachment existed. They passed each other on the Dover road, every day, for twenty-four years, never exchanging any other greeting than this; and yet, when one died, the other pined away, and soon afterwards followed him!

'Vell, George,' said Mr Weller, senior, taking off his upper coat, and seating himself with his accustomed gravity. 'How is it? All right behind, and full inside?'

'All right, old feller,' replied the embarrassed gentleman.

'Is the grey mare made over to any body?' inquired Mr Weller, anxiously. George nodded in the affirmative.

'Vell, that's all right,' said Mr Weller. 'Coach taken care on, also?'

'Con-signed in a safe quarter,' replied George, wringing the heads off half-a-dozen shrimps, and swallowing them without any more ado.

'Wery good, wery good,' said Mr Weller. 'Alvays see to the drag ven you go down hill. Is the vay-bill all clear and straight for'erd?'

'The schedule, sir,' said Pell, guessing at Mr Weller's meaning, 'the schedule is as plain and satisfactory as pen and ink can make it.'

Mr Weller nodded in a manner which bespoke his inward approval of these arrangements; and then, turning to Mr Pell, said, pointing to his friend George:

'Ven do you take his cloths off?'

'Why,' replied Mr Pell, 'he stands third on the opposed list, and I should think it would be his turn in about half an hour. I told my clerk to come over and tell us when there was a chance.'

Mr Weller surveyed the attorney from head to foot with great admiration, and said emphatically:

'And what'll you take, sir?'

'Why, really,' replied Mr Pell, 'you're very —. Upon my word and honour, I'm not in the habit of —. It's so very early in the morning, that, actually, I am almost —. Well, you may bring me three penn'orth of rum, my dear.'

The officiating damsel, who had anticipated the order before it was given, set the glass of spirits before Pell, and retired.

'Gentlemen,' said Mr Pell, looking round upon the company, 'Success to your friend! I don't like to boast, gentlemen; it's not my way; but I can't help saying, that, if your friend hadn't been fortunate enough to fall into hands that — but I won't say what I was going to say. Gentlemen, my service to you.' Having emptied the glass in a twinkling, Mr Pell smacked his lips, and looked complacently round on the assembled coachmen, who evidently regarded him as a species of divinity.

'Let me see,' said the legal authority. 'What was I a-saying, gentlemen?'

'I think you was remarkin' as you wouldn't have no objection to another 'o the same, sir,' said Mr Weller, with grave facetiousness.

'Ha, ha!' laughed Mr Pell. 'Not bad, not bad. A professional man, too! At this time of the morning, it would be rather too good a—. Well, I don't know, my dear – you *may* do that again, if you please. Hem!'

This last sound was a solemn and dignified cough, in which Mr Pell observing an indecent tendency to mirth in some of his auditors, considered it due to himself to indulge.

'The late Lord Chancellor, gentlemen, was very fond of me,' said Mr Pell.

'And wery creditable in him, too,' interposed Mr Weller.

'Hear, hear,' assented Mr Pell's client. 'Why shouldn't he be?'

'Ah! Why, indeed!' said a very red-faced man, who had said nothing yet, and who looked extremely unlikely to say anything more. 'Why shouldn't he?'

A murmur of assent ran through the company.

'I remember, gentlemen,' said Mr Pell, 'dining with him on one occasion; – there was only us two, but every thing as splendid as if twenty people had been expected – the great seal on a dumb-waiter⁵ at his right hand, and a man in a bag-wig and suit of armour guarding the mace with a drawn sword and silk stockings – which is perpetually done, gentlemen, night and day; when he said, "Pell," he said, "no false delicacy, Pell. You're a man of talent; you can get any body through the Insolvent Court, Pell; and your country should be proud of you." Those were his very words. "My Lord," I said, "you flatter me." – "Pell," he said, "if I do, I'm damned."'

'Did he say that?' inquired Mr Weller.

'He did,' replied Pell.

'Vell, then,' said Mr Weller, 'I say Parliament ought to ha' took it up; and if he'd been a poor man, they *would* ha' done it.'

'But, my dear friend,' argued Mr Pell, 'it was in confidence.'

'In what?' said Mr Weller.

'In confidence.'

'Oh! wery good,' replied Mr Weller, after a little reflection. 'If he damned his-self in confidence, o'course that was another thing.'

'Of course it was,' said Mr Pell. 'The distinction's obvious, you will perceive.'

'Alters the case entirely,' said Mr Weller. 'Go on, sir.'

'No, I will not go on, sir,' said Mr Pell, in a low and serious tone. 'You have reminded me, sir, that this conversation was private – private and confidential, gentlemen. Gentlemen, I am a professional man. It may be that I am a good deal looked up to, in my profession – it may be that I am not. Most people know. I say nothing. Observations have already been made, in this room, injurious to the reputation of my noble friend. You will excuse me, gentlemen; I was imprudent. I feel that I have no right to mention this matter without his concurrence. Thank you, sir; thank you.' Thus delivering himself, Mr Pell thrust his hands into his pockets, and, frowning grimly around, rattled three-halfpence with terrible determination.

This virtuous resolution had scarcely been formed, when the boy and the blue bag, who were inseparable companions, rushed violently into the room, and said (at least the boy did, for the blue bag took no part in the announcement) that the case was coming on directly. The intelligence was no sooner received than the whole party hurried across the street, and began to fight their way into Court – a preparatory ceremony, which has been calculated to occupy, in ordinary cases, from twenty-five minutes to thirty.

Mr Weller, being stout, cast himself at once into the crowd, with the desperate hope of ultimately turning up in some place which would suit him. His success was not quite equal to his expectations; for having neglected to take his hat off, it was knocked over his eyes by some unseen person, upon whose toes he had alighted with considerable force. Apparently, this individual regretted his impetuosity immediately afterwards; for, muttering an indistinct exclamation of surprise, he dragged the old man out into the hall, and, after a violent struggle, released his head and face.

'Samivel!' exclaimed Mr Weller, when he was thus enabled to behold his rescuer.

Sam nodded.

'You're a dutiful and affectionate little boy, you are, ain't you?' said Mr Weller, 'to come a bonnetin'⁶ your father in his old age?'

'How should I know who you wos?' responded the son. 'Do you s'pose I wos to tell you by the weight o' your foot?'

'Vell, that's wery true, Sammy,' replied Mr Weller, mollified at once; 'but wot are you a doin' on here? Your gov'nor can't do no good here, Sammy. They won't pass that werdick, they won't pass it, Sammy.' And Mr Weller shook his head, with legal solemnity.

'Wot a perwerse old file it is!' exclaimed Sam, 'alvays a goin' on about werdicks and alleybis, and that. Who said anything about the werdick?'

Mr Weller made no reply, but once more shook his head most learnedly.

'Leave off rattlin' that 'ere nob o' yourn, if you don't want it to come off the springs altogether,' said Sam impatiently, 'and behave reasonable. I vent all the vay down to the Markis o' Granby, arter you, last night.'

'Did you see the Marchioness o' Granby, Sammy?' inquired Mr Weller, with a sigh.

'Yes, I did,' replied Sam.

'How wos the dear creetur a lookin'?'

'Wery queer,' said Sam. 'I think she's a injurin' herself gradually vith too much o' that 'ere pine-apple rum, and other strong medicines o' the same natur.'

'You don't mean that, Sammy?' said the senior, earnestly.

'I do, indeed,' replied the junior. Mr Weller seized his son's hand, clasped it, and let it fall. There was an expression on his countenance in doing so – not of dismay or apprehension, but partaking more of the sweet and gentle character of hope. A gleam of resignation, and even of cheerfulness, passed over his face too, as he slowly said, 'I ain't quite certain, Sammy; I wouldn't like to say I wos altogether positive, in case of any subsekent disappintment, but I rayther think, my boy, I rayther think, that the shepherd's got the liver complaint!'

'Does he look bad?' inquired Sam.

'He's uncommon pale,' replied his father, ''cept about the nose, wich is redder than ever. His appetite is wery so-so, but he imbibes wunderful.'

Some thoughts of the rum appeared to obtrude themselves on Mr Weller's mind, as he said this; for he looked gloomy and thoughtful; but he very shortly recovered, as was testified by a perfect alphabet of winks, in which he was only wont to indulge when particularly pleased.

'Vell, now,' said Sam, 'about my affair. Just open them ears o' yourn, and don't say nothin' till I've done.' With this brief preface, Sam related, as succinctly as he could, the last memorable conversation he had had with Mr Pickwick.

'Stop there by himself, poor creetur!' exclaimed the elder Mr Weller, 'without nobody to take his part! It can't be done, Samivel, it can't be done.'

'O' course it can't,' asserted Sam: 'I know'd that, afore I came.'

'Wy, they'll eat him up alive, Sammy,' exclaimed Mr Weller.

Sam nodded his concurrence in the opinion.

'He goes in rayther raw, Sammy,' said Mr Weller metaphorically, 'and he'll come out, done so ex-ceedin' brown, that his most familiar friends won't know him. Roast pigeon's nothin' to it, Sammy.'

Again Sam Weller nodded.

'It oughtn't to be, Samivel,' said Mr Weller, gravely.

'It mustn't be,' said Sam.

'Cert'nly not,' said Mr Weller.

'Vell now,' said Sam, 'you've been a prophecyin' away, wery fine, like a red-faced Nixon⁷ as the sixpenny books gives picters on.'

'Who wos he, Sammy?' inquired Mr Weller.

'Never mind who he was,' retorted Sam; 'he warn't a coachman; that's enough for you.'

'I know'd a ostler o' that name,' said Mr Weller, musing.

'It warn't him,' said Sam. 'This here gen'l'm'n was a prophet.'

'Wot's a prophet?' inquired Mr Weller, looking sternly on his son.

'Wy, a man as tells what's a goin' to happen,' replied Sam.

'I wish I'd know'd him, Sammy,' said Mr Weller. 'P'raps he might ha' throw'd a small light on that 'ere liver complaint as we wos a speakin' on, just now. Hows'ever, if he's dead, and ain't left the bisness to nobody, there's an end on it. Go on, Sammy,' said Mr Weller, with a sigh.

'Well,' said Sam, 'you've been a prophecyin' avay, about wot'll happen to the gov'nor if he's left alone. Don't you see any vay o' takin' care on him?'

'No, I don't, Sammy,' said Mr Weller, with a reflective visage.

'No vay at all?' inquired Sam.

'No vay,' said Mr Weller, 'unless' – and a gleam of intelligence lighted up his countenance as he sunk his voice to a whisper, and applied his mouth to the ear of his offspring: 'unless it is getting him out in a turn-up bedstead, unbeknown to the turnkeys, Sammy, or dressin' him up like a old 'ooman vith a green vail.'

Sam Weller received both of these suggestions with unexpected contempt, and again propounded his question.

'No,' said the old gentleman; 'if he von't let you stop there, I see no vay at all. It's no thoroughfare, Sammy, no thoroughfare.'

'Well, then, I'll tell you wot it is,' said Sam, 'I'll trouble you for the loan of five-and-twenty pound.'

'Wot good 'ull that do?' inquired Mr Weller.

'Never mind,' replied Sam. 'P'raps you may ask for it, five minits artervards; p'raps I may say I von't pay, and cut up rough. You von't think o' arrestin' your own son for the money, and sendin' him off to the Fleet, will you, you unnat'ral wagabone?'

At this reply of Sam's, the father and son exchanged a complete code of telegraphic nods and gestures, after which, the elder Mr Weller sat himself down on a stone step, and laughed till he was purple.

'Wot a old image it is!' exclaimed Sam, indignant at this loss of time. 'What are you a settin' down there for, con-wertin' your face

into a street-door knocker,[8] wen there's so much to be done.
Where's the money?'

'In the boot, Sammy, in the boot,' replied Mr Weller, composing
his features. 'Hold my hat, Sammy.'

Having divested himself of this incumbrance, Mr Weller gave his
body a sudden wrench to one side, and, by a dexterous twist,
contrived to get his right hand into a most capacious pocket, from
whence, after a great deal of panting and exertion, he extricated a
pocket-book of the large octavo size, fastened by a huge leathern
strap. From this ledger he drew forth a couple of whip-lashes, three
or four buckles, a little sample-bag of corn, and finally a small roll
of very dirty banknotes: from which he selected the required
amount, which he handed over to Sam.

'And now, Sammy,' said the old gentleman, when the whip-
lashes, and the buckles, and the samples, had been all put back, and
the book once more deposited at the bottom of the same pocket,
'Now, Sammy, I know a gen'l'm'n here, as'll do the rest o' the
bisness for us, in no time – a limb o' the law, Sammy, as has got
brains like the frogs,[9] dispersed all over his body, and reachin' to
the wery tips of his fingers; a friend of the Lord Chancellorship's,
Sammy, who'd only have to tell him what he wanted, and he'd lock
you up for life, if that wos all.'

'I say,' said Sam, 'none o' that.'

'None o' wot?' inquired Mr Weller.

'Wy, none o' them unconstitootional ways o' doing it,' retorted
Sam. 'The have-his-carcase,[10] next to the perpetual motion, is vun
of the blessedest things as wos ever made. I've read that 'ere in the
newspapers, wery of'en.'

'Well, wot's that got to do vith it?' inquired Mr Weller.

'Just this here,' said Sam, 'that I'll patronise the inwention, and
go in, that vay. No visperin's to the Chancellorship, I don't like the
notion. It mayn't be altogether safe, vith reference to gettin' out
agin.'

Deferring to his son's feeling upon this point, Mr Weller at once
sought the erudite Solomon Pell, and acquainted him with his desire
to issue a writ, instantly, for the sum of twenty-five pounds, and
costs of process; to be executed without delay upon the body of one
Samuel Weller; the charges thereby incurred, to be paid in advance
to Solomon Pell.

The attorney was in high glee, for the embarrassed coach-horser
was ordered to be discharged forthwith. He highly approved of
Sam's attachment to his master; declared that it strongly reminded

him of his own feelings of devotion to his friend, the Chancellor; and at once led the elder Mr Weller down to the Temple, to swear the affidavit of debt, which the boy, with the assistance of the blue bag, had drawn up on the spot.

Meanwhile, Sam, having been formally introduced to the white-washed gentleman and his friends, as the offspring of Mr Weller, of the Belle Savage, was treated with marked distinction, and invited to regale himself with them in honour of the occasion; an invitation which he was by no means backward in accepting.

The mirth of gentlemen of this class is of a grave and quiet character, usually; but the present instance was one of peculiar festivity, and they relaxed in proportion. After some rather tumultuous toasting of the Chief Commissioner and Mr Solomon Pell, who had that day displayed such transcendent abilities, a mottled-faced gentleman in a blue shawl proposed that somebody should sing a song. The obvious suggestion was, that the mottled-faced gentleman, being anxious for a song, should sing it himself; but this the mottled-faced gentleman sturdily, and somewhat offensively, declined to do. Upon which, as is not unusual in such cases, a rather angry colloquy ensued.

'Gentlemen,' said the coach-horser, 'rather than disturb the harmony of this delightful occasion, perhaps Mr Samuel Weller will oblige the company.'

'Raly, gentlemen,' said Sam, 'I'm not wery much in the habit o' singin' without the instrument; but anythin' for a quiet life, as the man said wen he took the sitivation at the lighthouse.'

With this prelude, Mr Samuel Weller burst at once into the following wild and beautiful legend, which, under the impression that it is not generally known, we take the liberty of quoting. We would beg to call particular attention to the monosyllable at the end of the second and fourth lines, which not only enables the singer to take breath at those points, but greatly assists the metre.

ROMANCE

I.

Bold Turpin vunce, on Hounslow Heath,
His bold mare Bess bestrode – er;
Ven there he see'd the Bishop's coach
A-coming along the road – er.
So he gallops close to the orse's legs,
And he claps his head vithin;

And the Bishop says, 'Sure as eggs is eggs,
This here's the bold Turpin!'

Chorus.

And the Bishop says, 'Sure as eggs is eggs,
This here's the bold Turpin!'

II.

Says Turpin, 'You shall eat your words,
With a sarse of leaden bul-let;'
So he puts a pistol to his mouth,
And he fires it down his gul-let.
The coachman, he not likin' the job,
Set off at a full gal-lop.
But Dick put a couple of balls in his nob,
And perwailed on him to stop.

Chorus (sarcastically).

But Dick put a couple of balls in his nob,
And perwailed on him to stop.[11]

'I maintain that that 'ere song's personal to the cloth,' said the mottled-faced gentleman, interrupting it at this point. 'I demand the name o' that coachman.'

'Nobody know'd,' replied Sam. 'He hadn't got his card in his pocket.'

'I object to the introduction o' politics,' said the mottled-faced gentleman. 'I submit that, in the present company, that 'ere song's political; and, wot's much the same, that it ain't true. I say that that coachman did *not* run away; but that he died game – game as pheasants; and I won't hear nothin' said to the contrairey.'

As the mottled-faced gentleman spoke with great energy and determination: and as the opinions of the company seemed divided on the subject: it threatened to give rise to fresh altercation, when Mr Weller and Mr Pell most opportunely arrived.

'All right, Sammy,' said Mr Weller.

'The officer will be here at four o'clock,' said Mr Pell. 'I suppose you won't run away meanwhile, eh? Ha! ha!'

'P'raps my cruel pa 'ull relent afore then,' replied Sam, with a broad grin.

'Not I,' said the elder Mr Weller.

'Do,' said Sam.

'Not on no account,' replied the inexorable creditor.

'I'll give bills for the amount, at sixpence a month,' said Sam.

'I won't take 'em,' said Mr Weller.

'Ha, ha, ha! very good, very good,' said Mr Solomon Pell, who was making out his little bill of costs; 'a very amusing incident indeed! Benjamin, copy that.' And Mr Pell smiled again, as he called Mr Weller's attention to the amount.

'Thank you, thank you,' said the professional gentleman, taking up another of the greasy notes as Mr Weller took it from the pocket-book. 'Three ten and one ten is five. Much obliged to you, Mr Weller. Your son is a most deserving young man, very much so indeed, sir. It's a very pleasant trait in a young man's character, very much so,' added Mr Pell, smiling smoothly round, as he buttoned up the money.

'Wot a game it is!' said the elder Mr Weller, with a chuckle. 'A reg'lar prodigy son!'

'Prodigal, prodigal son, sir,' suggested Mr Pell, mildly.

'Never mind, sir,' said Mr Weller, with dignity. 'I know wot's o'clock, sir. Wen I don't, I'll ask you, sir.'

By the time the officer arrived, Sam had made himself so extremely popular, that the congregated gentlemen determined to see him to prison in a body. So, off they set; the plaintiff and defendant walking arm-in-arm; the officer in front; and eight stout coachmen bringing up the rear. At Serjeants' Inn Coffee-house the whole party halted to refresh, and, the legal arrangements being completed, the procession moved on again.

Some little commotion was occasioned in Fleet Street, by the pleasantry of the eight gentlemen in the flank, who persevered in walking four abreast; it was also found necessary to leave the mottled-faced gentleman behind, to fight a ticket-porter,[12] it being arranged that his friends should call for him as they came back. Nothing but these little incidents occurred on the way. When they reached the gate of the Fleet, the cavalcade, taking the time from the plaintiff, gave three tremendous cheers for the defendant, and, after having shaken hands all round, left him.

Sam, having been formally delivered into the warden's custody, to the intense astonishment of Roker, and to the evident emotion of even the phlegmatic Neddy, passed at once into the prison, walked straight to his master's room, and knocked at the door.

'Come in,' said Mr Pickwick.

Sam appeared, pulled off his hat, and smiled.

'Ah, Sam, my good lad!' said Mr Pickwick, evidently delighted to see his humble friend again; 'I had no intention of hurting your feelings yesterday, my faithful fellow, by what I said. Put down your hat, Sam, and let me explain my meaning, a little more at length.'

'Won't presently do, sir?' inquired Sam.

'Certainly,' said Mr Pickwick; 'but why not now?'

'I'd rayther not now, sir,' rejoined Sam.

'Why?' inquired Mr Pickwick.

''Cause – ' said Sam, hesitating.

'Because of what?' inquired Mr Pickwick, alarmed at his follower's manner. 'Speak out, Sam.'

''Cause,' rejoined Sam; ''cause I've got a little bisness as I want to do.'

'What business?' inquired Mr Pickwick, surprised at Sam's confused manner.

'Nothin' partickler, sir,' replied Sam.

'Oh, if it's nothing particular,' said Mr Pickwick, with a smile, 'you can speak with me first.'

'I think I'd better see arter it at once,' said Sam, still hesitating.

Mr Pickwick looked amazed, but said nothing.

'The fact is,' said Sam, stopping short.

'Well!' said Mr Pickwick. 'Speak out, Sam.'

'Why, the fact is,' said Sam, with a desperate effort, 'P'raps I'd better see arter my bed afore I do anythin' else.'

'*Your bed*!' exclaimed Mr Pickwick, in astonishment.

'Yes, my bed, sir,' replied Sam. 'I'm a pris'ner. I was arrested, this here wery arternoon, for debt.'

'You arrested for debt!' exclaimed Mr Pickwick, sinking into a chair.

'Yes, for debt, sir,' replied Sam. 'And the man as puts me in, 'ull never let me out, till you go yourself.'

'Bless my heart and soul!' ejaculated Mr Pickwick. 'What do you mean?'

'Wot I say, sir,' rejoined Sam. 'If it's forty year to come, I shall be a pris'ner, and I'm very glad on it, and if it had been Newgate, it would ha' been just the same. Now the murder's out, and, damme, there's an end on it!'

With these words, which he repeated with great emphasis and violence, Sam Weller dashed his hat upon the ground, in a most unusual state of excitement; and then, folding his arms, looked firmly and fixedly in his master's face.

CHAPTER 44

Treats of divers little Matters which occurred in the
Fleet, and of Mr Winkle's mysterious Behaviour; and
shows how the poor Chancery Prisoner obtained his
Release at last

Mr Pickwick felt a great deal too much touched by the warmth of
Sam's attachment, to be able to exhibit any manifestation of anger
or displeasure at the precipitate course he had adopted, in voluntarily consigning himself to a debtor's prison, for an indefinite
period. The only point on which he persevered in demanding any
explanation, was, the name of Sam's detaining creditor; but this Mr
Weller as perseveringly withheld.

'It ain't o' no use, sir,' said Sam, again and again. 'He's a malicious, bad-disposed, vorldly-minded, spiteful, windictive creetur,
with a hard heart as there ain't no soft'nin'. As the wirtuous
clergyman remarked of the old gen'l'm'n with the dropsy, ven he
said, that upon the whole he thought he'd rayther leave his property
to his vife than build a chapel vith it.'

'But consider, Sam,' Mr Pickwick remonstrated, 'the sum is so
small that it can very easily be paid; and having made up my mind
that you shall stop with me, you should recollect how much more
useful you would be, if you could go outside the walls.'

'Wery much obliged to you, sir,' replied Mr Weller gravely; 'but
I'd rayther not.'

'Rather not do what, Sam?'

'Wy, I'd rayther not let myself down to ask a favour o' this here
unremorseful enemy.'

'But it is no favour asking him to take his money, Sam,' reasoned
Mr Pickwick.

'Beg your pardon, sir,' rejoined Sam; 'but it 'ud be a wery great
favour to pay it, and he don't deserve none; that's where it is, sir.'

Here Mr Pickwick, rubbing his nose with an air of some vexation,
Mr Weller thought it prudent to change the theme of the discourse.

'I takes my determination on principle, sir,' remarked Sam, 'and
you takes yours on the same ground; wich puts me in mind o' the
man as killed his-self on principle, wich o' course you've heerd on,
sir.' Mr Weller paused when he arrived at this point, and cast a
comical look at his master out of the corners of his eyes.

'There is no "of course" in the case, Sam,' said Mr Pickwick, gradually breaking into a smile, in spite of the uneasiness which Sam's obstinacy had given him. 'The fame of the gentleman in question, never reached my ears.'

'No, sir!' exclaimed Mr Weller. 'You astonish me, sir; he wos a clerk in a gov'ment office, sir.'

'Was he?' said Mr Pickwick.

'Yes, he wos, sir,' rejoined Mr Weller; 'and a wery pleasant gen'l'm'n too – one o' the precise and tidy sort, as puts their feet in little India-rubber fire-buckets[1] wen it's wet weather, and never has no other bosom friends but hare-skins; he saved up his money on principle, wore a clean shirt ev'ry day on principle; never spoke to none of his relations on principle, 'fear they shou'd want to borrow money of him; and wos altogether, in fact, an uncommon agreeable character. He had his hair cut on principle vunce a fortnight, and contracted for his clothes on the economic principle – three suits a year, and send back the old uns. Being a wery reg'lar gen'l'm'n, he din'd ev'ry day at the same place, where it wos one and nine to cut off the joint, and a wery good one and nine's worth he used to cut, as the landlord often said, with the tears a tricklin' down his face: let alone the way he used to poke the fire in the vinter time, which wos a dead loss o' four-pence ha'penny a day: to say nothin' at all o' the aggrawation o' seein' him do it. So uncommon grand with it too! "Post arter[2] the next gen'l'm'n," he sings out ev'ry day ven he comes in. "See arter the Times, Thomas; let me look at the Mornin' Herald, wen it's out o' hand; don't forget to bespeak the Chronicle; and just bring the 'Tizer,[3] vill you:" and then he'd set vith his eyes fixed on the clock, and rush out, just a quarter of a minit afore the time, to way-lay the boy as was a comin' in with the evenin' paper, wich he'd read with sich intense interest and perseverance as worked the other customers up to the wery confines o' desperation and insanity, 'specially one i-rascible old gen'l'm'n as the vaiter wos always obliged to keep a sharp eye on, at sich times, fear he should be tempted to commit some rash act with the carving knife. Vell, sir, here he'd stop, occupyin' the best place for three hours, and never takin' nothin' arter his dinner, but sleep, and then he'd go away to a coffee-house a few streets off, and have a small pot o' coffee and four crumpets, arter wich he'd walk home to Kensington and go to bed. One night he wos took very ill; sends for a doctor; doctor comes in a green fly, with a kind o' Robinson Crusoe set o' steps,[4] as he could let down wen he got out, and pull up arter him wen he got in, to perwent the necessity o' the coachman's gettin' down, and thereby undeceivin' the public by lettin' 'em see that it wos only a livery coat as he'd got on, and not the trousers to match. "Wot's the matter?" says the doctor. "Wery ill," says the patient. "Wot have you been a eatin' on?" says the doctor. "Roast weal," says the patient. "Wot's the last thing you dewoured?" says the doctor. "Crumpets," says the patient. "That's it!" says the doctor. "I'll send you a box of pills directly, and don't you never take no more of 'em," he says. "No more o' wot?" says the patient – "Pills?" "No; crumpets," says the doctor. "Wy?" says the patient, starting up in bed; "I've eat four crumpets, ev'ry night for fifteen year, on principle." "Well, then, you'd better leave 'em off, on principle," says the doctor. "Crumpets is wholesome, sir," says the patient. "Crumpets is *not* wholesome, sir," says the doctor, wery fierce. "But they're so cheap," says the patient, comin' down a little, "and so wery fillin' at the price." "They'd be dear to you, at any price; dear if you wos paid to eat 'em," says the doctor. "Four crumpets a night," he says, "vill do your business in six months!" The patient looks him full in the face, and turns it over in his mind for a long time, and at last he says, "Are you sure o' that 'ere, sir?" "I'll stake my professional reputation on it," says the doctor. "How many crumpets, at a sittin', do you think 'ud kill me off at once?" says the patient. "I don't know," says the doctor. "Do you think half a crown's wurth 'ud do it?" says the patient. "I think it might," says the doctor. "Three shillins' wurth 'ud be sure to do it, I s'pose?" says the patient. "Certainly," says the doctor. "Wery good," says the patient; "good night." Next mornin' he gets up, has a fire lit, orders in three shillins' wurth o' crumpets, toasts 'em all, eats 'em all, and blows his brains out.'

'What did he do that for?' inquired Mr Pickwick abruptly; for he was considerably startled by this tragical termination of the narrative.

'Wot did he do it for, sir?' reiterated Sam. 'Wy in support of his great principle that crumpets wos wholesome, and to show that he wouldn't be put out of his way for nobody!'

With such like shiftings and changings of the discourse, did Mr Weller meet his master's questioning on the night of his taking up his residence in the Fleet. Finding all gentle remonstrance useless, Mr Pickwick at length yielded a reluctant consent to his taking lodgings by the week, of a bald-headed cobbler, who rented a small slip-room in one of the upper galleries. To this humble apartment Mr Weller moved a mattress and bedding, which he hired of Mr Roker; and, by the time he lay down upon it at night, was as much at home as if he had been bred in the prison, and his whole family had vegetated therein for three generations.

'Do you always smoke arter you goes to bed, old cock?' inquired Mr Weller of his landlord, when they had both retired for the night.

'Yes, I does, young bantam,' replied the cobbler.

'Will you allow me to in-quire wy you make up your bed under that 'ere deal table?' said Sam.

' 'Cause I was always used to a four-poster afore I came here, and I find the legs of the table answer just as well,' replied the cobbler.

'You're a character, sir,' said Sam.

'I haven't got anything of the kind belonging to me,' rejoined the cobbler, shaking his head; 'and if you want to meet with a good one, I'm afraid you'll find some difficulty in suiting yourself at this register office.'

The above short dialogue took place as Mr Weller lay extended on his mattress at one end of the room, and the cobbler on his, at the other; the apartment being illumined by the light of a rush candle, and the cobbler's pipe, which was glowing below the table, like a red-hot coal. The conversation, brief as it was, predisposed Mr Weller strongly in his landlord's favour; and raising himself on his elbow he took a more lengthened survey of his appearance than he had yet had either time or inclination to make.

He was a sallow man – all cobblers are; and had a strong bristly beard – all cobblers have. His face was a queer, good-tempered, crooked-featured piece of workmanship, ornamented with a couple of eyes that must have worn a very joyous expression at one time, for they sparkled yet. The man was sixty, by years, and Heaven knows how old by imprisonment, so that his having any look approaching to mirth or contentment, was singular enough. He was a little man, and, being half doubled up as he lay in bed, looked about as long as he ought to have been without his legs. He had a great red pipe in his mouth, and was smoking, and staring at the rush-light, in a state of enviable placidity.

'Have you been here long?' inquired Sam, breaking the silence which had lasted for some time.

'Twelve year,' replied the cobbler, biting the end of his pipe as he spoke.

'Contempt?' inquired Sam.

The cobbler nodded.

'Well, then,' said Sam, with some sternness, 'wot do you persevere in bein' obstinit for, vastin' your precious life away, in this here magnified pound? Wy don't you give in, and tell the Chancellorship that you're wery sorry for makin' his court contemptible, and you won't do so no more?'

The cobbler put his pipe in the corner of his mouth, while he smiled, and then brought it back to its old place again; but said nothing.

'Wy don't you?' said Sam, urging his question strenuously.

'Ah,' said the cobbler, 'you don't quite understand these matters. What do you suppose ruined me, now?'

'Wy,' said Sam, trimming the rush-light, 'I s'pose the beginnin' wos, that you got into debt, eh?'

'Never owed a farden,' said the cobbler; 'try again.'

'Well, perhaps,' said Sam, 'you bought houses, wich is delicate English for goin' mad: or took to buildin', wich is a medical term for bein' incurable.'

The cobbler shook his head and said, 'Try again.'

'You didn't go to law, I hope?' said Sam, suspiciously.

'Never in my life,' replied the cobbler. 'The fact is, I was ruined by having money left me.'

'Come, come,' said Sam, 'that von't do. I wish some rich enemy 'ud try to vork *my* destruction in that 'ere vay. I'd let him.'

'Oh, I dare say you don't believe it,' said the cobbler, quietly smoking his pipe. 'I wouldn't if I was you; but it's true for all that.'

'How wos it?' inquired Sam, half induced to believe the fact already, by the look the cobbler gave him.

'Just this,' replied the cobbler; 'an old gentleman that I worked for, down in the country, and a humble relation of whose I married – she's dead, God bless her, and thank Him for it! – was seized with a fit and went off.'

'Where?' inquired Sam, who was growing sleepy after the numerous events of the day.

'How should I know where he went?' said the cobbler, speaking through his nose in an intense enjoyment of his pipe. 'He went off dead.'

'Oh, that indeed,' said Sam. 'Well?'

'Well,' said the cobbler, 'he left five thousand pound behind him.'

'And wery gen-teel in him so to do,' said Sam.

'One of which,' continued the cobbler, 'he left to me, 'cause I'd married his relation, you see.'

'Wery good,' murmured Sam.

'And being surrounded by a great number of nieces and nevys, as was always a quarrelling and fighting among themselves for the property, he makes me his executor, and leaves the rest to me: in trust, to divide it among 'em as the will prowided.'

'Wot do you mean by leavin' it on trust?' inquired Sam, waking up a little. 'If it ain't ready money, were's the use on it?'

'It's a law term, that's all,' said the cobbler.

'I don't think that,' said Sam, shaking his head. 'There's wery little trust at that shop. Hows'ever, go on.'

'Well,' said the cobbler: 'when I was going to take out a probate[5] of the will, the nieces and nevys, who was desperately disappointed at not getting all the money, enters a caveat[6] against it.'

'What's that?' inquired Sam.

'A legal instrument, which is as much as to say, it's no go,' replied the cobbler.

'I see,' said Sam, 'a sort of brother-in-law o' the have-his-carcase. Well.'

'But,' continued the cobbler, 'finding that they couldn't agree among themselves, and consequently couldn't get up a case against the will, they withdrew the caveat, and I paid all the legacies. I'd hardly done it, when one nevy brings an action to set the will aside. The case comes on, some months afterwards, afore a deaf old gentleman, in a back room somewhere down by Paul's Churchyard; and arter four counsels had taken a day a-piece to bother him regularly, he takes a week or two to consider, and read the evidence in six vollums, and then gives his judgment that how the testator was not quite right in his head, and I must pay all the money back again, and all the costs. I appealed; the case come on before three or four very sleepy gentlemen, who had heard it all before in the other court, where they're lawyers without work; the only difference being, that, there, they're called doctors, and in the other place delegates, if you understand that; and they very dutifully confirmed the decision of the old gentleman below. After that, we went into Chancery, where we are still, and where I shall always be. My lawyers have had all my thousand pound long ago; and what between the estate, as they call it, and the costs, I'm here for ten thousand, and shall stop here, till I die, mending shoes. Some gentlemen have talked of bringing it afore parliament, and I dare say would have done it, only they hadn't time to come to me, and I hadn't power to go to them, and they got tired of my long letters, and dropped the business. And this is God's truth, without one word of suppression or exaggeration, as fifty people, both in this place and out of it, very well know.'

The cobbler paused to ascertain what effect his story had

produced on Sam; but finding that he had dropped asleep, knocked the ashes out of his pipe, sighed, put it down, drew the bedclothes over his head, and went to sleep too.

Mr Pickwick was sitting at breakfast, alone, next morning (Sam being busily engaged in the cobbler's room, polishing his master's shoes and brushing the black gaiters) when there came a knock at the door, which, before Mr Pickwick could cry 'Come in!' was followed by the appearance of a head of hair and a cotton-velvet cap, both of which articles of dress he had no difficulty in recognising as the personal property of Mr Smangle.

'How are you?' said that worthy, accompanying the inquiry with a score or two of nods; 'I say – do you expect anybody this morning? Three men – devilish gentlemanly fellows – have been asking after you down stairs, and knocking at every door on the Hall flight; for which they've been most infernally blown up by the collegians that had the trouble of opening 'em.'

'Dear me! How very foolish of them,' said Mr Pickwick, rising. 'Yes; I have no doubt they are some friends whom I rather expected to see, yesterday.'

'Friends of yours!' exclaimed Smangle, seizing Mr Pickwick by the hand. 'Say no more. Curse me, they're friends of mine from this minute, and friends of Mivins's too. Infernal pleasant, gentlemanly, dog, Mivins's, isn't he?' said Smangle, with great feeling.

'I know so little of the gentleman,' said Mr Pickwick, hesitating, 'that I—'

'I know you do,' interposed Smangle, clasping Mr Pickwick by the shoulder. 'You shall know him better. You'll be delighted with him. That man, sir,' said Smangle, with a solemn countenance, 'has comic powers that would do honour to Drury Lane Theatre.'

'Has he indeed?' said Mr Pickwick.

'Ah, by Jove he has!' replied Smangle. 'Hear him come the four cats in the wheelbarrow – four distinct cats, sir, I pledge you my honour. Now you know that's infernal clever! Dam'me, you can't help liking a man, when you see these traits about him. He's only one fault – that little failing I mentioned to you, you know.'

As Mr Smangle shook his head in a confidential and sympathising manner at this juncture, Mr Pickwick felt that he was expected to say something, so he said 'Ah!' and looked restlessly at the door.

'Ah!' echoed Mr Smangle, with a long-drawn sigh. 'He's delightful company, that man is, sir. I don't know better company anywhere; but he has that one drawback. If the ghost of his grandfather, sir, was to rise before him this minute, he'd ask him for the loan of his acceptance on an eighteenpenny stamp.'

'Dear me!' exclaimed Mr Pickwick.

'Yes,' added Mr Smangle; 'and if he'd the power of raising him again, he would, in two months and three days from this time, to renew the bill!'

'Those are very remarkable traits,' said Mr Pickwick; 'but I'm afraid that while we are talking here, my friends may be in a state of great perplexity at not finding me.'

'I'll show 'em the way,' said Smangle, making for the door. 'Good day. I won't disturb you while they 're here, you know. By-the-bye—'

As Smangle pronounced the last three words, he stopped suddenly, re-closed the door which he had opened, and, walking softly back to Mr Pickwick, stepped close up to him on tip-toe, and said in a very soft whisper:

'You couldn't make it convenient to lend me half-a-crown till the latter end of next week, could you?'

Mr Pickwick could scarcely forbear smiling, but managing to preserve his gravity, he drew forth the coin, and placed it in Mr Smangle's palm; upon which, that gentleman, with many nods and winks, implying profound mystery, disappeared in quest of the three strangers, with whom he presently returned; and having coughed thrice, and nodded as many times, as an assurance to Mr Pickwick that he would not forget to pay, he shook hands all round, in an engaging manner, and at length took himself off.

'My dear friends,' said Mr Pickwick, shaking hands alternately with Mr Tupman, Mr Winkle, and Mr Snodgrass, who were the three visitors in question, 'I am delighted to see you.'

The triumvirate were much affected. Mr Tupman shook his head deploringly; Mr Snodgrass drew forth his handkerchief, with undisguised emotion; and Mr Winkle retired to the window, and sniffed aloud.

'Mornin', gen'l'm'n,' said Sam, entering at the moment with the shoes and gaiters. 'Avay vith melincholly,[7] as the little boy said ven his school-missis died. Velcome to the College, gen'l'm'n.'

'This foolish fellow,' said Mr Pickwick, tapping Sam on the head as he knelt down to button up his master's gaiters: 'This foolish fellow has got himself arrested, in order to be near me.'

'What!' exclaimed the three friends.

'Yes, gen'l'm'n,' said Sam, 'I'm a – stand steady, sir, if you please – I'm a pris'ner, gen'l'm'n. Con-fined, as the lady said.'

'A prisoner!' exclaimed Mr Winkle, with unaccountable vehemence.

'Hallo, sir!' responded Sam, looking up. 'Wot's the matter, sir?'

'I had hoped, Sam, that—nothing, nothing,' said Mr Winkle, precipitately. There was something so very abrupt and unsettled in Mr Winkle's manner, that Mr Pickwick involuntarily looked at his two friends, for an explanation.

'We don't know,' said Mr Tupman, answering this mute appeal aloud. 'He has been much excited for two days past, and his whole demeanour very unlike what it usually is. We feared there must be something the matter, but he resolutely denies it.'

'No, no,' said Mr Winkle, colouring beneath Mr Pickwick's gaze; 'there is really nothing. I assure you there is nothing, my dear sir. It will be necessary for me to leave town, for a short time, on private business, and I had hoped to have prevailed upon you to allow Sam to accompany me.'

Mr Pickwick looked more astonished than before.

'I think,' faltered Mr Winkle, 'that Sam would have had no objection to do so; but, of course, his being a prisoner here, renders it impossible. So I must go alone.'

As Mr Winkle said these words, Mr Pickwick felt, with some astonishment, that Sam's fingers were trembling at the gaiters, as if he were rather surprised or startled. Sam looked up at Mr Winkle, too, when he had finished speaking; and though the glance they exchanged was instantaneous, they seemed to understand each other.

'Do you know anything of this, Sam?' said Mr Pickwick, sharply.

'No, I don't sir,' replied Mr Weller, beginning to button with extraordinary assiduity.

'Are you sure, Sam?' said Mr Pickwick.

'Wy, sir,' responded Mr Weller; 'I'm sure so far, that I've never heerd anythin' on the subject afore this moment. If I makes any guess about it,' added Sam, looking at Mr Winkle, 'I haven't got any right to say what it is, 'fear it should be a wrong 'un.'

'I have no right to make any further inquiry into the private affairs of a friend, however intimate a friend,' said Mr Pickwick, after a short silence; 'at present let me merely say, that I do not understand this at all. There. We have had quite enough of the subject.'

Thus expressing himself, Mr Pickwick led the conversation to different topics, and Mr Winkle gradually appeared more at ease, though still very far from being completely so. They had all so much to converse about, that the morning very quickly passed away; and when, at three o'clock, Mr Weller produced upon the little dining table, a roast leg of mutton and an enormous meat pie, with sundry dishes of vegetables, and pots of porter, which stood upon the chairs or the sofa-bedstead, or where they could, everybody felt disposed to do justice to the meal, notwithstanding that the meat had been purchased, and dressed, and the pie made, and baked, at the prison cookery hard by.

To these, succeeded a bottle or two of very good wine, for which a messenger was dispatched by Mr Pickwick to the Horn Coffee-house, in Doctors' Commons. The bottle or two, indeed, might be more properly described as a bottle or six, for by the time it was drunk, and tea over, the bell began to ring for strangers to withdraw.

But, if Mr Winkle's behaviour had been unaccountable in the morning, it became perfectly unearthly and solemn when, under the influence of his feelings, and his share of the bottle or six, he prepared to take leave of his friend. He lingered behind, until Mr Tupman and Mr Snodgrass had disappeared, and then fervently clenched Mr Pickwick's hand, with an expression of face in which deep and mighty resolve was fearfully blended with the very concentrated essence of gloom.

'Good night, my dear sir!' said Mr Winkle between his set teeth.

'Bless you, my dear fellow!' replied the warm-hearted Mr Pickwick, as he returned the pressure of his young friend's hand.

'Now then!' cried Mr Tupman from the gallery.

'Yes, yes, directly,' replied Mr Winkle. 'Good night!'

'Good night,' said Mr Pickwick.

There was another good night, and another, and half-a-dozen more after that, and still Mr Winkle had fast hold of his friend's hand, and was looking into his face with the same strange expression.

'*Is* anything the matter?' said Mr Pickwick at last, when his arm was quite sore with shaking.

'Nothing,' said Mr Winkle.

'Well then, good night,' said Mr Pickwick, attempting to disengage his hand.

'My friend, my benefactor, my honoured companion,' murmured Mr Winkle, catching at his wrist. 'Do not judge me harshly; do not, when you hear that, driven to extremity by hopeless obstacles, I —'

'Now then,' said Mr Tupman, re-appearing at the door. 'Are you coming, or are we to be locked in?'

'Yes, yes, I am ready,' replied Mr Winkle. And with a violent effort he tore himself away.

As Mr Pickwick was gazing down the passage after them in silent astonishment, Sam Weller appeared at the stair-head, and whispered for one moment in Mr Winkle's ear.

'Oh certainly, depend upon me,' said that gentleman aloud.

'Thankee, sir. You won't forget, sir?' said Sam.

'Of course not,' replied Mr Winkle.

'Wish you luck, sir,' said Sam, touching his hat. 'I should very much liked to ha' joined you, sir; but the gov'ner o' course is pairamount.'

'It is very much to your credit that you remain here,' said Mr Winkle. With these words they disappeared down the stairs.

'Very extraordinary,' said Mr Pickwick, going back into his room, and seating himself at the table in a musing attitude. 'What *can* that young man be going to do?'

He had sat ruminating about the matter for some time, when the voice of Roker, the turnkey, demanded whether he might come in.

'By all means,' said Mr Pickwick.

'I've brought you a softer pillow, sir,' said Roker, "instead of the temporary one you had last night.'

'Thank you,' said Mr Pickwick. 'Will you take a glass of wine?'

'You're wery good, sir,' replied Mr Roker, accepting the proffered glass. 'Yours, sir.'

'Thank you,' said Mr Pickwick.

'I'm sorry to say that your landlord's wery bad to-night, sir,' said Roker, setting down the glass, and inspecting the lining of his hat preparatory to putting it on again.

'What! The Chancery prisoner!' exclaimed Mr Pickwick.

'He won't be a Chancery prisoner wery long, sir,' replied Roker, turning his hat round, so as to get the maker's name right side upwards, as he looked into it.

'You make my blood run cold,' said Mr Pickwick. 'What do you mean?'

'He's been consumptive for a long time past,' said Mr Roker, 'and he's taken wery bad in the breath to-night. The doctor said, six months ago, that nothing but change of air could save him.'

'Great Heaven!' exclaimed Mr Pickwick; 'has this man been slowly murdered by the law for six months!'

'I don't know about that,' replied Roker, weighing the hat by the brims in both hands. 'I suppose he'd have been took the same, wherever he was. He went into the infirmary, this morning; the doctor says his strength is to be kept up as much as possible; and the warden's sent him wine and broth and that, from his own house. It's not the warden's fault, you know, sir.'

'Of course not,' replied Mr Pickwick hastily.

'I'm afraid, however,' said Roker, shaking his head, 'that it's all up with him. I offered Neddy two six penn'orths to one upon it just now, but he wouldn't take it, and quite right. Thankee, sir. Good night, sir.'

'Stay,' said Mr Pickwick earnestly. 'Where is this infirmary?'

'Just over where you slept, sir,' replied Roker. 'I'll show you, if you like to come.' Mr Pickwick snatched up his hat without speaking, and followed at once.

The turnkey led the way in silence; and gently raising the latch of the room-door, motioned Mr Pickwick to enter. It was a large, bare, desolate room, with a number of stump bedsteads made of iron: on one of which lay stretched, the shadow of a man: wan, pale, and ghastly. His breathing was hard and thick, and he moaned painfully as it came and went. At the bedside, sat a short old man in a cobbler's apron, who, by the aid of a pair of horn spectacles, was reading from the Bible aloud. It was the fortunate legatee.

The sick man laid his hand upon his attendant's arm, and motioned him to stop. He closed the book, and laid it on the bed.

'Open the window,' said the sick man.

He did so. The noise of carriages and carts, the rattle of wheels, the cries of men and boys, all the busy sounds of a mighty multitude instinct with life and occupation, blended into one deep murmur, floated into the room. Above the hoarse loud hum, arose, from time to time, a boisterous laugh; or a scrap of some jingling song, shouted forth, by one of the giddy crowd, would strike upon the ear, for an instant, and then be lost amidst the roar of voices and the tramp of footsteps; the breaking of the billows of the restless sea of life, that rolled heavily on, without. Melancholy sounds to a quiet listener at any time; how melancholy to the watcher by the bed of death!

'There is no air here,' said the sick man faintly. 'The place pollutes it. It was fresh round about, when I walked there, years ago; but it grows hot and heavy in passing these walls. I cannot breathe it.'

'We have breathed it together, for a long time,' said the old man. 'Come, come.'

There was a short silence, during which the two spectators approached the bed. The sick man drew a hand of his old fellow prisoner towards him, and pressing it affectionately between both his own, retained it in his grasp.

'I hope,' he gasped after a while: so faintly that they bent their ears close over the bed to catch the half-formed sounds his pale lips gave vent to: 'I hope my merciful Judge will bear in mind my heavy punishment on earth. Twenty years, my friend, twenty years in this hideous grave! My heart broke when my child died, and I could not even kiss him in his little coffin. My loneliness since then, in all this noise and riot, has been very dreadful. May God forgive me! He has seen my solitary, lingering death.'

He folded his hands, and murmuring something more they could not hear, fell into a sleep – only a sleep at first, for they saw him smile.

They whispered together for a little time, and the turnkey, stooping over the pillow, drew hastily back. 'He has got his discharge, by G – !" said the man.

He had. But he had grown so like death in life, that they knew not when he died.

CHAPTER 45

Descriptive of an Affecting Interview between Mr Samuel Weller and a Family Party. Mr Pickwick makes a Tour of the diminutive World he inhabits, and resolves to mix with it, in future, as little as possible

A few mornings after his incarceration, Mr Samuel Weller, having arranged his master's room with all possible care, and seen him comfortably seated over his books and papers, withdrew to employ himself for an hour or two to come, as he best could. It was a fine morning, and it occurred to Sam that a pint of porter in the open air would lighten his next quarter of an hour or so, as well as any little amusement in which he could indulge,

Having arrived at this conclusion, he betook himself to the tap. Having purchased the beer, and obtained, moreover, the day-but-one-before-yesterday's paper, he repaired to the skittle-ground, and seating himself on a bench, proceeded to enjoy himself in a very sedate and methodical manner.

First of all, he took a refreshing draught of the beer, and then he looked up at a window, and bestowed a Platonic wink[1] on a young lady who was peeling potatoes thereat. Then he opened the paper, and folded it so as to get the police reports outwards; and this being a vexatious and difficult thing to do, when there is any wind stirring, he took another draught of the beer when he had accomplished it. Then, he read two lines of the paper, and stopped short, to look at a couple of men who were finishing a game at rackets, which being concluded, he cried out 'wery good' in an approving manner, and looked round upon the spectators, to ascertain whether their sentiments coincided with his own. This involved the necessity of looking up at the windows also; and as the young lady was still there, it was an act of common politeness to wink again, and to drink to her good health in dumb show, in another draught of the beer, which Sam did; and having frowned hideously upon a small boy who had noted this latter proceeding with open eyes, he threw one leg over the other, and, holding the newspaper in both hands, began to read in real earnest.

He had hardly composed himself into the needful state of abstraction, when he thought he heard his own name proclaimed in some distant passage. Nor was he mistaken, for it quickly passed from mouth to mouth, and in a few seconds the air teemed with shouts of 'Weller!'

'Here!' roared Sam, in a stentorian voice. 'Wot's the matter? Who wants him? Has an express come to say that his country-house is a-fire?'

'Somebody wants you in the hall,' said a man who was standing by.

'Just mind that'ere paper and the pot, old feller, will you?' said Sam. 'I'm a comin'. Blessed, if they was a callin' me to the bar, they couldn't make more noise about it!'

Accompanying these words with a gentle rap on the head of the young gentleman before noticed, who, unconscious of his close vicinity to the person in request, was screaming 'Weller!' with all his might, Sam hastened across the ground, and ran up the steps into the hall. Here, the first object that met his eyes was his beloved father sitting on a bottom stair, with his hat in his hand, shouting out 'Weller!' in his very loudest tone, at half-minute intervals.

'Wot are you a roarin' at?' said Sam impetuously, when the old gentleman had discharged himself of another shout; 'makin' yourself so precious hot that you looks like a aggrawated glass-blower. Wot's the matter?'

'Aha!' replied the old gentleman, 'I began to be afeerd that you'd gone for a walk round the Regency Park,[2] Sammy.'

'Come,' said Sam, 'none o' them taunts agin the wictim o' avarice, and come off that 'ere step. Wot are you a settin' down there for? I don't live there.'

'I've got such a game for you, Sammy,' said the elder Mr Weller, rising.

'Stop a minit,' said Sam, 'you're all vite behind.'

'That's right, Sammy, rub it off,' said Mr Weller, as his son dusted him. 'It might look personal here, if a man walked about with whitevash[3] on his clothes, eh, Sammy?'

As Mr Weller exhibited in this place unequivocal symptoms of an approaching fit of chuckling, Sam interposed to stop it.

'Keep quiet, do,' said Sam, 'there never vos such a old picter-card[4] born. Wot are you bustin' vith, now?'

'Sammy,' said Mr Weller, wiping his forehead, 'I'm afeerd that vun o' these days I shall laugh myself into a appleplexy, my boy.'

'Vell, then, wot do you do it for?' said Sam. 'Now; wot have you got to say?'

'Who do you think's come here with me, Samivel?' said Mr Weller, drawing back a pace or two, pursing up his mouth, and extending his eyebrows.

'Pell?' said Sam.

Mr Weller shook his head, and his red cheek expanded with the laughter that was endeavouring to find a vent.

'Mottled-faced man, p'r'aps?' suggested Sam.

Again Mr Weller shook his head.

'Who then?' asked Sam.

'Your mother-in-law,' said Mr Weller; and it was lucky he did say it, or his cheeks must inevitably have cracked, from their most unnatural distension.

'Your mother-in-law, Sammy,' said Mr Weller, 'and the red-nosed man, my boy; and the red-nosed man. Ho! ho! ho!'

With this, Mr Weller launched into convulsions of laughter, while Sam regarded him with a broad grin gradually overspreading his whole countenance.

'They've come to have a little serious talk with you, Samivel,' said Mr Weller, wiping his eyes. 'Don't let out nothin' about the unnat'ral creditor, Sammy.'

'Wot, don't they know who it is?' inquired Sam.

'Not a bit on it,' replied his father.

'Vere are they?' said Sam, reciprocating all the old gentleman's grins.

'In the snuggery,'⁵ rejoined Mr Weller. 'Catch the red-nosed man a goin' any vere but vere the liquors is; not he, Samivel, not he. Ve'd a wery pleasant ride along the road, from the Markis this mornin', Sammy,' said Mr Weller, when he felt himself equal to the task of speaking in an articulate manner. 'I drove the old piebald in that 'ere little shay-cart as belonged to your mother-in-law's first wenter, into vich a harm-cheer wos lifted for the shepherd; and I'm blest,' said Mr Weller, with a look of deep scorn: 'I'm blest if they didn't bring a portable flight o' steps out into the road a front o' our door, for him to get up by.'

'You don't mean that?' said Sam.

'I *do* mean that, Sammy,' replied his father, 'and I vish you could ha' seen how tight he held on by the sides wen he did get up, as if he wos afeerd o' being precipitayted down full six foot, and dashed into a million o' hatoms. He tumbled in at last, however, and avay ve vent; and I rayther think, I say I rayther think, Samivel, that he found his-self a little jolted wen ve turned the corners.'

'Wot, I s'pose you happened to drive up agin a post or two?' said Sam.

'I'm afeerd,' replied Mr Weller, in a rapture of winks, 'I'm afeerd I took vun or two on 'em, Sammy; he wos a flyin' out o' the harm-cheer all the way.'

Here the old gentleman shook his head from side to side, and was seized with a hoarse internal rumbling, accompanied with a violent swelling of the countenance, and a sudden increase in the breadth of all his features; symptoms which alarmed his son not a little.

'Don't be frightened, Sammy, don't be frightened,' said the old gentleman, when, by dint of much struggling, and various convulsive stamps upon the ground, he had recovered his voice. 'It's only a kind o' quiet laugh as I'm a tryin' to come, Sammy.'

'Well, if that's wot it is,' said Sam, 'you'd better not try to come it agin. You'll find it rayther a dangerous inwention.'

'Don't you like it, Sammy?' inquired the old gentleman.

'Not at all,' replied Sam.

'Well,' said Mr Weller, with the tears still running down his cheeks, 'it 'ud ha' been a wery great accommodation to me if I could ha' done it, and 'ud ha' saved a good many vords atween your mother-in-law and me, sometimes; but I am afeerd you're right, Sammy: it's too much in the appleplexy line – a deal too much, Samivel.'

This conversation brought them to the door of the snuggery, into which Sam – pausing for an instant to look over his shoulder, and cast a sly leer at his respected progenitor, who was still giggling behind – at once led the way.

'Mother-in-law,' said Sam, politely saluting the lady, 'wery much obliged to you for this here wisit. Shepherd, how air you?'

'Oh, Samuel!' said Mrs Weller. 'This is dreadful.'

'Not a bit on it, mum,' replied Sam. 'Is it, shepherd?'

Mr Stiggins raised his hands, and turned up his eyes, till the whites – or rather the yellows – were alone visible; but made no reply in words.

'Is this here gen'l'm'n troubled vith any painful complaint?' said Sam, looking to his mother-in-law for explanation.

'The good man is grieved to see you here, Samuel,' replied Mrs Weller.

'Oh, that's it, is it?' said Sam. 'I was afeerd, from his manner, that he might ha' forgotten to take pepper vith that'ere last cowcumber he eat. Set down, sir, ve make no extra charge for the settin' down, as the king remarked wen he blowed up his ministers.'

'Young man,' said Mr Stiggins, ostentatiously, 'I fear you are not softened by imprisonment.'

'Beg your pardon, sir,' replied Sam; 'wot was you graciously pleased to hobserve?'

'I apprehend, young man, that your nature is no softer for this chastening,' said Mr Stiggins, in a loud voice.

'Sir,' replied Sam, 'you're wery kind to say so. I hope my natur is *not* a soft vun, sir. Wery much obliged to you for your good opinion, sir.'

At this point of the conversation, a sound, indecorously approaching to a laugh, was heard to proceed from the chair in which the elder Mr Weller was seated; upon which Mrs Weller, on a hasty consideration of all the circumstances of the case, considered it her bounden duty to become gradually hysterical.

'Weller,' said Mrs W. (the old gentleman was seated in a corner); 'Weller! Come forth.'

'Wery much obleeged to you, my dear,' replied Mr Weller; 'but I'm quite comfortable vere I am.'

Upon this, Mrs Weller burst into tears.

'Wot's gone wrong, mum?' said Sam.

'Oh, Samuel!' replied Mrs Weller, 'your father makes me wretched. Will nothing do him good?'

'Do you hear this here?' said Sam. 'Lady wants to know vether nothin' 'ull do you good.'

'Wery much indebted to Mrs Weller for her po-lite inquiries, Sammy,' replied the old gentleman. 'I think a pipe vould benefit me a good deal. Could I be accommodated, Sammy?'

Here Mrs Weller let fall some more tears, and Mr Stiggins groaned.

'Hallo! Here's this unfort'nate gen'l'm'n took ill agin,' said Sam, looking round. 'Were do you feel it now, sir?'

'In the same place, young man,' rejoined Mr Stiggins: 'in the same place.'

'Were may that be, sir?' inquired Sam, with great outward simplicity.

'In the buzzim, young man,' replied Mr Stiggins, placing his umbrella on his waistcoat.

At this affecting reply, Mrs Weller, being wholly unable to suppress her feelings, sobbed aloud, and stated her conviction that the red-nosed man was a saint; whereupon Mr Weller, senior, ventured to suggest, in an undertone, that he must be the representative of the united parishes of Saint Simon Without, and Saint Walker Within.[6]

'I'm afeerd, mum,' said Sam, 'that this here gen'l'm'n, with the twist in his countenance, feels rayther thirsty, with the melancholy spectacle afore him. Is it the case, mum?'

The worthy lady looked at Mr Stiggins for a reply; that gentleman, with many rollings of the eye, clenched his throat with his right hand, and mimicked the act of swallowing, to intimate that he was athirst.

'I am afraid, Samuel, that his feelings have made him so, indeed,' said Mrs Weller, mournfully.

'Wot's your usual tap, sir,' replied Sam.

'Oh, my dear young friend,' replied Mr Stiggins, 'all taps is vanities!'

'Too true, too true, indeed,' said Mrs Weller, murmuring a groan, and shaking her head assentingly.

'Well,' said Sam, 'I des-say they may be, sir; but which is your partickler wanity. Vich wanity do you like the flavour on, best, sir?'

'Oh, my dear young friend,' replied Mr Stiggins, 'I despise them all. If,' said Mr Stiggins, 'if there is any one of them less odious than another, it is the liquor called rum. Warm, my dear young friend, with three lumps of sugar to the tumbler.'

'Wery sorry to say, sir,' said Sam, 'that they don't allow that particular wanity to be sold in this here establishment.'

'Oh, the hardness of heart of these inveterate men!' ejaculated Mr Stiggins. 'Oh, the accursed cruelty of these inhuman persecutors!'

With these words, Mr Stiggins again cast up his eyes, and rapped his breast with his umbrella; and it is but justice to the reverend gentleman to say, that his indignation appeared very real and unfeigned indeed.

After Mrs Weller and the red-nosed gentleman had commented on this inhuman usage in a very forcible manner, and had vented a variety of pious and holy execrations against its authors, the latter recommended a bottle of port wine, warmed with a little water, spice, and sugar, as being grateful to the stomach, and savouring less of vanity than many other compounds. It was accordingly ordered to be prepared. Pending its preparation the red-nosed man and Mrs Weller looked at the elder W. and groaned.

'Well, Sammy,' said that gentleman, 'I hope you'll find your spirits rose by this here lively wisit. Wery cheerful and improvin' conwersation, ain't it, Sammy?'

'You're a reprobate,' replied Sam; 'and I desire you won't address no more o' them ungraceful remarks to me.'

So far from being edified by this very proper reply, the elder Mr Weller at once relapsed into a broad grin; and this inexorable conduct causing the lady and Mr Stiggins to close their eyes, and rock themselves to and fro on their chairs, in a troubled manner, he furthermore indulged in several acts of pantomime, indicative of a desire to pummel and wring the nose of the aforesaid Stiggins: the performance of which, appeared to afford him great mental relief. The old gentleman very narrowly escaped detection in one instance; for Mr Stiggins happening to give a start on the arrival of the negus, brought his head in smart contact with the clenched fist with which Mr Weller had been describing imaginary fireworks in the air, within two inches of his ear, for some minutes.

'Wot are you a reachin' out your hand for the tumbler in that 'ere sawage way for?' said Sam, with great promptitude. 'Don't you see you've hit the gen'l'm'n?'

'I didn't go to do it, Sammy,' said Mr Weller, in some degree abashed by the very unexpected occurrence of the incident.

'Try an in'ard application, sir,' said Sam, as the red-nosed gentleman rubbed his head with a rueful visage. 'Wot do you think o' that, for a go o' wanity warm, sir?'

Mr Stiggins made no verbal answer, but his manner was expressive. He tasted the contents of the glass which Sam had placed in his hand; put his umbrella on the floor, and tasted it again: passing his hand placidly across his stomach twice or thrice; he then drank the whole at a breath, and smacking his lips, held out the tumbler for more.

Nor was Mrs Weller behind-hand in doing justice to the composition. The good lady began by protesting that she couldn't touch a drop – then took a small drop – then a large drop – then a great many drops; and her feelings being of the nature of those substances which are powerfully affected by the application of strong waters, she dropped a tear with every drop of negus, and so got on, melting the feelings down, until at length she arrived at a very pathetic and decent pitch of misery.

The elder Mr Weller observed these signs and tokens with many manifestations of disgust, and when, after a second jug of the same, Mr Stiggins began to sigh in a dismal manner, he plainly evinced his disapprobation of the whole proceedings, by sundry incoherent ramblings of speech, among which frequent angry repetitions of the word 'gammon' were alone distinguishable to the ear.

'I'll tell you wot it is, Samivel, my boy,' whispered the old gentleman into his son's ear, after a long and steadfast contemplation of his lady and Mr Stiggins; 'I think there must be somethin' wrong in your mother-in-law's inside, as vell as in that o' the red-nosed man.'

'Wot do you mean?' said Sam.

'I mean this here, Sammy,' replied the old gentleman, 'that wot they drink, don't seem no nourishment to 'em; it all turns to warm water, and comes a' pourin' out o' their eyes. 'Pend upon it, Sammy, it's a constitootional infirmity.'

Mr Weller delivered this scientific opinion with many confirmatory frowns and nods; which, Mrs Weller remarking, and concluding that they bore some disparaging reference either to herself or to Mr Stiggins, or to both, was on the point of becoming infinitely worse, when Mr Stiggins, getting on his legs as well as he could, proceeded to deliver an edifying discourse for the benefit of the company, but more especially of Mr Samuel, whom he adjured in moving terms to be upon his guard in that sink of iniquity into which he was cast; to abstain from all hypocrisy and pride of heart; and to take in all things exact pattern and copy by him (Stiggins),

The Red-nosed man Discourseth

in which case he might calculate on arriving, sooner or later at the comfortable conclusion, that, like him, he was a most estimable and blameless character, and that all his acquaintance and friends were hopelessly abandoned and profligate wretches. Which consideration, he said, could not but afford him the liveliest satisfaction.

He furthermore conjured him to avoid, above all things, the vice of intoxication, which he likened unto the filthy habits of swine, and to those poisonous and baleful drugs which being chewed in the mouth, are said to filch away the memory. At this point of his discourse, the reverend and red-nosed gentleman became singularly incoherent, and staggering to and fro in the excitement of his eloquence, was fain to catch at the back of a chair to preserve his perpendicular.

Mr Stiggins did not desire his hearers to be upon their guard against those false prophets and wretched mockers of religion, who, without sense to expound its first doctrines, or hearts to feel its first principles, are more dangerous members of society than the common criminal; imposing, as they necessarily do, upon the weakest and worst informed, casting scorn and contempt on what should be held most sacred, and bringing into partial disrepute large bodies of virtuous and well conducted persons of many excellent sects and persuasions. But as he leant over the back of the chair for a considerable time, and closing one eye, winked a good deal with the other, it is presumed that he thought all this, but kept it to himself.

During the delivery of the oration, Mrs Weller sobbed and wept at the end of the paragraphs: while Sam, sitting cross-legged on a chair and resting his arms on the top-rail, regarded the speaker with great suavity and blandness of demeanour; occasionally bestowing a look of recognition on the old gentleman, who was delighted at the beginning, and went to sleep about half-way.

'Brayvo; wery pretty!' said Sam, when the red-nosed man having finished, pulled his worn gloves on: thereby thrusting his fingers through the broken tops till the knuckles were disclosed to view. 'Wery pretty.'

'I hope it may do you good, Samuel,' said Mrs Weller solemnly.

'I think it vill, mum,' replied Sam.

'I wish I could hope that it would do your father good,' said Mrs Weller.

'Thankee, my dear,' said Mr Weller, senior. 'How do *you* find yourself arter it, my love?'

'Scoffer!' exclaimed Mrs Weller.

'Benighted man!' said the reverend Mr Stiggins.

'If I don't get no better light than that 'ere moonshine o' yourn, my worthy creetur,' said the elder Mr Weller, 'it's wery likely as I shall continey to be a night coach till I'm took off the road altogether. Now, Mrs We, if the piebald stands at livery much longer, he'll stand at nothin' as we go back, and p'raps that 'ere harm cheer 'ull be tipped over into some hedge or another, with the shepherd in it.'

At this supposition, the reverend Mr Stiggins, in evident consternation, gathered up his hat and umbrella, and proposed an immediate departure, to which Mrs Weller assented. Sam walked with them to the lodge-gate, and took a dutiful leave.

'A-do, Samivel,' said the old gentleman.

'Wot's a-do?' inquired Sammy.

'Well, good bye, then,' said the old gentleman.

'Oh, that's wot you're a aimin' at, is it?' said Sam. 'Good bye!'

'Sammy,' whispered Mr Weller, looking cautiously round; 'my duty to your gov'ner, and tell him if he thinks better o' this here bis'ness, to commoonicate vith me. Me and a cab'net-maker has dewised a plan for gettin' him out. A pianner, Samivel, a pianner!' said Mr Weller, striking his son on the chest with the back of his hand, and falling back a step or two.

'Wot do you mean?' said Sam.

'A pianner forty, Samivel,' rejoined Mr Weller, in a still more mysterious manner, 'as he can have on hire; vun as von't play, Sammy.'

'And wot 'ud be the good o' that?' said Sam.

'Let him send to my friend, the cab'net-maker, to fetch it back, Sammy,' replied Mr Weller. 'Are you avake, now?'

'No,' rejoined Sam.

'There ain't no vurks in it,' whispered his father. 'It 'ull hold him easy, vith his hat and shoes on, and breathe through the legs, vich his holler. Have a passage ready taken for 'Merriker. The 'Merrikin gov'ment will never give him up, ven they find as he's got money to spend, Sammy. Let the gov'ner stop there, till Mrs Bardell's dead, or Mr Dodson and Fogg's hung (wich last ewent I think is the most likely to happen first, Sammy), and then let him come back and write a book about the 'Merrikins[7] as'll pay all his expenses and more, if he blows 'em up enough.'

Mr Weller delivered this hurried abstract of his plot with great vehemence of whisper; then, as if fearful of weakening the effect of the tremendous communication, by any further dialogue, he gave the coachman's salute, and vanished.

Sam had scarcely recovered his usual composure of countenance, which had been greatly disturbed by the secret communication of his respected relative, when Mr Pickwick accosted him.

'Sam,' said that gentleman.

'Sir,' replied Mr Weller.

'I am going for a walk round the prison, and I wish you to attend me. I see a prisoner we know coming this way, Sam,' said Mr Pickwick, smiling.

'Wich, sir?' inquired Mr Weller; 'the gen'l'm'n vith the head o' hair, or the interestin' captive in the stockin's?'

'Neither,' rejoined Mr Pickwick. 'He is an older friend of yours, Sam.'

'O' mine, sir?' exclaimed Mr Weller.

'You recollect the gentleman very well, I dare say, Sam,' replied Mr Pickwick, 'or else you are more unmindful of your old acquaintances than I think you are. Hush! not a word, Sam, not a syllable. Here he is.'

As Mr Pickwick spoke, Jingle walked up. He looked less miserable than before, being clad in a half-worn suit of clothes, which, with Mr Pickwick's assistance, had been released from the pawnbroker's. He wore clean linen too, and had had his hair cut. He was very pale and thin, however; and as he crept slowly up, leaning on a stick, it was easy to see that he had suffered severely from illness and want, and was still very weak. He took off his hat as Mr Pickwick saluted him, and seemed much humbled and abashed at sight of Sam Weller.

Following close at his heels, came Mr Job Trotter, in the catalogue of whose vices, want of faith and attachment to his companion could at all events find no place. He was still ragged and squalid, but his face was not quite so hollow as on his first meeting with Mr Pickwick, a few days before. As he took off his hat to our benevolent old friend, he murmured some broken expressions of gratitude, and muttered something about having been saved from starving.

'Well, well,' said Mr Pickwick, impatiently interrupting him, 'you can follow with Sam. I want to speak to you, Mr Jingle. Can you walk without his arm?'

'Certainly, sir – all ready – not too fast – legs shaky – head queer – round and round – earthquaky sort of feeling – very.'

'Here, give me your arm,' said Mr Pickwick.

'No, no,' replied Jingle; 'won't indeed – rather not.'

'Nonsense,' said Mr Pickwick; 'lean upon me, I desire, sir.'

Seeing that he was confused and agitated, and uncertain what to do, Mr Pickwick cut the matter short by drawing the invalided stroller's arm through his, and leading him away, without saying another word about it.

During the whole of this time, the countenance of Mr Samuel Weller had exhibited an expression of the most overwhelming and absorbing astonishment that the imagination can portray. After looking from Job to Jingle, and from Jingle to Job in profound silence, he softly ejaculated the words, 'Well, I *am* damn'd!' Which he repeated at least a score of times: after which exertion, he appeared wholly bereft of speech, and again cast his eyes, first upon the one and then upon the other, in mute perplexity and bewilderment.

'Now, Sam!' said Mr Pickwick, looking back.

'I'm a comin', sir,' replied Mr Weller, mechanically following his master; and still he lifted not his eyes from Mr Job Trotter, who walked at his side, in silence.

Job kept his eyes fixed on the ground for some time. Sam, with his glued to Job's countenance, ran up against the people who were walking about, and fell over little children, and stumbled against steps and railings, without appearing at all sensible of it, until Job, looking stealthily up, said:

'How do you do, Mr Weller?'

'It *is* him!' exclaimed Sam: and having established Job's identity beyond all doubt, he smote his leg, and vented his feelings in a long shrill whistle.

'Things has altered with me, sir,' said Job.

'I should think they had,' exclaimed Mr Weller, surveying his companion's rags with undisguised wonder. 'This is rayther a change for the worse, Mr Trotter, as the gen'l'm'n said, wen he got two doubtful shillin's and sixpenn'orth o' pocket pieces for a good half-crown.'

'It is, indeed,' replied Job, shaking his head. 'There is no deception now, Mr Weller. Tears,' said Job, with a look of momentary slyness, 'tears are not the only proofs of distress, nor the best ones.'

'No, they ain't,' replied Sam, expressively.

'They may be put on, Mr Weller,' said Job.

'I know they may,' said Sam; 'some people, indeed, has 'em always ready laid on, and can pull out the plug wenever they likes.'

'Yes,' replied Job; 'but *these* sort of things are not so easily counterfeited, Mr Weller, and it is a more painful process to get them up.' As he spoke, he pointed to his sallow sunken cheeks, and, drawing up his coat sleeves, disclosed an arm which looked as if the bone could be broken at a touch: so sharp and brittle did it appear, beneath its thin covering of flesh.

'Wot have you been a doin' to yourself?' said Sam, recoiling.

'Nothing,' replied Job.

'Nothin'!' echoed Sam.

'I have been doin' nothing for many weeks past,' said Job; 'and eating and drinking almost as little.'

Sam took one comprehensive glance at Mr Trotter's thin face and wretched apparel; and then, seizing him by the arm, commenced dragging him away with great violence.

'Where are you going, Mr Weller?' said Job, vainly struggling in the powerful grasp of his old enemy.

'Come on,' said Sam; 'come on!' He deigned no further explanation until they reached the tap; and then called for a pot of porter, which was speedily produced.

'Now,' said Sam, 'drink that up, ev'ry drop on it, and then turn the pot upside down, to let me see as you've took the med'cine.'

'But, my dear Mr Weller,' remonstrated Job.

'Down vith it!' said Sam, peremptorily.

Thus admonished, Mr Trotter raised the pot to his lips, and, by gentle and almost imperceptible degrees, tilted it into the air. He paused once, and only once, to draw a long breath, but without raising his face from the vessel, which, in a few moments thereafter, he held out at arm's length, bottom upward. Nothing fell upon the ground but a few particles of froth, which slowly detached themselves from the rim, and trickled lazily down.

'Well done!' said Sam. 'How do you find yourself arter it?'

'Better, sir. I think I am better,' responded Job.

'O' course you air,' said Sam, argumentatively. 'It's like puttin' gas in a balloon. I can see with the naked eye that you gets stouter under the operation. Wot do you say to another o' the same dimensions?'

'I would rather not, I am much obliged to you, sir,' replied Job, 'much rather not.'

'Vell, then, wot do you say to some wittles?' inquired Sam.

'Thanks to your worthy governor, sir,' said Mr Trotter, 'we have half a leg of mutton, baked, at a quarter before three, with the potatoes under it to save boiling.'

'Wot! Has *he* been a purwidin' for you?' asked Sam, emphatically.

'He has, sir,' replied Job. 'More than that, Mr Weller; my master being very ill, he got us a room – we were in a kennel before – and paid for it, sir; and come to look at us, at night, when nobody should know. Mr Weller,' said Job, with real tears in his eyes, for once, 'I could serve that gentleman till I fell down dead at his feet.'

'I say!' said Sam, 'I'll trouble you, my friend! None o' that!'

Job Trotter looked amazed.

'None o' that, I say, young feller,' repeated Sam, firmly. 'No man serves him but me. And now we're upon it, I'll let you into another secret besides that,' said Sam, as he paid for the beer. 'I never heerd, mind you, nor read of in story-books, nor see in picters, any angel in tights and gaiters – not even in spectacles, as I remember, though that may ha' been done for anythin' I know to the contrairey – but mark my vords, Job Trotter, he's a reg'lar thorough-bred angel for all that; and let me see the man as wenturs to tell me he knows a better vun.' With this defiance, Mr Weller buttoned up his change in a side pocket, and, with many confirmatory nods and gestures by the way proceeded in search of the subject of discourse.

They found Mr Pickwick, in company with Jingle, talking very earnestly, and not bestowing a look on the groups who were congregated on the racket-ground; they were very motley groups too, and worth the looking at, if it were only in idle curiosity.

'Well,' said Mr Pickwick, as Sam and his companion drew nigh, 'you will see how your health becomes, and think about it meanwhile. Make the statement out for me when you feel yourself equal to the task, and I will discuss the subject with you when I have considered it. Now, go to your room. You are tired, and not strong enough to be out long.'

Mr Alfred Jingle, without one spark of his old animation – with nothing even of the dismal gaiety which he had assumed when Mr Pickwick first stumbled on him in his misery – bowed low without speaking, and, motioning to Job not to follow him just yet, crept slowly away.

'Curious scene this, is it not, Sam?' said Mr Pickwick, looking good-humouredly round.

'Wery much so, sir,' replied Sam. 'Wonders 'ull never cease,' added Sam, speaking to himself. 'I'm wery much mistaken if that 'ere Jingle worn't a doin' somethin' in the water-cart way!'[8]

The area formed by the wall in that part of the Fleet in which Mr Pickwick stood, was just wide enough to make a good racket court;

one side being formed, of course, by the wall itself, and the other by that portion of the prison which looked (or rather would have looked, but for the wall) towards St Paul's Cathedral. Sauntering or sitting about, in every possible attitude of listless idleness, were a great number of debtors, the major part of whom were waiting in prison until their day of 'going up' before the Insolvent Court should arrive; while others had been remanded for various terms, which they were idling away, as they best could. Some were shabby, some were smart, many dirty, a few clean; but there they all lounged, and loitered, and slunk about, with as little spirit or purpose as the beasts in a menagerie.

Lolling from the windows which commanded a view of this promenade, were a number of persons, some in noisy conversation with their acquaintance below, others playing at ball with some adventurous throwers outside, others looking on at the racket-players, or watching the boys as they cried the game. Dirty slipshod women passed and re-passed, on their way to the cooking-house in one corner of the yard; children screamed, and fought, and played together, in another; the tumbling of the skittles, and the shouts of the players, mingled perpetually with these and a hundred other sounds; and all was noise and tumult – save in a little miserable shed a few yards off, where lay, all quiet and ghastly, the body of the Chancery prisoner who had died the night before, awaiting the mockery of an inquest. The body! It is the lawyer's term for the restless whirling mass of cares and anxieties, affections, hopes, and griefs, that make up the living man. The law *had* his body; and there it lay, clothed in grave clothes, an awful witness to its tender mercy.

'Would you like to see a whistling-shop, sir?' inquired Job Trotter.

'What do you mean?' was Mr Pickwick's counter inquiry.

'A vistlin' shop, sir,' interposed Mr Weller.

'What is that, Sam? A bird-fancier's?' inquired Mr Pickwick.

'Bless your heart, no, sir,' replied Job; 'a whistling-shop, sir, is where they sell spirits.' Mr Job Trotter briefly explained here, that all persons, being prohibited under heavy penalties from conveying spirits into debtors' prisons, and such commodities being highly prized by the ladies and gentlemen confined therein, it had occurred to some speculative turnkey to connive, for certain lucrative considerations, at two or three prisoners retailing the favourite article of gin, for their own profit and advantage.

'This plan you see, sir, has been gradually introduced into all the prisons for debt,' said Mr Trotter.

'And it has this wery great advantage,' said Sam, 'that the turnkeys takes wery good care to seize hold o' ev'ry body but them as pays 'em, that attempts the willainy, and wen it gets in the papers they're applauded for their wigilance; so it cuts two ways – frightens other people from the trade, and elewates their own characters.'

'Exactly so, Mr Weller,' observed Job.

'Well, but are these rooms never searched, to ascertain whether any spirits are concealed in them?' said Mr Pickwick.

'Cert'nly they are, sir,' replied Sam; 'but the turnkeys knows beforehand, and gives the word to the wistlers, and you *may* wistle for it wen you go to look.'

By this time, Job had tapped at a door, which was opened by a gentleman with an uncombed head, who bolted it after them when they had walked in, and grinned; upon which Job grinned, and Sam also; whereupon Mr Pickwick, thinking it might be expected of him, kept on smiling to the end of the interview.

The gentleman with the uncombed head appeared quite satisfied with this mute announcement of their business, and, producing a flat stone bottle, which might hold about a couple of quarts, from beneath his bedstead, filled out three glasses of gin, which Job Trotter and Sam disposed of in a most workmanlike manner.

'Any more?' said the whistling gentleman.

'No more,' replied Job Trotter.

Mr Pickwick paid, the door was unbolted, and out they came; the uncombed gentleman bestowing a friendly nod upon Mr Roker, who happened to be passing at the moment.

From this spot, Mr Pickwick wandered along all the galleries, up and down all the staircases, and once again round the whole area of the yard. The great body of the prison population appeared to be Mivins, and Smangle, and the parson, and the butcher, and the leg, over and over, and over again. There were the same squalor, the same turmoil and noise, the same general characteristics, in every corner; in the best and the worst alike. The whole place seemed restless and troubled; and the people were crowding and flitting to and fro, like the shadows in an uneasy dream.

'I have seen enough,' said Mr Pickwick, as he threw himself into a chair in his little apartment, 'My head aches with these scenes, and my heart too. Henceforth I will be a prisoner in my own room.'

And Mr Pickwick steadfastly adhered to this determination. For three long months he remained shut up, all day; only stealing out at night, to breathe the air, when the greater part of his fellow prisoners were in bed or carousing in their rooms. His health was beginning to suffer from the closeness of the confinement, but neither the often-repeated entreaties of Perker and his friends, nor the still more frequently-repeated warnings and admonitions of Mr Samuel Weller, could induce him to alter one jot of his inflexible resolution.

CHAPTER 46

Records a touching Act of delicate Feeling, not unmixed with Pleasantry, achieved and performed by Messrs Dodson and Fogg

It was within a week of the close of the month of July, that a hackney cabriolet, number unrecorded, was seen to proceed at a rapid pace up Goswell Street; three people were squeezed into it besides the driver, who sat in his own particular little dickey at the side; over the apron were hung two shawls, belonging to two small vixenish-looking ladies under the apron; between whom, compressed into a very small compass, was stowed away, a gentleman of heavy and subdued demeanour, who, whenever he ventured to make an observation, was snapped up short by one of the vixenish ladies before-mentioned. Lastly, the two vixenish ladies and the heavy gentleman were giving the driver contradictory directions, all tending to the one point that he should stop at Mrs Bardell's door; which the heavy gentleman, in direct opposition to, and defiance of, the vixenish ladies, contended was a green door and not a yellow one.

'Stop at the house with the green door, driver,' said the heavy gentleman.

'Oh! You perwerse creetur!' exclaimed one of the vixenish ladies. 'Drive to the ouse with the yellow door, cabmin.'

Upon this, the cabman, who in a sudden effort to pull up at the house with the green door, had pulled the horse up so high that he nearly pulled him backward into the cabriolet, let the animal's fore legs down to the ground again, and paused.

'Now vere am I to pull up?' inquired the driver. 'Settle it among yourselves. All I ask is, vere?'

Here the contest was renewed with increased violence; and the horse being troubled with a fly on his nose, the cabman humanely employed his leisure in lashing him about on the head, on the counter-irritation principle.

'Most wotes carries the day!' said one of the vixenish ladies at length. 'The ouse with the yellow door, cabmin.'

But after the cabriolet had dashed up, in splendid style, to the house with the yellow door: 'making,' as one of the vixenish ladies triumphantly said, 'acterrally more noise than if one had come in one's own carriage' – and after the driver had dismounted to assist the ladies in getting out – the small round head of Master Thomas Bardell was thrust out of the one-pair window of a house with a red door, a few numbers off.

'Aggrawatin' thing!' said the vixenish lady last mentioned, darting a withering glance at the heavy gentleman.

'My dear, it 's not my fault,' said the gentleman.

'Don't talk to me, you creetur, don't,' retorted the lady. 'The house with the red door, cabmin. Oh! If ever a woman was troubled with a ruffinly creetur, that takes a pride and a pleasure in disgracing his wife on every possible occasion afore strangers, I am that woman!'

'You ought to be ashamed of yourself, Raddle,' said the other little woman, who was no other than Mrs Cluppins.

'What have I been a doing of?' asked Mr Raddle.

'Don't talk to me, don't, you brute, for fear I should be perwoked to forgit my sect and strike you!' said Mrs Raddle.

While this dialogue was going on, the driver was most ignominiously leading the horse, by the bridle, up to the house with the red door, which Master Bardell had already opened. Here was a mean and low way of arriving at a friend's house! No dashing up, with all the fire and fury of the animal; no jumping down of the driver; no loud knocking at the door; no opening of the apron with a crash at the very last moment, for fear of the ladies sitting in a draught; and then the man handing the shawls out, afterwards, as if he were a private coachman! The whole edge of the thing had been taken off; it was flatter than walking.

'Well, Tommy,' said Mrs Cluppins, 'How's your poor dear mother?'

'Oh, she's very well,' replied Master Bardell. 'She's in the front parlour, all ready. I'm ready too, I am.' Here Master Bardell put his hands in his pockets, and jumped off and on the bottom step of the door.

'Is anybody else a goin', Tommy?' said Mrs Cluppins, arranging her pelerine.

'Mrs Sanders is going, she is,' replied Tommy, 'I'm going too, I am.'

'Drat the boy,' said little Mrs Cluppins. 'He thinks of nobody but himself. Here, Tommy, dear.'

'Well,' said Master Bardell.

'Who else is a goin', lovey?' said Mrs Cluppins in an insinuating manner.

'Oh! Mrs Rogers is a goin',' replied Master Bardell, opening his eyes very wide as he delivered the intelligence.

'What! The lady as has taken the lodgings!' ejaculated Mrs Cluppins.

Master Bardell put his hands deeper down into his pockets, and nodded exactly thirty-five times, to imply that it was the lady lodger, and no other.

'Bless us!' said Mrs Cluppins. 'It's quite a party!'

'Ah, if you knew what was in the cupboard, you'd say so,' replied Master Bardell.

'What is there, Tommy?' said Mrs Cluppins, coaxingly. 'You'll tell *me*, Tommy, I know.'

'No, I won't,' replied Master Bardell, shaking his head, and applying himself to the bottom step again.

'Drat the child!' muttered Mrs Cluppins. 'What a prowokin' little wretch it is! Come, Tommy, tell your dear Cluppy.'

'Mother said I wasn't to,' rejoined Master Bardell, 'I'm a goin' to have some, I am.' Cheered by this prospect, the precocious boy applied himself to his infantile treadmill, with increased vigour.

The above examination of a child of tender years, took place while Mr and Mrs Raddle and the cab-driver were having an altercation concerning the fare: which, terminating at this point in favour of the cabman, Mrs Raddle came up tottering.

'Lauk, Mary Ann! what's the matter?' said Mrs Cluppins.

'It's put me all over in such a tremble, Betsy,' replied Mrs Raddle. 'Raddle ain't like a man; he leaves everythink to me.'

This was scarcely fair upon the unfortunate Mr Raddle, who had been thrust aside by his good lady in the commencement of the dispute, and peremptorily commanded to hold his tongue. He had no opportunity of defending himself, however, for Mrs Raddle gave unequivocal signs of fainting; which, being perceived from the parlour window, Mrs Bardell, Mrs Sanders, the lodger, and the lodger's servant, darted precipitately out, and conveyed her into the house: all talking at the same time, and giving utterance to various expressions of pity and condolence, as if she were one of the most suffering mortals on earth. Being conveyed into the front parlour, she was there deposited on a sofa; and the lady from the first floor running up *to* the first floor, returned with a bottle of sal volatile,[1] which, holding Mrs Raddle tight round the neck, she applied in all womanly kindness and pity to her nose, until that lady with many plunges and struggles was fain to declare herself decidedly better.

'Ah, poor thing!' said Mrs Rogers, 'I know what her feelin's is, too well.'

'Ah, poor thing! so do I,' said Mrs Sanders: and then all the ladies moaned in unison, and said *they* knew what it was, and they pitied her from their hearts, they did. Even the lodger's little servant, who was thirteen years old, and three feet high, murmured her sympathy.

'But what's been the matter?' said Mrs Bardell.

'Ah, what has decomposed you, ma'am?' inquired Mrs Rogers.

'I have been a good deal flurried,' replied Mrs Raddle, in a reproachful manner. Thereupon the ladies cast indignant looks at Mr Raddle.

'Why, the fact is,' said that unhappy gentleman, stepping forward, 'when we alighted at this door, a dispute arose with the driver of the cabrioily—' A loud scream from his wife, at the mention of this word, rendered all further explanation inaudible.

'You'd better leave us to bring her round, Raddle,' said Mrs Cluppins. 'She'll never get better as long as you're here.'

All the ladies concurred in this opinion; so Mr Raddle was pushed out of the room, and requested to give himself an airing in the back yard. Which he did for about a quarter of an hour, when Mrs Bardell announced to him with a solemn face that he might come in now, but that he must be very careful how he behaved towards his wife. She knew he didn't mean to be unkind; but Mary Ann was very far from strong, and, if he didn't take care, he might lose her when he least expected it, which would be a very dreadful reflection for him afterwards; and so on. All this, Mr Raddle heard with great submission, and presently returned to the parlour in a most lamb-like manner.

'Why, Mrs Rogers, ma'am,' said Mrs Bardell, 'you've never been introduced, I declare! Mr Raddle, ma'am; Mrs Cluppins, ma'am; Mrs Raddle, ma'am.'

—'Which is Mrs Cluppins's sister,' suggested Mrs Sanders.

'Oh, indeed!' said Mrs Rogers, graciously; for she was the lodger, and her servant was in waiting, so she was more gracious than intimate, in right of her position. 'Oh, indeed!'

Mrs Raddle smiled sweetly, Mr Raddle bowed, and Mrs Cluppins said 'she was sure she was verry happy to have a opportunity of being known to a lady which she had heerd so much in faviour of, as Mrs Rogers.' A compliment which the last-named lady acknowledged with graceful condescension.

'Well, Mr Raddle,' said Mrs Bardell; 'I'm sure you ought to feel very much honoured at you and Tommy being the only gentlemen to escort so many ladies all the way to the Spaniards,[2] at Hampstead. Don't you think he ought, Mrs Rogers, ma'am?'

'Oh, certainly, ma'am,' replied Mrs Rogers; after whom all the other ladies responded 'Oh, certainly.'

'Of course I feel it, ma'am,' said Mr Raddle, rubbing his hands, and evincing a slight tendency to brighten up a little. 'Indeed, to tell you the truth, I said, as we was a coming along in the cabrioily —'

At the recapitulation of the word which awakened so many painful recollections, Mrs Raddle applied her handkerchief to her eyes again, and uttered a half-suppressed scream; so Mrs Bardell frowned upon Mr Raddle, to intimate that he had better not say anything more, and desired Mrs Rogers's servant, with an air, to 'put the wine on.'

This was the signal for displaying the hidden treasures of the closet, which comprised sundry plates of oranges and biscuits, and a bottle of old crusted port — that at one and nine — with another of the celebrated East India sherry at fourteenpence, which were all produced in honour of the lodger, and afforded unlimited satisfaction to everybody. After great consternation had been excited in the mind of Mrs Cluppins, by an attempt on the part of Tommy to recount how he had been cross-examined regarding the cupboard then in action, (which was fortunately nipped in the bud by his imbibing half a glass of the old crusted 'the wrong way,' and thereby endangering his life for some seconds,) the party walked forth, in quest of a Hampstead stage. This was soon found, and in a couple of hours they all arrived safely in the Spaniards Tea-gardens, where the luckless Mr Raddle's very first act nearly occasioned his good lady a relapse; it being neither more nor less than to order tea for seven, whereas (as the ladies one and all remarked), what could have been easier than for Tommy to have drank out of anybody's cup — or everybody's, if that was all — when the waiter wasn't looking: which would have saved one head of tea, and the tea just as good!

However, there was no help for it, and the tea-tray came, with seven cups and saucers, and bread and butter on the same scale. Mrs Bardell was unanimously voted into the chair, and Mrs Rogers being stationed on her right hand, and Mrs Raddle on her left, the meal proceeded with great merriment and success.

'How sweet the country is, to-be-sure!' sighed Mrs Rogers; 'I almost wish I lived in it always.'

'Oh, you wouldn't like that, ma'am,' replied Mrs Bardell, rather hastily; for it was not at all advisable, with reference to the lodgings, to encourage such notions; 'you wouldn't like it, ma'am.'

'Oh! I should think you was a deal too lively and sought-after, to be content with the country, ma'am,' said little Mrs Cluppins.

'Perhaps I am, ma'am. Perhaps I am,' sighed the first-floor lodger.

'For lone people as have got nobody to care for them, or take care of them, or as have been hurt in their mind, or that kind of thing,' observed Mr Raddle, plucking up a little cheerfulness, and looking round, 'the country is all very well. The country for a wounded spirit, they say.'

Now, of all things in the world that the unfortunate man could have said, any would have been preferable to this. Of course Mrs Bardell burst into tears, and requested to be led from the table instantly; upon which the affectionate child began to cry too, most dismally.

'Would anybody believe, ma'am,' exclaimed Mrs Raddle, turning fiercely to the first-floor lodger, 'that a woman could be married to such a unmanly creetur, which can tamper with a woman's feelings as he does, every hour in the day, ma'am?'

'My dear,' remonstrated Mr Raddle, 'I didn't mean anything, my dear.'

'You didn't mean!' repeated Mrs Raddle, with great scorn and contempt. 'Go away. I can't bear the sight on you, you brute.'

'You must *not* flurry yourself, Mary Ann,' interposed Mrs Cluppins. 'You really must consider yourself, my dear, which you never do. Now go away, Raddle, there's a good soul, or you'll only aggravate her.'

'You had better take your tea by yourself, sir, indeed,' said Mrs Rogers, again applying the smelling-bottle.

Mrs Sanders, who according to custom was very busy with the bread and butter, expressed the same opinion, and Mr Raddle quietly retired.

After this, there was a great hoisting up of Master Bardell, who was rather a large size for hugging, into his mother's arms: in which operation he got his boots in the tea-board, and occasioned some confusion among the cups and saucers. But that description of fainting fits, which is contagious among ladies, seldom lasts long; so when he had been well kissed, and a little cried over, Mrs Bardell recovered, set him down again, wondered how she could have been so foolish, and poured out some more tea.

It was at this moment, that the sound of approaching wheels was heard, and that the ladies, looking up, saw a hackney-coach stop at the garden-gate.

'More company!' said Mrs Sanders.

'It's a gentleman,' said Mrs Raddle.

'Well, if it ain't Mr Jackson, the young man from Dodson and Fogg's!' cried Mrs Bardell. 'Why, gracious! Surely Mr Pickwick can't have paid the damages.'

'Or hoffered marriage!' said Mrs Cluppins.

'Dear me, how slow the gentleman is,' exclaimed Mrs Rogers: 'Why doesn't he make haste!'

As the lady spoke these words, Mr Jackson turned from the coach where he had been addressing some observations to a shabby man in black leggings, who had just emerged from the vehicle with a thick ash stick in his hand, and made his way to the place where the ladies were seated; winding his hair round the brim of his hat as he came along.

'Is anything the matter? Has anything taken place, Mr Jackson?' said Mrs Bardell, eagerly.

'Nothing whatever, ma'am,' replied Mr Jackson. 'How de do, ladies? I have to ask pardon, ladies, for intruding – but the law, ladies – the law.' With this apology Mr Jackson smiled, made a comprehensive bow, and gave his hair another wind. Mrs Rogers whispered Mrs Raddle that he was really an elegant young man.

'I called in Goswell Street,' resumed Jackson, 'and hearing that you were here, from the slavey, took a coach and came on. Our people want you down in the city directly, Mrs Bardell.'

'Lor!' ejaculated that lady, starting at the sudden nature of the communication.

'Yes,' said Jackson, biting his lip. 'It's very important and pressing business, which can't be postponed on any account. Indeed, Dodson expressly said so to me, and so did Fogg. I've kept the coach on purpose for you to go back in.'

'How very strange!' exclaimed Mrs Bardell.

The ladies agreed that it *was* very strange, but were unanimously of opinion that it must be very important, or Dodson and Fogg would never have sent; and further, that the business being urgent, she ought to repair to Dodson and Fogg's without any delay.

There was a certain degree of pride and importance about being wanted by one's lawyers in such a monstrous hurry, that was by no means displeasing to Mrs Bardell, especially as it might be reasonably supposed to enhance her consequence in the eyes of the first-floor lodger. She simpered a little, affected extreme vexation and hesitation, and at last arrived at the conclusion that she supposed she must go.

'But won't you refresh yourself after your walk, Mr Jackson?' said Mrs Bardell, persuasively.

'Why, really there ain't much time to lose,' replied Jackson; 'and I've got a friend here,' he continued, looking towards the man with the ash stick.

'Oh, ask your friend to come here, sir,' said Mrs Bardell. 'Pray ask your friend here, sir.'

'Why, thankee, I'd rather not,' said Mr Jackson, with some embarrassment of manner. 'He's not much used to ladies' society, and it makes him bashful. If you'll order the waiter to deliver him anything short, he won't drink it off at once, won't he! – only try him!' Mr Jackson's fingers wandered playfully round his nose, at this portion of his discourse, to warn his hearers that he was speaking ironically.

The waiter was at once despatched to the bashful gentleman, and the bashful gentleman took something; Mr Jackson also took something, and the ladies took something, for hospitality's sake. Mr Jackson then said he was afraid it was time to go; upon which, Mrs Sanders, Mrs Cluppins, and Tommy (who it was arranged should accompany Mrs Bardell: leaving the others to Mr Raddle's protection), got into the coach.

'Isaac,' said Jackson, as Mrs Bardell prepared to get in: looking up at the man with the ash stick, who was seated on the box, smoking a cigar.

'Well?'

'*This* is Mrs Bardell.'

'Oh, I know'd that, long ago,' said the man.

Mrs Bardell got in, Mr Jackson got in after her, and away they drove. Mrs Bardell could not help ruminating on what Mr Jackson's friend had said. Shrewd creatures, those lawyers. Lord bless us, how they find people out!

'Sad thing about these costs of our people's, ain't it,' said Jackson,

when Mrs Cluppins and Mrs Sanders had fallen asleep; 'your bill of
costs I mean?'

'I'm very sorry they can't get them,' replied Mrs Bardell. 'But if
you law-gentlemen do these things on speculation, why you must
get a loss now and then, you know.'

'You gave them a *cognovit*[3] for the amount of your costs, after
the trial, I'm told?' said Jackson.

'Yes. Just as a matter of form,' replied Mrs Bardell.

'Certainly,' replied Jackson, drily. 'Quite a matter of form. Quite.'

On they drove, and Mrs Bardell fell asleep. She was awakened,
after some time, by the stopping of the coach.

'Bless us!' said the lady. 'Are we at Freeman's Court?'

'We're not going quite so far,' replied Jackson. 'Have the goodness to step out.'

Mrs Bardell, not yet thoroughly awake, complied. It was a
curious place: a large wall, with a gate in the middle, and a gas-
light burning inside.

'Now ladies,' cried the man with the ash stick, looking into the
coach, and shaking Mrs Sanders to wake her, 'Come!' Rousing her
friend, Mrs Sanders alighted. Mrs Bardell, leaning on Jackson's
arm, and leading Tommy by the hand, had already entered the
porch. They followed.

The room they turned into, was even more odd-looking than the
porch. Such a number of men standing about! And they stared so!

'What place is this?' inquired Mrs Bardell, pausing.

'Only one of our public offices,' replied Jackson, hurrying her
through a door, and looking round to see that the other women
were following. 'Look sharp, Isaac!'

'Safe and sound,' replied the man with the ash stick. The door
swung heavily after them, and they descended a small flight of steps.

'Here we are, at last. All right and tight, Mrs Bardell!' said
Jackson, looking exultingly round.

'What do you mean?' said Mrs Bardell, with a palpitating heart.

'Just this,' replied Jackson, drawing her a little on one side; 'don't
be frightened, Mrs Bardell. There never was a more delicate man
than Dodson, ma'am, or a more humane man than Fogg. It was
their duty, in the way of business, to take you in execution for them
costs; but they were anxious to spare your feelings as much as they
could. What a comfort it must be, to you, to think how it's been
done! This is the Fleet, ma'am. Wish you good night, Mrs Bardell.
Good night, Tommy!'

As Jackson hurried away in company with the man with the ash

Mrs Bardell encounters Mr Pickwick in the prison

stick, another man with a key in his hand, who had been looking on, led the bewildered female to a second short flight of steps leading to a doorway. Mrs Bardell screamed violently; Tommy roared; Mrs Cluppins shrunk within herself; and Mrs Sanders made off, without more ado. For, there, stood the injured Mr Pickwick, taking his nightly allowance of air; and beside him leant Samuel Weller, who, seeing Mrs Bardell, took his hat off with mock reverence, while his master turned indignantly on his heel.

'Don't bother the woman,' said the turnkey to Weller: 'she's just come in.'

'A pris'ner!' said Sam, quickly replacing his hat. 'Who's the plaintives? What for? Speak up, old feller.'

'Dodson and Fogg,' replied the man; 'execution on cognovit for costs.'

'Here Job, Job!' shouted Sam, dashing into the passage. 'Run to Mr Perker's, Job. *I* want him directly. I see some good in this. Here's a game. Hooray! were's the gov'nor!'

But there was no reply to these inquiries, for Job had started furiously off, the instant he received his commission, and Mrs Bardell had fainted in real down-right earnest.

CHAPTER 47

Is chiefly devoted to matters of Business, and the
temporal Advantage of Dodson and Fogg.
Mr Winkle re-appears under extraordinary
circumstances. Mr Pickwick's Benevolence proves
stronger than his Obstinacy

Job Trotter, abating nothing of his speed, ran up Holborn: sometimes in the middle of the road, sometimes on the pavement, sometimes in the gutter, as the chances of getting along, varied with the press of men, women, children, and coaches, in each division of the thoroughfare; regardless of all obstacles, he stopped not for an instant until he reached the gate of Gray's Inn. Notwithstanding all the expedition he had used, however, the gate had been closed a good half hour when he reached it, and by the time he had discovered Mr Perker's laundress, who lived with a married daughter, who had bestowed her hand upon a non-resident waiter, who occupied the one-pair of some number in some street closely adjoining to some brewery somewhere behind Gray's Inn Lane, it was within fifteen minutes of closing the prison for the night. Mr Lowten had still to be ferreted out from the back parlour of the Magpie and Stump; and Job had scarcely accomplished this object, and communicated Sam Weller's message, when the clock struck ten.

'There,' said Lowten, 'it's too late now. You can't get in to-night; you've got the key of the street, my friend.'

'Never mind me,' replied Job. 'I can sleep anywhere. But won't it be better to see Mr Perker to-night, so that we may be there, the first thing in the morning?'

'Why,' responded Lowten, after a little consideration, 'if it was in anybody else's case, Perker wouldn't be best pleased at my going up to his house; but as it's Mr Pickwick's, I think I may venture to take a cab and charge it to the office.' Deciding on this line of conduct, Mr Lowten took up his hat, and begging the assembled company to appoint a deputy chairman during his temporary absence, led the way to the nearest coach-stand. Summoning the cab of most promising appearance, he directed the driver to repair to Montague Place, Russell Square.[1]

Mr Perker had had a dinner party that day, as was testified by the appearance of lights in the drawing-room windows, the sound of an improved grand piano, and an improvable cabinet voice issuing therefrom, and a rather overpowering smell of meat which pervaded the steps and entry. In fact a couple of very good country agencies happening to come up to town, at the same time, an agreeable little party had been got together to meet them: comprising Mr Snicks the Life Office Secretary, Mr Prosee the eminent counsel, three solicitors, one commissioner of bankrupts, a special pleader from the Temple, a small-eyed peremptory young gentleman, his pupil, who had written a lively book about the law of demises,[2] with a vast quantity of marginal notes and references; and several other eminent and distinguished personages. From this society, little Mr Perker detached himself, on his clerk being announced in a whisper; and repairing to the dining-room, there found Mr Lowten and Job Trotter looking very dim and shadowy by the light of a kitchen candle, which the gentleman who condescended to appear in plush shorts and cottons for a quarterly stipend, had, with a becoming contempt for the clerk and all things appertaining to 'the office,' placed upon the table.

'Now, Lowten,' said little Mr Perker, shutting the door, 'what's the matter? No important letter come in a parcel, is there?'

'No, sir,' replied Lowten. 'This is a messenger from Mr Pickwick, sir.'

'From Pickwick, eh?' said the little man, turning quickly to Job. 'Well, what is it?'

'Dodson and Fogg have taken Mrs Bardell in execution for her costs, sir,' said Job.

'No!' exclaimed Perker, putting his hands in his pockets, and reclining against the sideboard.

'Yes,' said Job. 'It seems they got a cognovit out of her, for the amount of 'em, directly after the trial.'

'By Jove!' said Perker, taking both hands out of his pockets, and striking the knuckles of his right against the palm of his left, emphatically, 'those are the cleverest scamps I ever had anything to do with!'

'The sharpest practitioners I ever knew, sir,' observed Lowten.

'Sharp!' echoed Perker. 'There's no knowing where to have them.'

'Very true, sir, there is not,' replied Lowten; and then, both master and man pondered for a few seconds, with animated countenances, as if they were reflecting upon one of the most beautiful and ingenious discoveries that the intellect of man had ever made. When they had in some measure recovered from their trance of admiration, Job Trotter discharged himself of the rest of his commission. Perker nodded his head thoughtfully, and pulled out his watch.

'At ten precisely, I will be there,' said the little man. 'Sam is quite right. Tell him so. Will you take a glass of wine, Lowten?'

'No, thank you, sir.'

'You mean yes, I think,' said the little man, turning to the sideboard for a decanter and glasses.

As Lowten *did* mean yes, he said no more on the subject, but inquired of Job, in an audible whisper, whether the portrait of Perker, which hung opposite the fire-place, wasn't a wonderful likeness, to which, Job of course replied that it was. The wine being by this time poured out, Lowten drank to Mrs Perker and the children, and Job to Perker. The gentleman in the plush shorts and cottons considering it no part of his duty to show the people from the office out, consistently declined to answer the bell, and they showed themselves out. The attorney betook himself to his drawing-room, the clerk to the Magpie and Stump, and Job to Covent Garden Market to spend the night in a vegetable basket.

Punctually at the appointed hour next morning, the good-humoured little attorney tapped at Mr Pickwick's door, which was opened with great alacrity by Sam Weller.

'Mr Perker, sir,' said Sam, announcing the visitor to Mr Pickwick, who was sitting at the window in a thoughtful attitude. 'Wery glad you've looked in accidentally, sir. I rather think the gov'nor wants to have a word and a half with you, sir.'

Perker bestowed a look of intelligence on Sam, intimating that he understood he was not to say he had been sent for: and beckoning him to approach, whispered briefly in his ear.

'You don't mean that 'ere, sir?' said Sam, starting back in excessive surprise.

Perker nodded and smiled.

Mr Samuel Weller looked at the little lawyer, then at Mr Pickwick, then at the ceiling, then at Perker again; grinned, laughed outright, and finally, catching up his hat from the carpet, without further explanation, disappeared.

'What does this mean?' inquired Mr Pickwick, looking at Perker with astonishment. 'What has put Sam into this most extraordinary state?'

'Oh, nothing, nothing,' replied Perker. 'Come, my dear sir, draw up your chair to the table. I have a good deal to say to you.'

'What papers are those?' inquired Mr Pickwick, as the little man deposited on the table a small bundle of documents tied with red tape.

'The papers in Bardell and Pickwick,' replied Perker, undoing the knot with his teeth.

Mr Pickwick grated the legs of his chair against the ground; and throwing himself into it, folded his hands and looked sternly – if Mr Pickwick ever could look sternly – at his legal friend.

'You don't like to hear the name of the cause?' said the little man, still busying himself with the knot.

'No, I do not indeed,' replied Mr Pickwick.

'Sorry for that,' resumed Perker, 'because it will form the subject of our conversation.'

'I would rather that the subject should be never mentioned between us, Perker,' interposed Mr Pickwick, hastily.

'Pooh, pooh, my dear sir,' said the little man, untying the bundle, and glancing eagerly at Mr Pickwick out of the corners of his eyes. 'It must be mentioned. I have come here on purpose. Now, are you ready to hear what I have to say, my dear sir? No hurry; if you are not, I can wait. I have this morning's paper here. Your time shall be mine. There!' Hereupon, the little man threw one leg over the other, and made a show of beginning to read with great composure and application.

'Well, well,' said Mr Pickwick, with a sigh, but softening into a smile at the same time. 'Say what you have to say; it's the old story I suppose?'

'With a difference, my dear sir; with a difference,' rejoined Perker, deliberately folding up the paper and putting it into his pocket again. 'Mrs Bardell, the plaintiff in the action, is within these walls, sir.'

'I know it,' was Mr Pickwick's reply.

'Very good,' retorted Perker. 'And you know how she comes here, I suppose; I mean on what grounds, and at whose suit?'

'Yes; at least I have heard Sam's account of the matter,' said Mr Pickwick, with affected carelessness.

'Sam's account of the matter,' replied Perker, 'is, I will venture to say, a perfectly correct one. Well now, my dear sir, the first question I have to ask, is, whether this woman is to remain here?'

'To remain here!' echoed Mr Pickwick.

'To remain here, my dear sir,' rejoined Perker, leaning back in his chair and looking steadily at his client.

'How can you ask me?' said that gentleman. 'It rests with Dodson and Fogg; you know that, very well.'

'I know nothing of the kind,' retorted Perker, firmly. 'It does *not* rest with Dodson and Fogg; you know the men, my dear sir, as well as I do. It rests solely, wholly, and entirely with you.'

'With me!' ejaculated Mr Pickwick, rising nervously from his chair, and reseating himself directly afterwards.

The little man gave a double knock on the lid of his snuff-box, opened it, took a great pinch, shut it up again, and repeated the words, 'With you.'

'I say, my dear sir,' resumed the little man, who seemed to gather confidence from the snuff; 'I say, that her speedy liberation or perpetual imprisonment rests with you, and with you alone. Hear me out, my dear sir, if you please, and do not be so very energetic, for it will only put you into a perspiration and do no good whatever. I say,' continued Perker, checking off each position on a different finger, as he laid it down; 'I say that nobody but you can rescue her from this den of wretchedness; and that you can only do that, by paying the costs of this suit – both of plaintiff and defendant – into the hands of these Freeman's Court sharks. Now pray be quiet, my dear sir.'

Mr Pickwick, whose face had been undergoing most surprising changes during this speech, and who was evidently on the verge of a strong burst of indignation, calmed his wrath as well as he could. Perker, strengthening his argumentative powers with another pinch of snuff, proceeded.

'I have seen the woman, this morning. By paying the costs, you can obtain a full release and discharge from the damages; and further – this I know is a far greater object of consideration with you, my dear sir – a voluntary statement, under her hand, in the form of a letter to me, that this business was, from the very first, fomented, and encouraged, and brought about, by these men, Dodson and Fogg; that she deeply regrets ever having been the instrument of annoyance or injury to you; and that she entreats me to intercede with you, and implore your pardon.'

'If I pay her costs for her,' said Mr Pickwick, indignantly. 'A valuable document, indeed!'

'No "*if*" in the case my dear sir,' said Perker, triumphantly. 'There is the very letter I speak of. Brought to my office by another woman at nine o'clock this morning, before I had set foot in this place, or held any communication with Mrs Bardell, upon my honour.' Selecting the letter from the bundle, the little lawyer laid it at Mr Pickwick's elbow, and took snuff for two consecutive minutes, without winking.

'Is this all you have to say to me?' inquired Mr Pickwick, mildly.

'Not quite,' replied Perker. 'I cannot undertake to say, at this moment, whether the wording of the cognovit, the nature of the ostensible consideration, and the proof we can get together about the whole conduct of the suit, will be sufficient to justify an indictment for conspiracy. I fear not, my dear sir; they are too clever for that, I doubt. I do mean to say, however, that the whole facts, taken together, will be sufficient to justify you, in the minds of all reasonable men. And now, my dear sir, I put it to you. This one hundred and fifty pounds, or whatever it may be – take it in round numbers – is nothing to you. A jury has decided against you; well, their verdict is wrong, but still they decided as they thought right, and it *is* against you. You have now an opportunity, on easy terms, of placing yourself in a much higher position than you ever could, by remaining here; which would only be imputed, by people who didn't know you, to sheer dogged, wrongheaded, brutal obstinacy: nothing else, my dear sir, believe me. Can you hesitate to avail yourself of it, when it restores you to your friends, your old pursuits, your health and amusements; when it liberates your faithful and attached servant, whom you otherwise doom to imprisonment for the whole of your life; and above all, when it enables you to take the very magnanimous revenge – which I know, my dear sir, is one after your own heart – of releasing this woman from a scene of misery and debauchery, to which no man should ever be consigned, if I had my will, but the infliction of which on any woman, is even more frightful and barbarous. Now I ask you, my dear sir, not only as your legal adviser, but as your very true friend, will you let slip the occasion of attaining all these objects, and doing all this good, for the paltry consideration of a few pounds finding their way into the pockets of a couple of rascals, to whom it makes no manner of difference, except that the more they gain, the more they'll seek, and so the sooner be led into some piece of knavery that must end in a crash? I have put these considerations to you, my dear sir, very feebly and imperfectly, but I ask you to think of them. Turn them over in your mind as long as you please. I wait here most patiently for your answer.'

Before Mr Pickwick could reply; before Mr Perker had taken one twentieth part of the snuff with which so unusually long an address imperatively required to be followed up; there was a low murmuring of voices outside, and then a hesitating knock at the door.

'Dear, dear,' exclaimed Mr Pickwick, who had been evidently roused by his friend's appeal; 'what an annoyance that door is! Who is that?'

'Me, sir,' replied Sam Weller, putting in his head.

'I can't speak to you just now, Sam,' said Mr Pickwick. 'I am engaged, at this moment, Sam.'

'Beg your pardon, sir,' rejoined Mr Weller. 'But here's a lady here, sir, as says she's somethin' wery partickler to disclose.'

'I can't see any lady,' replied Mr Pickwick, whose mind was filled with visions of Mrs Bardell.

'I vouldn't make too sure o' that, sir,' urged Mr Weller, shaking his head. 'If you know'd who was near, sir, I rayther think you'd change your note. As the hawk remarked to himself with a cheerful laugh, ven he heerd the robin red-breast a singin' round the corner.'

'Who is it?' inquired Mr Pickwick.

'Will you see her, sir?' asked Mr Weller, holding the door in his hand as if he had some curious live animal on the other side.

'I suppose I must,' said Mr Pickwick, looking at Perker.

'Well then, all in to begin!' cried Sam. 'Sound the gong, draw up the curtain, and enter the two con-spiraytors.'

As Sam Weller spoke, he threw the door open, and there rushed tumultuously into the room, Mr Nathaniel Winkle: leading after him by the hand, the identical young lady who at Dingley Dell had worn the boots with the fur round the tops, and who, now a very pleasing compound of blushes and confusion and lilac silk and a smart bonnet and a rich lace veil, looked prettier than ever.

'Miss Arabella Allen!' exclaimed Mr Pickwick, rising from his chair.

'No,' replied Mr Winkle, dropping on his knees, 'Mrs Winkle. Pardon, my dear friend, pardon?'

Mr Pickwick could scarcely believe the evidence of his senses, and perhaps would not have done so, but for the corroborative testimony afforded by the smiling countenance of Perker, and the bodily presence, in the background, of Sam and the pretty housemaid; who appeared to contemplate the proceedings with the liveliest satisfaction.

'Oh, Mr Pickwick!' said Arabella, in a low voice, as if alarmed at the silence. 'Can you forgive my imprudence?'

Mr Pickwick returned no verbal response to this appeal; but he took off his spectacles in great haste, and seizing both the young lady's hands in his, kissed her a great number of times – perhaps a greater number than was absolutely necessary – and then, still retaining one of her hands, told Mr Winkle he was an audacious young dog, and bade him get up. This, Mr Winkle, who had been for some seconds scratching his nose with the brim of his hat, in a penitent manner, did; whereupon Mr Pickwick slapped him on the back several times, and then shook hands heartily with Perker, who, not to be behind-hand in the compliments of the occasion, saluted both the bride and the pretty housemaid with right good will, and, having wrung Mr Winkle's hand most cordially, wound up his demonstrations of joy by taking snuff enough to set any half dozen men with ordinarily constructed noses, a sneezing for life.

'Why, my dear girl,' said Mr Pickwick, 'how has all this come about? Come! Sit down, and let me hear it all. How well she looks, doesn't she Perker?' added Mr Pickwick, surveying Arabella's face with a look of as much pride and exultation, as if she had been his daughter.

'Delightful, my dear sir,' replied the little man. 'If I were not a married man myself, I should be disposed to envy you, you dog.' Thus expressing himself, the little lawyer gave Mr Winkle a poke in the chest, which that gentleman reciprocated; after which they both laughed very loudly, but not so loudly as Mr Samuel Weller, who

Mr Winkle returns under extraordinary circumstances

had just relieved his feelings by kissing the pretty housemaid, under cover of the cupboard-door.

'I can never be grateful enough to you, Sam, I am sure,' said Arabella, with the sweetest smile imaginable. 'I shall not forget your exertions in the garden at Clifton.'

'Don't say nothin' wotever about it, ma'm,' replied Sam. 'I only assisted natur', ma'm; as the doctor said to the boy's mother, arter he'd bled him to death.'

'Mary, my dear, sit down,' said Mr Pickwick, cutting short these compliments. 'Now then; how long have you been married, eh?'

Arabella looked bashfully at her lord and master, who replied, 'Only three days.'

'Only three days, eh?' said Mr Pickwick. 'Why, what have you been doing these three months?'

'Ah, to be sure!' interposed Perker; 'come! Account for this idleness. You see Pickwick's only astonishment is, that it wasn't all over, months ago.'

'Why the fact is,' replied Mr Winkle, looking at his blushing young wife, 'that I could not persuade Bella to run away, for a long time. And when I had persuaded her, it was a long time more, before we could find an opportunity. Mary had to give a month's warning, too, before she could leave her place next door, and we couldn't possibly have done it without her assistance.'

'Upon my word,' exclaimed Mr Pickwick, who by this time had resumed his spectacles, and was looking from Arabella to Winkle, and from Winkle to Arabella, with as much delight depicted in his countenance as warm-heartedness and kindly feeling can communicate to the human face: 'upon my word! you seem to have been very systematic in your proceedings. And is your brother acquainted with all this, my dear?'

'Oh, no, no,' replied Arabella, changing colour. 'Dear Mr Pickwick, he must only know it from you – from your lips alone. He is so violent, so prejudiced, and has been so – so anxious in behalf of his friend, Mr Sawyer,' added Arabella, looking down, 'that I fear the consequences dreadfully.'

'Ah, to be sure,' said Perker gravely. 'You must take this matter in hand for them, my dear sir. These young men will respect you, when they would listen to nobody else. You must prevent mischief, my dear sir. Hot blood, hot blood.' And the little man took a warning pinch, and shook his head doubtfully.

'You forget, my love,' said Mr Pickwick, gently, 'you forget that I am a prisoner.'

'No, indeed I do not, my dear sir,' replied Arabella. 'I never have forgotten it. I have never ceased to think how great your sufferings must have been in this shocking place. But I hoped that what no consideration for yourself would induce you to do, a regard to our happiness, might. If my brother hears of this, first, from you, I feel certain we shall be reconciled. He is my only relation in the world, Mr Pickwick, and unless you plead for me, I fear I have lost even him. I have done wrong, very, very wrong, I know.' Here poor Arabella hid her face in her handkerchief, and wept bitterly.

Mr Pickwick's nature was a good deal worked upon, by these same tears; but when Mrs Winkle, drying her eyes, took to coaxing and entreating in the sweetest tones of a very sweet voice, he became particularly restless, and evidently undecided how to act. As was evinced by sundry nervous rubbings of his spectacle-glasses, nose, tights, head, and gaiters.

Taking advantage of these symptoms of indecision, Mr Perker (to whom, it appeared, the young couple had driven straight that morning) urged with legal point and shrewdness that Mr Winkle, senior, was still unacquainted with the important rise in life's flight of steps which his son had taken; that the future expectations of the said son depended entirely upon the said Winkle, senior, continuing to regard him with undiminished feelings of affection and attachment, which it was very unlikely he would, if this great event were long kept a secret from him; that Mr Pickwick, repairing to Bristol to seek Mr Allen, might, with equal reason, repair to Birmingham to seek Mr Winkle, senior; lastly, that Mr Winkle, senior, had good right and title to consider Mr Pickwick as in some degree the guardian and adviser of his son, and that it consequently behoved that gentleman, and was indeed due to his personal character, to acquaint the aforesaid Winkle, senior, personally, and by word of mouth, with the whole circumstances of the case, and with the share he had taken in the transaction.

Mr Tupman and Mr Snodgrass arrived, most opportunely, in this stage of the pleadings, and as it was necessary to explain to them all that had occurred, together with the various reasons pro and con, the whole of the arguments were gone over again, after which everybody urged every argument in his own way, and at his own length. And, at last, Mr Pickwick, fairly argued and remonstrated out of all his resolutions, and being in imminent danger of being argued and remonstrated out of his wits, caught Arabella in his arms, and declaring that she was a very amiable creature, and that he didn't know how it was, but he had always been very fond of her from the first, said he could never find it in his heart to stand in the way of young people's happiness, and they might do with him as they pleased.

Mr Weller's first act, on hearing this concession, was to despatch Job Trotter to the illustrious Mr Pell, with an authority to deliver to the bearer the formal discharge which his prudent parent had had the foresight to leave in the hands of that learned gentleman, in case it should be, at any time, required on an emergency; his next proceeding was, to invest his whole stock of ready money, in the purchase of five-and-twenty gallons of mild porter: which he himself dispensed on the racket ground to everybody who would partake of it; this done, he hurra'd in divers parts of the building until he lost his voice, and then quietly relapsed into his usual collected and philosophical condition.

At three o'clock that afternoon, Mr Pickwick took a last look at his little room, and made his way, as well as he could, through the throng of debtors who pressed eagerly forward to shake him by the hand, until he reached the lodge steps. He turned here, to look about him, and his eye lightened as he did so. In all the crowd of wan, emaciated faces, he saw not one which was not the happier for his sympathy and charity.

'Perker,' said Mr Pickwick, beckoning one young man towards him, 'this is Mr Jingle, whom I spoke to you about.'

'Very good, my dear sir,' replied Perker, looking hard at Jingle. 'You will see me again, young man, to-morrow. I hope you may live to remember and feel deeply, what I shall have to communicate, sir.'

Jingle bowed respectfully, trembled very much as he took Mr Pickwick's proffered hand, and withdrew.

'Job you know, I think?' said Mr Pickwick, presenting that gentleman.

'I know the rascal,' replied Perker, good-humouredly. 'See after your friend, and be in the way to-morrow at one. Do you hear? Now, is there anything more?'

'Nothing,' rejoined Mr Pickwick. 'You have delivered the little parcel I gave you for your old landlord, Sam?'

'I have, sir,' replied Sam. 'He bust out a cryin', sir, and said you wos wery gen'rous and thoughtful, and he only wished you could have him innokilated for a gallopin' consumption, for his old friend as had lived here so long, wos dead, and he'd noweres to look for another.'

'Poor fellow, poor fellow!' said Mr Pickwick. 'God bless you, my friends!'

As Mr Pickwick uttered this adieu, the crowd raised a loud shout. Many among them were pressing forward to shake him by the hand, again, when he drew his arm through Perker's, and hurried from the prison: far more sad and melancholy, for the moment, than when he had first entered it. Alas! how many sad and unhappy beings had he left behind!

A happy evening was that, for, at least, one party in the George and Vulture; and light and cheerful were two of the hearts that emerged from its hospitable door next morning. The owners thereof were Mr Pickwick and Sam Weller, the former of whom was speedily deposited inside a comfortable post coach, with a little dickey behind, in which the latter mounted with great agility.

'Sir,' called out Mr Weller to his master.

'Well, Sam,' replied Mr Pickwick, thrusting his head out of the window.

'I wish them horses had been three months and better in the Fleet, sir.'

'Why, Sam?' inquired Mr Pickwick.

'Wy, sir,' exclaimed Mr Weller, rubbing his hands, 'how they would go if they had been!'

CHAPTER 48

Relates how Mr Pickwick, with the Assistance of Samuel Weller, essayed to soften the heart of Mr Benjamin Allen, and to mollify the wrath of Mr Robert Sawyer

Mr Ben Allen and Mr Bob Sawyer sat together in the little surgery behind the shop, discussing minced veal and future prospects, when the discourse, not unnaturally, turned upon the practice acquired by Bob the aforesaid, and his present chances of deriving a competent independence from the honourable profession to which he had devoted himself.

' – Which, I think,' observed Mr Bob Sawyer, pursuing the thread of the subject, 'which, I think, Ben, are rather dubious.'

'What's rather dubious?' inquired Mr Ben Allen, at the same time sharpening his intellects with a draught of beer. 'What's dubious?'

'Why, the chances,' responded Mr Bob Sawyer.

'I forgot,' said Mr Ben Allen. 'The beer has reminded me that I forgot, Bob – yes; they *are* dubious.'

'It's wonderful how the poor people patronise me,' said Mr Bob Sawyer, reflectively. 'They knock me up, at all hours of the night; they take medicine to an extent which I should have conceived impossible; they put on blisters and leeches with a perseverance worthy of a better cause; they make additions to their families, in a manner which is quite awful. Six of those last-named little promissory notes,[1] all due on the same day, Ben, and all intrusted to me!'

'It's very gratifying, isn't it?' said Mr Ben Allen, holding his plate for some more minced veal.

'Oh, very,' replied Bob; 'only not quite so much so, as the confidence of patients with a shilling or two to spare, would be. This business was capitally described in the advertisement, Ben. It is a practice, a very extensive practice – and that's all.'

'Bob,' said Mr Ben Allen, laying down his knife and fork, and fixing his eyes on the visage of his friend: 'Bob, I'll tell you what it is.'

'What is it?' inquired Mr Bob Sawyer.

'You must make yourself, with as little delay as possible, master of Arabella's one thousand pounds.'

'Three per cent. consolidated Bank annuities, now standing in her name in the book or books of the Governor and Company of the Bank of England,' added Bob Sawyer, in legal phraseology.

'Exactly so,' said Ben. 'She has it when she comes of age, or marries. She wants a year of coming of age, and if you plucked up a spirit she needn't want a month of being married.'

'She's a very charming and delightful creature,' quoth Mr Robert Sawyer, in reply; 'and has only one fault that I know of, Ben. It happens, unfortunately, that that single blemish is a want of taste. She don't like me.'

'It's my opinion that she don't know what she does like,' said Mr Ben Allen, contemptuously.

'Perhaps not,' remarked Mr Bob Sawyer. 'But it's my opinion that she does know what she doesn't like, and that's of more importance.'

'I wish,' said Mr Ben Allen, setting his teeth together, and speaking more like a savage warrior who fed on raw wolf's flesh which he carved with his fingers, than a peaceable young gentleman who ate minced veal with a knife and fork, 'I wish I knew whether any rascal really has been tampering with her, and attempting to engage her affections. I think I should assassinate him, Bob.'

'I'd put a bullet in him, if I found him out,' said Mr Sawyer, stopping in the course of a long draught of beer, and looking malignantly out of the porter pot. 'If that didn't do his business, I'd extract it afterwards, and kill him that way.'

Mr Benjamin Allen gazed abstractedly on his friend for some minutes in silence, and then said:

'You have never proposed to her, point-blank, Bob?'

'No. Because I saw it would be of no use,' replied Mr Robert Sawyer.

'You shall do it, before you are twenty-four hours older,' retorted Ben, with desperate calmness. 'She *shall* have you, or I'll know the reason why. I'll exert my authority.'

'Well,' said Mr Bob Sawyer, 'we shall see.'

'We *shall* see, my friend,' replied Mr Ben Allen, fiercely. He paused for a few seconds, and added in a voice broken by emotion, 'You have loved her from a child, my friend. You loved her when we were boys at school together, and, even then, she was wayward, and slighted your young feelings. Do you recollect, with all the eagerness of a child's love, one day pressing upon her acceptance, two small caraway-seed biscuits and one sweet apple, neatly folded into a circular parcel with the leaf of a copybook?'

'I do,' replied Bob Sawyer.

'She slighted that, I think?' said Ben Allen.

'She did,' rejoined Bob. 'She said I had kept the parcel so long in the pockets of my corduroys, that the apple was unpleasantly warm.'

'I remember' said Mr Allen, gloomily. 'Upon which we ate it ourselves, in alternate bites.'

Bob Sawyer intimated his recollection of the circumstance last alluded to, by a melancholy frown; and the two friends remained for some time absorbed, each in his own meditations.

While these observations were being exchanged between Mr Bob Sawyer and Mr Benjamin Allen; and while the boy in the grey livery, marvelling at the unwonted prolongation of the dinner, cast an anxious look, from time to time, towards the glass door, distracted by inward misgivings regarding the amount of minced veal which would be ultimately reserved for his individual cravings; there rolled soberly on through the streets of Bristol, a private fly, painted of a sad green colour, drawn by a chubby sort of brown horse, and driven by a surly-looking man with his legs dressed like the legs of a groom, and his body attired in the coat of a coachman. Such appearances are common to many vehicles belonging to, and maintained by, old ladies of economic habits; and in this vehicle, sat an old lady who was its mistress and proprietor.

'Martin!' said the old lady, calling to the surly man, out of the front window.

'Well?' said the surly man, touching his hat to the old lady.

'Mr Sawyer's,' said the old lady.

'I was going there,' said the surly man.

The old lady nodded the satisfaction which this proof of the surly man's foresight imparted to her feelings; and the surly man giving a smart lash to the chubby horse, they all repaired to Mr Bob Sawyer's together.

'Martin!' said the old lady, when the fly stopped at the door of Mr Robert Sawyer late Nockemorf.

'Well?' said Martin.

'Ask the lad to step out, and mind the horse.'

'I'm going to mind the horse myself,' said Martin, laying his whip on the roof of the fly.

'I can't permit it, on any account,' said the old lady; 'your testimony will be very important, and I must take you into the house with me. You must not stir from my side during the whole interview. Do you hear?'

'I hear,' replied Martin.

'Well; what are you stopping for?'

'Nothing,' replied Martin. So saying, the surly man leisurely descended from the wheel, on which he had been poising himself on the tops of the toes of his right foot, and having summoned the boy in the grey livery opened the coach-door, flung down the steps, and thrusting in a hand enveloped in a dark wash-leather glove, pulled out the old lady with as much unconcern in his manner as if she were a bandbox.[2]

'Dear me!' exclaimed the old lady. 'I am so flurried, now I have got here, Martin, that I'm all in a tremble.'

Mr Martin coughed behind the dark wash-leather glove, but expressed no sympathy; so the old lady, composing herself, trotted up Mr Bob Sawyer's steps, and Mr Martin followed. Immediately on the old lady's entering the shop, Mr Benjamin Allen and Mr Bob Sawyer, who had been putting the spirits and water out of sight, and upsetting nauseous drugs to take off the smell of the tobacco-smoke, issued hastily forth in a transport of pleasure and affection.

'My dear aunt,' exclaimed Mr Ben Allen, 'how kind of you to look in upon us! Mr Sawyer, aunt; my friend Mr Bob Sawyer whom I have spoken to you about, regarding – you know, aunt.' And here Mr Ben Allen, who was not at the moment extraordinarily sober, added the word 'Arabella,' in what was meant to be a whisper, but which was an especially audible and distinct tone of speech, which nobody could avoid hearing, if anybody were so disposed.

'My dear Benjamin,' said the old lady, struggling with a great shortness of breath, and trembling from head to foot: 'don't be alarmed, my dear, but I think I had better speak to Mr Sawyer, alone, for a moment. Only for one moment.'

'Bob,' said Mr Ben Allen, 'will you take my aunt into the surgery?'

'Certainly,' responded Bob, in a most professional voice. 'Step this way, my dear ma'am. Don't be frightened ma'am. We shall be able to set you to rights in a very short time, I have no doubt, ma'am. Here, my dear ma'am. Now then!' With this, Mr Bob Sawyer having handed the old lady to a chair, shut the door, drew another chair close to her, and waited to hear detailed the symptoms of some disorder from which he saw in perspective a long train of profits and advantages.

The first thing the old lady did, was to shake her head a great many times, and begin to cry.

'Nervous,' said Bob Sawyer complacently. 'Camphor-julep[3] and water three times a-day, and composing draught at night.'

'I don't know how to begin, Mr Sawyer,' said the old lady. 'It is so very painful and distressing.'

'You need not begin, ma'am,' rejoined Mr Bob Sawyer. 'I can anticipate all you would say. The head is in fault.'

'I should be very sorry to think it was the heart,' said the old lady, with a slight groan.

'Not the slightest danger of that, ma'am,' replied Bob Sawyer. 'The stomach is the primary cause.'

'Mr Sawyer!' exclaimed the old lady, starting.

'Not the least doubt of it, ma'am,' rejoined Bob, looking wondrous wise. 'Medicine, in time, my dear ma'am, would have prevented it all.'

'Mr Sawyer,' said the old lady, more flurried than before, 'this conduct is either great impertinence to one in my situation, sir, or it arises from your not understanding the object of my visit. If it had been in the power of medicine, or any foresight I could have used, to prevent what has occurred, I should certainly have done so. I had better see my nephew at once,' said the old lady, twirling her reticule indignantly, and rising as she spoke.

'Stop a moment, ma'am,' said Bob Sawyer; 'I'm afraid I have not understood you. What *is* the matter, ma'am?'

'My niece, Mr Sawyer,' said the old lady: 'your friend's sister.'

'Yes, ma'am,' said Bob, all impatience; for the old lady, although much agitated, spoke with the most tantalising deliberation, as old ladies often do. 'Yes, ma'am.'

'Left my home, Mr Sawyer, three days ago, on a pretended visit to my sister, another aunt of hers, who keeps the large boarding-school just beyond the third mile-stone where there is a very large laburnum tree and an oak gate,' said the old lady, stopping in this place to dry her eyes.

'Oh, devil take the laburnum tree! ma'am,' said Bob, quite forgetting his professional dignity in his anxiety. 'Get on a little faster; put a little more steam on, ma'am, pray.'

'This morning,' said the old lady, slowly, 'this morning, she—'

'She came back, ma'am, I suppose,' said Bob, with great animation. 'Did she come back?'

'No, she did not; she wrote,' replied the old lady.

'What did she say?' inquired Bob, eagerly.

'She said, Mr Sawyer,' replied the old lady – 'and it is this, I want you to prepare Benjamin's mind for, gently and by degrees; she said that she was – I have got the letter in my pocket, Mr Sawyer, but my glasses are in the carriage, and I should only waste your time if I attempted to point out the passage to you, without them; she said, in short, Mr Sawyer, that she was married.'

'What!' said, or rather shouted, Mr Bob Sawyer.

'Married,' repeated the old lady.

Mr Bob Sawyer stopped to hear no more; but darting from the surgery into the outer shop, cried in a stentorian voice, 'Ben, my boy, she's bolted!'

Mr Ben Allen, who had been slumbering behind the counter, with his head half a foot or so below his knees, no sooner heard this appalling communication, than he made a precipitate rush at Mr Martin, and, twisting his hand in the neck-cloth of that taciturn servitor, expressed an intention of choking him where he stood. This intention, with a promptitude often the effect of desperation, he at once commenced carrying into execution, with much vigour and surgical skill.

Mr Martin, who was a man of few words and possessed but little power of eloquence or persuasion, submitted to this operation with a very calm and agreeable expression of countenance, for some seconds; finding, however, that it threatened speedily to lead to a result which would place it beyond his power to claim any wages, board or otherwise, in all time to come, he muttered an inarticulate remonstrance and felled Mr Benjamin Allen to the ground. As that gentleman had his hands entangled in his cravat, he had no alternative but to follow him to the floor. There they both lay struggling, when the shop door opened, and the party was increased by the arrival of two most unexpected visitors: to wit, Mr Pickwick, and Mr Samuel Weller.

The impression at once produced on Mr Weller's mind by what he saw, was, that Mr Martin was hired by the establishment of Sawyer late Nockemorf, to take strong medicine, or to go into fits and be experimentalised upon, or to swallow poison now and then with the view of testing the efficacy of some new antidotes, or to do something or other to promote the great science of medicine, and gratify the ardent spirit of inquiry burning in the bosoms of its two young professors. So, without presuming to interfere, Sam stood perfectly still, and looked on, as if he were mightily interested in the result of the then pending experiment. Not so, Mr Pickwick. He at once threw himself on the astonished combatants, with his accustomed energy, and loudly called upon the by-standers to interpose.

This roused Mr Bob Sawyer, who had been hitherto quite paralysed by the frenzy of his companion. With that gentleman's assistance, Mr Pickwick raised Ben Allen to his feet. Mr Martin finding himself alone on the floor, got up, and looked about him.

'Mr Allen,' said Mr Pickwick, 'what is the matter, sir?'

'Never mind, sir!' replied Mr Allen, with haughty defiance.

'What is it?' inquired Mr Pickwick, looking at Bob Sawyer. 'Is he unwell?'

Before Bob could reply, Mr Ben Allen seized Mr Pickwick by the hand, and murmured, in sorrowful accents, 'My sister, my dear sir; my sister.'

'Oh, is that all!' said Mr Pickwick. 'We shall easily arrange that matter, I hope. Your sister is safe and well, and I am here, my dear sir, to—'

'Sorry to do anythin' as may cause an interruption to such wery pleasant proceedin's, as the king said wen he dissolved the parliament,' interposed Mr Weller, who had been peeping through the glass door; 'but there's another experiment here, sir. Here's a wenerable old lady a lyin' on the carpet waitin' for dissection, or galwinism,[4] or some other rewivin' and scientific inwention.'

'I forgot,' exclaimed Mr Ben Allen. 'It is my aunt.'

'Dear me!' said Mr Pickwick. 'Poor lady! Gently Sam, gently.'

'Strange sitivation for one o' the family,' observed Sam Weller, hoisting the aunt into a chair. 'Now, depitty Sawbones, bring out the wollatilly!'⁵

The latter observation was addressed to the boy in grey, who, having handed over the fly to the care of the street-keeper, had come back to see what all the noise was about. Between the boy in grey, and Mr Bob Sawyer, and Mr Benjamin Allen (who having frightened his aunt into a fainting fit, was affectionately solicitous for her recovery) the old lady was, at length, restored to consciousness; then Mr Ben Allen, turning with a puzzled countenance to Mr Pickwick, asked him what he was about to say, when he had been so alarmingly interrupted.

'We are all friends here, I presume?' said Mr Pickwick, clearing his voice, and looking towards the man of few words with the surly countenance, who drove the fly with the chubby horse.

This reminded Mr Bob Sawyer that the boy in grey was looking on, with eyes wide open, and greedy ears. The incipient chemist having been lifted up by his coat collar, and dropped outside the door, Bob Sawyer assured Mr Pickwick that he might speak without reserve.

'Your sister, my dear sir,' said Mr Pickwick, turning to Benjamin Allen, 'is in London; well and happy.'

'Her happiness is no object to me, sir,' said Mr Benjamin Allen, with a flourish of the hand.

'Her husband *is* an object to *me*, sir,' said Bob Sawyer. 'He shall be an object to me, sir, at twelve paces, and a very pretty object I'll make of him, sir – a mean-spirited scoundrel!' This, as it stood, was a very pretty denunciation, and magnanimous withal; but Mr Bob Sawyer rather weakened its effect, by winding up with some general observations concerning the punching of heads and knocking out of eyes, which were commonplace by comparison.

'Stay, sir,' said Mr, Pickwick; 'before you apply those epithets to the gentleman in question, consider, dispassionately, the extent of his fault, and above all remember that he is a friend of mine.'

'What!' said Mr Bob Sawyer.

'His name!' cried Ben Allen. 'His name!'

'Mr Nathaniel Winkle,' said Mr Pickwick.

Mr Benjamin Allen deliberately crushed his spectacles beneath the heel of his boot, and having picked up the pieces, and put them into three separate pockets, folded his arms, bit his lips, and looked in a threatening manner at the bland features of Mr Pickwick.

'Then it's you, is it, sir, who have encouraged and brought about this match?' inquired Mr Benjamin Allen at length.

'And it's this gentleman's servant, I suppose,' interrupted the old lady, 'who has been skulking about my house, and endeavouring to entrap my servants to conspire against their mistress. Martin!'

'Well?' said the surly man, coming forward.

'Is that the young man you saw in the lane, whom you told me about, this morning?'

Mr Martin, who, as it has already appeared, was a man of few words, looked at Sam Weller, nodded his head, and growled forth, 'That's the man!' Mr Weller, who was never proud, gave a smile of friendly recognition as his eyes encountered those of the surly groom, and admitted, in courteous terms, that he had 'knowed him afore.'

'And this is the faithful creature,' exclaimed Mr Ben Allen, 'whom I had nearly suffocated! Mr Pickwick, how dare you allow your fellow to be employed in the abduction of my sister? I demand that you explain this matter, sir.'

'Explain it, sir!' cried Bob Sawyer, fiercely.

'It's a conspiracy,' said Ben Allen.

'A regular plant,' added Mr Bob Sawyer.

'A disgraceful imposition,' observed the old lady.

'Nothing but a do,' remarked Martin.

'Pray hear me,' urged Mr Pickwick, as Mr Ben Allen fell into a chair that patients were bled in, and gave way to his pocket-handkerchief. 'I have rendered no assistance in this matter, beyond that of being present at one interview between the young people, which I could not prevent, and from which I conceived my presence would remove any slight colouring of impropriety that it might otherwise have had; this is the whole share I have taken in the transaction, and I had no suspicion that an immediate marriage was even contemplated. Though, mind,' added Mr Pickwick, hastily checking himself, 'mind, I do not say I should have prevented it, if I *had* known that it was intended.'

'You hear that, all of you; you hear that?' said Mr Benjamin Allen.

'I hope they do,' mildly observed Mr Pickwick, looking round, 'and,' added that gentleman: his colour mounting as he spoke: 'I hope they hear this, sir, also. That from what has been stated to me, sir, I assert that you were by no means justified in attempting to force your sister's inclinations as you did, and that you should rather have endeavoured by your kindness and forbearance to have supplied the place of other nearer relations whom she has never known, from a child. As regards my young friend, I must beg to add, that in every point of worldly advantage, he is, at least, on an equal footing with yourself, if not on a much better one, and that unless I hear this question discussed with becoming temper and moderation, I decline hearing any more said upon the subject.'

'I wish to make a wery few remarks in addition to wot has been put forard by the honorable gen'l'm'n as has jist give over,' said Mr Weller, stepping forth, 'wich is this here: a indiwidual in company has called me a feller.'

'That has nothing whatever to do with the matter, Sam,' interposed Mr Pickwick. 'Pray hold your tongue.'

'I ain't a goin' to say nothin' on that ere pint, sir,' replied Sam, 'but merely this here. P'raps that gen'l'm'n may think as there wos a priory 'tachment; but there worn't nothin' o' the sort, for the young lady said, in the wery beginnin' o' the keepin' company, that she couldn't abide him. Nobody's cut him out, and it 'ud ha' been jist the wery same for him if the young lady had never seen Mr Vinkle. That's wot I wished to say, sir, and I hope I've now made that 'ere gen'l'm'n's mind easy.'

A short pause followed these consolatory remarks of Mr Weller. Then Mr Ben Allen rising from his chair, protested that he would never see Arabella's face again: while Mr Bob Sawyer, despite Sam's flattering assurance, vowed dreadful vengeance on the happy bridegroom.

But, just when matters were at their height, and threatening to remain so, Mr Pickwick found a powerful assistant in the old lady, who, evidently much struck by the mode in which he had advocated her niece's cause, ventured to approach Mr Benjamin Allen with a few comforting reflections, of which the chief were, that after all, perhaps, it was well it was no worse; the least said the soonest mended, and upon her word she did not know that it was so very bad after all; what was over couldn't be begun, and what couldn't be cured must be endured: with various other assurances of the like novel and strengthening description. To all of these, Mr Benjamin Allen replied that he meant no disrespect to his aunt, or anybody there, but if it were all the same to them, and they would allow him to have his own way, he would rather have the pleasure of hating his sister till death, and after it.

At length, when this determination had been announced half a hundred times, the old lady suddenly bridling up and looking very majestic, wished to know what she had done that no respect was to be paid to her years or station, and that she should be obliged to beg and pray, in that way, of her own nephew, whom she remembered about five-and-twenty years before he was born, and whom she had known, personally, when he hadn't a tooth in his head? To say nothing of her presence on the first occasion of his having his hair cut, and assistance at numerous other times and ceremonies during his babyhood, of sufficient importance to found a claim upon his affection, obedience, and sympathies, for ever.

While the good lady was bestowing this objurgation on Mr Ben Allen, Bob Sawyer and Mr Pickwick had retired in close conversation to the inner room, where Mr Sawyer was observed to apply himself several times to the mouth of a black bottle, under the influence of which, his features gradually assumed a cheerful and even jovial expression. And at last he emerged from the room, bottle in hand, and, remarking that he was very sorry to say he had been making a fool of himself, begged to propose the health and happiness of Mr and Mrs Winkle, whose felicity, so far from envying, he would be the first to congratulate them upon. Hearing this, Mr Ben Allen suddenly arose from his chair, and, seizing the black bottle, drank the toast so heartily, that, the liquor being strong, he became nearly as black in the face as the bottle. Finally, the black bottle went round till it was empty, and there was so much shaking of hands and interchanging of compliments, that even the metal-visaged Mr Martin condescended to smile.

'And now,' said Bob Sawyer, rubbing his hands, 'we'll have a jolly night.'

'I am sorry,' said Mr Pickwick, 'that I must return to my inn. I have not been accustomed to fatigue lately, and my journey has tired me exceedingly.'

'You'll take some tea, Mr Pickwick?' said the old lady, with irresistible sweetness.

'Thank you, I would rather not,' replied that gentleman. The truth is, that the old lady's evidently increasing admiration, was Mr Pickwick's principal inducement for going away. He thought of Mrs Bardell; and every glance of the old lady's eyes threw him into a cold perspiration.

As Mr Pickwick could by no means be prevailed upon to stay, it was arranged at once, on his own proposition, that Mr Benjamin Allen should accompany him on his journey to the elder Mr Winkle's, and that the coach should be at the door, at nine o'clock next morning. He then took his leave, and, followed by Samuel Weller, repaired to the Bush. It is worthy of remark, that Mr Martin's face was horribly convulsed as he shook hands with Sam at parting, and that he gave vent to a smile and an oath simultaneously: from which tokens it has been inferred by those who were best acquainted with that gentleman's peculiarities, that he expressed himself much pleased with Mr Weller's society, and requested the honor of his further acquaintance.

'Shall I order a private room, sir?' inquired Sam, when they reached the Bush.

'Why, no, Sam,' replied Mr Pickwick; 'as I dined in the coffee room, and shall go to bed soon, it is hardly worth while. See who there is in the travellers' room, Sam.'

Mr Weller departed on his errand, and presently returned to say, that there was only a gentleman with one eye: and that he and the landlord were drinking a bowl of bishop together.

'I will join them,' said Mr Pickwick.

'He's a queer customer, the vun-eyed vun, sir,' observed Mr Weller, as he led the way. 'He's a gammonin' that 'ere landlord, he is, sir, till he don't rightly know wether he's a standing on the soles of his boots or the crown of his hat.'

The individual to whom this observation referred, was sitting at the upper end of the room when Mr Pickwick entered, and was smoking a large Dutch pipe, with his eye intently fixed on the round face of the landlord: a jolly looking old personage, to whom he had recently been relating some tale of wonder, as was testified by sundry disjointed exclamations of, 'Well, I wouldn't have believed it! The strangest thing I ever heard! Couldn't have supposed it possible!' and other expressions of astonishment which burst spontaneously from his lips, as he returned the fixed gaze of the one-eyed man.

'Servant, sir,' said the one-eyed man to Mr Pickwick. 'Fine night, sir.'

'Very much so indeed,' replied Mr Pickwick, as the waiter placed a small decanter of brandy, and some hot water before him.

While Mr Pickwick was mixing his brandy and water, the one-eyed man looked round at him earnestly, from time to time, and at length said:

'I think I've seen you before.'

'I don't recollect you,' rejoined Mr Pickwick.

'I dare say not,' said the one-eyed man. 'You didn't know me, but I knew two friends of yours that were stopping at the Peacock at Eatanswill, at the time of the Election.'

'Oh, indeed!' exclaimed Mr Pickwick.

'Yes,' rejoined the one-eyed man. 'I mentioned a little circumstance to them about a friend of mine of the name of Tom Smart. Perhaps you've heard them speak of it.'

'Often,' rejoined Mr Pickwick, smiling. 'He was your uncle, I think?'

'No, no; only a friend of my uncle's,' replied the one-eyed man.

'He was a wonderful man, that uncle of yours, though,' remarked the landlord shaking his head.

'Well, I think he was, I think I may say he was,' answered the one-eyed man. 'I could tell you a story about that same uncle, gentlemen, that would rather surprise you.'

'Could you?' said Mr Pickwick. 'Let us hear it, by all means.'

The one-eyed Bagman ladled out a glass of negus from the bowl, and drank it; smoked a long whiff out of the Dutch pipe; and then, calling to Sam Weller who was lingering near the door, that he needn't go away unless he wanted to, because the story was no secret, fixed his eye upon the landlord's and proceeded, in the words of the next chapter.

CHAPTER 49

Containing the Story of the Bagman's Uncle

'My uncle, gentlemen,' said the bagman, 'was one of the merriest, pleasantest, cleverest fellows that ever lived. I wish you had known him, gentlemen. On second thoughts, gentlemen, I *don't* wish you had known him, for if you had, you would have been all, by this time, in the ordinary course of nature, if not dead, at all events so near it, as to have taken to stopping at home and giving up company: which would have deprived me of the inestimable pleasure of addressing you at this moment. Gentlemen, I wish your fathers and mothers had known my uncle. They would have been amazingly fond of him, especially your respectable mothers; I know they would. If any two of his numerous virtues predominated over the many that adorned his character, I should say they were his mixed punch and his after supper song. Excuse my dwelling on these melancholy recollections of departed worth; you won't see a man like my uncle every day in the week.

'I have always considered it a great point in my uncle's character, gentlemen, that he was the intimate friend and companion of Tom Smart, of the great house of Bilson and Slum, Cateaton Street, City. My uncle collected for Tiggin and Welps, but for a long time he went pretty near the same journey as Tom; and the very first night they met, my uncle took a fancy for Tom, and Tom took a fancy for my uncle. They made a bet of a new hat before they had known each other half an hour, who should brew the best quart of punch and drink it the quickest. My uncle was judged to have won the making, but Tom Smart beat him in the drinking by about half a salt-spoon-full. They took another quart a-piece to drink each other's health in, and were staunch friends ever afterwards. There's a destiny in these things, gentlemen; we can't help it.

'In personal appearance, my uncle was a trifle shorter than the middle size; he was a thought stouter too, than the ordinary run of people, and perhaps his face might be a shade redder. He had the jolliest face you ever saw, gentlemen: something like Punch, with a handsomer nose and chin; his eyes were always twinkling and sparkling with good humour; and a smile – not one of your unmeaning wooden grins, but a real, merry, hearty, good-tempered smile – was perpetually on his countenance. He was pitched out of his gig once, and knocked, head first, against a mile-stone. There he lay, stunned, and so cut about the face with some gravel which had been heaped up alongside it, that, to use my uncle's own strong expression, if his mother could have revisited the earth, she wouldn't have known him. Indeed, when I come to think of the matter, gentlemen, I feel pretty sure she wouldn't, for she died when my uncle was two years and seven months old, and I think it's very likely that, even without the gravel, his top-boots would have puzzled the good lady not a little: to say nothing of his jolly red face. However, there he lay, and I have heard my uncle say, many a time, that the man said who picked him up that he was smiling as merrily as if he had tumbled out for a treat, and that after they had bled him, the first faint glimmerings of returning animation, were, his jumping up in bed, bursting out into a loud laugh, kissing the young woman who held the basin, and demanding a mutton chop and a pickled walnut. He was very fond of pickled walnuts, gentlemen. He said he always found that, taken without vinegar, they relished the beer.

'My uncle's great journey was in the fall of the leaf, at which time he collected debts, and took orders, in the north: going from London to Edinburgh, from Edinburgh to Glasgow, from Glasgow back to Edinburgh, and thence to London by the smack. You are to understand that his second visit to Edinburgh was for his own pleasure. He used to go back for a week, just to look up his old friends; and what with breakfasting with this one, lunching with that, dining with a third, and supping with another, a pretty tight week he used to make of it. I don't know whether any of you, gentlemen, ever partook of a real substantial hospitable Scotch breakfast, and then went out to a slight lunch of a bushel of oysters, a dozen or so of bottled ale, and a noggin or two of whiskey to close up with. If you ever did, you will agree with me that it requires a pretty strong head to go out to dinner and supper afterwards.

'But, bless your hearts and eye-brows, all this sort of thing was nothing to my uncle! He was so well seasoned, that it was mere child's play. I have heard him say that he could see the Dundee people out, any day, and walk home afterwards without staggering; and yet the Dundee people have as strong heads and as strong punch, gentlemen, as you are likely to meet with, between the poles. I have heard of a Glasgow man and a Dundee man drinking against each other for fifteen hours at a sitting. They were both suffocated, as nearly as could be ascertained, at the same moment, but with this trifling exception, gentlemen, they were not a bit the worse for it.

'One night, within four-and-twenty hours of the time when he had settled to take shipping for London, my uncle supped at the house of a very old friend of his, a Baillie[1] Mac something and four syllables after it, who lived in the old town of Edinburgh. There were the baillie's wife, and the baillie's three daughters, and the baillie's grown-up son, and three or four stout, bushy eye-browed, canny old Scotch fellows, that the baillie had got together to do honour to my uncle, and help to make merry. It was a glorious supper. There were kippered[2] salmon, and Finnan haddocks, and a lamb's head, and a haggis – a celebrated Scotch dish, gentlemen, which my uncle used to say always looked to him, when it came to table, very much like a cupid's stomach – and a great many other things besides, that I forget the names of, but very good things notwithstanding. The lassies were pretty and agreeable; the baillie's wife was one of the best creatures that ever lived; and my uncle was in thoroughly good cue. The consequence of which was, that the young ladies tittered and giggled, and the old lady laughed out loud, and the baillie and the other old fellows roared till they were red in the face, the whole mortal time. I don't quite recollect how many tumblers of whiskey toddy each man drank after supper; but this I know, that about one o'clock in the morning, the baillie's grown-up son became insensible while attempting the first verse of "Willie brewed a peck o' maut;"[3] and he having been, for half an hour before, the only other man visible above the mahogany, it occurred to my uncle that it was almost time to think about going: especially as drinking had set in at seven o'clock, in order that he might get home at a decent hour. But, thinking it might not be quite polite to go just then, my uncle voted himself into the chair, mixed another glass, rose to propose his own health, addressed himself in a neat and complimentary speech, and drank the toast with great enthusiasm. Still nobody woke; so my uncle took a little drop more – neat this time, to prevent the toddy from disagreeing with him – and, laying violent hands on his hat, sallied forth into the street.

'It was a wild gusty night when my uncle closed the baillie's door, and settling his hat firmly on his head, to prevent the wind from taking it, thrust his hands into his pockets, and looking upward, took a short survey of the state of the weather. The clouds were drifting over the moon at their giddiest speed: at one time wholly obscuring her: at another, suffering her to burst forth in full splendour and shed her light on all the objects around: anon, driving over her again, with increased velocity, and shrouding everything in darkness. "Really, this won't do," said my uncle, addressing himself to the weather, as if he felt himself personally offended. "This is not at all the kind of thing for my voyage. It will not do, at any price," said my uncle very impressively. Having repeated this, several times, he recovered his balance with some difficulty – for he was rather giddy with looking up into the sky so long – and walked merrily on.

'The baillie's house was in the Canongate, and my uncle was going to the other end of Leith Walk,[4] rather better than a mile's journey. On either side of him, there shot up against the dark sky, tall gaunt straggling houses, with time-stained fronts, and windows that seemed to have shared the lot of eyes in mortals, and to have grown dim and sunken with age. Six, seven, eight stories high, were the houses; story piled above story, as children build with cards – throwing their dark shadows over the roughly paved road, and making the dark night darker. A few oil lamps were scattered at long distances, but they only served to mark the dirty entrance to some narrow close, or to show where a common stair communicated, by steep and intricate windings, with the various flats above.

Glancing at all these things with the air of a man who had seen them too often before, to think them worthy of much notice now, my uncle walked up the middle of the street, with a thumb in each waistcoat pocket, indulging from time to time in various snatches of song, chaunted forth with such good will and spirit, that the quiet honest folk started from their first sleep and lay trembling in bed till the sound died away in the distance; when, satisfying themselves that it was only some drunken ne'er-do-weel finding his way home, they covered themselves up warm and fell asleep again.

'I am particular in describing how my uncle walked up the middle of the street, with his thumbs in his waistcoat pockets, gentlemen, because, as he often used to say (and with great reason too) there is nothing at all extraordinary in this story, unless you distinctly understand at the beginning that he was not by any means of a marvellous or romantic turn.

'Gentlemen, my uncle walked on with his thumbs in his waistcoat pockets, taking the middle of the street to himself, and singing, now a verse of a love song, and then a verse of a drinking one, and when he was tired of both, whistling melodiously, until he reached the North Bridge, which, at this point, connects the old and new towns of Edinburgh. Here he stopped for a minute, to look at the strange irregular clusters of lights piled one above the other, and twinkling afar off so high, that they looked like stars, gleaming from the castle walls on the one side and the Calton Hill on the other, as if they illuminated veritable castles in the air; while the old picturesque town slept heavily on, in gloom and darkness below: its palace and chapel of Holyrood, guarded day and night, as a friend of my uncle's used to say, by old Arthur's Seat,[5] towering, surly and dark, like some gruff genius, over the ancient city he has watched so long. I say, gentlemen, my uncle stopped here, for a minute, to look about him; and then, paying a compliment to the weather which had a little cleared up, though the moon was sinking, walked on again, as royally as before; keeping the middle of the road with great dignity, and looking as if he would very much like to meet with somebody who would dispute possession of it with him. There was nobody at all disposed to contest the point, as it happened; and so, on he went, with his thumbs in his waistcoat pockets, like a lamb.

'When my uncle reached the end of Leith Walk, he had to cross a pretty large piece of waste ground which separated him from a short street which he had to turn down, to go direct to his lodging. Now, in this piece of waste ground, there was, at that time, an enclosure belonging to some wheelwright[6] who contracted with the Post-office for the purchase of old worn-out mail coaches; and my uncle, being very fond of coaches, old, young, or middle-aged, all at once took it into his head to step out of his road for no other purpose than to peep between the palings at these mails – about a dozen of which, he remembered to have seen crowded together in a very forlorn and dismantled state, inside. My uncle was a very enthusiastic, emphatic sort of person, gentlemen; so, finding that he could not obtain a good peep between the palings, he got over them, and sitting himself quietly down on an old axletree,[7] began to contemplate the mail coaches with a deal of gravity.

'There might be a dozen of them, or there might be more – my uncle was never quite certain on this point, and being a man of very scrupulous veracity about numbers, didn't like to say – but there they stood, all huddled together in the most desolate condition imaginable. The doors had been torn from their hinges and removed; the linings had been stripped off: only a shred hanging here and there by a rusty nail; the lamps were gone, the poles had long since vanished, the iron-work was rusty, the paint was worn away; the wind whistled through the chinks in the bare wood work; and the rain, which had collected on the roofs, fell, drop by drop, into the insides with a hollow and melancholy sound. They were the decaying skeletons of departed mails, and in that lonely place, at that time of night, they looked chill and dismal.

'My uncle rested his head upon his hands, and thought of the busy bustling people who had rattled about, years before, in the old coaches, and were now as silent and changed; he thought of the numbers of people to whom one of those crazy mouldering vehicles had borne, night after night, for many years, and through all weathers, the anxiously expected intelligence, the eagerly looked-for remittance, the promised assurance of health and safety, the sudden announcement of sickness and death. The merchant, the lover, the wife, the widow, the mother, the schoolboy, the very child who tottered to the door at the postman's knock – how had they all looked forward to the arrival of the old coach. And where were they all now!

'Gentlemen, my uncle used to *say* that he thought all this at the time, but I rather suspect he learnt it out of some book afterwards, for he distinctly stated that he fell into a kind of doze, as he sat on the old axletree looking at the decayed mail coaches, and that he was suddenly awakened by some deep church-bell striking two. Now, my uncle was never a fast thinker, and if he had thought all these things, I am quite certain it would have taken him till full half-past two o'clock, at the very least. I am, therefore, decidedly of opinion, gentlemen, that my uncle fell into the kind of doze, without having thought about any thing at all.

'Be this, as it may, a church bell struck two. My uncle woke, rubbed his eyes, and jumped up in astonishment.

'In one instant after the clock struck two, the whole of this deserted and quiet spot had become a scene of most extraordinary life and animation. The mail coach doors were on their hinges, the lining was replaced, the iron-work was as good as new, the paint was restored, the lamps were alight, cushions and great coats were on every coach box, porters were thrusting parcels into every boot, guards were stowing away letter-bags, hostlers were dashing pails of water against the renovated wheels; numbers of men were rushing about, fixing poles into every coach; passengers arrived, portmanteaus⁸ were handed up, horses were put to; in short, it was perfectly clear that every mail there, was to be off directly. Gentlemen, my uncle opened his eyes so wide at all this, that, to the very last moment of his life, he used to wonder how it fell out that he had ever been able to shut 'em again.

'"Now then!" said a voice, as my uncle felt a hand on his shoulder, "You're booked for one inside. You'd better get in."

'"*I* booked!" said my uncle, turning round.

'"Yes, certainly."

'My uncle, gentlemen, could say nothing; he was so very much astonished. The queerest thing of all, was, that although there was such a crowd of persons, and although fresh faces were pouring in, every moment, there was no telling where they came from. They seemed to start up, in some strange manner, from the ground, or the air, and disappear in the same way. When a porter had put his luggage in the coach, and received his fare, he turned round and was gone; and before my uncle had well begun to wonder what had become of him, half-a-dozen fresh ones started up, and staggered along under the weight of parcels which seemed big enough to crush them. The passengers were all dressed so oddly too! Large, broad-skirted laced coats with great cuffs and no collars; and wigs, gentlemen, – great formal wigs with a tie behind. My uncle could make nothing of it.

'"Now, *are* you going to get in?"' said the person who had addressed my uncle before. He was dressed as a mail guard, with a wig on his head and most enormous cuffs to his coat, and had a lantern in one hand, and a huge blunderbuss⁹ in the other, which he was going to stow away in his little arm-chest. "*Are* you going to get in, Jack Martin?" said the guard, holding the lantern to my uncle's face.

'"Hallo!" said my uncle, falling back a step or two. "That's familiar!"

'"It's so on the way-bill," replied the guard.

'"Isn't there a "Mister" before it?" said my uncle. For he felt, gentlemen, that for a guard he didn't know, to call him Jack Martin, was a liberty which the Post-office wouldn't have sanctioned if they had known it.

'"No, there is not," rejoined the guard coolly.

'"Is the fare paid?" inquired my uncle.

'"Of course it is," rejoined the guard.

'"It is, is it?" said my uncle. "Then here goes! Which coach?"

'"This," said the guard, pointing to an old-fashioned Edinburgh and London Mail, which had the steps down, and the door open. "Stop! Here are the other passengers. Let them get in first."

'As the guard spoke, there all at once appeared, right in front of my uncle, a young gentleman in a powdered wig, and a sky-blue coat trimmed with silver, made very full and broad in the skirts, which were lined with buckram.[10] Tiggin and Welps were in the printed calico and waistcoat piece line, gentlemen, so my uncle knew all the materials at once. He wore knee breeches, and a kind of leggings rolled up over his silk stockings, and shoes with buckles; he had ruffles at his wrists, a three-cornered hat on his head, and a long taper sword by his side. The flaps of his waistcoat came half way down his thighs, and the ends of his cravat reached to his waist. He stalked gravely to the coach-door, pulled off his hat, and held it above his head at arm's length: cocking his little finger in the air at the same time, as some affected people do, when they take a cup of tea. Then he drew his feet together, and made a low grave bow, and then put out his left hand. My uncle was just going to step forward, and shake it heartily, when he perceived that these attentions were directed, not towards him, but to a young lady who just then appeared at the foot of the steps, attired in an old-fashioned green velvet dress with a long waist and stomacher. She had no bonnet on her head, gentlemen, which was muffled in a black silk hood, but she looked round for an instant as she prepared to get into the coach, and such a beautiful face as she disclosed, my uncle had never seen – not even in a picture. She got into the coach, holding up her dress with one hand; and, as my uncle always said with a round oath, when he told the story, he wouldn't have

The Ghostly passengers in the ghost of a mail

believed it possible that legs and feet could have been brought to such a state of perfection unless he had seen them with his own eyes.

'But, in this one glimpse of the beautiful face, my uncle saw that the young lady cast an imploring look upon him, and that she appeared terrified and distressed. He noticed, too, that the young fellow in the powdered wig, notwithstanding his show of gallantry, which was all very fine and grand, clasped her tight by the wrist when she got in, and followed himself immediately afterwards. An uncommonly ill-looking fellow, in a close brown wig and a plum-coloured suit, wearing a very large sword, and boots up to his hips, belonged to the party; and when he sat himself down next to the young lady, who shrunk into a corner at his approach, my uncle was confirmed in his original impression that something dark and mysterious was going forward, or, as he always said himself, that "there was a screw loose somewhere." It's quite surprising how quickly he made up his mind to help the lady at any peril, if she needed help.

' "Death and lightning!" exclaimed the young gentleman, laying his hand upon his sword as my uncle entered the coach.

' "Blood and thunder!" roared the other gentleman. With this, he whipped his sword out, and made a lunge at my uncle without further ceremony. My uncle had no weapon about him, but with great dexterity he snatched the ill-looking gentleman's three-cornered hat from his head, and, receiving the point of his sword right through the crown, squeezed the sides together, and held it tight.

' "Pink him behind!" cried the ill-looking gentleman to his companion, as he struggled to regain his sword.

' "He had better not," cried my uncle, displaying the heel of one of his shoes, in a threatening manner. "I'll kick his brains out, if he has any, or fracture his skull if he hasn't." Exerting all his strength, at this moment, my uncle wrenched the ill-looking man's sword from his grasp, and flung it clean out of the coach-window; upon which the younger gentleman vociferated "Death and lightning!" again, and laid his hand upon the hilt of his sword, in a very fierce manner, but didn't draw it. Perhaps, gentlemen, as my uncle used to say with a smile, perhaps he was afraid of alarming the lady.

' "Now, gentlemen," said my uncle, taking his seat deliberately, "I don't want to have any death, with or without lightning, in a lady's presence, and we have had quite blood and thundering enough for one journey; so, if you please, we'll sit in our places like quiet insides. Here, guard, pick up that gentleman's carving-knife."

'As quickly as my uncle said the words, the guard appeared at the coach-window, with the gentleman's sword in his hand. He held up his lantern, and looked earnestly in my uncle's face, as he handed it in: when, by its light, my uncle saw, to his great surprise, that an immense crowd of mail-coach guards swarmed round the window, every one of whom had his eyes earnestly fixed upon him too. He had never seen such a sea of white faces, red bodies, and earnest eyes, in all his born days.

'"This is the strangest sort of thing I ever had anything to do with," thought my uncle; "allow me to return you your hat, sir."

'The ill-looking gentleman received his three-cornered hat in silence, looked at the hole in the middle with an inquiring air, and finally stuck it on the top of his wig with a solemnity the effect of which was a trifle impaired by his sneezing violently at the moment, and jerking it off again.

'"All right!" cried the guard with the lantern, mounting into his little seat behind. Away they went. My uncle peeped out of the coach-window as they emerged from the yard, and observed that the other mails, with coachmen, guards, horses, and passengers, complete, were driving round and round in circles, at a slow trot of about five miles an hour. My uncle burnt with indignation, gentlemen. As a commercial man, he felt that the mail bags were not to be trifled with, and he resolved to memorialise the Post-office on the subject, the very instant he reached London.

'At present, however, his thoughts were occupied with the young lady who sat in the farthest corner of the coach, with her face muffled closely in her hood; the gentleman with the sky-blue coat sitting opposite to her; the other man in the plum-coloured suit, by her side; and both watching her intently. If she so much as rustled the folds of her hood, he could hear the ill-looking man clap his hand upon his sword, and could tell by the other's breathing (it was so dark he couldn't see his face) that he was looking as big as if he were going to devour her at a mouthful. This roused my uncle more and more, and he resolved, come what come might, to see the end of it. He had a great admiration for bright eyes, and sweet faces, and pretty legs and feet; in short, he was fond of the whole sex. It runs in our family, gentlemen – so am I.

'Many were the devices which my uncle practised, to attract the lady's attention, or at all events, to engage the mysterious gentlemen in conversation. They were all in vain; the gentlemen wouldn't talk, and the lady didn't dare. He thrust his head out of the coach-window at intervals, and bawled out to know why they didn't go faster? But he called till he was hoarse; nobody paid the least attention to him. He leant back in the coach, and thought of the beautiful face, and the feet and legs. This answered better; it wiled away the time, and kept him from wondering where he was going, and how it was that he found himself in such an odd situation. Not that this would have worried him much, any way – he was a mighty free and easy, roving, devil-may-care sort of person, was my uncle, gentlemen.

'All of a sudden the coach stopped. "Hallo!" said my uncle, "What's in the wind now?"

'"Alight here," said the guard, letting down the steps.

'"Here!" cried my uncle.

'"Here," rejoined the guard.

'"I'll do nothing of the sort," said my uncle.

'"Very well, then stop where you are," said the guard.

'"I will," said my uncle.

'"Do," said the guard.

'The other passengers had regarded this colloquy with great attention, and, finding that my uncle was determined not to alight, the younger man squeezed past him, to hand the lady out. At this moment, the ill-looking man was inspecting the hole in the crown of his three-cornered hat. As the young lady brushed past, she dropped one of her gloves into my uncle's hand, and softly whispered, with her lips, so close to his face that he felt her warm breath on his nose, the single word "Help!" Gentlemen, my uncle leaped out of the coach at once, with such violence that it rocked on the springs again.

'"Oh! You've thought better of it, have you?" said the guard when he saw my uncle standing on the ground.

'My uncle looked at the guard for a few seconds, in some doubt whether it wouldn't be better to wrench his blunderbuss from him, fire it in the face of the man with the big sword, knock the rest of the company over the head with the stock, snatch up the young lady, and go off in the smoke. On second thoughts, however, he abandoned this plan, as being a shade too melodramatic in the execution, and followed the two mysterious men, who, keeping the lady between them, were now entering an old house in front of which the coach had stopped. They turned into the passage, and my uncle followed.

'Of all the ruinous and desolate places my uncle had ever beheld, this was the most so. It looked as if it had once been a large house of entertainment; but the roof had fallen in, in many places, and the stairs were steep, rugged, and broken. There was a huge fire-place in the room into which they walked, and the chimney was blackened with smoke; but no warm blaze lighted it up now. The white feathery dust of burnt wood was still strewed over the hearth, but the stove was cold, and all was dark and gloomy.

'"Well," said my uncle, as he looked about him, "a mail travelling at the rate of six miles and a half an hour, and stopping for an indefinite time at such a hole as this, is rather an irregular sort of proceeding I fancy. This shall be made known. I'll write to the papers."

'My uncle said this in a pretty loud voice, and in an open unreserved sort of manner, with the view of engaging the two strangers in conversation if he could. But, neither of them took any more notice of him than whispering to each other, and scowling at him as they did so. The lady was at the farther end of the room, and once she ventured to wave her hand, as if beseeching my uncle's assistance.

'At length the two strangers advanced a little, and the conversation began in earnest.

'"You don't know this is a private room; I suppose, fellow?" said the gentleman in sky-blue.

'"No, I do not, fellow," rejoined my uncle. "Only if this is a private room specially ordered for the occasion, I should think the public room must be a *very* comfortable one;" with this my uncle sat himself down in a high-backed chair, and took such an accurate measure of the gentleman, with his eyes, that Tiggin and Welps could have supplied him with printed calico for a suit, and not an inch too much or too little, from that estimate alone.

'"Quit this room," said both the men together, grasping their swords.

'"Eh?" said my uncle, not at all appearing to comprehend their meaning.

'"Quit the room, or you are a dead man," said the ill-looking fellow with the large sword, drawing it at the same time and flourishing it in the air.

'"Down with him!" cried the gentleman in sky-blue, drawing his sword also, and falling back two or three yards. "Down with him!" The lady gave a loud scream.

'Now, my uncle was always remarkable for great boldness, and great presence of mind. All the time that he had appeared so indifferent to what was going on, he had been looking slyly about, for some missile or weapon of defence, and at the very instant when the swords were drawn, he espied, standing in the chimney corner, an old basket-hilted rapier[11] in a rusty scabbard. At one bound, my uncle caught it in his hand, drew it, flourished it gallantly above his head, called aloud to the lady to keep out of the way, hurled the chair at the man in sky-blue, and the scabbard at the man in plum-colour, and taking advantage of the confusion, fell upon them both, pell-mell.

'Gentlemen, there is an old story – none the worse for being true – regarding a fine young Irish gentleman, who being asked if he could play the fiddle, replied he had no doubt he could, but he couldn't exactly say, for certain, because he had never tried. This is not inapplicable to my uncle and his fencing. He had never had a sword in his hand before, except once when he played Richard the Third at a private theatre: upon which occasion it was arranged with Richmond that he was to be run through, from behind, without showing fight at all. But here he was, cutting and slashing with two experienced swordsmen: thrusting and guarding and poking and slicing, and acquitting himself in the most manful and dexterous manner possible, although up to that time he had never been aware that he had the least notion of the science. It only shows how true the old saying is, that a man never knows what he can do, till he tries, gentlemen.

'The noise of the combat was terrific; each of the three combatants swearing like troopers, and their swords clashing with as much noise as if all the knives and steels in Newport market[12] were rattling together, at the same time. When it was at its very height, the lady (to encourage my uncle most probably) withdrew her hood entirely from her face, and disclosed a countenance of such dazzling beauty, that he would have fought against fifty men, to win one smile from it, and die. He had done wonders before, but now he began to powder away like a raving mad giant.

'At this very moment, the gentleman in sky-blue turning round, and seeing the young lady with her face uncovered, vented an exclamation of rage and jealousy, and, turning his weapon against her beautiful bosom, pointed a thrust at her heart, which caused my uncle to utter a cry of apprehension that made the building ring. The lady stepped lightly aside, and snatching the young man's sword from his hand, before he had recovered his balance, drove him to the wall, and running it through him, and the panelling, up to the very hilt, pinned him there, hard and fast. It was a splendid example. My uncle, with a loud shout of triumph, and a strength that was irresistible, made his adversary retreat in the same direction, and plunging the old rapier into the very centre of a large red flower in the pattern of his waistcoat, nailed him beside his friend; there they both stood, gentlemen, jerking their arms and legs about, in agony, like the toy-shop figures that are moved by a piece of packthread.[13] My uncle always said, afterwards, that this was one of the surest means he knew of, for disposing of an enemy; but it was liable to one objection on the ground of expense, inasmuch as it involved the loss of a sword for every man disabled.

'"The mail, the mail!" cried the lady, running up to my uncle and throwing her beautiful arms round his neck; "we may yet escape."

'"*May* !" cried my uncle; "why, my dear, there's nobody else to kill, is there?" My uncle was rather disappointed, gentlemen, for he thought a little quiet bit of love-making would be agreeable after the slaughtering, if it were only to change the subject.

'"We have not an instant to lose here," said the young lady, "He (pointing to the young gentleman in sky-blue) is the only son of the powerful Marquess of Filletoville."

'"Well then, my dear, I'm afraid he'll never come to the title," said my uncle, looking coolly at the young gentleman as he stood fixed up against the wall, in the cockchafer fashion[14] I have described. "You have cut off the entail,[15] my love."

'"I have been torn from my home and friends by these villains," said the young lady, her features glowing with indignation. "That wretch would have married me by violence in another hour."

'"Confound his impudence!" said my uncle, bestowing a very contemptuous look on the dying heir of Filletoville.

'"As you may guess from what you have seen," said the young lady, "the party were prepared to murder me if I appealed to any one for assistance. If their accomplices find us here, we are lost. Two minutes hence may be too late. The mail!" With these words, overpowered by her feelings, and the exertion of sticking the young Marquess of Filletoville, she sunk into my uncle's arms. My uncle caught her up, and bore her to the house-door. There stood the mail, with four long-tailed, flowing-maned, black horses, ready harnessed; but no coachman, no guard, no hostler even, at the horses' heads.

'Gentlemen, I hope I do no injustice to my uncle's memory, when I express my opinion, that although he was a bachelor, he *had* held some ladies in his arms, before this time; I believe indeed, that he had rather a habit of kissing barmaids; and I know, that in one or two instances, he had been seen by credible witnesses, to hug a landlady in a very perceptible manner. I mention the circumstance, to show what a very uncommon sort of person this beautiful young lady must have been, to have affected my uncle in the way she did; he used to say, that as her long dark hair trailed over his arm, and her beautiful dark eyes fixed themselves upon his face when she recovered, he felt so strange and nervous that his legs trembled beneath him. But, who can look in a sweet soft pair of dark eyes, without feeling queer? *I* can't, gentlemen. I am afraid to look at some eyes I know, and that's the truth of it.

'"You will never leave me," murmured the young lady.

'"Never," said my uncle. And he meant it too.

'"My dear preserver!" exclaimed the young lady. "My dear, kind, brave preserver!"

'"Don't," said my uncle, interrupting her.

'"Why?" inquired the young lady.

'"Because your mouth looks so beautiful when you speak," rejoined my uncle, "that I'm afraid I shall be rude enough to kiss it."

'The young lady put up her hand as if to caution my uncle not to do so, and said – no, she didn't say anything – she smiled. When you are looking at a pair of the most delicious lips in the world, and see them gently break into a roguish smile – if you are very near them, and nobody else by – you cannot better testify your admiration of their beautiful form and colour than by kissing them at once. My uncle did so, and I honour him for it.

'"Hark!" cried the young lady, starting. "The noise of wheels and horses!"

'"So it is," said my uncle, listening. He had a good ear for wheels, and the trampling of hoofs; but there appeared to be so many horses and carriages rattling towards them, from a distance, that it was impossible to form a guess at their number. The sound was like that of fifty breaks, with six blood cattle in each.

'"We are pursued!" cried the young lady, clasping her hands. "We are pursued. I have no hope but in you!"

'There was such an expression of terror in her beautiful face, that my uncle made up his mind at once. He lifted her into the coach, told her not to be frightened, pressed his lips to hers once more, and then advising her to draw up the window to keep the cold air out, mounted to the box.

'"Stay, love," cried the young lady.

'"What's the matter?" said my uncle, from the coach-box.

'"I want to speak to you," said the young lady; "only a word. Only one word, dearest."

'"Must I get down?" inquired my uncle. The lady made no answer, but she smiled again. Such a smile, gentlemen! It beat the other one, all to nothing. My uncle descended from his perch in a twinkling.

'"What is it, my dear?" said my uncle, looking in at the coach window. The lady happened to bend forward at the same time, and my uncle thought she looked more beautiful than she had done yet. He was very close to her just then, gentlemen, so he really ought to know.

'"What is it, my dear?" said my uncle.

'"Will you never love any one but me; never marry any one beside?" said the young lady.

'My uncle swore a great oath that he never would marry any body else, and the young lady drew in her head, and pulled up the window. He jumped upon the box, squared his elbows, adjusted the ribands, seized the whip which lay on the roof, gave one flick to the off leader, and away went the four long-tailed flowing-maned black horses, at fifteen good English miles an hour, with the old mail coach behind them. Whew! How they tore along!

'The noise behind grew louder. The faster the old mail went, the faster came the pursuers – men, horses, dogs, were leagued in the pursuit. The noise was frightful, but, above all, rose the voice of the young lady, urging my uncle on, and shrieking, "Faster! Faster!"

'They whirled past the dark trees, as feathers would be swept before a hurricane. Houses, gates, churches, haystacks, objects of every kind they shot by, with a velocity and noise like roaring waters suddenly let loose. Still the noise of pursuit grew louder, and still my uncle could hear the young lady wildly screaming, "Faster! Faster!"

'My uncle plied whip and rein, and the horses flew onward till they were white with foam; and yet the noise behind increased; and yet the young lady cried "Faster! Faster!" My uncle gave a loud stamp on the boot in the energy of the moment, and – found that it was grey morning, and he was sitting in the wheelwright's yard, on the box of an old Edinburgh mail, shivering with the cold and wet and stamping his feet to warm them! He got down, and looked eagerly inside for the beautiful young lady. Alas! There was neither door nor seat to the coach. It was a mere shell.

'Of course, my uncle knew very well that there was some mystery in the matter, and that everything had passed exactly as he used to relate it. He remained staunch to the great oath he had sworn to the beautiful young lady: refusing several eligible landladies on her account, and dying a bachelor at last. He always said, what a curious thing it was that he should have found out, by such a mere accident as his clambering over the palings, that the ghosts of mail-coaches and horses, guards, coachmen, and passengers, were in the habit of making journeys regularly every night. He used to add, that he believed he was the only living person who had ever been taken as a passenger on one of these excursions. And I think he was right, gentlemen – at least I never heard of any other.'

'I wonder what these ghosts of mail-coaches carry in their bags,' said the landlord, who had listened to the whole story with profound attention.

'The dead letters,[16] of course,' said the Bagman.

'Oh, ah! To be sure,' rejoined the landlord. 'I never thought of that.'

CHAPTER 50

How Mr Pickwick sped upon his Mission, and how he was reinforced in the Outset by a most unexpected Auxiliary

The horses were put to, punctually at a quarter before nine next morning, and Mr Pickwick and Sam Weller having each taken his seat, the one inside and the other out, the postillion[1] was duly directed to repair in the first instance to Mr Bob Sawyer's house, for the purpose of taking up Mr Benjamin Allen.

It was with feelings of no small astonishment, when the carriage drew up before the door with the red lamp, and the very legible inscription of 'Sawyer, late Nockemorf,' that Mr Pickwick saw, on popping his head out of the coach-window, the boy in the grey livery very busily employed in putting up the shutters: the which, being an unusual and an un-business-like proceeding at that hour of the morning, at once suggested to his mind, two inferences; the one, that some good friend and patient of Mr Bob Sawyer's was dead; the other, that Mr Bob Sawyer himself was bankrupt.

'What is the matter?' said Mr Pickwick to the boy.

'Nothing's the matter, sir,' replied the boy, expanding his mouth to the whole breadth of his countenance.

'All right, all right!' cried Bob Sawyer suddenly appearing at the door, with a small leathern knapsack, limp and dirty, in one hand, and a rough coat and shawl thrown over the other arm. 'I'm going, old fellow.'

'You!' exclaimed Mr Pickwick.

'Yes,' replied Bob Sawyer, 'and a regular expedition we'll make of it. Here, Sam! Look out!' Thus briefly bespeaking Mr Weller's attention, Mr Bob Sawyer jerked the leathern knapsack into the dickey, where it was immediately stowed away, under the seat, by Sam, who regarded the proceeding with great admiration. This done, Mr Bob Sawyer, with the assistance of the boy, forcibly worked himself into the rough coat, which was a few sizes too small for him, and then advancing to the coach window, thrust in his head, and laughed boisterously.

'What a start it is, isn't it!' cried Bob, wiping the tears out of his eyes, with one of the cuffs of the rough coat.

'My dear sir,' said Mr Pickwick, with some embarrassment, 'I had no idea of your accompanying us.'

'No, that's just the very thing,' replied Bob, seizing Mr Pickwick by the lappel of his coat. 'That's the joke.'

'Oh, that's the joke?' said Mr Pickwick.

'Of course,' replied Bob. 'It's the whole point of the thing, you know – that, and leaving the business to take care of itself as it seems to have made up its mind not to take care of me.' With this explanation of the phenomenon of the shutters, Mr Bob Sawyer pointed to the shop, and relapsed into an ecstasy of mirth.

'Bless me, you are surely not mad enough to think of leaving your patients without anybody to attend them!' remonstrated Mr Pickwick in a very serious tone.

'Why not?' asked Bob, in reply. 'I shall save by it, you know. None of them ever pay. Besides,' said Bob, lowering his voice to a confidential whisper, 'they will be all the better for it; for, being nearly out of drugs, and not able to increase my account just now, I should have been obliged to give them calomel² all round, and it would have been certain to have disagreed with some of them. So it's all for the best.'

There was a philosophy, and a strength of reasoning, about this reply, which Mr Pickwick was not prepared for. He paused a few moments, and added, less firmly than before –

'But this chaise, my young friend, will only hold two; and I am pledged to Mr Allen.'

'Don't think of me for a minute,' replied Bob. 'I've arranged it all; Sam and I will share the dickey between us. Look here. This little bill is to be wafered on the shop door: "Sawyer, late Nocke-morf. Enquire of Mrs Cripps over the way." Mrs Cripps is my boy's mother. "Mr Sawyer's very sorry," says Mrs Cripps, "couldn't help it – fetched away early this morning to a consultation of the very first surgeons in the country – couldn't do without him – would have him at any price – tremendous operation." The fact is,' said Bob in conclusion, 'it'll do me more good than otherwise, I expect. If it gets into one of the local papers, it will be the making of me. Here's Ben; now then, jump in!'

With these hurried words, Mr Bob Sawyer pushed the postboy on one side, jerked his friend into the vehicle, slammed the door, put up the steps, wafered the bill on the street door, locked it, put the key in his pocket, jumped into the dickey, gave the word for starting, and did the whole with such extraordinary precipitation, that before Mr Pickwick had well began to consider whether Mr Bob Sawyer ought to go or not, they were rolling away, with Mr Bob Sawyer thoroughly established as part and parcel of the equipage.

So long as their progress was confined to the streets of Bristol, the facetious Bob kept his professional green spectacles on, and conducted himself with becoming steadiness and gravity of demean-our; merely giving utterance to divers verbal witticisms for the exclusive behoof and entertainment of Mr Samuel Weller. But when they emerged on the open road, he threw off his green spectacles and his gravity together, and performed a great variety of practical jokes, which were calculated to attract the attention of the passers-by, and to render the carriage and those it contained, objects of more than ordinary curiosity; the least conspicuous among these feats, being, a most vociferous imitation of a key-bugle, and the ostentatious display of a crimson silk pocket-handkerchief attached to a walking-stick, which was occasionally waved in the air with various gestures indicative of supremacy and defiance.

'I wonder,' said Mr Pickwick, stopping in the midst of a most sedate conversation with Ben Allen, bearing reference to the numer-ous good qualities of Mr Winkle and his sister: 'I wonder what all the people we pass, can see in us to make them stare so.'

'It's a neat turn-out,' replied Ben Allen, with something of pride in his tone. 'They're not used to see this sort of thing, every day, I dare say.'

'Possibly,' replied Mr Pickwick. 'It may be so. Perhaps it is.'

Mr Pickwick might very probably have reasoned himself into the belief that it really was: had he not, just then happening to look out of the coach window, observed that the looks of the passengers betokened anything but respectful astonishment, and that various telegraphic communications appeared to be passing between them and some persons outside the vehicle: whereupon it occurred to him that these demonstrations might be, in some remote degree, referable to the humorous deportment of Mr Robert Sawyer.

'I hope,' said Mr Pickwick, 'that our volatile friend is committing no absurdities in that dickey behind.'

'Oh dear, no,' replied Ben Allen. 'Except when he's elevated, Bob's the quietest creature breathing.'

Here a prolonged imitation of a key-bugle broke upon the ear, succeeded by cheers and screams, all of which evidently proceeded from the throat and lungs of the quietest creature breathing, or in plainer designation, of Mr Bob Sawyer himself.

Mr Pickwick and Mr Ben Allen looked expressively at each other, and the former gentleman taking off his hat, and leaning out of the coach window until nearly the whole of his waistcoat was outside it, was at length enabled to catch a glimpse of his facetious friend.

Mr Bob Sawyer was seated: not in the dickey, but on the roof of the chaise, with his legs as far asunder as they would conveniently go, wearing Mr Samuel Weller's hat on one side of his head, and bearing, in one hand, a most enormous sandwich, while, in the other, he supported a goodly-sized case-bottle,[3] to both of which he applied himself with intense relish: varying the monotony of the occupation by an occasional howl, or the interchange of some lively *badinage* with any passing stranger. The crimson flag was carefully tied in an erect position to the rail of the dickey; and Mr Samuel Weller, decorated with Bob Sawyer's hat, was seated in the centre thereof, discussing a twin sandwich, with an animated countenance, the expression of which betokened his entire and perfect approval of the whole arrangement.

This was enough to irritate a gentleman with Mr Pickwick's sense of propriety, but it was not the whole extent of the aggravation, for a stage-coach full, inside and out, was meeting them at the moment, and the astonishment of the passengers was very palpably evinced. The congratulations of an Irish family, too, who were keeping up with the chaise, and begging all the time, were of rather a boisterous

Mr Bob Sawyer's mode of travelling

description; especially those of its male head, who appeared to consider the display as part and parcel of some political, or other procession of triumph.

'Mr Sawyer!' cried Mr Pickwick, in a state of great excitement. 'Mr Sawyer, sir!'

'Hallo!' responded that gentleman, looking over the side of the chaise with all the coolness in life.

'Are you mad, sir?' demanded Mr Pickwick.

'Not a bit of it,' replied Bob; 'only cheerful.'

'Cheerful, sir!' ejaculated Mr Pickwick. 'Take down that scandalous red handkerchief, I beg. I insist, sir. Sam, take it down.'

Before Sam could interpose, Mr Bob Sawyer gracefully struck his colours, and having put them in his pocket, nodded in a courteous manner to Mr Pickwick, wiped the mouth of the case-bottle, and applied it to his own; thereby informing him, without any unnecessary waste of words, that he devoted that draught to wishing him all manner of happiness and prosperity. Having done this, Bob replaced the cork with great care, and looking benignantly down on Mr Pickwick, took a large bite out of the sandwich, and smiled.

'Come,' said Mr Pickwick, whose momentary anger was not quite proof against Bob's immovable self-possession, 'pray let us have no more of this absurdity.'

'No, no,' replied Bob, once more exchanging hats with Mr Weller; 'I didn't mean to do it, only I got so enlivened with the ride that I couldn't help it.'

'Think of the look of the thing,' expostulated Mr Pickwick; 'have some regard to appearances.'

'Oh, certainly,' said Bob, 'it's not the sort of thing at all. All over, governor.'

Satisfied with this assurance, Mr Pickwick once more drew his head into the chaise and pulled up the glass; but he had scarcely resumed the conversation which Mr Bob Sawyer had interrupted, when he was somewhat startled by the apparition of a small dark body, of an oblong form, on the outside of the window, which gave sundry taps against it, as if impatient of admission.

'What's this?' exclaimed Mr Pickwick.

'It looks like a case-bottle;' remarked Ben Allen, eyeing the object in question through his spectacles with some interest; 'I rather think it belongs to Bob.'

The impression was perfectly accurate; for Mr Bob Sawyer having attached the case-bottle to the end of the walking-stick, was battering the window with it, in token of his wish that his friends inside would partake of its contents, in all good fellowship and harmony.

'What's to be done?' said Mr Pickwick, looking at the bottle. 'This proceeding is more absurd than the other.'

'I think it would be best to take it in,' replied Mr Ben Allen; 'it would serve him right to take it in and keep it, wouldn't it?'

'It would,' said Mr Pickwick: 'shall I?'

'I think it the most proper course we could possibly adopt,' replied Ben.

This advice quite coinciding with his own opinion, Mr Pickwick gently let down the window and disengaged the bottle from the stick: upon which the latter was drawn up, and Mr Bob Sawyer was heard to laugh heartily.

'What a merry dog it is!' said Mr Pickwick, looking round at his companion with the bottle in his hand.

'He is,' said Mr Allen.

'You cannot possibly be angry with him,' remarked Mr Pickwick.

'Quite out of the question,' observed Benjamin Allen.

During this short interchange of sentiments, Mr Pickwick had, in an abstracted mood, uncorked the bottle.

'What is it?' inquired Ben Allen, carelessly.

'I don't know,' replied Mr Pickwick, with equal carelessness. 'It smells, I think, like milk-punch.'

'Oh, indeed?' said Ben.

'I *think* so,' rejoined Mr Pickwick, very properly guarding himself against the possibility of stating an untruth: 'mind, I could not undertake to say certainly, without tasting it.'

'You had better do so,' said Ben; 'we may as well know what it is.'

'Do you think so?' replied Mr Pickwick. 'Well; if you are curious to know, of course I have no objection.'

Ever willing to sacrifice his own feelings to the wishes of his friend, Mr Pickwick at once took a pretty long taste.

'What is it?' inquired Ben Allen, interrupting him with some impatience.

'Curious,' said Mr Pickwick, smacking his lips, 'I hardly know, now. Oh, yes!' said Mr Pickwick, after a second taste. 'It *is* punch.'

Mr Ben Allen looked at Mr Pickwick; Mr Pickwick looked at Mr Ben Allen; Mr Ben Allen smiled; Mr Pickwick did not.

'It would serve him right,' said the last-named gentleman, with some severity, 'it would serve him right to drink it every drop.'

'The very thing that occurred to me,' said Ben Allen.

'Is it indeed?' rejoined Mr Pickwick. 'Then here's his health!' With these words, that excellent person took a most energetic pull at the bottle, and handed it to Ben Allen, who was not slow to imitate his example. The smiles became mutual, and the milk-punch was gradually and cheerfully disposed of.

'After all,' said Mr Pickwick, as he drained the last drop, 'his pranks are really very amusing; very entertaining indeed.'

'You may say that,' rejoined Mr Ben Allen. In proof of Bob Sawyer's being one of the funniest fellows alive, he proceeded to entertain Mr Pickwick with a long and circumstantial account how that gentleman once drank himself into a fever and got his head shaved; the relation of which pleasant and agreeable history was only stopped by the stoppage of the chaise at the Bell at Berkeley Heath, to change horses.

'I say! We're going to dine here, aren't we?' said Bob, looking in at the window.

'Dine!' said Mr Pickwick. 'Why, we have only come nineteen miles, and have eighty-seven and a half to go.'

'Just the reason why we should take something to enable us to bear up against the fatigue,' remonstrated Mr Bob Sawyer.

'Oh, it's quite impossible to dine at half-past eleven o'clock in the day,' replied Mr Pickwick, looking at his watch.

'So it is,' rejoined Bob, 'lunch is the very thing. Hallo, you sir! Lunch for three, directly, and keep the horses back for a quarter of an hour. Tell them to put everything they have cold, on the table, and some bottled ale, and let us taste your very best Madeira.' Issuing these orders with monstrous importance and bustle, Mr Bob Sawyer at once hurried into the house to superintend the arrangements; in less than five minutes he returned and declared them to be excellent.

The quality of the lunch fully justified the eulogium which Bob had pronounced, and very great justice was done to it, not only by that gentleman, but Mr Ben Allen and Mr Pickwick also. Under the auspices of the three, the bottled ale and the Madeira were promptly disposed of; and when (the horses being once more put to) they resumed their seats, with the case-bottle full of the best substitute for milk-punch that could be procured on so short a notice, the key-bugle sounded, and the red flag waved, without the slightest opposition on Mr Pickwick's part.

At the Hop Pole at Tewkesbury, they stopped to dine; upon which occasion there was more bottled ale, with some more Madeira, and some Port besides; and here the case-bottle was replenished for the fourth time. Under the influence of these combined stimulants, Mr Pickwick and Mr Ben Allen fell fast asleep for thirty miles, while Bob and Mr Weller sang duets in the dickey.

It was quite dark when Mr Pickwick roused himself sufficiently to look out of window. The straggling cottages by the road-side, the dingy hue of every object visible, the murky atmosphere, the paths of cinders and brick-dust, the deep-red glow of furnace fires in the distance, the volumes of dense smoke issuing heavily forth from high toppling chimneys, blackening and obscuring everything around; the glare of distant lights, the ponderous waggons which toiled along the road, laden with clashing rods of iron, or piled with heavy goods – all betokened their rapid approach to the great working town of Birmingham.

As they rattled through the narrow thoroughfares leading to the heart of the turmoil, the sights and sounds of earnest occupation struck more forcibly on the senses. The streets were thronged with working-people. The hum of labour resounded from every house, lights gleamed from the long casement windows in the attic stories, and the whirl of wheels and noise of machinery shook the trembling walls. The fires, whose lurid sullen light had been visible for miles, blazed fiercely up, in the great works and factories of the town. The din of hammers, the rushing of steam, and the dead heavy clanking of engines, was the harsh music which arose from every quarter.

The postboy was driving briskly through the open streets, and past the handsome and well-lighted shops which intervene between the outskirts of the town and the Old Royal Hotel,[4] before Mr Pickwick had begun to consider the very difficult and delicate nature of the commission which had carried him thither.

The delicate nature of this commission, and the difficulty of executing it in a satisfactory manner, were by no means lessened by the voluntary companionship of Mr Bob Sawyer. Truth to tell, Mr Pickwick felt that his presence on the occasion, however considerate and gratifying, was by no means an honour he would willingly have sought; in fact, he would cheerfully have given a reasonable sum of money to have had Mr Bob Sawyer removed to any place at not less than fifty miles' distance, without delay.

Mr Pickwick had never held any personal communication with Mr Winkle, senior, although he had once or twice corresponded with him by letter, and returned satisfactory answers to his inquiries concerning the moral character and behaviour of his son; he felt nervously sensible that to wait upon him, for the first time, attended by Bob Sawyer and Ben Allen, both slightly fuddled,[5] was not the most ingenious and likely means that could have been hit upon to prepossess him in his favour.

'However,' said Mr Pickwick, endeavouring to re-assure himself, 'I must do the best I can. I must see him to-night, for I faithfully promised to do so. If they persist in accompanying me, I must make the interview as brief as possible, and be content to hope that, for their own sakes, they will not expose themselves.'

As he comforted himself with these reflections, the chaise stopped at the door of the Old Royal. Ben Allen having been partially awakened from a stupendous sleep, and dragged out by the collar by Mr Samuel Weller, Mr Pickwick was enabled to alight. They were shown to a comfortable apartment, and Mr Pickwick at once propounded a question to the waiter concerning the whereabout of Mr Winkle's residence.

'Close by, sir,' said the waiter, 'not above five hundred yards, sir. Mr Winkle is a wharfinger,' sir, at the canal, sir. Private residence is not – oh dear no, sir, *not* five hundred yards, sir.' Here the waiter blew a candle out, and made a feint of lighting it again, in order to afford Mr Pickwick an opportunity of asking any further questions, if he felt so disposed.

'Take anything now, sir?' said the waiter, lighting the candle in desperation at Mr Pickwick's silence. 'Tea or coffee, sir? Dinner, sir?'

'Nothing now.'

'Very good, sir. Like to order supper, sir?'

'Not just now.'

'*Very* good, sir.' Here, he walked softly to the door, and then stopping short, turned round, and said, with great suavity:

'Shall I send the chambermaid, gentlemen?'

'You may if you please;' replied Mr Pickwick.

'If *you* please, sir.'

'And bring some soda water,' said Bob Sawyer.

'Soda water, sir? Yes, sir.' With his mind apparently relieved from an overwhelming weight, by having at last got an order for something, the waiter imperceptibly melted away. Waiters never walk or run. They have a peculiar and mysterious power of skimming out of rooms, which other mortals possess not.

Some slight symptoms of vitality having been awakened in Mr Ben Allen by the soda water, he suffered himself to be prevailed upon to wash his face and hands, and to submit to be brushed by Sam. Mr Pickwick and Bob Sawyer having also repaired the disorder which the journey had made in their apparel, the three

started forth, arm in arm, to Mr Winkle's; Bob Sawyer impregnating
the atmosphere with tobacco smoke as he walked along.

About a quarter of a mile off, in a quiet, substantial-looking
street, stood an old red-brick house with three steps before the
door, and a brass plate upon it, bearing, in fat Roman capitals, the
words, 'Mr Winkle.' The steps were very white, and the bricks were
very red, and the house was very clean; and here stood Mr Pickwick,
Mr Benjamin Allen, and Mr Bob Sawyer, as the clock struck ten.

A smart servant girl answered the knock, and started on beholding the three strangers.

'Is Mr Winkle at home, my dear?' inquired Mr Pickwick.

'He is just going to supper, sir,' replied the girl.

'Give him that card if you please,' rejoined Mr Pickwick. 'Say I
am sorry to trouble him at so late an hour; but I am anxious to see
him to-night, and have only just arrived.'

The girl looked timidly at Mr Bob Sawyer, who was expressing
his admiration of her personal charms by a variety of wonderful
grimaces; and casting an eye at the hats and great-coats which hung
in the passage, called another girl to mind the door while she went
up stairs. The sentinel was speedily relieved; for the girl returned
immediately, and begging pardon of the gentlemen for leaving them
in the street, ushered them into a floor-clothed back parlour, half
office and half dressing-room, in which the principal useful and
ornamental articles of furniture, were a desk, a wash-hand stand
and shaving glass, a boot-rack and boot-jack, a high stool, four
chairs, a table, and an old eight-day clock. Over the mantel-piece
were the sunken doors of an iron safe, while a couple of hanging
shelves for books, an almanack,[7] and several files of dusty papers,
decorated the walls.

'Very sorry to leave you standing at the door, sir,' said the girl,
lighting a lamp, and addressing Mr Pickwick with a winning smile,
'but you was quite strangers to me; and we have such a many
trampers that only come to see what they can lay their hands on,
that really – '

'There is not the least occasion for any apology, my dear,' said
Mr Pickwick good humouredly.

'Not the slightest, my love,' said Bob Sawyer, playfully stretching
forth his arms, and skipping from side to side, as if to prevent the
young lady's leaving the room.

The young lady was not at all softened by these allurements, for
she at once expressed her opinion that Mr Bob Sawyer was an
'odous creetur;' and, on his becoming rather more pressing in his

attentions, imprinted her fair fingers upon his face, and bounced out of the room with many expressions of aversion and contempt.

Deprived of the young lady's society, Mr Bob Sawyer proceeded to divert himself by peeping into the desk, looking into all the table-drawers, feigning to pick the lock of the iron safe, turning the almanack with its face to the wall, trying on the boots of Mr Winkle, senior, over his own, and making several other humorous experiments upon the furniture, all of which afforded Mr Pickwick unspeakable horror and agony, and yielded Mr Bob Sawyer proportionate delight.

At length the door opened, and a little old gentleman in a snuff-coloured suit, with a head and face the precise counterpart of those belonging to Mr Winkle, junior, excepting that he was rather bald, trotted into the room with Mr Pickwick's card in one hand, and a silver candlestick in the other.

'Mr Pickwick, sir, how do you do?' said Winkle the elder, putting down the candlestick and proffering his hand. 'Hope I see you well, sir. Glad to see you. Be seated, Mr Pickwick, I beg sir. This gentleman is – '

'My friend, Mr Sawyer,' interposed Mr Pickwick, 'your son's friend.'

'Oh,' said Mr Winkle the elder, looking rather grimly at Bob. 'I hope *you* are well, sir.'

'Right as a trivet, sir,' replied Bob Sawyer.

'This other gentleman,' cried Mr Pickwick, 'is, as you will see, when you have read the letter with which I am entrusted, a very near relative, or I should rather say a very particular friend of your son's. His name is Allen.'

'*That* gentleman?' inquired Mr Winkle, pointing with the card towards Ben Allen, who had fallen asleep in an attitude which left nothing of him visible but his spine and his coat collar.

Mr Pickwick was on the point of replying to the question, and reciting Mr Benjamin Allen's name and honourable distinctions at full length, when the sprightly Mr Bob Sawyer, with a view of rousing his friend to a sense of his situation, inflicted a startling pinch upon the fleshy part of his arm, which caused him to jump up with a shriek. Suddenly aware that he was in the presence of a stranger, Mr Ben Allen advanced and, shaking Mr Winkle most affectionately by both hands for about five minutes, murmured, in some half-intelligible fragments of sentences, the great delight he felt in seeing him, and a hospitable inquiry whether he felt disposed to take anything after his walk, or would prefer waiting 'till dinner-time;' which done, he sat down and gazed about him with a petrified stare, as if he had not the remotest idea where he was, which indeed he had not.

All this was most embarrassing to Mr Pickwick, the more especially as Mr Winkle, senior, evinced palpable astonishment at the eccentric – not to say extraordinary – behaviour of his two companions. To bring the matter to an issue at once, he drew a letter from his pocket, and presenting it to Mr Winkle, senior, said:

'This letter, sir, is from your son. You will see, by its contents, that on your favourable and fatherly consideration of it, depend his future happiness and welfare. Will you oblige me by giving it the calmest and coolest perusal, and by discussing the subject afterwards, with me, in the tone and spirit in which alone it ought to be discussed? You may judge of the importance of your decision to your son, and his intense anxiety upon the subject, by my waiting upon you, without any previous warning, at so late an hour; and,' added Mr Pickwick, glancing slightly at his two companions, 'and under such unfavourable circumstances.'

With this prelude, Mr Pickwick placed four closely written sides of extra superfine wire-wove[8] penitence in the hands of the astounded Mr Winkle, senior. Then reseating himself in his chair, he watched his looks and manner: anxiously, it is true, but with the open front of a gentleman who feels he has taken no part which he need excuse or palliate.

The old wharfinger turned the letter over; looked at the front, back, and sides; made a microscopic examination of the fat little boy on the seal; raised his eyes to Mr Pickwick's face; and then, seating himself on the high stool, and drawing the lamp closer to him, broke the wax, unfolded the epistle, and lifting it to the light, prepared to read.

Just at this moment, Mr Bob Sawyer, whose wit had lain dormant for some minutes, placed his hands upon his knees, and made a face after the portraits of the late Mr Grimaldi,[9] as clown. It so happened that Mr Winkle, senior, instead of being deeply engaged in reading the letter, as Mr Bob Sawyer thought, chanced to be looking over the top of it at no less a person than Mr Bob Sawyer himself; rightly conjecturing that the face aforesaid was made in ridicule and derision of his own person, he fixed his eyes on Bob with such expressive sternness, that the late Mr Grimaldi's lineaments gradually resolved themselves into a very fine expression of humility and confusion.

'Did you speak, sir?' inquired Mr Winkle, senior, after an awful silence.

'No, sir,' replied Bob, with no remains of the clown about him, save and except the extreme redness of his cheeks.

'You are sure you did not, sir?' said Mr Winkle, senior.

'Oh dear yes, sir, quite,' replied Bob.

'I thought you did, sir,' rejoined the old gentleman, with indignant emphasis. 'Perhaps you *looked* at me, sir?'

'Oh, no! sir, not at all,' replied Bob, with extreme civility.

'I am very glad to hear it, sir,' said Mr Winkle, senior. Having frowned upon the abashed Bob with great magnificence, the old gentleman again brought the letter to the light, and began to read it seriously.

Mr Pickwick eyed him intently as he turned from the bottom line of the first page to the top line of the second, and from the bottom of the second to the top of the third, and from the bottom of the third to the top of the fourth; but not the slightest alteration of countenance afforded a clue to the feelings with which he received the announcement of his son's marriage, which Mr Pickwick knew was in the very first half-dozen lines.

He read the letter to the last word; folded it again with all the carefulness and precision of a man of business; and, just when Mr Pickwick expected some great outbreak of feeling, dipped a pen in the inkstand, and said as quietly as if he were speaking on the most ordinary counting-house topic:

'What is Nathaniel's address, Mr Pickwick?'

'The George and Vulture, at present,' replied that gentleman.

'George and Vulture. Where is that?'

'George Yard, Lombard Street.'

'In the City?'

'Yes.'

The old gentleman methodically indorsed the address on the back of the letter; and then, placing it in the desk, which he locked, said as he got off the stool and put the bunch of keys in his pocket:

'I suppose there is nothing else which need detain us, Mr Pickwick?'

'Nothing else, my dear sir!' observed that warm-hearted person in indignant amazement. 'Nothing else! Have you no opinion to express on this momentous event in our young friend's life? No assurance to convey to him, through me, of the continuance of your affection and protection? Nothing to say which will cheer and sustain him, and the anxious girl who looks to him for comfort and support? My dear sir, consider.'

'I will consider,' replied the old gentleman. 'I have nothing to say just now. I am a man of business, Mr Pickwick. I never commit myself hastily in any affair, and from what I see of this, I by no means like the appearance of it. A thousand pounds is not much, Mr Pickwick.'

'You're very right, sir,' interposed Ben Allen, just awake enough to know that he had spent *his* thousand pounds without the smallest difficulty. 'You're an intelligent man. Bob, he's a very knowing fellow this.'

'I am very happy to find that *you* do me the justice to make the admission, sir,' said Mr Winkle, senior, looking contemptuously at Ben Allen, who was shaking his head profoundly. 'The fact is, Mr Pickwick, that when I gave my son a roving license for a year or so, to see something of men and manners (which he has done under your auspices), so that he might not enter into life a mere boarding-school milk-sop to be gulled by everybody, I never bargained for this. He knows that, very well, so if I withdraw my countenance from him on this account, he has no call to be surprised. He shall hear from me, Mr Pickwick. Good night, sir. Margaret, open the door.'

All this time, Bob Sawyer had been nudging Mr Ben Allen to say something on the right side; Ben accordingly now burst, without the slightest preliminary notice, into a brief but impassioned piece of eloquence.

'Sir,' said Mr Ben Allen, staring at the old gentleman, out of a pair of very dim and languid eyes, and working his right arm vehemently up and down, 'you – you ought to be ashamed of yourself.'

'As the lady's brother, of course you are an excellent judge of the question,' retorted Mr Winkle, senior. 'There; that's enough. Pray say no more, Mr Pickwick. Good night, gentlemen!'

With these words the old gentleman took up the candlestick, and opening the room door, politely motioned towards the passage.

'You will regret this, sir,' said Mr Pickwick, setting his teeth close together to keep down his choler; for he felt how important the effect might prove to his young friend.

'I am at present of a different opinion,' calmly replied Mr Winkle, senior. 'Once again, gentlemen, I wish you a good night.'

Mr Pickwick walked, with angry strides, into the street. Mr Bob Sawyer, completely quelled by the decision of the old gentleman's manner, took the same course. Mr Ben Allen's hat rolled down the steps immediately afterwards, and Mr Ben Allen's body followed it directly. The whole party went silent and supperless to bed; and Mr Pickwick thought, just before he fell asleep, that if he had known Mr Winkle, senior, had been quite so much of a man of business, it was extremely probable he might never have waited upon him, on such an errand.

CHAPTER 51

In which Mr Pickwick encounters an old Acquaintance. To which fortunate circumstance the Reader is mainly indebted for matter of thrilling interest herein set down, concerning two great Public Men of might and power

The morning which broke upon Mr Pickwick's sight, at eight o'clock, was not at all calculated to elevate his spirits, or to lessen the depression which the unlooked-for result of his embassy inspired. The sky was dark and gloomy, the air was damp and raw, the streets were wet and sloppy. The smoke hung sluggishly above the chimney-tops as if it lacked the courage to rise, and the rain came slowly and doggedly down, as if it had not even the spirit to pour. A game-cock in the stable-yard, deprived of every spark of his accustomed animation, balanced himself dismally on one leg in a corner; a donkey, moping with drooping head under the narrow roof of an outhouse, appeared from his meditative and miserable countenance to be contemplating suicide. In the street, umbrellas were the only things to be seen, and the clicking of pattens and splashing of rain-drops, were the only sounds to be heard.

The breakfast was interrupted by very little conversation; even Mr Bob Sawyer felt the influence of the weather, and the previous day's excitement. In his own expressive language he was 'floored.' So was Mr Ben Allen. So was Mr Pickwick.

In protracted expectation of the weather clearing up, the last evening paper from London was read and re-read with an intensity of interest only known in cases of extreme destitution; every inch of the carpet was walked over, with similar perseverance; the windows were looked out of, often enough to justify the imposition of an additional duty[1] upon them; all kinds of topics of conversation were started, and failed; and at length Mr Pickwick, when noon had arrived, without a change for the better, rang the bell resolutely and ordered out the chaise.

Although the roads were miry, and the drizzling rain came down harder than it had done yet, and although the mud and wet splashed in at the open windows of the carriage to such an extent that the discomfort was almost as great to the pair of insides as to the pair of outsides, still there was something in the motion, and the sense of being up and doing, which was so infinitely superior to being pent in a dull room, looking at the dull rain dripping into a dull street, that they all agreed, on starting, that the change was a great improvement, and wondered how they could possibly have delayed making it, as long as they had done.

When they stopped to change at Coventry, the steam ascended from the horses in such clouds as wholly to obscure the hostler, whose voice was however heard to declare from the mist, that he expected the first Gold Medal from the Humane Society[2] on their next distribution of rewards, for taking the postboy's hat off; the water descending from the brim of which, the invisible gentleman declared must inevitably have drowned him (the postboy), but for his great presence of mind in tearing it promptly from his head, and drying the gasping man's countenance with a wisp of straw.

'This is pleasant,' said Bob Sawyer, turning up his coat collar, and pulling the shawl over his mouth to concentrate the fumes of a glass of brandy just swallowed.

'Wery,' replied Sam, composedly.

'You don't seem to mind it,' observed Bob.

'Vy, I don't exactly see no good my mindin' on it 'ud do, sir,' replied Sam.

'That's an unanswerable reason, anyhow,' said Bob.

'Yes, sir,' rejoined Mr Weller. 'Wotever is, is right,[3] as the young nobleman sveetly remarked wen they put him down in the pension list[4] 'cos his mother's uncle's vife's grandfather vunce lit the king's pipe vith a portable tinder-box.'

'Not a bad notion that, Sam,' said Mr Bob Sawyer approvingly.

'Just wot the young nobleman said ev'ry quarter-day arterwards for the rest of his life,' replied Mr Weller.

'Wos you ever called in,' inquired Sam, glancing at the driver, after a short silence, and lowering his voice to a mysterious whisper: 'wos you ever called in, ven you wos 'prentice to a sawbones, to wisit a postboy?'

'I don't remember that I ever was,' replied Bob Sawyer.

'You never see a postboy in that 'ere hospital as you *walked* (as they says o' the ghosts), did you?' demanded Sam.

'No,' replied Bob Sawyer. 'I don't think I ever did.'

'Never know'd a churchyard were there wos a postboy's tombstone, or see a dead postboy, did you?' inquired Sam, pursuing his catechism.

'No,' rejoined Bob, 'I never did.'

'No!' rejoined Sam, triumphantly. 'Nor never vill; and there's another thing that no man never see, and that's a dead donkey.⁵ No man never see a dead donkey, 'cept the gen'l'm'n in the black silk smalls as know'd the young 'ooman as kep a goat; and that wos a French donkey, so wery likely he warn't wun o' the reg'lar breed.'

'Well, what has that got to do with the postboys?' asked Bob Sawyer.

'This here,' replied Sam. 'Without goin' so far as to as-sert, as some wery sensible people do, that postboys and donkeys is both immortal, wot I say is this; that wenever they feels theirselves gettin' stiff and past their work, they just rides off together, wun postboy to a pair in the usual way; wot becomes on 'em nobody knows, but it's wery probable as they starts avay to take their pleasure in some other vorld, for there ain't a man alive as ever see, either a donkey or a postboy, a takin' his pleasure in this!'

Expatiating upon this learned and remarkable theory, and citing many curious statistical and other facts in its support, Sam Weller beguiled the time until they reached Dunchurch, where a dry postboy and fresh horses were procured; the next stage was Daventry, and the next Towcester; and at the end of each stage it rained harder than it had done at the beginning.

'I say,' remonstrated Bob Sawyer, looking in at the coach window, as they pulled up before the door of the Saracen's Head, Towcester, 'this won't do, you know.'

'Bless me!' said Mr Pickwick, just awaking from a nap, 'I'm afraid you're wet.'

'Oh you are, are you?' returned Bob. 'Yes, I am, a little that way. Uncomfortably damp, perhaps.'

Bob did look dampish, inasmuch as the rain was streaming from his neck, elbows, cuffs, skirts, and knees; and his whole apparel shone so with the wet, that it might have been mistaken for a full suit of prepared oilskin.⁶

'I *am* rather wet,' said Bob, giving himself a shake, and casting a little hydraulic shower around, like a Newfoundland dog just emerged from the water.

'I think it's quite impossible to go on to-night,' interposed Ben.

'Out of the question, sir,' remarked Sam Weller, coming to assist in the conference; 'it's a cruelty to animals, sir, to ask 'em to do it. There's beds here, sir,' said Sam, addressing his master, 'everything clean and comfortable. Wery good little dinner, sir, they can get ready in half an hour – pair of fowls, sir, and a weal cutlet; French beans, 'taturs, tart, and tidiness. You'd better stop vere you are, sir, if I might recommend. Take adwice, sir, as the doctor said.'

The host of the Saracen's Head opportunely appeared at this moment, to confirm Mr Weller's statement relative to the accommodations of the establishment, and to back his entreaties with a variety of dismal conjectures regarding the state of the roads, the doubt of fresh horses being to be had at the next stage, the dead certainty of its raining all night, the equally mortal certainty of its clearing up in the morning, and other topics of inducement familiar to innkeepers.

'Well,' said Mr Pickwick; 'but I must send a letter to London by some conveyance, so that it may be delivered the very first thing in the morning, or I must go forward at all hazards.'

The landlord smiled his delight. Nothing could be easier than for the gentleman to inclose a letter in a sheet of brown paper, and send it on, either by the mail or the night coach from Birmingham. If the gentleman were particularly anxious to have it left as soon as possible, he might write outside, 'To be delivered immediately,' which was sure to be attended to; or 'pay the bearer half-a-crown extra for instant delivery,' which was surer still.

'Very well,' said Mr Pickwick, 'then we will stop here.'

'Lights in the Sun,[7] John; make up the fire; the gentlemen are wet!' cried the landlord. 'This way, gentlemen; don't trouble yourselves about the postboy now, sir. I'll send him to you when you ring for him, sir. Now, John, the candles.'

The candles were brought, the fire was stirred up, and a fresh log of wood thrown on. In ten minutes' time, a waiter was laying the cloth for dinner, the curtains were drawn, the fire was blazing brightly, and everything looked (as everything always does, in all decent English inns) as if the travellers had been expected, and their comforts prepared, for days beforehand.

Mr Pickwick sat down at a side table, and hastily indited a note to Mr Winkle, merely informing him that he was detained by stress of weather, but would certainly be in London next day; until when he deferred any account of his proceedings. This note was hastily made into a parcel, and despatched to the bar per Mr Samuel Weller.

Sam left it with the landlady, and was returning to pull his master's boots off, after drying himself by the kitchen fire, when, glancing casually through a half-opened door, he was arrested by the sight of a gentleman with a sandy head who had a large bundle of newspapers lying on the table before him, and was perusing the leading article of one with a settled sneer which curled up his nose and all his other features into a majestic expression of haughty contempt.

'Hallo!' said Sam, 'I ought to know that 'ere head and them features; the eye-glass, too, and the broad-brimmed tile! Eatansvill to vit, or I'm a Roman.'

Sam was taken with a troublesome cough, at once, for the purpose of attracting the gentleman's attention; the gentleman starting at the sound, raised his head and his eye-glass, and disclosed to view the profound and thoughtful features of Mr Pott, of the Eatanswill Gazette.

'Beggin' your pardon, sir,' said Sam, advancing with a bow, 'my master's here, Mr Pott.'

'Hush, hush!' cried Pott, drawing Sam into the room, and closing the door, with a countenance of mysterious dread and apprehension.

'Wot's the matter, sir?' inquired Sam, looking vacantly about him.

'Not a whisper of my name,' replied Pott; 'this is a buff neighbourhood. If the excited and irritable populace knew I was here, I should be torn to pieces.'

'No! Vould you, sir?' inquired Sam.

'I should be the victim of their fury,' replied Pott. 'Now, young man, what of your master?'

'He's a stopping here to-night on his vay to town, vith a couple of friends,' replied Sam.

'Is Mr Winkle one of them?' inquired Pott, with a slight frown.

'No, sir. Mr Vinkle stops at home now,' rejoined Sam. 'He's married.'

'Married!' exclaimed Pott, with frightful vehemence. He stopped, smiled darkly, and added, in a low, vindictive tone: 'It serves him right!'

Having given vent to this cruel ebullition of deadly malice and cold-blooded triumph over a fallen enemy, Mr Pott inquired whether Mr Pickwick's friends were 'blue?' Receiving a most satisfactory answer in the affirmative from Sam, who knew as much about the matter as Pott himself, he consented to accompany him to Mr Pickwick's room, where a hearty welcome awaited him. An agreement to club dinners together was at once made and ratified.

'And how are matters going on in Eatanswill?' inquired Mr Pickwick, when Pott had taken a seat near the fire, and the whole party had got their wet boots off, and dry slippers on. 'Is the Independent still in being?'

'The Independent, sir,' replied Pott, 'is still dragging on a wretched and lingering career. Abhorred and despised by even the few who are cognizant of its miserable and disgraceful existence; stifled by the very filth it so profusely scatters; rendered deaf and blind by the exhalations of its own slime; the obscene journal, happily unconscious of its degraded state, is rapidly sinking beneath that treacherous mud which, while it seems to give it a firm standing with the low and debased classes of society, is nevertheless, rising above its detested head, and will speedily engulf it for ever.'

Having delivered this manifesto (which formed a portion of his last week's leader) with vehement articulation, the editor paused to take breath and looked majestically at Bob Sawyer.

'You are a young man, sir,' said Pott.

Mr Bob Sawyer nodded.

'So are you, sir,' said Pott, addressing Mr Ben Allen.

Ben admitted the soft impeachment.

'And are both deeply imbued with those blue principles, which, so long as I live, I have pledged myself to the people of these kingdoms to support and to maintain?' suggested Pott.

'Why, I don't exactly know about that,' replied Bob Sawyer. 'I am – '

'Not buff, Mr Pickwick,' interrupted Pott, drawing back his chair, 'your friend is not buff, sir?'

'No, no,' rejoined Bob, 'I'm a kind of plaid[8] at present; a compound of all sorts of colours.'

'A waverer,' said Pott, solemnly, 'a waverer. I should like to show you a series of eight articles, sir, that have appeared in the Eatanswill Gazette. I think I may venture to say that you would not be long in establishing your opinions on a firm and solid blue basis, sir.'

'I dare say I should turn very blue, long before I got to the end of them,' responded Bob.

Mr Pott looked dubiously at Bob Sawyer for some seconds, and, turning to Mr Pickwick, said:

'You have seen the literary articles which have appeared at intervals in the Eatanswill Gazette in the course of the last three months, and which have excited such general – I may say universal – attention and admiration?'

'Why,' replied Mr Pickwick, slightly embarrassed by the question, 'the fact is, I have been so much engaged in other ways, that I really have not had an opportunity of perusing them.'

'You should do so, sir,' said Pott, with a severe countenance.

'I will,' said Mr Pickwick.

'They appeared in the form of a copious review of a work on Chinese metaphysics, sir,' said Pott.

'Oh,' observed Mr Pickwick; 'from your pen, I hope?'

'From the pen of my critic, sir,' rejoined Pott with dignity.

'An abstruse subject I should conceive,' said Mr Pickwick.

'Very, sir,' responded Pott, looking intensely sage. 'He *crammed* for it, to use a technical but expressive term; he read up for the subject, at my desire, in the *Encyclopædia Britannica*.'

'Indeed!' said Mr Pickwick; 'I was not aware that that valuable work contained any information respecting Chinese metaphysics.'

'He read, sir,' rejoined Pott, laying his hand on Mr Pickwick's knee, and looking round with a smile of intellectual superiority, 'he read for metaphysics under the letter M, and for China under the letter C, and combined his information, sir!'

Mr Pott's features assumed so much additional grandeur at the recollection of the power and research displayed in the learned effusions in question, that some minutes elapsed before Mr Pickwick felt emboldened to renew the conversation; at length, as the Editor's countenance gradually relaxed into its customary expression of moral supremacy, he ventured to resume the discourse by asking:

'Is it fair to inquire what great object has brought you so far from home?'

'That object which actuates and animates me in all my gigantic labours, sir,' replied Pott, with a calm smile; 'my country's good.'

'I supposed it was some public mission,' observed Mr Pickwick.

'Yes, sir,' resumed Pott, 'it is.' Here, bending towards Mr Pickwick, he whispered in a deep hollow voice, 'A buff ball, sir, will take place in Birmingham to-morrow evening.'

'God bless me!' exclaimed Mr Pickwick.

'Yes, sir, and supper,' added Pott.

'You don't say so!' ejaculated Mr Pickwick.

Pott nodded portentously.

Now, although Mr Pickwick feigned to stand aghast at this disclosure, he was so little versed in local politics that he was unable to form an adequate comprehension of the importance of the dire conspiracy it referred to; observing which, Mr Pott, drawing forth the last number of the Eatanswill Gazette, and referring to the same, delivered himself of the following paragraph:

'HOLE-AND-CORNER BUFFERY

'A reptile contemporary has recently sweltered forth his black venom in the vain and hopeless attempt of sullying the fair name of our distinguished and excellent representative, the Honourable Mr Slumkey – that Slumkey whom we, long before he gained his present noble and exalted position, predicted would one day be, as he now is, at once his country's brightest honour, and her proudest boast: alike her bold defender and her honest pride – our reptile contemporary, we say, has made himself merry, at the expense of a superbly embossed plated coal-scuttle, which has been presented to that glorious man by his enraptured constituents, and towards the purchase of which, the nameless wretch insinuates, the Honourable Mr Slumkey himself contributed, through a confidential friend of his butler's, more than three-fourths of the whole sum subscribed. Why, does not the crawling creature see, that even if this be the fact, the Honourable Mr Slumkey only appears in a still more amiable and radiant light than before, if that be possible? Does not even *his* obtuseness perceive that this amiable and touching desire to carry out the wishes of the constituent body, must for ever endear him to the hearts and souls of such of his fellow townsmen as are not worse than swine; or, in other words, who are not as debased as our contemporary himself? But such is the wretched trickery of hole-and-corner Buffery! These are not its only artifices. Treason is abroad. We boldly state, now that we are goaded to the disclosure, and we throw ourselves on the country and its constables for protection – we boldly state that secret preparations are at this moment in progress for a Buff ball; which is to be held in a Buff town, in the very heart and centre of a Buff population; which is to be conducted by a Buff master of the ceremonies; which is to be attended by four ultra Buff members of parliament, and the admission to which, is to be by Buff tickets! Does our fiendish contemporary wince? Let him writhe, in impotent malice, as we pen the words, WE WILL BE THERE.'

'There, sir,' said Pott, folding up the paper quite exhausted, 'that is the state of the case!'

The landlord and waiter entering at the moment with dinner, caused Mr Pott to lay his finger on his lips, in token that he considered his life in Mr Pickwick's hands, and depended on his secrecy. Messrs. Bob Sawyer and Benjamin Allen, who had irreverently fallen asleep during the reading of the quotation from the Eatanswill Gazette, and the discussion which followed it, were roused by the mere whispering of the talismanic word 'Dinner' in their ears: and to dinner they went with good digestion waiting on appetite, and health on both, and a waiter on all three.

In the course of the dinner and the sitting which succeeded it, Mr Pott descending, for a few moments, to domestic topics, informed Mr Pickwick that the air of Eatanswill not agreeing with his lady, she was then engaged in making a tour of different fashionable watering-places with a view to the recovery of her wonted health and spirits; this was a delicate veiling of the fact that Mrs Pott, acting upon her often repeated threat of separation, had, in virtue of an arrangement negociated by her brother, the Lieutenant, and concluded by Mr Pott, permanently retired with the faithful body-guard upon one moiety or half-part of the annual income and profits arising from the editorship and sale of the Eatanswill Gazette.

While the great Mr Pott was dwelling upon this and other matters, enlivening the conversation from time to time with various extracts from his own lucubrations, a stern stranger, calling from the window of a stage-coach, outward bound, which halted at the inn to deliver packages, requested to know, whether, if he stopped short on his journey and remained there for the night, he could be furnished with the necessary accommodation of a bed and bedstead.

'Certainly, sir,' replied the landlord.

'I can, can I?' inquired the stranger, who seemed habitually suspicious in look and manner.

'No doubt of it, sir,' replied the landlord.

'Good,' said the stranger. 'Coachman, I get down here. Guard, my carpet-bag!'

Bidding the other passengers good night, in a rather snappish manner, the stranger alighted. He was a shortish gentleman, with very stiff black hair cut in the porcupine or blacking-brush[9] style, and standing stiff and straight all over his head; his aspect was pompous and threatening; his manner was peremptory; his eyes were sharp and restless; and his whole bearing bespoke a feeling of great confidence in himself, and a consciousness of immeasurable superiority over all other people.

This gentleman was shown into the room originally assigned to the patriotic Mr Pott; and the waiter remarked, in dumb astonishment at the singular coincidence, that he had no sooner lighted the candles than the gentleman, diving into his hat, drew forth a newspaper, and began to read it with the very same expression of indignant scorn, which, upon the majestic features of Pott, had paralysed his energies an hour before. The man observed too, that whereas Mr Pott's scorn had been roused by a newspaper headed The Eatanswill Independent, this gentleman's withering contempt was awakened by a newspaper entitled The Eatanswill Gazette.

'Send the landlord,' said the stranger.

'Yes, sir,' rejoined the waiter.

The landlord was sent, and came.

'Are you the landlord?' inquired the gentleman.

'I am, sir,' replied the landlord.

'Do you know me?' demanded the gentleman.

'I have not that pleasure, sir,' rejoined the landlord.

'My name is Slurk,' said the gentleman.

The landlord slightly inclined his head.

'Slurk, sir,' repeated the gentleman, haughtily. 'Do you know me now, man?'

The landlord scratched his head, looked at the ceiling, and at the stranger, and smiled feebly.

'Do you know me, man?' inquired the stranger, angrily.

The landlord made a strong effort, and at length replied: 'Well, sir, I do not know you.'

'Great Heaven!' said the stranger, dashing his clenched fist upon the table. 'And this is popularity!'

The landlord took a step or two towards the door; the stranger fixing his eyes upon him, resumed.

'This,' said the stranger, 'this is gratitude for years of labour and study in behalf of the masses. I alight wet and weary; no enthusiastic crowds press forward to greet their champion; the church-bells are silent; the very name elicits no responsive feeling in their torpid bosoms. It is enough,' said the agitated Mr Slurk, pacing to and fro, 'to curdle the ink in one's pen, and induce one to abandon their cause for ever.'

'Did you say brandy and water, sir?' said the landlord, venturing a hint.

'Rum,' said Mr Slurk, turning fiercely upon him. 'Have you got a fire anywhere?'

'We can light one directly, sir,' said the landlord.

'Which will throw out no heat until it is bed-time,' interrupted Mr Slurk. 'Is there anybody in the kitchen?'

Not a soul. There was a beautiful fire. Everybody had gone, and the house door was closed for the night.

'I will drink my rum and water,' said Mr Slurk, 'by the kitchen fire.' So, gathering up his hat and newspaper, he stalked solemnly behind the landlord to that humble apartment, and throwing himself on a settle by the fireside, resumed his countenance of scorn, and began to read and drink in silent dignity.

Now, some demon of discord, flying over the Saracen's Head at that moment, on casting down his eyes in mere idle curiosity, happened to behold Slurk established comfortably by the kitchen fire, and Pott slightly elevated with wine in another room; upon which the malicious demon, darting down into the last-mentioned apartment with inconceivable rapidity, passed at once into the head of Mr Bob Sawyer, and prompted him for his (the demon's) own evil purposes to speak as follows:

'I say, we've let the fire out. It's uncommonly cold after the rain, isn't it?'

'It really is,' replied Mr Pickwick, shivering.

'It wouldn't be a bad notion to have a cigar by the kitchen fire, would it?' said Bob Sawyer, still prompted by the demon aforesaid.

'It would be particularly comfortable, *I* think,' replied Mr Pickwick. 'Mr Pott, what do you say?'

Mr Pott yielded a ready assent; and all four travellers, each with his glass in his hand, at once betook themselves to the kitchen, with Sam Weller heading the procession to show them the way.

The stranger was still reading; he looked up and started. Mr Pott started.

'What's the matter?' whispered Mr Pickwick.

'That reptile!' replied Pott.

'What reptile?' said Mr Pickwick, looking about him for fear he should tread on some overgrown black beetle, or dropsical spider.[10]

'That reptile,' whispered Pott, catching Mr Pickwick by the arm, and pointing towards the stranger. 'That reptile Slurk, of the Independent!'

'Perhaps we had better retire,' whispered Mr Pickwick.

'Never, sir,' rejoined Pott, pot-valiant in a double sense, 'never.' With these words, Mr Pott took up his position on an opposite settle, and selecting one from a little bundle of newspapers, began to read against his enemy.

Mr Pott, of course, read the Independent, and Mr Slurk, of course, read the Gazette; and each gentleman audibly expressed his contempt of the other's compositions by bitter laughs and sarcastic sniffs; whence they proceeded to more open expressions of opinion, such as 'absurd,' 'wretched,' 'atrocity,' 'humbug,' 'knavery,' 'dirt,' 'filth,' 'slime,' 'ditch-water,' and other critical remarks of the like nature.

Both Mr Bob Sawyer and Mr Ben Allen had beheld these symptoms of rivalry and hatred, with a degree of delight which imparted great additional relish to the cigars at which they were puffing most vigorously. The moment they began to flag, the mischievous Mr Bob Sawyer, addressing Slurk with great politeness, said:

'Will you allow me to look at your paper, sir, when you have quite done with it!'

'You will find very little to repay you for your trouble in this contemptible *thing*, sir,' replied Slurk, bestowing a Satanic frown on Pott.

'You shall have this presently,' said Pott, looking up, pale with rage, and quivering in his speech, from the same cause. 'Ha! ha! you will be amused with this *fellow's* audacity.'

Terrific emphasis was laid upon this 'thing' and 'fellow;' and the faces of both editors began to glow with defiance.

'The ribaldry of this miserable man is despicably disgusting,' said Pott, pretending to address Bob Sawyer, and scowling upon Slurk.

Here, Mr Slurk laughed very heartily, and folding up the paper so as to get at a fresh column conveniently, said, that the blockhead really amused him.

'What an impudent blunderer this fellow is,' said Pott, turning from pink to crimson.

'Did you ever read any of this man's foolery, sir?' inquired Slurk, of Bob Sawyer.

'Never,' replied Bob; 'is it very bad?'

'Oh, shocking! shocking!' rejoined Slurk.

'Really! Dear me, this is too atrocious!' exclaimed Pott, at this juncture; still feigning to be absorbed in his reading.

'If you can wade through a few sentences of malice, meanness, falsehood, perjury, treachery, and cant,' said Slurk, handing the paper to Bob, 'you will, perhaps, be somewhat repaid by a laugh at the style of this ungrammatical twaddler.'[11]

'What's that you said, sir?' inquired Mr Pott, looking up, trembling all over with passion.

'What's that to you, sir?' replied Slurk.

'Ungrammatical twaddler, was it, sir?' said Pott.

'Yes, sir, it was,' replied Slurk; 'and *blue bore*, sir, if you like that better; ha! ha!'

Mr Pott retorted not a word to this jocose insult, but deliberately folded up his copy of the Independent, flattened it carefully down, crushed it beneath his boot, spat upon it with great ceremony, and flung it into the fire.

'There, sir,' said Pott, retreating from the stove, 'and that's the way I would serve the viper who produces it, if I were not, fortunately for him, restrained by the laws of my country.'

'Serve him so, sir!' cried Slurk, starting up. 'Those laws shall never be appealed to by him, sir, in such a case. Serve him so, sir!'

'Hear! hear!' said Bob Sawyer.

'Nothing can be fairer,' observed Mr Ben Allen.

'Serve him so, sir!' reiterated Slurk, in a loud voice.

Mr Pott darted a look of contempt, which might have withered an anchor.

'Serve him so, sir!' reiterated Slurk, in a louder voice than before.

'I will not, sir,' rejoined Pott.

'Oh, you won't, won't you, sir?' said Mr Slurk, in a taunting manner; 'you hear this, gentlemen! He won't; not that he's afraid; oh, no! he *won't*. Ha! ha!'

'I consider you, sir,' said Mr Pott, moved by this sarcasm, 'I consider you a viper. I look upon you, sir, as a man who has placed himself beyond the pale of society, by his most audacious, disgraceful, and abominable public conduct. I view you, sir, personally and politically, in no other light than as a most unparalleled and unmitigated viper.'

The indignant Independent did not wait to hear the end of this personal denunciation; for, catching up his carpet-bag which was well stuffed with moveables, he swung it in the air as Pott turned away, and, letting it fall with a circular sweep on his head, just at that particular angle of the bag where a good thick hair-brush happened to be packed, caused a sharp crash to be heard through-out the kitchen, and brought him at once to the ground.

'Gentlemen,' cried Mr Pickwick, as Pott started up and seized the fire-shovel, 'gentlemen! Consider, for Heaven's sake – help – Sam – here – pray, gentlemen – interfere, somebody.'

Uttering these incoherent exclamations, Mr Pickwick rushed between the infuriated combatants just in time to receive the carpet-bag on one side of his body, and the fire-shovel on the other. Whether the representatives of the public feeling of Eatanswill were blinded by animosity, or (being both acute reasoners) saw the advantage of having a third party between them to bear all the blows, certain it is that they paid not the slightest attention to Mr Pickwick, but defying each other with great spirit, plied the carpet-bag and the fire-shovel most fearlessly. Mr Pickwick would unques-tionably have suffered severely for his humane interference, if Mr Weller, attracted by his master's cries, had not rushed in at the moment, and, snatching up a meal-sack, effectually stopped the conflict by drawing it over the head and shoulders of the mighty Pott, and clasping him tight round the shoulders.

'Take avay that 'ere bag from the t'other madman,' said Sam to Ben Allen and Bob Sawyer, who had done nothing but dodge round the group, each with a tortoise-shell lancet in his hand, ready to bleed the first man stunned. 'Give it up, you wretched little creetur, or I'll smother you in it.'

Awed by these threats, and quite out of breath, the Independent suffered himself to be disarmed; and Mr Weller, removing the extinguisher from Pott, set him free with a caution.

'You take yourselves off to bed quietly,' said Sam, 'or I'll put you both in it, and let you fight it out vith the mouth tied, as I vould a dozen sich, if they played these games. And you have the goodness to come this here vay, sir, if you please.'

Thus addressing his master, Sam took him by the arm, and led him off, while the rival editors were severally removed to their beds by the landlord, under the inspection of Mr Bob Sawyer and Mr Benjamin Allen; breathing, as they went away, many sanguinary threats, and making vague appointments for mortal combat next day. When they came to think it over, however, it occurred to them that they could do it much better in print, so they recommenced deadly hostilities without delay; and all Eatanswill rung with their boldness – on paper.

They had taken themselves off in separate coaches, early next morning, before the other travellers were stirring; and the weather

The Rival Editors

having now cleared up, the chaise companions once more turned their faces to London.

CHAPTER 52

Involving a serious Change in the Weller Family, and the untimely Downfall of the red-nosed Mr Stiggins

Considering it a matter of delicacy to abstain from introducing either Bob Sawyer or Ben Allen to the young couple, until they were fully prepared to expect them, and wishing to spare Arabella's feelings as much as possible, Mr Pickwick proposed that he and Sam should alight in the neighbourhood of the George and Vulture, and that the two young men should for the present take up their quarters elsewhere. To this, they very readily agreed, and the proposition was accordingly acted upon; Mr Ben Allen and Mr Bob Sawyer betaking themselves to a sequestered pot-shop on the remotest confines of the Borough, behind the bar-door of which their names had in other days very often appeared, at the head of long and complex calculations worked in white chalk.

'Dear me, Mr Weller,' said the pretty housemaid, meeting Sam at the door.

'Dear *me* I vish it wos, my dear,' replied Sam, dropping behind, to let his master get out of hearing. 'Wot a sweet lookin' creetur you are, Mary!'

'Lor, Mr Weller, what nonsense you do talk!' said Mary. 'Oh! *don't*, Mr Weller.'

'Don't what, my dear?' said Sam.

'Why, that,' replied the pretty housemaid. 'Lor, do get along with you.' Thus admonishing him, the pretty housemaid pushed Sam against the wall, declaring that he had tumbled her cap, and put her hair quite out of curl.

'And prevented what I was going to say, besides,' added Mary. 'There's a letter been waiting here for you four days; you hadn't been gone away, half an hour, when it came; and more than that, it's got, immediate, on the outside.'

'Vere is it, my love?' inquired Sam.

'I took care of it, for you, or I dare say it would have been lost long before this,' replied Mary. 'There, take it; it's more than you deserve.'

With these words, after many pretty little coquettish doubts and fears, and wishes that she might not have lost it, Mary produced the letter from behind the nicest little muslin tucker possible, and handed it to Sam, who thereupon kissed it with much gallantry and devotion.

'My goodness me!' said Mary, adjusting the tucker, and feigning unconsciousness, 'you seem to have grown very fond of it all at once.'

To this Mr Weller only replied by a wink, the intense meaning of which no description could convey the faintest idea of; and, sitting himself down beside Mary on a window-seat, opened the letter and glanced at the contents.

'Hallo!' exclaimed Sam, 'wot's all this?'

'Nothing the matter, I hope?' said Mary, peeping over his shoulder.

'Bless them eyes o' yourn!' said Sam, looking up.

'Never mind my eyes; you had much better read your letter,' said the pretty housemaid; and as she said so, she made the eyes twinkle with such slyness and beauty that they were perfectly irresistible.

Sam refreshed himself with a kiss, and read as follows:

> 'Markis Gran
> By dorken
> Wens^{dy.}

'My dear Sammle,

'I am wery sorry to have the plessure of being a Bear of ill news your Mother in law cort cold consekens of imprudently settin too long on the damp grass in the rain a hearin of a shepherd who warnt able to leave off till late at night owen to his havin vound his-self up vith brandy and vater and not being able to stop his-self till he got a little sober which took a many hours to do the doctor says that if she'd svallo'd varm brandy and vater artervards insted of afore she mightn't have been no vus her veels wos immedetly greased and everythink done to set her agoin as could be inwented your farther had hopes as she vould have vorked round as usual but just as she wos a turnen the corner my boy she took the wrong road and vent down hill vith a welocity you never see and notvithstandin that the drag wos put on drectly by the medikel man it wornt of no use at all for she paid the last pike at twenty minutes afore six o'clock yesterday evenin havin done the jouney wery much under the reglar time vich praps was partly owen to her haven taken in wery little luggage by the vay your father says that if you vill come and see me Sammy he vill take it as a wery great favor for I am wery lonely Samivel n b he *vill* have it spelt that vay vich I say ant right and as there is sich a many things to settle he is sure your guvner wont object of course he vill not Sammy for I knows him better so he sends his dooty in which I join and am Samivel infernally yours

'TONY VELLER.'

'Wot a incomprehensible letter,' said Sam; 'who's to know wot it means, vith all this he-ing and I-ing! It ain't my father's writin', 'cept this here signater in print letters; that's his.'

'Perhaps he got somebody to write it for him, and signed it himself afterwards,' said the pretty house-maid.

'Stop a minit,' replied Sam, running over the letter again, and pausing here and there, to reflect, as he did so. 'You've hit it. The gen'l'm'n as wrote it wos a tellin' all about the misfortun' in a proper vay, and then my father comes a lookin' over him, and complicates the whole concern by puttin' his oar in. That's just the wery sort o' thing he'd do. You're right, Mary, my dear.'

Having satisfied himself on this point, Sam read the letter all over, once more, and, appearing to form a clear notion of its contents for the first time, ejaculated thoughtfully, as he folded it up:

'And so the poor creatur's dead! I'm sorry for it. She warn't a bad-disposed 'ooman, if them shepherds had let her alone. I'm wery sorry for it.'

Mr Weller uttered these words in so serious a manner, that the pretty house-maid cast down her eyes and looked very grave.

'Hows'ever,' said Sam, putting the letter in his pocket with a gentle sigh, 'it wos to be – and wos, as the old lady said arter she'd married the footman. Can't be helped now, can it, Mary?'

Mary shook her head, and sighed too.

'I must apply to the hemperor for leave of absence,' said Sam.

Mary sighed again. The letter was so very affecting.

'Good bye!' said Sam.

'Good bye,' rejoined the pretty housemaid, turning her head away.

'Well, shake hands, won't you?' said Sam.

The pretty housemaid put out a hand which, although it was a housemaid's, was a very small one, and rose to go.

'I shan't be wery long avay,' said Sam.

'You're always away,' said Mary, giving her head the slightest possible toss in the air. 'You no sooner come, Mr Weller, than you go again.'

Mr Weller drew the household beauty closer to him, and entered upon a whispering conversation, which had not proceeded far, when she turned her face round and condescended to look at him again. When they parted, it was somehow or other indispensably necessary for her to go to her room, and arrange the cap and curls before she could think of presenting herself to her mistress; which preparatory ceremony she went off to perform, bestowing many nods and smiles on Sam over the banisters as she tripped up stairs.

'I shan't be away more than a day, or two, sir, at the farthest,' said Sam, when he had communicated to Mr Pickwick the intelligence of his father's loss.

'As long as may be necessary, Sam,' replied Mr Pickwick, 'you have my full permission to remain.'

Sam bowed.

'You will tell your father, Sam, that if I can be of any assistance to him in his present situation, I shall be most willing and ready to lend him any aid in my power,' said Mr Pickwick.

'Thankee, sir,' rejoined Sam. 'I'll mention it, sir.'

And with some expressions of mutual goodwill and interest, master and man separated.

It was just seven o'clock when Samuel Weller, alighting from the box of a stage-coach which passed through Dorking, stood within a few hundred yards of the Marquis of Granby. It was a cold dull evening; the little street looked dreary and dismal; and the mahogany countenance of the noble and gallant Marquis seemed to wear a more sad and melancholy expression than it was wont to do, as it swung to and fro, creaking mournfully in the wind. The blinds were pulled down, and the shutters partly closed; of the knot of loungers that usually collected about the door, not one was to be seen; the place was silent and desolate.

Seeing nobody of whom he could ask any preliminary questions, Sam walked softly in. Glancing round, he quickly recognised his parent in the distance.

The widower was seated at a small round table in the little room behind the bar, smoking a pipe, with his eyes intently fixed upon the fire. The funeral had evidently taken place that day; for attached to his hat, which he still retained on his head, was a hatband measuring about a yard and a half in length, which hung over the top rail of the chair and streamed negligently down. Mr Weller was in a very abstracted and contemplative mood. Notwithstanding that Sam called him by name several times, he still continued to smoke with the same fixed and quiet countenance, and was only roused ultimately by his son's placing the palm of his hand on his shoulder.

'Sammy,' said Mr Weller, 'you're velcome.'

'I've been a callin' to you half a dozen times,' said Sam, hanging his hat on a peg, 'but you didn't hear me.'

'No, Sammy,' replied Mr Weller, again looking thoughtfully at the fire. 'I wos in a referee, Sammy.'

'Wot about?' inquired Sam, drawing his chair up to the fire.

'In a referee, Sammy,' replied the elder Mr Weller, 'regarding *her*, Samivel.' Here Mr Weller jerked his head in the direction of Dorking churchyard, in mute explanation that his words referred to the late Mrs Weller.

'I wos a thinkin', Sammy,' said Mr Weller, eyeing his son, with great earnestness, over his pipe; as if to assure him that however extraordinary and incredible the declaration might appear, it was nevertheless calmly and deliberately uttered. 'I wos a thinkin', Sammy, that upon the whole I wos wery sorry she wos gone.'

'Vell, and so you ought to be,' replied Sam.

Mr Weller nodded his acquiescence in the sentiment, and again fastening his eyes on the fire, shrouded himself in a cloud, and mused deeply.

'Those wos wery sensible observations as she made, Sammy,' said Mr Weller driving the smoke away with his hand, after a long silence.

'Wot observations?' inquired Sam.

'Them as she made, arter she was took ill,' replied the old gentleman.

'Wot was they?'

'Somethin' to this here effect. "Veller," she says, "I'm afeard I've not done by you quite wot I ought to have done; you're a wery kind-hearted man, and I might ha' made your home more comfortabler. I begin to see now," she says, "ven it's too late, that if a married 'ooman vishes to be religious, she should begin vith dischargin' her dooties at home, and makin' them as is about her cheerful and happy, and that vile she goes to church, or chapel, or wot not, at all proper times, she should be wery careful not to convert this sort o' thing into a excuse for idleness or self-indulgence. I *have* done this," she says, "and I've vasted time and substance on them as has done it more than me; but I hope ven I'm gone, Veller, that you'll think on me as I wos afore I know'd them people, and as I raly wos by natur"." "Susan," says I, – I wos took up wery short by this, Samivel; I von't deny it, my boy – "Susan," I says, "you 've been a wery good vife to me, altogether; don't say nothin' at all about it; keep a good heart my dear; and you'll live to see me punch that 'ere Stiggins's head yet." She smiled at this, Samivel,' said the old gentleman, stifling a sigh with his pipe, 'but she died arter all!'

'Vell,' said Sam, venturing to offer a little homely consolation, after the lapse of three or four minutes, consumed by the old gentleman in slowly shaking his head from side to side, and solemnly smoking; 'vell, gov'ner, ve must all come to it, one day or another.'

'So we must, Sammy,' said Mr Weller the elder.

'There's a Providence in it all,'[1] said Sam.

'O' course there is,' replied his father with a nod of grave approval. 'Wot 'ud become of the undertakers vithout it, Sammy?'

Lost in the immense field of conjecture opened by this reflection, the elder Mr Weller laid his pipe on the table, and stirred the fire with a meditative visage.

While the old gentleman was thus engaged, a very buxom-looking cook, dressed in mourning, who had been bustling about, in the bar, glided into the room, and bestowing many smirks of recognition upon Sam, silently stationed herself at the back of his father's chair, and announced her presence by a slight cough: the which, being disregarded, was followed by a louder one.

'Hallo!' said the elder Mr Weller, dropping the poker as he looked round, and hastily drew his chair away. 'Wot's the matter now?'

'Have a cup of tea, there's a good soul,' replied the buxom female, coaxingly.

'I von't,' replied Mr Weller, in a somewhat boisterous manner, 'I'll see you – ' Mr Weller hastily checked himself, and added in a low tone, 'furder fust.'

'Oh, dear, dear! How adversity does change people!' said the lady, looking upwards.

'It's the only thing 'twixt this and the doctor as shall change *my* condition,' muttered Mr Weller.

'I really never saw a man so cross,' said the buxom female.

'Never mind. It's all for my own good; vich is the reflection vith wich the penitent schoolboy comforted his feelin's ven they flogged him,' rejoined the old gentleman.

The buxom female shook her head with a compassionate and sympathising air; and, appealing to Sam, inquired whether his father really ought not to make an effort to keep up, and not give way to that lowness of spirits.

'You see, Mr Samuel,' said the buxom female, 'as I was telling him yesterday, he *will* feel lonely, he can't expect but what he should, sir, but he should keep up a good heart, because, dear me, I'm sure we all pity his loss, and are ready to do anything for him; and there's no situation in life so bad, Mr Samuel, that it can't be mended. Which is what a very worthy person said to me when my husband died.' Here the speaker, putting her hand before her mouth, coughed again, and looked affectionately at the elder Mr Weller.

'As I don't rekvire any o' your conversation just now, mum, vill you have the goodness to re-tire?' inquired Mr Weller in a grave and steady voice.

'Well, Mr Weller,' said the buxom female, 'I'm sure I only spoke to you out of kindness.'

'Wery likely, mum,' replied Mr Weller. 'Samivel, show the lady out, and shut the door arter her.'

This hint was not lost upon the buxom female; for she at once left the room, and slammed the door behind her, upon which Mr Weller, senior, falling back in his chair in a violent perspiration, said:

'Sammy, if I wos to stop here alone vun veek – only vun veek, my boy – that 'ere 'ooman 'ud marry me by force and wiolence afore it was over.'

'Wot! Is she so wery fond on you?' inquired Sam.

'Fond!' replied his father, 'I can't keep her away from me. If I was locked up in a fire-proof chest vith a patent Brahmin,[2] she 'd find means to get at me, Sammy.'

'Wot a thing it is, to be so sought arter!' observed Sam, smiling.

'I don't take no pride out on it, Sammy,' replied Mr Weller, poking the fire vehemently, 'it's a horrid sitiwation. I'm actiwally drove out o' house and home by it. The breath was scarcely out o' your poor mother-in-law's body, ven vun old 'ooman sends me a pot o' jam, and another a pot o' jelly, and another brews a blessed large jug o' camomile-tea, vich she brings in vith her own hands.' Mr Weller paused with an aspect of intense disgust, and, looking round, added in a whisper: 'They wos all widders, Sammy, all on 'em, 'cept the camomile-tea vun, as wos a single young lady o' fifty-three.'

Sam gave a comical look in reply, and the old gentleman having broken an obstinate lump of coal, with a countenance expressive of as much earnestness and malice as if it had been the head of one of the widows last-mentioned, said:

'In short, Sammy, I feel that I ain't safe anyveres but on the box.'

'How are you safer there than anyveres else?' interrupted Sam.

'''Cos a coachman's a privileged indiwidual,' replied Mr Weller, looking fixedly at his son. '''Cos a coachman may do vithout suspicion wot other men may not; 'cos a coachman may be on the wery amicablest terms with eighty mile o' females, and yet nobody think that he ever means to marry any vun among 'em. And wot other man can say the same, Sammy?'

'Vell, there's somethin' in that,' said Sam.

'If your gov'ner had been a coachman,' reasoned Mr Weller, 'do you s'pose as that 'ere jury 'ud ever ha' conwicted him, s'posin' it possible as the matter could ha' gone to that extremity? They dustn't ha' done it.'

'Wy not?' said Sam, rather disparagingly.

'Wy not!' rejoined Mr Weller; '''cos it 'ud ha' gone agin their consciences. A reg'lar coachman's a sort o' con-nectin' link betwixt singleness and matrimony, and every practicable man knows it.'

'Wot! You mean, they're gen'ral fav'rites, and nobody takes adwantage on 'em, p'raps?' said Sam.

His father nodded.

'How it ever come to that 'ere pass,' resumed the parent Weller, 'I can't say. Wy it is that long-stage coachmen possess such insiniwations, and is alvays looked up to – a-dored I may say – by ev'ry young 'ooman in ev'ry town he vurks through, I don't know. I only know that so it is. It's a reg'lation of natur – a dispensary, as your poor mother-in-law used to say.'

'A dispensation,' said Sam, correcting the old gentleman.

'Wery good, Samivel, a dispensation if you like it better,' returned Mr Weller; '*I* call it a dispensary, and it's alvays writ up so, at the places vere they gives you physic for nothin' in your own bottles; that's all.'

With these words, Mr Weller re-filled and re-lighted his pipe, and once more summoning up a meditative expression of countenance, continued as follows:

'Therefore, my boy, as I do not see the adwisability o' stoppin here to be marrid vether I vant to or not, and as at the same time I do not vish to separate myself from them interestin' members o' society altogether, I have come to the determination o' drivin' the Safety, and puttin' up vunce more at the Bell Savage, vich is my nat'ral-born element, Sammy.'

'And wot's to become o' the bis'ness?' inquired Sam.

'The bis'ness, Samivel,' replied the old gentleman, 'good-vill, stock, and fixters, vill be sold by private contract; and out o' the money, two hundred pound, agreeable to a rekvest o' your mother-in-law's to me a little afore she died, vill be inwested in your name in – wot do you call them things agin?'

'Wot things?' inquired Sam.

'Them things as is always a goin' up and down, in the City.'

'Omnibuses?' suggested Sam.

'Nonsense,' replied Mr Weller. 'Them things as is alvays a fluctooatin', and gettin' theirselves inwolved somehow or another vith the national debt, and the checquers bills, and all that.'

'Oh! the funds,' said Sam.

'Ah!' rejoined Mr Weller, 'the funs; two hundred pounds o' the money is to be inwested for you, Samivel, in the funs; four and a half per cent. reduced counsels,[3] Sammy.'

'Wery kind o' the old lady to think o' me,' said Sam, 'and I'm wery much obliged to her.'

'The rest vill be inwested in my name,' continued the elder Mr Weller; 'and ven I'm took off the road, it'll come to you, so take care you don't spend it all at vunst, my boy, and mind that no widder gets a inklin' o' your fortun', or you 're done.'

Having delivered this warning, Mr Weller resumed his pipe with a more serene countenance; the disclosure of these matters appearing to have eased his mind considerably.

'Somebody's a tappin' at the door,' said Sam.

'Let 'em tap,' replied his father, with dignity.

Sam acted upon the direction. There was another tap, and another, and then a long row of taps; upon which Sam inquired why the tapper was not admitted.

'Hush,' whispered Mr Weller, with apprehensive looks, 'don't take no notice on 'em, Sammy, it's vun o' the widders, p'raps.'

No notice being taken of the taps, the unseen visitor, after a short lapse, ventured to open the door and peep in. It was no female head that was thrust in at the partially opened door, but the long black locks and red face of Mr Stiggins. Mr Weller's pipe fell from his hands.

The reverend gentleman gradually opened the door by almost

imperceptible degrees, until the aperture was just wide enough to admit of the passage of his lank body, when he glided into the room and closed it after him with great care and gentleness. Turning towards Sam, and raising his hands and eyes in token of the unspeakable sorrow with which he regarded the calamity that had befallen the family, he carried the high-backed chair to his old corner by the fire, and, seating himself on the very edge, drew forth a brown pocket-handkerchief, and applied the same to his optics.

While this was going forward, the elder Mr Weller sat back in his chair, with his eyes wide open, his hands planted on his knees, and his whole countenance expressive of absorbing and overwhelming astonishment. Sam sat opposite him in perfect silence, waiting, with eager curiosity, for the termination of the scene.

Mr Stiggins kept the brown pocket-handkerchief before his eyes for some minutes, moaning decently meanwhile, and then, mastering his feelings by a strong effort, put it in his pocket and buttoned it up. After this, he stirred the fire; after that, he rubbed his hands and looked at Sam.

'Oh my young friend,' said Mr Stiggins, breaking the silence in a very low voice, 'here's a sorrowful affliction!'

Sam nodded, very slightly.

'For the man of wrath, too!' added Mr Stiggins; 'it makes a vessel's heart bleed!'

Mr Weller was overheard by his son to murmur something relative to making a vessel's nose bleed; but Mr Stiggins heard him not.

'Do you know, young man,' whispered Mr Stiggins, drawing his chair closer to Sam, 'whether she has left Emanuel anything?'

'Who's he?' inquired Sam.

'The chapel,' replied Mr Stiggins; 'our chapel; our fold, Mr Samuel.'

'She hasn't left the fold nothin', nor the shepherd nothin', nor the animals nothin',' said Sam, decisively; 'nor the dogs neither.'

Mr Stiggins looked slyly at Sam; glanced at the old gentleman, who was sitting with his eyes closed, as if asleep; and drawing his chair still nearer, said:

'Nothing for *me*, Mr Samuel?'

Sam shook his head.

'I think there's something,' said Stiggins, turning as pale as he could turn. 'Consider, Mr Samuel; no little token?'

'Not so much as the vorth o' that 'ere old umberella o' yourn,' replied Sam.

'Perhaps,' said Mr Stiggins, hesitatingly, after a few moments' deep thought, 'perhaps she recommended me to the care of the man of wrath, Mr Samuel?'

'I think that's wery likely, from what he said,' rejoined Sam; 'he wos a speakin' about you, jist now.'

'Was he, though?' exclaimed Stiggins brightening up. 'Ah! He's changed, I dare say. We might live very comfortably together now, Mr Samuel, eh? I could take care of his property when you are away – good care, you see.'

Heaving a long-drawn sigh, Mr Stiggins paused for a response. Sam nodded, and Mr Weller, the elder, gave vent to an extraordinary sound, which being neither a groan, nor a grunt, nor a gasp, nor a growl, seemed to partake in some degree of the character of all four.

Mr Stiggins, encouraged by this sound, which he understood to betoken remorse or repentance, looked about him, rubbed his hands, wept, smiled, wept again, and then, walking softly across the room to a well-remembered shelf in one corner, took down a tumbler, and with great deliberation put four lumps of sugar in it. Having got thus far, he looked about him again, and sighed grievously; with that, he walked softly into the bar, and presently returning with the tumbler half full of pine-apple rum, advanced to the kettle which was singing gaily on the hob, mixed his grog, stirred it, sipped it, sat down, and taking a long and hearty pull at the rum and water, stopped for breath.

The elder Mr Weller, who still continued to make various strange and uncouth attempts to appear asleep, offered not a single word during these proceedings; but when Stiggins stopped for breath, he darted upon him, and snatching the tumbler from his hand, threw the remainder of the rum and water in his face, and the glass itself into the grate. Then, seizing the reverend gentleman firmly by the collar, he suddenly fell to kicking him most furiously: accompanying every application of his top-boots to Mr Stiggins's person, with sundry violent and incoherent anathemas upon his limbs, eyes, and body.

'Sammy,' said Mr Weller, 'put my hat on tight for me.'

Sam dutifully adjusted the hat with the long hatband more firmly on his father's head, and the old gentleman, resuming his kicking with greater agility than before, tumbled with Mr Stiggins through the bar, and through the passage, out at the front door, and so into the street; the kicking continuing the whole way, and increasing in vehemence, rather than diminishing, every time the top-boot was lifted.

It was a beautiful and exhilarating sight to see the red-nosed man writhing in Mr Weller's grasp, and his whole frame quivering with anguish as kick followed kick in rapid succession; it was a still more exciting spectacle to behold Mr Weller, after a powerful struggle, immersing Mr Stiggins's head in a horse-trough full of water, and holding it there, until he was half suffocated.

'There!' said Mr Weller, throwing all his energy into one most complicated kick, as he at length permitted Mr Stiggins to withdraw his head from the trough, 'send any vun o' them lazy shepherds here, and I'll pound him to a jelly first, and drownd him artervards! Sammy, help me in, and fill me a small glass of brandy. I'm out o' breath, my boy.'

CHAPTER 53

Comprising the final Exit of Mr Jingle and Job Trotter; with a Great Morning of Business in Gray's Inn Square. Concluding with a Double Knock at Mr Perker's door

When Arabella, after some gentle preparation, and many assurances that there was not the least occasion for being low-spirited, was at length made acquainted by Mr Pickwick with the unsatisfactory result of his visit to Birmingham, she burst into tears, and sobbing aloud, lamented in moving terms that she should have been the unhappy cause of any estrangement between a father and his son.

'My dear girl,' said Mr Pickwick, kindly, 'it is no fault of yours. It was impossible to foresee that the old gentleman would be so strongly prepossessed against his son's marriage, you know. I am sure,' added Mr Pickwick, glancing at her pretty face, 'he can have very little idea of the pleasure he denies himself.'

'Oh my dear Mr Pickwick,' said Arabella, 'what shall we do, if he continues to be angry with us?'

'Why, wait patiently, my dear, until he thinks better of it,' replied Mr Pickwick, cheerfully.

'But, dear Mr Pickwick, what is to become of Nathaniel if his father withdraws his assistance?' urged Arabella.

'In that case, my love,' rejoined Mr Pickwick, 'I will venture to prophesy that he will find some other friend who will not be backward in helping him to start in the world.'

The significance of this reply was not so well disguised by Mr Pickwick but that Arabella understood it. So, throwing her arms round his neck, and kissing him affectionately, she sobbed louder than before.

'Come, come,' said Mr Pickwick, taking her hand, 'we will wait here a few days longer, and see whether he writes or takes any other notice of your husband's communication. If not, I have thought of half a dozen plans, any one of which would make you happy at once. There, my dear, there!'

With these words, Mr Pickwick gently pressed Arabella's hand, and bade her dry her eyes, and not distress her husband. Upon which, Arabella, who was one of the best little creatures alive, put her handkerchief in her reticule, and by the time Mr Winkle joined them, exhibited in full lustre the same beaming smiles and sparkling eyes that had originally captivated him.

'This is a distressing predicament for these young people,' thought Mr Pickwick, as he dressed himself next morning. 'I'll walk up to Perker's, and consult him about the matter.'

As Mr Pickwick was further prompted to betake himself to Gray's Inn Square by an anxious desire to come to a pecuniary settlement with the kind-hearted little attorney without further delay, he made a hurried breakfast, and executed his intention so speedily, that ten o'clock had not struck when he reached Gray's Inn.

It still wanted ten minutes to the hour when he had ascended the staircase on which Perker's chambers were. The clerks had not arrived yet, and he beguiled the time by looking out of the staircase window.

The healthy light of a fine October morning made even the dingy old houses brighten up a little: some of the dusty windows actually looking almost cheerful as the sun's rays gleamed upon them. Clerk after clerk hastened into the square by one or other of the entrances, and looking up at the Hall clock, accelerated or decreased his rate of walking according to the time at which his office hours nominally commenced; the half-past nine o'clock people suddenly becoming very brisk, and the ten o'clock gentlemen falling into a pace of most aristocratic slowness. The clock struck ten, and clerks poured in faster than ever, each one in a greater perspiration than his predecessor. The noise of unlocking and opening doors echoed and re-echoed on every side; heads appeared as if by magic in every window; the porters took up their stations for the day; the slipshod laundresses hurried off; the postman ran from house to house; and the whole legal hive was in a bustle.

'You're early, Mr Pickwick,' said a voice behind him.

'Ah, Mr Lowten,' replied that gentleman, looking round, and recognising his old acquaintance.

'Precious warm walking, isn't it?' said Lowten, drawing a Bramah[1] key from his pocket, with a small plug therein, to keep the dust out.

'You appear to feel it so,' rejoined Mr Pickwick, smiling at the clerk, who was literally red hot.

'I've come along rather, I can tell you,' replied Lowten. 'It went the half hour as I came through the Polygon.[2] I'm here before *him*, though, so I don't mind.'

Comforting himself with this reflection, Mr Lowten extracted the plug from the door-key, and having opened the door, replugged and repocketed his Bramah, and picked up the letters which the postman had dropped through the box. He then ushered Mr Pickwick into the office. Here, in the twinkling of an eye, he divested himself of his coat, put on a threadbare garment which he took out of a desk, hung up his hat, pulled forth a few sheets of cartridge[3] and blotting-paper in alternate layers, and sticking a pen behind his ear, rubbed his hands with an air of great satisfaction.

'There you see, Mr Pickwick,' he said, 'now I'm complete. I've got my office coat on, and my pad out, and let him come as soon as he likes. You haven't got a pinch of snuff about you, have you?'

'No, I have not,' replied Mr Pickwick.

'I'm sorry for it,' said Lowten. 'Never mind. I'll run out presently, and get a bottle of soda. Don't I look rather queer about the eyes, Mr Pickwick?'

The individual appealed to, surveyed Mr Lowten's eyes from a distance, and expressed his opinion that no unusual queerness was perceptible in those features.

'I'm glad of it,' said Lowten. 'We were keeping it up pretty tolerably at the Stump last night, and I'm rather out of sorts this morning. Perker's been about that business of yours, by the bye.'

'What business?' inquired Mr Pickwick. 'Mrs Bardell's costs?'

'No, I don't mean that,' replied Mr Lowten. 'About getting that customer that we paid the ten shillings in the pound to the bill discounter for, on your account – to get him out of the Fleet, you know – about getting him to Demerara.'[4]

'Oh? Mr Jingle?' said Mr Pickwick, hastily. 'Yes. Well?'

'Well, it's all arranged,' said Lowten, mending his pen. 'The agent at Liverpool said he had been obliged to you many times when you were in business, and he would be glad to take him on your recommendation.'

'That's well,' said Mr Pickwick. 'I am delighted to hear it.'

'But I say,' resumed Lowten, scraping the back of the pen preparatory to making a fresh split, '*what* a soft chap that other is!'

'Which other?'

'Why, that servant, or friend, or whatever he is; *you* know; Trotter.'

'Ah?' said Mr Pickwick, with a smile. 'I always thought him the reverse.'

'Well, and so did I, from what little I saw of him,' replied Lowten, 'it only shows how one may be deceived. What do you think of *his* going to Demerara, too?'

'What! And giving up what was offered him here!' exclaimed Mr Pickwick.

'Treating Perker's offer of eighteen bob a-week, and a rise if he behaved himself, like dirt,' replied Lowten. 'He said he must go along with the other one, and so they persuaded Perker to write again, and they've got him something on the same estate; not near so good, Perker says, as a convict would get in New South Wales, if he appeared at his trial in a new suit of clothes.'

'Foolish fellow,' said Mr Pickwick, with glistening eyes. 'Foolish fellow.'

'Oh, it's worse than foolish; it's downright sneaking, you know,' replied Lowten, nibbing the pen with a contemptuous face. 'He says that he's the only friend he ever had, and he's attached to him, and all that. Friendship's a very good thing in its way: we are all very friendly and comfortable at the Stump, for instance, over our grog, where every man pays for himself; but damn hurting yourself for anybody else, you know! No man should have more than two attachments – the first, to number one, and the second to the ladies; that's what I say – ha! ha!' Mr Lowten concluded with a loud laugh, half in jocularity, and half in derision, which was prematurely cut short by the sound of Perker's footsteps on the stairs: at the first approach of which, he vaulted on his stool with an agility most remarkable, and wrote intensely

The greeting between Mr Pickwick and his professional adviser was warm and cordial; the client was scarcely ensconced in the attorney's arm chair, however, when a knock was heard at the door, and a voice inquired whether Mr Perker was within.

'Hark!' said Perker, 'that's one of our vagabond friends – Jingle himself, my dear sir. Will you see him?'

'What do you think?' inquired Mr Pickwick, hesitating.

'Yes, I think you had better. Here, you sir, what's your name, walk in, will you?'

In compliance with this unceremonious invitation, Jingle and Job walked into the room, but, seeing Mr Pickwick, stopped short in some confusion.

'Well,' said Perker, 'don't you know that gentleman?'

'Good reason to,' replied Mr Jingle, stepping forward. 'Mr Pickwick – deepest obligations – life preserver – made a man of me – you shall never repent it, sir.'

'I am happy to hear you say so,' said Mr Pickwick. 'You look much better.'

'Thanks to you, sir – great change – Majesty's Fleet – unwholesome place – very,' said Jingle, shaking his head. He was decently and cleanly dressed, and so was Job, who stood bolt upright behind him, staring at Mr Pickwick with a visage of iron.

'When do they go to Liverpool?' inquired Mr Pickwick, half aside to Perker.

'This evening, sir, at seven o'clock,' said Job, taking one step forward. 'By the heavy coach from the city, sir.'

'Are your places taken?'

'They are, sir,' replied Job.

'You have fully made up your mind to go?'

'I have, sir,' answered Job.

'With regard to such an outfit as was indispensable for Jingle,' said Perker, addressing Mr Pickwick aloud, 'I have taken upon myself to make an arrangement for the deduction of a small sum from his quarterly salary, which, being made only for one year, and regularly remitted, will provide for that expense. I entirely disapprove of your doing anything for him, my dear sir, which is not dependent on his own exertions and good conduct.'

'Certainly,' interposed Jingle, with great firmness. 'Clear head – man of the world – quite right – perfectly.'

'By compounding with his creditor, releasing his clothes from the pawn-broker's, relieving him in prison, and paying for his passage,' continued Perker, without noticing Jingle's observation, 'you have already lost upwards of fifty pounds.'

'Not lost,' said Jingle, hastily. 'Pay it all – stick to business – cash up – every farthing. Yellow fever, perhaps – can't help that – if not – '. Here Mr Jingle paused, and striking the crown of his hat with great violence, passed his hand over his eyes, and sat down.

'He means to say,' said Job, advancing a few paces, 'that if he is not carried off by the fever, he will pay the money back again. If he lives, he will, Mr Pickwick. I will see it done. I know he will, sir,' said Job, with energy. 'I could undertake to swear it.'

'Well, well,' said Mr Pickwick, who had been bestowing a score or two of frowns upon Perker, to stop his summary of benefits conferred, which the little attorney obstinately disregarded, 'you must be careful not to play any more desperate cricket matches, Mr Jingle, or to renew your acquaintance with Sir Thomas Blazo, and I have little doubt of your preserving your health.'

Mr Jingle smiled at this sally, but looked rather foolish notwithstanding; so, Mr Pickwick changed the subject by saying,

'You don't happen to know, do you, what has become of another friend of yours – a more humble one, whom I saw at Rochester?'

'Dismal Jemmy?' inquired Jingle.

'Yes.'

Jingle shook his head.

'Clever rascal – queer fellow, hoaxing genius – Job's brother.'

'Job's brother!' exclaimed Mr Pickwick. 'Well, now I look at him closely, there *is* a likeness.'

'We were always considered like each other, sir,' said Job, with a cunning look just lurking in the corners of his eyes, 'only I was really of a serious nature, and he never was. He emigrated to America, sir, in consequence of being too much sought after here, to be comfortable; and has never been heard of since.'

'That accounts for my not having received the "page from the romance of real life," which he promised me one morning when he appeared to be contemplating suicide on Rochester Bridge, I suppose,' said Mr Pickwick, smiling. 'I need not inquire whether his dismal behaviour was natural or assumed.'

'He could assume anything, sir,' said Job. 'You may consider yourself very fortunate in having escaped him so easily. On intimate terms he would have been even a more dangerous acquaintance than – ' Job looked at Jingle, hesitated, and finally added, 'than – than – myself even.'

'A hopeful family yours, Mr Trotter,' said Perker, sealing a letter which he had just finished writing.

'Yes, sir,' replied Job. 'Very much so.'

'Well,' said the little man, laughing; 'I hope you are going to disgrace it. Deliver this letter to the agent when you reach Liverpool, and let me advise you, gentlemen, not to be too knowing in the West Indies. If you throw away this chance, you will both richly deserve to be hanged, as I sincerely trust you will be. And now you had better leave Mr Pickwick and me alone, for we have other matters to talk over, and time is precious.' As Perker said this, he looked towards the door, with an evident desire to render the leave-taking as brief as possible.

It was brief enough on Mr Jingle's part. He thanked the little attorney in a few hurried words for the kindness and promptitude with which he had rendered his assistance, and, turning to his benefactor, stood for a few seconds as if irresolute what to say or how to act. Job Trotter relieved his perplexity; for, with a humble and a grateful bow to Mr Pickwick, he took his friend gently by the arm, and led him away.

'A worthy couple!' said Perker, as the door closed behind them.

'I hope they may become so,' replied Mr Pickwick. 'What do you think? Is there any chance of their permanent reformation?'

Perker shrugged his shoulders doubtfully, but observing Mr Pickwick's anxious and disappointed look, rejoined:

'Of course there is a chance. I hope it may prove a good one. They are unquestionably penitent now; but then, you know, they have the recollection of very recent suffering fresh upon them. What they may become, when that fades away, is a problem that neither you nor I can solve. However, my dear sir,' added Perker, laying his hand on Mr Pickwick's shoulder, 'your object is equally honourable, whatever the result is. Whether that species of benevolence which is so very cautious and long-sighted that it is seldom exercised at all, lest its owner should be imposed upon, and so wounded in his self-love, be real charity or a worldly counterfeit, I leave to wiser heads than mine to determine. But if those two fellows were to commit a burglary to-morrow, my opinion of this action would be equally high.'

With these remarks, which were delivered in a much more animated and earnest manner than is usual in legal gentlemen, Perker drew his chair to his desk, and listened to Mr Pickwick's recital of old Mr Winkle's obstinacy.

'Give him a week,' said Perker, nodding his head prophetically.

'Do you think he will come round?' inquired Mr Pickwick.

'I think he will,' rejoined Perker. 'If not, we must try the young lady's persuasion, and that is what anybody but you, would have done at first.'

Mr Perker was taking a pinch of snuff with various grotesque contractions of countenance, eulogistic of the persuasive powers appertaining unto young ladies, when the murmur of inquiry and answer was heard in the outer office, and Lowten tapped at the door.

'Come in!' cried the little man.

The clerk came in, and shut the door after him, with great mystery.

'What's the matter?' inquired Perker.

'You're wanted, sir.'

'Who wants me?'

Lowten looked at Mr Pickwick, and coughed.

'Who wants me? Can't you speak, Mr Lowten?'

'Why, sir,' replied Lowten, 'it's Dodson; and Fogg is with him.'

'Bless my life!' said the little man, looking at his watch, 'I appointed them to be here, at half-past eleven, to settle that matter of yours, Pickwick. I gave them an undertaking on which they sent down your discharge; it's very awkward, my dear sir; what will you do? Would you like to step into the next room?'

The next room being the identical room in which Messrs. Dodson and Fogg were, Mr Pickwick replied that he would remain where he was: the more especially as Messrs. Dodson and Fogg ought to be ashamed to look him in the face, instead of his being ashamed to see them. Which latter circumstance he begged Mr Perker to note, with a glowing countenance and many marks of indignation.

'Very well, my dear sir, very well,' replied Perker, 'I can only say that if you expect either Dodson or Fogg to exhibit any symptom of shame or confusion at having to look you, or anybody else, in the face, you are the most sanguine man in your expectations that *I* ever met with. Show them in, Mr Lowten.'

Mr Lowten disappeared with a grin, and immediately returned ushering in the firm, in due form of precedence: Dodson first, and Fogg afterwards.

'You have seen Mr Pickwick, I believe?' said Perker to Dodson, inclining his pen in the direction where that gentleman was seated.

'How do you do, Mr Pickwick?' said Dodson in a loud voice.

'Dear me,' cried Fogg, 'how do you do, Mr Pickwick? I hope you are well, sir. I thought I knew the face,' said Fogg, drawing up a chair, and looking round him with a smile.

Mr Pickwick bent his head very slightly, in answer to these salutations, and, seeing Fogg pull a bundle of papers from his coat-pocket, rose and walked to the window.

'There's no occasion for Mr Pickwick to move, Mr Perker,' said Fogg, untying the red tape which encircled the little bundle, and smiling again more sweetly than before. 'Mr Pickwick is pretty well acquainted with these proceedings. There are no secrets between us, I think. He! he! he!'

'Not many, I think,' said Dodson. 'Ha! ha! ha!' Then both the partners laughed together – pleasantly and cheerfully, as men who are going to receive money, often do.

'We shall make Mr Pickwick pay for peeping,' said Fogg, with considerable native humour, as he unfolded his papers. 'The amount of the taxed costs is one hundred and thirty three, six, four, Mr Perker.'

There was a great comparing of papers, and turning over of leaves, by Fogg and Perker, after this statement of profit and loss. Meanwhile, Dodson said in an affable manner to Mr Pickwick:

'I don't think you are looking quite so stout as when I had the pleasure of seeing you last, Mr Pickwick.'

'Possibly not, sir,' replied Mr Pickwick, who had been flashing forth looks of fierce indignation, without producing the smallest effect on either of the sharp practitioners; 'I believe I am not, sir. I have been persecuted and annoyed by Scoundrels of late, sir.'

Perker coughed violently, and asked Mr Pickwick whether he wouldn't like to look at the morning paper? To which inquiry Mr Pickwick returned a most decided negative.

'True,' said Dodson, 'I dare say you *have* been annoyed in the Fleet; there are some odd gentry there. Whereabouts were your apartments, Mr Pickwick?'

'My one room,' replied that much-injured gentleman, 'was on the Coffee Room flight.'

'Oh, indeed!' said Dodson. 'I believe that is a very pleasant part of the establishment.'

'Very,' replied Mr Pickwick drily.

There was a coolness about all this, which, to a gentleman of an excitable temperament, had, under the circumstances, rather an exasperating tendency. Mr Pickwick restrained his wrath by gigantic efforts; but when Perker wrote a cheque for the whole amount, and Fogg deposited it in a small pocket-book with a triumphant smile playing over his pimply features which communicated itself likewise to the stern countenance of Dodson, he felt the blood in his cheeks tingling with indignation.

'Now, Mr Dodson,' said Fogg, putting up the pocket-book and drawing on his gloves, 'I am at your service.'

'Very good,' said Dodson, rising, 'I am quite ready.'

'I am very happy,' said Fogg, softened by the cheque, 'to have had the pleasure of making Mr Pickwick's acquaintance. I hope you don't think quite so ill of us, Mr Pickwick, as when we first had the pleasure of seeing you.'

'I hope not,' said Dodson, with the high tone of calumniated virtue. 'Mr Pickwick now knows us better, I trust: whatever your opinion of gentlemen of our profession may be, I beg to assure you, sir, that I bear no ill-will or vindictive feeling towards you for the sentiments you thought proper to express in our office in Freeman's Court, Cornhill, on the occasion to which my partner has referred.'

'Oh no, no; nor I,' said Fogg, in a most forgiving manner.

'Our conduct, sir,' said Dodson, 'will speak for itself, and justify itself I hope, upon every occasion. We have been in the profession some years, Mr Pickwick, and have been honoured with the confidence of many excellent clients. I wish you good morning, sir.'

'*Good* morning, Mr Pickwick,' said Fogg. So saying, he put his umbrella under his arm, drew off his right glove, and extended the hand of reconciliation to that most indignant gentleman: who, thereupon, thrust his hands beneath his coat-tails, and eyed the attorney with looks of scornful amazement.

'Lowten!' cried Perker at this moment. 'Open the door.'

'Wait one instant,' said Mr Pickwick, 'Perker, I *will* speak.'

'My dear sir, pray let the matter rest where it is,' said the little attorney, who had been in a state of nervous apprehension during the whole interview; 'Mr Pickwick, I beg!'

'I will not be put down, sir,' replied Mr Pickwick hastily. 'Mr Dodson, you have addressed some remarks to me.'

Dodson turned round, bent his head meekly, and smiled.

'Some remarks to me,' repeated Mr Pickwick, almost breathless; 'and your partner has tendered me his hand, and you have both assumed a tone of forgiveness and high-mindedness, which is an extent of impudence that I was not prepared for, even in you.'

'What, sir!' exclaimed Dodson.

'What, sir!' reiterated Fogg.

'Do you know that I have been the victim of your plots and conspiracies?' continued Mr Pickwick. 'Do you know that I am the man whom you have been imprisoning and robbing? Do you know that you were the attorneys for the plaintiff, in Bardell and Pickwick?'

'Yes, sir, we do know it,' replied Dodson.

'Of course we know it, sir,' rejoined Fogg, slapping his pocket – perhaps by accident.

'I see that you recollect it with satisfaction,' said Mr Pickwick, attempting to call up a sneer for the first time in his life, and failing most signally in so doing. 'Although I have long been anxious to tell you, in plain terms, what my opinion of you is, I should have let even this opportunity pass, in deference to my friend Perker's wishes, but for the unwarrantable tone you have assumed, and your insolent familiarity. I say insolent familiarity, sir,' said Mr Pickwick, turning upon Fogg with a fierceness of gesture which caused that person to retreat towards the door with great expedition.

'Take care, sir,' said Dodson, who, though he was the biggest man of the party, had prudently intrenched himself behind Fogg, and was speaking over his head with a very pale face. 'Let him assault you, Mr Fogg; don't return it on any account.'

'No, no, I won't return it,' said Fogg, falling back a little more as he spoke; to the evident relief of his partner, who by these means was gradually getting into the outer office.

'You are,' continued Mr Pickwick, resuming the thread of his discourse, 'you are a well-matched pair of mean, rascally, pettifogging robbers.'

'Well,' interposed Perker, 'is that all?'

'It is all summed up in that,' rejoined Mr Pickwick; 'they are mean, rascally, pettifogging robbers.'

'There!' said Perker in a most conciliatory tone. 'My dear sirs, he has said all he has to say. Now pray go. Lowten, *is* that door open?'

Mr Lowten, with a distant giggle, replied in the affirmative.

'There, there – good morning – good morning – now pray, my dear sirs, – Mr Lowten, the door!' cried the little man, pushing Dodson and Fogg nothing loath, out of the office; 'this way, my dear sirs, – now pray don't prolong this – dear me – Mr Lowten – the door, sir – why don't you attend?'

'If there's law in England, sir,' said Dodson, looking towards Mr Pickwick, as he put on his hat, 'you shall smart for this.'

'You are a couple of mean – '

'Remember, sir, you pay dearly for this,' said Fogg.

' – Rascally, pettifogging robbers!' continued Mr Pickwick, taking not the least notice of the threats that were addressed to him.

'Robbers!' cried Mr Pickwick, running to the stair-head, as the two attorneys descended.

'Robbers!' shouted Mr Pickwick, breaking from Lowten and Perker, and thrusting his head out of the staircase window.

When Mr Pickwick drew in his head again, his countenance was smiling and placid; and, walking quietly back into the office, he declared that he had now removed a great weight from his mind, and that he felt perfectly comfortable and happy.

Perker said nothing at all until he had emptied his snuff-box, and sent Lowten out to fill it, when he was seized with a fit of laughing, which lasted five minutes; at the expiration of which time he said that he supposed he ought to be very angry, but he couldn't think of the business seriously yet – when he could, he would be.

'Well, now,' said Mr Pickwick, 'let me have a settlement with you.'

'Of the same kind as the last?' inquired Perker, with another laugh.

'Not exactly,' rejoined Mr Pickwick, drawing out his pocket-book, and shaking the little man heartily by the hand, 'I only mean a pecuniary settlement. You have done me many acts of kindness that I can never repay, and have no wish to repay, for I prefer continuing the obligation.'

With this preface, the two friends dived into some very complicated accounts and vouchers, which, having been duly displayed and gone through by Perker, were at once discharged by Mr Pickwick with many professions of esteem and friendship.

They had no sooner arrived at this point, than a most violent and startling knocking was heard at the door; it was not an ordinary double knock, but a constant and uninterrupted succession of the loudest single raps, as if the knocker were endowed with the perpetual motion, or the person outside had forgotten to leave off.

'Dear me, what's that!' exclaimed Perker, starting.

'I think it is a knock at the door,' said Mr Pickwick, as if there could be the smallest doubt of the fact!

The knocker made a more energetic reply than words could have yielded, for it continued to hammer with surprising force and noise, without a moment's cessation.

'Dear me!' said Perker, ringing his bell, 'we shall alarm the Inn. Mr Lowten, don't you hear a knock?'

'I'll answer the door in one moment, sir,' replied the clerk.

The knocker appeared to hear the response, and to assert that it was quite impossible he could wait so long. It made a stupendous uproar.

'It's quite dreadful,' said Mr Pickwick, stopping his ears.

'Make haste, Mr Lowten,' Perker called out, 'we shall have the panels beaten in.'

Mr Lowten, who was washing his hands in a dark closet, hurried to the door, and turning the handle, beheld the appearance which is described in the next chapter.

CHAPTER 54

Containing some Particulars relative to the Double Knock, and other Matters: among which certain Interesting Disclosures relative to Mr Snodgrass and a Young Lady are by no means irrelevant to this History

The object that presented itself to the eyes of the astonished clerk, was a boy – a wonderfully fat boy – habited as a serving lad, standing upright on the mat, with his eyes closed as if in sleep. He had never seen such a fat boy, in or out of a travelling caravan; and this, coupled with the calmness and repose of his appearance, so very different from what was reasonably to have been expected of the inflicter of such knocks, smote him with wonder.

'What's the matter?' inquired the clerk.

The extraordinary boy replied not a word; but he nodded once, and seemed, to the clerk's imagination, to snore feebly.

'Where do you come from?' inquired the clerk.

The boy made no sign. He breathed heavily, but in all other respects was motionless.

The clerk repeated the question thrice, and receiving no answer, prepared to shut the door, when the boy suddenly opened his eyes, winked several times, sneezed once, and raised his hand as if to repeat the knocking. Finding the door open, he stared about him with astonishment, and at length fixed his eyes on Mr Lowten's face.

'What the devil do you knock in that way for?' inquired the clerk, angrily.

'Which way?' said the boy, in a slow and sleepy voice.

'Why, like forty hackney-coachmen,' replied the clerk.

'Because master said, I wasn't to leave off knocking till they opened the door, for fear I should go to sleep,' said the boy.

'Well,' said the clerk, 'what message have you brought?'

'He's down stairs,' rejoined the boy.

'Who?'

'Master. He wants to know whether you're at home.'

Mr Lowten bethought himself, at this juncture, of looking out of the window. Seeing an open carriage with a hearty old gentleman in it, looking up very anxiously, he ventured to beckon him; on which, the old gentleman jumped out directly.

'That's your master in the carriage, I suppose?' said Lowten. The boy nodded.

All further inquiries were superseded by the appearance of old Wardle, who, running up stairs and just recognising Lowten, passed at once into Mr Perker's room.

'Pickwick!' said the old gentleman. 'Your hand, my boy! Why have I never heard until the day before yesterday of your suffering yourself to be cooped up in jail? And why did you let him do it, Perker?'

'I couldn't help it, my dear sir,' replied Perker, with a smile and a pinch of snuff: 'you know how obstinate he is.'

'Of course I do, of course I do,' replied the old gentleman. 'I am heartily glad to see him, notwithstanding. I will not lose sight of him again, in a hurry.'

With these words, Wardle shook Mr Pickwick's hand once more, and, having done the same by Perker, threw himself into an arm-chair; his jolly red face shining again with smiles and health.

'Well!' said Wardle. 'Here are pretty goings on – a pinch of your snuff, Perker, my boy – never were such times, eh?'

'What do you mean?' inquired Mr Pickwick.

'Mean!' said Wardle. 'Why, I think the girls are all running mad; that's no news, you'll say? Perhaps it's not; but it's true, for all that.'

'You have not come up to London, of all places in the world, to tell us *that*, my dear sir, have you?' inquired Perker.

'No, not altogether,' replied Wardle; 'though it was the main cause of my coming. How's Arabella?'

'Very well,' replied Mr Pickwick, 'and will be delighted to see you, I am sure.'

'Black-eyed little jilt!' replied Wardle, 'I had a great idea of marrying her myself, one of these odd days. But I am glad of it too, very glad.'

'How did the intelligence reach you?' asked Mr Pickwick.

'Oh, it came to my girls, of course,' replied Wardle. 'Arabella wrote, the day before yesterday, to say she had made a stolen match without her husband's father's consent, and so you had gone down to get it when his refusing it couldn't prevent the match, and all the rest of it. I thought it a very good time to say something serious to *my* girls; so I said what a dreadful thing it was that children should marry without their parents' consent, and so forth; but, bless your hearts, I couldn't make the least impression upon them. They thought it such a much more dreadful thing that there should have been a wedding without bridesmaids, that I might as well have preached to Joe himself.'

Here the old gentleman stopped to laugh; and having done so to his heart's content, presently resumed.

'But this is not the best of it, it seems. This is only half the love-making and plotting that have been going forward. We have been walking on mines for the last six months, and they're sprung at last.'

'What do you mean!' exclaimed Mr Pickwick, turning pale; 'no other secret marriage, I hope?'

'No, no,' replied old Wardle; 'not so bad as that; no.'

'What then?' inquired Mr Pickwick; 'am I interested in it?'

'Shall I answer that question, Perker?' said Wardle.

'If you don't commit yourself by doing so, my dear sir.'

'Well then, you are,' said Wardle.

'How?' asked Mr Pickwick anxiously. 'In what way?'

'Really,' replied Wardle, 'you're such a fiery sort of young fellow that I am almost afraid to tell you; but, however, if Perker will sit between us to prevent mischief, I'll venture.'

Having closed the room-door, and fortified himself with another application to Perker's snuff-box, the old gentleman proceeded with his great disclosure in these words.

'The fact is, that my daughter Bella – Bella, who married young Trundle, you know.'

'Yes, yes, we know,' said Mr Pickwick impatiently.

'Don't alarm me at the very beginning. My daughter Bella, Emily having gone to bed with a headache after she had read Arabella's letter to me, sat herself down by my side the other evening, and began to talk over this marriage affair. "Well, pa," she says, "what do you think of it?" "Why, my dear," I said, "I suppose it's all very well; I hope it's for the best." I answered in this way because I was sitting before the fire at the time, drinking my grog rather thoughtfully, and I knew my throwing in an undecided word now and then, would induce her to continue talking. Both my girls are pictures of their dear mother, and as I grow old I like to sit with only them by me; for their voices and looks carry me back to the happiest period of my life, and make me, for the moment, as young as I used to be then, though not quite so light-hearted. "It's quite a marriage of affection, pa," said Bella, after a short silence. "Yes, my dear," said I, "but such marriages do not always turn out the happiest."'

'I question that, mind!' interposed Mr Pickwick, warmly.

'Very good,' responded Wardle, 'question anything you like when it's your turn to speak, but don't interrupt me.'

'I beg your pardon,' said Mr Pickwick.

'Granted,' replied Wardle. '"I am sorry to hear you express your opinion against marriages of affection, pa," said Bella, colouring a little. "I was wrong; I ought not to have said so, my dear, either," said I, patting her cheek as kindly as a rough old fellow like me could pat it, "for your mother's was one, and so was yours." "It's not that, I meant, pa," said Bella. "The fact is, pa, I wanted to speak to you about Emily."'

Mr Pickwick started.

'What's the matter now?' inquired Wardle, stopping in his narrative.

'Nothing,' replied Mr Pickwick. 'Pray go on.'

'I never could spin out a story,' said Wardle abruptly. 'It must come out, sooner or later, and it'll save us all a great deal of time if it comes at once. The long and the short of it is, then, that Bella at last mustered up courage to tell me that Emily was very unhappy; that she and your young friend Snodgrass had been in constant correspondence and communication ever since last Christmas; that she had very dutifully made up her mind to run away with him, in laudable imitation of her old friend and schoolfellow; but that having some compunctions of conscience on the subject, inasmuch as I had always been rather kindly disposed to both of them, they had thought it better in the first instance to pay me the compliment of asking whether I would have any objection to their being married in the usual matter-of-fact manner. There now, Mr Pickwick, if you can make it convenient to reduce your eyes to their usual size again, and to let me hear what you think we ought to do, I shall feel rather obliged to you!'

The testy manner in which the hearty old gentleman uttered this last sentence was not wholly unwarranted; for Mr Pickwick's face had settled down into an expression of blank amazement and perplexity, quite curious to behold.

'Snodgrass! Since last Christmas!' were the first broken words that issued from the lips of the confounded gentleman.

'Since last Christmas,' replied Wardle; 'that's plain enough, and very bad spectacles we must have worn, not to have discovered it before.'

'I don't understand it,' said Mr Pickwick, ruminating; 'I really cannot understand it.'

'It's easy enough to understand,' replied the choleric old gentleman. 'If you had been a younger man, you would have been in the secret long ago; and besides,' added Wardle after a moment's hesitation, 'the truth is, that, knowing nothing of this matter, I have rather pressed Emily for four or five months past, to receive favourably (if she could; I would never attempt to force a girl's inclinations) the addresses of a young gentleman down in our neighbourhood. I have no doubt that, girl-like, to enhance her own value and increase the ardour of Mr Snodgrass, she has represented this matter in very glowing colours, and that they have both arrived at the conclusion that they are a terribly persecuted pair of unfortunates, and have no resource but clandestine matrimony or charcoal.[1] Now the question is, what's to be done?'

'What have *you* done?' inquired Mr Pickwick.

'I!'

'I mean what did you do when your married daughter told you this?'

'Oh, I made a fool of myself of course,' rejoined Wardle.

'Just so,' interposed Perker, who had accompanied this dialogue with sundry twitchings of his watch-chain, vindictive rubbings of his nose, and other symptoms of impatience. 'That's very natural; but how?'

'I went into a great passion and frightened my mother into a fit,' said Wardle.

'That was judicious,' remarked Perker; 'and what else?'

'I fretted and fumed all next day, and raised a great disturbance,' rejoined the old gentleman. 'At last I got tired of rendering myself unpleasant and making everybody miserable; so I hired a carriage at Muggleton, and, putting my own horses in it, came up to town, under pretence of bringing Emily to see Arabella.'

'Miss Wardle is with you, then?' said Mr Pickwick.

'To be sure she is,' replied Wardle. 'She is at Osborne's hotel[2] in the Adelphi at this moment, unless your enterprising friend has run away with her since I came out this morning.'

'You are reconciled, then?' said Perker.

'Not a bit of it,' answered Wardle; 'she has been crying and moping ever since, except last night, between tea and supper, when she made a great parade of writing a letter that I pretended to take no notice of.'

'You want my advice in this matter, I suppose?' said Perker, looking from the musing face of Mr Pickwick to the eager countenance of Wardle, and taking several consecutive pinches of his favourite stimulant.

'I suppose so,' said Wardle, looking at Mr Pickwick.

'Certainly,' replied that gentleman.

'Well then,' said Perker, rising and pushing his chair back, 'my advice is, that you both walk away together, or ride away, or get away by some means or other, for I'm tired of you, and just talk this matter over between you. If you have not settled it by the next time I see you, I'll tell you what to do.'

'This is satisfactory,' said Wardle, hardly knowing whether to smile or be offended.

'Pooh, pooh, my dear sir,' returned Perker. 'I know you both a great deal better than you know yourselves. You have settled it already, to all intents and purposes.'

Thus expressing himself, the little gentleman poked his snuff-box, first into the chest of Mr Pickwick, and then into the waistcoat of Mr Wardle, upon which they all three laughed, but especially the two last-named gentlemen, who at once shook hands again, without any obvious or particular reason.

'You dine with me to-day,' said Wardle to Perker, as he showed them out.

'Can't promise, my dear sir, can't promise,' replied Perker. 'I'll look in, in the evening, at all events.'

'I shall expect you at five,' said Wardle. 'Now, Joe!' And Joe having been at length awakened, the two friends departed in Mr Wardle's carriage, which in common humanity had a dickey behind for the fat boy, who, if there had been a foot-board instead, would have rolled off and killed himself in his very first nap.

Driving to the George and Vulture, they found that Arabella and her maid had sent for a hackney-coach immediately on the receipt of a short note from Emily announcing her arrival in town, and had proceeded straight to the Adelphi. As Wardle had business to transact in the city, they sent the carriage and the fat boy to his hotel, with the information that he and Mr Pickwick would return together to dinner at five o'clock.

Charged with this message, the fat boy returned, slumbering as peaceably in his dickey, over the stones, as if it had been a down bed on watch-springs. By some extraordinary miracle he awoke of his own accord, when the coach stopped, and giving himself a good shake to stir up his faculties, went up stairs to execute his commission.

Now, whether the shake had jumbled the fat boy's faculties together, instead of arranging them in proper order, or had roused such a quantity of new ideas within him as to render him oblivious of ordinary forms and ceremonies, or (which is also possible) had proved unsuccessful in preventing his falling asleep as he ascended the stairs, it is an undoubted fact that he walked into the sitting-room without previously knocking at the door; and so beheld a gentleman with his arms clasping his young mistress's waist, sitting very lovingly by her side on a sofa, while Arabella and her pretty handmaid feigned to be absorbed in looking out of a window at the other end of the room. At sight of this phenomenon, the fat boy uttered an interjection, the ladies a scream, and the gentleman an oath, almost simultaneously.

'Wretched creature, what do you want here?' said the gentleman, who it is needless to say was Mr Snodgrass.

To this the fat boy, considerably terrified, briefly responded, 'Missis.'

'What do you want me for?' inquired Emily, turning her head aside, 'you stupid creature!'

'Master and Mr Pickwick is a going to dine here at five,' replied the fat boy.

'Leave the room!' said Mr Snodgrass, glaring upon the bewildered youth.

'No, no, no,' added Emily hastily. 'Bella, dear, advise me.'

Upon this, Emily and Mr Snodgrass, and Arabella and Mary, crowded into a corner, and conversed earnestly in whispers for some minutes, during which the fat boy dozed.

'Joe,' said Arabella, at length, looking round with a most bewitching smile, 'how do you do, Joe?'

'Joe,' said Emily, 'you're a very good boy; I won't forget you, Joe.'

'Joe,' said Mr Snodgrass, advancing to the astonished youth, and seizing his hand, 'I didn't know you before. There's five shillings for you, Joe!'

'I'll owe you five, Joe,' said Arabella, 'for old acquaintance sake, you know;' and another most captivating smile was bestowed upon the corpulent intruder.

The fat boy's perception being slow, he looked rather puzzled at first to account for this sudden prepossession in his favour, and stared about him in a very alarming manner. At length his broad face began to show symptoms of a grin of proportionately broad dimensions; and then, thrusting half-a-crown into each of his pockets, and a hand and wrist after it, he burst into a horse laugh: being for the first and only time in his existence.

'He understands us, I see,' said Arabella.

'He had better have something to eat, immediately,' remarked Emily.

The fat boy almost laughed again when he heard this suggestion. Mary, after a little more whispering, tripped forth from the group, and said:

'I am going to dine with you to-day, sir, if you have no objection.'

'This way,' said the fat boy, eagerly. 'There is such a jolly meat pie!'

With these words, the fat boy led the way down stairs; his pretty companion captivating all the waiters and angering all the chamber-maids as she followed him to the eating-room.

There was the meat-pie of which the youth had spoken so feelingly, and there were, moreover, a steak, and a dish of potatoes, and a pot of porter.

'Sit down,' said the fat boy. 'Oh, my eye, how prime! I am *so* hungry.'

Having apostrophised his eye, in a species of rapture, five or six times, the youth took the head of the little table, and Mary seated herself at the bottom.

'Will you have some of this?' said the fat boy, plunging into the pie up to the very ferules[3] of the knife and fork.

'A little, if you please,' replied Mary.

The fat boy assisted Mary to a little, and himself to a great deal, and was just going to begin eating when he suddenly laid down his knife and fork, leant forward in his chair, and letting his hands, with the knife and fork in them, fall on his knees, said, very slowly:

'I say! How nice you look!'

This was said in an admiring manner, and was, so far, gratifying; but still there was enough of the cannibal in the young gentleman's eyes to render the compliment a double one.

'Dear me, Joseph,' said Mary, affecting to blush, 'what do you mean?'

The fat boy gradually recovering his former position, replied with a heavy sigh, and remaining thoughtful for a few moments, drank a long draught of the porter. Having achieved this feat he sighed again, and applied himself assiduously to the pie.

Mary and the fat boy

'What a nice young lady Miss Emily is!' said Mary, after a long silence.

The fat boy had by this time finished the pie. He fixed his eyes on Mary, and replied:

'I knows a nicerer.'

'Indeed!' said Mary.

'Yes, indeed!' replied the fat boy, with unwonted vivacity.

'What's her name?' inquired Mary.

'What's yours?'

'Mary.'

'So's her's,' said the fat boy. 'You're her.' The boy grinned to add point to the compliment, and put his eyes into something between a squint and a cast, which there is reason to believe he intended for an ogle.

'You musn't talk to me in that way,' said Mary; 'you don't mean it.'

'Don't I though?' replied the fat boy; 'I say!'

'Well.'

'Are you going to come here regular?'

'No,' rejoined Mary, shaking her head, 'I'm going away again to-night. Why?'

'Oh!' said the fat boy in a tone of strong feeling; 'how we should have enjoyed ourselves at meals, if you had been!'

'I might come here sometimes perhaps, to see you,' said Mary, plaiting the table-cloth in assumed coyness, 'if you would do me a favour.'

The fat boy looked from the pie-dish to the steak, as if he thought a favour must be in a manner connected with something to eat; and then took out one of the half-crowns and glanced at it nervously.

'Don't you understand me?' said Mary, looking slyly in his fat face.

Again he looked at the half-crown, and said faintly, 'No.'

'The ladies want you not to say anything to the old gentleman about the young gentleman having been up stairs; and I want you too.'

'Is that all?' said the fat boy, evidently very much relieved as he pocketed the half-crown again. 'Of course I ain't a going to.'

'You see,' said Mary, 'Mr Snodgrass is very fond of Miss Emily, and Miss Emily's very fond of him, and if you were to tell about it, the old gentleman would carry you all away miles into the country, where you'd see nobody.'

'No, no, I won't tell,' said the fat boy, stoutly.

'That's a dear,' said Mary. 'Now it's time I went up stairs, and got my lady ready for dinner.'

'Don't go yet,' urged the fat boy.

'I must,' replied Mary. 'Good bye, for the present.'

The fat boy, with elephantine playfulness, stretched out his arms to ravish a kiss; but as it required no great agility to elude him, his fair enslaver had vanished before he closed them again; upon which the apathetic youth ate a pound or so of steak with a sentimental countenance, and fell fast asleep.

There was so much to say up stairs, and there were so many plans to concert for elopement and matrimony in the event of old Wardle continuing to be cruel, that it wanted only half an hour of dinner when Mr Snodgrass took his final adieu. The ladies ran to Emily's bedroom to dress, and the lover taking up his hat, walked out of the room. He had scarcely got outside the door, when he heard Wardle's voice talking loudly, and looking over the banisters, beheld him, followed by some other gentlemen, coming straight up stairs. Knowing nothing of the house, Mr Snodgrass in his confusion stepped hastily back into the room he had just quitted, and passing from thence into an inner apartment (Mr Wardle's bed-chamber), closed the door softly, just as the persons he had caught a glimpse of, entered the sitting-room. These were Mr Wardle, Mr Pickwick, Mr Nathaniel Winkle, and Mr Benjamin Allen, whom he had no difficulty in recognising by their voices.

'Very lucky I had the presence of mind to avoid them,' thought Mr Snodgrass with a smile, and walking on tiptoe to another door near the bedside; 'this opens into the same passage, and I can walk, quietly and comfortably, away.'

There was only one obstacle to his walking quietly and comfortably away, which was that the door was locked and the key gone.

'Let us have some of your best wine to-day, waiter,' said old Wardle, rubbing his hands.

'You shall have some of the very best, sir,' replied the waiter.

'Let the ladies know we have come in.'

'Yes, sir.'

Devoutly and ardently did Mr Snodgrass wish that the ladies could know *he* had come in. He ventured once to whisper 'Waiter!' through the keyhole, but as the probability of the wrong waiter coming to his relief, flashed upon his mind, together with a sense of the strong resemblance between his own situation and that in which another gentleman had been recently found in a neighbouring hotel (an account of whose misfortunes had appeared under the head of

'Police' in that morning's paper), he sat himself on a portmanteau, and trembled violently.

'We won't wait a minute for Perker,' said Wardle, looking at his watch; 'he is always exact. He will be here, in time, if he means to come; and if he does not, it's of no use waiting. Ha! Arabella!'

'My sister!' exclaimed Mr Benjamin Allen, folding her in a most romantic embrace.

'Oh, Ben, dear, how you do smell of tobacco,' said Arabella, rather overcome by this mark of affection.

'Do I?' said Mr Benjamin Allen, 'Do I, Bella? Well, perhaps I do.'

Perhaps he did; having just left a pleasant little smoking party of twelve medical students, in a small back parlour with a large fire.

'But I am delighted to see you,' said Mr Ben Allen. 'Bless you, Bella!'

'There,' said Arabella, bending forward to kiss her brother; 'don't take hold of me again, Ben dear, because you tumble me so.'

At this point of the reconciliation, Mr Ben Allen allowed his feelings and the cigars and porter to overcome him, and looked round upon the beholders with damp spectacles.

'Is nothing to be said to me?' cried Wardle with open arms.

'A great deal,' whispered Arabella, as she received the old gentleman's hearty caress and congratulation. 'You are a hard-hearted, unfeeling, cruel, monster!'

'You are a little rebel,' replied Wardle, in the same tone, 'and I am afraid I shall be obliged to forbid you the house. People like you, who get married in spite of everybody, ought not to be let loose on society. But come!' added the old gentleman aloud, 'Here's the dinner; you shall sit by me. Joe; why, damn the boy, he's awake!'

To the great distress of his master, the fat boy was indeed in a state of remarkable vigilance; his eyes being wide open, and looking as if they intended to remain so. There was an alacrity in his manner, too, which was equally unaccountable; every time his eyes met those of Emily or Arabella, he smirked and grinned; once, Wardle could have sworn he saw him wink.

This alteration in the fat boy's demeanour, originated in his increased sense of his own importance, and the dignity he acquired from having been taken into the confidence of the young ladies; and the smirks, and grins, and winks, were so many condescending assurances that they might depend upon his fidelity. As these tokens were rather calculated to awaken suspicion than allay it, and were somewhat embarrassing besides, they were occasionally answered by a frown or shake of the head from Arabella, which the fat boy considering as hints to be on his guard, expressed his perfect understanding of, by smirking, grinning, and winking, with redoubled assiduity.

'Joe,' said Mr Wardle, after an unsuccessful search in all his pockets, 'is my snuff-box on the sofa?'

'No, sir,' replied the fat boy.

'Oh, I recollect; I left it on my dressing-table this morning,' said Wardle. 'Run into the next room and fetch it.'

The fat boy went into the next room; and having been absent about a minute, returned with the snuff-box, and the palest face that ever a fat boy wore.

'What's the matter with the boy!' exclaimed Wardle.

'Nothen's the matter with me,' replied Joe, nervously.

'Have you been seeing any spirits?' inquired the old gentleman.

'Or taking any?' added Ben Allen.

'I think you're right,' whispered Wardle across the table. 'He is intoxicated, I'm sure.'

Ben Allen replied that he thought he was; and as that gentleman had seen a vast deal of the disease in question, Wardle was confirmed in an impression which had been hovering about his mind for half an hour, and at once arrived at the conclusion that the fat boy was drunk.

'Just keep your eye upon him for a few minutes,' murmured Wardle. 'We shall soon find out whether he is or not.'

The unfortunate youth had only interchanged a dozen words with Mr Snodgrass: that gentleman having implored him to make a private appeal to some friend to release him, and then pushed him out with the snuff-box, lest his prolonged absence should lead to a discovery. He ruminated a little with a most disturbed expression of face, and left the room in search of Mary.

But Mary had gone home after dressing her mistress, and the fat boy came back again more disturbed than before.

Wardle and Mr Ben Allen exchanged glances.

'Joe!' said Wardle.

'Yes, sir.'

'What did you go away for?'

The fat boy looked hopelessly in the face of everybody at table, and stammered out, that he didn't know.

'Oh,' said Wardle, 'you don't know, eh? Take this cheese to Mr Pickwick.'

Now, Mr Pickwick being in the very best health and spirits, had been making himself perfectly delightful all dinner-time, and was at this moment engaged in an energetic conversation with Emily and Mr Winkle: bowing his head, courteously, in the emphasis of his discourse, gently waving his left hand to lend force to his observations, and all glowing with placid smiles. He took a piece of cheese from the plate, and was on the point of turning round to renew the conversation, when the fat boy, stooping so as to bring his head on a level with that of Mr Pickwick, pointed with his thumb over his shoulder, and made the most horrible and hideous face that was ever seen out of a Christmas pantomime.

'Dear me!' said Mr Pickwick, starting, 'what a very – eh?' He stopped, for the fat boy had drawn himself up, and was, or pretended to be, fast asleep.

'What's the matter?' inquired Wardle.

'This is such an extremely singular lad!' replied Mr Pickwick, looking uneasily at the boy. 'It seems an odd thing to say, but upon my word I am afraid that, at times, he is a little deranged.'

'Oh! Mr Pickwick, pray don't say so,' cried Emily and Arabella, both at once.

'I am not certain, of course,' said Mr Pickwick, amidst profound silence, and looks of general dismay; 'but his manner to me this moment was really very alarming. Oh!' ejaculated Mr Pickwick, suddenly jumping up with a short scream. 'I beg your pardon, ladies, but at that moment he ran some sharp instrument into my leg. Really he is not safe.'

'He's drunk,' roared old Wardle, passionately. 'Ring the bell! Call the waiters! He's drunk.'

'I ain't,' said the fat boy, falling on his knees as his master seized him by the collar. 'I ain't drunk.'

'Then you're mad; that's worse. Call the waiters,' said the old gentleman.

'I ain't mad; I'm sensible,' rejoined the fat boy, beginning to cry.

'Then, what the devil do you run sharp instruments into Mr Pickwick's legs for?' inquired Wardle, angrily.

'He wouldn't look at me,' replied the boy. 'I wanted to speak to him.'

'What did you want to say?' asked half a dozen voices at once.

The fat boy gasped, looked at the bedroom door, gasped again, and wiped two tears away with the knuckle of each of his forefingers.

'What did you want to say?' demanded Wardle, shaking him.

'Stop!' said Mr Pickwick; 'allow me. What did you wish to communicate to me, my poor boy?'

'I want to whisper to you,' replied the fat boy.

'You want to bite his ear off, I suppose,' said Wardle. 'Don't come near him; he's vicious; ring the bell, and let him be taken down stairs.'

Just as Mr Winkle caught the bell-rope in his hand, it was arrested by a general expression of astonishment; the captive lover, his face burning with confusion, suddenly walked in from the bedroom, and made a comprehensive bow to the company.

'Hallo!' cried Wardle, releasing the fat boy's collar, and staggering back, 'What's this!'

'I have been concealed in the next room, sir, since you returned,' explained Mr Snodgrass.

'Emily, my girl,' said Wardle, reproachfully, 'I detest meanness and deceit; this is unjustifiable and indelicate in the highest degree. I don't deserve this at your hands, Emily, indeed!'

'Dear papa,' said Emily, 'Arabella knows – everybody here knows – Joe knows – that I was no party to this concealment. Augustus, for Heaven's sake, explain it!'

Mr Snodgrass, who had only waited for a hearing, at once recounted how he had been placed in his then distressing predicament; how the fear of giving rise to domestic dissensions had alone prompted him to avoid Mr Wardle on his entrance; how he merely meant to depart by another door, but, finding it locked, had been compelled to stay against his will. It was a painful situation to be placed in; but he now regretted it the less, inasmuch as it afforded him an opportunity of acknowledging, before their mutual friends, that he loved Mr Wardle's daughter, deeply and sincerely; that he was proud to avow that the feeling was mutual; and that if thousands of miles were placed between them, or oceans rolled their waters, he could never for an instant forget those happy days, when first – and so on.

Having delivered himself to this effect, Mr Snodgrass bowed again, looked into the crown of his hat, and stepped towards the door.

'Stop!' shouted Wardle. 'Why, in the name of all that's—'

'Inflammable,' mildly suggested Mr Pickwick, who thought something worse was coming.

'Well – that's inflammable,' said Wardle, adopting the substitute; 'couldn't you say all this to me in the first instance?'

'Or confide in me?' added Mr Pickwick.

'Dear, dear,' said Arabella, taking up the defence, 'what is the use of asking all that now, especially when you know you had set your covetous old heart on a richer son-in-law, and are so wild and fierce besides, that everybody is afraid of you, except me. Shake hands with him, and order him some dinner, for goodness gracious sake, for he looks half-starved; and pray have your wine up at once, for you'll not be tolerable until you have taken two bottles at least.'

The worthy old gentleman pulled Arabella's ear, kissed her without the smallest scruple, kissed his daughter also with great affection, and shook Mr Snodgrass warmly by the hand.

'She is right on one point at all events,' said the old gentleman, cheerfully. 'Ring for the wine!'

The wine came, and Perker came up stairs at the same moment. Mr Snodgrass had dinner at a side table, and, when he had despatched it, drew his chair next Emily, without the smallest opposition on the old gentleman's part.

The evening was excellent. Little Mr Perker came out wonderfully, told various comic stories, and sang a serious song which was almost as funny as the anecdotes. Arabella was very charming, Mr Wardle very jovial, Mr Pickwick very harmonious, Mr Ben Allen very uproarious, the lovers very silent, Mr Winkle very talkative, and all of them very happy.

CHAPTER 55

Mr Solomon Pell, assisted by a Select Committee of Coachmen, arranges the Affairs of the elder Mr Weller

'Samivel,' said Mr Weller, accosting his son on the morning after the funeral, 'I've found it, Sammy. I thought it wos there.'

'Thought wot wos were?' inquired Sam.

'Your mother-in-law's vill, Sammy,' replied Mr Weller. 'In wirtue o' vich, them arrangements is to be made as I told you on, last night, respectin' the funs.'

'Wot, didn't she tell you were it wos?' inquired Sam.

'Not a bit on it, Sammy,' replied Mr Weller. 'We wos a adjestin' our little differences, and I wos a cheerin' her spirits and bearin' her up, so that I forgot to ask anythin' about it. I don't know as I should ha' done it indeed, if I had remembered it,' added Mr Weller, 'for it's a rum sort o' thing, Sammy, to go a hankerin' arter anybody's property, ven you're assistin' 'em in illness. It's like helping an outside passenger up, ven he's been pitched off a coach, and puttin' your hand in his pocket, vile you ask him vith a sigh how he finds hisself, Sammy.'

With this figurative illustration of his meaning, Mr Weller unclasped his pocket-book, and drew forth a dirty sheet of letter paper, on which were inscribed various characters crowded together in remarkable confusion.

'This here is the dockyment, Sammy,' said Mr Weller. 'I found it in the little black teapot, on the top shelf o' the bar closet. She used to keep bank notes there, 'afore she vos married, Samivel. I've seen her take the lid off, to pay a bill, many and many a time. Poor creeter, she might ha' filled all the teapots in the house vith vills, and not have inconwenienced herself neither, for she took wery little of anythin' in that vay lately, 'cept on the Temperance nights, ven they just laid a foundation o' tea to put the spirits a-top on!'

'What does it say?' inquired Sam.

'Jist vot I told you, my boy,' rejoined his parent. 'Two hundred pound vurth o' reduced counsels to my son-in-law, Samivel, and all the rest o' my property, of ev'ry kind and description votsoever to my husband, Mr Tony Veller, who I appint as my sole eggzekiter.'

'That's all, is it?' said Sam.

'That's all,' replied Mr Weller. 'And I s'pose as it's all right and satisfactory to you and me as is the only parties interested, ve may as vell put this bit o' paper into the fire.'

'Wot are you a-doin' on, you lunatic?' said Sam, snatching the paper away, as his parent, in all innocence, stirred the fire preparatory to suiting the action to the word. 'You're a nice eggzekiter, you are.'

'Vy not?' inquired Mr Weller, looking sternly round, with the poker in his hand.

'Vy not!' exclaimed Sam. ''Cos it must be proved, and probated, and swore to, and all manner o' formalities.'

'You don't mean that?' said Mr Weller, laying down the poker.

Sam buttoned the will carefully in a side pocket; intimating by a look, mean-while, that he did mean it, and very seriously too,

'Then I'll tell you wot it is,' said Mr Weller, after a short meditation, 'this is a case for that 'ere confidential pal o' the Chancellorship's. Pell must look into this, Sammy. He's the man for a difficult question at law. Ve'll have this here, brought afore the Solvent Court directly, Samivel.'

'I never did see such a addle-headed old creetur!' exclaimed Sam, irritably, 'Old Baileys, and Solvent Courts, and alleybis, and ev'ry species o' gammon alvays a runnin' through his brain! You'd better get your out o' door clothes on, and come to town about this bisness, than stand a preachin' there about wot you don't understand nothin' on.'

'Wery good, Sammy,' replied Mr Weller, 'I'm quite agreeable to anythin' as vill hexpedite business, Sammy. But mind this here, my boy, nobody but Pell – nobody but Pell as a legal adwiser.'

'I don't want anybody else,' replied Sam. 'Now, are you a-comin'?'

'Vait a minit, Sammy,' replied Mr Weller, who, having tied his shawl with the aid of a small glass that hung in the window, was now, by dint of the most wonderful exertions, struggling into his upper garments. 'Vait a minit, Sammy; ven you grow as old as your father, you von't get into your veskit quite as easy as you do now, my boy.'

'If I couldn't get into it easier than that, I'm blessed if I'd vear vun at all,' rejoined his son.

'You think so now,' said Mr Weller, with the gravity of age, 'but you'll find that as you get vider, you'll get viser. Vidth and visdom, Sammy, alvays grows together.'

As Mr Weller, delivered this infallible maxim – the result of many years' personal experience and observation – he contrived, by a dexterous twist of his body, to get the bottom button of his coat to perform its office. Having paused a few seconds to recover breath, he brushed his hat with his elbow, and declared himself ready.

'As four heads is better than two, Sammy,' said Mr Weller, as they drove along the London Road in the chaise cart, 'and as all this here property is a wery great temptation to a legal gen'l'm'n, ve'll take a couple o' friends o' mine vith us, as'll be wery soon down upon him if he comes anythin' irreg'lar; two o' them as saw you to the Fleet that day. They're the wery best judges,' added Mr Weller in a half whisper, 'the wery best judges of a horse, you ever know'd.'

'And of a lawyer too?' inquired Sam.

'The man as can form a ackerate judgment of a animal, can form a ackerate judgment of anythin',' replied his father; so dogmatically, that Sam did not attempt to controvert the position.

In pursuance of this notable resolution, the services of the mottled-faced gentleman and of two other very fat coachmen – selected by Mr Weller, probably, with a view to their width and consequent wisdom – were put into requisition; and this assistance having been secured, the party proceeded to the public-house in Portugal Street, whence a messenger was despatched to the Insolvent Court over the way, requiring Mr Solomon Pell's immediate attendance.

The messenger fortunately found Mr Solomon Pell in court, regaling himself, business being rather slack, with a cold collation of an Abernethy biscuit and a saveloy. The message was no sooner whispered in his ear than he thrust them in his pocket among various professional documents, and hurried over the way with such alacrity, that he reached the parlour before the messenger had even emancipated himself from the court.

'Gentlemen,' said Mr Pell, touching his hat, 'my service to you all. I don't say it to flatter you, gentlemen, but there are not five other men in the world, that I'd have come out of that court for, to-day.'

'So busy, eh?' said Sam.

'Busy!' replied Pell; 'I'm completely sewn up, as my friend the late Lord Chancellor many a time used to say to me, gentlemen, when he came out from hearing appeals in the House of Lords. Poor fellow! he was very susceptible of fatigue; he used to feel those appeals uncommonly. I actually thought more than once that he'd have sunk under 'em; I did indeed.'

Here Mr Pell shook his head and paused; on which, the elder Mr Weller, nudging his neighbour, as begging him to mark the attorney's high connections, asked whether the duties in question produced any permanent ill effects on the constitution of his noble friend.

'I don't think he ever quite recovered them,' replied Pell; 'in fact I'm sure he never did. "Pell," he used to say to me many a time, "how the blazes you can stand the head-work you do, is a mystery to me." – "Well," I used to answer, "I hardly know how I do it, upon my life." – "Pell," he'd add, sighing, and looking at me with a little envy – friendly envy, you know, gentlemen, mere friendly envy; I never minded it – "Pell, you're a wonder; a wonder." Ah! you'd have liked him very much if you had known him, gentlemen. Bring me three penn'orth of rum, my dear.'

Addressing this latter remark to the waitress in a tone of subdued grief, Mr Pell sighed, looked at his shoes, and the ceiling; and, the rum having by that time arrived, drunk it up.

'However,' said Pell, drawing a chair to the table, 'a professional man has no right to think of his private friendships when his legal assistance is wanted. By the bye, gentlemen, since I saw you here before, we have had to weep over a very melancholy occurrence.'

Mr Pell drew out a pocket-handkerchief, when he came to the word weep, but he made no further use of it than to wipe away a slight tinge of rum which hung upon his upper lip.

'I saw it in the Advertiser, Mr Weller,' continued Pell. 'Bless my soul, not more than fifty-two! Dear me – only think.'

These indications of a musing spirit were addressed to the mottled-faced man, whose eyes Mr Pell had accidentally caught; on which, the mottled-faced man, whose apprehension of matters in general was of a foggy nature, moved uneasily in his seat, and opined that indeed, so far as that went, there was no saying how things *was* brought about; which observation, involving one of those subtle propositions which it is difficult to encounter in argument, was controverted by nobody.

'I have heard it remarked that she was a very fine woman, Mr Weller,' said Pell in a sympathising manner.

'Yes, sir, she wos,' replied the elder Mr Weller, not much relishing this mode of discussing the subject, and yet thinking that the attorney, from his long intimacy with the late Lord Chancellor, must know best on all matters of polite breeding.

'She wos a wery fine 'ooman, sir, ven I first know'd her. She wos a widder, sir, at that time.'

'Now, it's curious,' said Pell, looking round with a sorrowful smile; 'Mrs Pell was a widow.'

'That's very extraordinary,' said the mottled-faced man.

'Well, it is a curious coincidence,' said Pell.

'Not at all,' gruffly remarked the elder Mr Weller. 'More widders is married than single wimin.'

'Very good, very good,' said Pell, 'you're quite right, Mr Weller. Mrs Pell was a very elegant and accomplished woman; her manners were the theme of universal admiration in our neighbourhood. I was proud to see that woman dance; there was something so firm and dignified, and yet natural, in her motion. Her cutting,' gentlemen, was simplicity itself. Ah! well, well! Excuse my asking the question, Mr Samuel,' continued the attorney in a lower voice, 'was your mother-in-law tall?'

'Not wery,' replied Sam.

'Mrs Pell was a tall figure,' said Pell, 'a splendid woman, with a noble shape, and a nose, gentlemen, formed to command and be majestic. She was very much attached to me – very much – highly connected, too. Her mother's brother, gentlemen, failed for eight hundred pounds, as a Law Stationer.'

'Vell,' said Mr Weller, who had grown rather restless during this discussion, 'vith regard to bis'ness.'

The word was music to Pell's ears. He had been revolving in his mind whether any business was to be transacted, or whether he had been merely invited to partake of a glass of brandy and water, or a bowl of punch, or any similar professional compliment, and now the doubt was set at rest without his appearing at all eager for its solution. His eyes glistened as he laid his hat on the table, and said:

'What is the business upon which – um? Either of these gentlemen wish to go through the court? We require an arrest; a friendly arrest will do, you know; we are all friends here, I suppose?'

'Give me the dockyment, Sammy,' said Mr Weller, taking the will from his son, who appeared to enjoy the interview amazingly. 'Wot we rekvire, sir, is a probe o' this here.'

'Probate, my dear sir, probate,' said Pell.

'Well, sir,' replied Mr Weller sharply, 'probe and probe it, is wery much the same; if you don't understand wot I mean, sir, I dessay I can find them as does.'

'No offence I hope, Mr Weller,' said Pell, meekly. 'You are the executor I see,' he added, casting his eyes over the paper.

'I am, sir,' replied Mr Weller.

'These other gentlemen, I presume, are legatees, are they?' inquired Pell with a congratulatory smile.

'Sammy is a leg-at-ease,' replied Mr Weller; 'these other gen'l'm'n is friends o' mine, just come to see fair; a kind of umpires.'

'Oh!' said Pell, 'very good. I have no objections, I'm sure. I shall want a matter of five pound of you before I begin, ha! ha! ha!'

It being decided by the committee that the five pound might be advanced, Mr Weller produced that sum; after which, a long consultation about nothing particular, took place, in the course whereof Mr Pell demonstrated to the perfect satisfaction of the gentlemen who saw fair, that unless the management of the business had been intrusted to him, it must all have gone wrong, for reasons not clearly made out, but no doubt sufficient. This important point being despatched, Mr Pell refreshed himself with three chops, and liquids both malt and spirituous, at the expense of the estate; and then they all went away to Doctors' Commons.

The next day, there was another visit to Doctors' Commons, and a great to do with an attesting hostler, who, being inebriated, declined swearing anything but profane oaths, to the great scandal of a proctor and surrogate. Next week, there were more visits to Doctors' Commons, and there was a visit to the Legacy Duty Office besides, and there were treaties entered into, for the disposal of the lease and business, and ratifications of the same, and inventories to be made out, and lunches to be taken, and dinners to be eaten, and so many profitable things to be done, and such a mass of papers accumulated, that Mr Solomon Pell, and the boy, and the blue bag to boot, all got so stout that scarcely anybody would have known them for the same man, boy, and bag, that had loitered about Portugal Street, a few days before.

At length all these weighty matters being arranged, a day was fixed for selling out and transferring the stock, and of waiting with that view upon Wilkins Flasher, Esq., stock-broker, of somewhere near the Bank, who had been recommended by Mr Solomon Pell for the purpose.

It was a kind of festive occasion, and the parties were attired accordingly. Mr Weller's tops were newly cleaned, and his dress was arranged with peculiar care; the mottled-faced gentleman wore at his button-hole a full-sized dahlia with several leaves; and the coats of his two friends were adorned with nosegays of laurel and other evergreens. All three were habited in strict holiday costume; that is to say, they were wrapped up to the chins, and wore as many clothes as possible, which is, and has been, a stage-coachman's idea of full dress ever since stage coaches were invented.

Mr Pell was waiting at the usual place of meeting at the appointed time; even Mr Pell wore a pair of gloves and a clean shirt much frayed at the collar and wristbands by frequent washings.

'A quarter to two,' said Pell, looking at the parlour clock. 'If we are with Mr Flasher at a quarter past, we shall just hit the best time.'

'What should you say to a drop o' beer, gen'l'm'n?' suggested the mottled-faced man.

'And a little bit o' cold beef,' said the second coachman.

'Or a oyster,' added the third, who was a hoarse gentleman, supported by very round legs.

'Hear, hear!' said Pell; 'to congratulate Mr Weller, on his coming into possession of his property: eh? ha! ha!'

'I'm quite agreeable, gen'l'm'n,' answered Mr Weller. 'Sammy, pull the bell.'

Sam complied; and the porter, cold beef, and oysters being promptly produced, the lunch was done ample justice to. Where

Mr Weller and his friends drinking to Mr Pell

everybody took so active a part, it is almost invidious to make a distinction; but if one individual evinced greater powers than another, it was the coachman with the hoarse voice, who took an imperial pint of vinegar with his oysters, without betraying the least emotion.

'Mr Pell, sir,' said the elder Mr Weller, stirring a glass of brandy and water, of which one was placed before every gentleman when the oyster shells were removed, 'Mr Pell, sir, it wos my intention to have proposed the funs on this occasion, but Samivel has vispered to me – '

Here Mr Samuel Weller, who had silently eaten his oysters with tranquil smiles, cried 'Hear!' in a very loud voice.

' – Has vispered to me,' resumed his father, 'that it vould be better to dewote the liquor to vishin' you success and prosperity, and thankin' you for the manner in which you've brought this here business through. Here's your health, sir.'

'Hold hard there,' interposed the mottled-faced gentleman, with sudden energy, 'your eyes on me, gen'l'm'n!'

Saying this, the mottled-faced gentleman rose, as did the other gentlemen. The mottled-faced gentleman reviewed the company, and slowly lifted his hand, upon which every man (including him of the mottled countenance) drew a long breath, and lifted his tumbler to his lips. In one instant the mottled-faced gentleman depressed his hand again, and every glass was set down empty. It is impossible to describe the thrilling effect produced by this striking ceremony. At once dignified, solemn, and impressive, it combined every element of grandeur.

'Well, gentlemen,' said Mr Pell, 'all I can say is, that such marks of confidence must be very gratifying to a professional man. I don't wish to say anything that might appear egotistical, gentlemen, but I'm very glad, for your own sakes, that you came to me: that's all. If you had gone to any low member of the profession, it's my firm conviction, and I assure you of it as a fact, that you would have found yourselves in Queer Street² before this. I could have wished my noble friend had been alive to have seen my management of this case. I don't say it out of pride, but I think – however, gentlemen, I won't trouble you with that. I'm generally to be found here, gentlemen, but if I'm not here, or over the way, that's my address. You'll find my terms very cheap and reasonable, and no man attends more to his clients than I do, and I hope I know a little of my profession besides. If you have any opportunity of recommending me to any of your friends, gentlemen, I shall be very much obliged to you, and so will they too, when they come to know me. *Your* healths, gentlemen.'

With this expression of his feelings, Mr Solomon Pell laid three small written cards before Mr Weller's friends, and, looking at the clock again, feared it was time to be walking. Upon this hint Mr Weller settled the bill, and, issuing forth, the executor, legatee, attorney, and umpires, directed their steps towards the City.

The office of Wilkins Flasher, Esquire, of the Stock Exchange, was in a first floor up a court behind the Bank of England; the house of Wilkins Flasher, Esquire, was at Brixton, Surrey; the horse and stanhope of Wilkins Flasher, Esquire, were at an adjacent livery stable; the groom of Wilkins Flasher, Esquire, was on his way to the West End to deliver some game; the clerk of Wilkins Flasher, Esquire, had gone to his dinner; and so Wilkins Flasher, Esquire, himself, cried, 'Come in,' when Mr Pell and his companions knocked at the counting-house door.

'Good morning, sir,' said Pell, bowing obsequiously. 'We want to make a little transfer, if you please.'

'Oh, come in, will you?' said Mr Flasher. 'Sit down a minute; I'll attend to you directly.'

'Thank you, sir,' said Pell, 'there's no hurry. Take a chair, Mr Weller.'

Mr Weller took a chair, and Sam took a box, and the umpires took what they could get, and looked at the almanack and one or two papers which were wafered against the wall, with as much open-eyed reverence as if they had been the finest efforts of the old masters.

'Well, I'll bet you half a dozen of claret on it; come!' said Wilkins Flasher, Esquire, resuming the conversation to which Mr Pell's entrance had caused a momentary interruption.

This was addressed to a very smart young gentleman who wore his hat on his right whisker, and was lounging over the desk, killing flies with a ruler. Wilkins Flasher, Esquire, was balancing himself on two legs of an office stool, spearing a wafer-box with a pen-knife, which he dropped every now and then with great dexterity into the very centre of a small red wafer that was stuck outside. Both gentlemen had very open waistcoats and very rolling collars, and very small boots, and very big rings, and very little watches, and very large guard chains, and symmetrical inexpressibles, and scented pocket-handkerchiefs.

'I never bet half a dozen,' said the other gentleman. 'I'll take a dozen.'

'Done, Simmery, done!' said Wilkins Flasher, Esquire.

'P. P.,³ mind,' observed the other.

'Of course,' replied Wilkins Flasher, Esquire. Wilkins Flasher, Esquire, entered it in a little book, with a gold pencil-case, and the other gentleman entered it also, in another little book with another gold pencil-case.

'I see there's a notice up this morning about Boffer,' observed Mr Simmery. 'Poor devil, he's expelled the house!'

'I'll bet you ten guineas to five, he cuts his throat,' said Wilkins Flasher, Esquire.

'Done,' replied Mr Simmery.

'Stop! I bar,' said Wilkins Flasher, Esquire, thoughtfully. 'Perhaps he may hang himself.'

'Very good,' rejoined Mr Simmery, pulling out the gold pencil-case again. 'I've no objection to take you that way. Say, makes away with himself.'

'Kills himself, in fact,' said Wilkins Flasher, Esquire.

'Just so,' replied Mr Simmery, putting it down. '"Flasher – ten guineas to five, Boffer kills himself." Within what time shall we say?'

'A fortnight?' suggested Wilkins Flasher, Esquire.

'Con-found it, no;' rejoined Mr Simmery, stopping for an instant to smash a fly with the ruler. 'Say a week.'

'Split the difference,' said Wilkins Flasher, Esquire. 'Make it ten days.'

'Well; ten days,' rejoined Mr Simmery.

So, it was entered down in the little books that Boffer was to kill himself within ten days, or Wilkins Flasher, Esquire, was to hand over to Frank Simmery, Esquire, the sum of ten guineas; and that if Boffer did kill himself within that time, Frank Simmery, Esquire, would pay to Wilkins Flasher, Esquire, five guineas, instead.

'I'm very sorry he has failed,' said Wilkins Flasher, Esquire. 'Capital dinners he gave.'

'Fine port he had too,' remarked Mr Simmery. 'We are going to send our butler to the sale to-morrow, to pick up some of that sixty-four.'

'The devil you are!' said Wilkins Flasher, Esquire. 'My man's going too. Five guineas my man outbids your man.'

'Done.'

Another entry was made in the little books, with the gold pencil-cases; and Mr Simmery having, by this time, killed all the flies and taken all the bets, strolled away to the Stock Exchange to see what was going forward.

Wilkins Flasher, Esquire, now condescended to receive Mr Solomon Pell's instructions, and having filled up some printed forms, requested the party to follow him to the Bank: which they did: Mr Weller and his three friends staring at all they beheld in unbounded astonishment, and Sam encountering everything with a coolness which nothing could disturb.

Crossing a court-yard which was all noise and bustle; and passing a couple of porters who seemed dressed to match the red fire engine which was wheeled away into a corner; they passed into an office where their business was to be transacted, and where Pell and Mr Flasher left them standing for a few moments, while they went up stairs into the Will Office.

'Wot place is this here?' whispered the mottled-faced gentleman to the elder Mr Weller.

'Counsel's Office,' replied the executor in a whisper.

'Wot are them gen'l'men a settin' behind the counters?' asked the hoarse coachman.

'Reduced counsels, I s'pose,' replied Mr Weller. 'Ain't they the reduced counsels, Samivel?'

'Wy, you don't suppose the reduced counsels is alive, do you?' inquired Sam, with some disdain.

'How should I know?' retorted Mr Weller; 'I thought they looked wery like it. Wot are they, then?'

'Clerks,' replied Sam.

'Wot are they all a eatin' ham sangwidges for?' inquired his father

''Cos it's in their dooty,' I suppose, replied Sam, 'it's a part o' the system; they're alvays a doin' it here, all day long!'

Mr Weller and his friends had scarcely had a moment to reflect upon this singular regulation as connected with the monetary system of the country, when they were rejoined by Pell and Wilkins Flasher, Esquire, who led them to a part of the counter above which was a round black board with a large 'W.' on it.

'Wot's that for, sir?' inquired Mr Weller, directing Pell's attention to the target in question.

'The first letter of the name of the deceased,' replied Pell.

'I say,' said Mr Weller, turning round to the umpires. 'There's somethin' wrong here. We's our letter – this won't do.'

The referees at once gave it as their decided opinion that the business could not be legally proceeded with, under the letter W, and in all probability it would have stood over for one day at least, had it not been for the prompt, though, at first sight, undutiful behaviour of Sam, who, seizing his father by the skirt of the coat, dragged him to the counter, and pinned him there, until he had affixed his signature to a couple of instruments; which from Mr Weller's habit of printing, was a work of so much labour and time, that the officiating clerk peeled and ate three Ripstone pippins while it was performing.

As the elder Mr Weller insisted on selling out his portion forthwith, they proceeded from the Bank to the gate of the Stock Exchange, to which Wilkins Flasher, Esquire, after a short absence, returned with a cheque on Smith, Payne, and Smith,[4] for five hundred and thirty pounds; that being the sum of money to which Mr Weller at the market price of the day, was entitled, in consideration of the balance of the second Mrs Weller's funded savings. Sam's two hundred pounds stood transferred to his name, and Wilkins Flasher, Esquire, having been paid his commission, dropped the money carelessly into his coat pocket, and lounged back to his office.

Mr Weller was at first obstinately determined on cashing the cheque in nothing but sovereigns: but it being represented by the umpires that by so doing he must incur the expense of a small sack to carry them home in, he consented to receive the amount in five-pound notes.

'My son,' said Mr Weller as they came out of the banking-house, 'my son and me has a wery particular engagement this arternoon, and I should like to have this here bis'ness settled out of hand, so let's jest go straight away someveres, vere ve can hordit the accounts.'

A quiet room was soon found, and the accounts were produced and audited. Mr Pell's bill was taxed by Sam, and some charges were disallowed by the umpires; but, notwithstanding Mr Pell's declaration, accompanied with many solemn asseverations that they were really too hard upon him, it was by very many degrees the best professional job he had ever had, and one on which he boarded, lodged, and washed, for six months afterwards.

The umpires having partaken of a dram, shook hands and departed, as they had to drive out of town that night. Mr Solomon Pell, finding that nothing more was going forward, either in the eating or drinking way, took a friendly leave, and Sam and his father were left alone.

'There!' said Mr Weller, thrusting his pocket-book in his side pocket. 'Vith the bills for the lease, and that, there's eleven hundred and eighty pound here. Now, Samivel, my boy, turn the horses' heads to the George and Wulter!'

CHAPTER 56

An important Conference takes place between Mr
Pickwick and Samuel Weller, at which his Parent
assists. An old Gentleman in a snuff-coloured Suit
arrives unexpectedly

Mr Pickwick was sitting alone, musing over many things, and thinking among other considerations how he could best provide for the young couple whose present unsettled condition was matter of constant regret and anxiety to him, when Mary stepped lightly into the room, and, advancing to the table, said, rather hastily:

'Oh, if you please, sir, Samuel is down stairs, and he says may his father see you?'

'Surely,' replied Mr Pickwick.

'Thank you, sir,' said Mary, tripping towards the door again.

'Sam has not been here long, has he?' inquired Mr Pickwick.

'Oh no, sir,' replied Mary eagerly. 'He has only just come home. He is not going to ask you for any more leave, sir, he says.'

Mary might have been conscious that she had communicated this last intelligence with more warmth than seemed actually necessary, or she might have observed the good-humoured smile with which Mr Pickwick regarded her, when she had finished speaking. She certainly held down her head, and examined the corner of a very smart little apron, with more closeness than there appeared any absolute occasion for.

'Tell them they can come up at once, by all means,' said Mr Pickwick.

Mary, apparently much relieved, hurried away with her message.

Mr Pickwick took two or three turns up and down the room; and rubbing his chin with his left hand as he did so, appeared lost in thought.

'Well, well,' said Mr Pickwick at length, in a kind but somewhat melancholy tone, 'it is the best way in which I could reward him for his attachment and fidelity; let it be so, in Heaven's name. It is the fate of a lonely old man, that those about him should form new and different attachments and leave him. I have no right to expect that it should be otherwise with me. No, no,' added Mr Pickwick more cheerfully, 'it would be selfish and ungrateful. I ought to be happy to have an opportunity of providing for him so well. I am. Of course I am.'

Mr Pickwick had been so absorbed in these reflections, that a knock at the door was three or four times repeated before he heard it. Hastily seating himself, and calling up his accustomed pleasant looks, he gave the required permission, and Sam Weller entered, followed by his father.

'Glad to see you back again, Sam,' said Mr Pickwick. 'How do you do, Mr Weller?'

'Wery hearty, thankee, sir,' replied the widower; 'hope I see *you* well, sir.'

'Quite, I thank you,' replied Mr Pickwick.

'I wanted to have a little bit o' conwersation with you, sir,' said Mr Weller, 'if you could spare me five minits or so, sir.'

'Certainly,' replied Mr Pickwick. 'Sam, give your father a chair.'

'Thankee, Samivel, I've got a cheer here,' said Mr Weller, bringing one forward as he spoke; 'uncommon fine day it's been, sir,' added the old gentleman, laying his hat on the floor as he sat himself down.

'Remarkably so indeed,' replied Mr Pickwick. 'Very seasonable.'

'Seasonablest veather I ever see, sir,' rejoined Mr Weller. Here, the old gentleman was seized with a violent fit of coughing, which, being terminated, he nodded his head and winked and made several supplicatory and threatening gestures to his son, all of which Sam Weller steadily abstained from seeing.

Mr Pickwick, perceiving that there was some embarrassment on the old gentleman's part, affected to be engaged in cutting the leaves of a book that lay beside him, and waited patiently until Mr Weller should arrive at the object of his visit.

'I never see sich a aggerawatin' boy as you are, Samivel' said Mr Weller, looking indignantly at his son; 'never in all my born days.'

'What is he doing, Mr Weller?' inquired Mr Pickwick.

'He von't begin, sir,' rejoined Mr Weller; 'he knows I ain't ekal to ex-pressin' myself ven there's anythin' partickler to be done, and yet he'll stand and see me a settin' here takin' up your walable time, and makin' a reg'lar spectacle o' myself, rayther than help me out vith a syllable. It ain't filial conduct, Samivel,' said Mr Weller, wiping his forehead; 'wery far from it.'

'You said you'd speak,' replied Sam; 'how should I know you wos done up at the wery beginnin'?'

'You might ha' seen I warn't able to start,' rejoined his father; 'I'm on the wrong side of the road, and backin' into the palins, and all manner of unpleasantness, and yet you von't put out a hand to help me. I'm ashamed on you, Samivel.'

'The fact is, sir,' said Sam, with a slight bow, 'the gov'ner's been a drawin' his money.'

'Wery good, Samivel, wery good,' said Mr Weller, nodding his head with a satisfied air, 'I didn't mean to speak harsh to you, Sammy. Wery good. That's the vay to begin. Come to the pint at once. Wery good indeed, Samivel.'

Mr Weller nodded his head an extraordinary number of times, in the excess of his gratification, and waited in a listening attitude for Sam to resume his statement.

'You may sit down, Sam,' said Mr Pickwick, apprehending that the interview was likely to prove rather longer than he had expected.

Sam bowed again and sat down; his father looking round, he continued,

'The gov'ner, sir, has drawn out five hundred and thirty pound.'

'Reduced counsels,' interposed Mr Weller, senior, in an under tone.

'It don't much matter vether it's reduced counsels, or wot not,' said Sam; 'five hundred and thirty pound is the sum, ain't it?'

'All right, Samivel,' replied Mr Weller.

'To vich sum, he has added for the house and bisness – '

'Lease, good-vill, stock, and fixters,' interposed Mr Weller.

– 'As much as makes it,' continued Sam, 'altogether, eleven hundred and eighty pound.'

'Indeed!' said Mr Pickwick. 'I am delighted to hear it. I congratulate you, Mr Weller, on having done so well.'

'Vait a minit, sir,' said Mr Weller, raising his hand in a deprecatory manner. 'Get on, Samivel.'

'This here money,' said Sam, with a little hesitation, 'he's anxious to put someveres, vere he knows it'll be safe, and I'm wery anxious too, for if he keeps it, he'll go a lendin' it to somebody, or inwestin' property in horses, or droppin' his pocket-book down a airy, or makin' a Egyptian mummy of his-self in some vay or another.'

'Wery good, Samivel,' observed Mr Weller, in as complacent a manner as if Sam had been passing the highest eulogiums on his prudence and foresight. 'Wery good.'

'For vich reasons,' continued Sam, plucking nervously at the brim of his hat; 'for vich reasons, he's drawd it out to-day, and come here vith me to say, leastvays to offer, or in other vords to –'

' – To say this here,' said the elder Mr Weller, impatiently, 'that it ain't o' no use to me. I'm a goin' to vork a coach reg'lar, and ha'nt got noveres to keep it in, unless I vos to pay the guard for takin' care on it, or to put it in vun o' the coach pockets, vich 'ud be a temptation to the insides. If you'll take care on it for me, sir, I shall be wery much obliged to you. P'raps,' said Mr Weller, walking up to Mr Pickwick and whispering in his ear, 'P'raps it'll go a little vay towards the expenses o' that 'ere conwiction. All I say is, just you keep it till I ask you for it again.' With these words, Mr Weller placed the pocket-book in Mr Pickwick's hands, caught up his hat, and ran out of the room with a celerity scarcely to be expected from so corpulent a subject.

'Stop him, Sam!' exclaimed Mr Pickwick, earnestly. 'Overtake him; bring him back instantly! Mr Weller – here – come back!'

Sam saw that his master's injunctions were not to be disobeyed; and catching his father by the arm as he was descending the stairs, dragged him back by main force.

'My good friend,' said Mr Pickwick, taking the old man by the hand; 'your honest confidence overpowers me.'

'I don't see no occasion for nothin' o' the kind, sir,' replied Mr Weller, obstinately.

'I assure you, my good friend, I have more money than I can ever need, far more than a man at my age can ever live to spend,' said Mr Pickwick.

'No man knows how much he can spend, till he tries,' observed Mr Weller.

'Perhaps not,' replied Mr Pickwick; 'but as I have no intention of trying any such experiments, I am not likely to come to want. I must beg you to take this back, Mr Weller.'

'Wery well,' said Mr Weller with a discontented look. 'Mark my vords, Sammy. I'll do somethin' desperate vith this here property; somethin' desperate!'

'You'd better not,' replied Sam.

Mr Weller reflected for a short time, and then, buttoning up his coat with great determination, said:

'I'll keep a pike.'[1]

'Wot!' exclaimed Sam.

'A pike,' rejoined Mr Weller, through his set teeth; 'I'll keep a pike. Say good bye to your father, Samivel. I dewote the remainder o' my days to a pike.'

This threat was such an awful one, and Mr Weller besides appearing fully resolved to carry it into execution, seemed so deeply mortified by Mr Pickwick's refusal, that that gentleman, after a short reflection, said:

'Well, well, Mr Weller, I will keep the money. I can do more good with it, perhaps, than you can.'

'Just the wery thing, to be sure,' said Mr Weller, brightening up; 'o' course you can, sir.'

'Say no more about it,' said Mr Pickwick, locking the pocket-book in his desk; 'I am heartily obliged to you, my good friend. Now sit down again. I want to ask your advice.'

The internal laughter occasioned by the triumphant success of his visit, which had convulsed not only Mr Weller's face, but his arms, legs, and body also, during the locking up of the pocket-book, suddenly gave place to the most dignified gravity as he heard these words.

'Wait outside a few minutes, Sam, will you?' said Mr Pickwick.

Sam immediately withdrew.

Mr Weller looked uncommonly wise and very much amazed, when Mr Pickwick opened the discourse by saying:

'You are not an advocate for matrimony, I think, Mr Weller?'

Mr Weller shook his head. He was wholly unable to speak; vague thoughts of some wicked widow having been successful in her designs on Mr Pickwick, choked his utterance.

'Did you happen to see a young girl down stairs when you came in just now with your son?' inquired Mr Pickwick.

'Yes. I see a young gal,' replied Mr Weller, shortly.

'What did you think of her, now? Candidly, Mr Weller, what did you think of her?'

'I thought she wos wery plump, and vell made,' said Mr Weller, with a critical air.

'So she is,' said Mr Pickwick, 'so she is. What did you think of her manners, from what you saw of her?'

'Wery pleasant,' rejoined Mr Weller. 'Wery pleasant and conformable.'

The precise meaning which Mr Weller attached to this last-mentioned adjective, did not appear; but, as it was evident from the tone in which he used it that it was a favourable expression, Mr Pickwick was as well satisfied as if he had been thoroughly enlightened on the subject.

'I take a great interest in her, Mr Weller,' said Mr Pickwick.

Mr Weller coughed.

'I mean an interest in her doing well,' resumed Mr Pickwick; 'a desire that she may be comfortable and prosperous. You understand?'

'Wery clearly,' replied Mr Weller, who understood nothing yet.

'That young person,' said Mr Pickwick, 'is attached to your son.'

'To Samivel Veller!' exclaimed the parent.

'Yes,' said Pickwick.

'It's nat'ral,' said Mr Weller, after some consideration, 'nat'ral, but rayther alarmin'. Sammy must be careful.'

'How do you mean?' inquired Mr Pickwick.

'Wery careful that he don't say nothin' to her,' responded Mr Weller. 'Wery careful that he ain't led avay, in a innocent moment, to say anythink as may lead to a conwiction for breach. You're never safe vith 'em, Mr Pickwick, ven they vunce has designs on you; there's no knowin' vere to have 'em; and vile you're a-considering of it, they have you. I wos married fust, that vay myself, sir, and Sammy wos the consekens o' the manoover.'

'You give me no great encouragement to conclude what I have to say,' observed Mr Pickwick, 'but I had better do so at once. This young person is not only attached to your son, Mr Weller, but your son is attached to her.'

'Vell,' said Mr Weller, 'this here's a pretty sort o' thing to come to a father's ears, this is!'

'I have observed them on several occasions,' said Mr Pickwick, making no comment on Mr Weller's last remark; 'and entertain no doubt at all about it. Supposing I were desirous of establishing them comfortably as man and wife in some little business or situation, where they might hope to obtain a decent living, what should you think of it, Mr Weller?'

At first, Mr Weller received, with wry faces, a proposition involving the marriage of anybody in whom he took an interest; but, as Mr Pickwick argued the point with him, and laid great stress on the fact that Mary was not a widow, he gradually became more tractable. Mr Pickwick had great influence over him, and he had been much struck with Mary's appearance; having, in fact, bestowed several very unfatherly winks upon her, already. At length he said that it was not for him to oppose Mr Pickwick's inclination, and that he would be very happy to yield to his advice; upon which, Mr Pickwick joyfully took him at his word, and called Sam back into the room.

'Sam,' said Mr Pickwick, clearing his throat, 'your father and I have been having some conversation about you.'

'About you, Samivel,' said Mr Weller, in a patronising and impressive voice.

'I am not so blind, Sam, as not to have seen, a long time since, that you entertain something more than a friendly feeling towards Mrs Winkle's maid,' said Mr Pickwick.

'You hear this, Samivel?' said Mr Weller in the same judicial form of speech as before.

'I hope, sir,' said Sam, addressing his master: 'I hope there's no harm in a young man takin' notice of a young 'ooman as is undeniably good-looking and well-conducted.'

'Certainly not,' said Mr Pickwick.

'Not by no means,' acquiesced Mr Weller, affably but magisterially.

'So far from thinking there is anything wrong, in conduct so natural,' resumed Mr Pickwick, 'it is my wish to assist and promote your wishes in this respect. With this view, I have had a little conversation with your father; and finding that he is of my opinion—'

'The lady not bein' a widder,' interposed Mr Weller in explanation.

'The lady not being a widow,' said Mr Pickwick, smiling. 'I wish to free you from the restraint which your present position imposes upon you, and to mark my sense of your fidelity and many excellent qualities, by enabling you to marry this girl at once, and to earn an independent livelihood for yourself and family. I shall be proud, Sam,' said Mr Pickwick, whose voice had faltered a little hitherto, but now resumed its customary tone, 'proud and happy to make your future prospects in life, my grateful and peculiar care.'

There was a profound silence for a short time, and then Sam said, in a low husky sort of voice, but firmly withal:

'I'm very much obliged to you for your goodness, sir, as is only like yourself; but it can't be done.'

'Can't be done!' ejaculated Mr Pickwick in astonishment.

'Samivel!' said Mr Weller, with dignity.

'I say it can't be done,' repeated Sam in a louder key. 'Wot's to become of you, sir?'

'My good fellow,' replied Mr Pickwick, 'the recent changes among my friends will alter my mode of life in future, entirely; besides, I am growing older, and want repose and quiet. My rambles, Sam, are over.'

'How do I know that 'ere, sir?' argued Sam. 'You think so now! S'pose you wos to change your mind, vich is not unlikely, for you've the spirit o' five-and-tventy in you still, what 'ud become on you vithout me. It can't be done, sir, it can't be done.'

'Wery good, Samivel, there's a good deal in that,' said Mr Weller, encouragingly.

'I speak after long deliberation, Sam, and with the certainty that I shall keep my word,' said Mr Pickwick, shaking his head. 'New scenes have closed upon me; my rambles are at an end.'

'Wery good,' rejoined Sam. 'Then, that's the wery best reason wy you should alvays have somebody by you as understands you, to keep you up and make you comfortable. If you vant a more polished sort o' feller, vell and good, have him; but vages or no vages, notice or no notice, board or no board, lodgin' or no lodgin', Sam Veller, as you took from the old inn in the Borough, sticks by you, come what come may; and let ev'rythin' and ev'rybody do their wery fiercest, nothin' shall ever perwent it!'

At the close of this declaration, which Sam made with great emotion, the elder Mr Weller rose from his chair, and, forgetting all considerations of time, place, or propriety, waved his hat above his head, and gave three vehement cheers.

'My good fellow,' said Mr Pickwick, when Mr Weller had sat down again, rather abashed at his own enthusiasm, 'you are bound to consider the young woman also.'

'I do consider the young 'ooman, sir,' said Sam. 'I have considered the young 'ooman. I've spoke to her. I've told her how I'm sitivated; she's ready to vait till I'm ready, and I believe she vill. If she don't, she's not the young 'ooman I take her for, and I give her up vith readiness. You've know'd me afore, sir. My mind's made up, and nothin' can ever alter it.'

Who could combat this resolution? Not Mr Pickwick. He derived, at that moment, more pride and luxury of feeling from the disinterested attachment of his humble friends, than ten thousand protestations from the greatest men living could have awakened in his heart.

While this conversation was passing in Mr Pickwick's room, a little old gentleman in a suit of snuff-coloured clothes, followed by a porter carrying a small portmanteau, presented himself below; and after securing a bed for the night, inquired of the waiter whether one Mrs Winkle was staying there, to which question the waiter, of course, responded in the affirmative.

'Is she alone?' inquired the little old gentleman.

'I believe she is, sir,' replied the waiter; 'I can call her own maid, sir, if you—'

'No, I don't want her,' said the old gentleman quickly. 'Show me to her room without announcing me.'

'Eh, sir?' said the waiter.

'Are you deaf?' inquired the little old gentleman.

'No, sir.'

'Then listen, if you please. Can you hear me now?'

'Yes, sir.'

'That's well. Show me to Mrs Winkle's room, without announcing me.'

As the little old gentleman uttered this command, he slipped five shillings into the waiter's hand, and looked steadily at him.

'Really, sir,' said the waiter, 'I don't know, sir, whether—'

'Ah! you'll do it, I see,' said the little old gentleman. 'You had better do it at once. It will save time.'

There was something so very cool and collected in the gentleman's manner, that the waiter put the five shillings in his pocket, and led him up stairs without another word.

'This is the room, is it?' said the gentleman. 'You may go.'

The waiter complied, wondering much who the gentleman could be, and what he wanted; the little old gentleman waiting till he was out of sight, tapped at the door.

'Come in,' said Arabella.

'Um, a pretty voice at any rate,' murmured the little old gentleman; 'but that's nothing.' As he said this, he opened the door and walked in. Arabella, who was sitting at work, rose on beholding a stranger – a little confused – but by no means ungracefully so.

'Pray don't rise, ma'am,' said the unknown, walking in, and closing the door after him. 'Mrs Winkle, I believe?'

Arabella inclined her head.

'Mrs Nathaniel Winkle, who married the son of the old man at Birmingham?' said the stranger, eyeing Arabella with visible curiosity.

Again, Arabella inclined her head, and looked uneasily round, as if uncertain whether to call for assistance.

'I surprise you, I see, ma'am,' said the old gentleman.

'Rather, I confess,' replied Arabella, wondering more and more.

'I'll take a chair, if you'll allow me, ma'am,' said the stranger.

He took one; and drawing a spectacle-case from his pocket, leisurely pulled out a pair of spectacles, which he adjusted on his nose.

'You don't know me, ma'am?' he said, looking so intently at Arabella that she began to feel alarmed.

'No, sir,' she replied timidly.

'No,' said the gentleman, nursing his left leg; 'I don't know how you should. You know my name, though, ma'am.'

'Do I?' said Arabella, trembling, though she scarcely knew why. 'May I ask what it is?'

'Presently, ma'am, presently,' said the stranger, not having yet removed his eyes from her countenance. 'You have been recently married, ma'am?'

'I have,' replied Arabella, in a scarcely audible tone, laying aside her work, and becoming greatly agitated as a thought, that had occurred to her before, struck more forcibly upon her mind.

'Without having represented to your husband the propriety of first consulting his father, on whom he is dependent, I think?' said the stranger.

Arabella applied her handkerchief to her eyes.

'Without an endeavour, even, to ascertain, by some indirect appeal, what were the old man's sentiments on a point in which he would naturally feel much interested?' said the stranger.

'I cannot deny it, sir,' said Arabella.

'And without having sufficient property of your own to afford your husband any permanent assistance in exchange for the worldly advantages which you knew he would have gained if he had married agreeably to his father's wishes?' said the old gentleman. 'This is what boys and girls call disinterested affection, till they have boys and girls of their own, and then they see it in a rougher and very different light!'

Arabella's tears flowed fast, as she pleaded in extenuation that she was young and inexperienced; that her attachment had alone induced her to take the step to which she had resorted; and that she had been deprived of the counsel and guidance of her parents almost from infancy.

'It was wrong,' said the old gentleman in a milder tone, 'very wrong. It was foolish, romantic, unbusiness-like.'

'It was my fault; all my fault, sir,' replied poor Arabella, weeping.

'Nonsense,' said the old gentleman; 'it was not your fault that he fell in love with you, I suppose? Yes it was though,' said the old gentleman, looking rather slyly at Arabella. 'It was your fault. He couldn't help it.'

This little compliment, or the little gentleman's odd way of paying it, or his altered manner - so much kinder than it was, at first - or all three together, forced a smile from Arabella in the midst of her tears.

'Where's your husband?' inquired the old gentleman, abruptly; stopping a smile which was just coming over his own face.

'I expect him every instant, sir,' said Arabella. 'I persuaded him, to take a walk this morning. He is very low and wretched at not having heard from his father.'

'Low, is he?' said the old gentleman. 'Serve him right!'

'He feels it on my account, I am afraid,' said Arabella; 'and indeed, sir, I feel it deeply on his. I have been the sole means of bringing him to his present condition.'

'Don't mind it on his account, my dear,' said the old gentleman. 'It serves him right. I am glad of it – actually glad of it, as far as he is concerned.'

The words were scarcely out of the old gentleman's lips, when footsteps were heard ascending the stairs, which he and Arabella seemed both to recognise at the same moment. The little gentleman turned pale, and making a strong effort to appear composed, stood up, as Mr Winkle entered the room.

'Father!' cried Mr Winkle, recoiling in amazement.

'Yes, sir,' replied the little old gentleman. 'Well, sir, what have you got to say to me?'

Mr Winkle remained silent.

'You are ashamed of yourself, I hope, sir?' said the old gentleman.

Still Mr Winkle said nothing.

'Are you ashamed of yourself, sir, or are you not?' inquired the old gentleman.

'No, sir,' replied Mr Winkle, drawing Arabella's arm through his. 'I am not ashamed of myself, or of my wife either.'

'Upon my word!' cried the old gentleman, ironically.

'I am very sorry to have done anything which has lessened your affection for me, sir,' said Mr Winkle; 'but I will say, at the same time, that I have no reason to be ashamed of having this lady for my wife, nor you of having her for a daughter.'

'Give me your hand, Nat,' said the old gentleman in an altered voice. 'Kiss me, my love. You *are* a very charming little daughter-in-law after all!'

In a few minutes' time Mr Winkle went in search of Mr Pickwick, and returning with that gentleman, presented him to his father, whereupon they shook hands for five minutes incessantly.

'Mr Pickwick, I thank you most heartily for all your kindness to my son,' said old Mr Winkle, in a bluff straightforward way. 'I am a hasty fellow, and when I saw you last, I was vexed and taken by surprise. I have judged for myself now, and am more than satisfied. Shall I make any more apologies, Mr Pickwick?'

'Not one,' replied that gentleman. 'You have done the only thing wanting to complete my happiness.'

Hereupon, there was another shaking of hands for five minutes longer, accompanied by a great number of complimentary speeches, which, besides being complimentary, had the additional and very novel recommendation of being sincere.

Sam had dutifully seen his father to the Belle Sauvage, when, on returning, he encountered the fat boy in the court, who had been charged with the delivery of a note from Emily Wardle.

'I say,' said Joe, who was unusually loquacious, 'what a pretty girl Mary is, isn't she? I am *so* fond of her, I am!'

Mr Weller made no verbal remark in reply; but eyeing the fat boy for a moment, quite transfixed at his presumption, led him by the collar to the corner, and dismissed him with a harmless but ceremonious kick. After which, he walked home, whistling.

CHAPTER 57

In which the Pickwick Club is finally dissolved, and everything concluded to the satisfaction of everybody

For a whole week after the happy arrival of Mr Winkle from Birmingham, Mr Pickwick and Sam Weller were from home all day long, only returning just in time for dinner, and then wearing an air of mystery and importance quite foreign to their natures. It was evident that very grave and eventful proceedings were on foot; but various surmises were afloat, respecting their precise character. Some (among whom was Mr Tupman) were disposed to think that Mr Pickwick contemplated a matrimonial alliance; but this idea the ladies most strenuously repudiated. Others, rather inclined to the belief that he had projected some distant tour, and was at present occupied in effecting the preliminary arrangements; but this again was stoutly denied by Sam himself, who had unequivocally stated when cross-examined by Mary that no new journeys were to be undertaken. At length, when the brains of the whole party had been racked for six long days, by unavailing speculation, it was unanimously resolved that Mr Pickwick should be called upon to explain his conduct, and to state distinctly why he had thus absented himself from the society of his admiring friends.

With this view, Mr Wardle invited the full circle to dinner at the Adelphi; and, the decanters having been twice sent round, opened the business.

'We are all anxious to know,' said the old gentleman, 'what we have done to offend you, and to induce you to desert us and devote yourself to these solitary walks.'

'Are you?' said Mr Pickwick. 'It is singular enough that I had intended to volunteer a full explanation this very day; so, if you will give me another glass of wine, I will satisfy your curiosity.'

The decanters passed from hand to hand with unwonted briskness, and Mr Pickwick looking round on the faces of his friends, with a cheerful smile, proceeded:

'All the changes that have taken place among us,' said Mr Pickwick, 'I mean the marriage that *has* taken place, and the marriage that *will* take place, with the changes they involve, rendered it necessary for me to think, soberly and at once, upon my future plans. I determined on retiring to some quiet pretty neighbourhood in the vicinity of London; I saw a house which exactly suited my fancy; I have taken it and furnished it. It is fully prepared for my reception, and I intend entering upon it at once, trusting that I may yet live to spend many quiet years in peaceful retirement, cheered through life by the society of my friends, and followed in death by their affectionate remembrance.'

Here Mr Pickwick paused, and a low murmur ran round the table.

'The house I have taken,' said Mr Pickwick, 'is at Dulwich. It has a large garden, and is situated in one of the most pleasant spots near London. It has been fitted up with every attention to substantial comfort; perhaps to a little elegance besides; but of that you shall judge for yourselves. Sam accompanies me there. I have engaged, on Perker's representation, a housekeeper – a very old one – and such other servants as she thinks I shall require. I propose to consecrate this little retreat, by having a ceremony in which I take a great interest, performed there. I wish, if my friend Wardle entertains no objection, that his daughter should be married from my new house, on the day I take possession of it. The happiness of young people,' said Mr Pickwick, a little moved, 'has ever been the chief pleasure of my life. It will warm my heart to witness the happiness of those friends who are dearest to me, beneath my own roof.'

Mr Pickwick paused again: Emily and Arabella sobbed audibly.

'I have communicated, both personally and by letter, with the club,' resumed Mr Pickwick, 'acquainting them with my intention. During our long absence, it had suffered much from internal dissensions; and the withdrawal of my name, coupled with this and other circumstances, has occasioned its dissolution. The Pickwick Club exists no longer.

'I shall never regret,' said Mr Pickwick in a low voice, 'I shall never regret having devoted the greater part of two years to mixing with different varieties and shades of human character: frivolous as my pursuit of novelty may have appeared to many. Nearly the whole of my previous life having been devoted to business and the pursuit of wealth, numerous scenes of which I had no previous conception have dawned upon me – I hope to the enlargement of my mind, and the improvement of my understanding. If I have done but little good, I trust I have done less harm, and that none of my adventures will be other than a source of amusing and pleasant recollection to me in the decline of life. God bless you all!'

With these words, Mr Pickwick filled and drained a bumper with a trembling hand, and his eyes moistened as his friends rose with one accord, and pledged him from their hearts.

There were very few preparatory arrangements to be made for the marriage of Mr Snodgrass. As he had neither father nor mother, and had been in his minority a ward of Mr Pickwick's, that gentleman was perfectly well acquainted with his possessions and prospects. His account of both was quite satisfactory to Wardle – as almost any other account would have been, for the good old gentleman was overflowing with hilarity and kindness – and a handsome portion having been bestowed upon Emily, the marriage was fixed to take place on the fourth day from that time: the suddenness of which preparations reduced three dress-makers and a tailor to the extreme verge of insanity.

Getting post-horses to the carriage, old Wardle started off, next day, to bring his mother up to town. Communicating his intelligence to the old lady with characteristic impetuosity, she instantly fainted away; but being promptly revived, ordered the brocaded silk gown to be packed up forthwith, and proceeded to relate some circumstances of a similar nature attending the marriage of the eldest daughter of Lady Tollimglower, deceased, which occupied three hours in the recital, and were not half finished at last.

Mrs Trundle had to be informed of all the mighty preparations that were making in London, and being in a delicate state of health was informed thereof through Mr Trundle, lest the news should be too much for her; but it was not too much for her, inasmuch as she at once wrote off to Muggleton, to order a new cap and a black satin gown, and moreover avowed her determination of being present at the ceremony. Hereupon, Mr Trundle called in the doctor, and the doctor said Mrs Trundle ought to know best how she felt herself, to which Mrs Trundle replied that she felt herself quite equal to it, and that she had made up her mind to go; upon which the doctor, who was a wise and discreet doctor, and knew what was good for himself as well as for other people, said that perhaps if Mrs Trundle stopped at home she might hurt herself more by fretting, than by going, so perhaps she had better go. And she did go; the doctor with great attention sending in half a dozen of medicine, to be drunk upon the road.

In addition to these points of distraction, Wardle was intrusted with two small letters to two small young ladies who were to act as bridesmaids; upon the receipt of which, the two young ladies were driven to despair by having no 'things' ready for so important an occasion, and no time to make them in – a circumstance which appeared to afford the two worthy papas of the two small young ladies rather a feeling of satisfaction than otherwise. However, old frocks were trimmed, and new bonnets made, and the young ladies looked as well as could possibly have been expected of them. And as they cried at the subsequent ceremony in the proper places, and trembled at the right times, they acquitted themselves to the admiration of all beholders.

How the two poor relations ever reached London – whether they walked, or got behind coaches, or procured lifts in wagons, or carried each other by turns – is uncertain; but there they were, before Wardle; and the very first people that knocked at the door of Mr Pickwick's house, on the bridal morning were the two poor relations, all smiles and shirt collar.

They were welcomed heartily though, for riches or poverty had no influence on Mr Pickwick; the new servants were all alacrity and readiness; Sam was in a most unrivalled state of high spirits and excitement; Mary was glowing with beauty and smart ribands.

The bridegroom, who had been staying at the house for two or three days previous, sallied forth gallantly to Dulwich Church to meet the bride, attended by Mr Pickwick, Ben Allen, Bob Sawyer, and Mr Tupman; with Sam Weller outside, having at his button-hole a white favour, the gift of his lady love, and clad in a new and gorgeous suit of livery invented for the occasion. They were met by the Wardles, and the Winkles, and the bride and bridesmaids, and the Trundles; and the ceremony having been performed, the coaches rattled back to Mr Pickwick's to breakfast, where little Mr Perker already awaited them.

Here, all the light clouds of the more solemn part of the proceedings passed away; every face shone forth joyously; nothing was to be heard but congratulations and commendations. Everything was so beautiful! The lawn in front, the garden behind, the miniature conservatory, the dining-room, the drawing-room, the bed-rooms, the smoking-room, and above all the study with its pictures and easy chairs, and odd cabinets, and queer tables, and books out of number, with a large cheerful window opening upon a pleasant lawn and commanding a pretty landscape, dotted here and there with little houses almost hidden by the trees; and then the curtains, and the carpets, and the chairs, and the sofas! Everything was so beautiful, so compact, so neat, and in such exquisite taste, said everybody, that there really was no deciding what to admire most.

And in the midst of all this, stood Mr Pickwick, his countenance lighted up with smiles, which the heart of no man, woman, or child, could resist: himself the happiest of the group: shaking hands, over and over again with the same people, and when his own hands were not so employed, rubbing them with pleasure: turning round in a different direction at every fresh expression of gratification or curiosity, and inspiring everybody with his looks of gladness and delight.

Breakfast is announced. Mr Pickwick leads the old lady (who has been very eloquent on the subject of Lady Tollimglower), to the top of a long table; Wardle takes the bottom; the friends arrange themselves on either side; Sam takes his station behind his master's chair; the laughter and talking cease; Mr Pickwick, having said grace, pauses for an instant, and looks round him. As he does so, the tears roll down his cheeks, in the fulness of his joy.

Let us leave our old friend in one of those moments of unmixed happiness, of which, if we seek them, there are ever some, to cheer our transitory existence here. There are dark shadows on the earth, but its lights are stronger in the contrast. Some men, like bats or owls, have better eyes for the darkness than for the light. We, who have no such optical powers, are better pleased to take our last parting look at the visionary companions of many solitary hours, when the brief sunshine of the world is blazing full upon them.

———

It is the fate of most men who mingle with the world, and attain even the prime of life, to make many real friends, and lose them in the course of nature. It is the fate of all authors or chroniclers to create imaginary friends, and lose them in the course of art. Nor is this the full extent of their misfortunes; for they are required to furnish an account of them besides.

In compliance with this custom – unquestionably a bad one – we subjoin a few biographical words, in relation to the party at Mr Pickwick's assembled.

Mr and Mrs Winkle, being fully received into favour by the old gentleman, were shortly afterwards installed in a newly-built house, not half a mile from Mr Pickwick's. Mr Winkle, being engaged in the City as agent or town correspondent of his father, exchanged his old costume for the ordinary dress of Englishmen, and presented all the external appearance of a civilised Christian ever afterwards.

Mr and Mrs Snodgrass settled at Dingley Dell, where they purchased and cultivated a small farm, more for occupation than profit. Mr Snodgrass, being occasionally abstracted and melancholy, is to this day reputed a great poet among his friends and acquaintance, although we do not find that he has ever written anything to encourage the belief. There are many celebrated characters, literary, philosophical, and otherwise, who hold a high reputation on a similar tenure.

Mr Tupman, when his friends married, and Mr Pickwick settled, took lodgings at Richmond, where he has ever since resided. He walks constantly on the Terrace during the summer months, with a youthful and jaunty air which has rendered him the admiration of the numerous elderly ladies of single condition, who reside in the vicinity. He has never proposed again.

Mr Bob Sawyer, having previously passed through the Gazette,[1] passed over to Bengal, accompanied by Mr Benjamin Allen; both gentlemen having received surgical appointments from the East India Company. They each had the yellow fever fourteen times, and then resolved to try a little abstinence; since which period, they have been doing well.

Mrs Bardell let lodgings to many conversable single gentlemen, with great profit, but never brought any more actions for breach of promise of marriage. Her attorneys, Messrs. Dodson and Fogg, continue in business, from which they realise a large income, and in which they are universally considered among the sharpest of the sharp.

Sam Weller kept his word, and remained unmarried, for two years. The old housekeeper dying at the end of that time, Mr Pickwick promoted Mary to the situation, on condition of her marrying Mr Weller at once, which she did without a murmur.

From the circumstance of two sturdy little boys having been repeatedly seen at the gate of the back garden, there is reason to suppose that Sam has some family.

The elder Mr Weller drove a coach for twelve months, but being afflicted with the gout, was compelled to retire. The contents of the pocket-book had been so well invested for him, however, by Mr Pickwick, that he had a handsome independence to retire on, upon which he still lives at an excellent public-house near Shooter's Hill,[2] where he is quite reverenced as an oracle: boasting very much of his intimacy with Mr Pickwick, and retaining a most unconquerable aversion to widows.

Mr Pickwick himself continued to reside in his new house, employing his leisure hours in arranging the memoranda which he afterwards presented to the secretary of the once famous club, or in hearing Sam Weller read aloud, with such remarks as suggested themselves to his mind, which never failed to afford Mr Pickwick great amusement. He was much troubled at first, by the numerous applications made to him by Mr Snodgrass, Mr Winkle, and Mr Trundle, to act as godfather to their offspring; but he has become used to it now, and officiates as a matter of course. He never had occasion to regret his bounty to Mr Jingle; for both that person and Job Trotter became, in time, worthy members of society, although they have always steadily objected to return to the scenes of their old haunts and temptations. Mr Pickwick is somewhat infirm now; but he retains all his former juvenility of spirit, and may still be frequently seen, contemplating the pictures in the Dulwich Gallery,[3] or enjoying a walk about the pleasant neighbourhood on a fine day. He is known by all the poor people about, who never fail to take their hats off, as he passes, with great respect. The children idolise him, and so indeed does the whole neighbourhood. Every year, he repairs to a large family merry-making at Mr Wardle's; on this, as on all other occasions, he is invariably attended by the faithful Sam, between whom and his master there exists a steady and reciprocal attachment which nothing but death will terminate.

NOTES

Like many editors of this novel, I am indebted to the 'Notes on *The Pickwick Papers*' by T. W. Hill, published in *The Dickensian* 44 and 45 (1948–9). I have also been greatly helped by the work of other *Pickwick* editors and Dickens scholars (acknowledged by surname in several of the notes below): Robert Patten, in his edition of the novel for the Penguin English Library (1972); M.K.A. Beisiegel, *Notes on Dickens' Pickwick Papers* (1912); Percy Fitzgerald, *The Pickwickian Dictionary and Cyclopaedia* (1903); N. Bentley, M. Slater & N. Burgis (eds), *The Dickens Index* (1990). Especial thanks are due to Michael Flavin, my Research Assistant, and to the General Editor, Michael Slater, for his advice.

Readers of this edition should be aware that there is a separate Glossary to explain terms relating to **modes of transport, food and drink** and **clothing** (see pp. 812–15).

DEDICATION TO MR SERJEANT TALFOURD, M.P.

1. **(xxxv) Talfourd:** Thomas Noon Talfourd (1795–1854) was a lawyer, Member of Parliament and writer. He was elected to Parliament by the constituency of Reading in 1835, coincidentally the same constituency which invited Dickens to stand as its MP in 1841. 'Serjeant' was the title given to a certain class of barristers who had the exclusive right to present cases in the Court of Common Pleas. Talfourd was the author of the play, *Ion* (1836), and an edition of Charles Lamb's letters (1837). He and Dickens became close friends, having first met in 1837, and Talfourd may have been the model for Tommy Traddles in *David Copperfield*.

2. **(xxxv) copyright:** In May 1837 Talfourd introduced his Copyright Bill in Parliament, though it did not pass into law until 1842. Dickens's gratitude for Talfourd's campaign would have been greatly strengthened by the end of *Pickwick*'s run, when countless plagiarisms, stage adaptations and commercial exploitations of the novel made him increasingly aware that he was a valuable literary property, and that his future livelihood and that of his family would depend on the legal protection afforded to his work. Talfourd's Bill extended the copyright period to forty-two years or

seven years after the author's death, whichever was longer. This was, of course, for the United Kingdom only; international copyright was non-existent.

PREFACE TO THE FIRST EDITION (1837)

1. **(xxxviii)** **a very dear young friend:** Mary Hogarth, Dickens's sister-in-law. Mary died in May 1837, at the age of seventeen.

2. **(xxxvii)** **the gentleman:** Hablot Knight Browne ('Phiz').

PREFACE TO THE CHARLES DICKENS EDITION (1867)

1. **(xxxix)** **Morning Chronicle:** daily newspaper founded in 1769. Dickens served as a reporter on the paper from 1834 to 1836.

2. **(xxxix)** **Monthly Magazine:** Founded in 1769, the magazine carried the first of Dickens's published stories, 'A Dinner at Poplar Walk' (December 1833), as well as several other tales by him.

3. **(xxxix)** **some pieces ... published in two volumes:** The reference is to Dickens's *Sketches by Boz* (First Series), which had just been published in two volumes by John Macrone in February 1836. Dickens would have been twenty-four (not 'three and twenty') when he met William Hall, the 'managing partner' of the publishing firm Chapman and Hall.

4. **(xxxix)** MR GEORGE CRUIKSHANK: George Cruikshank (1792–1878), prolific caricaturist and book illustrator, was engaged by the publisher John Macrone to design plates for *Sketches by Boz* (First and Second Series). He also illustrated *Oliver Twist*.

5. **(xxxix)** **Furnival's Inn:** one of the old Inns of Chancery. It was situated in Holborn and Dickens occupied chambers there in 1834–7, when it had ceased to be a legal community.

6. **(xxxix)** **Westminster Hall:** an ancient building next to the House of Commons. From the early thirteenth century it housed the Royal Courts of Justice.

7. **(xxxix)** MR SEYMOUR: Robert Seymour (?1798–1836). Popular illustrator, noted particularly for his comic sporting pictures. He was a key figure in the plans for *Pickwick* and his suicide on 20 April 1836 had a considerable impact on the direction the novel was subsequently to take.

8. **(xxxix)** 'NIMROD CLUB': Nimrod was the legendary mighty hunter, great-grandson of Noah (Genesis 10:8–9).

9. **(xl)** MR EDWARD CHAPMAN: Chapman, along with William Hall,

founded the publishing company of Chapman and Hall in 1830 at 186 Strand, London. The success of the company was closely linked to its association with Dickens. In 1938 Chapman and Hall was sold to Methuen. In 1849 Chapman told John Forster (the future biographer of Dickens) that he had been responsible for suggesting a model for the appearance of Mr Pickwick, 'a fat old beau who would wear, in spite of the ladies' protests, drab tights and black gaiters' (Forster, *The Life of Charles Dickens* [1872], Book I, Chapter 5).

10. (xl) **twenty-four pages:** actually Number 1 was twenty-six pages.

11. (xl) **some intangible and incoherent assertions:** In this and the subsequent paragraph Dickens rebuts the allegations made by Seymour's widow that her husband had had an unacknowledged part to play in originating incidents and characters in *Pickwick*.

12. (xl) **only twenty-four pages:** Dickens is incorrect here, as Patten points out. The first two numbers of *Pickwick* were complete by the time of Seymour's death: that is, a total of fifty printed pages.

13. (xli) **Old Mortality:** a novel by Sir Walter Scott, published in 1816 as part of the *Tales of my Landlord* series. The novel, set in the late seventeenth century, dramatises political and religious conflicts.

14. (xli) **Exeter Hall, or Ebenezer Chapel:** Exeter Hall, in the Strand, was the venue for meetings of the Evangelical movement. Dickens was always impatient with what he saw as misguided Evangelical zealotry. 'Ebenezer Chapel' is here used as a contemptuous generic term for dissenting sects.

15. (xli) **in the words of Swift:** the reference is to the opening maxim of Swift's 'Thoughts on Various Subjects' (*Miscellanies in Prose and Verse*, 1711).

16. (xlii) **Fleet Prison:** the debtors' prison; see Chapter 40, n. 6.

17. (xlii) **Poor Laws:** Dickens no doubt has uppermost in his mind the 1834 Poor Law Amendment Act, which introduced a more bureaucratic organisation of care for the poor and established workhouses with living conditions sufficiently grim to dissuade the poor from entering. He had launched his famous attack on these initiatives in *Oliver Twist* (1838).

18. (xlii) **Schools, on the broad principles of Christianity:** Dickens is referring to the controversies over the structure and educational ideology of state-aided educational institutions, especially to the issue of how far established or dissenting religious bodies should have control over schools.

CHAPTER I

1. (3) **May 12, 1827:** The internal dating is notoriously awry; for example, in 1827 Jingle could hardly have known about, let alone participated in, the July 1830 French revolution, as he boasted. Dodson and Fogg's letter to Pickwick advising him of the prosecution for breach of promise of marriage is dated August 1830, even though it comes three months after the novel's action begins. Other anachronisms were noted in 'corrigenda' for the first single volume edition in 1837.

2. (3) **Tittlebats:** 'Variant of sticklebat, of childish origin' (*OED*). The use of the juvenile terms serves to satirise, undercut or otherwise qualify Pickwick's achievement.

3. (3) **Hampstead Ponds ... Camberwell:** The majestic roll-call of names ironically disguises the fact that these London locations are all within a few miles of each other. The Ponds on Hampstead Heath, Highgate and Hornsey are close together in north London; Brixton and Camberwell were then suburban villages in south London, the latter close to Dulwich where Pickwick eventually retires.

4. (3) **advancement of knowledge:** a satirical reference to the Society for the Diffusion of Useful Knowledge (founded in 1826) and the British Association for the Advancement of Science (founded in 1831, four years later than the date of *Pickwick*'s action). Dickens produced parodies of the latter's proceedings in *The Mudfog Papers* (1837–8).

5. (5) **Swing:** the fictitious name 'Captain Swing' used by disaffected labourers during the agricultural unrest of 1830–1; the introduction of machinery jeopardised their jobs and they wrote threatening letters to landlords and farmers, signed 'Swing', followed often by the firing of their ricks. Another anachronism in the novel.

6. (8) **used the word in its Pickwickian sense:** a reference to Parliamentary satire. Lord Brougham in 1823 attacked Canning using opprobrious terms, which he then said he was using only in their 'Parliamentary sense' and had not meant them in the ordinary way.

7. (8) **MS. authorities:** abbreviation of Latin, *manu scriptum*, i.e. manuscript.

CHAPTER 2

1. (9) **St Martin's-le-Grand:** a street next to St Paul's Cathedral, a few hundred metres south of Goswell Street.

2. (9) **Golden Cross:** a coaching inn on the corner of St Martin's Lane and the Strand.

3. (9) **bob ... shilling:** 'Bob' is slang for a shilling; this was the minimum possible cab fare. Under the old British currency £1 = twenty shillings and one shilling = twelve pence. The slang for a sixpenny piece was 'tanner' or 'bender'. Two coins represented fractions of a penny, the halfpenny or 'ha'penny', and the farthing (a quarter of a penny, or fourth-thing). A 'crown' was a five-shilling coin; half-a-crown was a coin to the value of two shillings and sixpence. A florin was a two-shilling coin. The value of a guinea was twenty-one shillings.

4. (9) **Pentonwil:** Pentonville, then a prosperous suburb in north London.

5. (13) **fives:** fists, probably from 'a bunch of fives'.

6. (13) **pig's whisper ... gammon:** slang expressions for, respectively, a short space of time, humbug or nonsense.

7. (14) **somebody else's head off there:** Charles I was executed in 1649, on one of the balconies of the Banqueting House in Whitehall. His equestrian statue stands at the top of Whitehall.

8. (14) **revolution of July:** The revolution of 1830 in France overthrew the Bourbon dynasty and brought Louis-Philippe d'Orléans to the throne.

9. (14) **A remarkable instance ... 1830:** footnote added by Dickens in the Cheap Edition of 1847.

10. (20) **way of the sun ... heeltaps:** from right to left, the proper direction for passing port around the table; buttonholes conventionally appear on the left lapel of men's coats; heel-taps is the term for the liquor left at the bottom of a glass after drinking.

11. (20) **Bacchus:** Greek god of wine.

12. (22) **the Dragon (called by courtesy a woman):** The gold sovereign coin (to the value of a pound) had the head of the monarch on one side and St George and the Dragon on the other side, where, on other coins, the figure of Britannia is represented; hence 'the woman'.

13. (22) **cheval glass:** a full-length moveable mirror, hinged on a frame.

14. (22) **quadrilles:** a square dance usually performed by four couples.

15. (23) **nobs:** slang for 'nobility'.

16. (23) **the yard:** the naval dockyard at nearby Chatham.

17. (24) **Alexander Selkirks:** Selkirk, the supposed model for Robinson
Crusoe, was a Scottish sailor marooned on a South Pacific island. William
Cowper (1731–1800) wrote a poem 'Verses supposed to be written by
Alexander Selkirk', which began, 'I am monarch of all I survey . . .'

18. (25) **knock you up:** slang for 'call on you'.

19. (25) **a shuffler . . . poltroon:** respectively, a shifty character and a
spiritless coward.

20. (26) **Boots:** boot-boy, a lowly servant at an inn or hostelry, responsible for cleaning the footwear of the clientele.

21. (31) **Twopenny Postman:** 'Before the introduction of the Penny
Post in 1840 the charge for local delivery of letters in London was twopence'
(*Dickens Index*).

22. (32) **satisfaction pistols:** duelling pistols; from the conventional
expression of 'satisfying' one's honour by a duel.

23. (32) **newspapers . . . loadings:** refers to the practice of loading
firearms by pouring gunpowder down the barrel, ramming in a wad of
paper to secure the powder, and then inserting the shot.

CHAPTER 3

1. (38) **black-eyed Susan:** *Black-eyed Susan, or All in the Downs* was
a popular melodrama by Douglas Jerrold, based on a ballad by John Gay,
first performed in 1829 (another of the novel's anachronisms).

2. (39) **Dance of Death:** a well-known subject for painters. The most
famous version was the series of woodcuts (1523–6) by Hans Holbein.

3. (40) **playing in the last piece . . . a benefit night:** A single evening's
entertainment at a popular theatre would consist of several different items,
such as songs and short dramatic pieces. On 'benefit nights', the proceeds
from ticket sales would go to a single nominated performer.

4. (43) **gibing:** speaking with a sneer.

CHAPTER 4

1. (48) **New River Head:** a north London reservoir, built in the seventeenth century, from which (as Dickens's elaborately extended metaphor
indicates) water was 'laid on' for the city's inhabitants.

2. (49) **Lines:** The Chatham Lines are an open space on the top of a steep hill, overlooking Chatham dockyards. Equipped with mock fortifications, the Lines were used for spectacular military manœuvres

3. (49) **a mine was to be sprung:** A mine is a subterranean passage or gallery, used either as a means of gaining entry by besiegers, or as a location in which gunpowder is placed in order to blow up an enemy's fortifications.

4. (49) **curvetting:** a movement involving the horse's standing up on its back legs and then, as its forelegs come down, quickly raising the hind legs, so that all four legs are briefly off the ground.

5. (50) **sally-port:** a gate in a fortified building from which troops could issue quickly to mount an assault.

6. (58) **quiz:** here meaning a teasing or satirical person.

CHAPTER 5

1. (63) **hostler:** a stable-man.

2. (66) **quickset:** a hedge or thicket.

3. (70) **eight-day clock:** so-called because it required winding once every week.

CHAPTER 6

1. (71) **brought up in the way she should go ... when old:** an echo of Proverbs 22:6: 'Train up a child in the way he should go: and when he is old, he will not depart from it.'

2. (73) **rubber:** a set of three or five games (here applied to the card game 'whist').

3. (73) **Pope Joan ... whist:** Pope Joan is a card game for any number of players, with cards and a circular tray something like a roulette-cloth. The old-fashioned 'Long whist' rather than the modern whist game is the version being played at Dingley Dell.

4. (74) **fish:** refers to the small counters used in scoring games, which were sometimes shaped like fish. The term derives from the French word '*fiche*', meaning 'pin' or 'peg'.

CHAPTER 7

1. (85) **cows ... stone crop:** A 'cow' is a Kentish dialect version of 'cowl', here referring to the hood-shaped coverings on chimneys; 'pan-tiles'

are curved roofing tiles; 'stone crop' is 'sedum acre', a plant which grows on rocks and old walls.

2. (86) **a second Robinson Crusoe:** the eponymous hero of Daniel Defoe's novel carried a pistol and rifle.

3. (87) **Lambert:** Daniel Lambert (1770–1809) weighed just over 740 pounds at the time of his death.

4. (87) **cap:** a small metal container on a gun, holding a small amount of gunpowder. Caps first appeared in 1825, which may, from an extremely charitable point of view, explain Winkle's unfamiliarity with them.

5. (90) **sale of livings ... abolishing Sunday trading:** A 'living', in the ecclesiastical sense used here, is the granting to a clergyman of paid responsibility for a parish. On the matter of 'Sunday trading', Dickens was a lifelong opponent of the stricter forms of Sabbatarianism, which forbad Sunday trading and restricted the forms of entertainment and leisure available to the labouring classes on their one weekly day of rest, though often left the wealthy still enjoying the services of their own staff.

6. (91) **corn-factor:** a dealer in grain.

7. (91) **diffusion of ... useful knowledge:** see Chapter 1, n. 4.

8. (92) **notch:** keep the score; from the old practice of keeping count by cutting notches in a stick.

9. (97) **Diogenes:** a Greek Cynic philosopher, who lived in a tub in order to show his contempt for the comforts of life.

10. (98) **song:** refers to a song by the dramatist John O'Keeffe (1747–1833), which has the following lines:
> The Glasses sparkle on the Board,
> The Wine is ruby bright.

CHAPTER 8

1. (100) **jessamine:** jasmine.

2. (106) **perturbed spirit:** echo of Hamlet's line to the ghost of his father: 'Rest, rest, perturbed spirit!' (*Hamlet*, Act II, Sc. 1).

3. (109) **Fielding:** Thomas Fielding (pseudonym of John Wade), whose *Select Proverbs of all Nations* (1824) records the saying that 'man is fire', etc.

4. (112) **cut:** snub, refuse to recognise.

CHAPTER 9

1. (118) **Mich'lmas:** Michaelmas, the feast of St Michael, 29 September.

CHAPTER 10

1. (124) **the Borough:** an area of London immediately south of the River Thames, comprising Southwark and parts of Bermondsey, Lambeth and Rotherhithe.

2. (125) **Jack Ketch:** generic name for executioner. John Ketch was public hangman in England, 1663–86.

3. (126) **Warren ... Day and Martin:** rival shoe-blacking producers; see Chapter 33, n. 7.

4. (126) **Doctors' Commons:** Doctors' Commons was an ancient college of lawyers. Its members had to be Doctors of Law of either Oxford or Cambridge Universities and had the sole right of appearing in ecclesiastical (including divorce), probate and admiralty courts.

5. (126) **Old Bailey Proctors:** The Old Bailey is the Central Criminal Court of London and its adjacent region. Proctors undertook the functions of solicitors or attorneys.

6. (126) **blunt:** slang for 'money'.

7. (127) **In hurry, post-haste ... I come back:** the first two lines from a song in Kane O'Hara's *Tom Thumb* (1781). O'Hara's comic opera was adapted from Henry Fielding's play *Tom Thumb*.

8. (128) **mizzle:** slang for 'disappear suddenly' (*OED*).

9. (128) **Vicar General:** an official who deputised for the Archbishop of Canterbury at Doctors' Commons.

10. (131) *amicus curiæ*: Latin for 'a friend of the court'.

11. (131) *ad captandum*: Latin for 'designed to captivate'; here meaning a bribe.

12. (131) **George Barnwell:** Barnwell and Adolphus were well-known reporters of King's Bench trials. Sam assumes, mistakenly, that Perker is about to refer to George Lillo's play *The History of George Barnwell, or the London Merchant* (1731). The 'young ooman' would be Millwood, who enticed Barnwell to murder and robbery.

13. (131) **scragging:** hanging.

CHAPTER 11

1. (139) **porter's knot:** twisted or knotted rope worn by porters over their shoulders to spread the weight of heavy loads.

CHAPTER 12

1. (159) **Up to snuff:** knowing, or sharp. Weller thereafter puns on the word 'snuff'.

2. (159) **farden:** farthing; see Chapter 2, n. 3.

3. (160) **seedsman:** a sower or dealer in seeds.

CHAPTER 13

1. (161) **schedules A and B:** list of boroughs in the 1832 Reform Bill. Schedule A listed boroughs which would cease to be Parliamentary constituencies; Schedule B listed boroughs which would return only one member.

2. (161) **Eatanswill:** The towns of Sudbury and Ipswich, both in Suffolk, claim to be the actual Eatanswill, with Sudbury reputedly having the stronger claim. The claim of Ipswich is somewhat diminished by the fact that it appears as itself in Chapter 22. The name Eatanswill may well have been inspired by Hogarth's 'Guzzledown', the electoral constituency whose candidate was Mr Punch, in the second of Hogarth's *Election* paintings.

3. (161) **our distinguished publishers:** Chapman and Hall.

4. (162) **to new skylight the market-place:** The market-place is an indoor, or at least covered, arena.

5. (168) *écarté*: a card game for two persons, in which the cards from two to six inclusive are discarded.

6. (168) **Twenty Eight:** The action of the novel is still supposed to be taking place in 1827.

7. (170) **where was you half baptized?:** Children in danger of imminent death undertook a shortened form of the 'Private Baptism of Children in Houses' ceremony. 'Half baptized' was the popular name for this practice. Figuratively, it was used to describe anyone who was lacking in worldly wisdom.

8. (171) **hustings:** temporary platforms on which Parliamentary candidates stood and sought nomination from the electors.

9. (174) **crier:** town crier.

CHAPTER 14

1. (179) **bagatelle-board ... skittle-ground:** Bagatelle is a kind of bar billiards, played on a table with holes on its surface for the balls to fall into, rather than margin pockets as for standard billiards. A skittle ground is a bowling alley.

2. (179) **'commercial room':** 'A room in an inn, hotel, etc., for the accommodation of commercial travellers and their customers' (*OED*).

3. (180) **watch-box:** 'A small wooden shelter resembling a sentry-box but furnished with a seat and a half-door, used by municipal watchman' (*OED*).

4. (180) **half a wafer:** a small adhesive disk, made of flour and gum, used to seal letters.

5. (180) **imperence:** 'A vulgar corruption of *impudence*, perhaps associated with *impertinence*' (*OED*).

6. (180) **Dutch pipe:** a long clay pipe, also known as a 'churchwarden'.

7. (181) **bagman:** 'A commercial traveller, whose business it is to show samples and solicit orders on behalf of manufacturers, etc. (*somewhat depreciatory*)' (*OED*).

8. (182) **two penny post-office pony:** see Chapter 2, n. 21.

9. (191) **cold larded fowl:** Larded dishes were stuffed with fat bacon, smeared with lard or otherwise greased.

CHAPTER 15

1. (195) **Doctor Faustus:** German astrologer and necromancer of the early sixteenth century. The legend that he sold his soul to the devil in exchange for greater knowledge of the mysteries of the universe was the subject of plays by Marlowe and Goethe.

2. (196) *fête champêtre*: a rural festival.

3. (196) **feasts of reason ... soul:** quotations from Alexander Pope's *The First Satire of the Second Book of Horace Imitated* (1733), ll. 127–8.

4. (197) **Minerva:** the Roman goddess of wisdom and the patroness of all the arts.

5. (197) **Plato, Zeno, Epicurus, Pythagoras:** Plato, philosopher of

ancient Greece, (c.429–c.347 BC). Zeno of Citium (c.300 BC), founder of the Stoic school of philosophy. Epicurus, Athenian philosopher (c.300 BC.), and Pythagoras, ancient Greek philosopher and mathematician of Samos (sixth century BC).

6. (201) **knout:** a particularly vicious kind of whip or scourge, formerly used in Russia as a means of punishment.

7. (203) **Count Smorltork:** based partly on Prince Pückler-Muskau and partly on Professor Friedrich von Raumer, who had both published recently books of travel in England. See K. Tillotson, 'Dickens's Count Smorltork', *TLS*, 22 December 1957.

8. (207) **Baker's patent:** A well-known kind of mangle; i.e. a machine for pressing clothes dry after washing.

9. (208) **Living Skellinton:** A gruesomely thin Frenchman, Claude Ambroise Seurat, was exhibited in London in 1825 as the 'Living Skeleton'.

CHAPTER 16

1. (210) **mother-in-law:** stepmother.

2. (211) **Right as a trivet:** A trivet was a three-footed stool or support. Weller is presumably using the phrase to express the solidity and firmness of Pickwick's proposal.

CHAPTER 17

1. (228) **a cast in his eye:** a slight squint.

2. (229) **ewer:** a jug with a wide spout.

3. (233) **Saracenic:** The Saracens were nomads of the Syro-Arabian desert who harassed the Syrian confines of the Greek and Roman empires. It was also used as a generic term for Arabs and non-Christians.

CHAPTER 18

1. (236) **Britannia metal:** a cheap metal alloy, mainly of tin and antimony.

2. (243) *Freeman's Court, Cornhill, August 28th, 1830:* close to the Bank of England, Freeman's Court was demolished in 1842 during the construction of the Royal Exchange. The date on the letter is another anachronism (see Chapter 1, n. 1).

3. (243) *Court of Common Pleas*: the court in which civil actions were tried.

CHAPTER 19

1. (248) **making a point**: Hunting dogs indicate the presence of game by standing rigidly and looking towards it.

2. (252) **Tyburn**: the place of public execution for Middlesex until 1783. It was situated at the junction of Oxford Street, Bayswater Road and Edgware Road.

3. (255) **rattan**: a tropical climbing plant, the stem of which could be cut to make a walking-stick. A rattan cane was carried by a master-at-arms and signified his disciplinary role.

4. (255) **spring guns**: loaded and cocked guns, the trigger of which was attached to a trip-wire; used to deter poachers and trespassers.

5. (256) **plebeian**: The 'plebs' were the Roman commoners.

6. (256) **wheel him to the pound**: The pound was a wooden-railed enclosure, used for confining stray animals.

CHAPTER 20

1. (259) **his Majesty's Attorneys ... High Court of Chancery**: Criminal cases were tried in the Court of King's Bench, the highest Common Law Court, and civil actions in the Court of Common Pleas. Chancery dealt with disputes over legacies and trusts, etc., and decided on grounds of equity, rather than precedent. The term 'solicitor' is now used for 'attorney'.

2. (260) **deal boxes**: boxes made of pine or firwood planks.

3. (260) **pomatum**: a perfumed ointment for skin and hair.

4. (260) **Somers Town**: an area of north-west London, including Euston and St Pancras districts.

5. (260) **lushey**: drunk.

6. (260) **knock up**: rouse up.

7. (261) **the Temple**: an area of London south of Fleet Street, where, in 1608, two Inns of Court were founded, Inner Temple and Middle Temple.

8. (261) **warrant of attorney**: the formal authorising of an attorney to act for a client.

9. (261) **the one-pair back:** a first-floor (in America second-floor) room at the rear of the house.

10. (265) *præcipe* ... **Capias:** '*Præcipere*' is Latin for 'to admonish'; the '*præcipe* book' refers to the note containing particulars of a writ. '*Capias*' is Latin for 'you may take, or arrest', and refers here to the writ formally authorising arrest.

11. (267) **Battledore and shuttlecock:** a game similar to Badminton played by two people who hit the feathered shuttlecock to each other with small rackets (battledores). The wrapper-design of *Bleak House* shows two lawyers playing the game with clients as shuttlecocks.

12. (271) **Blue Beard's:** Blue Beard was the central character in Charles Perrault's fairy-tale of the same name. Blue Beard kills and dismembers his wives.

13. (273) **pot-boy:** a boy or young man employed as a bartender.

14. (273) **tap:** tap-room, a room in a tavern in which alcoholic drinks are kept on tap.

15. (274) **out o' door:** the clerk appointed to run messages around town.

16. (274) **Mosaic:** This probably refers to 'Mosaic gold', an alloy used in the manufacture of cheap jewellery. According to T. W. Hill, the term was Dickens's appellation for a style of ostentatious jewellery favoured by certain Jews. For Percy Fitzgerald, the use of the capital 'M' denoted that it was not plain mosaic work, but jewellery of Jewish or Eastern class.

CHAPTER 21

1. (276) **German universities:** This would have been understood as nearly proverbial for Gothic sensation literature, such as *The Robber of the Rhine*; the ancient German universities were often used as settings for such romances.

2. (277) **Clifford's Inn:** the oldest of the Inns of Chancery, situated on the north side of Fleet Street.

3. (280) **the Marshalsea ... Newgate:** The Marshalsea was a prison in Borough High Street, Southwark, where Dickens's father was imprisoned for debt in 1824. It was closed in the 1840s, a fact recognised by Dickens in his footnote to the 1847 edition. Newgate was a London prison, rebuilt in 1782 and finally demolished in 1902–3 during construction of the Old Bailey.

4. (284) **turnkeys:** employees (usually of low rank) in a prison, in charge of the keys.

5. (290) **caption:** details of the authorisation of an indictment.

CHAPTER 22

1. (293) **new birth:** Dickens was criticised for this apparent assault on religion. However, he always defended the passage, insisting that it was directed against the misuse of religion, not religion itself.

2. (293) **half-a-crown:** see Chapter 2, n. 3.

3. (294) **to grub:** slang for 'to feed'.

4. (294) **a wessel of wrath:** 'vessel of wrath', Romans 9:22.

5. (295) **dog's-meat man:** Food for dogs was generally prepared from horse-flesh or from scraps of offal, and was sold by street dealers.

6. (297) **'Heads,' as the pieman says:** the practice of offering a free pie if the purchaser guessed correctly on the toss of a coin.

7. (299) **fortnight's napkin . . . coeval stockings:** The napkin is presumably unclean, not having been washed for some time. The word coeval, meaning 'of equal antiquity', suggests that the waiter's stockings are similarly unkempt.

8. (301) **japanned:** lacquered.

9. (304) **rushlight:** a rush candle.

10. (306) **Blunderbore:** the name of the man-eating giant in the fairy-tale 'Jack and the Beanstalk'.

11. (307) **the old patrol:** night-watchmen, superseded in 1829 by the Metropolitan Police.

CHAPTER 23

1. (315) **number four collection of hymns:** T. W. Hill conjectures that the reference is to the fourth of Isaac Watts's little hymn books, 'Moral Songs' (1730).

2. (315) **Chelsea water-works:** one of ten private undertakings that provided the capital with its water.

CHAPTER 24

1. (326) **a short truncheon, surmounted by a brazen crown:** the official insignia of the special constabulary.

2. (327) **gammon:** 'Ridiculous nonsense suited to deceive simple persons only' (*OED*).

CHAPTER 25

1. (333) **American aloe:** a large-leaf evergreen with no stem. Not an aloe, but the name for *Agave Americana*.

2. (334) **the Newgate Calendar:** a publication featuring accounts of prisoners held in Newgate; first issued in 1773.

3. (338) **Mr Perceval:** Spencer Perceval (1762–1812), Prime Minister who was, like Julius Caesar, assassinated.

4. (342) **Saugur Point:** on Saugur Island, Bay of Bengal; 'a sufficiently insalubrious spot', according to T. W. Hill.

5. (343) **grampus:** 'A person giving to puffing and blowing' (*OED*).

CHAPTER 26

1. (352) **young township . . . hinfant fernomenon:** 'Townskip' was 'a jocular name for a city urchin' (*OED*). The phrase 'infant phenomenon' subsequently appeared in *Nicholas Nickleby* (1838–9) as the stage name of Mr Crummles's daughter, Ninetta. Whereas Weller addresses his remark to a juvenile, in Miss Crummles's case it is merely a theatrical appellation as she is significantly older than her stage name implies.

2. (352) **flat candle:** flat candlestick with a tray to catch the wax drippings.

3. (352) **Dutch oven:** portable oven for placing in front of the fire

CHAPTER 27

1. (357) **The Marquis of Granby:** a popular name for an inn. The actual Marquis was born John Manners, in 1721, and died in 1770. He was a well-loved military figure.

2. (360) **It's all vanity:** 'Vanity of vanities, saith the Preacher, vanity of vanities; all is vanity' Ecclesiastes 1:2.

3. (360) **A man of wrath:** a biblical allusion, drawn from the Old Testament: Proverbs 19:19.

4. (361) **moral pocket handkerchiefs:** Improving texts and pictures were printed on handkerchiefs, often for propaganda purposes by missionaries. Two of these are illustrated in *The Dickensian* 6 (1910), pp. 129, 254.

5. (362) **nails in the horse's shoes:** a famous arithmetical problem: if the first nail costs a farthing and each additional nail costs double the price of the one before, what would be the total cost of shoeing one horse?

6. (363) **turncock:** a water-works official, responsible for water supply.

7. (364) **Walker:** Cockney expression of incredulity.

CHAPTER 28

1. (368) **key-bugle:** 'A bugle fitted with keys to increase the number of its sounds' (OED).

2. (371) **young dropsy:** having a morbid, taciturn disposition. Weller may also be punning on the fat boy's talent for handling 'a drop' of liquor.

3. (375) **hobbledehoys:** adolescent, and generally unmanageable, youth.

4. (376) **Horner:** Jack Horner, hero of the nursery rhyme 'Little Jack Horner sat in the corner, Eating his pudding and pie . . . .'

5. (377) **the cake was cut, and passed through the ring:** an old custom whereby the bride took off her wedding-ring and a piece of the cake passed through it, for luck.

6. (380) **poussette:** dancing round and round with joined hands.

7. (382) **Dutch clock:** a cheap kind of clock, made in Germany (Deutsch) from wood and brass.

8. (384) **snap-dragon:** a game in which the players try to snatch raisins from a bowl of burning brandy.

7. (384) **bowl of wassail:** supposedly derived from the Middle English 'waes-hail', 'be in good health'. The wassail cup or bowl, filled with spiced ale, was passed around the company during Christmas or New Year's festivities.

CHAPTER 29

1. (388) **gall and wormwood:** Lamentations 3:19.

2. (392) **he threw a somerset:** performed a somersault.

CHAPTER 30

1. (399) **barnacles:** spectacles.

2. (399) **Cubas:** Cuban cigars.

3. (409) **Guy's:** Guy's Hospital, in Southwark, was one of the major teaching hospitals.

CHAPTER 31.

1. (410) **Gower Street ... Tavistock Square:** At the time when *Pickwick Papers* was written, this was a recently constructed area inhabited largely by the professional classes. Dickens later had a house there (1851–60).

2. (410) **Adelphi Theatre:** The Adelphi opened on 18 October 1819 and became renowned for a kind of sensational melodrama known as 'Adelphi screamers'. Half-price admission was made available after the main piece of the evening had been performed.

3. (412) **shilling from his waistcoat pocket:** A token payment of one shilling for expenses ensured the presence of the witness in court.

4. (412) **settens:** sittings.

5. (412) **secrets of the prison-house:** from *Hamlet*, Act 1, Sc. 4.

6. (414) **burked:** The murderers William Burke and William Hare supplied corpses to the medical profession by suffocating their victims or ransacking graveyards.

7. (417) **Serjeant Snubbin:** The obsolete title 'serjeants-at-law' referred to members of a superior order of barristers.

8. (418) **Lincoln's Inn Old Square:** a square within the oldest of the Inns of Court.

9. (420) **forensic:** pertaining to or used in courts of law.

CHAPTER 32

1. (425) **clear-starchers:** those employed in stiffening linen with a colourless starch.

2. (425) **mantua-makers:** According to the *OED*, 'mantua' in this usage is a corruption of 'manteau', a loose upper garment worn by women. 'Mantua makers' became a general term for dress-makers.

3. (425) **mangling:** the squeezing dry and pressing of clothes after they have been laundered.

4. (425) **quarter-day:** a day marking the quarter of the year, when rent and similar payments were due.

5. (430) **Bartholomew's:** St Bartholomew's Hospital, in Little Britain. Founded in 1123, it is one of the major teaching hospitals.

6. (430) **four pair of stairs' window:** on the fourth (American fifth) floor.

7. (431) **cribbed:** slang for 'stole'.

8. (431) **croup:** a disease characterised by a rasping cough.

9. (432) **scorbutic:** afflicted with scurvy.

10. (432) *vingt-et-un* ... **'natural':** *Vingt-et-un* is a card game in which a player's hand should not exceed twenty-one (by counting the pips on the cards). A 'natural' is a count of exactly twenty-one recorded immediately after the initial deal to the players.

11. (433) **dropsical, bloated articles ... huge gouty leg:** drinking glasses, once fashionable but now obsolete. The drinking vessel was mounted on a large lump of glass.

CHAPTER 33

1. (439) **brockiley sprout, wot then?:** the head of broccoli, a type of cabbage. Dickens's phonetic spelling here is more or less the current standard pronunciation of 'broccoli'. Perhaps, since the word is Italian (diminutive of *brocco*, meaning 'stalk'), the second 'o' in 'broccoli' would have been more distinctly sounded as a short 'o'. Dickens's phoneticised Cockney 'wot', for 'what', reminds us that, properly sounded, 'what' has – or had – a slightly aspirated 'wh' sound.

2. (439) **the Mansion House:** one of the main stops used by coaches.

3. (440) **cads and drivers of short stages:** short stage coaches operated over short distances between fixed destinations. Cad is short for 'cadet', and was the popular term used for a coach or 'bus conductor'.

4. (440) **the church in Langham Place:** All Souls' church, designed by John Nash, was completed in 1824. Its conical spire was regarded by many as an architectual folly.

5. (440) **a cerulean elephant:** of a deep blue, azure colour.

6. (441) **Vell, my Prooshan Blue:** Sam is here referring to the colour of his father's face, which, in the elder man's excitement and agitation, has turned blue. The epithet is rather affectionate, as the Prussians were popular in Britain in the aftermath of the Napoleonic Wars. The actual Prussian Blue (ferrocyanide of iron) was discovered in Berlin in 1704, and is a rich, dark shade of blue.

7. (443) **Warren's blackin' ... Rowland's oil:** Warren's refers to the blacking factory (where Dickens worked for a while as a child), which employed hack poets to advertise its product. Mr Slum, in *The Old Curiosity Shop*, is evidently modelled on one of these poets (see *The Dickensian* 34, [1938], p. 199). Rowland's manufactured a macassar of oil for the hair.

8. (445) **profeel macheen:** an apparatus which produced a kind of silhouette portrait. One end of a piece of wire was passed over the features of the sitter, while a pencil fixed to the other end traced an outline on paper.

9. (447) **turpentine and bees'-vax:** furniture polish.

10. (448) *tic douloureux:* severe facial neuralgia.

11. (448) **corpilence:** a corruption of 'corpulence', meaning 'of bulky body'.

12. (450-1) **H. Walker ... Betsy Martin ... Thomas Burton:** joke names. *The Dickens Index* explains as follows: 'Walker!' or 'Hookey Walker' was a Cockney exclamation of incredulity; Betsy Martin, the one-eyed widow (cf. the expression, 'all my eye and Betty Martin', meaning 'nonsense' or 'humbug'); Burton-on-Trent was the centre of a famous brewing industry.

13. (451) **Mr Dibdin:** Charles Dibdin (1745–1814), dramatist and song-writer.

14. (452) **lath and plaster:** Lath is a thin strip of wood, used as a groundwork for plaster.

CHAPTER 34

1. (454) **faithful Report of the memorable Trial:** Much of the ensuing trial is a parody of the Melbourne vs Norton trial of June 1836, which

Dickens had reported. Melbourne, the Prime Minister, was accused of having an affair with the Hon. Mrs Caroline Norton.

2. (455) **Guildhall:** The Court of Common Pleas was held in Guildhall until 1873, whereafter it moved to Westminster, and subsequently to the Royal Courts of Justice in the Strand.

3. (455) **blue bag:** Solicitors and barristers carry blue bags, Serjeants and King's Counsels carry red bags.

4. (455) **the students' box:** 'That part of the Court reserved for law students who were preparing to enter the legal profession' (Hill).

5. (457) **prayed a *tales*:** *Tales* is the Latin plural of *talis*, meaning 'such'. The phrase *tales de circumstantibus* means 'such persons as those standing about'. Buzfuz is asking the court to complete the proper number of jurymen from persons who happened to be in the courtroom.

6. (458) **Epsom salts means oxalic acid; and syrup of senna, laudanum:** respectively, a magnesium sulphate preparation, a poisonous and sour acid, a mild laxative, and a preparation in which opium is the main ingredient.

7. (463) *alley tors* or *commoneys*: Alabaster ('alley') taws were marbles. They were more highly prized, because of the quality of their material, than 'commoneys', marbles made of baked clay covered with coloured glaze.

8. (464) **Garraway's:** a well-known coffee-house in Exchange Alley, Cornhill.

9. (464) **warming-pan:** a long-handled copper pan containing live coals for warming beds.

10. (465) **knuckle-down:** kneel down, in the proper position for playing marbles. The phrase is still used to exhort someone to concentrate and apply himself or herself to a task. 'Knuckles are correctly held down when playing marbles' (Beisiegel).

11. (465) **tip-cheese:** child's game. 'A small cylindrical piece of wood, sharpened at both ends, is laid on the ground, one end is then struck sharply with a stick, causing it to fly in the air, when it is again struck horizontally and hurled some distance' (Beisiegel).

12. (466) **back one pair of stairs:** see Chapter 20, n. 9.

13. (474) **magnifyin' gas microscopes:** These devices used gas to illu-

minate the object under examination. An advertisement for an exhibition of such devices was published in *The Dickensian* 5 (1909), p. 318.

CHAPTER 35

1. (479) **White Horse Cellar:** This was the main point of departure in London for coaches for the west of England. It was situated in Piccadilly.

2. (479) **a pewter half-crown:** Pewter is a grey alloy, usually consisting of tin and lead. The disputed coin is clearly counterfeit.

3. (482) **way-bill:** a list of passengers booked for seats on a coach.

4. (482) **the magic name of PICKWICK!:** The fictitious Pickwick confronts his historical namesake: Moses Pickwick was proprietor of the White Hart Hotel in Bath and of the coach which ran services between Bath and London.

5. (483) **the Kensington turnpike:** a modest two-and-a-half miles from the White Horse Cellar.

6. (484) **Westminster boys:** Boys at Westminster School wore knee-breeches.

7. (484) **curb chain:** a chain that curbs or restrains.

8. (485) **this morning at two o'clock:** i.e. at 2 p.m.

9. (487) **rappee:** a dark-coloured, coarse kind of snuff.

10. (489) **grand climacteric:** sixty-third year. According to astrologers, every seventh year in a person's life is a critical period; the sixty-third is traditionally the most momentous.

11. (489) **chalked floors, girandoles:** Fine chalk powder was sprinkled on unpolished ballrooms to ease the surface for dancing; girandoles are branched supports for candles.

CHAPTER 36

1. (494) **The great pump-room:** built in 1796–7.

2. (494) **a Tompion clock:** a clock made by Thomas Tompion, noted clock and watchmaker in the reign of Queen Anne.

3. (494) **a statue of Nash:** Beau Nash (1674–1761) is commemorated for his efforts to establish The Royal Mineral Water Hospital.

4. (494) **a deserving charity:** the Bath Hospital.

5. (496) **Pliny:** Gaius Plinius Secundus, A.D. 23–79, a naturalist who died of suffocation whilst investigating the volcanic Mount Vesuvius.

6. (501) **in the arms o' Porpus:** corruption of 'Morpheus', the god of Dreams (son of Sleep).

7. (501) **link-boy:** A link was a torch used for lighting people along the streets. A link-boy was employed to carry a link to assist passengers along the street.

8. (502) **bradawl:** small boring tool.

9. (503) **India-rubber ball:** made of an elastic, flexible material; bounces very hard.

10. (505) **washhand-stand:** 'A piece of furniture for holding the wash-hand basin, ewer, soap dish, etc.' (*OED*).

CHAPTER 37

1. (506) **he learnt writin' from the large bills:** The bills were, in effect, time-tables featuring details of the routes of the coaches and their times of arrival and departure. Many of the lines were written in capital letters.

2. (506) **the superscription:** the address.

3. (506) **swarry:** a misspelling of 'soirée'.

4. (506) **airy bell:** the bell for the basement, to summon the servants who were quartered down there. 'Airy' is slang for 'area', the sunken court giving access to the basement.

5. (507) **a copper time-piece:** a cheap watch, signified by the fact that the cover is copper, not silver.

6. (508) **the killibeate taste:** slang for 'chalybeate', the iron-impreg-nated waters of Bath.

7. (510) **kiver:** slang for 'cover'.

8. (510) **gaped:** yawned.

9. (515) **the frog hornpipe:** a comic, solo dance. This incident was later illustrated by 'Phiz' in the 1874 edition.

CHAPTER 38

1. (518) **The Bush:** Bristol's chief coaching inn, situated near the Guildhall, was demolished in 1864.

2. (519) **fire-irons:** implements such as tongs and poker, for tending a domestic fire.

3. (520) **King's-taxes:** Rates and taxes were often collected from tax-payers' houses by officials.

4. (520) **Church-rates:** a property tax levied for the maintenance of the church and its services; abolished in 1868.

5. (521) **to qualify it:** moderate its strength.

6. (521) **pipkin:** a small, earthenware cooking-pot.

7. (521) **flying the garter:** a game, similar to leap-frog, in which one player jumps from behind a line (garter) over another.

8. (525) **jorum:** a drinking-bowl.

9. (529) **pick-a-back:** also 'Piggy-back', carried on the back or shoulders, like a pack.

10. (529) **pennywinkle:** periwinkle; a small edible mollusc, now known as a 'winkle'.

11. (530) **fanteegs:** a state of excitement, anxiety or embarrassment.

CHAPTER 39

1. (535) **Lor do adun:** 'Lord, do have done'. Mary is urging Sam to stop.

2. (536) **the wandering Jew:** a popular legend dating from the thirteenth century, according to T. W. Hill. Just before his crucifixion Jesus was said to have told a Jew to wait for the Second Coming, and the Jew has wandered the world ever since.

3. (538) **Miss Sawbones:** A sawbones is a medical practitioner, usually a surgeon. Miss Allen's brother is a doctor, hence Sam's appellation.

4. (539) **lead in his head:** pieces of lead shot from a shotgun.

5. (540) **dark lantern:** a lantern with a sliding front, thereby enabling the light to be removed without extinguishing the candle.

6. (542) **coping:** the uppermost layer of masonry in a wall, often sloped to disperse rainwater.

7. (543) **Guy Fawkes:** the principal agent in the Gunpowder Plot of 1605, always associated with a dark lantern. A straw-stuffed effigy of Guy Fawkes is ritualistically burned on Guy Fawkes Day (5 November).

8. (543) **moistening his clay:** having a drink.

9. (545) **Scientific Associations:** another satirical reference, perhaps, to the British Association for the Advancement of Science (see Chapter 1, n. 4).

CHAPTER 40

1. (547) **Botany Bay:** a penal colony in New South Wales, Australia.

2. (550) **grazier:** 'One who grazes or feeds cattle for the market' (*OED*).

3. (550) **drover:** one who drives cattle to market, or a dealer in cattle.

4. (551) **Whitecross Street:** a debtors' prison near St Giles, Cripplegate, built in 1813. It was notoriously overcrowded.

5. (551) **ca-sa:** abbreviation of *capias ad satisfaciendum*, 'You may take (the accused into custody) pending satisfaction (over the plaintiff's claim).'

6. (551) **the Fleet:** a debtors' prison, located at the junction of Fleet Street and Farringdon Street. It was closed in 1842. On the general subject of debtors' prisons in this novel, see Angus Easson, 'Imprisonment for Debt in *Pickwick Papers*', *The Dickensian* 64 (1971), pp. 105–12.

7. (551) **habeas corpus:** a writ instructing that the person named therein be brought before the court; from the Latin: 'Let you [i.e. see that you] have the body [in court].'

8. (555) **tipstaff:** officer of the court, whose official status would be signified by his carrying a metal-tipped staff.

9. (536) **Dutch clock:** see Chapter 28, n. 7.

10. (538) **chummed:** To chum is to share a space, to live together.

11. (538) **an out-and-outer:** a perfect type of its kind.

CHAPTER 41

1. (561) **all-fours:** a simple card game for two players, called after the 'four' points, *high*, *low*, *Jack*, and *the game*.

2. (563) **rackets:** played by two persons, with rackets, who try to keep a ball rebounding from a wall; similar to squash.

3. (565) **cut:** in dancing, to twiddle the feet during a spring off the floor.

4. (569) **Portugal Street:** a street off Lincoln's Inn Fields, where there was a Court for Insolvent Debtors. John Dickens went through this Court to obtain his release from the Marshalsea in 1824. See also Chapter 43, n. 1.

CHAPTER 42

1. (574) **Fox-under-the-Hill:** a tavern on the bank of the Thames, much frequented by the coal heavers who worked on the barges near Adelphi Terrace.

2. (574) **street-keepers:** officials appointed locally to keep order in the streets.

3. (575) **horse chaunter: he's a leg now:** A chaunter, or 'chanter', sells horses fraudulently. A 'leg', short for 'blackleg', meant a swindler in the horse-racing business.

4. (575) **gleaning for pewter:** collecting up the empty (pewter) tankards.

5. (576) **a rig:** a prank.

6. (577) **three bob . . . a bender:** slang for (respectively) three shillings and sixpence (see Chapter 2, n. 3).

7. (583) **Spout:** the pawnbroker's shop. The spout was the lift or shoot by which deposited goods were sent from the shop front into the store. 'Uncle' is slang for pawnbroker.

8. (583) **Constable's Miscellany:** a popular periodical first published in 1826, full of accounts of shipwrecks, experiences on desert islands, prison escapes, and so on.

CHAPTER 43

1. (586) **Insolvent Court:** the Insolvent Debtors' Court. Imprisoned debtors could apply to it for release under the Insolvent Debtors Act. This

enabled imprisoned debtors to apply for their discharge provided that they surrendered all their property and stated all their liabilities and debts (which still had to be met).

2. (586) **Houndsditch:** a popular location for the sale of second-hand clothes, running from Aldgate up to Bishopsgate.

3. (587) **'the Rules':** a defined area outside the prison walls where prisoners in custody could live on condition of their being able to give security.

4. (587) **obelisk in St George's Fields:** An obelisk was erected in 1771 in honour of the then Lord Mayor of London. It stood in St George's Circus, just over half a mile south of Blackfriars Bridge.

5. (590) **dumb-waiter:** an item of dining-room furniture in which dishes could be stored prior to serving, thereby dispensing with the services of a waiter.

6. (591) **bonnetin':** the act of pulling or knocking a hat over a person's eyes.

7. (593) **Nixon:** *Nixon's Prophecies: the Original Predictions of Robert Nixon, commonly called the Cheshire Prophet* (1701). A cheap pamphlet edition had a portrait of the author with highly coloured cheeks.

8. (594) **con-wertin' your face into a street-door knocker:** Street-door knockers were sometimes fashioned in the shape and rough design of a person's face. In *A Christmas Carol* (1843), Scrooge sees the face of his erstwhile partner, Jacob Marley, in a door knocker.

9. (594) **brains like the frogs:** It was popularly believed that frogs had their brains dispersed throughout their nervous system.

10. (594) **have-his-carcase:** the Weller translation of *habeas corpus* (see above Chapter 40, n. 7).

11. (595–6) **Bold Turpin vunce ... to stop:** 'Turpin and the Bishop', a ballad by Horace Smith, published in 1825. Sam sings a variant of the first two verses of the ballad. Dick Turpin was a celebrated highwayman, hanged in York in 1739.

12. (597) **ticket-porter:** a London street-porter licensed by the City to carry messages and parcels. They displayed their 'tickets' or licences in the form of a badge.

CHAPTER 44

1. (600) **little India-rubber fire-buckets:** Sam Weller's idiosyncratic way of describing waterproof boots.

2. (600) **Post arter:** Sam's 'reg'lar gen'l'm'n' is asking for the *Morning Post* after the next gentleman has finished with it.

3. (600) **'Tizer:** the *Morning Advertiser*.

4. (600) **Robinson Crusoe set o' steps:** In Daniel Defoe's novel, the hero Robinson Crusoe constructs a short ladder for access to his hideaway; once inside, he could lift the ladder in after him.

5. (604) **probate:** the official validation of the will, prior to execution.

6. (604) **caveat:** a legal process undertaken in order to suspend proceedings.

7. (606) **Avay vith melincholly:** 'Away with melancholy': a lyric written to a melody from Mozart's *Magic Flute*. A mournful piece, but none the less a favourite with Dickens.

CHAPTER 45

1. (612) **Platonic wink:** Platonic love means a love of a pure, non-sensual kind. No doubt the term is meant ironically here.

2. (613) **Regency Park:** a popular name for Regent's Park.

3. (613) **whitevash:** To whitewash was to clear a debtor of his liabilities. Weller senior is concerned that his appearance may be inferred as a joke at the expense of the inmates of the prison.

4. (613) **picter-card:** Sam is comparing his father to a highly coloured court card in a deck of cards.

5. (614) **snuggery:** 'The bar-parlour in an inn or public-house' (*OED*).

6. (616) **Saint Simon Without, and Saint Walker Within:** Without and Within mean outside and inside the city boundaries. Mr Weller suggests that Stiggins might seem, to all outward appearances, a zealous pastor (the disciple Simon was called Simon the Zealot), but is inwardly an impostor ('Walker', see Chapter 27, n. 7).

7. (621) **a book about the 'Merrikins:** Mrs Frances Trollope made about £800 from her book *Domestic Manners of the Americans* (1832), which caused some offence to the Americans but was very popular in England.

8. (625) **somethin' in the water-cart way:** jocular reference to Jingle's weeping.

CHAPTER 46

1. (631) **sal volatile:** ammonium carbonate. It was compounded as an aromatic solution and employed as a restorative in fainting fits.

2. (632) **the Spaniards:** an inn and tea-garden, so-called because it was founded by a servant from the Spanish Embassy.

3. (636) *cognovit*: Latin for 'he acknowledges'; here, a document formally acknowledging that Dodson and Fogg are owed Mrs Bardell's court costs. Since she cannot pay them, the document enables the lawyers to avoid suing procedures and commit her directly to the Fleet.

CHAPTER 47

1. (639) **Montague Place, Russell Square:** Situated in Bloomsbury, this district was, in the early nineteenth century, largely the preserve of the professional classes.

2. (639) **demises:** transfers of land by lease or will.

CHAPTER 48

1. (651) **promissory notes:** written pledges to pay specified amounts.

2. (653) **bandbox:** a box constructed of fairly flimsy material, generally used for storing millinery.

3. (654) **Camphor-julep:** camphor, a medicine taken with julep drink to sweeten its taste.

4. (656) **galwinism:** Galvanism, named after Aloysius Galvani (1737–98), who, in his experiments on dead frogs, caused their legs to spasm by introducing an electric current.

5. (657) **wollatilly:** *sal volatile*; see Chapter 46, n. 1.

CHAPTER 49

1. (664) **Baillie:** Scottish municipal officer.

2. (664) **kippered:** dried and smoked.

3. (665) **Willie brewed a peck o' maut:** a song written by Robert Burns. It appeared in *The Scots Musical Museum* (1790).

4. (665) **Canongate . . . Leith Walk:** an eastward journey along Edinburgh's 'historic mile'.

5. (666) **Holyrood . . . Arthur's Seat:** Holyrood House lies at the foot of the Canongate. Arthur's Seat is a hill overlooking Edinburgh.

6. (667) **wheelwright:** a maker of wheels.

7. (667) **axletree:** the axle of a wheel.

8. (668) **portmanteaus:** travelling bags suitable for clothing.

9. (668) **blunderbuss:** a short gun, effective within a limited range without exact aim.

10. (669) **buckram:** a fabric, sometimes linen, generally stiffened or starched.

11. (675) **basket-hilted rapier:** a sword incorporating a defence for the swordsman's hand shaped roughly like a basket.

12. (675) **Newport market:** near Leicester Square. The meat market had its own slaughterhouse, hence the noise of knives.

13. (676) **packthread:** strong thread used for sewing or fastening.

14. (676) **cockchafer fashion:** A cockchafer is a type of insect or beetle. They were often pinned to boards by collectors.

15. (676) **entail:** the line of family succession.

16. (679) **the dead letters:** letters which were unclaimed or could not be delivered. A jocular follow-up to the landlord's question.

CHAPTER 50

1. (679) **postillion:** a horse-rider who rides one of the leading horses when four or more are used on a travelling carriage.

2. (680) **calomel:** mercurous chloride, a common medicinal preparation.

3. (682) **case-bottle:** a bottle designed to fit into a case, or (as is more probable in this instance) a bottle protected by a leather case.

4. (687) **Old Royal Hotel:** situated in Temple Row, in Birmingham city centre.

5. (687) **fuddled:** drunk.

6. (688) **wharfinger:** proprietor of a wharf; here, on the canal.

7. (689) **almanack:** a form of calendar containing a variety of astronomical, ecclesiastical and miscellaneous information.

8. (690) **extra super-fine wire-wove:** high quality writing paper.

9. (691) **Mr Grimaldi:** the celebrated clown, Joseph Grimaldi (1779–1837), whose *Memoirs* Dickens edited in 1838.

CHAPTER 51

1. (695) **additional duty:** The tax on windows was first imposed in 1695, and eventually abolished in 1851.

2. (695) **Humane Society:** The Royal Humane Society, formed in 1774, gave awards to individuals who saved people from drowning.

3. (695) **Wotever is, is right:** quotation from Alexander Pope's *Essay on Man* (1733), II, 294.

4. (695) **the pension list:** a periodic payment made by the state in recognition of past services.

5. (696) **dead donkey:** Sam alludes (improbably) to Laurence Sterne's *Sentimental Journey* (1768), 'Nampont. The Dead Ass'. Sterne, as a clergyman, wore 'black silk smalls'. According to T. W. Hill, it was an old Cockney superstition that donkeys live to such a great age that no one ever saw one dead.

6. (696) **oilskin:** a cloth which is waterproof, having been treated with oil.

7. (697) **Lights in the Sun:** The Sun is a room in the inn. It was customary to give individual names to the principal rooms.

8. (699) **plaid:** woollen cloth having a chequered or tartan pattern.

9. (703) **blacking-brush:** a shoe-brush. Slurk's hair is obviously somewhat thick and spiky.

10. (704) **dropsical spider:** swollen, bloated.

11. (706) **twaddler:** a writer of trash.

CHAPTER 52

1. (714) **There's a Providence in it all:** 'There's a special providence in the fall of a sparrow', *Hamlet*, Act v, Sc. 2.

2. (715) **patent Brahmin:** more properly known as a Bramah, a lock

and key invented by Joseph Bramah (1749–1814), of 124 Piccadilly, and patented in 1784.

3. (717) **counsels:** more properly known as 'Consols', itself a contraction of 'Consolidated Annuities'. They paid interest at three per cent and were introduced in 1751, to alleviate the National Debt.

CHAPTER 53

1. (722) **Bramah:** see Chapter 52, n. 2; Dickens here refers to the key.

2. (722) **Polygon:** a ring of houses (demolished in 1891) in Clarendon Square, Somers Town, north London.

3. (722) **cartridge:** a strong kind of paper.

4. (722) **Demerara:** a region of Guyana (then British Guiana) which produced cane-sugar.

5. (730) **pettifogging:** A 'fogger' is a fraudulent lawyer (Mr Fogg is aptly named); the prefix 'petti-', from the French '*petit*', denotes one who takes on small cases and employs mean practices.

CHAPTER 54

1. (736) **charcoal:** suicide by inhaling flames from a charcoal fire.

2. (736) **Osborne's hotel:** Osborne was the proprietor of the Adelphi Hotel in John Street, Adelphi.

3. (739) **ferules:** a ring or band strengthening the cutlery and placed at the end of the handle.

CHAPTER 55

1. (751) **cutting:** see Chapter 41, n. 3.

2. (755) **Queer Street:** an imaginary street where people whose solvency is doubtful are supposed to reside.

3. (757) **P.P.:** play or pay.

4. (759) **Smith, Payne, and Smith:** a banking house in Lombard Street. The manager was George Beadnell, the father of Dickens's adored Maria.

CHAPTER 56

1. (763) **pike:** a turnpike.

CHAPTER 57

1. (776) **passed through the Gazette:** having become bankrupt.

2. (777) **Shooter's Hill:** crosses Blackheath, becomes Watling Street and the main route to Dover.

3. (777) **Dulwich Gallery:** founded in the seventeenth century on the basis of a bequest of paintings by the Elizabethan actor and land speculator, Edward Alleyn.

GLOSSARY:

Modes of transport, items of clothing, food and drink

ABNERNETHY BISCUIT *a large biscuit, flavoured with caraway seeds*

BACK-HAIR *'The long hair at the back of a woman's head' (OED)*

BAG-WIG *a wig confining the hair in a silken bag*

BAROUCHE *a four-seater, four-wheel carriage with a half-top which could be raised or lowered*

BATH-CHAIR *a large chair on wheels for invalids*

BEAVER *a high hat for men, made of beaver's fur*

BISHOP *a drink consisting of wine, oranges or lemons, and sugar; also used to describe mulled and spiced port*

BLUCHERS *strong leather half-boots or high shoes, named after the Prussian commander Field-Marshal von Blücher, who distinguished himself at the Battle of Waterloo*

BRITISH HOLLANDS *gin; originally manufactured in Holland*

BROCADED GOWN *featuring an ornate design with a raised pattern*

CARPET BAG *a travelling bag*

CHAISE *a term applied to various travelling carriages*

CHARIOT *a chariot differs from a post-chaise in having a coach-box (a seat occupied by the driver)*

COCKADES *a ribbon or a rosette worn in the hat*

'COLD WITHOUT' *'cold spirits without water' (Patten)*

COMFORTERS *'a long woollen scarf worn round the throat as protection from the cold' (OED)*

DAMASK *a fabric of silk or linen featuring elaborate designs*

DANTZIC SPRUCE *a beer made from the buds of spruce-fir*

DICKEY *also known as a 'dicky-box', the seat in a carriage on which the driver sits. A dickey can, in addition, refer to a coach-seat for a servant or a guard*

DOG-CART *an open cart for ordinary driving, with space for a dog box, originally used by sportsmen*

DRABS *dull-coloured trousers*

DRIVING-BOXES *detachable boxes fitted to carriage seats to hold the driver's belongings*

EAST INDIA SHERRY *To enhance its maturity, sherry was often carried in butts on long voyages to the East and back.*

FALSE COLLAR *detachable*

FINNAN HADDOCKS *The fish (traditionally from Findhorn, Scotland) is cured in the smoke of peat earth, turf, or green wood.*

FLY 'a quick-travelling carriage' (OED)

FUSTIAN JACKET made from a coarse cloth derived from cotton and flax

GAITERS a covering for the ankle, or ankle and lower leg

GAMBOOGE TOPS Gambooge was a gum resin used as a pigment, giving a bright, yellow colour. 'Tops' refers to Top-boots

GIG a light, two-wheeled, two-seater, one-horse carriage

GLAZED STOCKS Stocks are stiff collars on military tunics. Often made of patent leather, they can have a shiny or 'glazed' look

GREEN FOIL SMALLS green cloth breeches

GROG 'a drink consisting of spirits and water' (OED)

GUILLOTINED CABRIOLET A cabriolet is a light, two-wheeled chaise driven by one horse, generally covered and with an apron to cover the arms and legs of the passenger. The guillotined version was uncovered.

HACKNEY COACH 'a four-wheeled coach, driven by two horses, and seated for six persons, kept for hire' (OED)

HARE-SKINS The dressed skin of the hare was worn with the fur side next to the chest as a protector.

HARD-BAKE 'a sweetmeat made of boiled sugar or treacle with blanched almonds; almond toffee' (OED)

HIGH-LOWS 'A boot laced or otherwise fastened up in front and reaching up over the ankle' (OED)

HOLLANDS Dutch gin

INDESCRIBABLES humorous euphemism for trousers

INDIA-RUBBER CLOAK the waterproof cloak patented by Charles Macintosh in 1823. 'Macintosh' or 'mac' is still used as the generic term for waterproof coats

INEXPRESSIBLES euphemism for trousers

KERSEY coarse woollen clothing

KNEE-CORDS knee-length trousers

LAWN SLEEVES sleeves of thin cotton or linen, forming part of the episcopal dress

MILK-PUNCH milk mixed with spirits

MIXTURE TROUSERS Mixture is 'a cloth of variegated or mottled fabric, usually of "quiet" colouring' (OED)

NAPLESS HAT worn or threadbare

NEGUS a drink made of wine and hot water, flavoured with lemon and spices; named after Colonel Francis Negus (d.1732)

NEW PATENT CABS the hansom cab, a two-seater cab introduced in the mid-1830s; another anachronism

OXFORD-MIXTURE TROUSERS made from a dark grey woollen cloth

PANTALOONS tight-fitting trousers fastened below the calf

PASTEBOARD CAPS probably pill-box caps, which were headgear of smart appearance, generally worn by cavalry officers

PATTENS *wooden sandals with high soles, to protect the wearer and his or her finer footwear from the mud and filth of the streets*

PELERINE *a short cape worn by women*

PELISSE *an informal, ankle-length garment*

PETTITOES *the little feet of suckling pigs*

PINE-APPLE RUM AND WATER *rum flavoured with, rather than made of, pineapple*

PLUSH SHORTS *worn by footmen and made of a material resembling velvet*

PO'-CHAY *a post-chaise (see below)*

PORTER *a dark beer*

POST-BOY *a post-boy drives, or rides postillion on, a post-chaise*

POST-CHAISE *a horse-drawn carriage for two to four persons, usually with a closed body with the driver or postillion riding on one of the horses*

POST-HORSES *horses kept at a post-house or inn, used for drawing travelling-carriages*

QUART POT *a pot capable of holding a quart, i.e. two pints*

RETICULE *a small handbag, usually made of some woven material (deriving from the Latin word for 'net')*

RIPSTONE PIPPIN *a dessert apple, named after its place of origin, Ribston Park, Yorkshire*

ROLLING COLLARS *probably collars of which the tops could be rolled up or down*

RUFFLES *ornamental frills on items of clothing, usually made of linen or another fine material*

SAVELOY *a cheap sausage, usually filled with fat or smoked meat scraps, and strongly flavoured to disguise the quality of the contents*

SEDAN CHAIR *a closed vehicle to seat one person, borne on two poles by two bearers, one in front and one behind*

SEIDLITZ POWDER *a compound which, when dissolved in water, effervesces and is drunk, like selzer-water, to alleviate a hangover*

SHAY *a post-chaise (see above)*

SHAY-CART *a post-chaise (see above)*

SMACK *small sailing ship, mainly for coastal waters*

SMOCK FROCK *a loose garment worn over the outer clothes*

SNUFF-COLOURED SUIT *a brown suit*

SPRING VANS *four-wheeled carts with springs to ease the jolting*

SRUB *Cockney for 'Shrub', a drink compounded of lemon and rum*

STANHOPE *a light, open, one-seater vehicle. It was first made for the Hon. and Rev. Fitzroy Stanhope (1787–1864) in 1825*

STOMACHER *an ornamental style of waistcoat worn by women*

SUGAR-LOAF HAT *a cone-shaped hat. A sugar-loaf is 'a moulded conical mass of hard refined sugar' (OED)*

SURTOUT *a man's great-coat or overcoat*

SWALLOW-TAILS *coats that ended in a pair of pointed or tapering skirts*

TAXED-CART *used by farmers and tradesmen, they were liable for a reduced rate of tax*

THUNDER-AND-LIGHTNING BUTTONS *loud and flashy, possibly combining two strongly contrasting colours*

TILE *slang for hat*

TOP-BOOTS *a high boot with a top of coloured leather, generally worn by gentlemen, yeomen and farmers*

TOPS *top-boots (see above)*

TUCKER *a piece of material worn as a frill around the neck*

TURNPIKE *toll-gate, where road tolls were levied on wheeled vehicles and cattle*

UNDRESS UNIFORM *military apparel, but not full regalia*

WASH-LEATHER GLOVES *made of a soft kind of leather which, in appearance though not quality, resembles chamois leather*

WELLINGTONS *originally a high boot, named after the style worn by the Duke of Wellington; applied later to shorter dress boots, and now only to rubber waterproof boots*

WHISKEY TODDY *whiskey, hot water and sugar*

YELLOW CURL PAPERS *For women to achieve the fashionable ringlet and corkscrew curls, the hair had to be screwed up in paper before going to bed*

APPENDIX A

The following lavish Advertisement, generally accepted as being Dickens's work, appeared in *The Athenaeum*, 26 March 1836. It reads like a missing section from the mock-heroic idiom of Chapter 1 of the novel; and is also of interest in telling us the founding date of the Pickwick Club: 1822.

On the 31st of March will be published, to be continued Monthly, price ONE SHILLING, THE FIRST NUMBER OF THE POSTHUMOUS PAPERS OF THE PICKWICK CLUB; CONTAINING A FAITHFUL RECORD OF THE PERAMBULATIONS, PERILS, TRAVELS, ADVENTURES, AND SPORTING TRANSACTIONS OF THE CORRESPONDING MEMBERS. EDITED BY 'BOZ.' AND EACH MONTHLY PART EMBELLISHED WITH FOUR ILLUSTRATIONS BY SEYMOUR.

The PICKWICK CLUB, so renowned in the annals of Huggin-lane, and so closely entwined with the thousand interesting associations connected with Lothbury and Cateaton-street, was founded in the year One Thousand Eight Hundred and Twenty-two, by Samuel Pickwick – the great traveller – whose fondness for the useful arts prompted his celebrated journey to Birmingham in the depth of winter; and whose taste for the beauties of nature even led him to penetrate to the very borders of Wales in the height of summer.

This remarkable man would appear to have infused a considerable portion of his restless and inquiring spirit into the breasts of other members of the Club, and to have awakened in their minds the same insatiable thirst for Travel which so eminently characterized his own. The whole surface of Middlesex, a part of Surrey, a portion of Essex, and several square miles of Kent, were in their terms examined, and reported on. In a rapid steamer, they smoothly navigated the placid Thames; and in an open boat they fearlessly crossed the turbid Medway. High-roads and by-roads, towns and villages, public convey-ances and their passengers, first-rate inns and road-side public houses, races, fairs, regattas, elections, meetings, market days – all the scenes that can possibly occur to enliven a country place, and at which different traits of character may be observed and recognized, were alike visited and beheld, by the ardent Pickwick and his enthusiastic followers.

The Pickwick Travels, the Pickwick Diary, the Pickwick Correspondence – in short, the whole of the Pickwick Papers, were carefully preserved, and duly registered by the secretary, from time to time, in the voluminous Transactions of the Pickwick Club. These transactions have been purchased from the patriotic secretary, at an immense expense, and placed in the hands of 'Boz,' the author of 'Sketches Illustrative of Every Day Life, and Every Day People' – a gentleman whom the publishers consider highly qualified for the task of arranging these important documents, and placing them before the public in an attractive form. He is at present deeply immersed in his arduous labours, the first fruits of which will appear on the 31st March.

Seymour has devoted himself, heart and graver, to the task of illustrating the beauties of Pickwick. It was reserved to Gibbon to paint, in colours that will never fade, the Decline and Fall of the Roman Empire – to Hume to chronicle the strife and turmoil of the two proud houses that divided England against herself – to Napier to pen, in burning words, the History of the War in the Peninsula – the deeds and actions of the gifted Pickwick yet remain for 'Boz' and Seymour to hand down to posterity.

From the present appearance of these important documents, and the probable extent of the selections from them, it is presumed that the series will be completed in about twenty numbers.

APPENDIX B

The following Address appeared in Number 10 (January 1837). The 'late eminent John Richardson' referred to was a celebrated fairground showman. He was born in the workhouse in 1761 and died a very wealthy man in 1837.

ADDRESS

Ten months have now elapsed since the appearance of the first number of the PICKWICK PAPERS. At the close of the year, and the conclusion of half his task, their Author may perhaps, without any unwarrantable intrusion on the notice of the Public, venture to say a few words for himself.

He has long been desirous to embrace the first opportunity of announcing that it is his intention to adhere to his original pledge of confining this work to twenty numbers. He has every temptation to exceed the limits he first assigned to himself, that brilliant success, an enormous and increasing sale, the kindest notice, and the most extensive popularity, can hold out. They are, one and all, sad temptations to an author, but he has determined to resist them; firstly, because he wishes to keep the strictest faith with his readers; and, secondly, because he is most anxious that when the POST-HUMOUS PAPERS OF THE PICKWICK CLUB form a complete work, the book may not have to contend against the heavy disadvantage of being prolonged beyond his original plan.

For ten months longer, then, if the Author be permitted to retain his health and spirits, the PICKWICK PAPERS will be issued in their present form, and will then be completed. By what fresh adventures they may be succeeded is no matter for present consideration. The Author merely hints that he has strong reason to believe that a great variety of other documents still lie hidden in the repository from which these were taken, and that they may one day see the light.

With this short speech, Mr Pickwick's Stage-Manager makes his most grateful bow, adding, on behalf of himself and publishers, what the late eminent Mr John Richardson, of Horsemonger Lane

Southwark, and the Yellow Caravan with the Brass Knocker, always said on behalf of himself and company, at the close of every performance –

'Ladies and gentlemen, for these marks of your favour, we beg to return you our sincerest thanks; and allow us to inform you, that we shall keep perpetually going on beginning again, regularly, until the end of the fair.'

December 1836

The following Address appeared in Number 15 (June 1837). The 'severe domestic affliction' refers to the death of Dickens's sister-in-law, Mary Hogarth, on 7 May, at the age of seventeen.

186, STRAND, *June 30,* 1837.

ADDRESS

The author is desirous to take the opportunity afforded him by his resumption of this work, to state once again what he thought had been stated sufficiently emphatically before, namely, that its publication was interrupted by a severe domestic affliction of no ordinary kind; that this was the sole cause of the non-appearance of the present number in the usual course; and that henceforth it will continue to be published with its accustomed regularity.

However superfluous this second notice may appear to many, it is rendered necessary by various idle speculations and absurdities which have been industriously propagated during the past month; which have reached the author's ears from many quarters, and have pained him exceedingly. By one set of intimate acquaintances, especially well informed, he has been killed outright; by another, driven mad; by a third, imprisoned for debt; by a fourth, sent per steamer to the United States; by a fifth, rendered incapable of any mental exertion for evermore – by all, in short, represented as doing anything but seeking in a few weeks' retirement the restoration of that cheerfulness and peace of which a sad bereavement had temporarily deprived him.

NOTICE TO CORRESPONDENTS

We receive every month an immense number of communications, purporting to be 'suggestions' for the Pickwick Papers. We have no doubt that they are forwarded with the kindest intentions; but as it is wholly out of our power to make use of any such hints, and as we really have no time to peruse anonymous letters, we hope the writers will henceforth spare themselves a great deal of unnecessary and useless trouble.

APPENDIX C:

Selected Re-etched Plates by Browne

The Breakdown

Mrs Bardell faints in Mr Pickwick's arms

The Election at Eatanswill

Mrs Leo Hunter's Fancy-dress déjeuné

DICKENS AND HIS CRITICS

As is the case with most of Dickens's novels, the history of the critical reception of *Pickwick Papers* begins a year and a half before the novel is completed. As pointed out in the Introduction, the earliest reviews treated it not as a novel but as a series of papers, a sequence of illustrated sketches. None of the reviewers had any confident idea that the work would be completed in twenty monthly numbers (nor indeed did Dickens in the early months), and so they responded to it as an open-ended series. Four days after the publication of the first monthly number, *The Atlas* (3 April 1836) received 'this strange publication' with contempt:

> The Pickwickians are essentially Cocknies of the true stamp, and the wit of the writer has no wider range than through that melancholy region of exhausted comicality, which Hood and Poole and Smith and Cruikshank have reaped, until they have left not a single laugh behind. The cuts [the engraved illustrations] are better than the letterpress, but the whole affair is excessively dull.

Other early reviewers were concerned to sort out just how to classify *Pickwick*, and many, like the *Atlas* reviewer, saw it as partly a rehash of the work of other popular writers of the time. *The News and Sunday Herald* (10 April 1836), in more complimentary mood, added to *The Atlas*'s list of Boz's Cockney antecedents Theodore Hook and Washington Irving:

> 'Boz' of Sketches celebrity has undertaken to chronicle the sayings and doings of a cockney fraternity yclept Pickwickians, whose whims and oddities he has Hook-ed in with facetious felicity and Hood-ed over with most risible ridicule. The plan is in some measure the same as that adopted in Irving's Bracebridge Hall, and the spirit of the author of 'Sketch Book' is not wanting in the development of the various peculiarities with which the Pickwickians are by no means sparingly gifted.

The *Morning Post* (11 May 1836) welcomed *Pickwick* in terms which were taken up by many other contemporary reviews as the book's popularity became increasingly irresistible. It recommended the London scenes in the early chapters as 'a rich treat to the lovers of the mental-picturesque' and went on to eulogise the author:

> 'Boz' is a shrewd observer of all the phases of citizenship, stationary or warding, waxing or waning, effulgent or eclipsed, and has the happiest knack in the world of combining the glowing outlines of personal sublimity with that recipient risibility of conception which makes them unconsciously waver into profiles of the ridiculous. His imitations of Parliamentary eloquence and etiquette in the proceedings of the Pickwick Club are particularly good.

The *Sunday Times* (12 June 1836) paid Dickens the sort of compliment he must have worked so hard to win. The reviewer acclaimed his style as 'that of Fielding and Smollett, and we can truly affirm that no modern writer has approached so nearly to those great originals'.

As pointed out in the Introduction, following Kathryn Chittick's observations, the growing success of *Pickwick* in the summer and autumn of 1836 was due not only to the eulogies of the reviewers but also to the substantial extracts from the book carried by the journals. These samples whetted the appetite of readers who had not yet bought any of *Pickwick*'s monthly numbers and turned them into devoted subscribers. *Pickwick* became the subject of conversation in every walk of life in 1837, as Mary Russell Mitford testifies in a letter to a friend (A. L'Estrange [ed.], *The Life of Mary Russell Mitford* [1870], 30 June 1837):

> So you have never heard of the *Pickwick Papers*! Well, they publish a number once a month and print 25,000. The bookseller has made 10,000l. by the speculation. It is fun – London life – but without anything unpleasant: a lady might read it all *aloud*; and it is so graphic, so individual, and so true, that you could curtsey to all the people as you met them in the streets. I did think there had not been a place where English is spoken to which 'Boz' had not penetrated. All the boys and girls talk his fun – the boys in the streets; and yet those who are of the highest taste like it the most. Sir Benjamin Brodie takes it to read in his carriage, between patient and patient; and Lord Denman studies *Pickwick* on the bench while the jury are deliberating. Do take some means to borrow the *Pickwick Papers*. It seems like not having heard of Hogarth, whom he resembles greatly, except that he takes a far more cheerful view, a Shakespearian view, of humanity.

John Forster's review in the *Examiner* (2 July 1837) endorsed the comparison of Boz with Fielding and called particular attention to the section dealing with the Fleet prison. He argued that in these scenes the young author showed a power and versatility unsuspected from the earlier numbers of the serial, and went on to comment on the increasing maturity of Dickens as a writer: 'We see in every succeeding work he takes in hand, a superior insight into the general principles of character joining itself to the old and exquisite representations of local peculiarities and humours; and we can rarely now find anything that approaches to caricature or exaggeration without finding also some very shrewd and sound truth concealed beneath it.'

Like the *Examiner*, most of the heavyweight journals of the period held their critical fire until the novel was almost finished. A long, discerning review of Dickens's early works, attributed to G. H. Lewes, appeared in the December 1837 issue of *National Magazine and Monthly Critic*. The reviewer addressed the issue of how *wide* Dickens's popularity was: his appeal cut right across class divisions. He also dismissed the old comparisons with Hook as useless and disparaging to Dickens's talents. He defended Dickens against charges of gross caricature and praised his satire (the Leo Hunter episode, the Eatanswill election, the Seventeen Foreign Learned Societies) and his stylistic verve:

> 'Boz's' satire is the finest that we ever read, because it is generally satire by *implication*, not personality – we do not say that it cuts so deep as Voltaire or Swift, or that it crushes like Hobbes – but it is pointed enough for its purpose, and has none of the bitter, withering tincture which forms so large a portion of satire in general; and it is done in that style that one might easily suppose an individual under the lash laughing at it himself, and feeling its deep truth at the same time – an effect very different to the satire of the great writers above-mentioned .... Then, too, his language, even on the most trivial points, has, from a peculiar collocation of the words, or some happy expression, a drollery which is spoiled by repeating or reading loud, because this drollery arises from so fine an association of ideas that the sound of the voice destroys it.

T. H. Lister in the *Edinburgh Review* (October 1838) felt that comparisons between Dickens and Fielding or Dickens and Smollett were, nearly a year after the close of *Pickwick*, now inappropriate. Dickens was *sui generis*. The comparison with Hogarth was more useful:

What was in painting, such very nearly is Mr Dickens in prose fiction. The same turn of mind – the same species of power displays itself strongly in each. Like Hogarth he takes a keen and practical view of life – is an able satirist – very successful in depicting the ludicrous side of human nature, and rendering its follies more apparent by humorous exaggeration – peculiarly skilful in his management of details, throwing in circumstances which serve not only to complete the picture before us, but to suggest indirectly antecedent events which cannot be brought before our eyes. Hogarth's cobweb over the poor-box, and the plan for paying off the national debt, hanging from the pocket of a prisoner in the Fleet, are strokes of satire very similar to some in the writings of Mr Dickens.

Dickens's readers always wanted more of Pickwick and the Wellers, and Dickens obliged them in 1840 by reintroducing those characters into *Master Humphrey's Clock*. He explained his motives with some disingenuousness in the September 1840 Preface to the first bound volume of the *Clock*: he had revived them 'not with any intention of re-opening an exhausted and abandoned mine, but to connect them in the thoughts of those whose favourites they had been, with the tranquil enjoyments of Master Humphrey'. In spite of *Pickwick*'s continuing popularity (over 31,000 copies of the Cheap Edition of 1847 sold in the first year alone), Dickens confided to his friend Dudley Costello on 25 April 1849, 'The world would not take another Pickwick from me, now.' Perhaps he was right. Perhaps the age had become too sober, too inhibited to giggle or guffaw with laughter at the antics of those characters. Edmund Gosse in *Father and Son* (1907) suspected he 'was the latest of the generation which accepted Mr Pickwick with an unquestioning and hysterical abandonment'. Half a century later John Middleton Murry recorded much the same experience when he wrote on Dickens in *Pencillings* (1923):

> Until the day when I read Mr Gosse's *Father and Son*, I was persuaded that the behaviour Mr Pickwick induced in me at the age of eight and nine was a clear proof of a peculiar madness. Even at that age I was half-ashamed of it. I used to begin to laugh before I had opened the book . . . . And I have never been able to read more than a few pages since then, because the helpless feeling of unquenchable Achene laughter takes hold of me. I dare not let go my sanity; I am afraid of a second childhood . . . . I cannot help believing that forty years hence it will happen again, and that the generations of childish Pickwick enthusiasts are perennial.

The publication of the Library Edition of Dickens's novel in 1858 was the occasion for a long critical essay in the *National Review* (October 1858) by Walter Bagehot. He had some shrewd remarks to make about Dickens's methods of characterisation and focused his comments on Pickwick himself:

> But his peculiar humour is even more indebted to his habit of vivifying external traits, than to his power of external observation. He, as we have explained, expands traits into people; and it is a source of true humour to place these, when so expanded, in circumstances in which only people – that is complete human beings – can appropriately act. The humour of Mr Pickwick's character is entirely of this kind. He is a kind of incarnation of simple-mindedness and what we may call obvious-mindedness. The conclusion which each occurrence or position in life most immediately presents to the unsophisticated mind is that which Mr Pickwick is sure to accept.... He is stated to have 'retired from business'. But no one can fancy what he was in business. Such guileless simplicity of heart and easy impressibility of disposition would soon have induced a painful failure amid the harsh struggles and the tempting speculations of pecuniary life. As he is represented in the narrative, however, nobody dreams of such antecedents. Mr Pickwick moves easily over all the surface of English life from Goswell Street to Dingley Dell, from Dingley Dell to the Ipswich elections, from drinking milk-punch in a wheelbarrow to sleeping in the approximate pound, and no one ever thinks of applying to him the ordinary maxims which we would apply to any common person in life, or to any common personage in fiction.... We are in a conventional world, where the mere maxims of common life do not apply, and yet which has all the amusing detail, and picturesque elements, and singular eccentricities of common life. Mr Pickwick is a personified ideal; a kind of amateur in life, whose course we watch through all the circumstances of ordinary existence, and at whose follies we are amused just as really skilled people are at the mistakes of an amateur in their art.

Bagehot's sense of the sublime simplicity of Pickwick as being at the heart of the comedy of this novel is echoed in G. K. Chesterton's exuberant chapter on *Pickwick* in his book *Charles Dickens* (1906): 'The round, moon-like face, the round, moon-like spectacles of Samuel Pickwick move through the tale as emblems of a certain spherical simplicity .... Pickwick's round face is like a round and honourable mirror, in which are reflected all the fantasies of earthly existence.' Incidentally, Chesterton's remarks about the spherical composition of Pickwick find an unlikely echo in a much more recent essay, *Illustration* (1992), by J. Hillis Miller. Miller examines a number of Phiz's plates for the novel in which Pickwick's ample waistcoated tummy seems to be the radiant focus, a 'counter-sun' in Miller's terms, which links up with mock-epic and more earnest references in the text to Pickwick's sunny optimism and benevolence (Pickwick in Chapter 2 'burst like another sun from his slumbers').

Chesterton also endorses some of Bagehot's points about the 'conventional' world of *Pickwick Papers* and argues that it belongs more with mythology than with the recognisably real world. In that mythological England, the novel's characters 'live statically, in a perpetual summer of being themselves':

> It was his [Dickens's] aim to show character hung in a kind of happy void, in a world apart from time – yes, and essentially apart from circumstance, though the phrase may seem odd in connection with the god-like horse-play of 'Pickwick'. But all the Pickwickian events, wild as they often are, were only designed to display the greater wildness of souls, or sometimes merely to bring the reader within touch, so to speak, of that wildness . . . . Once the great characters are face to face, the ladder by which they climbed is forgotten and falls down, the structure of the story drops to pieces, the plot is abandoned; the other characters deserted at every kind of crisis; the whole crowded thoroughfare of the tale is blocked by two or three talkers, who take their immortal ease as if they were already in Paradise. For they do not exist for the story; the story exists for them; and they know it.

The 'god-like horse-play' of *Pickwick* is a marvellously evocative phrase for the unrestrained fun of the book, which had captivated three generations of readers.

Forty years later, in the middle of the Second World War, a new generation of critics was trying to come to terms with the fictional world Dickens had created. George Orwell remarked that critics of different ideological persuasions had turned Dickens into a Catholic, or a Marxist, or a bourgeois sentimentalist or any number of personae, and his pioneering essay, 'Charles Dickens' (from *Inside the Whale* [1940]), tried to get a clearer perspective and recognise the complexity of Dickens and his relation to his age. He is astute on Dickens's methods of characterisation and plotting. Of the famous characters he says: 'They start off as magic-lantern slides and they end by getting mixed up in a third-rate movie.' The

essentially static nature of the characters, as he sees it, leads to the
following conclusion:

> Consequently his greatest success is *The Pickwick Papers*, which is not
> a story at all, merely a series of sketches; there is little attempt at
> development – the characters simply go on and on, behaving like
> idiots, in a kind of eternity. As soon as he tries to bring his characters
> into action, the melodrama begins.

Orwell's view, pungently argued, has been an influential one. How
seriously should *Pickwick* be taken, especially if it can't be granted
the status of a 'novel'. This is the beginning of a gradual turning of
critical attention to the middle and later novels, and one may
reasonably feel that over the second half of the twentieth century
Pickwick has received far less than its fair share of critical attention.

In the year after Orwell's essay, Edmund Wilson, in his essay
'Dickens: The Two Scrooges' (1941), offered a psychoanalytical
account of Dickens and his fiction. In a way that is symptomatic of
subsequent critical priorities in Dickens studies, Wilson's interest in
Pickwick is restricted to the dark tales scattered through the book
and to the deepening seriousness evident as Pickwick becomes
involved with the law and prison. Wilson declares that he will make
'no attempt to discuss at length the humour of the early Dickens':

> This is the aspect of his work that is best known, the only aspect that
> some people know. In praise of Dickens' humour, there is hardly
> anything new to say. The only point I want to make is that the humour
> of Dickens does differ from such humour as that of Aristophanes in
> being unable for ever to inhabit an empyrean of blithe intellectual
> play, of charming fancies and biting good sense. Dickens' laughter is
> an exhilaration which already [in *Pickwick*] shows a trace of the
> hysterical. It leaps free of the prison life; but gloom and soreness must
> always drag it back. Before he has finished *Pickwick* and even while
> he is getting him out of jail and preparing to unite the lovers, the
> prison will close in again on Dickens. While he is on the last
> instalments of *Pickwick*, he will begin writing *Oliver Twist* . . . .

Dickens's humour is the best-known aspect of his work, 'the only
aspect that some people know'. Half a century later, readers new to
Dickens may be forgiven for thinking the reverse is true: so
completely has the darker, more complex Dickens dominated
critical tastes that one almost forgets his identity as one of the
greatest comic novelists in the language.

Given the prioritisation of the later works, *Pickwick* has, since

Wilson's essay, been seen often as the inchoate preparation for Dickens's more mature handling of 'Condition-of-England' themes, as for example in William Axton's book *Circle of Fire: Dickens's Vision and Style and the Popular Victorian Theater* (1966). Axton views Pickwick and his club associates as epitomising 'the middle classes' pretensions to the paraphernalia of the aristocracy'. In their inability to distinguish form from substance, they are easy prey to Jingle's exploitations. Sam Weller and his father, on the other hand, represent a 'ruthless empiricism' which unmasks hypocrisy (Stiggins) and deflates specious authority (Sam in the witness box facing Buzfuz). The relevance of this critique to later novels, such as *Little Dorrit*, is clearly pointed.

Several critics have seen the relationship between Sam and Pickwick in broader allegorical terms, touched with biographical significance. Steven Marcus's chapter on *Pickwick* in his book *Dickens: From Pickwick to Dombey* (1965) argues that Sam is partly a surrogate for his author, representing 'a skeptical judgement of experience and Mr Pickwick's absolute and ideal morality'. The view that in this central relationship Dickens is projecting his own relationship with his father is endorsed and extended by Angus Wilson in *The World of Charles Dickens* (1970):

> Most first novels are patently autobiographical. *Pickwick* only *seems* to defy this rule. Indeed it seems to me that Professor Marcus's fruitful analysis of the novel can be pushed even farther than he extends it. In *Pickwick* surely Dickens relives the cruel months of his father's first imprisonment and solves them as he would like them to have been solved. In this fictional version of the young boy Dickens (Sam) stays with his father in the Marshalsea and yet guides and befriends him with the worldly knowledge he had so cruelly gained as he tramped the streets during his luncheon hours at Warren's.

Marcus had also argued that the dark tales in the novel represent an inversion of that central relationship: the benign, mutually protective parent-child relationship between Sam and Pickwick is radically altered to its opposite in these relatively unassimilated visions of 'terrible parents and violated children'. A similar view of the relation of the tales to the themes, modes and patterns of the main narrative is developed by Doreen Roberts in 'The Pickwick Papers and the Sex War' (*Dickens Quarterly*, September 1990). She argues that there is a 'formal clash of farce and melodrama, but a covert ideological cooperation between them' in the depiction of the power relations between men and women. In the main, farcical narrative men are forever fugitives from the dominant predatory widows and spinsters; in the melodramatic tales of the first half of the book, men turn on women and abuse them in a variety of ways. The tales exact a fierce revenge for the comic persecutions in the main narrative. By the time we reach the Fleet sections, farce and melodrama are no longer so formally discrete, and accordingly it is in the Fleet that 'we first meet a selection of the martyred, infinitely long-suffering women hitherto confined to the inset tales.'

Marcus's chapter on *Pickwick*, in offering a fabular or allegorical reading of the book, gives it a conceptual coherence that its formal shape lacks. A famous essay by W. H. Auden works in much the same way. In 'Dingley Dell and the Fleet' (*The Dyer's Hand and Other Essays* [1962]), Auden proposes *Pickwick* as an allegory of the Fall. Pickwick becomes 'the innocent adult who no longer lives in an imaginary Eden of his own but in the real and fallen world'. The two locations of Auden's title represent, respectively, Eden and the fallen world. Jingle plays his part as the 'serpent', but it is the Law which most powerfully precipitates the Fall:

> When he is found guilty, Mr Pickwick takes a vow that he will never pay the damages. In so doing he takes his first step out of Eden into the real world, for to take a vow is to commit one's future, and Eden has no conception of the future for it exists in a timeless present. In Eden, a man always does what he likes to do at the moment, but a man who takes a vow commits himself to doing something in the future, which, when the time comes, he may dislike doing. The consequence of Mr Pickwick's vow is that he has to leave his Eden of clean linen and polished silver for a Limbo of dirty crockery and rusty broken toasting forks where, in the eyes of the Law, he is a guilty man, a lawbreaker among other lawbreakers.

Pickwick was served well in the 1960s, in the work of Axton, Marcus and Auden. Their investigations, both psychoanalytical and archetypal in approach, reflect in part the influential work of Northrop Frye in *Anatomy of Criticism* (1957). Frye's later essay, 'Dickens and the Comedy of Humours' (in R. H. Pearce [ed.], *Experience in the Novel* [1968]), is one of the best things ever written on Dickens's comedy. Frye associates Dickens's characteristic mode of comedy with the 'New Comedy structure, which has come down to us from Plautus and Terence through Ben Jonson'. Characterisation in such comedy derives from the old 'Humours' tradition, where a character is identified with a single characteristic.

Pickwick is taken as a curious example of Dickens's adoption and 'Victorianising' of the New Comedy mode:

> The original scheme proposed to Dickens was a comedy of humors in its most primitive and superficial form: a situation comedy in which various stock types, including an incautious amorist (Tupman), a melancholy poet (Snodgrass), and a pedant (Pickwick) . . . get into one farcical adventure after another. This form is frequent in stories for children, and was represented in my childhood by now obsolete types of comic strip and silent movie comedies . . . . But although traces of the original scheme persist throughout *The Pickwick Papers*, it quickly turns inside out into a regular New Comedy story, which leads up in the regular way to a recognition scene and a reversal of direction in the plot at its most serious point, in the debtor's prison. The pedant becomes a man of principle, and the humor of pedantry is transferred to the law which entraps him. Thus the comedy of humors takes root in society, as Dickens sees society, instead of merely extending from one incident to another.

Steven Marcus returned to the novel in an absorbing essay 'Language into Structure: Pickwick Revisited' (*Daedalus: Journal of the American Academy of Arts and Sciences*, Winter 1972). In this essay Marcus sees in *Pickwick Papers* an exercise of something like pure linguistic self-indulgence, unprecedented in the English novel:

> It is language with the shackles removed from certain of its deeper creative powers, which henceforth becomes capable of a constant, rapid, and virtually limitless multiplication of its own effects and forms in new inventions and combinations and configurations. *Mutatis mutandis* it is the timely equivalent in written novelistic prose of the take-off into self-sustained growth . . . For Dickens has committed himself at the outset of *Pickwick Papers* to something like pure writing, to language itself.

It is not only the author-editor in his main narrative who makes this sort of commitment, for 'This kind of free, wild, inventive doodling language tends to break out in character after character' in the novel. Marcus's interest in the exuberant, quasi-autonomous language of *Pickwick* is followed up by Garrett Stewart in *Dickens and The Trials of Imagination* (1974). Stewart offers a very full diagnosis of the parodic function of the language in the novel: 'the ways in which Dickens puts under more direct fire the spoiled language of rhetoric and public address, whether its corrupt accents are heard in pulpit oratory, in Parliamentary declamation, in the written periods of the newspapers, or in the official "legalese" of the courts'. By the end of the novel not only has Pickwick's pompous language changed but so has the narrator's polyphonic performance. This is largely due, so Stewart argues, to the development and foregrounding of Sam Weller, the 'antidote to the "Pickwickian" stuffiness', the healthy, integrated liberator of imaginative life.

The totalising critical readings of *Pickwick*, characteristic of some of the best critiques of the 1960s, have always run side by side with another critical interest, in the constitution of the text itself, the 'making' of *Pickwick*, the circumstances of its publication, and its fragmentary, discontinuous nature as a consequence of the serialisation mode. Marcus's essay just referred to takes account of these circumstances and sees them as crucial in determining the kind of book *Pickwick* became. A good example of the fruits of scholarly investigation in this area is the chapter on *Pickwick* in *Dickens at Work* (1957) by John Butt and Kathleen Tillotson, where the interlacing of Dickens the journalist with Dickens the novelist is studied in close focus, as the building of the novel from month to month is traced. Even more detailed is James Kinsley's 'Introduction' to his Clarendon edition of the novel in 1986, a study which incorporates the planning and execution of the illustrations. Kathryn Chittick's chapter on the novel, '1836–1837: The qualifications of a novelist' in *Dickens and the 1830s* (1990) is a richly contextualised examination of Dickens's role in the production of *Pickwick*. Chittick (as I have remarked in the Introduction) reveals the extent to which Dickens's reading public and reviewers were oblivious to any *novelistic* design or aim in *Pickwick* as it appeared from month to month, and she sharpens the edge of the whole question of when exactly Dickens himself began to see his work as a novel. The whole issue of *genre* as far as *Pickwick* is concerned is connected with the 'materialist' critiques of this book as a publishing phenomenon. From the start, Dickens was a Chapman and Hall 'property'. He was enmeshed in the increasingly competitive, commercially sophisticated and technologically advanced world of early nineteenth-century publishing. N.N. Feltes explores the implications of this for the author, publisher and reader in his essay 'The Moment of *Pickwick*, or The Production of a Commodity Text' (*Literature and History* x, Autumn 1984). As he puts it:

> Chapman and Hall had bought Dickens's intellectual labour power for nineteen months, divided into monthly intervals; the forms of

control, initially imposed by capital and adjusted in the way we have seen, determined that the 'monthly something' should be a discrete, illustrated written text of a determinate length, produced regularly, and to be collected, complete, in a stated time.

In reviewing the critical history of *Pickwick*, one is struck by how little attention has been paid to the book's greatest claim to fame, its comedy. It is notoriously hard to write about comedy, to analyse what makes one laugh. Perhaps, as poor Gosse and Middleton Murry suspected, helpless laughter is an infantile response to a novel. But it is possible to take comedy seriously without being either purely celebratory or stuffily earnest. One hopes the time is coming when critics can address the subject more intensively; we are otherwise unlikely to understand the strong, enduring heartbeat of *Pickwick Papers*.

SUGGESTIONS FOR FURTHER READING

John Forster's *Life of Charles Dickens* (3 vols, 1872–4), in spite of its selective silences on some aspects of its subject's life, remains the classic, indispensable biography; the most recent edition is the two-volume Everyman edition, ed A. H. Hoppé (1969). The standard modern biography is Edgar Johnson's *Charles Dickens: His Tragedy and Triumph* (2 vols, 1952), but two more recent ones are also valuable: Fred Kaplan's *Dickens: A Biography* (1988) and Peter Ackroyd's remarkable *Dickens* (1990). Dickens's letters were first collected in three volumes of the limited Nonesuch Edition of Dickens's works (ed. Walter Dexter, 1938). These are being superseded by the magnificent Clarendon Press *Pilgrim Edition of the Letters of Charles Dickens*, eds M. House, G. Storey, K. Tillotson *et al.* (1965–in progress). The standard scholarly edition of *The Pickwick Papers* is by James Kinsley (Clarendon Press, 1986); Kinsley's Introduction offers a very full account of the composition of *Pickwick*. The Garland Annotated Bibliography of the novel is by Elliot Engel (1990).

The following list of suggested criticism on *Pickwick* includes some titles already featured in the section 'Dickens and his Critics' above:

W. H. Auden, 'Dingley Dell and the Fleet' (in *The Dyer's Hand and Other Essays*, 1962): influential reading of the novel as an allegory of the Fall of Man.

Kathryn Chittick, *Dickens and the 1830s* (1990): indispensable study of the evolution of *Pickwick* and its relation to the early Victorian publishing milieu.

George Ford, *Dickens and His Readers* (1965): a lively survey of the early reception of *Pickwick*.

Louis James, *Fiction for the Working Man 1830–50* (1963): includes a richly documented discussion of the impact of *Pickwick* on contemporary popular culture and the plagiarised serials spawned by the novel.

Steven Marcus, *Dickens: From Pickwick to Dombey* (1965): Marcus's chapter on *Pickwick* is a stimulating critique with a strong psychoanalytic bias, especially in investigating the patterns of parent-child relations dramatised both in the main narrative and in the interpolated tales.

Steven Marcus, 'Language into Structure: Pickwick Revisited' (*Daedalus*

101 [1972], pp. 183–202): penetrating and influential discussion of the extent to which 'language itself is spontaneously creating this novel' as a kind of autonomous energy.

Doreen Roberts, 'The Pickwick Papers and the Sex War' (Dickens Quarterly, September 1990): an adroit essay arguing for the ways in which the interpolated tales belong thematically and ideologically to the main narrative, in spite of their generic and formal discreteness.

Garrett Stewart, Dickens and the Trials of Imagination (1974): a substantial and eloquent critique of the novel, in part extending Marcus's study of its linguistic exuberance, but also discussing the tensions between Dickens's 'editorial masquerade' and the imaginative freedoms triumphantly realised in Dickens's acquiring his own comic voice.

TEXT SUMMARY

Chapter 1
The Pickwick Club resolves to constitute a Corresponding Society consisting of Pickwick, Tupman, Snodgrass and Winkle. They are to go out into the world and to send back from time to time reports of their adventures.

Chapter 2
The Pickwickians encounter the loquacious Jingle, who accompanies them on their journey to Rochester. At a Charity Ball Tupman, having borrowed Winkle's dress suit, innocently chooses to dance with a widow to whom Dr Slammer has been paying court. The next morning the jealous Doctor, identifying the coat with Winkle, sends his second to him to challenge him to a duel, which is called off at the last moment when the mistaken identity is discovered.

Chapter 3
The Pickwickians meet a dismal man who offers to tell them 'The Stroller's Tale', an account of the wretched decline and death of a poor pantomime actor. Dr Slammer and his friends appear, recognise the real culprits, Tupman and Jingle, but decline to pursue the duel when they realise Jingle is no 'gentleman'.

Chapter 4
The company attend a Field Day on Chatham Lines and meet new acquaintances, Mr Wardle and his family, whom they join for a picnic.

Chapter 5
Pickwick and his friends take up Wardle's invitation to visit Manor Farm, Dingley Dell, where they arrive after some trouble on the road with a refractory horse.

Chapter 6
A card-party at Manor Farm, at which the local clergyman tells the tale of 'The Convict's Return': the son of a violent drunkard is drawn into crime, in spite of his much abused mother's devotion to him, is caught and transported for many years. On his return to England and his native village, he finds his father and kills him in revenge.

Chapter 7
A day's shooting at Manor Farm. Winkle's ineptness with the gun causes him to wound Tupman, whose convalescence is comforted with some ardour by Rachael, Wardle's sister. There is a hard-fought cricket match between the Dingley Dellers and All-Muggleton.

Chapter 8
Tupman and Rachael continue their courtship. On the morning after a bibulous evening, Jingle, who is interested in Rachael's money, furtively discredits Tupman's motives with her and wins over her affections.

Chapter 9
Jingle and Rachael elope and are pursued to London by Wardle and Pickwick.

Chapter 10
At the White Hart Inn, joined by Wardle's lawyer, Perker, the pursuers catch up with Jingle, who has produced a marriage licence. Sam Weller, the Inn's 'Boots', is introduced. Jingle is persuaded, with a bribe, to give up his marital plans.

Chapter 11
Back at Dingley Dell, the grieving Tupman's absence is explained by his letter from Cobham (Kent), whither the Pickwickians travel. There Pickwick discovers a stone with a mysterious inscription, which excites his antiquarian and scholarly interests. That night he reads the tale 'A Madman's Manuscript', a macabre story told from the point of view of a deranged and violent man.

Chapter 12
Mrs Bardell, Pickwick's London landlady, misinterprets as a marriage proposal to herself Pickwick's fumbling explanation of his decision to employ Sam Weller as his manservant.

Chapter 13
The Pickwickians and Sam Weller attend a Parliamentary by-election at Eatanswill and witness the rivalry between the editors of the two local newspapers. Winkle warms to the wife of one of the editors, Mrs Pott.

Chapter 14
At a gathering at the local inn that evening, the company hear another tale, 'The Bagman's Story': Tom Smart, a commercial traveller, is attracted by the proprietress of a country inn, who has a sinister suitor. As a result of a supernatural intervention, Tom is able to eliminate his rival and marry her.

Chapter 15
Still at Eatanswill, the Pickwickians attend a fancy-dress *fête champetre*, hosted by Mrs Leo Hunter, and meet a variety of local and international celebrities, among whom, to their indignation, Jingle appears as Mr Charles Fitz-Marshall.

Chapter 16
The Pickwickians pursue Jingle to Bury St Edmunds and meet his accomplice, Job Trotter, who tells them of Jingle's plan to abduct a young lady from the nearby boarding-school. Pickwick resolves to scotch the plan, which turns out to be a confidence trick, and is discovered loitering in the school's grounds at night. The unexpected presence of Wardle eases the compromising situation.

Chapter 17
Pickwick, convalescing from rheumatism, reads another tale, 'The Parish Clerk', a farcical and sentimental story of young love thwarted but eventually resolved happily.

Chapter 18
Pickwick receives notice of a court action against him for breach of promise of marriage to Mrs Bardell.

Chapter 19
A shooting party, hosted by Wardle, is followed by a picnic on Capt. Boldwig's land. Pickwick, overcome by the effects of too much cold punch, falls asleep in a wheelbarrow and is discovered by Boldwig, who has him wheeled to the Pound and there exposed to public derision.

Chapter 20
Return to London, where Pickwick meets Dodson and Fogg, Mrs Bardell's lawyers. Sam Weller's father tells Pickwick that Jingle and Trotter have been seen in Ipswich.

Chapter 21
Pickwick hears some tales about the Inns of Court, including 'The Queer Client': an imprisoned debtor exacts a protracted and cruel revenge for the death, from heartbreak and poverty, of his wife and child.

Chapter 22
Pickwick goes to Ipswich in pursuit of Jingle. That night he inadvertently settles himself into the wrong bedroom in the inn, to the outrage of its middle-aged lady occupant. The latter is being courted by Mr Peter Magnus.

Chapter 23
Sam Weller meets Job Trotter again, outside an imposing mansion.

Chapter 24
Pickwick is discovered by Peter Magnus to have intruded into his lady-friend's bedroom. A duel is threatened. Pickwick's arrest is violently interrupted by Sam.

Chapter 25
At a formal hearing before the magistrate, Mr Nupkins, Sam tells Pickwick that the magistrate's house is now the haunt of Trotter and Jingle (still alias 'Captain Fitz-Marshall'). These two are exposed as impostors and the charges against Pickwick dropped. Sam takes a fancy to Mary, the Nupkinses' maid.

Chapter 26
Back in London, Sam visits Mrs Bardell's house and there learns that her lawyers are taking her case 'on speculation'.

Chapter 27
Sam goes to Dorking to visit his stepmother, who owns a public house there and who has become captivated by the attentions (largely mercenary) of a hypocritical clergyman, Mr Stiggins, much to the disgust of Sam's father.

Chapter 28
The Pickwickians journey down to Manor Farm for the Christmas festivities and wedding of one of Wardle's daughters. A Christmas Eve party is held in the old kitchen.

Chapter 29
Wardle tells 'The Story of the Goblins who Stole a Sexton': a misanthropic sexton, Gabriel Grubb, is visited by a large goblin who shows him various visions to persuade him of the wretchedness of his life and attitudes.

Chapter 30
Pickwick is introduced to two medical students, Bob Sawyer and Ben Allen. The company go skating and Pickwick falls through the ice.

Chapter 31
Back in London, Pickwick is served notice of the breach-of-promise trial, and enlists Serjeant Snubbin to defend him.

Chapter 32
Pickwick is guest at a bachelor party at Bob Sawyer's.

Chapter 33
Sam Weller composes a Valentine letter to Mary. He and his father attend a Temperance Association meeting to which a very drunk Stiggins is introduced.

Chapter 34
The trial: Bardell vs Pickwick. Damages of £750 awarded against Pickwick.

Chapter 35
Pending procedures for exacting the damages, which he refuses to pay, Pickwick and his club friends visit Bath.

Chapter 36
Pickwick finds the Legend of Prince Bladud, a romantic account of the founding of Bath. Winkle is accidentally involved in a compromising situation with the wife of the homicidally jealous Mr Dowler, and flees Bath.

Chapter 37
Sam attends a footman's soirée, and is sent in search of Winkle.

Chapter 38
Winkle, a refugee in Bristol, accidentally finds Bob Sawyer and Ben Allen and, to his mortification, learns of Sawyer's interests in Ben Allen's sister, Arabella. Reconciliation with Dowler.

Chapter 39
Sam and Pickwick liaise on Winkle's behalf with Arabella. Sam meets Mary again.

Chapter 40
Pickwick is committed to the Fleet Debtor's Prison for refusing to pay the damages.

Chapter 41
Pickwick learns what life is like in the Fleet.

Chapter 42
Pickwick discovers Job Trotter and Jingle are fellow prisoners.

Chapter 43
Sam arranges to have himself formally arrested for debt (to his father), so as to be able to join Pickwick in the Fleet.

Chapter 44
Winkle visits Sam and Pickwick in the Fleet and behaves in a strangely distracted manner.

Chapter 45
Sam is visited by his stepmother and Stiggins, who treats Sam to a pious and drunken homily.

Chapter 46
Mrs Bardell is brought to the Fleet as a prisoner, for failing to pay costs to Dodson and Fogg.

Chapter 47
Winkle and Arabella, newly and secretly wed, arrive and plead with Pickwick to intercede on their behalf with Arabella's brother and Winkle's father. Pickwick consents to pay all that is necessary to secure his own and Mrs Bardell's release.

Chapter 48
In Bristol, Bob Sawyer and Ben Allen are reconciled by Pickwick to Arabella's marriage.

Chapter 49
The 'Story of the Bagman's Uncle', who dreams he is involved in a romantic, swashbuckling adventure.

Chapter 50
Pickwick and Sam, with Ben Allen and a boisterous Bob Sawyer, journey from Bristol to Birmingham, to break the news of Winkle's wedding to his father, who then disinherits him.

Chapter 51
At their Towcester inn the company meet the rival Eatanswill editors, Pott and Slurk.

Chapter 52
Sam's stepmother dies. Sam visits Dorking, where his father's patience snaps and he dunks Stiggins in the horse-trough.

Chapter 53
Pickwick arranges for Jingle and Trotter to take passage to the West Indies, and in a final confrontation speaks his mind to Dodson and Fogg.

Chapter 54
Wardle arrives with news of the secret courtship between his daughter, Emily, and Snodgrass, who themselves are welcomed into the company and receive Wardle's blessing.

Chapter 55
Sam and his father receive the proceeds of Mrs Weller's will.

Chapter 56
Old Mr Weller entrusts his inheritance to Pickwick's care and learns of Sam's love for Mary. Winkle's father arrives, having regretted his earlier opposition to his son's marriage.

Chapter 57

Pickwick announces his decision to retire to Dulwich, and the Pickwick Club is dissolved. Snodgrass and Emily are married and so, eventually, are Sam and Mary, both of whom stay in Pickwick's service.

CHARLES DICKENS
IN EVERYMAN

*The Everyman Dickens is the most comprehensive paperback
edition available, with all the original illustrations*

Bleak House
edited by Andrew Sanders
A great mystery unravelled
£5.99

Great Expectations
edited by Robin Gilmour
*From Newgate prison to society
drawing rooms – Pip's hopes and
dreams of becoming a gentleman*
£3.99

Hard Times
edited by Grahame Smith
*Dickens's bleak vision of
mid-Victorian England*
£3.99

Oliver Twist
edited by Steven Connor
*An innocent's journey through
London's underworld*
£4.99

Martin Chuzzlewit
edited by Michael Slater
*Classic examination of greed
and hypocrisy, by turns disturbing
and hilarious*
£4.99

Nicholas Nickleby
edited by David Parker
*An exciting tale of the young
Nicholas making his way in
the world*
£5.99

The Old Curiosity Shop
edited by Paul Schlicke
*A story that has provoked more
extreme responses than anything
else Dickens wrote*
£5.99

A Tale of Two Cities
edited by Norman Page
*The classic English evocation
of the French Revolution*
£3.99

Holiday Romance and Other
Writings for Children
edited by Gillian Avery
'Holiday Romance', The Life of
Our Lord', 'A Child's History
of England', *available only in
Everyman*
£5.99

All books are available from your local bookshop or direct from:
Littlehampton Book Services Cash Sales, 14 Eldon Way, Lineside Estate,
Littlehampton, West Sussex BN17 7HE (*prices are subject to change*)

To order any of the books, please enclose a cheque (in sterling) made payable to
Littlehampton Book Services, or phone your order through with credit card details (Access,
Visa or Mastercard) on 01903 721596 (24 hour answering service) stating card number
and expiry date. (*Please add £1.25 for package and postage to the total of your order.*)

In the USA, for further information and a complete catalogue call 1-800-526-2778

CLASSIC FICTION
IN EVERYMAN

**The Impressions of
Theophrastus Such**
GEORGE ELIOT
*An amusing collection of character
sketches, and the only paperback
edition available*
£5.99

Frankenstein
MARY SHELLEY
*A masterpiece of Gothic terror in
its original 1818 version*
£3.99

East Lynne
MRS HENRY WOOD
*A classic tale of melodrama,
murder and mystery*
£7.99

**Holiday Romance and
Other Writings for Children**
CHARLES DICKENS
*Dickens's works for children,
including 'The Life of Our Lord'
and 'A Child's History of England',
with original illustrations*
£5.99

The Ebb-Tide
R. L. STEVENSON
*A compelling study of ordinary
people in extreme circumstances*
£4.99

The Three Impostors
ARTHUR MACHEN
*The only edition available
of this cult thriller*
£4.99

Mister Johnson
JOYCE CARY
*The only edition available of this
amusing but disturbing twentieth-
century tale*
£5.99

The Jungle Book
RUDYARD KIPLING
*The classic adventures of Mowgli
and his friends*
£3.99

Glenarvon
LADY CAROLINE LAMB
*The only edition available of the
novel which throws light on the
greatest scandal of the early nineteenth century – the infatuation of
Caroline Lamb with Lord Byron*
£6.99

**Twenty Thousand Leagues
Under the Sea**
JULES VERNE
*Scientific fact combines with
fantasy in this prophetic tale
of underwater adventure*
£4.99

All books are available from your local bookshop or direct from:
Littlehampton Book Services Cash Sales, 14 Eldon Way, Lineside Estate,
Littlehampton, West Sussex BN17 7HE (*prices are subject to change*)

To order any of the books, please enclose a cheque (in sterling) made payable to
Littlehampton Book Services, or phone your order through with credit card details (Access,
Visa or Mastercard) on 01903 721596 (24 hour answering service) stating card number
and expiry date. (*Please add £1.25 for package and postage to the total of your order.*)

In the USA, for further information and a complete catalogue call 1-800-526-2778

CLASSIC NOVELS
IN EVERYMAN

The Time Machine
H. G. WELLS

*One of the books which defined
'science fiction' – a compelling
and tragic story of a brilliant
and driven scientist*
£3.99

Oliver Twist
CHARLES DICKENS

*Arguably the best-loved of
Dickens's novels. With all the
original illustrations*
£4.99

Barchester Towers
ANTHONY TROLLOPE

*The second of Trollope's
Chronicles of Barsetshire,
and one of the funniest of all
Victorian novels*
£4.99

The Heart of Darkness
JOSEPH CONRAD

*Conrad's most intense, subtle,
compressed, profound and
proleptic work*
£3.99

Tess of the d'Urbervilles
THOMAS HARDY

*The powerful, poetic classic
of wronged innocence*
£3.99

Wuthering Heights and Poems
EMILY BRONTË

*A powerful work of genius – one of
the great masterpieces of literature*
£3.99

Pride and Prejudice
JANE AUSTEN

*Proposals, rejections, infidelities,
elopements, happy marriages –
Jane Austen's most popular novel*
£2.99

North and South
ELIZABETH GASKELL

*A novel of hardship, passion
and hard-won wisdom amidst the
conflicts of the industrial revolution*
£4.99

The Newcomes
W. M. THACKERAY

*An exposé of Victorian polite
society by one of the nineteenth-
century's finest novelists*
£6.99

Adam Bede
GEORGE ELIOT

*A passionate rural drama enacted
at the turn of the eighteenth
century*
£5.99

All books are available from your local bookshop or direct from:
Littlehampton Book Services Cash Sales, 14 Eldon Way, Lineside Estate,
Littlehampton, West Sussex BN17 7HE (*prices are subject to change*)

To order any of the books, please enclose a cheque (in sterling) made payable to
Littlehampton Book Services, or phone your order through with credit card details (Access,
Visa or Mastercard) on 01903 721596 (24 hour answering service) stating card number
and expiry date. (*Please add £1.25 for package and postage to the total of your order.*)

In the USA, for further information and a complete catalogue call 1-800-526-2778

ESSAYS, CRITICISM AND HISTORY
IN EVERYMAN

Essays and Poems
R. L. STEVENSON
Stevenson's hidden treasures
£4.99

The Rights of Man
THOMAS PAINE
*One of the great masterpieces
of English radicalism*
£4.99

Speeches and Letters
ABRAHAM LINCOLN
*A key document of the American
Civil War*
£5.99

Essays
FRANCIS BACON
*An excellent introduction to
Bacon's incisive wit and moral
outlook*
£4.99

Biographia Literaria
SAMUEL TAYLOR COLERIDGE
*A masterpiece of criticism,
marrying the study of literature
with philosophy*
£4.99

Selected Writings
JOHN RUSKIN
'An excellent selection'
The Guardian
£7.99

**Chesterton on Dickens:
Criticisms and Appreciations**
G. K. CHESTERTON
*A landmark in Dickens criticism,
rarely surpassed*
£4.99

History of His Own Time
BISHOP GILBERT BURNET
*A highly readable contemporary
account of the Glorious Revolution
of 1688*
£7.99

**Memoirs of the Life of Colonel
Hutchinson**
LUCY HUTCHINSON
*Biography by his wife of a man who
signed Charles I's death warrant*
£6.99

**Puritanism and Liberty: Being
the Army Debates (1647-49)
from the Clarke Manuscripts**
edited by A. S. P. Woodhouse
*A fascinating revelation of Puritan
minds in action*
£7.99

**The Embassy to Constantinople
and Other Writings**
LIUDPRAND OF CREMONA
*An insider's view of political
machinations in medieval Europe*
£5.99

All books are available from your local bookshop or direct from:
Littlehampton Book Services Cash Sales, 14 Eldon Way, Lineside Estate,
Littlehampton, West Sussex BN17 7HE *(prices are subject to change)*

To order any of the books, please enclose a cheque (in sterling) made payable to
Littlehampton Book Services, or phone your order through with credit card details (Access,
Visa or Mastercard) on 01903 721596 (24 hour answering service) stating card number
and expiry date. *(Please add £1.25 for package and postage to the total of your order.)*

In the USA, for further information and a complete catalogue call 1-800-526-2778

SHORT STORY COLLECTIONS
IN EVERYMAN

The Strange Case of Dr Jekyll and Mr Hyde and Other Stories
R. L. STEVENSON

An exciting selection of gripping tales from a master of suspense
£1.99

Nineteenth-Century American Short Stories
edited by Christopher Bigsby

A selection of the works of Henry James, Edith Wharton, Mark Twain and many other great American writers
£6.99

The Best of Saki
edited by MARTIN STEPHEN

Includes Tobermory, Gabriel Ernest, Svedni Vashtar, The Interlopers, Birds on the Western Front
£4.99

Souls Belated and Other Stories
EDITH WHARTON

Brief, neatly crafted tales exploring a range of themes from big taboo subjects to the subtlest little ironies of social life
£6.99

The Night of the Iguana and Other Stories
TENNESSEE WILLIAMS

Twelve remarkable short stories, each a compelling drama in miniature
£4.99

Selected Short Stories and Poems
THOMAS HARDY

Hardy's most memorable stories and poetry in one volume
£4.99

Selected Tales
HENRY JAMES

Stories portraying the tensions between private life and the outside world
£5.99

The Best of Sherlock Homes
ARTHUR CONAN DOYLE

All the favourite adventures in one volume
£4.99

The Secret Self 1: *Short Stories by Women*
edited by Hermione Lee

'A superb collection' The Guardian
£4.99

All books are available from your local bookshop or direct from:
Littlehampton Book Services Cash Sales, 14 Eldon Way, Lineside Estate,
Littlehampton, West Sussex BN17 7HE *(prices are subject to change)*

To order any of the books, please enclose a cheque (in sterling) made payable to
Littlehampton Book Services, or phone your order through with credit card details (Access,
Visa or Mastercard) on 01903 721596 (24 hour answering service) stating card number
and expiry date. *(Please add £1.25 for package and postage to the total of your order.)*

In the USA, for further information and a complete catalogue call 1-800-526-2778

FOREIGN LITERATURE IN TRANSLATION
IN EVERYMAN

A Hero of Our Time
MIKHAIL LERMONTOV
*The Byronic adventures of
a Russian army officer*
£5.99

L'Assommoir
ÉMILE ZOLA
*One of the most successful novels
of the nineteenth century and one
of the most scandalous*
£6.99

Poor Folk and **The Gambler**
FYODOR DOSTOYEVSKY
*These two short works of doomed
passion are among Dostoyevsky's
quintessential best. Combination
unique to Everyman*
£4.99

Yevgeny Onegin
ALEXANDER PUSHKIN
*Pushkin's novel in verse is Russia's
best-loved literary work. It con-
tains some of the loveliest Russian
poetry ever written*
£5.99

The Three-Cornered Hat
ANTONIO PEDRO DE ALARCÓN
*A rollicking farce and one of
the world's greatest masterpieces
of humour. Available only in
Everyman*
£4.99

Notes from Underground
and **A Confession**
FYODOR DOSTOYEVSKY *and*
LEV TOLSTOY
*Russia's greatest novelists ruthlessly
tackle the subject of their mid-life
crises. Combination unique to
Everyman*
£4.99

Selected Stories
ANTON CHEKHOV
edited and revised by Donald
Rayfield
*Masterpieces of compression and
precision. Selection unique to
Everyman*
£7.99

Selected Writings
VOLTAIRE
*A comprehensive edition of
Voltaire's best writings. Selection
unique to Everyman*
£6.99

Fontamara
IGNAZIO SILONE
*'A beautifully composed tragedy.
Fontamara is as fresh now, and as
moving, as it must have been when
first published.' London Standard.
Available only in Everyman*
£4.99

All books are available from your local bookshop or direct from:
Littlehampton Book Services Cash Sales, 14 Eldon Way, Lineside Estate,
Littlehampton, West Sussex BN17 7HE (*prices are subject to change*)

To order any of the books, please enclose a cheque (in sterling) made payable to
Littlehampton Book Services, or phone your order through with credit card details (Access,
Visa or Mastercard) on 01903 721596 (24 hour answering service) stating card number
and expiry date. (*Please add £1.25 for package and postage to the total of your order.*)

In the USA, for further information and a complete catalogue call 1-800-526-2778